de Gruyter Textl

European Fundamental Rights and Freedoms

edited by

Dirk Ehlers

with contributions by

Ulrich Becker   Thilo Marauhn
Christian Calliess   Eckhard Pache
Dirk Ehlers   Matthias Ruffert
Astrid Epiney   Frank Schorkopf
Christoph Grabenwarter   Christian Tietje
Jörg Gundel   Robert Uerpmann-Wittzack
Stefan Kadelbach   Christian Walter
Thorsten Kingreen   Bernhard W. Wegener
Peter von Wilmowsky

De Gruyter Recht · Berlin

∞ Printed on acid-free paper which falls within the guidelines of the ANSI
to ensure permanence and durability.

ISBN 978-3-89949-446-4

Bibliografische Information der Deutschen Nationalbibliothek

Die Deutsche Nationalbibliothek verzeichnet diese Publikation in der Deutschen Nationalbibliografie; detaillierte bibliografische Daten sind im Internet über http://dnb.d-nb.de abrufbar.

© Copyright 2007 by De Gruyter Rechtswissenschaften Verlags-GmbH, D-10785 Berlin

All rights reserved, including those of translation into foreign languages. No part of this book may be reproduced in any form or by any means, electronic or mechanical, including photocopy, recording, or any information storage and retrieval system, without permission in writing from the publisher.

Printed in Germany

Data Conversion: WERKSATZ Schmidt & Schulz GmbH, Gräfenhainichen
Printing and Binding: Hubert & Co., Göttingen
Cover Design: deblik, Berlin

Preface

The ever increasing relevance of European law which involves replacement or supplementation of and interaction with national law not only affects the states in Europe but also, and foremost, the citizens. The rights of the citizens in Europe are protected by the European Fundamental Rights and Freedoms. The aim of this textbook is to grasp and illustrate the meaning of these rights and to integrate it into a coherent system. For this purpose the book not only deals with the pertinent law of the European Union and the European Community, but also with the European Convention for the Protection of Human Rights and Fundamental Freedoms which, too, is becoming more and more important. In addition, the Charter of Fundamental Rights of the Union is covered. The Community Courts already refer to the Charter, which is not yet legally binding, as a concentrate of the constitutional traditions common to the Member States. Although the "constitutional concept", which consisted in replacing all existing Treaties by the Treaty establishing a Constitution for Europe, has been abandoned by the Brussels European Council of June 2007, the Council intends to provide Article 6 of the Treaty on European Union with a cross reference to the Charter, giving it legally binding value and setting out the scope of its application. The European Council agreed to convene an Intergovernmental Conference the mandate of which will be to reach all relevant decisions. The resulting Treaty is due to be ratified before the European Parliament elections in June 2009. In relation to the United Kingdom, the following declarations have been annexed to the Presidency Conclusions of the Council: "1. The Charter does not extend the ability of the Court of Justice, or any court or tribunal of the United Kingdom, to find that the laws, regulations or administrative provisions, practices or action of the United Kingdom are inconsistent with the fundamental rights, freedoms and principles that it reaffirms. 2. In particular, and for the avoidance of doubt, nothing in [Title IV] of the Charter creates justiciable rights applicable to the United Kingdom except in so far as the United Kingdom has provided for such rights in its national law." In case of an alteration of the Treaties governing the European Union, the impact of these reservations is yet to be seen. The European Union as well as all Member States must observe the general principles of Community law including the fundamental rights – as guaranteed by the European Convention for the Protection of Human Rights and Fundamental Freedoms and as they result from the constitutional traditions common to the Member States – when applying or implementing Community law. It can therefore not be assumed that the fundamental rights of the European Union will be of no relevance in the United Kingdom. Since the Brussels European Council took place after the editorial deadline of this book, reference is still made to the Treaty establishing a Constitution for Europe – a fact which, however, does not affect the substantial validity of the remarks. The book also takes into account those Protocols to the European Convention for the Protection of Human Rights and Fundamental Freedoms that have not yet entered into force.

Even though the different national laws of the EU Member States do not form part of the Community legal order, each interpretative approach to European law is necessarily influenced to some degree by the respective national law tradition. The present book was originally published in German (2nd ed, Berlin 2005). The authors are law professors in Germany, Austria and Switzerland. Hence, they teach and conduct research in countries with a predominantly continental school of thought focusing on the systematisation of

Preface

the law. The authors are convinced that legal academics as well as practitioners need to be informed about the different methodical approaches to European law and that pan-European perspectives should be developed. It was therefore their intent to translate the textbook into the English language.

While the book was primarily written for students, it is also addressed to other people and institutions that are concerned with European law. Since the impact of European law – most notably the guarantees of fundamental rights and freedoms – reaches far beyond the territorial boundaries of the EU, the authors hope that the book will also appeal to readers from outside Europe.

The concept of this textbook is a trifold one. Firstly, the book is aimed at a systematic description of the European Fundamental Rights and Freedoms. 'General Principles' therefore precede the remarks on specific guarantees. In addition each chapter uniformly distinguishes between the scope of protection of a fundamental guarantee, the interferences with this scope and their justification. In doing so, both the guarantees of the European Convention for the Protection of Human Rights and the guarantees of the fundamental rights of the European Union have been grouped according to subject areas. The need for a reduction of the complex subject matter notwithstanding, the authors have tried to cover all essential problems relating to the European Fundamental Rights and Freedoms. This entailed a certain degree of overlapping between the chapters that could not be entirely avoided. Accordingly, the problems covered within the 'General Principles' are also addressed in the chapters on the specific fundamental rights and freedoms. Since the European Convention for the Protection of Human Rights is referred to by Union and Community law, it is closely connected to the fundamental rights of the European Union. The editor and the authors have tried to accommodate this overlapping by cross-linking the chapters with each other. Finally, the textbook pursues a uniform didactic concept insofar as its systematic approach is complemented by the inclusion of model cases. These model problems and answers are mostly based on actual court decisions. Not only are they supposed to serve as a means of illustration, but shall also enable the reader to grasp the respective topic independently and to apply the underlying principles.

The authors have considered case-law and academic writing up to the end of the year 2006. While judgments of the European Court of Justice and of the Court of First Instance have been cited according to the European Court Reports, decisions of the European Court of Human Rights have generally been cited from the European Human Rights Reports. Where only a case number is given because a decision has not (yet) been published, the decision can be looked up online (ECJ: http://curia.europa.eu; ECtHR: http://www.echr.coe.int).

The extensive editorial work was carried out by members of my staff. I wish to express my sincere thanks to all of them. In particular, Christoph Lepper and Jan Stemplewitz have to be mentioned who where entrusted with the translation of my chapters and the co-ordination of the project. With her revision Alena Hermans substantively contributed to the linguistic quality of this book as a whole. The translation of complex legal texts always constitutes a risky venture – a fact which the authors have been aware of. Nevertheless, they hope to have achieved a presentable result. Feedback and critical comments are highly appreciated by both the editor and the authors. They can also be communicated by email (ehlersd@uni-muenster.de).

Münster, June 2007 *Dirk Ehlers*

Table of Contributors and Outline Table of Contents

Part I: The Notion of European Fundamental Rights and Freedoms

Dr. Christian Walter
Professor of Law at the University of Münster
§ 1   History and Development of European Fundamental Rights and Fundamental Freedoms   1

Part II: European Convention for the Protection of Human Rights and Fundamental Freedoms

Dr. Dirk Ehlers
Professor of Law at the University of Münster
§ 2   General Principles   25

Dr. Robert Uerpmann-Wittzack
Professor of Law at the University of Regensburg
§ 3   Personal Rights and the Prohibition of Discrimination   67

Dr. Thilo Marauhn
Professor of Law at the University of Gießen
§ 4   Freedom of Expression, Freedom of Assembly and Association   97

Dr. Bernhard W. Wegener
Professor of Law at the University of Erlangen-Nürnberg
§ 5   Economic Fundamental Rights   130

Dr. Dr. Christoph Grabenwarter
Justice of the Constitutional Court of Austria
Professor of Law at the Vienna University of Economics and Business Administration
§ 6   Fundamental Judicial and Procedural Rights   151

Part III: The Fundamental Freedoms of the European Communities

Dr. Dirk Ehlers
Professor of Law at the University of Münster
§ 7   General Principles   175

Dr. Astrid Epiney
Professor of Law at the University of Freiburg, Switzerland
§ 8   Free Movement of Goods   226

Dr. Ulrich Becker
Professor of Law at the Ludwig-Maximilians-Universität Munich
Director of the Max Planck Institute for Foreign and International Social Law
§ 9   Freedom of Movement for Workers   255

Dr. Christian Tietje
Professor of Law at the University of Halle
§ 10   Freedom of Establishment   281

Dr. Eckhard Pache
Professor of Law at the University of Würzburg
§ 11   The Free Movement of Services   309

Dr. Peter v. Wilmowsky
Professor of Law at the University of Frankfurt a.M.
§ 12   Freedom of Movement of Capital and Payments   331

Dr. Thorsten Kingreen
Professor of Law at the University of Regensburg
§ 13   Prohibition of Discrimination Due to Nationality   362

Part IV: The Fundamental Rights of the European Union

Dr. Dirk Ehlers
Professor of Law at the University of Münster
§ 14   General Principles   371

Dr. Frank Schorkopf
Privatdozent at the University of Bonn
§ 15   Human Dignity, Fundamental Rights of Personality and Communication .   399

Dr. Matthias Ruffert
Professor of Law at the University of Jena
§ 16   The Right to Pursue a Freely Chosen Occupation   430

Dr. Christian Calliess
Professor of Law at the University of Göttingen
§ 17   The Fundamental Right to Property   448

Dr. Thorsten Kingreen
Professor of Law at the University of Regensburg
§ 18   Basic Rights of Equality and Social Rights   466

Dr. Jörg Gundel
Professor of Law at the University of Bayreuth
§ 19   Judicial and Procedural Fundamental Rights   490

Dr. Christian Calliess
Professor of Law at the University of Göttingen
§ 20   The Charter of Fundamental Rights of the European Union   518

Part V: Citizenship Rights in Europe

Dr. Stefan Kadelbach
Professor of Law at the University of Frankfurt a.M.
§ 21   European Citizenship Rights   541

Contents

European Fundamental Rights and Freedoms

Table of Contributors and Outline Table of Contents VII
Contents IX
Table of Abbreviations XXI

PART I

The Notion of European Fundamental Rights and Freedoms

§ 1 History and Development of European Fundamental Rights and Fundamental Freedoms 1
    I. International and European Human Rights Protection 1
    II. History and Development of Human Rights Protection in the Context of the Council of Europe and the European Convention on HumanRights 2
        1. The Development of Human Rights Protection through the ECHR 3
        2. Human Rights Protection in the Council of Europe in General . . 9
    III. History and Development of Human Rights Protection within the EC/EU 11
        1. Early Jurisprudence 11
        2. Development and Legal Foundation of Human Rights of the EC/EU 11
        3. The Debate Concerning Accession to the ECHR 14
        4. Demands for a Catalogue of Human Rights of the EU and the European Charter of Fundamental Rights 15
        5. The Scope of Application of Fundamental Rights of the Union . 16
    IV. The Fundamental Freedoms of European Community Law 17
        1. Recognition of fundamental rights as subjective rights 18
        2. Interpretation of the Fundamental Freedoms as prohibitions of discrimination and prohibitions of limitations 19
        3. Complementing the free movement of persons with rights derived from the Union citizenship 21
        4. Horizontal Effect ("Drittwirkung") and Positive Obligations: Using Structural Human Rights Arguments for the Interpretation of the Fundamental Freedoms 21
    V. Consequences of the Treaty Establishing a Constitution for Europe . 23
    VI. Summary: Protection of Fundamental Rights and Fundamental Freedoms in a Multi-Layered Europe 23

PART II

The European Convention for the Protection of Human Rights and Fundamental Freedoms

§ 2	General Principles	25
	I. The Position and Status of the Convention within the Structure of International and National Law	25
	II. Functions of the Convention Rights	32
	1. Guarantee of the Status Negativus (Defensive or Liberty Rights)	33
	2. Guarantee of Equal Treatment and Equality before the Law	33
	3. Guarantee of the Status Positivus (Rights to Governmental Action / Positive Obligations)	34
	4. Guarantee of the Status Activus (Civic Rights)	36
	5. Guarantee of the Status Activus Processualis (Procedural Rights)	36
	6. The Objective Dimension of the Convention Rights	37
	III. Interpretation of the Convention	38
	IV. Beneficiaries of the Convention Rights	39
	V. Entities Bound by the Convention Rights	41
	1. Convention States of the Council of Europe	41
	2. International and Supranational Organisations	43
	3. Private Persons	45
	VI. Territorial scope	46
	VII. Temporal scope	46
	VIII. Guarantees and Limitations of the Convention Rights	48
	1. Stages of Scrutiny	48
	2. Applicability of the Convention	48
	3. Scope of Protection of the Convention Rights	49
	4. Interference with a Right or Freedom	49
	5. Justification of the Interference or Limitation	51
	6. Schematic Summary	54
	IX. Judicial protection	54
	1. Judicial Protection by the ECtHR	54
	2. Judicial Protection by National Courts	64
§ 3	Personal Rights and the Prohibition of Discrimination	67
	I. Protection of Privacy	67
	1. Private and Family Life, Home and Correspondence (Article 8 ECHR)	68
	2. Freedom of Thought, Conscience and Religion (Article 9 ECHR)	78
	II. Right to Personal Integrity	81
	1. Prohibition of Torture, Inhuman or Degrading Treatment or Punishment (Article 3 ECHR)	81
	2. Right to Life (Article 2 ECHR)	86

Contents

	III. Prohibition of Discrimination	92
	1. The Complementary Prohibition of Discrimination (Article 14 ECHR)	92
	2. Special Aspects of Equality	95
§ 4	Freedom of Expression, Freedom of Assembly and Association	97
	I. Freedom of Communication within the European Human Rights System	97
	II. Freedom of Opinion and Freedom of Information	98
	1. Scope of Protection	98
	2. Interference	105
	3. Justification	107
	III. Freedom of Assembly	118
	1. Scope of Protection	118
	2. Interference	119
	3. Justification	120
	IV. Freedom of Association	121
	1. Scope of Protection	122
	2. Interference	122
	3. Justification	123
	V. Freedom to Form and Join Trade Unions	124
	1. Scope of Protection	125
	2. Interference	127
	3. Justification	127
	VI. Conclusions	128
§ 5	Economic Fundamental Rights	130
	I. Introduction	130
	II. Protection of Property	131
	1. Scope of Protection of the Guarantee of Property	132
	2. Drawbacks of the Property Right	136
	3. Justification of Ownership Restrictions	140
	4. Ownership Law and other Guarantees of the ECHR	147
	III. Other Guarantees under Economic Law	148
	IV. Influence of the European Social Charter	149
§ 6	Fundamental Judicial and Procedural Rights	151
	I. The Protection of Liberty (Article 5 ECHR)	151
	1. The Right to Liberty and Security	152
	2. Types of Interference	153
	3. Rights Guaranteed to Individuals Deprived of their Liberty	157

II.	Fundamental Judicial Rights in Connection with Proceedings before Courts	160
	1. The Right to a Fair Trial pursuant to Article 6(1) of the ECHR	160
	2. Nulla poena sine lege (Article 7 of the ECHR)	169
	3. The Prohibition of Double Jeopardy	171
	4. Right of Appeal in Criminal Matters	172
	5. The Right to Compensation for Wrongful Conviction (Article 3 of the 7th Prot ECHR)	173
III.	Procedural Safeguards Relating to Expulsion of Aliens	173
IV.	The Right to an Effective Remedy	173

PART III

The Fundamental Freedoms of the European Communities

§ 7	General Principles	175
I.	The Nature and Position of the Fundamental Freedoms within the Structure of European Community Law	175
	1. The Significance of the Fundamental Freedoms	175
	2. The Different Fundamental Freedoms	176
	3. Direct Internalisation and Direct Effect of the Fundamental Freedoms	178
	4. The Fundamental Freedoms as Subjective Rights	179
	5. Supremacy of the Fundamental Freedoms	179
	6. Delineation from Other Rights Guaranteed by Primary Community Law	180
	7. Dogmatics of the Fundamental Freedoms	182
II.	Functions of the Fundamental Freedoms	183
	1. The Fundamental Freedoms as Equality Rights	183
	2. The Fundamental Freedoms as Liberty Rights	186
	3. The Fundamental Freedoms as Rights to Governmental Action	190
	4. The Fundamental Freedoms as Procedural Rights	192
	5. The Objective Dimension of the Fundamental Freedoms	193
III.	Beneficiaries of the Fundamental Freedoms	193
	1. Nationals of the Member States	194
	2. Legal Persons and Groups of Individuals within the Community	194
	3. Non-EU Citizens and Legal Persons / Groups of Individuals Outside the Community	196
IV.	Entities Bound by the Fundamental Freedoms	196
	1. Member States of the European Communities	197
	2. European Communities	197
	3. Private Individuals	198
V.	Territorial Scope of the Fundamental Freedoms	200
VI.	Temporal Scope of the Fundamental Freedoms	201

Contents

	VII. Scope of Protection, Interferences, Justification	201
	1. Scope of Protection of the Fundamental Freedoms	202
	2. Interference with the Fundamental Freedoms	207
	3. Justification of Interferences with the Fundamental Freedoms	213
	4. Schematic Summary	223
	VIII. Judicial Protection	224
	1. Avenues of Judicial Protection for the Individual	224
	2. Protection of the Fundamental Freedoms through Proceedings Instituted by the Commission or by the Member States	225
§ 8	Free Movement of Goods	226
	I. Scope of Protection	227
	II. Interference	229
	1. Addressees (Obligors)	229
	2. Import Restrictions and Measures Having Equivalent Effect (Article 28 TEC/Article III-153 DC)	232
	3. Quantitative Restrictions on Exports and Measures Having Equivalent Effect	239
	III. Justification	240
	1. Transversal Aspects	240
	2. Written Grounds of Justification	247
	3. Unwritten Grounds of Justification	249
	4. Proportionality	249
§ 9	Freedom of Movement for Workers	255
	I. Scope of Protection	256
	1. Preliminary Remarks	256
	2. Subject Matter of Protection	257
	3. Personal Scope of Protection	267
	4. Concurrences	270
	II. Interference	270
	1. Discrimination	271
	2. Limitations	273
	3. Addressees	275
	III. Justification	276
	1. Written Restrictions	276
	2. Unwritten Restrictions	277
	3. General Limits to Restrictability	278
§ 10	Freedom of Establishment	281
	I. Introduction	281
	1. The Basic Structure and Problems of the Freedom of Establishment within the System of the Fundamental Freedoms	281
	2. The Interplay between the Freedom of Establishment under Community Law and Public International Law	284

	II.	Scope of Protection	286
		1. Territorial Scope of Protection	286
		2. Personal Scope of Protection	286
		3. Subject Matter of Protection	287
		4. Exceptions to the applicability	296
	III.	Interference	298
		1. Discrimination	299
		2. Restrictions	300
	IV.	Justification	302
	V.	The Application of the Freedom of Establishment to Legal Persons According to Article 48 of the TEC (Article III-142 DC)	304
§ 11	The Free Movement of Services		309
	I.	Introduction	309
		1. The General Relevance of the Principle of the Freedom to Provide Services	309
		2. The Structure of the Freedom to Provide Services in the Community Law	310
		3. The Free Movement of Services beyond the Treaty	311
		4. Liberalisation of the Freedom to Provide Services and Secondary Legislation	312
		5. The New Strategy for the Internal Market	313
	II.	The Scope of Protection	314
		1. The Territorial Scope of Protection	314
		2. The Personal Scope of Protection	314
		3. The Subject Matter of Protection	315
	III.	Interference	320
		1. Obligors	321
		2. Discriminatory Rules	322
		3. Interferences with the Freedom to Provide Services	324
	IV.	Justification	326
		1. The Explicit Written Restrictions	326
		2. Unwritten Restrictions	327
		3. General Limits to the Restrictability of Rights and Freedoms	328
§ 12	Freedom of Movement of Capital and Payments		331
	I.	Scope of Protection	331
		1. Movement of Capital	331
		2. Relationship to the Other Fundamental Freedoms	332
		3. Crossing Borders	334
		4. Payments	335
	II.	Prohibition on Restrictions	336
	III.	Justification of Restrictions within the Community: The Subjects Protected by Article 58 of the TEC (Article III-158 DC) and the Mandatory Requirements	338

Contents

IV.	Regulatory Fields	340
	1. Tax Law: Capital Gains Tax	340
	2. Company Law	346
	3. Foreign Trade and Payments Legislation: Reporting Requirements	348
	4. Monetary Law	350
	5. The Law of Real Estate Transactions	351
	6. Security Interests	355
V.	Additional Restrictions With Regard to Third Countries	357
	1. Restrictions Pursuant to Article 57 of the TEC (Article III-157 DC): No Justification Needed	358
	2. Restrictions Pursuant to Article 59 of the TEC (Article III-159 DC): Temporary Measures Only	359
	3. Restrictions Pursuant to Article 60 of the TEC: Economic Sanctions	360
	4. Broader Interpretation of Article 58 of the TEC (Article III-158 DC) and of the Mandatory Requirements	360
VI.	Conclusion	361

§ 13 Prohibition of Discrimination Due to Nationality 362

    I. Sources of Law and Systematic Classification 362

    II. Structure of Review 363
       1. Scope of Protection 363
       2. Interference 367

PART IV

The Fundamental Rights of the European Union

§ 14 General Principles 371

    I. The Character and Position of the Fundamental Rights of the European Union within the Structure of International and National Law 371
       1. The Notion of Fundamental Rights 371
       2. The Necessity of Guaranteeing Fundamental Rights on the EU Level 372
       3. The Legal Foundation of the Fundamental Rights of the Union . 373
       4. The Relation between the Fundamental Rights of the Union and other Fundamental Guarantees 375
       5. Charter of Fundamental Rights of the Union 379

    II. Functions of the Fundamental Rights of the Union 382
       1. Guarantee of Liberty Rights 382
       2. Guarantee of Equality Rights 382
       3. Guarantee of Rights to Governmental Action / Positive Obligations 383

	4. Guarantee of the Citizens' Rights	383
	5. Guarantee of Procedural Rights	384
	6. The Objective Dimension of the Fundamental Rights of the Union	384
III.	Beneficiaries of the Fundamental Rights of the Union	385
	1. Natural Persons	385
	2. Entities with Legal Personality and Groups of Individuals	385
IV.	Entities Bound by the Fundamental Rights of the Union	386
	1. European Union and European Communities	386
	2. Member States of the European Union	387
	3. Private Persons	388
V.	Territorial and Temporal Scope of the Fundamental Rights of the Union	389
VI.	Guarantees of / Interferences with the Fundamental Rights of the Union	390
	1. Scope of Protection of the Fundamental Rights of the Union	390
	2. Interferences with the Fundamental Rights of the Union	391
	3. Justification of Interferences with the Fundamental Rights of the Union	391
	4. Schematic Summary	395
VII.	Judicial Protection	396
	1. Judicial Protection of the Individual	396
	2. Judicial Protection of the Institutions of the EC and the Member States	397
VIII.	Other Forms of Protection of Fundamental Rights in the EU	397

§ 15 Human Dignity, Fundamental Rights of Personality and Communication . 399

I.	Dignity of Man	400
	1. Scope of Protection	400
	2. Interference	403
	3. Justification	403
II.	Protection of the Personality	405
	1. Scope of Protection	405
	2. Interference	417
	3. Justification	417
III.	The Protection of Communication	418
	1. Scope of Protection	418
	2. Interference	425
	3. Justification	426
IV.	Freedom and Security – Outlook	427

Contents

§ 16	The Right to Pursue a Freely Chosen Occupation	430
	I. Scope of Protection	430
	1. Function, Significance and Sources of the Right to Pursue a Freely Chosen Occupation in EU Law	430
	2. Subject Matter of Protection	435
	3. Personal Scope of Protection	441
	II. Infringement	442
	III. Justification	443
	1. Restrictions of the Right to Pursue a Freely Chosen Occupation	444
	2. Requirements for a Restriction of the Right to Pursue a Freely Chosen Occupation in Conformity with Community Law	444
§ 17	The Fundamental Right to Property	448
	I. Position and Relevance of the Fundamental Right to Property in Community Law	448
	II. The Derivation and Dogmatic Structure of the Fundamental Right to Property under Community Law	449
	III. The European Fundamental Right to Property in Detail	453
	1. The Scope of Protection of the Fundamental Right to Property	453
	2. Impairment of the Scope of Protection	455
	3. Justification	458
	IV. Conclusion	464
§ 18	Basic Rights of Equality and Social Rights	466
	I. Rights to Equality	466
	1. Overview and System	466
	2. Norm Structure and Structure of Review	467
	3. The General Principle of Equality	469
	4. Specific Principles of Equality	471
	II. Social Rights	485
	1. Solidarity and Social Rights	485
	2. Typology of Social Rights	487
§ 19	Judicial and Procedural Fundamental Rights	490
	I. Overview	490
	1. Relevance of Judicial and Procedural Fundamental Rights in Community Law	490
	2. Sources of Community Law Procedural Fundamental Rights	491
	3. Obligors	493
	II. Fundamental Procedural Rights in Relation to the Community Institutions	494
	1. Fundamental Procedural Rights in Relation to the Community Administrative Organs	494
	2. Procedural Rights before the Community Tribunals	500

	III. Requirements of Community Procedural Fundamental Rights for Member States	506
	1. Applicability of Procedural Fundamental Rights to Member States' Actions	506
	2. Parallel Guarantees of Procedural Rights through Fundamental Freedoms	508
	3. Parallel Guarantee of Procedural Rights through the Requirement of Equal and Effective Protection (Article 10 TEC/Article I-5(2) DC)	508
	IV. Particular Problems in 'Tiered' Proceedings und 'Mixed' Decisions between National Authorities and EC-Commission	513
	1. The 'Tiered' Proceeding	513
	2. Problems of Judicial Protection in 'Mixed Decisions'	515
	V. Summary	517
§ 20	The Charter of Fundamental Rights of the European Union	518
	I. Introduction	518
	II. Contents and Restrictions of Fundamental Rights	520
	1. Overview of the Fundamental Rights Guaranteed by the Charter	520
	2. The Restrictions within the Charter of Fundamental Rights	524
	3. Comment	526
	III. On the Area of Application of the Charter of Fundamental Rights of the European Union	530
	IV. On the Legally Binding Nature of the Charter of Fundamental Rights of the European Union prior to the European Constitution Coming into Effect	533
	V. The European Agency for Fundamental Rights	538
	VI. Prospect	539

PART V

Citizenship Rights in Europe

§ 21	European Citizenship Rights	541
	I. Introduction	541
	II. Union Citizenship as a Matter of the European Union	542
	1. From Market Citizen to Union Citizen	542
	2. TEC Stipulations Relating to Union Citizenship	544
	III. Nationality, National Citizenship and Citizenship of the Union	546
	1. Nationality and National Citizenship	547
	2. Nationality as a Condition for Citizenship of the Union	549
	3. Citizenship of the Union as a Complement to National Citizenship	551

Contents

    IV. European Citizenship Rights 552
        1. Freedom of Movement 552
        2. Political Rights 556
        3. Right to Diplomatic and Consular Protection (Article 20 TEC/
           Article I-10(2)(c) DC) 564
        4. Citizenship of the Union and the Prohibition on Discrimination
           (Article 12 TEC/Articles I-4(2), III-123 DC) 568

    V. Concluding Remarks 572

Decisions of the European Court of Human Rights 575

Decisions of the European Court of Justice 586

Table of Model Cases 606

Index 609

Table of Abbreviations

A
ACD	Decisions adopted by the Association Council
ACP States	African, Caribbean and Pacific States
AfP	Archiv für Presserecht
AG	Advocate General
AJCL	American Journal of Comparative Law
AJDA	L'Actualité Juridique – Droit Administratif
All ER	All England Reports
AöR	Archiv des öffentlichen Rechts
App No	Application Number
ArbuR	Arbeit und Recht
ArchVR	Archiv des Völkerrechts
Art	Article
Arts	Articles
AuA	Arbeit und Arbeitsrecht
AVR	Archiv des Völkerrechts

B
Beih	Beiheft (supplement)
BFH	Bundesfinanzhof (German Federal Court of Finance)
BGBl	Bundesgesetzblatt (Official Journal of the Federal Republic of Germany)
BGH	Bundesgerichtshof (German Federal Court of Justice)
BGHZ	Amtliche Sammlung der Entscheidungen des Bundesgerichtshofs in Zivilsachen (Official Reports of the German Federal Court of Justice in civil court matters)
Bull EC	Bulletin of the European Communities
BVerfG	Bundesverfassungsgericht (German Federal Constitutional Court)
BVerfGG	Bundesverfassungsgerichtsgesetz (German Federal Constitutional Court Act)
BVerfGE	Amtliche Sammlung der Entscheidungen des Bundesverfassungsgerichts (Official Reports of the German Federal Constitutional Court)
BVerfG-K	Kammerentscheidung des Bundesverfassungsgerichts (Decision of a chamber of the German Federal Constitutional Court)
BVerwG	Bundesverwaltungsgericht (German Federal Administrative Court)

C
CAP	Common Agricultural Policy
CD	Collection of Decisions
CDE	Cahiers du Droit Européen
cf	confer
CFI	Court of First Instance
CFR	Charter of Fundamental Rights of the European Union

XXI

CFSP	Common Foreign and Security Policy
ch	chapter
CMLR	Common Market Law Reports
CMLRev	Common Market Law Review
COCON	working party on consular cooperation (within the EU Council)
COM	Commission documents for the other institutions (*eg* legislative proposals)
CONV	Convention

D

DB	Der Betrieb
DC	Draft Constitution
DCSI	Diritto comunitario e degli scambi internazionali
DG	Directorate General
Dir	Directive
Dirs	Directives
DÖV	Die öffentliche Verwaltung
DR	Decisions and Reports
DuD	Datenschutz und Datensicherheit
Duke J. of Comp. & Int'l L	Duke Journal of Comparative and International Law
DV	Deutsche Verwaltung
DVBl	Deutsches Verwaltungsblatt

E

EA	Europaarchiv
EAC	Treaty establishing the European Atomic Energy Community
EAEC	European Atomic Energy Community
EC	European Community / European Communities
ECB	European Central Bank
ECHR	European Convention on the Protection of Human Rights and Fundamental Freedoms
ECJ	European Court of Justice
ECOSOC	United Nations Economic and Social Council
ECR	European Court Reports
ECSC	European Coal and Steel Community
ECtHR	European Court of Human Rights
ed	editor / edition
eds	editor / editions
EEA	European Economic Area
EEC	European Economic Community
eg	for example
EGV	Vertrag zur Gründung der Europäischen Gemeinschaft (see TEC)
EHRLR	European Human Rights Law Review
EHRR	European Human Rights Reports
EJIL	European Journal of International Law
ELJ	European Law Journal
ELR	European Law Report

Table of Abbreviations

ELRev	European Law Review
EMRK	Europäische Menschenrechtskonvention (see ECHR)
EP	European Parliament
EPL	European Public Law
ESA	European Space Agency
ESC	European Social Charter
ESC	European Social Charter
et al	et aliae
ETS	European Treaty Series
EU	European Union
EuGRZ	Europäische Grundrechtezeitschrift
EuR	Europarecht
EurCommHR	European Commission of Human Rights
EUV	Vertrag zur Gründung der Europäischen Union (see TEU)
EuZW	Europäische Zeitschrift für Wirtschaftsrecht
EVR	Europäischer Verwaltungsrechtsschutz
EWS	Europäisches Wirtschafts- und Steuerrecht

F

FAZ	Frankfurter Allgemeine Zeitung
ff	following
FRG	Federal Republic of Germany
FS	Festschrift

G

GAOR	UN General Assembly Official Records
GATS	General Agreement on Trade in Services
GDR	German Democratic Republic
GG	Grundgesetz (German Basic Law / Federal Constitution)
GmbHR	GmbH-Rundschau
GYIL	German Yearbook of International Law

H

HRLJ	Human Rights Law Journal

I

ICCPR	International Covenant on Civil and Political Rights
ICESCR	International Covenant on Economic, Social and Cultural Rights
ICLQ	International and Comparative Law Quarterly
ie	that is
ILM	International Legal Materials
IMF	International Monetary Fund
IPrax	Praxis des internationalen Privat- und Verfahrensrechts

J

JBl	Juristische Blätter
JöR	Jahrbuch des öffentlichen Rechts
JR	Juristische Rundschau

XXIII

JTDE	Journal des tribunaux – Droit européen
JURA	Juristische Ausbildung
JuS	Juristische Schulung
JZ	Juristenzeitung

K
KJ	Kritische Justiz
KritV	Kritische Vierteljahresschrift für Gesetzgebung und Rechtswissenschaft

L
LIEI	Legal Issues of Economic Integration

M
Maastr JECL	Maastricht Journal of European and Comparative Law
MJ	Maastricht Journal
MLR	Modern Law Review

N
NdsVBl	Niedersächsische Verwaltungsblätter
NHS	National Health Service
NJW	Neue Juristische Wochenschrift
No	Number
NQHR	Netherlands Quarterly of Human Rights
NVwZ	Neue Zeitschrift für Verwaltungsrecht
NW	Nordrhein-Westfalen
NZA	Neue Zeitschrift für Arbeitsrecht

O
OECD	Organisation for European Co-operation and Development
OJ	Official Journal
ÖJZ	Österreichische Juristen-Zeitung
OLAF	European Anti-Fraud Office
OLG	Oberlandesgericht (Higher Regional Court)
OSCE	Organisation for Security and Co-operation in Europe
OVG	Oberverwaltungsgericht (Higher Administrative Court)
ÖZÖR	Österreichische Zeitung für Öffentliches Recht
ÖZW	Österreichische Zeitschrift für Wirtschaftsrecht

P
p	page
para	paragraph
paras	paragraphs
PESC	Politique étrangère et de sécurité commune (see CFSP)
pp	pages
Prot	Protocol

R
RabelsZ	Rabels Zeitschrift für ausländisches und internationales Privatrecht
RdA	Recht der Arbeit

Table of Abbreviations

RDP	Revue de Droit Prospectif
Reg	Regulation
Regs	Regulations
RevMC	Revue du marché commun
RFDA	Revue française de droit administratif
RFDC	Revue française de droit constitutionnel
RGDIP	Revue Générale de Droit International Public
RIDPC	Rivista italiana di diritto pubblico comunitario
Riv Trim Dir Pubbl	Rivista trimestrale di diritto pubblico
RIW	Recht der internationalen Wirtschaft
RJD	Reports of Judgements and Decisions
RMC	Revue du Marché commun et de l'Union européenne
RMUE	Revue du Marché Unique européen
RTDE	Revue trimestrielle de droit européen
RTDH	Revue trimestrielle des droits de l'homme
RUDH	Revue Universelle des Droits des l'homme

S

sec	Section
secs	Sections
StPO	Strafprozessordnung (German Code of Criminal Procedure)
STuB	Steuern und Bilanzen
STuW	Steuer und Wirtschaft
SZIER	Schweizerische Zeitschrift für internationales und europäisches Recht

T

TEC	Treaty establishing the European Community
TEU	Treaty on European Union

U

UDHR	Universal Declaration of Human Rights
UN	United Nations
UNTS	United Nations Treaty Series
UPR	Umwelt- und Planungsrecht
UTR	Jahrbuch des Umwelt- und Technikrechts

V

v	versus
VBLBW	Verwaltungsblätter für Baden-Württemberg
VerfGH	Verfassungsgerichtshof (Constitutional Court)
VerwArch	Verwaltungsarchiv
VG	Verwaltungsgericht (Administrative Court)
VSSR	Vierteljahresschrift für Sozialrecht
VVDStRL	Veröffentlichungen der Vereinigung der deutschen Staatsrechtslehrer

W

WM	Zeitschrift für Wirtschaft- und Bankrecht
WTO	World Trade Organisation
WuW	Wirtschaft und Wettbewerb

Y
YECHR — Yearbook of the European Convention on Human Rights
YEL — Yearbook of European Law

Z
ZaöRV — Zeitschrift für ausländisches öffentliches Recht und Völkerrecht
ZBR — Zeitschrift für Beamtenrecht
ZEuP — Zeitschrift für europäisches Privatrecht
ZEuS — Zeitschrift für europarechtliche Studien
ZfA — Zeitschrift für Arbeitsrecht
ZfBR — Zeitschrift für deutsches und internationales Baurecht
ZfRV — Zeitschrift für Rechtsvergleichung, internationales Privatrecht und Europarecht
ZfV — Zeitschrift für Versicherungswesen
ZfZ — Zeitschrift für Zölle und Verbrauchsteuern
ZG — Zeitschrift für Gesetzgebung
ZGR — Zeitschrift für Unternehmens- und Gesellschaftsrecht
ZHR — Zeitschrift für das gesamte Handelsrecht und Wirtschaftsrecht
ZIP — Zeitschrift für Wirtschaftsrecht
ZNER — Zeitschrift für neues Energierecht
ZöR — Zeitschrift für öffentliches Recht
ZP — Zusatzprotokoll (see Prot)
ZPO — Zivilprozessordnung (German Code of Civil Procedure)
ZRP — Zeitschrift für Rechtspolitik
ZUM — Zeitschrift für Urheber- und Medienrecht
ZUR — Zeitschrift für Umweltrecht

Part I: The Notion of European Fundamental Rights and Freedoms

§ 1
History and Development of European Fundamental Rights and Fundamental Freedoms

Christian Walter

I. International and European Human Rights Protection

When understood in the context of international and supranational organisations, especially within the Council of Europe and the European Union, "European" fundamental rights and fundamental freedoms are a development of the period after World War II and form part of the then emerging international law of human rights. Among the **important milestones of international human rights protection** are the Universal Declaration of Human Rights adopted by the General Assembly of the United Nations on 10 December 1948, the European Convention for the Protection of Human Rights and Fundamental Freedoms of 4 November 1950 as well as the two 1966 Covenants on Human Rights which were developed within the United Nations: the International Covenant on Civil and Political Rights and the International Covenant on Economic, Social and Cultural Rights. This development in international law after World War II follows in the tradition of the famous human rights declarations of the times of Enlightenment, most importantly the French Declaration of 1789, the American Declaration of Independence of 1776 and the bills of rights which were declared within the New England States. From this perspective, the international protection of human rights is the continuation of a legal culture which originated in national constitutions.[1]

On the **European regional level,** the integration process after World War II spawned a number of international organisations with a variety of different aims and tasks.[2] As far as the development of fundamental rights and fundamental freedoms is concerned, the Council of Europe, the OSCE and the EC/EU are of importance. The protection of human rights within these three organisations differs in significant respects. The Council of Europe is the oldest among the three organisations. Founded in 1949, its main aim, according to Article 1 of its Statute, is to achieve a greater unity between its members for the purpose of safeguarding and realising the ideals and principles which are their common heritage. The Council of Europe mainly worked on the elaboration of legally binding treaties for the protection of human rights and on the handling of social questions.[3] In this context it has acquired a specific role as "guardian of human rights, rule of law and

---

[1] See in that context Hofmann [1989] NJW 3177; generally on the history of human rights and fundamental freedoms Oestreich *Geschichte der Menschenrechte und Grundfreiheiten im Umriss* (2nd ed, Berlin 1978); Betten/Grief *EU Law and Human Rights* (New York 1998) Chapter 1 and 2.

[2] See for survey Oppermann *Europarecht* (3rd ed, Munich 2005) § 3, paras 1–25 and Herdegen *Europarecht* (7th ed, Munich 2005) § 1, paras 6–12.

[3] See in detail the supporting documents in Oppermann (note 2) § 2, paras 9 ff.

democracy"[4]. In contrast to this, human rights protection within the OSCE in the 1970ies was characterised by its process-like way of working and the lack of hard legal obligations. Rather, the focus was on political obligations.[5] This characteristic was expressed in the former denomination of the current OSCE as "Conference on Security and Cooperation in Europe (CSCE)".[6] Both human rights protection on the basis of the legally binding treaties under the Council of Europe and the protection of human rights within the OSCE/CSCE framework aim at the protection of human rights against infringements emanating from Member States of the respective organisations.

3   In contrast to this, the discussion on the **protection of human rights within the EC/EU** is situated on a different level. Since 1 November 1993, the three European Communities (EC, ECSC[7] und EAC) have been institutionally brought together under the roof of the European Union. Most importantly, the sovereign power exercised by the EC influences the legal orders of the Member States and replaces to a considerable extent their national sovereign power. This has provoked a debate on the protection of fundamental rights against acts of European Community law. This implies that the focus is not on the protection of international human rights against interference by states, but rather on the protection and enforcement of human rights standards against a newly created, supranational sovereign power.

4   The following overview on the history and development of human rights and fundamental freedoms first deals with the protection of fundamental rights within the context of the Council of Europe, notably by the European Convention on Human Rights, and then describes and analyses the development of human rights protection in the EU context. It concludes with an analysis of the development of the fundamental freedoms in European Community law, which originally were primarily conceived as instruments against discrimination on the basis of nationality, but over time have gradually developed towards economic freedoms.

II. History and Development of Human Rights Protection in the Context of the Council of Europe and the European Convention on Human Rights

5   The Council of Europe sees its primary responsibility in the elaboration of legally binding treaty instruments for the protection of human rights. Among the more than 170 treaties which have been compiled within the Council of Europe[8], a great number deals with the protection of human rights. The most important of these treaties certainly is the Euro-

---

4 Wording in the declaration of The German Bundestag *50 Jahre Europarat: 50 Jahre europäischer Menschenrechtsschutz* BT-Drs 14/1568 of 9 September 1999, p 2.
5 In the Final Act of Helsinki (http://www.osce.org/about/15661.html) of 1975, the respect of human rights was anchored as an independent policy (principle VII) and basket III contained amongst others agreements concerning human contacts, see on this issue Hailbronner in: Graf Vitzthum (ed) *Völkerrecht* (3rd ed, Berlin 2004) sec 3, para 258.
6 The renaming to "Organisation for Security and Co-operation in Europe" took place after the political changes in Middle and Eastern Europe (*cf* summit declaration of Helsinki "The Challenges of Change", http://www.osce.org/documents/mcs/1992/07/4046_en.pdf; Bulletin of the Federal Government of Germany Nr 82 of 23 July 1992, 777, 781).
7 The ECSC-Treaty came out of force on 23 July 2002 (Art 97 ECSC-Treaty in the version of the Amsterdam Treaty); see Obwexer [2002] EuZW 517.
8 Klein (2001) 39 ArchVR 121, 123.

pean Convention for the Protection of Human Rights and Fundamental Freedoms (ECHR).

1. The Development of Human Rights Protection through the ECHR

The **European Convention on Human Rights**, which originally had only 10 Member States, has developed over the years into an international system of human rights protection in which the Member States participate and which may be functionally compared with national constitutional jurisdictions.[9] Some authors even argue that it may be qualified as a European Fundamental Rights Constitution.[10] The European Court of Human Rights uses the term "constitutional instrument of European Public Order"[11].

a) Drafting History

The idea of creating a European Convention on Human Rights including a Court for its implementation was first formed at the Congress of Europe organised by the International Committee of the Movements for European Unity. It was presided over by Winston Churchill. During the negotiations, the protection of property, the right of parents to educate their children and the right to free elections were excluded from the original draft.[12] Additionally, Member States were permitted to formulate reservations.[13] This implied that they themselves could determine the extent of their human rights obligations deriving from the Convention. The European Convention on Human Rights entered into force on 3 September 1953 after ten states had ratified the document. Among the big Western European states it was notably the French Republic which waited a long time before ratifying the Convention on 3 May 1974.

The most difficult step in the construction of a European mechanism of human rights protection was the creation of a procedure of individual complaints enabling individuals to claim a violation of their rights guaranteed under the Convention before a European organ of human rights protection. At the time, the Member States were not willing to grant individuals direct access to the European Court of Human Rights. The solution found was to admit direct individual complaints to the European Commission for Human Rights and leave it to the Commission and the Member State concerned whether to bring the case before the Court or not.[14] By contrast, a complaint brought by one Member State against another Member State was easily agreed upon because it remained within the traditional structures of international law as a law between states. As a result, the Convention provided two kinds of procedures: **state complaints** and **individual complaints**. While the procedure of state complaints was automatically accepted with accession to the Convention, the individual complaint procedure before the Commission and the submission to the Court was made subject to separate declarations of acceptance.[15]

---

9 Frowein *Collected Courses of the Academy of European Law Vol I Book 2* (Oxford 1990) pp 267, 278.
10 Hoffmeister (2001) 40 Der Staat 349, see also Walter (1999) 59 ZaöRV 961.
11 ECtHR *Loizidou* (1997) 23 EHRR 513, para 75; on this case Ress (1996) 56 ZaöRV 427.
12 In detail on the origins Brinkmeier [2000] MenschenRechtsMagazin, Themenheft „50 Jahre EMRK" 21, 26 ff; Partsch (1953/54) 15 ZaöRV 631, 633 ff; Janis/Kay/Bradley *European Human Rights Law* (2nd ed, Oxford 2000) pp 16 ff.
13 Giegerich (1995) 55 ZaöRV 713.
14 *Cf* list of institutions qualified for motion in Art 48 ECHR old version.
15 Art 25(1) and Art 46(1) ECHR old version.

9   The Commission and the Court took up their functions already in the 1950ies. The Commission was set up in 1954, after the necessary six declarations of acceptance (Article 25(4) of the ECHR old version) had been received. The creation of the Court was delayed due to the fact that Member States were even more reluctant to submit to the jurisdiction of the Court than to accept the individual complaint procedure before the Commission. It was only in 1958 that the necessary eight declarations of acceptance (Article 56 of the ECHR old version) were received.

b) Development of the Convention and Legal Practice of the Court and Commission

10 Over the years, the Convention was supplemented by **14 Additional Protocols (Prot ECHR)** which deal with both the substantive rights guaranteed and with the procedure before the Court and Commission. The protection of property, the right to educate one's children and the right to free elections, which had been in dispute during the negotiations on the Convention, were included in the 1st Prot ECHR (Articles 1 to 3). Further important additions were criminal law guarantees, such as the right not to be tried or punished twice (Article 4 of the 7th Prot ECHR), the right of appeal in criminal matters (Article 2 of the 7th Prot ECHR), the abolition of the death penalty in times of peace (Articles 1 and 2 of the 6th Prot ECHR) and, recently, its abolition in all circumstances (*ie* also in times of war, Article 1 of the 13th Prot ECHR). Further additions concerned the prohibition of imprisonment for debt (Article 1 of the 4th Prot ECHR), freedom of movement (Article 2 of the 4th Prot ECHR), prohibition of collective expulsion of aliens (Article 4 of the 4th Prot ECHR) as well as equality between spouses during marriage and in the event of its dissolution (Article 5 of the 7th Prot ECHR). In contrast to the Universal Declaration of Human Rights by the General Assembly of the United Nations (Article 7) and the International Covenant on Civil and Political Rights (Article 14, section 1), the European Convention for a long time did not contain a general equality clause. Article 14 of the ECHR is restricted to equality in respect of the rights guaranteed under the Convention.[16] With the entry into force of the 12th Prot ECHR on 1 April 2005, this situation has changed.

11 Both the 9th and 11th Prot ECHR altered the **procedure of the Strasbourg system** significantly and thus reflect the new role of the individual in international law. Under the 9th Prot ECHR, applicants who have started the procedure in front of the Commission were given the right to bring the case before the Court themselves.[17] The 11th Prot ECHR[18] amended the whole system by abolishing the Commission and the two-step-procedure. Since its entry into force on 1 November 1998, the European Court of Human Rights has been the sole judicial organ of control. In contrast to its predecessor, it now functions as a permanent institution. A further amendment which came with the 11th Prot ECHR is the compulsory jurisdiction of the Court, i.e. adherence to the Convention automatically implies acceptance of the Court's jurisdiction to hear individual complaints.[19] The former possibility of separate acceptance was abolished. By contrast, the role of the Committee

---

16 In detail Weiß [2000] MenschenRechtsMagazin, Themenheft „50 Jahre EMRK" 36, 43 ff.
17 http://www.echr.coe.int/Library/annexes/140E.pdf.
18 http://www.echr.coe.int/Library/annexes/155E.pdf.
19 Art 34 ECHR new version; in general on amendments by 6th Prot ECHR Schlette (1996) 56 ZaöRV 905; Blackburn in: Blackburn/Polakiewicz (eds) *Fundamental Rights in Europe* (Oxford 2001) pp 14 ff.

of Ministers[20] as a mechanism of observing compliance with the judgments was kept.[21] Similar to the procedure of constitutional complaint before the German Federal Constitutional Court, the overwhelming success of the individual complaint in the Strasbourg system is about to suffocate the Court. In 2001, 13.858 individual complaints were registered. During the same period 889 judgments were rendered and 8.989 applications were either declared inadmissible or struck from the list.[22] These figures led to an intensive debate of reform which resulted in the acceptance of the 14th Prot ECHR in May 2004.[23] Important changes concern the possibility of single-judge decisions on the admissibility of applications, a new hurdle on admissibility with the requirement for the applicant to demonstrate a "significant disadvantage" and the strengthening of the procedure concerning the supervision of execution of judgments. Under the 14th Prot, the Committee of Ministers has the possibility to refer to the Court questions of interpretation of its judgments and the question of whether a party has failed to fulfil its obligations of execution.

The decisive factor in the evolution of the system in the last 50 years was the only gradually growing acceptance of the **system of individual complaints**. Among the big European States only Germany – for obvious historical reasons – had accepted the Commission's competency to deal with individual complaints at an early stage. It was in 1966 that – with the UK – a second major European power followed suit. France accepted the individual complaint only in 1981. Under these circumstances of obvious reluctance on behalf of the Member States, it does not come as a surprise that the Commission and Court for a long time acted with "judicial self-restraint".[24] The reasons for such restraint today have largely been overcome. Therefore, the Court now rightly understands the Convention as a "living instrument which must be interpreted in the light of present-day conditions"[25]. This implies that the influence of the Strasbourg jurisprudence on the national legal systems of the Member States is growing steadily.[26] This fact is exemplified most impressively by France, which traditionally does not allow the retroactive control of laws already in force by its Constitutional Council. Today, the ordinary Courts conduct a so-called "contrôle de conventionnalité", *ie* a review of the conformity of laws with the European Convention on Human Rights. There have already been cases in which the application of (otherwise valid) laws was refused because the Courts decided that their application would violate the Convention.[27] The quasi-constitutional character of the judicial control exercised by the European Court of Human Rights is also evidenced by the fact that highly political issues are dealt with in Strasbourg, such as the criminal liabil-

12

---

20 Arts 13 ff Statute of the Council of Europe.
21 Art 46(2) ECHR new version.
22 Press release of the Court of 21 January 2002.
23 The 14th Prot ECHR has been duly ratified by all Member States except for Russia. The Russian Duma refused to ratify in December 2006, which brought the reform to a standstill, [2006] EuGRZ 704.
24 → to dogmatics of fundamental rights in the ECHR see § 2.
25 ECtHR *Tyrer* (1979–80) 2 EHRR 1, para 31; critical on the in his opinion too dynamic interpretation of the ECHR by the Court Buß [1998] DÖV 323, 328 ff.
26 Supporting documents and special problems with reference to Germany in Frowein [2002] NVwZ 29.
27 See for example the *Lorenzi* decision of the French Conseil d'Etat of 30 October 1998, RDP 1999, 649.

ity of the political leaders of the former GDR for the killings at the German-German border or the prohibition of political parties in Turkey.[28]

13 The **incorporation of the Convention into the British national system** through the Human Rights Act of 1998 was certainly a major step in the process of integrating the Convention into the national legal orders.[29] Under British constitutional law, without such incorporation an international treaty cannot produce rights and obligations for individuals. This had led to a comparatively high number of procedures against the UK.[30] Since the entry into force of the Human Rights Act on 2 October 2000, an impressive jurisprudence of British Courts has evolved which also enhances the international importance of the Convention.[31] Before 2 October 2000, domestic courts used the Convention mostly for construing statutory provisions whose meaning was unclear by presuming that the Parliament intended to legislate in conformity with the convention, not in conflict with it.[32] Now that the Human Rights Act is in force, however, domestic courts are required to apply the Convention directly within the justice system of the UK. Individuals claiming to be aggrieved by an act or omission on the part of a public authority can now challenge this act or omission in the courts and obtain remedy and just satisfaction.[33] However, while the Human Rights Act did not provide the Convention with legal priority over earlier or later domestic UK legislation, Sections 3 and 4 of the Human Rights Act do provide alternative methods for domestic courts. Pursuant to Section 3, courts are required to interpret national legislation in conformity with the Convention to the extent possible. In all other cases they may make a declaration of incompatibility, which, however, does not affect the validity and continuing operation of the provision in question. While this procedure on a formal level respects the principle of Parliament, a declaration of incompatibility by the judiciary nevertheless is able to exude considerable pressure on the authorities to bring the law in question into conformity with the Convention.[34]

14 Within the German legal order, the Convention has the rank of **ordinary federal law**. According to the jurisprudence of the Federal Constitutional Court, the rights guaranteed by the Convention have to be taken into account when interpreting the fundamental rights of the *Grundgesetz* (German Basic Law).[35] Attempts in the literature to develop arguments in favour of a binding force of the Convention beyond this jurisprudence[36]

---

28 ECtHR *Streletz, Kessler and Krenz* (2001) 33 EHRR 751; see Werle [2001] NJW 3001; Rau [2001] NJW 3008; ECtHR *Refah-Partisi* (2002) 35 EHRR 56; *ÖZDEP* (1999) 31 EHRR 675.
29 See Grote (1998) 58 ZaöRV 309; *cf* also the Irish European Convention on Human Rights Bill (No 26 of 2001) of 10 April 2001; Polakiewicz in: Blackburn/Polakiewicz (eds) *Fundamental Rights in Europe* (Oxford 2001) p 42.
30 Supporting documents in Grote (1998) 58 ZaöRV 309, 322 ff; Betten/Grief (note 1) pp 139 ff.
31 *Cf* chart by Raine/Walker in: Halliday/Schmidt (eds) *Human Rights brought home* (Oxford 2004) pp 123 ff.
32 *Cf* Blackburn (note 19), pp 949 ff for supporting documents.
33 Elaborately on these legal proceedings Blackburn (note 19) p 966.
34 Blackburn (note 19) pp 962–963.
35 *Bundesverfassungsgericht* (BVerfG – German Federal Constitutional Court) (1987) 74 BVerfGE 358, 370; (1991) 82 BVerfGE 106, 115.
36 With different approaches Bleckmann [1994] EuGRZ 149; Frowein *Der Europäische Grundrechtsschutz und die nationale Gerichtsbarkeit* (Berlin 1983) p 26; Ress in: FS Zeidler (Berlin 1987) pp 1775, 1790 ff; as well as supporting documents in Hoffmeister (2001) 40 Der Staat 349; Walter (1999) 59 ZaöRV 961.

have so far not been taken up by the Constitutional Court.[37] However, in 2004, the Constitutional Court came up with a new formula on how to implement decisions of the European Court of Human Rights into German jurisprudence. In the case in question, the Court of Appeal's dealing with the case had refused to follow a decision by the European Court of Human Rights. It stated that as a result of the status of the Convention as ordinary statutory law below the level of the constitution, the European Court of Human Rights was not functionally a higher-ranking one in relation to national German courts. For this reason it declared itself not to be bound by European Courts' interpretations of the Convention. The Federal Constitutional Court replied to this by clearly stressing that "the principle that the judge is bound by statute and law includes taking into account the guarantees of the European Convention for the Protection of Human Rights and Fundamental Freedoms and the decisions of the European Court of Human Rights as part of a methodologically justifiable interpretation of the law. Both a failure to consider a decision of the European Court of Human Rights and the 'enforcement' of such a decision in a schematic way, in violation of prior-ranking law, may therefore violate fundamental rights in conjunction with the principle of the rule of law."[38] This implies that non-compliance with a decision by the European Court of Human Rights may be brought before the Federal Constitutional Court as a violation of fundamental rights guaranteed in national constitutional law. It should not be overlooked, however, that in this decision the Federal Constitutional Court also stressed the priority of German constitutional law in case of a conflict with its obligations under the Convention[39].

More precisely, the Constitutional Court then defines that "taking into account means taking notice of the Convention provision as interpreted by the European Court of Human Rights and applying it to the case, provided the application does not violate prior-ranking law, in particular constitutional law. In any event, the Convention provision as interpreted by the European Court of Human Rights must be taken into account in making a decision; the court must at least duly consider it."[40]

15

In recent years, the European Court of Human Rights has repeatedly dealt with the questions regarding the extent of Convention duties in cases where Member States **transfer sovereign rights**, which until then were exercised at the national level, to international organisations.[41] In its most recent jurisdiction,[42] the Court requires the Member States to provide a level of protection equivalent to that of the ECHR. This was decided in several cases concerning protection against unfair dismissal by the European Space Agency (ESA).[43]

16

---

37 See in detail to the whole topic Grabenwarter (2000) 60 VVDStRL 290, 299 ff.
38 BVerfG (2005) 111 BVerfGE 307, 325–326; available in English at http://www.bverfg.de/entscheidungen/rs20041014_2bvr148104e.html; see the commentary by Cremer [2004] EuGRZ 683; cf also Blackburn (note 19) p 965 regarding obligations to UK domestic courts to take into account the Strasbourg decisions.
39 Frowein in: FS Delbrück (Berlin 2005) pp 279, 285; Hartwig [2005] German Law Journal No 5, http://www.germanlawjournal.com/article.php?id=600.
40 BVerfG (2005) 111 BVerfGE 307, 329.
41 In detail on the connected legal problems Winkler *Der Beitritt der Europäischen Gemeinschaften zur Europäischen Menschenrechtskonvention* (Baden-Baden 2000) pp 153 ff; → § 2 paras 31–32; § 14 para 14.
42 An early decision by the Commission to this issue is the case M, see Giegerich (1990) 50 ZaöRV 836.
43 ECtHR *Waite* (2000) 30 EHRR 261.

17 Until now, there is no decision which states a direct obligation of European Community organs by the Convention.[44] However, the European Court of Human Rights has qualified the European Parliament as "legislature" within the meaning of Article 3 of the 1st Prot ECHR and it stated that the UK violated this provision because it did not allow people residing in Gibraltar to participate in the European elections.[45] This jurisprudence may be viewed as an attempt by the Court to not only enforce the human rights obligations of the ECHR in the national legal orders of the Member States, but also to ensure that the Member States do not avoid their ECHR obligations by "fleeing into organisationally independent units on the trans-national level".[46] In order to do so, the Court has developed a positive obligation of Member States from Article 1 of the ECHR.[47]

18 In an important recent decision, the European Court of Human Rights followed a rather comprehensive way of controlling the human rights standard in the European Union. In the *Bosphorus*-case, the European Court of Human Rights had to rule indirectly on the compatibility with the Convention of a European regulation which enacted sanctions against the former Yugoslavia. While the Court in the end denied a violation of Article 1 of the 1st Prot ECHR, it nevertheless pointed out that the Member States are not free from their responsibility under Convention when they transfer sovereign rights to an international organisation. In fact, the Court set up a specific two-step test for dealing with such cases. On a first level, it stated that transfer of public authority to an international organisation is in compliance with obligations under the Convention "as long as the relevant organisation is considered to protect fundamental rights, as regards both the substantive guarantees offered and the mechanisms controlling their observance, in a manner which can be considered at least equivalent to that for what the Convention provides [...]. By "equivalent" the Court means "comparable".[48] If this condition is met, the Court works with a presumption of compatibility: "If such an equivalent protection is considered to be provided by the organisation, the presumption will be that a State has not departed from the requirements of the Convention when it does no more than implement legal obligations flowing from its membership of the organisation. However, any such presumption can be rebutted if, in the circumstances of a particular case, it is considered that the protection of Convention rights was manifestly deficient. In such cases, the interest of international co-operation would be outweighed by the Convention's role as a 'constitutional instrument of European public order' in the field of human rights."[49] The Court then states with respect to the EC that it fulfils the conditions of the presumption and that the presumption has not been rebutted in the case at hand. The test developed in this important decision could be applied to any other international organisation which has the power to directly affect individual rights. Such legal problems, created by globalisation

---

44 The case *Senator Lines* against the 15 EU Member States (*cf* the motion in (2000) 12 RUDH 191) became moot and was hence rejected as inadmissable; the same question however plays a role again in a case called Emesa Sugar (App No 62023/00).
45 ECtHR *Matthews* (1999) 28 EHRR 361.
46 Thus the wording of the German Federal Constitutional Court in a similar case [2001] DVBl 1130.
47 ECtHR *Matthews* (1999) 30 EHRR 361, paras 29 ff.
48 ECtHR *Bosphorus* (2006) 42 EHRR 1, para 155.
49 ECtHR *Bosphorus* (2006) 42 EHRR 1, para 156.

and internationalisation, will certainly require further developments in the theory and practice of European human rights[50].

2. *Human Rights Protection in the Council of Europe in General*

a) Treaty-based Human Rights Guarantees

Among the **human rights guaranteed in treaties created under the auspices of the Council of Europe**, some developments merit further elaboration. Already in 1961, the European Social Charter was adopted in which the Member States declared that they are resolved to "make every effort to improve the standard of living and to promote the social well-being of both their urban and rural populations"[51]. The Charter offers its Member States the possibility to choose five binding rights from a catalogue of seven (Article 20), and it maintains a surveillance procedure according to which Member States have to present biannual reports concerning the five rights chosen and, at appropriate intervals, concerning all other rights (Articles 21 and 22). These reports are examined by a Committee of Experts (Article 24). Just like the ECHR, the Social Charter has been supplemented by Additional Protocols. In 1996, these additions were combined in a revised Social Charter, which entered into force on 1 July 1999. Important European States like Spain or the UK have not yet ratified it. Germany is among the few States that did not even sign the revised text[52].

The **European Convention for the Prevention of Torture and Inhuman or Degrading Treatment or Punishment** of 26 November 1987 merits special attention because of its preventive mechanisms.[53] It establishes a Committee, the European Committee for the Prevention of Torture and Inhuman or Degrading Treatment or Punishment, which may visit any place where persons are deprived of their liberty by a public authority[54] and which reports on these visits, if the party concerned so agrees, even publicly. The most important element in the system established by the convention is the possibility of the Committee to make any recommendations it considers necessary (Article 10(1)). The Committee not only uses this possibility for recommendations concerning grievances which it has actually found. Additionally, it has used this competence in order to formulate general propositions for the prevention of inhuman or degrading treatment and has thus paved the way for preventive action against torture.

In recent years, the work of the Council of Europe on the codification of human rights protection has mainly focussed on the specific problems of **minority protection**. On 5 November 1992, the European Charter for Regional or Minority Languages was adopted, which is also subject to surveillance by a Committee of Experts. Additional protection is provided by the Framework Convention for the Protection of National Minorities of 1 February 1995.[55] This Framework Convention contains a comprehensive catalogue of

---

50 See Walter (2004) 129 AöR 39.
51 Thus the motivation after the fourth consideration in the preamble of the European Social Charter; ETS No 035.
52 ETS No 163.
53 Janis/Kay/Bradley (note 12) pp 93 ff.
54 Including psychiatric and other locked wards, *cf* Alleweldt [1998] EuGRZ 245, 247 with Giegerich (1990) 50 ZaöRV 836; Ovey/White *European Convention on Human Rights* (3rd ed, Oxford 2002) pp 87–88.
55 http://conventions.coe.int/Treaty/EN/Treaties/Html/157.htm.

minority rights[56] and a separate mechanism of control.[57] It entered into force in Germany on 1 February 1998. The protection of minorities within the Council of Europe creates special problems for France. The French Constitutional Council decided in 1997 that the constitutional principle of "unity of the Republic" prohibited its participation in the European Charter for European and Minority Languages[58]. Consequently, the Framework Convention was not even signed by France.

22   A further recent area of codification concerns **medical and bioethical issues**. In this regard the Convention on Human Rights and Biomedicine of 4 April 1997 and Additional Protocol on the Prohibition of Cloning of Human Beings of 12 January 1998 deserve mentioning. As it considers the level of protection to be insufficient, Germany has maintained a rather critical attitude towards the work of the Council of Europe in this area. Neither the Convention nor the Additional Protocol was signed by Germany.

b) The Work of the Parliamentary Assembly after 1989/1990

23   Together with the Committee of Ministers, the **Parliamentary Assembly** is one of the central organs of the Council of Europe.[59] It acquired an important role in the supervision and promotion of human rights in the years after the end of the Cold War. Already in 1949, the Committee of Ministers committed itself to using its right in Article 4 of the Statute to invite new members to the Council only in close co-operation with the Parliamentary Assembly. The Parliamentary Assembly used this right of participation in order to review the standard of human rights protection in the membership candidates among the former Middle- and East-European states. In doing so, it sent rapporteurs into the respective states that had the task of reviewing the national legal orders in terms of their conformity with the human rights standards of the Council of Europe. The Parliamentary Assembly also started to formally note the intention of the candidate to become a member of the European Convention on Human Rights and its willingness to accept the individual complaint procedure (which was still necessary at the time). Later, the Parliamentary Assembly supplemented these conditions of admittance with a surveillance procedure which was designed to monitor the execution of the obligations after the state concerned was admitted to membership in the Council of Europe. During the war in Chechnya, this practice had the consequence that the Parliamentary Assembly questioned Russia's membership in the Council of Europe.[60] Due to the implementation of these procedures, the Parliamentary Assembly has acquired a particular renown for the implementation and promotion of human rights standards in the Middle- and East-European States after the end of the Cold War. Today, the Parliamentary Assembly is also concerned with human rights infringements committed in the fight against terrorism. Its investigation into secret detentions lead in June 2006 to a report that uncovered "a global spider's web" of CIA detentions involving several Member States.[61]

---

56 See in detail Hofmann [2000] MenschenRechtsMagazin 63.
57 On this Hofmann [1999] ZEuS 379.
58 Decision No 99–412 DC of 15 June 1999; available at http://www.conseil-constitutionnel.fr/decision/1999/99412/index.htm.
59 The Parliamentary Assembly assembles members of national parliaments (*cf* Art 25 of the Statute of the Council of Europe); see diagram in Blackburn/Polakiewicz (note 19) p 23.
60 See Recommendation 1444 (2000) of 27 January 2000 and Resolution 1221 (2000) of 29 June 2000; in general Bowring (2000) 11 Helsinki Monitor 53.
61 "Alleged secret detentions and unlawful inter-state transfers of detainees involving Council of

III. History and Development of Human Rights Protection within the EC/EU

In contrast to the ECHR, which aims at assuring a minimum standard of human rights protection against the public power of the Member States, the question of **human rights protection in the EC/EU** deals with the issue of the protection of fundamental rights against a non-state public power (→ § 14 paras 4 ff).

1. Early Jurisprudence

In its early jurisprudence, the European Court in Luxemburg created the impression of a lack of sensitivity towards the issue of human rights protection[62]. It refused as inadmissible complaint about violations of national human rights standards by European Community law without really addressing the human rights issue behind these disputes[63]. This approach by the Court was compelling from a strictly legal point of view because the Court can neither interpret national norms, nor can it apply them against European Community law. However, the combination of the (correct) decision that Article 14 of the Basic Law was inapplicable when confronted with European Community law with the statement that European Community law "does not contain any general principle, express or otherwise guaranteeing the maintenance of vested rights."[64], necessarily provoked doubts as to the protection of property in European Community law (→ more specifically § 17).

2. Development and Legal Foundation of Human Rights of the EC/EU

The Court changed this restrictive jurisprudence in the late 1960ies and considered human rights to be part of European Community law as **general principles of law**. The development starts with the *Stauder* judgment[65]. This case concerned the dispensing of butter to social welfare recipients at reduced prices. In order to avoid abuse, European Community law required the Member States to make sure that the beneficiaries received this butter only if they presented – according to the German version of the text – "a voucher issued in their name". In the other languages, the term "individualised voucher" was used. Stauder, the plaintiff in the case, was of the opinion that it was incompatible with his human rights to disclose his name, and thus his identity, when purchasing butter at the lower price. In view of the different linguistic versions, the Court concluded that only an individualisation was required, not the mentioning of the name. After having thus interpreted the Community norm in question, the Court adds – as a supplementary consideration,

---

Europe member states" Report of 12 June 2006, Doc. 10957 (2006), http://www.coe.int/T/E/Com/Files/Events/2006-cia/.

62 See to the following also Kühling in: von Bogdandy (ed) *Europäisches Verfassungsrecht* (Heidelberg 2003) pp 583, 586 ff.

63 *Cf* for example ECJ *Ruhrkohlen-Verkaufsgesellschaft* [1960] ECR 857, 920 ff; *Sgarlata* [1965] ECR 279, 312 (not allowing the express provisions of the Treaty to be overridden by a plea which was founded upon other principles, even if those were fundamental principles which were common to the legal systems of all the Member States); also *cf* Craig/de Burca *EU Law* (3rd ed, Oxford 2003) pp 319 ff.

64 ECJ *Ruhrkohlen-Verkaufsgesellschaft* [1960] ECR 887, 921.

65 ECJ *Stauder* [1969] ECR 419; Betten/Grief (note 1) pp 56–57; Weatherill *Cases and Materials on EU Law* (7th ed, Oxford 2006) pp 69 ff.

which strictly speaking would not have been necessary – a very brief deduction of the legal basis of human rights in European Community law:

27 "Interpreted in this way, the provision at issue contains nothing capable of prejudicing the fundamental human rights enshrined in the general principles of Community law as protected by the Court."

28 A **more elaborate legal reasoning** was presented by Advocate General *Römer,* who followed arguments presented in legal literature at the time when he concluded, "that general qualitative concepts of national constitutional law, in particular fundamental rights recognized by national law, must be ascertained by means of a comparative evaluation of laws, and such concepts, which form an unwritten constituent part of Community law, must be observed in making secondary Community law."[66]

29 The important difference to the reasoning rejected by the Court in its earlier jurisprudence lies in the fact that the reasoning adopted by the Advocate General does not seek the basis of human rights protection in the human rights standards of a specific Member State, nor does it apply national human rights directly, but only considers them as a **secondary source of cognition** ("Rechtserkenntnisquelle") for determining the unwritten Community human rights standards. (→ § 14 para 8). The Court confirmed this legal construction in 1970 in its *Internationale Handelsgesellschaft* case. In this decision, the Court stressed that the supremacy of European Community law was also valid when confronted with national constitutional law, including its human rights guarantees. However, in addition the Court states that human rights protection is assured on the European level by the Court itself, a European human rights standard based on **"constitutional traditions common to the Member States"**.[67]

30 In 1974, with the *Nold* decision, the Court added to the "constitutional traditions common to the Member States" a further source of cognition for Community human rights standards. In this case, the Court decided that **international treaties** concluded by the Member States may "supply guidelines which should be followed within the framework of Community law"[68]. This rather cautious wording was strengthened in the following years with respect to the **ECHR**. Today, it serves as the basis for a rather comprehensive reception of the jurisprudence of the European Court of Human Rights in Strasbourg (ECtHR) by the European Court of Justice in Luxemburg. The ECJ has repeatedly highlighted the special significance of the ECHR as opposed to other international human rights treaties.[69] Also, the ECJ today as a matter of course relies on precedents from Strasbourg when confronted with the interpretation of the ECHR in order to develop corresponding Community human rights standards. An impressive example may be found regarding the right to a procedure within reasonable time. In this area, a rather elaborate jurisprudence by the ECtHR concerning Article 6(1) of the ECHR exists[70]. The ECJ adopted this jurisprudence offhandedly in a case concerning the duration of procedure before the Court of

---

66 ECJ *Stauder* [1969] ECR 419, 427–428; Craig/de Burca (note 63) p 321.
67 ECJ *Internationale Handelsgesellschaft* [1970] ECR 1125, para 4.
68 ECJ *Nold* [1974] ECR 491, para 13.
69 For example ECJ *Annibaldi* [1997] ECR I-7493, para 12; as far as the specific importance of the ECHR is concerned, the Court itself considers its decision *Johnston* [1986] ECR 1651, para 18 to be fundamental, see *ERT* [1991] ECR I-2925, para 41; see also Betten/Grief (note 1) pp 90 ff; Steiner/Woods *EC Law* (8th ed, Oxford 2003) pp 157 ff.
70 See in detail Peukert in: Frowein/Peukert *Europäische Menschenrechtskonvention* (2nd ed, Kehl 1996) Art 6 EMRK, paras 136 ff.

First Instance. The relevant passage creates the impression that the ECJ felt itself to be bound by the Strasbourg jurisprudence[71]. However, the natural manner in which the ECJ adopts the Strasbourg case-law should not obscure the legal construction of Community human rights. In spite of several propositions in the literature[72], the ECJ has until now refused to accept the ECHR as formally binding on the EC/EU. Under the current legal construction, the conclusion is inevitable that the ECHR is no more than a secondary source of cognition for the determination of Community human rights. It does not constitute a source of Community law by itself.[73] The Court has stressed this point explicitly on several occasions.[74] Due to this comparative approach, divergence of interpretation can not be avoided completely. This holds even more true when the Luxemburg Court has to deal with a question of human rights interpretation which has not yet been decided in Strasbourg.[75]

On the basis of the two sources of cognition just described (constitutional traditions common to the Member States and international human rights treaties, notably the ECHR), the ECJ and the Court of First Instance have developed a rather comprehensive **catalogue of unwritten human rights** (→ comprehensively §§ 14–19). The German Federal Constitutional Court, which was initially rather sceptical regarding human rights protection by the ECJ and hence claimed a right to human rights protection against Community law (Decision *Solange I*)[76], decided in 1986, that the level of human rights protection guaranteed by the ECJ was generally equivalent to its own standard of protection (Decision *Solange II*).[77] Henceforth, constitutional complaints and requests for judicial review of statutory provisions which are directed against European Community law have been considered inadmissible. Some doubts as to the continued validity of this jurisprudence, which had been created by the wording of the Maastricht-judgment[78], were dissolved in 2000 by the Court's decision concerning the Common Organisation of the Market in Bananas.[79]

31

---

71 ECJ *Baustahlgewebe* [1998] ECR I-8417, para 29; see, however, also the opposite tendency in ECJ *Emesa Sugar* [2000] ECR I-665, paras 4 ff; see also the critical remarks by Krüger/Polakiewicz [2001] EuGRZ 92, 98.
72 See for example Hilf in: Recht zwischen Umbruch und Bewahrung (Berlin 1995) pp 1193, 1197–1198; further supporting documents to be found at Kingreen in: Calliess/Ruffert *Kommentar des Vertrages über die Europäische Union* (2nd ed, Neuwied 2002) Art 6 EUV, para 38.
73 Kingreen (note 72) Art 6 EUV, para 35; → § 14 para 9.
74 CFI *Mannesmann-Röhrenwerke AG* [2001] ECR II-729, para 59; *Mayr-Melnhof v Commission* [1998] ECR II-1751, paras 311–312.
75 That might be an explanation for the most conspicuous divergence so far that can be ascertained in the case law of both courts: The ECJ decided in 1989 under explicit use of Art 8 ECHR, that the fundamental right of the inviolability of the home does not apply to the protection of business offices (ECJ *Hoechst* [1989] ECR 2859, para 18). The ECtHR, which had to deal with the same legal question not earlier than in 1992, decided exactly contrary, ECtHR *Niemitz* (1993) 17 EHRR 97, para 29.
76 BVerfG *Solange I* [1974] 2 CMLR 540; see for introduction: Betten/Grief (note 1) pp 64 ff.
77 BVerfG *Solange II* [1987] 3 CMLR 225.
78 BVerfG *Maastricht* [1994] 1 CMLR 57.
79 BVerfG *Bananas Case* (2001) 102 BVerfGE 147; see in this context the assessment in Nicolaysen/Nowak [2001] NJW 1233, 1235–1236 and in Aziz [2003] ConWEB No 3, http://les1.man.ac.uk/conweb.

32 In 1993, the jurisprudential construction adopted by the ECJ for the foundation of Community human rights found a partial[80] formal basis in the Treaty on European Union (TEU). According to **Article 6(2) of the TEU**, the Union "shall respect fundamental rights, as guaranteed by the European Convention for the Protection of Human Rights and Fundamental Freedoms signed in Rome on 4 November 1950 and as they result from the constitutional traditions common to the Member States, as general principles of Community law."

3. The Debate Concerning Accession to the ECHR

33 In spite of the legal guarantees created by this jurisprudence, the situation without a written catalogue of human rights was considered insufficient in many places.[81] This brought about both ambitions for the creation of an autonomous Community law human rights catalogue[82] and intentions to **accede formally to the ECHR**. In favour of acceding to the ECHR, it has been and still is argued that this would avoid a duplication of European human rights standards and allow for a single institutional mechanism of control of the standards exercised by the European Court of Human Rights in Strasbourg.[83] The Commission had already proposed accession of the Community to the ECHR in a memorandum dating from 1979.[84] The European Parliament had also favoured such proposals.[85]

34 There are, however, several obstacles to formal accession.[86] On the side of the ECHR, the problem is that the Convention only allows "members of the Council of Europe" to accede,[87] whereas the Statute of the Council of Europe only provides membership for "states".[88] The 14th Prot ECHR envisages an amendment of the Convention in this respect in explicitly allowing accession of the European Union to the ECHR. Regarding European Community law, the question of the Community's competence for concluding a human rights treaty was raised. When the ECJ was asked by the Council to render an advisory opinion on the issue, the Court answered in the negative, arguing that competence in external relations was dependent on a corresponding internal competence vis à vis the Member States.[89] The Court argued that while it was true that respect of fundamental

---

80 Besides the fundamental principles which are common to the legal systems of all the Member States, Article 6(2) of the TEU only refers to the European Convention on Human Rights, while the earlier case law of the ECJ in general mentioned international treaties on the protection of human rights concluded by the Member States as a source of legal cognition and highlighted the ECHR only as one especially important treaty amongst others; also *cf* Betten/Grief (note 1) pp 130 ff.
81 See instead of others Kokott (1996) 121 AöR 599, 602.
82 On this forthwith under para 35.
83 See for example Wildhaber [2000] Zeitschrift für schweizerisches Recht 123, 134.
84 [1979] EuGRZ 330; see the comments by Bieber [1979] EuGRZ 338.
85 Resolution of 27 April 1979, [1979] EuGRZ 257; also see resolution of 18 January 1994 regarding the accession of the Community to the European Convention on Human Rights, [1994] OJ C 44/32.
86 Betten/Grief (note 1) pp 115 ff; Gaja in: Alston (ed) *The EU and human rights* (Oxford 1999) pp 793 ff.
87 Art 59(2)(i) ECHR.
88 Art 4(i) of the Statute of the Council of Europe; proposals for solutions to this problem can be found in the Memorandum of the Commission [1979] EuGRZ 330, 337 (para VII); see also Bernhardt in: Festschrift für Ulrich Everling (Baden-Baden 1995) pp 103 ff; Krüger/Polakiewicz [2001] EuGRZ 92, 102.
89 ECJ *AETR* [1971] ECR 263, paras 15 ff.

human rights guarantees was a condition for the legality of Community and Union action, a formal accession of the Union to the ECHR would entail so fundamental a change in the structure of the system of judicial protection, that accession could not be based on the residual **legislative power** of Article 235 of the TEC (Article 308 TEC/Article I-18 DC).[90] Hence an amendment of the founding treaties would have been necessary. Such an amendment was neither included in Amsterdam nor in Nice. Instead, the Member States opted for the adoption of an autonomous catalogue of human rights of the European Union, namely the Charter of Fundamental Rights of the European Union[91]. With the deliberations on a **"Treaty Establishing a Constitution for Europe"**, this reticence was abandoned. While earlier versions only provided for the possibility of accession or spoke of a political intention ("the Union shall seek accession")[92], the text adopted on 29 October 2004 in Rome uses in its German and French versions the indicative mode ("die Union tritt bei"), while the English version contains an instruction ("the Union shall accede")[93]. Irrespective of the divergence in the different languages, it seems clear that the mere use of the indicative mode cannot automatically bring about the accession to the ECHR with the entry into force of the Treaty Establishing a Constitution for Europe, because the procedure provided for accession to the ECHR has to be respected. Nevertheless, the explicit political intention to accede to the ECHR contained in Article I-9 of the Treaty Establishing a Constitution for Europe remains remarkable.

4. Demands for a Catalogue of Human Rights of the EU and the European Charter of Fundamental Rights[94]

The political demands for a human rights catalogue, which finally led to the proclamation of the **Charter of Fundamental Rights of the European Union** on the occasion of the European Council on 7 December 2000 in Nice,[95] were not new. With the "Declaration of fundamental rights and freedoms", the European Parliament had already adopted the first comprehensive human rights catalogue of European Community law in 1989.[96] This declaration does not only contain classical freedoms such as those enshrined in the ECHR, but also social rights such as a right to education (Article 16) or a right to social welfare (Article 15). A comparable catalogue, including corresponding social rights, may also be found in the European Parliament Resolution on the Constitution of the European Union, which the European Parliament adopted on 10 February 1994.[97]

The text of the European Charter of Fundamental Rights adopted in Nice was not negotiated in the usual form of an inter-governmental conference, but by a **"Convention"**. This implied a new form of participation of national Parliaments and the public in general. The Convention instituted by the European Council of Tampere (Finland) consisted of 15 members sent by national governments, 16 members of the European Parliament,

---

90 ECJ *Opinion 2/94* [1996] ECR I-1759, para 35.
91 Grabenwarter in: Tradition und Weltoffenheit des Rechts (Berlin 2002) pp 1129, 1148 ff.
92 In detail Grabenwarter [2004] EuGRZ 563, 569.
93 Art I-9 DC.
94 → Elaborate to the European Charter of Fundamental Rights § 20; see for an introduction: Carolan *EU Law for Irish Students* (Dublin, 2004) pp 124–125; Steiner/Woods (note 69) pp 162 ff.
95 [2000] OJ C364/1.
96 [1989] OJ C120/51.
97 [1994] OJ C61/155.

30 members of national Parliaments and a Commissioner as representative of the Commission. This departure from the traditional form of intergovernmental collaboration may be qualified as a step of "constitutional significance"[98] and bestows a degree of (parliamentary) legitimacy upon the Charter which until then was unknown to the European level.[99] However, the European Council of Nice confined itself to a mere formal proclamation and refused to accord the Charter a formal legal status or even to integrate it into the binding primary law of the Union. Consequently, the proclamation of the Charter implies a political commitment to common European standards of human rights protection, but **does not create legally binding obligations for the Community organs.**

37 However, it would mean underestimating the indirect legal effects of the Charter if one were to qualify it as currently irrelevant to the development of European human rights protection because of its lacking binding character[100]. The Charter contains the **most modern systematisation of fundamental rights** and, because of the composition of the Convent and the principle of consensus which was largely followed in its deliberations, must be viewed as an authoritative representation of the human rights standards of the European Union. Already for this reason alone one may safely assume that the Charter will be groundbreaking in the future. The systematising effects which it brings about are already visible in the fact that the Advocates General at the European Court of Justice frequently refer to the Charter in their conclusions in order to confirm a result which they have reached by using the traditionally accepted sources of cognition. In January 2002, the Court of First Instance for the first time used the Charter in a similar manner in order to confirm human rights which it had developed from the constitutional traditions common to the Member States[101]. In June 2006, the European Court of Justice followed suit.[102] According to the decisions of the European Council of 23 June 2007 the Charter will become binding by an explicit reference in Art 6(2) of the TEU.

5. The Scope of Application of Fundamental Rights of the Union

38 Based on a review of their historical development, the human rights of the European Union could initially be understood as a means of binding the Community organs to a common human rights standard. **Article 6(2) of the TEU,** according to which *"the Union respects the fundamental rights ..."*[103], expresses quite clearly that the Union (and hence also the EC) are the addressees of the obligation. However, in view of the supranational character of Community law and the close interlocking between Community law and national law of the Member States, the question of the exact reach of Community human rights obligations, and especially their extension towards acts of the Member States, could not remain unanswered.[104] The Court distinguished two groups of cases in which Member States have to respect Community human rights: 1) in situations where their national authorities apply European Community law, and 2) when they lawfully restrict the funda-

---

98 *Cf* Leinen/Schönlau (2001) 24 integration 26.
99 Bernsdorff [2001] NdsVBl 177, 178.
100 Kühling (note 62) pp 583, 593 ff.
101 CFI *max.mobil Telekommunikation Service GmbH* [2002] ECR II-313, para 48.
102 ECJ *Parliament v Council* [2006] ECR I-5769, paras 38 and 58.
103 Emphasis added.
104 See in this context Ruffert [1995] EuGRZ 518; → § 14 paras 33 ff.

mental freedoms guaranteed in European Community law.[105] Apart from these cases, the Court stated explicitly in 1998 that the fundamental rights of the European Union may not "in themselves have the effect of extending the scope of the Treaty provisions beyond the competencies of the Community".[106]

Furthermore, in its **foreign relations,** the Union pursues elements of what may be called a human rights policy. The agreements of association which the Community has concluded with several states contain human rights clauses in which the continued collaboration is made subject to the respect of certain minimum standards of protection.[107] However, beyond this rather limited area, there is no specific human rights policy of the European Union.[108]

Recently, the Court of First Instance decided, whether the European Community had to consider **human rights while implementing sanctions agreed upon in the United Nations Security Council.** In the *Yusuf* case, the complainant had been listed in a Commission Regulation ordering that financial funds and economic resources belonging to certain individuals be frozen. These "smart" sanctions combating international terrorism had been prescribed by Security Council Resolutions. The Court of First Instance refused to indirectly review the lawfulness of Security Council resolutions on the basis of Community law human rights guarantees. However, it saw itself "empowered to check, indirectly, the lawfulness of the resolutions of the Security Council with regard to *jus cogens*, understood as a body of higher rules of public international law binding all subjects of international law, including the bodies of the United Nations".[109] One may doubt that *jus cogens* provides for an appropriate standard of human rights protection in such cases, since it comprises only some of the most fundamental norms of international law, such as the prohibition of genocide or slavery. As a consequence, the rights invoked by *Yusuf*, *ie* the right to the use of property and right to a fair hearing and to effective judicial remedy, were not held to be violated even though the Court of First Instance, in this particular decision, already showed a rather wide conception of *jus cogens*.

IV. The Fundamental Freedoms of European Community Law

According to Article 14(2) of the TEC (Article III-130(2) DC), the common market is characterised by the free movement of goods, persons, services and capital. The so-called market or **fundamental freedoms** are central pillars of European Community law. The term "fundamental freedoms" is not expressly used in the treaties, but has long been used in the German legal literature.[110] Since the early 1980ies it has also been used by the Euro-

---

105 ECJ *Wachauf* [1989] ECR 2609, para 19; *ERT* [1991] ECR I-2925, paras 42–43; in detail Kingreen (note 72) Art 6 EUV, paras 56 ff
106 ECJ *Grant* [1998] ECR I-621, para 45; the Treaty establishing a Constitution for Europe in Art II-111 also contains such a restraint.
107 Elaborating on these clauses: Hoffmeister *Menschenrechts- und Demokratieklauseln in den vertraglichen Außenbeziehungen der Europäischen Gemeinschaft* (Berlin 1998); Simma/Aschenbrenner/Schulte in: Alston (ed) *The EU and human rights* (Oxford 1999) pp 571 ff.
108 See on the one hand Alston/Weiler in: Alston (ed) *The EU and human rights* (Oxford 1999) pp 3 ff and on the other hand von Bogdandy [2001] JZ 157.
109 CFI *Yusuf* [2005] ECR II-3533, paras 226 ff, para 276 and 277.
110 On this term see Kingreen in: von Bogdandy (ed) *Europäisches Verfassungsrecht* (Heidelberg 2003) pp 631 ff.

pean Court of Justice[111] and has found its way into non-German legal writing.[112] This implies a certain restriction and change of meaning as compared to earlier usage. Back in 1950, the ECHR qualified its human rights guarantees as "fundamental freedoms" as well. Irrespective of certain fundamental rights implications, which are inherent especially in the provisions concerning free movement of persons in the TEC[113], it is obvious that there exists a difference in meaning between the use of the term "fundamental freedom" in the context of the ECHR versus that of the TEC. The ECHR uses the term with respect to rights guaranteed in a catalogue of fundamental rights, while the use of the term in European Community law refers to transnational economic freedoms necessary to establish a common market.

42 The fundamental freedoms formed an integral part of the TEC right from the beginning. Their exact content and meaning has been clarified and developed over the years in the jurisprudence of the European Court of Justice. Gradually, they have been extended from mere prohibitions of discrimination on the basis of nationality to far reaching prohibitions of limitations which show clear elements of **economic fundamental rights**. Furthermore, the provisions concerning free movement of persons and the Union citizenship have merged into a general right of free movement. The most **important mile-stones of this development** are: 1) recognition of the fundamental freedoms as subjective rights of the individual with their direct applicability in the national legal orders as a necessary consequence; 2) extension of their scope of application to comprehensive prohibitions of discriminations and limitations; 3) supplementing the free movement of workers with guarantees derived from the freedom of movement inherent in the Union citizenship (Article 18 TEC/Article I-10 DC), and, finally, 4) use of legal arguments derived from fundamental rights, notably "horizontal effect" (*Drittwirkung*) and "positive obligations".

1. Recognition of fundamental rights as subjective rights

43 The recognition of the fundamental freedoms as **subjective rights of the individual** in the decision *van Gend & Loos* in 1963 is central to the entire further development of Community law. Today, the principle of direct applicability of primary Community law (→ *cf* § 7 para 7) has become so natural a part of European law, that the position held by the Dutch and Belgian governments at the time, that it was up to the national law of the Member State concerned to decide on the direct applicability of European Community law, seems hard to fathom. If one compares the attitude of the two governments with the arguments presented by the Court in its decision, the enormous qualitative step of European law becomes clear which was made with the recognition of the fundamental freedoms as subjective rights.[114] According to the decision of the ECJ in *van Gend & Loos,* the Community "constitutes a new legal order of international law for the benefit of which the states have limited their sovereign rights, albeit within limited fields, and the subjects of which com-

---

111 ECJ *Casati* [1981] ECR 2595, para 8; see in detail Pfeil *Historische Vorbilder und Entwicklung des Rechtsbegriffs der „Vier Grundfreiheiten" im Europäischen Gemeinschaftsrecht* (Frankfurt aM 1998) pp 4 ff.
112 Supporting documents in Pfeil (note 111) pp 6 ff; Barnard *The Substantive Law of the EU* (Oxford 2004) pp 17 ff.
113 Oppermann *Europarecht* (note 2) § 6, para 31.
114 Kingreen *Die Struktur der Grundfreiheiten des Europäischen Gemeinschaftsrechts* (Berlin 1999) p 24; Weatherill (note 65) pp 99 and 114; Barnard (note 112) p 39.

prise not only Member States but also their nationals." The Court ruled that it was the purpose of the Treaty to create individual rights: "These rights arise not only where they are expressly granted by the Treaty, but also by reason of obligations which the Treaty imposes in a clearly defined way upon individuals as well as upon the Member States and upon the institutions of the Community."[115]

In the years following this decision, the **direct applicability** of the fundamental freedoms (and of other provisions which create such "clearly defined obligations") led to the consequence that European Community law greatly influenced the internal legal orders of the Member States. The practical importance of this jurisprudence and its effects on the national legal orders are witnessed by the fact that the most controversial decisions of the ECJ did not concern the distribution of competencies between the Community and its Member States, but concerned the implications of the fundamental freedoms and the consequences of the direct applicability of Community law.[116]

2. Interpretation of the Fundamental Freedoms as prohibitions of discrimination and prohibitions of limitations[117]

The development just described was accelerated and intensified by the fact that the Court interpreted the fundamental freedoms as comprehensive economic freedoms, which not only prohibited **direct and indirect discriminations** based on nationality, but also any other measures which could lead to a barrier of free movement of goods or persons between the Member States. The wording of the Treaty shows significant differences between the fundamental freedoms guaranteed. While the provisions concerning the free movement of goods and of services and the free movement of capital and payments explicitly prohibit limitations (see Article 28 and Article 49(1) TEC/Article III-153 and Article III-144 DC), the free movement of workers and the freedom of establishment seem to be limited to a prohibition of discrimination on grounds of nationality (Article 39(2) and Article 43 TEC/Article III-133 and Article III-137 DC). However, over the years, the ECJ has interpreted all fundamental freedoms in a similar manner and construed them as prohibiting both discriminations based on nationality and limitations. All in all, it is fair to say that the jurisprudence concerning the free movement of goods has functioned as a pace setter for the other fundamental freedoms.

The comprehensive prohibition of limitations regarding the **free movement of goods** was formulated in the *Dassonville* case. According to the henceforth so-called *Dassonville*-formula, measures equivalent to quantitative limitations within the meaning of Article 28 of the TEC refer to any national regulation which is capable "of hindering, directly or indirectly, actually or potentially, intra-community trade".[118] The wording chosen by the Court indicates that even limitations to the free movement of goods which are not discriminatory fall within the scope of application of Article 28 of the TEC. In its final result, this extensive interpretation of the prohibition of trade limitations would have meant that in principle any product which was lawfully produced and/or sold in one Member State

---

115 ECJ *van Gend & Loos* [1963] ECR 3, 12.
116 See for example ECJ *Kohll* [1998] ECR I-1931; *Decker* [1998] ECR I-1831; *Kreil* [2000] ECR I-69.
117 → in detail § 7 paras 18 ff.
118 ECJ *Dassonville* [1974] ECR 837, para 5.

could have been exported and traded in any other Member State.[119] In an attempt to avoid such a far reaching consequence, the Court decided in the *Cassis de Dijon* case that "obstacles to movement (...) as being necessary in order to satisfy mandatory requirements relating in particular to the effectiveness of fiscal supervision, the protection of public health, the fairness of commercial transactions and the defence of the consumer" are to be excluded from the scope of application of Article 28 of the TEC.[120] In a similar manner, the decision in *Keck* and *Mithouard*, according to which selling arrangements[121], eg shop opening hours[122] or the requirement that certain medicines be sold only in pharmacies[123], also do not fall within the scope of application of Article 28 of the TEC, tries to limit the consequences of the broad *Dassonville*-formula. To summarise the development with respect to the free movement of goods, it is characterised by an extension of its scope of application in a first phase and a restriction of the consequences generated by this in a second phase.

47 A similar development can be observed concerning the **other fundamental freedoms**. As far as the free movement of services is concerned, which already according to the wording of the Treaty is not restricted to a prohibition of discrimination, this was indicated in the Court's first decision regarding that freedom.[124] In the *Alpine Investments* case, the Court indicated that the restrictive approach taken in *Keck* with respect to the free movement of goods may in principle also be applied to the free movement of services.[125] Furthermore, the Court extended the reach of the freedom of establishment from a mere prohibition of discrimination to a general prohibition of limitations.[126] Finally, in the much debated *Bosman* decision, the Court applied the principles just described with respect to the free movement of workers. In that decision it also indicated that it is not only the general idea of a prohibition of limitations which may be applied, but also its restriction by the *Keck*-formula.[127] Overall, there seems to be a development towards a common legal structure in the jurisprudence of the Court concerning the four fundamental freedoms.[128]

---

119 Epiney in: Calliess/Ruffert *Kommentar des Vertrages über die Europäische Union* (2nd ed, Neuwied 2002) Art 28 EGV, para 16; Barnard (note 112) pp 87 ff; Steiner/Woods (note 69) pp 222 ff.
120 ECJ *Cassis de Dijon* [1979] ECR 649, para 8.
121 ECJ *Keck* [1993] ECR I-6097, para 16.
122 ECJ *Punta casa* [1994] ECR I-2355, paras 12–13.
123 ECJ *Deutscher Apothekerverband* [2003] ECR I-14887, para 73.
124 ECJ *van Binsbergen* [1974] ECR 1299, para 10.
125 ECJ *Alpine Investments* [1995] ECR I-1141, paras 33 ff.
126 *Cf* the recapitulating elaboration of the principles in ECJ *Gebhard* [1995] ECR I-4165, paras 37 ff, as well as the description of the developments in the case law regarding the freedom of establishment in Bröhmer in: Calliess/Ruffert *Kommentar des Vertrages über die Europäische Union* (2nd ed, Neuwied 2002) Art 43 EGV, paras 22 ff; *cf* however also there paras 30–31 on criticism regarding the usage of the term "discrimination"; also see Da Cruz Vilaca in: Andenas/Roth (eds) *Services and Free Movement in EU Law* (Oxford 2004) pp 25 ff.
127 ECJ *Bosman* [1995] ECR I-4921, para 103; see more explicitly in this respect also the opinion by AG Lenz (para 206); also see the discussion of this problem and the different positions taken in Ganten *Die Drittwirkung der Grundfreiheiten* (Augsburg 2000) pp 124–129.
128 Hilf/Pache [1996] NJW 1169, 1172; Kingreen (note 114) pp 61–62; also see Classen [1995] EWS 97 ff; Roth in: Andenas/Roth (eds) *Services and Free Movement in EU Law* (Oxford 2004) pp 1–2.

3. Complementing the free movement of persons with rights derived from the Union citizenship

The right to **freedom of movement in Article 18 of the TEC** (Article I-10 DC) provides for a general right to freely move within the territory of the Member States, i.e. irrespective of the exercise of economic activities[129]. According to the jurisprudence of the Court, this provision is directly applicable at least in connection with the prohibition of discrimination.[130] The almost unanimous position in the literature is also that it is directly applicable.[131] In combination with the prohibition of discrimination contained in Article 12 of the TEC (Article I-4(2) DC), it works as a catalyst for equal treatment of all Union citizens as far as social rights are concerned. A telling example is the decision of the ECJ in the *D'Hoop* case: A Belgian citizen was denied a certain social right (an interim allowance for transition from education to profession) because she had completed her secondary schooling not in Belgium, but in another Member State. The Court qualified this as an unjustified discrimination based on the use of the general right to freedom of movement guaranteed in Article 18 of the TEC. Irrespective of whether one sees the development rather negatively as a "gateway for an almost unlimited application of Article 12 of the TEC"[132], or welcomes it as a strengthening of individual rights[133], this jurisprudence turns the right to freedom of movement contained in the Union citizenship into a fall-back fundamental right for all cases which, for lack of economic activities, do not fall within the scope of application of either the free movement of workers or the freedom of establishment.

4. Horizontal Effect ("Drittwirkung") and Positive Obligations: Using Structural Human Rights Arguments for the Interpretation of the Fundamental Freedoms[134]

With the decision in the *Bosman* case, the ECJ confirmed its earlier jurisprudence, according to which the fundamental freedoms are not only binding on the Member States and any organ exercising public power, but also on **private entities**. However, the extent of their binding force on private persons was left unclear. The decisions in *Walrave*[135] and *Bosman* applied the freedom of services and the free movement of workers to sports federations and other associations which have the power to set collective rules for employees. Therefore, it was often assumed in the literature that such a **direct horizontal effect ("Dritt-**

---

129 Kadelbach in: von Bogdandy (ed) *Europäisches Verfassungsrecht* (Heidelberg 2003) pp 539, 552–553 (for English version see http://www.jeanmonnetprogram.org/papers/03/030901.html); Steiner/Woods (note 69) p 383.
130 ECJ *Grzelczyk* [2001] ECR I-6193, paras 30 ff; *D'Hoop* [2002] ECR I-6191, paras 25 ff; *Baumbast* [2002] ECR I-7091, paras 84 ff; *Trojani* [2004] ECR I-7573, paras 31 ff; also see the differing opinion of AG Geelhoed, ECJ *Trojani* [2004] ECR I-7573, paras 66 ff.
131 Supporting documents in Kadelbach (note 129) pp 539, 553; recently Streinz, *Europarecht* (7th ed, München 2005) paras 955 ff; also see Scheuing [2003] EuR 744, 759 ff; critical regarding the methodology of the ECJ: Hailbronner [2004] NJW 2185, 2186 ff; also cf Steiner/Woods (note 69) p 384.
132 Bode [2002] EuZW 637, 639.
133 Thus the tendency in Borchardt [2000] NJW 2057, 2058.
134 → in detail § 7 paras 45–46.
135 ECJ *Walrave* [1974] ECR 1405, paras 17 ff.

wirkung") would be restricted to cases where the private entities concerned had a certain general regulatory power.[136] As far as the free movement of goods is concerned, the ECJ – after some initial uncertainties – refused in its constant jurisprudence to rely on direct horizontal effect ("*Drittwirkung*") for private persons.[137] However, in summer 2000, in the *Angonese* case, the Court accepted a direct horizontal effect ("*Drittwirkung*") of the free movement of workers even against a private entity which was not an association for the exercise of collective interests.[138] One should not expect this to be the last word on direct "*Drittwirkung*"[139]. The decision has been criticised in the literature.[140] Furthermore, in contrast to the *Bosman* case, it concerned a situation of discrimination and hence does not necessarily allow any conclusion as to the possible answer of the Court had it been confronted with a merely restrictive and not a discriminatory measure. Finally the general problem remains of how to develop a general doctrine of "*Drittwirkung*" which is applicable in a similar manner to all fundamental freedoms.

50   It must also be taken into account that the doctrine of **"positive obligations"** (in particular an obligation to protect[141]), which has been developed in the context of free movement of goods, intends to pursue similar aims.[142] When French farmers again and again violently blocked the import of agricultural products from Spain and other Member States of the EC into France, the Court was confronted with a problem similar to that of direct horizontal effect. Just as in the "*Drittwirkung*"-situation, the case concerned enforcing the fundamental freedoms against limitations caused by private actions. In contrast to its jurisprudence concerning the free movement of workers, the Court did not directly apply the fundamental freedoms against the private person, but preferred to derive from the free movement of goods a positive obligation of the state to forestall limitations to the free movement of goods by private persons. It decided that France had violated its obligations under the TEC because it had not taken action against the recurrent violent protests of the farmers.[143] This approach leads to the same factual result: The application of the fundamental freedoms guaranteed by the Treaty is also ensured against obstacles emanating from private persons. However, the result is not reached by a direct horizontal effect of the Treaty provisions concerned against the interfering private persons, but indirectly by construing a corresponding duty of the Member States to forestall the interference.

---

136 Streinz/Leible [2000] EuZW 459 ff with further supporting documents; Jarass in: Andenas/Roth (eds) *Services and Free Movement in EU Law* (Oxford 2004) pp 152–153; Steiner/Woods (note 69) pp 300 and 336.
137 In detail the elaborate analysis of the case law in Ganten (note 127) pp 34–45; Jaensch *Die unmittelbare Drittwirkung der Grundfreiheiten* (Baden-Baden 1997) pp 45–64; also see Streinz/Leible [2000] EuZW 459, 460.
138 ECJ *Angonese* [2000] ECR I-4139, paras 31, 36.
139 Kingreen (note 110) pp 631, 677 ff.
140 Streinz/Leible [2000] EuZW 459, 464 ff; Snell in: Andenas/Roth (eds) *Services and Free Movement in EU Law* (Oxford 2004) pp 228 ff.
141 Opinion AG Stix-Hackl, ECJ *Coname* C-231/03, para 48.
142 See comparative to the dogmatic grounds of positive obligations Jaeckel *Schutzpflichten im deutschen und europäischen Recht* (Baden-Baden 2001) pp 222 ff; Barnard (note 112) pp 68 ff; Steiner/Woods (note 69) pp 518–519.
143 ECJ *Commission v France* [1997] ECR I-6959, paras 30 ff; on this case Szczekalla [1998] DVBl 219.

The terminology and the doctrines used show the extent to which the interpretation and application of the fundamental freedoms borrows from the general principles developed in the context of fundamental rights: Positive obligations and direct or indirect horizontal effect ("*Drittwirkung*") are terms taken from the general doctrine of fundamental rights, and they thus exemplify that the fundamental freedoms today have moved quite far from their original function to abolish discriminations based on nationality.[144] In fact, the jurisprudence of the ECJ has turned them substantially into economic fundamental rights.[145]

V. Consequences of the Treaty Establishing a Constitution for Europe

The Treaty Establishing a Constitution for Europe, which was signed in Rome on 29 October 2004, does not alter the developments described in the preceding paragraphs. Rather, it provides for their consequent continuation. If it enters into force, the Charter of Fundamental Rights will become binding Treaty law (*cf* already above para 37) and the wording of Article I-9 suggests that a swift accession of the Union to the ECHR may then be expected. As far as the doctrine concerning the interpretation and application of the fundamental freedoms is concerned, no fundamental changes to the developments described here are to be expected.

VI. Summary: Protection of Fundamental Rights and Fundamental Freedoms in a Multi-Layered Europe

Although the various developments within the ECHR and the EU are mutually interdependent, they do not occur within a single European legal order, but on different levels. This poses limits to generalisations. However, the following lines of development may be summarised:

1) Since 1945, national protection of fundamental rights has been supplemented with a growing intensity by international human rights guarantees. With the structure of human rights protection which was established by the ECHR in November 1998 in the 11th Prot ECHR and all the following amendments, the European Court of Human Rights has taken over functions similar to those of a constitutional court with respect to human rights protection in Europe.

2) A supra-national legal order which interrelates as closely with the national legal orders of its Member States as the one created by the TEC requires an autonomous mechanism of human rights protection. Currently, such a mechanism is provided for in the jurisprudence of the ECJ. Until now, the EC/EU has not formally acceded to the ECHR, but the jurisprudence of the ECJ in Luxembourg and the one of the European Court of Human Rights in Strasbourg assure largely corresponding standards of control. However, they cannot provide for an identical level of protection. Before the entry into force of the Treaty Establishing a Constitution for Europe, the European Charter of Fundamental Rights

---

144 *Cf* for example the description of the purpose of a prohibition of measures which have an equivalent effect in Art 28 TEC in Ipsen *Europäisches Gemeinschaftsrecht* (Tübingen 1972) paras 588–589.
145 Against a freedom-based understanding and for a material term of discrimination *cf* Kingreen (note 114) pp 72 and 118 ff.

does not create binding effects. Nevertheless, even without such binding effects it contains the most modern systematics of fundamental rights in Europe. For this reason it is used by the Advocates General and the Court of First Instance in order to confirm results of interpretation at which they have arrived in application of the traditional jurisprudence concerning the determination of Community human rights obligations. Soon after the entry into force of the 14th Prot ECHR to the ECHR and the Treaty Establishing a Constitution for Europe, an accession of the Union to the ECHR is likely to occur.

3) In recent years, the European Court of Human Rights in Strasbourg has tried to enforce the human rights obligations contained in the Convention not only with respect to the internal legal orders of the Member States, but it forces the Member States to respect the standards in their external relations as well when creating new subjects of international law to which they transfer sovereign rights.

4) Due to their interpretation as general prohibitions on limitations, the fundamental freedoms guaranteed in European Community law (free movement of goods, free movement of workers, freedom of establishment and freedom of services) have gradually been transformed into rights of economic freedom. As far as the free movement of persons is concerned, they are supplemented by the guarantees for a general right to freedom of movement for Union citizens which is contained in Article 18 of the TEC. Combined with the prohibition of discrimination in Article 12 of the TEC, this right can be qualified as a fall-back fundamental right for all cases which for their lack of any economic connection do not fall into the scope of application of either the free movement of workers or the freedom of establishment.

Part II: The European Convention for the Protection of Human Rights and Fundamental Freedoms

§ 2
General Principles

Dirk Ehlers

Leading cases: ECtHR *Niemietz* (1993) 17 EHRR 97; *Guerra* (1998) 26 EHRR 357; *Waite and Kennedy* (2000) 30 EHRR 261; *Matthews* (1999) 28 EHRR 361; *Krenz* (2001) 33 EHRR 31; *Refah Partisi* (2002) 35 EHRR 3; *Caroline von Hannover* (2005) 40 EHRR 1; BVerfG [2004] NJW 3407.

Further reading: Frowein/Peukert (eds) *Europäische Menschenrechtskonvention* (2nd ed, Kehl 1996); Grabenwarter *Europäisches und nationales Verfassungsrecht* (2001) 60 VVDStRL 290; Grabenwarter *Europäische Menschenrechtskonvention* (2nd ed, Munich 2005); Ovey/White *Jacobs & White – The European Convention on Human Rights* (4th ed, Oxford 2006); Schilling *Internationaler Menschenrechtsschutz* (Tübingen 2004); Meyer-Ladewig *Konvention zum Schutz der Menschenrechte und Grundfreiheiten* (Baden-Baden 2003); Peters *Einführung in die Europäische Menschenrechtskonvention* (Munich 2003); Karl *Internationaler Kommentar zur Europäischen Menschenrechtskonvention* (looseleaf, Cologne/Berlin/Bonn/Munich)

I. The Position and Status of the Convention within the Structure of International and National Law

Case 1 – Problem: (ECtHR *von Hannover* (2005) 40 EHHR 1)
The applicant (Caroline von Hannover) is the eldest daughter of the late Prince Rainer III of Monaco. She is president of several humanitarian and cultural foundations, however, does not perform any function within or on behalf of the Principality. She feels she is being continuously observed in her private life by so-called paparazzi and seeks injunctions against the publication of certain photographs in the German tabloid press. Her actions before the German courts as well as a constitutional complaint to the *Bundesverfassungsgericht* (BVerfG – German Federal Constitutional Court) were only in part successful. The applicant now turns to the ECtHR and asserts a violation of the right to respect for private and family life as guaranteed by Article 8 of the Convention.

Fundamental or human rights of the individual limiting the exercise of public power are nowadays recognised on a universal, regional and national level. At least in the western world, the latter is now regarded as a matter of course.

On a **universal** level, some of the most prominent sources of human rights, besides a large number of specific conventions (*eg* against torture, slavery, genocide and child labour)[1], are the **Universal Declaration of Human Rights** (UDHR)[2] adopted by the Gen-

---

1 *Cf* compilation by Centre for Human Rights Geneva (ed) *Human Rights: A Compilation of International Instruments* (New York 1988); Malanczuk *Akehurst's Modern Introduction to International Law* (7th ed, London 1999) pp 216 ff.
2 General Assembly Resolution 217(A) III.

eral Assembly of the United Nations on 10 December 1948, the **International Covenant on Civil and Political Rights** (ICCPR) and the **International Covenant on Economic, Social and Cultural Rights** (ICESCR) of 19 December 1966[3]. The UDHR contains a catalogue of the most important civil, social and political rights, such as the right to life and liberty, the prohibition of slavery and torture, the right to equality before the law and to an effective remedy by a competent national tribunal for acts violating fundamental rights. At the same time, it recognises limitations as are determined by law solely for the purpose of securing due recognition and respect for the rights and freedoms of others and for the purpose of meeting the just requirements of morality, public order and the general welfare in a democratic society (Article 29). Whether or not the Declaration – which entered into force by way of passing a resolution and not through a source of international law – creates internationally binding obligations has been a matter of some debate.[4] In either case, it contributes to the creation and development of customary international law. In addition, the UDHR is being referred to by numerous other human rights instruments, for example in the preamble of the European Convention for the Protection of Human Rights and Fundamental Freedoms (ECHR) – without thereby being incorporated into the ECHR. The UDHR sets a minimum standard of human rights and fundamental freedoms against which the level of human rights protection in different states and regions can be measured. From a political perspective, the observance of such standards is monitored by a sub-commission of the United Nations Commission on Human Rights.[5] The protection of human rights has been hedged by means of international law through the adoption of, *inter alia,* the ICCPR and the ICESCR which both came into force in 1976. Today, the two Covenants are in force in approximately 75 % of existing states, including the Member States of the Council of Europe. The ICCPR essentially repeats the liberal guarantees contained in the UDHR, although it tends to be more specific and only partly allows for limitations of the guaranteed rights (*cf* Articles 9, 12). However, there is no absolute congruence between the two. In contrast to the UDHR, the ICCPR contains provisions on the death penalty[6], but – unlike Article 17 of the UDHR – no right to own property. In times of public emergency, the ICCPR permits certain rights to be suspended (Article 4). Contrary to the ICCPR, the ICESCR – the result of an initiative by the socialist states of the time – does not impose any directly enforceable duties on the Convention States, but rather makes economic, social and cultural promises of a more objective nature. A mandatory periodic reporting system serves to enforce the rights guaranteed under the Covenants (Article 40 ICCPR; Article 16 ICESCR). The reports delivered under the ICCPR are assessed and analysed by the Human Rights Committee (Article 28 ICCPR), which consists of 18 elected independent members. For the reports under the ICESCR, this task has been assigned to the Committee on Economic, Social and Cultural Rights, a body of independent experts established under ECOSOC Resolution 1985/17 of 28 May 1985 to carry out the monitoring functions assigned to the United Nations Economic and

---

3 999 UNTS 171; 999 UNTS 3.
4 *Cf* Stein/Buttlar *Völkerrecht* (11th ed, Cologne 2005) para 1006 ff; Hailbronner in: Graf Vitzthum (ed) *Völkerrecht* (3rd ed, Berlin/New York 2004) 3. Abschnitt, paras 222–223; Epping in: Ipsen (ed) *Völkerrecht* (5th ed, Munich 2004) § 7, para 10.
5 *Cf* Schilling *Internationaler Menschenrechtsschutz* (Tübingen 2004) para 6.
6 *Cf* Art 6 ICCPR, as well as the 2nd Optional Protocol to the ICCPR of 15 December 1989 concerning the abolition of the death penalty, 999 UNTS 302.

Social Council (ECOSOC) in Part IV of the Covenant.[7] In addition, the ICCPR (but not the ICESCR) provides for an optional *state* complaint procedure (Article 41) as well as an optional complaint procedure for *individuals* (Optional Protocol to the ICCPR of 19 December 1966)[8]. In both cases, the review is undertaken by the Human Rights Committee in quasi-judicial proceedings. The Committee prepares a report on the facts of the complaint (but not on violations of the Covenant)[9] or, with regard to individual communications, forwards its (non-binding) views and conclusions to the State Party concerned.[10] Most European states have signed or acceded to both the ICCPR and the Optional Protocol – some with certain reservations.[11] However, the state complaint procedure has never been used to date. The possibility for an individual complaint will generally not be of great interest to Europeans either, as the ECHR provides for judicial protection that is by far more effective (*cf* paras 50 ff). This does not mean, however, that the UN Covenants can be disregarded in Europe. Rather, they affect the ECHR in various respects. The ICCPR, for example, guarantees rights that had not been included in the ECHR and were only taken up in the 7th Protocol to the ECHR in order to bring the level of protection under the Convention up to the standards of the ICCPR.

Regional guarantees of human rights can be found, for example, in the American Convention on Human Rights, the African Charta on Human and Peoples' Rights, and the Arab Charta on Human Rights.[12] Particular regard should be had to the **European Convention for the Protection of Human Rights and Fundamental Freedoms** (ECHR) of 4 November 1950[13], which is the oldest convention on human rights in modern times, aiming to secure – together with the OSCE ($\rightarrow$ § 1 para 2) and the law of the European Union (para 9) – a minimum standard of human rights and fundamental freedoms in Europe.

The ECHR was adopted by the **Council of Europe**. The Council constitutes an organisation under international law formed by European states in 1949 for the purpose of safeguarding and realising the ideals and principles which are their common heritage and facilitating their economic and social progress.[14] Until the beginning of 2006, **46 European states** (including such large countries like the Russian Federation and Turkey, both situated on the fringes of Europe) have joined this organisation. In exercising its mandate, the Council of Europe has passed nearly **200 conventions and agreements**. In 1961, for example, the Council adopted the European Social Charter as a social counterpart to the ECHR which has, however, not yet been ratified by all Member States. According to Article 20 of the Charter, signatory states undertake to accept as binding at least 10 out of the 19 rights-conferring articles (or 45 numbered paragraphs therefrom), and to prepare regular reports on the accepted provisions (Article 21), which are examined by a Committee of Experts (Articles 24–25). The by far most important convention, however, is the ECHR.

---

7 *Cf* Hailbronner (note 4) para 227. For more details as to the reports and their deficiencies see Schilling (note 5) paras 478 ff.
8 999 UNTS 171.
9 Art 41(1)(h)(ii) ICCPR.
10 Art 5(4) Opt Prot ICCPR, 999 UNTS 302. More detailed as to the complaint procedure Schilling (note 5) paras 487 ff.
11 *Cf* http://www.ohchr.org/english/countries/ratification/5.htm (last accessed 31 May 2007).
12 *Cf* the overview by Ipsen in: Ipsen (ed) *Völkerrecht* (5th ed, Munich 2004) § 49 paras 16 ff; see also Wittinger [1999] JURA 405.
13 ETS No 005.
14 Art 1(a) Statute of the Council of Europe, ETS No 001.

Under Article 3 of the Statute of the Council of Europe, every member of the Council of Europe must already accept the principles of the rule of law and of the enjoyment by all persons within its jurisdiction of human rights and fundamental freedoms. In order to affirm and vitalise these general principles, the ECHR – being strongly influenced by the UDHR – was signed in Rome on 4 November 1950. It came into force on 3 September 1953 after ten states had deposited their instruments of ratification.[15] Only the **English** and **French** texts are equally authentic and authoritative.[16] To this day, the Convention has been modified or revised by fourteen protocols.[17] While the 1st Protocol protects property rights, the right to education and the right to free elections by secret ballot, the 3rd Protocol primarily concerns the freedom of movement and the prohibition of certain types of expulsions from the territory of the Contracting States. The 6th Protocol provides for the abolition of the death penalty during times of peace. This ban was then extended by the 13th Protocol to include times of war. Modifications to the judicial and procedural guarantees were made by the 7th Protocol. The 12th Protocol contains a more general prohibition of discrimination which is supposed to complement the prohibition under Article 14 of the ECHR. Protocols 12 and 14 have yet to enter into force. The above-mentioned Protocols have also modified the procedural review of alleged violations of the Convention. The 11th Protocol, which came into force on 1 November 1998, is of special importance in this regard, as it restructured the institutional framework of the ECHR and thereby simplified the judicial enforcement of the Convention guarantees (para 51). A permanent court now attends to both the admissibility and merits phases of the applications (paras 51 ff).[18] This, as well as the fact that now almost 800 million people from Iceland to Vladivostok are potential applicants to the Court, will further increase the importance of the ECHR in the future. At the same time, however, the demands on the European Court of Human Rights (ECtHR) grow continuously.[19] In 2004 alone, the ECtHR received nearly 41,000 applications. For the Court to be able to cope with this workload, the 14th Protocol was designed to further improve and optimise the system of judicial protection. In particular, simple cases can be finally disposed of by single judges (*cf* new version of Article 27 ECHR).

6   When the Convention was initially signed, several states made reservations pursuant to Article 57 of the ECHR. Similarly, not all Protocols have been ratified by all Member States of the Council of Europe.[20] Therefore, the Member States' obligations under international law differ in respect of the Convention. Article 53 of the ECHR provides that nothing in the Convention shall be construed as limiting or derogating from any of the human rights and fundamental freedoms which may be ensured under the laws of any High Contracting Party or under any other agreement to which it is a party.[21] This provi-

---

15 Art 59(2) ECHR.
16 *Cf* Declaration after Art 59(4) ECHR.
17 *Cf* the overview by *Frowein* in: Frowein/Peukert (eds) *Europäische Menschenrechtskonvention* (2nd ed, Kehl 1996) Einführung EMRK, para 2.
18 *Cf* Ovey/White *Jacobs & White – The European Convention on Human Rights* (4th ed, Oxford 2006) pp 8–10 on the old system of protection.
19 *Cf* Ovey/White (note 18) pp 519 ff.
20 See http://conventions.coe.int.
21 A similar provision can be found in Article II-113 of the DC (for the relation between fundamental rights of the European Union on the one hand and international guarantees or domestic fundamental rights in the Member States on the other).

General Principles §2 I

sion allows Member States some leeway to afford a higher level of fundamental rights protection than the ECHR. However, this leeway is inherently limited whenever the relationship between the state and private individuals also concerns a third (private) party with conflicting interests equally protected under the ECHR. In this scenario, the farther reaching protection of one individual can only be maintained, if the protection of the other does not fall short of the standard guaranteed under the Convention. This normally requires the degree of human rights protection in multipolar relationships to be aligned with the respective levels set by the ECHR.[22]

The Convention itself does not lay down for the Contracting States any particular manner for ensuring within their internal law the effective implementation of the provisions of the Convention.[23] Although Article 1 of the ECHR creates no obligation to incorporate the Convention into domestic law, the substance of the Convention rights and freedoms must be secured under the domestic legal order – in some form or another – to everyone within the jurisdiction of the respective Contracting State. Consequently, the **rank** and **status** of the ECHR **within the domestic legal order** of the Contracting States differs greatly.[24] The approaches range from according the ECHR a rank superior to the constitution (*eg* the Netherlands), equal to the constitution (*eg* Austria), superior to ordinary acts of parliament (*eg* Belgium, Luxembourg, France) and equal to ordinary acts of parliament (*eg* Italy, Greece). The status of the ECHR in the United Kingdom was for a long time somewhat special:[25] until its incorporation into national law through the Human Rights Act 1998 (which came into force on 2 October 2000), the Convention was binding on the United Kingdom only under international law, but not domestically.[26] In Germany, the ECHR and its Protocols have the status of ordinary federal acts of parliament[27] in as much as they have been formally approved by the federal legislature pursuant to Article 59(2) of the *Grundgesetz* (GG – German Basic Law / Federal Constitution). However, certain guarantees of the ECHR (*eg* the prohibition of torture and slavery, Articles 3 and 4(1) ECHR) may well be taken to reflect general principles of international law.[28] Pur-

7

---

22 This problem surfaced in the *Open Door* case: Under the Irish Constitution, unborn life enjoys a higher degree of protection than under the ECHR. For an abortion counselling service, this would have led to a decrease in protection of the right to freedom of expression below the level guaranteed by the ECHR. In order to ensure a protection of freedom of expression consistent with the Convention, the further-reaching domestic protection of the unborn life had to recede. ECtHR *Open Door* (1993) 15 EHRR 244; *cf* Grabenwarter (2001) 60 VVDStRL 290, 298–299.
23 ECtHR *Swedish Engine Drivers' Union* (1979-80) 1 EHRR 617, para 50; *James* (1986) 8 EHRR 123, para 84; Geiger *Grundgesetz und Völkerrecht – Die Bezüge des Staatsrechts zum Völkerrecht und Europarecht* (3rd ed, Munich 2002) § 72 VI 1.
24 *Cf* Ress in: Maier (ed) *Europäischer Menschenrechtsschutz* (Heidelberg 1982) pp 260 ff, Frowein (note 17) Einführung EMRK, para 6; see also Grabenwarter (2001) 60 VVDStRL 290, 299 ff; Ovey/White (note 18) p 19.
25 Frowein (note 17) Einführung EMRK, para 6; Grabenwarter *Europäische Menschenrechtskonvention* (2nd ed, Munich 2005) § 3, para 9; Ovey/White (note 18) pp 34–37; Grote [1998] ZaöRV 309.
26 *Cf* Ovey/White (note 18) p 34; Grote [1998] ZaöRV 309.
27 *Cf Bundesverfassungsgericht* (BVerfG – German Federal Constitutional Court) (1987) 74 BVerfGE 358, 370; (1990) 82 BVerfGE 106, 120; [2004] NJW 3407, 3408; Uerpmann *Die Europäische Menschenrechtskonvention und die deutsche Rechtsprechung* (Berlin 1993) pp 72 ff; Oppermann *Europarecht* (3rd ed, Munich 2005) paras 25–26. *Contra* Bleckmann [1994] EuGRZ 149, 152.
28 Likewise Grabenwarter (2001) 60 VVDStRL 290, 306.

suant to Article 25(ii) of the Basic Law, such principles take priority over ordinary legislation and may consequently not be overridden by the legislature. Though conflicting federal acts of parliament are not automatically void, they must not be applied.[29] Since the ECHR is only given the status of ordinary legislation, the *lex posterior* rule would in principle permit the federal legislature to diverge from the ratifying act through any subsequent piece of legislation. However, the Basic Law's openness towards, and commitment to, international law[30] calls for an interpretation and application of statutes that is consistent with Germany's international obligations, even if the statute in question has been adopted subsequently to an international treaty. There is a presumption that the legislature – save for express wording to the contrary – did not intend to depart from such obligations or to permit breaches of the same.[31] A question that remains to be solved relates to which rules govern the interpretation of the ECHR in Germany. The answer largely depends on the manner in which international law is being given force within the domestic legal order. Generally speaking, two approaches are being argued in Germany (and most countries that recognise a dualistic structure of international and domestic law). While the first approach considers that any provision of international law must be "transformed" into national law (with the consequence that its interpretation follows domestic rules of interpretation), proponents of the **application model** see the ratification of international norms as the state's authorisation of their direct application within the domestic legal system (without translating them into national provisions).[32] The latter view should be preferred.[33] According to the *Bundesverfassungsgericht* (BVerfG – German Federal Constitutional Court), the ECHR – apart from its direct impact on ordinary legislation – must also be taken into account for the interpretation of the Basic Law itself, as long as this does not lead to a restriction or curtailment of the national level of fundamental rights protection. Consequently, the **jurisprudence of the European Court for Human Rights** (ECtHR) serves as a guide to the interpretation of the content and scope of fundamental rights and principles under the Basic Law.[34] The BVerfG, for example, revised its opinion on the legality of a special fire brigade levy imposed only on men after the ECtHR[35] had delivered a judgment to the contrary.[36] Indirectly, the ECHR is thereby accorded a **quasi-constitutional rank**.

---

29 As to the priority in application *cf* Streinz in: Sachs (ed) *Grundgesetz* (4th ed, Munich 2007) Art 25, para 93.
30 BVerfG [2004] NJW 3407, 3408.
31 See the BVerfG's seminal decision in (1987) 74 BVerfGE 358, 370. More detailed as to an interpretation in conformity with the Convention (with further differentiations) Uerpmann (note 27) pp 48 ff.
32 For more details see Cassese *International Law* (2nd ed, Oxford 2005) pp 220 ff; O'Connell *International Law* (2nd ed, London 1970) pp 56 ff.
33 *Cf* BVerfG (1977) 46 BVerfGE 342, 363, 403–404; (1987) 75 BVerfGE 223, 244–245. See, however, also BVerfG [2004] NJW 3407, 3408 ("transformed"). More detailed Steinberger in: Isensee/Kirchhof (eds) *Handbuch des Staatsrechts der Bundesrepublik Deutschland* (Volume 7, Heidelberg 1992) § 173 para 42; Schweitzer *Staatsrecht III* (8th ed, Heidelberg 2004) paras 423, 441 ff; Geiger (note 23) § 29 II 3, 32 II 2.
34 BVerfG (1987) 74 BVerfGE 358, 370; [2004] NJW 3407, 3408.
35 *Cf* ECtHR *Schmidt* (1994) 18 EHRR 513.
36 *Cf* the first judgment in BVerfG (1961) 13 BVerfGE 167 in contrast to the second decision in BVerfG (1995) BVerfGE 92, 91.

General Principles   § 2 I

Case 1 – Answer:
The application is admissible (Articles 34, 35 ECHR). It will also succeed on the merits of   8
the case, if the decisions of the German courts violate the applicant's right to respect for private and family life guaranteed under Article 8(1) of the Convention. The concept of private life extends to aspects relating to personal identity, such as a person's name or a person's picture. The publication of photos of the applicant in her daily life either on her own or with other people falls within the scope of her private life. In interpreting Sections 22, 33 of the *Kunsturheberrechtsgesetz* (German Copyright (Arts Domain) Act) and balancing the public's interest in being informed (Article 5(1)(ii) Basic Law) against the legitimate interests of the applicant in the protection of her private life (Articles 2(1), 1(1) Basic Law), the German courts ruled that the applicant, as a figure of contemporary society "*par excellence*", enjoyed the protection of her private life even outside her home but only if she was in a secluded place out of the public eye. Otherwise, freedom of the press, even the entertainment press, outweighed the applicant's interests. The ECtHR did not agree with this result. The Court considered that the decisive factor in balancing the protection of private life against freedom of expression should lie in the contribution that the published photos and articles make to a debate of general interest. As the photos showed the applicant pursuing activities of a purely private nature, their sole purpose was to satisfy the curiosity of a particular readership. Although the right of the public to be informed can, in certain special circumstances, even extend to aspects of the private life of public figures, the applicant was no such public figure. Therefore, the ECtHR found that there had been a violation of the right to respect for private and family life.

Finally, the ECHR has a profound impact on the **European Union** and the **European Communities**. Pursuant to Article 6(2) of the TEU, the Union observes the fundamental rights   9
as guaranteed by the ECHR and as they result from the constitutional traditions common to the Member States, as general principles of Community law. This protection of fundamental rights and freedoms not only applies to the EU itself, but also to the European Communities as part of the EU (Article 1(3) TEU) and to their institutions (Article 46(d) TEU). However, the ECHR does not create any direct obligations under EU and EC law. Firstly, the ECHR only binds states in the Council of Europe, of which neither the EU nor the European Communities are members.[37] Secondly, a strict legal commitment to the ECHR (and the case-law generated thereunder) cannot be inferred from the provisions of the TEU, since such a commitment would not be compatible with the obligation to merely "observe" fundamental rights and the concurrent commitment to the common constitutional traditions. Both the ECHR and the constitutional traditions common to the Member States rather serve – as they did in the past[38] – as subsidiary means for the determination of the general principles of Community law. The legal position will be fundamentally different, if (or when) the Charter of Fundamental Rights of the Union enters into force (→ § 14 para 13). Insofar as the Charter contains rights which correspond to rights guaranteed by the ECHR, the meaning and scope of those rights shall be the same as those laid down by the Convention (Article II-112(3) of the DC). No provision of the Charter is to be interpreted as restricting or adversely affecting human rights and funda-

---

37 *Cf* paras 30 ff.
38 ECJ *Internationale Handelsgesellschaft* [1970] ECR 1125, paras 3 ff; *Nold* [1974] ECR 491, para 13.

§ 2 II   Dirk Ehlers

mental freedoms as recognised, in their respective fields of application, by the ECHR (Article II-113 of the DC). Article 17(2) of the 14th Protocol to the ECHR (which has yet to enter into force) allows the EU to accede to the ECHR, which is in turn provided for in Article I-9(2) of the DC. An accession to the ECHR is not meant to alter any of the competences of the Union laid out in the Treaties. Should the EU accede, the Convention would be directly and unreservedly applicable. This would, however, lead to the question whether the ECJ or the ECtHR will have the final say on fundamental rights issues. For a more detailed discussion of this point see paras 31–32; → § 14 para 13. As to the latest developments *cf* the preface.

10 The following sections will deal with the functions of the Convention rights (paras 11 ff), the interpretation of the Convention (para 21), its beneficiaries (paras 22 ff) and entities bound (paras 27 ff), as well as its territorial (para 35) and temporal scope (para 36). After examining the guarantees and limitations of the Convention rights (paras 38 ff), this chapter concludes with some remarks on their judicial (procedural) protection (paras 50 ff).

II. Functions of the Convention Rights

Case 2 – Problem: (ECtHR *Guerra* (1998) 26 EHRR 357)
11 The applicants live in the proximity of a chemical factory, in which numerous accidents – including severe arsenic poisoning – have occurred in the past. The local authorities are under a statutory obligation to inform the public about the hazards of the factory as well as safety measures and procedures to be followed in the event of an accident. After they denied – with the approval of the national courts – to provide such information with reference to an ongoing investigation, the applicants would like to know whether it is advisable to lodge a complaint with the ECtHR.

12 The rights guaranteed under the Convention can be described as **subjective rights,** *ie* normative obligations which (also) serve the fulfilment and protection of individual interests and, for this purpose, accord their beneficiaries the legal power to enforce those interests in a court of law. Following the classifications by *G Jellinek*[39] fundamental guarantees are often distinguished – as regards their content – according to the status they protect. The *status negativus* is secured by defensive or liberty rights (1), the *status positivus* by rights to governmental action (3), the *status activus* by civic rights (4) and the *status activus processualis*[40] by other procedural rights (5). These different angles of protection can also be attributed to the various guarantees of the ECHR. Beyond this, equality rights (2) require a separate consideration, as well as the role of the Convention rights in contributing to an objective legal order (6). For the respective contents of the individual guarantees see the following chapters.[41]

---

39 Jellinek *System der subjektiven öffentlichen Rechte* (2nd ed, Tübingen 1919) pp 87, 94 ff.
40 *Cf* Häberle (1971) 30 VVDStRL 43, 80–81.
41 See also Grabenwarter (note 25) §§ 20 ff; Peters *Einführung in die Europäische Menschenrechtskonvention* (Munich 2003) §§ 5 ff; Meyer-Ladewig *Konvention zum Schutz der Menschenrechte und Grundfreiheiten* (Baden-Baden 2003) pp 42 ff.

1. Guarantee of the Status Negativus (Defensive or Liberty Rights)

The ECHR primarily protects the freedom of the individual by guaranteeing a certain sphere of liberty and by conferring a right to be free from unlawful governmental interferences as well as a right to reversal of such interferences where this remains possible. The Convention firstly deals with the protection of life (Article 2 ECHR; → § 3 paras 48 ff) including the prohibition of the death penalty (Articles 1, 2 6th Prot ECHR, Article 1 13th Prot ECHR; → § 3 paras 54–55), physical integrity (Article 3 ECHR; → § 3 paras 38 ff) and general freedom (Article 4 ECHR, Article 1 4th Prot ECHR) as well as the freedom of movement (Article 2 4th Prot ECHR[42]). Furthermore, the ECHR guarantees the right to respect for private and family life (Article 8 ECHR; → § 3 paras 3 ff), education (Article 2 1st Prot ECHR[43]), marriage (Article 12 ECHR; → § 3 para 11), freedom of thought, conscience and religion (Article 9 ECHR; → § 3 paras 31 ff), freedom of expression, assembly and association (Articles 10, 11 ECHR; → § 4 paras 4 ff) and the right to property (Article 1 1st Prot ECHR[44]; → § 5 paras 3 ff). Notwithstanding the prohibition of slavery and forced labour (Article 4 ECHR), the Convention does not contain any general right to pursue a freely chosen occupation, nor a right to asylum. However, by interpreting Article 10 of the ECHR to protect commercial information,[45] the ECtHR partially compensates the lack of a right to freedom of profession. Finally, the ECHR does not guarantee any overarching general right to freedom of action, as recognised, for example, by Article 2(1) of the German Basic Law.

13

2. Guarantee of Equal Treatment and Equality before the Law[46]

Equality rights do not guarantee any particular status, but rather ensure equality before the law for the purpose of averting state interferences, participating in benefits provided, or granting procedural and civic rights. The ECHR does not guarantee any general equality right as such, but only prohibits – as an accessory right – discrimination (*ie* differential treatment of comparable sets of circumstances) as regards the enjoyment of the rights and freedoms set forth in the Convention (Article 14 ECHR; → § 3 paras 66 ff).[47] The term 'Convention' in Article 14 of the ECHR must be understood as to include the several Protocols. Article 5 of the 7th Protocol to the Convention contains a special equality right providing that spouses shall enjoy equality of rights and relationships of a private law character between them, and in their relations with their children, as to marriage, during marriage and in the event of its dissolution. The Convention is triggered if the complaint of discrimination falls within the sphere of a protected Convention right. Article 14 of the ECHR enumerates prohibited grounds of discrimination. This list is,

14

---

42 Unlike Article 11 of the German Basic Law (*cf* BVerfG *Elfes* (1957) 6 BVerfGE 32, 35–36; (1986) 72 BVerfGE 200, 245), Article 2(2) of the 4th Protocol to the ECHR also protects the right to leave a country or to emmigrate.
43 The provision includes the freedom to establish private schools; *cf* ECtHR *Kjeldsen* (1979–80) 1 EHRR 711, para 50.
44 According to the ECtHR, the right to inheritance is protected by Art 1 Prot 1 ECHR; *cf* ECtHR *Marckx* (1979–80) 1 EHRR 330; → § 5 para 19.
45 *Cf* ECtHR *Autronic AG* (1990) 12 EHRR 485; Frowein (note 17) Art 10 EMRK, para 12.
46 See also Ovey/White (note 18) pp 412 ff.
47 Thereby, the ECHR falls short of other human rights instruments, *eg* Art 7 UDHR or Art 26 ICCPR.

however, not exhaustive.[48] According to the ECtHR, the Convention does not prohibit every difference in treatment *per se*, but only such discriminatory measures which have no objective and reasonable justification.[49] A difference of treatment in the exercise of a right laid down in the Convention must pursue a legitimate aim and conform to the principle of proportionality, *ie* the means employed must be proportionate to the legitimate aim. The density of review is rather low, since the ECtHR generally[50] accords the Contracting States a certain margin of appreciation (paras 43, 67).[51] Due to the accessory nature of the right to freedom from discrimination, the Court often does not determine whether there has been a violation of Article 14 if it finds that a substantive Article of the Convention has been breached. Article 14 only unfolds its full effect when a clear inequality of treatment in the enjoyment of the right in question constitutes a fundamental aspect of the case.[52] While a restriction of ecclesiastic bell-ringing to certain times can be justified under Article 9(2) of the ECHR, such a provision must not be directed against specific religious groups.[53] Considering the far-reaching catalogue of Convention rights, the effect of Article 14 in conjunction with substantive provisions of the ECHR will often come close to a general right of equality. Article 1 of the 12th Protocol to the ECHR creates a general, non-accessory prohibition of discrimination. Pursuant to paragraph 1 of the provision the enjoyment of any right set forth by law shall be secured without discrimination on any ground as listed in Article 14 of the Convention. Paragraph 2 adds that no one shall be discriminated against by any public authority on any of these grounds. Thus far, the Protocol has not been ratified by a sufficient number of Member States and has therefore not yet entered into force. If it does – which is difficult to foresee at present – the prohibition of discrimination will cover any right and not only those guaranteed under the Convention itself.

3. Guarantee of the Status Positivus (Rights to Governmental Action / Positive Obligations)

a) Original and derivative rights to governmental action

15   Article 1 of the ECHR requires the Contracting States to secure to those within their jurisdiction the rights guaranteed by the Convention. This requirement is not necessarily limited to a prohibition of state measures which interfere with those rights, but can also include **positive obligations** on the state to take steps to ensure their observation.[54] Such rights to governmental action (*eg* to realise certain liberties) can be subdivided into **original** and **derivative** rights.[55] While the first group concerns rights which oblige the state to take measures that were previously inexistent, the latter guarantees access to already exist-

---

48 See *eg* ECtHR *Pretty* (2002) 35 EHRR 1, paras 87 ff (discrimination of persons with disabilities).
49 ECtHR *Belgian Linguistics Case* (1979–80) 1 EHRR 252, para 10; see also generally Ovey/White (note 18) p 416.
50 On exceptions to this rule *cf* Grabenwarter (note 25) § 26, paras 10 ff.
51 *Cf* Peters (note 41) pp 217 ff.
52 ECtHR *Chassagnou* (2000) 29 EHRR 615, para 89.
53 Peukert in: Frowein/Peukert (eds) *Europäische Menschenrechtskonvention* (2nd ed, Kehl 1996) Art 14 EMRK, para 4.
54 Ovey/White (note 18) p 51; Reid *A Practitioner's Guide to the European Convention on Human Rights* (2nd ed, London 2004) para I-064.
55 On this distinction *cf* Martens (1971) 30 VVDStRL 7, 21 ff.

ing institutions or benefits. Apart from Article 3 of the 7th Protocol to the ECHR which provides that – under certain circumstances – an individual is to be compensated for wrongful conviction of a criminal offence, the Convention does not contain any other provision that expressly grants original rights to governmental action. The right to education (Article 2 Prot 1 ECHR) is generally interpreted to only guarantee access to existing public schools or educational programmes. Consequently, the right cannot be relied upon to demand the establishment of new schools or programmes.[56] However, it can be inferred from this provision that the state is under an enforceable duty to provide for some form of generally accessible school system at all. The same principle applies to a number of other guarantees that require further normative, organisational or procedural shaping. For example, the right to an effective remedy (Article 13 ECHR) presupposes the existence of a competent national body which can be called upon in case of a violation of rights and freedoms set forth in the Convention. The right to free assistance of an interpreter (Article 6(3)(e) ECHR) can only be realised, if the state maintains an interpreter service. Often, liberty rights also obligate the state to create procedural safeguards. The right to respect for private and family life (Article 8 ECHR) has been construed to comprise a right of access to records, a right to be heard and a right to information.[57] Furthermore, liberty rights require the state to provide for effective mechanisms to terminate an (unlawful) interference or to reverse its consequences.[58] **Derivative rights** to governmental action primarily arise from an application of the principle of equal treatment (para 14) which also includes equal *preferential* treatment.

b) Right to Protection against Unlawful Private Interference[59]

Much like the German Federal Constitutional Court and the European Court of Justice (→ § 7 para 31; → § 14 para 35), the ECtHR – under certain well-defined prerequisites – derives from liberty rights (and other Convention rights) an obligation of the Contracting States to protect individuals from unlawful **private interference** with the guaranteed sphere of the Convention rights.[60] Article 2(1) of the ECHR enjoins the state not only to refrain from the intentional and unlawful taking of life, but also to take appropriate steps to safeguard the lives of those within its jurisdiction. The state's obligation in this respect extends beyond its primary duty to secure the right to life by putting in place effective criminal law provisions to deter the commission of offences against the person, backed up by a law-enforcement machinery for the prevention, suppression and sanctioning of breaches of such provisions. It may also imply a positive obligation on the authorities to take preventive operational measures to protect an individual whose life is at risk from the criminal acts of another individual.[61] The prohibition of torture requires states to take

16

---

56 *Cf* Frowein (note 17) Art 2 1.ZP EMRK, para 2; Meyer-Ladewig (note 41) Art 2 1.ZP EMRK, para 4. Where a state has provided for primary education in a certain language, it must also offer appropriate secondary education, *cf* ECtHR *Cyprus v Turkey* (2002) 35 EHRR 731, para 277.
57 *Cf* Ovey/White (note 18) pp 286 ff, 294 with further references.
58 Grabenwarter (note 25) § 19, para 6.
59 See also Ovey/White (note 18) pp 51–52.
60 More detailed Szczekalla *Die sogenannten grundrechtlichen Schutzpflichten im deutschen und europäischen Recht* (Berlin 2002) pp 712 ff; Streuer *Die positiven Verpflichtungen des Staates* (Baden-Baden 2003) pp 191 ff.
61 *Cf* ECtHR *Osman* (2000) 29 EHRR 245, para 115; *Streletz, Kessler and Krenz* (2001) 33 EHRR 751, para 86.

measures which ensure that individuals are not subjected to torture or inhuman or degrading treatment, including such ill-treatment administered by private individuals.[62] Article 8(1) of the ECHR not only obliges the state to abstain from unlawful interferences with private and family life, home and correspondence, but also imposes a positive duty to take reasonable and appropriate measures to secure respect for these rights.[63] In many cases the Court also derives positive duties on the part of the Contracting States from the general obligation to respect human rights under Article 1 of the Convention.[64] Protective duties not only bind the state, but also correspond with a subjective right of the individual concerned. The scope of these obligations largely depends on the individual circumstances of the case. Where they are in issue, the state has a considerable margin of appreciation as to how it wishes to regulate a particular area.[65] In particular, positive obligations must be interpreted in a way that does not impose an impossible or disproportionate burden on national authorities.[66]

4. Guarantee of the Status Activus (Civic Rights)[67]

17 By and large, the drafters of the ECHR refrained from including civic rights in the Convention. The only such right is contained in Article 3 of the 1st Protocol to the Convention obligating the Contracting States to hold free elections at reasonable intervals by secret ballot, under conditions which will ensure the free expression of the opinion of the people in the choice of the legislature. The ECtHR's case-law under this provision has further shaped the right to vote and to stand for election.[68] One example is the Court's approach to derive from Article 3 the principle of equality of citizens even though the provision does not mention equal suffrage.[69] The ECHR neither requires full equivalency of each vote, *ie* that each votes carries the same weight, nor a particular electoral system.

5. Guarantee of the Status Activus Processualis (Procedural Rights)

18 The Convention places particular emphasis on procedural guarantees (→ § 6 paras 32 ff) which in part go well beyond those contained, for example, in the German Constitution.[70] This shows how other legal systems and codifications ascribe more importance to procedure than does the German law.[71] In detail, Article 5 of the Convention protects against unlawful detentions,[72] **Article 6** contains rights to a fair judicial process, Article 7 enuncia-

---

62 ECtHR *Z et al v United Kingdom* (2002) 34 EHRR 97, para 73.
63 ECtHR *Hatton* (2002) 34 EHRR 1, para 95; → § 3 paras 26–27; ECtHR *X and Y v The Netherlands* (1986) 8 EHRR 235, para 23. See also Ovey/White (note 18) p 243.
64 *Cf* documentation by Szczekalla (note 60) p 727 (footnote 69).
65 Ovey/White (note 18) p 244.
66 ECtHR *Osman* (2000) 29 EHRR 245, para 116; *Abdulaziz* (1985) 7 EHRR 471, para 67; *Ilaşcu* (2005) 40 EHRR 1030, para 332.
67 See also Ovey/White (note 18) pp 388 ff.
68 In respect of prisoners' rights see ECtHR *Hirst* (2004) 38 EHRR 825.
69 *Cf* for example ECtHR *Mathieu-Mohin* (1988) 10 EHRR 1, para 54; for the right to vote see also para 37.
70 Grabenwarter (2001) 60 VVDStRL 290, 312.
71 *Cf* Ehlers [2004] DVBl 1441, 1446, 1449; more detailed Harlow in: Alston (ed) *The EU and Human Rights* (Oxford 2004) pp 187–188.
72 *Cf* ECtHR *K.-F.* (1998) 26 EHRR 390 → § 6 paras 3 ff.

tes the principle of *"nulla poena sine lege"*[73], and Article 13 guarantees a right to an effective remedy. These provisions have been expanded by the 7th Protocol to the Convention, which, *inter alia*, contains procedural safeguards relating to the expulsion of aliens, a right of appeal in criminal matters and a right not to be tried or punished twice (*"ne bis in idem"*). In addition, the ECHR's substantive provisions themselves may require certain procedural protections or a specific application of the national procedural law (para 15). For example, the ECtHR developed from Article 8 of the Convention the right to a fair process for obtaining a planning permission to enable a gypsy to live in caravans on her own land.[74] Altogether the Court has succeeded in establishing a common European standard of "fair trial", which is being enhanced continuously.[75] Ascertaining the exact meaning of the Convention's procedural guarantees generally necessitates consultation of the authoritative French and English texts of the Convention. The right to a fair hearing guaranteed by Article 6 of the ECHR has proven to be the provision which is invoked most frequently – and which has also been found breached most frequently.[76] It has been repeatedly relied upon by the ECtHR to criticize an overlong duration of court proceedings.[77] The Court interprets Article 13 of the Convention to require a national complaint procedure, if the state courts fail to determine a case within reasonable timeframe.[78]

6. The Objective Dimension of the Convention Rights

Besides – and irrespective of – the protection of subjective rights of the individual, the ECHR also has an objective dimension,[79] *ie* imposes objective requirements on the Contracting States. The states are bound under international law to interpret and apply their respective national laws in conformity with the Convention. This obligation is incumbent on all state authorities, regardless of whether an individual actually invokes the rights conferred by the ECHR. **19**

Case 2 – Answer:
An individual application (Article 34 ECHR) will succeed on the merits of the case, if one of the applicants' Convention rights has been violated. In the case at hand, the Court might consider a violation of the right to life (Article 2(1) ECHR), the freedom to receive information (Article 10(1)(ii) ECHR) and the right to respect for private and family life (Article 8(1) ECHR). Since the applicants do not complain of state interference but rather assert an obligation on part of the state to disseminate information, the abovementioned provisions can only have been breached if they accord a right to governmental action. Considering the circumstances of the case, such an interpretation of Article 2(1) of the ECHR is rather unlike- **20**

---

73 *Cf* ECtHR *Streletz, Kessler and Krenz* (2001) 33 EHRR 751 → § 6 paras 53 ff.
74 ECtHR *Buckley* (1997) 23 EHRR 101, para 76.
75 Oppermann (note 27) para 53; Grabenwarter (2001) 60 VVDStRL 290, 312.
76 *Cf* Peukert (note 53) Art 6 EMRK, para 3.
77 *Cf* ECtHR *Probstmeier* App No 20950/92; *Pammel* (1998) 26 EHRR 100; *Kind* App No 44324/98, para 51. See also Reid (note 54) paras IIA-134 ff.
78 *Cf* ECtHR *Kudla* (2002) 35 EHRR 198. See also Meyer-Ladewig [2001] NJW 2679; Schmidt-Aßmann in: Horn *et al* (eds) *Recht im Pluralismus – Festschrift Schmitt-Glaeser* (Berlin 2003) pp 331 ff; Gundel [2004] DVBl 17.
79 *Cf* ECtHR *Ireland v United Kingdom* (1979–80) 2 EHRR 25, para 239; *Loizidou* (1995) 20 EHRR 99, para 75.

ly. As regards the freedom to receive information the ECtHR has on a number of occasions recognised that the public has a right to receive information as a corollary of the specific function of journalists which is to impart information and ideas on matters of public interest (see *eg* ECtHR *Observer* (1992) 14 EHRR 153, para 59). However, Article 10(1)(ii) of the ECHR cannot generally be construed as imposing on a state positive obligations to collect and disseminate information on its own motion. Other than for journalists, the ECtHR sees the primary object and purpose of this provision in prohibiting a government to restrict a person from receiving information that others wish or may be willing to impart to him. In contrast, Article 8(1) of the Convention has consistently been interpreted not only to compel the state to abstain from unlawful interferences with private and family life; but also to impose positive obligations inherent in effective respect for private or family life. Since the ECtHR considers severe environmental pollution to adversely affect private and family life, it found that the state was under a duty to inform the applicants about the risks they and their families might run if they continued to live in a town particularly exposed to danger in the event of an accident at the factory. The ongoing investigation did not justify the retention of such information, since further delays would unacceptably burden the applicants. Consequently, the state did not fulfil its obligation to secure the applicants' right to respect for their private and family life, in breach of Article 8 of the Convention.

III. Interpretation of the Convention

21 For the interpretation of the ECHR as well as the determination of the effects of rulings by the ECtHR, the English and French texts are equally authentic (para 5). Where these texts differ, the meaning which best reconciles the texts must be adopted (*cf* Article 33(4) of the Vienna Convention on the Law of Treaties). Just like any other international treaty, the ECHR must be interpreted autonomously in the light of its object and purpose (*cf* Article 31(1) of the Vienna Convention on the Law of Treaties). Due to its character aimed at permanently limiting the powers of the state, the ECHR – similar to the law of the European Union – requires a **dynamic** (in contrast to a static historical) **interpretation** committed to the principle of effectiveness ("*effet utile*").[80] Accordingly, the ECtHR has confirmed on many occasions that the Convention is a "living instrument which must be interpreted in the light of present day conditions". It is meant to guarantee rights that are not "theoretical or illusory" but "practical and effective".[81] Use of the preparatory work to the ECHR is therefore of importance only in relation to the interpretation of reservations made by the Member States. On a systematic level, regard must be had to the interaction between the Convention, the Protocols, the Statute and other agreements concluded by the Council, as well as to the embedding of the ECHR in general international law. Where the Convention refers to the domestic law of the Contracting States (*eg* Article 12 ECHR: "according to the national laws"), the latter may not negate the essential (core) content of the right or freedom in question.[82]

---

80 Reid (note 54) paras I-057, I-066.
81 ECtHR *Tyrer* (1979–80) 2 EHRR 1, para 31; *Airey* (1979–80) 2 EHRR 305, para 24.
82 *Cf* ECtHR *Rees* (1987) 9 EHRR 56; Reid (note 54) para I-059.

IV. Beneficiaries of the Convention Rights

Case 3 – Problem: (ECtHR *Matthews* (1999) 28 EHRR 361)
The applicant is a citizen of the United Kingdom resident in Gibraltar. She applied to be registered as a voter at the elections to the European Parliament. Her application was declined with reference to Annex II of the EC Act on Direct Elections of 20 September 1976 limiting the franchise for European parliamentary elections to the United Kingdom. Gibraltar is a dependent territory of the United Kingdom which forms part of Her Majesty the Queen's Dominions, but not part of the United Kingdom itself. The Treaty establishing the European Communities (TEC) applies to Gibraltar by virtue of Article 299(4) TEC (Article IV-440 DC). However, the Treaty of Accession of 1972 by which the United Kingdom acceded to the EEC provides that Gibraltar is excluded from certain parts of the TEC. In particular, Gibraltar does not form part of the customs territory of the Community and is treated as a third country for the purposes of the Common Commercial Policy. Although Gibraltar is not part of the United Kingdom in domestic terms, its citizens are treated as "nationals" within the meaning of the TEC. With her individual application against the United Kingdom the applicant claims a violation of Article 3 of the 1st Protocol to the ECHR. The provision guarantees free elections at reasonable intervals by secret ballot, under conditions which will ensure the free expression of the opinion of the people in the choice of the legislature.

It follows from Article 1 of the ECHR that the Convention (including the Protocols) generally protects "**everyone**" within the jurisdiction of the Contracting States. The protection is consequently not limited to individuals of any particular nationality (in contrast, for example, to some of the German fundamental rights that only apply to German citizens).[83] However, the respective scope of a right may be inherently limited to a particular group, *eg* the right to marry (Article 12 ECHR) only applies to "men and women of marriageable age", Article 3(2) of the 4th Protocol to the ECHR provides that everyone has the right to enter the territory of the state "of which he is a national", and only "aliens" are protected by certain procedural safeguards relating to expulsion (Article 1 of the 7th Protocol to the Convention).[84] Aside from such qualifications, the meaning of "everyone" can be deduced from Article 34 (*cf* para 56) which provides that the ECtHR may receive applications "from any person, non-governmental organisation or group of individuals claiming to be the victim of a violation […] of the rights set forth in the Convention and the protocols thereto".

As far as the right to life is concerned, Article 2 of the ECHR could (and probably should) be interpreted as to also protect unborn life[85]. In the case of *Vo*, the ECtHR con-

---

83 Frowein (note 17) Art 1 EMRK, para 3.
84 Both the prohibition of torture and inhuman or degrading treatment in Article 3 of the ECHR as well as the right to respect for private and family life (Article 8) may render the extradition or expulsion of aliens unlawful if, for example, they were liable to suffer inhuman treatment or punishment in the state to which they are to be sent. Ovey/White (note 18) pp 101 ff; Reid (note 54) paras IIB-148 ff; See also ECtHR *Dragan* App No 33743/03; *Ghiban* App No 11163/03; *cf* Grabenwarter (2001) 60 VVDStRL 290, 314; → § 3 para 44.
85 Considered but left undecided in ECtHR *Vo* (2005) 40 EHRR 259, para 85. In *X v United Kingdom* (1980) 19 DR 244, the (former) European Commission on Human Rights suggested that the term 'everyone' did not alone extend to the unborn child, but went on to consider whether 'life' could be interpreted as including 'unborn life'. See also Ovey/White (note 18) p 69; Reid (note 54) para IIB-004.

sidered this issue, however, left it undecided.[86] Similarly, there is no clear case law on the question whether the ECHR contains a right to or prohibition of abortion.[87] **Age** or legal capacity is irrelevant to the protection under the Convention. In case of conflict between the Convention rights of minors and the equally protected right to parenting (Article 2(ii) of the 1st Protocol to the ECHR) the state must balance the conflicting interests in a proportional manner. As to the procedural enforcement of the protection of minors *cf* para 59. Even a **post-mortem** protection by the ECHR seems possible, though this point has yet to be decided by the ECtHR. In the event of the death of an applicant, his or her heirs may continue the proceedings before the Court if they have a legitimate interest in doing so.[88]

25 The Convention protects foundations, trusts, associations and groups of individuals of any kind provided that they are **non-governmental**. It is irrelevant whether or not they are equipped with legal personality, according to which national law they are organised, and where they have their seat or registered office.[89] Consequently, **legal persons under private law** may also invoke the guarantees of the ECHR. However, many rights under the Convention only protect spheres of personal liberty which are solely applicable to natural persons (*eg* the right to life, the protection against torture, the right to personal liberty or the right to respect for private and family life). Nevertheless, the ECtHR[90] – in contrast to the ECJ[91] – has interpreted the right to respect for home (Article 8(1) ECHR) to encompass business premises (→ § 3 para 13). In this respect, Article 8 also protects non-natural persons. The rights of non-governmental organisations or groups of individuals must be distinguished from the (personal) rights of those constituting the group or organisation. Accordingly, groups of individuals or non-governmental organisations cannot invoke the rights of their members.[92] They may, however, under certain circumstances rely on their own rights even after their dissolution (in particular, if the dissolution constitutes the result of the alleged violation).[93]

26 Governmental groups or organisations do not come within the protective ambit of the Convention. The **state** does not benefit from, but is bound by the Convention rights. This holds true even if the state avails itself of private law patterns of organisation, or if its

---

86 ECtHR *Vo* (2005) 40 EHRR 259, para 85.
87 The Commission took the view that German legislation restricting the availability of medical termination of pregnancies did not constitute a violation of Article 8 of the Convention, *cf* EurCommHR *Brüggemann and Scheuten* (1981) 3 EHRR 244.
88 *Cf* Peukert (note 53) Art 25 EMRK, para 13.
89 See also Partsch in: Bettermann/Neumann/Nipperdey (eds) *Die Grundrechte* (Volume I/1, Berlin 1966) pp 235, 295; Gornig *Äußerungsfreiheit und Informationsfreiheit als Menschenrechte* (Berlin 1988) p 284.
90 ECtHR *Niemietz* (1993) 16 EHRR 97, paras 29 ff; *Société Colas Est (2004) 39 EHRR 373*, para 41.
91 ECJ *Hoechst* [1989] ECR 2859, para 18. In more recent judgments, the ECJ has expressly taken note of the ECtHR's view on this subject matter; see *eg* ECJ *Roquette frères* [2002] ECR I-9011, para 29. Nonetheless, it remains unclear whether the ECJ is prepared to give up its position established in *Hoechst*.
92 *Cf* documentation by Rogge in: Karl (ed) *Internationaler Kommentar zur Europäischen Menschenrechtskonvention* (loose-leaf, Cologne/Berlin/Bonn/Munich) Art 25, para 140; Rogge [1996] EuGRZ 341, 343; Peukert (note 53) Art 25 EMRK, para 16; Ovey/White (note 18) p 483; EurCommHR *Norris* App No 10581/83, (1984) 44 DR 132.
93 *Cf* documentation by Peukert (note 53) Art 25 EMRK, para 17.

General Principles

actions are governed by private law (*eg* when entering into contracts of sale).[94] Therefore, Article 1 of the 1st Protocol to the ECHR does not protect, for example, municipal property.[95] On the other hand, it would go too far to entirely exclude from the ECHR's applicability all legal persons under public law.[96] Incorporated religious groups, for example, should be regarded as non-governmental organisations or groups of individuals, since they represent institutions of society rather than the state (unless they are organised as state churches).[97] The same principle applies to public broadcasting corporations.[98] Many other questions remain largely unanswered. At least those state-run entities whose activities can be directly attributed to a sphere protected by fundamental rights and freedoms (*eg* the expression of opinion by state universities in the exercise of their scientific mandate)[99] should be able to invoke the applicable guarantees.[100] As regards institutions with both private and public shareholders or members (*eg* mixed public-private companies[101]) the law of the European Community tends to ask which side exercises effective control (→ § 14 para 28). The same could apply for the ECHR.[102] In contrast, private persons or bodies acting in the performance of a public power or duty conferred upon them cannot rely on the Convention, because they are exercising sovereign powers on behalf of the state.

V. Entities Bound by the Convention Rights

1. Convention States of the Council of Europe

Article 1 of the ECHR requires the **High Contracting Parties** to secure to everyone within their jurisdiction the rights and freedoms defined in the Convention. The High Contracting Parties to the ECHR are all Member States of the Council of Europe that have ratified the Convention (Article 59 ECHR) – Convention States. The contractual obligation engages all branches of government (legislative, executive and judicial) and applies on all intra-state levels irrespective of the form and manner in which the state may act. It includes individuals acting in the performance of a public power or duty, as well as those (private) entities that are either owned by the state or at least (directly or indirectly) controlled

27

---

94 Peukert (note 53) Art 25 EMRK, para 16.
95 *Contra* Tettinger in: Baur *et al* (eds) *Europarecht, Energierecht, Wirtschaftsrecht – Festschrift für Bodo Börner zum 70. Geburtstag* (Cologne 1992) pp 625, 633 ff, who argues that all public entities with legal personality can invoke the right to protection of property, since Article 1(1) of the 1st Protocol to the ECHR provides that "every natural and legal person is entitled to the peaceful enjoyment of his possessions". *Cf* also Stern *Das Staatsrecht der Bundesrepublik Deutschland* (Volume III/1, Munich 1988) p 1103. However, the ECtHR's decision cited by Tettinger concerned an entity with legal personality under private, not public law.
96 Contrast Oppermann (note 27) para 31.
97 *Cf* Ehlers in: Sachs (ed) *Grundgesetz* (4th ed, Munich 2007) Art 140 GG/137 WRV, para 23.
98 *Cf* Grabenwarter (note 25) § 17, para 5.
99 *Cf* BVerfG (1971) 31 BVerfGE 314, 322; (1975) 39 BVerfGE 302, 314.
100 *Cf* Grabenwarter (note 25) § 17, para 5.
101 For the position under German law see Schmidt-Aßmann in: Jayme *et al* (eds) *Festschrift für Hubert Niederländer* (Heidelberg 1991) pp 383 ff.
102 See also Barden *Grundrechtsfähigkeit gemischt-wirtschaftlicher Unternehmen* (Munich 2002) pp 185 ff.

by the same[103] (cf para 26). Although the institutional and organisational framework for churches and other incorporated religious groups differs greatly between the Convention States, ecclesiastical institutions should be attributed to the non-governmental sphere unless they are organised as state churches or exercise state power (cf para 26)[104]. The state is strictly responsible for every violation of the Convention, even if there was no possibility to exert influence in a decision making process (eg in regard to decisions by an independent judiciary) or if government officials acted contrary to prior instructions.[105] Not only positive action but also omission by the state (eg the refusal to provide free assistance of an interpreter, Article 6(3)(e) ECHR) can lead to a violation of the Convention.[106] According to the ECtHR, breaches of **supranational law** may also trigger liability under the ECHR. In certain circumstances, the refusal by a domestic court to refer a case to the ECJ for a preliminary ruling (Article 234 TEC; II-369 DC) may infringe the principle of fair trial as set forth in Article 6(1) of the Convention, in particular where such refusal appears to be arbitrary.[107] Similarly, the non-observance of a directly applicable EC Directive has been found to infringe the right to protection of property under Article 1 of the 1st Protocol to the ECHR.[108] Due to the subsidiary character of individual applications under Article 34 of the Convention (para 56), judicial protection by the ECtHR may, however, only be sought if all remedies under domestic and Community law have been exhausted.

28 A state is **not responsible** for acts of sovereign power on its territory where such power is in fact exercised by another state.[109] In this case, only the other state is liable under the ECHR – provided that it is a party to the Convention.[110] The situation is most likely to arise in the field of transnational administrative action on the basis of international or Community law. For example, the Convention Implementing the Schengen Agreement under certain circumstances empowers national police forces to take cross-border measures.[111] The ECHR imposes liability only on the state that crossed the border, not on the state on whose territory the measures were taken.

---

103 Cf Ehlers in: Erichsen/Ehlers (eds) *Allgemeines Verwaltungsrecht* (13th ed, Berlin 2006) § 1, para 4.
104 Cf *Aston Cantlow and Wilmcote with Billesley Parochial Chuch Council v Wallbank* [2004] 1 AC 546 (HL), para 167 (per Lord Rodger of Earlsferry).
105 Cf ECtHR *Ireland v United Kingdom* (1979–80) 2 EHRR 25, para 159.
106 Cf examples by Frowein (note 17) Art 1 EMRK, para 11.
107 ECtHR *Coëme* App No 32492/96, para 114; *Desmots* App No 41358/98; *Dotta* App No 38399/97.
108 Cf ECtHR *S. A. Jacquers Dangeville* App No 36677/97, RJD 2002-III; cf more detailed Breuer [2003] JZ 433.
109 See also ECtHR (Grand Chamber) *Maltzan et al* (2006) 42 EHRR 92, para 81: No responsibilty for acts committed by occupying forces or for those perpetrated by a later succeeded state (eg the former German Democratic Republic). However, a state remains reponsible for acts committed on parts of its territory where its exercise of sovereign power is only partially limited, cf ECtHR *Ilaşcu* (2005) 40 EHRR 1030, para 313.
110 Cf Partsch (note 89) p 299; ECtHR *Ilaşcu* (2005) 40 EHRR 1030, paras 314 ff.
111 Cf Arts 40, 41 Convention Implementing the Schengen Agreement.

2. International and Supranational Organisations

a) Direct Obligations

Since the ECHR has its roots in the Statute of the Council of Europe (*cf* Article 1(b) of the Statute), the **institutions of the Council** themselves are bound by the Convention and the Protocols thereto (as long as these are not modified or terminated by later agreements).[112] It would be contradictory if the institutions of the Council that adopted the ECHR did not have to abide by its standards. The effect of this obligation, however, is rather limited as the Council of Europe has not been vested with any governmental powers. At least the Council is obliged – as can be deduced from Article 3 of the Statute (para 5) – to only accept new members which generally (*ie* subject to reservations[113]) accept the principles of the rule of law and of the enjoyment by all persons within their jurisdiction of human rights and fundamental freedoms.

29

Of greater importance is the question whether other international or supranational organisations that do exercise governmental powers within the territorial scope of the Convention (para 35) are bound by the ECHR. At present, there can be no direct obligations under the Convention, as only members of the Council of Europe, *ie* only sovereign states (*cf* Article 4 and 5 of the Statute of the Council of Europe), are allowed to accede to the ECHR pursuant to Article 59(1) of the Convention.[114] Community law prevents an (often contemplated) accession of the **European Community** which presently lacks the competence to join an international organisation committed to the protection of fundamental human rights and freedoms.[115] Insofar as the law of the European Community and Union refers to the ECHR, the Convention only serves as a subsidiary means for the determination of the general principles of Community law, and not as a source of law (*cf* para 9; → § 14 para 8). This situation will change, should the 14th Protocol to the ECHR enter into force (para 9). Pursuant to Article 17(2) of the Protocol, the European Union may accede to the Convention – which in turn is provided for in Article I-9(2) of the DC. Furthermore, the Charter of Fundamental Rights of the Union provides that the meaning and scope of the rights contained in the Charter may not fall below the standard set by the ECHR (→ § 14 para 13; *cf* para 9).

30

b) Indirect Obligations

Even though the ECHR does not impose any direct obligations on international or supranational organisations, the High Contracting States still remain bound by the Convention if they transfer sovereign rights or powers to such organisations. This tends to lead to a collision between the applicable international or supranational law on the one hand and the provisions of the ECHR (which also apply domestically) on the other. In order to avoid such conflict, the former[116] European Commission on Human Rights (EurCommHR) adopted a position loosely based on the *Solange II* decision[117] by the German Federal

31

---

112 See also Partsch (note 89) pp 299–300.
113 Article 57 ECHR.
114 *Cf* ECtHR *Matthews* (1999) 28 EHRR 361.
115 ECJ *Opinion 2/94* [1996] ECR I-1759.
116 *Cf* para 51.
117 BVerfG *Solange II* [1987] 1 CMLR 225. See also → § 14 para 14; Craig/de Búrca *EU law* (3rd ed, Oxford 2003) pp 289 ff.

Constitutional Court: an individual application under Article 34 of the Convention is deemed inadmissible, if the law of the international or supranational organisation provides a level of protection of fundamental rights which is comparable to the protection guaranteed by the ECHR.[118] The Commission found this to be the case for the law of the European Community and thereby ultimately denied a responsibility of the Convention States for acts of the EC.[119]

32 Initially, the ECtHR did not subscribe to this view. In a decision of 15 November 1996, the Court held that a Contracting State is not relieved of its responsibility under the Convention for acts implementing provisions of Community law into national law only because such implementation is mandatory.[120] This position has since been clarified in more recent decisions. Although the ECHR does not preclude the transfer of sovereign rights or powers to international or supranational organisations, the Contracting States nevertheless remain responsible for compliance with the Convention rights. They must ensure that the international or supranational legal order guarantees a standard of protection comparable to the ECHR. Failure to do so violates the Convention. According to the Court, the Contracting States' responsibility also persists in relation to European Community law. Since the ECHR is intended to guarantee not "theoretical or illusory" rights, but rights that are "practical and effective", and since the effects of Community law correspond to the effects of national law within the Member States, the Convention rights must, in their entirety, be protected against violations through acts of the EC.[121] The ECtHR thereby went far beyond the position of the German Constitutional Court. While the latter only reviews EC law for compatibility with certain inalienable principles protected under the German Constitution itself, the ECtHR required EC law (or any other international or supranational law) to effectively protect the Convention rights (→ § 14 para 13). Otherwise, the Contracting States were still held liable for any deficiencies. The Court thus indirectly reviewed acts of the EC via the responsibility of the EC Member States for the observance and protection of the Convention rights.[122] In its *Bosphorus* decision of 30 June 2005, however, the Court changed its position and more or less aligned itself with the view originally taken by the EurCommHR (and the *Solange* approach of the German Federal Constitutional Court). Where a Convention State transfers sovereign rights to an international organisation and where such organisation protects human rights both in regard to content and judicial supervision in a way comparable to the Convention – as accepted by the ECtHR for the European Community –, the Court now presumes that a state does not depart from the requirements of the Convention if it does no more than implement legal obligations flowing from the membership of the organisation. This presumption can (only) be rebutted by demonstrating that the protection of the Convention

---

118 *Cf* EurCommHR *M. & Co* App No 13258/87. For more details see Giegerich (1990) 50 ZaöRV 836; Craig/de Búrca (note 117) pp 289 ff.
119 Lenz [1999] EuZW 311.
120 ECtHR *Cantoni* App No 17862/91, RJD 1996-V, 1614, para 30.
121 *Cf* ECtHR *Waite* (2000) 30 EHRR 261; ECtHR *Matthews* (1999) 28 EHRR 361. For more details see para 21.
122 See also Lenz [1999] EuZW 311, 313; Grabenwarter/Pabel in: Stern/Tettinger (eds) *Die Europäische Grundrechte-Charta im wertenden Verfassungsvergleich* (Berlin 2005) pp 85–88.

General Principles   § 2 V 3

rights was in fact "manifestly deficient".[123] Outside any strict international commitments, the Convention States remain fully responsible under the ECHR – especially for acts involving the exercise of discretion when implementing international obligations (eg EC Directives). Consequently, the ECtHR still reserves for itself the final say in determining ECHR-compatibility of any act of sovereign authority by the Convention States in Europe.

What has yet to be answered is whether such responsibility also extends to measures of the EC institutions taken independently of the Member States. In the case of *Senator Lines GmbH* the applicant commenced proceedings before the ECtHR against all EU Member States (simultaneously), alleging that the EC courts' denial of granting interim relief pending a decision on his appeal against a fine imposed by the EU Commission violated Article 6 of the Convention. The ECtHR rejected the application on other grounds (the fine, which was neither paid nor enforced, was later quashed) without making any determination on its general admissibility.[124] For states which are both member of the Council of Europe as well as the European Union, a responsibility to ensure that acts of the EC comply with the Convention may lead to serious problems. If they implement or apply Community law which is – according to the ECtHR – in breach of the Convention, they violate the ECHR. On the other hand, choosing not to follow Community law would mean to ignore its primacy over national law and thereby to breach treaty obligations vis-à-vis the other EU Member States.[125] Considering the reference to the ECHR in Article 6(2) of the TEU, the principle to be considerate of the Member States' international obligations (as can be derived from Article 10 of the TEC), the subordination clause in Article 307(1) of the TEC for obligations arising from agreements prior to an accession to the EC, and the principle to prefer an interpretation favourable to international law[126], the fundamental rights of the Union should be given a meaning compatible with the obligations of the Member States under the ECHR.[127] This will be ensured by Article II-112(3) of the Draft Constitution. Should the EU accede to the ECHR, the Convention will apply directly as part of EU law anyway. It would then be difficult to argue that the ECtHR should not have the last word on questions involving the compatibility of Community law with the Convention.

33

3. Private Persons

Contrary to isolated views,[128] the Convention rights have **no direct (horizontal) effect** on private individuals.[129] This already follows from Article 1 of the ECHR and is confirmed

34

---

123 ECtHR *Bosphorus* (2006) 42 EHRR 1, para 156.
124 ECtHR *Senator Lines GmbH* (2004) 39 EHRR 13.
125 On the supremacy of EC law *cf* ECJ *Costa v E.N.E.L.* [1964] ECR 584, 593.
126 Schmalenbach in: Calliess/Ruffert (eds) *Kommentar des Vertrages über die Europäische Union und des Vertrages zur Gründung der Europäischen Gemeinschaft* (2nd ed, Neuwied 2002) Art 307 EGV, para 15.
127 Grabenwarter (2001) 60 VVDStRL 290, 331–332.
128 *Bundesgerichtshof* (BGH – German Federal Court of Justice) (1958) 27 BGHZ 284, 285–286.
129 See also Szczekalla (note 60) pp 900, 906. Similar to the position in Germany (*cf* Pieroth/Schlink *Grundrechte – Staatsrecht II* (22nd ed, Heidelberg 2006) paras 177 ff) a "direct horizontal effect" cannot be deduced from the fact that the state decides disputes between private individuals through its court system. For a discussion (in common law jurisdictions) and for further references see Stemplewitz (2006) 4 New Zealand Journal of Public and International Law 197.

by the provisions in Articles 33 and 34, which only envisage applications against the Contracting States and not against private persons. However, many rights under the Convention – for example the prohibition of slavery or servitude (Article 4(1) ECHR), the right to marry (Article 12 ECHR) and the right to equality between spouses (Article 5 7th Prot ECHR) – also (and in particular) affect private law. As has been mentioned above (para 19), the Convention rights may require the state to protect private persons against unlawful interferences by other private individuals. The state is primarily obligated to enact domestic legislation which does not permit rights-infringing behaviour by third parties.[130] At least in one case the ECtHR went even further and held a Convention State responsible for corporal punishment by a private school headmaster, *ie* the Court reviewed private conduct which was then attributed to the state.[131]

VI. Territorial scope

35 Pursuant to Article 1 of the ECHR, the Contracting States guarantee the rights and freedoms to everyone within their "jurisdiction". Jurisdiction normally coincides with the **territory** of a state. However, the territorial scope of the Convention goes further. For example, a state is responsible for acts of its diplomatic and consular representatives abroad. The same responsibility arises when, as a consequence of military action, a state exercises "effective control" over an area outside its national territory.[132] The Court reasoned – unconvincingly – that this prerequisite was not met in the case of aerial bombings outside of occupied territories.[133] The decision of a Contracting State to expel or extradite a person may engage the responsibility of that state under the Convention, even if a rights- infringing measure occurs in the receiving state.[134] Furthermore, the so-called "colonial clause" in Article 56 of the ECHR as well as other provisions in the Protocols (Article 4 1st Prot ECHR, Article 5 4th Prot ECHR, Article 5 6th Prot ECHR, Article 6 7th Prot ECHR) enable a Contracting State to extend the Convention to all or any of the territories for whose international relations it is responsible (*eg* Netherlands Antilles, Falkland Islands, *etc*).

VII. Temporal scope

36 Since the Convention has no retroactive effect,[135] it is binding on each Contracting State **from the date of ratification** for the duration of the accession (provided that no reservation to the contrary has been made, *cf* para 39). Article 58 of the ECHR sets out rules governing the denunciation of the Convention by a Contracting State. For events prior to 3 September 1953 (the Convention's date of entry into force) or prior to the subsequent accession of a certain state, the Convention does not apply unless the event has consequences which may raise the question of a continuing violation.[136]

---

130 *Cf* ECtHR *Young, James and Webster* (1982) 4 EHRR 38, para 49.
131 ECtHR *Costello-Roberts* (1994) 19 EHRR 112, paras 27–28.
132 ECtHR *Drozd* (1992) 14 EHRR 745, para 91; *Loizidou* (1997) 23 EHRR 513, para 52; *Ilaşcu* (2005) 40 EHRR 1030, paras 314 ff.
133 ECtHR *Banković* App No 52207/99, paras 67 ff.
134 ECtHR *Soering* (1989) 11 EHRR 439, para 91; *cf* also *Bundesverwaltungsgericht* (German Federal Administrative Court – BVerwG) (2005) 122 BVerwGE 271.
135 Ovey/White (note 18) pp 21 ff.
136 ECtHR *De Becker* (1979–80) 1 EHRR 43; Reid (note 54) para I-043.

Case 3 – Answer:
The admissible individual application is well founded, if one of the applicant's guaranteed rights under the Convention has been breached. The only provision in question here is Article 3 of the 1st Protocol to the ECHR guaranteeing the right to participate in free elections of the legislature. A violation of this right requires that the act complained of falls within the scope of protection of the right and constitutes an unjustifiable interference therewith (*cf* paras 40 ff). The scope of protection can only be affected, if (1) the applicant is a beneficiary of the right, (2) the United Kingdom is the proper addressee of the respective obligation under the Convention, and (3) if Gibraltar comes within the territorial ambit of the ECHR and the 1st Protocol respectively. Furthermore, the requirements of Article 3 of the 1st Protocol must be met. The provision generally accords every (adult) person within the jurisdiction of a legislature the right to participate in parliamentary elections. The applicant is therefore to be regarded as a beneficiary of the Convention right. In the present case, the United Kingdom might escape liability for not holding elections for the European Parliament in Gibraltar, as Annex II of the EC Act on Direct Elections of 20 September 1976 itself excludes an election on this territory. Since the EC is not a member of the Council of Europe, its acts are not (directly) subject to review by the ECtHR. However, the Convention States may not absolve themselves from their responsibility under the ECHR by transferring sovereign rights or powers to international or supranational organisations. Hence, they remain liable for the observance of the Convention rights and freedoms even after such a transfer. However, in the case of *Bosphorus* (2006) 42 EHRR 1 the ECtHR decided that mere compliance with legal obligations flowing from EC law may disengage a Contracting State's responsibility under the Convention, if, and in as much as, the EC can be considered to protect fundamental rights and freedoms in a manner at least equivalent to that for which the ECHR provides. The presumption for such an equivalent level of protection to exist can only be rebutted, if, in the circumstances of a particular case, the protection of Convention rights appears manifestly deficient. However, while in the *Bosphorus* case the interference with a Convention right was a direct (and inevitable) consequence of complying with mandatory EC obligations, Annex II of the EC Act on Direct Elections was adopted *unanimously* by the Council, *ie* voluntarily by the United Kingdom. In contrast to a Commission decision, the EC Act of Direct Elections does not impose any strictly binding obligations on the Member States. In accordance with Article 190(4)(ii) of the TEC, the EC Act on Direct Elections was only "recommend[ed] to Member States for adoption in accordance with their respective constitutional requirements". Hence, the United Kingdom was not obliged to exclude residents of Gibraltar from the franchise for European parliamentary elections and is consequently bound by Article 3 of the 1st Protocol also in relation to such elections. By way of declaration pursuant to Article 4 of 1st Protocol and Article 56 of the ECHR, the United Kingdom extended the territorial application of the Convention and the 1st Protocol to Gibraltar. Finally, the European Parliament must be regarded as a "legislature", for there is no reason which could justify excluding it from the ambit of the elections referred to in Article 3 of Protocol No 1 on the ground that it is a supranational, rather than a purely domestic, representative organ. The European Parliament represents "the principle form of democratic, political accountability in the Community". However, the right to free elections is not guaranteed in an absolute form, but is subject to limitations (and further normative shaping). Then again, such restrictions may not touch upon the essential content of the right to vote. This line was crossed in the case at hand, as the citizens of Gibraltar were denied any opportunity to influence the composition of the European Parliament. Consequently, the individual application was successful.

VIII. Guarantees and Limitations of the Convention Rights

1. Stages of Scrutiny

38 In Germany, the process of scrutinising governmental action for compatibility with fundamental rights is typically subdivided into three stages – **scope of protection, interference** and **justification**.[137] This pattern was primarily developed for the defensive function of liberty rights, and even there not as a matter of course. It entails a tendency to perceive rights and freedoms as naturally unlimited (in contrast to guarantees that are bestowed by law and therefore often inherently limited, but at the same time designed for true realisation).[138] Furthermore, it seems questionable whether the approach can adequately deal with such rights and freedoms which *a priori* require further normative shaping (*eg* freedom of association or the right to (respect for) property). Nevertheless, the pattern is mostly used – with certain modifications[139] – also in relation to other types of fundamental rights or freedoms (*ie* equality rights, rights to governmental action, civic and procedural rights). As regards the ECHR, there appears to be no detailed systematic pattern of review thus far. Although the German approach is debatable, it still covers the same issues that arise under the Convention. It therefore seems appropriate to at least use the German pattern as a basis for fundamental rights scrutiny under the ECHR.[140] An additional and separate point is the applicability of the Convention. The respective scope of protection of a right can be interpreted rather broadly – likewise should the existence of an interference with the right in question not be determined too narrowly. In return, the Convention States are given considerable leeway on the level of justification (*cf* para 68). It is, however, equally possible to proceed on a two-stage basis (after having established the applicability of the Convention), *ie* to first ask whether a right or freedom has been interfered with and then to determine the lawfulness of such interference. Any pattern of review should, of course, never be understood as being compulsory or unalterable. For example, for determining whether the prohibition of discrimination (Article 14 ECHR) has been breached, it would be sufficient (assuming that the Convention is applicable) to examine whether there has been differential treatment and whether such treatment can be justified. With respect to procedural rights it is generally advisable to determine the applicability of a specific guarantee and then to scrutinise the observance of the procedure required.

2. Applicability of the Convention

39 Prior to entering into the actual process of reviewing governmental action for compliance with the ECHR, the Convention or relevant Protocol must first be found applicable. While the Protocols to the Convention only enter into force after they have been **ratified** by a sufficient number of Convention States (and then only bind those states which did in fact ratify them), the ECHR itself applies, in principle, to all Contracting States. However,

---

137 *Cf* for example Starck in: von Mangoldt/Klein/Starck (eds) *Das Bonner Grundgesetz* (Volume 1, 4th ed, Berlin 1999) Art 1, paras 228 ff; Dreier in: Dreier (ed) *Grundgesetz* (Volume 1, 2nd ed, Tübingen 2004) paras 119 ff; Jarass in: Jarass/Pieroth *Grundgesetz* (8th ed, Munich 2006) Vorb vor Art 1, paras 14 ff; Pieroth/Schlink (note 129) paras 195 ff.
138 *Cf* critical appraisal by Hoffmann-Riem [2004] Der Staat 203, 226 ff.
139 *Cf* Jarass (note 137) vor Art 1, paras 15 ff.
140 Likewise Grabenwarter (note 25) § 18; Peters (note 41) p 257.

General Principles § 2 VIII 4

pursuant to Article 57 of the ECHR every state may, at the time of signing the Convention (or Protocol) or when depositing its instrument of ratification, make a **reservation** (within the meaning of Article 2(1)(d) of the Vienna Convention on the Law of Treaties)[141] in respect of any particular provision of the Convention to the extent that a law *then in force* in its territory is not in conformity with the provision. Reservations exclude the respective legal obligation under the Convention. They are not permitted in relation to the provision abolishing the death penalty (Article 4 of the 6th Protocol and Article 3 of the 13th Protocol to the ECHR). Furthermore, they may not be of a general character, *ie* "couched in terms that [are] too vague or broad for it to be possible to determine their exact meaning and scope"[142]. The reservation must contain a brief statement of the law concerned (Article 57(2) ECHR). The validity of the (unfortunately numerous[143]) reservations is subject to review by the ECtHR.[144] Since the Court has developed a rather restrictive stance in interpreting the prerequisites of Article 57 of the Convention, many reservations prove to be invalid or at least of limited effect.[145] The right of derogation from the Convention in emergency situations (Article 15 ECHR) does not affect the applicability of the Convention, but only allows the Contracting States to temporarily act contrary to their obligations (para 44).

3. Scope of Protection of the Convention Rights

The **scope of protection** of a Convention right circumscribes a delimited part of reality in which certain conduct is protected (*eg* the expression of an opinion), whereas the **content of a right** describes the legal guarantee itself (*eg* the right to freely express opinions). The Convention also protects so-called "negative" liberties or freedoms, *eg* the freedom not to practise any religion.[146] As to the interpretation of the Convention see para 21. Those who have effectively renounced their rights under the ECHR cannot rely on its protection. The same applies to applicants abusing its guarantees (Article 17 ECHR; *cf* para 44). An abuse of the right to freedom of expression guaranteed by Article 10 of the ECHR lies, for example, in the denial of the holocaust.[147] A renunciation is not effective, if it adversely affects the rights of others or is contrary to the public interest.[148]

40

4. Interference with a Right or Freedom

The Convention rights do not shield against any kind of disadvantage within their respective area of application, but only against unjustified state interferences (or limitations). Such interferences require a sufficiently close connection between the state measure and the detriment suffered by the beneficiary of the right affected. The ECHR speaks of

41

---

141 As to the permissibility of reservations under international law *cf* Article 19 of the Vienna Convention on the Law of Treaties.
142 ECtHR *Belilos* (1988) 10 EHRR 466, paras 52 ff.
143 *Cf* the documentation by Frowein (note 17) pp 893 ff.
144 See for example ECtHR *Belilos* (1988) 10 EHRR 466, para 50; *Eisenstecken* (2002) 34 EHRR 860, paras 28–29.
145 *Cf* ECtHR *Schmautzer* (1996) 21 EHRR 511. See also Grabenwarter (2001) 60 VVDStRL 290, 297–298.
146 As to the freedom of religion *cf* Frowein (note 17) Art 9 EMRK, para 2; → see also § 3 paras 31 ff.
147 ECtHR *Garaudy* App No 65831/01, RJD 2003-IX.
148 Likewise Grabenwarter (note 25) § 18, para 30.

49

"restrictions" (*eg* in Articles 9(2) and 11(2) ECHR) and "interferences" (*cf* Articles 8(2) and 10(1) ECHR). A systematic approach to the issue of interferences with the Convention rights has not been developed thus far. The ECtHR tends to proceed on a case-by-case basis[149] and generally does not differentiate between intentional and unintentional, direct and indirect, *de jure* and *de facto*, or imperative and non-imperative infliction of disadvantages.[150] It sporadically requires an act of law[151] or a certain intensity of the measure in question[152]. In order to secure an effective protection of the rights under the Convention, there is, in principle, agreement not to make particularly high demands on demonstrating the existence of an interference or limitation.[153] For example, the contribution to interfering acts of others (*eg* extradition to a state where the person is threatened to suffer inhuman or degrading punishment) may also trigger responsibility under the Convention.[154] Likewise, a failure to fulfil positive obligations incumbent on the Contracting States is to be treated as an interference with the right concerned.[155]

42   Interferences or limitations must be distinguished from other forms of legal regulation, particularly from **further shaping of the Convention rights** by the national legislature. When, for example, Article 12 of the ECHR guarantees the right to marry "according to the national laws governing [its] exercise", the enactment of appropriate legislation by the Contracting States does not constitute an interference with Article 12, but rather renders possible the realisation of the right. Such a predisposition for normative refinement can be identified in many Convention rights (*eg* the right to respect for property and the right to free elections, Articles 1 and 3 of the 1st Protocol to the ECHR), even though the respective wording of the provisions does not always expressly point to it. However, normative shaping can turn into an interference or limitation, if the national provisions fall below the minimum standard guaranteed by the Convention, or if they restrict a pre-existing legal position.[156]

---

149 *Cf* Weber-Dürler (1998) 57 VVDStRL 57, 86.
150 More restrictive Villiger *Handbuch der EMRK* (2nd ed, Zurich 1999) para 542 (excluding indirect disadvantages).
151 According to the EurCommHR, medical examinations or vaccinations only constitute an interference with Article 8 of the Convention, if they are carried out on the basis of a mandatory order (critical as to this distinction Wildhaber/Breitenmoser in: Karl (ed) *Internationaler Kommentar zur Europäischen Menschenrechtskonvention* (loose-leaf, Cologne/Berlin/Bonn/Munich) Art 8, para 64). It is generally accepted that also *de facto* measures (*eg* the collection and storage of personal data, *cf* Frowein (note 17) Art 8 EMRK, para 5) may constitute an interference.
152 For a measure to come withtin the ambit of prohibited torture (Article 3 ECHR), it must attain a minimum level of severity (ECtHR *Ireland v United Kingdom* (1979–80) 2 EHRR 25, para 162). Governmental acts of minor effect are said to fall below the threshold for restrictions within the meaning of Article 8(2) ECHR (Wildhaber/Breitenmoser (note 151) Art 8, para 61). See also ECtHR *López Ostra* (1995) 20 EHRR 277, where the Court held that only severe environmental pollution may affect the right to respect for private and family life protected under Article 8(1) of the Convention.
153 *Cf* Roth *Faktische Eingriffe in Freiheit und Eigentum* (Berlin 1994) pp 58 ff.
154 *Cf* Frowein (note 17) Art 3 EMRK, paras 18 ff. In addition, cases of extradition virtually always involve an interference with the right to respect for private and family life protected under Article 8(1) of the ECHR; *cf* for example ECtHR *Adam* App No 43359/98.
155 *Cf* ECtHR *López Ostra* (1995) 20 EHRR 277, paras 54 ff. Critical as to the previous case law Wildhaber/Breitenmoser (note 151) Art 8, paras 13, 55 ff.
156 As to the position under German law *cf* BVerfG (1975) 39 BVerfGE 1, 42 ff; (1981) 57 BVerfGE

General Principles

5. Justification of the Interference or Limitation

a) Restrictability of the Convention Rights

Not every governmental act or omission which interferes with a right or freedom guaranteed under the Convention necessarily amounts to a breach of the Convention. Rather, a measure can be justified, if the state may restrict the Convention right. Similar to the German Basic Law, the ECHR distinguishes between rights that are guaranteed **unreservedly**, and those which are **subject to restrictions**. The former group is an exception. In Germany, such rights can only be restricted by way of other (conflicting) constitutional guarantees, which either serve as a limit to the scope of protection or, mostly, as a restriction of the other right (then, however, requiring a concretising statutory basis).[157] The same should apply to the ECHR,[158] even though the problem is less likely to arise due to the lower level of protection under the Convention.[159] It must therefore be assumed that the prohibition of torture and slavery (Article 3, Article 4(1) ECHR) is not open to any restrictions at all (→ § 3 para 45). On various occasions, however, the ECtHR has recognised inherent, intrinsic or implicit restrictions in order to exclude trivial complaints[160] or to allow the Convention States to regulate the general conditions for the exercise of a right[161] (*eg* the right to vote[162] or the right to access to court[163]). In truth, these cases generally lack an act of interference, as they primarily concern the interpretation of substantive requirements of a right, the recognition of a regulatory mandate for the Contracting States, or the determination of a minimum threshold for limitations. For example, the prohibition of inhuman or degrading treatment (Article 3 ECHR) does not exclude the use of physical force in every form. If recourse to physical force is made "strictly necessary" by a prisoner's own conduct,[164] there is no inhuman or degrading treatment.[165] In other words, the necessary balancing act must often be performed already in relation to the scope of protection or the interference, and not necessarily on the level of justification. In summary, leaving aside the (extremely rare) case of conflicting Convention law, the rights and freedoms contained in the ECHR may only be limited according to designated provisions in the Convention.[166] These can be subdivided into general and specific restriction provisions.

b) General Provisions on the Restriction of Convention Rights

Articles 15–17 of the ECHR contain general provisions on the restriction of Convention rights. Under **Article 15(1)**, any High Contracting Party may, in time of war or other

---

295, 320 ff; Ehlers (1992) 51 VVDStRL 211, 225; Bethge (1998) 57 VVDStRL 7, 29–30; Scherzberg *Grundrechtsschutz und „Eingriffsintensität"* (Berlin 1989) pp 208 ff.
157 *Cf* Sachs in: Sachs (ed) *Grundgesetz* (4th ed, Munich 2007) Vor Art 1, paras 118 ff.
158 The fact that the second paragraphs of Articles 8–11 ECHR expressly permit restrictions "for the protection of the rights and freedoms of others" should not be taken to imply that conflicting Convention rights are irrelevant.
159 There is apparently no ECtHR case-law on this point.
160 *Cf* Wildhaber/Breitenmoser (note 151) Art 8, paras 579–580.
161 *Cf* para 37.
162 ECtHR *Ahmed* (2000) 29 EHRR 1, para 75; *Mathieu-Mohin* (1988) 10 EHRR 1, para 52.
163 ECtHR *Fogarty* (2002) 34 EHRR 302, para 33.
164 *Cf* ECtHR *Tekin* (2001) 31 EHRR 95, paras 52–53.
165 Peters (note 41) § 6 III treats this as a question of justification.
166 See also the discussion by Ovey/White (note 18) pp 219–220 on inherent limitations.

public emergency, take measures derogating from its obligations under the Convention to the extent strictly required by the exigencies of the situation, provided that such measures are not inconsistent with its other obligations under international law. The existence of a public emergency requires "an exceptional situation of crisis or emergency which affects the whole population and constitutes a threat to the organized life of the community of which the state is composed"[167] and which cannot adequately be dealt with by employing normal measures permitted under the Convention.[168] By reason of their direct and continuous contact with the pressing needs of the moment, the national authorities are left a wide margin of appreciation.[169] The derogation from the obligations under the Convention must conform to the principle of proportionality. Due to the savings provision in Article 53 of the ECHR (cf para 6), Article 15(1) does not permit breaches of human rights and fundamental freedoms guaranteed under domestic law. The rights referred to in Article 15(2) are non-derogable. Pursuant to paragraph 3 of the same Article, the Contracting State must keep the Secretary General of the Council of Europe fully informed of the measures taken and the reasons therefor. Article 15 has played a role in a considerable number of cases (Greece, Cyprus, Turkey, Northern Ireland).[170] **Article 16** of the ECHR allows the Contracting States to impose restrictions on political activities of aliens irrespective of the prohibition of discrimination in Article 14 of the Convention. The antiquated provision (unknown to other human rights covenants) should probably not apply to citizens of EU Member States.[171] **Article 17** seeks to prevent abuses of the Convention (para 39) and therefore precludes "enemies of freedom" from invoking its guarantees for any activity aimed at the destruction of the rights and freedoms or at their limitation to a greater extent that is provided for in the Convention itself. This means that the state may prohibit and punish an abusive exercise of fundamental rights. At the same time, however, the state is barred from imposing more stringent restrictions than envisaged by the ECHR.

c) Specific Provisions on the Restriction of Convention Rights

45 Specific restriction provisions only permit a limitation of the particular right or freedom for which they have been formulated. They, too, show a number of common characteristics.

aa) Requirement of a Legal Basis

46 Restrictable Convention rights are subject only to limitations **prescribed by or in accordance with law** (cf Articles 5, 8–11 ECHR; Article 1 of the 1st Protocol; Article 2 of the 4th Protocol; Article 2 of the 7th Protocol). Exactly what requirements "law" must meet in this context has not yet been entirely resolved.[172] As the reference is to national law, differences

---

167 ECtHR *Lawless (No 2)* (1979–80) 1 EHRR 13, para 28 of the judgment; see also Ovey/White (note 18) pp 443 ff.
168 Ovey/White (note 18) p 443.
169 ECtHR *Ireland v United Kingdom* (1979–80) 2 EHRR 25, para 207.
170 More detailed Stein in: Maier (ed) *Europäischer Menschenrechtsschutz* (Heidelberg 1982) pp 135 ff.
171 Cf ECtHR *Piermont* (1995) 20 EHRR 301, para 64; Frowein (note 17) Art 16 EMRK, para 1; Grabenwarter (2001) 60 VVDStRL 290, 333.
172 Cf Weiß *Das Gesetz im Sinne der Europäischen Menschenrechtskonvention* (Berlin 1996).

General Principles   § 2 VIII 5

in the Contracting States' legal systems must be taken into account.[173] A formal Act of Parliament is not required. With regard to common law countries, the ECtHR has also accepted unwritten law.[174] However, the law must be accessible as well as sufficiently precise and clear in its terms to enable citizens to foresee its consequences.[175]

bb) Pursuance of a Legitimate Aim

The provisions on the restriction of Convention rights list **specified legitimate aims** for which the rights may be limited. For example, a limitation of the freedom to manifest one's religion must serve the protection of public order, health or morals, or the protection of the rights and freedoms of others (Article 9(2) ECHR). As Article 18 of the ECHR expressly (re-)emphasises, the restrictions shall not be applied for any purpose other than those for which they have been prescribed. Article 1 of the 1st Protocol to the Convention permits the deprivation of property subject to conditions provided for by law, however, does not further specify those conditions. As a minimum, adequate exigencies of the common welfare should be required. 47

cc) Proportionality of the Interference

Many provisions for restriction under the Convention contain the requirement that an interference with the affected right must be "necessary in a democratic society".[176] Little by little, the ECtHR developed this phrase to embrace the principle of proportionality, noting that the adjective "necessary" is not synonymous with "indispensable".[177] The principle of proportionality[178] is understood in the sense most fully developed within German law.[179] The Court differentiates – just as the German courts and, for some time now, the ECJ (→ § 7 para 96; → § 14 para 48) – between the **suitability** of the state measure to the desired objective,[180] its **necessity** (in the sense that no less restrictive option was available)[181] and the **adequateness** of the measure in relation to the aim being pursued (proportionality *stricto sensu*)[182]. Other than in the case of Community law, it is often that last step, *ie* the juxtaposition and balancing of the interests of the Convention States on the one hand and of the applicants on the other, which is of particular importance. This concept of proportionality is probably one of the most important German contributions to the European legal system in recent history. The principle of proportionality serves as a general limit to the restrictability of Convention rights even where the ECHR or its Protocols do not expressly require the limitation to be "necessary". 48

---

173 In this sense Grabenwarter (note 25) § 18, para 8; see also Ovey/White (note 18) p 223.
174 ECtHR *Sunday Times* (1979–80) 2 EHRR 245, para 47; see also EurCommHR *Klass* App No 15473/89.
175 *Cf* ECtHR *Kruslin* (1990) 12 EHRR 547, para 30; *Herczegfalvy* (1993) 15 EHRR 437, paras 88, 91; *Rekvényi* (2000) 30 EHRR 519, paras 34 ff. See also Ovey/White (note 18) pp 223 ff.
176 *Cf* paragraphs 2 of Articles 8–11 ECHR.
177 ECtHR *Handyside* (1979–80) 1 EHRR 737, para 48; see also Reid (note 54) para I-062.
178 See generally Ovey/White (note 18) pp 222, 232 ff.
179 *Cf* Craig/de Búrca (note 117) p 373; Grabenwarter (2001) 60 VVDStRL 290, 308. For more details see → § 14 para 48.
180 *Cf* ECtHR *Groppera Radio AG* (1990) 12 EHRR 321, para 70.
181 ECtHR *Barthold* (1985) 7 EHRR 383, paras 52 ff. See also ECtHR *Dudgeon* (1982) 4 EHRR 149, para 58.
182 *Cf* ECtHR *Moustaquim* (1991) 13 EHRR 802, para 46.

6. Schematic Summary

49 In summary, the question whether a Convention right has been infringed should be dealt with as follows (at least in the case of liberty rights):

  I. Applicability of the Convention
   1. Entry into force of the Convention provision
   2. Ratification of the Convention provision by the Contracting State
   3. No reservations made

  II. Scope of protection of the Convention right
   1. Subject matter of the right
   2. Personal scope of protection
      Beneficiaries and entities bound by the Convention
   3. Territorial scope
      Extraterritorial effects
   4. Temporal scope

  III. Interference with the Convention right
      Exclusion of distant or marginal interferences

  IV. Justification of the interference
   1. Conflicting substantive provisions of the Convention
   2. General provisions on the restriction of Convention rights
      a) Article 15 ECHR
      b) Article 16 ECHR
      c) Article 17 ECHR
   3. Specific provisions on the restriction of Convention rights
      a) Requirement of a legal basis
         Accessibility, foreseeability, sufficient clarity and precision
      b) Legitimate aim
      c) Proportionality of the interference to the aim pursued
         Suitability, necessity and adequateness (proportionality *stricto sensu*)

IX. Judicial protection

1. Judicial Protection by the ECtHR

Case 4 – Problem: (ECtHR *K.-F.* (1998) 26 EHRR 390)

50 The applicant (a German citizen) had been arrested by German police officers on the strong suspicion of rent fraud and had been taken to a local police station so that his identity could be checked. Since the police officers found that there was a risk he could abscond, they provisionally held him in custody until the next morning. The period of detention amounted to 12 hours and 45 minutes. The Public Prosecutor's Office later discontinued the criminal proceedings against the applicant on the ground that it could not be proved that he had not intended to pay the rent owed. As a consequence, the applicant lodged a complaint with the Public Prosecutor's Office against the police officers alleging false imprisonment, attempted coercion and insulting behaviour. These proceedings were also discontinued. The applicant unsuccessfully applied for an order by the *Oberlandesgericht* (OLG – Regional Court of Appeal) to prosecute the police officers. The Court found that the discontinuation of the proceedings was justified, there being insufficient cause to bring a prosecution for false imprisonment and coercion. The *Bundesverfassungsgericht* (BVerfG – German Federal Con-

General Principles   § 2 IX 1

> stitutional Court) declined to accept a constitutional complaint for adjudication. The applicant then lodged an individual application against the Federal Republic of Germany with the ECtHR. Is the application admissible and well-founded?

Fundamental rights and freedoms can only unfold their full protection, if compliance   51
with them can be enforced through an independent judiciary. In the case of international guarantees, an international jurisdiction is required. The 11th Protocol to the ECHR[183], which entered into force on 11 November 1998, fundamentally restructured and simplified the – previously complicated and drawn-out – process of protecting human rights and fundamental freedoms under the Convention.[184] While under the old system of protection the European Court of Human Rights had to collaborate with the European Commission of Human Rights and the Committee of Ministers, the ECtHR now acts as a **permanent Court** (Article 19(ii) ECHR) and solely handles both the admissibility and merits phases of an application. The European Commission of Human Rights was dissolved; the Committee of Ministers (Articles 13 ff of the Statute of the Council of Europe) only supervises the execution of the Court's judgments (Article 46(2) ECHR). The ECtHR consists of a number of judges equal to that of the High Contracting Parties to the Convention (Article 20 ECHR) who are elected by the Parliamentary Assembly from a list of candidates nominated by the respective Contracting State (Article 22 ECHR) for a period of six years (Article 23(1) ECHR). The judges are required to be of high moral character and must either possess the qualifications required for appointment to high judicial office or be jurisconsults of recognised competence (Article 21(1) ECHR). They exercise a full-time office (Article 21(3) ECHR) and may be re-elected (Article 23(1)(ii) ECHR). Under Article 27 of the Convention, the ECtHR may sit in Committees of three judges, Chambers of seven judges, and in a Grand Chamber of seventeen judges.[185] The judge who is a national of any state being party to the proceedings sits as an *ex officio* member of the Chamber or Grand Chamber. The Plenary Court (Article 26 ECHR) is only concerned with administrative tasks (*eg* electing the President and Vice-Presidents of the Court, setting up Chambers). The organisation and administration of the Court, as well as the proceedings before it, are governed by Rules of Court adopted in 1998. The Court's jurisdiction is mandatory for all Contracting States (*ie* not subject to reservations).[186] Unlike the European Court of Justice (Article 222 TEC / Article III-354 DC), the European Court of Human Rights is not assisted by Advocates-General.

In order to secure and improve the effectiveness of the control system in view of the   52
Court's constantly increasing caseload (para 5), the Council of Europe drafted the 14th Protocol to the ECHR, which has yet to enter into force. In particular, the Court will be able to sit in a single-judge formation. The single judge may then finally declare inadmissible or strike out of the Court's list of cases an application submitted under Article 34 of the Convention, where such a decision can be taken without further examination (Article 27 ECHR as amended by the Protocol). The following paragraphs are based on the law currently in force. However, the 14th Protocol is being referred to where it will bring about substantial changes.

---

183 ETS No 155.
184 *Cf* Ovey/White (note 18) pp 8–11; Reid (note 54) paras I-002–I-003; → § 1 para 11.
185 On the composition of the Committes and Chambers see Rules 24 ff of the Rules of Court.
186 Initially, recognition of the jurisdiction was (technically) optional under former Article 46 of the Convention. *Cf* Schlette [1996] ZaöRV 905, 941.

a) Inter-State Cases

53 The ECHR currently provides for two forms of judicial proceedings – inter-state cases (Article 33 ECHR) and individual applications (Article 34 ECHR). In the future, the Committee of Ministers shall also be able to refer matters to the Court (para 54).

54 The inter-state proceedings allow each Contracting State to refer to the ECtHR any alleged breach of the Convention and the Protocols thereto by another Contracting Party. The applicant state is neither required to only pursue its own rights, nor does it have to demonstrate any particular interest in the outcome of the case. Although the number of inter-state cases is small, the procedure is seen as an effective means for securing a minimum standard of human rights protection in all Convention States.[187]

b) Advisory Opinions at the Request of the Committee of Ministers

55 Under the present Article 47 of the Convention, the ECtHR has jurisdiction to give **advisory opinions** at the request of the Committee of Ministers on legal questions concerning the interpretation of the Convention and its accompanying Protocols. The 14th Protocol to the ECHR provides that the Committee may refer to the Court questions concerning the execution and interpretation of final judgments as well as matters where it considers that a state refuses to abide by such a judgment (Article 46 Nos 3, 4 ECHR as amended by the Protocol). In the latter case, the Committee must first serve formal notice on the State Party considered to be in breach of its obligations.

c) Individual Application

56 The individual application (Article 34 ECHR), which can be regarded as an extraordinary right of appeal,[188] is of much greater relevance. It does not have any suspensive effect; however, the ECtHR may indicate to the parties any interim measure which it considers should be adopted in the interests of the parties or of the proper conduct of the proceedings before it (Rule 39 of the Rules of Court).[189] Normally, the Court will only make use of this power in cases involving allegations of (impending) breaches of Article 2 and/or 3 of the Convention.[190]

aa) Admissibility Requirements[191]

(1) Form, Language

57 Pursuant to Rule 45(1) of the ECtHR's Rules of Court, the application must be signed by the applicant or the applicant's representative. It can be lodged either in one of the official

---

[187] *Cf* Frowein [1996] JuS 845, 846. Examples of more recent cases are ECtHR *Denmark v Turkey* App No 34382/97; *Cyprus v Turkey* (2002) 35 EHRR 731.

[188] *Cf* von Stackelberg/von Stackelberg *Das Verfahren der deutschen Verfassungsbeschwerde und der europäischen Menschenrechtsbeschwerde* (Cologne 1988) pp 87 ff; Peukert (note 53) Art 25 EMRK, para 2; Rogge (note 92) Art 25, para 82.

[189] The Rules of Court have been adopted by the ECtHR pursuant to Article 26(d) of the Convention.

[190] *Cf* ECtHR *Cruz Varas* (1992) 14 EHRR 1, para 53.

[191] *Cf* also Ovey/White (note 18) pp 478 ff; Reid (note 54) paras I-029 ff; Grabenwarter (note 25) § 13; Peters (note 41) § 35; Rogge (note 92) Art 25, paras 1–70.

languages of the Court (**English** or **French**) or in one of the official languages of the Contracting States (Rule 34(2) of the Rules of Court).

(2) Compatibility with the ECHR

Article 35(3) of the ECHR directs the Court to declare inadmissible any individual application which it considers **incompatible** with the Convention or the Protocols thereto. The provision thereby defines the boundaries within which the Court is empowered to act. It comprises four requirements which relate to the personal (*ratione personae*), territorial (*ratione loci*), temporal (*ratione temporis*) and material (*ratione materiae*) scope of the Convention and its Protocols. It would also be possible to attribute these points to the requirement of legal standing (para 63).

58

(a) Capacity to Take Legal Action and to be Party to the Proceedings

Firstly, the applicant must be **capable of taking legal action** and of **being party to the proceedings**. Secondly, the respondent state must be bound by the Convention right concerned. An individual application may be lodged by any natural person, non-governmental organisation or group of individuals (even those without legal personality). For a definition of the beneficiaries of the Convention see paras 22 ff. Both the ECHR and the Rules of Court do not contain any specific requirements as regards the ability to plead before the Court. Hence, everyone who is factually capable of doing so may take part in the proceedings.[192] This may even be a legally incapacitated person or a minor,[193] although cases concerning children will normally be brought by parents or guardians. There is no strict requirement to be represented by counsel, at least in the pre-hearing phase of an application. However, the Court will generally direct that the applicant be represented following notification of the application to the respondent Contracting Party (Rule 36(2) of the Rules of Court). Where an applicant dies during the examination of a case, his heirs or next of kin may pursue the application on his behalf, if they have a legitimate interest in doing so.[194] An application may be brought only against a state which is bound by the Convention right in question and only in respect of measures for which the state is in some way responsible (paras 27 ff).

59

(b) As to the **territorial** scope of the Convention see para 35.

60

(c) The **temporal** scope of the Convention is determined according to general principles of the law of international treaties (para 36).

61

(d) The dispute giving rise to the application must fall within the subject matter of the Convention. All other issues concerning the compatibility of the application with the ECHR should be addressed either under the issue of legal standing (para 63) or the question whether the application is directed against an entity bound by the Convention (paras 58, 27 ff).

62

---

192 *Cf* Murswiek [1986] JuS 8, 9.
193 *Cf* ECtHR *A v United Kingdom* (1999) 27 EHRR 611.
194 *Cf* EurCommHR *Ensslin, Bader and Raspe* App No 7572/76, (1979) 14 DR 64, para 1; ECtHR *Jėčius* App No 34578/97, RJD 2000-IX, 237, para 41.

(3) Legal Standing

63 Pursuant to Article 34 of the ECHR, the applicant must further claim to be the victim of a violation by one of the High Contracting Parties of the rights set forth in the Convention or the Protocols thereto. It is common ground that the applicant must claim a violation of his or her own rights.[195] By "victim" Article 34 means the person directly affected by the act or omission which is in issue.[196] The applicant must substantiate that there is at least the possibility of a violation of his or her rights.[197] This relatively low threshold for legal standing is supported by the fact that, *inter alia*, only "manifestly ill-founded" applications must be declared inadmissible (Article 35(3) ECHR). If the application is directed against a legal provision without challenging an individual measure of implementation, the applicant must be directly (*ie* personally and currently) affected by the law itself (and not just its implementation).[198] Where a measure ceases to affect the applicant, the Court may nevertheless examine the case, unless the Convention State has acknowledged the violation and (if appropriate) paid compensation.[199]

(4) Exhaustion of Domestic Remedies

64 Article 35(1) of the ECHR stipulates that the ECtHR may only deal with the application "after all domestic remedies have been exhausted". The term "remedies" also includes informal steps – provided that they are sufficient and adequate to afford redress in respect of the breach alleged.[200] Considering that the state is to be given an opportunity to put matters right through its own legal system and that the machinery of protection established by the Convention is only subsidiary to the national systems safeguarding human rights, the applicant must have raised the complaint "in substance" before the national judicial or administrative authorities.[201] If the applicant's complaint relates to an unreasonable length of proceedings (Article 6(1)(i) ECHR), the exhaustion of remedies depends on whether he or she could have expedited the proceedings or at least obtained compensation for its excessive duration.[202] The applicant is not required to first pursue actions for damages against the state if these are insufficient to remedy his or her complaint.[203] Due to its extraordinary character, an application for a new trial or re-hearing is not to be counted among the effective "remedies".[204] Although the applicant must have generally exhausted all domestic remedies prior to petitioning to the ECtHR, it may in

---

195 *Cf* Reid (note 54) para I-065; Schmidt-Aßmann in: Schoch/Schmidt-Aßmann/Pietzner (eds) *Verwaltungsgerichtsordnung* (loose-leaf, Munich 2005) Einl, para 147.
196 ECtHR *Groppera Radio AG* (1990) 12 EHRR 321, para 47; *cf* Peukert (note 53) Art 25 EMRK, para 20. See also Rogge (note 92) Art 25, paras 214 ff.
197 *Cf* for example Pieroth/Schlink (note 129) paras 1129 ff; Wahl/Schütz in: Schoch/Schmidt-Aßmann/Pietzner (eds) *Verwaltungsgerichtsordnung* (loose-leaf, Munich 2005) § 42 II, paras 64 ff.
198 *Cf* ECtHR *Marckx* (1979–80) 2 EHRR 330, para 27.
199 Peukert (note 53) Art 25 EMRK, para 29; Reid (note 54) para I-042; Villiger (note 150) § 9, paras 149–150.
200 Schmidt-Aßmann (note 184) Einl, para 148.
201 *Cf* Villiger (note 150) § 7, paras 133–134; Ovey/White (note 18) pp 485–487; Reid (note 54) paras I-037 ff; ECtHR *Akdivar* (1997) 23 EHRR 143, para 65.
202 ECtHR *Tomé Mota* App No 32082/96, RJD 1999-IX, 402.
203 ECtHR *Hornsby* (1997) 24 EHRR 250, para 37; *Iatridis* (2000) 30 EHRR 97.
204 Peters (note 41) p 242.

certain cases be sufficient if the last domestic decision is delivered even after the application has been filed (but before the ECtHR has made a determination as regards the admissibility).[205] Domestic remedies will only be exhausted, if the applicant has unsuccessfully appealed – where this was possible – to the highest competent court. This may also include special remedies such as, for example, a constitutional complaint to the German Federal Constitutional Court, if such remedies are capable of redressing the alleged violation of the Convention.[206] According to the ECtHR, structural or institutional changes resulting from the conclusion of international treaties by the Convention States must be taken into account when interpreting the Convention.[207] Therefore, **remedies under the law of the European Community** can also be regarded as "domestic" for the purposes of Article 35(1) of the ECHR.[208] In any case, remedies required to be exhausted are only those which are not merely theoretically but practically available or accessible to the applicant, and which are sufficient to effectively redress the complaint.[209] The requirement of accessibility must be given particular attention in the cases of persons detained, lacking sufficient financial means or incapable of speaking the language of the Convention State. If national case law shows that a formally available remedy has no reasonable chance of success, an applicant is not obliged to try it.[210] If an appeal only permits the national court to deal with questions of law but not with factual issues, the exhaustion of domestic remedies depends on whether the application in fact challenges questions of fact.[211] In borderline cases, the ECtHR tends to adopt a view that enhances rather than curtails the level of judicial protection. Where the respondent state does not raise the objection of non-exhaustion of domestic remedies during the admissibility phase of an application, the Court may declare that the state is estopped from relying on the objection at a later stage (*cf* Rule 55 of the Rules of Court).[212]

(5) Time-limit[213]

The application must be filed within a period of **six months** from the date on which the final domestic decision was taken. (Article 35(1) ECHR). Time starts running from the day after the applicant became aware of the act or decision of which he or she complains.[214] If the decision must be formally served on the applicant (*eg* in the case of court judgments), the six-month period is generally counted from the date on which the written version of the decision was served and not from the date when it was initially announced or delivered.[215] As a general rule, the date of introduction of the application is considered

---

205 Grabenwarter (note 25) § 13, para 22.
206 *Cf* Peukert (note 53) Art 26 EMRK, para 28.
207 ECtHR *Matthews* (1999) 28 EIIRR 361, para 39.
208 Grabenwarter (2001) 60 VVDStRL 290, 335.
209 *Cf* ECtHR *Dalia* (2001) 33 EHRR 625, para 38; ECtHR *Stögmüller* (1979–80) 1 EHRR 155, para 11.
210 Ovey/White (note 18) p 486; Peters (note 41) p 244.
211 *Cf* ECtHR *Civet* (2001) 31 EHRR 871, paras 43 ff.
212 *Cf* Villiger (note 150) § 7, para 114. *Cf* ECtHR *Artico* (1981) 3 EHRR 1, paras 27 ff; *Granger* (1990) 12 EHRR 469, para 38.
213 See also Ovey/White (note 18) p 487–488.
214 Ovey/White (note 18) p 487.
215 *Cf* ECtHR *Worm* (1998) 25 EHRR 454, paras 31–32; Meyer-Ladewig (note 41) Art 35, paras 19 ff; Reid (note 54) para I-031.

to be the date of the first communication from the applicant and not the date of its receipt by the Court (Article 47(5) of the Rules of Court). The Court may for good cause decide that a different date should be considered to be the date of introduction (*eg* if the communication was obviously backdated).[216] The applicant must at least summarily communicate the object of the application before the time-limit expires. In principle, the six-month period cannot be suspended – unless the applicant was factually incapable of complying with the time-limit (*eg* due to being detained in solitary confinement).

(6) Other Admissibility Requirements

66 Articles 34 and 35 of the ECHR impose a number of further admissibility criteria, which partly overlap with the requirements discussed above. The application may not be filed anonymously (Article 35(2)(a) ECHR) and must not constitute an abuse of process (Article 35(3) ECHR)[217]. In addition, Article 35(2)(b) of the ECHR requires that it has not already been examined by the Court or submitted to another procedure of international investigation or settlement. This means that the application must have neither been the subject of any previous final decision by the ECHR (*res judicata*), nor be pending for decision before any other international court or tribunal (*litis pendentia*).[218] Both the applicant as well as the facts and the content of the complaint must be identical. Applicants are already considered 'identical' if they pursue the same legal interests and are sufficiently closely connected to each other.[219] The 14th Protocol to the Convention will enable the Court to declare applications inadmissible where it considers that the applicant has not suffered any significant disadvantage, unless respect for human rights as defined by the Convention and the Protocols thereto requires an examination of the case on the merits. An application may also not be rejected on this ground if the complaint has not been duly considered by a domestic tribunal (Article 35(2)(b) ECHR as amended by the 14th Protocol). Finally, the applicant must demonstrate that there is a need for legal protection.[220]

bb) Proceedings

67 The proceedings before the ECtHR in the case of individual applications comprise multiple stages. Subject to the President of the Section directing that the case be considered by a Chamber, the Judge Rapporteur decides whether the application is to be considered by a Committee or by a Chamber (Rule 49(3)(b) of the Rules of Court). Where an application appears to be clearly inadmissible, the Rapporteur will refer it to a Committee of the Chamber (Article 27(1)(ii) ECHR) for a decision on its admissibility. After entry into

---

216 In practice, the Court therefore regularly uses the date of the postmark.
217 Since the latter point is, however, closely intertwined with the actual content of the Convention right in question, the Court will only deal with on examining the merits of an application, see ECtHR *Bosphorus* (2006) 42 EHRR 1, para 102.
218 Reid (note 54) para I-047.
219 *Cf* EurCommHR *Rudolf Hess* [1982] EuGRZ 15, para 2 (re-application by relatives of the victim); *Cereceda Martin* (1993) 15 EHRR CD18 (application of members of an association who had already appeared as applicants in other proceedings). In both cases, the Commission declared the applications inadmissible.
220 *Cf* EurCommHR *Darby* App No 11581/85, (1989) 56 DR 166; Peukert (note 53) Art 25 EMRK, para 38.

force of the 14th Protocol to the ECHR, a single judge may finally declare inadmissible an individual application, where such a decision can be taken without further examination (para 52), unless the application concerns the High Contracting Party in respect of which he or she has been elected. Until then, the Committee may reject or strike out of its list of cases (Article 37 ECHR) any individual application which it unanimously considers to be inadmissible without further examination (Article 28 ECHR). If no negative decision is taken, the appropriate **Chamber** must decide on the admissibility and merits of the application (Article 29 ECHR). Pursuant to Article 29(3) of the ECHR, the decision on admissibility shall be taken separately unless the Court, in exceptional cases, decides otherwise. Once an application is declared admissible, Article 38 of the ECHR directs the Court to pursue the examination of the case, undertake an investigation (if need be), and to place itself at the disposal of the parties with a view to securing a friendly settlement (which would result in the application being struck out of the list of cases). In principle, the proceedings are conducted in public (Article 40 ECHR). Only where a case raises a serious question affecting the interpretation of the Convention or where the resolution of a question might be inconsistent with a previous judgment of the Court, the Chamber may – at any time before it has rendered its judgment – relinquish jurisdiction in favour of the Grand Chamber, unless one of the parties to the case objects (Article 30 ECHR).[221] Furthermore, any one of the parties may, within three months of the judgment of a Chamber, "in exceptional cases" request that the case be referred to the Grand Chamber (Article 43(1) ECHR). Pursuant to Article 43(2) of the ECHR, a panel of five judges of the Grand Chamber shall accept the request if the case raises a serious issue. In this case, the Grand Chamber – as an internal appellate body[222] – decides by way of final judgment (Article 43(3) ECHR). Even at this stage, the Grand Chamber may still declare an application inadmissible.[223] (*cf* Article 35(4)(ii) ECHR)

cc) Examination on the Merits and the Effects of a Decision by the ECtHR

An individual application submitted under Article 34 of the Convention is well-founded, if one of the applicant's Convention rights has been violated (paras 38 ff). The density of judicial review is – compared to Germany – somewhat lower, primarily because the ECtHR accords the Contracting States "margins of appreciation" in a rather generous fashion. The actual wording of the provisions of the Convention is often given little significance. As regards the margins of appreciation, their respective scope may vary depending on the legal or factual issue in question. For example, the Court leaves a considerably wider margin to national authorities when it comes to complying with positive obligations under the Convention. Other relevant factors are the importance of the aim pursued, the presence or absence of common European standards and the intensity of the potential

---

221 The parties' right of objection seems anomalous.
222 It is problematic that according to Article 27(3)(ii) of the ECHR the composition of the Grand Chamber includes the President of the Chamber which rendered the judgment and the judge who sat in respect of the State Party concerned, *ie* two judges who have already been involved in the judgment that is being scrutinised by the Grand Chamber. Critical as to this provision Schlette [1999] JZ 219, 225–226.
223 ECtHR *Bosphorus* (2006) 42 EHRR 1, para 103; see also Art 35(4)(ii) ECHR: "at any stage of the proceedings."

encroachment on the sovereignty of the Convention State concerned.[224] Furthermore, the Court is generally prepared to grant the Contracting Parties more leeway in relation to the substantive questions, if this is compensated by procedural or organisational safeguards.[225]

69 Final decisions of the ECtHR, which are of **declaratory** nature (as can be deduced from Article 41 of the ECHR[226]), are binding on the parties to the proceedings. The respondent state is **bound under international law** to abide by a judgment (Article 46(1) ECHR). However, the Court neither has the power to reverse measures that violate the Convention (*eg* domestic judicial determinations), nor is it competent to demand any specific actions by the Contracting State (aside from imposing an obligation to pay just satisfaction pursuant to Article 41 of the ECHR).[227] In certain cases, however, the ECtHR held that the nature of the violation left no choice as regards the appropriate measure to be taken and, for example, ordered the respondent state to secure the release of an incarcerated applicant at the earliest possible date.[228] The Convention is silent on the legal effects of the Court's decisions withtin the domestic legal systems. They must hence be determined according to national law. The Contracting Parties must ensure that their internal legal order is compatible with the Convention. Consequently, it is for the respondent state to remove any obstacles in its domestic legal system that might prevent the applicant's situation from being adequately redressed.[229] Firstly, the breach of the Convention must be terminated; secondly, reparation must be made for the consequences of the breach; and thirdly, measures must be taken to avoid the recurrence of a similar breach in the future. Legislative, administrative or other governmental acts incompatible with the Convention can usually be repealed or reversed. More problematic are incompatible domestic court decisions. If the national proceedings have yet to be completed, the domestic courts are obliged – within the limits of acceptable methods of interpretation – to adopt a decision that is compatible with the Convention as expressed in the opinion of the ECtHR (paras 74–75). Where a domestic decision is no longer subject to appeal, the principle of *restitutio in integrum* (putting the injured party, as far as possible, in the same situation as he or she enjoyed prior to the violation of the Convention) would generally require the reopening of the proceedings, especially in criminal cases. However, the

---

224 *Cf* ECtHR *Refah Partisi* (2002) 35 EHRR 56, paras 40–41; Ovey/White (note 18) p 54; Reid (note 54) para I-055.
225 For more details on the doctrine of margins of appreciation see Ovey/White (note 18) pp 232–239; Reid (note 54) para I-055; Yourow *The Margin of Appreciation Doctrin in the Dynamics of the European Human Rights Jurisprudence* (The Hague 1996); Rupp-Swienty *Die Doktrin von der margin of appreciation in der Rechtsprechung des Europäischen Gerichtshofs für Menschenrechte* (Munich 1999); Arai-Takahashi *The Margin of Appreciation Doctrine and the Principle of Proportionality in the Jurisprudence of the ECHR* (Antwerp 2002); Rubel *Die Gewährung von Entscheidungsfreiräumen in der Rechtsprechung des Europäischen Gerichtshofs für Menschenrechte und des Europäischen Gerichtshofs* (Hamburg 2005).
226 See also ECtHR *Assanidze* (2004) 39 EHRR 653, para 202.
227 Settled case-law (in Germany) *cf* BVerfG [1986] NJW 1425; [2004] NJW 3407, 3409; see also Uerpmann (note 27) pp 172 ff; Dörr in: Sodan/Ziekow (eds) *Nomos-Kommentar zur Verwaltungsgerichtsordnung* (2nd ed, Baden-Baden 2006) EVR, para 286; Ehlers *Die Europäisierung des Verwaltungsprozessrechts* (Cologne 1999) pp 139–140.
228 ECtHR *Assanidze* (2004) 39 EHRR 653, paras 203–204; *Ilaşcu* (2005) 40 EHRR 46, para 490.
229 ECtHR *Assanidze* (2004) 39 EHRR 653, para 198; BVerfG [2004] NJW 3407, 3409.

General Principles §2 IX 1

ECtHR does not impose any general obligation on the Contracting States to provide for such mechanisms within their national legal systems – particularly since the principle of legal certainty is also recognised under the Convention.[230] Nevertheless, the adoption of some procedure for reopening cases if an applicant was successful before the ECtHR would be desirable.[231] Where a final domestic decision has not yet been executed, Article 46 of the ECHR bars any execution in favour of the Convention State.[232] If the internal law of the High Contracting Party concerned allows only partial reparation to be made, the ECtHR may, if necessary, afford **just satisfaction** to the injured party (Article 41 ECHR).[233] This requires the applicant to show that he or she has suffered a loss causally connected to the breach of the Convention. Both pecuniary and non-pecuniary losses are recoverable[234] – even if the applicant is not a natural person.[235] In determining the amount of compensation, damages already awarded under the law of the European Union are to be taken into account.[236] The ECtHR considers reparation under national law to be insufficient, if the applicant is required to again call upon the national courts for realising an existing entitlement to damages.[237]

Case 4 – Answer:
The admissibility of the application could be in doubt, since the applicant did not exhaust all available domestic remedies. He neither sought judicial review of his arrest nor of the detention, but only initiated proceedings against the police officers. According to the ECtHR, the purpose of the rule of exhaustion of domestic remedies (Article 34 ECHR) is to afford the Contracting States the opportunity of preventing or putting right the violations alleged against them before those allegations are submitted to the ECtHR. Nevertheless, the only remedies that must be exhausted are those that are effective and capable of redressing the alleged violation (para 63; ECtHR *Remli* (1996) 22 EHRR 253, para 33). Furthermore, the rule is to be applied with some degree of flexibility and without excessive formalism. In the case at hand, the ECtHR held that the applicant had met the requirements of Article 34 by lodging a complaint against the officers and subsequently applying to the OLG to have a prosecution brought against them on the grounds that his arrest and

70

---

230 Predominant opinion (in Germany); *cf Bundesfinanzhof* (BFH – German Federal Tax Court) [1978] DVBl 501; BVerwG [1998] DÖV 924; BVerfG [2004] NJW 3407, 3410.
231 *Cf* ECtHR *Öcalan* (2005) 41 EHRR 985 (Grand Chamber), para 210, in which the Court considered that where an individual has been convicted by a court which did not meet the Convention requirements of independence and impartiality, a retrial or a reopening of the case, if requested, represents in principle an "appropriate" way of redressing the violation. See also Recommendation by the Committee of Ministers No R (2000) 2 of 19 January 2000 and Pache/Bielitz [2006] DVBl 325.
232 *Cf* Frowein [1986] JuS 845, 850.
233 *Cf* Dannemann *Schadensersatz bei Verletzung der Europäischen Menschenrechtskonvention* (Cologne 1994); for details see Reid (note 54) paras III-001 ff.
234 *Cf* for example ECtHR *Smith and Grady* (2001) 31 EHRR 24, paras 12-13; Ossenbühl *Staatshaftungsrecht* (5th ed, Munich 1998) pp 527 ff.
235 *Cf* ECtHR *Comingersoll* (2001) 31 EHRR 772, para 35.
236 ECtHR *Hornsby* App No 18357/91, RJD 1998-II (Just Satisfaction), para 18; Grabenwarter (2001) 60 VVDStRL 290, 335–336.
237 ECtHR *Papamichalopoulos* (1996) 21 EHRR 439, para 40; *Scollo* (1996) 22 EHRR 514, para 50; *Barberà* App No 10590/83, (1994) Série A, Vol 285-C (Just Satisfaction), para 17; *Neumeister* (1979–80) 1 EHRR 136 (Just Satisfaction), para 30.

> detention had been unlawful. Since the OLG at least in part examined the lawfulness of the police actions, the remedy taken by the applicant was effective and adequate to deal with the complaint. The applicant could not be expected to have used other remedies. The application is well-founded, if Article 5(1)(c) of the Convention was breached. Although there was reasonable suspicion that the applicant had committed an offence, the arrest and detention must have been lawful. Under German law (Section 163c(3) of the *Strafprozessordnung* (StPO – Code of Criminal Procedure)), a person may be provisionally held in custody for up to 12 hours in order to check his or her identity. This maximum period had been exceeded by 45 minutes. Consequently, the ECtHR found that there had been a violation of Article 5(1)(c) of the Convention, but only afforded the applicant 10,000 German Marks (approximately 5,000 Euro) in respect of costs and expenses.

dd) Schematic Summary

71 In summary, it is advisable to examine the admissibility of individual applications according to the following check-list:

1. Proper form and language
2. Compatibility of the application with the ECHR
   a) *Ratione personae*
      Beneficiaries of and entities bound by the Convention
   b) *Ratione loci*
   c) *Ratione temporis*
   d) *Ratione materiae*
      Applicability of the Convention right(s)
3. Legal standing
4. Exhaustion of domestic remedies
5. Time-limit
6. Other admissibility requirements
   a) No anonymity
   b) No *res judicata*
   c) No proceedings pending before international courts or tribunals
   d) No abuse of process
   e) Significant disadvantage
      After entry into force of Article 35(3)(b) ECHR as amended by the 14th Protocol to the ECHR
   f) Need for legal protection

72 As regards the examination of the merits, see paras 38 ff.

2. Judicial Protection by National Courts

Case 5 – Problems:
73 a) (High Court *Venables & Thompson v News Group Newspapers* [2001] 1 All ER 908): In 1993, when they were ten years old, the claimants killed a two-year old boy. The circumstances of the killing were particularly shocking and were widely publicised in the media. The claimants were convicted of murder by an English court and sentenced to be detained during Her Majesty's pleasure. At the conclusion of the trial, the judge imposed injunctions restricting the publication of information about the claimants other than their names and

backgrounds. Those injunctions were based on jurisdictions which only applied to minors. In 2000 the claimants reached the age of 18. It was likely that the Parole Board would shortly afterwards make a decision on the claimants' reintegration into the community. In proceedings against three newspaper groups, the claimants seek permanent injunctions protecting information regarding changes in their physical appearances since their detention and the new identities that would probably be given to them on their release. They allege that the intended publication of their future whereabouts and description of their appearances would endanger their lives in view of threats that had been made against them. While the newspapers argue that there is no legal basis for the Court to grant such injunctions in respect of adults, the claimants contend that such a jurisdiction can be found in the law of confidence, taking into account the right to life and the prohibition against torture and inhumane or degrading treatment guaranteed by Article 2 and 3 of the ECHR. Can the Court rely on the Convention for granting the requested injunctions?

b) (BVerfG (2004) 111 BVerfGE 307): The complainant is the father of a child born illegitimate that was given up for adoption by foster parents with whom the child has been living since its birth. Since 1999, the complainant has unsuccessfully endeavoured in a number of judicial proceedings to be given custody and to be granted a right of access. In response to his individual application, the ECtHR held that the decision on custody and the exclusion of the right of access violated Article 8 of the ECHR. Following this decision, the complainant's re-application before the German courts was ultimately declined by the Regional Court of Appeal, which held that the ECtHR's judgment was only binding on the Federal Republic of Germany, but not on the independent German judiciary. In his constitutional complaint against the decision of the Regional Court of Appeal, the complainant alleges a violation of his fundamental right under Article 6 of the Basic Law. Is the complaint well-founded?

Since the ECHR and its Protocols confer subjective rights on the individual against the respective Contracting State, those rights can (and must) be enforced (primarily) before the domestic courts of the state concerned. As shown above (para 69), the national courts are bound to pay due regard – within the limits of acceptable methods of interpretation – to the Contracting State's obligations under the Convention as well as to the decisions of the ECtHR.[238]

Case 5 – Answers:
a) Since the inherent jurisdiction of the Family Division of the High Court to protect minors is no longer applicable to the claimants and since there is no specific statutory or common law power in respect of protecting adults, the Court can only grant the injunctions if an existing jurisdictional basis is extended to cover the case at hand. Such a basis could lie in the common law of confidence – interpreted in light of the guarantees of the European Convention. The ECHR has been incorporated into the English legal system by the Human Rights Act 1998. Pursuant to Section 6(1) of the Act it is unlawful for any public authority to act in way which is incompatible with a Convention right (as set out in Schedule 1 of the Act). Although operating in the public domain and fulfilling a public service, the defendant newspapers do not come within the definition of "public authority". Consequently, the Convention rights are not directly enforceable against them. That is not, however, the end of the matter, as the Court itself is a public authority (cf Section 6(3) of the Act) and must there-

---

238 For German courts see BVerfG [2004] NJW 3407, 3411.

fore act in a way compatible with the Convention and have regard to the jurisprudence of the ECtHR (*cf* Section 2 of the Act). Under certain circumstances, the Convention imposes positive obligations on the Contracting States to actively protect the rights of individuals (*cf* ECtHR *X and Y v The Netherlands* (1986) 8 EHRR 235, para 23). These obligations also extend to the judicial branch of government requiring, where necessary, the provision or adoption of a regulatory framework of adjudicatory and enforcement machinery in order to ensure an appropriate level of protection. They do not, however, encompass the creation of a free-standing cause of action against other private individuals based directly upon the articles of the Convention. Rather, the duty on the courts is to act compatibly with the Convention rights in adjudicating upon existing common and statutory law causes of action. Hence, in determining whether or not to grant the injunctions based on the law of confidence, the Court must pay due regard both to the claimants' rights to protection against inhumane or degrading treatment as well as the newspapers' right to freedom of expression as guaranteed by the ECHR.

b) A constitutional complaint can only be used to assert a violation of German fundamental rights guaranteed by the Basic Law. Consequently, the complainant will only be successful before the Federal Constitutional Court, if the decision of the Regional Court of Appeal violates his fundamental right to protection of the family and to the upbringing of his child as guaranteed by Article 6 of the Basic Law. Although the right also guarantees access to one's own children, it is subject to restrictions. However, in restricting fundamental rights, the essence of those rights and the principle of the rule of law must be observed. In particular, Article 20(3) of the Basic Law provides that the judiciary shall be bound by law and justice. This obligation includes the observance of the ECHR and the decisions by the ECtHR. While the German Court could have given due consideration to the ECtHR's judgment when interpreting Article 6 of the Basic Law, it erroneously proceeded on the assumption that it was not bound by the judgment. The decision of the Regional Court of Appeal therefore not only violated Article 8 of the ECHR, but also Article 6 of the Basic Law. The German Federal Constitutional Court consequently upheld the complaint.

§ 3
Personal Rights and the Prohibition of Discrimination*

Robert Uerpmann-Wittzack

Leading Cases: ECtHR *Soering* (1989) 11 EHRR 439; *Niemietz* (1993) 16 EHRR 97; *Guerra* (1998) 26 EHRR 357.

Further Reading: Breitenmoser *Der Schutz der Privatsphäre gemäß Art 8 EMRK* (Basel 1986); Brötel *Schutz des Familienlebens* (1999) 63 RabelsZ 580; Hailbronner *Art 3 EMRK – ein neues europäisches Konzept der Schutzgewährung?* [1999] DÖV 617; Heselhaus/Marauhn *Straßburger Springprozession zum Schutz der Umwelt* [2005] EuGRZ 549; Kälin *Tragweite und Begründung des Abschiebungshindernisses von Art 3 EMRK bei nichtstaatlicher Gefährdung* in: Hailbronner/Klein (eds) *Einwanderungskontrolle und Menschenrechte* (Heidelberg 1999) pp 49–52; Kley-Struller *Der Schutz der Umwelt durch die Europäische Menschenrechtskonvention* [1995] EuGRZ 507; Kugelmann *Individualkommunikation* [2003] EuGRZ 16; Mock *Le droit au respect de la vie privée et familiale, du domicile et de la correspondance (article 8 CEDH) à l'aube du XXIe siècle* (1998) 10 RUDH 237; Schmidt-Radefeldt *Ökologische Menschenrechte* (Baden-Baden 2000) pp 55–200; Schöbener *Die „Lehrerin mit Kopftuch" – europäisch gewendet!* [2003] Jura 186; Wolfrum (ed) *Gleichheit und Nichtdiskriminierung im nationalen und internationalen Menschenrechtsschutz* (Berlin 2003).

The following section deals with some of the **core guarantees** of the European Convention on Human Rights, in particular the rights to private life and personal integrity and the prohibition of discrimination. This section is not supposed to impart detailed knowledge on these guarantees, but rather to create an understanding of the basic structures and to enable the reader to work independently with the guarantees. The ECHR is, like the *Grundgesetz* (German Basic Law) and other European constitutions, part of a common European culture of fundamental rights.[1] Despite significant differences, guarantees of the ECHR also show strong parallels with national fundamental rights norms. The following contribution pays special attention to the similarities and differences with regard to German constitutional law. Some concepts which have been developed by German constitutional jurisprudence and scholarship may be transferred to the ECHR quite easily. On the other hand, the ECHR has impacted some areas in which the German fundamental rights have remained vague. This is the case, for instance, with the protection of foreigners against expulsion and deportation. These areas of application will be given particular attention.

1

I. Protection of Privacy

Case 1 – Problem:
The Turkish citizen M was born in Munich and brought up there by his parents. He knew Turkey only from holiday stays and hardly spoke any Turkish. Before he was even fourteen years old, he repeatedly committed criminal offences. After his fourteenth birthday, he continued to commit further criminal offences such as theft, breaking and entering, robbery,

2

---

* Translated by Alice Lees and revised by the author.
1 Uerpmann *Die Europäische Menschenrechtskonvention und die deutsche Rechtsprechung* (Berlin 1993) pp 117–130.

physical harm, coercion and trespass. Within four years he was sentenced to a youth offenders institution for a total of more than three years. As a consequence he was expelled and deported in accordance with the German Immigration Act. Is this expulsion and deportation in accordance with the Convention?

1. Private and Family Life, Home and Correspondence (Article 8 ECHR)

a) Scope of Protection

aa) Private Life

3   Article 8(1) of the ECHR contains four different scopes of protection, *ie* private life, family life, home and correspondence. The **right to private life** is the broadest of all four. The other scopes of protection are to a large degree specific expressions of the right to private life. The respect for private life is often invoked in the absence of more specific guarantees. Article 8(1) of the ECHR shows similarities in this regard with Article 2(1) of the Basic Law. Article 2(1) of the Basic Law protects the free development of personality. This is understood in a very broad sense to cover any human activity and to convey a *prima facie* protection against any intrusion by the state. A special aspect of this freedom is the general right to personality, which is derived both from Article 2(1) and from the protection of human dignity under Article 1(1) of the Basic Law. While the ECHR does not contain a general right to freedom, the right to private life, according to Article 8(1) of the ECHR, accepts functions which Article 2(1) of the Basic Law and particularly the general right to personality fulfil in Germany. For example, both the Basic Law and the ECHR protect the private life of VIP's from the overpowering intrusion of the press. In the Basic Law, the general right to personality protects their interests[2], while on the European level Article 8 of the ECHR intervenes[3]. A similar approach is taken for data protection. Whereas in Germany the right to self-determination over personal data is enshrined in the general right to personality[4], the ECHR relies on the right to respect for private life[5]. Moreover, the ECtHR has emphasised that the principle of self-determination forms the basis of the guarantees of Article 8 of the ECHR.[6] This, too, shows the proximity to Article 2(1) of the Basic Law.

4   The ECtHR has expressly abstained from a definition of private life.[7] It follows a casuistic approach, as is typical Convention practice. Whereas continental constitutional

---

2 *Bundesverfassungsgericht* (BVerfG – German Federal Constitutional Court) (1986) 73 BVerfGE 118, 201; (1998) 97 BVerfGE 125, 146; (1999) 101 BVerfGE 361, 379.
3 ECtHR *von Hannover* (2005) 40 EHRR 1; Court of Appeal (England & Wales) *Douglas v Hello!* [2001] 2 All ER 289; *cf* Amelung/Vogenauer [2002] ZeuP 341; Theusinger [2001] ZRP 529.
4 BVerfG *Census* (1983) 65 BVerfGE 1, 42 ff; *cf* Kunig [1993] Jura 595.
5 ECtHR *Amann* (2000) 30 EHRR 843, para 65; Mock (1998) 10 RUDH 237, 241; but see *Bundesgericht* (Swiss Federal Court) [1999] EuGRZ 53 with regard to taxation data; see also ECtHR *Knauth* App No 41111/98 (decision on admissibility) with regard to the use of information contained in the files of the former GDR secret service.
6 ECtHR *Pretty* (2002) 35 EHRR 1, para 61; *Van Kück* (2003) 37 EHRR 973, para 69; with regard to *Pretty* see also Fassbender [2004] Jura 115.
7 ECtHR *Niemietz* (1993) 16 EHRR 97, para 29; see also Merrills/Robertson *Human Rights in Europe* (4th ed, 2001 Manchester) p 138; Mock (note 5) p 239.

law jurisprudence and scholarship try to develop definitions for constitutional terms, similar definitions do not exist with regard to the ECHR. Therefore, no attempts at definitions will be made here. Instead it seems more adequate to impart **guidelines** which may be useful **for casuistic reasoning**.

The concept of private life is to be **construed broadly**. It does not only include an inner sphere of personal existence, but also social relationships and contacts to the outside world. Private life has to be distinguished from the public, state-related sphere. The exercise of public functions does not belong to private life. Outside of the state's sphere, however, professional occupations may also fall within the scope of Article 8(1) of the ECHR. Many people come into contact with the outside world within their professional spheres. There are some professions where a clear distinction between private life and occupation is scarcely possible. In the *Niemietz* case, the ECtHR held that the searching of a law firm, including its files, by public authorities amounted to an intrusion into private life.[8] Under most national constitutions and under European Union law (→ § 16), lawyers would probably discuss this case as an interference with the freedom of occupation. Although the ECHR does not guarantee freedom of occupation, Article 8(1) of the ECHR may provide a protection from specific intrusions into occupational practice. The fact that private life and correspondence are guaranteed in the same Article confirms this broad interpretation. No distinction is made between private and business correspondence. Since correspondence can be conceived as a special expression of private life (para 3), it follows that private life should likewise be understood in a broad way.

Private life also includes **communication with other people**.[9] Here though, it is difficult to draw a clear line between private life and correspondence.[10] As mentioned above (para 3), the protection of private life is the broader concept. Where circumstances are protected as correspondence by Article 8(1) of the ECHR, it is therefore not necessary to invoke the protection of private life. Traditional correspondence by mail obviously falls within the scope of protection of correspondence. However, this classification appears doubtful with regard to telephone conversations. If the notion of correspondence is widely construed, telephone calls may be covered. Otherwise they will be protected as a part of private life. The ECtHR has not decided on this point. In the relevant decisions it cites both private life and correspondence.[11] This indecisiveness is unsatisfactory from the point of view of legal theory. On the other hand, the distinction between correspondence and private life is not relevant for the outcome of a case because both private life and correspondence are subject to the same restriction provision (paras 20 ff). It is therefore inconsequential how new forms of communication are qualified. There are good reasons to qualify the transfer of emails as correspondence within the meaning of Article 8(1) of the ECHR.[12] Otherwise they would be protected in any case as a part of private life. In contrast to freedom of expression (→ § 4 paras 6 ff), Article 8 protects the confidentiality

---

8 ECtHR *Niemietz* (1993) 16 EHRR 97, paras 29 ff; *cf* Kunig/Uerpmann-Wittzack *Übungen im Völkerrecht* (2nd ed, Berlin 2006) pp 210–211.
9 Kugelmann [2003] EuGRZ 16, 21.
10 With regard to correspondence see below para 14.
11 ECtHR *Klass et al* (1979–80) 2 EHRR 214, para 41; *Malone* (1985) 7 EHRR 173, para 64; *Lüdi* (1993) 15 EHRR 14, para 39; *Amann* (2000) 30 EHRR 843, para 44.
12 Mock (note 5) p 243.

of individual communication, while Article 10 of the ECHR protects the contents of the communication.[13]

7   The **physical living conditions** of a certain place are another part of private life. If inhabitants are exposed to poisonous gases emitted by a factory, as was the case in the *Guerra* case, this threatens their private life.[14] In this respect, Article 8(1) of the ECHR contains elements of a right to environmental protection[15]. The right to private life is equally at stake when a person is torn away from his or her social surroundings by deportation measures.[16] Article 8(1) of the ECHR is relevant in this instance particularly as a limit for **expulsion and deportation** in Immigration Law. In fact, the ECHR grants foreigners neither a right to entry nor a right to stay. Article 3 of the 4th Prot ECHR only prohibits the expulsion of own nationals and Article 4 of the same Protocol merely protects aliens from collective expulsion. Article 1 of the 7th Prot ECHR, which is not in force in Germany, the United Kingdom and some other important members of the Council of Europe, confines itself to some procedural safeguards relating to expulsions. However, these selective rules do not preclude the provision of additional protection against expulsion and deportation measures through the general guarantees laid down in Article 8 of the ECHR.

8   Private life has a strong **social component**. People are protected in their respective social spheres. The protection also applies to the inner sphere of personality, sexual identity and sexual self-determination. If state authorities refuse to correct the civil status register and the official identity documents of a post-operative transsexual, this amounts to an interference with private life[17]. Homosexuality also falls within the scope of protection of private life[18]. Regulations which make rape and other infringements of sexual self-determination a punishable offence serve to protect private life as well[19]. Personal identity, which is protected as part of the right to private life, includes the knowledge of your own descent. On the other hand, the right of a mother to remain anonymous is likewise protected by Article 8(1) of the ECHR. Thus the decision to permit or to prohibit **anonymous births** touches upon a conflict of the rights of the mother and the child under Article 8(1) of the ECHR. In addition, the public interest to avoid abortions and the uncontrolled abandoning of children has to be taken into consideration. The ECtHR therefore reviewed the French rule on anonymous birth under Article 8 of the ECHR, but concluded that the French solution fell within the national margin of appreciation.[20]

---

13   Kugelmann (note 9) p 24; → § 4 para 22.
14   ECtHR *Guerra* (1998) 26 EHRR 357, para 57; see also *López Ostra* (1995) 20 EHRR 277.
15   *Cf* more detailed Schmidt-Radefeldt *Ökologische Menschenrechte* (Baden-Baden 2000) pp 105 ff; see also Heselhaus/Marauhn [2005] EuGRZ 546; Kley-Struller [1995] EuGRZ 507, 512.
16   Mock (note 5) p 241; nor does the ECtHR make a clear destintion between private and family life; see ECtHR *Mehemi* (2000) 30 EHRR 739, paras 23 ff; *Baghli* (2001) 33 EHRR 799, paras 32 ff.
17   ECtHR *B v France* (1994) 16 EHRR 1, paras 44–63; *Goodwin* (2002) 35 EHRR 447, paras 71 ff.
18   ECtHR *Dudgeon* (1982) 4 EHRR 149, paras 37 ff; *Norris* (1991) 13 EHRR 186, para 38; *Smith & Grady* (2000) 29 EHRR 493, para 70; Ovey/White *Jacobs & White – The European Convention on Human Rights* (3rd ed, Oxford 2002) pp 240–244.
19   ECtHR *X and Y v The Netherlands* (1986) 8 EHRR 235, para 22; *cf* below para 26.
20   ECtHR *Odièvre* (2004) 38 EHRR 871, paras 28–29, 40 ff; *cf* Lux-Wesener [2003] EuGRZ 2003, 555; Wittinger [2003] NJW 2138.

bb) Family Life

Family life is also a **broad concept**.[21] A marital connection is not necessary.[22] The relationship between an individual parent and his or her child is also included. Actual social contact is protected independently from legal recognition. Thus, the relationship of children born out of wedlock to their fathers falls within the scope of Article 8 of the ECHR even if parentage has not yet been legally established. Moreover, the relationship of children to their adoptive or foster-parents constitutes family life.[23] If a child, after a separation of his or her parents, lives with only one parent, the family bond with the other parent will not be broken, provided that both remain in contact.[24] Mere descent is not sufficient to establish family life. There must be actual contact or at least a desire for contact. Relationships with more distant family members such as grandparents or aunts are protected under the same conditions.[25]

The ECJ stressed that **stable homosexual relationships** do not fall within the scope of protection of the right to a family life.[26] In view of the expanse of the family concept, which does not require formal legal connections, this seems doubtful.[27] By all means, family life is indeed at stake if children grow up in such a relationship. Besides, every long-term relationship falls at least within the scope of private life and is thus protected by Article 8(1) of the ECHR.

The Convention does **not** claim an **equal status of unmarried** and especially of same sex **couples** with traditional marriage. This follows from Article 12 of the ECHR, which guarantees the right to marriage. In conformity with the wording, the ECtHR retains the traditional concept of marriage as a long-term relationship between two partners of different sexes.[28] It has recently expressed doubts, however, as to whether sex can always be determined biologically.[29] In the *Goodwin* case, a recognised male-to-female transsexual was refused marriage to a man. The ECtHR saw a violation of the right to marry according to Article 12 of the ECHR.[30] In general, however, this Article is of little importance compared with the right to family life under Article 8(1) of the ECHR.

In practice, the right to family life plays an important role in **child custody**, access and care proceedings.[31] **Immigration** law is another important field of application when the right to joining one's family in the country of immigration or expulsion is at stake.[32]

---

21 *Cf* more detailed Fahrenhorst *Familienrecht und Europäische Menschenrechtskonvention* (Paderborn/München 1994) pp 94 ff.
22 *Bundesgerichtshof* (BGH – German Federal Court of Justice) [2001] NJW 2472, 2475.
23 Mock (note 5) p 241.
24 ECtHR *Ciliz* App No 29192/95, para 59; *Elsholz* (2002) 34 EHRR 1412, paras 43–44.
25 Mock (note 5) pp 241–242.
26 ECJ *Grant* [1998] ECR I-621, paras 33–35.
27 Wittinger *Familien und Frauen im regionalen Menschenrechtsschutz* (Baden-Baden 1999) pp 42–45.
28 ECtHR *Rees* (1987) 9 EHRR 56, para 49; *cf* Fahrenhorst (note 21) pp 204–212.
29 ECtHR *Goodwin* (2002) 35 EHRR 447, para 100.
30 ECtHR *Goodwin* (2002) 35 EHRR 447, paras 101–104; *cf* Henrich [2004] FamRZ 173, 174; consenting ECJ *K.B. v National Health Service* [2004] ECR I-541, para 33.
31 *Cf* the decisions quoted in note 24 and in para 28; see generally Ovey/White (note 18) pp 228–231; Fahrenhorst (note 21) pp 191 ff; Brötel *Der Anspruch auf Achtung des Familienlebens* (Baden-Baden 1991) pp 175 ff.
32 *Eg* ECtHR *Mehemi* (2000) 30 EHRR 739; *Baghli* (2001) 33 EHRR 799; see generally Ovey/White (note 18) pp 233–238; Caroni *Privat- und Familienleben zwischen Menschenrecht und Migration* (1999) pp 107 ff.

cc) Home

13 A home is an enclosed space where private life is realised. As professional activities may fall within the scope of private life (para 5), it is consistent to qualify business premises where such activities take place as a home within the meaning of Article 8 of the ECHR. The ECtHR did so in the Niemietz case[33]. The French term "domicile", which is equally authentic (→ § 2 para 5), is more ready to support this interpretation than the English wording. Under the German Constitutional law, however, the term "Wohnung", which is as narrow as the term "home", is also understood to include business premises.[34] The more restrictive position, which the ECJ adopted in the *Hoechst* case[35], appears to be outdated. Premises are protected against every form of intrusion. **Bugging operations** are also regarded interferences with a person's home.[36] While a clear distinction between home and private life may be difficult, this is without relevance for the outcome of a case, since the same restriction provision applies to both guarantees.

dd) Correspondence

14 Lastly, Article 8(1) of the ECHR protects **correspondence**. Written communication[37] which is transmitted via a recognised method of delivery from one person to another is regarded as correspondence[38]. It does not matter whether the documents are delivered by state postal authorities or by private firms. Article 8 protects the process of transmitting information, *ie* the stage during which a third person could access the documents relatively easily. Messages which have not yet been sent or which have already been received are not considered to be correspondence.[39] Such messages are nevertheless covered by the broader term "private life" and thus enjoy the protection of Article 8.

15 The Convention rights also apply where persons are in special positions in which they are subordinate to state authority, such as the military, school or prison (*besonderes Gewaltverhältnis*[40]). Therefore, even the correspondence of **prisoners** is protected by Article 8(1) of the ECHR.[41] This means *inter alia* that a State must not interfere with correspondence between a prisoner and the ECtHR.[42]

b) Interference

16 The **general principles** on interferences (→ § 2 para 41) also apply to Article 8. Searching of a flat, confiscation of personal documents and wire-tapping by public authorities are typical interferences. The publication of pictures of celebrities by the press does not

---

33 ECtHR *Niemietz* (1993) 16 EHRR 97, paras 30–33.
34 See BVerfG (1971) 32 BVerfGE 54, 69 ff with regard to Article 13 of the German Basic Law.
35 ECJ *Hoechst* [1989] ECR 2859, para 18; → § 13 paras 35, 38; → § 14 paras 16 ff.
36 ECtHR *Khan* (2001) 31 EHRR 1016, para 25.
37 Regarding telephone conversations see above para 6.
38 Frowein in: Frowein/Peukert *Europäische Menschenrechtskonvention* (2nd ed, Kehl 1996) Art 8 EMRK, para 34.
39 Mock (note 5) p 243.
40 *Cf* von Münch in: von Münch/Kunig (eds) *Grundgesetz-Kommentar Band I* (5th ed, München 2000) Vorbem Art 1–19, para 59.
41 Ovey/White (note 18) pp 247 ff; Jacobs/White *The European Convention on Human Rights* (2nd ed, Oxford 1996) pp 297–299.
42 ECtHR *Petra* (2001) 33 EHRR 105, paras 35 ff; Mock (note 5) pp 243–244.

Personal Rights and the Prohibition of Discrimination　　　　　　　　　　§ 3 I 1

amount to an interference, since the private press is not bound by the Convention (→ § 2 para 34). There is, however, a duty to protect VIP's and other persons against excessive media coverage (paras 26–27).

Expulsion and deportation hinder a person from further living within his or her actual private sphere. Therefore, both acts constitute interferences with the right to private life. If expulsion or deportation disrupts family ties, then family life is at stake. Whereas this seems quite clear with regard to Article 8 of the ECHR, it is rather controversial whether the corresponding Article 6(1) of the Basic Law is to be invoked in these situations. In cases of expulsion and deportation, German courts generally do not establish an interference with the right to family life, but rather grant recourse to a duty to protect.[43] This unconvincing jurisprudence is likely to be motivated by insufficient restriction provisions. Unlike Article 8 of the ECHR, Article 6(1) of the Basic Law is not subject to any restriction provision, *ie* under German constitutional law, the right to family life is guaranteed unreservedly. Therefore, interferences with Article 6(1) of the Basic Law can only be justified under the theory of inherent constitutional restrictions, which is quite difficult (→ § 2 para 42). A narrow concept of interference circumvents these problems. As Article 8(2) of the ECHR contains reasonable restrictions, no such problems arise.

17

Child custody cases require a differentiated approach.[44] It constitutes an interference if a court withdraws child custody from a divorced parent. If, however, one parent denies the other his right to contact with the child, there is no state interference. Rather, the courts will have to invoke the duty to protect inherent in Article 8 of the ECHR.[45]

18

In the field of **environmental protection** it is also difficult to delimitate defence against state interference from a duty to protect. There is an interference if the state directly causes the environmental burden. This is true, for instance, for burdens which emanate from an army training area. On the other hand, private conduct which threatens the environment is, in principle, not attributable to the state. The situation becomes more difficult if hazardous private conduct is covered by a licence or permission granted by the state. If the state repeals the preventative ban by means of a licence in an individual case, it could possibly fall short of the duty to protect. This alone does not constitute an interference.[46] The licence only interferes with Article 8(1) of the ECHR if it imposes obligations on a third party. Section 14 of the *Bundesimmissionsschutzgesetz* (German Federal Immission Protection Law) is an example of this. This area is disputed in the German discussion on basic rights. The concept of interference is less developed in the Convention, but it points into the same direction. In the *Hatton* case, the ECtHR had to judge **noise from night flights** into London Heathrow Airport and found that permission for private night flights does not constitute an interference. Instead, the Chamber considered whether the United Kingdom had sufficiently taken into account its positive obligations to secure the applicants' right under Article 8(1).[47] In *López Ostra*, the ECtHR had to judge a difficult mix-

19

---

43 BVerfG (1979) 51 BVerfGE 386, 396–397; left open in (1987) 76 BVerfGE 1, 46; *cf* Pieroth/Schlink *Grundrechte, Staatsrecht II* (21st ed, Heidelberg 2005) para 651.
44 ECtHR *Ciliz* App No 29192/95, para 62.
45 *Eg* ECtHR *Ignaccolo-Zenide* (2001) 31 EHRR 212, para 94.
46 Jaeckel *Schutzpflichten im deutschen und europäischen Recht* (Baden-Baden 2001) p 150.
47 ECtHR *Hatton* (2002) 34 EHRR 1, para 95; *cf* Kuck [2002] NVwZ 307; the Grand Chamber, however, attached hardly any importance to this distinction in its subsequent judgment, see ECtHR *Hatton* (2003) 37 EHRR 611, paras 98, 119.

ture of different kinds of state conduct.[48] A liquid and solids **waste management plant** was erected by a group of tanneries on a site owned by the local authorities. The group of tanneries obtained state subsidies for their project. The plant started operating without the necessary authorisation. Different remedial measures by the authorities had only limited success. There was no authorisation which could have made private conduct attributable to the state. The remedial measures by the authorities had a protective character, even if they were insufficient. As long as these measures did not worsen the situation, they did not amount to an interference. One might ask whether the subsidies through which the state promoted the installation of the plant could establish the responsibility of the state for the operation of the plant. This cannot be answered, however, without analysing in detail the purpose of the subsidies and the conditions under which they were granted. The ECtHR showed little interest in these questions. It did not decide on whether there was an interference. Rather, it limited itself to weighing and balancing the conflicting interests, which is common practice both when justifying an interference and when examining a duty to protect (para 27). After the protective measures had been declared to be insufficient, the question of whether there had even been an interference seized to be important.

c) Justification

20 An interference with Article 8(1) of the ECHR can only be justified according to Article 8(2) of the ECHR. The **limitation requirements** match those of Articles 9 to 11 of the ECHR in their structure.[49] The ECtHR examines a justification carefully in three steps (→ § 2 paras 44–47). The infringement must be (aa) in accordance with the law, (bb) pursue a legitimate aim and (cc) be necessary in a democratic society, *ie* proportionate.

aa) Requirement of a Legal Basis

21 According to the 2nd paragraphs of Articles 9 to 11 of the ECHR, any restriction must be "prescribed by law". Article 8(2) of the ECHR, however, only states that restrictions must be "in accordance with the law". Whereas Articles 9 to 11 of the ECHR clearly require a legal basis for any interference (so-called **reservation of statute**[50]), the different wording of Article 8(2) of the ECHR could signify that state authorities must respect existing national laws, but that they can act even in the absence of a legal basis (simple **supremacy of statute**[51]). In the French version, however, which is equally authentic, the words "*prévu par la loi*", which are equivalent to "prescribed by law", are used invariably in the 2nd paragraphs of Articles 8 to 11 of the ECHR. So there are good reasons to conclude that a legal basis is needed also for interferences with Article 8 of the ECHR. This corresponds to the case-law of the ECtHR.[52]

22 The French term "*loi*" seems to indicate that any interference must have a statutory basis. This would be in accordance with the Constitutional tradition of Continental Europe, but would run counter to the common law tradition which is found in some Convention states. In consequence, "*loi*" has to be understood in the larger sense of the English

---

48 ECtHR *López Ostra* (1995) 20 EHRR 277, paras 51–52.
49 *Cf* more detailed Ovey/White (note 18) pp 198 ff.
50 In German constitutional theory: *Vorbehalt des Gesetzes*.
51 In German constitutional theory: *Vorrang des Gesetzes*.
52 *Eg* ECtHR *Petra* (2001) 33 EHRR 105, paras 36–39.

term "law", which also covers **unwritten law**[53]. It is necessary, in any case, that the legal basis for an interference is sufficiently accessible and foreseeable.[54] Statutes and other legal acts which are published in an official journal will, in general, easily meet this test. The term "foreseeable" implies a certain degree of legal certainty in the interpretation of the law. Through these criteria, the ECtHR strengthens the **rule of law**.

As a consequence of the requirement of a legal basis, there is a breach of Article 8 of the ECHR whenever an interference is not covered by the relevant national laws. However, scrutiny by the ECtHR is reduced in this respect. The interpretation and application of national law is primarily a matter of national authorities[55]. The European Court will only intervene if national law is handled in an arbitrary manner. The relationship between the ECtHR and the national courts is similar to that of the German Federal Constitutional Court and other German courts. The ECtHR, which is a kind of European Constitutional Court, limits itself, as does the German Federal Constitutional Court, to reviewing decisions with regard to **specific violations of the Constitution**, *ie* the ECHR.

23

bb) Legitimate Aim

Interferences with Article 8(1) of the ECHR are only lawful if they pursue one of the aims which are listed **exhaustively** in Article 8(2) of the ECHR. German Constitutional theory would call this a qualified requirement of a statutory basis (*qualifizierter Gesetzesvorbehalt*). The list contains autonomous European terms, which cannot be defined by reverting to specific national concepts. It would be inadequate, for instance, to interpret the terms "national security, public safety" and "prevention of disorder" in light of the concept of "public security and order", which constitutes the foundation of German Police Law. The aims listed in Article 8(2) of the ECHR are very broad. The ECtHR has refrained from putting them in concrete form. Mostly, the Court limits itself to stating that a given interference pursues one or more legitimate aims.[56] It is hard to imagine that the legal justification of an interference will ever fail due to the absence of a legitimate aim.[57]

24

cc) Proportionality

Finally, the interference must be "necessary in a democratic society". The ECtHR requests a "pressing social need" and conducts a **proportionality test**[58]. This test corresponds in essence to the German **three-step approach**: The interference must be suitable to promote the legitimate aim, it must be necessary in the sense that no less restrictive but equally suitable option is available, and it must be adequate, *ie* proportionate *stricto sensu* (→ § 2 para 47). National authorities enjoy a **margin of appreciation** with regard to the question of whether a measure is necessary and adequate.[59] Given their acquaintance with the local

25

---

53 ECtHR *Sunday Times* (1979–80) 2 EHRR 245, para 47.
54 ECtHR *Sunday Times* (1979–80) 2 EHRR 245, para 49.
55 Schokkenbroek (1998) 19 HRLJ 30, 33; see also ECtHR *X and Y v The Netherlands* (1986) 8 EHRR 235, para 29.
56 *Eg* ECtHR *Niemietz* (1993) 16 EHRR 97, para 36; *Ciliz* App No 29192/95, para 65; *Elsholz* (2002) 34 EHRR 1412, para 47.
57 Mock (note 5) pp 245–246.
58 *Eg* ECtHR *Baghli* (2001) 33 EHRR 799, para 45.
59 *Cf* Ovey (1998) 19 HRLJ 10 ff; Schokkenbroek (note 55) p 31.

situation, they are best placed to judge the subtle differences. The domestic decision is only subject to a limited review by the ECtHR. However, the degree of review is variable. It depends on the circumstances of the individual case[60]. The way of reasoning is similar to that of the German Federal Constitutional Court. In particular, the standard of review is stricter the more serious the interference is[61]. It is not unusual for the ECtHR to regard an interference as disproportionate[62].

d) Duty to Protect

26 Throughout the ECHR, the **duty to protect** (→ § 2 para 16) is most developed in Article 8 of the ECHR. Whereas Articles 9 to 12 of the ECHR simply guarantee rights, Article 8(1) of the ECHR expressly requires "respect for" the rights laid down there. This makes the duty to protect particularly clear. The leading case of the ECtHR, *X and Y v The Netherlands*[63], concerned the criminal protection of a mentally handicapped woman from sexual abuse. The Dutch law at that time required a personal complaint by the person concerned, which could not take place here because of her mental incapacity. Furthermore, the Dutch law did not allow representation in the complaint process, which meant that the massive interference with sexual self-determination could not be criminally punished in this case. According to the ECtHR, this loophole constituted a violation of the duty to protect private life under Article 8 of the ECHR. In the meantime, the duty to protect has gained particular importance in the field of environmental protection[64].

27 It is difficult to establish a **violation of the duty to protect**. Article 8(2) of the ECHR only applies to interferences and therefore cannot be used. Whereas any interference must have a legal basis, a duty to protect may oblige the state to take positive measures even if they are not prescribed by law. Rather, it is essential to strike a **fair balance** between the interests protected by Article 8 of the ECHR on the one hand and the conflicting legitimate interests of the state on the other hand. This operation of weighing and balancing is common both to the justification of an interference and to the scrutiny of a duty to protect.[65] Possible conflicting interests, which may restrict a duty to protect, include but are not limited to those listed in Article 8(2) of the ECHR. If the media covers the private life of VIP's, for instance, the duty to protect private life is limited by freedom of the press and, more generally, of the media as contained in Article 10 of the ECHR (→ § 4 para 17). In the process of weighing and balancing, the state authorities enjoy a certain margin of appreciation, which is, however, limited by European control. In the sensational case of *Caroline von Hannover*, a chamber of the ECtHR held the protection of celebrities from the publication of photos concerning their private life in higher regard than did the German Federal Constitutional Court.[66]

---

60 Mock (note 5) pp 245–246; Starmer *European Human Rights Law* (London 1999) p 189.
61 ECtHR *Kutzner* (2002) 35 EHRR 653, para 67.
62 *Eg* ECtHR *Niemietz* (1993) 16 EHRR 97, para 37.
63 ECtHR *X and Y v The Netherlands* (1986) 8 EHRR 235, paras 23–30.
64 See the leading cases above note 14 and para 51; see also Brötel (1999) 63 RabelsZ 580, 591–593 with regard to family law and child custody.
65 *Cf* ECtHR *López Ostra* (1995) 20 EHRR 277, para 51; *Ciliz* App No 29192/95, para 61; *Odièvre* (2004) 38 EHRR 871, para 40.
66 ECtHR *von Hannover* (2005) 40 EHRR 1, paras 56 ff; against BVerfG (1999) 101 BVerfGE 361, 379 ff; *cf* Heldrich [2004] NJW 2634.

Personal Rights and the Prohibition of Discrimination §3 I 1

e) Procedural Aspects

In recent ECtHR case-law on child custody, **procedural aspects** are emerging as being important[67]. The protection of family life implies that the state must take the will of all affected family members into account without patronising them.[68] In proceedings in which the state interferes with the right to family life, all family members must be sufficiently involved. As it is often difficult to assess the truth of child statements, it can even prove necessary to consult psychological expertise.[69] Long lasting child custody and contact proceedings can lead to alienation between the child and the parent, which creates a *fait accompli*. For this reason, Article 8 of the ECHR also provides a right to a speedy decision.[70] Furthermore, the ECtHR has relied on procedural aspects where substantial review is limited by a margin of appreciation granted to the national authorities. An example is the protection against aircraft noise.[71] The review of administrative and, where necessary, of court procedure is meant to compensate for the deficits in the review of the substance of the case. The idea that fundamental rights imply guarantees on proceedings with a view to their full realisation and safeguarding is well known from German constitutional law[72].

28

The ECHR also provides for special and far-reaching **procedural guarantees** in its Article 6(1) (→ § 6 paras 30 ff). For systematic reasons, procedural guarantees should primarily be derived from Article 6 of the ECHR. As far as Article 6 of the ECHR is applicable, it is not necessary to derive additional and unwritten guarantees from Article 8 of the ECHR. The ECtHR, however, takes the opposite approach. In the *Elsholz* case, for example, the Court first established a violation of Article 8 of the ECHR due to inadequate proceedings[73] and then briefly stated that the same circumstance lead to a violation of Article 6(1) of the ECHR[74]. In *Haase*, the ECHR even refrains completely from a scrutiny under Article 6(1) of the ECHR.[75] Thus, Article 6(1) of the ECHR is bereft of any autonomous meaning. As Article 6(1) of the ECHR only deals with judicial proceedings, no conflict of norms arises where the ECtHR derives requirements for administrative proceedings from Article 8 of the ECHR, as in *Hatton* with regard to the protection from noise at Heathrow airport[76].

29

Case 1 – Answer:
As M lives with his parents, he enjoys the right to respect for family life under Article 8(1) of the ECHR. As far as not his family life but the rest of his personal living sphere in Munich is concerned, he can assert the protection of his private life. The expulsion order and the –

30

---

67 See generally Brötel [1999] DeuFamR 143.
68 ECtHR *W v United Kingdom* (1988) 10 EHRR 29, paras 62 ff; *Ciliz* App No 29192/95, paras 66–71; *Görgülü* App No 74969/01, paras 52–53; Wittinger (note 27) p 282.
69 ECtHR *Elsholz* (2002) 34 EHRR 1412, para 52; *Sommerfeld* (2004) 38 EHRR 756, paras 68 ff (Grand Chamber).
70 ECtHR *Sylvester* (2003) 37 EHRR 417, para 60.
71 ECtHR *Hatton* (2003) 37 EHRR 611, paras 103–104, 128 (Grand Chamber).
72 Von Münch (note 40) paras 25–27.
73 ECtHR *Elsholz* (2002) 34 EHRR 1412, paras 52–53.
74 ECtHR *Elsholz* (2002) 34 EHRR 1412, para 66.
75 ECtHR *Haase* (2005) 40 EHRR 430, para 108; see also Brötel (note 6454) p 593 who gives Article 8 priority under the concept of speciality.
76 See above note 71.

following deportation make the continuation of his family and private life in Munich impossible and therefore constitute an interference with both rights.

This interference could be justified in accordance with Article 8(2) of the ECHR. The Immigration Act fulfils the Convention requirement for a legal basis. The prevention of crime is a legitimate aim listed in Article 8(2) of the ECHR. One might also consider the aspects of prevention of disorder or the protection of the rights and freedoms of others. There are doubts, however, as to whether expulsion and deportation are necessary in a democratic society. The search for a pressing social need leads to a proportionality test. The scarcity of reported facts does not permit a detailed analysis here. Given the previous criminal acts, it seems probable that M would continue committing criminal acts in the future. Expulsion and deportation is a suitable means of avoiding further criminal acts in Germany. In light of the long list of previous acts, it is difficult to assume that there is a milder but equally suitable means.

The outcome of the case therefore depends on the proportionality test *stricto sensu*, where the protected interest of M to stay has to be weighed and balanced against the interest of the state to make him leave the country. The unusual accumulation of partly serious criminal acts stands in favour of expulsion and deportation. On the other hand, M is, despite his foreign nationality, at home in Germany. He has only lived in Germany and speaks hardly any Turkish. Apparently, German is his mother tongue. Expulsion and deportation would be the same to him as a German being deported. If he were German, he could not be expelled from Germany despite his criminal acts according to Article 3(1) of the 4th Prot ECHR. German Courts would have to resolve the problem by means of criminal law on the one hand whilst also considering the need to help young people by social work on the other. The formal lack of German nationality alone does not justify treating M differently from other settled inhabitants. The case shows parallels to *Mehemi*, in which the ECtHR considered the deportation of a foreign offender of the second generation of immigrants as disproportionate.[77] In *Baghli*, the ECtHR held the deportation of an Algerian born in France as permissible.[78] In this case, however, the appellant was of age, maintained no relationship with his relatives living in France and had carried out his military service in Algeria.[79] The link to his state of residence was by far less tight than that of M in Case 1.

2. *Freedom of Thought, Conscience and Religion (Article 9 ECHR)*

a) Scope of Protection

31   Article 9 of the ECHR protects **thought, conscience and religion**. Whereas the corresponding terms of Article 4(1, 2) of the Basic Law have been defined by constitutional jurisprudence and scholarship[80], there are no generally recognised definitions for the Convention terms[81]. The scope of both provisions is nevertheless largely the same. Article 9 of the ECHR does not only protect inner convictions and beliefs (so-called *forum internum*) but also the expression of these convictions and beliefs (so-called *forum externum*). According to the German Federal Constitutional Court, Article 4(1, 2) of the Basic Law guarantees

---

77   ECtHR *Mehemi* (2000) 30 EHRR 739, paras 35–37.
78   ECtHR *Baghli* (2001) 33 EHRR 799, paras 46–49.
79   See also the analysis of ECtHR case-law in BVerfG [2004] NVwZ 852, 853–854 (Chamber).
80   *Cf* Mager in: von Münch/Kunig (eds) *Grundgesetz-Kommentar Band I* (5th ed, München 2000) Art 4, paras 12 ff.
81   With regard to the case-law approach followed by the ECtHR see above para 4.

not only the manifestation in the narrow sense but also the right to adjust one's whole life according to one's religion or philosophy of life.[82] Article 9(1) of the ECHR is clearer because it expressly refers to the manifestation of a religion or belief in practice and observance. If, for example, a teacher wants to wear a headscarf, this falls within the scope of protection of Article 9(1) of the ECHR.[83] The same is true for special forms of slaughtering according to Muslim or Jewish rites.[84] The right of parents to bring up their children in conformity with religious and philosophical convictions enjoys an additional protection under Article 2(2) of the 1st Prot ECHR.[85] Like Article 4 of the Basic Law, Article 9(1) of the ECHR protects negative freedoms, *ie* the right to have no beliefs or convictions, alongside positive freedoms. As the ECtHR phrased, atheists, agnostics and sceptics are also protected.[86] Furthermore, a claim under Article 9 of the ECHR may be raised not only by individual believers but also by religious communities.[87]

b) Interference

It is sometimes difficult to establish an **interference**. In this respect there are, however, hardly differences compared to other human rights norms. Problems are solved in a similar way under the ECHR and under German Constitutional law. In *Cha'are Shalom Ve Tsedek*, for example, the ECtHR saw no interference in the denial of the authorisation to slaughter because the believers had sufficient possibilities to provide themselves with kosher meat from other sources.[88] The German Federal Administrative Court argued similarly, but more rigorously and dogmatically consistent with respect to Article 4(1)(ii) of the Basic Law. It put forward that no religious rule prescribes the consumption of kosher meat. If the state prohibits the **religious slaughter**, the possibility remains for the believers to go back to meat imports or to avoid meat completely.[89] The German Federal Constitutional Court, however, did not completely follow this rigid line. It put forward that the forced renunciation of meat is no reasonable alternative and that in case of meat imports it is less certain whether the meat really is kosher.[90] So it comes close to the position of the ECtHR.

It is debatable whether **deportation** amounts to an interference with Article 9 of the ECHR if the other state does not respect the deported person's freedom of thought or conscience. As an incriminating act of the state, deportation can interfere with Convention rights, as has already been seen with respect to Article 8 of the ECHR (para 17). However, the act of deportation in itself is neutral in respect of the scope of protection of

---

82 BVerfG (1971) 32 BVerfGE 98, 106–107; but see Mager (note 80) Art 4, para 17.
83 ECtHR *Dahlab* App No 42393/98 (decision on admissibility); *cf* Schobener [2003] Jura 186; see also *Verwaltungsgericht Stuttgart* (Administrative Tribunal of Stuttgart) [2002] NVwZ 959, 960.
84 ECtHR *Cha'are Shalom Ve Tsedek* App No 27417/95, paras 73–74; *cf* in a perspective of comparative law Pabel [2002] EuGRZ 220.
85 *Cf* Dujmovitis in: Grabenwarter/Thienel (eds) *Kontinuität und Wandel in der EMRK* (Kehl 1998) pp 139, 153–154.
86 ECtHR *Dahlab* App No 42393/98 (decision on admissibility).
87 ECtHR *Cha'are Shalom Ve Tsedek* App No 27417/95, para 72.
88 ECtHR *Cha'are Shalom Ve Tsedek* App No 27417/95, paras 80–83.
89 *Bundesverwaltungsgericht* (BVerwG – German Federal Administrativ Court) (1995) 99 BVerwGE 1; see also Trute [1996] Jura 462, 465–466.
90 BVerfG (2002) 104 BVerfGE 337, 350–351.

Article 9 of the ECHR. The freedoms protected by Article 9 of the ECHR are restricted in the other state without this being the intent of the deporting state. Therefore, deportation should not be qualified as an interference with Article 9 of the ECHR even if a person's belief or religion is threatened abroad. That does not mean that deportation could not be contrary to Article 9 of the ECHR. The **duty to protect** inherent in Article 9 of the ECHR hinders deportation at least in cases where there is a serious interference with the freedom of religion abroad.[91] Alternatively, deportation, which exposes a person to massive restrictions of his or her freedom of religion, can be seen as inhuman in the sense of Article 3 of the ECHR (para 41). This would also provide a protection from deportation (paras 44, 47).

c) Justification

34 The rights under Article 9(1) of the ECHR are only in part restrictable. Article 9(2) of the ECHR contains a **qualified reservation** (para 24) with regard to the freedom to manifest one's religion or belief. Thus, only the *forum externum* may be restricted, while the *forum internum* is guaranteed without reservations and restrictions.[92] This distinction makes sense. It takes into account both the indefeasibility of internal convictions and the need to subject human behaviour which has an effect on other people to legal rules. In this respect, the system of restriction provisions, as provided for by the Convention, is superior to that contained in the Basic Law. Whilst it is widely accepted that Article 4(1, 2) of the Basic Law is not subject to any restriction provision, its guarantees are to a large extent qualified by inherent Constitutional limitations[93].

35 Article 9(2) of the ECHR corresponds to Article 8(2) of the ECHR, which has been treated above (paras 20 ff). Any restriction must be prescribed by law, it must be to protect one of the listed legitimate aims and it must be "necessary in a democratic society". In the case of a Muslim **teacher** who wanted to teach in a headscarf, the German Federal Constitutional Court decided that it was up to the legislature to decide upon the fundamental public conflict between supporters and opponents of the **Muslim headscarf** in the process of public parliamentary debate and to enact a special statute on this subject if necessary.[94] The principle of statutory reservation has a double foundation, *ie* promoting democracy and the rule of law. In a democracy, parliament, which has been elected by the people, should decide on interferences with human rights. Under the rule of law, legal certainty is important, and individuals should know in advance which interferences with their rights are allowed. In its headscarf-decision, the German Federal Constitutional Court emphasised the democratic aspect, whereas the ECHR generally focuses more on the accessibility and forseeability of a law (para 22), *ie* on legal certainty and the **rule of law**. Therefore, the strict reservation of substantial decisions for the parliament, as emphasised by the German Federal Constitutional Court, cannot be transferred to the ECHR.

36 The fact that the **catalogue of legitimate aims** is shorter than in Article 8(2) of the ECHR coincides with the status of the freedom of religion. However, the slight difference between the catalogues is hardly able to have any practical meaning in light of the expanse of the grounds for justification. If, for example, authorities prevent a Muslim teacher

---

91 *Cf* BVerwG (2000) 111 BVerwGE 223, 229–230.
92 Dujmovitis (note 85) p 141, 152.
93 But see Mager (note 80) para 93.
94 BVerfG (2003) 108 BVerfGE 282, 310 ff; *cf* Baer/Wrase [2003] JuS 1162.

from appearing in front of a class in a headscarf, the "rights and freedoms of others", *ie* the pupils and perhaps their parents, are at stake. The state, wanting to protect school children from religious influence, pursues a legitimate aim. In *Dahlab*, the ECtHR referred in addition to the "interests of public safety" and the "protection of public order".[95] This shows how little the catalogue of legitimate aims serves as a filter for the justification.

It is essential to strike a **fair balance** between the right protected under the Convention and the legitimate aim which justifies an interference.[96] In this process, the state authorities have a margin of appreciation. Where state and religion are as strictly separated as in Turkey, the ECtHR has even accepted a ban on headscarves for female students at University.[97] This decision is not transferable to similar situations in Germany. State and religion are less divided in Germany. Moreover, a ban on headscarves in Germany would affect a religious minority. Human rights gain a special importance where minorities have to be protected. On the other hand, clothing regulations for teaching staff that represent the state are easier to justify than those for students.

II. Right to Personal Integrity

1. Prohibition of Torture, Inhuman or Degrading Treatment or Punishment (Article 3 ECHR)

Case 2 – Problem: (ECtHR *D v United Kingdom* (1997) 24 EHRR 423)
D, a drug courier who is ill with aids, is imprisoned in the United Kingdom. His illness is aptly treated there. At the end of his imprisonment, D is to be deported to his Caribbean home land of St. Kitts and Nevis. He will not be able to continue with his aids therapy and care there. This will dramatically shorten his life expectancy. Can D be deported?

a) Scope of Protection

Article 3 of the ECHR prohibits **torture, inhuman or degrading treatment** and punishment. Unlike Article 3(1) of the Charter of Fundamental Rights of the European Union, the ECHR does not guarantee physical and mental integrity as such. Article 3 of the ECHR covers important, but not all aspects of personal integrity. For example, a blood test carried out on suspicion of drunk driving is outside the scope of Article 3 of the ECHR. Such a test may, however, interfere with the far-reaching protection of private life under Article 8 of the ECHR as explained above (paras 3 ff).[98] On the other hand, there can be degrading treatment even without interference with physical integrity. Thus, a statute discriminating on grounds of race which forces members of a certain group to wear an identification badge in public interferes with Article 3 of the ECHR.[99] This example shows the close link between Article 3 of the ECHR and the protection of human dignity as laid down in Article 1 of the Charter of Fundamental Rights of the European Union

---

95 ECtHR *Dahlab* App No 42393/98 (decision on admissibility); *cf* Schöbener (note 83) p 186.
96 See Dujmovitis (note 85) pp 141 ff with regard to the ECtHR case-law.
97 ECtHR *Şahin* (2005) 41 EHRR 109, paras 112 ff (Grand Chamber).
98 Frowein (note 38) Art 3 EMRK, para 14.
99 *Cf* Frowein (note 38) Art 3 EMRK, para 9.

and in Article 1(1) of the Basic Law[100]. Under the German Constitutional law, which does not know an explicit ban on torture and other inhuman or degrading treatment, such a statute would run counter to the prohibition of racial discrimination under Article 3(3)(i) of the Basic Law. Moreover, the general right to personality (para 3) would be pertinent.

40 Article 1(1)(i) of the United Nations Convention against Torture and Other Cruel, Inhuman or Degrading Treatment or Punishment of 10 December 1984[101] provides a **definition of torture**. According to this Article, torture means "any act by which severe pain or suffering, whether physical or mental, is intentionally inflicted on a person for such purposes as obtaining from him or a third person information or a confession, punishing him for an act he or a third person committed or is suspected of having committed, or intimidating or coercing him or a third person, or for any reason based on discrimination of any kind, when such pain or suffering is inflicted by or at the instigation of or with the consent or acquiescence of a public official or other person acting in an official capacity." This UN definition is not binding on the ECtHR. Nevertheless, it can be accepted as a meaningful description, and therefore the ECtHR refers to this definition[102]. Three criteria must be emphasised: (1) Interference must attain a minimum level of severity to be qualified as torture. (2) Intent is required. Torture is inflicted with the purpose to manipulate the mind of the person being tortured or of a third party. This could be to obtain a confession, to terrorise others, to frighten and to create a feeling of insecurity. (3) Finally, the conduct must be directly or at least indirectly attributable to a state. Torture in this narrow sense is seldom found in the states of the ECHR. However, even in Europe there are incidents which amount to torture. This is particularly the case in police custody.[103]

41 **Inhuman** or **degrading treatment** must reach a certain severity, although it remains below the threshold of torture. Inhumanity and degradation are assessed through a grading system, whereby degrading treatment is the mildest form. A clear distinction between the alternatives of inhumanity and degradation is neither necessary nor possible. The establishment of inhuman or degrading treatment requires an assessment of the individual case. Important criteria are the severity and length of the interference. Over the course of time, case groups have developed. In 1978, the ECtHR qualified corporal punishment on the Isle of Man as degrading in *Tyrer*[104]. In the *Soering* case in 1989, the ECtHR decided that detention on death row for many years could conflict with Article 3 of the ECHR in light of the conditions of detention.[105] During the last few years, the ECtHR has extended the scope of protection of Article 3 of the ECHR, mainly in deportation cases. Deportation can be a violation of the Convention if the person being deported is threatened with persecution by the state or by private groups in his or her home state.[106] One requirement is the existence of substantial reasons which establish a real danger.[107]

---

100 *Cf* Meyer-Ladewig [2004] NJW 981, 982; in ECJ *Omega* [2004] ECR I-9609 the concept of human dignity was analysed in detail by AG Stix-Hackl.
101 1465 UNTS 85.
102 ECtHR *Salman* (2005) 41 EHRR 8, para 114.
103 *Eg* ECtHR *Selmouni* (2000) 29 EHRR 403, paras 96–105; *Salman* (2005) 41 EHRR 8, para 114.
104 ECtHR *Tyrer* (1979–80) 2 EHRR 1, paras 29–35.
105 ECtHR *Soering* (1989) 11 EHRR 439, paras 105–111.
106 Kälin in: Hailbronner/Klein (eds) *Einwanderungskontrolle und Menschenrechte* (Heidelberg 1999) pp 49, 54–55.
107 Trechsel in: Barwig/Brinkmann *et al* (eds) Ausweisung im demokratischen Rechtsstaat (Baden-Baden 1996) pp 223, 237–240; see also ECtHR *H.L.R.* (1998) 26 EHRR 29, para 37.

The terms of Article 3 of the ECHR are subject to **dynamic interpretation**.[108] They are the manifestation of a common European standard which continues to evolve. Measures that were still considered permissible at the time of the creation of the ECHR in 1950, such as corporal punishment on the Isle of Man, have been considered to be degrading since as early as 1978[109].

Questions of proof frequently arise in the context of violations of Article 3 in police custody. As a rule, the relevant conduct of the state must be positively established. Where mistreatment in police custody is concerned, the responding state is often the only party that could secure the necessary evidence. This induced the ECtHR to alleviate the burden of proof some years ago. If a person is in good health when taken into custody and leaves with injuries, the state is obliged to provide a plausible explanation.[110] If the state is not able to do so, the ECtHR will find a violation of Article 3 of the ECHR. This comes close to *prima facie* evidence.[111] As a result, states are obligated to record any injuries and their causes during the period of detention in order to avoid a conviction of torture or inhuman or degrading treatment.

42

b) Interference

By definition, torture only exists when **state organs** inflict pain or suffering. Inhuman or degrading treatment must also stem from the state in order to constitute an interference.

43

It is disputed whether and when **extradition or deportation** can be classed as an interference. Contrary to the view of the 9th Senate of the German Federal Administrative Court[112], it hardly seems possible to rely on the conduct of the third party state. Often this third party state is not even a contracting party to the ECHR. Besides that, the question is not whether the third party state acts contrary to the ECHR, but whether the act of extradition or deportation violates the ECHR.[113] It has to be established whether the extradition or deportation is inhuman or degrading in light of its consequences.[114] One might object that the extraditing or deporting state is not responsible for the threat occurring in the other state. In this hypothesis, the duty not to interfere with Article 3 of the ECHR would give no protection against deportation, only a duty to protect would do so[115]. This solution, however, is not satisfactory either. While a duty to protect does not depend on any pre-conduct of a Convention state such as extradition or deportation, the Convention outlaws precisely extradition and deportation that exposes a person to inhuman or degrading conditions. This state conduct qualifies as an interference. The analysis concentrates on the conduct of the Convention state; it is irrelevant where the danger comes

44

---

108 Kälin (note 106) pp 57 ff; but see Hailbronner (1999) DÖV 617, 620–621 within the special context of immigration law.
109 ECtHR *Tyrer* (1979–80) 2 EHRR 1, para 31.
110 ECtHR *Ribitsch* (1996) 21 EHRR 573, para 34; *Selmouni* (2000) 29 EHRR 403, para 87; *cf* Rudolf [1996] EuGRZ 497.
111 Rudolf (note 110) pp 500–501.
112 BVerwG (1995) 99 BVerwGE 331, 334–335; (1997) 105 BVerwGE 187, 188 ff; (2000) 111 BVerwGE 223, 227.
113 Starmer (note 60) p 509; Trechsel (note 107) p 234.
114 Kälin (note 106) pp 63–67.
115 *Cf* Jaeckel (note 46) pp 162–163.

from in the third party state[116]. Persecution by the third party state makes the extradition or deportation by the Convention state as much a violation of the Convention as persecution by private persons or other inhuman living conditions.

c) Justification

45 The guarantee of Article 3 of the ECHR may not be restricted and according to Article 15(2) of the ECHR may also not be derogated from in times of emergency. If there is an adequate reason to interfere with the personal integrity of a person, the interference will not be qualified as inhuman, degrading or even as torture. If, by contrast, a treatment falls within the scope of Article 3 of the ECHR, **no justification** is possible and the violation is established definitively. Article 3 of the ECHR has an absolute character in this sense.[117] The ECHR does not have a parallel concept to the German inherent constitutional restrictions[118]. This concept is the expression of an inadequate system of restriction provisions within the Basic Law. The German Constitution contains some fundamental freedoms without any provision for restriction. As these freedoms, such as freedom of religion and freedom of artistic expression, must obviously be subject to certain restrictions, it was necessary to construe inherent Constitutional restrictions. The guarantees of the ECHR show extensive provisions for restriction, which make inherent limitations unnecessary. Article 3 of the ECHR, by contrast, is a right which may not be restricted at all. Limitations are only discussed in **exceptional cases**. Such a case occurred in 2002 in Frankfurt am Main.[119] The vice president of the police threatened a kidnapper with torture in order to find out where he was hiding the kidnapped boy. Afterwards it was discovered that the boy had already been killed. Other scenarios concern terrorist attacks. With respect to the protection of human dignity under Article 1(1) of the Basic Law, it has been argued that in such cases the state duty to protect the dignity of the victim is weighed up against the human dignity of the perpetrator.[120] This proposal touches on the absoluteness of human dignity. Anyhow, it may not be applied to the ECHR, where the coherent system of provisions for restriction leaves no room for inherent Convention limitations. In addition, the danger of abuse should forbid any attempt to justify torture even in exceptional cases. It would be an unacceptable excess, for instance, if states used torture on mere suspicion in order to combat international terrorism. It is typical that even in the Frankfurt case, torture finally turned out to be no suitable means of saving the kidnapped boy, who, in fact, had died before. Even if torture is always illegal, one might, however, in extreme cases, consider the possibility of exempting a perpetrator of torture from criminal prosecution.[121]

---

116 Gusy [1993] ZAR 63, 66; see also Alleweldt *Schutz vor Abschiebung bei drohender Folter oder unmenschlicher oder erniedrigender Behandlung oder Strafe* (Berlin 1996) pp 15, 26.
117 ECtHR *Selmouni* (2000) 29 EHRR 403, para 95.
118 Jacobs/White (note 41) p 299; but see § 2 para 42.
119 The facts are reported by Welsch [2003] BayVBl 481, 482.
120 Wittreck [2003] DÖV 873, 879 ff.
121 *Cf* Wittreck (note 120) p 876; but see Hilgendorf [2004] JZ 331, 338–339; see also Articles 4 ff of the UN Convention against Torture (note 101), which oblige a state to prosecute cases of torture under its criminal law.

d) Protective Mechanisms

Violations of the Convention can give rise to an application to the ECtHR under Article 33 of the ECHR (→ § 2 paras 43 ff). This is also true for Article 3. However, procedures before the ECtHR only deal with **individual violations**. Experience has shown that the risk of torture, inhuman or degrading treatment is particularly high where state authorities hold people in custody. In these situations, the proof of torture or inhuman or degrading treatment is especially difficult. In addition, persons who have been intimidated by state officials will often dread bringing the matter before court.[122] In the last few years, the ECtHR has reacted to the problems of evidence by lightening the burden of proof (para 42). This notwithstanding, there were good reasons to ensure the protection of persons in state custody by an additional preventative mechanism. For this reason, the **European Convention for the Prevention of Torture and Inhuman or Degrading Treatment or Punishment** was adopted on 26 November 1987.[123] The Convention takes up, both in the preamble and with the wording, the substantial prohibition contained in Article 3 of the ECHR[124], and it establishes a European Committee for the Prevention of Torture and Inhuman or Degrading Treatment or Punishment[125]. The Committee is made up of independent members from all contracting states.[126] The Committee's task is to visit prisons and other detention centres and make reports on its findings.[127] In fact, the Committee has uncovered some alarming situations and has been able to achieve improvements.[128] The protective mechanisms of the ECHR are only complemented and not diminished by the Convention of 1987.[129]

46

Case 2 – Answer:
The deportation of D could amount to inhuman treatment and thus violate Article 3 of the ECHR. Contrary to the view of the German Federal Administrative Court[130], there is no need to establish whether the state of St Kitts and Nevis will treat D in an inhuman way. What matters is the conduct of the British state authority, which has to be qualified under Article 3 of the ECHR. Deportation of D would have concrete and most serious consequences. It would definitely expose him to an early death. In the light of present day conditions, a state act which would interrupt an ongoing, vitally important medical treatment is in principle inhuman. The deportation therefore interferes with Article 3 of the ECHR. As there is no justification for inhuman treatment, D must not be deported.
For Germany, Section 60(5) of the *Aufenthaltsgesetz* (German Immigration Statute) makes it clear that national authorities have to respect deportation impediments which follow from the ECHR. The same would be true even without a special provision in the German Immigration Statute[131].

47

---

122 Alleweldt [1998] EuGRZ 245, 246.
123 ETS No 126, modified by two additional protocols of 4 November 1993, ETS No 151, 152.
124 Alleweldt (note 122) p 248.
125 Art 1 of the Convention (note 123).
126 Arts 4 f of the Convention (note 123).
127 Arts 7 ff of the Convention (note 123).
128 *Cf* Alleweldt (note 122) pp 249 ff and, with special regard to Turkey, *idem* [2000] EuGRZ 193, 194.
129 Art 17(2) of the Convention (note 123).
130 See above note 112.
131 *Cf* BVerwG (1995) 99 BVerwGE 331, 333.

2. Right to Life (Article 2 ECHR)

Case 3 – Problem:

48 Terrorists had barricaded themselves within a flat. The police blocked the pavement in front of the residential building before a special forces command stormed the building. During an exchange of fire, an uninvolved passer-by on the other side of the street got killed before the terrorists met their own deaths. A short administrative investigation on the reasons for the death of the passer-by led to the official result that the lethal shot had been fired by the terrorists. The deadly bullet was never found. Witnesses to the crime and in particular the police involved were not questioned. All attempts by the husband of the passer-by at reaching a judicial investigation of the incident failed. When he appealed to the ECtHR, the government declared that the circumstances of the death of the passer-by could no longer be resolved. How will the ECtHR decide?

a) Scope of Protection

49 Article 2(1)(i) of the ECHR protects **human life**. Life ends with death, and it seems proper to rely on the occurrence of brain death in this regard. The beginning of protection is more difficult to determine. While protection exists from birth, the protection of **unborn life** is disputed. The Austrian Constitutional Court has rejected protection of unborn children with reference to the restriction provisions.[132] According to the Austrian Constitutional Court, it would be absurd if the ECHR under certain circumstances permitted the killing of born persons. but imposed a strict ban on abortion even in case of special indications. This is not convincing, because the provisions for restriction only apply in case of state interference with human life[133]. If a private doctor performs an abortion following the wish of the pregnant woman, there is no interference. Thus, Article 2(1)(ii) and Article 2(2) would not hinder an abortion undertaken by private persons. In consequence, there is no compelling reason to leave unborn lives outside the scope of protection.[134] This notwithstanding, in *Vo v France,* the Grand Chamber of the ECtHR followed in essence the restrictive position. According to the Grand Chamber, the determination of the beginning of life falls into the **margin of appreciation** of the individual states as long as a general European consensus is lacking.[135] Indeed, it is not up to the ECtHR to establish new legal standards in an area where, due to medical and technical developments such as stem cell research, a consensus among European states cannot be perceived[136]. Nevertheless, the solution of the ECtHR is met with concerns. The margin of appreciation is a useful concept for the justification stage.[137] In *Vo*, however, the ECtHR placed the scope of protection at the disposal of the member states, although it should be common ground that even unborn life must at least enjoy some protection.[138]

---

132 *Österreichischer Verfassungsgerichtshof* (Austrian Constitutional Court) [1975] EuGRZ 74, 78.
133 Kneihs in: Grabenwarter/Thienel (eds) *Kontinuität und Wandel in der EMRK* (Kehl 1998) pp 21, 37–38.
134 Frowein (note 38) Art 2 EMRK, para 3; Lux-Wesener (note 20) p 562; but see Kneihs (note 133) pp 40–41.
135 ECtHR *Vo* (2005) 40 EHRR 259, paras 81 ff (Grand Chamber).
136 *Cf* Trechsel in: Benedek/Isak/Kicker (eds) *Development and Developing International and European Law* (Frankfurt am Main 1999) pp 671, 672–673.
137 Peters *Einführung in die Europäische Menschenrechtskonvention* (München 2003) p 25.
138 *Cf* Lux-Wesener (note 20) p 558.

Contrary to other rights to freedom, Article 2(1)1 of the ECHR does not include the negative freedom not to live.[139] The right to life under the ECHR covers as little a right to **suicide** or to active **euthanasia** as does the Basic Law.[140] That does not rule out the fact that self-determination over one's own life falls into the scope of protection of Article 8(1) of the ECHR (paras 3 ff). A state can restrict euthanasia, however, in accordance with Article 8(2) to protect the right to life of the other person.[141] As the right to life according to Article 2(1)(i) of the ECHR may not be renounced, the state is allowed to disregard the will of the person wanting to die in prohibiting euthanasia. Above all, the danger of abuse is an important reason for prohibiting euthanasia.

Article 1 of the ECHR limits the **territorial scope** of all Convention rights, including the right to life. This limitation *ratione loci* is mainly relevant for military operations abroad. A leading case is *Banković*, where the ECtHR had to deal with the NATO air raids on Belgrade during the Kosovo conflict.[142] According to Article 1 of the ECHR, the Convention rights only apply to those who are within the jurisdiction of a Convention state. Understood in a broad sense, this would only mean that the ECHR applies to any exercise of state power by Convention states. In this case, however, the express reference to jurisdiction would be superfluous because it is a self-evident truth that state responsibility is linked to an act of the state[143]. Rather, the term "jurisdiction" implies a certain competence of the state. The jurisdiction of a state is legally limited, above all, by territory. The ECHR therefore applies to extraterritorial acts only in exceptional cases.[144] Following *Banković*, the primordial goal of the ECHR is to protect individuals who stay within the European Convention states, but not to limit foreign policy and military actions of Convention states around the world. A military operation abroad *per se* establishes no jurisdiction over the people who live there, which would open up the area of application of the Convention according to Article 1 of the ECHR. As a consequence, attacks abroad which kill people do not fall into the scope of protection of Article 2 of the ECHR.[145] However, jurisdiction within the meaning of Article 1 of the ECHR is established in cases of military occupation, when the Convention state effectively controls the state power in a foreign area.[146] Thus, the ECtHR did not hesitate in holding Turkey responsible for a violation of Article 2 of the ECHR in Northern Cyprus.[147] Moreover, the fact that Cyprus is a party to the ECHR meant that the population of Northern Cyprus already found themselves within the territorial scope of the ECHR. This was a further reason for applying Article 2 of the ECHR. One might reproach the ECtHR for applying a double standard

---

139 ECtHR *Pretty* (2002) 35 EHRR 1; *cf* Fassbender (note 6) p 115.
140 *Cf* Kunig in: von Münch/Kunig (eds) *Grundgesetz-Kommentar Band I* (5th ed, München 2000) Art 2, para 20 with regard to German constitutional law.
141 ECtHR *Pretty* (2002) 35 EHRR 1.
142 ECtHR *Banković* App No 52207/99 (Grand Chamber, decision on admissibility).
143 *Cf* Arts 1 ff of the Draft Articles on Responsibility of States for Internationally Wrongful Acts adopted by the International Law Commission in 2001, UN Doc A/65/10, pp 43 ff; Schröder in: Graf Vitzthum (ed) *Völkerrecht* (3rd ed, Berlin 2004) Sec 7, para 13.
144 Frowein (note 38) Art 1 EMRK, para 4.
145 But see Breuer [2003] EuGRZ 449, 450–451; Rüth/Trilsch (2003) 97 AJIL 168, 171.
146 *Cf* more detailed Krieger (2002) 62 ZaöRV 669, 673 ff with regard to operations of German armed forces abroad.
147 ECtHR *Cyprus v Turkey* (2002) 35 EHRR 731, paras 75 ff, 131 ff; *Loizidou* (1997) 23 EHRR 513, paras 52 ff.

to the conduct of Convention states. By strengthening the territorial link, the ECtHR creates a European justice area in which an exemplary standard of human rights is realised, whereas malpractice of European state power outside this area is exempted from any control. On the other hand, it would certainly ask too much of the ECtHR should military operations outside the Convention area also be investigated.[148]

b) Interference

52 To the extent that Article 2 of the ECHR is a defensive right against interference (→ § 2 para 13), it prohibits killings that can be **attributed to the state**. Non-intentional killing also interferes with Article 2 of the ECHR[149]. In particular, there is an interference if state use of firearms leads to death, no matter whether the death was intended or merely an unintentional consequence. There is no interference, however, if the death is caused by private conduct or natural events. Abortion is an example of this (para 49). Nor does self-defence by private persons interfere with Article 2 of the ECHR, even though the duty to protect private life may oblige states to restrict private self-defence (paras 62–63). In cases where it remains unclear whether state authorities are responsible for a killing, no interference and, in consequence, no violation of the defensive right can be established. According to the ECtHR, the death must be attributed to the state without reasonable doubt.[150]

53 In principle, it is necessary to prove all circumstances which establish the state's responsibility for a death. If a person dies in police custody, however, such evidence is frequently as difficult to obtain as in cases of torture or inhuman treatment, which have been discussed above (para 42). The ECtHR therefore modifies the **burden of proof** in such cases.[151] If a person is in good health when taken into custody and the dead body later shows injuries, it is up to the state to explain this. If under these circumstances the state is not capable of providing evidence that the death occurred without state influence, then an interference is established.

54 It is debatable whether the **extradition** of a person interferes with the right to life if that person then faces a **death sentence** in the country of destination. It is true that the extraditing state sets a necessary condition for a later conviction and execution. Moreover, the extradition is carried out with the specific aim of criminal prosecution and execution of the sentence. If the state extradites despite the risk of the death sentence, it at least accepts the consequences. Hence there are good reasons to establish an interference. If this indirect attribution of a killing was deemed to be insufficient, Article 2 of the ECHR would become relevant as the source of a duty to protect. Moreover, one might consider a solution through Article 3 of the ECHR. One may easily qualify extradition despite the threat of the death penalty as inhuman treatment. The ECtHR decided differently in 1989 in *Soering*[152]. However, at the time of that case the UK had not yet ratified the 6th Prot ECHR which prohibits the death penalty. After the entry into force of the 6th Prot ECHR, the case must be decided differently[153].

---

148 *Cf* Shelton (2003) 13 Duke J of Comp & Int'l L 95, 128.
149 ECtHR *Oğur* (2001) 31 EHRR 912, para 78; *Salman* (2005) 41 EHRR 8, para 98.
150 ECtHR *Ergi v Turkey* (2001) 32 EHRR 388, para 78.
151 ECtHR *Salman* (2005) 41 EHRR 8, paras 100–103.
152 ECtHR *Soering* (1989) 11 EHRR 439, paras 101–103.
153 *Cf* Trechsel (note 136) p 678.

c) Justification

Article 2 of the ECHR does not contain one single restriction provision, but **several exceptions and limitations** are spread out over paragraph 1(ii) and paragraph 2. Both clauses are not in tune with one another in terms of their wording, which makes interpretation more difficult. The provisions of restrictions are complemented by the prohibition of the death penalty in the 6th and 13th Prot ECHR.

aa) Restriction and Prohibition of the Death Penalty

The **death penalty** was not yet prohibited by the Convention in 1950. Article 2(1)(ii) of the ECHR merely provides special justification requirements. The imposition of the death penalty is faced with the requirement of a statutory basis and is reserved for courts. In addition, the penalty is limited to crimes, *ie* to offences which are particularly serious.

Article 1 of the 6th Prot ECHR of 28 April 1983 abolishes the imposition and enforcement of the death penalty. In accordance with Article 2 of the 6th Prot ECHR, exceptions are permissible only in times of war. Beyond this, Article 3 of the 6th Prot ECHR states that the prohibition may not be derogated from under Article 15 of the ECHR in times of emergency (→ § 2 para 43). Furthermore, Article 4 of the 6th Prot ECHR excludes reservations under Article 57 of the ECHR. The 13th Protocol of 3 May 2002 finally abolishes the exceptions even for times of war. Thus, the **prohibition** of the death penalty **becomes absolute**. This Protocol is up to now in force for 36 out of the 46 Convention states.[154] Based on this development, the ECtHR considered in *Öcalan* that even Convention states who have not yet ratified the 6th Prot ECHR could have impliedly waived Article 2(1)(ii) of the ECHR, at least with regard to the imposition of the death penalty in times of peace.[155] This reasoning is highly problematic and practically irrelevant, as only Russia has still not ratified the 6th Prot ECHR and even this state no longer uses the death penalty.

bb) Defence of Persons

According to Article 2(2)(a) of the ECHR, killing is justified if it results from a use of force which is absolutely necessary to defend a person from unlawful violence. That concerns, above all, the use of firearms by the police. It is remarkable that this restriction provision does not require a legal basis, but simply lays down substantial requirements.[156] The text is geared towards the **protection of human beings**. The defence of material assets does not justify deadly shots under Article 2 of the ECHR. One may ask whether Article 2(2) of the ECHR can ever justify **intentional killing**. Article 2(1)(ii) of the ECHR could argue against that, for this sentence prohibits intentional killing with the exception of the death penalty. In consequence, paragraph 2 appears to deal only with unintentional killing. It hardly appears coherent, however, to allow the purely repressive killing of a person within the framework of criminal law on the one hand, but to exclude without exception the purposeful killing to save another person's life on the other hand. Therefore, paragraph 2 and

---

154 As of 29 March 2006; for updated information see http://conventions.coe.int/.
155 ECtHR *Öcalan* (2003) 37 EHRR 238, paras 189–198 (Chamber); *Öcalan* (2005) 41 EHRR 985, Judgment of 12 May 2005, para 162–165 (Grand Chamber); *cf* Breuer (note 145) p 453; Kühne [2003] JZ 670, 673–674; Künzli (2004) 17 LJIL 141, 152 ff.
156 Trechsel (note 136) p 681.

paragraph 1(ii) should be applied independently from one another. Even the purposeful killing of a person can be justified by Article 2(2)(a) of the ECHR[157].

59 Article 2(2) of the ECHR requires that the use of force is "absolutely necessary". Whereas an interference with Article 8(2) of the ECHR must simply be "necessary in a democratic society" (para 25), Article 2(2) of the ECHR qualifies the necessity by the adjective "absolute", thereby intensifying justification requirements[158]. This means that the use of force is subject to a particularly strict **proportionality test**. A purposeful shot should be preceded, for instance, by a warning shot unless this would jeopardise the success of the defence in a given case. The higher the risk of the aggressor being killed, the greater the danger which is to be averted must be.

cc) Further Restrictions

60 Article 2(2) of the ECHR recognises **further cases** in which state power leading to death can be justified. *Litera* b mentions the use of force to effect a lawful arrest or to prevent the escape of a person lawfully detained and *litera* c mentions the use of force for the purpose of quelling a riot or insurrection. In both cases, the strict proportionality test applies which has already been mentioned with regard to *litera* a (para 59). It is particularly difficult to justify intentional fatal shots at this point.

61 A final exception is to be found in Article 15 of the ECHR. This provision, which is seldom used, permits, under narrow conditions laid down in paragraphs 1 and 2, the restriction of Convention rights in times of **war and public emergency** (→ § 2 para 43). Under these conditions, Article 15(2) of the ECHR allows death resulting from lawful acts of war. The Convention refers to the legal standards of International humanitarian law, as laid down in the four Geneva Red Cross Conventions of 1949 and in the first Protocol to this Convention of 1977[159]. Military operations abroad which do not fall within the territorial scope of the ECHR (para 51) need not be justified under Article 15(2) of the ECHR.

d) Duty to Protect

62 If the death does not result from state conduct but from private acts or from natural phenomena, there is no interference with the defensive or liberty right. Rather, the **duty to protect** which is enshrined in Article 2(1)(i) of the ECHR is at stake.[160] States must not only take preventative measures in order to protect individual lives.[161] The state must also protect life by means of criminal law, *ie* killing must be made a punishable offence and actually prosecuted[162].

63 In Germany at least there have been serious doubts whether Article 2 of the ECHR limits private **self-defence**. In principle, Article 2 of the ECHR obliges the state to restrict the right to self-defence, so that the life of the aggressor will be sufficiently protected.[163]

---

157 ECtHR *McCann et al* (1996) 21 EHRR 97, paras 148, 199; Kneihs (note 133) pp 33–34.
158 ECtHR *Oğur* (2001) 31 EHRR 912, para 78; *Salman* (2005) 41 EHRR 8, para 98; Kneihs (note 133) pp 31 ff.
159 *Cf* Bothe in: Graf Vitzthum (ed) *Völkerrecht* (3rd ed, Berlin 2004) Sec 8, paras 56 ff.
160 *Cf* Ovey/White (note 18) pp 51–53.
161 See ECtHR *Cyprus v Turkey* (2002) 35 EHRR 731, para 219 with regard to medical care.
162 Trechsel (note 136) pp 673 ff.
163 German scholars of criminal law largely ignore this duty to protect; see Lenckner/Perron in:

However, the narrow limits to the restrictability of Article 2(1), which are laid out in Article 2(2)(a) of the ECHR (para 58), do not apply in this context. Therefore, the defence of material assets with life-threatening force can be accepted under certain circumstances without violating the state's duty to protect. The state must intervene, however, in case of extreme disparity between the material assets which give rise to self-defence and the threat to life. In the process of weighing and balancing, which is inherent to the duty to protect (para 27), one may also look to the standards set out in Article 2(2) of the ECHR[164], even though this restriction provision is not directly applicable. Given the attention which German scholars pay to the problem of self-defence under the ECHR, it is quite astonishing that there is no pertinent case-law[165]. One reason may be that relevant cases are not brought before court in the first place.

The **criminal protection** must not only exist on paper but must also be effectively implemented. This entails that the state, in instances where the cause of death is not clear from the outset, initiates an investigation to clarify the cause of death and provide evidence.[166] The investigation must be suitable to lead to the identification and punishment of the persons responsible.[167] This presupposes that the investigation authorities are sufficiently independent.[168] State investigation is particularly important if a person dies in state custody.[169] Altogether, the ECtHR has derived procedural requirements from the duty to protect which are similar to those of Article 8 of the ECHR (para 28).[170]

64

Case 3 – Answer:
There is doubt as to the admissibility of the appeal because the husband has not had his own right to life violated. However, in the interests of an effective legal protection by the Convention, violations of Article 2 of the ECHR must be able to be examined by the ECtHR. In case of a killing, close relatives of the victims, such as the husband, are therefore considered to be a victim in the sense of Article 34(i) of the ECHR, which gives them legal standing before the ECtHR (→ § 2 para 62)[171].

65

The killing of the passer-by falls within the scope of protection of Article 2(1)(i) of the ECHR. It cannot be established without reasonable doubt, however, that the fatal shot was fired by a police officer. In this respect there is no interference which could be attributed to the state (para 52). Whereas the defensive or liberty right to life is not at stake, Article 2 of the ECHR also provides for a duty to protect (para 62). It is not difficult to foresee that with an operation of this kind, ricocheted shots could reach the opposite side of the street. The

---

Schönke/Schröder (eds) *Strafgesetzbuch* (26th ed, München 2001) § 32, para 62; Tröndle/Fischer *Strafgesetzbuch* (52nd ed, München 2004) § 32, para 21; Kleinknecht/Meyer-Goßner *Strafprozessordnung* (47 ed, München 2004) A 4 MRK, Art 2, para 3; all with further references.
164 Kneihs (note 133) pp 38–39; see also Frowein (note 38) Art 2 EMRK, paras 2, 11.
165 Uerpmann (note 1) pp 25–26.
166 ECtHR *Salman* (2005) 41 EHRR 8, para 104; *cf* more detailed Ovey/White (note 18) pp 48–51.
167 ECtHR *Oğur* (2001) 31 EHRR 912, para 88; *Grams* App No 33677/96 (decision on admissibility).
168 ECtHR *Oğur* (2001) 31 EHRR 40, para 91.
169 ECtHR *Salman* (2005) 41 EHRR 8, para 105.
170 Grabenwarter *Europäische Menschenrechtskonvention* (2nd ed, München 2005) pp 120–121, → § 19 para 9.
171 Meyer-Ladewig *Konvention zum Schutz der Menschenrechte und Grundfreiheiten* (Baden-Baden 2003) Art 34, para 12.

police would therefore have had to block off the area in order to protect the uninvolved passer-by. Reasons which could justify the lack of action by the police are not to be found. The duty to protect arising from Article 2 of the ECHR is therefore violated. Furthermore, in unclear cases of death, a state is bound under Article 2 of the ECHR to undertake sufficient efforts to investigate possible perpetrators (para 64). This duty is even more relevant if the fatal shot was possibly fired by state organs. The criminal prosecution authorities, who did not even interrogate the involved police forces, failed to fulfil this duty. Therefore, the ECtHR will also find a violation of Article 2 in this regard.[172]

III. Prohibition of Discrimination

Case 4 – Problem: (ECtHR *Schmidt* (1994) 18 EHRR 513)

66 In Baden-Württemberg and Bavaria, men were required to serve as firemen until the mid 1990s. Men who did not perform this service had to pay a fire service levy. In fact, no one was obliged against his will to serve in the voluntary fire brigade, however, the fire service levy was an important financial source. Women were not obliged to perform this service and therefore had no duty to pay the levy. A man from Baden-Württemberg challenged his obligation to pay the levy with an appeal to the Court in Strasbourg.

1. The Complementary Prohibition of Discrimination (Article 14 ECHR)

a) Complementary Character

67 Article 14 of the ECHR is a **complementary equality clause**. Since it is linked to "the enjoyment of the rights and freedoms set forth in this convention", the prohibition of discrimination only applies to state conduct which falls within the scope of protection of another Convention right.[173] It does not matter, however, if the other right has actually been violated or not. There is not even a need to establish an interference with the other right.[174] Guarantees which are laid down in the Protocols to the ECHR also trigger Article 14 of the ECHR. Whereas Article 14 of the ECHR in its wording only refers to Convention rights, the additional Protocols contain special provisions which give Protocol rights the full status of Convention rights[175]. Due to the complementary character of Article 14 of the ECHR, the ECtHR must not review discrimination in fields that are not covered by the Convention. That is true, above all, in the area of social rights. The ECHR differs in this respect from the International Covenant on Civil and Political Rights (ICCPR) of 19 December 1966 (→ § 2 para 3). Article 26 ICCPR is autonomous according to its wording. Correspondingly, the UN Human Rights Committee (HRC) applies it also in the area of social rights.[176] The complementary character at one time may have seemed appropriate. Today, it is increasingly anachronistic. Therefore, the 12th Prot ECHR was concluded on 4 November 2000.[177] Article 1 of this Protocol takes up the wording of

---

172 *Cf* ECtHR *Ergi v Turkey* (2001) 32 EHRR 388, paras 77 ff.
173 ECtHR *Odièvre* (2004) 38 EHRR 871, para 54.
174 ECtHR *Cha'are Shalom Ve Tsedek* App No 27417/95, paras 86–87.
175 See Art 5 Prot 1 ECHR, Art 6 Prot 4 ECHR, Art 6 Prot 6 ECHR, Art 7 Prot 7 ECHR.
176 UN HRC *Zwaan-de-Vries* (1988) 9 HRLJ 256 (257–258); but see Kunig/Uerpmann-Wittzack (note 8) pp 237–238.
177 ETS No 177.

Article 14 of the ECHR, but transforms the guarantee into a general prohibition of discrimination, without, however, replacing Article 14 of the ECHR.[178] The Protocol entered into force on 1 April 2005, but as of today has only been ratified by 13 out of the 46 Convention states[179]. Important states, such as France, Poland and the United Kingdom, have not even signed it.

The complementary character **reduces** the **significance** of Article 14 of the ECHR. If a right to freedom is violated, the ECtHR frequently abstains from reviewing whether an unequal treatment exists.[180] If the interference with a right to freedom is justified, then there will often also be good reasons for an unequal treatment. Article 14 of the ECHR is therefore seldom used.

68

b) Differential Treatment

Article 14 of the ECHR prohibits discrimination, *ie* unjustified **differential treatment**. The provision lists characteristics which are in principle inadmissible as grounds for unequal treatment. This corresponds to the special clause on equality in Article 3(3) of the Basic Law. By using the words "such as", Article 14 of the ECHR makes it clear that the list is not exhaustive. Any discrimination for whatever reason or, as Article 14 of the ECHR stipulates, "on any ground", is prohibited.[181] In particular, the prohibition of discrimination is not restricted to personal characteristics.[182] While Article 14 in the English version is specially geared towards differences due to "status", the equally authentic French version does not refer to status, but to different situations. Accordingly, the ECtHR has reviewed possible differences between open sea fishing and coastal fishing under Article 14 of the ECHR.[183] The Convention guarantee therefore comes close to a **general clause of equality,** such as Article 3(1) of the Basic Law. The standard of review is essentially the same for both provisions, except for the complementary character of Article 14 of the ECHR. Both norms are best examined in two stages, *ie* differential treatment and justification (→ § 2 para 37).

69

c) Justification

Prohibited discrimination only exists if the established differential treatment is not **justified**. In Germany, the concept of legal equality is quite elaborately differentiated. The general equality clause of Article 3(1) of the Basic Law is complemented by specific equality clauses such as Article 3(3), which provide for a strict standard of review. Even within the general equality clause, the German Federal Constitutional Court has established different standards of review, ranging from a mere protection against arbitrary differentiation to a strict proportionality test in cases where inalienable personal characteristics, such as sexual orientation, are at stake. Under the so-called new formula, the German Federal Constitutional Court asks whether there are differences of such weight that they are able

70

---

178 Ovey/White (note 18) pp 358–359; Trechsel in: Wolfrum (ed) *Gleichheit und Nichtdiskriminierung im nationalen und internationalen Menschenrechtsschutz* (Berlin 2003) pp 119, 122–124.
179 As of 29 March 2006; for updated information see http://conventions.coe.int/.
180 *Eg* ECtHR *X and Y v The Netherlands* (1986) 8 EHRR 235, para 32; *Smith & Grady* (2000) 29 EHRR 493, para 115.
181 Bayefsky (1990) 11 HRLJ 1, 5–6.
182 But see Peters (note 137) pp 216–217.
183 ECtHR *Posti & Rahko* (2003) 37 EHRR 158, paras 79 ff.

to justify the unequal legal consequences.[184] In the ECHR, specific equality clauses are virtually unknown.[185] With regard to the general equality clause, though, both the ECtHR and the German Federal Constitutional Court apply, in essence, a similar standard of review.[186] There must be a **legitimate aim** that is able to justify the differential treatment, and the unequal treatment must be **proportionate** to the aim pursued.[187] In assessing these requirements, domestic authorities enjoy a **margin of appreciation** which varies according to the seriousness of the differential treatment[188]. Moreover, one may assume that the reasons for discrimination which are expressly incriminated by Article 14 of the ECHR, such as sex or race, are particularly severe. The closer a given reason for distinction comes to these mentioned in Article 14 of the ECHR, the higher the justification requirements are. As a rule, justification requirements become stricter if inalienable, individual-related characteristics of a person are concerned.[189] Therefore, discrimination due to gender is only justified in very rare exceptions.[190] This does not exclude affirmative actions to compensate for actual disadvantaging of women. Unlike Article 3(2) of the Basic Law,[191] the ECHR does not charge national authorities with realising equality within the social sphere or with combating factual discrimination. If the Member State sets itself a goal of actual equality, this can nevertheless justify unequal treatment burdening men if this is necessary in order to promote full and effective equality.[192] The 12th Prot ECHR (para 67) has confirmed this in the 3rd recital of its preamble.[193]

71   Equality under the ECHR can presumably fully develop only under the 12th Protocol. Until now, the solutions of the ECtHR have been strongly characterised by **liberty rights**. This is exemplified by the case-law concerning transsexuals. While courts in Germany predominantly relied upon Article 3(1) of the Basic Law[194], the ECtHR mostly referred to Article 8[195]. This also shows that liberty rights and equality rights are functionally equivalent up to a certain point.

Case 4 – Answer:
72   Case 4 obviously deals with a problem of discrimination. As up to now the ECHR knows no autonomous prohibition of discrimination, it is necessary to examine first whether another Convention right is concerned. Article 4(2) of the ECHR prohibits forced or compulsory labour. Fire service duty can be seen as such. Article 4(3)(d) of the ECHR exempts work or service which forms part of common civic obligations from the prohibition. The

---

184 BVerfG (1993) 88 BVerfGE 87, 96–97; *cf* Bryde/Kleindiek [1999] Jura 36.
185 But see below paras 73 ff.
186 *Cf* Walter in: Wolfrum (ed) *Gleichheit und Nichtdiskriminierung im nationalen und internationalen Menschenrechtsschutz* (Berlin 2003) pp 253, 255 ff.
187 ECtHR *Dahlab* App No 42393/98 (decision on admissibility).
188 *Cf* Ovey/White (note 18) pp 356–358.
189 See also BVerfG (1993) 88 BVerfGE 87, 96.
190 Wittinger (note 27) pp 163–164.
191 *Cf* BVerfG (1992) 85 BVerfGE 191, 206–207, Osterloh in: Sachs (ed) *Grundgesetz* (3rd ed, Munich 2003) Art 3, paras 261 ff.
192 Wittinger (note 27) p 165.
193 *Cf* Wittinger [2001] EuGRZ 272, 279.
194 *Cf* BVerfG (1993) 88 BVerfGE 87, 96 ff.
195 ECtHR *Van Kück* (2003) 37 EHRR 973, para 91 is particularly clear in this regard; see also above para 8.

ECtHR concluded from this exception that Article 4(2) was not violated. The next question was whether Article 14 of the ECHR read in conjunction with Article 4 of the ECHR could be considered. If one considers the wording of Article 4, civic obligation work in the sense of Article 4(3) of the ECHR is not even included in the scope of protection of Article 4(2) of the ECHR. Consequently, Article 14 of the ECHR would be inapplicable. The ECtHR held a different view. Since civic obligations are dealt with in Article 4(3)(d) of the ECHR, they fall within the ambit of the Convention. Article 14 of the ECHR therefore applies. This seems an appropriate solution. The Court makes sure that Article 14 of the ECHR only applies to discriminations that have a link to other Convention rights without exaggerating the concept of complementarity.

Taken alone, the liability for levy infringes neither Article 4 of the ECHR nor any other Convention right. Nevertheless, the ECtHR applied Article 14 because of the close link to the underlying civic obligation.

Fire service duty that is limited to one sex is clearly differential treatment. Through the service duty, the liability for the levy is equally connected to sex. It therefore also constitutes differential treatment.

With regard to justification, a distinction has to be made between the fire service duty and the levy. The ECtHR at first expressed some doubt as to the justification of the civic obligation. It demanded objective and sensible reasons as well as an appropriate relationship between means and purpose. It was made clear that strict requirements are to be placed on discrimination on the basis of gender. The fact that other states of the Federal Republic of Germany also have fire service duty for women and that women in the south of Germany do and have done voluntary service argues against justification. The ECtHR left this issue unsolved because the civic obligation only existed on paper. Therefore, only the justification for the levy is relevant. Because nobody had to do the service against his will, the levy had no compensating function, but a purely financial effect. The decision to enlist only men to finance the voluntary fire service had no sufficient reasons. Therefore, the liability to pay levy was contrary to the Convention.

The German Federal Constitutional Court used the decision of the ECtHR as an opportunity to hold that the fire service levy, which up to that point was held to be constitutional[196], is in fact contrary to the Basic Law[197]. Under the Basic Law, the reasoning is much easier than under the ECHR. Article 3(3)(i) of the Basic Law prohibits any form of gender discrimination. The levy, which puts a burden only on men, obviously interferes with this right. Short of justification, Article 3(3)(i) of the Basic Law is violated.

2. Special Aspects of Equality

Some aspects of equality are found outside Article 14 of the ECHR. Article 5 of the 7th Prot ECHR, which guarantees **equality between spouses**, is a specific equality clause. The provision has played no meaningful role so far.[198] It scarcely complements the Convention guarantees, but does not limit them either[199]. For Andorra, Belgium, Germany, the Netherlands, Spain, Turkey and the United Kingdom, the whole Protocol is not in force. Within the Convention itself, the procedural guarantees of Article 6 of the ECHR (→ § 6 paras 33 ff) contain the strongest elements of equality.

---

196 See BVerwG [1994] BayVBl 315; see also Rozek [1993] BayVBl 646 with a critical analysis of former case-law.
197 BVerfG (1995) 92 BVerfGE 91.
198 *Cf* Wittinger (note 27) pp 177–179.
199 ECtHR *Burghartz* (1994) 18 EHRR 101, para 22.

74 The most important example is Article 6(3)(e) of the ECHR, which grants the right to an **interpreter free of charge** in criminal proceedings. Taken literally, Article 6(3)(e) of the ECHR contains a procedural guarantee which shall ensure a fair trial without showing components of equality. At least in Germany, initially the opinion prevailed that freedom of charge should only be granted until the end of the proceeding. The convict was burdened with court costs including costs for interpretation. To ensure a fair trial it is sufficient in principle if the interpreter is initially paid for by the state, so that the demand for an interpreter cannot be denied on grounds of costs. In *Luedicke* the ECtHR decided, however, that even the convict should not be burdened with the interpreter costs.[200] This decision is consistent if Article 6(3)(e) of the ECHR is construed as a specific equality right. Beyond the provision's primary function of ensuring an effective defence, the accused who does not have a good command of the language of the court should be released from all additional financial burdens. Those who are not proficient in a given language are thus put on a par with those who command this language.[201]

75 The principle of **fair trial** also shows aspects of a special equality clause. This is particularly true for the principle of equality of arms, which, according to the ECtHR, emanates from the concept of fair trial and which constitutes a standard of review for the respective rights of all parties to a litigation[202].

---

200 ECtHR *Luedicke* (1979–80) 2 EHRR 149, paras 38 ff.
201 *Cf* ECtHR *Luedicke* (1979–80) 2 EHRR 149, paras 34 ff and especially para 42, where the Court alludes to this argument.
202 ECtHR *Borgers* (1993) 15 EHRR 92, para 24.

§ 4
Freedom of Expression, Freedom of Assembly and Association

Thilo Marauhn

I. Freedom of Communication within the European Human Rights System

Since communication with fellow human beings is an essential element of an individual's personality, the protection of freedom of expression as well as freedom of assembly and association is of utmost importance in any human rights instrument. However, the protection of freedom of communication does not only serve the individual. Unhampered communication also is of societal and political importance since without such communication, democracy is inconceivable. In interpreting pertinent provisions of the Convention, the European Court of Human Rights has embraced this idea, arguing that freedom of expression "constitutes one of the essential foundations of a democratic society and one of the basic conditions for its progress and for each individual's self-fulfilment".[1] While the Convention does not protect freedom of communication as such, its Articles 9,[2] 10 and 11 of the ECHR establish distinct interrelated freedoms extending across the different modes of communication in real life.

A closer look at the wording of Article 10 of the ECHR reveals that it specifies several communicative liberties: freedom of opinion, freedom of information, freedom of the press and freedom of broadcasting, television and film.[3] The inclusion of the freedom to hold opinions and to receive and impart information as a separate part of the freedom of expression acknowledges that communication is not a unilateral activity but an interactive process, even though the reciprocity of dialogues is hard to grasp in legal terms.[4] Article 10 of the ECHR is followed by Article 11 of the ECHR which guarantees freedom of assembly, freedom of association and trade union rights, in particular. According to the European Court of Human Rights, the rights guaranteed by Article 11 of the ECHR are closely associated with Articles 9 and 10. The Court, however, considers freedom of assembly and association as *leges speciales*[5] and builds on jurisprudence of the US Supreme Court in this regard. The US Supreme Court derived the freedom of association from the freedom of opinion as guaranteed by the US Constitution's First Amendment.[6] It follows that freedom of assembly and association must be considered in light of the rights guaranteed in Articles 9 and 10 of the ECHR.[7]

---

1 ECtHR *Handyside* (1979–80) 1 EHRR 737, para 49; *Lingens* (1986) 8 EHRR 407, para 41; *Oberschlick* (1998) 25 EHRR 357, para 58; *Observer* (1992) 14 EHRR 153, para 59; *Feldek* App No 29032/95, para 83.
2 This chapter does not address Art 9 ECHR. For a discussion of religious liberty in Europe and of pertinent Strasbourg jurisprudence see Evans *Religious liberty and international law in Europe* (Cambridge 1997), and, recently, Langlaude (2006) 55 ICLQ 929–944.
3 Grabenwarter *Europäische Menschenrechtskonvention* (Munich/Vienna 2003) Art 23, para 2.
4 This was already pointed out by Müller *Grundrechte in der Schweiz* (3rd ed, Bern 1999) p 184.
5 ECtHR *Ezelin* (1992) 14 EHRR 362, para 35: "In the circumstances of the case, this provision (*ie* Article 10) is to be regarded as a lex generalis in relation to Article 11 (…), a lex specialis, so that it is unnecessary to take it into consideration separately".
6 United States Supreme Court *NAACP v Alabama ex rel Patterson* (1958) 357 US 449.
7 ECtHR *United Communist Party of Turkey* (1998) 26 EHRR 121, para 42: "The Court reiterates

3 It is true that there is no formal hierarchy among the rights and freedoms guaranteed by the ECHR, except for non-derogable rights. However, freedom of expression and freedom of assembly and association can be considered to be elementary for the enjoyment of all other freedoms included in the ECHR. The main argument is that without free communication, there is no effective defence of fundamental freedoms.[8] In order to further pluralism and tolerance, Strasbourg jurisprudence has paid tribute thereto by broadly interpreting the scope of Articles 10 and 11 of the ECHR and by considering limitations permissible only under narrow circumstances. A sharp distinction between the various freedoms included in Articles 10 and 11 of the ECHR is neither possible nor necessary since the provisions are designed to comprehensively protect human discourse.[9] However, differences are taken into account when evaluating the proportionality of limitations.[10]

II. Freedom of Opinion and Freedom of Information

Leading cases: ECtHR *Handyside* (1979–80) 1 EHRR 737; *Lingens* (1986) 8 EHRR 407; *Müller* (1991) 13 EHRR 212; *Groppera Radio AG* (1990) 12 EHRR 321; *Oberschlick* (1998) 25 EHRR 357; *Open Door* (1993) 15 EHRR 244; *Informationsverein Lentia* (1993) 17 EHRR 93; *Otto-Preminger-Institut* (1995) 19 EHRR 34; *Vogt* (1996) 21 EHRR 295; *Observer* (1991) 14 EHRR 153; *markt intern* (1990) 12 EHRR 161; *Janowski* (2000) 29 EHRR 705; *Bladet Tromsø* (1999) 29 EHRR 125; *Özgür Gündem* (2001) 31 EHRR 1082; *Feldek* App No 29032/95; *von Hannover* (2005) 40 EHRR 1.

Further reading: Calliess *Werbung, Moral und Europäische Menschenrechtskonvention* [2000] AfP 248; Cram *Automatic Reporting Restrictions in Criminal Proceedings and Article 10 of the ECHR* [1998] EHRLR 742; Engel *Einwirkungen des europäischen Menschenrechtsschutzes auf Meinungsäußerungsfreiheit und Pressefreiheit – insbesondere auf die Einführung von innerer Pressefreiheit* [1994] AfP 1; Frowein/Peukert (eds) *Europäische Menschenrechtskonvention. Kommentar* (2nd ed, Kehl/Strassbourg/Arlington 1996); Gornig *Äußerungsfreiheit und Informationsfreiheit als Menschenrechte* (Berlin 1988); Grabenwarter *Europäische Menschenrechtskonvention* (Munich/Vienna 2003) pp 267 ff; Hoffmeister *Art. 10 EMRK in der Rechtsprechung des Europäischen Gerichtshofs für Menschenrechte 1994–1999* (2000) 27 EuGRZ 358; Kirby *Opinion: Freedom of information* [1998] EHRLR 245; Malinverni *Freedom of Information in the European Convention on Human Rights and the International Covenant on Civil and Political Rights* [1983] HRLJ 443; Peters *Einführung in die Europäische Menschenrechtskonvention* (Munich 2003) §§ 9–14; Thorgeirsdóttir *Journalism Worthy of the Name* (2004) 22 NQHR 601.

1. Scope of Protection

a) Freedom to Hold Opinions

4 The freedom to hold opinions as guaranteed by Article 10(1)(ii) of the ECHR is the basis for and the generic notion of the right to freedom of expression as incorporated in Article 10(1)(i) of the ECHR.[11] Similar to the freedom of thought as guaranteed by Article 9 of

---

that notwithstanding its autonomous role and particular sphere of application, Article 11 must also be considered in the light of Article 10".

8 *Cf* Peukert *Die Kommunikationsrechte im Lichte der Rechtsprechung der Organe der Europäischen Menschenrechtskonvention (EMRK)* in: Däubler-Gmelin (ed) *Gegenrede – Aufklärung, Kritik, Öffentlichkeit. Festschrift für Ernst Gottfried Mahrenholz* (Baden-Baden 1994) pp 277–301.

9 ECtHR *Barthold* (1985) 7 EHRR 383, para 42: "All these various components overlap to make up a whole, the gist of which is the expression of "opinions" and the imparting of "information" on a topic of general interest. It is not possible to dissociate from this whole those elements which go more to manner of presentation than to substance ...".

10 Villiger *Handbuch der Europäischen Menschenrechtskonvention (EMRK)* (2nd ed, Zurich 1999) p 390.

11 Guradze *Die Europäische Menschenrechtskonvention* (Berlin 1968) p 142.

the ECHR, the freedom to hold opinions protects the internal formation of an opinion, the *forum internum*. In order to safeguard this internal sphere, the government is, inter alia, barred from wilful indoctrination of its citizens.[12] Likewise, a continuous and systematic one-sided information policy or one-sided reporting in government-controlled mass media can be considered to be contrary to the Convention.[13]

While the German Federal Constitutional Court, in an effort to separate a factual statement from the voicing of an opinion, has interpreted the core concept of "opinion" (as included in Article 5 of the *Grundgesetz* (GG – German Basic Law)) by vaguely paraphrasing it,[14] the ECHR has avoided any abstract definition of "opinion" so far. Such definitional reluctance may be criticized. However, synonyms and transcriptions lacking the necessary precision are not only deficient from a methodological point of view, but also run the risk of blending the problems related to the scope of protection on the one hand and the legitimacy of an interference on the other. Besides, the ECHR can avoid distinguishing between imparting facts and communicating opinions by simply referring to the wording of Article 10 of the ECHR which speaks of "freedom of expression". This notion is broad enough to cover both factual statements and opinions.[15]

5

b) Freedom of Expression

Freedom of expression includes both the freedom of an individual to express an opinion and to impart information and ideas (sometimes characterised as active freedom of information[16]). Considering the authentic English ("freedom of expressions") and French ("liberté d'expression") text, freedom of expression is not limited to communicating "opinions" but also covers statements of fact.

6

While assessing each individual case separately, the ECHR has generally interpreted freedom of expression as covering all forms of expression, any medium and any content (facts, opinions, entertainment,[17] *etc*). The right to freedom of expression even includes content which may offend, shock or disturb the State or any sector of the population.[18] Article 10 of the ECHR is not limited to information and ideas that are favourably receiv-

7

---

12 ECtHR *Kjeldsen* (1979–80) 1 EHRR 711, para 53: "The State is forbidden to pursue an aim of indoctrination that might be considered as not respecting parents' religious and philosophical convictions".
13 Similarly, Frowein in: Frowein/Peukert (eds) *Europäische Menschenrechtskonvention* (2nd ed, Kehl 1996) Art 10, para 4.
14 *Cf* BVerfG (1983) 61 BVerfGE 1, 8–9.
15 For a critique of the jurisprudence of the German Federal Constitutional Court see Erichsen [1996] JURA 84. – The European Court on Human Rights, nevertheless, distinguishes between opinion and statements of fact in the context of whether or not a limitation can be justified under the Convention; *cf* Peters *Einführung in die Europäische Menschenrechtskonvention* (Munich 2003) p 39.
16 See above (note 15) Peters pp 70 ff.
17 ECtHR *Groppera Radio AG* (1990) 12 EHRR 321, para 55: "… the Court considers that both broadcasting of programmes over the air and cable retransmission of such programmes are covered by the right enshrined in the first two sentences of Article 10 sec 1 (Art 10-1), without there being any need to make distinctions according to the content of the programmes".
18 ECtHR *Handyside* (1979–80) 1 EHRR 737, para 49: "… it is applicable not only to "information" or "ideas" that are favourably received or regarded as inoffensive or as a matter of indifference, but also to those that offend, shock or disturb the State or any sector of the population".

ed or regarded as inoffensive. According to the jurisprudence of the ECHR, open intellectual discourse is at the heart of the freedom of expression. This necessitates the maintenance of pluralism in the information sector.

8   Apart from political expression, the ECHR considers commercial statements to be covered by Article 10(1) of the ECHR,[19] including criticism of business practices[20] and commercial publicity[21]. Such a broad interpretation can at best be criticized by arguing that successful advertising does not require a conscious consumer. Placing incentives on the market in order to convince the consumer does not presuppose open discourse, which is deemed to be at the heart of Article 10(1) of the ECHR.[22] However, neither the wording nor the context of Article 10(1) of the ECHR suggest a restrictive reading of the scope of protection, which would only be based on the view that commercial expression does not need to be privileged vis-à-vis other commercial activities.

9   Article 10(1) of the ECHR does not only protect the content and substance of expression, but also its form and illustration.[23] Even acts which simply express disapproval of the activities of others are protected by Article 10(1) of the ECHR.[24] Neither form nor illustration of expression require advance authorisation. Article 10(1)(iii) of the ECHR, however, serves as a limit by stating that certain broadcasting, television or cinema enterprises are subject to prior approval.

c) Freedom of Information

10   Article 5(1)(i) of the Basic Law protects the freedom of every person to inform herself or himself from generally accessible sources. By contrast, Article 10(1)(i) of the ECHR does not qualify sources of information, but simply guarantees "freedom ... to receive ... information and ideas". The German Federal Constitutional Court has considered such sources to be "generally accessible" which are technologically appropriate and designed to inform the general public. According to the jurisprudence of the German Federal Constitutional Court, sources remain "generally accessible" notwithstanding measures taken to prevent their dissemination.[25] Thus, the Court has taken a broad view of what is "generally accessible". However, there has long been a certain reluctance vis-à-vis the freedom of

---

19 For a detailed analysis see Nolte [1999] RabelsZ 507; see also Lester of Herne Hill/Pannick *Advertising and Freedom of Expression in Europe. Joint Opinion on the Scope and Effect of the European Convention on Human Rights, Marketing Commission of the ICC* (1984).
20 ECtHR *markt intern* (1990) 12 EHRR 161, para 35.
21 ECtHR *Barthold* (1985) 7 EHRR 383, para 58. See also ECtHR *Casado Coca* (1994) 18 EHRR 1, para 35 where the Court saw no violation of Art 10 ECHR because the prohibition against advertising by lawyers was not absolute; however, the Court clearly stated that "Article 10 does not apply solely to certain types of information or ideas or forms of expression ..., in particular those of a political nature; it also encompasses artistic expression ..., information of a commercial nature ... and even light music and commercials transmitted by cable ...".
22 Thus arguing in favour of a more restrictive definition, Ipsen *Staatsrecht II, Grundrechte* (7th ed, Neuwied 2004) para 394.
23 Frowein (note 13) Art 10, para 5.
24 ECtHR *Steel* (1999) 28 EHRR 603, paras 7 and 92; *Hashman and Harrup* (2000) 30 EHRR 241, para 28: "It is true that the protest took the form of impeding the activities of which they disapproved, but the Court considers nonetheless that it constituted an expression of opinion within the meaning of Article 10 ...".
25 BVerfG (1970) 27 BVerfGE 83; (1973) 33 BVerfGE 52, 65; (1994) 90 BVerfGE 27, 32.

information in the German constitutional and legislative tradition insofar as claims to information against the State are concerned. Only recently – as part of the development towards an information society –has it become accepted that the freedom of information is a precondition for rational formation of opinion and decision-making within a democratic polity.[26] Freedom of information, however, is not only conducive to the establishment of a democratic society; an open information society supports self-development of the individual and has the potential to increase the efficiency of a polity by raising its problem-solving capacity and innovative ability.[27]

Unfortunately, the Convention organs so far have taken a rather narrow view on the freedom to receive information – even though the text is open to a broader approach. In particular, they have rejected the idea that public authorities are under an obligation to actively inform the citizen.[28] While the Court has sought to protect the role of the media as intermediary and has made it clear that the general public is entitled to receive any pertinent information,[29] it, nevertheless, reads Article 10(1)(i) of the ECHR as only guaranteeing the right to receive information from generally accessible sources.[30] Within these limits, the individual is entitled to receive information, news and ideas without governmental interference – which is of particular importance for broadcasting. In contrast to Article 5(1)(i) of the Basic Law, Article 10(1)(i) of the ECHR expressly guarantees this right "regardless of frontiers". This includes the use of pertinent receivers, subject to the provisions of Article 10(1)(iii) and (2) of the ECHR.[31]

11

Until today, there is still no interpretative consensus on whether Article 10(1) of the ECHR goes beyond the (passive) freedom to receive and includes the (active) freedom to acquire information. It is noteworthy that Article 10(1) of the ECHR insofar differs from Article 19(2) of the ICCPR and from Article 13(1) of the ACHR. Nevertheless, this difference in wording may be considered an editorial lapse rather than a deliberate choice in light of an ECHR draft that expressly included a right to actively acquire information.[32] It seems, however, plausible to include the freedom to acquire information in Article 10(1) of the ECHR by reference to the object and purpose of this provision, since without such freedom there can be no effective reception or impartation of opinions.[33] Finally, the Convention does not intend to devalue the freedom of expression by leaving the freedom to search for information unprotected.

12

---

26 Only in 2005, the German legislature adopted an Act to Regulate Access to German Federal Government Information (BGBl I 2005, 2722); for an analysis *cf* Kugelmann [2005] NJW 3609.
27 See above Müller (note 4) pp 278–279.
28 ECtHR *Guerra* (1998) 26 EHRR 357, para 53: "That freedom cannot be construed as imposing on a State, in circumstances such as those of the present case, positive obligations to collect and disseminate information of its own motion". Even in a case where the information requested had been specified by the applicant, the Court was not willing to derive a positive obligation from Art 10(1) ECHR: "Also in the circumstances of the present case, Article 10 does not embody an obligation on the State concerned to impart the information in question to the individual" (ECtHR *Gaskin* (1990) 12 EHRR 36, para 52).
29 ECtHR *Sunday Times* (1979–80) 2 EHRR 245, para 65.
30 ECtHR *Lingens* (1986) 8 EHRR 407, para 41; *Leander* (1987) 9 EHRR 433, para 74.
31 See above Villiger (note 10) p 413.
32 For a discussion of the draft see Gornig *Äußerungsfreiheit und Informationsfreiheit als Menschenrechte* (Berlin 1989) p 291.
33 This argument was developed, among others, by Probst *Art 10 EMRK – Bedeutung für den Rundfunk in Europa* (Baden-Baden 1996) pp 24–25.

13 Article 10 of the ECHR does not expressly prohibit censorship. An interference with free expression, however, is only permissible subject to Article 10(2) of the ECHR.[34] Thus, even though Article 10(1)(iii) of the ECHR permits licensing requirements for broadcasting, television or cinema (*sic!*), this does not allow pre-censorship for programmes.[35]

d) Freedom of the Arts

Case 1 – Problem: (ECtHR *Müller* (1991) 13 EHRR 212)
14 M, an artist, produced three huge paintings on the spot as part of an exhibition. The three paintings depicted homosexual acts and sodomy. On the day of the opening of the exhibition, a father complained after his minor daughter had reacted intensely to the paintings. The paintings were subsequently seized by the authorities on the ground that they were obscene. Moreover, M was prosecuted. Swiss authorities even ordered the destruction of the paintings.

15 Freedom of the arts is not expressly included in Article 10 of the ECHR. Nevertheless, the arts generally, and paintings in particular, are a form of expression covered by Article 10(1) of the ECHR. The artist's creative activities communicate his or her worldview as well as his or her thoughts about society.[36] Thus, there is general interpretative agreement that Article 10 of the ECHR also covers freedom of the arts. This includes the making of the object of art as well as its reception by the general public and thus also protects the interpretation, the dissemination and the exhibition of works of art.[37]

Case 1 – Answer:
16 The activities of M, the making of as well as the exhibition of the paintings are all covered by the scope of Article 10(1) of the ECHR.
The imposition of fines, the seizure, the confiscation and the eventual destruction of the paintings are interferences with the freedom of expression enjoyed by the artist.
In order to be lawful, such interferences must be prescribed by law and must pursue one of the objectives listed in Article 10(2) of the ECHR. In this particular case, one could refer to the protection of public morals. When assessing whether or not such interference can be justified, States enjoy a wide margin of appreciation. Whereas the imposition of fines may meet the requirements of the proportionality principle, this can not be argued with regard to the eventual destruction of the paintings. Such a destruction would deprive M of the chance to exhibit the paintings at another place where they might be welcome. This appears to result in a disproportionate interference. Even a return of the paintings will not change the fact that the threat of their destruction was disproportionate (the Strasbourg Court, however, regarded this threat to be proportionate).

---

34 *Cf* ECtHR *Cyprus v Turkey* (2002) 35 EHRR 731, indicating that censorship with regard to school textbooks amounts to a violation of Art 10 ECHR.
35 Along the same lines see above Gornig (note 32) p 294.
36 ECtHR *Müller* (1991) 13 EHRR 212, para 70. See also ECtHR *Wingrove* (1997) 24 EHRR 1; *Otto-Preminger-Institut* (1995) 19 EHRR 34.
37 ECtHR *Otto-Preminger-Institut* (1995) 19 EHRR 34, para 56.

e) Freedom of the Press and of the Media

Freedom of the press is not expressly listed in Article 10(1) of the ECHR. However, it is an integral part of the freedom of expression and of the freedom to receive and impart information.[38] The Convention thus follows the traditional approach of international human rights instruments which implicitly protect the freedom of the press even though they do not expressly mention it. The ECHR has continuously emphasized the democratic function of the press when informing the general public about issues of general interest.[39] The role of the press as a public watchdog meant to inform the public of deficiencies, mistakes and illegal activities in politics and society has been taken up for the establishment of a comprehensive protection of freedom of the press.[40] Freedom of the press includes critical debate of commercial activities of individual undertakings.[41] In general, there are three categories to be distinguished: traditional press coverage including expression of opinions, dissemination of opinions voiced by others and dissemination of facts and materials. These distinctions have an impact on the assessment of due diligence in the context of press and media law.[42] **17**

Undoubtedly, freedom of the press includes all editorial work irrespective of the method of reproduction.[43] So far, however, it is not totally clear whether and in how far the related infrastructure of the press (including sales and distribution)[44] is also covered by Article 10(1) of the ECHR. Given that the ECHR has considered means of transmission and receivers as being protected by Article 10(1) of the ECHR[45] and bearing in mind **18**

---

38 The only explicit reference to the press in the Convention is in Art 6(1)(ii) ECHR: "Judgment shall be pronounced publicly but the press and public may be excluded from all or part of the trial in the interests of morals, public order or national security in a democratic society, where the interests of juveniles or the protection of the private life of the parties so require, or to the extent strictly necessary in the opinion of the court in special circumstances where publicity would prejudice the interests of justice".
39 ECtHR *Sunday Times* (1979–80) 2 EHRR 245, para 65: "... freedom of expression constitutes one of the essential foundations of a democratic society; subject to section 2 of Article 10, it is applicable not only to information or ideas that are favourably received or regarded as inoffensive or as a matter of indifference, but also to those that offend, shock or disturb the State or any sector of the population ... These principles are of particular importance as far as the press is concerned".
40 ECtHR *Sunday Times (No 2)* (1992) 14 EHRR 229, para 50; *Thorgeirson* (1992) 14 EHRR 843, para 63; *Observer* (1992) 14 EHRR 153, para 59.
41 ECtHR, *markt intern* (1990) 12 EHRR 161, para 35; see also ECtHR *Weber* (1990) 12 EHRR 508; *VGT Verein gegen Tierfabriken* (2002) 34 EHRR 159.
42 On these distinctions see Hoffmeister (2000) 27 EuGRZ 358; on due diligence see also ECtHR *Özgür Gündem* (2001) 31 EHRR 1082, para 58: "While the press must not overstep the bounds set, inter alia, for the protection of the vital interests of the State, such as the protection of national security or territorial integrity against the threat of violence or the prevention of disorder or crime, it is nevertheless incumbent on the press to convey information and ideas on political issues, even divisive ones. Not only has the press the task of imparting such information and ideas; the public has a right to receive them. Freedom of the press affords the public one of the best means of discovering and forming an opinion of the ideas and attitudes of political leaders".
43 See above Villiger (note 10) p 405.
44 The German Federal Constitutional Court includes sales and distribution as part of freedom of the press according to Art 5(1)(ii) Basic Law BVerfG (1988) 77 BVerfGE 346, 353–354.
45 ECtHR *Autronic AG* (1990) 12 EHRR 485, para 47.

that freedom of the press does not only protect the individual medium but also the press as a whole, it is important to point out that an interference with sales and marketing can have a major impact on the press as such. Interpreting Article 10(1) of the ECHR in light of its object and purpose necessitates the inclusion of media infrastructure as part of freedom of the press.[46]

19 It has been discussed whether Article 10(1) of the ECHR includes an obligation imposed upon the national legislature to introduce a right of counterstatement. Counterstatements were already well known at the time the ECHR was drafted. Nevertheless, nothing was included in the ECHR to this end. Thus, it seems to be rather difficult to argue in favour of a right of counterstatement on the basis of Article 10 of the ECHR. However, what seems reasonable is an interpretation relying on Articles 8 and 10 of the ECHR which grants a right to counterstatement in the case of serious violations of personal rights by the media.[47] It seems even more convincing to establish such a right solely on the basis of Article 8(1) of the ECHR[48] and to consider it as a particular instrument to protect the reputation of others according to Article 10(2) of the ECHR.[49]

20 Article 10(1)(iii) of the ECHR implicitly confirms that the scope of protection of Article 10(1) ECHR as a whole extends to the freedom of broadcasting, television and film. This includes the production, transmission and reception of programmes. The provision does not differentiate according to the medium of transmission but covers all modalities thereof (airwaves, cable, satellite, *etc*). With regard to broadcasting, television and film it is noteworthy that Article 10(1) of the ECHR is not limited to national broadcasting but explicitly protects the international flow of information since the freedom is granted "regardless of frontiers".

21 As far as broadcasting is independent of its organizational and institutional setting, the only problem of scope relates to public broadcasting. Commercial broadcasting undoubtedly enjoys the protection of Article 10(1) of the ECHR.[50] It is, however, accepted that public broadcasting must enjoy a sufficient degree of freedom from governmental interference.[51] Otherwise freedom of broadcasting would prove ineffective in situations of public broadcasting monopolies which were widespread in Europe until the 1970s.

22 As to scope, finally, the applicability of Article 10(1) of the ECHR to new media has to be addressed. In order to reach a proper assessment in this regard, it is helpful to bear in mind that the Convention distinguishes between individual (Article 8 ECHR) and mass communication (Article 10 ECHR). In light of this distinction, it seems plausible to differentiate along the same lines with regard to new media.[52] Thus, Email communication should evidently be covered by Article 8 of the ECHR, whereas the presentation of information on a website should rather be protected by Article 10 of the ECHR. Difficulties occur with regard to forms of communication which are not unequivocally individual or mass communication. Thus, a discussion forum can be assessed depending on whether or

---

46 For the position of a publisher under the Convention see ECtHR *NEWS Verlags GmbH & Co. KG* (2001) 31 EHRR 246, para 39.
47 Frowein (note 13) Art 10, para 16.
48 Malinverni [1983] HRLJ 443–460.
49 This is at least the approach adopted by the German Federal Constitutional Court with regard to the parallel provision of Art 5(2) Basic Law; see BVerfG (1983) 63 BVerfGE 131, 142–143.
50 Reference may be made to ECtHR *Autronic AG* (1990) 12 EHRR 485, para 47 → § 2 para 26.
51 See above Frowein (note 13) Art 10, para 19.
52 *Cf* Grote (1999) 27 KritV 29.

not it is moderated or open. However, with regard to interactive media pertinent distinctions become increasingly blurred. This is a particular problem under the ECHR because the Convention lacks a catch-all clause. It thus seems to be difficult to construe an abstract freedom of internet use to fill in the (perceived or real) gap.[53] On the other hand, the Convention does not intend to leave certain freedoms of communication unprotected. Thus, it may be argued that decisions are best taken on a case-by-case basis, holding either Article 8 or Article 10 of the ECHR applicable.[54] Such an approach can also pay tribute to the different limitation clauses attached to those freedoms.

2. Interference

Case 2 – Problem: (ECtHR *Wille* (2000) 30 EHRR 558)
W, a national of L and, at the relevant time, a member of the government of L, had been involved in a controversy between the Head of State and the government of L on political competences in connection with a plebiscite. Later, W was appointed President of L's Administrative Court for a fixed term of office. When L, in the context of a series of lectures, expressed the view that the Constitutional Court was competent to decide on the interpretation of the Constitution in case of disagreement between government and parliament, the Head of State sent a letter to W, stating that W was disqualified from holding a public office. When L was proposed by parliament for a further term of office as President of the Administrative Court, the Head of State did not appoint him. The applicant complains that the letter sent by the Head of State, informing him that he would not appoint him to public office, should he be proposed by parliament, violated his right to freedom of expression as guaranteed by Article 10 of the Convention.

Article 10(2) of the ECHR lays down criteria for permissible governmental interference with the freedoms stipulated in Art. 10(1) of the ECHR. The provision explicitly names some types of interferences, namely formalities, conditions, restrictions and penalties. However, it is not possible to develop a clear-cut typology of permissible interferences on the basis of this list. Rather, a useful starting point is that not each and every limitation of the guarantees amounts to an interference which needs a justification based on the Convention. It is common ground that at least those governmental acts which directly and substantially affect the individual must be justified. This concept of „interference" covers executive orders prohibiting publications. Consequently, the ECHR does not accept precensorship since this potentially reverses rule and exception.[55] Other "traditional" types of "interference" are disciplinary, administrative and penal sanctions imposed with regard to acts of communication.[56]

---

53 For a discussion of German law *cf* Mecklenburg [1997] ZUM 525.
54 On the multimedia debate *cf* Dörr *Festschrift Kriele* (Munich 1997) pp 1417 ff; see also Bröhmer *Die innerstaatliche und europarechtliche Bedeutung von Art. 10 EMRK für die Medienordnung* in: *Europäisches Medienrecht – Fernsehen und seine gemeinschaftsrechtliche Regelung* (Saarbrücken/Munich/Berlin 1998) pp 79 ff.
55 In its decision in the case of *Observer,* the ECHR did not outrule any preventive controls but applied strict scrutiny in this regard; see ECtHR *Observer* (1992) 14 EHRR 153, para 60. For an evaluation of this ruling see above Frowein (note 13) Art 10, para 24; see above also Probst (note 33) p 25.
56 See above Villiger (note 10) pp 391–392.

25 Narrow views of what constitutes an "interference" which were traditionally applied to Articles 8 to 11 of the ECHR[57] are increasingly questioned in the context of freedom of expression. Today, there is a tendency to even take into consideration indirect sanctions such as banning someone from a profession or claims for damages. Their chilling effect on future speech is considered to be as serious as direct forms of interference.[58] Restrictive readings of interferences are, however, more fundamentally questioned: commentators have taken up the idea of horizontal effect ("Drittwirkung") of freedom of expression,[59] and the ECHR had to consider whether factual intimidation already amounts to an interference needs to be justified[60].

26 If biased reporting and indoctrination of public broadcasting already amounts to an interference with freedom of opinion,[61] it is necessary to discuss whether the growing power of private media and the concentration of the media industry can affect freedom of opinion in a similar way. The Convention as such does not single out the idea of "Drittwirkung". Consequently, the Strasbourg organs have so far taken a reserved position,[62] which is not likely to be abandoned in the near future. On the other hand, the concept of "positive obligations", which has been applied less in the context of Article 10 of the ECHR[63], but rather with regard to Article 8 of the ECHR (→ comp § 3 para 26 *et seq*), provides sufficient leeway to safeguard pluralism which is so essential for a democratic society as referred to in Article 10(2) of the ECHR.[64] In one of the cases under consideration, positive obligations gave rise to a careful balancing of individual and community interests within the framework of Article 10(1) of the ECHR rather than discussing the limitations clause of Article 10(2) of the ECHR.[65]

27 If indirect sanctions are already considered to be more subtle forms of interfering with freedom of expression, this is even more so in the case of threatening sanctions which may be imposed irrespective of conventional freedoms. In finding an interference, the ECHR does not primarily consider whether the content of the threat is contrary to the Convention or whether the threat as such has any direct legal effect. What is decisive is whether the measure in question suppresses freedom of expression.[66] Opening up the notion of "interference" on the basis of earlier jurisprudence[67] the ECHR has meanwhile confirmed that attempts at factual intimidation amount to an interference.[68] Taking these

---

57 See above Villiger (note 10) p 344; see also Grabenwarter (note 3) Art 18, paras 5–6; for further details.
58 For further details *cf* Frowein (note 13) Art 10, para 36.
59 See above Probst (note 33) pp 27–28; Peukert *Festschrift Mahrenholz* (Baden-Baden 1994) pp 285–286; → § 2, para 34.
60 See ECtHR *Hashman and Harrup* (2000) 30 EHRR 241; *Steel* (1999) 28 EHRR 603.
61 See above Frowein (note 13) Art 10, para 4.
62 For further details see above Probst (note 33) p 27; see also EurCommHR *Rommelfanger v Germany* (1989) 62 RJD 151.
63 But see EurCommHR *T v United Kingdom* (1983) 49 RJD 49, 5.
64 On pluralism as one of the foundations of freedom of opinion and freedom of the press in a democratic society see ECtHR *Informationsverein Lentia* (1994) 17 EHRR 93, para 38.
65 This was the approach taken by the Court in ECtHR *Gaskin* (1990) 12 EHRR 36, para 42 and in *Powell and Rayner* (1990) 12 EHRR 355, para 41.
66 Hoffmeister [2000] EuGRZ 358, 359.
67 See, among others, ECtHR *Lingens* (1986) 8 EHRR 407, para 44; *Barfod* (1991) 13 EHRR 493, para 29.
68 ECtHR *Wille* (2000) 30 EHRR 558, paras 44 ff.

developments into account means to first apply the traditional notion of "interference" and then broaden it with regard to case-specific risks for individual freedoms.

Case 2 – Answer:
Prima facie, the case looks like access to public service. Such an individual right, however, is not included in the Convention. Nevertheless, civil servants can complain about dismissal if this act potentially violates a conventional freedom. In our case, the freedom of opinion is pertinent. Regarding the letter sent to W by the Head of State, it must be discussed whether the declaration of intent therein amounts to an interference. It has to be noted in this context that the letter was intended to criticize W and to discourage him from making further statements. While the decision of the Head of State not to appoint W as such does not violate the Convention, the threat uttered in the letter is intended to suppress W's freedom of opinion.
If one accepts that the measure was provided by law and served a legitimate purpose it only remains to assess the proportionality of the incriminated measure. While W was under an obligation to exercise self-restraint when commenting on political decisions, it has to be noted that the statement was made in the context of an academic lecture and that it did not affect W's conduct of office at all. Thus, the measure was not necessary in a democratic society. Hence, Article 10 of the ECHR was violated.

3. Justification

Interferences with any of the freedoms guaranteed by Article 10(1) of the ECHR are only permissible if they are prescribed by law, adopted in pursuance of one of the objectives listed in Article 10(2) of the ECHR and "necessary in a democratic society". All of these conditions must be met. It is noteworthy that the list of objectives that may be legitimately pursued is the most extensive one compared to other rights and freedoms guaranteed by the Convention.[69] Furthermore, it is unusual that Article 10(2) of the ECHR starts of by giving reasons for such limitations: the exercise of freedom of expression "carries with it duties and responsibilities". Whereas the ECHR in an early case argued that it could not overlook the "duties" and "responsibilities" of a person making use of the freedoms guaranteed by Article 10(1) of the ECHR[70], it later made it clear that the introductory phrase does not constitute an independent limitation of Article 10(1) of the ECHR.[71] It may be argued that, originally, the introductory formula only provided some legitimacy to address the specific risks of mass media.[72]

a) Situations in which a Restriction May Be Justifiable

One of the most important situations in which a restriction may be justifiable according to Article 10(2) of the ECHR is the **protection of the reputation of others**. Since defamation laws can have a serious impact on the freedom of expression, this clause must be interpreted restrictively and can only be applied after a careful analysis of the facts. Any other approach would place freedom of speech as one of the essential backbones of

---

69 Along the same lines see above Frowein (note 13) Art 10, para 23.
70 ECtHR *Handyside* (1979–80) 1 EHRR 737, para 49.
71 ECtHR *Thorgeirson* (1992) 14 EHRR 843, para 46.
72 See above Probst (note 33) p 28.

democracy at risk.[73] Only a restrictive interpretation of defamation laws will contain the dangers described as having a "chilling effect" on so many occasions by the U.S. Supreme Court[74]. Future speech should not be put at risk by an extensive application of defamation laws. On the other hand the ECHR that defamation laws contribute to law and order ("*Rechtsfrieden*").[75] The Court, adopting a functional approach, has established broader limits for political speech than in the case of criticism of private individuals.[76] This is a matter of proportionality. Special problems arise in the case of public bodies and institutions. While it at first recognized the need to protect their reputation[77], the ECHR meanwhile seems to have distanced itself from this line of argument. Thus, the Court considered the imposition of criminal proceedings against a conscript in the perceived interest of national security and public safety because of collective defamation of the Greek armed forces to be disproportionate.[78] By declaring that the functions to be performed by the armed forces merit judicial protection, the Court implicitly seems to reject the idea of protecting the reputation of state organs and other public bodies.[79]

31 Closely related to defamation laws is the **protection of rights of others**. This partly overlaps with the protection of the reputation of others. However, it is much broader. Thus, the ECHR has accepted that interferences may be justified in pursuit of protecting the religious beliefs of others[80] as well as their privacy[81]. Furthermore, the protection of rights of others may be relevant with regard to commercial speech. Measures adopted against unfair competition may easily be attributed to the protection of rights of others.[82] Recently, the ECHR has even considered the right to effective democracy as a right of others.[83] Thus, the protection of the rights of others develops into a kind of blanket clause.

---

73 For a differentiated approach see above Peukert (note 59) pp 294 ff; likewise see above Frowein (note 13) Art 10, para 32.
74 On the "chilling effect" see United States Supreme Court *NAACP v Alabama ex rel Patterson* (1958) 357 US 449; for German doctrine and jurisprudence *cf* Grimm [1995] NJW 1703; on the ECHR *cf* ECtHR *Thorgeirson* (1992) 14 EHRR 843, para 68 and Prepeluh [2001] ZaöRV 771, 819–820.
75 ECtHR *Lingens* (1986) 8 EHRR 407, para 36.
76 ECtHR *Lingens* (1986) 8 EHRR 407, para 42; *Oberschlick* (1998) 25 EHRR 357, para 59; see above also Peukert (note 59) pp 294 ff.
77 ECtHR *Thorgeirson* (1992) 14 EHRR 843, para 59; *Castells* (1992) 14 EHRR 445, para 46.
78 ECtHR *Grigoriades* (1999) 27 EHRR 464, para 47; on the applicability of Art 10 ECHR to members of the armed forces see ECtHR *Vereinigung demokratischer Soldaten Österreichs* (1995) 20 EHRR 56, para 36.
79 Thus, the explicit argument of Judge *Jambrek* in his separate opinion in the case of ECtHR *Grigoriades* (1999) 27 EHRR 464, paras 3–4. For details on the reputation of the armed forces, Nolte [1996] AfP 313.
80 ECtHR *Otto-Preminger-Institut* (1995) 19 EHRR 34, paras 47–48; *Wingrove* (1997) 24 EHRR 1, paras 52 ff.
81 See ECtHR *Tammer* (2003) 37 EHRR 857, paras 68–69; *von Hannover* (2005) 40 EHRR 1, paras 63–66 (clearly taking a different approach than the German Federal Constitutional Court, BVerfG (2000) 101 BVerfGE 361, 390–391). Earlier already Frowein (note 13) Art 10, para 33, referring to Art 8 ECHR.
82 ECtHR *Barthold* (1985) 7 EHRR 383; *markt intern* (1990) 12 EHRR 161; *Casado Coca* (1994) 18 EHRR 1.
83 ECtHR *Ahmed* (1997) 24 EHRR 278, para 54; early indications in *Bowman* (1998) 26 EHRR 1, para 38; for some discussions see Hoffmeister [2000] EuGRZ 358, 360.

The admissibility and exigency of political speech is particularly sensitive with respect to the interests of **national security, territorial integrity** and **public safety**. The distribution of pamphlets including a call for desertion and specific advice to this end may be easily considered as endangering national security.[84] The same applies to the distribution of propaganda material of unconstitutional organizations[85], although pertinent governmental reactions may also be adopted by reference to the protection of the rights of others. On the other hand, it is doubtful to consider the publication of the memoirs of a former secret service agent as endangering national security, in particular, if it is rather the reputation of the secret service and not national security that seems to be at stake.[86] In its recent case-law concerning Turkey, the ECHR addressed the protection of territorial integrity. The Court recognized that measures against separatist pro-Kurdish propaganda may be justified for reasons of protecting both territorial integrity as well as national security.[87]

32

The **prevention of disorder or crime** goes beyond the protection of public order. It includes the protection of societal groups and non-state institutions, their internal functioning and their structure.[88] On the one hand, reference may be made to the protection of the armed forces[89] and prisons,[90] on the other hand, non-state actors have been protected by reference to rules of professional conduct[91] (in the context of commercial speech). In as far as hate speech, in particular the spread of racist propaganda[92] or the Auschwitz lie,[93] cannot be attributed to any of the other objectives listed in Article 10(2) of the ECHR, a related interference may be justified by reference to the prevention of disorder. These cases have to be distinguished from what has been argued in the context of the organization of a country's broadcasting system. This may be legitimately developed on the basis of Article 10(1)(iii) of the ECHR. License requirements for undertakings pursuing pertinent commercial activities may be based on this provision. Nevertheless, the requirements of Article 10(2) of the ECHR must also be met in such a case, and reference to the prevention of disorder is advisable.[94] It is noteworthy that among the limitation clauses of Articles 8 to 11 of the ECHR only Article 8(2) of the ECHR explicitly refers to "the economic well-being of the country".

33

---

84 EurCommHR *Arrowsmith* (1981) 3 EHRR 218, paras 38–39.
85 EurCommHR *Kühnen* (1988) 56 RJD 205, 209.
86 Thus the criticism of Frowein (note 13) Art 10, para 2, positioning himself against EctHR *Observer* (1992) 14 EHRR 153, paras 56 and 69; see also the dissenting opinions of Judges *Petitti* und *Morenilla* in this case.
87 See ECtHR *Arslan* (2001) 31 EHRR 264, paras 40, 48–49.
88 See above Frowein (note 13) Art 10, para 30.
89 ECtHR *Engel* (1979–80) 1 EHRR 647, para 98.
90 ECtHR *Golder* (1979–80) 1 EHRR 524, para 45 (on Art 8(2) ECHR). See also Laeuchli/Bosshard *Die Meinungsfreiheit gem Art 10 EMRK unter Berücksichtigung der neueren Entscheidungen und der neuen Medien* (Bern 1990) pp 165 ff.
91 Also ECtHR *Casado Coca* (1994) 18 EHRR 1.
92 ECtHR *Jersild* (1995) 19 EHRR 1, paras 33–35.
93 EurCommHR *X v Germany* (1982) 29 RJD 194; *Remer* (1995) 82 RJD 117. In an obiter dictum, the Court has meanwhile argued that the so-called Auschwitz lie is not protected by Article 10 ECHR because of Article 17 ECHR, see ECtHR *Lehideux and Isorni* (2000) 30 EHRR 665, para 47.
94 On the interrelationship between Art 10(1)(iii) ECHR and Art 10(2) ECHR, see below (para 54).

34 One of the more difficult objectives listed in Article 10(2) of the ECHR is the **protection of morals**. Since it is open to broad interpretation, its scope must be limited by reference to the principle of proportionality. State practice demonstrates that public authorities, probably due to its flexibility and its lack of precision, seem to prefer reference to the protection of morals even in cases when reference to the **protection of health** is plausible. The protection of morals has thus been relied upon when dealing with pornographic literature and videos. Sometimes reference to morals was combined with an argument to protect the rights of others, meaning religious beliefs. The main issue is that the protection of morals is a controversial issue and that ideas about its content differ widely. There is no European conception of morals. Due to the multitude of differing conceptions, the ECHR is less qualified to assess a pertinent situation than national and local authorities.[95] In this context, the national authorities' „margin of appreciation" („marge d'appreciation")[96] is of importance and will be analysed more closely when discussing the principle of proportionality below.

35 The objective of **preventing the disclosure of information received in confidence** has so far not received much attention by the Convention organs. In the context of governmental activities there is a close connection to issues of national security.[97] Whether and in how far the objective of preventing the disclosure of information can also be relied upon in order to protect confidential business information needs to be re-considered in light of new technological developments. It is noteworthy that municipal regulation of telecommunications includes rules on protecting the confidentiality of individual communication. Since Article 8 ECHR only provides limited protection of private communication against interference by non-state actors (even if drawing on positive obligations), there seems to be little room for conflicting principles emerging from Articles 8 and 10 of the ECHR.[98] Only if and in so far as private communication is protected by national legislation, those protective measures may amount to an interference with the freedoms included in Article 10(1) of the ECHR which then has to be assessed against Article 10(2) of the ECHR.

36 From a German perspective, the objective of **maintaining the authority and impartiality of the judiciary** has never been of primary importance. The objective was included in order to safeguard the common law instrument of "contempt of court".[99] Recently, however, the objective has sometimes been taken up in the context of media reporting on court proceedings (read together with the prevention of disorder).[100]

b) The Requirement of a Legal Basis for the Interference

Case 3 – Problem: (ECtHR *Steel* (1999) 28 EHRR 603)
37 A, an animal-rights activist, took part in a protest against a grouse shoot. She walked in front of a member of the shoot as he lifted his shotgun to take aim and thus prevented him

---

95 ECtHR *Handyside* (1979–80) 1 EHRR 737, para 48; *Müller* (1991) 13 EHRR 212, para 34.
96 For a general discussion of the doctrine of margin of appreciation see Brems [1996] ZaöRV 240; on the margin of appreciation as applied to freedom of the press *cf* Prepeluh [2001] ZaöRV 771.
97 See above Laeuchli/Bosshard (note 90) p 180. See also EurCommHR *X v Germany* App No 4247/69 = (1970) 13 YECHR 888.
98 On Art 8 ECHR and its relevance for cryptography, *cf* Diregger [1998] DuD 28.
99 ECtHR *Sunday Times* (1979-80) 2 EHRR 245, paras 56–57.
100 ECtHR *Worm* (1998) 25 EHRR 454, para 49. For a comparative perspective see Gehring [2000] ZRP 197.

from firing. A was arrested for "breach of the peace". She was found guilty, a fine was imposed and the Court ordered her to agree to be bound over for 12 months. She refused and was committed to prison for 28 days. A argues that her freedom of opinion as guaranteed by Article 10 of the ECHR was thus violated.

What is normally required in order to justify an interference is a general and abstract rule authorizing public authorities to adopt pertinent measures. This rule, whether written or unwritten, must have the force of law. It must further be accessible and predictable ($\rightarrow$ § 2 para 46). Problems normally only occur when a broad notion of "interference" is applied. Thus, if factual attempts at intimidation qualify as interferences,[101] it will be difficult to identify a legal basis for such interferences within the meaning of Article 10(2) of the ECHR. As can be gathered from the jurisprudence of the ECHR, this does not necessarily imply the illegality of the measure taken, since Article 10(2) of the ECHR seems to have been drafted with formal and not factual measures in mind. Thus, with regard to factual interferences it may be permissible to abandon the requirement of a legal basis for the interference if at least the principle of proportionality is met.[102]

38

Case 3 – Answer:
First, it has to be discussed whether the freedom of opinion is at all applicable. A did not say anything to the participant in the shoot. She just performed an act of protest. It can, however, not be disputed that opinions can be communicated by both words and deeds. The arrest and the court ruling therefore constitute interferences with the freedom of opinion.
The second problem in our case is the justification of the interferences. Even though "breach of the peace" is very general, it has been specified over years by jurisprudence and police practice. This meets the requirements of Article 10(2) of the ECHR.
The objectives pursued by the court ruling were the prevention of disorder and the protection of the rights of others. In addition, the imprisonment also served to maintain the authority of the judiciary.
Since the municipal court – given that A refused to be bound over – could legitimately expect her to continue her protest activities, 28 days of imprisonment can still be considered to be proportionate in the case.

39

c) The Principle of Proportionality

Similar to the other limitation clauses of Articles 8, 9 and 11 of the ECHR, governmental interference with the freedom guaranteed, *ie* freedom of expression, is not justified by mere reference to a legitimate aim. Rather, the act must be "necessary in a democratic society" in order to be compatible with the Convention. Whether or not the principle of proportionality has been met is for the Convention organs to decide. In light of the importance of freedom of expression for a democratic society, the assessment of whether or not the interference is proportionate is of utmost importance (generally on the prin-

40

---

101 See above (paras 23 ff).
102 Similarly, Hoffmeister [2000] EuGRZ 358–359. Alternatively, the requirements as to clarity and preciseness of the statutory basis maybe reduced; for such an approach see above Grabenwarter (note 3) Art 23, para 20. This basically seems to be compatible with the rule of law, see Degenhart *Staatsrecht I* (20th ed, Heidelberg 2004) para 281.

ciple of proportionality → § 2 para 48).[103] First of all, this necessitates that the objectives which are considered as legitimate aims of governmental interference have to be interpreted narrowly. Furthermore, any interference must be well reasoned. This means that, in principle, Article 10 of the ECHR must be read as an assumption in favour of the permissibility of the expression under scrutiny.[104] While this is convincing prima facie, it leads to a differentiation resulting from the interrelationship between a democratic society and freedom of expression: the ECHR seems to privilege political speech when applying the principle of proportionality[105] and thus adopts a functional interpretation of Article 10 of the ECHR.[106] But even if one doesn't share the resulting discrimination of commercial and other forms of non-political speech, it must be admitted that the ECHR does not make this distinction when defining the scope of protection, but rather in the context of the proportionality, i.e. in the context of a possible justification of interferences. Only such an approach seems to be methodologically viable. There is no resulting differentiation with regard to the scope of Article 10(1) of the ECHR.

41 Even though Strasbourg jurisprudence – in contrast to German constitutional doctrine – does not normally distinguish between appropriateness, necessity and reasonableness as sub-categories of proportionality, there are indications that the underlying elements of such differentiation are taken into account when applying Article 10(2) of the ECHR. It is plausible to first assess the appropriateness and necessity of interferences.

42 An executive order preventing publication is inappropriate (even ineffective) if – as in the case of a former secret service agent – the material has already been published abroad (in the case under consideration, in the United States).[107] The same seems to apply to a prohibition to disseminate information in Ireland about British abortion clinics if interested women can obtain the information without any major difficulties otherwise (e.g. by consulting British phone books or journals).[108]

43 The necessity of interferences can be doubtful in cases of indirect sanctions. For purposes of illustration, reference is made to the Strasbourg organs' case-law on banning someone from a profession. Early jurisprudence of the ECHR was not really convincing when arguing that there was no violation of Article 10 of the ECHR because the Convention does not include rights of access to public service. This reasoning overlooked that it was not access to public service which was at issue (one of the cases concerned the withdrawal of a probationary appointment of a teacher because of fraudulent misrepresentation,[109] in another case a civil servant was removed from office because of fascist statements[110]), but the extent of obligations of loyalty which may be imposed on civil servants.

---

103 ECtHR *Thorgeirson* (1992) 14 EHRR 843, para 63; *Castells* (1992) 14 EHRR 445, para 42.
104 See above Frowein (note 13) Art 10, para 26.
105 For a parallel assessment see above Villiger (note 10) p 400 and Brems [1996] ZaöRV 240, 274–275. Occasionally, the margin of appreciation was strictly limited even in the context of business life; see Prepeluh [2001] ZaöRV 771, 805.
106 On the interrelationship between the theory of human rights and the interpretation of pertinent norms still appropriate: Böckenförde [1974] NJW 1529.
107 Not really convincing ECtHR *Observer* (1992) 14 EHRR 153, paras 66 ff. For a critique thereof see above Frowein (note 13) Art 10, para 27.
108 ECtHR *Open Door* (1993) 15 EHRR 244, para 55; for detailed analyses of this ruling and a parallel ruling of the ECJ see Zimmermann [1993] NJW 2966 and Langenfeld/Zimmermann [1992] ZaöRV 259.
109 ECtHR *Glasenapp* (1987) 9 EHRR 25.
110 ECtHR *Kosiek* (1987) 9 EHRR 328.

Looking back at those early court rulings, it seems likely that the ECHR did not want to address the hard issues during the Cold War. Only after the end of the (ideological) conflict between East and West, the ECHR adopted a critical approach to the extent of loyalty requirements and ruled that obligations of loyalty may in principle be imposed, but their application must take into account the functions performed by the civil servant. Mere membership of a political party doesn't seem to be sufficient for removal from office, which would thus be disproportionate.[111] Other disciplinary measures might have met the principle of proportionality, in particular, the element of necessity. Taking another example, the award of extremely high amounts of damages in defamation cases can not be considered to be necessary and thus is also disproportionate.[112]

Apart from appropriateness and necessity, several differentiations have been developed when applying the principle of proportionality in the context of Article 10(2) of the ECHR. These differentiations concern political speech, defamation laws, the margin of appreciation when protecting morals, and the criteria applied to interferences with broadcasting.

44

d) Political Speech

Strasbourg jurisprudence provides a relatively high level of protection for political speech: An "interference" which more or less prevents political criticism is generally regarded as disproportionate and thus contrary to the Convention. On several occasions, the Court has considered a municipal rule on the need to demonstrate that value judgements are "true" as disproportionate in political discourse. Sometimes the ECHR qualified expressions as value judgments even though they had been considered to be statements of fact by municipal courts.[113] In particular, the ECHR considered the requirement to prove correctness when reporting about rumours and narratives on police abusiveness to be disproportionate[114]. Furthermore, the sentencing of a Danish journalist who had included racist statements of interviewees in a broadcast reportage, even though he had – according to the views taken by the ECHR – distanced himself from them, was likewise held to be disproportionate.[115] More generally, the ECHR has made it clear that statements of fact may not be made without any substantiation nor maliciously.[116]

45

Interference with expressions of a commercial character is subject to less scrutiny;[117] there is more leeway for reliance on the doctrine of margin of appreciation. Thus, statements of fact[118] or the remittance of newspaper articles[119] can be restricted by rules

46

---

111 ECtHR *Vogt* (1996) 21 EHRR 205.
112 ECtHR *Tolstoy Miloslavsky* (1995) 20 EHRR 442.
113 It can be argued today that if proof of validity (truth) is required by municipal law, this normally will amount to a violation of Article 10 ECHR; *cf* ECtHR *Lingens* (1986) 8 EHRR 407, para 46; *Oberschlick* (1998) 25 EHRR 357, para 63; *Schwabe* App No 13704/88, para 34; *Unabhängige Initiative Informationsvielfalt* (2003) 37 EHRR 710, paras 45–46. These rulings have to be distinguished from the case of *Castells* (1992) 14 EHRR 445, para 48 which concerned facts the validity of which can in principle be assessed and which were not made part of the proceedings in the case at hand.
114 ECtHR *Thorgeirson* (1992) 14 EHRR 843, para 65.
115 ECtHR *Jersild* (1995) 19 EHRR 1, paras 33–36.
116 ECtHR *Thorgeirson* (1992) 14 EHRR 843, paras 63, 67.
117 See also Calliess [2000] AfP 248 and Grabenwarter [2002] ÖZW 1.
118 ECtHR *markt intern* (1990) 12 EHRR 161, paras 35–36.
119 ECtHR *Jacubowski* (1995) 19 EHRR 64, paras 26–30; there was a strong dissenting opinion in

against unfair competition without qualifying such interference as disproportionate. To a limited extent, this also applies to rules of professional conduct and the prohibition of adverts based thereupon. The ECHR takes a sceptical position on a broad interpretation of rules of professional conduct in this regard. Rather, it underlines the participation of competent individuals in public discourse and assesses the admissibility of interferences according to whether the advertising effect was primary or secondary (for a law firm or a doctor's practice).[120]

e) Defamation Laws and Due Diligence of the Press

Case 4 – Problem: (ECtHR *Bladet Tromsø* (2000) 29 EHRR 125)

47 A journal had published a report written by a government inspector on his observations made on a ship during the seal hunting season. The ship was named in the report. In the report, the inspector had stated that individual members of the crew whose names were also mentioned had taken off the fur of seals still alive and had violated other provisions related to seal hunting. The publication of the article was part of a series of articles which gave a voice to all interested parties. However, at the time of publication, the journal was aware that the government had blocked public access to the report in order to carefully examine all criminal charges raised against members of the crew. Eventually, both the inspector and the journal were fined because they were not able to prove that the statements made in the report were indeed true. The inspector and the journal subsequently complained that their rights under Article 10 of the ECHR had been violated.

48 Generally speaking, politicians cannot complain about being harshly criticized. However, given that Strasbourg jurisprudence strictly applies the principle of proportionality in the context of defamation laws,[121] it is *prima facie* surprising that the Convention organs assess the proportionality of political speech rather than of the act of interference. Pertinent jurisprudence tends to reverse the relationship between rule and exception, and must thus be assessed in critical terms.

49 Typically, the ECHR raises the question whether criticism could have been voiced differently while having the same effect. With regard to the form of expression, the Court requires an assessment of whether or not personal attacks were indispensable.[122] Consequently, the Court does not protect false statements of fact, libellous propositions, unnecessary incisiveness, and value judgements lacking a factual basis since governmental interference with any of these usually is proportionate.[123] While the case-law as such can

---

the Court in this particular case. See also ECtHR *markt intern* (1990) 12 EHRR 161, paras 35–36 and Calliess [1996] EuGRZ 293, 295.

120 Thus the argument presented by Villiger (note 10) p 404, referring to ECtHR *Barthold* (1985) 7 EHRR 383, para 58; but see also ECtHR *Casado Coca* (1994) 18 EHRR 1, paras 55–56, where the ECHR was not prepared to further attack rules of professional conduct on the basis of Art 10(2) ECHR in light of a lack of consensus across Europe. In its ruling in the case of EurCommHR *Schöpfer* (1996) 22 EHRR 184, paras 30–34, the Court considered a fine imposed on a lawyer as proportionate because he had attacked the courts in a press conference rather than bringing the case before the courts in the first place.

121 Settled jurisprudence since ECtHR *Lingens* (1986) 8 EHRR 407, para 46.

122 ECtHR *Barfod* (1991) 13 EHRR 493, paras 33–35; for a critique see above Frowein (note 13) Art 10, para 25.

123 ECtHR *De Haes* (1998) 25 EHRR 1, para 47; *Unabhängige Initiative Informationsvielfalt* (2003) 37 EHRR 710, para 47.

be considered convincing, the methodological approach of the ECHR nevertheless deserves criticism.

With regard to reproducing statements of fact or materials received from others, the ECHR imposes an obligation of due diligence on the press. This has direct repercussions on the proportionality of governmental interference. On the one hand, the Court has accepted that there is no need for protecting confidential information if the information is already available elsewhere.[124] In the case of anonymous informants, the interest in protecting them and their identity prevails if the person concerned will only be marginally affected.[125] In so far, the press is hardly subject to any due diligence obligations. This may, however, be different if the press anonymously receives material. In principle, the Court then requires that the journalist at least assesses the authenticity of the material before publication,[126] unless there are special reasons to relieve the press of such a due diligence obligation, e.g. the general reliability of the information received.[127] The publication of libellous statements of fact may be permissible even if their validity cannot be assessed ex post.[128]

Case 4 – Answer:
It is fairly obvious that Article 10 of the ECHR is applicable, that there were interferences, and that the aim pursued by the government was to protect the reputation of others. What needs closer scrutiny is whether the imposition of a fine met a pressing social need, whether it was proportionate to the aim pursued, and whether the reasons given by the authorities were sufficient. Thereby it has to borne in mind that the publication of the report was part of a series of articles and that, hence, there was no intention on the side of the inspector and the journal.
The right of journalists to disseminate information is, however, only protected by Article 10 of the ECHR in as far they act in good faith, rely upon established facts, and respect professional ethics (this is already an application of the principle of proportionality). In this case it is critical whether the journal had good reasons not to cross-check the validity of the statements included in the report. This depends on the form and on the intensity of the statements. While some of the charges were grave, their negative impact was mitigated because they were not addressed against the crew as a whole. Furthermore, since it was a government sponsored report, the journal could to a certain extent rely upon its correctness. Were the press – under those circumstances – obliged to perform its own research into the matter, this would question its capacity as a public watchdog.
Thus, there can hardly be any doubt that the journal acted in good faith. Hence, the imposition of the fine was disproportionate.

f) The Margin of Appreciation when Protecting Morals and Religious Beliefs

The ECHR has always pointed out that there is no European conception of morals. Thus, municipal authorities are – in principle – in a better position to assess the reasonableness of pertinent interferences with any of the freedoms included in Article 10(1) of the

---

124 ECtHR *Vereniging Weekblad Bluf!* (1995) 20 EHRR 189, paras 44 ff.
125 ECtHR *Goodwin* (1996) 22 EHRR 123, paras 42–45.
126 ECtHR *Fressoz and Roire* (2001) 31 EHRR 28, paras 53–55.
127 ECtHR *Bladet Tromsø* (2000) 29 EHRR 125, para 66.
128 Prepeluh [2001] ZaöRV 771, 801; Hoffmeister [2000] EuGRZ 358, 366.

ECHR. Hence, the Court accepted the assessment made by English courts on the morally damaging effect of a disputed publication on children and youngsters.[129] Similarly, the Court relied on the margin of appreciation with regard to religious beliefs. The Court explicitly stated that it is impossible to agree on religious beliefs in a given society within Europe.[130] Even though there is little room for governmental interference with freedom of expression in political (and other public) discourse, the Court accepts that it is primarily for the municipal authorities to assess whether or not the protection of religious beliefs necessitates interferences with freedom of expression. The Court argues that municipal authorities are directly and continuously in touch with local groups and other parts of civil society.[131] The reluctance of Strasbourg organs in this regard can be illustrated by reference to the case of a Belgian national who was prosecuted for distributing a journal that was freely available in the Netherlands. The Commission itself considered this interference to be proportionate.[132]

53   The Court's ruling in the – already mentioned – case of an artist who had created and exhibited pornographic paintings is less convincing. The painter was not only to be prosecuted, but his paintings should be destroyed. Whereas the Commission only considered the prosecution to be proportionate, the ECHR regarded both the prosecution and the order of destruction as proportionate.[133] Even though the paintings were not destroyed and were returned to the plaintiff several months before (*sic!*) the Court's ruling, the ECHR failed to comprehensively assess the reasonableness of such interferences. The only acceptable reasoning may be that it would be to ask too much of the Court to develop uniform approaches to morals among all High Contracting Parties. Thus, whenever confronted with morals or religious beliefs, the Court refers to the doctrine of margin of appreciation and avoids a careful assessment of proportionality.

g) Yardsticks with Regard to Interferences in Broadcasting

54   With regard to broadcasting, the substance of Article 10(1)(iii) of the ECHR is relevant. Clearly, there is sufficient leeway for the High Contracting Parties to regulate the technical aspects of broadcasting. In this regard, Article 10(1)(iii) of the ECHR can even be the basis for implementing international telecommunications law.[134] When doing so, the principle of proportionality has to be respected. Thus, the ECHR ruled that the refusal of Swiss authorities to license the reception of USSR radio transmissions was disproportionate since the Court could not identify reasons to prohibit the reception of transmissions addressed to the general public in the USSR.[135] Similarly, limitations on the establishment of individual receivers based on building and conservation laws will at least be subject to strict scrutiny (based on the principle of proportionality) if a collective receiver does not

---

129 ECtHR *Handyside* (1979–80) 1 EHRR 737, para 52.
130 ECtHR *Otto-Preminger-Institut* (1995) 19 EHRR 34, para 50; See also Grabenwarter [1995] ZaöRV 128.
131 ECtHR *Wingrove* (1997) 24 EHRR 1, para 58; see on this case Kolonovits in: Grabenwarter/Thienel (eds) *Kontinuität und Wandel der EMRK* (Kehl 1998) pp 169 ff.
132 EurCommHR *X, Y and Z v United Kingdom* App No 21830/93.
133 ECtHR *Müller* (1991) 13 EHRR 212, paras 35–36 and 43.
134 ECtHR *Groppera Radio AG* (1990) 12 EHRR 321, paras 60–61.
135 ECtHR *Autronic AG* (1990) 12 EHRR 485, para 63.

provide equivalent possibilities.[136] Whenever the essence of the freedom of information is affected, interferences are likely to be disproportionate.[137]

In as far as regulations go beyond addressing the technical aspects of broadcasting, the ECHR has subjected licensing requirements to the provisions of Article 10(2) of the ECHR. This may be difficult to accept from a methodological perspective. However, it pays tribute to technological progress and socio-economic change when interpreting Article 10(1)(iii) of the ECHR restrictively and thus including freedom of private broadcasting into freedom of expression[138]. This is not only appropriate, but – on the contrary – a state monopoly on broadcasting would seem to be disproportionate.[139] Whenever a High Contracting Party has eased its traditional state monopoly on broadcasting and introduced a licensing system for private broadcasting, the licensing as such has to be assessed against the provisions of Article 10(2) of the ECHR. This does not prevent governments from including aspects other than those of a technological nature when deciding on the license, such as the objectives pursued by the undertaking, cultural pluralism, the specifics of the political organization of the state (*eg* a federal state) as well as non-technical obligations arising from international treaties.[140] In as far as the government pursues objectives not listed in Article 10(2) of the ECHR, the Court considers this to be permissible and covered by Article 10(1)(iii) of the ECHR,[141] but requires compliance with the other criteria incorporated in Article 10(2) of the ECHR, in particular the requirement of a legal basis for the interference and the principle of proportionality.[142] 55

While Article 10 of the ECHR does not explicitly include other requirements with regard to the organization of broadcasting, some may be taken from the jurisprudence of the Convention organs. In particular, the ECHR has accepted the principle of media pluralism and has incorporated this into the protection of the rights of others within Article 10(2) of the ECHR.[143] However, the Convention organs – in contrast to the German Federal Constitutional Court[144] – have always been reluctant to impose broadcasting standards on the High Contracting Parties. In particular, the Court has refrained from imposing a positive obligation on governments in so far. Thus, there is no risk that Strasbourg will transform freedom of broadcasting (and media) into an obligation.[145] 56

---

136 ECtHR *Autronic AG* (1990) 12 EHRR 485, para 47; see also the decisions of the European Commission of Human Rights EurCommHR *Radio X. S. and W. v Switzerland* (1984) 37 RJD 236; *A v Switzerland* (1984) 38 RJD 219, para 49; *Ebner* App No 13253/87, para 3.
137 See above Laeuchli-Bosshard (note 90) pp 31 ff; Villiger (note 10) p 413.
138 In general Engel *Privater Rundfunk vor der Europäischen Menschenrechtskonvention* (Baden-Baden 1993).
139 ECtHR *Informationsverein Lentia* (1994) 17 EHRR 93, paras 39, 41–43; see also the settlement in EurCommHR *Telesystem Tirol Kabeltelevision* (1997) 24 EHRR 11, as well as the ruling in the case of ECtHR *Radio ABC* (1998) 25 EHRR 185, paras 31–33. In another case ECtHR *Tele 1 Privatfernsehgesellschaft MBH* (2002) 34 EHRR 181.
140 See above Frowein (note 13) Art 10, para 19
141 ECtHR *Informationsverein Lentia* (1994) 17 EHRR 93, para 32.
142 ECtHR *Groppera Radio AG* (1990) 12 EHRR 321; *Informationsverein Lentia* (1994) 17 EHRR 93, para 32.
143 ECtHR *Groppera Radio AG* (1990) 12 EHRR 321, paras 69–70; affirmative see above Probst (note 33) p 26.
144 *Cf* Stock [1997] JZ 583.
145 For a critique of the jurisprudence of the Federal Constitutional Court see Engel [1994] AfP 185.

III. Freedom of Assembly

Leading cases: ECtHR *Plattform Ärzte für das Leben* (1988) 13 EHRR 204; *Ezelin* (1992) 14 EHRR 362; *Cisse* App No 51346/99; EurCommHR *Stankov* (1998) 26 EHRR 103; *Rassemblement jurassien* (1979) 17 RJD 93.

Further reading: Fitzpatrick/Taylor [1998] EHRLR 292; Grabenwarter *Europäische Menschenrechtskonvention* (Munich/Vienna 2003) 296; Peters *Einführung in die Europäische Menschenrechtskonvention* (Munich 2003) § 15.

57 As with the freedom of expression, the freedom of assembly, included in Article 11(1) of the ECHR, is of ultimate importance for a democratic society. The formation of an assembly is not only a particular form of expression. It overcomes isolation, establishes an idea of togetherness and allows the formation and transmission of individual as well as collective opinions. Thus, freedom of assembly supports freedom of expression and is an essential factor in the forefront of institutionalized political decision-making within a democratic society.[146] Freedom of assembly protects the organizers as well as the participants thereof.

58 **Case 5 – Problem:** (EurCommHR *Stankov* (1998) 26 EHRR 103)
S chaired an organization which had been established in order to unite a particular ethnic minority on the basis of religion and culture and with the intent to gain governmental recognition as a minority. After the courts had turned down efforts to register the organization because they considered the organization's activities to threaten national unity and to further ethnic hatred, S and his organization – over a period of several years – were not allowed to hold assemblies and to organize celebrations at historic monuments. When S brought the matter before the courts, they argued that the organization was illegal and that there had been concerns that its activities would endanger public safety and the rights of others. S and his organization complained about a violation of their rights guaranteed by Article 11 of the ECHR.

1. Scope of Protection

59 No definition of what an assembly is was included in Article 11(1) of the ECHR. However, commentators and jurisprudence agree that an assembly means the coming together of individuals in order to impart ideas among themselves or with others and to discuss or to symbolically express opinions.[147] In the absence of a common awareness, a common objective or a minimum of organization, there is no assembly. A simple gathering of people is not an assembly. Although freedom of assembly contributes to democracy, its scope of protection should not be limited to political meetings. There is no reason why social gatherings should only be protected by Article 8 of the ECHR[148] even though they may contribute to the formation of opinions.[149]

60 Article 11(1) of the ECHR protects various forms of assemblies, their preparation and their realisation: assemblies of a public or private character, open air as well as in-door

---

146 ECtHR *Young, James and Webster* (1982) 4 EHRR 38, para 57; *Ezelin* (1992) 14 EHRR 362, para 37.
147 ECtHR *Plattform „Ärzte für das Leben"* (1991) 13 EHRR 204, para 12.
148 But see above Frowein (note 13) Art 11, para 2 and Grabenwarter (note 2) Art 23, para 47.
149 See above Müller (note 4) pp 327–328.

assemblies, stationary assemblies or processions, short or long-lasting assemblies. Freedom of assembly is not only protected in private premises or on private property. Rather, public places are of importance for the implementation of freedom of assembly, since they effectively facilitate collective expression.[150] Article 11(1) of the ECHR thus does not only guarantee freedom of assembly, but also encompasses the broader notion of freedom of demonstration. The latter includes so-called "sit-ins".[151] Thus, the occupation of a church, tolerated by the church council, by a group of illegal immigrants has been considered to be an assembly.[152] In contrast to Article 8 of the German Basic Law, which guarantees freedom of assembly "without prior notification or permission", mere requirements of authorization and notification with regard to public places are not considered as interferences with freedom of assembly under the ECHR.[153]

Being an indispensable part of a democratic society based on the rule of law, Article 11(1) of the ECHR only protects peaceful forms of communication. The wording of Article 11 of the ECHR explicitly refers to "freedom of peaceful assembly". Given that provocations are an essential form of expression during demonstrations, however, only extreme cases of violence can be considered to be outside the scope of Article 11(1) of the ECHR a priori. An assembly is not peaceful if the organizers plan to violently enforce their objectives. In contrast, an assembly remains peaceful notwithstanding violent activities on the margins of a demonstration or attempts of extremists to undermine the assembly.[154]

It is noteworthy that Article 11(1) of the ECHR imposes a positive obligation on governments to actively protect demonstrations. Otherwise fear of violent counter-demonstrations would in practice prevent the exercise of the rights and freedoms included in Article 11(1) of the ECHR.[155] The choice of means is left to the government, however. This positive obligation has an impact on the admissibility of counter-demonstrations. It is arguable that counter-demonstrations are considered to be outside the scope of protection of Article 11(1) of the ECHR if they exclusively aim at the disruption of another demonstration. Nevertheless, it is preferable to assess the protection of counter-demonstrations on the basis of Article 11(2) of the ECHR.

2. Interference

Whereas a licence requirement with regard to assemblies on public places is not considered to be an interference, a prohibition of an assembly constitutes an interference with the freedom of assembly. Other limitations of freedom of assembly which concern the preparation, organization and implementation of assemblies easily qualify as interferences. Likewise, disciplinary and penal sanctions related to participation in a demonstration must be considered an interference.[156]

---

150 EurCommHR *Rassemblement jurassien* (1979) 17 RJD 93, para 3.
151 EurCommHR *G v Germany* (1989) 60 RJD 256, para 2.
152 ECtHR *Cisse* App No 51346/99, paras 35–39.
153 EurCommHR *Rassemblement jurassien* (1979) 17 RJD 93, para 3.
154 ECtHR *Ezelin* (1992) 14 EHRR 362, para 39; EurCommHR *Christians against Racism and Facism* (1980) 21 RJD 138, para 4.
155 ECtHR *Plattform „Ärzte für das Leben"* (1991) 13 EHRR 204, para 32.
156 ECtHR *Ezelin* (1992) 14 EHRR 362, para 39. See, however, also ECtHR *Cisse* App No 51346/99, para 40.

3. Justification

64 Article 11(2)(i) of the ECHR follows the model of the limitation clauses included in Articles 8 to 10 of the ECHR. Interferences with freedom of assembly are justified, if they "are prescribed by law", if they serve one of the aims listed in Article 11(2)(i) of the ECHR and if they "are necessary in a democratic society". All conditions must be equally met.

a) Permissible Aims

65 Among the aims listed in Article 11(2)(i) of the ECHR, measures adopted in the interest of public safety are of particular importance. The other objectives (national security,[157] the protection of health or morals, the protection of the rights and freedoms of others) are of limited relevance in practice.

b) Principle of Proportionality

66 The application of the principle of proportionality is decisive also with regard to the freedom of assembly. It is necessary to distinguish between the justification of direct and indirect interferences as well as between an assembly ban and more modest measures.

67 Indirect interferences require strict scrutiny in so far as disciplinary and penal sanctions can only be imposed under narrow circumstances and with regard to persons who commit reproachable acts themselves. In light of the prime importance of freedom of assembly, the rights of other participants can not be legitimately encroached upon.[158]

68 Direct interferences, in particular assembly bans, are only permissible under exceptional circumstances. A prohibition of public events over a period of two days in the context of the partly violent conflict with regard to the establishment of the canton Jura in Switzerland was considered proportionate by the then Commission.[159] Even a prohibition of demonstrations in the City of London over a period of two months was considered to be proportionate. However, the Commission underlined the exceptional character of such a general prohibition.[160]

69 When assessing the permissibility of interferences below the threshold of an assembly ban, the proportionality of direct measures has to be evaluated on the basis of a balancing of individual and public interests involved. This necessitates taking into consideration the freedom as such, the extent of governmental interference and the possibility to adopt less intrusive measures. In case of substantial effects on public order it is permissible to limit the choice of the assembly's venue and the route of a demonstration or procession.[161]

---

157 *Cf* EurCommHR *A. Association and H.* (1984) 36 RJD 187; *Stankov* (1998) 26 EHRR 103.
158 ECtHR *Ezelin* (1992) 14 EHRR 362, para 53; see also EurCommHR *X v Germany* (1982) 29 RJD 194, para 2.
159 EurCommHR *Rassemblement jurassien* (1979) 17 RJD 93, para 11.
160 EurCommHR *Christians against Racism and Facism* (1980) 21 RJD 138, para 5.
161 On the prohibition of a demonstration on Trafalgar Square in London, see EurCommHR *Negotiate Now* (1995) 81 RJD 146.

c) Special Restrictions Imposed on Civil Servants

The special restrictions for civil servants, which are listed in Article 11(2)(ii) of the ECHR, have so far had little practical relevance – if so, then mostly in the context of the freedom of association, where they will be discussed in detail. In a case concerning disciplinary measures taken against a Dutch soldier, the ECHR – on the basis of the facts of the case – argued that the individual had not been prosecuted because of participation in the assembly, but for other reasons.[162]

Case 5 – Answer:
Since there were no indications that the organizers of the assemblies intended to apply physical force, Article 11 of the ECHR is applicable in scope. It is further obvious that there were interferences. Given a statutory basis, the governmental acts were intended to serve accepted objectives, including national security and the prevention of disorder. What is questionable is whether the act was indeed necessary in a democratic society.
Given the close interrelationship between Articles 10 and 11 of the ECHR, it is particularly problematic that the prohibition of assemblies was based on the opinions and views held by the organizers and participants. There is no doubt that individuals are in principle entitled to set up groups for the promotion of their "regional" characteristics. Also, the joint intention to be accepted as a minority in itself is not sufficient to interfere with the rights included in Article 11 of the ECHR. Furthermore, refusal to register the organization as such does not call for systematic prohibitions to hold assemblies.
Neither the presumed use of arms nor the dangers for public order could be proven sufficiently in the case under consideration. The only demonstrable matter was the dissemination of separatist ideas. This, however, is not sufficient to legitimize a prohibition of assemblies. In a democratic society based on the rule of law, political ideas aiming at changing the existing order must be permissible as long as they are to be implemented peacefully.
Thus, the interferences were not necessary in a democratic society. Hence, Article 11 of the ECHR was violated.

IV. Freedom of Association

Leading cases: ECtHR *Le Compte et al* (1982) 4 EHRR 1; *United Communist Party of Turkey* (1998) 26 EHRR 121; *Chassagnou* (1999) 29 EHRR 615; *Refah Partisi (the Welfare Party)* (2003) 37 EHRR 1.

Further reading: Grabenwarter *Europäische Menschenrechtskonvention* (Munich/Vienna 2003) 305; Klein [2001] ZRP 397; Koch [2002] DVBl 1388; Tomuschat in: MacDonald/Matscher/Petzold (eds) *The European System for the Protection of Human Rights* (Dordrecht 1993) p 493; Wildhaber *Politische Parteien, Demokratie und Art. 11 EMRK* in: Bovenschulte (ed) *Festschrift für Dian Schefold* (Baden-Baden 2001) p 257.

Case 6 – Problem: (ECtHR *Refah Partisi* (2003) 37 EHRR 1)
W was established as a political party in Turkey in 1983. Having had a turn-out of 22% in the 1995 parliamentary elections, W became the strongest faction in the national parliament and joined a coalition government. In early 1998, the Turkish Constitutional Court dissolved W, arguing that it had become a centre of anti-secular activities in Turkey. In its reasoning, the Turkish Constitutional Court stressed that secularism was an indispensable pre-condition of democracy. Representatives of W had questioned the separation of state and reli-

---
162 ECtHR *Engel* (1979–80) 1 EHRR 647, para 108.

> gion on many occasions. They had called upon members of parliament who were party members to engage in a "holy war" and to introduce the sharia. In addition, the Constitutional Court withdrew members of the parliament who were members of W the status as parliamentarians, prohibiting them to take up any functions in a different party for a period of 5 years.

1. Scope of Protection

73 The freedom of association protects the formation of collective entities by individuals for any lawful purpose. The legal system of each state party must provide for such a possibility. It must offer procedures and forms. However, there is no right to have particular forms and legal constructs offered by municipal law. In principle, member states are free to regulate the conditions for granting legal personality. In particular, Article 11(1) of the ECHR does not include a right to establish public law institutions. Even in the case of forced membership, the ECHR does not acknowledge interferences with Article 11(1) of the ECHR unless pertinent legislation at the same time excludes the establishment of similar associations under private law.[163]

74 While Article 11(1) of the ECHR may be generally relevant for company law, the details of its effects on this area of the law are subject to controversy, e.g. whether the government is free to introduce new categories of legal personality or not to do so.[164] In contrast, freedom of association has recently gained increasing importance as freedom to establish political parties. Even if they are subject to special regimes according to national legislation, political parties enjoy the protection of Article 11(1) of the ECHR. This protection even covers parties that are considered unconstitutional by the state concerned.[165]

75 Apart from their establishment, Article 11(1) of the ECHR covers some of the activities of associations, at least in the case of trade unions and federations of employers.[166] This does, however, not include the attainment of the association's objectives.[167]

76 Even though Article 11(1) of the ECHR (in contrast to Article 20(2) of the Universal Declaration on Human Rights) does not explicitly mention a negative freedom of association, the ECHR considers this to be part of freedom of association.[168] This is particularly relevant in the case of the freedom not to join trade unions.

2. Interferences

77 Interferences with the freedom of association can affect many different addressees and can take a broad variety of forms. Both the dissolution of an association and the prohibition of some of its activities qualify as interferences. Similarly, the imposition of sanctions by national law merely on account of membership or non-membership must be considered as interferences. This applies in particular to employment monopolies of trade unions

---

163 ECtHR *Le Compte et al* (1982) 4 EHRR 1, para 65.
164 *Cf* on this Marauhn [1999] RabelsZ 537, 550.
165 Grabenwarter (Fn 3) § 23 para 61 with reference to ECtHR *United Communist Party of Turkey* (1998) 26 EHRR 121, para 27. *Cf* ECtHR *The Socialist Party* (1999) 27 EHRR 51, para 29.
166 ECtHR *National Union of Belgian Police* (1979–80) 1 EHRR 578, paras 38–39.
167 EurCommHR *Association X v Sweden* (1977) 9 RJD 5, para 52.
168 ECtHR *Sigurjonsson* (1993) 16 EHRR 462, para 35; *cf* also *Chassagnou* (2000) 29 EHRR 615, para 103.

("closed shop")[169], which will also be addressed below. It also applies to the non-employment or dismissal from civil service because of membership in a non-prohibited (i.e. still constitutional) political party.[170]

3. Justification

As with the freedom of assembly, interferences with the freedom of association are only permissible if they are provided by law,[171] if they serve one of the purposes listed in Article 11(2)(i) of the ECHR and if they are necessary in a democratic society. It is not without problems to refer to „national security" and "public safety" in the context of defending national cultural traditions and national historic or cultural symbols. Such interferences will normally be contrary to the Convention, even though the ECHR in a case concerning Greece did not rule this out from the very beginning, but only considered the governmental action taken to be disproportionate.[172] In general, the legitimacy of objectives pursued by governmental interferences is assessed like cases on freedom of assembly.

The principle of proportionality has gained particular prominence in recent years in cases concerning the establishment and the continuance of political parties. A party cannot be dissolved merely on account of its name[173], nor because of its critique of the government and its support for minorities.[174] The situation is different if the party pursues unconstitutional objectives, in particular objectives that are contrary to human rights standards or to democratic governance. In such cases the state enjoys a wide margin of appreciation which the ECHR will not scrutinize.[175] In the case of Vogt v Germany, the Court found a violation of the freedom of association because the complainant was dismissed as a civil servant simply because of her membership in the German Communist Party, whereas the Federal Constitutional Court had not dissolved the party.[176] While the ECHR had not ruled out the possibility to explicitly apply Article 11(2)(ii) of the ECHR to German teachers, it may be argued that a prohibition of membership in a particular political party can be covered by this part of the limitation clause in exceptional cases if provided by law and if not applied in an arbitrary manner.[177]

Case 6 – Answer:
The freedom of association is obviously applicable in this case. The dissolution of W clearly amounts to an interference. The governmental measures are only justified if provided by

---

169 ECtHR *Young, James and Webster* (1982) 4 EHRR 38, paras 49 and 51–53.
170 ECtHR *Vogt* (1996) 21 EHRR 205, para 44. Prohibiting a chairman of a party to hold a similar position in another party in the future also constitutes an interference; ECtHR *Özdep* (2001) 31 EHRR 674, para 27.
171 ECtHR *N.F. v Italy* (2002) 35 EHRR 106, para 26, 31–32. In this case the ECtHR considered an act which served as the legal basis for sanctioning a judge who had joined a Masonic Loge to be so vague and thus not foreseeable for the affected individual, that it found that in fact no legal basis existed.
172 ECtHR *Sidiropoulos* (1999) 27 EHRR 633, para 47.
173 ECtHR *United Communist Party of Turkey* (1998) 26 EHRR 121, para 54.
174 ECtHR *Halkin Emeği Partisi* (2003) 36 EHRR 59, paras 56–57 and 60.
175 ECtHR *Refah Partisi* (2003) 37 EHRR 1, paras 8–83.
176 ECtHR *Vogt* (1996) 21 EHRR 205, paras 60–61, 66 ff.
177 EurCommHR *Council of Civil Service Unions* (1988) 10 EHRR 269.

law, if one of the objectives listed in Article 11(2)(i) of the ECHR is pursued and if this is necessary in a democratic society (*ie* proportionate). The Turkish Constitutional Court is empowered by statute to dissolve political parties that violate the Constitution. It is noteworthy that the Constitution includes an equal treatment clause and the principle of a democratic and secular republic. Thus, the measure is provided by law. Also, it cannot be disputed that several of the objectives listed in Art 11(2) of the ECHR are being pursued. According to established jurisprudence, there must be sufficient proof of an endangering of democracy before the government can take actions. The measures of party officers must be attributable to the party. This is the case if they reflect a particular model of society which the party aspires to. The Turkish Constitutional Court in particular referred to the introduction of the sharia (which would be contrary to religious freedom) and to the ambivalent attitude towards the use of force in pursuing their objectives. This eventually led the ECHR to hold that the dissolution of the party could be considered to meet the principle of proportionality.

V. Freedom to Form and Join Trade Unions

Leading cases: ECtHR *National Union of Belgian Police* (1975) 1 EHRR 578; *Swedish Engine Drivers' Union* (1979–80) 1 EHRR 617; *Young, James and Webster* (1981) 4 EHRR 38; *Gustafsson* (1996) 22 EHRR 409; EurCommHR *Council of Civil Service Unions* (1988) 10 EHRR 269.

Further reading: Hendy *The Human Rights Act, Article 11, and the right to strike* [1998] EHRLR 582; Marauhn *Die wirtschaftliche Vereinigungsfreiheit zwischen menschenrechtlicher Gewährleistung und privatrechtlicher Ausgestaltung. Zur Bedeutung von Art 11 EMRK für das kollektive Arbeitsrecht und das Gesellschaftsrecht* (1999) 63 RabelsZ 537; Wildhaber *Die Koalitionsfreiheit gemäß Art 11 EMRK* (1976) 19 GYIL 238.

81 Apart from freedom of assembly and freedom of association, Article 11(1) of the ECHR – in parallel to Article 20 and Article 23 No. 4 of the Universal Declaration on Human Rights – guarantees freedom to form and join trade unions. This explicit guarantee of freedom of association for trade unions does not mean to privilege one element of freedom of association at the expense of others.[178] Rather, it is a clarification that trade unions enjoy freedom of association irrespective of whether or not they qualify as associations according to national law.[179]

Case 7 – Problem: (ECtHR *Gustafsson* (1996) 22 EHRR 409)
82 G was owner of a restaurant. He refused to join the Federation of Hotels and Restaurants. Thus, his employees were not subject to any of the pertinent collective agreements. G even refused to sign a special agreement. As a consequence thereof, the unions boycotted him, among other means by preventing deliveries to G's restaurant. G then asked the government to intervene. However, the government referred him to the courts. Any complaints against the government's inaction remained futile. Following the boycott, G had to give up his restaurant. G argues that his freedom of association was violated by the government's inaction.

---

178 See above Frowein (note 13) Art 11, para 9.
179 Van Dijk/van Hoof *Theory and Practice of the European Convention on Human Rights* (2nd ed, Deventer 1990) p 431; Tomuschat in: MacDonald/Matscher/Petzold (eds) *The European System for the Protection of Human Rights* (Dordrecht 1993) pp 493–494.

1. Scope of Protection

The freedom to form and join trade unions as included in Article 11 of the ECHR does not only protect the individual, but also the association as such, thus fulfilling two functions. Trade unions enjoy protection of their activities, as may be drawn from the wording of Article 11 of the ECHR: "for the protection of his interests". Primarily, the provision is directed against the state and its organs. Article 11(1) of the ECHR does not in itself impose obligations on private individuals and corporations. One might, however, argue in favour of indirect horizontal effect ("mittelbare Drittwirkung") in the sense that there is an obligation to protect individuals against interferences from third persons, including trade unions.[180] If governmental institutions act as employers themselves, Article 11 of the ECHR is directly applicable.[181]

83

a) Individual Freedom to Form and Join Trade Unions

An essential element of Article 11(1) of the ECHR is the individual freedom to form and join trade unions. While the article doesn't mention employers' federations, it is today beyond doubt that they are also included in Article 11(1) of the ECHR.[182] The Court even considers associations of medical practitioners to be covered by Article 11(1) of the ECHR.[183] In contrast, however, forced associations under public law are not subject to Article 11(1) of the ECHR.[184] Finally, the freedom to join trade unions only applies subject to the statutes of the union itself, since the union enjoys a degree of autonomy on the basis of Article 11(1) of the ECHR.[185]

84

The primary importance of Strasbourg jurisprudence in respect of the conventional freedom to form and join trade unions is its recognition of negative freedom of association. Pertinent case-law was first developed in dealing with so-called "closed shop" arrangements. While a private employer who concludes an agreement with a trade union in order to only employ members of that trade union is basically protected by freedom of contract, governmental recognition of such a system by tolerating dismissals directly concerns the employees' freedom not to join a trade union, thus his or her negative freedom of association.[186] Strasbourg jurisprudence points out that there has never been an explicit ruling on the conformity of "closed shop" arrangements with the Convention.[187] It is along these lines that the Court in a case where the employer could have continued to work for his employee in a different position did not find a violation of Article 11(1) of the ECHR.[188] Furthermore, the Court holds Article 11(1) of the ECHR applicable in the case of a boycott initiated by trade unions and intended to force the employee into an

85

---

180 Cf see above Frowein (note 13) Art 11, para 15; Tomuschat (note 179) pp 504 ff; van Dijk/van Hoof (note 179) pp 435, 437–438; ECtHR *Young, James and Webster* (1982) 4 EHRR 38, para 49. Cf also Wildhaber *Festschrift Vischer* (Zurich 1983) pp 349, 358–359.
181 ECtHR *Swedish Engine Drivers' Union* (1979–80) 1 EHRR 617, para 37; *Schmidt and Dahlström* (1979–80) 1 EHRR 632, para 33.
182 See above Frowein (note 13) Art 11, para 1; Tomuschat (Fn 179) p 494.
183 ECtHR *Le Compte et al* (1982) 4 EHRR 1, para 65.
184 ECtHR *Le Compte et al* (1982) 4 EHRR 1, paras 62 ff; *Albert and Le Compte* (1983) 5 EHRR 533, paras 43–44.
185 EurCommHR *Cheall* (1986) 8 EHRR 74.
186 Thus correctly described in Tomuschat (note 179) pp 502–503.
187 ECtHR *Young, James and Webster* (1982) 4 EHRR 38, para 61.
188 ECtHR *Sibson* (1994) 17 EHRR 193.

agreement with the trade union or into other collective agreements.[189] Such measures are subject to the negative freedom of association. It may be argued, however, that the government is only obliged to intervene if the boycott indeed leads to demonstrable effects on freedom of association.

b) Collective Freedom to Form and Join Trade Unions, in particular Freedom of Collective Bargaining and Freedom of Collective Action

86   As already indicated, Article 11 of the ECHR covers both individual and collective trade union freedom. This follows directly from the wording of the Convention. Strasbourg jurisprudence developed the trade union freedom extensively in the 1970s.[190] However, Article 11(1) of the ECHR does not include a specific right of trade unions vis-à-vis private or public employers to be consulted in professional matters, nor does it grant trade unions a right to have collective labour agreements concluded.[191] In contrast to Article 6 of the European Social Charter, the Court only grants trade unions a right to be heard,[192] in other words, they must have the possibility to operate in public[193]. This hardly allows clear definitions on the scope of trade union rights within Article 1(1) of the ECHR.[194] Likewise, Article 11 of the ECHR does not allow for clear statements on industrial co-determination.[195] This is easily acceptable since trade union rights are to a large extent specified in agreements and treaties concluded under public international law.

87   A separate issue is whether or not Article 11 of the ECHR includes a right to strike. The ECHR has argued that the right to strike is one of the most important collective measures. However, at the same time the Court has underlined that there are limitations, some of which are included in the European Social Charter. In principle, the Court argues that collective measures are protected by Article 11 of the ECHR, but are subject to a wide margin of appreciation. From this it can be gathered that it may be permissible to provide alternatives to strikes for trade unions without violating Article 11 of the ECHR.[196] However, as a general statement this is not convincing. What is decisive is to safeguard the purpose of trade union activities because they are at the heart of the freedom to form and join trade unions as included in Article 11 of the ECHR. In principle, trade unions should not enjoy the freedoms included in Article 11 of the ECHR to a lesser degree than individuals. At the very least, trade union rights must extend to such activities and functions which the individual employee cannot perform.[197] Total exclusion of the right to strike would thus not be compatible with Article 11 of the ECHR.[198]

---

189 ECtHR *Gustafsson* (1996) 22 EHRR 409.
190 In detail *Wildhaber* [1976] GYIL 238.
191 ECtHR *National Union of Belgian Police* (1979–80) 1 EHRR 578, para 38; *Swedish Engine Drivers' Union* (1979–80) 1 EHRR 617, para 39.
192 ECtHR *National Union of Belgian Police* (1979–80) 1 EHRR 578, para 39.
193 See above Frowein (note 13) Art 11, para 11.
194 Frowein in: Vassilouni (ed) *Aspects of the protection of individual and social rights* (Athens 1995) p 203, 213.
195 Öhlinger *Verfassungsrechtliche Probleme der Mitbestimmung der Arbeitnehmer im Unternehmen* (Vienna 1982) pp 145–146.
196 Thus the assessment of Villiger (note 10) pp 417–418.
197 Thus convincingly Tomuschat (note 179) pp 500–501.
198 See above Frowein (note 13) Art 11, para 13; Frowein (note 194) p 213. Likewise Hendy [1998] EHRLR 582, 587, 608.

Freedom of Expression, Freedom of Assembly and Association § 4 V 3

2. Interference

There are different categories of interferences with the freedom to form and join trade **88** unions. Strasbourg jurisprudence has not only dealt with direct interferences, such as a ban on trade unions, but also indirect interferences, including sanctions attached to trade union membership or non-membership. Occasionally, even forced membership in a private association of self-employed individuals qualified as an interference, in the case of a taxi-driver who lost his concession after having left the federation of taxi-drivers.[199] Also, a trade union initiated boycott in order to force an employer into a collective agreement has been considered to be an interference by the ECHR.[200]

3. Justification

Neither individual nor collective freedoms to form and join trade unions are unlimited **89** according to Article 11 of the ECHR. Interferences are only compatible with the Convention if they are provided by law, if they pursue one of the objectives listed in Article 11(1)(i) of the ECHR and if the governmental act is necessary in a democratic society. As far as the objectives pursued are concerned, reference may be made to the above commentary on these in the context of freedom of assembly and association.

In the case of trade union rights, Article 11(2)(ii) of the ECHR enjoys a degree of pro- **90** minence. This provision is a difficult one for several reasons. First, the question arises who belongs to the governing body of the state, which is named alongside the armed forces and the police. This broad wording entails uncertainty as to the scope of this provision. However, taking up jurisprudence of the then European Commission on Human Rights, it may be argued that this only applies to persons who perform vital functions for the protection of national security.[201] It seems that a functional approach is the only valid one in this context.[202] Thus, a prohibition to form and join trade unions for members of a British military IT centre was held to be in conformity with Article 11 of the ECHR.[203] On the other hand, the Court has explicitly left it open whether or not German teachers employed as civil servants (*Beamte*) are subject to this part of the limitation clause.[204]

It is not only the personal scope of Article 11(2)(ii) of the ECHR which causes prob- **91** lems. There is also a debate as to whether the provision takes away the rights guaranteed in Article 11 of the ECHR or whether it only limits the enjoyment of those rights. One may argue that a comprehensive prohibition is acceptable as long as the proportionality principle is met.[205] On the other hand, there is a categorical difference between the exercise and the existence of particular rights. This argues in favour of limitations of the exercise only.[206] In an unpublished decision, the then European Commission on Human Rights held that the prohibition imposed on Belgian policemen with regard to the formation and joining of trade unions was in conformity with Article 11 of the ECHR, in light of Article

---

199 ECtHR *Sigurjonsson* (1993) 16 EHRR 462, para 35.
200 ECtHR *Gustafsson* (1996) 22 EHRR 409, paras 44–45.
201 EurCommHR *Council of Civil Service Unions* (1988) 10 EHRR 269.
202 See above Tomuschat (note 179) p 511.
203 On the complaints brought to the International Labour Organisation in this *context cf* Mills [1997] EHRLR 35, 41.
204 ECtHR *Vogt* (1996) 21 EHRR 205, para 68.
205 Thus apparently Frowein (note 13) Art 11, para 18.
206 Velu/Ergec *La convention européenne des droits de l'homme* (Brussels 1990) p 659.

127

11(2)(ii) of the ECHR. This ruling was harshly criticized because it withheld trade union rights from the policemen although it might have been sufficient to only limit the exercise of these rights.[207]

92 Finally, the question arises whether measures based on Article 11(2)(ii) of the ECHR must also be provided by law. Whereas the then European Commission on Human Rights once argued that limitations based on this clause must only as such be lawful,[208] there seems to be a tendency today to consider Article 11(1)(ii) of the ECHR as only replacing the permissible objectives listed in the preceding sentence, not, however, the other requirements, including the necessity of a "law".[209] This definitely applies to the principle of proportionality.[210] Beyond this, notwithstanding the differences in wording, any limitation based on this clause must also be provided by law[211] if the protection of freedom of association and assembly are generally to be upheld.

Case 7 – Answer:
93 First, it must be discussed whether the case concerns trade union rights at all. Given that the boycott aimed at forcing G into a collective agreement, this is plausible. G was confronted with two alternatives: either becoming a member of the pertinent employers' association or signing a separate agreement. Such alternatives are an interference with the freedom of association. Thus, the case is within the scope of Article 11 of the ECHR:
However, we can only confirm that there has been an interference if the government is under an obligation to act. Such a positive obligation only exists if the government's inaction has real effects on freedom of association. Force, even if leading to damages, is not sufficient to be considered an interference according to Article 11 of the ECHR. In this particular case, there are at least serious doubts as to the proportionality of governmental inaction.[212] This amounts to a violation.

VI. Conclusions

94 The high importance of communicative freedom within the ECHR is reflected in the comprehensive protection provided for by different freedoms. The network set up by the various freedoms in Articles 10 and 11 of the ECHR is designed to avoid loopholes. The ECHR argues that the guarantees included in Article 11 of the ECHR are *leges speciales* vis-à-vis those laid down in Article 10 of the ECHR. The Court argues that assemblies and associations are particular modes of expressing an opinion.[213] Within Article 11(1) of the ECHR, freedom to form and join trade unions is a sub-category of freedom of association.

95 Apart from the freedom to form and join trade unions, which has to be read in light of the European Social Charter and other public international law instruments related there-

---

207 See above Van Dijk/van Hoof (note 179) p 439 (with further reference to the decision of the Commission).
208 EurCommHR *Council of Civil Service Unions* (1988) 10 EHRR 269.
209 Thus convincingly Tomuschat (note 179) p 512.
210 Expressly van Dijk/van Hoof (Fn 179) p 439.
211 Villiger (note 10) p 419 obviously takes this view as well.
212 The ECtHR did however not find a violation in this case, *cf* ECtHR *Gustafsson* (1996) 22 EHRR 409, paras 54–55.
213 ECtHR *Ezelin* (1992) 14 EHRR 362, para 35.

to, all freedoms should be broadly interpreted. Only in doing so, the democratic function of the freedoms guaranteed in Articles 10 and 11 of the ECHR can be safeguarded even though the two Articles do not explicitly mention democracy as the underlying value of the two Articles. Interferences can also be indirect in character. Then, there must be differentiations in the context of justification. Indirect measures necessitate higher scrutiny both with respect to the objectives pursued and with regard to the principle of proportionality.

If and in how far communicative freedoms can be applied to business and economics is subject to an intense discussion. Some authors argue that – notwithstanding the broad wording – economic freedoms are not included. They refer to the history of the Convention and to the need to distinguish between form and substance. Both arguments are not convincing. Freedom of association by its very nature is a political as well as an economic right. Furthermore, Strasbourg jurisprudence has confirmed the applicability of Article 10 of the ECHR to business and economics.[214] Freedom of communication is not a mere exercise right. This is obvious in the case of the freedom of association, which at least in part must cover the object and purpose of the association.[215] Finally, none of the arguments in favour of a restrictive interpretation of the said freedoms is convincing. Given the broad wording, Articles 10 and 11 of the ECHR also include an economic dimension.

96

---

214 ECtHR *markt intern* (1990) 12 EHRR 161, para 26; *cf* also ECtHR *Casado Coca* (1994) 18 EHRR 1, para 35
215 See above Frowein (note 13) Art 11, para 7 – the constitutional law parallel is of interest here: according to the German Federal Constitutional Court, Art 9 (1) GG also protects the self-advertising presentation of an association (BVerfG (1992) 84 BVerfGE 372).

§ 5
Economic Fundamental Rights

Bernhard Wegener

Leading cases[1]: ECtHR *Handyside* (1979-80) 1 EHRR 737; *Sporrong and Lönnroth* (1983) 5 EHRR 35; *James* (1986) 8 EHRR 123; *Lithgow* (1986) 8 EHRR 329; *AGOSI* (1987) 9 EHRR 1; *Tre Traktörer AB* (1991) 13 EHRR 309; *Pine Valley* (1993) 16 EHRR 379; *Jahn* App No 46720/99, 72203/01 and 72552/01.

Further reading: van den Broek *The Protection of Property Rights under the European Convention on Human Rights* (1986) Legal Issues of European Integration 52; Coban *Protection of Property Rights within the European Convention on Human Rights* (Aldershot 2004); Condorelli in: Pettiti/Decaux/Imbert (eds) *La Convention Européenne des droits de l'homme* (Paris 1999) p 971; von Danwitz in: von Danwitz/Depenheuer/Engel (eds) *Bericht zur Lage des Eigentums* (Berlin 2002) p 215; Dutertre/van der Velde (eds) *Yearbook of the European Convention on Human Rights Volume 41A* (The Hague 1998) p 178; Fiedler *Die Europäische Menschenrechtskonvention und der Schutz des Eigentums* [1996] EuGRZ 354; Frowein in: Pfeiffer (ed) *Festschrift für Heinz Rowedder zum 75. Geburtstag* (Munich 1994) p 49; Frowein/Peukert (eds) *Europäische Menschenrechtskonvention* (2nd ed, Kehl 1996); Gelinsky *Der Schutz des Eigentums gemäß Art 1 des 1. ZP zur EMRK* (Berlin 1996); Grabenwarter *Europäische Menschenrechtskonvention* (2nd ed, Munich 2005) p 358; Hartwig *Der Eigentumsschutz nach Art 1 des 1. ZP zur EMRK* [1999] RabelsZ 63, 561; Harris/O'Boyle/Warbrick *Law of the European convention on human rights* (London 1995) p 516; Loof *The Right to Property* (Maastricht 2000); Mittelberger *Der Eigentumsschutz nach Art 1 des 1. ZP zur EMRK im Lichte der Rechtsprechung der Straßburger Organe* (Bern 2000); Mittelberger *Die Rechtsprechung des ständigen Europäischen Gerichtshofs für Menschenrechte zum Eigentumsschutz* [2001] EuGRZ 364; Müller-Michaels *Grundrechtlicher Eigentumsschutz in der Europäischen Union* (Berlin 1997) p 62; Peters *Einführung in die Europäische Menschenrechtskonvention* (Munich 2003) pp 193–201; Peukert *Der Schutz des Eigentums nach Art 1 des 1. ZP zur EMRK* [1981] EuGRZ 97; Reininghaus *Eingriffe in das Eigentumsrecht nach Art 1 des 1. ZP zur EMRK* (Berlin 2002); Schutte *The European Fundamental Right of Property* (Deventer 2004); Sermet *The European Convention on Human Rights and Property Rights* (Strasbourg 1990).

I. Introduction

1   The protection of **economic fundamental rights** by international law is not clearly defined. On the contrary, international regulations on fundamental rights often provide no such guarantees. Although Article 17 of the UN Human Rights Declaration of 1948 contained a guarantee of property rights,[2] no agreement was reached in the preliminary negotiations on the European Convention on Human Rights (ECHR), which was ratified in 1950 without any such guarantee. It was only two years later that the right to property was laid

---

1   The cases can be downloaded from the ECtHR website (http://www.echr.coe.int/).
2   "1. Everyone has the right to own property alone as well as in association with others. 2. No one shall be arbitrarily deprived of his property." As to the original intention of the law Commission of the advisory assembly of the European Council, to suggest a property guarantee by reference to Article 17 of the Universal Declaration of Human Rights and as to further details of the history of Art 1 Prot 1 ECHR *cf* Peukert [1981] EuGRZ 97 with further references; van den Broek [1986] Legal Issues of European Integration 52, 53 ff; Coban *Protection of Property Rights within the European Convention on Human Rights* (Aldershot 2004) pp 123 ff; Schutte *The European Fundamental Right of Property* (Deventer 2004) pp 13 ff.

down in Protocol 1 to the ECHR, which was signed on 20 March 1952.[3] Other than the right to property, the European Convention on Human Rights is almost totally without further guarantees of economic and social fundamental rights.[4] In particular, there is no independent regulation of the freedom to practise one's chosen profession.[5]

The main reasons for these omissions were – apart from the historical variations in regimes – the differences in national expectations about how to form an economic order as well as concerns about overregulation by international law and the loss of national freedom in favour of a *"gouvernement de juges"* in the area of economic constitution and economic politics.[6] In view of the growing European and global equalization of economic and social orders, these issues have certainly become less divisive over the last decades. But the restraint regarding the regulation of international guarantees of economic freedom, which also resulted in the somewhat restricted formulation of the corresponding guarantees,[7] was due to the rather cautious approach of the ECtHR in the past.[8] However, the number of confirmed violations of fundamental rights has been increasing significantly for some time.[9]

II. Protection of Property

Article 1 of Protocol 1 to the ECHR, which was ratified by 43 of the 46 member states of the Council of Europe,[10] guarantees the "Protection of Property"[11] as follows:

"Every natural or legal person is entitled to the peaceful enjoyment of his possessions. No one shall be deprived of his possessions except in the public interest and subject to the conditions provided for by law and by the general principles of international law. The preceding provisions shall not, however, in any way impair the right of a State to enforce

---

3 As to the history of the ECHR and the 1st Protocol to the ECHR *cf* Robertson *Human Rights in Europe* (Manchester 1977) pp 5 ff; von Danwitz in: von Danwitz/Depenheuer/Engel (eds) *Bericht zur Lage des Eigentums* (Berlin 2002) pp 220 ff.
4 Frowein in: MacDonald/Matscher/Petzold (eds) *The European System for the Protection of Human Rights* (Dordrecht/Boston/London 1993) p 515.
5 See also paras 12 and 61.
6 With regard to the guarantee of protection of property see also: Fiedler [1996] EuGRZ 354: "politically delicate", "scope of disposal originally reserved to the state", "substantial lifeblood".
7 See also the corresponding evaluation of the property guarantee in Art 1 Prot 1 ECHR by Harris/O'Boyle/Warbrick *ECHR* (London 1995) p 516: "a much qualified right, allowing the state a wide power to interfere with property".
8 Mittelberger [2001] EuGRZ 364, 366 is even more critical when he speaks about a "phase ..., in which the court came to results not absolutely favorable to the property protection in Europe"; for criticism in other respects see also Fromont in: Fiedler (ed) *Verfassungsrecht und Völkerrecht, Gedächtnisschrift für Wilhelm Karl Geck* (Cologne/Munich 1989) pp 213 ff; Dolzer in: Fürst (ed) *Festschrift für Wolfgang Zeidler* (Berlin 1987) p 1679.
9 With respect to the older case law on Art 1 Prot 1 ECHR, Clements, in his *European Human Rights – Taking A Case Under The Convention* (London 1994) p 201, states "Article 1 of the First Protocol is frequently invoked, but violations are seldom found". Frowein disagrees in: Pfeiffer (ed) *Festschrift für Heinz Rowedder zum 75. Geburtstag* (Munich 1994) p 49, according to which a consistent body of case law been developed since the 1980s.
10 The three states who did not ratify Prot 1 ECHR are Switzerland (a member since 1963), Andorra (a member since 1994) and Monaco (a member since 2004).
11 Heading of Art 1 Prot 1 ECHR.

such laws as it deems necessary to control the use of property in accordance with the general interest or to secure the payment of taxes or other contributions or penalties."[12]

5 The fundamental right provided here differs from the corresponding guarantees under national constitutional law primarily in that it is not linked to a particular legal structure of property ownership and economics. Hence, it is less predefined by private law than the guarantees under national law.[13] Nevertheless this does not mean that Article 1 of the 1st Prot ECHR is not a constitutional guarantee.[14]

6 Whether a violation of the fundamental right has occurred can essentially be determined according to these three points: (1.) scope of protection, (2.) infringement and (3.) justification.[15]

1. Scope of Protection of the Guarantee of Property

Case 1 – Problem: (ECtHR *Gaygusuz* (1997) 23 EHRR 364)
7 G is a Turkish citizen and worked as an employee in Austria for eleven years. After losing his job, he received unemployment benefit. When this expired, he claimed welfare payments (*Notstandshilfe*), which are paid under Austrian law for an indefinite period to people who are no longer eligible for unemployment benefit. His claim was rejected because, according to Austrian law, welfare payments are only made to Austrian citizens.

a) General Remarks

8 Property under Article 1 of the 1st Prot ECHR means not only ownership of movables or land, but basically all acquired rights ("*wohlerworbene vermögenswerte Rechte*", "*droits acquis*").[16] This includes shares in a company[17] and similar assets[18]. The case law[19] has

---

12 Protocols to the Convention for the Protection of Human Rights and Fundamental Freedoms, signed on 20.3.1952, *Bundesgesetzblatt* (BGBl – German Official Federal Gazette) II 1956, 1879.
The use of the different terms "possessions/property" and "proprieté/biens" in the English and French versions respectively is frequently criticized, although both words have the same meaning. In its first decision on property rights, the ECtHR emphasized that the both terms had the same substance, see ECtHR *Handyside* (1979–80) 1 EHRR 737; also *Marckx* (1979–80) 2 EHRR 330 and Peukert in: Frowein/Peukert (eds) *Europäische Menschenrechtskonvention* (2nd ed, Kehl 1996) Art 1 1. ZP, para 4.
Numerous examples of ECtHR case law on the term "possessions" can be found in the *Yearbook of the European Convention on Human Rights Volume 41A* (1998) pp 178, 179 ff.
13 Similarly Grabenwarter *Europäische Menschenrechtskonvention* (2nd ed, Munich 2005) p 359; on the particular meanings of the terms in ECHR as opposed to their definitions in the law systems of the Member states of the Council of Europe: ECtHR *Holy Monasteries* (1995) 20 EHRR 1, paras 52 ff.
14 Grabenwarter (note 13) p 359.
15 For the function and limitations of this approach → § 2 para 38; also Schutte (note 2) p 28.
16 Frowein (note 9) pp 49–50; as to the wide scope of protection of the property guarantee according to Art 1 Prot 1 ECHR see also Coban (note 2) pp 145 ff; Schutte (note 2) pp 35 ff.
17 Cf ECtHR *Lithgow* (1986) 8 EHRR 329.
18 As to the question whether assets as such fall into the scope of application of Art 1 Prot 1 ECHR, see Müller-Michaels *Grundrechtlicher Eigentumsschutz in der Europäischen Union* (Berlin 1997) p 69; for a dissenting opinion see von Danwitz (note 3) pp 233 ff.
19 Until 31.10.1998, the ECHR was enforced by the European Commission of Human Rights (created in 1954) and the former – limited – Court of Human Rights (created in 1959). The new Court,

broadly interpreted the ECHR to include such rights, even when they are not covered by the law of the state against which the appeal is brought.[20]

According to the explicit phrasing of Article 1(1) of the 1st Prot ECHR, not only individuals, but also legal[21] persons[22] can acquire property rights. In this case it is debatable[23] whether the interpretation of the property right in the ECHR can solely be attributed to its function as a protector of "human rights".[24]

b) Protection of Acquired Property, Not of Acquisition

Mere expectations and prospects of acquisition are not legally substantiated assets and, as such, are not covered by the term property.[25] Neither is the expectation that an asset which has become worthless over time will once again become valuable – the expectation itself cannot meet the definition of property.[26] In this respect, according to the procedures of the Commission,[27] the right to acquire property is not protected.[28] Legal positions based on a contract or tort are protected[29] because as assets they are property within the meaning of Article 1 of the 1st Prot ECHR.

c) Goodwill

The property right in Article 1 of the 1st Prot ECHR also covers the business relationships which a company or an entrepreneur has formed in the past and which have an influence on the value of business (exceeding the mere intrinsic value).[30] The protection of this so-

---

as instituted by Prot 11 ECHR on 1.11.1998, consists of four Chambers, selected by the four sections of the Court, and a Great Chamber, which consists of the President, the Vice-Presidents, the Section Presidents and a rotating selection of judges.

20 ECtHR *Sporrong and Lönnroth* (1983) 5 EHRR 35; *Tre Traktörer AB* (1991) 13 EHRR 309; *Former King of Greece et al v Greece* (2001) 33 EHRR 516; Harris/O'Boyle/Warbrick (note 7) pp 516, 517 ff; Gelinsky *Der Schutz des Eigentums gemäß Art 1 1. ZP zur EMRK* (Berlin 1996) p 200; Coban (note 2) p 148.

21 As to the protection of property of legal persons under public law see Grabenwarter (note 13) p 362; Müller-Michaels (note 18) p 70.

22 On the (debateable) meaning of the provisions concerning the registered office and incorporation of international companies: Engel [1993] ZEuP 150.

23 Similarly Frowein (note 9) p 49; van Dijk/van Hoof (eds) *Theory and Practice of the European Convention on Human Rights* (2nd ed, Deventer 1990) p 454.

24 Gelinsky (note 20) pp 36 ff; on other aspects of this point: Riedel *Theorie des Menschenrechtsstandards* (Berlin 1986) pp 65 ff, 118 ff.

25 Harris/O'Boyle/Warbrick (note 7) p 517; Sermet *The European Convention on Human Rights and Property Rights* (Strasbourg 2000) p 8; Coban (note 2) pp 150 ff.

26 ECtHR *Prince Hans Adam II of Liechtenstein* App No 42527/98, in more detail Gattini [2002] EJIL 513.

27 See the references in Peukert (note 12).

28 Villiger *Handbuch der Europäischen Menschenrechtskonvention unter besonderer Berücksichtigung der schweizerischen Rechtslage* (2nd ed, Zürich 1999) para 669.

29 See von Danwitz (note 3) pp 227 ff; also Grabenwarter (note 13) p 360; Coban (note 2) pp 150 ff.

30 According to Gelinsky (note 20) p 28 a recognition of this legal concept is found for the first time in ECtHR *Van Marle* (1986) 8 EHRR 483; as to the legal property protection of the "established clientele" of a lawyer and a tax consultant, see also ECtHR *Döring* App No 37595/97, RJD 1999-VIII and *Olbertz* App No 37592/97, RJD 1999-V.

called "**goodwill**"[31] has become increasingly relevant especially for the rather complex judgements concerning the revocation of a business licence. Such a revocation cannot be considered as an infringement of property rights if the granting of the licence was from the very beginning dependent on certain conditions being met. On the other hand, some protection could possibly be derived from the adverse effects on the "goodwill" caused by the revocation.[32]

12   With this broad definition of the concept of "goodwill", the ECtHR is seeking to achieve a complete and effective protection of fundamental rights through the interpretation of the very restricted catalogue of the economic fundamental rights guaranteed by the ECHR. Therefore, scopes of protection have been assigned to the property right that are – at least from a national perspective – already protected by the freedoms of occupational choice and general activity, which are not guaranteed by the Convention.

d) Claims under Public Law

13   The inclusion of claims under public law into the scope of protection of the property right is of particular practical relevance, but is also somewhat controversial.[33] Such claims include, for example, claims based on social insurance, public servants' claims concerning salary law or claims for restitution for unlawful duties. The jurisdiction of the German Federal Constitutional Court (*Bundesverfassungsgericht*) acknowledges a protection of claims based on social insurance law, if they are "assigned as of private utility to the legal entity in the manner of an exclusive right", "based on non negligible personal contributions of the insured person" and serve "him to make a living".[34]

14   The decisions of the **EurCommHR** tend, on the contrary, not to include assets based on public law in the property right's scope of protection.[35] The **EurCommHR** has ruled that claims involving (at least in part) a claimant's own contributions – *eg* entitlements to a pension – should not, in principle, be covered.[36] An exception should be made only where there is a direct correlation between the contributions paid and the amount of the entitlement to a pension or annuity, *ie* where the beneficiary has an "identifiable share in the fund". This would not be the case where contributions collected from younger members of a community are used to finance the pensions of older or surviving members.[37]

---

31 Coban (note 2) pp 152 ff; van den Broek [1986] Legal Issues of European Integration 52, 70 ff; for a criticism of the recognition of "goodwill" as a protected property see Hartwig [1999] RabelsZ 63, 566, who is concerned about a transformation of the property guarantee into a safeguard of future speculations, see also von Danwitz (note 3) p 233.
32 ECtHR *Tre Traktörer AB* (1991) 13 EHRR 309; See also ECtHR *Fredin (No 1)* (1991) 13 EHRR 784; Summarised in Gelinsky (note 20) pp 27 ff.
33 Sermet (note 25) p 5; Coban (note 2) pp 155 ff; van den Broek [1986] Legal Issues of European Integration 52, 67 ff.
34 *Bundesverfassungsgericht* (BVerfG – German Federal Constitution Court) (1985) 69 BVerfG 272, 300; see also BVerfG (1980) 53 BVerfGE 257; (1987) 72 BVerfGE 9, 18; (1988) 75 BVerfGE 78; (1988) 76 BVerfGE 220, 235; on the traditionally far more reserved decisions of the Austrian Constitutional Court see Pech in: Grabenwarter/Thienel (eds) *Kontinuität und Wandel der EMRK: Studien zur Europäischen Menschenrechtskonvention* (Kehl 1998) pp 233 ff.
35 Criticism from *Gelinsky* (note 20) pp 29 ff, 36 ff; Pech (note 34) pp 233 ff.
36 As to the dissenting view *cf* van Dijk/van Hoof (note 23) pp 455 ff.
37 EurCommHR *X v The Netherlands* App No 4130/69, (1972) 38 CD 9; confirmed in: *Vos* App No 10971/84, (1985) 43 DR 190, 191 ff; *Kleine Staarmann* App No 10503/83, (1985) 42 DR 162,

But even where a claim under public law falls within the scope of the property right 15
according to these principles, it may still be outside of the Commission's jurisdiction. Accepting the necessity of budgetary policy, the Commission decided that even where a person is entitled to benefits from a state pension fund, the determination of the actual amount of the entitlement is not covered by the property right's scope of protection.[38]

If in the past the EurCommHR was inclined towards a broader inclusion of claims 16
under public law into the scope of the property right,[39] this point of view has been confirmed by, among others,[40] the ECtHR in its controversial judgment in the *Gaygusuz* case.[41]

Case 1 – Answer:
G can successfully enforce his claim based on Article 1 of the 1st Prot 1 ECHR (in conjunc- 17
tion with the general prohibition of discriminatory practices in Article 14 ECHR)[42] only if the social security benefit (*Notstandshilfe*) applied for constitutes property in terms of this provision. At least according to the older rulings of the Convention bodies, claims based on public law can only be considered as property if they rely, at least in part, on the actual contributions of the insured party and the insured party has at least an identifiable share in the fund. Although this is debatable in the case of welfare payments under Austrian law,[43] the ECtHR accepted a violation of the property right in that particular case – apparently deciding that the provision that citizenship was a prerequisite to benefit entitlement was clearly discriminatory.[44]

e) Intellectual Property

The rights commonly considered to be intellectual property rights, such as copyrights, 18
patents, publishing rights, trademarks and other proprietary rights, preclude use by third persons for economic gain and are alienable. According to prevailing opinion, these rights are also covered by the term "property" according to Article 1 of the 1st Prot ECHR.[45] The Commission thus confirmed that a patent obtained under Dutch law was "property".[46]

166; rightly critical as to the basic and obviously too formal distinction between capital accumulation procedure and rate assessment between generations: von Danwitz (note 3) p 235.
38 EurCommHR *Müller* App No 6849/72, (1976) 1 DR 50, 31.
39 Peukert (note 12) paras 17 ff.
40 For the other references see von Danwitz (note 3) p 236, note 100.
41 See Pech (note 34) p 233, 241, according to whom, with regards to this decision, there are "no doubts at all", that "the core claims on the social security system, *ie* pensions, sickness benefits and accident insurance, now fall within the scope of protection of the property guarantee of Art 1 Prot 1 ECHR".
42 As to the legal concept and function of this combination see para 57.
43 See Hailbronner [1997] JZ 397, 398, who understands benefit to mean not only those payments partially funded from insurance contributions, but also welfare payments. In this respect – as Hailbronner rightly argues – a classification as a legally protected claim hardly seems justified. For claims to unemployment benefit and the scope of protection of the property right according to Art 14 *Grundgesetz* (German Basic Law) see BVerfG (1987) 72 BVerfGE 9, 18; (1987) 74 BVerfGE 203, 213.
44 ECtHR *Gaygusuz* (1997) 23 EHRR 364.
45 Peukert [1981] EuGRZ 97, 103; Gelinsky (note 20) p 32; Riedel (note 24) p 69; Sermet (note 25) p 8; Coban (note 2) pp 149 ff.
46 EurCommHR *Smith Kline v Netherlands* App No 12633/87, (1990) 66 DR 70, 79.

f) Right of Succession

19 Other than Article 14 of the *Grundgesetz* (German Basic Law), Article 1 of the 1st Prot ECHR does **not explicitly** refer to the right of succession. Nevertheless, the ECtHR regards the owner's right to dispose of his assets as he chooses to be covered by the scope of protection of Article 1 of the 1st Prot ECHR.[47] It explicitly refused the request of a potential heir to make a ruling on legal succession under the property right. It held that Article 1 of the 1st Prot ECHR protects only the actual property of living persons, not the expectation of an inheritance.[48]

2. Drawbacks of the Property Right

20 **Case 2 – Problem:** (based on ECtHR *Sporrong and Lönnroth* (1983) 5 EHRR 35)
S owned a number of parcels of land on which the local authority had a compulsory purchase option. The option was combined with an order prohibiting the building of new buildings on the land parcels. Compensation for renovations performed on the existing buildings in the meantime, or for losses resulting from the uncertainty caused by the option, is precluded under national law. The initial option was valid for a period of three years. During this time the local authority did not exercise its option to buy. However, at the end of the period, the option was extended by another 20 years at the local authority's request. After more than 20 years the option to purchase was cancelled due to changes in planning regulations for urban developments. S had, in the meantime, tried several times to sell the properties and had cancelled necessary renovations. S complained of a loss of rent, and considered the compulsory purchase option to violate her property right.

21 At least the earlier judgements of both the ECtHR and EurCommHR distinguish between **three different forms of encroachment**: expropriations, usage regulating measures and other interventions.[49] The distinction is made by considering the objectives of the respective measure and the degree of intervention. It is of no significance whether the intervention was deliberate or if it was an incidental consequence caused by governmental action. Also its legality or illegality plays no role in the classification.[50]

22 **Case 3 – Problem:** (based on ECtHR *AGOSI* (1987) 9 EHRR 1)
In 1975, the German gold trading company A sold Krügerrand gold coins with a value of £ 120,000 to the British citizen X. Title was retained until full payment had been made. Because the payment was not made, the contract was subsequently found to be invalid and the coins remained the property of A. However, X took the coins – without A's knowledge – to Great Britain. The import of the coins was illegal under to British Law and the coins were seized by customs. A sought compensation from the British authorities. The authorities denied his claim, arguing that the coins were legally seized and the property was forfeit under the applicable regulations.

---

47 ECtHR *Marckx* (1979–80) 2 EHRR 330.
48 ECtHR *Marckx* (1979–80) 2 EHRR 330.
49 For criticism of the older decisions, which contain a separate category of "other encroachments", and on the newer trends in the decisions of the ECtHR see paras 32 ff; see also Schutte (note 2) p 29.
50 Gelinsky (note 20) p 200.

a) Expropriations

Whereas the German Federal Constitutional Court traditionally leans towards a strict interpretation of the term **expropriation**,[51] the ECtHR tends to uphold[52] the rights of the owner against governmental intervention with a more generous interpretation of the scope of application of Article 1(1)(ii) of the 1st Prot ECHR. The Court states that the Convention shall protect "tangible and enforceable" rights.[53]

The test whether a national measure constitutes expropriation under Article 1(1)(ii) of the 1st Prot ECHR does not require a formal transfer of property. To ensure effective protection of property, many other situations must also be covered.[54] When considering restrictions on use under Article 1(2) of the 1st Prot ECHR, it is particularly important whether the affected assets can continue to be used in an economically reasonable manner.[55] Additionally, national restrictions on use can also be determined under the expropriation rule of Article 1(1)(ii) of the 1st Prot ECHR if the measures are preparatory to a compulsory purchase order and are therefore not simply designed to regulate the use of the property.[56]

Recently, the ECtHR has been increasingly occupied with examining the legality of expropriations in the context of the European post-war systems. The end of the cold war and changes of regime in the Middle and Eastern European states have raised serious issues of coping with the (in-)justice practised there.

Case 4 – Problem: (based on ECtHR Jahn App No 46720/99)[57]
A inherited a piece of land before the political change in eastern Germany in 1989 under the land reform laws of the former GDR. The land reform took place in the Soviet occupied zone between 1945 and 1949. Large pieces of real estate were seized and converted into property trusts, out of which small parcels of land were assigned to landless or land-poor farmers (so-called New Farmers). The "ownership" of these parcels of land could generally be bequeathed to descendants under GDR law, but was restricted in many ways. The land could not be disposed of freely. Regulations regarding change in ownership at the time of the GDR decreed that land parcels be reincorporated into the property trust and allowed the transfer to third parties only under the condition that those parties agreed to use the

---

51 See BVerfG [2001] WM 775.
52 For the other differences between the guarantee of Art 14 of the German Basic Law and that of Art 1 Prot 1 ECHR see Grabenwarter (note 13) p 359, who rightly also points out factors of a weaker property protection in Art Prot 1 ECHR.
53 ECtHR *Jahn* App No 46720/99.
54 See ECtHR *Jahn* App No 46720/99; further examples in Coban (note 2) pp 178 ff; for the difference between formal and de facto encroachments see Grabenwarter (note 13) pp 362 ff.
55 As to the differentiation between the formal expropriation and the regulation of use see also Mittelberger *Der Eigentumsschutz nach Art 1 des 1. ZP zur EMRK im Lichte der Rechtsprechung der Straßburger Organe* (Bern 2000) pp 92 ff; on the differentiation between de facto expropriation and regulation of use see also Müller-Michaels (note 18) pp 74 ff, as well as Mittelberger (note 55) pp 86 ff.
56 On expropriation according to Art 1(1)(ii) Prot 1 ECHR generally: Peukert [1988] EuGRZ 510; Gelinsky (note 20) pp 42 ff; van den Broek [1986] Legal Issues of European Integration 52, 72 ff; *Yearbook of the European Convention on Human Rights Volume 41A* (1998) p 172, 184 ff.
57 The "Jahn" decision is hotly debated in the German literature, see Cremer [2004] EuGRZ 134; Kämmerer [2004] DVBl 995; Hornickel [2004] NVwZ 567.

land for agricultural purposes. The "Modrow Law", which came into force on 16 March 1990, removed all restrictions on the disposal of land and gave the occupants full ownership. The first free elections in the GDR took place on 18 March 1990. On 22 July 1992, a new law enacted by the federal legislator of then reunified Germany came into force in the former GDR. According to this law, land allocated under the land reform generally becomes the property of the person who was registered as the owner in the land register on 15 March 1990, or to their heirs. The latter, however, is only the case if there is no other person with a stronger entitlement and who asserts this claim. Should the owner have died who was registered in the land register at the time when the Modrow Law came into effect, the fiscal authorities of the federal state in which the land lies shall be deemed to have superior title if the heir did not work in agriculture and forestry on 15 March 1990. In 1994 A, who did not at any time work in agriculture and forestry, was entered as the owner of the land in the land register. In 1996, A was ordered to transfer his land without charge to the federal state of L.

b) Measures Concerning Restrictions on Use

27   Generally **restrictions on use** are measures which, although they constrain the owner, have at least some "substance".[58] The ECtHR for example judged the refusal of police co-operation in the eviction of a tenant who was refusing to vacate a property as violating Article 1(2) of the 1st Prot ECHR.[59]

28   The ECtHR also held that there were certain circumstances where restrictions on use according to Article 1(2) of the 1st Prot ECHR can result in a complete forfeiture of ownership, for example where the confiscation is taken to enforce the restriction of use.[60]

29   Besides the restrictions on use, in a further subgroup Article 1(2) of the 1st Prot ECHR contains authorisations for the imposition of **duties**, especially taxes and fines.[61]

30   According to the decisions of the courts, Member States are not obligated to **compensate** owners when imposing restrictions of use according to Article 1(2) of the 1st Prot ECHR. This corroborates the general community limits on ownership familiar from German national law.[62] As under Article 14(1)(ii) of the German Basic Law, even when it has been determined by the ECHR that the restriction of use is permissible, compensation could exceptionally be awarded, *eg* when inequitable hardship could not otherwise be avoided. This is already moving towards the determination of compensation using the principle of reasonableness.[63]

---

58 As the to the notion and the requirements for the regulation of use see Hartwig (note 31) pp 569 ff; von Danwitz (note 3) pp 243 ff; van den Broek [1986] Legal Issues of European Integration 52, 76; Coban (note 2) pp 180 ff; *Yearbook of the European Convention on Human Rights Volume 41A* (1998) pp 172, 191 ff; Mittelberger (note 55) pp 66, 69 ff, who also mentions numerous examples for typical cases of application of change of use.
59 ECtHR *Immobiliare Saffi* (2000) 30 EHRR 756, in more detail Peters *Einführung in die Europäische Menschenrechtskonvention* (Munich 2003) p 197.
60 The often criticized judgment ECtHR *AGOSI* (1987) 9 EHRR 1. With regard to the classification of such "seizures" into the category of the regulation of use see Gelinsky (note 20) pp 47 ff, 54.
61 Also von Danwitz (note 3) p 246; Mittelberger (note 55) p 71; Müller-Michaels (note 18) p 73; Coban (note 2) pp 182 ff; Sermet (note 25) p 13; van den Broek [1986] Legal Issues of European Integration 52, 76.
62 As to this parallel see Frowein (note 9) pp 49–50.
63 See paras 45 ff.

Case 3 – Answer:
The forfeiture of the Krügerrand gold coins affects property protected by Article 1(1) of the 1st Prot ECHR. Although the coins are permanently confiscated from the owner, the ECtHR does not consider this to be an expropriation, but instead views it as the legal consequence of the import restriction. Because the latter is merely a regulation of use, the seizure is judged to comply with Article 1(2) of the 1st Prot ECHR.[64]

31

c) "Miscellaneous" Encroachments

The acceptance by the ECtHR of a single self-contained category **miscellaneous encroachments** according to Article 1(1)(i) of the 1st Prot ECHR[65] is often disputed in literature. According to some, the introductory sentence of the Article 1 of the 1st Prot ECHR describes only the scope of protection for the guarantee of ownership and subsequently created opportunities for intervention need to be justified. It may restrict, but cannot facilitate, intervention.[66] In its more recent judgements, the ECtHR seems to favour this opinion insofar as it considers the explicit differentiation between individual encroachment types to be superfluous, at least in complex cases. Instead it measures the encroachment by means of the basic standard of Article 1(1)(i) of the 1st Prot ECHR, establishing the freedom of property ownership.[67] In more recent decisions it furthermore mentions three "rules" to be found in Article 1 of the 1st Prot ECHR, of which the second (expropriating encroachments according to Article 1(1)(ii) of the 1st Prot ECHR) and the third (regulations on use according to Article 1(2) of the 1st Prot ECHR) concern specific limitations on the right of ownership, which shall be interpreted considering the general principle of the first rule (Article 1(1)(i) of the 1st Prot ECHR).[68] An examination of "miscellaneous encroachments" based solely on the first rule shall only be considered if the intervention rules in the second and/or third rules cannot be applied.[69]

32

As far as the ECtHR accepts miscellaneous encroachments of ownership, they have to be combined with a **compensation rule** or at least with **other measures** provided by national law to make up for losses. As a result, there are higher demands on the justification of miscellaneous encroachments than on the measures regulating use.[70]

33

Case 2 – Answer:
The compulsory purchase option did not constitute a dispossession in the sense of Article 1(1)(ii) of the 1st Prot ECHR. No such dispossession ever took place and, after the can-

34

---

64 ECtHR *AGOSI* (1987) 9 EHRR 1. According to Frowein (note 9) pp 49, 65, the company received fifty percent of the coins' value, paid after the judgment.
65 See ECtHR *Sporrong and Lönnroth* (1983) 5 EHRR 35; see also the dissenting opinions expressed by eight of the judges. More recently: ECtHR *Beyeler (No 2)* (2003) 36 EHRR 46. As to the differentiation, see also Mittelberger [2001] EuGRZ 364, 366; on the "other interventions" see also van den Brock [1986] Legal Issues of European Integration 52, 76 ff
66 Gelinsky (note 20) pp 86 ff; of different opinion is Peters (note 59) p 198, who basically affirms the fundamental idea of creating a catchall element.
67 ECtHR *Beyeler (No 2)* (2003) 36 EHRR 46, para 106; the late use of a preemptive right of purchase for a painting of Van Gogh; see also ECtHR *Broniowski* (2005) 40 EHRR 495.
68 See for example ECtHR *Former King of Greece et al v Greece* (2001) 33 EHRR 516.
69 ECtHR *James* (1986) 8 EHRR 123; as to the subsidiarity of the first rule see also the *Yearbook of the Convention on Human Rights* (1998) pp 172, 193 ff.
70 Gelinsky (note 20) p 203.

cellation of the option, is no longer expected to take place. At no time did the terms of the compulsory purchase order restrict S's ownership rights to such an extent that they effectively constituted a dispossession. The ECtHR was nevertheless unable to classify the compulsory purchase order as a regulation of the "use of property" in the sense of Article 1(2) of the 1st Prot ECHR. The order was never intended to restrict or control the use. In its initial stages (*ie* before confirmation), a dispossession could only be classified as an "other restriction" under Article 1(1)(i) of the 1st Prot ECHR.[71] As a matter of fact, the compulsory purchase order was a violation of the ownership right under the ECHR because of its excessive duration and the preclusion of any reparation for the assets damaged as a consequence.[72]

3. Justification of Ownership Restrictions

35 According to the text of Article 1 of the 1st Prot ECHR and the case law of the Convention bodies, the interference with ownership rights can be justified according to **three cumulative** prerequisites. The corresponding government measures must be lawful, serve the public interest and be reasonable.[73]

Case 5 – Problem: (based on ECtHR *Handyside* (1979–80) 1 EHRR 737)
36 The British publisher H printed an English version of a Danish book with the title "The Little Red Schoolbook". The book is a reference book for pupils and deals with general issues concerning education and tuition. About 10 % of the book deal with sex education issues. The book was seized by the British police. In the resulting proceedings before the British courts H was fined due to violations of the Obscene Publications Act. Additionally, the confiscation and destruction of the books was ordered.

a) Legality of the Restrictions

37 According to Article 1(1)(ii) of the 1st Prot ECHR, a dispossession is permitted only according to the provisions enacted by law and the general rules of public international law.[74] Even Article 1(2) of the 1st Prot ECHR only allows a **lawful regulation of use**. The

---

71 As to the criticism on this dogmatic classification see paras 32 ff.
72 ECtHR *Sporrong and Lönnroth* (1983) 5 EHRR 35. As to the fact that a reclassification of farmland which takes an unreasonably long time may prove to be – apart from a violation of Art 6 ECHR – an additional infringement of Art 1(1) Prot 1 ECHR: ECtHR *Poiss* (1991) 13 EHRR 414; as to the negation of the extremely long compensation procedure of a compulsory purchase: ECtHR *Papachelas* (2000) 30 EHRR 923.
73 There are differing opinions as to whether these requirements can be applied consistently for all three forms of property encroachment. Grabenwarter (note 13) pp 365 ff as well as Müller-Michaels (note 18) pp 78 ff differentiate as to the justification of property interventions between the particular encroachments. There is no special significance attributed to the requirement to observe the "conditions provided by the general principles of international law" in the matter of expropriation, see Art 1(1) Prot 1 ECHR, so the conditions for a justification of regulations on use and expropriations resemble each other to some extent. It is also debateable whether there should be partially different requirements for each of the conditions. On this issue, and in particular on whether the "public interest" (para 1) is to be equated with the "general interest", see (para 2), Mittelberger (note 55) pp 115 ff. Similarly: von Danwitz (note 3) pp 250 ff; Schutte (note 2) p 34; van den Broek [1986] Legal Issues of European Integration 52, 78 ff; Coban (note 2) pp 175 and 194 ff as well as Sermet (note 25) pp 15 ff, who differentiates between public interest and general interest.
74 This criterion is nevertheless of relatively little importance in the decision making process of the

definition of the term ownership and the grounds for deprivation therefore require a sufficiently precise legal foundation, which must also allow sufficient scope for likely governmental interventions.[75] According to the recent case law of the ECtHR, the legality of an infringement of ownership is the first and most important requirement for its justification.[76] Further, the ECtHR decided that a continuous suspension of property rights shall be contrary to the Convention if it is held to be in violation of national laws.[77] The Court itself, however, has only restricted authority to judge such cases because of the peculiarities of the respective national laws.[78] In the first instance it is the responsibility of the national authorities and courts to interpret and apply the national law and, if necessary, to judge its constitutionality.[79] The ECtHR can therefore only rule on the question whether the interpretation of the applicable norms was "arbitrary".[80] Nevertheless, ambiguities in the applicable national laws are not inevitably to the detriment of the appellant. On the contrary, the criterion of the legality of the infringement must be clearly and precisely defined and be able to be consistently applied.[81]

b) Protection of the Public Interest

Article 1(1)(ii) of the 1st Prot ECHR permits expropriations in the "**public interest**". Article 1(2) of the 1st Prot ECHR permits the justification of property usage restrictions in the "**interests of the general public**". Both terms are understood in case law and in literature as identical.[82] Also for "other interventions", the ECtHR requires a justification of the respective measure as being in the public interest.[83] At the same time, the ECtHR allows national authorities broad discretion to determine the general public interest of a restriction of property use because of their "immediate familiarity" with the local situation or with the "respective social needs".[84] Judicial review by the ECtHR is restricted to the verification of whether the motives of the legislator appear to be "clearly unfounded".[85] The preferential treatment of private third parties can also be in the "public inter-

38

ECtHR, because international law deals with expropriation rules only with regard to the property of foreign nationals. The ECtHR refuses to deal with referrals (which are recognized by and referred to in international law). See Weiß *Die europäische Konvention zum Schutze der Menschenrechte und Grundfreiheiten* (Frankfurt aM 1954) p 20. On the limitations on and requests for compensation arising from expropriations of citizens' property, see ECtHR *James* (1986) 8 EHRR 123.
75 Mittelberger [2001] EuGRZ 364, 367; the term "law", however, is to be understood in a wider sense, comprising also rules developed by case law, see Schutte (note 2), pp 53 ff.
76 ECtHR *Iatridis* (2000) 30 EHRR 97; *Former King of Greece et al v Greece* (2001) 33 EHRR 516.
77 ECtHR *Iatridis* (2000) 30 EHRR 97, upholding of an eviction order despite contrary decisions by the national jurisdiction.
78 ECtHR *Håkansson and Sturesson* (1991) 13 EHRR 1.
79 ECtHR *Former King of Greece et al v Greece* (2001) 33 EHRR 516.
80 ECtHR *Jahn* App No 46720/99.
81 ECtHR *Hentrich* (1994) 18 EHRR 440; *Lithgow* (1986) 8 EHRR 329; *Beyeler (No 2)* (2003) 36 EHRR 46, para 109.
82 See ECtHR *James* (1986) 8 EHRR 123; Peukert (note 12) para 48; Mittelberger [2001] EuGRZ 364, 367; Coban (note 2) p 175; dissenting opinion Sermet (note 25) pp 15 ff.
83 ECtHR *Beyeler (No 2)* (2003) 36 EHRR 46, para 111.
84 *Cf* ECtHR *Wiesinger* (1993) 16 EHRR 258, with reference to *Fredin (No 1)* (1991) 13 EHRR 784; and *Raimondo* (1994) 18 EHRR 237; see Schutte (note 2) pp 55 ff.
85 ECtHR *James* (1986) 8 EHRR 123.

est". Such preferential treatment is unlawful only if it is the sole purpose of the mandatory measure and an advancement of other public interests cannot be identified.[86]

39 However, a handover of property into **communal use** is not necessary. In fact, sociopolitical or economic considerations can entitle the legislator to redistribute assets in favour of particular parts of the population.[87] It appears so far that the ECtHR has only once ruled that a restriction of property usage was not in the public interest.[88]

Case 5 – Answer:

40 The seizure of the books and the order for their confiscation and destruction infringe on H's property right as protected by Article 1 of the 1st Prot ECHR. Because the seizure, confiscation and destruction are themselves a consequences of a ban on obscene publications, they are considered by the ECtHR to be the result of the application of a national regulation. This does not constitute an expropriation, but simply a regulation on the use of property as per Article 1(2) of the 1st Prot ECHR.[89] According to the opinion of the ECtHR, however, this second paragraph appoints the contracting states as the sole judges of the necessity of intervention and allows them plenty of scope for interpretation. The Court therefore feels that it is unable to deviate from the judgement of the national courts on the morality of the schoolbook.[90]

c) Proportionality of the Encroachment

41 According to the ECHR, the bottom line for the protection of fundamental rights, and therefore the central judicial tool for the evaluation of national property encroachments,[91] is the issue of the **proportionality** of the encroachment.[92] According to case law, the ECtHR considers the test of proportionality as an unwritten requirement of Article 1 of the 1st Prot ECHR.[93]

aa) Legitimate Purpose

42 According to the case law of the ECtHR, every property encroachment must be for a reasonable **purpose**.[94] The examination of this point corresponds with the question as to

---

86 Cf *Österreichischer Verfassungsgerichtshof* (VerfGH – Austrian Constitutional Court) [1990] EuGRZ 425, according to which the refusal of an export licence for copper wire clippings cannot be justified solely because a domestic manufacturer would lose a cheap domestic source of supply and would have to obtain the copper on the world market at significantly higher prices.
87 ECtHR *James* (1986) 8 EHRR 123.
88 ECtHR *Raimondo* (1994) 18 EHRR 237, no public interest in a delay in the payment of compensation ordered by the court in respect of unlawfully confiscated property.
89 See para 28, especially footnote 60.
90 ECtHR *Handyside* (1979–80) 1 EHRR 737.
91 See von Danwitz (note 3) p 252, as to the growing significance of the principle of legality. Also von Danwitz accentuates the fundamental importance of the principle of reasonableness as a decisive factor, p 253.
92 See Cremona in: Beyerlein (ed) *Recht zwischen Umbruch und Bewahrung: Völkerrecht, Europarecht, Staatsrecht; Festschrift für Rudolf Bernhardt* (Berlin 1995) p 323; Eissen in: Pettiti/Decaux/Imbert (eds) *La Convention Européenne des droits de l'homme* (Paris 1999) pp 65 ff; Fiedler [1996] EuGRZ 354, 355; Schutte (note 2) pp 56 ff; → § 2 para 48.
93 Mittelberger [2001] EuGRZ 364, 368 ff.
94 ECtHR *Beyeler (No 2)* (2003) 36 EHRR 46, para 111.

Economic Fundamental Rights

whether a measure is in the "public interest" according to Article 1(1)(ii) of the 1st Prot ECHR.[95]

bb) Necessity

Until now, the decisions of the courts have placed no particular emphasis on the necessity of a governmental property restriction due to the broad **discretion**[96] granted to the member states.[97] Shortly before its disbandment, the Commission even determined that Article 1 of the 1st Prot ECHR contained no criteria at all regarding necessity.[98] The ECtHR has also been accused of not sufficiently considering in its case law whether the contested property encroachments could have been alleviated or avoided altogether by the use of alternative measures.[99] Indeed, the ECtHR clearly stated that no "requirement of strict necessity" could be found in Article 1 of the 1st Prot ECHR. According to the Court's opinion, the simple existence of alternative measures does not mean that a national measure is unjustified. This is to be taken as just "one aspect among others" that must be considered in order to determine whether the chosen measures can be deemed to be reasonable and appropriate for the achievement of the stated goal. Within these boundaries, the Court does not consider itself to be competent to determine whether a measure is the best solution to the problem, or whether the power of discretion granted to the national authorities should have been exercised differently.[100]

43

cc) Equitable Balance of Interests

The case law of the Courts therefore focuses on the question of whether there is an "**equitable balance**" between the demands of the public interest and the requirements for the effective protection of individual rights.[101] The Court must thus consider the actual details of the individual cases in determining the suitability and reasonableness of national measures.[102]

44

dd) Claims for Compensation

Case 6 – Problem: (based on ECtHR *James* (1986) 8 EHRR 123)
There are special legal provisions that allow "long-time tenants" to buy a house in which they have lived and which they have maintained in good condition in order to avoid the contractual agreed reversion of the property to the landlord. Under these provisions the purchase price payable to the former landlord is significantly below the property's true market value.

45

---

95 See above para 38.
96 See especially ECtHR *Handyside* (1979–80) 1 EHRR 737.
97 Mittelberger [2001] EuGRZ 364, 368 even says that the criterion of necessity was "of no importance".
98 See ECtHR *Former King of Greece et al v Greece* (2001) 33 EHRR 516.
99 Gelinsky (note 20) p 203 with reference to the decision ECtHR *AGOSI* (1987) 9 EHRR 1.
100 ECtHR *James* (1986) 8 EHRR 123.
101 English/French: "proper balance"/"juste équilibre", see ECtHR *Wiesinger* (1993) 16 EHRR 258; similarly for the evaluation of the relationship between expropriation and compensation ECtHR *Holy Monasteries* (1995) 20 EHRR 1, para 70: "fair balance". As to the "dangers of arbitrary results" arising from the use of this term Fiedler [1996] EuGRZ 354, 355.
102 See for this ECtHR *Hentrich* (1994) 18 EHRR 440. For a complete overview, critical however of the (lack of) control achieved in case law see Gelinsky (note 20) pp 202 ff.

46   Article 1 of the 1st Prot ECHR contains – in contrast to Article 14 of the German Basic Law – no explicit provision on the necessity of compensation. The conditions provided by the general rules of public international law, to which the Article refers, contain a **compensation duty** only for those national measures which concern the property of foreign nationals.[103]

47   Nevertheless, since the decision on *James*, the ECtHR considers the expropriation or other (virtual) complete confiscation of property from domestic citizens without compensation as justifiable only in exceptional cases[104] and refers to the principle of proportionality.[105] Where the expropriation was lawful and not arbitrary, the lack of compensation alone does not make it improper.[106] It is further necessary to determine whether the complainant had to bear a disproportionate or excessive burden.

48   Conversely, a legally designated compensation can alleviate the hardship of an expropriation or a restriction on use to such an extent that the measures are altogether proportional.[107] It is a prerequisite, however, that the compensation provided is actually received by the affected owners and that it is of some value to them. For example, the ECtHR considered the granting of permission to hunt on other people's land to be inadequate compensation for the legally imposed duty to allow others to hunt on one's own property. For people who, like the complainants, oppose hunting for ethical reasons, the offer of such compensation is worthless.[108]

49   The **obligation to provide compensation**[109] applies to citizens as well as to foreign nationals.[110] The ECtHR and the Commission also rely on the criterion of equitable balance to ascertain the necessary level of the compensation. This does not mean that in every case the full market value of the expropriated property has to be paid.[111] For example, compensation may be waived for losses caused by inflation which occur before the compensation is paid.[112] According to the case law of the ECtHR, there is only an obligation to pay "appropriate" compensation.[113] The Court however does not accept those rulings which reduce compensation across the board with reference to absolute legal presumptions. For

---

103 On the dogmatic weaknesses of this reasoning see von Danwitz (note 3) pp 221, 255 with further references; on the protection of direct investments abroad by the ECHR Ruffert [2000] *German Yearbook of International Law* 116; on the protection of property rights of tenants Schwelb [1964] *American Journal of Comparative Law* 518.
104 ECtHR *James* (1986) 8 EHRR 123: "the protection of the right of property ... would be largely illusionary and ineffective in the absence of any equivalent principle"; see also ECtHR *Holy Monasteries* (1995) 20 EHRR 1; *Former King of Greece et al v Greece* (2001) 33 EHRR 516. More detailed as to the meaning of the compensation requirement also for cases of de-facto-expropriation: Frowein (note 9) pp 49, 58 ff; Fiedler [1996] EuGRZ 354, 355 ff.
105 von Danwitz (note 3) p 256.
106 ECtHR *Jahn* App No 46720/99, para 83.
107 ECtHR *Former King of Greece et al v Greece* (2001) 33 EHRR 516.
108 ECtHR *Chassagnou* (2000) 29 EHRR 615.
109 In more detail: *Riedel* [1988] EuGRZ 333 ff; Coban (note 2) pp 210 ff.
110 Nevertheless, the ECtHR does not accept the application of the strict compensation rules resulting from the "rules in general international law" as referred to by Art 1(1)(i) Prot 1 ECHR to expropriations of citizens. A "discrimination against citizens" in the field of expropriation compensation is therefore allowed; see ECtHR *James* (1986) 8 EHRR 123.
111 ECtHR *James* (1986) 8 EHRR 123.
112 ECtHR *Lithgow* (1986) 8 EHRR 329; more detailed Gelinsky (note 20) pp 144 ff.
113 See Peters (note 59) pp 195 ff; Sermet (note 25) pp 20 ff.

this reason, a Greek compensation regulation was overturned according to which the construction of a major national thoroughfare was deemed to bring an increase in value to every affected resident; this increase was then taken into account when calculating compensation for the partial expropriation of property. Even practical administrative considerations cannot justify such a system because of its "excessive inflexibility".[114]

The ECtHR simply requires that the level of compensation be "reasonably commensurate" with the value of the expropriated property.[115] The ECtHR thereby grants Member States plenty of leeway for the determination of the amount of compensation. Therefore, the "social" or "socialising" character[116] of the governmental measure can be taken into account, provided that it meets the principles of a "democratic society".[117] Accordingly, expropriating measures for the purposes of the enforcement of economic and agricultural reforms are better accepted than other expropriations, even when there is little or no compensation.

Case 6 – Answer:
The legal requirement to sell a house which had previously been rented amounts to a property expropriation according to Article 1(1)(ii) of the 1st Prot ECHR. This expropriation is, however, found to be in the "public interest", even if it favours a third party. The expropriation was therefore not contrary to the Convention on the grounds that inadequate compensation was provided for the former owner. Although the ECtHR is of the opinion that compensation should be paid, its level need not match the market price. The hardships which could arise from the application of a general expropriation measure in particular cases are to be accepted in the interests of uniformity, legal certainty and the speed of the expropriation.[118]

The derivation of the compensation duty from the principle of proportionality makes it possible to identify a group of compensable usage regulations. So far, however, the ECtHR has not yet done this.[119]

Even though the ECtHR is willing to take national peculiarities such as German reunification and its corresponding difficulties into account,[120] it still applies high standards to infringements of property rights. It does not distinguish according to the way in which the property was acquired, but instead asks whether the property existed at the time when the ECHR came into effect. This leads to differences in case law between the German Federal

---

114 ECtHR *Papachelas* (2000) 30 EHRR 923 with further references.
115 ECtHR *Lithgow* (1986) 8 EHRR 329: "an amount reasonably related to its value"/"raisonnablement en rapport avec la valeur du bien"; for a further differentiation of the criteria used see Condorelli in: Pettiti/Decaux/Imbert (eds) *La Convention Européenne des droits de l'homme* (Paris 1999) pp 990 ff.
116 Similarly ECtHR *James* (1986) 8 EHRR 123: "greater social justice"/"justice social".
117 For these formulas see ECtHR *Lithgow* (1986) 8 EHRR 329; opposing with reference to a "class specific collectivization" and the perpetuation of the communist land reform of 1945–1949: Fiedler [1996] EuGRZ 354, 356.
118 ECtHR *James* (1986) 8 EHRR 123; see also ECtHR *Lithgow* (1986) 8 EHRR 329 on the limitation of the amount of compensation in the nationalisation of particular industries.
119 Similarly: Weber in: Bröhmer (ed) *Der Grundrechtsschutz in Europa* (Baden-Baden 2002) p 115. Weber – like Peters (note 59) p 194 – however sticks to the differentiation between expropriation and usage regulation compensation – defined precisely by the liability to pay compensation.
120 ECtHR *Jahn* App No 46720/99, para 89.

Constitutional Court concerning Article 14 of the German Basic Law and the ECtHR concerning Article 1 of the 1st Prot ECHR.[121]

Case 4 – Answer:

54   The order requiring A to transfer his land without charge to the federal state L is considered an expropriation according to Article 1(1)(ii) of the 1st Prot ECHR. A became full owner after the cancellation of the restrictions regarding the land reform parcels. This property law became a part of the law of the Federal Republic of Germany at the time of German reunification and now falls within the scope of the ECHR. The legitimacy of full ownership acquired this way cannot be challenged by the fact that the Federal Government subsequently decided that the property was wrongfully acquired. The decisive factor is that A was registered in the land register after the German reunification and could then make free use of his property.

The expropriation is indeed legal. The criteria of accessibility, accuracy and predictability were met by the legal regulation; the interpretation of the relevant rules by the German courts and the affirmation of the constitutionality by the German Federal Constitutional Court were not arbitrary. In addition, the ECtHR does not doubt that the intention of the legislator serves the public interest, as it aims to untangle the ownership questions in connection with the land reform and to correct the consequences of the Modrow Law.

However, the intervention is not proportional because A has no right to compensation. The ECtHR stated that it was well aware of the "infinitely great challenge" which the German legislator faced in transforming a socialist property order into one of a market economy. Nevertheless it does not consider A's acquisition of the property to be "unlawful". In the Court's opinion, A legally acquired full ownership of the land with the enactment of the Modrow Law. While the German legislator was permitted to amend the Modrow Law two

---

121 In contrast to the ECtHR, which affirmed the confiscation of the property according to Art 1(1)(ii) Prot 1 ECHR, the German Federal Constitutional Court had denied the expropriation under Art 14 of the German Basic Law (BVerfG [2001] WM 775). The German Federal Constitutional Court interprets Art 233, §§ 11(3), 12(2), (3) of the *Einführungsgesetz zum Bürgerlichen Gesetzbuch* (EGBGB – Introductory Act to the Civil Code) as a rule on the determination of substance and limitations of property in the sense of Art 14(1)(ii) of the German Basic Law. Expropriation is the State's acquisition of the property of individuals. Its aim is the total or partial expropriation of a particular property protected by Art 14(1)(i) of the German Basic Law in order to achieve specific public aims. By contrast, Art 233, §§ 11 to 16 EGBGB aims to correct the repeal of the laws on change of ownership (*Besitzwechselvorschriften*) without transitional provisions and to create clear conditions for the ownership of estates originating from the land reform. The legislator may also, according to Art 14(1)(ii) of the German Basic Law, in certain circumstances and when undertaking a general reorganisation of a particular field of law, annul pre-existing legal positions which are protected by the property guarantee.

The German Federal Constitutional Court decided that the substance and limitations of ownership were correctly determined because A could not reasonably expect to be allowed to maintain title to a property which he had acquired only because of a failure to transpose the regulations of the *Deutsche Demokratische Republik* (German Democratic Republic – GDR) on change of possession. Nor could there be a general expectation that the legal provisions of the GDR would not continue to develop over time with a view towards the possible reunification of the two German states, unless there was a particular reason for the belief that the law of the GDR would exceptionally stay in force. The basic fundamental law positions obtained before accession to the German Basic Law could not be expected to be afforded the same extensive protection as the rights obtained under the German Basic Law.

years later, he was not entitled to carry out such an expropriation in favour of the state without providing reasonable compensation to the affected party.
The ECtHR does not feel that the amount of compensation due can be decided yet. The unusual circumstances of the acquisition of property and the injustices which the former owners of the land reform parcels suffered when they were expropriated in 1945[122] could lead to a reduction of the compensation payable[123].

4. Ownership Law and other Guarantees of the ECHR

Case 7 – Problem: (based on ECtHR *Pine Valley* (1993) 16 EHRR 379)
The Company H acquires a plot of land which is not part of an accepted construction zone, but for which special planning permission has been given for the construction of a department store. The planning permission is registered in a public register. After the acquisition of the land, the planning permission is rescinded by the highest state court in a test case. While a law subsequently corrects the nullity for many other similar cases and re-establishes the effect of the originally unlawfully issued special planning permission, this is not the case for the property of H.

55

The protection of property guaranteed by Article 1 of the 1st Prot ECHR is **reinforced** in special cases by further guarantees of the ECHR.

56

For example, the **prohibition of discrimination** according to Article 14 of the ECHR (general → § 3 paras 66 ff) fulfils such a function. The clause has "no independent meaning" according to the case law of the Court. Rather, it only serves to protect the individual from an unjustified discrimination in respect of the usage of the freedoms provided by other regulations of the Convention and the amending protocols. Where the Court recognizes that a violation of the freedom of property guaranteed by Article 1 of the 1st Prot ECHR has occurred, it generally considers an additional determination as to whether a violation of the prohibition of discrimination has also occurred to be superfluous. Such a

57

---

122 The Grand Chamber of the ECtHR has ruled that the complaints of former owners, expropriated between 1945 and 1949 in the Soviet occupation zone or in the GDR after 1949, are inadmissible (ECtHR *Von Maltzan* (2006) 42 EHRR 92). These owners felt that their property rights had been violated according to Art 1 Prot 1 ECHR by the German law concerning compensation and reorganisation of 1994 (*Entschädigungs- und Ausgleichsgesetz*) and a decision by the German Federal Constitutional Court from 22.11.2000 (BVerfG (2001) 102 BVerfGE 254), because they were of the opinion that the amount of compensation which they had been paid was far below the real value of their unlawfully expropriated goods. The ECtHR dismissed the claimants' application for the return of the property or for compensation payments corresponding to the actual (current) value of the property. There was no legal basis for the application and no relevant case law. The complainants had not proved that they were the owners of the property and therefore their claims were not actionable. The ECtHR declined to examine the circumstances of the expropriations or their enduring consequences. The Federal Republic of Germany (FRG) was responsible neither for deeds during the Soviet occupation nor for those of the GDR, even as the legal successor of the GDR. The ECtHR has allowed the FRG broad discretion in the definition of the compensation rules.
123 In a case similar to the Jahn-Case, the Grand Chamber confirmed the existence of a property infringement (see ECtHR *Broniowski* (2005) 40 EHRR 495). Nevertheless the Great Panel, in an 11:6 decision from 30.6.2005, decided, contrary to many expectations, that there was no property violation in the Jahn-case (ECtHR *Jahn* App No 46720/99).

determination is only required if a clear discrimination concerning the exercise of the property right constitutes a substantial part of the case. The Court judged a French law to violate Article 1(1) of the 1st Prot ECHR in conjunction with Article 14 of the ECHR because it was clearly discriminatory in that it required smallholders to allow third parties access for the purpose of hunting, while exempting owners of larger estates from this requirement.[124]

58 One function strengthening the protection of property can be found most notably in the regulation of the **right to a fair trial** in Article 6 of the ECHR.[125]

Case 7 – Answer:
59 Although the planning permission was invalid from the outset, the ECtHR considers the determining judgment to be an infringement of H's property rights. When considering the unlawfulness of the permission and H's awareness of the legal confusions, the Court considered the nullification of the permission to be appropriate and as such not subject to compensation. A duty for compensation due to unjustified discrimination results, however, from Article 1(1)(i), (2) of the 1st Prot ECHR in conjunction with the discrimination prohibition contained in Article 14 of the ECHR.[126]

III. Other Guarantees under Economic Law

60 In contrast to the UN Universal Declaration of Human Rights, the ECHR does not provide any **economic fundamental rights** in addition to the property law. Only a rather unimportant special case is covered by Article 1 of the 4th Prot ECHR: it prohibits the imprisonment of someone due to an "inability to fulfil a contractual obligation". While the institution of the Debtor's Prison[127] is contrary to the Convention, this does not mean that imprisonment for contempt, which is expressly acknowledged by Article 5(1)(b) of the ECHR, is prohibited.[128] The custodial sentence in order to enforce a judgment according to section 901 of the *Zivilprozessordnung* (ZPO – German Code of Civil Procedure) and similar regulations are not affected by Article 1 of the 4th Prot ECHR.[129]

61 A guarantee of important economic fundamental rights, such as freedom of profession or economic freedom, is also missing.[130] The latter cannot possibly be derived from a general freedom of action. According to prevailing opinion, there is no trace of that in

---

124 See ECtHR *Chassagnou* (2000) 29 EHRR 615.
125 As to Art 6 ECHR → § 6 paras 33 ff. As to the relevance of Art 6(1) ECHR for property related processes, see above in footnote 72. Specifically on the function of Art 6 ECHR in the EC antitrust law: Weiß [1997] EWS 253, 255 ff; also on the protection of business premises by Art 8 ECHR.
126 ECtHR *Pine Valley* (1993) 16 EHRR 379.
127 The meaning of the provisions is defined in the 11th Protocol to the ECHR, which has introduced the heading "Prohibition of imprisonment for debt".
128 Villiger (note 28) para 682.
129 EurCommHR *X v Germany* App No 4445/70, (1970) 37 CD 119; cited according to Frowein/Peukert (note 12) Art 1 4. ZP.
130 Frowein in: Frowein/Peukert (eds) *Europäische Menschenrechtskonvention* (2nd ed, Kehl 1996) Art 4 EMRK.

Economic Fundamental Rights § 5 IV

the Convention.[131] Up until now, the Convention bodies have continued to withstand the occasional calls for an expansion of the economic fundamental rights.[132]

IV. Influence of the European Social Charter

Case 8 – Problem: (based on *Bundesverwaltungsgericht* (BVerwG – German Federal Administrative Court) (1993) 91 BVerwGE 327)
T, a Turkish citizen, has lived in Baden-Württemberg for several years with her Turkish husband, who works as an employee. She applied for state child benefit for their child. Her application was refused by the competent authority, because the appropriate state guidelines provide for the payment of the benefit only to citizens of the EU Member States.

62

According to the above allegation, the ECHR provides little protection other than for the classical economic fundamental rights. In particular, it does not contain any **rights to state benefits** (→ see § 2 para 15). These are instead contained in the European Social Charter (ESC)[133] passed by the Council of Europe as a counterpart to the ECHR concerning social rights,[134] but in a structurally reduced variation.[135] The rights contained in the Social Charter, such as the right to work (Article 1 ESC), right to a fair remuneration (Article 4 ESC), right to social security (Article 12 ESC) and right to social security (Article 13 ESC) or the right to form associations (Article 5 ESC) and the right to strike (Article 6 IV ESC) are merely detailed as stipulations which must be transposed into national law by the contracting states.

63

This follows from Part III of the annex to the ESC[136]. According to this, the Charter contains "legal obligations of an international character, the application of which is submitted solely to the supervision provided for in Part IV". The conditions laid down in Article 21 to 29 of the ESC provide however – other than the ECHR – for neither regulatory nor judicial controls within the individual contracting states, but merely a procedure for reporting, examination and recommendation at an intergovernmental level. The establishment of a European Social Security Court of Justice inspired by the Parliamentary Assembly of the Council of Europe, or of a chamber of the ECtHR responsible for the supervision of the compliance with the rules contained in the ESC, has not been realised in the recent revision of the ESC.[137] According to prevailing opinion, **no individual rights** can be derived directly from the provisions of the ESC.[138]

64

---

131 Laule [1996] EuGRZ 357, 362; Peukert (note 12) Art 5 EMRK, paras 7 ff; see → § 2 para 13, § 3 para 3.
132 On that particularly see Melchior in: MacDonald/Matscher/Petzold (eds) *The European System for the Protection of Human Rights* (Dordrecht/Boston/London 1993) pp 593, 599 ff.
133 See *Bundesgesetzblatt* (BGBl – German Official Federal Gazette) II 1964, 1262.
134 Hailbronner [1997] JZ 397, 398.
135 On ESC generally see Agnelli/Berenstein and others *Die Europäische Sozialcharta – Wege zu einer europäischen Sozialordnung* (Baden-Baden 1978). On the criticism by the labour unions on the judicial weakness of the ESC see Gabaglio/Fonteneau/Lörcher [1997] ArbuR 345 ff.
136 The appendix is – according to Art 38 ESC – a binding part of the Charter itself.
137 On this and the modifications effected by the "European Social Charter (revised)", which entered into force on 1.7.1999, but has not yet been ratified by Germany, see Dötsch [2001] AuA 27.
138 See *Bundesverwaltungsgericht* (BVerwG – German Federal Admininistrative Court) (1983) 65 BVerwGE, 188, 196; (1983) 66 BVerwGE 268, 274; *Bundesarbeitsgericht* (BAG – German

65 Due not only to the weaknesses in the area of legal enforcement, but also to reasons relating to content, the rights provided by the ESC are considered to be, at least in part, severely restricted. The ESC detailed "primary, fundamental (pre-existing) minimum standards for legal institutions of social security" and, in contrast to the social security law of the EC, is not aimed at changing the law of the Member States.[139] Whether this position can be maintained in view of the wide-ranging obligatory provisions of the ESC and the reservations which even contracting states like the Federal Republic of Germany have,[140] is indeed doubtful.[141]

Case 8 – Answer:

66 T is not entitled to be paid state child benefit. In particular there is no such claim under Article 16 of the ESC. It is true that the contractual states are obliged to promote the economic, legal and social protection of family life, especially through social and family benefits. The regulation, however, does not establish an individually enforceable claim for a particular type of assistance because of the mere international law character of the ESC. Although both Turkey and Germany are contacting states of the ESC and have recognized the relevant obligations as binding, there is no obligation on the state authorities, not even in conjunction with the equal treatment principle according to Article 3(1) of the German Basic Law, to amend the regulations so that child benefit (which is provided by the various states on a voluntary legal basis) is also payable to Turkish citizens.[142]

Federal Labour Court) [1985] JZ 445, for a dissenting view see Konzen [1986] JZ 157; *Verwaltungsgerichtshof* (VGH – Higher Administrative Court) Mannheim [2000] DÖV 874; Wengler *Die Unanwendbarkeit der Europäischen Sozialcharta im Staat* (Bad Homburg 1969) pp 11 ff; Pischel *Die Bedeutung der europäischen Sozialcharta für das Recht in der Bundesrepublik Deutschland* (Würzburg 1966); Harris (ed) *The European Social Charter* (New York 1984) p 290; Zuleeg (1975) 35 ZaöRV 341, 352. For the tentative attempt to justify a differing point of view see Lörcher [1991] EuZW 395.

139 Eichenhofer in: Oetker/Preis (eds) *Europäisches Arbeits- und Sozialrecht*, B 1200 (Heidelberg 1995) para 4.

140 The German Federal Republic has made use of the option in Art 20 ESC of an only limited ratification of the Charter and has not consented to Art 4(4) (right to a reasonable period of notice for termination of employment), Art 7(1) (minimum age of employment 15 years), Art 8(2) (ban on giving a woman notice of dismissal during maternity leave) and Art 8(4),(5) (special rules on night work and dangerous work for female employees) as well as Art 10(4) (financial support for retraining and reintegration of the unemployed); see Art 1 of the transposition of the ESC: *Bundesgesetzblatt* (BGBl – German Official Federal Gazette) II 1964, 1262.

141 For a more positive – yet also older – evaluation of the "practical consequences of the European Social Charter" see Fuchs in: Agnelli/Berenstein and others (eds) *Die Europäische Sozialcharta – Wege zu einer europäischen Sozialordnung* (Baden-Baden 1978) pp 289 ff, with further references.

142 See BVerwG (1993) 91 BVerwGE 327, 330 with further references; in contrast from the court of lower instance: VGH Mannheim [1993] NVwZ-RR 83.

§ 6
Fundamental Judicial and Procedural Rights

Christoph Grabenwarter

Leading cases: ECtHR *Deumeland* (1986) 8 EHRR 448; *Amuur* (1996) 22 EHRR 533; *Streletz, Kessler and Krenz* (2001) 33 EHRR 31; *Fischer* App No 37950/97.[1]

Further reading: Frowein in: Mahoney (ed) *Protection des droits de l'homme: la perspective européenne* (Cologne et al 2000) p 545; Grabenwarter *Verfahrensgarantien in der Verwaltungsgerichtsbarkeit* (Vienna 1997); Murdoch (1993) 42 ICLQ 494; Trechsel in: Macdonald/Matscher/Petzold (eds) *The European System for the Protection of Human Rights* (Dordrecht et al 1993) p 277.

The following chapter deals with those guarantees of the ECHR that contain **procedural rights** in a wider sense. Compared to the fundamental rights of the *Grundgesetz* (German Basic Law), the ECHR includes a far larger number of fundamental procedural rights. They are – influenced by Anglo-American law – both more detailed in their wording and more extensive in their use within jurisprudence than the classic civil rights and freedoms. It is therefore not surprising that the respective constitutional orders of numerous Member States have been significantly influenced by the ECHR especially in this field.[2] Not coincidentally, the *Bundesverfassungsgericht* (BVerfG – German Federal Constitutional Court) defined the importance of the ECHR within German law when discussing the presumption of innocence, which is explicitly embodied in the ECHR, but not in the Basic Law.[3]

The term of fundamental judicial and procedural rights summarises in fact different legal law positions that however share a common point of reference: the principle of effective legal protection as an expression of a European constitutional law principle of legality.[4]

I. The Protection of Liberty (Article 5 ECHR)

Lead by the structure of regulation used in the Basic Law, the content of Article 5 of the ECHR can be divided into three parts. Article 5(1)(i) of the ECHR contains the general guarantee of individual liberty (comparable to Article 2(2)(ii) of the Basic Law), the second sentence of paragraph 1 includes the conditions governing the legality of certain acts of interference (comparable to Article 104(1) of the Basic Law), while finally Article 5(2) to (5) of the ECHR comprises particular procedural guarantees related to deprivations of liberty (comparable to Article 104(2) and (3) of the Basic Law). In Article II-66, the Treaty establishing a Constitution for Europe (Draft Constitution – DC) recognises the right to liberty and security.[5]

---

1 Current judgements of the European Court of Human Rights can be retrieved from the internet under http://www.echr.coe.int/.
2 For example *cf* Grabenwarter in: Cremer (ed) *Tradition und Weltoffenheit des Rechts* (Berlin 2002) pp 1129–1131.
3 BVerfG (1987) 74 BVerfGE 358, 370; (1991) 82 BVerfGE 106, 115.
4 Grabenwarter *Verfahrensgarantien in der Verwaltungsgerichtsbarkeit* (Vienna 1997) pp 696 ff.
5 Concerning the extent of guarantee *cf* Grabenwarter [2001] DVBl 1, 4.

Case 1 – Problem: (ECtHR *Amuur* (1996) 22 EHRR 533)
On 9 March 1992, Somali citizens arrive from Syria at the airport Paris-Orly. Because their passports are forged, they are denied entry into French territory. A return to Syria is not possible. The Somalis apply for asylum and are held in a part of a hotel near the airport which is used as a "transit lounge". Their application is unsuccessful. On 29 March 1992, after diplomatic negotiations, they are sent back to Syria, which is not a member of the Convention relating to the Status of Refugees. There was no legal basis for the holding of asylum applicants at the hotel. The refugees assert that their detention in the transit zone therefore constituted a violation of their right of personal freedom in accordance with Article 5(1) of the ECHR. Is this assertion justified?

1. The Right to Liberty and Security

The **scope of protection** of Article 5 of the ECHR comprises – apart from the prohibition of arbitrary arrest and deprivation of liberty (subsection 1)[6] – the guarantee of a judicial control of deprivation of liberty. Article 5 of the ECHR is also applicable to short-term deprivation of liberty.[7] When judging whether a deprivation of liberty in the sense of Article 5 of the ECHR exists, the concrete situation of the individuals affected must be taken into account.[8]

Although the terms "liberty and security" are listed separately in Article 5(1) of the ECHR, the right to security has only gained minor significance of its own.[9] The right to security can provide a certain extent of protection against state-interventions outside the sovereign territory of a Member State, but does not oblige the Member States of the Convention to grant individuals whose security is endangered within their country of origin a right of entry or non-expulsion or a general right of asylum. With regard to the scope of protection of Article 5 of the ECHR, there are difficulties to delimit it from the guarantee of freedom of movement of Article 2 of the 4th Prot ECHR, which protects the freedom of movement, the choice of residence and the right to leave the country. According to the jurisprudence of the ECtHR, the concrete circumstances of the individual cases as they result from the respective restriction, especially its type, duration and effects, are to be considered.[10] Furthermore, the scope of protection of Article 5(1) of the ECHR does not

---

6 ECtHR *Amuur* (1996) 22 EHRR 533, para 42; *Winterwerp* (1979–80) 2 EHRR 387, para 37; *Lawless (No 3)* (1979–80) 1 EHHR 15, para 14; *Lukanov* (1997) 24 EHRR 121, para 41.
7 Villiger *Handbuch der Europäischen Menschenrechtskonvention* (Zürich 1999) pp 494 ff.
8 ECtHR *X v United Kingdom* (1983) 5 EHRR 192 (Just Satisfaction), para 41; *Guzzardi* (1981) 3 EHRR 333, para 92; *Engel* (1979–80) 1 EHRR 647, para 59.
9 Within the judgment ECtHR *Bozano* (1987) 9 EHRR 297, paras 54, 60, the "right of security" is mentioned without further consequences; van Dijk/van Hoof *Theory and Practice of the European Convention on Human Rights* (3rd ed, The Hague et al 1998) pp 344–345; Kopetzki in: Machacek/Pahr/Stadler (eds) *Grund- und Menschenrechte in Österreich* (Volume III, Kehl am Rhein 1997) pp 261, 290; Trechsel [1980] EuGRZ 514, 518; Trechsel in: Macdonald/Matscher/Petzold (eds) *The European System for the Protection of Human Rights* (Dordrecht et al 1993) pp 282–283. In the judgment ECtHR *Öcalan* (2003) 37 EHRR 238, para 88, the ECtHR considered the right to security to be affected if an arrest by the institutions of a Member State of the Convention occurred within the territory of another state.
10 ECtHR *Amuur* (1996) 22 EHRR 533, para 42; *Guzzardi* (1981) 3 EHRR 333, para 92; *Engel* (1979–80) 1 EHRR 647, para 58.

cover the conditions of detention.[11] Legal questions raised in this context are to be examined first and foremost according to Article 3 of the ECHR.[12]

2. Types of Interference

An interference with Article 5(1) of the ECHR occurs in **any case of deprivation of liberty** by a state organ, while an exhaustive list of permissible restrictions of personal freedom is included in Article 5(1)(a–f) of the ECHR. These exemptions must be interpreted strictly.[13] The control of the conditions under which restrictions are permissible is primarily carried out by the national courts. The ECtHR only examines the respective individual case, but not the applicable national law on which it is based. As an exception, however, the ECHR itself – as for example in Article 5(1) of the ECHR – refers to national law.[14]

To be justified, an interference must rely on a **legal basis**, take place in compliance with the procedural rules of national law and be justified in a substantive sense, which means that it must comply with one of the exemptions listed in Article 5(1)(a–f) of the ECHR. The national written and unwritten law must be sufficiently precise to allow the citizen – if need be, with legal advice – to foresee the consequences which a given action may entail.[15] Settled case-law regarding the interpretation of procedural rules fulfils the requirement of a legal base.[16] Concerning the compliance with national procedural law, the ECtHR requires both that the national law generally agrees with the ECHR and was also obeyed in the individual case.[17] The substantive lawfulness of detention is – as mentioned above – governed by Article 5(1)(a–f) of the ECHR.

a) Conviction

Convictions subject to Article 5(1)(a) of the ECHR include criminal or disciplinary offences and a finding of guilt.[18] The "court" defined by Article 5(1)(a) of the ECHR must be independent from the executive.[19] It is decisive that the detention follows the conviction, not only in terms of time but also of a sufficient causal connection between conviction and deprivation of liberty,[20] while in this context, "detention" describes the period from the first instance conviction on – even before the judgement comes into force.[21] Ar-

---

11 ECtHR *Vittorio* App No 44955/98, para 16; on that → § 3 paras 37 ff.
12 With regard to the problem of arrest conditions for mentally ill and drug addicted individuals *cf* para 16.
13 ECtHR *Lukanov* (1997) 24 EHRR 121, para 41; *Quinn* (1996) 21 EHRR 529, para 42; *Ciulla* (1991) 13 EHRR 346, para 41; *Bouamar* (1989) 11 EHRR 1, para 43.
14 ECtHR *Winterwerp* (1979–80) 2 EHRR 387, para 46; always differing *cf Ringeisen* (1979–80) 1 EHRR 455, para 97.
15 ECtHR *Steel* (1999) 28 EHRR 603, para 54.
16 ECtHR *Laumont* (2003) 36 EHRR 625, para 51.
17 ECtHR *Kemmache (No 3)* (1995) 19 EHRR 349, para 37.
18 ECtHR *B v Austria* (1991) 13 EHRR 20, para 38; Villiger (note 7) para 330; Kopetzki (note 9) p 323; Trechsel (note 9) p 297; Trechsel [1980] EuGRZ 514, 518, 523 ff.
19 ECtHR *Engel* (1979–80) 1 EHRR 647, para 68.
20 ECtHR *B v Austria* (1991) 13 EHRR 20, para 38; *Monnell* (1988) 10 EHRR 205, para 40; *Weeks* (1988) 10 EHRR 293, para 42; *Bozano* (1987) 9 EHRR 297, para 53.
21 ECtHR *B v Austria* (1991) 13 EHRR 20, para 36; *Wemhoff* (1979–80) 1 EHRR 55, para 9; *differing opinion* Reindl in: Grabenwarter (ed) *Kontinuität und Wandel der EMRK* (Kehl am Rhein

ticle 5(1)(a) of the ECHR cannot be construed to grant a right of suspension of the detention, *eg* in the case of a life sentence.[22]

b) Non-compliance with the Orders of a Court or to Secure the Fulfilment of a Legal Obligation

10   If the **reason for detention** is "non-compliance with the lawful order of a court or ... any obligation prescribed by law" pursuant to Article 5(1)(b) of the ECHR, the term "court" corresponds with that used in Article 5(1)(a).[23] The conduct of an administrative body can also amount to an "order of a court" in this regard.[24] While detention due to non-compliance with the orders of a court has a repressive character,[25] detention due to non-fulfilment of an obligation prescribed by law (*eg* duty to carry a passport[26]) does not have a punitive character, because the reason for detention ceases to exist as soon as the affected individual fulfils the obligation.[27] To avoid a too extensive interpretation of Article 5(1)(b) of the ECHR, the jurisprudence prescribes that deprivation of liberty subject to Article 5(1)(b) of the ECHR shall be lawful only in cases where the law permits the detention of a person to compel him to fulfil a specific and concrete obligation which he has until then failed to satisfy.[28]

c) Preventive Custody and Detention on Remand

11   **Preventive custody and detention on remand** according to Article 5(1)(c) of the ECHR serves the protection of criminal investigation and never occurs outside a criminal context.[29] Detention on remand lasts from the arrest until the first instance court judgement.[30] It is its purpose to bring the affected individual before the competent legal authority.[31] The term "legal authority" corresponds with that of the "judge" or "judicial officer" pursuant to Article 5(3) of the ECHR. The ECHR demands only that the arrested person is immediately brought before a judge (Article 5(3) of the ECHR), not, however, that detention on remand itself must be ordered by a court.[32] The content of the offence is determined by national law.[33]

1998) pp 45, 48: until the first instance judgment enters into legal force, the arrest is considered to be detention on remand in the sense of Art 5 I lit c ECHR.
22 Villiger (note 7) paras 332 ff; Concerning the legality of re-established imprisonment of individuals who are given a life-long prison sentence, also *cf* ECtHR *Weeks* (1988) 10 EHRR 293, paras 42, 50 ff; *Stafford* (2002) 35 EHRR 1121, para 81.
23 *Cf* (para 8).
24 Peukert in: Frowein/Peukert (eds) *Europäische Menschenrechtskonvention* (2nd ed, Kehl am Rhein et al 1996) Art 5 EMRK, para 67.
25 Peukert (note 24) Art 5 EMRK, para 64.
26 EurCommHR DR 52, 111, 118.
27 EurCommHR DR 25, 15, 81; Kopetzki (note 9) p 330.
28 ECtHR *Engel* (1979–80) 1 EHRR 647, para 69.
29 ECtHR *Ciulla* (1991) 13 EHRR 346, para 38.
30 *Cf* Meyer-Ladewig *Konvention zum Schutz der Menschenrechte und Grundfreiheiten* (Baden-Baden 2006) Art 5, para 12; *differing opinion* Reindl (note 21) pp 46 ff.
31 ECtHR *Murray* (1995) 19 EHRR 193, para 68; *Ireland v United Kingdom* (1979–80) 2 EHRR 25, para 199; *Lawless (No 3)* (1979–80) 1 EHRR 15, paras 13–14.
32 ECtHR DR 9, 210, 212.
33 Peukert (note 24) Art 5 EMRK, para 72, on the question of whether this includes mere misdemeanours and administrative offences ("Ordnungsunrecht").

As cumulative **conditions** for the lawfulness of the detention, Article 5(1)(c) of the ECHR lists the purpose of bringing the arrested person before court as well as the suspicion or risk that he might commit an offence or flee after having done so. If one of these conditions is not met, Article 5(1)(c) of the ECHR is violated.[34]

12

The central requirement for detention on remand is a *reasonable suspicion* of having committed an offence.[35] When the arrest first takes place, this suspicion alone is a sufficient reason for detention; however, if detention on remand is to endure,[36] it must meet the further conditions set out in Article 5(3) of the ECHR.[37] Should the national law provide a higher threshold, that more demanding provision is deciding.[38] This results in the fact that – besides the reasonable suspicion and the danger of flight expressly mentioned in Article 5(1)(c) of the ECHR – other typical grounds for detention, like danger of collusion or danger of recurrence, also become relevant in Convention law, provided that they are sufficient grounds for detention on remand according to national law.[39] The existence of a reasonable suspicion shall be presumed if satisfactory evidence exists objectively indicating that the affected individual could have committed the offence.[40] It is not required that the investigation of the facts of the case has already been completed. The examination of those conditions by the ECtHR is limited to the control whether the available evidence would have satisfied an objective observer that the person concerned may have committed an offence.[41]

13

Furthermore, the **arrest** of a person effected for the purpose of bringing him before the competent legal authority is lawful if it is necessary to prevent the affected person from committing an offence. Article 5(1)(c) of the ECHR does not necessarily require that a danger of recurrence exists; a mere *risk of execution* is sufficient. In this case, the existence of concrete reasons indicating the imminent execution of a specific offence is a precondition for detention.[42]

14

Finally, also the *risk of flight* after the execution of an offence constitutes a lawful ground for arrest. Since, however, Article 5(1)(c) of the ECHR also permits detention in case of reasonable suspicion without further grounds for arrest, this alternative is applied only where the legality of the continuance of detention on remand is concerned.[43]

15

---

34 *Cf* ECtHR *Murray* (1995) 19 EHRR 193, para 55; *Fox* (1991) 13 EHRR 157, para 32; *Guzzardi* (1981) 3 EHRR 333, para 102.
35 For details *cf* Grabenwarter *Europäische Menschenrechtskonvention* (3rd ed, Munich 2007) § 21, para 8.
36 ECtHR *Stögmüller* (1979 80) 1 EHRR 155, para 4; *De Jong* (1986) 8 EHRR 20, para 44.
37 *Cf* paras 21 ff.
38 Villiger (note 7) para 346.
39 ECtHR *Kemmache (No 3)* (1995) 19 EHRR 349, para 42; EurCommHR DR 34, 119, 124.
40 Concerning the special case of fight against terrorism: *Cf* ECtHR *Fox* (1991) 13 EHRR 157, para 32; *Murray* (1995) 19 EHRR 193, paras 50–51; *O'Hara* (2002) 34 EHRR 812, para 34.
41 ECtHR *Erdagöz* (2001) 32 EHRR 443, paras 51–52; *Fox* (1991) 13 EHRR 157, para 34; EurCommHR DR 88-B, 94, 113; DR 16, 111, 118; DR 54, 35, 38; Peukert (note 24) Art 5 EMRK, paras 75 ff.
42 ECtHR *Guzzardi* (1981) 3 EHRR 333, paras 102–103.
43 For more details *cf* Reindl *Untersuchungshaft und Menschenrechtskonvention* (Vienna 1997) pp 65 ff.

d) Detention of Minors

16 The detention of **minors** (lit d) includes measures taken by welfare services and the juvenile court,[44] so that an interim custody measure lasting to the decision on possible disciplinary measures is permissible as well.[45] A parental decision in favour of a psychiatrical children's hospital however does not fall within the scope of application of Article 5 of the ECHR.[46] A deprivation of liberty pursuant to lit d can also be ordered by an administrative authority.[47]

e) Detention of Invalid and Vagrants

17 Concerning the accommodation of **invalid people or vagrants** in accordance with Article 5(1)(e) of the ECHR, the margin of discretion rests first and foremost with the national authorities,[48] as Article 5(1)(e) of the ECHR itself includes no substantive limitations. Article 5(1)(e) of the ECHR permits the apprehension in case of infectious diseases, which have to be asserted by an objective medical expertise,[49] alcohol or drug addiction as well as mental illness.

18 The *dangerousness* of the affected person which justifies the detention can be directed towards the general public or the arrested individual himself.[50] The spreading of an infectious disease can constitute such a danger.[51]

19 Article 5(1) of the ECHR also demands the existence of a proportionate correlation between the grounds for a justified deprivation of liberty and the conditions of detention.[52] Consequently, Article 5(1)(e) of the ECHR may also impose the indirect obligation to provide a sufficient number of places in such institutions on the Member States.[53]

f) Prevention of Unauthorised Entry into National Territory, Detention with a view to Deportation or Extradition

20 Article 5(1)(f) of the ECHR provides **three grounds for detention**: On the one hand, the prevention of unauthorised entry into national territory, on the other hand, imminent deportation or extradition. The legitimacy of this kind of detention requires, apart from the compliance with procedural and substantive provisions, the observance of the overall aim of Article 5 of the ECHR.[54] The measure must comply with national as well as inter-

---

44 ECtHR *Bouamar* (1989) 11 EHRR 1, paras, 50, 52.
45 ECtHR *Bouamar* (1989) 11 EHRR 1, para 50.
46 ECtHR *Nielsen* (1989) 11 EHRR 175, para 72.
47 Villiger (note 7) para 335.
48 ECtHR *Herczegfalvy* (1993) 15 EHRR 437, para 63; *Luberti* (1984) 6 EHRR 440, para 27; *X v United Kingdom* (1982) 4 EHRR 188, para 43; *Winterwerp* (1979–80) 2 EHRR 387, para 40.
49 ECtHR *Ashingdane* (1985) 7 EHRR 528, para 37; *X v United Kingdom* (1982) 4 EHRR 188, para 40; *Winterwerp* (1979–80) 2 EHRR 387, para 39.
50 ECtHR *Guzzardi* (1981) 3 EHRR 333, para 98.
51 Kopetzki (note 9) p 333.
52 ECtHR *Reid* (2003) 37 EHRR 211, para 48.
53 ECtHR *Brand* App No 49902/99, paras 65–66; *Morsink* App No 48865/99, paras 48–49. In elder precedents, *Bizzotto* App No 22126/93, paras 32 ff, the ECHR had refused to state a violation of Art 5 I ECHR, for according to its former opinion, an illegitimate detention of drug addicted offenders does not alter the lawfulness of the arrest itself. *Cf* Grabenwarter (note 35) § 21, para 12.
54 ECtHR *Chahal* (1997) 23 EHRR 413, para 129.

national law.[55] To avoid a falsification of the ground for detention, an apprehension in cases of deportation or extradition may be conducted for this purpose only.[56] Unlike Article 5(1)(c) of the ECHR, Article 5(1)(f) of the ECHR merely requires that pending proceedings of extradition or deportation exist. It is irrelevant for Article 5 of the ECHR if the extradition in itself is lawful.[57] However, the ECtHR must also observe further requirements provided by national law.[58]

Case 1 – Answer:
As the asylum seekers are refused entry into France and a return to Syria is impossible before diplomatic negotiations between France and Syria have been completed – which means that it is only theoretically possible – their detention constitutes a restriction of liberty which is equivalent to a deprivation of liberty. Moreover Syria did not ratify the Geneva Convention. Thus the refugees lacked guarantees comparable to those in France. The scope of protection of Article 5(1) of the ECHR is affected; the detention represents an interference with the fundamental right. Since there is no sufficient legal basis for the measure, Article 5(1) of the ECHR was violated.[59]

21

3. Rights Guaranteed to Individuals Deprived of their Liberty

a) Right to Information

Pursuant to Article 5(2) of the ECHR everyone who is arrested shall be informed promptly, in a language which he understands, of the reasons of his arrest. According to the wording, the state's **duty to inform** only applies to the "arrest". However, this guarantee applies for any kind of deprivation of liberty provided in Article 5(1) of the ECHR.[60]

22

Form and scope of the right to information depend on the individual circumstances. In any case, information must be given in a language understandable for the arrested person and has to explain the factual and legal reasons for the arrest.[61] The information shall afford the arrested person the opportunity to gain effective legal protection pursuant to Article 5(4) of the ECHR. The arrested person must be informed "promptly"[62] which should usually not extend the term of 24 hours, while the individual circumstances must be taken into account.[63]

23

---

55 EurCommHR DR 12, 14, 27.
56 ECtHR *Chahal* (1997) 23 EHRR 413, para 112.
57 The legitimacy of the proceedings of deportation or extradition is governed by Art 1, Prot 7 ECHR, *cf* para 64.
58 ECtHR *Slivenko* (2004) 39 EHRR 490 (Grand Chamber), para 151.
59 ECtHR *Amuur* (1996) 22 EHRR 533, paras 48, 53; the ECtHR further emphasizes that the conditions for the refugees' stay were no subject of judicial control and that the individuals were had no access to legal, humanitarian, or social care; *cf* Kriebaum in: Grabenwarter (ed) *Kontinuität und Wandel der EMRK* (Kehl am Rhein 1998) pp 71 ff.
60 ECtHR *Van der Leer* (1990) 12 EHRR 567, paras 27–28; *X v United Kingdom* (1982) 4 EHRR 188, para 66; EurCommHR DR 16, 111, 117; DR 34, 119, 124; differing in: ECtHR *Keus* (1991) 13 EHRR 700, para 22.
61 ECtHR *Fox* (1991) 13 EHRR 157, para 40; *Van der Leer* (1990) 12 EHRR 567, para 27–28; *X v United Kingdom* (1982) 4 EHRR 188, para 66; EurCommHR DR 16, 111, 117.
62 ECtHR *Fox* (1991) 13 EHRR 157, para 40.
63 Villiger (note 7) para 351; ECtHR *Murray* (1995) 19 EHRR 193, para 78 (3 hours); *Van der Leer* (1990) 12 EHRR 567, para 31 (accidental noticing of reasons for arrest is not sufficient); *Fox* (1991) 13 EHRR 157, para 42 (7 hours); EurCommHR DR 21, 250, 253–254; DR 30, 93, 95.

b) Reasonable Duration of Arrest and Bringing Before a Judge or other Officer pursuant to Article 5(3) of the ECHR

24 Article 5(3) of the ECHR complements Article 5(1)(c) of the ECHR which governs the detention on remand and includes two **guarantees**: the bringing before judge and – in case of continuation of the interim custody – the execution of expeditious proceedings combined with a rapid attainment of a judgment.

The arrested person shall be brought before a judge or a judicial officer. The states can declare either a court or an administrative authority to be competent.[64] It is, however, required that the judge or judicial officer is independent from the executive[65] and has to be entitled to issue definite, binding decisions.[66] The ECtHR demands that the authority exercises "special diligence" during the proceedings when determining the reasons for arrest.[67]

25 The **bringing before a judge or** judicial officer has been effected "immediately" if a period of 24 to 48 hours[68] – in some cases up to four days[69] – is not exceeded.

26 The lawful duration of detention on demand depends on the facts of the individual case; it could be extended for suspects of terrorist offences.[70] A period of six days without a judicial review has however been regarded as being to long.[71] Assessing the issue if an arrest lasted for a "reasonable period" is first and foremost part of the national courts' jurisdiction.[72] It must be assessed in each case according to its special features whether public interest outweighs the rule of respect for individual liberty.[73]

27 At first, the persistence of reasonable suspicion that the person arrested has committed an offence is a condition *sine qua non* for the lawfulness of the continued detention,[74] but after a certain lapse of time it no longer suffices. It then becomes necessary to review whether other grounds, such as seriousness of the offence, disturbance of the public order, danger of flight, danger of collusion, danger of recurrence, or securing the proper con-

---

64 ECtHR *Schiesser* (1979–80) 2 EHRR 417, para 27.
65 ECtHR *Schiesser* (1979–80) 2 EHRR 417, para 31.
66 ECtHR *Yankov* (2005) 40 EHRR 854, para 166; *Nikolova* (2001) 31 EHRR 64, para 51.
67 ECtHR *Belchev* App No 39270/98, para 74; *J.G. v Poland* App No 36258/97, para 51; *Labita* App No 26772/95, paras 152–153.
68 *Cf* Villiger (note 7) para 358.
69 ECtHR *Brogan* (1989) 11 EHRR 117, para 62.
70 ECtHR *Brogan* (1989) 11 EHRR 117, para 61.
71 ECtHR *O'Hara* (2002) 34 EHRR 812, para 46 (6 days); *Aksoy* (1997) 23 EHRR 533, para 78 (14 days); *Demir* (2001) 33 EHRR 1056, para 40 (16 and 23 days); *Sakik* (1998) 26 EHRR 662, para 45 (12 and 14 days).
72 ECtHR *Van der Tang* (1996) 22 EHRR 363, para 55; *Yağci* (1995) 20 EHRR 505, para 50; *Mansur* (1995) 20 EHRR 535, para 52; *Tomasi* (1993) 15 EHRR 1, para 84; *Toth* (1992) 14 EHRR 551, para 67; *Kemmache (No 1 and 2)* (1992) 14 EHRR 520, para 45; *Letellier* (1992) 14 EHRR 83, para 35; *Neumeister* (1979–80) 1 EHRR 91, para 5; *Wemhoff* (1979–80) 1 EHRR 55, para 12; with regard to the existing difference to Art 6 ECHR: ECtHR *Stögmüller* (1979–80) 1 EHRR 155, para 5.
73 ECtHR *Ilowiecki* (2003) 37 EHRR 546, para 58; *Scott* (1997) 24 EHRR 391, para 74; *Van der Tang* (1996) 22 EHRR 363, para 55; *W v Switzerland* (1994) 17 EHRR 60, para 30; *cf* ECtHR *Wemhoff* (1979–80) 1 EHRR 55, para 10.
74 ECtHR *Ilowiecki* (2003) 37 EHRR 546, para 59; *B v Austria* (1991) 13 EHRR 20, para 42; *Stögmüller* (1979–80) 1 EHRR 155, para 4.

duct of proceedings, exist.[75] Provided that sufficient grounds for a continuation of detention exist, the ECtHR reviews as a second step whether the national authorities carried out the proceedings with the required diligence[76], in particular whether they made rapid progresses with the investigations and did not delay the proceedings for reasons relating to inner-authority difficulties.[77]

c) Right to Judicial Review of Remand in Detention Pursuant to Article 5(4) of the ECHR

The right of *judicial review of remand in detention* guaranteed in Article 5(4) of the ECHR reflects the Anglo-Saxon "**Habeas-Corpus-doctrine**". The guarantee of Article 5(4) of the ECHR is applicable to all forms of detention that Article 5(1) of the ECHR provides. The review of the arrest's lawfulness is measured by the standards of both domestic and international law.[78] **28**

A review of remand in detention must be requested.[79] A right to judicial review always exists where an administrative body has ordered the apprehension.[80] If, however, a court has ordered the arrest, one must differentiate between detention following a conviction and pre-trial detention. The review of detention ordered by Article 5(4) of the ECHR is in principle always incorporated in the sentence of the competent court.[81] In case the detention continues, a right to review of detention only exists if new, recent circumstances could retroactively challenge the detention's lawfulness.[82] **29**

A review of remand in detention shall be conducted "at reasonable intervals".[83] The reviewing body has to possess judicial character.[84] Apart from acting in an advisory capacity, it also has to be entitled to issue definite decisions. During proceedings of review, not all procedural guarantees subject to Article 6 of the ECHR have to be fulfilled. Yet fundamental guarantees like the principle of equality of arms[85] are to be ensured. In detail, the **30**

---

75 ECtHR *G.K. v Poland* App No 38816/97, para 84; *Muller* App No 21802/93, para 35; *Van der Tang* (1996) 22 EHRR 363, para 55; *W v Switzerland* (1994) 17 EHRR 60, para 30; *Tomasi* (1993) 15 EHRR 1, para 84; *Clooth* (1992) 14 EHRR 717, para 36; *Toth* (1992) 14 EHRR 551, para 67; *Kemmache (No 1 and 2)* (1992) 14 EHRR 520, para 45; *Letellier* (1992) 14 EHRR 83, para 35; *G.K. v Poland* App No 38816/97, para 84.
76 ECtHR *Zannouti* App No 42211/98, para 46; *Kreps* App No 34097/96, paras 42 ff.
77 ECtHR *Matwiejczuk* App No 37641/97, para 85; *Toth* (1992) 14 EHRR 551, para 76–77.
78 ECtHR *Chahal* (1997) 23 EHRR 413, para 127; *Weeks* (1988) 10 EHRR 293, para 57.
79 ECtHR *De Wilde* (1979–80) 1 EHRR 373, para 82–83; *Bouamar* (1989) 11 EHRR 1, para 55, Villiger (note 7) para 366.
80 ECtHR *Luberti* (1984) 6 EHRR 440, para 31; *Engel* (1979–80) 1 EHRR 647, para 77; *De Wilde* (1979–80) 1 EHRR 373, paras 76–77.
81 ECtHR *König* App No 39753/98, para 19; *Pérez* (1996) 22 EHRR 153, para 30.
82 ECtHR *Winterwerp* (1979–80) 2 EHRR 387, para 55; *Van Droogenbroeck* (1982) 4 EHRR 443, paras 45 ff; *Pérez* (1996) 22 EHRR 153, para 30; EurCommHR DR 40, 5, 26; Villiger (note 7) para 368.
83 ECtHR *Winterwerp* (1979–80) 2 EHRR 387, para 55; regarding this topic compare *Hirst* App No 40787/98, paras 37 ff.
84 ECtHR *Brannigan* (1994) 17 EHRR 539, para 58.
85 ECtHR *Hristov* App No 35436/97, para 118; *Schöps* App No 25116/94, para 44.

adjudication demands an oral hearing,[86] the right to legal assistance,[87] the giving of grounds for the detention as well as the right of extensive access to the file documents.[88]

d) Right to Compensation

31 Article 5(5) of the ECHR provides for a compensation payment for a detention contrary to the ECHR. The provision establishes direct claims for private individuals.[89] The prerequisites for a damage claim are that the affected person was arrested under violation of Article 5(1) to (4) and that the individual has consequently sustained a financial or non-pecuniary damage.[90] The applicability of Article 5(5) is not dependant on a domestic finding that the detention infringed the Convention.[91] According to settled case law of the ECtHR, Article 5(5) is violated if the person injured has an enforceable claim for compensation neither before nor after the finding of the breach of the Convention.[92] Concerning the calculation of the non-pecuniary damage, the principles of Article 41 of the ECHR apply.[93]

II. Fundamental Judicial Rights in Connection with Proceedings before Courts

1. The Right to a Fair Trial pursuant to Article 6(1) of the ECHR

32 Article 6(1) of the ECHR constitutes the **central part** of fundamental judicial rights within the ECHR. The guarantee of fair trial included therein can be divided into organisational and procedural guarantees. An element of the organisational guarantees is the right of access to a trial authority provided with certain minimal guarantees (b). The procedural guarantees contain – apart from the general guarantee of a fair trial including particular procedural rights applicable in criminal proceedings (c) – the rule of open court (d) as well as the rule of reasonable duration of proceedings (e). Article II-107 and Article II-108 of the DC also contain corresponding legal guarantees, yet do not possess the limitations which Article 6 of the ECHR features for its scope of protection.

a) Scope of Protection of Article 6(1) of the ECHR

33 Unlike in the case of any other fundamental right of the ECHR, the circumscription of the scope of protection has received considerable attention within jurisprudence and literature. Article 6(1) of the ECHR guarantees **fundamental procedural rights** for any pro-

---

86 ECtHR *G.K. v Poland* App No 38816/97, para 93–94; *Nikolova* (2001) 31 EHRR 64, para 58; *Winterwerp* (1979–80) 2 EHRR 387, para 60.
87 Peukert (note 24) Art 5 EMRK, para 143.
88 ECtHR *Garcia Alva* (2003) 37 EHRR 335, para 42; *Lietzow* App No 24479/94, para 47; *Schöps* App No 25 116/94, para 44. Concerning the same *cf* Kieschke/Osterwald [2002] NJW 2003.
89 Charrier *Code de la Convention européenne des Droits de l'Homme* (Paris 2000) Art 5, para 45.
90 ECtHR *Brogan* (1989) 11 EHRR 117, para 67; *Wassink* App No 12535/86, para 38; *Keus* (1991) 13 EHRR 700, para 29; *Tsirlis* (1998) 25 EHRR 198, paras 64 ff; EurCommHR DR 19, 213, 219; DR 42, 127, 131; DR 52, 236, 242; DR 77-A, 98, 107; DR 81-B, 130, 133.
91 ECtHR *Wynne (No 2)* (2004) 38 EHRR 864, para 31; *Thynne, Wilson and Gunnel* (1991) 13 EHRR 666, para 82.
92 ECtHR *Fox* (1991) 13 EHRR 157, para 46; *Brogan* (1989) 11 EHRR 117, para 67.
93 Villiger (note 7) para 374.

ceedings in which a decision either on civil rights or on the validity of a criminal charge is to be made.

The meaning of the term "**civil rights**" is defined on the basis of comparative law by a distinction between civil and public law referring to the content of law; in this context, the conventional continental formation of the concept is decisive. The term covers not only private-law disputes in the traditional sense, but certain proceedings under public law as well which affect contractual relations[94] or pecuniary rights[95] ("Jurisprudence of effect"). In proceedings on claims and contributions of social security, a consideration of private and public law aspects of the dispute has to be conducted ("Jurisprudence of consideration").[96] In order to determine the applicability to public servants, the nature of the public servant's duties and responsibilities – according to recent case law of the ECtHR – is decisive. If the public servant was entitled to exercise powers conferred by public law, the dispute is regularly not covered by this fundamental right.[97] Finally, also proceedings which concern assets or are based on alleged violations that affect assets are covered – notwithstanding administrative jurisdiction – by the scope of protection of Article 6 of the ECHR.[98] This includes the right which is subject to the specific procedure, not only its effect on assets.[99]

Excluded from the scope of protection are disputes deriving from the hard core of **public** law, including matters concerning nationality, asylum proceedings, proceedings settling the aliens' right of residence or right to vote as well as proceedings referring to revenue law which concern the extent of the obligation to pay taxes.[100]

In the end, also the delimitation of **criminal** disputes refers to the substance of a right, for the ECtHR chooses the national law as the starting point and allocates any criminal proceedings according to national law to the scope of protection. Furthermore, all proceedings for which an allocation to the fundamental right makes sense because of the *nature of contravention* as well as *form and seriousness of sanctions*, are covered by Article 6 of the ECHR, while only one of these three criteria has to exist.[101] It is decisive that the scope of application ratione materiae and personae of the offence is not restricted from the outset to specific groups of people. Regarding the legal consequences, preventive or repressive sanctions must be imminent. According to this criterion, for instance administrative and regulatory offence law is – unlike disciplinary law – covered by Article 6 of the ECHR.[102] Disciplinary law is covered by Article 6 of the ECHR only if the third criterion of a severe sanction is complied with. That is the case if the weight of all expected

---

94 ECtHR *König* (1979–80) 1 EHRR 170, para 90.
95 ECtHR *Editions Périscope* (1992) 14 EHRR 597, para 40.
96 ECtHR *Schouten* (1995) 19 EHRR 432, para 51; *Deumeland* (1986) 8 EHRR 448, paras 60 ff.
97 ECtHR *Pellegrin* (2001) 31 EHRR 651, paras 64 ff. Concerning the definition, the ECtHR refers temporarily to the exception of Art 39 IV TEC; with regard to this problem, *cf* Widmaier [2002] ZBR 244, 252 ff.
98 ECtHR *Paskhalidis et al* App No 20416/92, para 30; *Editions Périscope* (1992) 14 EHRR 597, para 40; *cf* Grabenwarter (note 4) pp 44 ff.
99 ECtHR *Bodén* (1988) 10 EHRR 36, para 32.
100 Taken from the jurisprudence of the ECtHR *Pierre-Bloch* (1998) 26 EHRR 202, paras 45 ff; *Maaouia* (2001) 33 EHRR 1037, paras 35 ff; *Ferrazzini* (2002) 34 EHRR 1068, para 29; as well as the proofs given in Grabenwarter (note 4) pp 49 ff.
101 For more details *cf* Grabenwarter (note 35) § 24, paras 12 ff.
102 ECtHR *Öztürk* (1984) 6 EHRR 409, paras 47 ff.

negative consequences which are at stake for the affected person is considerable.[103] In caselaw, this is presumed in cases of more than minor prison sentences as well as prison sentences for the failure to pay a fine.[104] Also the withdrawal of an occupational license as usually the most serious sanction of disciplinary law of the liberal professions justifies the applicability of Article 6 of the ECHR from a criminal law point of view.[105] Finally, the term "charge" is also subject to an autonomous interpretation according to the Convention, while the ECtHR presupposes that a "criminal charge" is existent at the moment the competent authority gives to the affected individual an official notification of an allegation that he has committed a criminal offence.[106]

b) Access to an Independent and Impartial Tribunal

37 The right of access to an independent and impartial tribunal established by law constitutes an **organisational guarantee**. By means of the requirement of a legal basis, ad hoc-interference by the executive in the judicial organisation shall be avoided; indirectly, it also serves judicial independence. This *requirement of a legal basis* covers the court's composition, its remaining organisation as well as its competency.[107] The *independence* of the court requires (in principal) the impossibility to discharge or transfer its members, their occupational freedom as well as a certain minimal term of office. The independence is – at the same time – a prerequisite for the court's impartiality.[108] A court is *impartial* only if the judge of the court in question is prejudiced neither in objective nor in subjective respects. A *subjective test* is geared to the personal relation between the particular judge and the proceeding's party; it is presumed as long as the contrary has not been proved. The affected individual can waive the court's impartiality.[109] If one of the court's members makes a racist remark during proceedings against an African immigrant, this can destroy the impartiality of the court in this respect.[110] An *objective test* abstracts from individuals and asks the abstract question if – according to the organisational and procedural rights and especially the extent and nature of measures taken by the judge before the proceedings – a prejudice has to be presumed.[111] Finally, the court must have *full jurisdiction* both on questions of facts and on questions of law.[112]

The access to a tribunal is not an absolute right, but is subject to **limitations** which are permitted as long as they pursue legitimate aims and if there is a reasonable relationship of proportionality between the means employed and the aim sought to be achieved. The limitations may not obstruct the access to a tribunal to such an extent that the very essence

---

103 ECtHR *Ezeh and Conners* (2004) 39 EHRR 1 (Grand Chamber), para 130.
104 ECtHR *Weber* (1990) 12 EHRR 508, paras 22, 34.
105 Grabenwarter (note 4) pp 100–101; *Austrian Constitutional Court* (11506/1987); the jurisprudence of the ECHR does not answer the question of whether bans from a profession represent sufficiently serious sanctions, but approves the applicability of Art 6 ECHR, as the imposition of a ban from a profession constitutes – according to the ECHR – a decision on a civil right; *eg* ECtHR *Diennet* App No 18160/91, para 28; *Le Compte et al* (1982) 4 EHRR 1, para 53.
106 ECtHR *Deweer* (1979–80) 2 EHRR 439, para 46.
107 For more details *cf* Grabenwarter (note 35) § 24, para 21.
108 Peukert (note 24) Art 6 EMRK, para 129.
109 For more details *cf* Grabenwarter (note 35) § 18, para 29–30.
110 ECtHR *Remli* (1996) 22 EHRR 253, paras 47–48.
111 ECtHR *De Cubber* (1985) 7 EHRR 236, para 26; *Morel* (2001) 33 EHRR 1118, para 45.
112 *Cf* ECtHR *Zumtobel* (1994) 17 EHRR 116, para 29.

of the right is impaired.[113] In other words, the right to access to a tribunal can be subject to limitations which – taking into account the aim pursued – comply with the principle of proportionality. With regard to the question of legitimate aim and the legal factors taken into consideration within the proportionality test, the case-law of the ECtHR provides several references. Beginning with the *Golder*-case, the settled case-law of the ECtHR states that the right of access to a tribunal calls for state regulation which may vary in time and place according to the needs and resources of the community and of individuals.[114]

By limiting the access to the court, various aims can be pursued that can differ according to the nature of limitation, the nature of the tribunal and the respective legal system. They may aim to protect against abusive and repeated actions[115], to avoid a multiplicity of claims and proceedings brought by individual shareholders in the context of a large-scale nationalisation measure,[116] or to protect the independence of reporting systems of organs controlling the management of certain joint-stock companies.[117] A further group of possible limitations is constituted by the requirements the national procedural law provides for the admissibility of actions or appeals, like time limits, mandatory representation by lawyer, provisions of form, approval of conducting a case,[118] securities for court costs or fees for lodging an action.[119] Furthermore, the grant of immunity according to international law[120] and parliamentary immunity can form an appropriate limitation of access to a tribunal.[121]

c) The Right to a Fair Trial

The right to a "fair hearing" expresses the principle of **fair trial**. It includes a multitude of partial guarantees focussing on a course of proceedings in which the parties can represent their point of view under basically equal conditions.[122] This right particularly demands that the affected individual can represent his legal position effectively.

First, **partial guarantees**, like the principle of equality of arms, the right of access to the file, the right to adversarial proceedings and the obligation to state reasons for a decision belong to the principle of a fair trial. Moreover, the rights of the defendant embodied both in Article 6(3) and (2) of the ECHR and developed by the case-law, *eg* the principle of *nemo tenetur*, are regarded as being an expression of the principle of fair hearing. In some cases, the Court is satisfied with the finding that the procedure in ques-

---

113 ECtHR *Ashingdane* (1985) 7 EHRR 528, para 57; *Lithgow* (1986) 8 EHRR 329, para 194; *Philis* (1991) 13 EHRR 741, para 59; Villiger (note 7) para 431.
114 ECtHR *Ashingdane* (1985) 7 EHRR 528, para 57; *Lithgow* (1986) 8 EHRR 329, para 194; *Philis* (1991) 13 EHRR 741, para 59; Villiger (note 7) para 431.
115 ECtHR *Ashingdane* (1985) 7 EHRR 528, para 58.
116 ECtHR *Lithgow* (1986) 8 EHRR 329, para 197.
117 ECtHR *Fayed* (1994) 18 EHRR 393, para 70.
118 ECtHR *Ashingdane* (1985) 7 EHRR 528, para 59.
119 ECtHR *Kreuz* App No 28249/95, paras 61 ff (Imposition of a fee for lodging an action to the amount of an average annual salary as an excessive impediment of the access to the court).
120 ECtHR *Waite* (2000) 30 EHRR 261, paras 59 ff.
121 *Cf* Matscher [1980] ÖZÖR 20–21.
122 Miehsler/Vogler in: Golsong/Karl (eds) *Internationaler Kommentar zur Europäischen Menschenrechtskonvention* (loose-leaf, Cologne et al) Art 6, para 341.

tion all in all does not meet the conditions of a fair hearing, although none of the partial guarantees is considered to be violated in particular.[123]

aa) The Principle of Equality of Arms

39 The principle of equality of arms is inherent in the principle of fair trial pursuant to Article 6(1) of the ECHR and at the same time constitutes a special expression of the principle of equality.[124] It demands that each party must be afforded a reasonable opportunity to present his case – including his evidence – under conditions that do not place him at a substantial disadvantage vis-à-vis his opponent.[125] This means that the opposing parties in principle have to be treated equally with regard to the procedural law. It is not important whether the opponent has actually exploited the advantage, but only whether such an advantage exists in the abstract and the party was able to exploit it.[126]

bb) Right to adversarial proceedings

40 A guarantee corresponding to Article 103(1) of the Basic Law is also derived from Article 6 of the ECHR. It is a condition for an effective conduct of judicial hearing that the parties have knowledge of the files' content and especially about the observations filed and the evidence adduced by the opposing party.[127] In this context and with respect to the principle of equality of arms, it is also important which possibilities the opponent was given to make observations in response. If one of the parties had advance knowledge of the other parties' arguments so that the first was able to make observations on them, then this will always amount to a violation of Article 6 of the ECHR.[128] Provided that the certain evidence is not disclosed to the defendant for the purpose of protecting conflicting interests, such as the safeguard of public interest or witness protection, the limitation of the defence's rights must be sufficiently counterbalanced by procedural guarantees in order to ensure that the accused has overall received a fair hearing.[129] The affected person also has to be enabled to challenge the authenticity and the use of evidence obtained by the breach of another right of the Convention at each stage of jurisdiction.[130] The right to receive a reasoned decision is connected to the right to be heard. The extent of the obligation to state reasons fundamentally depends on the concrete procedural situation and the respective legal system. Hence the extent of the obligation to state reasons depends on the respective national legal system.[131] From the point of view of the procedural situation, it is decisive what the litigants submitted within the proceedings, if it was a decision of the first or any higher instance, and finally, how precise the applied legal provisions are. In case of discretionary decisions, the obligation to state reasons is regularly more demanding.[132]

---

123 Similar in ECtHR *Van Kück* (2003) 37 EHRR 973, paras 55 ff, 62 ff.
124 *Cf* Grabenwarter (note 4) pp 596–597.
125 ECtHR *Dombo Beheer* (1994) 18 EHRR 213, para 33; *Ankerl* (2001) 32 EHRR 1, para 38.
126 ECtHR *Borgers* (1993) 15 EHRR 92, paras 27–28.
127 ECtHR *Brandstetter* (1993) 15 EHRR 378, paras 66–67; *Ruiz-Mateos* (1993) 16 EHRR 505, para 63.
128 ECtHR *Ruiz-Mateos* (1993) 16 EHRR 505, para 67.
129 ECtHR *Atlan* (2002) 43 EHRR 833, paras 40–41; *Rowe and Davis* (2000) 30 EHRR 1, para 61.
130 ECtHR *Khan* (2001) 31 EHRR 1016, paras 38 ff.
131 ECtHR *Hiro Balani* (1994) 19 EHRR 566, para 27.
132 ECtHR *De Moor* (1994) 18 EHRR 372, para 55; *H v Belgium* (1988) 10 EHRR 399, para 53.

cc) Specific Rights of the Accused

Article 6(3) of the ECHR contains a non-exhaustive enumeration of the rights of the accused.[133] It is made clear in the jurisprudence of the ECtHR that these rights are part of the concept of fair hearing pursuant to Article 6(1) of the ECHR. All these guarantees are characterised by the idea of the **effectiveness** of the defence, whether a certain element of time is prescribed,[134] disadvantages resulting from language difficulties of the defendant are outweighed,[135] contact with the defender is guaranteed,[136] economic disadvantages for the legal assistance are reimbursed[137] or effectiveness and equality of arms are protected within the trial process.[138]

41

Especially concerning testimonial and expert evidence, the ECtHR has developed an extensive jurisprudence. According to Article 6(3)(d) of the ECHR, the accused has the right to ask or to let his legal representative ask the witnesses for the prosecution questions and to obtain the attendance and examination of witnesses for the defence on the same conditions valid for witnesses for the prosecution. When determining of the court's obligations to attend witnesses and experts, one must ask – according to the jurisprudence of the ECtHR – if the denial of a summons or non-admission of rights to question can be justified by legitimate reasons. In this respect, it is necessary to balance the importance of these reasons with the disadvantages for the defendant.[139]

42

The right to remain silent and not to incriminate oneself ("*nemo tenetur*") is included in the rights of the defendant.[140] The principle of "*nemo tenetur*" is not explicitly mentioned in Article 6 of the ECHR, but is considered as part of the main aspect of a fair hearing by the ECtHR. In this context the court always refers to the close connection between this main aspect and the presumption of innocence subject to Article 6(2) of the ECHR.[141] It is incumbent upon the prosecution authority to prove a criminal case against the accused without resorting to evidence obtained through methods of coercion or oppression in defiance of the will of the accused.[142] The guarantee is not restricted to oral testimony[143]

43

---

133 A systematic comparison between the procedural guarantees within the German criminal law and guarantees of the ECHR can be found in Eisele [2004] JR 12.
134 Prompt information of nature and cause of the accusation – Art 6(3)(a)ECHR; adequate time and facilities for the preparation of the defence – lit b.
135 "Understandable language" of the information of the charge – Art 6(3)(a) ECHR; free assistance of an interpreter– lit e.
136 Art 6(3)(c) ECHR.
137 Counsel for the defence paid by the legal aid fund – Art 6(3)(c) ECHR; free assistance of an interpreter – lit e.
138 Right of the accused to be present and to defend himself – lit c; equality of arms in case of testimonial evidence – lit d.
139 For more details *cf* Grabenwarter (note 4) pp 636 ff. Contains extensive examples from the jurisprudence of the ECtHR.
140 BVerfG (1975) 38 BVerfGE 105, 114–115; (1981) 55 BVerfGE 144, 150; (1982) 56 BVerfGE 37, 43; Dreier in: Dreier (ed) *Grundgesetz-Kommentar* (Volume 1, Tübingen 1996) Art 1 I, para 81. Explanation concerning the whole matter Müller [2001] EuGRZ 546.
141 ECtHR *Heaney* App No 34720/97 RJD 2000-XII, para 40; *Saunders* (1997) 23 EHRR 313, para 68; *Murray* (1996) 22 EHRR 29, paras 46, 58.
142 ECtHR *Heaney* App No 34720/97 RJD 2000-XII, para 40; *Serves* (1999) 28 EHRR 265, para 46; *Saunders* (1997) 23 EHRR 313, para 68.
143 The right is not confined to statements of admission of wrongdoing or to remarks which are directly incriminating but also includes statements that do not appear to be incriminating at first

but also includes a forced personal delivery of evidence.[144] The results of breath-, blood-, urine-, or tissue-tests which were obtained through the use compulsory powers, but the existence of which does not depend on the will of the accused, are not protected.[145] Moreover, it is not an absolute right.[146] Thus, *eg* drawing an adverse inference from an accused's silence on certain conditions is consistent with the guarantee.[147] The ECtHR, for example, denies a violation of Article 6(1) of the ECHR if a criminal investigation is conducted against unknown offenders and not against the person required to give information at the time of his refusal to give information, and is at best commenced as a result of the (denied) information against that person, provided that the link with the criminal proceeding stays remote and hypothetical.[148]

44 Finally, the rights of the accused also include the principle of presumption of innocence, even though it is autonomously settled outside of the guarantee of fair trial. The BVerfG has presumed the existence of a respective requirement under the rule of law according to the Basic Law with express reference to Article 6(2) of the ECHR.[149] The rule of presumption of innocence has more than just one dimension. In the preliminary stages and during criminal proceedings, statements of state authorities and courts according to which a certain person has committed a crime are prohibited as long as the person has not been convicted.[150] Moreover, Article 6(2) of the ECHR forbids that the accused – although the proceedings have been closed and his guilt therefore has not been determined – is bound to pay the costs of the proceedings as doubt is therefore in this case left open as to the accused's innocence.[151] Even if doubts as to that person's innocence were expressed in an acquittal or the accused was acquitted for mere want of evidence, once an acquittal has become final, the voicing of any suspicions of guilt is incompatible with the principle of the presumption of innocence.[152] Finally, the state has an obligation to protect the accused against prejudging media reports.[153]

---

sight. What is of the essence in this context is the use to which evidence obtained under compulsion is put in the course of the criminal trial (ECHR *Saunders* (1997) 23 EHRR 313, para 71).
144 ECtHR *Funke* (1993) 16 EHRR 297, para 44 (differing from Art 14 § 3 g ICCPR).
145 ECtHR *Heaney* App No 34720/97 RJD 2000-XII, para 40; *Saunders* (1997) 23 EHRR 313, para 69; Villiger (note 7) para 502.
146 ECtHR *Heaney* App No 34720/97 RJD 2000-XII, para 47; *Condron* (2001) 31 EHRR 1, para 56; *Murray* (1996) 22 EHRR 29, para 47; *cf* ECtHR *Randall* App No 44014/98 (decision on admissibility), para 2.
147 ECtHR *Beckles* (2003) 36 EHRR 162, paras 53 ff; *cf Ashworth/Strange* [2004] EHRLR 121, 134 ff; ECtHR *Condron* (2001) 31 EHRR 1, para 61–62; *Murray* (1996) 22 EHRR 29, paras 50–51, 54; *cf* ECtHR *Randall* App No 44014/98 (decision on admissibility), para 2. *Cf* Kühne [1996] EuGRZ 571. In connection with the right to consult a defense counsel ECtHR *Magee* (2001) 31 EHRR 822, para 43.
148 ECtHR *WEH* (2005) 40 EHRR 890, paras 53 ff (denial of testimony about the driver of a vehicle on part of the vehicle's owner – holder of a licence – according to Austrian law).
149 BVerfG (1987) 74 BVerfGE 358, 370.
150 ECtHR *Schenk* (1991) 13 EHRR 242, para 51; *Allenet de Ribemont* (1995) 20 EHRR 557, para 41.
151 Starting with ECtHR *Sekanina* (1994) 17 EHRR 221, paras 29 ff; on that Pilnacek [2001] ÖJZ 546; recently ECtHR *Asan Rushiti* (2001) 33 EHRR 1331, paras 31–32.
152 ECtHR *Asan Rushiti* (2001) 33 EHRR 1331, paras 31–32; the situation is different, however, if the proceedings are abandoned without a final verdict on guilt or innocence (*cf* also decision on admissibility ECtHR *Reinmüller* App No 69169/01).
153 EurCommHR DR 14, 112–113.

Fundamental Judicial and Procedural Rights   § 6 II 1

d) Public Trial

Article 6 of the ECHR provides for a **public trial** in two different respects: On the one hand, it demands a hearing open to the public, and on the other hand, the final decision of the court which ends the proceedings shall be pronounced publicly. However, it is explicitly mentioned that the press may be excluded from attending all or part of the trial. Journalists perform the role of a professional public according to Article 6(1) of the ECHR, for they primarily contribute – by means of their reporting – to the publication of the proceedings. This reporting, however, has to be distinguished from the question of whether tape recordings or film reports are admissible in court. While the provision that decisions shall be made in public is guaranteed without reservations, the public conduct of proceedings is governed by a directly applicable limitation clause: The entire process or parts of it can be closed to the public in the interests of morals, public order or national security in a democratic society, where the interests of juveniles or the protection of the private life of the parties so require or in special circumstances where publicity would prejudice the interests of justice (in the latter case to the extent strictly necessary in the opinion of the court). This limitation clause shows many parallels to the limitation clauses subject to Articles 8 to 11 of the ECHR.[154]   45

In addition, the case-law has developed further reasons for which a trial or the pronouncement of a judgement can be **closed to public**. In case of a public trial, the settled case law presumes that a violation of fundamental right is excluded if the affected party to the proceeding has waived the right. A waiver of that kind is presumed if made voluntarily and in an unequivocal manner. According to the case-law of the ECtHR, not only an express statement, but also a tacit conduct can comply with the criterion of an unequivocal waiver.[155] In case of criminal proceedings, however, the unambiguousness of a waiver is scrutinized in a stricter way than in civil proceedings: In the former, the waiver has to be declared expressly.[156] In civil proceedings on the other hand, a right to request a public hearing exists if such a hearing is not provided for by national law, but is at the court's discretion. A tacit waiver is consequently only precluded if the law explicitly excludes a hearing and a request will have no success.[157] In cases in which a hearing is held exclusively upon a request or alternatively upon a request or ex officio, the ECtHR demands a request especially if in the practice of the court and comparable others such proceedings are usually conducted without a hearing.[158]   46

As an exception, a waiver is not sufficient to justify the omission of a hearing if this would run counter to the public interest.[159] In the appeal procedure, the hearing can be omitted without a waiver unless the importance and necessity of a hearing for the taking and consideration of evidence as well as for the solution of legal questions or the significance of the outcome of the proceeding for the affected person makes it necessary.[160]

---

154 For more details and differences *cf* Grabenwarter (note 4) pp 481 ff.
155 ECtHR *Schuler-Zgraggen* (1993) 16 EHRR 405, para 58; *Håkansson und Sturesson* (1991) 13 EHRR 1, para 66; *Le Compte et al* (1982) 4 EHRR 1, para 59.
156 ECtHR *Baischer* (2003) 37 EHRR 964, para 26.
157 ECtHR *Diennet* App No 18160/91, para 31; *H v Belgium* (1988) 10 EHRR 399, para 54.
158 ECtHR *Fredin (No 2)* App No 18928/91, para 22; *Fischer* (1995) 20 EHRR 349, para 44; *cf* Grabenwarter (note 35) § 24, para 35.
159 ECtHR *Håkansson und Sturesson* (1991) 13 EHRR 1, para 66; *Pauger* (1998) 25 EHRR 105, para 62.
160 *Cf* Grabenwarter (note 4) p 526 with further references.

47 The ECtHR has limited the right to the *public pronouncement* of the judgments pursuant to Article 6(1) of the ECHR by means of a teleological reduction to a right to a publication of the judgement in order to meet the standard of judgment publication valid in the Member States. Here it is sufficient if the purpose to ensure the scrutiny of the judiciary is served just as well by the way in which the judgment is published as by a public pronouncement.[161] The provisions governing the restriction of hearings are not applicable to the publication of judgements. The right to respect for privacy according to Article 8 of the ECHR can be complied with if decisions are published anonymously.

e) The Reasonable-Time Requirement

48 According to Article 6(1) of the ECHR, the tribunal shall make its decision "within a **reasonable time**". This guarantee is, on the one hand, part of effective legal protection, but on the other hand, its relation to the individual guarantees of fair trial is strained, as an increase of procedural rights always elongates the proceeding.[162] Especially in criminal proceedings, the time during which the outcome is still uncertain should be kept as short as possible. The period to be taken into account begins to run, in civil proceedings, when the action is filed,[163] in criminal proceedings, however, it starts prior the moment the case coming before a trial court, at the time first steps of criminal investigation were made outwardly.[164] In case of administrative court proceedings, the duration of the preceding administrative proceeding may have to be taken into account as well. The concluding decision of the court of ultimate resort and of the following proceeding before a constitutional court always constitutes the end of the proceedings.[165] The jurisprudence assesses the reasonableness of the length of proceeding **in each instance according to the circumstances of the case**, having regard to four criteria.[166]

49 *Importance at stake for the applicant*: If the outcome of a proceeding is of great importance for the affected person, a violation occurs already after a shorter period of time. A great importance is assumed in criminal proceedings in case of arrest of the applicant, in civil proceedings in cases of family law or of proceedings involving the affected person's income, such as proceedings concerning employment law[167] or tort[168] as well as decisions on pension claims.[169]

50 *Degree of complexity of the case*: If a proceeding shows a particular degree of complexity with regard to facts and legal issues, a comparably longer duration of the proceeding can be justified (*eg* complex cases involving business offences[170] and environmental criminal law[171]).

---

161 ECtHR *Pretto* (1984) 6 EHRR 182, para 27.
162 ECtHR *König* (1979–80) 1 EHRR 170, para 100.
163 ECtHR *Editions Périscope* (1992) 14 EHRR 597, para 43.
164 ECtHR *Hennig* App No 41444/98, para 32; *Manzoni* App No 19218/91, para 16; *Corigliano* (1983) 5 EHRR 334, para 34; *Eckle* (1983) 5 EHRR 1, para 73; *cf* also Leigh in: Weissbrodt/Wolfrum (eds) *The Right to a Fair Trial* (Berlin et al 1997) p 653.
165 ECtHR *Klein* (2002) 34 EHRR 415, para 29. Critical remarks by Breuer [2002] NJW ("Sonderheft Weber" / supplement) 6.
166 *Cf* for example ECtHR *Deumeland* (1986) 8 EHRR 448, paras 78 ff.
167 ECtHR *Kormacheva* App No 53084/99, para 56.
168 ECtHR *Krastanov* (2005) 41 EHRR 1137, para 70.
169 ECtHR *Süssmann* (1998) 25 EHRR 64, para 61.
170 *Cf* ECtHR *Lislawska* App No 37761/97, para 47.
171 *Cf* ECtHR *Smirnova* (2004) 39 EHRR 450, para 86.

Behaviour of the applicant: If the applicant delayed the procedure by his behaviour, this fact has to be considered in assessing the duration of proceedings. However, the applicant cannot be blamed for making full use of the remedies available to him.[172] Above all in criminal proceedings, it is not required that the accused cooperates actively with criminal prosecution authorities.[173]

Conduct of the competent authorities: Finally, it is decisive whether authorities and courts of the state have conducted the proceedings rapidly or showed longer periods of inactivity. Short- or long-term overburdening of courts can also be chargeable to the state. The case-law stresses the duty of states to organise their judicial systems in a way to meet the requirements of Article 6 of the ECHR.[174] Consequently, the responsibility for a failure of the court to revoke a tardy expert appointed by the court[175] as well as for a failure to take proper measures against the repeated absence of witnesses and the accused in court[176] can be considered to lie with the authorities. In this context, it has to be considered that according to Article 13 of the ECHR, the Member States of the Convention are also obliged to provide for an effective remedy against an unreasonably long duration of proceedings.[177]

2. Nulla poena sine lege (Article 7 of the ECHR)

Case 2 – Problem: (ECtHR *K.-H.W. v Germany* (2003) 36 EHRR 1081)
50-year-old W had enlisted to serve in the People's Army of the former German Democratic Republic from 1970 to 1973. On 15 February 1972, he killed a refugee who had tried to get from the Eastern to the Western part of Berlin by swimming across the River Spree with five short bursts of two shots each. He received congratulations, the decoration of achievement of frontier troops of the German Democratic Republic and a financial award of 150 Mark. On 17 June 1993, the juvenile department of the Berlin district court convicted him according to the law in effect in the German Democratic Republic at the time of incident, but then applied the less severe criminal law of the Federal Republic of Germany and punished him according to §§ 212, 213 of the *Strafgesetzbuch* (German Criminal Code) and §§ 1, 105 I No 1 of the *Jugendgerichtsgesetz* (German Code of Criminal Procedure in Cases dealing with Juvenile Delinquency). Does the conviction meet the provisions of the Convention?

The principle of "nulla poena sine lege" (no penalty without a law) in Article 7 of the ECHR contains a **prohibition against retroactive criminal legislation** and an **obligation to define an offence clearly**. This guarantee's scope of application corresponds with that of Article 6 of the ECHR, which means that it includes not only the criminal law but also administrative and regulatory offence law and parts of disciplinary law. Article 103(2) the Basic Law contains a fundamental right similar to Article 7 of the ECHR. Article II-109 of the DC goes beyond Article 7 of the ECHR in that it stipulates the imposition of

---

172 ECtHR *Girardi* App No 50064/99, para 56; *Poiss* (1988) 10 EHRR 231, para 57; *Pretto* (1984) 6 EHRR 182, para 34; *cf* on the other hand however ECtHR *Smirnova* (2004) 39 EHRR 450, para 86.
173 ECtHR *Eckle* (1983) 5 EHRR 1, para 82.
174 ECtHR *Philis (No 2)* (1998) 25 EHRR 417, para 40; *Podbielski* App No 27916/95, para 38.
175 *Cf* ECtHR *Rachevi* App No 47877/99, para 90; *Wohlmeyer Bau GmbH* App No 20077/02, para 52.
176 ECtHR *Kuśmierek* App No 10675/02, para 65.
177 For more details *cf* para 68.

lighter penalties if national legislation has established such penalty after the committing of the crime (Article II-109(1)(3) DC), and furthermore requires the degree of penalty to comply with the principle of proportionality pursuant to Article II-109(3).

55 The prohibition of retroactive effect follows from the wording of Article 7 of the ECHR. According to that, no one shall be held guilty of any criminal offence on account of any act or omission which did not constitute a criminal offence under national or international law at the time of the commission of the offence. National courts enjoy a certain degree of discretion when assessing the question of whether the applicant's acts, at the time when they were committed, constituted offences. It is primarily for the national courts to interpret and apply domestic law.[178] Especially concerning possible justifications subject to domestic law, the ECtHR considers whether the accused himself was involved in the establishment of the State practice deemed to justify the conduct which has given rise to his conviction. An accused person is – according to the ECtHR – not entitled to justify such conduct simply by showing that it did in fact take place and therefore formed a practice.[179] The reference to international law in Article 7(2) of the ECHR refers to international criminal law offences of war crimes, genocide etc.[180]

56 Apart from the prohibition of retrospective application, Article 7 of the ECHR also demands a *clear definition of the offence based on a legal norm*. Only a law may define an offence and prescribe a penalty. The law may not be construed extensively to an accused's disadvantage, for instance by use of analogy. Consequently, the criminal offence has to be established explicitly by law. The requirement is met if one can gather from the respective provision's wording, with the help of judicial interpretation if necessary, for which acts and omissions an individual can be held responsible according to criminal law. Thus Article 7 of the ECHR cannot be read as outlawing the gradual clarification of criminal liability through judicial interpretation from case to case, provided that the resultant development is consistent with the essence of the offence and could reasonably be foreseen.[181] The ECtHR considers a conviction to be foreseeable even in cases where at the time the respective legal system existed, the State practice not only provided impunity for the future accused, but imposed negative consequences on the affected person in case he failed to conduct the behaviour which later became liable to prosecution.

Case 2 – Answer:

57 Since W was convicted for an act or omission, Article 7 of the ECHR applies. It is questionable if the killing at the Berlin Wall was liable to prosecution at the time it was committed. There was no doubt that the killing fulfilled the elements of the relevant offence of the Criminal Code of the GDR (manslaughter). The question is whether the applicant's conduct can be justified. From a correct point of view, such grounds of justification were established by the State practice of the GDR – although it did not meet the standards of a constitutional state – where the frontier soldiers on duty had to expect investigations conducted by a military prosecutor in case of a successful escape. The ECtHR is of a different opinion. It acknowledges that such state practice existed. It argues, however, that the reason

---

178 ECtHR *Streletz, Kessler and Krenz* (2001) 33 EHRR 751, paras 49, 51, 66.
179 ECtHR *Streletz, Kessler and Krenz* (2001) 33 EHRR 751, para 74.
180 Harris/O'Boyle/Warbrick *Law of the European Convention on Human Rights* (London 1996) p 277; Kreicker *Art 7 EMRK und die Gewalttaten an der deutsch-deutschen Grenze* (Baden-Baden 2002) pp 81–82.
181 ECtHR *S W v United Kingdom* App No 20166/92, Série A Vol 335-B, paras 34 ff.

of State that formed the basis of this State practice was limited by the principles enunciated in the Constitution and legislation of the GDR itself, while it must be considered that the right to life was already the supreme value in the hierarchy of human rights at the time when the offence was committed.[182] This State practice obviously infringed both the fundamental rights enshrined in the constitution of the GDR and the obligation of international law to respect human rights, which was established inter alia by the ratification of the International Covenant of Civil and Political Rights. With this opinion, the ECtHR misjudges – as the BVerfG did before – that the International Covenant of Civil and Political Rights had not been transposed into national law of the GDR and therefore could not have any legal impact on the frontier soldiers.[183] The ECtHR also argued that a conviction was *foreseeable*. On the one hand, W as a young soldier was exposed to the indoctrination of young recruits by the People's Army and risked the initiation of criminal investigations in case of a successful escape. On the other hand, neither the constitution nor the Criminal Code of the GDR were obscure provisions; therefore, the principle that "ignorance of the law is no excuse" was applicable to W too. In addition to that, W had enlisted voluntarily for three years and he knew – like any other citizen of the GDR – the border-policing policy. So he had to know that the enlistment included the possibility to be posted at the border and to be obliged to shoot at unarmed refugees. Furthermore, an ordinary soldier could not refer to an order "fully and blindly" that obviously violated not only the very own legal maxims of the GDR, but also the human rights protected by international law, especially the right to life, which is the supreme value in the hierarchy of human rights. Therefore, W's conviction did not violate Article 7 of the ECHR. By using this line of argumentation – as the BVerfG did before – the ECtHR referred to the *Radbruch* Formula by varying and rephrasing it in terms of international law. Arguments derived from legal doctrine, however, are not to be found.[184]

3. *The Prohibition of Double Jeopardy*

Article 4 of the 7th Prot ECHR contains the **prohibition of double jeopardy** (*"ne bis in idem"*). Although Germany has signed the 7th additional protocol, it has not ratified it up to now. The guarantee can be found in the Basic Law as one of the so-called rights equal to fundamental rights in Article 103(3) of the Basic Law.[185] Article II-110 of the DC comprises a right corresponding to Article 4 of the 7th Prot ECHR, according to which no one shall be liable to be tried or punished again in criminal proceedings for an offence for which he or she has already been finally acquitted or convicted within the Union in accordance with the law. Article 4 of the 7th Prot ECHR says that "no one shall be liable to be tried or punished again in criminal proceedings under the jurisdiction of the same State for an offence for which he has already been finally acquitted or convicted in accordance with the law and penal procedure of that State." Article 4 of the 7th Prot ECHR has no international application, but only protects against a renewed penalty or trial by the "same" state.[186] In order for the provision to unfold, the "blocking effect" of the guarantee is applicable only where a criminal procedure has been definitely concluded by final

58

---

182 ECtHR *Streletz, Kessler and Krenz* (2001) 33 EHRR 751, para 72.
183 *Cf* already Dreier [1997] JZ 421, 425.
184 Critical remarks concerning the judgement Rau [2001] NJW 3008, as well as Roellecke [2001] NJW 3024–3025.
185 *Cf* BVerfG (1954) 3 BVerfGE 248, 250 ff; (1988) 75 BVerfGE 1, 8 ff.
186 Concerning the international validity of the guarantees of the Basic Law, *cf* Specht *Die zwischenstaatliche Geltung des ne bis in idem* (Berlin et al 1999).

judgement or acquittal[187] and (two) criminal sanctions in the sense of the ECHR are at stake. Therefore, renewed sanctions of another kind (*eg* measures from disciplinary law) are not affected by the "blocking effect" of Article 4 of the 7th Prot ECHR.[188] The term "criminal" corresponds with the notion underlying Article 6 and 7 of the ECHR.[189] Provided that two criminal sanctions exist, it is questionable whether these were in fact imposed because of the same "offence".[190] It is not decisive that the sanctions are based on the same conduct.[191] The mere fact that a conduct constitutes more than one offence is not contrary to the prohibition of double jeopardy.[192] However, two different offences can encompass one and the same criminal wrongdoing. It constitutes a violation if the same person was convicted because of the same conduct according to the same offence, or two different but – with regard to substantive aspects – in fact at least partially identical offences.[193] The Court examines whether the offences at issue have the same essential elements.[194] If they are identical, this denotes a concurrence of laws and therefore a violation. There is no contravention if the criminal offences stand in a relation of ideal coincidence of offences.[195]

59 Article 4(2) of the 7th additional protocol clarifies that the principle of *ne bis in idem* shall not prevent the re-opening of the case, if there is evidence of new or newly discovered facts, or if there has been a fundamental defect in the previous proceedings,[196] which could affect the outcome of the case.[197]

4. Right of Appeal in Criminal Matters

60 According to Article 2 of the 7th Prot ECHR, everyone convicted of a criminal offence by a tribunal shall have the right to have his conviction or sentence reviewed by a higher tribunal. The reviewing tribunal does not need to have the same extent of jurisdiction as a tribunal in the sense of Article 6 of the ECHR. Tribunals of last resort or entitled to decide on the admissibility or dismissal of an appeal also meet this condition.[198] Moreover, national legislation may prescribe exceptions with regard to offences of a minor character or in cases in which the person concerned was tried in the first instance by the highest tribunal or was convicted following an appeal against acquittal (Article 2(2) of the 7th Prot ECHR).

---

187 ECtHR *Fischer* App No 37950/97, para 22; *Gradinger* App No 15963/90, para 53.
188 Council of Europe *Explanatory Report relating to Protocol No 7* [1985] HRLJ 82, para 32.
189 Charrier (note 89) p 352; Van Dijk/Van Hoof (note 9) p 690; *cf* above para 56.
190 *Cf* ECtHR *Oliveira* App No 25711/94, paras 26–27; *Fischer* App No 37950/97, paras 23 ff. *The ECtHR's judgement Gradinger* App No 15963/90, para 55 *is out-dated*.
191 *But equally still in* ECtHR *Gradinger* App No 15963/90, para 55.
192 ECtHR *Fischer* App No 37950/97, para 25.
193 ECtHR *Fischer* App No 37950/97, paras 25, 29.
194 ECtHR *Fischer* App No 37950/97, para 25.
195 ECtHR *Oliveira* App No 25711/94, para 26.
196 Frowein/Peukert in: Frowein/Peukert (eds) *Europäische Menschenrechtskonvention* (2nd ed, Kehl am Rhein et al 1996) Art 4 7.ZP EMRK, para 3, name the threat or bribery of witnesses or judges as examples.
197 ECtHR *Nikitin* (2005) 41 EHRR 149, paras 45 ff.
198 ECtHR *Hubner* App No 34311/96 (decision on admissibility).

Fundamental Judicial and Procedural Rights § 6 IV

5. *The Right to Compensation for Wrongful Conviction (Article 3 of the 7th Prot ECHR)*

In case of a final conviction and a revision of the proceeding resulting in a determination of the convict's innocence, Article 3 of the 7th Prot ECHR provides for a state obligation to compensate for that part of the unjustified punishment already served. It is doubtful whether the affected person should be refused all kinds of compensation if the withholding of relevant facts has to be attributed to other persons as well.[199] There is no obligation to compensate if the affected person is entirely responsible for the fact that newly discovered facts were not disclosed in time. Therefore, Article 3 of the 7th Prot ECHR does not apply in cases where the charge is dismissed or the accused person is acquitted either by the court of first instance or, on appeal, by a higher tribunal.[200] Moreover, the defendant's innocence must be unambiguously established afterwards by the judgement repealing the final conviction or by the act of clemency abolishing judgement.[201] **61**

III. Procedural Safeguards Relating to Expulsion of Aliens

Article 1 of the 7th Prot ECHR contains several procedural guarantees concerning the **expulsion of aliens**. As a minimum standard, an alien lawfully resident in the territory of a State shall not be expelled therefrom except in pursuance of a decision reached in accordance with law. In addition, the provision prescribes certain rights as minimum procedural guarantees which are contained in Article 6(1) and (3) of the ECHR in a fully developed form. It shall be allowed to an alien to submit reasons against his expulsion, to have his case reviewed, and to be represented for these purposes before the competent authority.[202] Pursuant to Article 1(2) of the 7th Prot ECHR, an alien may exceptionally be expelled before the exercise of his rights when such expulsion is necessary in the interests of public order or is grounded on reasons of national security. **62**

IV. The Right to an Effective Remedy

According to **Article 13 of the ECHR**, each person who claims a violation of his rights and freedoms under the Convention has the right to an "effective remedy" before a national authority. Article 13 of the ECHR can be invoked only in conjunction with other provisions of the ECHR or one of its additional protocols. As is the case with Article 19(4) of the Basic Law, it is not a prerequisite that the Convention be in fact violated; it is sufficient that the applicant claims to be the victim of a violation.[203] The alleged violation must however be an arguable one.[204] Article II-107 of the DC includes a similar guarantee, although its scope of application is broader as it includes in a general manner the rights and freedoms guaranteed by the law of the Union. **63**

The national authority can consist of a court, especially a constitutional court. It may not necessarily be a judicial authority but, if it is not, it is decisive that its powers and the **64**

---

199 Van Dijk/Van Hoof (note 9) p 689 propose a partial compensation in cases like that.
200 Explanatory Report (1985) 5 HRLJ 85.
201 Frowein/Peukert in: Frowein/Peukert (eds) *Europäische Menschenrechtskonvention* (2nd ed, Kehl am Rhein et al 1996) Art 3 7.ZP EMRK, para 1.
202 For more details *cf* Wiederin *Aufenthaltsbeendende Maßnahmen im Fremdenpolizeirecht* (Vienna 1993), pp 85 ff.
203 ECtHR *Klass et al* (1979–80) 2 EHRR 214, para 64.
204 ECtHR *Boyle and Rice* (1988) 10 EHRR 425, para 52.

procedural guarantees are effective before the authority.²⁰⁵ Moreover, Article 13 of the ECHR does not oblige the Member States to introduce a constitutional procedure permitting the validity of laws to be challenged for non-observance of fundamental rights.²⁰⁶ The crucial requirement is that access to the respective authority is granted and that the latter is obliged to issue a decision and that the decision provides adequate redress for any violation that has already occurred. Such a remedial measure may consist in a repeal of the contested measure or any compensation.

65 The **extent** of the obligations arising from Article 13 of the ECHR depends on the right of the Convention in connection to which it is invoked. Thus, where an individual has an arguable claim that he has been tortured, Article 13 in conjunction with Article 3 of the ECHR entails, in addition to the State obligation following from Article 3 of the ECHR to carry out a thorough and effective investigation, a right of the affected individual to access to the investigation procedure and to payment of compensation where appropriate.²⁰⁷ A finding of a violation of a substantive right under the Convention is not a prerequisite for the application of Article 13 of the ECHR. Article 13 of the ECHR must be interpreted as guaranteeing an effective remedy to everyone who claims that his rights under the Convention have been violated.²⁰⁸ Provided that this condition is met, the ECtHR examines a possible breach of Article 13 of the ECHR notwithstanding its findings that no right invoked has been infringed,²⁰⁹ provided that a violation of another right under the Convention is arguable.²¹⁰

66 Contrary to earlier case-law of the ECtHR²¹¹, it is not excluded to apply Article 13 of the ECHR also in cases where a violation of a procedural guarantee embodied in Article 5(4) or Article 6(1) of the ECHR is claimed. For example, in case of complaints for an alleged violation of the requirement under Article 6(1) of the ECHR to hear a case within a reasonable time, a violation of Article 13 of the ECHR shall be considered in addition.²¹² With regard to alleged violations of the right to life following from Article 2 of the ECHR, the Court presumes a Member States' obligation deriving from Article 13 of the ECHR to introduce a mechanism for establishing any liability of State officials and bodies.²¹³ Furthermore, financial and non-pecuniary compensation flowing from the breach must be available to the victim.²¹⁴ In such cases, the ECtHR declares a violation of both Article 2 of the ECHR and Article 13 of the ECHR.²¹⁵

---

205 ECtHR *Silver* (1983) 5 EHRR 347, para 113.
206 ECtHR *James* (1986) 8 EHRR 123, para 85; *Lithgow* (1986) 8 EHRR 329, para 206.
207 ECtHR *Aksoy* (1997) 23 EHRR 553, para 98.
208 ECtHR *Klass et al* (1979–80) 2 EHRR 214, para 64.
209 ECtHR *Costello-Roberts* (1994) 19 EHRR 112, para 59.
210 ECtHR *Powell and Rayner* (1990) 12 EHRR 355, para 33; *Boyle and Rice* (1988) 10 EHRR 425, para 52; *Leander* (1987) 9 EHRR 433, para 77.
211 ECtHR *Airey* (1979–80) 2 EHRR 305, para 35; *Sporrong and Lönnroth* (1983) 5 EHRR 35, para 88.
212 ECtHR *Horvat* App No 51585/99, para 63; *Kudla* (2002) 35 EHRR 198, para 149.
213 ECtHR *Buldan* App No 28298/95, paras 103 ff; *Nuray Şen (No 2)* App No 25354/94, para 191; *Tekdağ* App No 27699/95, para 96; *T.P. and K.M. v United Kingdom* (2002) 34 EHRR 42, para 107; *Kaya* (1998) 28 EHRR 1, para 107.
214 ECtHR *Edwards* (2002) 35 EHRR 487, para 97; *Z et al v United Kingdom* (2002) 34 EHRR 97, para 109; *Kaya* (1998) 28 EHRR 1, para 107.
215 *Cf* ECtHR *TekdaTekdağ* App No 27699/95, paras 95 ff; *Tepe* (2004) 39 EHRR 29, paras 195 ff; *Edwards* (2002) 35 EHRR 487, paras 96 ff; *Z et al v United Kingdom* (2002) 34 EHRR 97, paras 108 ff.

Part III: The Fundamental Freedoms of the European Communities

§ 7
General Principles

Dirk Ehlers

Leading Cases: ECJ *van Gend & Loos* [1963] ECR 1; *Costa* [1964] ECR 584; *Dassonville* [1974] ECR 837; *van Binsbergen* [1974] ECR 1299; *Walrave* [1974] ECR 1405; *Cassis de Dijon* [1979] ECR 649; *Vlassopoulou* [1991] ECR I-2357; *Keck* [1993] ECR I-6097; *Alpine Investments* [1995] ECR I-1141; *Gebhard* [1995] ECR I-4165; *Bosman* [1995] ECR I-4921; *Familiapress* [1997] ECR I-3689; *Commission v France* [1997] ECR I-6959; *Angonese* [2000] ECR I-4139; *Elf-Aquitaine* [2002] ECR I-4781; *Carpenter* [2002] ECR I-6279; *Schmidberger* [2003] ECR I-5659; *DocMorris* [2003] ECR I-14887; *Omega* [2004] ECR I-9609.

Further Reading: Barnard *The Substantive Law of the EU – The Four Freedoms* (Oxford 2004); Craig/ de Búrca *EU law* (3rd ed, Oxford 2003) pp 580 ff; Frenz *Handbuch Europarecht – 1. Europäische Grundfreiheiten* (Berlin 2004); Jarass *Elemente einer Dogmatik der Grundfreiheiten* [1995] EuR 202; Jarass *Elemente einer Dogmatik der Grundfreiheiten II* [2000] EuR 705; Kingreen *Die Struktur der Grundfreiheiten des Europäischen Gemeinschaftsrechts* (Berlin 1999); Kingreen in: von Bogdandy (ed) *Europäisches Verfassungsrecht* (Heidelberg 2003) pp 630 ff.

I. The Nature and Position of the Fundamental Freedoms within the Structure of European Community Law

1. The Significance of the Fundamental Freedoms

The European Community (EC) is primarily understood as a framework for economic and monetary union including a common market.[1] The activities of the Community include, *inter alia*, the realisation of an internal market characterised by the abolition of obstacles to the free movement of goods, persons, services and capital (Article 3(1)(c) TEC/Articles I-3(2), I-4(1) DC). These four freedoms can be described as the **'support columns'** on which the **economic constitution of the Community** rests.[2] They are of particular relevance where national rules impede trade between Member States. Accordingly, the German import ban on beer that has not been brewed in accordance with German purity laws,[3] the restrictions on the establishment of companies that have been incorporated under the law of another Member State in order to transfer their actual centre of administration to Germany immediately afterwards,[4] the refusal to reimburse the costs for me-

1

---

1 *Cf* already Art 2 TEC (Art I-2, I-3 DC). For a definition of "common market" see Craig/de Búrca *EU law* (3rd ed, Oxford 2003) p 580; Barnard *The Substantive Law of the EU – The Four Freedoms* (Oxford 2004) pp 10 ff.
2 *Cf* also Kingreen *Die Struktur der Grundfreiheiten des Europäischen Gemeinschaftsrechts* (Berlin 1999) p 13. As to the constitutional character of the Community treaties *cf* Pernice [2000] DVBl 1751, 1753; Huber [2000] DVBl 1754–5.
3 ECJ *Commission v Germany* [1987] ECR 1227.
4 ECJ *Centros* [1999] ECR I-1459; *Überseering* [2002] ECR I-9919; *Inspire Art* [2003] ECR I-10155.

dical care that has been rendered in another Member State[5] and the requirement of governmental approval as regards land purchase on the part of foreign nationals or as regards the alienation of shares in a company[6] have been declared incompatible with the fundamental freedoms. The same applies to certain types of agreements that have been concluded between private parties – *eg* the rules of the transfer system in European professional football[7]. All this indicates that the legislative and political discretion of the Member States as well as the freedom of contract of private persons – especially in the field of economic and social law – are significantly shortened by the fundamental freedoms.

2. The Different Fundamental Freedoms

2 Although the term 'fundamental freedom' is not explicitly mentioned in the current version[8] of the TEC[9] it is widely accepted that one can distinguish between four to six (depending on the method of counting) freedoms: the free movement of goods (Articles 23, 28, 29 TEC/Articles III-151, III-153 DC; → § 8), the free movement of persons including the freedom of movement for workers (Article 39 TEC/Article III-133 DC; → § 9) and the freedom of establishment (Article 43 TEC/Article III-137 DC; → § 10), the free movement of services (Article 49 TEC/Article III-144 DC; → § 11) and the free movement of capital and payments (Article 56 TEC/Article III-156 DC; → § 12).

3 The **free movement of goods** is primarily concerned with the free flow of products – *ie* both tangible and other objects which are capable of forming the subject of commercial transactions[10] – between the Member States.[11] In order to be protected, products have to either originate or be in free circulation in the Member States (Article 23(2) TEC/Article III-151(2) DC).[12] While Article 25 of the TEC (Article III-151(4) DC) prohibits customs duties on imports and exports including charges having equivalent effect (so-called 'tariff' barriers to trade), quantitative restrictions on imports and exports as well as measures having equivalent effects are prohibited by Articles 28 and 29 of the TEC (Article III-153 DC) ('non-tariff' barriers to trade).

---

5 ECJ *Kohll* [1998] ECR I-1931 (*cf* para 88); *Geraets-Smits* [2001] ECR I-5473; *Müller-Fauré* [2003] ECR I-4509.
6 As to the compatibility of "golden shares" with the free movement of capital *cf* ECJ *Commission v Portugal* [2002] ECR I-4731; *Commission v France* [2002] ECR I-4781.
7 ECJ *Bosman* [1995] ECR I-4921.
8 Treaty of Nice of 26 February 2001 ([2002] OJ C325/1–184) as amended by the Accession Treaty of 16 April 2003 ([2003] OJ L236/17).
9 However, the term is used (with a different meaning) in the ECHR (European Convention for the Protection of Human Rights and Fundamental Freedoms) as well as in Article 6(2) of the TEU. *Cf* also Art I-4(1) DC.
10 *Eg* electricity.
11 *Cf* Jarass [1995] EuR 202, 205.
12 Products originate in the Community if they are wholly obtained, produced or substantially processed or worked in a Member State of the EC, *cf* Articles 23 ff of the Customs Code (Council Regulation 2913/92, [1992] OJ L302/1). Products coming from a third country are considered to be in free circulation in a Member State if the import formalities have been complied with, if any customs duties or charges have been levied, and if they have not benefited from a total or partial drawback of such duties or charges (Article 24 TEC/Article III-151(3) DC).

General Principles   § 7 I 2

The free movement of persons including the **freedom of movement for workers** and the   4
freedom of establishment primarily applies to situations in which citizens of the Union
(Article 17 TEC/Article I-10 DC) or (concerning the freedom of establishment) companies (Article 48 TEC/Article III-142 DC; → § 10 paras 62 ff) are planning to permanently relocate to another Member State in order to take up and pursue economic activities – either employed or self-employed on the basis of a fixed establishment. The freedom of movement for workers confers, *inter alia*, the right to apply for employment that is offered in another Member State, to move freely within the territory of the Member States for this purpose and to remain in the territory of the Member State after having been employed.[13] Additionally, members of the worker's family[14] (→ § 9 para 29) as well as his or her employer[15] are protected. While the freedom of movement for workers primarily concerns employees,[16] the freedom of establishment applies to the self-employed[17] and also covers the formation and management of undertakings including agencies and subsidiaries (Article 43(2) TEC/Article III-137(2) DC). It protects against undue regimentation by the state of origin[18] as well as the host Member State[19].

The **freedom to provide services** covers services which are normally performed for remu-   5
neration insofar as they are not governed by the provisions relating to freedom of movement for goods, capital and persons (Article 50 TEC/Article III-145 DC; → § 11 para 20).[20] It is not only applicable to situations in which the service itself "crosses the border" (*eg* telecommunication services),[21] but also where the provider (active freedom to provide services) and/or the recipient (passive freedom to provide services) temporarily travel to another Member State in order to provide or receive the service in question.[22] In this respect the freedom to provide services also protects the free movement of persons. This protection covers both providers and recipients.[23]

The **free movement of capital** guarantees the unimpeded transfer of money and similar   6
assets between Member States (primarily for the purpose of investment). All payments

---

13 *Cf* Art 39(3)(a), (b), (d) TEC (Art III-133(a), (b), (d) DC); → § 9 paras 19 ff.
14 As to the worker's children *cf* ECJ *Baumbast* [2002] ECR I-7091, para 52.
15 ECJ *Clean Car* [1998] ECR I-2521, paras 16 ff; → § 9 para 28.
16 *Cf* Art 1(1) Council Regulation 1612/68, [1968] OJ 257/2 ("activity as an employed person").
17 Activities of self-employed prostitutes are also protected, *cf* ECJ *Jany* [2001] ECR I-8615, paras 32 ff.
18 *Cf* for example ECJ *de Lasteyrie du Saillant* [2004] ECR I-2409 (prohibition of an increase in the value of securities in the event of the transfer of residence for tax purposes).
19 *Cf* for example ECJ *Inspire Art* [2003] ECR I-10155 (formation of a company in another Member State in order to circumvent the provisions of domestic company law).
20 *Cf* Müller-Graf in: Streinz (ed) *EUV/EGV. Vertrag über die Europäische Union und Vertrag zur Gründung der Europäischen Gemeinschaft* (Munich 2003) Art 49 EGV, paras 15 ff; Holoubek in: Schwarze (ed) *EU-Kommentar* (Baden-Baden 2000) Art 50 EGV, paras 5 ff.
21 Barnard (note 1) p 333.
22 *Cf* Roth in: Dauses (ed) *Handbuch des EU-Wirtschaftsrechts* (loose-leaf, Munich) E I, para 100; Kluth in: Calliess/Ruffert (eds) *Kommentar des Vertrages über die Europäische Union und des Vertrages zur Gründung der Europäischen Gemeinschaft* (2nd ed, Neuwied 2002) Art 50 EGV, paras 24–25.
23 Even activities of prostitutes are protected, *cf* ECJ *Commission v Italy* [2003] ECR I-721, paras 12 ff.

that involve cross-border scenarios are covered by the free movement of payments (→ § 12 para 6).[24] As to the relationship between the different fundamental freedoms *cf* para 57.

3. Direct Internalisation and Direct Effect of the Fundamental Freedoms

7   The body of European Community law constitutes an **autonomous Community legal order** which – while existing independently from national legal orders – is directly internalised within the legal systems of the Member States.[25] Due to this **direct internalisation**, rules of Community law must be fully and uniformly applied in all Member States from their entry into force. This can either be derived from the principle of autonomy of the Community legal order[26] or from the fact that the Member States transferred governmental powers on the EC. The direct internalisation of the EC legal order must be distinguished from what is commonly described as **direct effect** or direct application (**applicability**) of Community law.[27] According to a broad definition one can already speak of direct effect or applicability of EC law where any of the entities that are subject to a domestic legal system have to observe Community law. This includes, for example, the legislature of a Member State that has to implement EC directives. Mostly, however, a narrower definition of direct effect of EC law is employed. According to this narrow approach it is decisive whether or not Community law confers rights (or imposes duties) on the citizens of the Union and on other individuals.[28] The assessment of this requirement necessarily involves the interpretation of the rules of Community law in question.[29] All fundamental freedoms impose unconditional[30] duties on the entities that are bound by them (paras 42 ff). All fundamental freedoms are therefore directly applicable within the domestic legal systems.[31] Admittedly, all relevant **secondary Community law** – unless violating primary Community law – takes priority in application: the most specific source of law that

---

24   *Cf* Bröhmer in: Calliess/Ruffert (eds) *Kommentar des Vertrages über die Europäische Union und des Vertrages zur Gründung der Europäischen Gemeinschaft* (2nd ed, Neuwied 2002) Art 56 EGV, paras 5, 22; → § 12 para 6; Sedlaczeck in: Streinz (ed) *EUV/EGV. Vertrag über die Europäische Union und Vertrag zur Gründung der Europäischen Gemeinschaft* (Munich 2003) Art 56 EGV, paras 7 ff.

25   Explicit provisions to the contrary notwithstanding (*eg* transitional provisions in the event of an accession of new Member States); *cf* note 33.

26   Oppermann *Europarecht* (2nd ed, Munich 1999) para 672; Borchardt *Die rechtlichen Grundlagen der Europäischen Union* (3rd ed, Heidelberg 2006) para 148.

27   A uniform usage of the terms can neither be found in the case-law of the ECJ nor in academic writing. *Cf* for example Jarass/Beljin *Casebook, Grundlagen des EG-Rechts* (Baden-Baden 2003) pp 55 ff; Ruffert in: Calliess/Ruffert (eds) *Kommentar des Vertrages über die Europäische Union und des Vertrages zur Gründung der Europäischen Gemeinschaft* (2nd ed, Neuwied 2002) Art 249 EGV, para 18.

28   ECJ *van Gend & Loos* [1963] ECR 1, 11 ff; *Simmenthal II* [1978] ECR 629, 643–4; Kadelbach *Allgemeines Verwaltungsrecht unter europäischem Einfluß* (Tübingen 1999) pp 57 ff; Borchardt (note 26) para 149.

29   Direct effect does not depend on provisions explicitly providing for such an effect, *cf* ECJ *van Gend & Loos* [1963] ECR 1, 11 ff.

30   The former transition periods (Art 7(1), Arts 31, 33, 35, Art 48(1), Art 52(1), Art 59(1), Art 67 EEC-Treaty) have all expired.

31   Barnard (note 1) p 261.

General Principles §7 I 5

covers the case in question has to be applied.³² Only where secondary Community law does not exhaustively regulate a certain matter, the fundamental freedoms have a direct impact. However, secondary Community law always has to conform to and must be interpreted in light of the fundamental freedoms. Unfortunately, the case-law of the ECJ falls short of this principle because the Court rarely scrutinises secondary Community law for its compatibility with the fundamental freedoms. Apparently, the ECJ has never nullified secondary Community law for violation of the fundamental freedoms. It therefore seems that the ECJ applies double standards and places weaker demands on the Community legislator than on the Member States. If new Member States accede to the EC, transitional provisions can be included in the accession treaties (or in the TEC/TEU). With regard to the accession of the 10 new Member States on 1 May 2004 such transitional provisions were included concerning the applicability of some of the fundamental freedoms (para 49).³³

4. The Fundamental Freedoms as Subjective Rights

A free movement of goods, persons, services and capital between Member States (Article 3(1)(c) TEC/Article I-4 DC) can only develop if the fundamental freedoms not only bind the Member States but also accord the individual a legal power to enforce his or her interests protected by the same. Since the judgment of the ECJ in *van Gend & Loos*³⁴ a consensus has been reached that the fundamental freedoms not only serve as general limits to governmental action but that they are also designed to protect each individual economic subject. Hence, the fundamental freedoms are **subjective rights** (*ie* normative obligations which also serve the fulfilment and protection of individual interests and, for this purpose, accord their beneficiaries the legal power to enforce those interests in a court of law).³⁵ This means that the guarantees of the fundamental freedoms can be enforced both in the Community courts and in the courts of the Member States (paras 99 ff).

8

5. Supremacy of the Fundamental Freedoms

The principles governing the relationship between Community law and the domestic law of the Member States also apply to the fundamental freedoms. In case of conflict between Community law and national law Community law takes precedence – according to the ECJ Community law takes precedence under all circumstances,³⁶ according to the *Bundesverfassungsgericht* (BVerfG – German Federal Constitutional Court) the supremacy of

9

---

32 ECJ *Cassis de Dijon* [1979] ECR 649, para 8; *Vanacker* [1993] ECR I-4947, para 9; *Daimler Chrysler* [2001] ECR I-9897, para 32; von Bogdandy [2001] JZ 157, 166; Oexle [2003] AbfallR 284, 288. Where secondary Community law prohibits a certain behaviour, the fundamental freedoms are nevertheless applicable (*contra* ECJ *DocMorris* [2003] ECR I-14887, para 52) – in these cases, the provisions of secondary Community law function as a justification of interferences with the fundamental freedoms.
33 *Cf* Art 24 Act of Accession read in conjunction with Annexes IV–XIV, [2003] OJ L236/33, 987.
34 *Cf* note 29; ECJ *van Gend & Loos* [1963] ECR 1, 11.
35 As to the conditions under which subjective rights can be derived from EC law see generally Ehlers *Die Europäisierung des Verwaltungsprozeßrechts* (Cologne 1999) pp 47 ff; Ehlers [2004] DVBl 1441, 1445–6.
36 *Cf* ECJ *Costa v E.N.E.L.* [1964] ECR 584; *Internationale Handelsgesellschaft* [1970] ECR 1125, para 3; *Factortame* [1990] ECR I-2433, para 18.

179

Community law is subject to certain conditions developed in its *Solange*-decisions[37]. In any case, Community law only takes **precedence in application**.[38] This means that conflicting national law remains in force but becomes inapplicable to situations in which Community law is directly applicable. All governmental branches that are concerned with such a case (including trial courts and public authorities[39]) are obliged to ignore conflicting national law – this may even apply to private individuals bound by Community law (para 45).

6. Delineation from Other Rights Guaranteed by Primary Community Law

10 Apart from the fundamental freedoms, numerous other rights are guaranteed by primary Community law (*ie* the Treaties including protocols and annexes, the unwritten general principles of Community law and customary law supplementing the Treaties). These guarantees, which are distinct from the fundamental freedoms, can be divided into written and unwritten rights.

a) Written Rights

aa) The General Prohibition of Discrimination as per Article 12 of the TEC (Article I-4(2) DC)

11 Within the scope of application of the TEC Article 12 (Article I-4(2) DC) prohibits any discrimination on grounds of nationality "without prejudice to any special provisions" contained in the Treaty (→ § 13). As already indicated by this reservation, Article 12 of the TEC applies independently only to "situations governed by Community law in respect of which the Treaty lays down no specific prohibition of discrimination".[40] Consequently, Article 12 of the TEC is of **subsidiary nature**, *ie* the fundamental freedoms take precedence in application.[41] Since the provision only prohibits discrimination on grounds of nationality, it does not take precedence over the general right to equality before the law (Article II-80 DC) either.[42] For the purposes of Article 12 of the TEC, the provisions concerning the citizenship of the Union also fall inside the scope of application of the Treaty. The ECJ therefore concluded that citizens of the Union can rely on Article 12 of the TEC in all situations that fall within the scope of Community law if they reside legally in the territory of a Member State (→ § 21 para 85).[43] This also means that foreign citizens of

---

37 BVerfG *Solange I* [1974] 2 CMLR 540; *Solange II* [1987] 3 CMLR 225; *Maastricht* [1994] 1 CMLR 57; *Bananas Case* (2000) 102 BVerfGE 147. See also → § 14 para 14.
38 ECJ *Nimz* [1991] ECR I-297, para 19; BVerfG (1988) 75 BVerfGE 223, 244; (1992) 85 BVerfGE 191, 204; Jarass/Beljin [2004] NVwZ 1. As to the exceptions (nullity) *cf* Ehlers in: Erichsen/Ehlers (eds) *Allgemeines Verwaltungsrecht* (13th ed, Berlin 2006) § 2, para 107.
39 *Cf* ECJ *Costanzo* [1989] ECR 1839, paras 28 ff. *Cf* the criticism raised by Schmidt-Aßmann in: Ehlers/Krebs (eds) *Grundfragen des Verwaltungsrechts und Kommunalrechts* (Berlin 2000) pp 1, 17 ff.
40 ECJ *Skanavi* [1996] ECR I-929, para 20. See, however, also ECJ *Collins* [1993] ECR I-5145, para 17.
41 As to the fundamental freedoms in their function as prohibitions of discrimination *cf* paras 19 ff.
42 *Cf* ECJ *Hochstrass* [1980] ECR 3005, paras 7–8.
43 ECJ *Grzelczyk* [2001] ECR I-6193, paras 34 ff; see the criticism raised by Kluth (note 22) Art 18 EGV, para 5 (reliance on Article 12 of the TEC only where there is a substantial link between the (potentially) protected behaviour and the purpose of residence and where the behaviour in question is aimed at the attainment of this purpose); Hailbronner [2004] NJW 2185.

the Union may not be treated inferior to nationals of the respective Member State while exercising their right to move freely (Article 18 TEC/Article I-10(2)(a) DC).[44] It is disputed whether or not the provision has "direct horizontal effect". This, however, has to be determined according to the same standards that apply to the fundamental freedoms (paras 45–46). As regards the question whether or not Article 12 of the TEC allows any restrictions *cf* → § 13 para 19.

bb) Specific Equality Rights

Beside Article 12 of the TEC (Article I-4(2) DC) the EC-Treaty grants many other **specific equality rights**. These rights mostly deal with the prohibition of inferior treatment of foreign citizens of the Union vis-à-vis nationals of the Member States or with the prevention of a distortion of competition within the common market. Reference can be made, for example, to the prohibitions contained in Articles 25,[45] 31,[46] 72,[47] 90[48] and 294 of the TEC (Articles III-151(4), III-155, III-237, III-170(1) DC) which (also) serve the fulfilment and protection of individual interests. Being more specific than the fundamental freedoms, these provisions take priority in application (*leges speciales*).

Some provisions of the Treaty are concerned with other forms of discrimination: As per Article 34(2)(ii) of the TEC (Article III-228(2)(ii) DC) any discrimination between producers or consumers within the Community shall be excluded as regards the common organisation of agricultural markets. Article 141 of the TEC (Article III-214 DC) is particularly important. It ensures – with direct effect[49] – the principle of equal pay for male and female workers even with regard to non-governmental employers (irrespective of whether or not only nationals of the same Member State are concerned). In addition, it defines other requirements concerning the **equality between women and men** in working life (→ § 18 paras 21 ff).[50] The subject matters of these provisions are not identical to those of the fundamental freedoms. Hence, these specific equality rights can be applied concurrently. The Charter of Fundamental Rights of the Union guarantees a general prohibition of discrimination (Article II-80 DC) as well as numerous novel equality rights (Articles II-81 ff DC).

cc) Other Rights

The EC-Treaty furthermore contains guarantees that do not address the individual as an economic subject but as a **citizen of the Union** (Article 17 TEC/Article I-10 DC). Reference can be made to the right to move and reside freely (Article 18 TEC/Article I-10(2)(a) DC), the right to vote and stand as a candidate at municipal elections and in elections to the

---

44 ECJ *Bidar* [2005] ECR I-2119. See the criticism raised by Kluth (note 22) Art 18 EGV, para 5.
45 *Cf* ECJ *van Gend & Loos* [1963] ECR 3, 11 ff.
46 *Cf* ECJ *Manghera* [1976] ECR 91, paras 15–16.
47 *Cf* ECJ *Commission v Germany* [1992] ECR I-3141, paras 13 ff.
48 *Cf* ECJ *Lütticke* [1966] ECR 205, 214 ff.
49 ECJ *Defrenne II* [1976] ECR 455, paras 4 ff.
50 German provisions which automatically favour equally-qualified women competing with men for promotion within the civil service (*cf* ECJ *Kalanke* [1995] ECR I-3051, paras 21 ff; *Marschall* [1997] ECR I-6363, paras 23 ff; *Badeck* [2000] ECR I-1875) as well as the exclusion of women from service in the armed forces (*cf* ECJ *Sirdar* [1999] ECR I-7403; *Kreil* [2000] ECR I-69) have so far only been scrutinised against their consistency with secondary Community law.

European Parliament (Article 19 TEC/Article I-10(2)(b) DC), the entitlement to protection by diplomatic or consular authorities in third countries (Article 20 TEC/Article I-10(2)(c) DC) and the right to petition (Article 21 TEC/Article I-10(2)(d) DC). Besides, Article 255 TEC (Article III-358 DC) contains a right of access to documents of the Community institutions. These guarantees supplement the (more economy-oriented) fundamental freedoms (→ detailed § 21).

b) Unwritten Rights

15 The fundamental freedoms must be distinguished from the unwritten **general principles of Community law** which the ECJ has derived case-by-case on the basis of Article 220(1) of the TEC from the constitutional traditions common to the Member States and from international treaties – in particular the European Convention for the Protection of Human Rights and Fundamental Freedoms. The general principles of Community law particularly comprise the **fundamental rights of the Union** (→ § 14 paras 5 ff) which have lately been codified in the Charter of Fundamental Rights of the European Union (Articles II-61 ff DC; → § 20 – not yet entered into force; *cf*, however, the preface). The fundamental rights of the Union are primarily binding on the Communities and the EU. However, where Member States apply Community law they are also bound by the fundamental rights of the Union (→ § 14 paras 31 ff). As a consequence, the scope of the fundamental freedoms and of the fundamental rights of the Union may overlap. According to the view taken here, the fundamental freedoms – in as much as they are applicable (*ie* the requirement of a cross-border scenario) – are specific kinds of fundamental rights that take priority in application over the more general fundamental rights of the Union.[51] This is also in line with Article II-112(2) of the DC stipulating that the rights recognised by the Charter for which provision is made in other parts of the Constitution shall be exercised under the conditions and within the limits defined by these relevant parts (as to the United Kingdom *cf* the preface). Even where the fundamental freedoms are applied, the fundamental rights of the Union still function as general limits to their restrictability – *ie* where the justification of an interference with the fundamental freedoms is scrutinised (para 94; → § 14 para 12): Interferences with the fundamental freedoms that are inconsistent with the fundamental rights of the Union constitute a violation of the fundamental freedoms. On the other hand, the fundamental rights of the Union might conflict with the fundamental freedoms. In this case, the conflict has to be resolved by balancing both types of guarantees against each other (para 86; → § 14 para 12).

7. Dogmatics of the Fundamental Freedoms

16 Although the fundamental freedoms are of vital importance for the common market in the EC, no consensus has yet been reached on their dogmatic structure. The ECJ does not always follow a clear line either. However, according to the view taken here, all fundamental freedoms share the same basic structure. This 'universal structure' requires uniform dogmatic solutions. In this respect one can speak of a 'convergence' of the fundamental freedoms.[52] Consequently, the following section will examine those aspects which are common to all fundamental freedoms without focusing on the different freedoms individually.

---

51 *Cf* also → § 14 para 12.
52 Considerably more reluctant as to such a 'convergence' Steinberg [2002] EuGRZ 13.

General Principles §7 II 1

Firstly, the functions of the fundamental freedoms (paras 17 ff), their beneficiaries (paras 36 ff), the entities bound by them (paras 42 ff), their territorial (para 48) and temporal scope (para 49) will be analysed. Thereafter, the scope of protection, interferences with and restrictions of the fundamental freedoms will be examined (paras 50 ff). Finally, the issue of judicial protection will be addressed (paras 99 ff).

II. Functions of the Fundamental Freedoms

Case 1 – Problem: (ECJ *DocMorris* [2003] ECR I-14887)
The Netherlands-based firm DocMorris runs an approved online pharmacy involving the distribution of medicinal products the sale of which is restricted to pharmacies in some Member States (*eg* Germany). DocMorris is offering those products for sale to – *inter alia* – consumers in Germany over the internet. The *Apothekerverband* (German association of pharmacists) was convinced that this practice violates the *Arzneimittelgesetz 1998* (German Law on Medicinal Products) and filed an application for an injunction with a German *Landgericht* (Regional Court). The Court had doubts concerning the compatibility of the relevant provisions of the Law on Medicinal Products with European Community law. It therefore requested the ECJ to give a preliminary ruling as per Article 234 of the TEC (Article III-369 DC) on the compatibility of the provisions in question with Article 28 of the TEC (Article III-153 DC). 17

Various functions can be attributed to the fundamental freedoms. Firstly, it is debatable whether they not only function as equality rights (paras 19 ff) but also as liberty rights (paras 24 ff) conferring defensive rights on the individual. The fundamental freedoms might furthermore function as rights to governmental action (paras 28 ff) and as procedural rights (para 34). In addition to that, they might also possess an objective dimension (*ie* fundamental freedoms as normative obligations that cannot be judicially enforced by the individual) – para 35. On the other hand, it appears to be clear that the fundamental freedoms do not function as (European) citizenship rights.[53] 18

1. The Fundamental Freedoms as Equality Rights

a) Prohibition of Discrimination

The various **prohibitions of discrimination** that can be derived from the fundamental freedoms sectorally specify the general prohibition of discrimination contained in Article 12 of the TEC (Article I-4(2) DC).[54] The internal market cannot be established if Member States treat citizens of other Member States inferior to their own nationals concerning cross-border transactions. Accordingly, Article 30(ii) of the TEC (Article III-154(ii) DC) determines that restrictions on imports or exports, which may be justified under certain circumstances, shall not constitute "a means of arbitrary discrimination". The free move- 19

---

[53] See, however, also ECJ *Commission v Austria* [2004] ECR I-8291: denying workers who are nationals of other Member States of the EU or the European Economic Area the right to stand for election to workers' chambers violates Article 39 of the TEC (Article III-133 DC).
[54] *Cf* Epiney *Umgekehrte Diskriminierungen* (Cologne 1995) p 7; Meyer *Das Diskriminierungsverbot des Gemeinschaftsrechts als Grundsatznorm und Gleichheitsrecht* (Frankfurt am Main 2002) pp 29–30; see, however, also Plötscher *Der Begriff der Diskriminierung im Europäischen Recht* (Berlin 2003) p 136.

183

ment for workers prescribes "the abolition of any discrimination based on nationality" (Article 39(2) TEC/*cf* Article III-133(2) DC), the right of establishment allows EU nationals to take up and pursue activities in another Member State "under the conditions laid down for its own nationals" (Article 43(2) TEC/Article III-137(2) DC) and the freedom to provide services enables its beneficiaries to temporarily stay in another Member State "under the same conditions as are imposed by that State on its own nationals" (Article 50(3) TEC/Article III-145(3) DC). The free movement of capital and payments protects against restrictions "between Member States and between Member States and third countries" (Article 56(1), (2) TEC/Article III-155(1), (2) DC). Such restrictions can also and foremost be discriminatory measures.

b) Standard of Comparison

20 Determining whether a measure is discriminatory within the meaning of the fundamental freedoms requires an authoritative standard of comparison. The fundamental freedoms deal with measures "between Member States".[55] They are aimed at market access, not at a complete unification of markets within the EC. According to the convincing case-law of the ECJ[56] the fundamental freedoms – in contrast to the fundamental rights of the Union – therefore only apply to actual (and not purely hypothetical[57]) **cross-border scenarios**.[58] Hence, a comparison has to be made between purely internal situations and situations involving more than one Member State.[59] The fundamental freedoms are not applicable to other kinds of discrimination. In particular, purely internal situations cannot be reviewed under the fundamental freedoms.[60] This implies that a (pure) 'reverse discrimination' by the Member States (*ie* discrimination against the Member State's own nationals in favour of foreign citizens of the Union) is not prohibited by the fundamental freedoms.[61] Even if – contrary to the view taken here – a prohibition of 'reverse discrimination' could be derived from Article 12 of the TEC (Article I-4(2) DC) read in conjunction with the provisions on the citizenship of the Union,[62] the fundamental freedoms would take priority in application as *leges speciales*. Germany is therefore not violating Community law, for example, by applying its strict purity laws on beer to German breweries only. As a general rule, such a 'reverse discrimination' is not violating German constitutional guarantees against discrimination either.

21 The prohibition of discrimination following from the fundamental freedoms proscribes an inferior treatment of **foreign citizens of the Union** vis-à-vis the Member State's own nationals. However, the prohibition of discrimination **also** benefits **nationals** within their

---

55 See for example Art 28 TEC (Art III-153 DC).
56 *Cf* for example ECJ *Steen I* [1992] ECR I-341, para 9; *Steen II* [1994] ECR I-2715, para 9. For further references see Lackhoff *Die Niederlassungsfreiheit des EGV – nur ein Gleichheits- oder auch ein Freiheitsrecht?* (Berlin 2000) p 55 with note 167.
57 ECJ *Moser* [1984] ECR 2539, para 18; *Kremzow* [1997] ECR I-2629, para 16.
58 *Contra* (*inter alia*) Epiney (note 54) pp 201, 203, 209–10; Lackhoff (note 56) pp 55 ff, 67 ff.
59 A cross-border scenario can always be assumed where Community measures – in contrast to national measures – are scrutinised.
60 The differentiation between internal situations and cross-border scenarios can be difficult in the individual case. *Cf* for example Kingreen (note 2) pp 140 ff.
61 *Cf* for example Streinz *Europarecht* (7th ed, Heidelberg 2005) para 813.
62 *Eg* Borchardt (note 26) para 244. See the appropriate criticism raised by Kingreen → § 18 paras 13 ff; Kadelbach → § 21 paras 83 ff.

Member States, if by reason of their conduct they are in a situation which may be regarded as equivalent to that of a person from another Member State enjoying the rights and liberties guaranteed by the Treaty.[63] One can speak of a cross-border scenario where, for example, nationals (including companies that have been incorporated under the law of the Member State in question) want to export goods to another Member State,[64] where they want to leave their state of origin in order to accept offers of employment, to set up agencies or to provide services in other Member States,[65] where nationals want to provide services in other Member States without leaving their state of origin or where they want to conduct capital transactions or payments involving other Member States. In such situations nationals can rely on the fundamental freedoms in relation to their Member State of origin. In addition, former residence in another Member State may suffice. Where nationals of one Member State have obtained a professional qualification in another Member State they may invoke the free movement of persons in their Member State of origin in order to take up the profession concerned.[66] The fundamental freedoms furthermore benefit the contracting parties of those who exercise these guarantees:[67] the free movement for employees also benefits employers[68]; the freedom to provide services also benefits recipients (para 5). If, for example, tourists originating from another Member State have to pay higher admission charges to state-owned museums than nationals of the Member State in question, these tourists can invoke the free movement of services.[69] As already mentioned above, the free movement of persons also protects (domestic or foreign) family members of its (primary) beneficiaries (para 4). Measures that do not benefit the whole population of the Member State in question but only a certain group of nationals, *eg* residents in particular parts of the national territory, are nevertheless discriminatory vis-à-vis foreign EU citizens.[70] Many German authors speak of a 'prescription of equal treatment with nationals' instead of a 'prohibition of discrimination'.[71] However, both terms are not synonymous – the prohibition of discrimination does not affect so called 'reverse discrimination' (para 20).

c) Forms of Discrimination

One can distinguish between **overt**, direct and *de jure* discrimination on the one hand and **covert**, indirect, *de facto* discrimination on the other.[72] In case of overt discrimination, national measures (*eg* statutes) explicitly differentiate between domestic and cross-border scenarios – putting cross-border scenarios at a disadvantage (*eg* by focusing on the state of origin of goods or on the nationality of persons). Covertly discriminating measures do

22

---

63 ECJ *Knoors* [1979] ECR 399, para 24; *Asscher* [1996] ECR I-3089, para 32.
64 As to a transfer of the central management and control of a company to another Member State *cf* ECJ *Daily Mail* [1988] ECR 5483.
65 ECJ *Ciola* [1999] ECR I-2517; *Vestergaard* [1999] ECR I-7641, para 20.
66 *Cf* ECJ *Knoors* [1979] ECR 399, paras 24–25; *Broekmeulen* [1981] ECR 2311, para 19.
67 Jarass [2000] EuR 705, 708.
68 ECJ *Clean Car* [1998] ECR I-2521, paras 16 ff.
69 ECJ *Commission v Spain* [1994] ECR I-911, para 10; *Commission v Italy* [2003] ECR I-721, paras 14–15.
70 ECJ *Angonese* [2000] ECR I-4139, para 41; *Commission v Italy* [2003] ECR I-721, para 14.
71 *Cf* for example Frenz *Handbuch Europarecht – 1. Europäische Grundfreiheiten* (Berlin 2004) paras 2103 ff.
72 The terms are used synonymously. More detailed Plötscher (note 54).

not address goods or persons that originate from other[73] Member States as such but typically put a greater burden on cross-border scenarios,[74] for example if consumer goods have to be labelled in the language of the region where the product is placed on the market[75]. Provisions that differentiate according to the place of residence or employment can also be covertly discriminating, since they will usually have a greater impact on foreign citizens of the Union than on persons that live or work in the Member State concerned.[76] The ECJ employs a very broad concept of discrimination. It is irrelevant whether or not the Member State actually intends to discriminate. The distinction between overt and covert discrimination is particularly important in relation to the justification of interferences with the fundamental freedoms (cf paras 80 ff).

d) The Effects of the Prohibition of Discrimination

23 Where the prohibition of discrimination applies, it confers a **defensive right** on the individual – ie a right to forbearance or a right to elimination of discriminatory practices where the infliction of disadvantages is at question. Where a discriminatory practice excludes individuals from particular benefits, the prohibition of discrimination entails a right to a renewed, non-discriminatory allocation of the benefit in question or even **a right to receive the benefit** (para 30).

2. *The Fundamental Freedoms as Liberty Rights*

24 The free movement of goods and persons as protected by the fundamental freedoms cannot only be impaired by discriminatory measures but also by indistinctly applicable measures, which apply to both nationals and foreign citizens of the Union. In Germany, for example, running a business as a craftsman requires – as a general rule – passing a so-called 'master craftsman qualifying examination'.[77] If this requirement were also applicable to foreign citizens of the Union,[78] who want to render services as craftsmen in Germany on a permanent basis, one would not necessarily assume a covert discrimination. However, the requirement of a 'master craftsman certificate' would almost exclude foreign citizens of the Union from the German market: most Member States do not provide for a 'master craftsman qualifying examination' and it cannot be expected from experienced craftsmen to pass such an examination before rendering services in Germany. The requirement of a 'master craftsman certificate' for foreign citizens of the Union would therefore violate the freedom of establishment and the freedom to provide services (as well as secondary Community law[79]) as the fundamental freedoms not only entail a prohibition of discrimination but also a **prohibition of limitation**. This already found expression in the

---

73 Or – where only nationals of one Member State are involved in a cross-border scenario – *domestic* goods or persons.
74 Cf ECJ *Sotgiu* [1974] ECR 153, paras 11–12; *Beentjes* [1988] ECR 4635, para 30; *O'Flynn* [1996] ECR I-2617, paras 17 ff; *DocMorris* [2003] ECR I-14887, paras 74–75 (cf case 1).
75 Cf ECJ *Colim* [1999] ECR I-3175.
76 Cf the case-law cited by Plötscher (note 54) p 116.
77 Cf secs 1, 7 *Handwerksordnung* (German Regulation of Crafts).
78 Which is not the case. Cf sec 9 Regulation of Crafts.
79 Cf for example Directive of the European Parliament and of the Council 1999/42/EC, [1999] OJ L201/77.

wording of the relevant Treaty provisions.[80] The ECJ was at first hesitant to attribute a prohibition of limitation to the fundamental freedoms. In 1974, however, the Court broadened the concept of the fundamental freedoms as regards the free movement of goods and services. In its judgment in the leading case *Dassonville* (which is still valid today) the ECJ defined measures having equivalent effect (Article 28 TEC/Article III-153 DC) as "all trading rules enacted by Member States which are capable of hindering, directly or indirectly, actually or potentially, intra-Community trade"[81]. According to the ECJ, limitations to be abolished pursuant to the freedom to provide services (Article 49 TEC/Article III-144 DC) are all requirements imposed on the person providing the service which may prevent or otherwise obstruct his or her activities.[82] The issue whether or not a prohibition of limitation can also be attributed to the free movement of persons was subject to intense debate.[83] In its *Bosman*-judgment[84] (concerning the transfer-system in European professional football) the ECJ answered this question in the affirmative as regards the freedom of movement for workers. In various judgments of the mid-nineties the right of establishment was interpreted correspondingly.[85] One can speak of a limitation of the free movement of persons where there is neither overt nor covert discrimination against cross-border scenarios but where the crossing of the border itself is impeded.[86] Even measures that are less favourable to nationals than to foreign citizens of the Union might constitute such an impediment.[87] The fact that indistinctly applicable measures are also to be abolished under the free movement of capital and payments (Article 56 TEC/Article III-156 DC) is supported by the clear wording of the relevant provisions ("all restrictions").[88] In summary, a limitation of the fundamental freedoms occurs where national measures are "liable to hinder or make less attractive the exercise of fundamental freedoms guaranteed by the Treaty".[89]

Since all fundamental freedoms not only entail a prohibition of discrimination but also a prohibition of limitation they can be characterised as **liberty rights**. This concept of the

25

---

80 Only the wording of the provisions on the freedom of movement for workers is slightly different.
81 ECJ *Dassonville* [1974] ECR 837, para 5 – Dassonville.
82 ECJ *van Binsbergen* [1974] ECR 1299, paras 10 ff.
83 Arguments in favour of a prohibition of limitation were already raised by Ehlers [1990] NVwZ 810, 811; Behrens [1992] EuR 145, 151 ff; Roth (note 22) E I, paras 69 ff. *Cf* more detailed Barnard (note 1) pp 238 ff.
84 ECJ *Bosman* [1995] ECR I-4921, paras 92 ff.
85 *Cf* notably ECJ *Kraus* [1993] ECR I-1663, paras 16–17; *Gebhard* [1995] ECR I-4165, paras 34 ff; as to the decision in *Gebhard* see Ehlers/Lackhoff [1996] JZ 467, 468. More detailed Lackhoff (note 56) pp 358 ff.
86 As to the establishment of branches by companies see ECJ *Centros* [1999] ECR I-1459. In its decision in *Graf* [2000] ECR I-493, para 23, the ECJ found an indistinctly applicable provision on the entitlement to compensation on termination of employment to constitute a limitation of the freedom of movement for workers because it might preclude or deter a national of a Member State from leaving his country of origin. See also Jarass [2000] EuR 705, 711.
87 *Cf* ECJ *Lehtonen* [2000] ECR I-2681, paras 47 ff: transfer deadlines for basketball players possibly violate the freedom of movement for workers – even if stricter transfer deadlines apply to domestic players.
88 More detailed on the concept of limitation with regard to the free movement of capital (which has not been sufficiently clarified by the ECJ so far) Bröhmer (note 24) Art 56 EGV, paras 16 ff.
89 ECJ *Gebhard* [1995] ECR I-4165, para 37. *Cf* also *Guiot* [1996] ECR I-1905, para 10; *Arblade* [1999] ECR I-8453, para 33; *Mazzoleni and ISA* [2001] ECR I-2189, para 22.

fundamental freedoms is still disputed.[90] However, given the general prohibition of discrimination as per Article 12 of the TEC (Article I-4(2) DC) there would not have been any need for the inclusion of the fundamental freedoms if they did not entail further protection. Apart from that, a more far-reaching access to national markets cannot be achieved without the fundamental freedoms being understood as liberty rights. Since the fundamental freedoms are only applicable to cross-border scenarios (para 20) the application of the prohibition of limitation requires **transnationality** as well. However, where cross-border scenarios do come within the ambit of protection, they are protected comprehensively (*ie* irrespective of whether the measure in question is discriminatory). Accordingly, the impact of Community law on the legal systems of the Member States increases substantially. In its decision in *Carpenter* the ECJ even found a deportation order against a national of the Philippines who resided illegally in the UK to violate the freedom to provide services of her husband – a UK national: the separation of Mr and Mrs Carpenter would be detrimental to their family life (which is protected by Article 9(1) of the ECHR and also by the fundamental rights of the Union) and, therefore, to the conditions under which Mr Carpenter exercises his freedom to provide services (→ § 11 para 56).[91] On such a basis, the fundamental freedoms apply to almost any national rule with cross-border effects. However, there always has to be an adequate link between the national rule in question and the situation that is covered by the fundamental freedoms – *ie* application of the fundamental freedoms to the benefit of the internal market[92]. Whether in *Carpenter* such a link existed between the protection of family life and the freedom to provide services appears to be highly questionable.[93]

26 The prohibition of limitation entails defensive rights – *ie* **rights to forbearance** and **rights to elimination of unlawful interferences** – where the entities bound by the fundamental freedoms are about to violate the prohibition of limitation or where such a violation has already been established. As regards the relationship between discrimination and limitation *cf* para 78.

Case 1 – Answer:
27 There appear to be no objections to the admissibility of the request for a preliminary ruling as per Article 234(1)(a), (2) of the TEC (Article III-369(1)(a), (2) DC).
1. Scope of protection of the free movement of goods: Article 28 of the TEC (Article III-153 DC) prohibits quantitative restrictions on imports and all measures having equivalent effect between Member States. The restrictive provisions of the Law on Medicinal Products affect trade between Member States (*cf* paras 19 ff, 24–25, 55 as regards the requirement of a cross-border scenario). With regard to the scope of protection of the free

---

90 Arguing for an understanding of the fundamental freedoms as (mere) prohibitions of discrimination *eg* Kingreen (note 2) pp 115 ff; Kingreen in: von Bogdandy (ed) *Europäisches Verfassungsrecht* (Heidelberg 2003) pp 652 ff. *Cf* also Jarass [1995] EuR 202, 216 ff, who (now) characterises the fundamental freedoms as (also) entailing a prohibition of limitation ([2000] EuR 705, 710 ff). Arguing for a distinction between fundamental freedoms and fundamental rights Gebauer *Die Grundfreiheiten des EG-Vertrages und Gemeinschaftsgrundrechte* (Berlin 2004) pp 346 ff.
91 ECJ *Carpenter* [2002] ECR I-6279, para 39.
92 *Cf* Gebauer (note 90) pp 308 ff, 346 ff.
93 *Cf* also Puth [2002] EuR 860, 865 ff; Mager [2003] JZ 204, 206–7; Kingreen [2004] EuGRZ 570, 573.

movement of goods the ECJ distinguishes between medicinal products that are authorised for sale in Germany by German authorities and products that are not. Pursuant to section 73(1) of the Law on Medicinal Products, products that are not authorised for sale may not be brought into German territory regardless of the method of distribution that is pursued in the individual case. According to the ECJ, section 73 of the Law on Medicinal Products cannot be seen as a measure having equivalent effect in terms of Article 28 of the TEC (Article III-153 DC) because it merely implements Article 6(1) of Directive 2001/83/EC. This view appears to be questionable: the compatibility of restrictive measures with secondary Community law does not prevent these measures from falling inside the scope of protection of a fundamental freedom – furthermore, secondary Community law itself has to be scrutinised against the fundamental freedoms. As regards the prohibition of mail-order sales of medicines that are authorised in Germany, the ECJ finds – after noting that the distribution of medicinal products is not regulated exhaustively by secondary Community law – that this prohibition falls inside the scope of protection of the free movement of goods pursuant to Article 28 of the TEC (Article III-153 DC).

2. Interference with the free movement of goods: The ECJ scrutinises the prohibition of mail-order sales of medicinal products the sale of which is restricted to pharmacies (section 43(1) of the Law on Medicinal Products) not against the prohibition of discrimination but against the prohibition of limitation which is contained in Article 28 of the TEC (Article III-153 DC). The requirements of the *Dassonville* formula (para 72) according to which all measures capable of hindering directly or indirectly, actually or potentially, intra-Community trade are to be regarded as measures having equivalent effect to quantitative restrictions are fulfilled. As the ECJ held in *Keck*, rules merely governing arrangements for the sale of products are not regarded as quantitative restrictions (para 75). However, *Keck* only covers rules which apply to all relevant traders operating in the national territory (as it is the case here) and which affect in the same manner, in law and in fact, the marketing of both domestic products and those from other Member States. According to the ECJ, the second requirement is not satisfied by the Law on Medicinal Products because of pharmacies in Germany still being able to sell the products in question in their dispensaries so that they are not affected by the prohibition of mail-order sales in the same manner as pharmacies outside Germany. One can object to this view because the prohibition of mail-order sales does not affect (medicinal) products but their distribution. Following the ECJ, the prohibition contained in section 43(1) of the Law on Medicinal Products represents a measure having equivalent effect.

3. Justification of the interference: A justification of interferences with the fundamental freedoms under Article 30 of the TEC (Article III-154 DC) is not possible where the subject matter in question is regulated exhaustively by secondary Community law (otherwise the harmonisation of the law of the Member States could be circumvented). However, since mail-order sales of medicinal products are not regulated exhaustively, section 43(1) of the Law on Medicinal Products can be based on the "protection of health and life" as a ground for justification under Article 30 of the TEC (Article III-154 DC). Furthermore, an interference with the fundamental freedoms has to be proportional. In particular, the national measure has to be necessary to achieve the desired objective. With regard to this, the ECJ distinguishes between medicinal products that are only available on prescription and products that are not. As regards medicines that are available without prescription the potential risks are small – adequate information and advice can also be given over the internet. In contrast, the sale of medicines that are available only on prescription requires personal customer contact. Section 43(1) of the Law on Medicinal Products therefore violates Article 28 of the TEC (Article III-153 DC) insofar as it applies to medicinal products which are authorised for sale in Germany and which are available without prescription.

3. The Fundamental Freedoms as Rights to Governmental Action

Case 2 – Problem: (ECJ *Commission v France* [1997] ECR I-6959)

28 After having delivered a reasoned opinion, the Commission brings an action before the ECJ for a declaration that the French Republic has violated Article 28 of the TEC (Article III-153 DC). The Commission refers to numerous violent acts committed by private individuals and by protest movements of French farmers directed against lorries that transport fruits and vegetables from Spain or Italy to France. The French government stresses that it has adopted all measures open to it in order to ensure the free movement of goods on its territory.

29 One can distinguish between original (para 33) and derivative (para 30) rights to governmental action as well as rights aimed at governmental protection (para 31).

a) Derivative Rights to Governmental Action

30 Derivative rights to governmental action are based on the prohibition of discrimination. They convey an **entitlement** to existing benefits (granted by the state) to individuals that are excluded from those benefits in a discriminatory manner. Since the fundamental freedoms are primarily understood as equality rights this function can be regarded as a matter of course. However, in case of a discriminatory exclusion from benefits derivative rights to governmental action do not necessarily lead to the granting of these benefits. Under German law, for example, it is accepted that a violation of equality rights can be eliminated in three different ways: The access to the benefit in question can be extended, the benefit can be withdrawn entirely or the allocation of the benefit can be re-regulated. The individual has a right to claim the benefit in exceptional cases only – *ie* where an entitlement to the benefit is guaranteed by the Constitution or by statutory law, where the legislator has created a complex system of allocation and obviously wants to maintain it or in case of self-commitment by the state.[94] As regards Community law, this concept requires some modification because it is unlikely for Member States to eliminate a violation of the fundamental freedoms by putting their own nationals at a disadvantage. If, for example, a Member State excludes foreign citizens of the Union from assistance covering maintenance costs of students, one does not expect the Member State in question to stop granting this assistance to its own nationals in order to restore equality. In addition, Member States also have to eliminate any temporary preferential treatment of their own nationals. Accordingly, the prohibition of discrimination as it is contained in the fundamental freedoms entails the right to claim benefits where and insofar as foreign citizens of the Union are excluded in a discriminatory manner from benefits that are granted to nationals.[95] However, it remains possible for the Member States to re-regulate the allocation of benefits in accordance with the fundamental freedoms.

b) Rights to Governmental Protection

31 Under certain requirements, liberty rights in German law are understood as conferring a right to claim governmental **protection against unlawful interferences by private indivi-**

---

94 *Cf* also Pieroth/Schlink *Grundrechte* (22nd ed, Heidelberg 2006) paras 485–486.
95 *Cf* also Kingreen (note 2) p 192; Frenz (note 71) para 184.

duals.[96] The same effect can be attributed to the fundamental freedoms.[97] Restrictions on trade do not only emanate from the Member States or from the EC itself but also from private individuals. As 'guarantors' of the fundamental freedoms[98] the Member States (or the EC) are, at least in principle, obliged to take steps against such restrictions. However, this general rule does not apply to situations in which restrictive conduct by private individuals is itself protected by fundamental rights. Accordingly, the failure to ban a demonstration which amounts to a restriction of the free movement of goods (demonstration organised by an environmental group on the Brenner motorway, the effect of which was to completely close that motorway) can be necessary in order to protect the protesters' right to freedom of expression and freedom of assembly.[99] Where Member States are obliged to protect against interferences by private individuals, this obligation can also entail the right to claim such governmental protection. The decision on *how* to provide protection, though, is subject to discretion on the part of the Member States. A duty to intervene in a particular manner only arises in exceptional cases. It has yet to be sufficiently clarified under which circumstances a right to claim certain protective measures or a lawful decision thereon emerges.[100] However, it appears to be reasonable to grant such a right where the failure to provide protection amounts to a limitation of the fundamental freedom in question. One has to distinguish between duties to protect that can be derived from the fundamental freedoms and those arising from the fundamental rights of the Union (or from domestic guarantees) (→ § 14 para 22). Exercise of the latter can lead to a justified limitation of the fundamental freedoms (para 86).

Case 2 – Answer:
The admissibility of the action brought before the ECJ does not appear to be questionable. The Commission has observed the procedure prescribed by Article 226 of the TEC (Article III-360 DC). The action is well-founded if the French Republic has violated Article 28 of the TEC (Article III-153 DC). An impediment to the free movement of goods cannot only emanate from positive acts but also from a failure to act on the part of the Member States – especially where private individuals are restricting the flow of trade. The decision on which measures are to be taken in such a situation is subject to discretion on the part of the Member States who are solely responsible for the maintenance of public security within their territory. In the present case, however, the French Republic has obviously and insistently refused to take adequate and efficient measures in order to prevent violent acts from being committed. The ECJ therefore convincingly found that the French Republic has violated Article 28 of the TEC (Article III-153 DC).

32

---

96 *Cf* the case-law cited by Sachs in: Sachs (ed) *Grundgesetz* (4th ed, Munich 2007) Vor Art 1 GG, para 35 with note 69. More detailed Dietlein *Die Lehre von den grundrechtlichen Schutzpflichten* (Berlin 1992) pp 51 ff; see also the criticism raised by Isensee in: Hübner (ed) *Festschrift für Bernhard Großfeld zum 65. Geburtstag* (Heidelberg 1999) pp 485, 500 ff.
97 Frenz (note 71) paras 190 ff. *Cf* more detailed Van den Bogaert in: Barnard/Scott (eds) *The Law of the Single European Market – Unpacking the Premises* (Oxford 2002) pp 123 ff.
98 *Cf* Burgi [1999] EWS 327, 329–30.
99 ECJ *Schmidberger* [2003] ECR I-5659. More detailed Kadelbach/Petersen [2002] EuGRZ 213.
100 More detailed on the duties to protect that can be derived from the fundamental freedoms and on the consequences thereof Schwarze [1998] EuR 53; Szczekalla [1998] DVBl 219; Burgi [1999] EWS 327; Kühling [1999] NJW 403.

c) Original Rights to Governmental Action

33 Regardless of the right to claim governmental protection and the rights to procedural guarantees (which are covered below) the fundamental freedoms **neither** convey a right to claim the **creation** of new **benefits** to be granted by the state, **nor** a right to claim the creation of new **public facilities**. Such original rights to governmental action are not provided for within the inner structure of the fundamental freedoms. To reinterpret the fundamental freedoms as containing such guarantees would mean to overextend their character (*ie* the prohibition of discrimination and limitation) as well as to substantially limit the political margin of the Member States and to drastically widen the power of the Community courts. A different conclusion might be reached in exceptional cases.[101]

4. The Fundamental Freedoms as Procedural Rights

34 The fundamental freedoms also convey **procedural guarantees**. Neither legal academics nor the courts have thus far paid much attention to this dimension of the fundamental freedoms. A reason for this may be the fact that the prohibition of discrimination and limitation themselves often have procedural implications, without necessitating a derivation of separate procedural rights. If, for example, a lawyer from another Member State is not admitted to legal practice in Germany for not having passed the *Staatsexamen* (German Bar Exam), this rejection constitutes a limitation of the freedom of establishment or a discrimination. The limitation or discrimination is justified if German law provides for a procedure in the course of which the equivalence of a degree obtained in the Member State of origin is examined and if the foreign lawyer is given an opportunity to demonstrate the required knowledge of German law in a supplementary examination (other than the *Staatsexamen*). However, one can arrive at the same result by directly deriving a right to the above-mentioned procedural precautions from the freedom of establishment if admission to legal practice requires certain professional qualifications under national law. Accordingly, in its decision in *Vlassopoulou* the ECJ found that the examination in question "must be carried out … in accordance with a procedure which is in conformity with the requirements of Community law".[102] Either line of legal argumentation demonstrates that the fundamental freedoms often entail procedural rights.[103] In many cases, these rights are further enhanced by rights to governmental protection. Where Community law is directly applicable and entails subjective rights, the ECJ also considers beneficiaries to be entitled to **effective judicial protection**.[104] Member States are therefore obliged to provide for the possibility of interim relief if an effective application of Community law so requires.[105] In this context, the ECJ primarily refers to Article 10 of the

---

101 The formation of a legal person in another Member State, for example, may not be rendered impossible by entirely repudiating the concept of legal persons within a domestic legal system.
102 ECJ *Vlassopoulou* [1991] ECR I-2357, para 22.
103 *Cf*, for example, ECJ *Commission v Italy* [1996] ECR I-2691, paras 8 ff; *CO.NA.ME.* [2005] ECR I-7287, para 21.
104 *Cf* ECJ *Johnston* [1986] ECR 1651, paras 18–19; *Heylens* [1987] ECR 4097, para 14; *Kühne* [2001] ECR I-9517, para 57; *Unión de Pequeños Agricultores* [2002] ECR I-6677, para 39; Tonne *Effektiver Rechtsschutz durch staatliche Gerichte als Forderung des europäischen Gemeinschaftsrechts* (Cologne 1997) pp 200 ff; Ehlers [2004] DVBl 1441–2.
105 *Cf* ECJ *Factortame* [1990] ECR I-2433, para 19.

General Principles §7 III

TEC (Article I-5(2) DC). However, where the effectiveness of Community rules (*effet utile*) is at question, this principle can also be derived from the fundamental freedoms.

5. The Objective Dimension of the Fundamental Freedoms

The objective dimension of the fundamental freedoms (*ie* fundamental freedoms as normative obligations that cannot be judicially enforced by the individual) is hardly covered in academic articles or textbooks. Some authors explicitly object to such a dimension of the fundamental freedoms.[106] However, while subjective rights can only be derived from legal rules that possess an objective dimension, not every normative obligation that is binding on the state corresponds to a subjective right of the individual – legal rules with an objective dimension therefore possibly but not necessarily entail subjective rights. The fundamental freedoms possess an **objective dimension**. Due to their character as normative obligations they have an impact on all areas of law of the Member States as well as on secondary Community law. Accordingly, the whole body of law of the Member States (including private law) as well as secondary Community law has to be applied and interpreted in accordance with and conforming to the fundamental freedoms.[107] In addition, the fundamental freedoms oblige both the Member States and the EC to offer governmental protection under certain conditions (para 31) and to provide for certain procedural safeguards (para 34). The fundamental freedoms shall take effect to the largest extent possible (*effet utile*). Hence, they even impose normative obligations on the Member States (and on the EC) where these obligations cannot be judicially enforced by the individual.[108] It seems, that the objective dimension of the fundamental freedoms was decisive, for example, in *Carpenter* (para 25) as the action by Mrs Carpenter against her deportation order was successful because of a violation of her husband's freedom to provide services – regardless of Mrs Carpenter not being a beneficiary of the freedom to provide services. Under no circumstances do the fundamental freedoms create or expand the jurisdiction of the EC. Where the Communities wish to specify or expand the scope of the fundamental freedoms or to harmonise relevant Member States' laws, the Treaty provisions that enable the institutions to define and implement the fundamental freedoms (*eg* Articles 40, 44, 47, 52, 53 TEC/Articles III-134, III-138, III-141, III-147, III-148 DC) have to be utilised.

35

III. Beneficiaries of the Fundamental Freedoms

Case 3 – Problem:
The major German city K is the sole shareholder in a limited company which provides manifold services in the fields of public transportation, energy supply, water supply and consultancy. For the future the company plans to provide its services not only in K but also in other Member States of the EC. However, according to German domestic law local au-

36

---

106 Kingreen (note 2) pp 200–1. Frenz (note 71) paras 213 ff, now shares the view taken here.
107 *Cf* also Jarass [1991] EuR 211, 222; Jarass [1995] EuR 202, 211; Zuleeg (1993) 53 VVDStRL 154, 165 ff.
108 As to the objective dimension of fundamental rights in general Hesse *Grundzüge des Verfassungsrechts der Bundesrepublik Deutschland* (20th ed, Heidelberg 1999) § 9, paras 290 ff. Critical as to such an objective dimension Cremer *Freiheitsgrundrechte – Funktionen und Strukturen* (Tübingen 2003) pp 198 ff.

> thorities may not pursue economic activities outside their territory. The competent German supervisory authority therefore ordered K to refrain from providing services in other Member States. K would like to know whether this order is in accordance with the fundamental freedoms.

1. Nationals of the Member States

37 Beneficiaries of the fundamental freedoms are first and foremost all **nationals of the Member States**. As regards the freedom of movement for workers, the freedom of establishment and the free movement of services this follows from Articles 39(2), 43(1), 49(1) of the TEC (Articles III-133(2), III-137(1), III-144 DC). The same principle, however, also applies to the free movement of goods, capital and payments. As a general rule[109], the Member States independently decide on the granting and deprivation of nationality. In some cases, even citizens of overseas or dependent territories such as Gibraltar or Martinique[110] count as nationals of the relevant Member State (*cf* more detailed para 48). The fundamental freedoms primarily cover foreign citizens of the Union – in case of a crossborder scenario (para 20) the nationals of the Member State concerned are protected as well. Where someone not only possesses the nationality of a Member State but also the nationality of a third country he or she is fully covered by the fundamental freedoms.[111] Stricter requirements apply with regard to some guarantees: *eg* as per Article 43(1)(ii) of the TEC (Article III-137(1)(ii) DC) the setting up of agencies is only protected if it is undertaken by nationals who are established in the territory of any Member State. It is irrelevant whether or not the nationals of the Member States are of full age or whether or not they are of legal capacity. These categories are only relevant when it comes to the judicial enforcement of the fundamental freedoms (paras 99 ff).

2. Legal Persons and Groups of Individuals within the Community

38 In the field of the freedom of establishment and the free movement of services, Articles 48(1), 55 of the TEC (Article III-142(1), III-150 DC) explicitly put **companies** on a par with natural persons that are nationals of a Member State. The Treaty refers to companies that are constituted under civil or commercial law, including cooperative societies and other legal persons governed by public or private law, save for those which are non-profit making (Article 48(2) TEC/Article III-142(2) DC). Incorporation – *ie* formation of an entity that has legal personality distinct from its members – is not required. Any form of organisation that is predefined by law can suffice. Hence, a partnership under the *Bürgerliches Gesetzbuch* (German Civil Code) is covered by the fundamental freedoms although its (full) legal capacity still being doubted.[112] It follows from the mentioning of

---

109 As to the exceptions *cf* Wölker/Grill in: von der Groeben/Schwarze (eds) *Vertrag über die Europäische Union und Vertrag zur Gründung der Europäischen Gemeinschaft. Kommentar* (6th ed, Baden-Baden 2004) Vorb Art 39–41 EGV, para 49.
110 More detailed Wölker/Grill (note 109) Vorb Art 39–41 EGV, paras 51 ff.
111 *Cf* ECJ *Micheletti* [1992] ECR I-4239, para 11.
112 Predominant opinion; *cf* Randelzhofer in: Grabitz/Hilf (eds) *Das Recht der Europäischen Union* (loose-leaf, Munich) Art 58 EGV, para 3. See the criticism raised by Bröhmer (note 24) Art 48 EGV, para 4. As to the legal capacity of partnerships under the Civil Code *cf Bundesgerichtshof* (BGH – German Federal Supreme Court) (2001) 146 BGHZ 341.

cooperative societies and legal persons governed by public law that the Treaty pursues a broad concept of 'profit making'. Any form of economic activity involving the offer of services normally provided for remuneration in the interest of (partial) cost recovery is sufficient.[113] Not only foundations and associations but also **legal persons governed by public law** which are under governmental control as well as the Member States themselves – insofar as they want to engage in economic activities in other Member States – are counted among 'legal persons'. However, 'companies or firms' are only treated in the same way as natural persons if they were formed in accordance with the law of a Member State and if they have their registered office, central administration or principal place of business within the Community (Article 48(1) TEC/Article III-142(1) DC). The nationality of partners or shareholders[114] and the existence of an effective and stable link with the economy of a Member State are both irrelevant.[115] In situations covered by Article 43(1)(ii) of the TEC (Article III-137(1)(ii) DC) the company has to be established within the Community.

The concept of an internal market cannot be realised if companies within the meaning of Article 48(2) of the TEC (Article III-142(2) DC) are not protected by the free **movement** of **goods**, **capital** and **payments**. Consequently, the principles that have been mentioned above with regard to the freedom of establishment and the free movement of services also apply to the other freedoms. According to the case-law of the ECJ, even the freedom of movement for workers applies to non-natural persons. In the view of the Court, employers can rely on Article 39 of the TEC (Article III-133 DC) if they are kept from employing, in the Member State in which they are established, workers who are nationals of another Member State.[116] In this regard, it is irrelevant whether the employer in question is a natural or a legal person.

Case 3 – Answer:
It emanates from Article 55 (Article III-150 DC) read in conjunction with Article 48 of the TEC (Article III-142 DC) that legal persons governed by public or private law, save for those which are non-profit making, can rely on the fundamental freedoms. Hence, public enterprises are beneficiaries of the fundamental freedoms. They can rely on the fundamental freedoms vis-à-vis other Member States without any restrictions. As regards private undertakings, the four freedoms of the TEC also entail a right (vis-à-vis the Member State of establishment) to leave the domestic market in order to engage in economic activities in other Member States. According to a widespread opinion the same applies to public enterprises.[117] However, this view cannot be followed.[118] Community law is not concerned with

---

113 *Cf* also Oppermann (note 26) para 1586; Scheuer in: Lenz/Borchardt (eds) *EU- und EG-Vertrag. Kommentar* (4th ed, Cologne 2006) Art 48 EGV, para 1.
114 *Cf* Ahlt/Deisenhofer *Europarecht* (3rd ed, Munich 2003) pp 193–4.
115 Lackhoff (note 56) pp 193–4.
116 ECJ *Clean Car* [1998] ECR I-2521, paras 19 ff.
117 *Cf* Nagel *Gemeindeordnung als Hürde?* (Baden-Baden 1999) pp 48 ff; Nagel [2000] NVwZ 758, 761; Becker [2000] ZNER 259, 261; Schwintowski [2001] NVwZ 607, 610, 612; Jarass *Kommunale Wirtschaftsunternehmen im Wettbewerb* (Stuttgart 2002) pp 41 ff.
118 *Cf* also Manthey *Bindung und Schutz öffentlicher Unternehmen durch die Grundfreiheiten des europäischen Gemeinschaftsrechts* (Frankfurt am Main 2001) pp 115 ff; Weiß [2002] DVBl 564; Ehlers in: Wurzel/Schraml/Becker (eds) *Rechtspraxis der kommunalen Unternehmen* (Munich 2005) B, para 12.

the internal organisation of the Member States – it always addresses a Member State as a whole. As a consequence, EC law does not protect political or administrative subdivisions of a state against each other where the Member State as a whole has to comply with the requirements of Community law. The prohibition of extraterritorial economic activities pursued by local authorities, which does not affect economic activities by private undertakings, is a matter of internal governmental organisation as well. In any case – even under the (mistaken) assumption that the fundamental freedoms are applicable to the territorial restrictions in question – these restrictions are justified. Hence, the fundamental freedoms do not confer on public enterprises (vis-à-vis the Member State of establishment) a right to leave the domestic market in order to engage in economic activities in other Member States.

3. Non-EU Citizens and Legal Persons/Groups of Individuals Outside the Community

41 Under certain conditions even non-EU citizens or legal persons and groups of individuals outside the Community can rely on the fundamental freedoms. For instance **products coming from third countries** which are in free circulation in at least one Member State fall inside the scope of protection of the free movement of goods (Articles 23(2), 24 TEC/Article III-151(2), (3) DC). As a matter of coherence, it appears to be reasonable to also include in the scope of protection all persons trading these products – regardless of their nationality.[119] The same can be argued with regard to the free movement of capital and payments because of all restrictions on the movement of capital "between Member States and third countries" being prohibited in the interest of a free circulation of capital – regardless of its origin – within the Community.[120] Finally, **family members** (who may be non-EU citizens) of all beneficiaries of the freedom of movement for workers and the freedom of establishment are protected by the said guarantees including the legal power to independently enforce those interests in a court of law (para 4).[121] A (partial) enjoyment of the fundamental freedoms for non-EU citizens can also be provided for through association agreements.[122]

IV. Entities Bound by the Fundamental Freedoms

42 **Case 4 – Problem:** (ECJ *Angonese* [2000] ECR I-4139)
The claimant in proceedings pending before an Italian court is an Italian national whose mother tongue is German and who went to study in Austria. In response to a notice published in the local newspapers he applied to take part in a competition for a post with a private banking undertaking in Bolzano (the defendant). One of the conditions for entry to the

---

119 Likewise Jarass [2000] EuR 705, 708. *Contra* Kingreen (note 2) p 79, who points out that the free movement of goods can be the subject matter of agreements establishing an association according to Article 310 of the TEC (Article III-324 DC).
120 Likewise (as to the result) Schürmann in: Lenz/Borchardt (eds) *EU- und EG-Vertrag. Kommentar* (4th ed, Cologne 2006) Art 56 EGV, para 15.
121 Likewise Brechmann in: Calliess/Ruffert (eds) *Kommentar des Vertrages über die Europäische Union und des Vertrages zur Gründung der Europäischen Gemeinschaft* (2nd ed, Neuwied 2002) Art 39 EGV, para 8; Lackhoff (note 56) p 182. As to the freedom to provide services *cf*, however, para 25 (decision in *Carpenter*).
122 *Cf*, for example, Decision 1/80 of the EEC-Turkey Association Council (partial freedom of movement for Turkish workers).

competition was possession of an official certificate of bilingualism, which can only be issued by the public authorities of the province of Bolzano. Since the claimant did not produce such a certificate he was not admitted to the competition. The Italian court seized of the case decided to stay proceedings and referred to the ECJ the question whether it was compatible with Article 39 of the TEC (Article III-133 DC) to make the admission of candidates for a competition organised to fill posts in a company governed by private law conditional on possession of a particular type of official certificate of bilingualism.

1. Member States of the European Communities

The fundamental freedoms are first and foremost binding on the Member States. Since they have direct effect in the domestic legal orders (para 7), the concept of 'Member State' is a functional one in this context. It covers any **authority vested with governmental powers**. Not only federal governments, state and local authorities as well as other legal persons governed by public law which are under governmental control – *eg* professional bodies[123] – but also legal persons governed by private law which are (directly or indirectly) held in their entirety by a legal person governed by public law are included. The four freedoms are binding on the Member State of the recipient of the good, service or payment or in which establishment is intended, as well as on the Member State of origin.[124] The Member States are bound irrespective of the form and manner in which they act (*eg* acts of parliament, judicial decisions *etc*).[125] In addition, any organisation or body that is subject to control by a Member State and whose acts are therefore attributable to said state is bound by the fundamental freedoms.[126] As an example, one can speak of 'Member State control' where officials of the body in question – which is not formally a part of state administration – are appointed by the government and remunerated out of the state budget.[127] The same applies to bodies which are vested with "special powers beyond those which result from the normal rules applicable to relations between individuals".[128]

43

2. European Communities

Beside the Member States, the **European Communities** themselves – including their **institutions** – are also bound by the fundamental freedoms.[129] This is due to the fact that measures of the European Communities can impede the internal market as well. In addition, the fundamental freedoms shall be observed 'communitywide'. Forming a part of primary Community law, the fundamental freedoms take supremacy over secondary Community

44

---

123 As to professional bodies which are equipped with governmental authority *cf* ECJ *Royal Pharmaceutical Society* [1989] ECR 1295, paras 15–16; *Hünermund* [1993] ECR I-6787, 6821.
124 Jarass [2000] EuR 705, 714.
125 *Cf* ECJ *Commission v Ireland* [1982] ECR 4005, paras 3 ff.
126 *Cf* ECJ *Apple and Pear Development Council* [1983] ECR 4083, paras 16–17; *Hennen Olie* [1990] ECR I-4625, paras 16 ff; Craig/de Búrca (note 1) p 625.
127 ECJ *Hennen Olie* [1990] ECR I-4625, para 15.
128 *Cf* ECJ *Foster* [1990] ECR I-3313, para 18.
129 *Cf* ECJ *Rewe* [1984] ECR 1229, para 18; *Meyhui* [1994] ECR I-3879, para 11; *Swedish Match* [2004] ECR I-11900, para 59; Jarass [1995] EuR 202, 211; Schwemer *Die Bindung des Gemeinschaftsgesetzgebers an die Grundfreiheiten* (Frankfurt am Main 1995) p 45; Kingreen/Störmer [1998] EuR 263, 277.

law in case of conflicts (Article 249(1) TEC: "in accordance with the provisions of this Treaty"; Article I-33(1) DC: "in accordance with Part III").[130] Furthermore, it would be contradictory for the Communities to assign duties to the Member States which are not binding on the Communities themselves. However, in the past – as far as is apparent – neither the ECJ nor the CFI have ever found a Community measure to violate the fundamental freedoms.[131] As to the criticism against this reluctance *cf* para 7.

3. Private Individuals

45 There is still ambiguity about whether or not the fundamental freedoms can be binding on private individuals. In any case, the ECJ found private individuals to be directly bound (*ie* **direct horizontal effect / *Drittwirkung***) with regard to the freedom of movement for workers, the freedom to provide services and the general prohibition of discrimination pursuant to Article 12 of the TEC (Article I-4(2) DC).[132] The Court wants to prevent private individuals – exercising their freedom of contract – from establishing limitations of the fundamental freedoms which the Member States would be barred from imposing. However, the relevant cases were primarily concerned with the protection of individuals against powerful private associations (sporting associations in particular).[133] In its more recent case-law, the ECJ seems to go further by generally recognising horizontal effects of the fundamental freedoms vis-à-vis private individuals – at least to a certain extent.[134]

46 However, the assumption of direct horizontal effects of the fundamental freedoms appears to be **problematic**. The wording of the relevant provisions ("between Member States") often presupposes some form of governmental action. The explicit grounds for possible restrictions on the fundamental freedoms (public policy and security in particular) are also geared to governmental action. It seems highly debatable whether private individuals can justify alleged restrictions on the fundamental freedoms on these grounds (as accepted by the ECJ[135]) because private individuals generally pursue different objectives than public bodies or governmental agencies. The fundamental freedoms certainly offer protection against **provisions of private law** that are discriminatory or that interfere with liberty rights, since such provisions can be attributed to the respective Member State. However, where **genuine private action** is alleged to interfere with the fundamental freedoms, many arguments support the assumption that the fundamental freedoms merely entail a right to claim governmental protection (by the Member States or by the EC)

---

130 As to the fact that secondary Community law takes priority in application *cf* para 7. See, however, also von Bogdandy [2001] JZ 157, 166, who interprets the case-law of the ECJ as only prohibiting *manifest* violations of primary Community law on the part of the Community legislator.
131 *Cf* ECJ *Denkavit* [1984] ECR 2171, paras 13 ff; *Meyhui* [1994] ECR I-3879, paras 9 ff; *Kieffer* [1997] ECR I-3629, paras 24 ff.
132 *Cf* ECJ *Walrave* [1974] ECR 1405, paras 16 ff; *Donà* [1976] ECR 1333, paras 17 ff; *Bosman* [1995] ECR I-4921, para 84; *Lehtonen* [2000] ECR I-2681; Craig/de Búrca (note 1) p 771. As to the free movement of goods *cf* ECJ *Dansk Supermarked* [1981] ECR 181, paras 16 ff (see the comments by Roth in: Due (ed) *Festschrift für Ulrich Everling, Band II* (Baden-Baden 1995) pp 1231, 1234–5), as to the freedom of establishment ECJ *van Ameyde* [1977] ECR 1091, para 28.
133 *Cf* Herdegen *Europarecht* (8th ed, Munich 2006) para 284.
134 *Cf* para 47. See also ECJ *Clean Car* [1998] ECR I-2521, paras 19 ff.
135 See in particular ECJ *Bosman* [1995] ECR I-4921, paras 86–87.

General Principles	§ 7 IV 3

against such unlawful interferences by private third parties (para 31).[136] Apart from that, protection against action by private individuals is only granted by the competition rules (Articles 81 ff TEC[137]/Articles III-161 ff DC) and by secondary Community law.

Case 4 – Answer:
I. Admissibility of the request for a preliminary ruling: The request for a preliminary ruling seeks an authoritative interpretation of Article 39 of the TEC (Article III-133 DC) – ie interpretation of the Treaty in terms of Article 234(1)(a) of the TEC (Art III-369(1)(a) DC). The admissibility of the request is questionable because a decision of the ECJ might not be necessary in the present case. The fundamental freedoms of the TEC are only applicable to cross-border scenarios (para 20). Since the claimant has been resident in the province of Bolzano since his birth without ever having conducted economic activities in other Member States and in the absence of any direct relevance of his studies in Austria for the present legal dispute, the case might have no connection with Community law. However, according to settled case-law of the ECJ it is for the national courts alone, which are seized of a case and which must assume responsibility for the judgment to be given, to determine both the need for a preliminary ruling and the relevance of the questions which they refer to the Court. A reference for a preliminary ruling from a national court may be rejected only if it is "quite obvious" that the interpretation of Community law sought by that court bears no relation to the actual nature of the case or the subject-matter of the main proceedings (cf ECJ Cabour [1998] ECR I-2055, para 21). In the present case the ECJ does not assume "obviousness" in this sense.

II. Compatibility of the requirement to possess an official certificate of bilingualism with Article 39 of the TEC (Article II-133 DC): The requirement to possess an official certificate of bilingualism can only be scrutinised against Article 39 of the TEC if this provision is binding on private individuals (here: a private banking undertaking in Bolzano). Although the banking undertaking in question cannot be classified as a private institution with enhanced social relevance and special powers, the ECJ assumes the prohibition of discrimination on grounds of nationality as per Article 39 of the TEC (Article III-133 DC) to be binding on private individuals. The Court bases this assumption on three arguments: the wording of Article 39 of the TEC (Article III-133 DC) does not explicitly negate a direct horizontal effect (1), the freedom of movement for workers cannot only be impeded by governmental action but also by private individuals (2), the uniform application of Community law requires an interpretation of Article 39 of the TEC (Article III-133 DC) in line with Article 12 (Article I-4(2) DC) and 141 of the TEC (Article III-214 DC) which prohibit discrimination of any kind regardless of its 'origin' (3). According to this view – which is by no means of compelling persuasiveness – the defendant is bound by Article 39 of the TEC

---

[136] Criticism against the case-law of the ECJ is also raised by Jaensch *Die unmittelbare Drittwirkung der Grundfreiheiten* (Baden-Baden 1997) pp 81 ff; Kluth (1997) 122 AoR 557, 568 ff; Streinz/Leible [2000] EuZW 459, 464 ff; Kadelbach/Petersen [2002] EuGRZ 213, 220. Arguing for a direct horizontal effect Steindorff in· Badura (ed) *Wege und Verfahren des Verfassungslebens – Festschrift für Peter Lerche* (Munich 1993) pp 575, 581 ff; Ganten *Die Drittwirkung der Grundfreiheiten* (Berlin 2000) pp 56 ff; Wernicke *Die Privatwirkung im europäischen Gemeinschaftsrecht* (Baden-Baden 2002) pp 201 ff; Parpart *Die unmittelbare Bindung Privater an die Personenverkehrsfreiheit im europäischen Gemeinschaftsrecht* (Munich 2003) pp 185 ff.

[137] The competition rules do not prohibit every kind of anti-competitive behaviour but only such private action that potentially affects trade between Member States. In addition, other requirements must be fulfilled (perceptible distortion of competition, behaviour by an undertaking, dominant position), cf Streinz/Leible [2000] EuZW 459, 464.

(Article III-133 DC). Furthermore, the requirement to possess a particular type of language-certificate as one condition for entry to the competition for a post with the defendant constitutes a (covert) discrimination, because persons who are not resident in the province of Bolzano have little chance of acquiring the diploma in question. Hence, nationals of other Member States are put at a disadvantage vis-à-vis individuals who are resident in the province of Bolzano. In the view of the ECJ, the said discrimination is not justified: Even though requiring an applicant for a post to have a certain level of linguistic knowledge may be legitimate and possession of a diploma such as the certificate in question may constitute a criterion for assessing that knowledge, the fact that it is impossible to submit proof of the required linguistic knowledge by any other means, in particular by equivalent qualifications obtained in other Member States, must be considered disproportionate in relation to the aim pursued. Accordingly, the ECJ found the admission practice of the defendant to be incompatible with Article 39 of the TEC (Article III-133 DC).

V. Territorial Scope of the Fundamental Freedoms

48 The territorial scope of protection of the TEC – including the fundamental freedoms – is defined in Article 299 of the TEC (Article IV-440 DC). It ties in with the **national territory of the Member States** – *ie* the part of the earth's surface, soil, airspace and waters which falls under the territorial jurisdiction of the Member States pursuant to the principles of international law[138]. Since the territorial scope of the TEC therefore depends on the territory of the Member States, one can speak of a flexible course of the frontier of the Treaty. As soon as the sovereign territory of a Member State changes (*eg* after the German Unification), the scope of application of the TEC including the fundamental freedoms is automatically extended (subject to any contractual provisions to the contrary). Some overseas departments and other territories of the Member States fall inside the scope of the TEC (Article 299(2), (4), (5) TEC/Article IV-440(2), (4), (5) DC) whereas others (Article 299(3) TEC read in conjunction with Annex 2/Article IV-440(3) DC) as well as the European mini states (*eg* Andorra, Monaco, San Marino, Vatican City) are partially or fully excluded from its application.[139] Article 299(6) of the TEC (Article IV-440(6) DC) lays down some particularities. Pursuant to the said provision the Treaty does not apply in full to the Channel Islands and the Isle of Man. Article 2 of Protocol 3 to the Act of Accession annexed to the Treaty of Accession of 1972[140], by which the United Kingdom became a member of the EEC, lays down that nationals of the Channel Islands and the Isle of Man shall not benefit from Community provisions relating to the free movement of persons and services. As a consequence, nationals of the said territories do not have the legal power to enforce the guarantees relating to the free movement of persons and services in a court of law. The fundamental freedoms apply to all legal relations that have a territorial connection with the Community either due to their place of conclusion or due to the place where they unfold their effects.[141] Furthermore, the fundamental freedoms even

---

138 *Cf* Graf Vitzthum in: Graf Vitzthum (ed) *Völkerrecht* (3rd ed, Berlin 2004) 5. Abschnitt, para 15; Ipsen *Völkerrecht* (5th ed, Munich 2004) § 5, para 4.
139 *Cf* also the protocols to the Community treaties.
140 [1972] OJ L73.
141 With regard to a cycling federation that (also) pursues activities outside the Community *cf* ECJ *Walrave* [1974] ECR 1405, paras 28–29.

apply to legal relations outside the Community if these relations are **strongly connected with the law of a Member State** and – as a consequence – with the relevant rules of EC law. Accordingly, the ECJ found that a Belgian national working for the German embassy in Algiers could rely on the freedom of movement for workers.[142] Where Member States have exploitation rights outside their territorial waters they are nevertheless bound by the rules relating to the free movement of persons and the freedom to provide services.[143]

VI. Temporal Scope of the Fundamental Freedoms

The Treaty establishing the European Economic Community entered into force on **1 January 1958**. With the expiration of the transition periods the fundamental freedoms became directly applicable (para 7). As regards new Member States, details concerning the entry into force of the fundamental freedoms are laid down in the accession treaties (para 7). Pursuant to Article 312 of the TEC (Article IV-446 DC) the Treaty is concluded for an **unlimited period**. In contrast to Article I-60 of the DC, the Treaty as it stands today does not provide for a voluntary withdrawal from the Community and/or the Union. However, since the Member States remain the 'Masters of the Treaties'[144], an exceptional termination according to the (narrow) rules of international law (Articles 60 ff of the Vienna Convention on the Law of Treaties) is possible. In contrast, there exists no possibility to exclude a Member State. At the most, a temporary suspension of rights resulting from Community and/or Union membership can be justified (a suspension of the fundamental freedoms only makes sense where Member States benefit from their application).[145] As a basic principle, the temporal dimension of the interpretation of the fundamental freedoms is determined by their date of entry into force and by the date at which they became directly applicable.[146] However, in rare exceptions (*ie* cases involving a risk of serious economic repercussions by reason of an objective and significant uncertainty regarding the implications of Community provisions[147]) the effects of a decision of the ECJ relating to the fundamental freedoms may be restricted to the future in order to give effect to the general principle of legal certainty which is inherent in the Community legal order.[148]

49

VII. Scope of Protection, Interferences, Justification

Up to now, there is no commonly accepted pattern according to which a measure can be scrutinised against its consistency with the fundamental freedoms. Nevertheless, it appears to be suitable – similar to the pattern which is used with regard to the fundamental rights of the European Union (→ § 14 para 51) – to assess whether the situation in question falls within the scope of protection of a fundamental freedom (paras 51 ff), whether there is an interference (paras 66 ff) and whether this interference is justified (paras 80 ff).

50

---

142 ECJ *Boukhalfa* [1996] ECR I-2253, paras 15 ff.
143 *Cf* Streinz (note 61) para 108.
144 *Contra* Pernice [2000] DVBl 1751.
145 *Cf* Art 7 TEU and Art 309 TEC (Art I-51 DC).
146 *Cf* ECJ *Roders* [1995] ECR I-2229, para 42; *Commission v France* [1998] ECR I-5325, para 46.
147 ECJ *Roders* [1995] ECR I-2229, para 43; *Grzelczyk* [2001] ECR I-6193, para 53.
148 ECJ *Buchner* [2000] ECR I-3625, para 39.

1. Scope of Protection of the Fundamental Freedoms

Case 5 – Problem: (ECJ *Bleis* [1991] ECR I-5627)
51 The German national B had applied to the French Ministry of Education to be registered for an external competition for the "Certificate of Aptitude as a Secondary School Teacher in German". Her application was refused on the ground of her nationality. The French court seized of the case referred to the ECJ the question whether employment as a secondary school teacher constitutes employment in the public service within the meaning of Article 39(4) of the TEC (Article III-133(4) DC).

52 The fundamental freedoms can only unfold their protection if the positive act or omission in question falls within their scope of protection (including the subject matter of protection as well as the personal, territorial and temporal scope of protection).

a) Subject Matter of Protection

53 A situation is covered by the subject matter of protection of the fundamental freedoms if the following **five conditions** are satisfied:

aa) Applicability of the Fundamental Freedoms

54 First of all, the fundamental freedoms need to be **applicable** to the situation in question. This is not the case where secondary Community law exhaustively regulates the subject matter (para 6). However, if such secondary Community law exists, its validity has to be reviewed: secondary Community law inconsistent with the fundamental freedoms is unlawful. In this respect, the fundamental freedoms serve as the standard of review even where secondary Community law exhaustively regulates the subject matter in question.

bb) Cross-border Element

55 In addition, the situation in question must involve a cross-border element (*cf* paras 19 ff, 24–25).

cc) Protected Behaviour

56 Furthermore, only **certain types of behaviour** of individuals are protected: *ie* behaviour relating to the free movement of goods, the activities of workers, the freedom of establishment, the free movement of services and the free movement of capital and payments (*cf* paras 2 ff). The corresponding guarantees have to be interpreted autonomously (*ie* independently from the standards of national law). The ECJ prefers a contextual-purposive approach to interpretation guided by the principle of effectiveness of Community law (*effet utile*). As a consequence, the scope of protection of the fundamental freedoms is construed broadly, the restrictability of the fundamental freedoms is construed narrowly.

57 Each fundamental freedom has its own distinct scope of protection. Accordingly, the definition of the scope of protection of a fundamental freedom also serves as its **delineation from other guarantees**. Product marketing, for example, can be regarded both as an

ancillary aspect of the distribution of goods[149] and as a service[150]. Where a situation falls within the scope of protection of more than one fundamental freedom, the different guarantees are in principle applicable in parallel. This is particularly the case if the situation in question can be divided into different parts. If, for example, an English company wants to set up a subsidiary in Germany in order to provide services in Belgium, both the freedom of establishment and the freedom to provide services are applicable because the activities of the company can be divided accordingly. Keeping in mind the different purposes of the fundamental freedoms, the applicability of one fundamental freedom does not necessarily foreclose the application of another even where the situation in question is indivisible.[151] The transfer of capital to another Member State for setting up a company, for example, is regarded as being covered by the free movement of capital as well as by the freedom of establishment.[152] However, if a situation due to its **predominant characteristics** clearly falls within the scope of one particular fundamental freedom, it is not covered by any other freedom which is of "completely secondary relevance" to the case.[153] Hence, the transportation of relocation goods within the course of office relocations from one Member State to another for the purpose of activities as a self-employed person as well as corresponding direct investments solely fall within the scope of protection of the freedom of establishment – the free movement of goods and the free movement of capital are not triggered. Furthermore, it is significant for the delineation of the fundamental freedoms from each other (and from other guarantees) whether or not one guarantee can be considered as *lex specialis* vis-à-vis the others. The freedom to provide services, for example, is of mere subsidiary character: 'Services' within the meaning of the TEC are only services that "are not governed by the provisions relating to freedom of movement for goods, capital and persons" (Article 50(1) TEC/Article III-145(1) DC). According to Article 305 of the TEC the provisions of the Treaty establishing the European Atomic Energy Community take priority in application over the provisions of the TEC (including the fundamental freedoms).[154]

dd) No Abusive Exercise of the Fundamental Freedoms

In numerous decisions the ECJ held that an abusive or fraudulent availment of the provisions of Community law (including the fundamental freedoms) is not permitted.[155] One

---

149 As to the incompatibility of a discriminatory prohibition of advertising with the free movement of goods *cf* para 79.
150 *Cf* for example ECJ *Alpine Investments* [1995] ECR I-1141.
151 The case-law of the ECJ is ambiguous. In some of its decisions the Court finds the scopes of protection of Articles 39, 43 and 49 of the TEC (Articles III-133, 137, 144 DC) to be mutually exclusive (ECJ *Gebhard* [1995] ECR I-4165, para 20). On the other hand, the ECJ speaks of a violation of 'Articles 48, 52' (today: Articles 39, 43 TEC/Articles III-133, 137 DC) – ECJ *Commission v France* [1996] ECR I-1307, para 24; *Commission v Ireland* [1997] ECR I-3327, para 16. Sharing the view taken here Müller-Graff in: von der Groeben/Schwarze (eds) *Vertrag über die Europäische Union und Vertrag zur Gründung der Europäischen Gemeinschaft. Kommentar* (6th ed, Baden-Baden 2004) Art 28 EGV, para 332.
152 *Cf* ECJ *Svensson* [1995] ECR I-3955, paras 8 ff; *Commission v Belgium* [2002] ECR I-4809, paras 58–59; Frenz (note 71) para 371.
153 *Cf* for example ECJ *Schindler* [1994] ECR I-1039, paras 20 ff; *van Schaik* [1994] ECR I-4837, para 14; *Canal Satélite* [2002] ECR I-607, para 31; *Omega* [2004] ECR I-9609, para 24.
154 Such a provision has not been included in the DC.
155 *Cf* in particular ECJ *Centros* [1999] ECR I-1459, para 24 (with numerous further references).

§ 7 VII 1   Dirk Ehlers

can speak of **abuse** if someone seeks unjust advantages with the help of cross-border commercial transactions. However, such 'abuse' should not be assumed lightly. In many cases, an abusive exercise of the fundamental freedoms is not protected due to "intrinsic" limits to their scope of protection which owe their existence to the principle of consistency of Community law. Drug dealers, for example, cannot rely on the free movement of goods, because this would be incompatible with human dignity (Article II-61 DC) and the Member States' obligation to grant governmental protection against unlawful interferences by private individuals. Whether situations of this kind are labelled as a 'misuse of rights' is a question of terminology. The assessment if a particular exercise of the fundamental freedoms is abusive mostly results in a mere analysis of the substantive scope of the freedom in question (*eg* by carefully examining the existence or non-existence of a cross-border scenario).[156] The main concept of the fundamental freedoms is to enable private individuals to benefit from cross-border commercial transactions. Accordingly, everyone is free to set up a company in the Member State which provides the most advantageous legal framework – even if the company does not pursue its economic activities there. The formation of a company in this manner does not constitute abusive or fraudulent behaviour.[157] After all, it is primarily the responsibility of the Member States to take measures which prevent their own nationals from an abusive exercise of Community law that leads to a circumvention of domestic law. The main issue is therefore not the scope of protection but the justification of interferences with the fundamental freedoms.[158]

ee) Non-applicability of Sectoral Exceptions

59   A situation is furthermore not protected by the fundamental freedoms if it is covered by a **sectoral exception** to the respective scope of protection.

60   The EC-Treaty contains various **explicit** sectoral exceptions. The free movement of workers, for example, does not apply to employment in the public service (Article 39(4) TEC/Article III-133(4) DC; → § 9 para 27). Likewise, the provisions governing the freedom of establishment and the freedom to provide services do not apply to activities which are connected, even occasionally, with the exercise of official authority in the Member State concerned (Article 45(1) read in conjunction with Article 55 TEC/Article III-139(1) read in conjunction with Article III-150 DC; → § 10 para 42; → § 11 para 33). Furthermore, the Council may, acting by a qualified majority on a proposal from the Commission, rule that the provisions of the Chapter governing the freedom of establishment and the freedom to provide services shall not apply to certain activities (Article 45(2) read in conjunction with Article 55 TEC/Article III-139(2) read in conjunction with Article III-150 DC). Pursuant to Article 86(2)(i) of the TEC (Article III-166(2)(i) DC), undertakings entrusted with the operation of services of general economic interest or having the character of a revenue producing monopoly are only subject to the rules of the Treaty insofar as the application of these rules does not obstruct the performance, in law or in fact, of the particular tasks assigned to them.

61   Some authors do not interpret the said provisions as sectoral exceptions to the subject matter of protection but as **explicit provisions on the restriction of the fundamental free-**

---

156 *Cf* Opinion AG La Pergola, ECJ *Centros* [1999] ECR I-1459, para 20.
157 ECJ *Inspire Art* [2003] ECR I-10155, paras 132 ff.
158 *Cf* ECJ *Centros* [1999] ECR I-1459, para 20.

doms. This view is based on the assumption that limits to the subject matter of protection of a right or freedom are characterised by an abstract determination not involving any balancing of conflicting guarantees whereas restrictions on the fundamental freedoms have to be proportional.[159] This view, however, does not appear to be convincing.[160] Firstly, the wording of the said Treaty provisions is clear and leaves no room for ambiguity ("shall not apply", "shall be subject to the rules ... insofar as"). Secondly, a comparison of Article 45 and 46 of the TEC (Articles III-139, III-140 DC) reveals that the EC-Treaty distinguishes between sectoral exceptions and provisions on the restriction of the fundamental freedoms. The wording of Article 46 of the TEC (Article III-140 DC) is clearly concerned with the justification of interferences. If Article 45 of the TEC (Article III-139 DC) was to be interpreted as a provision on the restriction of the fundamental freedoms as well, the drafting of two separate provisions would not have made any sense. Finally, sectoral exceptions to the scope of protection of a right or freedom (just as undefined legal terms) can very well be subjected to a balancing process. This process, however, is not identical to the one employed with regard to provisions on the restriction of a right or freedom: It is not primarily aimed at a reconciliation of conflicting guarantees but at a purposive interpretation of sectoral exceptions in the light of the relevant Treaty provisions. Accordingly, the ECJ found that the exceptions "cannot be given a scope which would exceed the objective for which ... [they were] inserted".[161]

Since the sectoral exceptions to the fundamental freedoms form part of substantive Community law, their scope is determined by Community law alone – and not by the laws of the Member States.[162] It is widely accepted, that the **provisions** in question have to be **construed narrowly** due to their character as exceptions. Hence, employment in the public service within the meaning of Article 39(4) of the TEC (Article III-133(4) DC) only includes posts "which involve direct or indirect participation in the exercise of powers conferred by public law and duties designed to safeguard the general interests of the state or of other public authorities".[163] A position as a judge, soldier or policemen, for example, qualifies as a post in the public service whereas governmental employees working in the field of research, education, health care or energy and water supply are not included.[164] One can only speak of an exercise of official authority within the meaning of Article 45(1) of the TEC (Article III-139(1) DC) where the person in question is vested with the power to give unilaterally binding orders.[165] As regards the application of Article 86(2) of the TEC

---

159 *Cf* notably Jarass [1995] EuR 202, 221–2; Jarass in: Due (ed) *Festschrift für Ulrich Everling, Band I* (Baden-Baden 1995) pp 593, 604–5; Jarass [2000] EuR 705, 717–8.
160 *Cf* Ehlers [1990] NVwZ 810, 812; Kingreen (note 2) pp 76–77; Streinz (note 61) para 825; Lackhoff (note 56) pp 152–3.
161 *Cf* ECJ *Reyners* [1974] ECR 631, paras 42–43. *Cf* also ECJ *Commission v Greece* [1988] ECR 1637 \t 61, para 10.
162 *Cf* for example (with regard to Art 39(4) TEC/Art III-133(4) DC) ECJ *Commission v Belgium* [1980] ECR 3881.
163 ECJ *Commission v Belgium* [1980] ECR 3881, para 10; *Commission v Greece* [1996] ECR I-3285. According to the predominant opinion among legal scholars *both* requirements have to be fulfilled. *Cf* Brechmann (note 121) Art 39 EGV, para 107; Schneider/Wunderlich in: Schwarze (ed) *EU-Kommentar* (Baden-Baden 2000) Art 39 EGV, para 135; → § 9 para 27.
164 *Cf* Schneider/Wunderlich (note 163) Art 39 EGV, para 140 (with further references to case-law).
165 *Cf* also Opinion AG Mayras, ECJ *Reyners* [1974] ECR 631. More detailed Jarass [1993] RIW 1, 4; Tiedje/Troberg in: von der Groeben/Schwarze (eds) *Vertrag über die Europäische Union und*

§ 7 VII 1   Dirk Ehlers

(Article III-166(2) DC) it has likewise been stressed that any exception to the applicability of the Treaty provisions must be 'necessary'.[166] However, this already follows from Article 86(2)(ii) of the TEC (Article III-166(2)(ii) DC) according to which the development of trade may not be affected to such an extent as would be contrary to the interests of the Community.

63   It is a moot point whether there are not only written but also **unwritten sectoral exceptions**. Since its seminal decision in the case of *Cassis de Dijon* of 1979[167] the ECJ consistently held that the fundamental freedoms can be justifiably limited and restricted on the grounds of so called 'mandatory requirements' (which correspond to a public-interest objective[168]). The question whether 'mandatory requirements' are sectoral exceptions to the subject matter of protection of the fundamental freedoms or provisions on their restriction is a matter of debate.[169] No explicit statement on this point can be found in the case-law of the ECJ. However, in its judgment in *Cassis* the Court seems to understand 'mandatory requirements' as (negative) conditions for the applicability of Article 30 of the TEC (now Article 28 TEC/Article III-153 DC). In contrast to this, the ECJ explicitly speaks of 'justification' in other (more recent) decisions.[170] Since 'mandatory requirements' have to be scrutinised against their consistency with the principle of proportionality in each individual case, it appears to be advisable to understand them as provisions on the restriction of the fundamental freedoms (thereby putting emphasis on the question of justification of interferences).

b) Personal, Territorial and Temporal Scope of Protection

64   The fundamental freedoms do not protect each and every 'individual' (paras 36 ff). In addition, they are only applicable to situations that fall within their territorial (para 48) and temporal (para 49) scope of protection. Further details on this can be found above.

Case 5 – Answer:
65   The admissibility of the request for a preliminary ruling pursuant to Article 234 of the TEC (Article III-369 DC) appears to be unquestionable. Employment in the public service within the meaning of Article 39(4) of the TEC (Article III-133(4) DC) must be understood as a series of posts which involve direct or indirect participation in the exercise of powers conferred by public law and duties designed to safeguard the general interests of the state or of other public authorities and which, because of that fact, presume on the part of those occupying them the existence of a special relationship of allegiance to the state and reciprocity of rights and duties which form the foundation of the bond of nationality. Due to its cha-

---

Vertrag zur Gründung der Europäischen Gemeinschaft. Kommentar (6th ed, Baden-Baden 2004) Art 45 EGV, paras 7 ff; Lackhoff (note 56) p 158.
166 *Cf* only von Burchard in: Schwarze (ed) *EU-Kommentar* (Baden-Baden 2000) Art 86 EGV, paras 51 ff, 71 ff.
167 ECJ *Cassis de Dijon* [1979] ECR 649.
168 ECJ *Familiapress* [1997] ECR I-3689, para 8.
169 Arguing for a classification as sectoral exceptions to the subject matter of protection *eg* Jestedt/Kaestle [1994] EWS 26, 27; Schilling [1994] EuR 50, 52; Ahlt/Deisenhofer (note 114) p 172. Arguing for a classification as provisions on restriction Hirsch [1999] ZEuS 503, 511; Lecheler/Gundel *Übungen im Europarecht* (Berlin 1999) pp 107, 109–10; Jarass [2000] EuR 705, 719.
170 *Cf* for example ECJ *Familiapress* [1997] ECR I-3689, para 18; *De Agostini* [1997] ECR I-3843.

racter as an exception to the principle established by the freedom of movement for workers, Article 39(4) of the TEC (Article III-133(4) DC) has to be construed narrowly so that its consequences do not go beyond what is indispensable to preserve the interests it aims to protect. Educational tasks of a teacher generally do not involve the exercise of official authority. Furthermore, the position as a teacher does not necessarily require a special relationship of allegiance to the state. Consequently, employment as a secondary school teacher does not constitute employment in the public service within the meaning of Article 39(4) of the TEC (Article III-133(4) DC).

2. Interference with the Fundamental Freedoms

Case 6 – Problem: (ECJ *Mars* [1995] ECR I-1923)
The limited company M imports ice-cream bars from France to Germany (the bars are lawfully produced by an American undertaking in France for distribution throughout Europe). As part of a publicity campaign the quantity of each product was increased by 10 % and the bars presented in wrappers marked "+ 10 %". However, the coloured part of the wrapping ("+ 10 %") occupies considerably more than 10 % of the total surface area of the wrapping. A German association for combating unfair competition brings an action before the German courts in order to prevent the "+ 10 %" marking from being used in Germany. The association contends that the campaign violates German competition law. According to the association, consumers are bound to assume that the advantage indicated by the "+ 10 %" marking comes without any increase in price. In order to avoid misleading consumers, all retailers would have to maintain the previously charged price. However, such a form of price fixing constitutes a breach of German competition law. On the other hand, the association contends that the way in which the "+ 10 %" marking is incorporated into the presentation is misleading because it gives the impression that the product has been increased by a quantity corresponding to the coloured part of the new wrapping. The German court seized of the case is inclined to rule against the defendant (M). It is in doubt, however, as to the conformity of this result with Article 28 of the TEC (Article III-153 DC).

66

a) Acts (or Omission) by an Entity Bound by the Fundamental Freedoms

Only positive acts or omissions undertaken by an entity bound by the fundamental freedoms can interfere with the scope of protection. It is equally possible, however, to deal with this requirement already under the heading 'scope of protection'. Omissions can only be put on a par with positive acts if the relevant entity is under a legal duty to take the requested action. Such a duty can arise, for example, from rights to governmental protection (para 31) or from procedural guarantees (para 34). According to the case-law of the ECJ, not only the Member States and the EC but also private individuals qualify as entities bound by the fundamental freedoms – at least under certain conditions (*cf* more detailed paras 42 ff).

67

b) Mode of Interference

aa) Requirement of a 'limitation' or 'discrimination'

Only positive acts or omissions in the form of a limitation (paras 24 ff) or discrimination (paras 19 ff) represent an interference with the fundamental freedoms.

68

bb) Existence of 'Discrimination' or 'Limitation'

(1) Concept of 'Discrimination'

69 The ECJ assumes a very broad concept of discrimination (para 22). One can speak of discrimination where national law or those who enforce it treat – either inevitably or typically – a cross-border scenario less favourably than corresponding internal cases. In other words, the prohibition of discrimination **restrains Member States from putting cross-border sceanrios at a disadvantage**.[171] It therefore leads – not necessarily but as a general rule – to an equal treatment of foreign citizens of the Union vis-à-vis nationals of the Member State in question (Member States, however, are free to discriminate against their own nationals in favour of foreign citizens of the Union).[172] The fundamental freedoms are only concerned with discrimination of cross-border scenarios – other forms of less favourable treatment (*eg* gender discrimination without any cross-border connection) are irrelevant. Hence, a difference in treatment is relevant to the fundamental freedoms if it is based on a criterion with cross-border connection or cross-border effects (*eg* nationality, residence, language *etc*). Both overt and covert discrimination of cross-border scenarios has to be scrutinised against its consistency with the fundamental freedoms (para 22) – regardless of whether

70 – discriminatory effects were intended or not,
 – *de jure* or *de facto* discrimination is at question,
 – direct or indirect discrimination is contended,
 – the measure in question has actual or only potential effects,
 – the discriminatory effects in question are of a severe or rather marginal nature.[173]

71 However, highly remote causal connections between a measure and discriminatory effects can be disregarded.[174] This is even more the case if acts by private individuals are scrutinised.

(2) Concept of 'Limitation'

72 The broad concept of discrimination as it has been described above corresponds to an equally broad concept of limitation. This can be demonstrated in particular by considering the case-law on the free movement of goods. Article 28 of the TEC (Article III-153 DC) not only prohibits quantitative restrictions on imports (which are hardly found today) but also all measures having equivalent effect. According to the **Dassonville formula** adopted by the ECJ "all trading rules enacted by Member States which are capable of hindering, directly or indirectly, actually or potentially, intra-Community trade are to be considered as measures having equivalent effect".[175] Hence, the predictability of the effects of a measure as well as its finality and legal nature are irrelevant. On the other hand, even hindrances that are not yet effective as well as marginal interferences with the

---

171 *Cf* for example ECJ *Cowan* [1989] ECR 195, paras 10 ff; Jarass [1995] EuR 202, 216.
172 See, however, Lackhoff (note 56) pp 222 ff, who argues for a right to (also) remain free from discrimination by one's own Member State.
173 *Cf* Gebauer (note 90) pp 353–4.
174 The state of the law is similar to the principles which apply to limitations. *Cf* the following remarks.
175 *Cf* ECJ *Dassonville* [1974] ECR 837, para 5.

scope of protection are to be considered as limitations. Consequently, solely the impact and effects of a measure are decisive.[176] One can already speak of a limitation where the (transnational) exercise of the free movement of goods is impeded in any way or rendered less attractive. The same applies to the other fundamental freedoms (para 24). Up to now, there is no case-law of the ECJ on whether the *Dassonville* formula is also applicable to interferences by private individuals.

The very broad concept of limitation as it is employed by the ECJ led to an extremely large number of national measures that had to be scrutinised for justification as regards their respective interferences with the fundamental freedoms. The Court, for example, even considered the Welsh rules prohibiting retailers from opening their premises on Sunday[177] and the (former) German prohibition of advertising using price comparisons[178] as limitations of the free movement of goods. Although it is improbable that the closure of certain types of shops on Sundays will cause consumers to refrain altogether from purchasing products which are available on week-days, the fact remains that such a prohibition may have negative repercussions on the volume of sales and hence on the volume of imports.[179]   73

In order to counter a massive overflow of cases that involve the fundamental freedoms and in order to prevent a corresponding overload on its part, the ECJ tried to narrow the applicability of the fundamental freedoms in three different ways: In its decision in ***Cassis***, the Court found that limitations of the fundamental freedoms have to be accepted if they are necessary in order to satisfy mandatory requirements.[180] However, according to the view taken here, such 'mandatory requirements' do not curtail the scope of the fundamental freedoms but are provisions on their restriction (para 63). In its decision in ***Keck***, the ECJ for the first time established 'real' exceptions to the scope of the fundamental freedoms.[181] Furthermore, the Court stressed in numerous decisions that there has to be a **certain degree of proximity** between the measure in question and the alleged effects on interstate trade. Accordingly, there is no interference with the fundamental freedoms where the restrictive effects that a measure might have are too uncertain and indirect.[182] The exact outline of this "rule of remoteness", which narrows the applicability of the *Dassonville* formula, has not been sufficiently clarified so far – it has to be redefined for each individual case.[183] Furthermore, the ECJ does not require an 'appreciability' of limitations.[184]   74

---

176 Craig/de Búrca (note 1) pp 615 ff.
177 ECJ *Torfaen Borough Council* [1989] ECR 3851; *cf* also ECJ *Marchandise* [1991] ECR I-1027; *B & Q* [1992] ECR I-6635.
178 ECJ *Yves Rocher* [1993] ECR I-2361, paras 11–12; *cf* also ECJ *Oosthoek* [1982] ECR 4575, paras 14–15.
179 ECJ *Conforama* [1991] ECR I-997, para 8.
180 ECJ *Cassis de Dijon* [1979] ECR 649.
181 ECJ *Keck* [1993] ECR I-6097, paras 14 ff. *Cf* the comments by *eg* Behrens [1992] EuR 145; Roth [1995] ZIIR 78, 86–87; Oliver *Free movement of goods in the European Community* (4th ed, London 2003) pp 122 ff; Oliver (1999) 36 CMLRev 97.
182 *Cf* notably ECJ *Semeraro* [1996] ECR I-2975, para 32; also *CMC Motorradcenter* [1993] ECR I-5009, para 9; *Peralta* [1994] ECR I-3453, para 24; *BASF* [1999] ECR I-6269, para 16; *Graf* [2000] ECR I-493, paras 24–25.
183 *Cf* more detailed Becker [1994] EuR 162, 170; Ebenroth in: Salje (ed) *Festschrift für Helmut Pieper* (Hamburg 1998) pp 133, 142; Oliver (1999) 36 CMLRev 97; Deckert/Schroeder [2001] JZ 88, 90.
184 *Cf* Ehlers (note 118) B, para 10; Frenz (note 71) paras 419–20.

75   The exceptions to the scope of the fundamental freedoms as they have been developed by the ECJ in its decision in *Keck* (→ § 8 paras 37 ff) deserve special attention. In *Keck* the Court refused to scrutinise a French law prohibiting the sale of goods at a loss against its consistency with Article 28 of the TEC (Article III-153 DC). In contrast to its previous jurisprudence, the ECJ found that national provisions restricting or prohibiting certain selling arrangements do not represent measures having equivalent effect as they do not hinder trade between Member States within the meaning of the *Dassonville* judgment. However, according to the Court this exception only covers national provisions which apply to all affected traders operating within the national territory (criterion of universality) and which affect in the same manner, in law and in fact, the marketing of domestic products and those from other Member States (criterion of neutrality).[185] It is still unsolved whether or not (and how) the criterion of neutrality can be distinguished from the concept of discrimination. Where a measure can be deemed discriminatory, its further classification as a limitation is irrelevant – a fact that argues for the distinctness of the concept of discrimination from the criterion of neutrality. The concept of discrimination appears to be narrower than the criterion of neutrality (in spite of a relatively broad concept of discrimination being appropriate): Double burdens resulting from a parallel applicability of the rules of different Member States, for example, may notably impede the marketing of products from other Member States. In contrast, the concept of discrimination is only concerned with effects resulting from the application of the rules of one domestic legal order alone (paras 19 ff).[186] The ECJ is vested with the power to authoritatively decide whether the requirements adopted in *Keck* are fulfilled.[187]

76   The ruling in *Keck*, which has been affirmed in numerous subsequent decisions,[188] requires a differentiation between **product-** and **sales-related measures**. In contrast to the former, the latter do not constitute interferences with the free movement of goods if they apply indistinctly. Such a differentiation can be very difficult and must therefore not be drawn schematically.[189] Restrictions on advertising, for example, mostly constitute selling arrangements within the meaning of *Keck*. Where, however, the advertising forms part of the product itself (*cf* paras 66, 79) or where national provisions generally prohibit the advertising of certain products altogether, a different assessment is necessary.[190] As a general rule, measures which impede access for out-of state goods to the domestic market always have to be scrutinised against Article 28 of the TEC (Article III-153 DC). In contrast, the Member States are free to take indistinctly applicable measures governing the distribution of goods which have been granted access to the market.[191]

---

185 ECJ *Keck* [1993] ECR I-6097, para 16.
186 *Cf* also Plötscher (note 54).
187 *Cf* the criticism raised by Lenz [2004] NJW 332–3.
188 *Cf* the references to case-law by Müller-Graff (note 151) Art 28 EGV, para 255; Epiney in: Calliess/Ruffert (eds) *Kommentar des Vertrages über die Europäische Union und des Vertrages zur Gründung der Europäischen Gemeinschaft* (2nd ed, Neuwied 2002) Art 28 EGV, para 29.
189 *Cf* also Kingreen (note 2) p 125; Becker in: Schwarze (ed) *EU-Kommentar* (Baden-Baden 2000) Art 28 EGV, para 49; → § 8 paras 37 ff.
190 *Cf* Stein [1995] EuZW 435, 436.
191 As the Court found in *Keck*, national rules restricting or prohibiting certain selling arrangements only fall outside the scope of Article 28 of the TEC if they do not prevent access to the market for products from other Member States or impede such access any more than they impedes the

General Principles §7 VII 2

It has not been sufficiently clarified so far whether or not the rule in *Keck* applies to the **other fundamental freedoms**. It seems to be most easily transferable to the freedom to provide services: cases in which a service itself is intended to "cross the border" are concerned with the mobility of an economic asset which resembles a tangible product (→ *contra* § 11 para 50). Accordingly, in its decision in *Alpine Investments* (dealing with a prohibition of cross-border cold calling by telephone) the ECJ made use of the criteria developed in *Keck* with regard to the freedom to provide services.[192] Moreover, the main concept underlying the rule in *Keck* seems to be applicable to all four fundamental freedoms insofar as it is aimed at narrowing the (extremely) broad scope of the fundamental freedoms in cases that do not involve questions concerning market access (*ie* questions of 'whether' economic activities can be pursued) but only questions concerning market behaviour (*ie* questions of 'how' to pursue economic activities).[193] At any rate, in order to benefit from the rule in *Keck* measures have to constitute (neutral and universal) limitations that indistinctly apply to all affected traders. 77

cc) Differentiation between Discrimination and Limitation

The **relationship** between the **prohibition of discrimination** and the **prohibition of limitation** can neither be clearly inferred from the existing case-law nor from academic writing. In many cases, a limitation also includes (at least covert) discrimination and vice versa. In the case of *Cassis de Dijon*[194], for example, which was concerned with a limitation of the free movement of goods for alcoholic beverages by means of the fixing of a minimum alcohol content, the national measure in question technically constituted an indistinctly applicable measure. In fact, however, the fixing of a minimum alcohol content put domestic production at an advantage because of the latter already being attuned to the national standard which allowed a marketing of domestic products without additional costs for adjustment.[195] On the other hand, there are also non-discriminatory limitations of the fundamental freedoms: *eg* generally applicable transfer rules in professional sports,[196] national legislation denying compensation on termination of employment to all workers (irrespective of their nationality) who voluntarily end their contract of employment,[197] or national rules according to which undertakings established in another Member State (as well as domestic undertakings) are obliged to pay its workers the minimum remuneration laid down by the national rules of the host State when providing services there.[198] A viola- 78

---

access of domestic products. *Cf* also ECJ *Gourmet International* [2001] ECR I-1795; Becker (note 189) Art 28 EGV, para 49.
[192] ECJ *Alpine Investments* [1995] ECR I-1141, paras 33 ff. *Cf* also ECJ *DocMorris* [2003] ECR I-14887 (*cf* case 1).
[193] *Cf* with regard to the freedom of movement for workers Brechmann (note 121) Art 39 EGV, para 49; with regard to the freedom of establishment Schlag in: Schwarze (ed) *EU-Kommentar* (Baden-Baden 2000) Art 43 EGV, para 33, with regard to the free movement of capital Bröhmer (note 24) Art 56 EGV, para 20. Sharing the view taken here Barnard (note 1) pp 238 ff; Deckert/Schroeder [2001] JZ 88.
[194] ECJ *Cassis de Dijon* [1979] ECR 649.
[195] Gundel [2001] JURA 79, 83.
[196] *Cf* ECJ *Bosman* [1995] ECR I-4921, para 99. According to Epiney (note 54) pp 61–62, it is not possible to draw a distinction between covert discrimination and limitation.
[197] ECJ *Graf* [2000] ECR I-493, paras 15 ff.
[198] ECJ *Portugaia Construções* [2002] ECR I-787, paras 16 ff.

tion of the prohibition of limitation (alone) is even conceivable where Member States treat their own nationals less favourably than foreign citizens of the Union.[199] In cases which involve overt discrimination, the ECJ tends to refrain from commenting on the existence or non-existence of a limitation.[200] In contrast, the Court often gives its sole attention to the prohibition of limitation where the measure in question constitutes both a limitation and covert discrimination by impeding access to a market or profession (*ie* interferences with the core guarantees of the fundamental freedoms).[201] In the case of interferences with rather subsidiary guarantees of the fundamental freedoms (*eg* regulation of details relating to the exercise of a self-employed occupation), the Court often solely examines whether the measures constitute discrimination.[202] It follows from the rule in *Keck* that, for example, certain selling arrangements can only be scrutinised against their consistency with the fundamental freedoms if they are discriminatory (*ie* non-universal or non-neutral selling arrangements). All this led to the assumption that the prohibition of limitation and the prohibition of (*de facto*) discrimination do not overlap: the fundamental freedoms contain a prohibition of limitation in relation to their core guarantees and a prohibition of discrimination in relation to their (rather) subsidiary guarantees.[203] However, according to the view taken here, the prohibition of discrimination and the prohibition of limitation can **coincide**. This view is supported by the wording of the fundamental freedoms (which primarily indicates a prohibition of discrimination), by the difficulties arising from a distinction between core- and subsidiary guarantees and by the fact that at least overt discrimination cannot be regarded as immaterial in the case of restrictions on (market) access. If and insofar as the prohibition of discrimination coincides with the prohibition of limitation, both concepts have to be applied separately. Nevertheless, a clear distinction is dispensable where the recognised grounds for justification of interferences are identical (*cf* paras 80 ff).

Case 6 – Answer:
The ice-cream bars are produced in France. Hence, they qualify as products originating in a Member State (Article 23(2) TEC/Article III-151(2) DC) even though they are produced by an American undertaking. A governmental prohibition of the distribution of the products in Germany (resulting from German competition law as applied by the courts) constitutes a measure having equivalent effect according to the *Dassonville* formula because of hindering intra-Community trade. It cannot be regarded as a (mere) selling arrangement in terms of the rule in *Keck* because it clearly constitutes a product-related measure: the disputed advertising is placed on the wrappers of the ice-cream bars – the prohibition in question forces M to modify its product by developing a new wrapping. The grounds for justification of inter-

---

199 *Cf* Hirsch [1999] ZEuS 503, 509, who refers to ECJ *Schöning* [1998] ECR I-47 (the case dealt with a collective agreement on remuneration applicable to public sector employees which took into account only periods of employment completed in the national public service but not periods of comparable employment completed in the public service of another Member State).
200 *Cf* for example ECJ *Commission v Spain* [1994] ECR I-911, para 10.
201 An example is the decision in *Cassis de Dijon*.
202 *Cf* for example ECJ *Ciola* [1999] ECR I-2517, paras 14 ff.
203 *Cf* Lecheler/Gundel (note 169) pp 177–8; see also Jarass [2000] EuR 705, 711, who categorises all interferences with the core guarantees of the fundamental freedoms as limitations – irrespective of whether they involve a less favourable treatment in the individual case. See also Eilmannsberger [1999] JBl 347.

ferences pursuant to Article 30 of the TEC (Article III-154 DC) (*cf* paras 83 ff) are not applicable. The (indistinctly applicable) limitation is not justifiable on the grounds of mandatory requirements either. The publicity campaign does not impair the interests of consumers. Prices have not been increased. Furthermore, a reasonably circumspect consumer is capable of distinguishing between the size of the "+ 10 %" marking and the actual increase in quantity. Where retailers are indirectly forced during the "+ 10 %" campaign to maintain the price previously charged, such a form of price fixing serves the interests of consumer protection. The prohibition of the publicity campaign can therefore not be justified on grounds of mandatory requirements. At any rate, a prohibition of the campaign would constitute a disproportional interference with the free movement of goods. Accordingly, the German court has to dismiss the action brought against M.

3. Justification of Interferences with the Fundamental Freedoms

National measures which constitute an interference with the fundamental freedoms are not *per se* incompatible with Community law. In each case it has to be examined whether or not the interference is justified. The justification will succeed if the interferences in question has a legal basis (paras 81–82), if it is covered by a written (paras 83 ff), unwritten (paras 88 ff) or other (paras 86–87) authorisation to restrict the fundamental freedoms and if the general limits to restrictability (paras 92 ff) are observed. **80**

a) Existence of a Legal Basis for Interferences
aa) Secondary Community Law as a Legal Basis

According to the case-law of the ECJ, the fundamental freedoms do not apply to situations that are **exhaustively regulated** by **secondary Community law** (paras 7, 54). This position of the Court is, however, only insofar in accord with the view taken here as secondary Community law repeats or defines the scope of protection of the fundamental freedoms – *ie* in case of a 'definition of' rather than an 'interference with' the fundamental freedoms. Either way, secondary Community law has to be scrutinised against its consistency with the fundamental freedoms. This is also and foremost true for secondary Community law which authorises to interfere with the fundamental freedoms. Where interferences can be justified on grounds that are (directly or indirectly[204]) laid down in provisions of secondary Community law, these provisions alone – and not provisions of domestic law – function as restrictions on the fundamental freedoms. **81**

bb) Statutory Basis in National Law

The ECJ found that "in all the legal systems of the Member States, any intervention by the public authorities in the sphere of private activities of any person, whether natural or legal, must have a legal basis".[205] The Court thus recognised the **requirement of a legal basis** as a general principle of Community law.[206] However, the decision in *Hoechst* dealt **82**

---

204 Grounds for justification are *indirectly* laid down in provisions of secondary Community law where such grounds are laid down in national provisions that owe their existence to a directive of the EC.
205 ECJ *Hoechst* [1989] ECR 2859, para 19.
206 → As to the requirement of a legal basis *cf* also § 14 para 44.

with interferences with a fundamental right of the Union. Up to now, there is no clear case-law of the ECJ on whether the requirement of a legal basis also applies to interferences with the fundamental freedoms. If the principle of legality can be deemed a general principle of (Community) law, though, and if the fundamental freedoms can be regarded as a specific kind of fundamental rights of the Union (para 15), the requirement of a legal basis must be likewise applicable.[207] This view is supported by the wording of Article 46(1) of the TEC (Article III-140 DC) which only allows for restrictions on the freedom of establishment by means of "provisions laid down by law, regulation or administrative action". Exactly what requirements a "legal basis" must meet in this context has not yet been resolved.[208] With regard to common law countries the European Court of Human Rights has also accepted unwritten law as a legal basis for interferences with the Convention rights (→ § 2 para 46). The same could apply to the fundamental freedoms. At any rate, interferences with the fundamental freedoms must have a legal basis that is sufficiently precise and clear in its terms.

b) Written Authorisation to Restrict the Fundamental Freedoms

83 The EC-Treaty provides for **explicit authorisation to restrict** each of the fundamental freedoms (Article 30, 39(3), 46 read in conjunction with 55, 57(1), 58(1) TEC/Article III-154, III-133(3), III-140 read in conjunction with III-150, III-157(1), III-158(1) DC). All provisions at least allow for interferences on grounds of public policy and (or) security. With regard to the free movement of goods the Treaty contains a long list of other grounds for (justifiable) interferences (public morality, the protection of health and life, national treasures, the protection of industrial and commercial property). The freedom of movement for workers, the freedom of establishment and the freedom to provide services can be justifiably limited on grounds of, *inter alia*, public health (the latter two only allow for such limitation in case of special treatment for foreign nationals). Interferences with the free movement of capital and payments are particularly justifiable in relation to transactions with third countries (Article 57 TEC/Article III-157 DC) as well as on fiscal grounds. However, this is without prejudice to the applicability of restrictions on the freedom of establishment (Article 58(2) TEC/Article III-158(2) DC). The provisions on the restriction of the fundamental freedoms apply to all modes of interferences.

84 The actual purpose of a law often does not fully correspond to the intent of the legislator as expressed therein. Hence, in order to determine the purpose of a law, its *objective* aim has to be assessed.[209] Where Member States pursue aims which are contrary to (secondary) Community law, these aims cannot serve as justification for interferences with the fundamental freedoms.

85 At first sight, the justifiability of interferences on grounds of "public policy and (or) security" appears to be a blanket clause for the justification of national measures. It is settled case-law of the ECJ, however, that the concept of "public policy and (or) security" has to be construed narrowly.[210] This can be particularly deduced from the exceptional

---

207 Jarass [1995] EuR 202, 222, comes to the same conclusion.
208 *Cf* also Jarass [1995] EuR 202, 222; Kingreen (note 2) p 153.
209 *Cf* Cremer [2004] NVwZ 668, 673.
210 *Cf* for example ECJ *Van Duyn* [1974] ECR 1337, para 18; *Bauhuis* [1977] ECR 5, paras 12 ff; *Commission v Ireland* [1981] ECR 1625, para 7; *Commission v Greece* [1991] ECR I-1361, para 9. *Cf* also Craig/de Búrca (note 1) p 626.

character of the said concept. Public policy and public security may be relied on only if there is a genuine and sufficiently serious threat to fundamental national interests,[211] which either affects a fundamental interest of society[212] (public policy) or the internal or external security of the state (public security). Consumer protection, for example, does not come under 'public policy and public security'.[213] The particular circumstances justifying recourse to the concept of public policy and (or) security may vary from one country to another and from one period to another. Hence, the ECJ allows the competent national authorities a margin of appreciation within the limits imposed by the TEC.[214] Where national law has been completely harmonised by means of secondary Community law the justification of interferences depends on the latter and not on national law.[215] As a general rule, however, the fundamental freedoms are not applicable in this case (para 54). See para 46 on the utilisation of the provisions on the restriction of the fundamental freedoms with regard to interferences by private individuals.

c) Other Community Law as Restrictions on the Fundamental Freedoms

Not only provisions that explicitly authorise restrictions on the fundamental freedoms but also other provisions of Community law may partially limit the fundamental freedoms. The **fundamental rights of the Union**, for instance, may conflict with the fundamental freedoms (→ § 14 para 12) – both sets of rights forming a part of primary Community law. In its decision in *Schmidberger* (→ § 8 paras 15, 21), for example, the ECJ found an interference with the free movement of goods by means of the non-intervention of the Austrian authorities in a blockade of the Brenner motorway to be justified because the demonstrators made use of their rights to freedom of expression and assembly. According to the Court, the protection of the fundamental rights is a legitimate interest which, in principle, justifies a proportional non-fulfillment of certain other obligations imposed by Community law.[216] In this view, the fundamental rights not only conduce to the implementation of the written or unwritten authorisation to restrict the fundamental freedoms. They rather have their own (independent) significance. It is, however, immaterial whether the fundamental rights are understood as independent restrictions on the fundamental freedoms or as a means for the interpretation of the provisions on restriction discussed above. The ECJ has not sufficiently clarified whether or not the above-mentioned concept only applies to the fundamental rights of the Union and not to fundamental rights guaranteed under national law. Since allowable restrictions on the fundamental freedoms have to be defined by Community law alone, only fundamental rights of the Union can be considered as independent restrictions.[217] Nevertheless, national fundamental guarantees may have an impact insofar as they assist in a more precise interpretation of the explicit Treaty provisions on restriction (*eg* interpretation of the terms 'public policy' or 'public security') or in a more precise interpretation of unwritten authorisations to restrict the fundamental

86

---

211 *Cf* Becker (note 189) Art 30 EGV, para 11.
212 ECJ *Scientologie* [2000] ECR I-1335, para 17.
213 *Cf* ECJ *Kohl* [1984] ECR 3651, paras 18–19.
214 ECJ *Van Duyn* [1974] ECR 1337, para 18; *Bouchereau* [1977] ECR 1999, para 33; *Omega* [2004] ECR I-9609, para 31.
215 *Cf* ECJ *DocMorris* [2003] ECR I-14887, para 102.
216 ECJ *Schmidberger* [2003] ECR I-5659, para 74.
217 *Cf* also Kadelbach/Petersen [2002] EuGRZ 213, 215–16.

freedoms. It has to be kept in mind, though, that it is not the task of the ECJ or the CFI to scrutinise national measures against their consistency with fundamental rights guaranteed under national law.

87 Apart from the fundamental rights of the Union, **other primary Community law** may, under certain conditions, function as a basis for justification of interferences with the fundamental freedoms as well. A national law which, for example, reserves a proportion of a public supply contract to undertakings located in a particular region of the national territory not only constitutes a measure having equivalent effect but also a state aid. In such a case, the parallel application of Article 28 (Article III-153 DC) and 87 of the TEC (Article III-167 DC) brings about the risk of a circumvention of the special rules (on justification) contained in Articles 87 ff of the TEC (Articles III-167 ff DC). It therefore appears to be advisable to evaluate a case of the said kind as follows: While the question on *whether* state aid may be granted is *solely* governed by Articles 87 ff of the TEC (Articles III-167 ff DC), the *exact terms* of the state aid *also* have to be scrutinised against their consistency with Articles 28 ff of the TEC (Articles III-153 ff DC).[218]

d) Unwritten Authorisation to Restrict the Fundamental Freedoms

Case 7 – Problem: (ECJ *Kohll* [1998] ECR I-1931)
88 According to Luxembourg law the costs incurred in connection with medical treatment provided in another Member State are only reimbursed by social security institutions if an authorisation has been granted prior to receiving the treatment or if the insured person suffers an emergency. K is a citizen of Luxembourg. He is planning to receive dental treatment in Germany. However, his social security institution is not willing to grant the necessary authorisation. K wants to know whether this is compatible with the fundamental freedoms.

aa) Development of the Case-law

89 If on the one hand the fundamental freedoms not only contain a broad prohibition of discrimination but also a broad prohibition of limitation and if on the other hand the provisions on restriction are construed narrowly, only a very small political scope is left to the Member States. This, however, falls short of the regulatory concept underlying the fundamental freedoms. In its decision in *Cassis de Dijon*, the ECJ therefore accepted **mandatory requirements** invoked by the Member States as unwritten grounds for the justification of interferences (paras 63, 74). Among these requirements, particular emphasis has been put on the effectiveness of fiscal supervision, the protection of public health, the fairness of commercial transactions and consumer protection. Nevertheless, other policy aims which correspond to a public-interest objective – except for aims of a purely economic nature[219] – also qualify as mandatory requirements. Where secondary Community law applies to the situation in question, the mandatory requirements must, however, also be scrutinised thereagainst. Although the unwritten grounds for the justification of interferences had initially been developed with regard to the free movement of goods, they were later also applied to the other fundamental freedoms (using a slightly different termi-

---

218 *Cf* Ehlers [1992] JZ 199. Seemingly *contra* ECJ *Du Pont de Nemours Italiana* [1990] ECR I-889, paras 22 ff.
219 *Cf* ECJ *Decker* [1998] ECR I-1831, para 39; *Schutzverband gegen unlauteren Wettbewerb* [2000] ECR I-151, para 33.

nology[220]). The *Cassis* **principles** have been accused of bringing about a contradiction, because a narrow interpretation of the explicit provisions on restriction and the negation of applying them analogously is not consistent with an extensive acceptance of unwritten grounds for the justification of interferences.[221] Critics argue that it is methodically more accurate to construe the written grounds for justification such as "public policy" and "public security" broadly.[222] However, the approach of the Court appears to be convincing, if the written grounds for justification are applied to any form of interferences, whereas unwritten authorisations are only applied to certain kinds of interferences (*cf* the remarks below).

bb) Unwritten Grounds for the Justification of Discriminatory Interferences

The *Cassis* **principles** were developed for **indistinctly applicable measures**, *ie* for non-discriminatory limitations only.[223] In many of its more recent decisions, the ECJ also found **covert discrimination** to be (potentially) justifiable by mandatory requirements.[224] Consequently, some authors argue that any type of discrimination can be justified by such requirements.[225] This view, however, is not convincing. Since overt discrimination constitutes a serious interference and since it is diametrically opposed to the concept of an internal market, overt discrimination can only be justified on the grounds of a written authorisation to restrict the fundamental freedoms. On the other hand, it can be assumed – in line with most of the recent case-law – that mandatory requirements which correspond to a public-interest objective qualify as grounds for the justification of covert discrimination.[226] Apart from the fact that it is difficult to draw a clear distinction between limitations and *de facto* discrimination, an exhaustive list of grounds for the justification of *de facto* discrimination would be just as inadequate as it is in relation to "mere" limitations.[227] At any rate, the proportionality test (para 96) serves as a corrective.

90

---

220 *Cf* with regard to the freedom of movement for workers *eg* ECJ *O'Flynn* [1996] ECR I-2617, para 19: "objective considerations"; with regard to the freedom of establishment and the freedom to provide services ECJ *Säger* [1991] ECR I-4221, paras 15 ff; *Familiapress* [1997] ECR I-3689, para 8: "public-interest objective"; *Kohll* [1998] ECR I-1931, para 41; *Pfeiffer* [1999] ECR I-2835, para 19: "overriding requirements in the general interest"; *Müller-Fauré* [2003] ECR I-4509, para 73.
221 *Cf* Kingreen (note 2) pp 52, 120–1.
222 *Cf* Schweitzer/Hummer *Europarecht* (6th ed, Neuwied 2003) para 1135.
223 *Cf* for example ECJ *Commission v Ireland* [1981] ECR 1625, para 10; *Schindler* [1994] ECR I-1039, paras 51 ff; *Läärä* [1999] ECR I-6067, para 31.
224 *Cf* ECJ *Vestergaard* [1999] ECR I-7641, paras 21 ff; *Commission v Italy* [2003] ECR I-721, paras 21 ff; *Burmanjer* [2005] ECR I-4133, para 32; *cf* also ECJ *Preussen Elektra* [2001] ECR I-2099, para 73 (see the comments by Frenz (note 71) paras 492 ff); Nowak/Schnitzler [2000] EuZW 627; Nowak (2002) 93 VerwArch 368, 374; Gundel [2001] JURA 79 – with numerous references to case-law; seemingly *contra* ECJ *Ciola* [1999] ECR I-2517, para 16 (discriminatory measures can only be justified "if they can be brought within the scope of an express derogation").
225 *Cf* Weiß [1999] EuZW 493, 497; Hakenberg in: Lenz/Borchardt (eds) *EU- und EG-Vertrag. Kommentar* (4th ed, Cologne 2006) Art 49/50 EGV, para 26; Leible in: Grabitz/Hilf (eds) *Das Recht der Europäischen Union* (loose-leaf, Munich) Art 28 EGV, para 20; → § 8 para 61.
226 Sharing the view taken here: Boger *Die Anwendbarkeit der Cassis-Formel auf Ungleichbehandlungen im Rahmen der Grundfreiheiten* (Berlin 2004) pp 197 ff.
227 Gundel [2001] JURA 79, 83.

Case 7 – Answer:

91 While Community law does not abridge the powers of the Member States to organise their social security systems, they must nevertheless comply with the fundamental freedoms when exercising those powers. The requirement of prior authorisation has cross-border effects and affects the freedom to provide services (Article 49 TEC/Article III-144 DC) of both provider (medical practitioner) and recipient (K). The Luxembourg law does not constitute an overt discrimination because it differentiates on the basis of the place of treatment and not on the basis of the nationality of the provider or recipient (costs incurred in connection with medical treatment that is provided in Luxembourg by foreign practitioners are reimbursed). However, the rules typically put nationals of other Member States at a disadvantage. They are therefore indirectly discriminatory. Although insured persons are not prevented from approaching a provider of services established in another Member State, they are deprived of reimbursement of the costs incurred so that the measure in question substantially impedes access to medical services abroad. Hence, the Luxembourg law also constitutes a limitation. It could be justified on the basis of Article 46 of the TEC read in conjunction with Article 55 of the TEC (Article III-140 DC read in conjunction with Article III-150 DC) or on the basis of mandatory requirements which correspond to a public-interest objective. The rules in question are aimed at the protection of public health, at the provision of a balanced medical and hospital service and at preserving the financial balance of the social security scheme. These aspects are altogether relevant and do not constitute aims of a purely economic nature. However, a serious threat to the said interests does not become apparent in the case at hand. This is also true with regard to the protection of the financial balance of the social security system, if the reimbursement of the costs of medical treatment conforms to the tariffs of the state of insurance. Consequently, the Luxembourg law in question may not be applied.[228]

e) General Limits to the Restrictability of the Fundamental Freedoms

Case 8 – Problem: (ECJ *Omega* [2004] ECR I-9609)

92 Omega, a German company which runs amusement arcades, operates an installation known as a "Laserdrome" in which it offers games with the object of firing on human targets using a laser beam or other technical devices in order to hit sensory tags fixed to jackets worn by the other players. Games of this kind are common in the UK. Omega is authorised by a British company to operate Laserdromes in Germany and uses equipment and technology supplied by this company. The competent German authority is convinced of the games in question being inhuman. It therefore issued an order against Omega, prohibiting it from operating the Laserdrome. The *Bundesverwaltungsgericht* (BVerwG – German Federal Administrative Court), which is finally seized of the case, refers to the ECJ the question whether the prohibition of the games is compatible with the fundamental freedoms.

93 Where Community law allows for interferences with the fundamental freedoms these interferences are again themselves subject to certain limits – *ie* the general limits to restric-

---

[228] The fundamental freedoms also apply to health insurance schemes which provide for benefits in kind (such as the German system), ECJ *Geraets-Smits* [2001] ECR I-5473, para 55. With regard to the British NHS the Court found that Article 49 of the TEC does *not* preclude reimbursement of the cost of hospital treatment to be provided in another Member State from being made subject to the grant of prior authorisation, ECJ *Watts* [2006] ECR I-4325, para 113. See also ECJ *Müller-Fauré* [2003] ECR I-4509.

tability. These are limitations which apply to the entities bound by the fundamental freedoms (first and foremost the Member States) when restricting the exercise of the fundamental freedoms (*eg* on the grounds of mandatory requirements). The general limits to restrictability are the fundamental rights of the Union and all other provisions of primary Community law (para 94), the provisions of secondary Community law (para 95) and most notably the principle of proportionality (para 96).

aa) Fundamental Rights of the Union / Other Provisions of Primary Community Law

The fundamental freedoms can only be justifiably interfered with, if the measures in question comply with all requirements of primary Community law. If the EC, for example, wants to interfere with the fundamental freedoms, it has to act within the limits of the **powers conferred upon it by the Treaty** (Article 5 TEC/Article I-11 DC). Furthermore, the Communities as well as the Member States (when applying Community law) have to act in accordance with the **fundamental rights of the Union** (para 15). The fundamental rights of the Union do not necessarily conflict with the fundamental freedoms (para 86); as the case may be they can also strengthen the protection which emanates from the fundamental freedoms (§ 14 para 12). Accordingly, the Court found that provisions on the restriction[229] as well as mandatory requirements[230] "must be interpreted in the light of the general principles of law and in particular of fundamental rights". The "maintenance of press diversity" and "consumer protection", for instance, both qualify as mandatory requirements. Nevertheless, the prohibition on the sale of periodicals containing prize competitions on such grounds has to be scrutinised against its consistency with the freedom of expression as one of the fundamental rights of the Union. This can be deduced from the principle of uniformity of the Community legal order.[231] In its decision in *Carpenter* (para 25), the ECJ found an interference with the freedom to provide services to be incompatible with Community law because it violated the fundamental right to respect for family life. The Union as well as the Member States (when applying Community law) are indeed directly bound by the fundamental rights of the Union. This is, however, only true with regard to situations to which Community or Union law applies. Where the fundamental rights of the Union limit the restrictability of the fundamental freedoms (§ 14 para 12), they do not function as independent "restrictions on the restrictions" but as a means for interpreting the recognised grounds for the justification of interferences. It is neither for the ECJ nor for the CFI to scrutinise interferences with the fundamental freedoms against their consistency with fundamental rights guaranteed under national law (para 86).

94

bb) Secondary Community Law

The above mentioned principles concerning the fundamental rights of the Union similarly apply to secondary Community law. A measure which is compatible with secondary Community law may still be in breach of the fundamental freedoms (*cf* para 54). However, a Member State (or private entity that is bound by the fundamental freedoms) cannot justifiably interfere with the fundamental freedoms where and as far as valid secondary Com-

95

---

229 ECJ *ERT* [1991] ECR I-2925, para 43.
230 ECJ *Familiapress* [1997] ECR I-3689, para 24.
231 Lackhoff (note 56) pp 459–60; see the criticism raised by Kingreen (note 2) pp 166 ff.

munity law prohibits such interferences (*eg* by providing for harmonising measures which only accept certain restrictions in relation to the policy objective in question[232]). As regards the Member States, this follows from the principle of supremacy of Community law (para 9). If the subject matter in question is **exhaustively** and justifiably **regulated** by secondary Community law, the Member States lack the power to enact laws to the contrary.[233] Due to the *lex specialis* principle (para 54), the fundamental freedoms are not applicable to these cases anyway.

cc) Principle of Proportionality

96 Finally, it is settled case-law of the ECJ that interferences with the fundamental freedoms have to be proportional.[234] The need for a proportionality test can be deduced either from the provisions on restriction which require "justified" measures (Articles 30, 39(3), 46 read in conjunction with 55, 58(1) TEC/Articles III-154, III-133(3), III-140 read in conjunction with III-150, III-158(1) DC) or from the term "mandatory" requirements or grounds which correspond to a public-interest objective. Incidentally, the principle of proportionality (which can also be referred to as the prohibition of excessive means[235]) constitutes a general principle of Community law which not only concerns the division of competences between the EC and its Member States[236] but also – and foremost – the fundamental rights including the fundamental freedoms because it can be derived from the liberty rights (as regards the future state of the law *cf* Article II-112(1) DC; → § 14 para 48) as well as from the principle of rule of law (Article I-2 DC). In most cases – the same applies to German law – the proportionality test is the crucial point when scrutinising interfering measures. For a measure to be proportional it must first be aimed at legitimate objectives. Furthermore, the means employed have to be legitimate as such. Interfering measures finally have to be suitable, necessary and adequate (proportional *stricto sensu*) means for attaining the desired objective.[237] The concept of suitability requires a means that (at least) advances the objective. A means is necessary if there is no less restrictive but equally effective option for attaining the aim pursued. Measures are considered adequate if they bear a well-balanced and carefully weighted relation to the significance and importance of the fundamental freedom in question. Compared to German standards, the ECJ and the CFI employ a 'low-key' proportionality test in relation to interferences with the fundamental freedoms (*cf* also → § 14 para 49). Since secondary Community law is hardly scrutinised against its consistency with the fundamental freedoms (para 7), its proportionality is normally not tested either. Although the ECJ found private individuals to be directly bound by the fundamental freedoms under certain circumstances (para 45), it has not clarified

---

232 *Cf* ECJ *Schumacher* [1989] ECR 617, paras 7 ff; *Commission v Germany* [1994] ECR I-2039, paras 12 ff; *Ortscheit* [1994] ECR I-5243, para 14; *Hedley Lomas* [1996] ECR I-2553, paras 18 ff.
233 Jarass [2000] EuR 705, 719–20. See, however, Art 95(4) TEC.
234 *Cf* only Craig/de Búrca (note 1) pp 371 ff; Pache [1999] NVwZ 1033; Jarass [2000] EuR 705, 721 ff; Schwab *Der Europäische Gerichtshof und der Verhältnismäßigkeitsgrundsatz* (Frankfurt am Main 2002); Koch *Der Grundsatz der Verhältnismäßigkeit in der Rechtssprechung des Gerichtshofs der Europäischen Gemeinschaften* (Berlin 2003); Frenz (note 71) paras 523 ff – each with numerous references to case-law.
235 As to the terminology *cf* Krebs [2001] JURA 228.
236 Art 5(3) TEC (Art I-11(4) DC).
237 *Cf* also ECJ *Schräder* [1989] ECR 2237, para 21; *MacQuen* [2001] ECR I-837, paras 31–32.

the implications of the proportionality test in these cases so far. Where Member States interfere with the fundamental freedoms they are – in the majority of cases – vested with a wide margin of appreciation. Some decisions resemble the Wednesbury test in English law (according to which measures are merely examined for their reasonableness and rationality).[238] However, the intensity of scrutiny correlates with the importance of the national interests that are affected. Stricter standards, for example, tend to be applied with regard to interferences with the free movement of goods, services, capital or payments (in contrast to interferences with the free movement for workers or the freedom of establishment) as well as with regard to overt discrimination (in contrast to indistinctly applicable interferences).[239] This appears to be due to the fact that the interests of the Member States are particularly strongly affected by the free movement for workers and the freedom of establishment. In contrast, Member States can hardly give any convincing reasons for overt discrimination. Above all, in many cases in which legitimate aims are pursued the ECJ usually confines itself to applying a mere two-stage test (*ie* measures are examined for their suitability and necessity but not for their adequateness).[240] In the vast majority of cases, the examination for the necessity of a measure – *ie* the question whether there is a less restrictive but equally effective option for attaining the aim pursued – is decisive. The fact that one Member State imposes stricter rules than another does not necessarily entail that the rules of the former are not necessary.[241] However, with regard to the freedom to provide services, for example, national rules of the host Member State are not necessary where the legitimate objective in question is already attained by equivalent requirements imposed by the Member State of origin.[242] The repeated control of persons or products is therefore dispensable where sufficient control has already been exercised by the Member State of origin.[243] Interferences with the freedom of establishment of a company formed in another Member State on grounds of protecting creditors against a lack of minimum capital are not necessary if the company publicly indicates that it is governed by foreign law. If so, potential creditors are put on sufficient notice that the company is covered by rules in respect of minimum capital and directors' liability which differ from domestic legislation.[244]

---

238 *Cf* von Dannwitz [2003] EWS 393, 397.
239 *Cf* also Jarass [2000] EuR 705, 723.
240 Characteristically ECJ *Inspire Art* [2003] ECR I-10155, para 133 with further references. See the criticism raised, for example, by von Dannwitz [2003] EWS 393, 395 ff. In some cases the Court speaks of adequateness when examining a measure for its necessity, *cf* ECJ *Commission v Spain* [2003] ECR I-4381, para 69, *Loi Evin* [2004] ECR I-6613, paras 35–36; Frenz (note 71) para 534.
241 *Cf* ECJ *Alpine Investments* [1995] ECR I-1141, paras 50 ff; *Broede* [1996] ECR I-6511, para 42; *Zenatti* [1999] ECR I-7289, para 34; *Mac Quen* [2001] ECR I-837, paras 33–34; *Loi Evin* [2004] ECR I-6613, para 37.
242 *Cf* ECJ *Säger* [1991] ECR I-4221, paras 15 ff; *Houtwipper* [1994] ECR I-4249, para 19; *Gebhard* [1995] ECR I-4165, paras 38–39.
243 ECJ *Vlassopoulou* [1991] ECR I-2357, paras 15 ff.
244 *Cf* ECJ *Inspire Art* [2003] ECR I-10155, para 135; more detailed DeDiego *Die Niederlassungsfreiheit von Scheinauslandsgesellschaften in der Europäischen Gemeinschaft* (Berlin 2004) pp 124 ff.

Case 8 – Answer:
The prohibition of the games possibly violates the freedom to provide services (Article 49 TEC/Article III-144 DC) and the free movement of goods (Article 28 TEC/Article III-153 DC). 1. Scope of protection of the freedom to provide services: The fundamental freedoms are only applicable to cross-border scenarios. The present facts constitute a cross-border scenario because Omega operates its "Laserdrome" under a format developed and marketed by a British company. The subject matter of protection of the freedom to provide services covers services which are normally provided for remuneration, insofar as they are not governed by the provisions relating to freedom of movement for goods, capital and persons (Article 50(1) TEC/Article III-145(1) DC). The marketing of the British laser game corresponds to this definition. Since the provider (British company) as well as the recipient (Omega) can rely on the freedom to provide services, the present case falls within the scope of protection of the said fundamental freedom.
2. Scope of protection of the free movement of goods: The technical equipment used in the Laserdrome constitutes a product. Purchasing the equipment in Britain therefore falls within the scope of the free movement of goods as protected by Article 28 of the TEC (Article III-153 DC). The prohibition of the laser games is likely to prevent Omega from purchasing the equipment. However, according to the case-law of the ECJ, a national measure which affects both the freedom to provide services and the free movement of goods is examined in relation to only one of those two fundamental freedoms if it is clear that, in the circumstances of the case, one of those freedoms is entirely secondary in relation to the other and may be attached to it (ECJ *Schindler* [1994] ECR I-1039, para 22). In the circumstances of the present case, the aspect of the freedom to provide services prevails over that of the free movement of goods: the importation of goods is only restricted as regards equipment specifically designed for the prohibited variant of the laser game; the said restriction is an unavoidable consequence of the restriction imposed with regard to the services which are provided by the British company.
3. Interference with the freedom to provide services: The prohibition order has been issued by the German authority irrespective of the nationality of the provider or recipient of the services in question. Hence, it does not constitute a discriminatory measure, but rather a limitation of the free circulation of services.
4. Justification of the interference: The prohibition order has been issued under powers conferred by section 14(1) of the *Ordnungsbehördengesetz Nordrhein-Westfalen* (German Law governing the North Rhine-Westphalia Police authorities). It has to be examined, however, whether section 14(1) corresponds to one of the recognised authorisations to restrict the freedom to provide services. Pursuant to Article 55 read in conjunction with Article 46 of the TEC (Article III-150 read in conjunction with Article III-140 DC) interferences with the freedom to provide services are justifiable on grounds of public policy. The concept of public policy is construed narrowly. It requires a genuine and sufficiently serious threat to fundamental interests of society. There can be "no doubt" that the objective pursued by the German authority – *ie* the protection of human dignity – is compatible with Community law. It is being immaterial in this respect that in Germany the principle of respect for human dignity has a particular status as an independent fundamental right which is protected by Article 1(1) of the *Grundgesetz* (Basic Law – German Federal Constitution).[245] The prohibition order is also suitable for the protection of human dignity. It is also 'necessary' if the desired objective cannot be attained with the help of measures which are less restrictive on the free circulation of services. In this respect, it is not indispensable, however, that the

---

245 *Cf* also Art II-61 DC.

restrictive measure in question corresponds to a conception of the fundamental rights that is shared by all Member States. Hence, the prohibition order is not lacking its necessity just because laser games of the said kind are common in the UK. It rather has to be examined whether the measure goes beyond what is necessary in order to attain the aim pursued by the competent national authority. No less restrictive means appears to be available here: the order only prohibits a certain type of laser games the object of which is to fire on human targets and thus play at killing people. The adequateness of the measure does not appear to be questionable either. Consequently, the prohibition of the laser game does not violate the freedom to provide services.

4. Schematic Summary

In summary, a measure should be scrutinised for its consistency with the fundamental freedoms as follows: 98

I. Scope of protection
  1. Subject matter of protection
     a) No secondary Community law that regulates the subject matter in question exhaustively while being consistent with primary Community law
     b) Cross-border scenario
     c) The scenario in question is protected by a fundamental freedom
        (where applicable: delineation of the fundamental freedoms from each other)
     d) No abusive exercise of the fundamental freedoms
  2. Personal scope of protection
  3. Territorial scope of protection
  4. Temporal scope of protection
II. Interference with the fundamental freedoms
  1. Act (or omission) by an entity that is bound by the fundamental freedoms
     (this issue can also be dealt with under the headline 'personal scope of protection')
  2. Existence of 'discrimination'
     a) Overt discrimination
     b) Covert discrimination
  3. Existence of a 'limitation'
     a) *Dassonville* formula (or equivalent formulas)
     b) No exclusion of a limitation according to *Keck*
     c) Rule of remoteness
III. Justification of the interference
  1. Requirement of a legal basis which authorises to interfere with a fundamental freedom
     a) Secondary Community law
     b) Statutory basis in national law
  2. Written authorisation to restrict the fundamental freedoms
  3. Other Community law as restrictions on the fundamental freedoms
  4. Unwritten authorisation to restrict the fundamental freedoms
     a) Overt discrimination (only justifiable on the basis of a written authorisation)
     b) Covert discrimination (also justifiable on the basis of an unwritten authorisation)
     c) Limitations (also justifiable on the basis of an unwritten authorisation)

5. General limits to the restrictability of the fundamental freedoms
   a) Observance of the fundamental rights of the Union and of all other provisions of primary Community law
   b) Observance of secondary Community law
   c) Observance of the principle of proportionality

VIII. Judicial Protection

1. Avenues of Judicial Protection for the Individual

99 Since the fundamental freedoms are directly applicable (para 7) and since they bestow (subjective) rights on their beneficiaries (para 8), the individual can seek judicial protection against violations of the fundamental freedoms. If **national measures** are challenged, the courts of the relevant Member State have (exclusive) jurisdiction. The division of jurisdiction among the courts of a Member State is governed by national procedural law.[246]

100 National courts may – and under certain circumstances must – request the ECJ to give a preliminary ruling pursuant to Article 234 of the TEC (Article III-369 DC) where the interpretation of the fundamental freedoms gives rise to ambiguity.

101 National measures that violate the fundamental freedoms can at the same time infringe fundamental rights guaranteed under national law. Where, for example, foreign citizens of the Union are covered by the personal scope of protection of the fundamental rights guaranteed under the Basic Law,[247] interferences that constitute a violation of the fundamental freedoms cannot be justified due to the fact that Community law takes precedence in application over conflicting domestic law. Accordingly, violations of the fundamental freedoms can be subjected to judicial review by way of a constitutional complaint to the *Bundesverfassungsgericht* (BVerfG – German Federal Constitutional Court) if – and in as much as – the measures in question also violate the fundamental rights guaranteed under the Basic Law. This again reveals the strong interlocking between domestic legal systems and the Community legal order.

102 As a general rule, the individual has to challenge measures of a Member State before the courts of that particular state. However, this is not true where a Member State pursues activities in other Member States without exercising official authority there. Pursuant to Article 5 No 5 of Council Regulation 44/2001[248] English courts, for example, would have to decide cases that arise from the operation of German public enterprises which pursue their economic activities from an agency situated in England. Such cases might also involve questions relating to the fundamental freedoms.

103 Where private individuals contend a **violation of Community law by the institutions of the EC**, they have to bring an action for annulment under Article 230(4) of the TEC (Article III-364(4) DC) which will be tried by the CFI (Article 225 TEC/Article III-358 DC). However, private individuals can only institute proceedings against decisions addressed to them or against decisions which, although in the form of a regulation or a decision addressed to another person, are of direct and individual concern to them. As re-

---

246 As to the impact of Community law on German procedural law *cf* Ehlers [2004] DVBl 1441.
247 More detailed as to foreign citizens of the Union being covered by the personal scope of protection Wernsmann [2000] JURA 657.
248 [2001] OJ L12/1.

General Principles §7 VIII 2

gards the future state of the law *cf* Article III-365(4) DC (individuals will, *inter alia*, be able to institute proceedings against a regulatory act which is of direct concern to the individual and does not require implementing measures).

2. Protection of the Fundamental Freedoms through Proceedings Instituted by the Commission or by the Member States

Not only individuals personally affected by a violation but also the Commission can ensure the observance of the fundamental freedoms on the part of the Member States by instituting an infringement procedure under Article 226 of the TEC (Article III-360 DC). Similarly, the Member States are able to bring an action before the ECJ (Article 227 TEC/Article III-361 DC) if they consider that another Member State has violated the fundamental freedoms. The institutions of the EC as well as the Member States can also bring an action for annulment under Article 230(2) and (3) of the TEC (Article III-364(2) and (3) DC).

104

§ 8
Free Movement of Goods

Astrid Epiney

Leading cases: ECJ *Dassonville* [1974] ECR 837; *Cassis de Dijon* [1979] ECR 649; *Keck* [1993] ECR I-6097; *Mars* [1995] ECR I-1923; *de Agostini* [1997] ECR I-3843; *DocMorris* [2003] ECR I-14887.

Further reading: Ahlfeld *Zwingende Erfordernisse im Sinne der Cassis-Rechtsprechung des Europäischen Gerichtshofs zu Art. 30 EGV* (Baden-Baden 1997); Frenz *Handbuch Europarecht. Band 1. Europäische Grundfreiheiten* (Berlin 2004); Füller *Grundlagen und inhaltliche Reichweite der Warenverkehrsfreiheiten nach dem EG-Vertrag* (Baden-Baden 2000); Hoffmann *Die Grundfreiheiten des EG-Vertrags als koordinationsrechtliche und gleichheitsrechtliche Abwehrrechte* (Baden-Baden 2000); Kingreen *Die Struktur der Grundfreiheiten des Europäischen Gemeinschaftsrechts* (Berlin 1999); Millarg *Die Schranken des freien Warenverkehrs in der EG* (Baden-Baden 2001).

1 According to the conception of the TEC, the free movement of goods is guaranteed by a whole set of rules:

2 Articles 25 ff of the TEC contain the provisions relevant to the customs union. Specifically, these provisions prohibit **custom duties on imports and exports** as well as **charges having equivalent effect** (Article 25 TEC/Article III-151 IV DC) on the one hand and permit the introduction of a **common customs tariff** in relation to third states (Article 26 TEC/Article III-151 V DC) on the other hand. While Article 25 of the TEC (Article III-151 IV DC) has direct effect and confers corresponding rights on individuals, featuring[1] the same characteristics as the Fundamental Freedoms[2] in this respect, the common customs tariff is (necessarily) introduced by secondary community law.[3]

3 The **prohibition of quantitative restrictions on imports and exports** and of **measures having equivalent effect** (Articles 28–30 TEC/Articles III-153–154 DC) complements the prohibition on tariff trade barriers set forth in Article 25 of the TEC (Article III-151 IV DC) by prohibiting trade barriers of non-tariff nature, thereby contributing substantially to the opening of the markets in terms of the cross-border circulation of goods.

4 Lastly, Article 31 of the TEC (Article III-155 DC) provides for the **transformation of state trade monopolies**. This provision – which complements the prohibition of tariff and non-tariff barriers – seeks to prevent restrictions of the effectiveness of the rules on the free movement of goods caused by the dealings of state trade monopolies.[4]

5 Due to the nature and focus of this volume, the following observations are limited to the aspect named in second place, which is also by far the most important in the (judicial) practice. As to the scope of Articles 28 and 29 of the TEC, one can distinguish – accord-

---

1 The notion of custom duties is relatively clear whereas the notion of measures having equivalent effect raises several questions. As to this, with further references to case-law, *cf* Epiney in: Bieber/Epiney/Haag (eds) *Die Europäische Union* (6th ed, Baden-Baden 2004) § 13, paras 20 ff.
2 As to the notion → § 7 para 7.
3 *Cf* more detailed Voß in: Grabitz/Hilf (eds) *Das Recht der Europäischen Union* (loose-leaf, Munich) Art 23 EGV, paras 17 ff.
4 However, while state trade monopolies are not forbidden, they are (also) subject to the rules of the free movement of goods. *Cf* more detailed on the provision and its interpretation by the ECJ, with further references, Epiney in: Calliess/Ruffert (eds) *Kommentar EUV/EGV* (2nd ed, Neuwied 2002) Art 31 EGV.

ing to the aforementioned general doctrines (→ § 7 paras 50 ff) – between (I.) the scope of protection, (II.) interference and (III.) justification. Those problems that have already been discussed generally will only be touched upon, so that the emphasis will lie on questions particularly relevant or specific to the movement of goods.

I. Scope of Protection

The **territorial scope of applicability** of Articles 28 and 29 of the TEC (Article III-153 DC) results from Article 299 of the TEC (Article IV-440 DC) and therefore corresponds with the scope of the TEC.[5]

The **subject matter of protection** of Articles 28 and 29 of the TEC (Article III-153 DC) can be drawn from Article 23(2) of the TEC (Article III-151(2) DC). In consequence, two aspects are of significance:

First of all, "**goods**" must be concerned. This term is not defined in the Treaty; however, it has been clarified to a certain extent by the case-law of the ECJ.[6] Accordingly, goods are to be understood as movable physical objects which generally have a monetary value and can thus be the objects of commercial transactions. However, in some cases the ECJ has taken a more pragmatic point of view, *eg* it has considered waste materials to be "goods"[7] in order to avoid delimitation problems – a monetary value is sometimes, but not always, attributed to waste, and this estimation is also quite susceptible to change. Electric current and gas are also considered to be goods[8], which is appropriate in view of their transferability and practical handling as goods with monetary value. However, it must be pointed out that these delimitation problems are not of great practical relevance, given that the free movement of services (Article 49 TEC/Article III-144 DC) would apply should Article 28 of the TEC (Article III-153 DC) be found not to be relevant.

Even if movables are concerned, the quality as a good and therefore the relevance of Articles 28 and 29 of the TEC (Article III-153 DC) may be negated if the movable as such is insignificant and of no or of a fairly negligible value, particularly because the main focus of the commercial activity lies in another field. For instance, the confiscation of lottery tickets and corresponding promotion materials following the application of a general prohibition of lotteries does not primarily concern the free movement of goods, but rather the free movement of services, since the distribution of advertising materials is inseparably linked with the running of lotteries.[9] However, a product should be considered a good if it acts as a "storage container", such as gramophone records.[10]

Secondly, the merchandise must either originate **from the Member States** or – in case of goods from third states – has to be **circulating freely between Member States**. The proof of the status of the merchandise as a Community good is regulated in detail in the Customs Code.[11]

---

5 More detailed → § 7 para 48.
6 For instance, *cf* ECJ *Jägerskiöld* [1999] ECR I-7319, paras 30 ff.
7 ECJ *Commission v Belgium* [1992] ECR I-4431, paras 22 ff.
8 ECJ *Almelo* [1994] ECR I-1477, para 28; *Preussen Elektra* [2001] ECR I-2099, paras 68 ff.
9 ECJ *Schindler* [1994] ECR I-1039, paras 22–23.
10 On this and as to the delimitation from "inventions" Voß (note 3) Art 23 EGV, para 12.
11 On this, more detailed, Voß (note 3) Art 23 EGV, paras 16 ff.

11   The question whether certain merchandise should not be given the status of a good **for ethical reasons** has not yet been definitively answered.[12] This problem is relevant when it comes to corpses as well as embryos or stem cells and can also arise accordingly within the scope of other Fundamental Freedoms. Ultimately, strong arguments suggest that the notion of goods should not be categorically restricted from an ethical point of view: First of all, the question of the possible scope of such a restriction can hardly be answered in a general abstract manner and hence predictably: The views as to what is and is not "ethical" differ considerably, as is exemplified by the current discussion regarding stem cells. Furthermore, and particularly, the systematics of Articles 28 ff of the TEC (Article III-153 DC) rely on the assumption that such problems are to be resolved in the framework of justification, given that Article 28 of the TEC (Article III-153 DC) generally does not pay regard to the legal classification of a certain product in a Member State. Rather, this aspect is considered at the level of justification (Article 30 TEC/Article III-154 DC and mandatory requirements, particularly public order). Therefore, it is more reasonable to resolve any ethical problems arising from trade with certain products at this level; in doing so, the Member States' diverse solutions to such questions may be considered as well.

12   Furthermore, in this context, there are **special rules** regarding specific goods and **general exemptions**: The former exist for goods subject to the Treaty on the European Atomic Energy Community (EAEC), which also prescribes the abolition of internal barriers. One might contemplate applying the provisions of the TEC at least as subsidiary law[13] in cases where the concrete guarantees of the TEC reach further.[14] As to agricultural products, the rules on the free movement of goods are (amongst others) applicable so long as Articles 33–38 of the TEC (Articles III-227-232 DC) do not prescribe something else (Article 32(2) TEC/Article III-226(2) DC). Finally, trade with arms, munitions and war materials can be restricted in accordance with Article 296(1)(b) of the TEC (Article III-436(1)(b) DC).

13   Pursuant to the case-law of the ECJ, the applicability of Articles 28 ff of the TEC (Article III-153 ff DC) also presupposes a **cross-border situation**.[15] Accordingly, so-called "reverse discrimination" – ie such cases in which, due to the application of community law (eg Article 28 TEC/Article III-153 DC), domestic products are treated less advantageously than goods imported from other Member States of the EU – is admissible in view of community law. However, in consideration of the development of community law – especially the newly introduced aim to establish a "boundless" single market – it does not seem appropriate any more to make border crossing a required precondition for the applicability of community law. A more differentiated approach would be more adequate. Thus, the absence of a cross-border element should certainly be taken into consideration at the level of justification when applying Article 28 of the TEC (Article III-153 DC), but it should not *a priori* exclude the application of this provision.[16] Finally, the case-law of

---

12 On this problem Frenz *Handbuch Europarecht Bd I* (Berlin 2004) paras 701–702.
13 *Cf* Voß (note 3) Art 23 EGV, para 14.
14 Thus, the EAEC Treaty for instance only contains a prohibition of quantitative restrictions, but not of measures having equivalent effect.
15 On this, already more detailed → § 7 paras 20, 25; from case-law, particularly regarding Art 28 TEC, *cf* ECJ *Mathot* [1987] ECR 809, para 12; *Rousseau* [1987] ECR 995, para 7.
16 More detailed on this approach Epiney *Umgekehrte Diskriminierungen* (Cologne 1995) especially pp 200 ff; also on this issue Hammerl *Inländerdiskriminierung* (Berlin 1997).

Free Movement of Goods §8 II 1

the ECJ, which defines the notion of a cross-border element more and more broadly[17], also serves to illustrate that a "frontier crossing" is a rather questionable requirement for the application of the provision.

II. Interference

Both Articles 28 and 29 of the TEC (Article III-153 DC) prohibit quantitative restrictions on imports and exports as well as measures having equivalent effect. However, because their respective scopes differ with respect to their contents the two provisions shall be discussed separately (paras 22–46, 47–50).[18] *A priori*, both of the provisions only apply on condition that an obligor takes action (paras 15–21).

1. Addressees (Obligors)

> **Case 1 – Problem:** (ECJ *Schmidberger* [2003] ECR I-5659)
> On the Brenner Motorway, a central north-south transit axis, a demonstration was held in 1998 by environmentalists who were opposed to the (increasing) transit traffic. The demonstration was not prohibited by the competent Austrian authorities (even though a corresponding request was filed) and lead to a 30 hour blockade of the motorway. The Austrian authorities provided detailed information about the demonstration some time in advance and suggested various detours. Eugen Schmidberger, a freight forwarder, sued the Republic of Austria before the *Oberlandesgericht* (Regional Court of Appeal – OLG) of Innsbruck and requested compensation for the specified loss of earnings resulting from the fact that he could not use his lorries during the period in question. During the course of the proceedings, the OLG Innsbruck raises the question whether the Republic of Austria violated its Community law obligations by not having prohibited the demonstration.

The primary addressees of Articles 28 ff of the TEC (Article III-153 DC) are the **Member States**, which generate the most significant part by far of the limitations of these Fundamental Freedoms in practice. However, as a result of Article 10 of the TEC (Article I-5 II DC), in certain cases the Member States are also obliged to intervene against trade barriers that emanate from individuals.[19] Judging by the phrasing in recent case-law,[20] it remains unclear whether, in order for Article 28 read in conjunction with Article 10 of the TEC (Article III-153 read in conjunction with Article I-5 II DC) to apply, it suffices that the actions of individuals lead to any kind of – even minimal – interference with the free movement of goods, or whether a certain level of interference is required. In any case, within the scope of justification, other interests must be taken into account, especially fundamental human rights guarantees.

It is also considered a state measure when individuals assert their industrial property rights: Although the holder of the right has to assert his claim, the subsequent measures restricting imports – confiscation, prohibition of marketing under certain conditions or

14

15

16

17

---

17 From recent case-law *cf* especially ECJ *Carpenter* [2002] ECR I-6279, paras 28 ff; *Garcia Avello* [2003] ECR I-11613.
18 At least based on case-law and the herewith represented point of view.
19 ECJ *Commission v France* [1997] ECR I-6959, paras 24 → More detailed on this § 7 para 43.
20 ECJ *Schmidberger* [2003] ECR I-5659.

229

the like – are imposed by state organs (authorities or courts).[21] Moreover, it is irrelevant whether the respective state measure is of an imperative character or not; only the discriminatory or limiting effect is decisive.[22] Consequently, the ECJ found an advertising campaign initiated by Irish authorities promoting the purchase of domestic products to constitute a measure having equivalent effect to an import restriction.[23]

18   Finally, also the **Community organs** themselves have to abide by the requirements of Articles 28 ff of the TEC (Article III-153 ff DC)[24] as a direct result of the hierarchy of norms (primary law has priority over secondary law).

19   Whether and to which extent **individuals** are bound[25] by Articles 28 ff of the TEC (Article III-153 ff DC) has not (yet) been completely clarified, as is the case with the other Fundamental Freedoms (→ § 7 paras 42-43). Meanwhile, the relevant case-law seems to assume that Articles 28 ff of the TEC (Article III-153 ff DC) have no extensive horizontal effect.[26] However, recent case-law also emphasises that certain formally private enterprises have to comply with the requirements of Article 28 of the TEC in some cases. This concerns formally private enterprises which were established on the basis of legal provisions, are required by law to reach specified objectives, have to comply with certain public law provisions and are financed by means of mandatory contributions by certain persons. Such enterprises have to comply with the requirements of Article 28 of the TEC if they introduce a regulation concerning all businesses of the respective economic branch which has an effect on intra-community trade equivalent to that of a provision originating from the state.[27] In these cases the ECJ apparently holds that the actions of these private companies may be attributed to the state.[28]

20   In any case, a denial of an extensive horizontal effect seems well-grounded within the framework of Articles 28 ff of the TEC (Article III-153 ff DC) – in particular when considering the function and objectives of Articles 28 ff of the TEC (Article III-153 ff DC) within the entire system of the Treaty: First of all, these provisions are essentially meant to complement the prohibition of custom duties and measures having equivalent effect with the ban on non-tariff barriers. Furthermore, in order to efficiently realise the free movement of goods, it is not absolutely necessary to include individual behaviours, these being subject to other provisions of the Treaty, namely the rules of competition (Articles 81-82 TEC/Article III-161 DC). In addition, the fact that the ECJ now seems to attribute

---

21 From case-law, *cf* for instance ECJ *Ideal Standard* [1994] ECR I-2789, paras 33–34; *Haag II* [1990] ECR I-3711, paras 8–9; among literature only Leible in: Grabitz/Hilf (eds) *Das Recht der Europäischen Union* (loose-leaf, Munich) Art 29 EGV, para 6.
22 On this, *cf* below.
23 ECJ *Commission v Ireland* [1981] ECR 1625, para 12.
24 ECJ *Meyhui* [1994] ECR I-3879, para 11.
25 Individuals are (as a matter of course) addressees of Articles 28 ff of the TEC insofar as they can invoke these provisions.
26 ECJ *Commission v Ireland* [1982] ECR 4005, paras 6 ff; *Bayer* [1988] ECR 5249, para 11; the contrary statement in ECJ *Dansk Supermarked* [1981] ECR 181, paras 17–18 has subsequently not been taken up by the Court, so that it can be assumed that the ECJ is from now on opposed to a horizontal effect; also ECJ *Commission v France* [1997] ECR I-6959, paras 24 ff is likely to follow this approach, given the circumstance, that the ECJ did not even address the issue of a possible responsibility of the private parties, rather indicates that it rejects a horizontal effect.
27 ECJ *Commission v Germany* [2002] ECR I-9977.
28 However, concerning open questions raised by this decision, *cf* Epiney [2004] NVwZ 555, 561.

Free Movement of Goods   § 8 II 1

an extensive horizontal effect[29] to the framework of Article 39 of the TEC presents problems of a general nature: Such a horizontal effect would probably not take into account the (also relevant) private autonomy and freedom of contract and, in this respect, could even exceed the function of the Fundamental Freedoms – not to mention the subsequent problems concerning implementation and application, for instance at the level of justification. It therefore seems more convincing to follow the approach – dominating in case-law – of limiting the horizontal effect to sets of rules which have a similar legal or factual binding force as state norms:[30] While this approach enables the efficient enforcement of the Fundamental Freedoms in the problematic areas, it also guarantees sufficient protection as the state duty to protect applies in all other cases. Insofar, this more recent case-law is principally convincing, since it apparently negates a general horizontal effect of Article 28 of the TEC (Article III-153 DC) in favor of an attribution of individuals' actions to the State. Hence it supports a commitment to Article 28 of the TEC (Article III-153 DC) only under the following conditions: The state must pursue a public task by means of private law and control the company in different aspects, while at the same time the regulation originating from the company must have the same effect on the intra-community movement of goods as a state regulation.

Case 1 – Answer:
Austria's decisions (no prohibition of the demonstration on the Brenner motorway and authorisation of the manifestation, respectively) could constitute a breach of Article 28 in conjunction with Article 10 of the TEC. These provisions oblige the Member States to take the necessary measures to ensure that the possibility of exercising the right of the free movement of goods is not compromised by the behaviour of (other) individuals. In the present case, such an interference has occured, since the blockade of the motorway impedes the freight forwarder from transporting the goods within an economically reasonable period of time; hindering or fully preventing the transit of goods constitutes a violation of Article 28 of the TEC. Therefore, the authorisation of the demonstration in question represents a measure which has the equivalent effect to a quantitative import restriction. However, this limitation of the free movement of goods can be justified by the protection of fundamental human rights, namely the freedom of free speech and of assembly, as guaranteed in Articles 10, 11 of the ECHR. These principles represent legitimate interests, which are generally suitable to justify a restriction of the free movement of goods. Accordingly, two interests – the realisation of the free movement of goods on the one side and the aforesaid fundamental human rights on the other – are in conflict and must be balanced in consideration of all the circumstances in each individual case. In the present case the following facts must be emphasised: The demonstration was authorised; the motorway was blocked (only) once for 30 hours; the blockade was geographically limited; the demonstration was not against the trade with goods of a certain kind or origin; the authorities had taken various accompanying measures in order to limit the jamming of road traffic; and, finally, a simple prohibition of the assembly would have meant an unacceptable interference with the freedom of assembly. In addition, had stricter requirements been imposed on the demonstration, they could have deprived it of an essential part of its impact. Considering all these circumstances, the appreciation of values by the Austrian authorities in the present case is not unjustifiable, so that they have not gone beyond their wide scope of discretion. Therefore, Articles 28, 10 of the TEC have not been violated.

21

---

29 ECJ *Angonese* [2000] ECR I-4139; → § 9 para 46.
30 *Cf* already ECJ *Walrave* [1974] ECR 1405; *cf* also ECJ *Bosman* [1995] ECR I-4921.

2. Import Restrictions and Measures Having Equivalent Effect (Article 28 TEC/Article III-153 DC)

a) Quantitative Restrictions

22 First of all, Article 28 of the TEC (Article III-153 DC) prohibits **import restrictions**. This applies to measures which restrict the import of goods according to their quantity or value.[31] Usually in practice, import restrictions assume the form of contingents; however, bans on imports and transits – as the most severe form of restriction – are also included. This leads to the conclusion that other measures, which do not directly restrict the import itself – particularly such measures that set up certain requirements as to the condition of the goods – are to, or can, respectively, be seen as measures having equivalent effect.[32]

23 Import restrictions by definition constitute cases of (direct) discrimination; non-discriminatory measures are therefore to be examined from the perspective of measures having equivalent effect.

24 In the meantime, however, quantitative restrictions on imports have become exceptional (*eg* environmentally motivated measures for the protection of species), so that their practical relevance is negligible.

b) Measures Having Equivalent Effect

> **Case 2 – problem:** (ECJ *Gourmet International* [2001] ECR I-1795)
> 25 In Sweden, there is a ban on advertising for alcoholic beverages in newspapers and magazines as well as in radio and television. Based on this prohibition, the *Konsumentombudsman* (consumer ombudsman) demanded the competent court to forbid Gourmet International Products AB (GIP) to publish advertisements for alcoholic beverages in newspapers, magazines, radio and television. The court would like to allow the claim; however, it has doubts as to the compatibility of such a ban with Article 28 of the TEC.

26 Central for the scope and relevance of Article 28 of the TEC (Article III-153 DC) is the prohibition of **measures having equivalent effect to import restrictions**. Their inclusion in the scope of Article 28 of the TEC (Article III-153 ff DC) must be seen against the background that the free movement of goods often is, or can be, hindered by non-quantifiable measures just as "effectively" – though not as "visible" – than by restrictions on imports.

27 Against this background, the **impact of a measure** is the most decisive factor in determining the notion of measures having equivalent effect: If a measure entails the same or similar consequences for the import of goods from other Member States as import restrictions, it is covered by Article 28 of the TEC (Article III-153 DC). By determining the "whether" and "how" of a discrimination, several forms of measures having equivalent effect can be distinguished.

---

31 ECJ *Geddo* [1973] ECR 865, para 7.
32 Among case-law *cf* for instance ECJ *Commission v United Kingdom* [1983] ECR 203, paras 21–22; *Commission v Germany* [1989] ECR 229, paras 4–5. More detailed on the delimitation *cf*, with further references, Epiney (note 4) Art 28 EGV, paras 8 ff.

aa) Direct Discrimination

Firstly, all measures which explicitly differentiate according to the origin of the goods (inland on the one hand, the other Member States on the other hand) are covered by the notion of measures having equivalent effect. Examples from practical experience in this context are, for instance, mandatory health inspections for imported goods[33] or labelling obligations only for imported goods[34].

bb) Indirect Discrimination

Indirectly discriminating measures are also forbidden, meaning such measures which, though apparently linked to a "neutral" criterion, in effect mainly concern and, as the case may be, discriminate against imported goods (→ on this generally § 7 para 22). In detail, the delimitation between indirect discrimination and the restrictions which will be dealt with below is problematic and hardly practicable when employing generally applicable criteria, at least within the scope of applicabilty of the Fundamental Freedoms.[35] However, this distinction is of no practical relevance, at least within the scope of Article 28 of the TEC (Article III-153 DC), since the reasons of justification are the same for indirect discrimination and restrictions.[36]

There is a point of view partly held in literature[37] which states that in the "core area" of the Fundamental Freedoms – *eg* the access itself to an occupation within the frame of Article 39 of the TEC (Article III-133 DC) – restrictions are generally prohibited, whereas in the "marginal areas" – *eg* regulating the exercise of an occupation within the scope of Article 39 of the TEC (Article III-133 DC) – only discriminations (in the broad sense of the term) are prohibited. However, at least in connection with Article 28 of the TEC (Article III-153 DC), this view is of no significance when one considers the relevant case-law (which is mostly adopted in literature): After all, Article 28 of the TEC (Article III-153 DC) is generally to be interpreted as a prohibition of restrictions, and the state of facts is limited as a result of the so-called *Keck* formula, so that it is neither appropriate nor necessary to differentiate according to "core and marginal areas" of the Fundamental Freedoms. Besides, such a differentiation already presents problems in its approach: First of all, it implies that within the core area, there generally is a severe interference with the rights of the concerned individuals. However, this is not necessarily the case, since *eg* certain employment modalities could possibly at least factually lead to access limitations. Closely related to this is the consideration that the core and marginal areas are often very difficult to separate.

In light of these problems, no delimitation between indirect discrimination and restrictions will be employed in the following, and the problem areas will be dealt with in connection with the discussion on the restrictions.

---

33 *Cf* the facts of the case in ECJ *Commission v Germany* [1989] ECR 3997.
34 *Cf* the facts of the case in ECJ *Commission v Ireland* [1981] ECR 1625.
35 As to Art 12 TEC and the hereby relevant criteria Epiney (note 16) p 102 ff.
36 *Cf* below paras 48 ff → § 7 para 90.
37 *Cf* for instance Lecheler/Gundel *Übungen im Europarecht* (Berlin 1999) p 177; in the same direction probably also Jarass [2000] EuR 705, 711.

cc) Restrictions

32 Non-discriminatory measures, which "only" **restrict the free movement of goods**, generally also fall within the scope of Article 28 of the TEC (Article III-152 DC), which already makes sense insofar as they can generate similar effects to import restrictions. Rules about product quality or advertising might be named as examples of this.

33 However, the conditions under which such a restriction must be assumed need further specification, since otherwise all measures which in some way relate to the free movement of goods could fall under Article 28 of the TEC (Article III-153 DC). The point of reference still is the so-called *Dassonville* **formula**: According to this formula, a measure having an equivalent effect is defined as any trading rule enacted by a Member State "which is capable of hindering directly or indirectly, actually or potentially, intra-community trade".[38] The decicive factor is therefore the restrictive effect of the measure. Consequently, the mere capability of a measure to have restrictive effects on trade is significant while it is irrelevant whether these effects have actually occurred or not.[39]

34 A possible consequence of this **broad scope of the notion of measures having equivalent effect** is that goods which were lawfully produced in one Member State can be imported and marketed in other Member States even though they do not correspond to their national standards (particularly product and approval requirements). Of course, possible grounds of justification remain reserved. Furthermore, even rules which are not directly related to products, such as provisions on manufacturing and marketing, can be subject to the *Dassonville* formula, because they are also in principle capable of having (negative) effects on the volume of (certain) imported products. Hence it also becomes clear that the consistent application of the *Dassonville* formula results in a considerable widening of the scope of Article 28 of the TEC (Article III-153 DC), which means that there is hardly any state measure which cannot fall within its scope, since numerous provisions could have repercussions, at least indirectly and potentially, on the import of products. As a result, a hardly limitable amount of national provisions can, or could, be assessed on the basis of Community law, concretely Article 28 of the TEC (Article III-153 DC).

35 Against this background, the judiciary has developed different approaches to limit the scope of Article 28 of the TEC (Article III-153 DC) in comparison to the wide definition of the *Dassonville* formula.

36 First of all, in several judgements the Court denied a **sufficiently close relation to the free movement of goods**. For instance, the ECJ denied the presence of a measure having an effect equivalent to import restrictions in its decision on the German prohibition to bake at night (prohibition to deliver bread rolls before 6 o'clock in the morning) on the grounds that it was a national sales regime without a cross-border effect, and that it could therefore not compromise trade between Member States.[40] Nor did the Court consider Article 28 of the TEC (Article III-153 DC) to be relevant regarding the Belgian prohibition of serving alcohol during night-time: As the measure was said not to be linked in any way with the import of goods, it was not capable of hindering trade between Member States.[41] On similar grounds, the Court refused to apply the standard of Article 28 of the TEC (Article III-153 DC) in order to assess the prohibition of Sunday shop

---

38 ECJ *Dassonville* [1974] ECR 837, para 5.
39 Explicitly ECJ *Prantl* [1984] ECR 1299, para 20.
40 ECJ *Oebel* [1981] ECR 1993, para 10.
41 ECJ *Blesgen* [1982] ECR 1211, para 9.

Free Movement of Goods §8 II 2

opening.[42] These judgements are particularly interesting because in all cases an indirect and potential interference with the import volume of products could hardly be denied, so that solely on the base of the *Dassonville* formula the relevance of Article 28 of the TEC (Article III-153 DC) should have been affirmed. This is especially striking in the case of the Belgian prohibition of serving alcohol at night, because the whole purpose of this measure is precisely to decrease the demand and hence the imports. From this "early" case-law[43] – "early" because prior to the *Keck* case-law[44] – it can only be deduced that especially for measures which are not (directly or indirectly) discriminating, potential market losses and following repercussions on the volume of imported products are not in every case sufficient in order for Article 28 of the TEC (Article III-153 DC) to be applicable. However, in this early stage the criteria according to which the scope of the *Dassonville* formula should be limited had not yet emerged clearly.

Insofar, the **Keck ruling** from 1993[45] introduced a certain, also dogmatic, clarification. 37
The subject-matter of the judgement was the French prohibition of resale of certain goods at a loss, which could not be judged by the standard of Article 28 of the TEC (Article III-153 DC). The Court reasoned that "**certain selling arrangements**" did not fall within the scope of Article 28 of the TEC (Article III-153 DC) if they fulfilled two conditions. Firstly, they have to apply to all concerned economic actors active within the Member State, and secondly, the marketing of domestic and imported products must be affected in the same manner, both in fact and in law.[46] Thus, the *Keck* case-law limits already the scope of Article 28 of the TEC (Article III-153 DC) – contrary to the previously developed so-called *Cassis de Dijon* case-law, which from a dogmatic point of view must be located at the level of justification.[47]

However, since the ECJ did not define the notion of „certain selling arrangements", 38
soon the question arose which national measures exactly should not fall within the scope of applicability of Article 28 of the TEC (Article III-153 DC). Certain indications can be deduced from the *Keck* formula itself, but also from **subsequent case-law**, in which primarily the following aspects are of importance:

Measures which in some way relate to the **quality of products** per se (including their 39
packaging, at least if it is inseparably connected to the product) do not constitute selling arrangements. For instance, the prohibition of labelling the wrapping of a chocolate bar under certain circumstances with the addition "+ 10%" must be considered as a measure having equivalent effect and is to be assessed on the basis of Article 28 of the TEC (Article III-153 DC).[48] Similarly, the prohibition of marketing certain products under a certain name is not to be seen as a selling arrangement in the sense of the *Keck* formula, for instance the prohibition of marketing cosmetics under the name "Clinique".[49] Also,

---

42 ECJ *Torfaen Borough Council* [1989] ECR 3851, para 14.
43 In addition to the mentioned decisions, *cf* the further references in Middeke *Nationaler Umweltschutz im Binnenmarkt* (Cologne 1994) pp 132–133, in consideration of the different approaches to their dogmatic classification; in detail on the relevant case-law also Hammer *Handbuch zum freien Warenverkehr* (Vienna 1998) pp 35 ff.
44 *Cf* in the text below in the next paragraph.
45 ECJ *Keck* [1993] ECR I-6097.
46 ECJ *Keck* [1993] ECR I-6097, para 16.
47 *Cf* below para 53 ff and → § 7 para 63.
48 ECJ *Mars* [1995] ECR I-1923, paras 12–13.
49 ECJ *Clinique* [1994] ECR I-317; *cf* also ECJ *Graffione* [1996] ECR I-6039.

235

due to the close connection with the product for sale, the prohibition of proffering prizes in magazines or other printed papers is to be considered a measure having equivalent effect to import restrictions.[50]

40   Measures which determine the **marketing of a product**, however, without being "connected" to it, are generally to be seen as selling arrangements. Accordingly, the obligation to sell baby food only in pharmacies must be classified as a selling arrangement.[51] The ECJ also considers the regulation of the opening hours of petrol stations to constitute a selling arrangement.[52]

41   When it comes to **borderline cases**, according to the ECJ it depends on whether a certain measure already impedes or restricts the **market access** of a product, in other words, whether it has the effect that the product in question cannot even enter the market of the concerned Member State, or that its access is hindered, so that there is an inequality of treatment between domestic and imported products in this regard.[53] In the case of distribution-related advertising, for instance, the focus is not set on the market access of the product, since this is guaranteed "boundlessly", but rather on the manner in which the product is marketed. Consequently, according to the case-law of the ECJ, the prohibition of television advertisement for certain goods must in principle be qualified as a selling arrangement, except in cases where such a prohibition has stronger effects on products from other Member States.[54]

42   In this context, one must recall that a measure generally does not constitute a selling arrangement if it has different effects on domestic and imported products, thus if it directly or indirectly discriminates the latter. This was the case with a rule of the Austrian Trade, Commerce and Industry Regulation Act, which held that only those vendors may offer groceries for sale "on the move" who also operate a fixed establishment in the concerning or an adjacent administrative district, since this rule entailed that foreign vendors were prevented from accessing this spectrum of the Austrian market.[55] The ECJ reasoned similarly with regard to the very comprehensive Swedish prohibition of advertising alcohol: Such a regulation was said to entail that the market access for products from other Member States was impeded to a larger extent than for the domestic products which were already better established anyway.[56] Also the German prohibition of mail order trading for pharmaceutical products does not constitute a selling arrangement according to the ECJ, since it affects foreign pharmacies (and therefore the imported products), which as such are not active in the German market, more substantially than domestic pharmacies; for the former, the

---

50 ECJ *Familiapress* [1997] ECR I-3689, para 12; → § 14 paras 31, 38.
51 ECJ *Commission v Greece* [1995] ECR I-1621, para 15.
52 ECJ *t'Heukske* [1994] ECR I-2199, paras 13 ff.
53 In this direction for instance ECJ *Commission v Greece* [1995] ECR I-1621, paras 11–12; *Alpine Investments* [1995] ECR I-1141, para 37; now explicitly in ECJ *Gourmet International* [2001] ECR I-1795, para 18: According to the considerations in the *Keck* ruling, "national provisions restricting or prohibiting certain selling arrangements only fall outside of Article 28 TEC, if they are not by nature such as to prevent the access of products of another Member State to the market or to impede access any more than they impede the access of domestic products".
54 ECJ *Leclerc* [1995] ECR I-179, paras 20 ff; *de Agostini* [1997] ECR I-3843, paras 39–40.
55 ECJ *Schutzverband gegen unlauteren Wettbewerb* [2000] ECR I-151, para 9. Very critical of this decision against the background of the – according to his opinion – too broad interpretation of the notion of indirect discrimination Gundel [2000] EuZW, 311–312.
56 ECJ *Gourmet International* [2001] ECR I-1795, paras 20–21; *cf* also below the answer to case 2.

internet as a means of access to the German market was said to be considerably more important than for the latter.[57] Altogether, there is thus a tendency in case-law not to consider those marketing and advertising rules as selling arrangements that have a noticeable impact on the sales volume of the concerning goods and which directly or indirectly influence the level of recognition of products, since they are a stronger "burden" to imported products due to the generally better market launch of national products.

Not all **delimitation problems**[58] can, however, be solved with these indications, as is exemplified by the general prohibition of advertisements for a certain product (*eg* alcohol or tobacco). On the one hand, the relevant judgements of the ECJ emphasise, as already mentioned, that television advertising for instance constitutes a selling arrangement,[59] since the access to the market itself is not restricted and the possibility of selling the corresponding products remains possible without limitation; beyond this, a material discrimination between imported and domestic products is apparently rejected. On the other hand, however, the ECJ points out that a measure always has equivalent effect if the (complete) prohibition of a form of sales promotion for a product in a Member State has unfavourable effects on products from other Member States.[60] This seems to be reasonable insofar as a quasi general prohibition on advertising is likely to entail that particularly newly launched products can hardly be established. Since new domestic products can probably also only be launched in the market with considerable difficulties, the effects of such a measure approach those of a market access restriction. It still remains open where exactly to draw the line between both cases. Insofar, the rulings of the ECJ could absolutely have turned out differently with respect to non-product related advertising.

43

However, the **approach of the ECJ** can also be **questioned** independently of such delimitation problems. If one departs from the assumption that the whole purpose of Article 28 of the TEC (Article III-153 DC) is primarily to ensure that products originating from different Member States can circulate freely within the Union territory, it makes sense to judge depending on whether the framework for the marketing or distribution of products is regulated generally or whether it is a matter of subjecting certain products in some manner to a particular regulation. The latter is, however, always the case if a national provision does not concern all products, but only a **delimitable product group** – such as, for instance, baby food, tobacco, alcohol etc. This approach also suggests itself against the background that – as exemplified by the restriction of selling certain products only in certain specialised locations – numerous provisions, which as such do not affect market access and are not discriminatory either, can cause quite significant losses of market shares for the economic actors and are, as to their effects, insofar absolutely comparable with directly product-related provisions. Moreover, with the approach presented here, it is also possible to resolve borderline cases without problems: For instance, in the case of the mentioned general prohibition to advertise, the purpose is precisely to regularise a certain delimitable product or product group, which by these standards amounts to a measure having equivalent effect.

44

---

57 ECJ *DocMorris* [2003] ECR I-14887.
58 For which different approaches have also been pointed out in literature; for an overview of the different represented approaches *cf* Epiney (note 4) Art 28 EGV, para 35, with further references.
59 ECJ *Leclerc* [1995] ECR I-179, paras 20 ff; *cf* also ECJ *Hünermund* [1993] ECR I-6787, paras 19ff.
60 ECJ *de Agostini* [1997] ECR I-3843, para 40; likewise ECJ *Gourmet International* [2001] ECR I-1795, paras 20–21.

45 Furthermore, any kind of **"noticeability"** of the measure or a "proximity" between the measure and the interfering effect are irrelevant in any case:[61] In the end, this only serves to weaken the criterion of the suitability of a measure to deploy restrictive effects on trade, the outlines of which, however, are apparently unclear and can hardly be predictably concretised. Besides, the "minor intensity" of a measure must anyway be considered at the level of justification within the frame of the proportionality test. However, the case-law of the ECJ is not always clear in this regard: While the ECJ sometimes seems to consider a sort of noticeability or proximity between the measure and the restrictive effect to be necessary,[62] other rulings indicate that this is precisely not the case, for instance, when the answer to the question whether a provision had a restrictive effect – which was doubtable – is exclusively based on its legal content, not, however, on the requirement of some kind of noticeability.[63]

Case 2 – Answer:

46 A prohibition on advertising such as the one in the case at hand generally concerns alcohol, thus also imported alcohol, so that insofar the scope of applicability of Articles 28 ff of the TEC becomes relevant (*cf* also Article 23(2) TEC). The judgement in question is a state measure. Furthermore, it constitutes a measure having equivalent effect in the sense of the *Dassonville* formula, because a ban on advertising can – and even should – lead to the reduction of sales (also) of imported alcohol, thus to an interference with intra-community trade. It might, however, be questionable whether there is a selling arrangement in the sense of the *Keck* formula in the case at hand. In principle, the prohibition does not represent a product related but a sales related measure, since only the marketing method is regulated and the advertising is also not inseparably connected to the product. Furthermore, the market access of alcohol as such is not affected; marketing still remains possible. Insofar, one could assume that the prohibition constitutes a selling arrangement. However, in view of the fact that the Swedish prohibition does not only ban one form of sales promotion of a product, but basically hinders the producers and importers from almost every kind of distribution of advertising aimed at consumers, and that – especially when stimulants such as alcohol are concerned – social traditions play an important role while selecting beverages, it must be considered that the comprehensive ban on advertising in question has stronger effects on products from other Member States than on domestic products. Consequently, there is an obstacle to the free movement of goods between the Member States and Article 28 of the TEC is applicable. However, the prohibition could be justified on grounds of health protection (Article 30 of the TEC) since it is supposed to contribute to the battle against alcoholism. In the facts of the case there are no indications that the prohibition does not meet the standards of the principle of proportionality; for this purpose, an examination of the legal and factual circumstances would be necessary, which is to be carried out by the national court requesting the preliminary ruling.

---

61 Apparently different → § 7 para 74; as presented here for instance Füller *Grundlagen und inhaltliche Reichweite der Warenverkehrsfreiheiten nach dem EG-Vertrag* (Baden-Baden 2000) pp 111 ff; Leible (note 21) Art 28 EGV, para 15; *cf* with reference to recent case-law also Epiney [1999] NVwZ 1076, 1077; more detailed on the problem also Keßler *Das System der Warenverkehrsfreiheit im Gemeinschaftsrecht* (Berlin 1997) pp 21 ff.
62 *Cf* for instance ECJ *Semeraro* [1996] ECR I-2975, paras 32–33; *CMC Motorradcenter* [1993] ECR I-5009, paras 8 ff; *Peralta* [1994] ECR I-3453, para 24; *BASF* [1999] ECR I-6269, para 16.
63 ECJ *Schutzverband gegen unlauteren Wettbewerb* [2000] ECR I-151, paras 25 ff; *cf* also ECJ *Commission v France* [1998] ECR I-6197, paras 16 ff; opposed to a "noticeability test" probably

3. Quantitative Restrictions on Exports and Measures Having Equivalent Effect

According to Article 29 of the TEC (Article III-153 DC), **quantitative restrictions on exports** and **measures having equivalent effect** are prohibited. The purpose of the ban of Article 29 of the TEC (Article III-153 DC) corresponds with the one of Article 28 of the TEC (Article III-153 DC) insofar as it aims at avoiding the hindrance of the free movement of goods which arises when Member States saturate the demand on their intrastate markets by means of restrictions on exports.[64] Insofar, it is absolutely possible to tie in with the principles developed within the scope of Article 28 of the TEC (Article III-153 DC) when interpreting Article 29 of the TEC (Article III-153 DC).[65] 47

However, the *Dassonville* **formula** must be **narrowed** against the background of the approaches developed within the framework of Article 28 of the TEC (Article III-153 DC), given that its "complete" application would ultimately mean that almost every production or distribution provision would violate Article 29 of the TEC (Article III-153 DC), since it regularly affects intra-community trade at least indirectly and potentially, as such provisions exert negative influence on manufacturing costs. Therefore, also the ECJ acts on the assumption that Article 29 of the TEC (Article III-153 DC) is only applicable to such measures which "have as their specific object or effect the restriction of patterns of exports and thereby the establishment of a difference in treatment between the domestic trade of a Member State and its export trade in such a way as to provide a particular advantage for national production or for the domestic market of the state in question at the expense of the production or of the trade of other Member States".[66] In the subsequent case-law, this approach was confirmed, while it was not required anymore that the advantage for the domestic market of the respective state comes along with a disadvantage for the production of other Member States. 48

This approach is convincing because sales on the domestic market are only favoured in the case of special provisions concerning exports or – in the words of the ECJ, respectively – provisions having "the specific effect of restricting patterns of export"; therefore, it is only under this condition that trade between Member States is actually affected.[67] 49

Ultimately, this restrictive interpretation of the notion of measures having equivalent effect within the scope of Article 29 of the TEC (Article III-153 DC) leads to the consequence that this rule only includes a prohibition of those measures which distinguish between products for the domestic market and products destined for export. Accordingly, general measures applicable to all products are a priori excluded from the scope of Article 29 of the TEC (Article III-153 DC). In this sense only discriminating measures are 50

---

also ECJ *Prantl* [1984] ECR 1299, para 20; *Yves Rocher* [1993] ECR I-2361, paras 17 ff; *Bluhme* [1998] ECR I-8033, para 22; *EDSrl* [1999] ECR I-3845.
64 As to the purpose of Article 29 TEC *cf* Müller-Graff in: von der Groeben/Schwarze (eds) *Kommentar zum Vertrag über die Europäische Union und zur Gründung der Europäischen Gemeinschaft* (6th ed, Baden-Baden 2003) Art 29 EGV, para 1.
65 Leible (note 21) Art 29 EGV, paras 2 ff; Müller-Graff (note 64) Art 29 EGV, paras 1 ff.
66 ECJ *Groenveld* [1979] ECR 3409, para 7; from recent case-law ECJ *EDSrl* [1999] ECR I-3845, para 10; *Belgium v Spain* [2000] ECR I-3123, paras 36 ff with regard to the requirement of bottling wine emanating from a certain region in precisely this region in order to be able to use the respective denomination of origin.
67 More detailed Epiney (note 1) § 13, paras 79–80; of a different opinion however Füller (note 61) pp 244 ff.

therefore included, whereas the differentiation has to tie in with the destination of the goods.

III. Justification

51 In case of a quantitative restriction to imports and exports or a measure having equivalent effect – which entails that the elements of Article 28 or 29 of the TEC (Article III-153 DC) are met – the respective measure is generally prohibited. However, Community law provides for possibilities of justification, whereas one can distinguish between grounds of justification explicitly held in the Treaty (2.) and unwritten grounds of justification (so-called "mandatory requirements") (3.). Both categories have in common that the principle of proportionality must be observed (4.). Moreover, there are a number of common questions which arise for all grounds of justification and which will therefore be discussed conjointly (1.).

52 The purpose of the possibility of deviating from the fundamental prohibition held in Articles 28 and 29 of the TEC (Article III-153 DC) consists in guaranteeing that the application of these provisions does not lead to the non-observance of certain protection concerns. Insofar, it is **not** a matter of **a general protection clause** (in favour of the Member States) or of "extracting" certain objectively defined areas from the scope of applicability of the rules on the free movement of goods, but it is only the **pursuit of certain protection targets** and therewith the **safeguarding of certain objects of legal protection**[68] which are allowed – in consideration of the requirements determined under Community law. These principles also entail that the objects of protection – whether explicitly regulated in the Treaty or unwritten – have to be interpreted pursuant to Community law principles as **Community law terms**. However, the related notions, in their turn, partly refer to concepts of the Member States, particularly the concepts of public order and public morality. But here Community law also sets boundaries insofar as the "filling in" of the content of these notions by the Member States must remain within a certain scope.[69]

1. Transversal Aspects

a) No Secondary Legislation

53 A justification can a priori only come into question on condition that the respective field is not regulated by **secondary legislation**.[70] This restriction, which is only relevant for Member States' provisions, results from the purpose of the possibility available to the Member States of reverting to the justification grounds of Article 30 of the TEC (Article III-154 DC) as well to as to the mandatory requirements: If the respective object of legal protection is (already) protected by Community law provisions, there is no necessity for an autonomous protection by the Member States, given that otherwise the existing Commu-

---

68 Explicitly for instance in ECJ *Commission v Germany* [1979] ECR 2555, para 5.
69 Anyhow, this "scope concept" implies that the contents of public order, for instance, (can) vary in the different Member States, as exemplified by lotteries which are (partly) forbidden in some Member States but admitted in others; cf the facts of the case in ECJ *Schindler* [1994] ECR I-1039; *Familiapress* [1997] ECR I-3689.
70 ECJ *Hedley Lomas* [1996] ECR I-2553, para 18; *Decker* [1998] ECR I-1831, para 42–43; → § 7 para 95.

nity harmonisation would be undermined. In other words, in these cases Community law acts on the assumption that the protection of the respective object of legal protection should be taken into consideration in secondary legislation. This view is confirmed by the rules in Articles 95(4) ff of the TEC (Article III-172 ff DC), which precisely (as an exception) allow the Member States to – under certain (narrowly defined) circumstances – apply a higher protection standard also within the scope of applicability of Community secondary legislation.

However, this restriction to the possibility of invoking Article 30 of the TEC (Article III-154 DC) and the mandatory requirements is (of course) only applicable insofar as a completed harmonisation actually exists,[71] whereas the conclusive character[72] of a community law provision must always be denied if the protection of the respective legally protected good is not regulated exhaustively.[73]

According to the case-law of the ECJ[74], the prohibition of reverting to the general justification grounds of primary Community law in case of an exhaustive provision of secondary Community law must be understood as "absolute" insofar as it also applies when the attainment of the protection level aimed at by secondary law is not possible because other Member States do not meet the Community law requirements – even in cases in which the relevant act of Community law does not provide for a control or sanction procedure.[75] This approach corresponds to the principle usually applied by the ECJ that the non-observance of Community law by another Member State does not have any influence on one's own obligation to respect Community law. However, the question arises whether the application of this in principle mandatory view is also imperative and appropriate for the constellation discussed here: The whole purpose of the possibility of justification according to Article 30 of the TEC (Article III-154 DC) and by means of the mandatory requirements is the protection of the respective objects of legal protection. This concern is no longer relevant when the Community legislator himself defines the protection level; however, it is renewed when the underlying protection standard is not – or cannot be, respectively – reached. Insofar, it is no longer the "typical" constellation in which a Member State wants to replace the Community provisions by its own conceptions or protection standard or that a Member State refuses to comply with its Community obligations under reference to the non-observance of the Treaty obligations by another Member State, so that the right to revert to Article 30 of the TEC (Article III-154 DC) or the mandatory requirements could have at least been admitted in cases of serious and clear violations of secondary legislation by other Member States.[76]

54

55

---

71 *Cf* ECJ *Commission v Germany* [1998] ECR I-6871, paras 26 ff; *Ortscheit* [1994] ECR I-5243, para 14

72 However, the question as to the exhaustive character of a provision can sometimes be difficult to answer; on this *cf* Slot [1996] ELR 378; comprehensively in Furrer *Sperrwirkung des sekundären Gemeinschaftsrechts auf die nationalen Rechtsordnungen* (Baden-Baden 1994).

73 *Cf* the examples from case-law in ECJ *Denkavit* [1991] ECR I-3069, paras 16 ff; *Compassion in World Farming* [1998] ECR I-1251, paras 26 ff; *Ortscheit* [1994] ECR I-5243, paras 13 ff.

74 ECJ *Hedley Lomas* [1996] ECR I-2553, para 19.

75 This problem essentially arises in the admittedly limited situation of restrictions on exports.

76 Of a different opinion Müller-Graff (note 64) Art 30 EGV, paras 14, 32.

b) The Relation of Article 30 of the TEC to the "Mandatory Requirements",
Scope of Applicability of the Grounds of Justification and Dogmatic Classification

56 As already mentioned initially, Community law contains explicit justification grounds held in the Treaty, which are laid down in Article 30 of the TEC (Article III-154 DC), as well as unwritten grounds of justification. The latter were developed by the ECJ in its *Cassis de Dijon* case-law[77]. This regulation raises the question as to the relation of the two categories of grounds of justification, their respective scope of applicability as well as the dogmatic classification of the mandatory requirements as grounds of exclusion or as grounds of justification.

57 The **case-law of the ECJ** with regard to these questions can be summarised in the following points:

Article 30 of the TEC – as an **exemption provision** – is to be interpreted narrowly, and the listing of the named grounds of justification is of an **exhaustive character**.[78] This approach excludes, quasi analogous to Article 30 of the TEC (Article III-154 DC), the development of further grounds of justification.

58 Nevertheless, it became clear quite soon that the grounds of justification listed in Article 30 of the TEC (Article III-154 DC) are not sufficient in order to guarantee the efficient protection of important objects of legal protection, given that the list contained in Article 30 of the TEC (Article III-154 DC) originates form 1957 and that throughout the years the necessity emerged to also pursue other protection targets, such as consumer or environmental protection. Against this background, the ECJ emphasized in the – in this respect fundamental – *Cassis de Dijon* case[79] that barriers to trade imposed by national provisions must always be accepted if they are "necessary in order to satisfy mandatory requirements relating in particular to the effectiveness of fiscal supervision, the protection of public health, the fairness of commercial transactions and the defence of the consumer" which pursue a "purpose which is in the general interest and such as to take precedence over the requirements of the free movement of goods, which constitutes one of the fundamental rules of the Community".[80] Whilst it initially was questionable which was the relation between the **mandatory requirements** and the grounds of justification held in Article 30 of the TEC[81], the ECJ has in the meantime clarified that only those interests not already included in Article 30 of the TEC (Article III-154 DC) can be considered as mandatory requirements.[82]

59 The case-law regarding the question whether the mandatory requirements are to be seen as **grounds of exclusion** or as **grounds of justification** is not entirely clear. The formulations used by the Court seem to indicate that the first approach is preferred.[83]

---

77 ECJ *Cassis de Dijon* [1979] ECR 649.
78 ECJ *Commission v Greece* [1991] ECR I-1361, para 9; *Commission v Italy* [1982] ECR 2187, para 27.
79 This case dealt with a German provision according to which fruit liqueurs are only marketable as such if they have a minimum alcohol strength of 25 %, which was precisely not the case with the French liqueur "Cassis de Dijon".
80 ECJ *Cassis de Dijon* [1979] ECR 649, paras 8, 14.
81 Since the protection of health, which is already contained in Article 30 TEC, was also listed as an example for a mandatory requirement.
82 ECJ *Aragonesa* [1991] ECR I-4151, para 13.
83 *Cf* for instance ECJ *Aragonesa* [1991] ECR I-4151, para 13; *Commission v Germany* [1989] ECR

Free Movement of Goods §8 III 1

60 The fact that the ECJ obviously draws a conceptual distinction between the two constellations also shows when the Court states that the grounds of justification of Article 30 of the TEC (Article III-154 DC) can always be applicable – thus also for direct discrimination based on the origins of the goods –, whereas reverting to the mandatory requirements was found to be inadmissible for cases of direct discrimination;[84] however, it must be pointed out that precisely in the field of environmental protection directly discriminating provisions were on various occasions generally considered to be justifiable[85], so that insofar this case-law does not seem to be completely consistent.[86]

61 Anyhow, this case-law leads to various inconsistencies – apart from the fact that the ECJ partly had to put quite substantial effort into reasoning in order to in the end qualify (in reality) directly discriminating measures as non-directly discriminating, so that the justification possibilities based on environmental concerns could come into consideration:[87] Thus, the dogmatic classification of the mandatory requirements as grounds of exclusion seems to lead to certain doubts, given that the latter have a parallel function to grounds of justification and are moreover examined pursuant to the same principles. Furthermore, the restrictive effect on imports remains in the case of mandatory requirements as well, so that the elements of Articles 28 and 29 of the TEC (Article III-153 DC) are in fact fulfilled; insofar, their qualification as grounds of justification is more suitable. In close connection to this is the consideration that the exclusion of a justification possibility for direct discriminations by mandatory requirements does not seem appropriate: Thereby, a sufficient protection of the concerned objects of legal protection is impeded in certain cases, since it is precisely not *a priori* excluded that, for instance, considerations of environmental protection could also justify directly discriminating measures. The possibility of "abuses" can be met at the level of proportionality.[88] This view would also pay regard to the parallel functions of the justification possibilities enabled by Article 30 of the TEC (Article III-154 DC) and the mandatory requirements as well as their in fact par-

---

229, para 16; however, *cf* also ECJ *Familiapress* [1997] ECR I-3689, para 18, where the ECJ speaks of justification.

84 *Cf* for instance ECJ *Commission v Ireland* [1981] ECR 1625, para 11; *Schutzverband* [1983] ECR 127, para 11; *Commission v Belgium* [1992] ECR I-4431, paras 33 ff; probably also *Decker* [1998] ECR I-1831, paras 45 ff; in case of indirect discriminations (and anyhow in case of restrictions), however, the mandatory requiremetns can additionally also apply, *cf Schutzverband gegen unlauteren Wettbewerb* [2000] ECR I-151, paras 25 ff, which dealt with an indirect discrimination, the ECJ, however, did not fundamentally exclude the recourse to the mandatory requirement of the protection of the supplying of goods at short distance to the advantage of local businesses; similar *de Agostini* [1997] ECR I-3843, paras 44 ff; in this sense also already *Commission v Ireland* [1981] ECR 1625, paras 11 ff; however, the case-law is not completely clear in this regard, *cf* for instance *Cullet* [1985] ECR 305, paras 27 ff; recently also *Ciola* [1999] ECR I-2517, para 14.

85 ECJ *Sydhavnens* [2000] ECR I-3743, para 48; in fact also already in *Commission v Belgium* [1992] ECR I-4431, paras 34–35; *cf* also *Preussen Elektra* [2001] ECR I-2099, which concerned a distinction according to the domicile of the electricity producer, even though the ECJ did not explicitly address the question of the existence of a direct discrimination.

86 More detailed on this problem *cf* Heselhaus [2001] EuZW, 645.

87 As in the case of the Walloon import ban on waste, *cf* ECJ *Commission v Belgium* [1992] ECR I-4431, paras 33 ff.

88 *Cf* in this connection also Heselhaus [2001] EuZW 645, 648–649, who pleads for a particularly strict proportionality test in case of direct discriminations.

allel application and examination.[89] If one is to follow this approach, the emphasis set on the exhaustive character of Article 30 of the TEC (Article III-154 of the DC) lacks any sense whatsoever, since the grounds of justification held therein are in any case at least functionally completed by the mandatory requirements. All in all, a uniform justification dogmatic therefore seems to be most reasonable: In a first step it is examined whether the elements of Articles 28 or 29 of the TEC (Article III-153 of the DC) are fulfilled; subsequently, the relevance of a "public interest" (either a ground held in Article 30 of the TEC/Article III-154 of the DC or a "mandatory requirement") is examined; and in a third step the proportionality of the measure is questioned. As a result, the point of view presented here only leads to results deviant from the case-law of the ECJ when it comes to the question of the applicability of the mandatory requirements on direct discriminations.

c) Noneconomic Character

Case 3 – Problem: (ECJ *Evans* [1995] ECR I-563)

62   Diacetylmorphine is an opium derivative. The production and processing of this substance in Great Britain was so far only authorised for two pharmaceutical enterprises domiciled in Great Britain; as far as third parties were concerned, any import of the substance was prohibited. This regulation was supposed to secure that a reliable supply of diacetylmorphine, which is used as a pain reliever, was guaranteed and that illegal trade was cut off. However, it was partly suspected that this regulation served to secure the existence of the only admitted producer. The British Home Secretary now changed this practice under reference to (among other things) its incompatibility with Article 28 of the TEC, which causes the concerned pharmaceutical enterprises to take legal proceedings. The competent court referred the question whether the regulation was in accordance with Article 28 of the TEC to the ECJ for preliminary ruling.

63   A justification of a restriction to the free movement of goods can only come into consideration if the asserted grounds of justification are of a **noneconomic character**.[90] In the end, this equals a restriction to those grounds of public interest which can be asserted within the frame of Article 30 of the TEC (Article III-154 DC) or the mandatory requirements: As soon as the targeted objectives are of an economic character, an application of the mandatory requirements or of Article 30 of the TEC (Article III-154 DC) (where *eg* the public order might be of relevance) does not come into question. An economic character can be assumed when the adopted measures in fact serve to steer the economy, achieve economic policy objectives or to prevent economic disadvantages in general.

64   The exclusion of such grounds from the scope of applicability of Article 30 of the TEC (Article III-154 DC) as well as of the mandatory requirements results from the purpose of Articles 28 ff of the TEC (Articles III-153 ff DC): The "basic philosophy" of

---

89 → of another opinion § 7 para 90; likewise for instance Weiss [1999] EuZW, 493, 497; Leible (note 21) Art 28 EGV, para 20; Hakenberg *Grundzüge des Europäischen Wirtschaftsrechts* (Munich 1994) pp 99–100 even goes as far as to interpret the case-law in the sense that the ECJ now departs from an uniform notion of (in other words, it would not anymore depend on the existence of a direct or indirect discrimination), subsequently examines the existence of a (exclusionary) selling arrangement and then conducts an uniform justification test.
90 Constant case-law, *cf* for instance ECJ *Evans* [1995] ECR I-563, para 36; *Campus Oil* [1984] ECR 2727, paras 35–36; *Cullet* [1985] ECR 305, paras 30 ff; *Commission v Greece* [2001] ECR I-7915, para 21.

these provisions – as well as of the other Fundamental Freedoms – is precisely that restrictions to the free movement of factors of production are to be abolished, given that they are presumed to be opposed to economic efficiency. If this is the case, then measures which aim at economic objectives precisely by means which restrict trade cannot be covered by Article 30 of the TEC (Article III-154 DC) or the mandatory requirements. Otherwise, the possibilities of justification enabled by Article 30 of the TEC (Article III-154 DC) and the mandatory requirements could be "misused" in order to meet economic difficulties which might possibly arise (momentarily) due to the application of Articles 28 and 29 of the TEC (Article III-153–154 DC).

However, the prohibition on asserting economic grounds does not rule out that the primary protection target of a certain provision is pursued by means of economic policy measures. Thus, only the independent pursuit of economic targets for their own sake is excluded; however, if economic policy measures only constitute a "means to an end" and in fact serve other purposes, they can in principle fall within the scope of Article 30 of the TEC (Article III-154 DC) and the mandatory requirements. This can eg be the case if it is a matter of supplying the population with important pharmaceuticals for health protection reasons.[91] However, such measures might not meet the requirements of proportionality.[92]

It is, however, not possible to appeal to Article 30 of the TEC (Article III-154 DC) or the mandatory requirements if the public order is disturbed due to economic difficulties, which eg may occur in cases of boycott measures affecting imports from other Member States. For it would contradict the systematics of the Treaty to qualify the functioning of the Fundamental Freedoms as a disturbance of the public order and therewith factually make it subject to some sort of reservation of the general police blanket clause.

Case 3 – Answer:
The preliminary question is admissible even though the practice in question has already been changed: After all, the answer to the posed questions is supposed to enable the national court to assure itself that the change of the national practice was in fact necessary in order to meet the requirements of Community law.
Diacetylmophine is merchandise in the sense of Article 23(2) of the TEC, since it can be the object of trading transactions and is transported across borders for this purpose. The prohibition of the import of diacetylmorphine constitutes a quantitative restriction on imports for the purpose of Article 28 of the TEC, since the import of merchandise is limited according to its value or quantity or – as in the present case – even forbidden. A justification can only be considered for measures of a noneconomic nature, *ie* for such which do not serve to steer the economy or to reach economic policy targets. Precisely these, however, are in dispute when the existence of an enterprise is assured, so that this consideration cannot be taken to account in order to justify the restriction on imports. On the other hand, the regular supply to the country with a substance that is used for important medical purposes serves the protection of health (Article 30 of the TEC/Article III-154 DC) and therefore may in principle justify an hindrance to intra-community trade. However, the measure must comply with the principle of proportionality. In the case at hand, the facts of the case do not allow a conclusive determination (which, besides, is incumbent on the national court) whether a milder measure would have been possible.

---

91 ECJ *Evans* [1995] ECR I-563, paras 36–37; *cf* also *Campus Oil* [1984] ECR 2727, paras 34 ff; *Decker* [1998] ECR I-1831, paras 39 ff.
92 *Cf* below paras 79 ff.

d) The Question of the Necessity of a Territorial Reference

68 In the first instance, Article 30 of the TEC (Article III-154 DC) and the recognition of the mandatory requirements are of course supposed to secure that the defined protection objectives can be pursued and achieved within the territory of the respective Member State.[93] It is, however, not excluded that a Member State – by the means of national measures – also pursues targets which are in fact "residing" in the territory of another state. For instance, a prohibition of imports for endangered animal species can (only) be aimed at the protection of animals in another state. It is questionable whether the Member States can also pursue such "extraterritorial targets" by invoking Article 30 of the TEC (Article III-154 DC) or the mandatory requirements, or whether this is *a priori* excluded.

69 When considering the whole purpose of the possibilities of justification by means of the objects of legal protection held in Article 30 of the TEC (Article III-154 DC) and covered by the mandatory requirements, a general preclusion of such a pursuit of "extraterritorial protection interests" does not seem appropriate: This provision is precisely meant to enable the Member States to safeguard the concerned objects of legal protection, whereas the intensity of this protection generally lies within their scope of evaluation.[94] Then, however, there is no apparant reason why national measures should not in principle be able to safeguard objects of legal protection beyond their own territory. However, this possibility must find its limits where the sphere of competence of other (Member) states begins; thus, it would not be compatible with the conception of the justification possibilities enabled by Article 30 of the TEC (Article III-154 DC) and the mandatory requirements if a state was able to impose its concept of a certain domain on other states. In other words, it depends on the competence of the Member States to regulate the respective issues. Therefore, the Member States must also effectively demonstrate a protection interest of their own, the existence of which is precisely not to be determined in accordance with the territory. It rather depends on an (also) legally justifiable, "own" responsibility for the object of legal protection, which can also be the result of international integration or interdependence, respectively.[95]

e) The Significance of the Community Fundamental Human Rights

70 Measures taken by Member States or by the Community in order to safeguard objects of legal protection listed in Article 30 of the TEC (Article III-154 DC) or covered by the

---

93 Or also of the Community. This constellation shall however remain out of consideration in the following. It essentially raises the question of conformity of corresponding unilateral measures with the GATT/WTO-legislation. On this *cf*, with further references, Epiney [2000] DVBl 77 ff.
94 On this below paras 83 ff.
95 So far, the ECJ did not yet have to decide this question. In literature, the opinions reach from a fundamental inadmissibility of the pursuance of extraterritorial objects of legal protection (*"extraterritoriale Rechtsgüter"*) (Gornig/Silagi [1992] EuZW 753, 756; probably also Everling [1993] NVwZ 209, 211) over an exceptional admissibility in case of the existence of a global responsibility (*"globale Gesamtverantwortung"*) of the states for certain interests (Müller-Graff (note 64) Art 30 EGV, paras 37 ff; similar Weiher *Nationaler Umweltschutz und internationaler Warenverkehr* (Baden-Baden 1997) pp 99 ff) to the point of a connection with international protection interests (*"internationale Schutzinteressen"*), whereas in the case of their relevance a possibility of justification is given (as in Kahl *Umweltprinzip und Gemeinschaftsrecht* (Heidelberg 1993) pp 192–193; Middeke (note 43) pp 167–168).

Free Movement of Goods § 8 III 2

mandatory requirements can also affect other positions protected by fundamental human rights, for instance if the freedom of expression is limited due to measures which are supposed to preserve press diversity, but also already whenever economic freedom is affected.

The fundamental rights of the Union[96] (→ detailed § 14) obviously oblige the Community itself and its organs. But they also have binding effect on the Member States insofar as the latter apply or enforce Community law.[97] Moreover, the fundamental rights of the Union must also be observed in cases of Member State regulations which fall into the scope of applicability of Community law and which, as far as their admissibility is concerned, refer to Community notions – such as the relevant objects of protection in Article 30 of the TEC (Article III-154 DC) or within the frame of the mandatory requirements. It is probably against this background that the case-law of the ECJ must be seen, which emphasises that the Community law justification for Member State measures restricting the Fundamental Freedoms must be interpreted "in the light of fundamental rights".[98]

71

This fundamental applicability of the fundamental rights of the Union has repercussions primarily at two levels: Firstly, the object of legal protection invoked within the frame of Article 30 of the TEC (Article III-154 DC) or the mandatory requirements must be able to justify restrictions to the affected Fundamental right, which applies to most of the cases. Secondly, and above all, the effect on the respective Fundamental right must be considered at the level of proportionality. Suitability, necessity and proportionality in the narrow sense must also be examined with regard to the interference with the Fundamental human rights. In most cases, however, these aspects of the proportionality test will coincide with the "normal" review of proportionality, since it is precisely the measure restricting trade which constitutes an interference with the respective Fundamental human right.[99]

72

2. Written Grounds of Justification

Article 30 of the TEC (Article III-154 DC) allows for the implementation of measures which actually infringe Articles 28 and 29 of the TEC (Article III-153 DC) by virtue of a range of grounds listed in detail. As already mentioned,[100] the ECJ assumes – on the basis of a narrow interpretation of the individual grounds of justification – that the list con-

73

---

96 With regard to the protection of fundamental human rights in the EU cf Kokott (1996) 121 AöR 599; against the background of the "proclamation" of the Charter of Fundamental Rights for instance Besselink [2001] MJ 68; von Bogdandy [2001] JZ 157; Calliess [2001] EuZW 261; Weber [2000] GYIL 101.
97 More detailed on the question of the binding effect of the fundamental human rights of the Community cf Epiney (note 16) pp 125 ff; from case-law particularly ECJ ERT [1991] ECR I-2925, para 43; Commission v Germany [1992] ECR I-2575, para 23; Familiapress [1997] ECR I-3689, para 21; → § 14 paras 33 ff.
98 ECJ Commission v Germany [1992] ECR I-2575, para 23; Familiapress [1997] ECR I-3689, para 24. In literature, this approach of the ECJ is mostly followed. Cf for instance Holznagel Rundfunkrecht in Europa (Tübingen 1996) p 156; Becker in: Schwarze EU-Kommentar (Baden-Baden 2000) Art 30 EGV, para 62; very critical however Kingreen Die Struktur der Grundfreiheiten des Europäischen Gemeinschaftsrechts (Berlin 1999) p 164; similar Störmer (1998) 123 AöR 541, 567. More detailed on the problem Schaller Die EU-Mitgliedstaaten als Verpflichtungsadressaten der Gemeinschaftsgrundrechte (Baden-Baden 2003) pp 79 ff; Wallrab Die Verpflichteten der Gemeinschaftsgrundrechte (Baden-Baden 2004) pp 43 ff.
99 → probably likewise § 7 para 94.
100 Above paras 57 ff.

tained in Article 30 of the TEC (Article III-154 DC) is exhaustive. In detail, four groups of exceptions can be distinguished, whereas in the following – on the basis of the relevant case-law – only a short overview on the significance of the individual exceptions will be given.[101]

74   The objects of protection of **public morality, order and security** refer to different aspects of the public order: In the end, this is a matter of observing the significant fundamental rules of a community[102], whereas public order represents a sort of generic term and public safety[103] and morality[104] take up specific aspects thereof.[105]

75   The **protection of health and life of humans, animals and plants** – which is of great significance in the case-law of the ECJ – only covers such measures which aim at the protection of humans, plants and animals as such; thus – always in accordance with the case-law of the ECJ – a direct relation to the named objects of protection is necessary, whereas with regard to the named objects of legal protection, only measures or concerns, respectively, of indirect effect (eg such which primarily serve consumer or environmental protection) are covered by the "mandatory requirements".[106]

76   The objects of protection which are the **national treasures possessing artistic, historic or archaeological value** refer to the interest of the Member States of preserving certain works of art or other objects which are significant for the national identity. In the ECJ's case-law, this protection interest has not played any role so far.[107]

77   The **protection of industrial and commercial property** refers to such legal instruments which are destined to protect industrial or commercial legal positions. According to the case-law of the ECJ, this primarily includes patent rights[108], trademark rights[109] and copyrights[110], but also denominations of origin and geographical indications of provenance[111].

78   In detail, the interpretation of these objects of legal protection poses numerous questions which, however, cannot be examined more closely in this context.[112]

---

101 For more details, particularly regarding the relevant case-law, refer to the commentary literature. From monograph literature Millarg *Die Schranken des freien Warenverkehrs in der EG. Systematik und Zusammenwirken von Cassis-Rechtsprechung und Art 30 EG-Vertrag* (Baden-Baden 2001) pp 139 ff.
102 For instance the prevention of fraud in connection with the granting of export aid ECJ *Deutsche Milchkontor* [1994] ECR I-2757, para 44.
103 Public morality in fact concerns the protection system of the state in order to maintain its monopoly of power, but also the protection of the existence of the state as well as of its central institutions; *cf* for instance ECJ *Richardt* [1991] ECR I-4621, paras 22 ff.
104 Public safety refers to moral conceptions which the coexistence of the population should comply with; *cf* ECJ *Conegate* [1986] ECR 1007, para 14; *Henn and Darby* [1979] ECR 3795.
105 *Cf* Müller-Graff (note 64) Art 30 EGV, para 49. In the same direction probably also ECJ *Campus Oil* [1984] ECR 2727, para 33.
106 Among case-law *cf* for instance ECJ *Bluhme* [1998] ECR I-8033; *van Harpegnies* [1998] ECR I-5121; *Commission v Germany* [1987] ECR 1227.
107 As to the arising questions of interpretation *cf*, with further references, Epiney (note 4) Art 30 EGV, para 37.
108 ECJ *Thetford* [1988] ECR 3585, paras 14–15.
109 ECJ *Hoffmann-La Roche* [1978] ECR 1139, paras 7–8.
110 ECJ *Basset* [1987] ECR 1747, paras 11 ff.
111 ECJ *Delhaize* [1992] ECR I-3669, para 10; *Belgium v Spain* [2000] ECR I-3123, para 50; *Exportur* [1992] ECR I-5529, para 25.
112 More detailed *cf*, with numerous references from case-law, Epiney (note 4) Art 30 EGV, paras 39 ff.

3. Unwritten Grounds of Justification

As already mentioned[113], in its *Cassis de Dijon*[114] judgement the ECJ developed the principle that restrictions on trade can also be justified by so-called mandatory requirements relating to the public good, whereas the ECJ assumes that these can only apply to indirect discriminations and restrictions, not, however, to direct discriminations.[115]

The ECJ has applied the original Cassis formula in numerous rulings and has partly also developed it further[116], especially by the explicit acceptance of other mandatory requirements, such as environmental protection[117], securing the financial balance of social security systems[118], cultural purposes[119] or also securing the conditions under which goods are supplied at short distance in relatively isolated areas of a Member State[120].

However, the mandatory requirements are not enumerated exhaustively ("in particular"), so that *a priori* all public interests can be subsumed thereunder, always provided that they can be recognised as such from a Community law point of view; hence, they must not in particular be of an economic character.[121]

4. Proportionality

Case 4 – Problem: (ECJ *Belgium v Spain* [2000] ECR I-3123)
According to the relevant Spanish provisions, in order to legitimately use the denomination of origin "Rioja" for wine coming from the homonymous region, the wine must (among other things) have been bottled in the producing region. Belgium sued the Spanish State before the ECJ due to this aspect of the origin regulation. Spain claims that the requirement of bottling in the producing region itself is necessary in order to be able to guarantee the quality of the wine, whereas Belgium argues that it constitutes an illegal restriction on the free circulation of goods.

If there is a ground of justification (either one listed in Article 30 of the TEC or a mandatory requirement), the respective (national or Community) measure must still comply with the principle of proportionality, *ie* the respective measure must be suitable to pursue the target, constitute the mildest means – in other words, comply with the principle of necessity – and be appropriate (proportionate in the narrow sense of the term).[122] This prin-

---

113 *Cf* above paras 57 ff.
114 ECJ *Cassis de Dijon* [1979] ECR 649.
115 *Cf* above paras 57 ff.
116 *Cf* the overview on case-law in Ahlfeld *Zwingende Erfordernisse im Sinne der Cassis-Rechtsprechung des Europäischen Gerichtshofs zu Art 30 EGV* (1997) pp 85 ff; Millarg (note 101) pp 163 ff.
117 ECJ *Commission v Denmark* [1988] ECR 4607, paras 8–9; *Commission v Belgium* [1992] ECR I-4431.
118 ECJ *Decker* [1998] ECR I-1831, para 39.
119 ECJ *Cinéthèque* [1985] ECR 2605, paras 21 ff; *Commission v Netherlands* [1991] ECR I-4069, paras 29–30; *Veronica Omröp Organisatie* [1993] ECR I-487, paras 9–10; however, in this regard case-law is partly also rather reserved, *cf* for instance *Leclerc* [1985] ECR 1, paras 28 ff, with regard to Art 49 TEC.
120 ECJ *Schutzverband gegen unlauteren Wettbewerb* [2000] ECR I-151, para 34.
121 On this above para 61 ff.
122 Whereas the ECJ only exceptionally rejects a measure based on the appropriateness criterion.

ciple, which has been recognised in settled case-law, is ultimately based on the application of general principles of law and is also imperative against the background of the whole purpose of Articles 28 and 29 of the TEC (Article III-153 DC) as well as the recognised possibilities of justification, given that the restriction on the free movement of goods should be limited to the necessary degree and appropriately proportionate to the sought protection objective.

84 No further requirements can be drawn from Article 30(ii) of the TEC (Article III-154 DC), which determines that the measures taken under reference to Article 30 of the TEC (Article III-154 DC) may not constitute a means of arbitrary discrimination nor a disguised restriction on trade. Rather, these requirements ultimately correspond with the principle of proportionality.[123] It is also hardly imaginable that "arbitrary discriminations" or "disguised restrictions" to trade could be suitable and necessary.

85 However, a justification under Article 30 of the TEC (Article III-154 DC) or on the basis of the mandatory requirements can *a priori* only be considered provided that the objects of protection are at risk. This does however not mean that such a threat must be proved with one hundred per cent certainty (as far as this is at all possible). Thus, there may absolutely be an element of uncertainty; however, a substantiated and comprehensible description of the present endangerment is necessary. For instance, coli bacteria are an indication for pathogenic microorganisms, which can represent a substantial threat to health.[124] By contrast, it could not be established that the additives in certain beers pose a threat to health in view of the normal diet[125] of the German population.[126] Nor was the low nutritional value of a foodstuff found to constitute a health threat.[127] Furthermore, the ECJ held in a recent judgement regarding the compatibility of a Danish prohibition on trade with food products which had been enriched with vitamins and mineral nutrients, that, if there were scientific uncertainties as to a possible harmful effect of additives in a foodstuff, the Member States had the obligation to decide to which extent the protection of health of the population should be guaranteed. However, the existence of a health threat must be based on a detailed examination of the respective risk; a marketing prohibition may only be enacted if the asserted danger to public health can be considered to be sufficiently proven on the basis of the available scientific information, whereas the evaluation of the degree of probability of the harmful effects as well as the potential severity must also be taken into account.[128]

Cf (however, with regard to Art 12 TEC) ECJ *Pastoors* [1997] ECR I-1, paras 19 ff. With regard to the proportionality test within the frame of Art 28 TEC for instance *Decker* [1998] ECR I-1831, paras 39 ff; *Familiapress* [1997] ECR I-3689, paras 19 ff; *Bluhme* [1998] ECR I-8033; *Commission v Denmark* [1988] ECR 4607, paras 11 ff.

123 Whereas the case-law of the ECJ is not uniform in this respect. On this problem, with further references to literature and case-law, *cf* Epiney (note 4) Art 30 EGV, paras 47 ff.
124 ECJ *Melkunie* [1984] ECR 2367, para 17.
125 Which can in principle absolutely be considered. *Cf* ECJ *Heijn* [1984] ECR 3263, para 16; *Muller* [1986] ECR 1511, para 20.
126 ECJ *Commission v Germany* [1987] ECR 1227, para 49.
127 ECJ *Commission v Germany* [1989] ECR 229, para 10.
128 ECJ *Commission v Denmark* [2003] ECR I-9693; *cf* also *Commission v France* [2000] ECR I-1129, where the ECJ emphasises that the Member States can determine the applicable protection standard in the field of health protection.

a) The Discretion Enjoyed by the Member States

The principle of proportionality[129] regulates a means-end relation; in other words, the question is whether a certain measure is suitable, necessary and appropriate in view of the attainment of a certain goal. The requirement of proportionality, thus, does not answer the question as to the applicable level of protection or the aimed target, respectively, but presupposes its determination. In view of the circumstance that Article 30 of the TEC (Article III-154 DC) as well as the mandatory requirements can in principle only be applied in those cases in which there is precisely no determination of the protection level in Community legislation, it is incumbent on the Member States to decide which level of protection they want to apply; in other words, they can thus decide how far eg the protection of health or consumers shall reach.[130] This competence of the Member States also relates to uncertainty as to the facts, *eg* regarding the dangerousness of certain substances.[131]

However, it is questionable whether the competence of the Member States[132] also relates to the determination of the respective conceptions of the pursued protection policies, *ie* for instance the determination of the principles on the basis of which consumer protection is to be conceived. This problem can indeed – at least regarding certain policies, such as consumer protection – be of significant importance for the conduct of the proportionality test and its result: Thus, for instance, the necessity of a measure must be evaluated differently depending on whether the evaluation is based on the image of the "sensible consumer" or that of the "vulnerable" or "absent-minded" consumer.

Here, the ECJ at least partly applies the principle that the conception of the respective policy and consequently the basis for the proportionality test have to be determined pursuant to Community standards. Especially in the field of consumer protection (in connection with health protection), the ECJ refers to a Community concept of the "responsible" consumer, which at the level of the necessity test has the result that generally imperative provisions on product quality and a resulting prohibition on sales are not admissible, since compulsory marking constitutes the milder measure.[133]

However, this approach is not convincing: In those cases in which there is no Community law regulation, the Member States in principle have the competence to determine the respective policies and to take the corresponding measures. This competence does not only relate to the "whether" of the pursuance of the corresponding aims, but also to the "how", which also includes – in addition to the determination of the protection level – the definition of the conceptions on which the respective policy is based. It is not apparent

---

129 Comprehensive on this principle in Communitly law, even though concerning legislation *cf* Emmerich-Fritsche *Der Grundsatz der Verhältnismäßigkeit als Direktive und Schranke der EG-Rechtsetzung* (Berlin 2000); *cf* also Jarass [2000] EuR 705, 721 ff.
130 Likewise also case-law. *Cf* for instance ECJ *Commission v Germany* [1987] ECR 1227, para 41; *Melkunie* [1984] ECR 2367, para 18; *Commission v France* [2000] ECR I-11499. From literature Ahlfeld (note 116) pp 62 ff; more detailed on the problem Epiney/Möllers *Freier Warenverkehr und nationaler Umweltschutz* (Cologne 1992), pp 70 ff.
131 *Cf* ECJ *Sandoz* [1983] ECR 2445, para 19; *van Bennekom* [1983] ECR 3883, para 6; *Muller* [1986] ECR 1511, para 20.
132 With regard to Community law provisions, the problem does not present itself in this form.
133 Constant case-law. *Cf* only ECJ *Commission v Germany* [1987] ECR 1227, paras 35 ff; *Cassis de Dijon* [1979] ECR 649, para 13; *van der Veldt* [1994] ECR I-3537, para 19; *Commission v Spain* [2003] ECR I-459; *Commission v Italy* [2003] ECR I-513.

why the Community's conception should be able to take the place of that of the Member States, since it is not a matter of the definition of Community notions, but of the setting of political priorities. Insofar, the case-law of the ECJ is not entirely unobjectionable. Anyhow, the relevant case-law has so far focused on the field of consumer protection, whereas other policy fields are obviously treated more generously.[134] Incidentally, the ECJ has recently tended to reduce the density of control, for instance if it states – with regard to a prohibition on selling a cream labelled "Lifting" – that such a regulation infringes the Treaty if an average consumer, reasonably well informed and reasonably observant and circumspect, expects the cream to have an effect comparable to surgical lifting.[135] The determination whether this is the case or not is left to the national court.[136]

b) The Requirements of Proportionality in Detail

90 As mentioned initially, the principle of proportionality includes the requirements of suitability, necessity and appropriateness.

91 Every measure is suitable if it is in principle able to reach the aimed target. Whether this condition is (probably[137]) fulfilled, must – where necessary – be determined by means of corresponding scientific investigations. The requirement of suitability of a measure is *eg* not fulfilled if a Member State considers imported goods of a certain quality to constitute a danger which it seeks to prevent, but does not take any measures with regard to comparable domestic goods.[138] A measure is also suitable if it does not manage to completely reach the aimed target, yet contributes – even if to a small extent – to its achievement, which is *eg* often the case with measures in the field of environmental protection. All in all, against this background the ECJ rarely denies the suitability of a measure.[139]

92 The necessity of a measure is always given when the sought protection target cannot be reached by measures less restrictive of the free movement of goods. However, the necessity test must always be based on the defined protection target. Necessity must, for instance, regularly be denied for the so-called "duplicated checks" – *eg* the requirement of technical analyses for imported products which have already been analysed in their country of origin and whose analysis results are accessible.[140] Also, the aims connected to import controls can often be reached in another manner, *eg* by marketing regulations or other control mechanisms.[141] In order to be able to affirm the necessity, it must be demonstrated in a justifiable manner that the also possible milder measure would not have been as effi-

---

134 Especially in the field of health protection, *cf* the references in note 131.
135 Which, of course, is not the case.
136 *Cf* ECJ *Lauder* [2000] ECR I-117.
137 As to uncertainties regarding the facts of the case, the Member States must also here have a certain scope of discretion. *Cf* more detailed Epiney (note 16) pp 303 ff.
138 ECJ *Conegate* [1986] ECR 1007, para 15; *cf* also ECJ *Commission v Italy* [1990] ECR I-4285, paras 6 ff.
139 However, *cf* also ECJ *Commission v Germany* [1989] ECR 229, para 10; *Cassis de Dijon* [1979] ECR 649, para 11; suitability was *eg* affirmed in the following cases: ECJ *Denkavit* [1991] ECR I-3069, para 23; *Aragonesa* [1991] ECR I-4151.
140 ECJ *van Harpegnies* [1998] ECR I-5121; *Commission v France* [1998] ECR I-6197, paras 22 ff; for further reading, *cf* the specifications regarding a system of prior authorisation in *Canal Satélite* [2002] ECR I-607.
141 *Cf eg* ECJ *Commission v Germany* [1994] ECR I-3303, para 25; *Commission v United Kingdom* [1988] ECR 547, paras 15 ff.

cient. However, when it comes to uncertainties regarding the facts, the Member States should also be afforded a certain margin of discretion. Thus, the ECJ points out that in case of difficulties relating to the question of the effectiveness of the measures, the necessity of the measure can already be assumed if there are no indications that the national measure goes beyond what is necessary in order to reach the aim.[142] Moreover, it should be recalled that here – as also in the following step, the appropriateness test – the violation of Fundamental human rights must, where necessary, be taken into account.

The appropriateness of a measure is a matter of balancing the impairment of the free movement of goods and, where applicable, the restriction of Fundamental human rights on the one side and the protection interest pursued by the measure on the other. As mentioned initially[143], a measure fails only in exceptional cases, if at all, due to the criterion of appropriateness.[144]

93

Case 4 – Answer:
Belgium's application for a declaration that the measure was infringing Community law is admissible (Article 227 of the TEC).

94

The measure in question constitutes a measure having equivalent effect to an export restriction (Article 29 TEC), since the export of unbottled wine certainly remains possible, but this wine may not carry the denomination of origin "Rioja". This, however, impairs its sales potential, since denominations of origin play an important role in terms of the marketing of products, especially where wine is concerned. Hence, the requirements of the *Dassonville* formula are met. Since this measure only concerns exported products (unbottled wine which is exported from the region), there is also a specific restriction on export patterns. For wine which has only been handled within the region and is bottled in approved wine cellars may still carry the denomination of origin.

Denominations of origin are industrial property rights. They are supposed to protect their holder from abuse of the denominations by third parties to their advantage. Furthermore, they should guarantee that the labelled product originates in a certain geographical area and features special qualities. Consequently, a justification pursuant to Article 30 of the TEC is possible in principle. However, the proportionality of the measure, particularly its necessity, is questionable: The starting point of the considerations is the circumstance that the bottling procedure is difficult and should only be conducted by persons or companies, respectively, with a vast expertise in order to prevent the wine from losing its quality and therefore its characteristics. This is also valid for the transportation of unbottled wine. Against this background, the ECJ acknowledges the necessity: The mentioned expertise is most likely to be existent in the companies of the concerned region, which have a a great amount of experience in handling wine of this quality. Therefore, there is a higher probability that the named procedures are conducted professionally in these regional companies. Furthermore,

---

142 ECJ *Kemikalieinspektionen* [2000] ECR I-5681, paras 40 ff; *Hetnonen* [1999] ECR I-3599, paras 36 ff; *cf* also *Commission v Belgium* [2000] ECR I-3123; *Consorzio del Prosciutto di Parma* [2003] ECR I-5121; *Ravil/Bellon* [2003] ECR I-5053.
143 *Cf* above paras 79 ff.
144 However, *cf* also ECJ *Canal Satélite* [2002] ECR I-607, where the ECJ – in connection with a system of prior authorisation for the initialisation of certain devices for the digital transmission or the digital reception of television signals over satellite – also refers to considerations attributable to the criterion of appropriateness, *eg* when it points out that an authorisation procedure, even if it meets the requirements of suitability and necessity, is still not compatible with Article 28 TEC if it hinders the market participants from exercising their freedoms.

the controls in other Member States are partly less strict than in Spain. Finally, compulsory marking alone would not be sufficient, since in the case of quality losses the reputation of all wines marketed under the denomination of origin "Rioja" would be affected. However, the fundamental approach of the ECJ is not convincing: It is not apparent why the bottling and transportation of Rioja should be more difficult than that of other quality wines, so that "companies from regions with quality wines" could have been used as a criterion. Above all, there are other methods of determining the qualification of companies which restrict the free movement of goods to a lesser extent, such as an admission procedure, an examination of the required expertise or regular inspections.

§ 9
Freedom of Movement for Workers

Ulrich Becker

Leading cases: ECJ *Walrave* [1974] ECR 1405; *Levin* [1982] ECR 1935; *Lawrie-Blum* [1986] ECR 2121; *Bosman* [1995] ECR I-4921

Traditionally, freedom of movement for workers is viewed as the supporting pillar of the **free movement of persons** in the EU – the most important rule enabling Union citizens (para 28) to go to other Member States and reside there. Its legal basis is Article 39 of the TEC (Article III-133 DC). This provision, along with the other fundamental freedoms, is directly applicable.[1] It confers the right to pursue an employment in another Member State and, in this context, is also a right of immigration and residence (paras 4 ff). Nevertheless, rights to freedom of movement also ensue from the other fundamental freedoms: the freedom of establishment (Article 43 TEC/Article III-137 DC), *ie* the right to take up and pursue activities as a self-employed person on a permanent basis in another Member State, and the freedom to provide services (Article 49 TEC/Article III-144 DC), *ie* the active freedom and the passive freedom to provide services, necessitating a temporary stay of the benefit provider and the benefit recipient, respectively, in a Member State other than the state of origin[2] (for definitions, *cf* para 35).

According to all of these rules, freedom of movement is linked to an economic activity and thus, for a long time, appeared only as a corollary to the market freedoms. That changed, however, with intensified efforts in the mid-1980s to create an internal market and, above all, to establish the European Union.[3] In an internal market, persons should be able to move about freely, irrespective of any intended purpose. Consequently, new rights in respect of freedom of movement were framed through secondary legislation – initially for retirees and students, and subsequently for all remaining persons.[4] The Treaty of Maastricht introduced a new part entitled **Citizenship of the Union** into the EC Treaty (Articles 17 ff TEC/Article I-10 DC; → *cf* more generally § 21). In this way, the general freedom of movement was given a (Community) constitutional basis (Article 18 TEC/Article I-10 DC).[5] This right is subsidiary to the specific economic rights of free move-

1

2

---

1 Just *cf* ECJ *Van Duyn* [1974] ECR 1337, paras 5 ff; → § 7 para 7.
2 For a fundamental view on the passive freedom to provide services, *cf* ECJ *Luisi and Carbone* [1984] ECR 377, paras 16–17.
3 On that development, Becker [1999] EuR 522.
4 For more details on the retirement of workers and self-employed persons, see Dir 90/365, [1990] OJ L180/28; regarding students, Dir 93/96, [1993] OJ L317/59 (amending Dir 90/366, [1990] OJ L180/30); regarding all remaining persons, Dir 90/364, [1990] OJ L180/26.
  These individual Directives are to be repealed with effect from 30-04-2006 and consolidated in Dir 2004/38, [2004] OJ L158/77, on the right of citizens of the Union and their family members to move and reside freely within the territory of the Member States.
5 *Cf* also Art 45 of the Charter of Fundamental Rights of the Union ([2000] OJ C364/1) (Art II-105 DC), which nevertheless has to be read in conjunction with Art 52(2) of the Charter (Art II-112 DC). Regarding Art 18 TEC (Art I-10 DC), see also Scheuing [2003] EuR 744.

ment and, hence, to Article 39 of the TEC (Article III-133 DC).[6] In the mean time, it has been decided by the ECJ that Article 18 of the TEC (Article I-10 DC) is directly applicable[7], although notable limitations in the form of secondary Community law remain.[8] Even so, a development towards a uniform right of free movement is foreseeable.[9]

I. Scope of Protection

1. Preliminary Remarks

3   Freedom of movement for workers is significantly influenced by **secondary Community law**. Even prior to the expiry of the transitional period set out in the EEC Treaty, divergent legal provisions in the Member States concerning non-nationals had made it seem necessary to enact pertinent Community legal instruments in order to provide cross-border recourse to the rights of free movement.[10] Apart from the aforementioned freedom of movement directive (Directive 2004/38/EC)[11], regulations governing freedom of movement for workers (Regulation 1612/68)[12] and their right to remain (Regulation 1251/70)[13] are still of importance today. Some of these provisions give concrete substance to the scope of protection of, and restrictions on, Article 39 of the TEC (Article III-133 DC), while others go beyond this Treaty provision in terms of their content. They in turn must

---

6   *Cf* ECJ *Calfa* [1999] ECR I-11. Conversely, Art 18 TEC (Art I-10 DC) is likely to precede the derivation of a right of residence from Art 12 TEC (Art III-123 DC) (*cf* ECJ *Gravier* [1985] ECR 593, paras 19 ff).

7   ECJ *Trojani* [2004] ECR I-7573; in conjunction with Art 12 TEC (Art III-123 DC), Union citizenship confers rights in residence; *cf* ECJ *Martínez Sala* [1998] ECR I-2691; *Grzelczyk* [2001] ECR I-6193. Stressing the fundamental rights character of Art 18 TEC (Art I-10 DC), ECJ *Yiadom* [2000] ECR I-9265, paras 23–24. On the case-law, see also Castro Oliveira [2002] CMLR 77, 78 ff.

8   *Cf* reference to implementing provisions in Art 18(1) TEC (Art I-10 DC); ECJ *Kaba* [2000] ECR I-2623, paras 30 ff.

9   *Cf* Dir 2004/38 (note 4).

10 On this development, just *cf* Wölker/Grill in: von der Groeben/Schwarze (eds) *Kommentar zum Vertrag über die Europäische Union und Vertrag zur Gründung der Europäischen Gemeinschaft Bd I* (6th ed, Baden-Baden 2003) Art 40 EGV, paras 3 ff.

11 *Cf* note 4. The Directives on the abolition of restrictions on residence (notably Dir 68/360, [1968] OJ L257/13, on the abolition of restrictions on movement and residence within the Community for workers of Member States and their families; and Dir 73/148, [1973] OJ L172/14, on the abolition of restrictions on movement and residence within the Community for nationals of Member States with regard to establishment and the provision of services) and on the reservation of *ordre public* (Dir 64/221, [1964] OJ L56/850, on the co-ordination of special measures concerning the movement and residence of foreign nationals which are justified on grounds of public policy, public security or public health) are to be repealed through Dir 2004/38 with effect from 30-04-2006.

12 Reg 1612/68, [1968] OJ L257/2, on the freedom of movement for workers within the Community.

13 Reg 1251/70, [1970] OJ L142/24, of the Commission on the right of workers to remain in the territory of a Member State after having been employed in that State. Concerning the right to remain after a self-employed activity, *cf* Dir 75/34, [1974] OJ L14/10 – this Directive is likewise to be repealed with effect from 30-04-2006 through Dir 2004/38 (note 4). *Cf* also ECJ *Givane* [2003] ECR I-345.

be interpreted in the light of the fundamental freedoms,[14] and their close links to the free movement of workers suggest that they be taken into account when describing scope of protection and restrictions in the following.[15] It should be noted, however, that the scope of application of secondary Community legislation can deviate from that of Article 39 of the TEC (Article III-133 DC); in so far, Community law embodies differing concepts of "worker".[16]

2. Subject Matter of Protection

a) Concept of Worker

Case 1 – Problem: (ECJ *Bettray* [1989] ECR 1621)
On account of his drug addiction, the German citizen B, who had entered the Netherlands back in 1980, was employed there in 1983 for an unlimited duration by a municipal work association in accordance with the Social Employment Law to perform certain services on a remunerative basis. The activity served the purpose of restoring his capacity for work and was intended to give B the opportunity to engage in paid work under conditions that came as close as possible to paid employment under normal conditions. When B applied for a residence permit, the application was rejected by the Netherlands authorities on grounds that B was not regarded as an "employed person" and could therefore not derive a right of residence from Article 39 of the TEC (Article III-133 DC). His activity, it was held, was a special form of engagement of a social nature, B's productivity was very low and, consequently, his remuneration was largely financed by subsidies from public funds.

The concept of worker is of central importance for determining the subject matter (and not only the personal scope) of protection of Article 39 of the TEC (Article III-133 DC).[17] According to the settled case-law of the ECJ, it represents a Community law concept that is interpreted from within itself. In principle, this could be taken for granted on the basic assumption that Community law constitutes an autonomous legal system. But because the national legal systems of all Member States likewise acknowledge the worker concept, the temptation thus being great to adopt national approaches to its interpretation, the ECJ has time and again felt obliged to declare that national authorities and courts are not allowed to invoke their own, additional requirements in applying Article 39 of the TEC (Article III-133 DC).[18] A second **principle of interpretation**, not only of significance to the concept of worker, is that Article 39 of the TEC (Article III-133 DC) is to

---

14 *Cf* early on ECJ *Royer* [1976] ECR 497, paras 24 ff.
15 Note that secondary Community law could restrict the scope of application of the fundamental freedoms, thus *cf* ECJ *Hocsman* [2000] ECR I-6623, paras 29–30. On the substantive effect *cf* also Weatherill/Beaumont *EU Law* (3rd ed, 1999) pp 626 ff.
16 Thus, *eg*, the coordination of social legislation through Reg 1408/71, [1971] OJ L149/2, is based on its own concept of worker, which makes reference to national social security systems and is in part broader, in part narrower than that of Art 39 TEC; the meanwhile adopted Reg 883/2004, [2004] OJ L166/1, amending this Regulation is expected to enter into force in 2007. But *cf* also for a parallel interpretation, insofar as no express derogations exist, ECJ *Mengner* [1995] ECR I-4741, paras 18 ff.
17 *Cf* also Colneric *Une communauté de droit: Festschrift für Gil Carlos Rodríguez Iglesias* (2003) pp 385 ff.
18 Just *cf* ECJ *Levin* [1982] ECR 1035, paras 11 ff; *Brown* [1988] ECR 3205, paras 22 ff.

be interpreted broadly rather than restrictively with a view to the elementary importance of this fundamental freedom and the attendant Treaty objectives:[19] According to the ECJ, the point is to help the provisions on freedom of movement attain their full effect[20] (*effet utile* principle).

6 Workers are characterised by the fact that they (1) pursue an economic activity (2) as an employed person and (3) receive remuneration in return for their activity, unless (4) a qualification of their activity as contrary to public policy precludes them from the scope of protection.

7 **(1)** The requirement of an **economic activity** reflects the general reference of all fundamental freedoms to the economic sphere. It is contrasted by purely social[21], possibly also cultural and sporting activities. Nevertheless, this limitation must not be taken to indicate that certain sectors as a whole are precluded from the application of the fundamental freedoms. Rather, exceptions exist only if the given activity is not pursued in the form of an economic exchange relationship.[22] Thus, for instance, employment with a social insurance institution is naturally a worker activity. Moreover, the circumstance that certain areas of society such as sports and culture bear distinct features, or that certain occupations are subject to particular regulations owing to their reference to common welfare, does not restrict the scope of protection of freedom of movement for workers, but at most has a bearing on the justification of any interference therewith. Accordingly, professional sportsmen[23] and persons active on behalf of religious or philosophical associations[24] can be workers just like lawyers and physicians.[25] That, however, is unlikely to apply to (unpaid) voluntary work, even if an expense allowance is awarded. Open as yet is the definition of amateur athletes.[26]

8 The status of an employed person (whether wage or salary earner, or active in the private or public sector; *cf* also para 27) or the scope of the activity and its productivity (*cf* also para 10) are irrelevant. The ECJ merely demands that the employed person pursue an "effective and genuine activity" that is not regarded as "purely marginal and ancillary".[27] Part-time activities and every other activity on an employed basis sufficiently meet these criteria; definitional problems primarily have to do with the additional requirements of the duty to comply with directions and remunerativeness.

---

19 *Cf* ECJ *Kempf* [1986] ECR 1741, paras 13 ff; *Lawrie-Blum* [1986] ECR 2121, paras 16 ff; *Ninni-Orasche* [2003] ECR I-13187, paras 23 ff.
20 ECJ *Levin* [1982] ECR 1035, paras 15 ff: "effectiveness".
21 Such as the security function of social benefit institutions, *cf* most recently ECJ *INAIL* [2002] ECR I-691.
22 The protection of entire institutions, such as those of existing social security systems, can only occur through a restriction of prohibitions of limitation or more lenient justification requirements. Even the removal of social activities from the scope of application by referring to only individual legal relationships is not uncontested.
23 *Cf* ECJ *Walrave* [1974] ECR 1405; *Bosman* [1995] ECR I-4921; *Lehtonen* [2000] ECR I-2681.
24 *Cf* ECJ *Steymann* [1988] ECR 6159, paras 11 ff.
25 *Cf* Dir 93/16/EEC, [1993] OJ L165, to facilitate the free movement of doctors and the mutual recognition of their diplomas, certificates and other evidence of formal qualifications; this Directive is to be repealed with effect from 20-10-2007 and consolidated in Dir 2005/36, [2005] OJ L255/22, on the Recognition of Professional Qualifications.
26 With reference to the freedom to provide services, *cf* ECJ *Deliège* [2000] ECR I-2549.
27 ECJ *Levin* [1982] ECR 1035, paras 17 ff.

(2) The pursuit of an activity as an employed person requires that he or she perform services for and **under the direction** of another person. This criterion simultaneously distinguishes the freedom of movement for workers from the freedom of establishment and the freedom to provide services, both of which presuppose a self-employed activity (*cf* also para 35).[28] The ECJ has generally held that self-employment depends on "all the factors and circumstances characterising the arrangements between the parties, such as, for example, the sharing of the commercial risks of the business, the freedom for a person to choose his own working hours and to engage his own assistants".[29] These elements distinguish entrepreneurial action, which on its part is above all shaped by the assumption of entrepreneurial risk. According to the pertinent case-law, remuneration in the form of a "share" in earnings, for example, does not preclude the concept of worker,[30] whereas the necessary "subordination" will be lacking if the director of a company is simultaneously the sole shareholder.[31] There are other constellations in which a relaxing of the duty to comply with directions may cause difficulty. Thus, the ECJ has quite rightly pointed out that in the case of family employment relationships, it will depend on how they are effectively carried out.[32] The Court has nevertheless refrained from clarifying the decisive criteria, thus reflecting the sparse nature of its overall judicature in matters of distinguishing between activities as employed or self-employed persons – compared with labour and social court rulings in Germany. Given that the criterion of being bound by directions is recognised by both legal systems and is of essential relevance in qualifying an activity as an employment relationship, national court rulings can – with all due caution (paras 4 ff) – largely be applied to this subject matter.[33]

(3) The remuneration received **in return for** the activity performed by the employed person does not have to suffice to make a living. Nor must it conform to collectively agreed provisions or meet a prescribed minimum wage; the form in which it is paid is irrelevant. That, however, in connection with the liberally applied remaining criteria, can lead to situations whose conformity with the economic orientation of the fundamental freedoms appears doubtful at first glance. Indeed, the worker status is already satisfied by a minor employment of 12 hours a week or less.[34] A merely very short term of employment nevertheless casts doubts on whether an economic activity is actually performed in such case.[35] In any event, the applicability of Article 39 of the TEC (Article III-133 DC) is not ruled out merely because public funds are needed to obtain supplementary means of subsist-

---

28 National law requires such distinctions, *ie* under labour, social and tax law; *cf, eg*, Dupeyroux *Droit de la sécurité sociale* (15th ed, Paris 2005) pp 445 ff; Wikeley/Ogus *The law of social security* (5th ed, London 2002) pp 96 ff; Schulin/Igl *Sozialrecht* (7th ed, Düsseldorf 2002) pp 71 ff.
29 ECJ *Agegate* [1989] ECR 4459, paras 36 ff.
30 ECJ *Agegate* [1989] ECR 4459, paras 36 ff.
31 ECJ *Asscher* [1996] ECR I-3089, paras 26 ff.
32 ECJ *Meeusen* [1999] ECR I-3289, paras 15 ff.
33 That, at least, is confirmed by the previous rulings of the ECJ, although it should be noted that in individual cases, even judgments within Germany may indeed vary. In taking the approach advocated here, the classification of employees with managerial functions, which is often considered indistinct, no longer poses any great problems.
34 *Cf* ECJ *Kempf* [1986] ECR 1741, paras 12 ff; *Rinner-Kühn* [1989] ECR 2743, paras 13 ff; *Mengner* [1995] ECR I-4741, paras 18 ff.
35 On the limited duration of casual employment, *cf* ECJ *Raulin* [1992] ECR I-1027, paras 14 ff.

ence;[36] even minor activities convey a right of residence and claims to social benefits. Article 39 of the TEC (Article III-133 DC) contains no restrictions here because its scope of application would be curtailed to too great an extent if it demanded the earning of minimum means of subsistence – which are difficult to define in the first place and, moreover, would not be in keeping with the tendency towards a more general right of free movement (paras 1 ff).

11 Employment for the purpose of occupational training constitutes a worker activity, whereas the pursuit of studies does not. The situation is questionable in the case of trainees. They are deemed workers if their preparatory training is completed "under the conditions of genuine and effective activity as an employed person", this depending on whether the expended period of time suffices to develop occupational skills.[37]

12 (4) In principle, the concept of worker is not precluded by the circumstance that an activity is viewed as being contrary to **public policy** – unless this characterisation is attended by a comprehensive ban on access to the labour market. That was doubted by the *Bundesverwaltungsgericht* (BVerwG – German Federal Administrative Court) in the case of prostitution pursued as an economic activity.[38] After initially proceeding from a merely implicit protection through the fundamental freedoms,[39] the ECJ has recently declared that prostitution concerns an economic activity which, though regulated in the Member States, is not fundamentally prohibited.[40] Any restrictions are therefore subject to justification (para 47).

Case 1 – Answer:
13 Workers are persons engaged in an employment relationship. According to the case-law of the ECJ, the essential feature of an employment relationship is that for a certain period of time, a person performs services for and under the direction of another person in return for which he receives remuneration. In the given case, B performed services in return for remuneration, meaning that an exception to the scope of application cannot be assumed. Whether that activity concerned a specific, legally constituted form of employment is irrelevant. Nevertheless, the ECJ does demand that the actual performance of the activity can be regarded as an "effective and genuine economic activity". That criterion was contradicted by the purpose of the employment and its execution – which served to reintegrate B. In other words, B was to regain the capacity to take up a regular economic activity later on. Persons engaged under the scheme set up by the Social Employment Law are not selected on the basis of their capacity to perform a certain activity; rather, the work assigned to them is adapted to their physical and mental possibilities. And finally, the entire social employment scheme is designed for the sole purpose of restoring or improving the capacity for work of the persons concerned. B was therefore not a worker within the meaning of Article 39 of the TEC (Article III-133 DC).[41]

---

36 ECJ *Kempf* [1986] ECR 1741, paras 14 ff.
37 ECJ *Bernini* [1992] ECR I-1071, paras 15 ff.
38 *Cf* (1990) 60 BVerwGE 284, 289 ff.
39 ECJ *Adoui* [1982] ECR 1665, paras 5 ff.
40 ECJ *Jany* [2001] ECR I-8615.
41 The fact that remuneration is paid from public funds does not oppose the concept of worker. Regarding employment relationships under the former German Federal Social Assistance Act (in the given case, with full weekly working hours and a net salary equivalent to a comparable engagement in the regular labour market), *cf* ECJ *Birden* [1998] ECR I-7747, paras 25 ff.

b) Temporal Scope

A worker is a person engaged in an employment relationship. The protection afforded under Article 39 of the TEC (Article III-133 DC) thus spans the duration of activity as an employed person. But what applies if an employment relationship has yet to be established (1) or, vice versa, if the employment relationship has been terminated (2)?

14

(1) Article 39(3)(a) of the TEC (Article III-133(3)(a) DC) expressly grants workers the right to accept offers of employment actually made. Quite obviously, then, an employment relationship need not exist beforehand; its conclusion must only be intended. In this way, **free access** to employment is guaranteed. This includes the rights of entry and residence and the right of equal treatment when applying for employment[42] (paras 19 ff). Entry thereby need not be geared towards specific, already advertised employment offers. It has not been regulated so far, however, for what duration employment may be sought in another Member State and, conversely, from what point in time a taking up of employment is deemed to have failed and, hence, no longer enables a right of residence to be derived from Article 39 of the TEC (Article III-133 DC).[43] The ECJ has accepted the interpretation that such is the case if employment has not been found over a period of six months.[44] Persons seeking employment will not have to abide by substantially shorter temporal limits,[45] although the decisive factor will always be whether the individual concerned has genuine prospects of finding work.

15

(2) On termination of their employment relationship, workers have a **right to remain** pursuant to Article 39(3)(d) of the TEC (Article III-133(3)(d) DC), which is substantiated by Regulation 1251/70 (para 3). The basic idea is that workers should be allowed to stay in their habitual living environment also after they have withdrawn from working life. Accordingly, the right to remain is linked to a termination of employment upon reaching retirement age or to a permanent incapacity for work, and presupposes prior employment of a specific duration.[46] Migrant workers who have become unemployed may not be treated differently from any national worker in a comparable situation in terms of their occupational reintegration.[47] Their status as workers and, in particular, the duration of their

16

---

42 In such cases, much speaks in favour of granting equal treatment also in taxation and social matters (paras 19 ff). As regards the seeking of employment, cf also Art 5 Reg 1612/68 (note 12). That does not mean, however, that following an unsuccessful search for employment, meanstested social benefits could not be linked to the requirement of residence (as a justifiable general interest), provided this concerns affiliation with the labour market; in this way, social tourism as an excuse for seeking employment is precluded; cf ECJ *Collins* [2004] ECR I-2703.
43 Cf also Barnard *The substantive law of the EU* (Oxford 2004) p 266.
44 ECJ *Antonissen* [1991] ECR I-745, paras 21 ff.
45 Taking a different view (ie that 3 months suffice), Magiera [1987] DÖV 221, 223–224; statement of the UK in ECJ *Antonissen* [1991] ECR I-745, para 19. At any rate, a termination of residence may not ensue automatically upon expiry of a 3-month term; cf ECJ *Commission v Belgium* [1997] ECR I-1035, paras 18 ff.
46 Cf more detailed Art 2 Reg 1251/70 (note 13), which under certain conditions also provides for a right to remain in the event of prolongation of an activity as an employed person in another Member State. Regarding evidence concerning the requirements and the 2-year term for the exercise of the right to remain, cf Arts 4 and 5 Reg 1251/70.
47 Art 7(1) Reg 1621/68 (note 12).

sustained right of residence depend on the given circumstances and, moreover, are not explicitly regulated by secondary Community legislation.[48]

17 If employment is terminated for reasons other than those cited above, the worker status is forfeited along with the attendant rights. Nevertheless, there are exceptions to this principle.[49] Based on the acknowledgement that workers from other Member States enjoy a right of access to national vocational schools and retraining facilities,[50] the ECJ has concluded that also university students are entitled in exceptional cases to the social advantages granted to workers if there is a connection between their studies and a previous occupational activity.[51] Irrespective of the duration of employment, the underlying intent is to secure[52] a right of residence and a right to the promotion of university education.

Case 2 – Problem: (ECJ *Meeusen* [1999] ECR I-3289)

18 The Belgian national M is resident in Belgium but employed in the Netherlands, namely by a company whose director and sole shareholder is her husband. Their daughter T, who is 18 years old and is supported by M, likewise resides in Belgium and is commencing studies there. She applies to the relevant authorities for a basic grant under the Netherlands law on the financing of studies. The study finance is refused on the grounds that it is conditional on either Netherlands nationality or place of residence in the Netherlands.

c) Protected Activities

19 On a very fundamental scale, the protection afforded by Article 39 of the TEC (Article III-133 DC) – similar to all other fundamental freedoms – demands a cross-border element. Its purview does not extend to purely national circumstances,[53] meaning simultaneously that it does not cover reverse discrimination.[54] In terms of Article 39 of the TEC (Article III-133 DC), **border crossing** consists in persons moving to another Member State (or their intention to do so) in order to work there. Whether this occurs permanently, in that workers take up residence in the host State, or whether they remain resident in their

---

48 Details are contested, notably whether a distinction should be made between voluntary and involuntary unemployment; *cf* Craig/de Búrca *EU Law* (3rd ed, Oxford 2003), pp 732–733; Scheuer in: Lenz/Borchardt (eds) *EU- und EG-Vertrag – Kommentar* (3rd ed, Cologne 2003) Art 39 EGV, para 63; more detailed Randelzhofer/Forsthoff in: Grabitz/Hilf (eds) *Das Recht der Europäischen Union Bd II* (Munich 2003) Art 39 EGV, paras 45 ff. Regarding residence status in the event of involuntary unemployment, *cf* Art 7(3) Dir 2004/38 (note 4), observing that Art 7(2) Dir 68/360 (note 11) is to remain in force until 30-04-06.
49 Notably as regards the maintenance of rights acquired under the employment relationship, *cf* ECJ *Meints* [1997] ECR I-6689, paras 40 ff; *Commission v France* [1998] ECR I-5325, paras 41 ff.
50 Art 7(3) Reg 1612/68 (note 12).
51 ECJ *Lair* [1988] ECR 3161, paras 35 ff; for differentiation, *cf Raulin* [1992] ECR I-1027.
52 Nevertheless, provided that certain abuses are excluded, ECJ *Lair* [1988] ECR 3161, paras 43 ff; *cf* also *Brown* [1988] ECR 3205, paras 22 ff.
53 Just *cf* ECJ *Steen I* [1992] ECR I-341; *Kapasakalis* [1998] ECR I-4239.
54 That is by no means uncontested, but need not be expanded here; Burrows *Free movement in European Community Law* (Oxford 1987) pp 133–134; Weiss/Woolridge *Free movement of persons within the European Community* (The Hague 2002) p 41; restrictively, Epiney in: Bieber/Epiney/Haag (eds) *Die Europäische Union. Rechtsordnung und Politik* (6th ed, Baden-Baden 2005) paras 778 ff; → more detailed § 7 para 20.

Freedom of Movement for Workers §9 I 2

home State and commute to the host state as frontier workers,[55] is irrelevant. In addition, their employment must not necessarily be with a non-national enterprise; in particular, it suffices if they take up an activity with an international organisation.[56]

Article 39 of the TEC (Article III-133 DC) provides protection against measures adopted both by another Member State and by the home State, which on its part must not in principle impede cross-border employment (paras 41 ff).[57] At first glance, this Treaty article seems to incorporate differentiated provisions, which nonetheless interact with each other. Thus paragraph 1 sets out the general and comprehensive guarantee, which is then substantiated by various rights in paragraphs 2 and 3: the abolition of any discrimination in respect of working and employment conditions (1), which is supplemented by the entitlement to equality of treatment in terms of tax and social advantages (2), and the concomitant rights of entry and residence (3). To safeguard against any movement-related loss of social security rights, the coordination of national social benefit systems was established on the basis of Article 42 of the TEC (Article I-126 DC) (4).

(1) With regard to employment, remuneration and other **conditions of work and employment**, any discrimination based on nationality must be abolished (Article 39(2) TEC/Article III-133(2) DC). This prohibition of discrimination, which also applies to collectively agreed and individual contracts,[58] covers every aspect of occupational activity. For instance, it precludes the requirement of work permits by migrants and preferential recruitment procedures for a Member State's own nationals,[59] differential treatment as regards dismissal and reinstatement,[60] the withholding of ancillary benefits[61] as well as discrimination in respect of opportunities for promotion[62] or through the temporal limitation of employment relationships[63]. The requirement of equal treatment also refers to membership of trade unions and the exercise of related rights.[64]

(2) Article 7(2) of Regulation 1612/68 guarantees to workers who are citizens of the Union a fundamental **social right**, namely entitlement to "the same social and tax advantages as national workers".[65] Tax advantages include, for example, the deductibility of expenses,[66] tax refunds,[67] or splitting schemes for the joint assessment of spouses[68], it

20

21

22

---

55 For a definition, cf Art 1(b) Reg 1408/71 or, prospectively from 2007, Art 1(f) Reg 883/2004 (note 16).
56 Cf ECJ Ferlini [2000] ECR I-8081.
57 Just cf ECJ Scholz [1994] ECR I-50, paras 9 ff.
58 On the invalidity of discriminatory agreements, cf Art 7(4) Reg 1612/68 (note 12); on the direct applicability of more favourable provisions, ECJ Schöning [1998] ECR I-47.
59 On access to employment, cf more detailed Arts 1-6 Reg 1612/68 (note 12).
60 Cf Art 7(1) Reg 1612/68 (note 12).
61 Without distinguishing between prescribed and voluntary benefits, cf ECJ Sotgiu [1974] ECR 153.
62 ECJ Commission v Greece [1998] ECR I-1095; Schöning [1998] ECR I-47.
63 ECJ Allue II [1993] ECR I-4309; Spotti [1993] ECR I-5185.
64 Art 8 Reg 1612/68 (note 12); here, eg, ECJ Commission v Luxembourg [1994] ECR I-1891.
65 Whether this right is also valid for unemployed persons and persons seeking employment is not uncontested; cf Randelzhofer/Forsthoff (note 48) Art 39 EGV, para 159; but insofar as the worker status extends to these persons, its validity is indeed a mandatory consequence, leaving no room for differentiation. Moreover, the debate loses importance in light of the general right to freedom of movement (paras 2 ff). On the eligibility of family members, cf paras 28 ff below.
66 Cf ECJ Bachmann [1992] ECR I-249.
67 ECJ Biehl [1990] ECR I-1779; Schumacker [1995] ECR I-225.
68 ECJ Zurstrassen [2000] ECR I-3337.

being important in which State the earnings are subject to taxation. By no means is every form of discriminatory treatment of national and non-national workers ruled out in the levying of direct taxes; in particular, a limited tax liability can likewise limit the possibilities of allowing for tax deductions.[69]

23   The case-law of the ECJ on social advantages is scarcely manageable any longer.[70] The concept is interpreted broadly by the Court and comprises "all the advantages which, whether or not linked to a contract of employment, are generally granted to national workers primarily because of their objective status as workers or by virtue of the mere fact of their residence on the national territory and whose extension to workers who are nationals of other Member States therefore seems likely to facilitate the free movement of such workers within the Community."[71] Thus they embrace education allowances,[72] aid in support of subsistence such as social assistance or minimum income[73] as well as family allowances, including fare reductions[74] and the like. Social advantages need not only consist in monetary and in-kind benefits, however, but may involve the award of social positions. For instance, they include the right to use one's own language before court[75] and the right of residence for non-marital partners[76]. Nevertheless, citizenship rights and rights linked to a specific previous history in the home State remain exempted.[77] Participation in the housing market is regulated separately.[78]

24   (3) Pursuant to Article 39(3)(b) and (c) of the TEC (Article III-133(3)(b) and (c) DC), workers have the right to move freely within the Member States to accept offers of employment and to stay there for this purpose. By necessity, the guarantee of access to employment comprises the exit from the country of origin and the admission to the sovereign territory of the other Member State. **Entry and resident rights** are detailed in Directive 2004/38 (para 3). According to this Directive, the presentation of an ID card or passport, but not a visa or similar formality may be demanded.[79] Right of residence is

---

69 Regarding this and the limits of this principle, given a lack of appreciable income in the country of residence, ECJ *Schumacker* [1995] ECR I-225; *de Groot* [2002] ECR I-11819.
70 For a detailed overview, see Wölker/Grill (note 10) Art 39 EGV, paras 64 ff; *cf* also Weiss/Wooldridge (note 54) pp 56 ff; Barnard (note 43) pp 278 ff.
71 Just *cf* ECJ *Martínez Sala* [1998] ECR I-2691, paras 25 ff. In respect of Reg 1408/71 or, prospectively from 2007, Reg 883/2004 (note 16) (*cf* below in the text), delineation is no longer required.
72 Just *cf* ECJ *Matteucci* [1988] ECR 5589; on bridging grants, *cf Merida* [2004] ECR I-8471.
73 *Cf* ECJ *Lebon* [1987] ECR 2811.
74 ECJ *Cristini* [1975] ECR 1085.
75 ECJ *Mutsch* [1985] ECR 2681.
76 ECJ *Reed* [1986] ECR 1283. It is self-explanatory that this must include residence rights for non-national homosexual partners if these are also accorded to nationals. Nevertheless the Member States remain entitled to differentiate according to nationality and/or residence status as regards the prerequisites for permanent residence (also if derived); cf ECJ *Kaba* [2000] ECR I-2623, paras 30 ff.
77 Such as suffrage and assistance to victims of war.
78 Art 9 Reg 1612/68 (note 12).
79 Art 5(1) Dir 2004/38 (note 4) or, until 30-04-2006, Art 3 Dir 68/360 (note 11); however, third-country nationals can be required to obtain visas. The admissibility of border controls is not questioned by the provisions on freedom of movement as such, but only after these have been replaced by controls at the Community's external borders; *cf* ECJ *Wijsenbeek* [1999] ECR I-6207, paras 39 ff. *Cf* also Arts 61 and 62 TEC and the incremental incorporation of the Schengen Agreement in Community law. The Freedom of Movement Act/EU stipulates an obligation to

Freedom of Movement for Workers §9 I 2

confirmed by a residence permit, which only has declaratory character.[80] Any evidence which may be requested for its issue is regulated by secondary Community legislation.[81] A refusal of entry or of the granting and/or extension of a residence permit is subject to specific procedural law guaranties.[82]

(4) Social security systems bear a close reference to the national territory of the Member States: inclusion within a system is based on a territorial nexus in respect of either employment or residence.[83] Depending on the structure of the given systems, preconditions for the receipt of benefits are as a rule linked to procedures within the national territory, and the export of benefits is frequently restricted.[84] All of this may threaten the social security of migrant workers. Thus, by working in several Member States, they might acquire only brief pension qualifying periods, which as such do not suffice for benefit entitlement; or family circumstances in the home State might be left out of consideration, although they affect the granting of benefits in the State of employment, and so forth. In order to avoid such disadvantages resulting from freedom of movement, Article 42 of the TEC (Article I-126 DC) provides for a coordination of social security systems. Competence in social security matters remains with the Member States; harmonisation in terms of the creation of uniform requirements or benefits is not striven for. The objective, rather, is to bring the systems into line with each other and thus to avoid a loss of rights.

25

Given their significance, the initial **coordination** rules were established very early on and modelled on international law.[85] Today, coordination rests on the legal foundations of Regulation 1408/71 or, prospectively from 2007, Regulation 883/2004[86], which also embraces self-employed persons[87] and civil servants[88], thus exceeding the personal scope of Article 39 of the TEC (Article III-133 DC). In terms of its subject matter, coordination addresses benefits granted in the events of sickness and maternity,[89] invalidity, old age and

26

---

register under § 5 and a general obligation to provide proof of identity for entry and residence under § 8.
80 *Cf*, quite early on, ECJ *Royer* [1976] ECR 497, paras 30 ff. Not subject to permit is a merely 3 months' stay and the stays of frontier and seasonal workers, Art 6(1) Dir 2004/38 (note 4) or, until 30-04-2006, Art 8 Dir 68/360 (note 11).
81 Art 8(3) Dir 2004/38 (note 4) or, until 30-04-2006, Art 4(3) Dir 68/360 (note 11).
82 Art 15 Dir 2004/38 (note 4) or, until 30-04-2006, Arts 8 and 9 Dir 64/221 (note 11). Regarding this and the negation of the question whether the termination of a non-permitted stay of several months is deemed a refusal of entry, *cf* ECJ *Yiadom* [2000] ECR I-9265, paras 27 ff.
83 The most important exception is the extension to temporary activity abroad; nevertheless, Art 14(1) Reg 1408/71 or, prospectively from 2007, Art 12(1) Reg 883/2004 (note 16) provides for a temporal limit in these cases of so-called posting.
84 Where property rights have been acquired, these are not forfeited through a change of territory; protection is thus also afforded by the ECHR, *cf* ECtHR *Gaygusuz* (1997) 23 EHRR 364, paras 405 ff.
85 Reg No 3 and Implementing Reg No 4 of 1958, [1958] OJ 561 and 597, modelled on the former social insurance agreement and on ILO Convention No 102 concerning Minimum Standards of Social Security, http://www.ilo.org/ilolex/english/convdisp1.htm.
86 See note 16 along with Implementing Reg 574/72, [1972] OJ L74/1, as amended.
87 Included on the legal basis of ex Art 235 EEC Treaty (Art 308 TEC) through Reg 1390/81, [1981] OJ L143/1.
88 On the requirement of their inclusion, ECJ *Vougioukas* [1995] ECR I-4033.
89 Including long-term care insurance; on the qualification of benefits, ECJ *Molenaar* [1998] ECR I-843.

death, occupational accidents and diseases, and unemployment; it also includes death benefits as well as family benefits and allowances.[90] Without going into detail,[91] the Regulation lays down applicable law[92] and, roughly speaking, regulates the aggregation of insurance periods, the extensive equal treatment of non-national criteria[93] and the export of benefits[94].

d) Exemptions from Scope

27 Article 39(4) of the TEC (Article III-133(4) DC) – the wording is explicit in this respect – contains an exemption from its scope of protection: the guarantee of free movement does "not apply to employment in the public service" (→ § 7 paras 51 ff). Considering how many people in most European states, regardless of any specific status, are employed in the public service, it would appear that wide sections of the working world do not come under the ambit of Article 39 of the TEC (Article III-133 DC). The exemption must not, however, be interpreted in this sense. The ECJ made it clear quite early on that, instead, it must be construed narrowly as an exemption provision applying only to "posts which involve direct or indirect participation in the exercise of powers conferred by public law and duties designed to safeguard the general interests of the State or of other public au-

---

90 It is irrelevant how the national systems are organised; regarding functional equivalence, *cf* also ECJ *Paletta I* [1992] ECR I-3423, paras 16 ff. The Member States have submitted declarations on scope of application (Art 5 Reg 1408/71 or, prospectively from 2007, Art 9 Reg 883/2004 (note 16)), which are nevertheless binding only as regards the positive inclusion of systems but not those left unmentioned. Social security benefits are benefits granted in accordance with statutory provisions, without any discretionary review of personal need in the individual case, and refer to the risks set out in Art 4 Reg 1408/71 or, prospectively from 2007, Art 3 Reg 883/2004; regarding inclusion of the German child-raising allowance, *cf* ECJ *Hoever and Zachow* [1996] ECR I-4895, paras 20–21.
91 For an overview, *cf* Becker in: Schwarze (ed) *EU-Kommentar* (Baden-Baden 2000) Art 42 EGV, paras 12 ff; more detailed Fuchs (ed) *Europäisches Sozialrecht* (4th ed, Baden-Baden 2005) Titel III; Hervey *European Social Law and Policy* (London 1998). Meanwhile, the case-law of the ECJ on coordination rules is quite diversified, which is easy to review through a subject-matter search under the keyword "freedom of movement" in CELEX or in the case-law database of the ECJ.
92 For workers, this is, in principle, the law of the State of employment, Art 13(2) Reg 1408/71 or, prospectively from 2007, Art 11(3) Reg 883/2004 (note 16); upon loss of the worker status, residence becomes the governing criterion; *cf* ECJ *Kuusijaevi* [1998] ECR I-3419, paras 14 ff. Regarding the relationship to intergovernmental social law, Arts 6 and 7 Reg 1408/71 or, prospectively from 2007, Art 8 Reg 883/2004 (note 16); on the applicability of social insurance agreements, ECJ *Rönfeldt* [1991] ECR I-323; *Thévenon* [1995] ECR I-3813; *Kaske* [2002] ECR I-1261.
93 These are stipulated in special provisions and fundamentally conveyed through the prohibition of discrimination; *cf* Becker [2000] VSSR 221.
94 *Cf* Arts 10 and 10(a) Reg 1408/71 or, prospectively from 2007, Art 7 Reg 883/2004 (note 16); the export of benefits in the event of unemployment is limited to 3 months, Art 69 Reg 1408/71 or, prospectively from 2007, Art 64 Reg 883/2004. Benefits in kind are not exported; in the event of sickness, however, there is in-kind assistance, *ie* benefits are granted – at the expense of the State of employment – in other Member States pursuant to the provisions applicable there, Art 22 Reg 1408/71 or, prospectively from 2007, Arts 17 ff Reg 883/2004. This form of export is not to be confused with the effect of the fundamental freedoms on the social law principle of territoriality.

Freedom of Movement for Workers §9 I 3

thorities."[95] It is irrelevant in this context whether a Member State entrusts specific posts to public servants in accordance with national law or whether the employer is a body governed by public law[96]. Accordingly, freedom of movement does indeed apply, say, to public service in the school and university sector.[97] The situation for police, soldiers and judges is again a different one. The decisive criterion at all times is whether the given employment involves the exercise of powers conferred by public law towards safeguarding the general interests of the State. Thus, for instance, the healthcare system in general is not exempt from the application of Article 39 of the TEC (Article III-133 DC),[98] whereas activities in the sphere of benefit administration might well be.[99] Also, certain managerial functions within the administration may require a specific form of protection on account of their overriding importance.[100]

3. Personal Scope of Protection

a) Union Citizens and Members of Their Families

Although Article 39 of the TEC (Article III-133 DC) does not contain a provision to that effect, its personal scope of protection, in keeping with the general conception of the EC Treaty, initially applies only to **Union citizens** (Article 17 TEC/Article I-10 DC), *ie* persons having the nationality of an EU Member State.[101] To be noted here is that apart from the workers themselves, employers, too, can resist any interference with the free movement of workers.[102] 28

The protection of workers' free movement largely extends also to their **family members**. Under Community law, as elsewhere, it is founded on the protection of marriage and the 29

---

95 ECJ *Commission v Belgium* [1980] ECR 3881, paras 10 ff. Both prerequisites apply cumulatively, this being disputed, however; just *cf* more detailed Craig/de Búrca (note 48) pp 722 ff; Weiss/Wooldridge (note 54) pp 49–50; Schneider/Wunderlich in: Schwarze (ed) *EU-Kommentar* (Baden-Baden 2000) Art 39 EGV, paras 135 ff; on criticism of the case-law, Brechmann in: Calliess/Ruffert (eds) *Kommentar zu EUV und EGV* (2nd ed, Neuwied 2002) Art 39 EGV, paras 104 ff.
96 *Cf* ECJ *Anker* [2003] ECR I-10447, paras 62–63.
97 ECJ *Lawrie-Blum (student teachers)* [1986] ECR 2121; *Bleis (secondary school teachers)* [1991] ECR I-5627; *Commission v Luxembourg (elementary school teachers)* [1996] ECR I-3207.
98 Regarding hospital care-staff, *cf* ECJ *Commission v France* [1986] ECR 1725.
99 *Cf* Wölker/Grill (note 10) Art 39 EGV, para 161. Nevertheless, this exception is very broad and would have to include social insurance institutions, although comparable activities are also carried out by private insurance companies.
100 *Cf* ECJ *Commission v Italy* [1987] ECR 2625. On the entire issue, now *cf* also Jakobs in: Deppenheuer et al (eds) *Nomos und Ethos* (Berlin 2002) pp 507 ff.
101 That is, regardless of possible dual citizenship; for a general view, just *cf* Bleckmann *Europarecht* (6th ed, Cologne 1997) paras 1561 ff; Burrows (note 54) pp 124–125; Weiss/Wooldridge (note 54) p 41. At any rate, refugees and stateless persons are included in the protection under a number of secondary provisions; on Reg 1408/71 or, prospectively from 2007, Reg 883/2004 (note 16) and the requirement of cross-border elements, just *cf* most recently ECJ *Khalil* [2001] ECR I-7413. On the competence of the Member States for stipulating requirements governing the acquisition and loss of citizenship, ECJ *Kaur* [2001] ECR I-1237, paras 19 ff.
102 ECJ *Clean Car* [1998] ECR I-2521, paras 19 ff, with reference to the effectiveness of Art 39 TEC, on the one hand, and to the fact that also employers can rely on justification grounds, on the other.

family,[103] but is left to be dealt with by secondary legislation, at least as far as its specific substance is concerned. And that is currently leading to differentiation (cf also paras 1 ff). Indeed, whether family members are deemed Union citizens depends not on general prerequisites governing their subsequent immigration or on their rights to and in residence, but on the visa obligation.[104] As for workers' rights *in* residence, the question will always be whether these rights apply only to the person directly entitled to free movement or also to that person's dependants. On the central issue of claims to tax and social advantages (Article 7(2) Regulation 1612/68; cf paras 19 ff), the ECJ took the view that family members are entitled on their own merits.[105] The children of workers are granted the right to equal participation in general education and vocational training.[106] Hence, quotas on university admission[107] or exclusion from grants[108] are incompatible with that right. The receipt of a grant from the host State does not hinge on the Member State in which studies are pursued.[109]

b) Nationals of Third Countries

30 Apart from the aforementioned derived rights for family members, nationals of third countries in principle do not enjoy a right to free movement.[110] Nevertheless, the Agreement on the European Economic Area places the nationals of EEA members countries on an equal footing with Union citizens, so that freedom of movement for workers applies

---

103 But whether freedom of movement for dependants can thus be derived directly from Art 39 TEC (Art III-133 DC) appears questionable; rightly, the assertion of their own rights would, at least additionally, require recourse to the protection afforded by a fundamental right. In view of the relatively liberal case-law of the ECJ, this question is scarcely relevant in practice.

104 Art 5(2) Dir 2004/38 (note 4). On the requirements (granting of maintenance; age for subsequent entry of children under 21) and rights in general, cf Arts 10 and 11 Reg 1612/68 (note 12) and Art 4(4) Dir 68/360 (note 11); on the visa obligation, Art 3(2) Dir 68/360. Arts 10 and 11 Reg 1612/68 as well as Dir 68/360 are to be repealed through Dir 2004/38 with effect from 3 0-04-2006. On the status of the spouse despite living apart, ECJ *Diatta* [1985] ECR 567; on the requirement of an appropriate dwelling, ECJ *Commission v Germany* [1989] ECR 1263. On the (admissible) less favourable treatment of family members who are third-country nationals in respect of unlimited residence permits, ECJ *Kaba* [2000] ECR I-2623; now also *Kaba II* [2003] ECR I-2219.

105 Insofar as they meet the requirements of Art 10(1) Reg 1612/68 (note 12 – in force only until 30-04-2006), just cf ECJ *Deak* [1985] ECR 1873, paras 22 ff; *Bernini* [1992] ECR I-1071, paras 28 ff. For an application in favour of family relations stipulated under Art 10(2) Reg 1612/68, cf Schneider/Wunderlich (note 95) para 88. Nevertheless, as in the past, national workers must likewise be eligible for the advantage; cf ECJ *Taghavi* [1992] ECR I-4401, paras 11 ff.

106 Cf Art 12 Reg 1612/68 (note 12); the provision dispenses with the stipulation of an age-limit for subsequent entry and establishes an autonomous right of residence; cf also ECJ *Baumbast* [2002] ECR I-7091.

107 Cf ECJ *Commission v Belgium* [1988] ECR 5445.

108 Cf ECJ *Casagrande* [1974] ECR 773.

109 Irrespective of the residence requirement under Art 12 Reg 1612/68 (note 12), cf ECJ *Di Leo* [1990] ECR I-4185, paras 16 ff.

110 But also cf propositions for a European immigration concept: European Parliament legislative resolution on the proposal for a Council directive on the conditions of entry and residence of third-country nationals for the purpose of paid employment and self-employed economic activities, [2004] OJ C43/230.

within the entire **EEA**. The relevant agreement with Switzerland entered into force on 1 June 2002.[111]

Other third-country nationals are granted rights through **Association Agreements**.[112] Brief mention is to be made here only of the agreements with Turkey (1) and with the accession candidates in conjunction with the Union's eastern enlargement (2). The Treaty of Accession of ten Central and Eastern European States, signed on 16 April 2003, lays down that the regulations on the free movement of workers are valid with immediate effect for Malta and Cyprus, whereas the eight remaining accession States are subject to a transitional period from 1 May 2004.[113]

(1) For Turkish nationals residing in EU-member states, it is of great practical importance that the ECJ declared the Decisions adopted by the Association Council (ACDs) on the basis of the EEC-Turkey Association Agreement to form integral parts of Community law that are directly applicable, provided they meet the general requirements of being sufficiently precise and unconditional.[114] Thus, although Turkish workers are not entitled to first-time access, Article 6 of ACD 1/80 grants them residence rights once they have been duly employed.[115] Article 3 of ACD 3/80 lays down a prohibition of discrimination in the social security sphere which is likewise directly applicable.[116]

(2) The **Europe Agreements** with the countries of Central and Eastern Europe[117] did not establish a right to free movement for employed persons.[118] They nevertheless specified directly applicable prohibitions of discrimination that demand equal treatment with regard to working conditions.[119]

---

111 On this and on the text: http://www.europa.admin.ch/ba/d/index.htm.
112 *Cf* also ECJ *Kolpak* [2003] ECR I-4135; more detailed Weiss/Wooldridge (note 54) pp 201 ff.
113 *Eg*, see [2003] OJ L236/40 in conjunction with No 2 of Annex V: list according to Art 34 of the Act of Accession: Czech Republic, [2003] OJ L236/803; or [2003] OJ L236/40 in conjunction with No 2 of Annex XII: list according to Art 24 of the Act of Accession: Poland, [2003] OJ L236/875. On the previous practice and the limits governing transitional provisions, Becker *EU-Enlargements and Limits to Amendments of the E. C. Treaty* The Jean Monnet Working Papers No.15/01 (http://www.jeanmonnetprogram.org/papers/01/013801.html).
114 Fundamentally, ECJ *Sevince* [1990] ECR I-3461. On the Association Agreement, Weiss/Wooldridge (note 54) pp 205 ff.
115 *Cf* ECJ *Kus* [1992] ECR I-6781; *Bozkurt* [1995] ECR I-1475; *Nazli* [2000] ECR I-957; *Kurz* [2002] ECR I-10691; *Ayaz* [2004] ECR I-8765. Regarding family reunion, *cf* Art 7 ACD 1/80; most recently ECJ *Ergat* [2000] ECR I-487; *Eyup* [2000] ECR I-4747. More detailed Weiss/Wooldridge (note 54) pp 208 ff. Art 10(1) ACD 1/80 contains a prohibition of discrimination regarding working conditions, ECJ *Wählergruppe* [2003] ECR I-4301.
116 ECJ *Sürül* [1999] ECR I-2685, paras 48 ff; *Ozturk* [2004] ECR I-3605.
117 Bulgaria, [1994] OJ L358/1 and Romania, [1994] OJ L357/1; see now Treaty of Accession [2005] OJ L157.
118 Owing to the more extensive nature of the provisions on freedom of establishment and freedom to provide services, a distinction between self-employed and employed activities becomes necessary; on this and the use of criteria applicable to the EC Treaty, *cf* ECJ *Jany* [2001] ECR I-8615.
119 Accordingly, the temporal limitation (paras 38 ff) on employment contracts with Polish foreign-language assistants is likewise inadmissible; *cf* ECJ *Pokrzeptowicz-Meyer* [2002] ECR I-1049.

Case 2 – Answer:

34 M is a worker. The fact that she is married to the sole shareholder of a company is irrelevant as long as she is effectively bound by directions in the performance of her services (para 6). Although T is not a worker, she herself as a family member can invoke Article 7(2) of Regulation 1612/68, even if it does not expressly refer to dependants as beneficiaries (para 6). T easily fulfils all the requirements governing the status of dependent family members. Furthermore, study finance comes under the very broad concept of social advantages (paras 19 ff).

The only question is whether the grant of benefits is excluded because M is a frontier worker. The Netherlands authorities thus argued that in the given constellation there was no connection whatever to the purpose of Article 7(2) of Regulation 1612/68, being to facilitate the free movement of workers and the integration of migrant workers and their families in the host country. The ECJ did not follow this line of argumentation, holding that Article 7(2) of Regulation 1612/68 applied without restriction also to frontier workers. The objective of the provision was to protect against discrimination. The study finance therefore had to be granted to the children of migrant workers under the same conditions as those applicable to the children of national workers. Consequently, an additional residence requirement is deemed to infringe Community law.

4. Concurrences

35 Distinguishing the freedom of movement for workers from the freedom of establishment and the freedom to provide services (→ *cf* also § 10 paras 20 ff; § 11 para 36) is based on whether an activity is pursued by an employed or a self-employed person. Workers are persons who perform services for and under the direction of another person (paras 4 ff). In specific cases, it may be difficult to make this distinction, but as the fundamental freedoms are very similar in substance, the ECJ attaches no great importance to doing so.[120] Apart from that, the duration of an occupation as an employed person certainly plays a role as well. If workers become temporarily active in another Member State on behalf of their employers, *ie* are **posted**, any obstacles to their activity constitute an interference with the employer's freedom to provide services, such interference possibly being justified to protect the workers.[121] In such cases, the ECJ does not draw on freedom of movement for workers as an – additional – criterion of assessment, although integration in the State of employment, as demonstrated by the example of frontier workers, is not a requirement governing the concept of worker.

II. Interference

Case 3 – Problem: (ECJ *Terhoeve* [1999] ECR I-345)

36 T, a citizen of the Netherlands, worked for the first ten months of 1990 in the United Kingdom and then in the Netherlands. During all that time, he was compulsorily insured under the Netherlands social security system. His social security contributions were levied together

---

120 But regarding the Europe Agreements, *cf* paras 30 ff; on the distinction within the scope of Reg 1408/71 or, prospectively from 2007, Reg 883/2004 (note 16), ECJ *Banks* [2000] ECR I-2005.
121 ECJ *Rush Portuguesa* [1990] ECR I-1417; *Vander Elst* [1994] ECR I-3803; *Arblade* [1999] ECR I-8453; *Finalarte* [2001] ECR I-7831; *Portugaia Construções* [2002] ECR I-787.

with income tax, *ie* up to a maximum amount of NLG 9 300. As T had worked in two countries, the then valid legislation required the issue of two tax assessments for 1990, with the limit for the calculation of social insurance contributions applying separately in each case. In this way, he was required to pay social insurance contributions of NLG 9 300 solely for the period of employment abroad and an additional NLG 1 400 for the period of employment at home. T felt that his right to freedom of movement was violated by the assessment modalities. The Netherlands authorities argued that T could not invoke Community law as he lived in his home State, and was subject to social insurance and taxation there. Moreover, the assessment provisions applied equally to all persons socially insured in the Netherlands. Apart from that, social security law came under the power of the Member States, meaning they could therefore also regulate the procedure for levying social contributions.

1. Discrimination

a) Overt discrimination is directly linked to nationality. It represents the strongest form of interference and is therefore held to be permissible only if supported by written grounds of justification.[122] The prohibition of discrimination is expressly laid down in Article 39(2) of the TEC (Article III-133(2) DC) and is otherwise set out in secondary Community legislation. Meanwhile, occurrences of overt discrimination are relatively rare because the Member States have largely eliminated nationality-related elements of unequal treatment from their legal systems. In view of the immense diversity of relevant provisions, alone in the sphere of taxation and social law, and long periods of national sovereignty backed by laws concerning foreign nationals, it is perhaps understandable that this process has taken quite some time and that individual instances of formal discrimination persist until this day. But, on the other hand, given the level of European integration and the many efforts towards creating an internal market, not only for goods but also for persons, such discrimination is nonetheless unacceptable. That overt forms of discrimination are still encountered at all is attributable to various reasons. In part, the applicability of Community law provisions to certain legal positions had not been sufficiently clarified in the past,[123] or certain activities were considered to be especially delicate.[124] In part, there continue to exist forms of discrimination which only at second glance are recognisable as such and obviously seek to protect persons active in peripheral areas. Thus one of the last judgments (in proceedings concerning a Treaty infringement) taken by the ECJ on a matter of overt discrimination within the scope of Article 39 of the TEC (Article III-133 DC) concerned a national provision that required dentists wishing to practise their profession to register with the competent dental association, which in turn required that they reside in the district of that association.[125] In the event of a transfer of residence to another Mem-

37

---

122 *Cf* paras 49 ff and → § 7 paras 22, 79.
123 Thus, *eg*, as regards the applicability of the coordination rules to German child-raising allowance; *cf* ECJ *Hoever and Zachow* [1996] ECR I-4895. Similarly, on the refusal of study finance for studies abroad, *cf* ECJ *Di Leo* [1990] ECR I-4185.
124 *Eg*, regarding private security services, *cf* ECJ *Commission v Spain* [1998] ECR I-6717; regarding employment in shipping, ECJ *Commission v Belgium* [1993] ECR I-6295; regarding eligibility for election in professional associations, ECJ *ASTI* [1991] ECR I-3507.
125 Which already constitutes an infringement of freedom of movement for workers and freedom of establishment; *cf* below.

ber State, only the State's own nationals were entitled to retain membership of the association.[126] In the end, it was of little avail to the defendants to plead that the legal situation had meanwhile become so unclear as to render the discriminatory provisions inapplicable in practice.[127]

38   b) Much more widespread than overt discrimination are the instances of **covert discrimination** encountered in the law of professional rules and regulations, as well as in labour and social law, as these are customarily characterised by a territorial bias. In its rulings on freedom of movement for workers, the ECJ established quite early on that a legal provision which, if not formally but in fact, "essentially" or by a "great majority" affects or is "intrinsically liable" to affect foreign nationals constitutes a form of discrimination and, in the final result, favours a State's own nationals.[128] However, the Court has thereby neglected to state more precisely[129] or to differentiate with recognisable finality the exact measure for determining differing degrees of affectedness.[130] Covert discrimination, given that it is not linked directly to nationality, can have objective grounds and therefore be justified not only by written but also by unwritten restrictions[131] (paras 41 ff).

39   Within the scope of freedom of movement for workers, indirect forms of discrimination mostly rest on rules that require evidence of specific occupational qualifications[132], language skills[133] or residence in the national territory[134]. Such requirements are compatible with Community law only if they serve legal interests that objectively merit protection (paras 49 ff) and if they are proportional (paras 52 ff). But also other forms of unequal treatment can predominantly affect non-national workers.[135] Prohibited, for instance, are generally imposed levies which (only) for migrant workers remain without a benefit in return.[136] A further, repeatedly adjudicated example concerns the imposition of temporal limits on employment contracts with foreign-language assistants in cases where there is generally no such limit on the contracts with other university staff.[137] Exceptional treat-

---

126 ECJ *Commission v Italy* [2001] ECR I-541; *cf* also ECJ *Commission v Austria* [2004] ECR I-8291.
127 Because the obligation of Member States to observe Community law requires the establishment of a clear legal position.
128 ECJ *Sotgiu* [1974] ECR 153, paras 11 ff; *Kenny* [1978] ECR 1489, paras 16 ff.
129 On the above-cited circumscriptions, *cf* ECJ *Pinna* [1986] ECR 1, paras 24 ff; *Commission v United Kingdom* [1992] ECR I-5785, paras 42 ff; *O'Flynn* [1996] ECR I-2617, paras 20 ff.
130 In particular, the terms 'indirect', 'covert' ('hidden') or 'disguised' discrimination are used alongside each other and without any recognisable concept. Expediently, indirect discrimination ought to serve as the generic term, as the others require an additional finalising element. Whether this distinction should be of any significance to the review of the fundamental freedoms is another question – one that tends to be abnegated.
131 That is sufficiently explicit from the case-law, although it is not always quite clear which remarks refer to the assessment of the interference and which to the justification grounds; → § 7 para 79.
132 *Cf, eg*, ECJ *Fernández de Bobadilla* [1999] ECR I-4773, paras 28 ff; *MacQueen* [2001] ECR I-837, paras 23 ff.
133 Just *cf* ECJ *Groener* [1989] ECR 3967, paras 23 ff.
134 ECJ *Schöning* [1998] ECR I-47, paras 21 ff; *Clean Car* [1998] ECR I-2521, paras 30 ff.
135 *Cf, eg*, on the non-recognition of previous periods of employment abroad, paras 19 ff; on obstacles to recognition, ECJ *ÖGB* [2000] ECR I-10497.
136 *Cf* ECJ *Sehrer* [2000] ECR I-4585; *Commission v France* [2000] ECR I-1049. The ECJ nevertheless invokes the prohibition of limitation without closer examination. With reference to tax treatment, *cf* also ECJ *Merida* [2004] ECR I-8471, paras 23 ff.
137 ECJ *Allué I* [1989] ECR 1591; *Allué II* [1993] ECR I-4309. Also other instances of placing

ment of this kind usually has no grounds of justification. The ECJ moreover deems the requirement of residence with regard to social advantages (paras 19 ff) a form of indirect discrimination;[138] in cases where the function of the advantage produces no objective ground for a territorial limitation, this approach compels an export of benefits.[139]

According to the case-law of the ECJ, a violation of the prohibition of discrimination makes it necessary to apply the regulations which are valid for national beneficiaries in favour of the disadvantaged migrant workers. An ascertainment of unequal treatment can therefore result directly in the granting of advantages.[140] **40**

2. Limitations

a) Whether freedom of movement for workers, like the free movement of goods, embodies a prohibition of limitation to the effect that all obstacles to it, irrespective of any given discrimination, are to be viewed as interference with this freedom, was questioned for a long time and is still sometimes contested today. That is essentially attributed to two reasons – first of all, to the general difficulty of distinguishing indirect discrimination from limitations.[141] Nevertheless, the two forms of interference are characterised, at least in theory, by a crucial difference that permits their categorical distinction: limitations explicitly do not involve any comparison with the treatment of other persons. A second argument, related specifically to Article 39 of the TEC (Article III-133 DC), is that its provisions enumerate the protected rights, so that for this reason alone a general prohibition of limitation is not needed. On the other hand, paragraphs 2 and 3 have a substantiating function, and the general freedom of movement for workers is comprehensively guaranteed in paragraph 1 (paras 19 ff). **41**

At the latest since the famous *Bosman* judgment, the position of the ECJ has become clear: the Court, on the basis of general considerations, interprets Article 39 of the TEC (Article III-133 DC) as a prohibition of limitation. This is expressed by the formulation "that the provisions of the Treaty relating to freedom of movement for persons are intended to facilitate the pursuit by Community citizens of occupational activities of all kinds throughout the Community, and preclude measures which **might place** Community citizens **at a disadvantage** when they wish to pursue an economic activity in the territory of another Member State."[142] **42**

b) As with other prohibitions of limitation, the remaining problem in view of the diversity of possible forms of interference is to attempt some form of circumscription above the justification level. Especially when considering that also indirect and potentially **43**

---

foreign-language assistants in an inferior position under labour law are indirectly discriminatory; cf ECJ *Commission v Italy* [2001] ECR I-4923; on the Europe Agreements, cf paras 30 ff.
138 ECJ *Meints* [1997] ECR I-6689, paras 43 ff; also cf ECJ *Barth* [2004] ECR I-6483.
139 In this context, cf regarding funeral allowance ECJ *O'Flynn* [1996] ECR I-2617.
140 Cf ECJ *Schöning* [1998] ECR I-47, paras 33 ff; *Terhoeve* [1999] ECR I-345, paras 57 ff; → § 7 para 29.
141 The ECJ itself – in accordance with its general style of justification – does not distinguish explicitly here; instead, it often reverts to its own approaches in elaborating a prohibition of limitation, notably in cases of indirect discrimination; just cf ECJ *Sehrer* [2000] ECR I-4585, paras 32, 34 (see also above note 136).
142 ECJ *Bosman* [1995] ECR I-4921, paras 94 ff; prior to that *Kraus* [1993] ECR I-1663, paras 32 ff; more recently *Burbaud* [2003] ECR I-8219, paras 95 ff.

effective measures can have interference character, it seems questionable whether every obstacle of an only remotely indirect effect ought to prompt an examination of proportionality.[143] Here, a possible approach to differentiation could be not to demand a substantial effect, but to apply the so-called *Keck* case[144] to freedom of movement for workers. In doing so, however, it would scarcely seem conducive to make a formal distinction between rules governing admission to an occupation and those regulating its exercise. Rather, the decisive point in terms of the *Keck* judgment[145] must be whether the measure in question relates to the cross-border taking up and pursuit of an activity as an employed person, *ie* involves **access to employment**. Although the ECJ has not yet ventured to make a clear distinction, it recently emphasised in this sense that limitations will be prohibited, failing justification, if they "preclude or deter a national of a Member State from leaving his country of origin in order to exercise his right to freedom of movement".[146] Moreover, the Court held – here again in parallel to the free movement of goods – that very "uncertain and indirect" obstacles to the free movement of workers lack interference character.[147] The matter in controversy was a claim to compensation on termination of employment (= severance payment) which employees were not entitled to if they themselves had given notice. Not only the Court's findings but also its justifications based on access to employment are to be endorsed in this context, even if a clear criterion of distinction would be needed to warrant legal certainty.[148]

Case 3 – Answer:

44 That T is a worker is beyond question. The applicability of Article 39 of the TEC (Article III-133 DC) is questionable only under the aspect of cross-border elements. These are satisfied by the fact that T transferred his residence to another Member State, whereas it is not necessary that the interference with T's rights had to occur through a State other than the State of origin; nor does T's current residence play any role. According to the case-law of the ECJ, Article 39 of the TEC (Article III-133 DC) is intended to "facilitate the pursuit by Community citizens of occupational activities of all kinds throughout the Community" and therefore opposes measures "which might place Community nationals at a disadvantage when they wish to pursue an economic activity in the territory of another Member State." It also comprises the right to leave the country of origin to enter the territory of another Member State and to reside there in order to pursue an economic activity. The ECJ declares: "Provisions which preclude or deter a national of a Member State from leaving his country of origin in order to exercise his right to freedom of movement therefore constitute an obstacle to that freedom even if they apply without regard to the nationality of the workers concerned". Accordingly, the point is not whether the levying of social insurance contributions occurs in an overtly or covertly discriminatory manner. Nor is it relevant that the

---

143 The problem is well known from the fundamental rights doctrine; just *cf* Pieroth/Schlink *Grundrechte* (21th ed, Heidelberg 2005) paras 238 ff.
144 ECJ *Keck* [1993] ECR I-6097.
145 More detailed Becker [1994] EuR 162; Weatherill [1996] CMLR 885; *cf* also Craig/de Búrca (note 48) p 718.
146 ECJ *Graf* [2000] ECR I-493, paras 23 ff; in that context (relating to the loss of social security advantages), quite early on *Masgio* [1991] ECR I-1119, paras 18 ff.
147 ECJ *Graf* [2000] ECR I-493, paras 25 ff.
148 In the relevant literature, criticism tends to predominate, which is justified insofar as clear distinctions cannot be made using simple formulas; just *cf* Randelzhofer/Forsthoff (note 48) vor Art 39–55 EGV, paras 112 ff.

underlying provisions relate to a matter whose regulation comes under the competence of the Member States, given that the distribution of competence does not restrict the scope of applicability of Article 39 of the TEC (Article III-133 DC). Rather, the decisive fact resulting in an obstacle to T's free movement is that merely because of his employment in another Member State, T must pay higher social insurance contributions than if he had remained in the same Member State for the entire year, meaning that his higher contributions are not counter-balanced by higher benefits. Moreover, such treatment cannot be justified by referring to administrative practicability. T is subject to the same provisions as those applying to all other persons who are socially insured in the national territory throughout the course of a year (in that respect, an infringement of equal treatment was found; *cf* para 40).

3. Addressees

Who are the addressees of the fundamental freedoms – that is, who is bound by them? This question is one that belongs to the general fundamental freedoms doctrine. Appropriately, it can only be solved uniformly for all fundamental freedoms because the problem it poses affects the interpretation of all liberty rights. It follows that the answer essentially depends on the function of these rights and their impact on the configuration of legal relations between private persons. In so far, recourse can be taken to the general explanations (→ § 7 paras 42 ff).

Nevertheless, because important judgments of the ECJ on the horizontal effects of fundamental freedoms have been delivered with a particular view to Article 39 of the TEC (Article III-133 DC),[149] this case-law should be recalled, if only briefly, here. Proceeding from its judgment in the *Walrave* case, the Court has on several occasions stressed that also interference in the form of rules aimed at "collectively regulating gainful employment and services" can be prohibited by virtue of Article 39 of the TEC (Article III-133 DC).[150] While that ruling might still be explained by the concession of regulatory power to associations and comparable institutions in the framing of employment conditions, the ECJ clearly went beyond this approach in the *Angonese* case. An Italian national, because he had completed his degree in Austria, had been unable to produce a certificate of bilingualism which was required by a private bank and was issued only in the province of Bolzano. With reference to the general formulation of Article 39 of the TEC (Article III-133 DC), the Court elucidated the importance of this fundamental freedom and its potential obstruction by private parties. Thus it held that the prohibition of discrimination on grounds of nationality enshrined in Article 39 of the TEC (Article III-133 DC) also applied to private persons.[151] Conversely, private persons can likewise invoke the recognised justifications to oppose any contractual forms of interference with this right.[152]

---

149 Although the relevance of Art 39 TEC (Art III-133 DC) does not follow from an ostensibly greater scope of freedom vis-à-vis the free movement of goods. Such distinctions according to scopes of freedom make little sense. Of essential import, however, are the particular life circumstances covered by the rule. Working conditions are primarily defined by collective agreements, and it is no coincidence that labour relations play a special role in discussions about the horizontal effects of fundamental rights – in Germany as in other countries (*eg* Italy).
150 ECJ *Walrave* [1974] ECR 1405, paras 16 ff; *Bosman* [1995] ECR I-4921, paras 84 ff.
151 ECJ *Angonese* [2000] ECR I-4139, paras 30–31, 36–37. Whether the ECJ wanted to limit the horizontal effect to the prohibition of discrimination remains questionable.
152 ECJ *Clean Car* [1998] ECR I-2521, paras 24 ff.

III. Justification

1. Written Restrictions

47 The rights enshrined in Article 39(3) of the TEC (Article III-133(3) DC) can be restricted on "grounds of public policy, public security or public health". The positioning of these grounds in the Treaty seems to imply that they do not extend to the prohibition of discrimination laid down in Article 39(2) of the TEC (Article III-133(2) DC),[153] especially when considering that the consistent practice of the ECJ calls for a narrow interpretation of exemption provisions.[154] Nevertheless, the better arguments lead to the opposite result.[155] Freedom of movement is a uniform fundamental freedom (paras 19 ff) that is not amenable to differing justification options, depending on how they are formulated. Furthermore, the grounds cited expressly in Article 39(3) of the TEC (Article III-133(3) DC) are applicable to all fundamental freedoms and, according to the general doctrine, do not distinguish between limitation and discrimination in this respect. Accordingly, grounds of public policy, security and health can justify all forms of interference with these rights.[156] In practice, however, they above all come to bear in cases involving a termination of residence, notably expulsion and deportation.

48 Once again, the grounds of justification must be interpreted strictly. They involve autonomous concepts which, owing to their reference to national interests, concede a certain margin of assessment to Member States in filling them out. Recourse to the concept of public policy thus requires "a genuine and sufficiently serious threat ... affecting one of the fundamental interests of society".[157] Any reference to external or internal security must therefore seek to protect the Member State and/or, as far as is necessary, its institutions and important public services.[158] Within the scope of applicability of the freedom of movement, Directive 2004/38 (note 5)[159] contains important specifications in this regard[160] which, depending on the interpretation of primary Community law, can also be viewed as general limits to restrictability. Thus Article 27(1) of the Directive[161] stipulates that the reservation of public policy must not be "invoked to serve economic ends", and Article 27(2)[162] requires that recourse to the public order and public security be based on the "personal conduct" of the individual concerned.[163] Diseases having the potential to pose a threat to public health are listed in detail[164] in Article 29 of the Directive[165].

---

153 *Cf* Burrows (note 54) pp 141 ff.
154 Just *cf* ECJ *Calfa* [1999] ECR I-11, paras 21 ff.
155 See also Burrows (note 54) p 143.
156 More strictly so because overt forms of discrimination are not considered justifiable: Schneider/Wunderlich (note 95) Art 39 EGV, para 120–121.
157 ECJ *Bouchereau* [1977] ECR 1999, paras 33, 35; *Adoui* [1982] ECR 1665, paras 8 ff; *Olazabal* [2002] ECR I-10981.
158 Just *cf* ECJ *Campus Oil* [1984] ECR 2727, paras 35 ff; *Richardt* [1991] ECR I-4621, paras 22 ff.
159 Or, until 30-04-2006, Dir 64/221 (note 11).
160 On the procedural minimum requirements, *cf* paras 19 ff.
161 Or, until 30-04-2006, Art 2(2) Dir 64/221 (note 11).
162 Or, until 30-04-2006, Art 3(1) Dir 64/221 (note 11).
163 On the direct applicability of the latter provision, just *cf* ECJ *Van Duyn* [1974] ECR 1337, paras 13 ff (there, the ECJ commented on Dir 64/221, which nevertheless contains the same provisions (note 11)). According to the Court, criminal convictions do not suffice for a termination of residence.
164 Albeit, partly in reference to other, alterable rules.
165 Or, until 30-04-2006, in the appendix to Dir 64/221 (note 11).

2. Unwritten Restrictions

Case 4 – Problem: (ECJ *Lehtonen* [2000] ECR I-2681)
The Finnish professional basketball player L, who had played in the Finnish championship, was engaged by a Belgian club early in April, after the championship was over, in order to reinforce the team in the final stage of the Belgian championship. This engagement was only for the championship playoffs (*ie* the matches to determine the champion among the teams with the highest scores after the first phase of league games) and had been contracted after the deadline (28 February) set by the national Belgian basketball federation for transfers of players within the European zone. The deadline for players from outside the zone is somewhat later (31 March). For this reason, L's fielding was penalised by a deduction of points, and the federation threatened to impose additional penalties if L were to take part in further matches. Both the club and L considered the penalisation incompatible with the freedom of movement for workers, which also applies to sports. The federation countered that transfers within Belgium are subject to even stricter transfer regulations, which is factually correct. It added that not the employment with the club but only the fielding of belatedly engaged players is prohibited. If deadline regulations, which are also set by the international basketball association, were dispensed with, competition in sports could be improperly distorted.

Given that Article 39 of the TEC (Article III-133 DC), as well as other fundamental freedoms, can afford protection against limitations and indirect forms of discrimination – the threshold for such interference thus being relatively low – the large number of potentially affected legal interests makes it necessary to elaborate on the grounds of justification. Hence, justification is possible (only) on **imperative grounds** of general interest.[166] This applies at least to limitations[167] as well as to covert forms of discrimination[168], but not, according to the majority view, to the overt forms.[169]

Although the descriptor "imperative" (or "mandatory") would suggest otherwise, the range of legal interests meriting protection is broad indeed. Case-law examples refer to protection against the misuse of academic titles[170] or the protection of sporting activities, in particular competition sports – including competition among nations, which leads to the special protection of national teams.[171] More general objects of legal of protection include the maintenance of public institutions in the broad sense, *eg* well-functioning tax law or social benefit systems,[172] of collective bargaining schemes or of universities.[173] Such protection also extends to workers and consumers and, apparantly, in general to the pro-

---

166 → § 7 para 89; the positioning in legal doctrine is completely uncontested for freedom of movement for workers.
167 Just *cf* ECJ *Bosman* [1995] ECR I-4921.
168 Just *cf* ECJ *O'Flynn* [1996] ECR I-2617.
169 See para 37. That no doubt still conforms to the established court practice, even if breaks are ascertainable (the *Bosman* case, for instance, was concerned with special clauses applicable to non-nationals) and some points speak in favour of the opposite view; *cf* Becker (note 91) Art 30 EGV, paras 43–44.
170 ECJ *Kraus* [1993] ECR I-1663.
171 ECJ *Bosman* [1995] ECR I-4921.
172 *Cf, eg*, ECJ *Bachmann* [1992] ECR I-249.
173 ECJ *Allué II* [1993] ECR I-4309.

per exercise of occupational activity.[174] By contrast, the invoking of purely economic grounds, practical difficulties[175] or administrative simplifications[176] is fundamentally precluded. A further listing of examples can be dispensed with as all possible justifications cannot be cited conclusively. Moreover, imperative general interests constitute justifications which are pertinent to all fundamental freedoms and are thus defined according to general and comprehensive criteria.[177]

3. General Limits to Restrictability

52 The invoking of specific legal interests as grounds of justification is ruled out if the protection of these interests is already conclusively regulated under Community law (a). As for all remaining cases – these are no doubt still the majority – any interference must be proportional (b).

53 a) Apart from the substantiation of written restrictions under secondary Community law (para 47), the most important restrictions on Member State provisions governing the protection of legal interests are encountered in the recognition of occupational qualifications. Here we find profession-related **harmonisation rules** (sectoral Directives)[178] as well as horizontal rules on the recognition of diplomas and other qualifications.[179] These rules also refer to activities of employed persons and are based, inter alia, on Article 40 of the TEC (Article III-134 DC), but by no means cover all occupations.

54 b) Interference is deemed **proportional** only if it is appropriate, necessary and reasonable; in this respect, Article 39 of the TEC (Article III-133 DC) is not subject to any particularities (→ § 7 para 96). As for the density of control, it should generally be noted that some matters – such as direct taxation or social security – chiefly remain under the regulatory competence of the Member States, who are responsible for determining the level of protection.[180] This does not entail exemptions from scope but should permit Member States to maintain plausible limitations in order to avoid any risks for existing national institutions.

---

174 The ECJ obviously takes a liberal stance here, at least on the merits, for instance when it refrains from further defining the protected legal interest in the case of demands for certain qualifications. This may, however, be attributable to the fact that in the adjudicated cases, the interference was mostly disproportional anyway; just *cf* ECJ *Angonese* [2000] ECR I-4139.
175 *Cf* ECJ *Commission v Greece* [1998] ECR I-1095.
176 Though left open, this evidently also refers to the facilitation of tax levying in ECJ *Zurstrassen* [2000] ECR I-3337, paras 25 ff.
177 Regarding freedom of movement for persons, just *cf* ECJ *Ramrath* [1992] ECR I-3351; *Gebhard* [1995] ECR I-4165.
178 Applying to physicians, pharmacists, architects and lawyers; these sectoral Directives are to be repealed with effect from 20-10-2007 and consolidated in Dir 2005/36, [2005] OJ L255/22, on the Recognition of Professional Qualifications.
179 Dir 89/48, [1989] OJ L19/16 (general system for the recognition of higher-education diplomas); Dir 92/51, [1992] OJ L209/25 (second general system for the recognition of professional education and training); Dir 99/42, [1999] OJ L201/77 (recognition of qualifications); these individual Directives are to be repealed with effect from 20-10-2007 and consolidated in Dir 2005/36, [2005] OJ L255/22, on the Recognition of Professional Qualifications.
180 That applies in general, meaning differing levels of requirement in the Member States are not disproportional *per se*; *cf* ECJ *Zenatti* [1999] ECR I-7289, paras 34 ff.

Justifications of indirect discrimination (para 38) are often thwarted by the requirement of proportionality, for instance where language skills acquired abroad[181] or professional qualifications not covered by harmonisation[182] fail to be adequately taken into account. Nor are residence requirements, as a rule, in effect necessary.[183] Even where protection as such is deemed proportional, it must not be enforced by means of disproportional penalties.[184] Especially legal measures imposed on non-nationals, such as expulsion and deportation, must be in suitable proportion to the offences committed.[185]

Case 4 – Answer:
In the case of L, the ECJ had to adjudicate in a preliminary ruling. The judgment is already worth reading because it reconstructs the assessment of Article 39 of the TEC (Article III-133 DC) in an exemplary manner and thereby addresses recurrent standard problems.
(1) As regards scope of protection, it should be reiterated that exemptions from scope do not exist in the field of sports. The sole decisive criterion is that L pursues an economic activity and that said activity is "effective and genuine and not as such to be regarded as purely marginal and ancillary". This is not questioned in the case of professional sportsmen. L was moreover engaged in an employment relationship, thus performing services under the direction of another person in return for remuneration. Freedom of movement guarantees not only the conclusion of the employment contract but also the exercise of the activity; even if the prohibition in question is directed only at the clubs, it in fact affects the employment possibilities of its players. Hence, the objection that only the fielding of players is prohibited runs dry.
(2) Addressees of Article 39 of the TEC (Article III-133 DC) are not merely the Member States but also the associations that regulate professional activities through collective agreements; further comments on horizontal effects are unnecessary. As for the given interference, an instance of overt discrimination related to nationality is not on hand. Covert discrimination can likewise be ruled out in view of the preferential treatment of transfers from other States. Article 39 of the TEC (Article III-133 DC) nonetheless also prohibits unjustified limitations of freedom of movement. Here, the ECJ declares: "Those rules are nevertheless liable to restrict the freedom of movement of players who wish to pursue their activity in another Member State, by preventing Belgian clubs from fielding in championship matches basketball players from other Member States where they have been engaged after a specified date. Those rules consequently constitute an obstacle to freedom of movement for workers."
(3) Thus the question of justification remains to be examined. It can be based on both the written and the unwritten restrictions imposed by Article 39 of the TEC (Article III-133 DC). An impairment of the legal interests expressly protected therein is not evident. Even so, imperative grounds of general interests meriting protection also include "ensuring the regularity of sporting competitions". Any interference that seeks to do so must, however, be proportional. Since late transfers can distort the course of a championship and obstruct the comparability of prior results, they are suitable for creating equal conditions. Whether the

---

181 *Cf* ECJ *Groener* [1989] ECR 3967, paras 23–24; *Angonese* [2000] ECR I-4139, paras 44 ff.
182 *Cf* ECJ *Fernández de Bobadilla* [1999] ECR I-4773, paras 29 ff. For more details on inter-comparison in respect of Art 43 TEC, ECJ *Vlassopoulou* [1991] ECR I-2357.
183 Regarding, *eg*, security firms, *cf* with a view to the screening of staff, ECJ *Commission v Belgium* [2000] ECR I-1221, paras 32–33. The imposition of residence requirements on managers is partly inappropriate, partly unnecessary, *Clean Car* [1998] ECR I-2521, paras 34 ff.
184 *Cf, eg,* ECJ *Wijsenbeek* [1999] ECR I-6207, paras 44 ff.
185 Hence, a case-by-case examination is needed, and is also required under Dir 64/221 (note 11); *cf* ECJ *Calfa* [1999] ECR I-11. A disregard of formalities must not entail any severe consequences.

given transfer regulations are necessary remains doubtful nonetheless. This assessment essentially depends on the chosen point in time and its meaning for the further course of the championship. In the given case, the deadline of 28 February applied only to players from the European zone, while that of March 31 applied to players from certain non-member countries. Such differentiation suggests a disproportional limitation with respect to the European zone, unless the national court is able to find objective reasons (*ie* a threat to sporting competition) for the setting of different deadlines.

§ 10
Freedom of Establishment

Christian Tietje

Case law: ECJ *Vlassopoulou* [1991] ECR I-2357; *Factortame* [1991] I-3956; *Gebhard* [1995] ECR I-4165; *VT4* [1997] ECR I-3143; *Commission v Spain* [1998] ECR I-6717; *Centros* [1999] ECR I-1459; *Pfeiffer* [1999] ECR I-2835; *Meeusen* [1999] ECR I-3289; *Calfa* [1999] ECR I-11; *Inspire Art* [2003] I-10155; *Hughes de Lasteyrie du Saillant* [2004] I-2409.

Further reading: Craig/de Burca *EU Law, Text, Cases and Materials* (3rd ed, Oxford 2003) pp 772–799; Fairhurst/Vincenzi *Law of the European Community* (4th ed, Harlow 2003) pp 273–303; Kapteyn/Verlooren van Themaat *Introduction to the Law of the European Communities* (3rd ed, London/The Hague/Boston 1998) pp 730–747; Kingreen *Die Struktur der Grundfreiheiten des Europäischen Gemeinschaftsrechts* (Berlin 1999); Lackhoff *Die Niederlassungsfreiheit des EGV – nur ein Gleichheits- oder auch ein Freiheitsrecht?* (Berlin 2000); Lasok/Lasok *Law & Institutions of the European Union* (7th ed, London 2001), pp 515–530; Leible/Hoffmann *"Überseering" und das (vermeintliche) Ende der Sitztheorie* [2002] RIW 925; Lenaerts/van Nuffel *Constitutional Law of the European Union* (2nd ed, London 2005) pp 188–203; Mathijsen *A Guide to European Union Law* (8th ed, London 2004) pp 202–214; Mülbert/Schmolke *Die Reichweite der Niederlassungsfreiheit von Gesellschaften – Anwendungsgrenzen der Artt 43 ff. EGV bei kollisions- und sachrechtlichen Niederlassungshindernissen* (2001) 100 ZVglRWiss 233; Nachbaur *Niederlassungsfreiheit: Geltungsbereich und Reichweite des Art 52 EGV im Binnenmarkt* (Baden-Baden 1999); Pasternacki *Zur Abgrenzung von Niederlassungsfreiheit und Dienstleistungsfreiheit bei Niederlassungen mit Teilfunktion* (Frankfurt 2000); Schnichels *Reichweite der Niederlassungsfreiheit. Dargestellt am Beispiel des deutschen Internationalen Gesellschaftsrechts* (Baden-Baden 1995); Unzicker *Niederlassungsfreiheit der Kapitalgesellschaften in der Europäischen Union nach der Centros- und der Überseering-Entscheidung des EuGH* (Frankfurt 2004); von Halen *Das Gesellschaftsstatut nach der Centros-Entscheidung des EuGH: kollisionsrechtliche Tragweite, materiellrechtliche Folgen und gesellschaftsrechtliche Gestaltungsmöglichkeiten* (Heidelberg 2001).

I. Introduction

1. The Basic Structure and Problems of the Freedom of Establishment within the System of the Fundamental Freedoms

The common market[1] is a fundamental element of European integration and entails, according to Article 3(1)(c) of the TEC, "the abolition as between Member States, of obstacles to the free movement of goods, persons, services and capital". No mention is made of the freedom of establishment (*cf* also Article 14(2) DC). Provisions regarding the "freedom of establishment" can however be found in Part III, Title III of the TEC, which deals with fundamental freedoms. Hence the freedom of establishment, being part of the free movement of persons[2], is one of the fundamental freedoms of Community law. Thus, corresponding to the relevance of the fundamental freedoms within the legal order of the European Community as a whole, the European Court of Justice (ECJ) repeatedly pointed out that the freedom of establishment constitutes "a fundamental principle of the

1

---

1 On the notions "common market" and "single market" see Lenaerts/van Nuffel *Constitutional Law of the European Union* (2nd ed, London 2005) pp 139–140.
2 Kapteyn/Verlooren van Themaat *Introduction to the Law of the European Communities* (3rd ed, London/The Hague/Boston 1998), p 730; von Bogdandy in: Grabitz/Hilf (eds) *Das Recht der Europäischen Union* (loose-leaf, Munich) Art 14 EGV, para 9.

Treaty".[3] Seen against this background, the neglect to mention the freedom of establishment in Article 3(1)(c) of the TEC is of no mentionable consequence. This has now also become evident in Article I-4(1) of the Draft Constitution (DC), which explicitly refers to the freedom of establishment as one of the fundamental freedoms.

2   The reasoning behind the freedom of establishment as guaranteed by Article 43 of the TEC (Article III-137 DC) becomes evident from the role played by this guarantee in the integrational concept behind the TEC. Enabling European Union citizens (Article 17 TEC[4]/Article I-10 I DC) to make economically rational decisions largely free from government control is a central aim of the common market (Article 2(f) TEC) and the internal market (Article 14 TEC/Article III-130 II DC).[5] In the transnational sphere, encompassing the common market and the internal market (Article 299 TEC/Article IV-440 DC), this aim can only be realised if the free movement of commercial factors is largely guaranteed. Thus, the question of where, territorially, factors of production such as labour, administration or capital should be located ought to be decided purely on economically rational grounds. Hence, economic entities should be allowed to only make economically relevant decisions based on the – in their opinion – most advantageous conditions of a location.[6] However, the fundamental freedoms in the sense of the internal market as defined by Article 14 of the TEC (Article III-130(2) DC) do not require the complete abolition of legal borders within the Community, *ie* between the Member States. For the time being, the internal market, which necessarily continues to be segmented on a legal level – with the exception of an harmonization of laws *eg* under Article 44 of the TEC (Article III-138 DC) and Article 95 of the TEC (Article III-172 DC) – seeks to guarantee only the free movement of goods, persons, services and capital.[7]

3   Initially, the realisation of the fundamental freedoms was effected only through the destination principle. This principle, which is expressed in the prohibition of discrimination (Article 12 TEC/Article I-4(2) DC; see in detail → § 7 note 19), ensures "only" that goods, persons etc are not discriminated against *vis-à-vis* comparable goods, persons etc in the country of destination; it is thus a national treatment guarantee not concerned with the legal provisions of the country of origin. This initial concept changed only with the development of the country of origin principle.[8] This principle states, in its current form as a prohibition against any obstacle to freely exercise the fundamental freedoms,[9] that goods, persons, services and capital, though having to satisfy the legal requirements of the country of destination in order to establish their marketability, need not comply with the specific national laws of the country of destination. Since the *Cassis* judgement of the ECJ[10] it has been widely recognised that Member State measures which, though being

---

3 ECJ *Reyners* [1974] ECR I-631, para 42; *Watson* [1976] ECR I-1185, para 16; *Kraus* [1993] ECR I-1663, para 29.
4 For the development and meaning of this concept see O'Leary *The Evolving Concept of Community Citizenship – From Free Movement of Persons to Union Citizenship* (The Hague 1996).
5 Lenaerts/van Nuffel (note 1) p 140; von Bogdandy (note 2) para 10; Lackhoff *Die Niederlassungsfreiheit des EGV – nur ein Gleichheits- oder auch ein Freiheitsrecht?* (Berlin 2000) p 28.
6 Müller-Graff in: Grundmann/Kerber/Weatherill (eds) *Party Autonomy and the Role of Information in the Internal Market* (Berlin/New York 2001) pp 133–134; Lackhoff (note 5) p 28.
7 Mülbert/Schmolke (2001) 100 ZVglRWiss 233, 238.
8 For details see Kapteyn/Verlooren van Themaat (note 2) p 580.
9 → § 7 para 24.
10 ECJ *Cassis de Dijon* [1979] ECR 649.

indistinctly applicable, nonetheless restrict the free movement of goods, persons, services and capital, must be justified. From this it follows that the nature etc of such foreign economic factors must be recognised. Thus, there exists a rebuttable presumption in favour of marketability if the relevant legal requirements of the country of origin have been met.[11] This mechanism, which, as previously highlighted, results from the so-called prohibition of restriction or limitation doctrine, was a significant factor in the development of the country of destination principle in the common market.

Based on these general, liberal and thus welfare-enhancing realisations and consequences of the ratio behind the fundamental freedoms (which follow the theory of comparative advantages[12]) as a whole, the objective of the freedom of establishment can be determined in the next step. Firstly, the freedom of establishment serves to generally enable natural and legal persons to set up a foreign branch in any Member State without discrimination *vis-à-vis* nationals. Analogously to the axiomatic ratio behind the fundamental freedoms, it aims to foster the optimal allocation of resources based on rational economic decisions. In contrast to the freedom to provide services, an individual may decide to merely provide incidental services or to partially or entirely move his commercial activities in the sense of setting up a foreign base.[13]

For historical reasons, the freedom of establishment initially relied solely on the country of destination principle, which determines that within the scope of the establishment a natural or legal person must not be discriminated against compared to domestic nationals.[14] Meanwhile, however, this exclusive reference to the country of destination principle has been put into perspective by the general development of the fundamental freedoms as prohibitions of any restriction or obstacle.[15] However, although the country of origin principle is growing increasingly important for the freedom of establishment, it is not without its difficulties. The problem with the freedom of establishment as compared to the other freedoms is namely that the creation of an establishment is inextricably linked to numerous fiscal and company law etc provisions of the country of destination. The creation of an establishment is not merely an exclusively economic act, but usually also a complex legal event, since it necessarily entails partial or total integration in the legal system of the host state. Against this background, the indiscriminate adoption of the doctrine on prohibitions against any limitation of the fundamental freedoms faces the problem that it would entail a radical liberalisation of those Member State regulations pertaining to establishment. That the freedom of establishment in Article 43 of the TEC (Article III-137 DC) cannot and does not have such far-reaching effects is without doubt.[16] A far greater problem to legal theory and practice, however, is the question of where to draw the line between the country of origin and the country of destination principle, and how to classify this distinction dogmatically. The fundamental legal difficulties that arise when interpreting and applying Article 43 and Article 44 of the TEC (Article III-137 DC) can be attributed to this basic problem.

---

11 On the concept of mutual acceptance or recognition see Kapteyn/Verlooren van Themaat (note 2) pp 579–580.
12 On the theory of comparative advantages see *eg* Kenen *The International Economy* (4th ed, Cambridge 2000) pp 19–20.
13 Lackhoff (note 5) p 29.
14 On this historical concept see Lackhoff (note 5) p 214.
15 For details see below (para 51).
16 Mülbert/Schmolke [2001] 100 ZVglRWiss 233, 238–239.

2. The Interplay between the Freedom of Establishment under Community Law and Public International Law

6 Prior to taking a closer look at the dogmatic structure of the freedom of establishment under Community law, it is necessary to consider its interplay with the relevant provisions of public international law. In Europe the freedom of establishment has long been the subject of miscellaneous international regulations. Initially, this took the form of numerous bilateral treaties. However, their scope never reached that of Article 43 of the TEC (Article III-137 DC), since these treaties were routinely subject to reservations concerning national treatment, and were based on the principle of reciprocity.[17] Even the European Convention on Establishment of 13 December 1955[18], which was adopted in the Council of Europe, contains several exceptions which significantly reduce the effectiveness of its legal guarantees.[19]

7 The Association Agreement between the EC and Turkey[20] and the decisions taken under it by the Association Council have created a unique legal regime. The Agreement, its Protocols and the decisions taken by the Association Council are an "integral part of Community law",[21] but they do not necessarily enable Turkish nationals to directly rely upon the relevant legal provisions. The necessary direct applicability of the Association Agreement, which amongst others contains provisions regarding the freedom of establishment (Article 13), has been rejected by the ECJ.[22] The Court did, however, affirm the direct applicability of Article 41(1) of the Protocol to the Agreement, which prohibits the introduction of new restrictions to the freedom of establishment and the freedom to provide services.[23] According to this case law of the ECJ, a Turkish national who is legally exercising the freedom of establishment in a Member State may have a right of residence.[24] To date, the Association Council has not yet passed any additional resolutions to substantiate the freedom of establishment in the Association Agreement. So far it is only agreed that negotiations on the progressing liberalisation of the services sector will be entered into.[25]

8 In addition to the territorial scope of the EC Treaty, the provisions regarding the freedom of establishment also appear in the so-called Europe Agreements with central and eastern European countries. They all include, amongst others, a prohibition on the discriminatory restriction of the freedom of establishment, which is directly applicable.[26] The

---

17 For details see Troberg in: von der Groeben/Schwarze (eds) *Vertrag über die Europäische Union und Vertrag zur Gründung der Europäischen Gemeinschaft* (6th ed, Baden-Baden 2004) Vor Art 52 EGV, para 13.
18 CETS No 19.
19 For details see Council of Europe (ed) *Commentary on the European Convention on Establishment* (Strasbourg 1955).
20 [1964] OJ 217/3685; → § 9 para 32.
21 *Eg* ECJ *Demirel* [1987] ECR 3719; *Sevince* [1990] ECR I-3461, para 9.
22 ECJ *Demirel* [1987] ECR 3719.
23 ECJ *Savas* [2000] ECR I-2927, para 46.
24 For details see Randelzhofer/Forsthoff in: Grabitz/Hilf (eds) Das Recht der Europäischen Union (loose-leaf, Munich) Vor Art 39-55 EGV, para 33; Eeckhout *External Relations of the European Union – Legal and Constitutional Foundations* (Oxford 2004) pp 288–289.
25 Randelzhofer/Forsthoff (note 24) Vor Art 39–55 EGV, para 35.
26 ECJ *Gloszczuk* [2001] ECR I-6369, para 30; *Barkoci and Malik* [2001] ECR I-6557; *Jany* [2001] ECR I-8615, para 26.

corresponding provisions, which also establish rights of entry and residence,[27] remain in place even after these countries have joined the EU – but only to the extent that the Treaty of Accession allows for derogations from the level of protection granted by the fundamental freedoms of the EC Treaty during a transition period.[28]

A further dimension of the right of establishment has resulted from the coming into force of the Agreement Establishing the World Trade Organisation and the General Agreement on Trade in Services (GATS) as an integral part of the WTO Agreement. The GATS aims to liberalise services *inter alia* with regard to "commercial presence" in a country (Article I:2(c) GATS). Article XXVIII(d) GATS defines this as "any type of business or professional establishment in another country for the purpose of supplying a service. This can be done through the creation of a new company or the purchase of an existing one, or the creation of a branch or representative office". The thus well-regulated freedom of establishment of the GATS,[29] however, applies only to those services sectors in which the WTO members have explicitly entered into liberalisation commitments (Articles XVI and XX GATS). In addition, there is a possibility of, amongst others, restricting or requiring special types of legal entity or limiting the participation of foreign capital (Article XVI:2(e) and (f) GATS). In numerous services sectors the EC and its Member States have submitted to extensive commitments to liberalise *inter alia* the law of establishment in the sense of Article XVI GATS, while at the same time adhering to exceptions in some areas.[30]

Thus, in a first, doubtlessly expandable step, the GATS has effected a liberalisation of the law of establishment which is virtually of universal effect. However, this obligation on the EC and its Member States under international law does not, according to ECJ jurisprudence, have direct applicability, which means that no natural or legal person may rely on it and that secondary Community law cannot be invalid because of a violation of the GATS.[31] But since, despite this jurisprudence, the EC and its Member States are comprehensively bound by the GATS under international law and there is an obligation to interpret Community law or national law in conformity with WTO law,[32] the GATS law of establishment must be observed when interpreting Articles 43 et seq. of the TEC (Article III-137 DC) where the establishment pertains to natural or legal persons from third countries.[33]

Overall, this shows that an increasing amalgamation of Community law and international law is also taking place in the field of the law of establishment.

---

27 Opinion AG Maduro, ECJ *Panayotova* [2004] ECR I-11055, para 24.
28 For details see Annex V *et seq* Act concerning the conditions of accession of the Czech Republic, the Republic of Estonia, the Republic of Cyprus, the Republic of Latvia, the Republic of Lithuania, the Republic of Hungary, the Republic of Malta, the Republic of Poland, the Republic of Slovenia and the Slovak Republic and the adjustments to the Treaties on which the European Union is founded – Final act, [2003] OJ L 236/803
29 See also *eg* Footer/George in: Macrory/Appleton/Plummer (eds) *The World Trade Organization: Legal, Economic and Political Analysis Vol I* (New York 2005) pp 799, 825.
30 The details can be found in the schedule of specific commitments of the EC and the Member States, WTO Doc GATS/SC/31.
31 ECJ *Portugal v Council* [1999] ECR I-8395, para 47; *Parfums Christian Dior* [2000] ECR I-11307; for a critical assessment see *eg* Bronckers [2005] CMLRev 1313, 1342–1343.
32 ECJ *Hermès* [1998] ECR I-3603, para 28; *Parfums Christian Dior* [2000] ECR I-11307.
33 See below (paras 61–62).

II. Scope of Protection

12 As is the case with all fundamental freedoms under Community law, also where Article 43(1) of the TEC (Article III-137(1) DC) is concerned one must always first examine whether the measure's scope of protection covers a particular set of facts (→ § 7 para 50). In doing so, a distinction can be drawn between the territorial and personal scope of protection and the subject matter of protection.

1. Territorial Scope of Protection

13 The territorial scope of protection of Article 43(1) of the TEC (Article III-137(1) DC) reflects the territorial scope of application of Community law as a whole (Article 299 TEC/Article IV-440 DC). In addition, the scope of protection of Article 43(1) of the TEC (Article III-137(1) DC) may extend to cases concerning an establishment outside of the EC if the laws on which it is based, or their effects, create sufficiently close ties with Community law within the meaning of Article 299 of the TEC (Article IV-440 DC).[34] However, in light of the distinctive characteristics of establishment under Article 43(1) of the TEC (Article III-137(1) DC), which distinguish it in particular from the free movement of workers and the freedom to provide services, and which is rooted in the close integration in the legal system of a third country, this possibility of expanding the territorial scope of protection can be little more than a theoretical construct.

14 By contrast, the expansion of the territorial scope of protection may be of greater significance where it concerns territories outside of Article 299 of the TEC (Article IV-440 DC) in which the Member States, or the EC itself, may exercise particular rights by virtue of certain provisions of international law. This applies in particular to the exclusive economic zone according to Article 55 of the UNCLOS,[35] which is of significant economic interest. It is particularly this economic dimension – which the fundamental freedoms in general, and thus also the freedom of establishment, seek to realise – which argues in favour of the recognition of the territorial applicability of the freedom of establishment to the exclusive economic zone of the Member States concerned.[36]

2. Personal Scope of Protection

15 The personal scope of protection of Article 43(1) of the TEC (Article III-137(1) DC) in the first place includes natural persons who are nationals of one of the Member States of the EC. This becomes evident from the precise wording of the provision. Nationals of third countries may not directly rely on Article 43(1) of the TEC (Article III-137(1) DC),[37] although the freedom of establishment does have indirect legal effect for family members of Community citizens;[38] in addition, they are granted certain rights by the relevant secondary legislation.[39] Otherwise third country nationals continue to enjoy the rights

---

34 Kapteyn/Verlooren van Themaat (note 2) p 733.
35 UN Convention on the Law of the Sea, ILM 21 (1982) 1261; for details on the exclusive economic zone see *eg* Brownlie *Prinicples of Public International Law* (6th ed, Oxford 2003) pp 199–200.
36 For details see Lackhoff (note 5) pp 200–201.
37 Lenaerts/Van Nuffel (note 1) p 554.
38 ECJ *Singh* [1992] ECR I-4265, para 23; Schlag in: Schwarze (ed) *EU-Kommentar* (Baden-Baden 2000) Art 43 EGV, para 30, 50.
39 For details see Randelzhofer/Forsthoff (note 24) Vor Art 39-55 EGV; above para 9.

Freedom of Establishment § 10 II 3

derived from the mentioned international treaties which are an integral part of Community law.[40]

A particularly important aspect of the personal scope of protection of the freedom of establishment concerns its extension to legal persons. The applicability of the freedom of establishment to legal persons results from Article 48 of the TEC (Article III-142 DC). Since specific, complex problems arise concerning Article 48 of the TEC (Article III-142 DC) and the relevant scope of the law of establishment, this aspect will be addressed at a later point.[41]

16

3. Subject Matter of Protection

Case 1 – Problem: (ECJ *Factortame* [1991] ECR I-3956)
In the early 1980s, F, a Spanish operator of fishing vessels, registers a large number of his ships in the United Kingdom, hoping to share in the British fishing quota (so-called quota hopping). In order to curb this practice, a law is passed in the United Kingdom in 1988 under which all ships which sail under the British flag must be reregistered in the shipping register. Registration in the shipping register demands, *inter alia*, that the vessels be operated from the United Kingdom, and that their deployment be controlled and supervised from the UK. F operates his ships from Spain. Does the UK's new registration law violate Article 43(1) of the TEC (Article III-137(1) DC)?

17

Case 2 – Problem: (ECJ *Gebhard* [1995] ECR I-4165)
G, a German national, has been a member of the German Bar in Stuttgart since 1977. He is an associate in a law firm, but does not himself maintain a law office in Germany. Having worked as an associate in a law firm in Italy for some time, G opens his own firm in Milan in 1989. He operates it as an "avvocato", the Italian occupational title for independent lawyers. Permission for this has not been granted by the appropriate bar association. In consequence, the bar association of Milan initiates disciplinary proceedings against G, which result in him being disqualified from exercising his profession for a duration of six months. Does G come under the scope of protection of Article 43(1) of the TEC (Article III-137(1) DC)?

18

The subject matter of protection of Article 43(1) of the TEC (Article III-137(1) DC) is significantly defined by its delimitation from the scope of the freedom to provide services (Article 49 TEC/Article III-144 DC). It becomes obvious from the context of the EC Treaty that the two freedoms must be distinct. And, as previously pointed out, the freedom of establishment is marked by the peculiar tension between the country of origin principle and the country of destination principle. On the other hand, the country of destination principle, which in light of the ECJ's jurisprudence should also be of relevance to the freedom of establishment, is in fact hardly ever applied to the freedom to provide services; here the argument centres on the question whether and to what extent the doctrine of the prohibition of restriction applies to Article 49 of the TEC (Article III-144 DC).[42] However, in the case of the freedom of establishment, even the wording of Article 43(2) of the TEC (Article III-137(2) DC) says that it concerns such activities which

19

---

40 Above para 6.
41 Below para 60.
42 For details see Randelzhofer/Forsthoff (note 24) Art 49/50 EGV, para 68.

are exercised "under the conditions laid down for its own nationals by the law of the country where such establishment is effected". This reference to the country of destination principle is the starting point for the necessary, yet problematic, task of distinguishing the freedom of establishment from the freedom to provide services.

a) Economic Activity

20 Article 43(2) of the TEC (Article III-137(2) DC) to some extent describes the scope of the freedom of establishment, without, however, offering a legal definition. According to Article 43(2) of the TEC (Article III-137(2) DC), the freedom of establishment encompasses "the right to take up and pursue activities as self-employed persons and to set up and manage undertakings [...] under the conditions laid down for its own nationals by the law of the country where such establishment is effected". This definition can be further refined if one is to take a general[43] look at the distinction between the freedom of establishment and the freedom to provide services. Pursuant to Article 50(3) of the TEC (Article III-145(3) DC), the provision of services in other Member States[44] builds, in contrast to the freedom of establishment, on the temporary pursuit of activities. It follows from this in conjunction with the definition in Article 43(2) of the TEC (Article III-137(2) DC), that "the concept of establishment involves the actual pursuit of an economic activity through a fixed establishment in another Member State for an indefinite period".[45]

21 As this definition suggests, the concept of establishment must be interpreted broadly in order to give effect to this fundamental freedom (Article 10 TEC/Article I-5(2) DC).[46] Certain restrictions resulting from the ratio of the EC Treaty as a whole, and in particular from Article 43 of the TEC (Article III-137 DC), must however be observed. As is true of all fundamental freedoms, the scope of protection of the freedom of establishment, too, relates exclusively to economic matters, and, more specifically, to economic activity. This follows from the wording of Article 43(2) of the TEC in conjunction with Article 2 of the TEC (Article III-137(2) DC in conjunction with Article I-3 DC).[47] However, the economic concept relevant in this respect is decidedly vague, leaving open to discussion to what extent it is suitable to serve as a definitional element.[48] This becomes evident from ECJ decisions which hold that even cultural,[49] sporting,[50] and religious[51] activities may all fall within the scope of protection of the fundamental freedoms.

22 Against this background it has been suggested that "activities" in the sense of Article 43(2) of the TEC (Article III-137(2) DC) should apply to all goods and services which are

---

43 On the precise distinction between the freedom of establishment and the freedom to provide services see note 24 below.
44 On the different dimensions of the freedom to provide services see Lenaerts/Van Nuffel (note 1) pp 228–229.
45 ECJ *Factortame* [1991] ECR I-3956, para 20.
46 ECJ *Gebhard* [1995] ECR I-4165, para 25; *Broede* [1996] ECR I-6511, para 20; Lenaerts/van Nuffel (note 1) p 188; Randelzhofer/Forsthoff (note 24) Art 43 EGV, para 13; Geiger *EUV/EGV* (4th ed, Munich 2004) Art 43 EGV, para 1.
47 On Art 2 TEC see von Bogdandy (note 2) Art 2 EGV, para 13; Kapteyn/Verlooren van Themaat (note 2) pp 113–114.
48 For details see Lackhoff (note 5) pp 38–39.
49 *Eg* ECJ *Commission v Spain* [1994] ECR I-911, para 10.
50 *Eg* ECJ *Bosman* [1995] ECR I-4921, para 73.
51 *Eg* ECJ *Steymann* [1988] ECR 6159.

of monetary value, ie all economic activity.[52] However, this fails to take account of the fact that, for example, private economic pressure groups play an important role in the economic sphere without necessarily aiming at financial gain. Thus, the focus of Article 43(2) of the TEC (Article III(2) DC) is not primarily on financial gain, but rather on any activity which serves an economic end.[53] Solely gratuitous activities which have no economic element whatsoever, *eg* purely creative pursuits, do not fall within the scope of the freedom of establishment.[54]

It remains to be determined to what extent an alleged "gross social harmfulness" of an action precludes the application of the subject matter of protection of Article 43(1) of the TEC (Article III-137(1) DC).[55] In light of the increasingly distinct freedom-related dimension of the fundamental rights (→ § 7 note 24), however, any restriction of the scope of protection is in principle a cause for concern; thus, from a freedom-preserving perspective the only solution to the problem lies in a possible justification.[56]

23

b) Permanent and Stable Integration into the National Economy

To the extent that we are dealing with an economic activity within the meaning of Article 43(2) of the TEC (Article III-134(2) DC), we now need to determine and examine the criteria which, distinguishing it from the freedom to provide services, qualify such activity as an establishment, or even remove it from the scope of the fundamental freedoms altogether. The latter point regarding an exclusion from the scope of protection concerns the abuse of Community law.[57] According to the ECJ's permanent jurisprudence regarding the freedom of establishment, "a Member State is entitled to take measures designed to prevent certain of its nationals from attempting [to] improperly or fraudulently tak[e] advantage of provisions of Community law"[58]. As regards the freedom of establishment, the ECJ has emphasised that it cannot constitute an abuse if the rules of company law of the Member State chosen for the establishment are "the least restrictive".[59] On the other hand, if the freedom of establishment is relied upon in a case where objectively the aim is not a lasting and stable integration into the economy of the Member State in question, such circumstances do not fall within the scope of Article 43(1) of the TEC (Article III-137(1) DC).[60] Although the ECJ explained this with the definition of "establishment", such instances may also be explained by the exclusion of abusive behaviour.[61]

24

---

52 Lackhoff (note 5) pp 39–40; similar Schlag (note 38) Art 43 EGV, paras 21–22.
53 Convincingly Randelzhofer/Forsthoff (note 24) Art 43 EGV, para 18.
54 See, *eg,* Troberg (note 17) Art 52 EGV, para 31; Randelzhofer/Forsthoff (note 24) Art 43 EGV, para 20.
55 For details on the discussion see Schnichels *Reichweite der Niederlassungsfreiheit* (Baden-Baden 1995) p 29; the ECJ includes prostitution in the freedom to provide services and the freedom of establishment: ECJ *Jany* [2001] ECR I-8615, para 55; see also ECJ *Omega* [2004] ECR I-9609.
56 For the theoretical background of this approach see Alexy *A Theory of Constitutional Rights* (Oxford 2002).
57 See Randelzhofer/Forsthoff (note 24) Vor Art 39–55 EGV, para 122; Lenaerts/Van Nuffel (note 1) p 715.
58 ECJ *Centros* [1999] ECR I-1459, para 24.
59 ECJ *Centros* [1999] ECR I-1459, para 27.
60 ECJ *Factortame* [1991] ECR I-3956, para 34.
61 Similar Randelzhofer/Forsthoff (note 24) Art 43 EGV, para 21.

§ 10 II 3 Christian Tietje

Case 1 – Answer:

25 A violation of the freedom of establishment initially requires the applicability of Article 43(1) of the TEC (Article III-137(1) DC). Thus, the registration of fishing vessels in the United Kingdom would have to be an establishment within the meaning of Article 43 of the TEC (Article III-137 DC). The term "establishment", which must be given a broad interpretation, includes the actual exercise of economic activities by means of a lasting establishment for an indefinite period in another Member State. Accordingly, the registration of a vessel would need to stand in connection with an economic activity. This is clearly the case where fishing vessels are concerned. The thus possible applicability of Article 43(1) of the TEC (Article III-137(1) DC) cannot be precluded by the fact that the registration of a ship determines its nationality. In principle, questions of nationality and citizenship fall under Member State competence. However, since the registration of a vessel necessarily involves a natural or legal person not seeking a new nationality, but rather seeking to exercise his or its economic freedom within the meaning of Article 43 of the TEC (Article III-137 DC), the fundamental freedoms must be applied. Nonetheless, it must be observed that not the vessels themselves are protected by Article 43 of the TEC (Article III-137 DC), but only their operators as legal or natural persons. Thus, the application for registration must be made by a person wishing to create an establishment. As a result, the operator of a vessel which is to be registered may be required to at least operate and control this vessel from the location of the new establishment. This requirement can be justified by the otherwise possible abuse of the freedom of establishment in the form of quota-hopping. Consequently, the scope of protection of Article 43 of the TEC (Article III-137 DC) does not extend to the circumstances of this case.

26 To the extent that the subject matter of application of Article 43 of the TEC (Article III-137 DC) is not already precluded by circumstances such as those in the above case, the central element of the analysis of the subject matter of application of Article 43 of the TEC (Article III-137 DC) is the necessity to distinguish the creation of an establishment from the provision of services within the meaning of Articles 43 (Article III-137 DC) and 49, 50 of the TEC (Articles III-144 DC). The necessity to make this distinction has previously been explained; however, it remains uncertain how this distinction is to be effected. The main difficulty results from the unarguable awareness – expressed in Article 50(3) of the TEC (Article III-145(3) DC) – that the so called active freedom to provide services[62] is protected as well. Since this allows a service provider to stay in another Member State in order to pursue his business activities, the exercise of the active freedom to provide services is closely related to an establishment. This becomes particularly evident when considering that the exercise of the active freedom to provide services confers the right to maintain the necessary infrastructure (renting an office *etc*) in the location where the service is provided.[63]

---

62 See, *eg,* Kluth in: Calliess/Ruffert (eds) *Kommentar des Vertrages über die Europäische Union und des Vertrages zur Gründung der Europäischen Gemeinschaft* (2nd ed, Neuwied 2002) Art 50 EGV, para 24; Kapteyn/Verlooren van Themaat (note 2) p 750; → § 11 para 27.
63 ECJ *Gebhard* [1995] ECR I-4165, para 27: "the temporary nature of the activities in question has to be determined in light not only of the duration of the provision of the service, but also of its regularity, periodicity or continuity. The fact that the provision of services is temporary does not mean that the provider of services within the meaning of the Treaty may not equip himself with some form of infrastructure in the host Member State (including an office, chambers or con-

Freedom of Establishment § 10 II 3

27 Case law and doctrine largely agree that the freedom of establishment and the freedom to provide services can only be distinguished in the face of all the facts of a particular case. The duration and continuity of the activity pursued in another Member State are of particular significance, as well as the question whether the business activity is carried out through a fixed establishment in this Member State.[64] Chiefly charged with drawing this distinction is the national court dealing with Article 43 or 49, 50 of the TEC (Article III-137 or 144, 145 DC) in a particular case.[65]

28 Even if the application of these criteria can offer guidance in the attempt to distinguish the freedom of establishment from the freedom to provide services, the necessity to evaluate the overall picture remains. After all, neither "duration and continuity" nor "fixed establishment" are necessary or sufficient criteria. Regarding the lasting duration, this becomes evident from the fact that although Article 50(3) of the TEC (Article III-145(3) DC) speaks of the "temporary" pursuit of activities in relation to the provision of services, vastly varying temporal dimensions may occur depending on the specific service in question. The construction of a large industrial plant, for example, will take a long time; but the contractor will not necessarily wish to create an establishment within the meaning of Article 43(1) of the TEC (Article III-137(1) DC). A continuous, recurring activity – such as the labour performed by a blacksmith in another Member State –, which is performed without relocating offices or a workshop, is to be assessed in a similar way. Despite the fact that such services are steadily provided for a long period of time, the activities in these cases should not necessarily be regarded as giving rise to an establishment. In light of these, and similar, cases it becomes obvious that the permanence, or rather continuity, of the activity is in itself of little evidential value, and can only be one of several factors which are to be taken into account.[66]

29 Even the creation of a fixed establishment in another Member State does not alone offer conclusive evidence of an establishment within the meaning of Article 43 of the TEC (Article III-137 DC). One can also conceive of occupations not requiring a "permanent establishment", *eg* the migrant knife grinder. Furthermore, a permanent establishment may, as previously outlined, indeed be reconcilable with the provision of services within the meaning of Articles 49, 50 of the TEC (Articles III-144, 145 DC), if such infrastructure is essential to the particular service.

30 Duration and continuity of the activity or the creation of a permanent establishment are thus neither necessary nor sufficient classification criteria. What is, in contrast, of central importance, is the question whether a national of one Member State has integrated into the national economy of another Member State.[67] In this context it is irrelevant

---

sulting rooms) in so far as such infrastructure is necessary for the purposes of performing the services in question".

64 ECJ *Gebhard* [1995] ECR I-4165, para 27; Mathijsen *A Guide to European Union Law* (8th ed, London 2004) p 204; Fairhurst/Vincenzi *Law of the European Community* (4th ed, Harlow 2003) p 274; Randelzhofer/Forsthoff (note 24) Art 43 EGV, para 25; Lackhoff (note 5) p 134 (with further references in note 591) and pp 136–137.
65 ECJ *Broede* [1996] ECR I-6511, para 22; Lackhoff (note 5) p 137.
66 Critical with regard to the criterion of "duration" also Lackhoff (note 5) pp 135–136; Randelzhofer/Forsthoff (note 24) Art 43 EGV, para 26; on the criterion of "duration" as the "key demarcation" see Kapteyn/Verlooren van Themaat (note 2) p 750.
67 Opinion AG Darmon, ECJ *Daily Mail* [1988] ECR I-5483, para 3: "Establishment means integrating into a national economy"; Opinion AG Léger, ECJ *Gebhard* [1995] ECR I-4165, para 19.

whether the economic operator deliberately performs his services in another Member State in order to evade the laws and regulations of his home country and place of establishment. In earlier cases involving such constellations, the ECJ was quick to affirm that they were nonetheless subject to the provisions relating to the right of establishment.[68] However, in the meantime the Court has clarified that the associated problems must be addressed within the context of a possible justification, and thus do not preclude a particular case from falling within the scope of protection of the freedom of establishment or the freedom to provide services.[69]

31 For the purpose of drawing a distinction between establishment and the provision of services, the criteria which are to be taken into account can be arranged in the following categories:[70] The freedom of establishment is pertinent and supersedes the freedom to provide services where a national of one Member State creates an establishment in another Member State in order to provide services there.[71] In this case, the establishment is a condition precedent for the economic activity. The situation becomes more complicated where the service is not provided "by", but merely "via" the establishment. Here, the establishment does not serve the purpose of creating a service, but merely markets it. Following an, albeit unclear, ECJ judgement,[72] there is an opinion in the literature that even cases of this nature are instances of the freedom of establishment, rather than the freedom to provide services.[73] Meanwhile, the ECJ conceded in 1997 that the provisions regarding the freedom to provide services may apply even where the enterprise in question is located in the host Member State, thus denying an *a priori* priority of the provisions regarding the freedom of establishment in such circumstances.[74] In light of this conclusion one is led to assume that the service is created at the head office, while branch offices are merely concerned with the marketing and distribution of this service on a secondary level.[75] This view also provides the solution to the so-called accumulation problem. This describes a situation where, although there is a branch office in the Member State in which the service is rendered, this branch is not directly involved in the service activity. Even in this instance, the rules pertaining to the freedom to provide services remain applicable – otherwise the freedom to provide services would run idle, particularly regarding large multinationals with subsidiaries in several Member States.[76]

32 In conclusion it can be said that the clear distinction between establishment and the provision of services cannot be established by way of a definition. The appropriate distinction must be drawn on the basis of the facts of each individual case, which, in light of the individual circumstances, carry more or less weight. In this context, the ratio behind

---

68 ECJ *van Binsbergen* [1974] ECR 1299, para 13; *Commission v Germany* [1986] ECR I-3755, para 22.
69 ECJ *TV 10* [1994] ECR I-4795, para 15; see also Randelzhofer/Forsthoff (note 24) Art 43 EGV, para 36.
70 For further details see Randelzhofer/Forsthoff (note 24) Art 43 EGV, para 37.
71 ECJ *Steymann* [1988] ECR 6159, para 17; *Sodemare* [1997] ECR I-3395, para 37.
72 ECJ *Commission v Germany* [1986] ECR I-3755, para 21.
73 In this direction Behrens [1992] EuR 145, 151.
74 ECJ *VT4* [1997] ECR I-3143, para 20.
75 For a comprehensive analysis see Pasternacki *Zur Abgrenzung von Niederlassungsfreiheit und Dienstleistungsfreiheit bei Niederlassungen mit Teilfunktion* (Frankfurt 2000).
76 Randelzhofer/Forsthoff (note 24) Art 43 EGV, paras 43–44; also ECJ *VT4* [1997] ECR I-3143, para 20; Lackhoff (note 5) p 142; Roth [1990] RabelsZ 63, 108–109.

Article 43 of the TEC (Article III-137 DC), which is evident in the legal position created by the integration of a service provider in the national economy of another Member State, is of central and paramount significance.

c) Primary and Secondary Establishment as Manifestations of the Guarantee of the Subject Matter of Protection

As is evident from the wording of Article 43(1) of the TEC (Article III-137(1) DC), there are two protected forms of establishment: the establishment *per se*, and "the setting-up of agencies, branches or subsidiaries". Thus, Article 43(1) of the TEC (Article III-147 DC) guarantees both the so called primary and the secondary establishment.[77]

Primary establishment describes the cross-border change of residence of self-employed natural and, pursuant to Article 48 of the TEC (Article III-142 DC), of legal persons.[78] In contrast to services within the meaning of Articles 49, 50 of the TEC (Articles III-144, 145 DC), what is at issue here is the cross-border relocation or the incorporation of an economic entity. In order to determine where the head office of an entrepreneur or of a company (Article 48 TEC/Article III-142 DC) is located, the main focus of economic activity is of central importance.[79] However, in the case of legal persons within the meaning of Article 48 of the TEC (Article III-142 DC), the situation under company law is of greater importance than other circumstances. Therefore, the domicile of the registered office is decisive for the purpose of the establishment.[80]

A secondary establishment is characterised by the fact that an economic entity "whose registered office is situated in another Member State" sets up a branch, subsidiary or agency – the choice of the type of establishment being free.[81] Thus, for the purpose of analysing Article 43(2) of the TEC (Article III-137(2) DC), the precise form of the secondary establishment is of little significance, the listed examples serving merely as a collective description of any dependent economic activity.[82] The only controversial issue is whether the scope of Article 43(2) of the TEC (Article III-43(2) DC) is to be interpreted as including an economic presence which "does not take the form of a branch or agency, but consists merely of an office managed by the undertaking's own staff or by a person who is independent but authorised to act on a permanent basis for the undertaking, as would be the case with an agency".[83] In the cited judgement concerning an insurance agent, the ECJ answered this question in the affirmative. This meets the objection that, aside from the specific features of the insurance industry, an expansion of the scope of Article 43(2) of the TEC (Article III-137(2) DC) to agents and intermediaries in general would create a conflict within the system of the fundamental freedoms: To the extent that,

---

77 Kapteyn/Verlooren van Themaat (note 2) p 736; Schlag (note 38) Art 43 EGV, paras 19–20.
78 Roth in: Dauses (ed) *Handbuch des EU-Wirtschaftsrechts* (loose-leaf, Munich) para 35; Schlag (note 38) Art 43 EGV, para 19.
79 Eyles D*as Niederlassungsrecht der Kapitalgesellschaften in der Europäischen Gemeinschaft: die Überlagerung des deutschen Gesellschaftsrechts und Unternehmenssteuerrechts durch Europäisches Gemeinschaftsrecht* (Baden-Baden 1990) p 41; Randelzhofer/Forsthoff (note 24) Art 43 EGV, para 49; Schlag (note 38) Art 43 EGV, para 19.
80 ECJ *Centros* [1999] ECR I-1459, para 17; Randelzhofer/Forsthoff (note 24) Art 43 EGV, para 49.
81 ECJ *Commission v France* [1986] ECR 1725, para 22; *Saint-Gobain* [1999] ECR I-6161, para 42.
82 Lackhoff (note 5) pp 173–174.
83 ECJ *Commission v Germany* [1986] ECR I-3755, para 21.

as is regularly the case where agents and intermediaries are concerned, a service provider acts independently, the provisions of the freedom to provide services become applicable. This general conclusion, which results from the previously-discussed rationale of Articles 43 and 49, 50 of the TEC (Articles III-137 and 144, 145 DC), must then apply also to agents and intermediaries in the field of services. Otherwise a services intermediary would come within the ambit of Article 43(2) of the TEC (Article III-137(2) DC), while the freedom to provide services (Articles 49, 50 TEC/Articles III-144, 145 DC) would apply to a vendor of goods produced in another Member State. This kind of differing legal assessment of economically comparable circumstances is not justifiable.[84]

36   Another characteristic which is to be observed – that of domicile found in Article 43(2) of the TEC (Article III-137(2) DC) – does not, as might be assumed from a cursory reading of the provision, relate to the Member State in which the establishment is to be set up. Rather, it relates to residence in any one Member State of the Union. This serves to exclude natural and legal persons which, from an economic perspective, are "mainly or exclusively integrated into a non-EU economy".[85] Thus, where secondary establishment is concerned, what is important is not merely EU citizenship under Article 17(1) of the TEC (Article I-10 DC), but also the economic ties to the European Union. This is designed to ensure that persons seeking to rely on Article 43 of the TEC (Article III-137 DC) merely within the context of secondary establishment can be subject to legal supervision with regard to their main point of economic activity within the EU.[86]

d) Cross-border Cases

37   Another prerequisite for the subject matter of protection of Article 43 of the TEC (Article III-137 DC) is, as in the case with all fundamental freedoms, that the particular case has a cross-border element. The presence of this cross-border element must be determined on the basis of the criteria applicable to all fundamental freedoms, and thus falls within the general doctrine of the fundamental freedoms (→ § 7 notes 20, 25).

38   To clarify the legal and practical relevance of the freedom of establishment it may be pointed out that Article 43 of the TEC (Article III-137 DC) can also be used against the country of origin. This is of particular relevance in the so-called moving-out cases. In such cases, the exercise of the freedom of establishment in the host Member State is hampered by measures of the home country. These situations are of elevated significance where national tax provisions disadvantage companies which have their head office in one Member State, and secondary establishments in another. Regarding situations such as this, the ECJ has unequivocally held that the provisions regarding the freedom of establishment forbids the home country to hamper the establishment of its nationals, or of companies established under its laws, in another Member State, as long as they meet the requirements of Article 48 of the TEC (Article III-142 DC).[87] This applies also where the exercise of the freedom of establishment in the host Member State is limited by a restriction of the possibility to return to the home country.[88] These so-called return cases can,

---

84 Randelzhofer/Forsthoff (note 24) Art 43 EGV, para 59; different Troberg (note 17) Art 52 EGV, para 19; Roth (note 78) para 37; see also Lackhoff (note 5) p 174.
85 Randelzhofer/Forsthoff (note 24) Art 43 EGV, para 51.
86 Schlag (note 38) Art 43 EGV, para 29; see also ECJ *AMID* [2000] ECR I-11619, para 20.
87 ECJ *AMID* [2000] ECR I-11619; *de Lasteyrie du Saillant* [2004] ECR I-2409.
88 Randelzhofer/Forsthoff (note 24) Art 43 EGV, para 62.

according to the – disputed – case-law of the ECJ, lead to a situation where the legal position of someone making use of the freedom of establishment in another Member State is improved *vis-à-vis* that of other nationals of his country of origin.[89]

Despite this expansion of the criterion of the cross-border element, it remains to be determined whether this criterion should be preserved. This question especially concerns the problem of so-called reverse discrimination. Insofar as a cross-border element is mandatory, the fundamental freedoms do not apply to situations where home nationals receive less preferential treatment than the nationals of another Member State. With regard to the freedom of establishment this appears to be supported by the wording of Article 43(1) of the TEC (Article III-137(1) DC), since the first sentence of the provision talks of the "freedom of establishment of nationals of a Member State in the territory of another Member State". However, it must be observed that although the wording of Article 43(1) of the TEC (Article III-137(1) DC) initially requires a cross-border element, this does not preclude a future inclusion of purely national facts.[90] Thus, it can justifiably be argued that in light of the fundamental aims of the EC Treaty, as set out in Articles 2 and 3 of the TEC (Article I-3(3) DC), and the fundamental freedoms in general, reverse discrimination violates the free market principle of Community law (see also Article 4(1) TEC/Article I-3(3) DC).[91] To be sure, the ECJ has not yet taken the next logical step of interpreting Article 43(1) of the TEC (Article III-137(1) DC) as not at all requiring a cross-border element. Even in literature, an inclusion of reverse discrimination continues to be rejected.[92]

Case 2 – Answer:
Here, the sole problem is that the applicability of Article 43(1) of the TEC (Article III-137(1) DC) in favour of G requires his working as a lawyer in Italy to be regarded as an establishment, not as a service under Articles 49, 50 of the TEC (Articles III-144, 145 DC). The pursuit of G's activity in Italy can only fall within one of these two areas, since another category in the chapter on the free movement of persons, that of Article 39 of the TEC (Article III-133 DC), is inapplicable by reason of the fact that G is self-employed. In addition, it must be remembered that the freedom to provide services is subsidiary to the freedom of establishment, as is evident from the wording of Article 50(1) of the TEC (Article III-145 DC). Whether G's economic activity in Italy can be regarded as an establishment depends on the precise definition of the term establishment. According to the permanent jurisprudence of the ECJ, this term is to be given a broad interpretation. Insofar, an establishment is the stable and continuous participation in the economy of another Member State. As shown by the first sentence of Article 43(1) of the TEC (Article III-137(1) DC), it is neither relevant whether next to the economic activity in the host Member State there are further establishments in the country of origin, nor whether the establishment in question is a head office or a branch. Based on this Community law standard for the determination of the subject

---

89 ECJ *Singh* [1992] ECR I-4265, para 19; different Randelzhofer/Forsthoff (note 24) Art 43 EGV, para 62.
90 For details see Lackhoff (note 5) pp 73–74.
91 For details see Lackhoff (note 5) pp 82–83.
92 Randelzhofer/Forsthoff (note 24) Art 43 EGV, para 65 and Vor Art 39–55 EGV, para 49; Epiney in: Calliess/Ruffert (eds) *Kommentar des Vertrages über die Europäische Union und des Vertrages zur Gründung der Europäischen Gemeinschaft* (2nd ed, Neuwied 2002) Art 12 EGV, para 33; for details on the discussion see Kingreen *Die Struktur der Grundfreiheiten des Europäischen Gemeinschaftsrechts* (Berlin 1999) pp 84, 115; Lackhoff (note 5) p 67, with further references.

matter of application of Article 43(1) of the TEC (Article III-137(1) DC), the fact that G maintains a law office in Milan, where he advises Italian and other clients, supports the applicability of the rules on the freedom of establishment in G's favour. G provides his services from his law office in Milan, and does so not merely on a temporary, but apparently on a permanent basis. The thus applicable scope of protection of Article 43 of the TEC (Article III-137 DC) could only be rejected with the argument that G, in pursuing his professional activity as a lawyer, violated the relevant professional code. To this extent it must be debated whether the concept of establishment within the meaning of Article 43 of the TEC (Article III-137 DC) requires the integration into the national economy under the laws of the host Member State. However, the structure of the freedom of establishment as one of the fundamental freedoms argues against this. Whether and to what extent the laws of the host Member State must be observed in exercising the freedom of establishment is a question relating to the justification of a restriction of the scope of protection of Article 43 of the TEC (Article III-137 DC). If this matter arose at an earlier point, it would be for the Member States to determine the subject matter of the freedom of establishment autonomously. And since this would render the freedom of establishment ineffectual, the possibility of restricting the freedom of establishment by reason of national legal provisions must only be examined at the justification stage.[93] As a result, and in favour of G, Article 43(1) of the TEC (Article III-137(1) DC) is applicable in this case.

4. Exceptions to the applicability

Case 3 – Problem: (ECJ *Commission v Spain* [1998] ECR I-6717)

41 In Spain, a law is passed which requires private security companies to be constituted in Spain in order to carry on their activities. In contrast to the police or other state-controlled security service providers, security companies are not endowed with comparable imperative authoritiy. Does the Spanish law fall within the scope of Articles 43 and 48 of the TEC (Articles III-137 and 142 DC)?

42 An exception to the applicability of fundamental freedoms exists not only in relation to the free movement of workers (Article 39(4) TEC/Article III-133(4) DC), but also in relation to the freedom of establishment (Article 45 TEC/Article III-139 DC) where it concerns the exercise of official authority. Article 45 of the TEC (Article III-139 DC), too, is characterised by the fact that it precludes the application of the freedom of establishment. This is evident from the wording of Article 45 of the TEC (Article III-139 DC) ("shall not apply"), and is affirmed by a systematic reading of Article 46(1) of the TEC (Article III-140(1) DC), which provides for a justification ("shall not prejudice"). Even though this clearly identifies Article 45 of the TEC (Article III-139 DC) as an exception to the applicability, it is important to note that the terminology of the ECJ is not always consistent in this respect. Thus, although several judgements refer to Article 45 of the TEC[94] (Article III-139 DC) as a justification, it in fact remains an exception.[95]

43 It must be noted that, despite certain similarities, Article 45 of the TEC (Article III-133 DC) differs significantly from Article 39(4) of the TEC (Article III-133(4) DC). Next

---

93 ECJ *Gebhard* [1995] ECR I-4165, para 20.
94 *Eg* ECJ *Commission v Spain* [1998] ECR I-6717, para 32.
95 Randelzhofer/Forsthoff (note 24) Art 45 EGV para 3; Lackhoff (note 5) p 153; → § 7 para 52; different however Jarass [1995] EuR, 202, 221–222.

to the competence in Article 45(2) of the TEC (Article III-139(2) DC) to exclude certain activities from the provisions regarding the freedom of establishment through secondary law[96], this is already evident from the wording of the two provisions: Article 39(4) of the TEC (Article III-133(4) DC) mentions "employment in the public sector", and the focus of Article 45(1) of the TEC (Article III-139(1) DC) is on the "exercise of official authority". Thus, Article 39(4) of the TEC (Article III-133(4) DC) is concerned with public service employees or civil servants, while Article 45(1) of the TEC (Article III-139(1) DC) predominantly aims at private individuals.[97]

According to the general rules of interpretation in Community law, the exception in Article 45 of the TEC (Article III-139 DC) must be interpreted narrowly. As was held by the ECJ, the provision "must be interpreted in a manner which limits its scope to what is strictly necessary for safeguarding the interests which that provision allows the Member States to protect".[98] In addition, as in the context of Article 39(4) of the TEC (Article III-133(4) DC), the term "official authority" in Article 45(1) of the TEC (Article III-139(1) DC) is to be interpreted in accordance with the principles of Community law, since otherwise the Member States could decide over the application of Article 45 of the TEC (Article III-139 DC) without being subject to control under Community law.[99] However, this does not go to say that Community law conclusively determines the exercise of "public authority" within the meaning of Article 45(1) of the TEC (Article III-139(1) DC). Rather, it is merely a skeleton concept under Community law, the application of which depends, *inter alia*, on the national legal system in an individual case.[100]

44

Corresponding to the framework character of Article 45(1) of the TEC (Article III-139(1) DC), the ECJ does not offer a conclusive definition of the element of the "exercise of official authority". In order to determine the interplay between Community law and national law in the application of Article 45 of the TEC (Article III-139 DC), the question is whether the activity "constitute[s] a direct and specific connexion with the exercise of official authority".[101] This would only be the case where the activity is connected to the exercise of mandatory authority,[102] or is distinguished by territorial or other privileges.[103] However, this will not lead to a formalistic, abstract separation between the authority to pass administrative acts, and purely territorial actions. After all, the effectiveness of Article 43 of the TEC (Article III-137 DC) (Article 10 TEC/Article I-5(2) DC) can only be guaranteed if the facts of an individual case, independent of the terminological freedoms of the Member States, are examined in light of the ratio behind Article 45 of the TEC (Article III-139 DC).

45

---

96 Art 45(2) TEC (Art III-139(2) DC) has not been of any practical relevance so far, Geiger (note 46) Art 45 EGV, para 5.
97 Randelzhofer/Forsthoff (note 24) Art 45 EGV, para 1.
98 ECJ *Commission v Spain* [1998] ECR I-6717, para 34.
99 Opinion AG Lenz, ECJ *Commission v Greece* [1991] ECR I-5863, para 30; Roth (note 78) para 29; Lackhoff (note 5) p 154.
100 Lackhoff (note 5) pp 155–156.
101 ECJ *Reyners* [1974] ECR I-631, para 45; *Thijssen* [1993] ECR I-4047, para 8; *Commission v Spain* [1998] ECR I-6717, para 35.
102 ECJ *Commission v Spain* [1998] ECR I-6717, para 37.
103 Opinion AG Mayras, ECJ *Reyners* [1974] ECR I-631, p 665.

Case 3 – Answer:
46 The requirement that private security companies be of Spanish nationality *prima facie* falls within the scope of Articles 43 and 48 of the TEC (Articles III-137 and III-142 DC). It is, however, debatable whether in this particular case, by virtue of Article 45(1) of the TEC (Article III-139(1) DC), Article 43 of the TEC (Article III-137 DC) does not apply since the case concerns national regulations pertaining to security companies. This could be supported by the argument that private security services contribute to the maintenance of public security and order in general. It could furthermore be argued that private security companies need to be subject to strict national control, which could only be exercised effectively if the company has such close ties to the state as can only be established through its nationality.[104]

It can be argued against the applicability of the exception in Article 45(1) of the TEC (Article III-139(1) DC) that in light of the character of the provision as an exemption, and the significance of Article 43 of the TEC (Article III-137 DC) within the framework of norms designed to maintain the fundamental freedoms, the provision must be applied restrictively. The scope of Article 45(1) of the TEC (Article III-139(1) DC) would thus have to be restricted to activities that have a direct and specific connection with the exercise of official authority. The security companies affected by the Spanish provision operate on a civil law basis. They hold no mandatory powers comparable to those held by the regular national security organs (particularly the police force). Additionally, everyone is obliged by law to maintain public security anyway. From the point of view of the state, the authorities and duties of private security companies do not exceed this general public duty. Thus, private security companies do not distinctly and specifically share in the exercise of official authority in Spain. As a result, the exception in Article 45(1) of the TEC (Article III-139(1) DC) is inapplicable,[105] and Article 43(1) of the TEC (Article III-137(1) DC) continues to apply.

III. Interference

Case 4 – Problem: (ECJ *Pfeiffer* [1999] ECR I-2835)
47 The German retailer T operates subsidiaries in several EC Member States. For some years now, T has been promoting all his stores under the uniform logo of "TPlus". One of T's subsidiaries in Austria operates several retail stores under the label "TPlus Kaufen". The Austrian company "TPlus Leben", which had long registered this name as a trademark with the Austrian patent office, argues that its rights are being violated by the activities of "TPlus Kaufen". It thus asks the competent Austrian court to prohibit T's subsidiary from operating or advertising under the name of "TPlus Kaufen". This request is supported by § 9(1) of the Austrian *UWG* (Competition Code), according to which one must refrain from using names or notable descriptions of a company in a manner capable of causing confusion with the names or notable descriptions which another is authorised to use. In the current case, the requirements of this provision are met with regard to the registered trademark "TPlus Leben". However, the competent court is of the opinion that a decision against "TPlus Kaufen" would not be compatible with the freedom of establishment in Articles 43, 48 of the TEC (Articles III-137, 142 DC). Correct?

---

104 Thus the arguments of Spain, ECJ *Commission v Spain* [1998] ECR I-6717, para 26.
105 ECJ *Commission v Spain* [1998] ECR I-6717, para 34; *Commission v Belgium* [2000] ECR I-1221, paras 25–26.

1. Discrimination

In accordance with the, historically speaking, pre-eminent ratio behind the fundamental freedoms in general, Article 43 of the TEC (Article III-137 DC), too, aims first and foremost at prohibiting discrimination on the grounds of nationality. What kind of discrimination might be incompatible with Article 43 of the TEC (Article III-137 DC) can best be seen from the "General Programme for the Abolition of Restrictions on Freedom to Provide Services", which was passed in 1962 on the basis of Article 44 of the TEC (Article III-138 DC).[106] It lists various discriminatory restrictions of the freedom to provide services, including separate permit and residence requirements for foreign nationals. The ECJ repeatedly pointed out that the general programme provides "useful guidance" for the interpretation of Article 43 of the TEC (Article III-137 DC).[107]

48

At the same time, the ECJ restricts the prohibition of discrimination in Article 43 of the TEC (Article III-137 DC) not only to areas directly related to the freedom of establishment, but applies it to so-called peripheral provisions. These include, for example, a provision according to which the daughter of an EU national, who, while maintaining his nationality and residence, sets up an establishment in another Member State, is not eligible to receive a university grant. The ECJ regards a discriminatory regulation of this kind as "hinder[ing] nationals of other Member States in their pursuit of activities as self-employed persons" within the meaning of the freedom of establishment.[108] At the same time it must be noted that peripheral discrimination such as this is predominantly covered by Articles 12 and 17 of the TEC (Articles I-4(2) and I-10 DC). Since in recent times the ECJ has effectively applied the prohibition of discrimination in Article 12 of the TEC (Article I-4 DC) to measures not directly caught by the fundamental freedoms,[109] it is no longer necessary to employ the specific freedom. In order to guarantee that a meaningful distinction between Articles 12 and 43 of the TEC (Articles I-4(2) and III-137 DC) is maintained, the main focus must be on the core content, in terms of restricting one of the fundamental freedoms, of the discriminatory provision.[110]

49

Both open and indirect discrimination infringe Article 43 of the TEC (Article III-137 DC). As in the case with all fundamental freedoms, the question is whether the Member State measure explicitly distinguishes between home nationals and foreign nationals (direct or open discrimination), or whether – where no such direct discrimination exists – it typically affects foreign nationals to a greater extent (indirect discrimination).[111] Indirect discrimination in the area of the freedom of establishment is of particular significance with regard to tax law. Thus, the ECJ relied solely on indirect discrimination in a case where a Member State regulation rendered tax deductible only those research expenses

50

---

106 [1961] OJ 36.
107 Eg ECJ *Steinhauser* [1985] ECR I-1819, para 15; *Meeusen* [1999] ECR I-3289, para 27.
108 ECJ *Meeusen* [1999] ECR I-3289, para 27; for further references on similar cases see Randelzhofer/Forsthoff (note 24) Art 43 EGV, para 72.
109 ECJ *Grzelczyk* [2001] ECR I-6193.
110 See also Randelzhofer/Forsthoff (note 24) Art 43 EGV, para 73.
111 Kapteyn/Verlooren van Themaat (note 2) pp 736–738; Lackhoff (note 5) p 227; → § 7 para 22; eg ECJ *Baxter* [1999] ECR I-4809, para 10: "it follows from the case-law of the Court [...] that the rules regarding equality of treatment prohibit not only overt discrimination by reason of nationality or, in the case of a company, its seat, but all covert forms of discrimination which, by the application of other criteria of differentiation, lead in fact to the same result".

incurred by enterprises whose primary place of business was within the levying Member State. The ECJ held that this would typically put enterprises which maintain a secondary place of business in that Member State at a disadvantage, since in the majority of cases research units are located in the same Member State as the undertaking's enterprise's principal place of business.[112] For the purpose of this decision it must be noted that Article 43 of the TEC (Article III-137 DC) does not merely prohibit national treatment in the stricter sense, but also prohibits discrimination regarding the various forms of establishment covered by Article 43 of the TEC (Article III-137 DC). In this sense, Article 43 of the TEC (Article III-137 DC) ensures the freedom of choice – including cumulative choice – of the type of establishment.[113]

51 Whether indirect discrimination according to Article 43 of the TEC (Article III-137 DC) is on hand must be decided on the basis of the question of whether there is an "application of different rules to comparable situations or the application of the same rule to different situations".[114] The ECJ predominantly takes a single-tier approach to this test.[115] Irrespective of this, it is important to answer the core question of comparability, which routinely requires a value judgement,[116] already at the point of deciding whether the provision applies. Although the ECJ occasionally seems to pose the question of comparability at the point of justification,[117] this procedure is not convincing. After all, it is only if it has been established that the facts of a case are comparable that we can ask whether their unequal treatment is based on justifiable aspects. However, this problem of the justification of an unequal treatment of comparable circumstances must be secondary to the question of comparability.[118]

2. Restrictions

52 For the purpose of a uniform interpretation of the fundamental freedoms, which has also been described as the convergence of the fundamental freedoms,[119] Article 43 of the TEC (Article III-137 DC) not only establishes a prohibition of discrimination, but also a general prohibition of restriction (or limitation). In principle, this is now accepted by jurisprudence[120] and literature alike.[121] The ECJ describes the prohibition of restriction of Article 43 of the TEC (Article III-137 DC) thus: "[Article 43] of the Treaty require[s] the elimination of restrictions on freedom of establishment and freedom to provide services

---

112 ECJ *Baxter* [1999] ECR I-4809, para 10.
113 *Eg* ECJ *Royal Bank of Scotland plc* [1999] ECR I-2651, para 23.
114 ECJ *Schumacker* [1995] ECR I-225, para 30; *Wielockx* [1995] ECR I-2493, para 17; *Asscher* [1996] ECR I-3089, para 40; *Royal Bank of Scotland plc* [1999] ECR I-2651, para 26.
115 Randelzhofer/Forsthoff (note 24) Art 43 EGV, para 77.
116 On the theoretical background see Alexy (note 56); Schoch [1988] DVBl 863, 873–874.
117 ECJ *Saint-Gobain* [1999] ECR I-6161, para 44.
118 Different however Randelzhofer/Forsthoff (note 24) Art 43 EGV, para 77.
119 See Behrens [1992] EuR 145; Hobe/Tietje [1996] JuS 486, 489–490; Bröhmer in: Calliess/Ruffert (eds) *Kommentar des Vertrages über die Europäische Union und des Vertrages zur Gründung der Europäischen Gemeinschaft* (2nd ed, Neuwied 2002) Art 43 EGV, para 29; Koenig/Haratsch *Europarecht* (4th ed, Tübingen 2003) para 485.
120 ECJ *Vlassopoulou* [1991] ECR I-2357, para 15; *Commission v Italy* [2002] ECR I-305, para 22; *de Lasteyrie du Saillant* [2004] ECR I-2409.
121 Lenaerts/van Nuffel (note 1) p 188; Lasok/Lasok *Law & Institutions of the European Union* (7th ed, Reed Elsevier 2001) p 519–520; Lackhoff (note 5) p 249, with further references.

[...]. All measures which prohibit, impede or render less attractive the exercise of such freedoms must be regarded as constituting such restrictions"[122].

The allocation of so-called specific entry restrictions to the prohibition of restriction in Article 43 of the TEC (Article III-137 DC) is largely undisputed. These are Member State measures which, though not directly or indirectly differentiating between nationals and foreigners, have the actual effect of restricting or rendering less attractive the access to a certain market with the aim of creating an establishment. This applies, for example, to the prohibition of certain activities, the establishment or maintenance of statutory monopolies, a prohibition of multiple establishment and requirements pertaining to residence, permits, licenses, and qualifications.[123] Also covered by the prohibition of restriction in Article 43 of the TEC (Article III-137 DC) are Member State measures which impede the establishment of its nationals in another Member State – even if the impediment is insignificant or marginal.[124]

Regarding the mentioned Member State measures associated with the concept of restriction under Article 43 of the TEC (Article III-137 DC), the question arises whether the freedom of establishment covers every national regulation which is capable of directly or indirectly, actually or potentially affecting the freedom of establishment. This is problematic specifically with regard to the fact that any exercise of the freedom of establishment necessitates integration into the national legal system. Therefore it seems doubtful that every national regulation relating to establishment infringes Article 43 of the TEC (Article III-137 DC). The numerous arguments used to justify a thus modified or limited concept of 'restriction' within the meaning of Article 43 of the TEC (Article III-137 DC) shall not be comprehensively presented at this point.[125] They are all subject to the accusation that a limitation of the concept of restriction is closely tied to a very narrow market access criterion. If we are to take the ratio behind the fundamental freedoms, which today is regarded as ensuring the greatest possible freedom, seriously, market access can only – if at all – enter the equation where a particular freedom has an inherent transnational dimension.[126] This may be true of the movement of goods or services, thus justifying – at least in part – the Court's judgement in *Keck*.[127] However, Article 43(1) of the TEC (Article III-137(1) DC) does not necessarily demand a transnational element.[128] It serves economic activities realised by way of establishment as a whole. The aim of securing this freedom is based on the overriding objective in Article 4(1) of the TEC (Article I-3(3) DC) of creating an open market economy with free competition.[129] This requires the Member State to demonstrate the necessity of any market regulation. Were individual Member State measures to be removed from the scope of Article 43 of the TEC (Article III-137 DC), this imperative requirement of justification would be lost. It can only be

---

122 ECJ *Commission v Italy* [2002] ECR I-305, para 22.
123 For details see Craig/de Burca *EU Law, Text, Cases and Materials* (3rd ed, Oxford 2003) pp 777–782; Randelzhofer/Forsthoff (note 24) Art 43 EGV, para 90.
124 ECJ *de Lasteyrie du Saillant* [2004] ECR I-2409.
125 For details see Lackhoff (note 5) p 417 with further references.
126 Lackhoff (note 5) p 427.
127 ECJ *Keck* [1993] ECR I-6097, para 12.
128 Lackhoff (note 5) p 427.
129 For details on Article 4 TEC see, *eg,* Kapteyn/Verlooren van Themaat (note 2) pp 113–114; Bandilla in: Grabitz/Hilf (eds) *Das Recht der Europäischen Union* (loose-leaf, Munich) Art 4 EGV, paras 7–8.

maintained in the interest of spontaneous market development, and thus of the realisation of the fundamental freedoms,[130] if the scope of Article 43(1) of the TEC (Article III-137(1) DC), and the concept of restriction therein, continue to be interpreted broadly. Accordingly, the ECJ did not follow the argument that the broad interpretation of Article 43(1) of the TEC (Article III-137(1) DC) must not lead to a situation where Member States are required to justify any provision of their legislation, which would make the right of establishment less attractive.[131] The ECJ gave just as little weight to the argument that the provisions of so-called "integrated national regulatory systems"[132] such as the Member States' social security systems, are not considered restrictive.[133]

55 Moreover, this broad view of the freedom-ensuring role of Article 43 of the TEC (Article III-137 DC) does not cause the "legal systems of the Member States to be replaced with a uniform supranational law".[134] National legal systems continue to serve as the framework of regulation within the respective national markets. What has changed is merely the burden on the Member States to justify the regulation of their markets. This means that national law must comply with Article 43 of the TEC (Article III-137 DC) not on the first level, which asks if there has been a restriction, but on the second level, which demands that there has to be a justification. Only this structure can satisfy the freedom-oriented system of the fundamental freedoms as a whole, and thus also Article 43 of the TEC (Article III-137 DC).[135]

IV. Justification

56 Infringements of Article 43 of the TEC (Article III-137 DC) may be justified by Article 46(1) of the TEC (Article III-140(1) DC), and by mandatory requirements. Direct discrimination can only be justified under Article 46(1) of the TEC (Article III-140(1) DC). In the case of an indistinctly applicable restriction, both Article 46(1) of the TEC (Article III-140(1) DC) and the doctrine of mandatory requirements may be applied. As with all fundamental freedoms, it is disputed whether the mandatory requirements can also be applied to instances of covert or indirect discrimination, or if such cases are restricted to an application of Article 46(1) of the TEC (Article III-140(1) DC).[136]

57 Article 46(1) of the TEC (Article III-140(1) DC) is the only provision of the Treaty explicitly designed to justify restrictions of the freedom of establishment. However, the exception in Article 46(1) of the TEC (Article III-140(1) DC) must be interpreted restrictively.[137] The thus already limited scope of the provision is further restricted when its ratio is taken into account: Article 46(1) of the TEC (Article III-140(1) DC) refers to "special

---

130 See v Hayek *Individualism and the Economic Order* (Chicago 1948) p 16.
131 Opinion AG Mischo, ECJ *Pfeiffer* [1999] ECR I-2835, para 58; the ECJ did not address this issue in its judgement, and decided that the measure in question (the application of the Austrian UWG) was in violation of Article 43 TEC, ECJ *Pfeiffer* [1999] ECR I-2835, para 19; AG Mischo defended his opinion again in: ECJ *Deutsche Paracelsus Schulen* [2002] ECR I-6915, para 57.
132 Randelzhofer/Forsthoff (note 0) Art 43 EGV, para 106.
133 ECJ *Smits* [2001] ECR I-5473.
134 As argued by Randelzhofer/Forsthoff (note 24) Vor Art 39-55 EGV, para 92.
135 The scope of the doctrine of limiation is very disputed. For details see *eg* Randelzhofer/Forsthoff (note 24) Vor Art 39–55 EGV, para 87.
136 For details see → § 7 para 79.
137 ECJ *Calfa* [1999] ECR I-11, para 23.

treatment for foreign nationals". Since the primary aim of the fundamental freedoms is to eradicate within the common market special treatment tied to nationality requirements (Article 12(1) TEC/Article I-4(2) DC), foreign nationality cannot alone be the key to Article 46(1) of the TEC (Article III-137(1) DC). The ECJ has continually held that Article 46(1) of the TEC (Article III-140(1) DC) "permits Member States to adopt with respect to nationals of other Member States, and in particular on the grounds of public policy, measures which they cannot apply to their own nationals, inasmuch as they have no authority to expel the latter from the territory or to deny them access thereto." [138] This statement of the ECJ must be seen in conjunction with the prohibition under constitutional law (*eg* Article 16(2) of the *Grundgesetz* (German Basic Law / Federal Constitution)) and international law (Article 3 of the 4th Prot ECHR) of expelling and extraditing citizens. Due to this prohibition and despite Article 12 of the TEC (Article I-4 DC), significant differences between citizens and foreign nationals with regard to expulsion and extradition exist. Article 46(1) of the TEC (Article III-140(1) DC) refers exclusively to this distinction, which continues to exist. It is thus recognised that the provision must primarily apply to national aliens' law.[139]

The fundamental orientation toward aliens' law of Article 46(1) of the TEC (Article III-140(1) DC) is also reflected in the requirement that the question of whether the personal conduct of the person entitled to establishment created a threat to public order, public security or public health must be evaluated on a case-by-case basis; an isolated offence being insufficient.[140] Furthermore, the criteria of "public order, public security and public health" must be interpreted in conformity with Article 39(3) of the TEC (Article III-133(3) DC).[141] In the past, Directive 64/221[142] was used as an aid for their interpretation,[143] but as of 30 April 2004 these terms are clarified by Directive 2004/38.[144] The principle of proportionality serves as an additional limitation on the restriction.[145]

58

To the extent that an infringement of Article 43 of the TEC (Article III-137 DC) exists due to a prohibition of restriction, it may be justified by reason of mandatory requirements. This unwritten principle must be applied in accordance with the general principles of the fundamental freedoms, and thus does not require closer analysis at this point.[146] It should only be pointed out that the European Court of Justice has developed a large

59

---

138 ECJ *Calfa* [1999] ECR I-11, para 20.
139 Schlag (note 38) Art 46 EGV, para 3; Roth (note 78) para 72.
140 ECJ *Calfa* [1999] ECR I-11, para 25.
141 See also Lenaerts/van Nuffel (note 1) pp 191–192; Schneider/Wunderlich in: Schwarze (ed) *EU-Kommentar* (Baden-Baden 2000) Art 39 EGV para 123.
142 [1964] OJ 850.
143 Craig/de Burca (note 123) pp 825–841; Lenaerts/van Nuffel (note 1) pp 191 193; Schlag (note 38) Art 46 EGV, para 5.
144 Dir 2004/38/EC of the European Parliament and of the Council of 29 April 2004 on the right of citizens of the Union and their family members to move and reside freely within the territory of the Member States amending Reg (EEC) No 1612/68 and repealing Dir 64/221/EEC, 68/360/EEC, 72/194/EEC, 73/148/EEC, 75/34/EEC, 75/35/EEC, 90/364/EEC, 90/365/EEC and 93/96/EEC.
145 ECJ *Commission v Italy* [1996] ECR I-2691, para 26; Fairhurst/Vincenzi (note 64) p 284; Randelzhofer/Forsthoff (note 24) Art 46 EGV, para 21.
146 *Cf* more detailed → § 7 para 78; Randelzhofer/Forsthoff (note 24) Vor Art 39–55 EGV, para 154.

§ 10 V Christian Tietje

number of recognised objectives regarding the mandatory requirements.[147] In addition, the requirement that a measure "must be suitable for securing the attainment of the objective which they pursue; and [...] must not go beyond what is necessary in order to attain it"[148] corresponds to the prevailing case law of the ECJ.

Case 4 – Answer:
60 Since the German company T operates a secondary establishment in Austria, the case falls within the scope of Articles 43 and 48 of the TEC (Articles III-137 and III-142 DC). It is, however, questionable whether the freedom of establishment has been restricted. The application of the Austrian *Bundesgesetz gegen unlauteren Wettbewerb* (Austrian Act on Unfair Competition) does not amount to open discrimination since this law applies without distinction to national and foreign undertakings alike. Covert or indirect discrimination would exist if § 9 of the Act on Unfair Competition typically puts foreign undertakings, such as T, at a disadvantage. This, too, does not appear to be the case. Thus, the freedom of establishment could only be restricted if the application of a national provision makes the exercise of a fundamental freedom less attractive. T deliberately chose the logo in order to become known throughout Europe by its advertising campaign. The uniformity of T's Europe-wide campaign is impaired if it must be departed from in some of the Member States. This, in turn, necessarily affects the attractiveness of entering into economic activities in a Member State which does not permit the use of a Europe-wide logo. Therefore, the freedom of establishment has been restricted, as at least the access to the market is affected.
The violation of Article 43 of the TEC (Article III-137 DC) could, however, be justified. A justification under Article 46(1) of the TEC (Article III-140(1) DC) is out of the question since the provisions of the Act on Unfair Competition do not pertain exclusively to foreign nationals. This leaves only possible justification under one of the mandatory requirements. The protection under the laws of competition of business relations from the risk of confusion is one such mandatory requirement. The application of § 9(1) of the Act on Unfair Competition satisfies the requirement of proportionality, since only a prohibition can guarantee the attainment of the justified objective.[149] Thus, there is no violation of Articles 43 and 48 of the TEC (Articles III-137 and III-142 DC).

V. The Application of the Freedom of Establishment to Legal Persons According to Article 48 of the TEC (Article III-142 DC)

Case 5 – Problem: (ECJ *Überseering* [2002] ECR I-9919)
61 The BV company has been enlisted in the commercial register of Amsterdam since 1990. BV owns land in Düsseldorf, Germany. On behalf of BV, the NCC company carried out construction services on BV's property. On 1 January 1995, two natural persons acquired all shares in BV. From then on, BV's actual place of business has been Düsseldorf. In 1996, BV brought an action against NCC, claiming compensation for costs incurred in remedying alleged defects. The *Oberlandesgericht* (higher regional court) dismissed the action on the grounds that BV did not have legal capacity in Germany within the meaning of § 50 *ZPO* (German Code of Civil Procedure). This results from the fact that under German law, legal

---

147 For details see Randelzhofer/Forsthoff (note 24) Vor Art 39–55 EGV, para 161.
148 ECJ *Gebhard* [1995] ECR I-4165, para 37; *Pfeiffer* [1999] ECR I-2835, para 19; *de Lasteyrie du Saillant* [2004] ECR I-2409.
149 ECJ *Pfeiffer* [1999] ECR I-2835, para 22.

Freedom of Establishment **§ 10 V**

capacity must be established in conformity with the laws of the country in which a company has its registered office. In the present case this is Germany, and BV does not have legal capacity there, according to the applicable German law. Does this decision violate Articles 43 and 48 of the TEC (Articles III-137 and III-142 DC)?

Article 48 of the TEC (Article III-142 DC) causes Article 43 of the TEC (Article III-137 DC) to be applied to "companies or firms formed in accordance with the law of a Member State and having their registered office, central administration or principal place of business within the Community". The term 'company' – or legal persons[150] – at the centre of Article 48 of the TEC (Article III-142 DC) must not be interpreted according to restrictive Member State definitions, but according to Community law. As is evident from Article 48(2) of the TEC (Article III-142(2) DC), the concept must be given a broad interpretation. In this respect, it is crucial that an association is so independent from its members that it acts autonomously. Thus, eg, in Germany, an *OHG* (partnership) and a *GbR* (civil law association) are "legal persons" within the meaning of Article 48 of the TEC (Article III-142 DC), even though their status of "legal persons" is not entirely clear under German law.[151] **62**

The pivotal problem with Article 48 of the TEC (Article III-142 DC) lies in the determination of those conditions which make an entity a legal person within the described context. This mainly concerns the question of when a company is "formed in accordance with the law of a Member State". Since the Member States have not yet come to a uniform regulation regarding the mutual recognition of companies under Article 293 of the TEC, and the focus of Article 48(2) of the TEC (Article III-142(2) DC) is on "the companies or firms formed in accordance with the law of a Member State", it is for Member State law to decide whether the conditions in Article 48(2) of the TEC (Art III-142 II DC) are met. Of course this evaluation is subject to the principles of Community law. **63**

Foreign legal persons are evaluated under applicable conflict of laws principles (so called international company law) of the Member States. In this regard, the so called company statute decides which law must be applied to a particular company.[152] Two distinct approaches exist: Some countries (*eg* the US and the UK) rely on the so called incorporation theory, which points to the law of the country in which a company was incorporated. Under the so called real seat or head office theory[153] (which is applied in Germany, for example), the question is in which country the main seat of a company's management is located. **64**

In light of Article 48 of the TEC (Article III-142 DC), the application of the real seat theory led to the problem that the legal capacity of an enterprise which was incorporated in Member State A, but later moved its registered office to Member State B, is determined **65**

---

150 As shown by Article 48(2) TEC (Article III-142(2) DC), the terms "companies" and "legal persons" are identical in meaning, see Craig/de Burca (note 123) p 793; Fairhurst/Vincenzl (note 64) pp 285–286; Randelzhofer/Forsthoff (note 24) Art 48 EGV, para 7.
151 Randelzhofer/Forsthoff (note 24) Art 48 EGV, para 7; BGH [2001] ZIP 330.
152 Kindler in: *Münchener Kommentar zum BGB (Internationales Handels- und Gesellschaftsrecht; Art 50–237 EGBGB)* (3rd ed, München 1998) 'IntGesR', para 7; Großfeld in: Staudinger *EGBGB/IPR/IntGesR* (13th ed, Berlin 1998) 'EGBGB/IPR/IntGesR', para 16.
153 See Craig/de Burca (note 123) pp 793–798; Kindler (note 152) para 5; Großfeld (note 152) para 38; Kegel/Schurig *Internationales Privatrecht* (8th ed, München 2000) p 502.

under the laws of B. Should the undertaking not be considered as having legal capacity under the laws of Member State B, Article 48 of the TEC (Article III-142 DC) is inapplicable even though it was effectively incorporated, and gained legal capacity, in another Member State. This circumstance has led to the highly disputed question whether, and to what extent, Articles 43 and 48 of the TEC (Articles III-137(1) and 142 DC) restrict the application of the real seat theory.[154]

66 Without discussing at length the questions raised with regard to the relation between international company law and Articles 43 and 48 of the TEC (Articles III-137 and 142 DC), one must at least mention some of the arguments used in solving this problem: First of all, it should be pointed out that the unlimited application of national company law could cause an undertaking from a third country to be affected by Article 48 of the TEC (Article III-142 DC). This would be the case where an undertaking is incorporated in a third country, but has its registered office in a Member State which applies the incorporation theory. In light of the fundamental aim of the freedom of establishment, which is to reserve the rights in Article 43 of the TEC (Article III-137 DC) for Member State citizens,[155] this result seems unacceptable.[156] In addition, one must bear in mind that applying the Member States' international company law without restricting it through Community law could lead to the different treatment of identical circumstances by Member States following the real seat theory compared to those following the incorporation theory. This result would be incompatible with the principle of the uniform application of Community law.[157]

67 These aspects alone show that the unrestricted application of the Member States' international company law must be regarded as being incompatible with Articles 43 and 48 of the TEC (Art III-137, 142 DC). Therefore, the following Community law principle must apply also with regard to Article 48 of the TEC (Article III-142 DC): Although this matter falls within the competence of the Member States, Community law must nonetheless be taken into account.[158] Hence, the in principle permissible application of the Member States' international company law may not lead to a restriction of the rights granted by Article 43 of the TEC (Article III-137 DC). Thus, the freedom conferred by Article 43 of the TEC (Art III-137 DC) forms the basis for relieving the tension between international company law and Article 48 of the TEC (Article III-142 DC).[159]

68 It would not be a valid counter-argument to say that international company law, as demonstrated in Article 293 of the TEC, does not fall within the competence of the EC Treaty, and that the principle of subsidiarity (Article 5(2) TEC/Article I-11(3) DC) com-

---

154 See, eg, Rothe [2004] American University Law Review 1104–1141; Gildea [2004] Brooklyn Journal of International Law, 257–292; Lenaerts/van Nuffel (note 1) pp 189–190; Craig/de Burca (note 123) pp 793–796; Behrens [1999] IPrax 323; Ebke [1999] JZ 656; Forsthoff [2000] EuR 167; Kindler [1999] NJW 1993; Meilicke [2000] GmbHR 693; Roth [2000] ZGR 311; Sonnenberger/Großerichter [1999] RIW 721.
155 Above para 7.
156 Randelzhofer/Forsthoff (note 24) Art 48 EGV, para 16.
157 Randelzhofer/Forsthoff (note 24) Art 48 EGV, para 17.
158 Convincing: Opinion AG Colmer, ECJ *Überseering* [2002] ECR I-9919, para 39; similar Randelzhofer/Forsthoff (note 24) Art 48 EGV, para 18.
159 Randelzhofer/Forsthoff (note 24) Art 48 EGV, para 2; similarly ECJ *Inspire Art* [2003] ECR I-10155, paras 95–96; *Centros* [1999] ECR I-1459, para 14; *Daily Mail* [1988] ECR 5483, para 21; different however Kindler [1999] NJW 1993, 1996.

mands the exclusive competence in this area of the Member States.[160] These arguments fail since Article 293 of the TEC (Art III-269(2) lit c DC) – as is evident from a comparison with Article 295 of the TEC (Art III-425 DC) – does not contain a reservation of statutory powers in the area of international company law in favour of the Member States,[161] and the principle of subsidiarity has no place in the interpretation of the fundamental freedoms.[162]

Thus, the international company law of the Member States – in particular with regard to the status of companies – remains largely untouched by Article 48 of the TEC (Article III-142 DC). However, where a Member State seeks to establish, under application of its international company law, whether in accordance with Article 48(1) of the TEC (Article III-142(1) DC) a company was formed or continues to exist "in accordance with the law of a Member State", the general principles of Community law demand that the fundamental freedoms must be taken into account. To the extent that it is impossible to refer to the fundamental freedoms, in particular Article 43 of the TEC (Article III-137 DC), for the purpose of interpreting national law in conformity with Community law, the conflicting national law can only be justified by compelling reasons in the general interest.[163]

In addition, it should be pointed out that, strictly speaking, the illustrated ECJ decisions result in a situation in which not only Community law, but also public international law could greatly restrict the national applicability of the real seat theory. This applies first and foremost to the numerous Treaties on Friendship, Commerce and Navigation which require the reciprocal recognition of the legal capacity of companies. In this regard, the *BGH* (German Federal Supreme Court), in a judgement from 29 January 2003, held a corresponding clause in the German-American Treaty on Friendship, Commerce and Navigation of 1954 to be directly applicable, with the result that the legal status of a Florida company had to be determined according to US law.[164] Following ECJ jurisprudence, the German Court came to the following conclusion: "If national treatment, most-favoured nation treatment and the freedom of establishment are agreed upon and a company is accordingly granted the right to engage in economic activity in another country, it can not be denied the legal capacity there to which it is entitled under the law of the state where it was established. In particular, the freedom of establishment comprises the unrestricted recognition of legal capacity."[165]

This statement of the German Federal Supreme Court has direct consequences for the perhaps most significant international treaty restricting the application of the real seat theory – the GATS. According to the already briefly outlined regulations of the GATS,[166] foreign companies have the right to commercial presence in those services areas in which WTO members have undertaken specific liberalisation commitments. Commercial presence is defined as "any type of business or professional establishment through [amongst others] the constitution, acquisition or maintenance of a juridical person" (Article

---

160 See, *eg,* Kindler [1999] NJW 1993, 1997–1998.
161 Opinion AG Colmer, ECJ *Überseering* [2002] ECR I-9919, para 42.
162 Randelzhofer/Forsthoff (note 24) Art 48 EGV, para 14.
163 ECJ *Inspire Art* [2003] ECR I-10155, paras 95–96; *Überseering* [2002] ECR I-9919, paras 78–79; Opinion AG Colmer, ECJ *Überseering* [2002] ECR I-9919, para 43; *Centros* [1999] ECR I-1459, para 14.
164 BGH [2003] DB 818, 819.
165 BGH [2003] DB 818, 819.
166 (Paras 9–10).

XXVIII(d)(i) GATS). A juridical person is "any legal entity duly constituted or otherwise organized under applicable law" (Article XXVIII(l) GATS). From these determinations it directly follows that the legal capacity of a company which was effectively established in one WTO member state must be recognised in every other WTO member state to the extent that it deals in services. This leaves very little room for an application of the real seat theory.[167]

> **Case 5 – Answer:**
> The application of the real seat theory for the purpose of determining BV's company statute causes its legal capacity to be judged under German law. Since according to the *Oberlandesgericht* (*OLG* – Regional Court of Appeal) BV does not have legal capacity under German law, it can also not have the capacity to be a party to judicial proceedings within the meaning of section 50 of the *Zivilprozessordnung* (*ZPO* – German Code of Civil Procedure). This puts BV in a situation which, having been aware of the legal position, would have deterred it from moving its administrative office to Germany. Thus, the real seat theory makes the exercise of the freedom of establishment significantly less attractive to BV, and Articles 43 and 48 of the TEC (Articles III-137 and 142 DC) have been infringed. This remains unmitigated by the fact that the Member States retain the capacity to regulate in the field of international company law, since this competence does not absolve the Member States from their obligation to observe the fundamental freedoms.
> However, it is questionable whether the infringement of Articles 43 and 48 of the TEC (Articles III-137 and 142 DC) can be justified. The application of the real seat theory serves, among other objectives, the protection of creditors and employees.[168] It is unclear, however, why the interests at the heart of the real seat theory must cause a company which was effectively established in another Member State to be denied legal personality in Germany. This is a significant infringement of the freedom of establishment, since the company in question is suddenly robbed of its "legal assets".[169] It furthermore conflicts with the right to effective judicial protection (including civil law protection) – one of the fundamental principles of Community law.[170] Thus, the infringement of the right of establishment is disproportionate, and therefore cannot be justified.[171]

---

167 Different however Lehmann [2004] RIW 816.
168 For details see Opinion AG Colmer, ECJ *Überseering* [2002] ECR I-9919, para 50.
169 Opinion AG Colmer, ECJ *Überseering* [2002] ECR I-9919, para 57.
170 ECJ *Überseering* [2002] ECR I-9919, para 93.
171 For details on the possibility of a justification in a similar case see ECJ *Inspire Art* [2003] ECR I-10155, paras 131–132.

§ 11
The Free Movement of Services

Eckhard Pache

Leading cases: ECJ *Luisi and Carbone* [1984] ECR 377; *Tourist Guide* [1991] ECR I-682, I-718, I-735; *Schindler* [1994] ECR I-1039; *Alpine Investments* [1995] ECR I-1141; *Ciola* [1999] ECR I-2517; *Müller-Fauré* [2003] ECR I-4509; *Carpenter* [2002] ECR I-6279; *Commission v France* [2004] I-6569.

Further reading: Kluth in: Calliess/Ruffert (eds) *Kommentar des Vertrages über die Europäische Union und des Vertrages zur Gründung der Europäischen Union* (3rd ed, München 2007) Art 49 EGV, paras 2 ff; Fischer *Europarecht. Grundlagen des Europäischen Gemeinschaftsrechts in Verbindung mit deutschem Staats- und Verwaltungsrecht* (3rd ed, Munich 2001); Randelzhofer in: Grabitz/Hilf (eds) *Das Recht der Europäischen Union*, (loose-leaf, Munich) Art 49 EGV, paras 4 ff; Troberg/Tiedje in: von der Groeben/Schwarze (eds) *Kommentar zum EU-/EG-Vertrag* (6th ed, Baden-Baden 2003) Art 49 EGV, paras 4 ff; Hailbronner/Nachbauer *Die Dienstleistungsfreiheit in der Rechtsprechung des EuGH* [1992] EuZW 105; Kort *Schranken der Dienstleistungsfreiheit im europäischen Recht* [1996] JZ 132; Lenz *EG-Vertrag – Kommentar* (3rd ed, Cologne 2003); Nowak *Erweiterte Rechtfertigungsmöglichkeiten für mitgliedstaatliche Beschränkungen auf EG-Grundfreiheiten. Genereller Rechtsprechungswandel oder Sonderweg im Bereich der sozialen Sicherheit?* [2000] EuZW 627; Holoubek in: Schwarze (ed) *EU-Kommentar* (Baden-Baden 2000); Müller-Graff in: Streinz (ed) *EUV/EGV* (Munich 2003) Art 49 EGV, paras 1 ff; Trautwein *Der praktische Fall – Europarecht mit Völkerrecht: Schwangerschaftsabbruch in Irland. Fragen der gemeinschaftsrechtlichen Dienstleistungsfreiheit und der völkerrechtlich garantierten Freiheit der Meinungsäußerung* [1995] JuS 908.

I. Introduction

1. The General Relevance of the Principle of the Freedom to Provide Services

1 Article 49 of the TEC (Article III-144 of the DC) prohibits, within the framework of the provisions set out in the following Articles of the TEC, certain limitations of the freedom to provide services within the European Community. Nationals of Member States may provide services to persons established in other states of the Community so long as (1) they are self-employed, (2) they are offering their services on a temporary basis in the particular state, (3) those services are normally provided for remuneration, and (4) the activities are not governed by the provisions relating to the freedom of movement for goods, capital and persons.

2 The principle of the freedom to provide services is central to the effective functioning of the European internal market. Because of its increasingly important role for the political economy of the Community, the freedom to provide services must be considered as one of the fundamental Community rights. The composition of the economy of the EU has changed significantly over the past ten years. There has been an exceptional increase in the service sector, so that it now comprises a considerable percentage of the gross margin in the EU. Consequently, the role of the freedom to provide services has changed from a catchall element to a right with significant autonomous legal meaning. The service sector of the European internal market has become at least twice as important as the industrial sector, and is three times larger than social services and other services in the public sector. The European service sector has an enormous commercial relevance and a great growth potential for the EU and its 25 Member States. Thus, the proper functioning of

the service sector within the internal market is crucial for an increase in wealth and competition[1].

3   From this it follows that the freedom to provide services is a central principle of the fundamental freedoms governing the internal market. It must be read parallel to the Treaty provisions of the freedom of establishment (Article 43 TEC/Article III-137 DC), since both provisions seek to address similar problems. Hence, Article 55 of the TEC (Article III-150 DC) declares certain Treaty provisions pertaining to the freedom of establishment to be applicable to Article 49 of the TEC. Furthermore, the Treaty lays down for both of these fundamental freedoms that the self-employed may freely exercise cross border activity, since Article 43 of the TEC (Article III-137 DC) demands the abolition of limitations on the self-employed offering cross border services. Due to its product-related aspects, the freedom to provide services is also closely connected to the right of free movement of goods (Article 28 TEC/Article III-151 DC).

2. The Structure of the Freedom to Provide Services in the Community Law

4   Articles 49 through 55 of the TEC (Articles III-144 ff DC) set forth both general provisions on the right of freedom to provide services as well as more specific provisions, such as *eg* Article 51 of the TEC (Article III-146 DC). Articles 49 and 50 of the TEC (Articles III-144 and 145 DC) contain the most important basic provisions. Art. 49 of the TEC forbids all restrictions on the freedom to provide services. Article 50 of the TEC (Article III-145 DC) defines the term "service". Article 51(1) of the TEC (Article III-146(1) DC) states that the freedom to provide services in the field of transport shall be governed by the provisions of the title relating to transport and therefore confines the field of application of the Articles 49 ff of the TEC (Articles III-144 ff DC). Article 51(2) of the TEC (Article III-146(2) DC) creates an obligation to coordinate the Treaty provisions relating to the liberalisation of banking and insurance services connected with movements of capital with the secondary law of the free movement of capital[2]. Article 52 of the TEC (Article III-147 DC) authorises the Community institutions to issue directives in order to achieve the liberalisation of a specific service[3]. In Article 53 of the TEC (Article III-148 DC) the Member States declare their readiness to undertake the liberalisation of services beyond the extent required by directives. This rule has, however, lost its normative relevance altogether after the transitional period. In some respects, it already lacked importance during the transitional period[4]. Article 54 of the TEC (Article III-149 DC) was meant as a temporary regulation. It obliges the Member States to treat all persons providing services equally without distinction on grounds of nationality or residency until all limitations on freedom to provide services have been abolished. The chapter concerning

---

1 On the increasing importance of the free movement of services Hakenberg in: Lenz (ed) *EG-Vertrag – Kommentar* (3rd ed, Cologne 2003) Vor Art 49–55 EGV, para 3; Holoubek in: Schwarze (ed) *EU-Kommentar* (Baden-Baden 2000) Art 49 EGV, paras 2–4; Troberg/Tiedje in: von der Groeben/Schwarze (eds) *Kommentar zum EU-/EG-Vertrag* (6th ed, Baden-Baden 2003) Vor Art 49–Art 55 EGV, paras 2–6.
2 Kluth in: Calliess/Ruffert (eds) *Kommentar des Vertrages über die Europäische Union und des Vertrages zur Gründung der Europäischen Union* (3rd ed, München 2007) Art 51 EGV, para 2.
3 *Cf* para 11.
4 *Cf* Holoubek (note 1) Art 54 EGV, paras 1–2; Kluth (note 2) Art 54 EGV, paras 1–2.

the free movement of services ends with Article 55 of the TEC (Article III-150 DC), which refers to the provisions of the freedom of establishment.

Because "services" in Article 50(1) of the TEC (Article III-145(1) DC) is defined in the negative ("...in so far as they are not governed by the provisions relating to freedom of movement for goods, capital and persons ..."), the European Court of Justice and literature have posited that the free movement of services serves only as a fundamental freedom with a reserve function. In doing so, they have strictly distinguished the free movement of services from the other fundamental freedoms. Accordingly, if the provisions of the free movement of goods or the freedom of establishment are applicable, they take priority over the provisions of the free movement of services[5].

The freedom to provide services is directly effective; its implementation is not dependant on the issue of specific directives by the EU legislature. The court explained the direct effect of Article 49 of the TEC (Article III-144 DC) in the decision *van Binsbergen*[6]. This means that the national courts and authorities are bound to the provisions of Articles 49 ff of the TEC (Articles III-144 ff DC) and are required to allow nationals of Member States to provide services under the same conditions as those imposed on their own nationals[7]. Article 49 of the TEC (Article III-144 DC) provides a defensive right that enables an individual to combat any discriminatory national rule or other non-discriminatory rules.

Finally, the principle of supremacy of Community law[8] further supports the recognition of the freedom to provide services as a fundamental freedom. The principle of supremacy of Community law holds that national law that is incompatible with the Treaty ranks behind Community law and is no longer applicable[9].

3. The Free Movement of Services beyond the Treaty

The **Treaty establishing the European Atomic Energy Community (EAC)** contains regulations for specific types of services. For example, Article 97 of the EAC prohibits rules that hinder individuals and legal persons from participating in the construction of nuclear power plants in the Community. Articles 75, 98, 10 and 15 of the EAC are also of importance, though they are not applicable under Articles 49 ff of the TEC (Articles III-144 ff DC)[10].

In addition, specific treaties with some states of the former Eastern block expressly anticipated the possibility of an accession to the EU. These treaties provided for the step-by-step introduction and establishment of a free trade area designed to lead, after a period of time, to a complete liberalisation of trade within the Community[11]. In the field of free movement of services they prohibited only discriminatory rules with some facilitations regarding access to the European job market. After the accession of ten states of Eastern and Central Europe, however, the freedom to provide services has been liberalised to the full extent. Transitory agreements exist only for the building and handcrafts indus-

---

5 Holoubek (note 1) Art 49 EGV, para 12.
6 ECJ *van Binsbergen* [1974] ECR 1299, para 27.
7 Holoubek (note 1) Art 49 EGV, para 5; Kluth (note 2) Art 50 EGV, para 48.
8 → § 7 para 9.
9 *Cf* ECJ *Costa v E.N.E.L.* [1964] ECR 584.
10 Troberg/Tiedje (note 1) Vor Arts 49–55 EGV, para 33.
11 *Cf* Herrnfeld in: Schwarze (ed) *EU-Kommentar* (Baden-Baden 2000) Art 310 EGV, para 10.

tries which are linked with the so-called "2 plus 3 plus 2 rule" of the free movement of workers. This rule allows the Member States to take provisional measures during a transition period of two years. The Member States may prolong the application of the provisional measures for another three years following a survey by the Commission, and for another two years after that in case of serious disturbances of the employment market[12]. The subject matter of protection for these provisions is set forth in the codex of the OECD. The wording in the codex of the OECD, describing its objective to "liberalise current invisible operations," is even broader than the provisions set forth in the TEC. This codex regulates many transactions of the international trade, which partly applies to the free movement of services. The obligations to liberalise in this codex have much less weight than the provisions of the TEC, however[13].

10   In the field of international law, in 1994 the **General Agreement on Trade in Services** (GATS) established multilateral provisions for international trade in services which are enforceable by law. There is no danger of a collision between GATS and Community law, because the provisions of GATS do not go further than Articles 49 ff of the TEC (Articles III-144 ff DC).

4. Liberalisation of the Freedom to Provide Services and Secondary Legislation

11   Article 52(1) of the TEC (Article III-147(1) DC) is the central rule in the field of the liberalisation of services under secondary legislation. It also authorises the EU legislature **to harmonise the provisions of the TEC with secondary legislation** and partially regulates the procedures required to achieve harmonisation[14]. The secondary legislation is therefore separate from the guarantee of a minimum standard, and because of its direct effect, it is a very important instrument to realise the freedom to provide services. The authorisation in Article 52(1) of the TEC (Article III-147(1) DC) allows the Council to issue directives in order to achieve the liberalisation of a specific service. It replaces the former Article 63(1) of the TEC, which authorised the Council to establish a general program to abolish all obstacles of the freedom to provide services[15]. Based on Article 52(1) and 47, 55 of the TEC (Article III-147(1) and 141, 150 DC), the EU legislature has issued many directives for various industry branches and for liberal professions[16]. Many of those directives simultaneously abolish any obstacles to the free movement of services.

12   Some very important directives have been issued in the field of the liberalisation of the free movement of services during the past forty years. In 1977, the directive to facilitate the effective exercise of the freedom to provide services by lawyers[17] enabled lawyers to provide legal services in another Member State without requiring them to have a fixed establishment in that state[18]. In addition, the directive on the coordination of provisions concerning television broadcasting activities[19] established minimum standards concerning

---

12 [2003] OJ L236/803; to the problems concerning the free movement of services because of the liberalisation in the field of handcraft see Pechstein [2004] EuZW 167.
13 *Cf* Troberg/Tiedje (note 1) Vor Arts 49–55 EGV, para 35.
14 Kluth (note 2) Art 52 EGV, para 3.
15 To the history of the freedom to provide services Kluth (note 2) Art 52 EGV, paras 15 ff.
16 Kluth (note 2) Art 52 EGV, paras 22 ff. For an outline see CELEX, www.europa.eu.int/celex.
17 Dir 77/249, [1977] OJ L078/17.
18 A new directive was issued in 1988 which includes the freedom of establishment, compare Dir 98/5, [1998] OJ L077/36.
19 Dir 89/552, [1989] OJ L331/51.

advertising and the protection of minors. Finally, a directive concerning the posting of workers in the framework of the provision of services established minimum standards for employees who work in another Member State providing services on behalf of their employer[20]. This directive aims at ensuring fair competition in the field of cross border services and to improve employment protection.

5. The New Strategy for the Internal Market

The Commission has issued a new strategy in the field of services in order to eliminate the remaining obstacles to the freedom to provide services[21]. This strategy is meant to improve the functioning of the internal market in general and to ensure that a provider of services is able to offer his services in a Member State as easily as in his own state. In Lisbon in 1999, the European Council announced the new strategic goal: "To become the most competitive and dynamic knowledge-based economy in the world, capable of sustainable economic growth with more and better jobs and greater social cohesion"[22]. The internet and other elements of the information society have given the service sector a new vitality because of the reduced costs for the procurement and the transmission of information. Consequently, the potential for cross-border demand has increased rapidly. The strategy is based on a new approach which recognises that while services are divided into different sectors, they are also intricately intertwined and must therefore be provided and used in combination with one another. The harmonisation affects a wide variety of different service sectors that face the same problems. The Commission intends to identify a broad and systematic inventory of barriers that still prevent the proper functioning of the internal market, draw up measures to tackle the relevant legal and other barriers, and order the Member States to tear down these obstacles. This strategy provides a new framework for services that allows new provisions of law to be developed, which are flexible enough to allow new forms of services to develop without barriers. In 2002, as part of this strategy, the Commission published a report on the state of the internal market in services. This report contained an inventory of the current most important barriers and criticised the risks associated with a combination of different provisions for the service market. The report also revealed the fact that services are much more prone to being hindered by market barriers than the free movement of goods because of the complex and intangible nature of many services and the importance of the qualifications of the service provider[23]. Based on this report the Commission has proposed the development of a directive on services. This directive would basically follow the country of origin principle and would require the harmonisation of some related policies, such as consumer protection, as well as the development of administrative simplification measures. The directive would also require the introduction of measures for promoting the quality of services, such as voluntary certification of activities, quality charters or cooperation between the chambers of commerce and chambers of crafts[24].

13

---

20 Dir 69/71, [1997] OJ L018/1.
21 COM (2000) 888.
22 Cf the presidency conclusions: http://ue.eu.int/ueDocs/cms_Data/docs/pressData/en/EC/00100-r1.en0.htm.
23 COM (2002) 441.
24 COM (2004) 3.

II. The Scope of Protection

1. The Territorial Scope of Protection

14   The territorial scope of protection is, according to Article 299(1) of the TEC (Article III-440 DC), the sovereign territory of the Member States. According to Article 299(2) of the TEC (Article III-440(2) DC) the Treaty also applies to the French overseas departments, the Azores, Madeira and the Canary Islands.

2. The Personal Scope of Protection

15   Article 49 of the TEC (Article III-144 DC) generally applies to the nationals of the Member States, though the wording of Article 49 of the TEC (Article III-144 DC) specifically identifies the providers of services. Despite the wording, the provision applies to nationals of Member States providing services as well to the recipients of services who travel to another Member State for the purpose of obtaining services[25]. Unlike the provisions for the free movement of workers and the freedom of establishment, the freedom of services applies only to nationals of the Member States who are established in a state of the Community. This means that the scope of protection applies only if the two participants of the exchange of services are both established in one state of the Community[26]. It must be pointed out that the two participants of the exchange of services must be established in two different states, and if this is not the case, some other cross-border element must exist. For instance, the provider and the recipient of services may be established in the same Member State, but meet in another state to provide and receive the service[27]. It is not obligatory that the provider and the recipient of services are of two different nationalities. Article 49 of the TEC (Article III-144 DC) also applies to the family members of the person who makes use of the free movement of services. They hold derivative rights to enter and reside in a Member State for the duration of the provision of services in the state where the exchange of services takes place. However, since the establishment of the right to move and reside freely within the territory of the Member States for citizens of the Union according to Article 18 of the TEC (Article III-10 DC) and the development of secondary legislation (particularly Directives 90/364 EWG, 73/148 EWG) this derivative right has lost its importance.

16   The free movement of services does not apply to two nationals of a non-Community country, even if they reside in different Community states. Nationals of states that are not Member States are not protected by the Treaty. According to Article 49(2) of the TEC (Article III-144(2) DC) the Council may extend the provisions of the chapter to nationals of a non-Community country who provide services and who are established within the Community. This option has not yet been exercised, however[28].

17   Still problematic and controversial is the exchange of services between a citizen of the Union and a third state national who reside in different Community states. Companies or

---

25 *Cf* Randelzhofer/Forsthoff in: Grabitz/Hilf *Das Recht der Europäischen Union* (loose-leaf, Munich) Arts 49/50 EGV, para 15; *Holoubek* (note 1) Art 49 EGV, paras 29 ff.
26 Kluth (note 2) Art 50 EGV, para 33; Randelzhofer/Forsthoff (note 25) Art 49/50 EGV, paras 16, 18.
27 *Eg* the tourist guide cases, compare note 95.
28 *Cf* the proposal for a directive extending the free movement of services to Third Country nationals, [1999] OJ C76/17.

firms formed in accordance with the law of a Member State and having their registered office, central administration or principal place of business within the Community are, according to Articles 55, 48 of the TEC (Article III-150, 142 DC), to be treated in the same way as natural persons who are nationals of Member States.

3. The Subject Matter of Protection

There is no precise definition of "services" in Article 49 or in Article 50 of the TEC (Articles III-144, 145 DC). The jurisdiction of the European Court of Justice offers valuable clues for the interpretation of this term, however.

a) Definition of "Service"

Article 50 of the TEC (Article III-145 DC) contains some provisions that describe characteristics of the free movement of services. The first paragraph describes a service as something which is normally provided for remuneration. It excludes all economic activities that fall within the scope of the free movement of goods and the free movement of capital[29]. The second paragraph suggests different economic activities that constitute services, namely activities of an industrial or commercial character (*eg* building industry, travel agencies), activities of craftsmen (*eg* hairdressers and sanitation services) and activities of self-employed professions (*eg* lawyers, physicians and architects). This list is by no means exclusive or limiting but serves merely to provide examples of the variety of services that are included. The third paragraph describes a service as being a temporary activity. This vague description of the characteristics of services shows the difficulties encountered when attempting to find an exact definition for "services"[30].

The first characteristic of a service, according to Article 50(1) of the TEC (Article III-145 DC), is that it is "normally provided for remuneration". Remuneration is a valuable consideration for the provided service. It is not obligatory that the recipient of the service pays for the service, but there has to be certain closeness between the service and the remuneration or between provider and recipient of the service[31]. A service is not "provided for remuneration" if the service has been financed primarily by public funding[32]. Services are "normally provided for remuneration" if the provider expects a pecuniary reward. This means that the expectation of an economic benefit is the crucial factor[33]. It is also sufficient if an activity is only aimed at cost recovery. To recapitulate, services fall within the scope of Article 50 of the TEC (Article III-145 DC) if they can be associated with a business (also *cf* Article 2 TEC and Articles I-2, I-3 DC). Activities with low economic importance are services so long as their main purpose is to obtain a pecuniary reward[34]. From this it follows that the content of the services, may it be of a social, religious or charitable nature, is irrelevant. The economic activity does not have to fall into

---

29 On the distinction between the free movement of services and the other fundamental freedoms compare paras 34 ff.
30 Randelzhofer/Forsthoff (note 25) Arts 49/50 EGV, para 24.
31 ECJ *Bond van Adverteerders* [1988] ECR 2085, para 16; *Kohll* [1998] ECR I-1931; also *cf* Randelzhofer/Forsthoff (note 25) Arts 49/59 EGV, para 36; Hakenberg (note 1) Art 49/50 EGV, para 13.
32 ECJ *Humbel* [1988] ECR 5365, para 18; Holoubek (note 1) Art 50 EGV, para 8.
33 As an example for a service provided exclusively for social or political motives, *cf* ECJ *Grogan* [1991] ECR I-4685; to this subject matter Trautwein [1995] JuS 908.
34 ECJ *Corsica Ferries* [1989] ECR 4441.

one of the categories of Article 50(2) of the TEC (Article III-145(2) DC), which mentions activities of an industrial or commercial character, activities of craftsmen and activities of self-employed professions. Many modern activities, such as broadcasting services, activities of the media and telecommunication services can also be classified as services[35].

21 The freedom to provide services is also applicable to services related to the public sector. The Court of Justice has often dealt with obstacles caused by the preference of national service providers[36]. The general rule has been that public authorities are deemed to provide services if they participate like enterprisers in businesses. However, where they were merely fulfilling their duty in the social, cultural and educational fields financed by public dues, the Court has determined that public authorities were not providing services[37].

22 Services have to be carried out by individuals that are **self-employed** in order to fall under the scope of Article 49 of the TEC (Article III-144 DC). Articles 49 ff of the TEC (Articles III-144 ff DC) only apply if self-employed persons undertake the activities; the criterion of independence distinguishes the freedom to provide services from the free movement of workers[38].

23 Another very important criterion of the free movement of services is its **intangible nature**. This criterion serves to distinguish the freedom to provide services from the free movement of goods and will be outlined in greater detail below[39].

24 Finally, Article 50(3) of the TEC (Article III-145(3) DC) points out that the provider of services must pursue his activity only temporarily in the other Member State; he must not be economically integrated in the other Member State. The criterion of temporary activity distinguishes the freedom to provide services from the freedom of establishment[40].

b) Cross-border transaction

25 **Case 1 – Problem:** (ECJ *Luisi and Carbone* [1984] ECR 377)
The Italian nationals Luisi and Carbone, residents of Italy, acquired a huge amount of foreign currencies to finance their travels abroad and to cover the costs of medical treatment within the EC. Particularly Mrs Luisi had frequently undergone medical treatment in Germany. The Italian law applicable at that time allowed the export of foreign currencies only up to a certain maximum amount. When Luisi and Carbone sold more than the legal maximum they were fined by the Italian authorities. Luisi and Carbone then brought an action to contest the monetary fines. They argued that the Italian laws prohibiting the export of foreign currencies in excess of a maximum number infringed their rights under Articles 49 ff of the TEC (Articles III-144 DC). The question that the court considered was whether the limitations under Italian law were covered by the principle of the freedom to provide services.

---

35 For a survey of activities beholding by the European Court as services Hakenberg (note 1) Arts 49/50 EGV, paras 9–11.
36 *Cf* Hakenberg (note 1) Anh zu Arts 43–55 EGV, para 14.
37 Kluth (note 2) Art 50 EGV, para 12.
38 Concerning the difference between these two fundamental freedoms see para 35.
39 Concerning the difference between the free movement of services and the free movement of goods see para 38.
40 Concerning the difference between the free movement of services and the freedom of establishment see para 34.

Activities only fall within the scope of the free movement of services if a **cross-border element** exists. Cross-border provision of services can take place in three "constellations" or sets of circumstances:

Article 49 of the TEC (Article III-144 DC) primarily covers the "classic" case of providing cross-border services: the provider crosses a border temporarily to provide services in another Member State. A case in point is the architect, who travels to another Member State to inspect a site and to draw up a project, crossing the border for this purpose. For this case, Article 50(3) of the TEC (Article III-145(3) DC) expressly allows the provider to temporarily pursue his activity in the state where the service is to be provided under the same conditions as are imposed by that state on its own nationals. This constellation of the free movement of services is called the **freedom to provide services**.

Although Article 49 of the TEC (Article III-144 DC) does not expressly mention the recipient of the services, it also covers the **freedom to receive services**. In this case a recipient of services may temporarily go to another Member State in order to receive services. The European Court of Justice has decided that Articles 49 ff of the TEC (Articles III-144 ff DC) also cover the recipients of services[41]. A typical example of this constellation is touristic traveling: a tourist goes temporarily to another Member State in order to receive services, *eg* to visit a museum. It should be noted that the freedom to provide services does not guarantee the right of permanent residence in the other Member State[42].

Besides these two constellations, which focus on the persons involved in the transaction, there is a third constellation, which is characterised by a situation in which only the service itself crosses the border; the provider of services and the recipients, being located in different Member States, do not change their location. An example of this kind of constellation is the provision of financial services and insurance services. These services have recently become very important in the Community. They are currently also the cause of major challenges within the realm of the freedom to provide services because of the development of telecommunications systems that allow those services to be provided from any location[43].

The law is not settled about whether the freedom to provide services applies to activities by or for a third country national. From one point of view, the freedom to provide services is applicable if either one of the two persons participating in the transaction is a third country national[44]. According to the prevailing opinion, however, for the freedom to provide services to apply, the provider must be a national of a Member State who has actively solicited the business of a third country national. In addition, for the freedom to receive services to apply, the recipient of the services must be a national of a Member State who has gone to the third country of the service provider to receive services[45].

In this context it has to be mentioned that because of the all-embracing approach of the freedom to provide services, all methods of initiating a contract, including publicity and merchandising, fall within the scope of Articles 49 ff of the TEC (Articles III-144 ff DC). The Court of Justice has pointed out that the freedom to provide services would be

---

41 Compare Randelzhofer/Forsthoff (note 25) Arts 49/50 EGV, para 43; Holoubek (note 1) Art 49 EGV, paras 50–51.
42 ECJ *Steymann* [1988] ECR 6159.
43 *Cf* more detailed Holoubek (note 1) Art 49 EGV, paras 52–55; Randelzhofer/Forsthoff (note 25) Arts 49/50 EGV, paras 44–48.
44 Randelzhofer/Forsthoff (note 25) Arts 49/50 EGV, para 16.
45 Holoubek (note 1) Art 49 EGV, para 25.

fatuous if a particular nation's law, relating to advertising, for instance, could already restrict an offer of services[46].

Case 1 – Answer:

32 The question in the case of the Italian nationals Luisi and Carbone was whether the Italian provisions are applicable to Articles 49 ff of the TEC (Articles III-144 ff DC). First of all, the subject matter and the person affected fall within the scope of Articles 49 ff of the TEC. The transaction takes place in Germany and Italy and Mrs Luisi is an Italian resident. Medical treatment constitutes a "service", because it is provided by a self-employed person and because the services are provided for remuneration. Mrs Luisi did not go to Germany to provide services, but to receive them. Though Article 49 of the TEC does not mention the recipient of a service, this position is supported by the Treaty. The Court of Justice therefore held that the Treaty covered recipients, stating that this case was the necessary corollary to the freedom to provide services and was necessary to fulfil the objective of liberalising all gainful activity not covered by the other fundamental freedoms.

c) The Exception of Article 45 of the TEC (Article III-139 DC)

33 The freedom to provide services does not apply to activities within a state that are connected, even if only occasionally, with the exercise of official authority. Article 45 of the TEC (Article III-139 DC) is not a justification, but an exception to the general rule in favour of the freedom to provide services. For that reason, its subject matter of protection must be checked against a presumption in favour of the freedom to provide services. The activities falling under this exception must have a proximate and specific relation to the duties of governmental authorities[47]. It is important that this exception is not applied to activities of a mere technical nature, such as planning activities, or the development of software for the administration of systems for governmental authorities[48].

d) Differentiation between the Freedom to Provide Services and the other Fundamental Freedoms

34 As mentioned above, the criterion that the stay in another Member State has to be temporary is crucial for the differentiation between the freedom to provide services and the freedom of establishment. Basically, the temporary character of an activity depends on the duration, its frequency and its continuity. Anyone who carries out his activity in another Member State not temporarily, but in a stable and continuous way falls under the provisions of the freedom of establishment[49]. Note that if the provider of services has established a certain infrastructure in the other Member State (*eg* the rent of office rooms), that does not automatically exclude a temporary character of the service if that infrastructure is essential for the provision of the service. In one case the Court of Justice indicated that the provisions of Articles 49 ff of the TEC (Article III-144 DC) were applicable although the respective activity had been carried out for several years and it was probable that a certain degree of infrastructure had been developed[50].

---

46 ECJ *Alpine Investments* [1995] ECR I-1141, para 19.
47 ECJ *EDV-systems* [1989] ECR 4035, para 13.
48 *Cf* Holoubek (note 1) Art 55 EGV, para 2.
49 Holoubek (note 1) Art 50 EGV, para 12 and ECJ *Gebhard* [1995] ECR I-4165, para 27.
50 *Cf* ECJ *Schnitzer* [2003] ECR I-14847, para 2.

35 According to recent case law of the Court of Justice, the term "service" has been extended in regard to its duration. The Court has held that an activity can fall within the scope of Articles 49 ff of the TEC (Articles III-144 DC) even if it is carried out over a long period of time (up to several years), for instance, the provision of services during the course of a large construction project. Despite the apparently clear criterion that the service must be temporary, the nature of what constitutes "temporary" is not always well-defined[51]. Furthermore, at the beginning of an activity, it is difficult to judge whether a continuous activity in another Member State will be profitable. It is therefore important to check in each individual case whether the scope of the freedom to provide services is applicable[52].

36 Regarding the differentiation between the freedom to provide services and the **free movement of workers** (Articles 39 ff TEC/Articles III-133 ff DC), the decisive factor is whether the activity has been carried out by an individual who is self-employed or not. At first glance, a conflict between these two fundamental freedoms is scarcely imaginable because the criteria are relatively distinct. *Eg* an activity falls within the scope of Articles 49 ff of the TEC (Articles III-144 ff DC) if it is proven that the service provider is not bound by instructions concerning the choice of the activity, the working conditions and the remuneration[53]. The determination about whether an activity falls under the scope of the freedom to provide services or the free movement of workers becomes more problematic only in situations in which an employee of a company located in one Member State goes to another Member State to provide services on behalf of his employer. If that employee provides services on a temporary basis, the activity falls within the scope of Articles 49 ff of the TEC (Articles III-144 ff DC). If the employee works in the other Member State for a longer period of time, the activity does not fall within the scope of Articles 49 ff of the TEC (Articles III-144 ff DC) and the rules related to the free movement of workers become applicable instead. The crucial criterion for the differentiation is the duration of the activity in the other Member State.

37 Difficulties exist in differentiating between the freedom to provide services and the free movement of capital (Articles 56 ff TEC/Articles III-156 ff DC), especially regarding the transactions of banks and insurance companies. Activities of banks unrelated to the movement of capital (*eg* renting of lockers, providing consulting services relating to matters associated with real property) fall, in principle, within the scope of the freedom to provide services. Activities of banks and insurance companies beyond the mere movement of capital fall within the scope of Articles 49 ff and Article 51(2) of the TEC (Articles III-144 and 146(2) DC). If certain transactions fall both within the scope of the freedom to provide services and the free movement of capital, the general rule is that the nature of the transaction is determined by the main focus and purpose of the activity[54].

38 Distinguishing between the freedom to provide services and the free movement of goods (Articles 23 ff TEC/Articles III-151 ff DC) becomes necessary if the delivery of goods is connected to the provision of a service[55]. In this case it is no longer clear whether

---

51 To the criteria of duration Lackhoff *Die Niederlassungsfreiheit des EGV – nur ein Gleichheits- oder auch ein Freiheitsrecht?* (Berlin 2000) p 135.
52 → § 10 paras 1 ff.
53 *Cf* ECJ *Jany* [2001] ECR I-8615.
54 *Cf* Randelzhofer/Forsthoff (note 25) Arts 49/50 EGV, para 139.
55 Hakenberg (note 1) Arts 49/50 EGV, para 8.

the matter of the transaction is a tangible object (free movement of goods) or an immaterial object (freedom to provide services). One possible way to tackle the problem is to identify the different areas of activity and divide them into their different elements. Another is to find the main focus of the activity. The European Court of Justice has applied both of these methods in different cases. In one case concerning television services, the Court of Justice divided the different services into categories and then applied the provisions relevant to each of these categories of activities. The Court held that telecasts were services, but that the trade in all the materials, sound storage mediums, films and other products being used for the transmission of telecasts falls within the scope of the free movement of goods[56]. Fortunately, the case law of the Court of Justice is extensive and well-developed in areas where the nature of goods is difficult to discern, as is the case with rubbish or electricity, and thus facilitates the problem of whether the principle of freedom to provide services or the principle of the free movement of goods should be applied[57].

39 It is unnecessary to distinguish the freedom to provide services from the non-discrimination principle of Article 12 of the TEC (Article III-123 DC). According to Article 12 of the TEC (Article III-123 DC), any discrimination on grounds of nationality is prohibited. This prohibition applies to the whole subject matter of protection of Community law and therefore also covers the free movement of services. The Court of Justice construes the freedom to provide services as a *"lex specialis"* to Article 12 of the TEC (Article III-123 DC). A certain degree of uncertainty remains, however, in cases where the provision in question only marginally belongs to the scope of protection of the freedom to provide services. For the purpose of clarity it is more suitable to apply Articles 49 ff of the TEC (Articles III-144 ff DC) rather than Article 12 of the TEC (Article III-123 DC) to limitations that mainly concern the addressees of the freedom to provide services[58].

III. Interference

Case 2 – Problem: (ECJ *Ciola* [1999] ECR I-2517)
40 Mr Ciola was the owner of a boat harbour located in the part of Lake Constance belonging to Austria. After he applied to the proper authority for an alteration of certain provisions concerning the harbour, the authority issued a decision that prohibited the renting of embarkation points beyond a certain number to owners of boats with residence in a foreign country. This prohibition was justified on the grounds that harbour owners would likely discriminate against local residents because the locals were assumed to be less affluent than foreigners. Despite this prohibition, Mr Ciola rented two embarkation points to foreigners beyond the permitted quota and was consequently fined by the Austrian authorities. Mr Ciola brought an action to the Superior Administrative Court contesting the monetary fine. The Court of Justice issued a preliminary ruling concerning the question of whether the Austrian authority ruling was in conflict with the freedom to provide services.

---

56 ECJ *Sacchi* [1974] ECR 409.
57 *Cf* more detailed Randelzhofer/Forsthoff (note 25) Arts 49/50 EGV, para 26.
58 *Cf* Randelzhofer/Forsthoff (note 25) Art 49/50 EGV, paras 50 and 132–133.

Case 3 – Problem: (ECJ *Alpine Investments* [1995] ECR I-1141)
The Alpine Investment BV is a company located in the Netherlands that specialises in option trading. For publicity purposes the company practised the so called "cold calling" method for advertising, which means that they contact potential clients, without the clients' prior approval, to offer them several financial services. This activity was prohibited by the Dutch authorities on grounds of the Dutch rules governing publicity. Alpine Investments argued that this prohibition constituted an infringement of the freedom to provide services.

41

As is the case with the free movement of goods and the freedom of establishment, one can distinguish between different kinds of interferences with the freedom to provide services as well, namely discriminations and limitations. In this context, the obligors of the fundamental freedoms require closer attention.

42

1. Obligors

In general, the Member States are the Obligors of Article 49 of the TEC (Article III-144 DC). All the activities of governmental authorities are attributable to the Member State, including local self-administration entities such as chambers of crafts or chambers of self-employed professions[59]. All measures of the Member States that hinder or render less attractive the exercise of the provision or reception of services are prohibited.[60] Limitations can be based on legislation or on decisions in individual cases. The discrimination or other limitation can be initiated by the host state or by the state from which the activity originates[61].

43

The **Community institutions** can also be obligors of Articles 49 ff of the TEC (Articles III-144 DC). The Court of Justice has specifically stated that European institutions are prohibited from abusing the provisions on the freedom to provide services. The legislature of the Community must not foil the obligations of the Member States deriving from the fundamental freedoms by issuing legislation that leads to an increase of barriers for the internal market[62].

44

The question as to whether individuals can be obligors of Articles 49 ff of the TEC (Articles III-144 ff DC) and whether the TEC also applies to the legal relationships of individuals remains unsettled[63]. As a basic principle it is assumed that Article 49 of the TEC (Article III-144 DC) covers only interferences caused by states and not by individuals[64]. The prevailing opinion in the literature appears to bind individuals by the fundamental freedoms in cases where collective organisations are able to issue rules which their members, or employees, are obliged to follow[65]. In a recent decision, the European Court of Justice determined that employees of a private bank violated the free movement of workers (Articles 39 ff TEC/Articles III-144 ff DC) because the private bank had included

45

---

59 Müller-Graff in: Streinz (ed) *EUV/EGV. Vertrag über die Europäische Union und Vertrag zur Gründung der Europäischen Gemeinschaft* (Munich 2003) Art 49 EGV, para 61.
60 *Cf* H G Fischer (ed) *Europarecht. Grundlagen des Europäischen Gemeinschaftsrechts in Verbindung mit deutschem Staats- und Verwaltungsrecht* (3rd ed, Munich 2001) § 17, para 6.
61 *Cf* Holoubek (note 1) Art 49 EGV, para 38.
62 *Cf* Holoubek (note 1) Art 49 EGV, para 42.
63 *Cf* more detailed Randelzhofer/Forsthoff (note 25) Vor Art 39–55 EGV, paras 53 ff.
64 Holoubek (note 1) Art 49 EGV, para 40.
65 *Cf* ECJ *Bosman* [1995] ECR I-4921; → also § 7 paras 45–47.

discriminatory provisions in its job advertisements[66]. It remains doubtful if this decision means a further step towards an unrestricted application of the fundamental freedoms to individuals[67].

2. Discriminatory Rules

a) Direct Discriminations

46 Despite the fact that Article 49 of the TEC (Article III-144 DC) speaks expressly of limitations only to the freedom to provide services, this prohibition also covers all those inner-state provisions and practices which discriminate against nationals of other Member States on grounds of their nationality or because they do not have a permanent residence in the host state. Under this provision, service providers and recipients of services may pursue their activities under the same conditions as those imposed by that state on its own nationals (Article 50(3) TEC/Article III-145(3) DC). The state must not consider the nationality of the service provider or the recipient of services in a way that would discriminate against foreigners. Direct discrimination occurs when states assume that certain activities are reserved to the state's own nationals[68].

b) Indirect Discriminations

47 The term "discrimination" covers not only direct but also indirect discrimination[69]. Indirect discrimination occurs when provisions do not formally differentiate between a state's own nationals and those of other states, but regularly result in stronger negative impacts on the nationals of other Member States[70]. In the case *Corsica Ferries,* the price for the services of pilot boats along the Italian coast depended on whether the boat in question was admitted to regular use of the Italian coastal waters. If that was the case, the tariffs were lower. Traditionally, these special services in coastal shipping were carried out by Italian ship owners. For this reason the tariff in force favoured boats of Italian owners, resulting in an indirect discrimination[71]. Note that as a general rule it does not constitute discrimination if service providers of the same services are facing different conditions for their activities in different Member States; the different law systems in the Member States do not result in a discrimination as long as the law within a particular state is applied equally to the nationals of all Member States[72].

c) The Requirement of Residency in the Host State

48 The freedom to provide services can also be impacted by the requirement that an individual must be resident in the host state. Requiring a local office or private residency in the host state generally constitutes indirect discrimination since nationals of the host states

---

66 ECJ *Angonese* [2000] ECR I-4139.
67 *Cf* → § 7 paras 42 ff.
68 ECJ *Commission v Spain* [1994] ECR I-923.
69 *Eg* Müller-Graff (note 59) Art 49 EGV, paras 78–83.
70 *Cf* Kluth (note 2) Art 50 EGV, para 53.
71 ECJ *Corsica Ferries* [1994] ECR I-1783.
72 Kort [1996] JZ 132, 135.

will regularly satisfy this criterion[73]. A Member State is also not allowed to demand the same requirements for a service provider as for someone who wants to establish a new business in the Member State under the freedom of establishment. This would be counterproductive to the provisions of the TEC. The requirement that a service provider has to have an office or a private residence in the host state must have an objective justification in order to place a limitation on the freedom to provide services.

Case 2 – Answer:
Mr Ciola falls within the scope of Articles 49 ff of the TEC (Article III-144 ff DC) as no other fundamental freedom is applicable to the situation and because he carries out cross-border services for remuneration. The next question is whether the limitation Mr Ciola is subject to is direct or indirect. It would be a direct discrimination if there were an obvious differentiation between nationals and foreign nationals. In this case the reason for the differentiation is not the nationality *per se*, but the residence of the boat owners. Therefore, there is no direct discrimination. At first glance, the criterion of residence seems to be neutral. However, the limitation results in indirect discrimination since non-residents are mainly foreigners. The impact of the limitation therefore affects foreigners much more than nationals. The Court of Justice has pointed out in this case that national rules that treat individuals differently on the grounds of residence constitute indirect discrimination because of their negative impact especially on non-nationals.

Case 3 – Answer:
The activities of Alpine Investments fall within the scope of Articles 49 ff of the TEC (Articles III-144 ff DC). The services of the enterprise are provided for remuneration and do not fall within the scope of the other fundamental freedoms. Because Article 49 of the TEC (Article III-144 DC) also covers all methods for initiating a contract, including all publicity and merchandising, the fact that Alpine Investments was soliciting services rather than actually providing services is irrelevant. Because the service is offered by telephone, not only does the offer and acceptance of the service cross the border, but Alpine Investments also provides the service itself without any change of location. The next question is whether there is a limitation, either a discriminatory rule or an other rule which hinders the exercise of the free movement of services. The prohibition of "cold calling" does not differentiate between nationals and non-nationals; in fact it applies to both, nationals and non-nationals, similarly and is not discriminatory. Nevertheless it constitutes an obstacle to unrestricted publicity and the right to establish contact with potential clients. However, if this prohibition concerned merely the method for reaching clients, it might only be a modality of the provision of services and would therefore not be relevant according to the *"Keck"*-case law of the Court of Justice. In the *Keck* decision, the Court of Justice held that the prohibition of publicity by telephone was a mere modality of the free movement of goods under Articles 28 ff of the TEC (Articles III-153 ff DC). According to the Court, mere modalities do not fall within the scope of Articles 28 ff of the TEC (the free movement of goods) because they do not hinder the market access of goods to other Member States and the limitations do not have a stronger impact on foreigners. However, in the case of Alpine Investments, the Court of Justice distinguished the situation from the situation in Keck. In Alpine Investments the free movement of services is at issue, since both the solicitation and the pro-

---

[73] Concerning the early case law of the Court of Justice see Troberg/Tiedje (note 1) Art 49 EGV, para 36.

vision of services occur through cross-border telecommunications systems. The Court of Justice held that the prohibition in this case would not only concern the offers of Alpine Investment to nationals, but also their offers to foreign recipients of services which would have a negative impact on the market access in other Member States.

3. Interferences with the Freedom to Provide Services

a) Comprehensive Prohibition of Interferences

51 Similar to developments relating to the Free Movement of Goods, the Court of Justice recently decided that interferences other than discrimination can affect the freedom to provide services[74]. The Court of Justice dealt with this question for the first time in the *van Binsbergen* case. In this case a Dutch lawyer lost his right of action in court when he changed his residence from the Netherlands to Belgium. The Court held that all requirements relating to the nationality or residence of a service provider as well as limitations which in other respects hinder or render less attractive the exercise of the freedom to provide services were prohibited[75]. Since then, Article 49 of the TEC (Article III-144 DC) is seen to not only prohibit discrimination, but also any other limitations which differentiate in their treatment of national and non-national service providers[76].

52 The Court has determined that interferences can be based upon the actions of the state of the service provider or on the actions of the state of the recipient of services. In the former case it is mostly a matter of certain admission restrictions for an activity or its exercise. A case in point is the requirement of an official license or qualification to provide a service that does not exist in other Member States[77]. The state of the service provider is also not allowed to cause interferences. The Court of Justice has recently decided numerous cases in the field of broadcasting services concerning interferences regarding advertising or the times of broadcasting. The Court regularly decided that such requirements were limitations prohibited by Articles 49 ff of the TEC (Articles III-144 ff DC)[78].

53 To recapitulate, the Court of Justice has applied Articles 49 ff of the TEC (Articles III-144 ff DC) very broadly to bar limitations that hinder or render less attractive the exercise of the freedom to provide cross border services.

Case 4 – Problem: (ECJ *Carpenter* [2002] ECR I-6279)
54 Mrs Carpenter was a national of the Philippines. She entered the UK as a visitor and overstayed her leave. She married a UK national who was selling advertising space in journals to many advertisers in other Member States. Mrs Carpenter applied for permission to remain in the UK but her application was declined and a deportation order was issued against her. Is the deportation order a limitation of Articles 49 ff of the TEC (Articles III-144 ff DC)?

---

74 Concerning the development of the case law see Randelzhofer/Forsthoff (note 25) Arts 49/50 EGV, paras 89–90.
75 ECJ *van Binsbergen* [1974] ECR 1299.
76 *Cf* Fischer (note 60) § 17, para 5.
77 For case law *cf* Randelzhofer/Forsthoff (note 25) Arts 49/50 EGV, paras 114–116.
78 *Cf* Hakenberg (note 1) Art 49/50 EGV, para 23 with many links to case law.

b) Modification

The comprehensive prohibition of all kinds of interferences concerning the fundamental freedoms can sometimes cause problems. Many rules restricting the fundamental freedoms have only an indirect reference to or impact on economic activity, such as provisions for the purchase of real estate or the granting of loans[79]. This increases the possibility that decisions will be made politically. It may therefore be considered appropriate to confine the subject matter of protection of the freedom to provide services in a similar manner as with the free movement of goods[80]. In the field of the free movement of goods the Court of Justice held that non-discriminatory modalities of trade are no longer to be seen as limitations of the free movement of goods ("*Keck*-formula")[81]. The impact of an application of the *Keck*-formula to the freedom to provide services would be that only limitations concerning the market access are prohibited by the TEC. The European Court has not yet decided whether the *Keck*-formula should be applied to the other fundamental freedoms; therefore, their subject matter of protection is currently not restricted[82]. It is also questionable whether it is in fact necessary to limit the subject matter of protection of the other fundamental freedoms, since the broad scope of protection can be remedied on the level of justification by restrictions imposed to safeguard legitimate interests of the Member States, such as public policy, security or health within the European Community.

55

Case 4 – Answer:
The question was whether the action to deport Mrs Carpenter, a foreigner whose husband, a UK national, sold advertising space in journals throughout the Member States, fell within the scope of Articles 49 ff of the TEC (Articles III-144 ff DC). Generally, the family members of service providers also fall within the scope of Articles 49 ff of the TEC. According to Directive 73/148/EEC, the family of providers and recipients of services have the right to reside in the other Member State for the duration of the economic activities of the provider who falls within the scope of Articles 49 ff of the TEC. The directive does not cover third-country nationals, but the Court of Justice held that if Mrs Carpenter were deported, this would interfere with Mr Carpenter's exercise of the freedom to provide services. It is obvious that Mr Carpenter falls within the scope of protection of the freedom to provide services as Mr Carpenter provides cross-border services. The deportation order could be a limitation of Mr Carpenter's rights to exercise his freedom to provide services if the measure hindered him from carrying out his economic activities. The deportation of Mrs Carpenter would have had a negative impact on Mr Carpenter's activities because Mrs Carpenter had been caring for his children during his absence while he was working in other Member States. Although such limitations could be justified on grounds of public policy or security, since Mrs Carpenter's stay infringed UK law, the Court of Justice held that the deportation of Mrs Carpenter would interfere with Article 8 of the European Convention for the Protection for Human Rights and Fundamental Freedoms (ECHR) because Mr Carpenter has the right to maintain his family life and a deportation of his wife would be disproportional.

56

---

79 For details *cf* Roth in: Dauses (ed) *HdBEUWirtschR* (loose-leaf, Munich) § E1 para 107.
80 → § 8 para 1 ff.
81 ECJ *Keck* [1993] ECR I-6097.
82 *Cf* Randelzhofer/Forsthoff (note 25) Arts 49/50 EGV, paras 91–98; Holoubek (note 1) Art 49 EGV, para 60.

IV. Justification

Case 5 – Problem: (ECJ *Schindler* [1994] ECR I-1039)
57 The Schindler brothers were Dutch nationals working independently for the German *Süddeutsche Klassenlotterie* selling lottery tickets. They sent letters with advertisements and application forms from the Netherlands to recipients in other Member States. These mailings were confiscated by the British customs authorities on the grounds that they infringed the British prohibition of gambling. When the case came before the Court of Justice, the British authorities argued that Article 49 of the TEC (Article III-144 ff DC) does not apply to this rule because every lottery is affected by the prohibition, regardless of the nationality of the individuals selling the tickets. The British authorities argued that the prohibition was justified by overriding reasons in the general interest, in this case by the British social policy and the struggle against fraud.

Case 6 – Problem: (ECJ *Tourist Guide* [1991] ECR I-682, I-718, I-735)
58 Italy, France and Greece had rules requiring diplomas to provide evidence of professional experience for foreign tourist guides visiting other Member States with a party from their own Member State. The tourist guides argued that this requirement infringed their freedom to provide services.

1. The Explicit Written Restrictions

59 According to Articles 55 and 46 of the TEC (Articles III-150, 140 DC), provisions laid down by law, regulations or administrative actions that treat foreign nationals differently on grounds of public policy, public security or public health, are permitted. Article 46 of the TEC (Article III-140 DC) contains an explicit permission to derogate from the freedom to provide services, but this provision must be interpreted restrictively. The kind of restriction named in Article 46 of the TEC (Article III-140 DC) applies to all forms of services. Thus, special treatment of foreign nationals that restricts their freedom to provide services can be justified by Article 46 of the TEC (Article III-140 DC). These written restrictions cover only discrimination but not non-discriminatory rules[83]. The terms "public policy", "public security" and "public health" have been concretized in part by secondary law[84]. The Court of Justice conceives the term "public security" to comprise the fundamental interests of the Member States, like the maintaining of important public services and the effective functioning of the state,[85] while it has interpreted "public policy" to stand for basic rules concerning important interests of the state[86].

60 It remains in question whether Article 46 of the TEC (Article III-140 DC) also covers indirect discrimination or if indirect discrimination can only be justified by the unwritten restriction based on overriding reasons of general interest[87].

---

83 ECJ *Commission v Belgium* [1992] ECR I-6757.
84 Compare *eg* Dir 64/221/EWG, [1964] OJ 56/850. In detail Schlag in: Schwarze (ed) *EU-Kommentar* (Baden-Baden 2000) Art 46 EGV, paras 5–10; Randelzhofer/Forsthoff (note 25) Art 46 EGV, paras 14 ff.
85 *Cf* ECJ *Campus Oil* [1984] ECR 2727, para 3.
86 ECJ *Bouchereau* [1977] ECR 1999, paras 33 ff.
87 → § 7 paras 88 ff; Ehlers [2001] JURA 482, 487.

Case 5 – Answer:
The activities of the Schindler brothers fall within the scope of Articles 49 ff of the TEC (Articles III-144 ff DC). Though publicizing and sending letters with lottery tickets may have a close connection to the sale of goods, it nevertheless is a service activity because the brothers are providing the public with the opportunity to participate in the lottery. The activities of the Schindler brothers are provided for remuneration, which is the price of the lottery tickets, and the activity is occurring across national borders, because the tickets are offered in another Member State. The provisions for the freedom to provide services are therefore applicable. The next question is whether the British rules constitute a prohibited limitation of the freedom to provide services. The rules are of a non-discriminatory nature because they concern everyone, irrespective of the nationality of the person selling the lottery tickets. However, the rules hinder non-British lottery services from extending their services to British nationals. The rule could possibly be justified by the unwritten overriding reasons of general interest. The British law prohibiting gambling is designed to fight against fraud and to protect consumers. The Court of Justice held that the characteristics of lotteries do in fact provide sufficient justification for the British authorities to treat lotteries differently from the authorities in other Member States and that the authorities were permitted to take into account the sociocultural differences of their country. Therefore, the Court ruled that the British rule was justified.

2. Unwritten Restrictions

Non-discriminatory rules can be justified by overriding rules of general interest, but not by the specific written restrictions (Articles 46, 55 TEC/Articles III-140, 150 DC)[88]. The case law of the Court of Justice shows noticeable parallels to the "*Cassis de Dijon*" decision, which was the first decision to acknowledge that general interests can justify limitations on the free movement of goods[89]. The term "general interest" must be interpreted according to Community law, although the national authorities have been responsible for concretising the term in individual cases[90]. The Court of Justice has accepted many different public interests as overriding considerations of general interest and the catalogue is not closing. The Court has held, however, that the general interests must be of a non-economic kind. Mere economic interests cannot justify limitations on the fundamental freedoms[91].

Overriding rules of general interest can limit the freedom to provide services[92]: Consumer protection, the protection of trade[93], the functioning of the administration of justice[94], the functioning of the capital markets, political interests regarding culture like the protection of the national and artistic heritage[95], the protection of the financial balance of the public health system[96], and rules for the exercise of certain professions for the protection of the recipients of services[97] have all been held as permissible. The require-

---

[88] ECJ *van Binsbergen* [1974] ECR 1299, paras 10,12.
[89] On the exact contents and developments of the „*Cassis*"-case law → § 7 paras 89 ff.
[90] Hailbronner/Nachbauer [1992] EuZW 105, 110.
[91] ECJ *Kohll* [1998] ECR I-1931, para 41; Holoubek (note 1) Art 49 EGV, para 94.
[92] For an overview *cf* Müller-Graff (note 59) Art 49 EGV, paras 106–108.
[93] ECJ *de Agostini* [1997] ECR I-3843, para 53.
[94] ECJ *Reisebüro Broede* [1996] ECR I-6511, para 31.
[95] ECJ *Commission v France* [1991] ECR I-659, para 17.
[96] ECJ *Kohll* [1998] ECR I-1931, para 41.
[97] ECJ *van Wesemael* [1979] ECR 35, para 38.

ment of a residence or the establishment of a business in the host state need not automatically be an infringement of the freedom to provide services. The obligation to have a residence in the host state is acceptable if other important rules regarding the exercise of certain professions cannot be enforced[98].

3. General Limits to the Restrictability of Rights and Freedoms

64 **Case 7 – Problem:** (ECJ *Müller-Fauré* [2003] ECR I-4509)
While on holiday in Germany, Ms Müller-Fauré underwent dental treatment. When she returned from her holiday, she applied to the *Zwijndrecht Fund* for reimbursement of the costs of the treatment. According to Dutch law, costs for medical treatment are only reimbursable if the health fund has contractual relations with the health facility that treated the insured person or, if this is not the case, if the health fund has previously agreed to cover the costs. In this case, the health fund refused to reimburse Ms Müller-Fauré on grounds that she had voluntarily sought treatment by a dentist established in Germany while she was on holiday there because she lacked confidence in dental practitioners in the Netherlands. The court concerned in the matter held that, under the national legislation, such circumstances do not provide grounds for reimbursement without authorisation from the insured person's fund. Does the national legislation infringe Ms Müller-Fauré's rights under Articles 49 ff of the TEC (Articles III-144 ff DC)?

65 **Case 8 – Problem:** (ECJ *Loi Evin* [2004] ECR I-6613)
France issued new laws prohibiting direct or indirect advertising for certain alcoholic beverages. Indirect advertising includes, for instance, advertising on the tricots of players during sporting events and other forms of marketing that do not involve broadcasting exclusively for publicity. In the case of bi-national events taking place abroad, to comply with French law, French broadcasters had to use all available means to prevent the appearance of brand names of alcoholic beverages on their channels. In cases where this was impossible, the sporting event was not to be broadcast at all. Thus, a French broadcaster, at the time when it acquired the retransmission rights, had to inform its foreign partners of the requirements of French law. The Commission initiated an infringement procedure against France. The question to be addressed was whether the French rule was an infringement of Articles 49 ff of the TEC (Articles III-144 ff DC).

66 Derogations from Community law are generally limited, since they permit the Member States to deviate from observing the fundamental rights. In order for them to be permissible, these limits to Community law must reflect the basic rights of the Community, provisions of the primary law and the principle of proportionality[99]. It is especially important that the measures undertaken by the Member States to pursue general interests are proportional to the state goals. This means that the measures must be reasonably related to the goal, so that they are able to procure the desired result without overshooting the target. Note that the Court of Justice only looks at these two criteria (suitability and necessity) when examining the proportionality of a measure. The Court omits the criterion of proportionality in a stricter sense (adequateness), which tests whether the measures are adequate to actually procure the desired result. Questions of adequateness seem to be

---

98 ECJ *van Binsbergen* [1974] ECR 1299.
99 → § 7 paras 96 ff.

left by the Court of Justice to be answered the law court initiating the preliminary ruling[100]. In the field of limitations to the freedom to provide services, the requirements regarding the proportionality of a measure are relatively strict because of the temporary nature of the services, in contrast to establishments[101].

Newly introduced limitations to the free movement of services are considered disproportional if there are existing rules in the state of origin of the service provider which are already sufficient to pursue the aim. If permission for a certain activity has been granted by the authorities of the state of origin, this must be recognised by the host state to the extent that it is comparable to the requirements of the host state for the same activity[102]. Regulations developed by a host state requiring tourist guides from another Member State to obtain and provide diplomas when they give tours within the host state are also considered disproportional[103].

Case 6 – Answer:
The activities of a tourist guide must fall within the scope of applicability of Articles 49 ff of the TEC (Articles III-144 ff DC). The activities of a tourist guide are provided for remuneration. They are cross-border services if the tourist guide visits other Member States. The French provisions constitute a limitation of Articles 49 ff of the TEC (Articles III-144 ff DC) because they prevent foreign tourist guides from offering their services in other Member States. The limitation is not discriminatory because it also applies to tourist guides who are French nationals. The next question is whether the limitation may be justified on grounds of overriding reasons of general interest. One might argue that a thourough knowledge of a nation's cultural heritage is so important that the state is permitted to require all registered tour guides to have studied this subject extensively. However it is questionable whether the requirement of a diploma is proportional, since it would cause the total number of tourist guides to decline and consequently there would be far fewer guides capable of speaking the native languages of other Member States. While the dangers associated with having unskilled tourist guides are limited, the disadvantages ensuing if the limitation remains in place are far greater and are not to be underestimated. The Court held that the limitation of Article 49 ff of the TEC (Articles III-144 ff DC) could not be justified.

Case 7 – Answer:
Because Mrs Müller-Fauré went from the Netherlands to another Member State to receive health services, this case falls within the subject matter of protection of Articles 49 ff of the TEC (Articles III-144 ff DC). It is irrelevant that systems of social security fall within the competence of the courts and the administration of the Member States and not of the Community. The ruling that the health care system in the Netherlands was not obligated to pay for the dental services Mrs. Müller-Fauré received in Germany hinders the exercise of the freedom to provide services. The ruling also acts as an indirect discrimination because the obligation to seek authorisation for medical treatment arises only for services provided in another Member State. The Court of Justice examined the rules to determine whether they could have been justified by overriding reasons of general interest. In this case the Court deviated from its former case law. In prior cases, when discriminatory provisions were concerned, the Court had applied only the written limitations. The Court's decision contained some hints that in the fields of the other fundamental freedoms, there may be a trend to

---

100 ECJ *de Agostini* [1997] ECR I-3843, para 54; Holoubek (note 1) Art 49 EGV, para 95.
101 Fischer (note 60) § 17, para 20.
102 ECJ *van Wesemael* [1979] ECR 35, para 54; Hailbronner/Nachbauer [1992] EuZW 105, 110.
103 ECJ *Commission v Greece* [1991] ECR I-727.

treat discriminatory and non-discriminatory rules equally. The Court examined whether the protection of the systems of social security was sufficient justification for the rule, and found that the state had not proved that the rule was really necessary. There was no evidence to indicate that the financial impact of paying for services provided in other states would be so great as to represent a significant danger to the systems of social security. The Member States using such a system of social security must establish mechanisms for a subsequent refund of expenses. The Court indicated that the requirement of an authorisation in the case of a hospital stay would have been justified, however (ECJ *Smits and Peerbooms* [2001] ECR I-5473).

Case 8 – Answer:
The French measure prohibiting television advertising for alcoholic drinks is a limitation of the freedom to provide services. The ruling would require broadcasters to reject broadcasting an event if the sporting events contained advertising of alcoholic beverages, and the events could therefore possibly not be broadcasted in France. The broadcasting itself as well as the advertising for the events fall within the scope of Articles 49 ff of the TEC (Articles III-144 ff DC). The next question is whether the rule could be justified by the written limitation of health protection (Articles 55, 46 TEC/Articles III-150, 140 DC), because the rule could contribute to the fight against alcoholic excess. The level of health protection is a matter that remains with the Member States, but the rules they develop must respect the principle of proportionality. The Court determined that the rule was suitable to promote health protection, because it decreases the inducement to drink alcohol. The Court also found that the rule was necessary as it did not overshoot the target. The fact that publicity for alcoholic beverages is permitted in many Member States was found to be irrelevant.

§ 12
Freedom of Movement of Capital and Payments

Peter von Wilmowsky

Leading cases: ECJ *Bordessa* [1995] ECR I-361; *Konle* [1999] ECR I-3099; *Verkooijen* [2000] ECR I-4071; *Commission v France* [2002] ECR I-4781; *Manninen* [2004] ECR I-7477.

Further reading: Armbrüster [2003] JuS 224; Barnard *The Substantive Law of the EU* (Oxford, 2004) pp 461–482; Dautzenberg [2000] StuB 720; Fischer [2000] ZEuS 391; Glöckner [2000] EuR 592.

As do the other fundamental freedoms of the EC Treaty, the **freedom of movement of capital** (Article 56(1) TEC/Article III-156 DC) and the **freedom of payments** (Article 56(2) TEC/Article III-156 DC) contribute to the establishment of the common (or internal) market. They require the elimination of all restrictions which are not justified by overriding requirements of the common welfare.

I. Scope of Protection

1. Movement of Capital

To determine the scope of protection of the freedom of capital movement, one first must clarify what "**capital**" is. The term capital refers to proprietary rights.[1] These rights may lie in personal or real property, claims and other intangibles. Thus, rights in cash, real property, personal property, accounts receivable and other rights to performance, shares in companies (including partnerships, limited companies and stock companies), securities, intangible assets (such as copy rights, patents, utility-model patents, design patents, brand names and trade names) or (tradable) emission permits are included. Capital movement is both the creation and the transfer of these rights.[2] The following transactions illustrate the breadth of the spectrum of capital movement: the physical movement or transfer of cash;[3] foreign exchange transactions (*ie* the acquisition of a certain amount of foreign currency); the issuance of cheques and bills of exchange; the purchase of real estate;[4] the transfer of shares in companies; securities transactions (such as the issuance of and trade in stocks and bonds); the acquisition of interests in investment funds; forward exchange

1

2

---

1 From case-law *cf eg* ECJ *Bordessa* [1995] ECR I-361, para 13. From the legislation: Dir 88/361, Annex I, chapeau, [1988] OJ L178/5. (On the function of this Directive see *infra* para 8). From the literature: Kiemel in: von der Groeben/Schwarze (eds) *Vertrag über die Europäische Union und zur Gründung der Europäischen Gemeinschaft, Kommentar* (6th ed, Baden-Baden 2003) Art 56 EGV, para 1; Ress/Ukrow in: Grabitz/Hilf (eds) *Das Recht der Europäischen Union, Kommentar* (looseleaf, Munich) Art 56 EGV, para 13.
2 The ECJ describes capital movements as the "transfer of assets". See *eg* ECJ *Bordessa* [1995] ECR I-361, para 13. See also Ress/Ukrow (note 1) Art 56 EGV, para 32.
3 See *eg* ECJ *Bordessa* [1995] ECR I-361: Mr Bordessa, an Italian citizen, had concealed 50 million Pesetas (approximately EUR 300,000) in various places of his car in order to bring the money from Spain to France. He thereby violated the rules requiring prior authorization for the export of banknotes then in force in Spain. The ECJ held that these rules were inconsistent with the freedom of movement of capital.
4 ECJ *Konle* [1999] ECR I-3099, para 22; *Albore* [2000] ECR I-5965, para 14.

transactions; asset deals or share deals with respect to enterprises;[5] equity contributions when founding a company;[6] the provision of loans;[7] payments into savings deposits and other forms of financial investments;[8] insuring risks;[9] the establishment of claims;[10] the assignment of claims (and thus also factoring); the provision of security interests;[11] the acceptance of guarantees;[12] and entering into third party liabilities.[13] Capital movements also include gifts, inheritances and legacies.[14] The protection provided by the EC Treaty's freedom of capital movement extends to any and all acts taken by the party or the parties to accomplish the transaction.[15] In civil law, both the contract supporting the transaction and the acts directed at performance are covered.

2. Relationship to the Other Fundamental Freedoms

3 The Treaty provisions relating to the free movement of capital are not rendered inapplicable merely because another fundamental freedom applies. Conversely, the application of the freedom of movement of capital does not exclude the application of another fundamental freedom. The (individual) transaction may enjoy the protection of several funda-

---

5 Dir 88/361, Annex I, heading I, [1988] OJ L178/5.
6 In the case ECJ *Veronica Omröp Organisatie* [1993] ECR I-487, a Dutch broadcaster who received public funding as a non-commercial enterprise had founded a commercial broadcasting company with these funds in Luxembourg, for the purpose of producing programmes there which were intended to be relayed in the Netherlands by cable. The competent Dutch authority imposed fines and other sanctions against this conduct.
7 Dir 88/361, Annex I, headings VII and VIII, [1988] OJ L178/5; *cf* however also ECJ *Parodi* [1997] ECR I-3899, para 17 (also services).
8 Roth in: Dauses (eds) *Handbuch des EU-Wirtschaftsrechts* (loose-leaf, Munich) ch E I, para 110.
9 See Geiger (ed) *Vertrag über die Europäische Union und zur Gründung der Europäischen Gemeinschaft, Kommentar* (4th ed, Munich 2004) Art 51 EGV, para 5: The establishment of the claim resulting from an insurance contract is to be seen as capital movement. The prevailing legal opinion also considers insurance to be a service; further references to the case-law may be found in Randelzhofer/Forsthoff in: Grabitz/Hilf (eds) *Das Recht der Europäischen Union, Kommentar* (loose-leaf, Munich) Art 49/50 EGV, para 38.
10 See Müller *Kapitalverkehrsfreiheit in der Europäischen Union* (Berlin 2000) p 156. Other opinions on this matter may be found in Ohler [1996] WM 1801, 1805.
11 ECJ *Trummer* [1999] ECR I-1661, paras 19-24; Dir 88/361, Annex I, heading IX, [1988] OJ L178/5; von Wilmowsky *Europäisches Kreditsicherungsrecht* (Tübingen 1996) pp 77–93. A different opinion may be found in Opinion AG La Pergola, ECJ *Trummer* [1999] ECR I-1661, para 10.
12 *Oberlandesgericht* (OLG – Higher Regional Court) Düsseldorf [1995] WM 1993. But see Mankowski in: Lwowski (ed) *Entscheidungssammlung zum Wirtschafts- und Bankrecht* (loose-leaf, Frankfurt am Main) VII A § 108 ZPO 1.96 (provision of services), who presents a different opinion.
13 See ECJ *Scientologie* [2000] ECR I-1335: The background of this case is, among other things, the attempt by the British Church of Scientology to settle the outstanding tax debt of the organisation's French branch. Pursuant to the French law then in force, the competent French authority's prior authorization for foreign direct investments was required. The prior authorisation was denied. See Opinion AG Saggio, ECJ *Scientology* [2000] ECR I-1335, para 8.
14 Dir 88/361, Annex I, heading XI, [1988] OJ L178/5; on asset transfers for the benefit of third parties as a case for the application of the freedom of movement of capital see also von Hippel [2005] EuZW 7.
15 Dir 88/361, Annex I, heading XI, [1988] OJ L178/5.

Freedom of Movement of Capital and Payments § 12 I 2

mental freedoms. In this case they are to be applied concurrently.[16] If the capital transfer is for the purpose of establishing or operating a branch office, providing a service or having an employment, the freedom of establishment, the freedom of services or the freedom of workers, respectively, is applicable in addition to the freedom of movement of capital.[17] This **cumulative application** of several fundamental freedoms is not, however, without controversy. Some scholars argue that only a single fundamental freedom can be applied to any one transaction.[18] In order to establish the exclusivity of a single fundamental freedom, they favour subordinating the other affected freedoms and letting a single freedom govern the protection. The proponents of this view have significant difficulties in choosing which one of the several affected fundamental freedoms should be given priority. The freedom of establishment may serve as an example. This fundamental freedom is applicable in cases where a person founds or acquires a company, establishes a branch office or takes up another type of self-employment and in doing so acquires assets (specifically, shares in a company which convey an influence over the management, or means of production such as machines and real estate). If one believes that several fundamental freedoms may be cumulatively applicable, then this acquisition of assets – termed "investment" because it serves entrepreneurial purposes – enjoys the protection of not only the freedom of movement of capital, but also the freedom of establishment.[19] Those who advocate reducing the protection to a single fundamental freedom, however, must decide between the freedom of capital movement and the freedom of establishment. It is hardly surprising that the proponents of this theory suggest differing solutions. Some of them wish to grant priority to the freedom of movement of capital and to base the protection provided by the fundamental freedoms for the acquisition of assets associated with the right to establishment solely on Article 56 of the TEC (Article III-156 DC).[20] They refer to the Treaty reservation which makes the right of establishment subject to the provisions on the movement of capital (Article 43(2) TEC/Article III-137(2) DC). Others, by contrast, give priority to the freedom of establishment: Only the Treaty chapter on establishment is to be applicable to those movements of capital which are related to an establishment.[21] The doctrine of exclusivity has similar problems in cases where the movement

---

16 See generally on concurrently applicable fundamental freedoms → 7 para 57.
17 This is the prevailing view of courts and legal authors. From the case-law see eg ECJ *Svensson* [1995] ECR I-3955, paras 10–11 (concurrent application of the provisions relating to the freedom of movement of capital and freedom to provide services). From literature see, eg, Tiedje/Troberg in: von der Groeben/Schwarze (eds) *Vertrag über die Europäische Union und zur Gründung der Europäischen Gemeinschaft, Kommentar* (6th ed, Baden-Baden 2003) Art 43 EGV, paras 8–31; Streinz *Europarecht* (7th ed, Heidelberg 2005) paras 764–765; R Weber in: Lenz (ed) *EU- und EG-Vertrag, Kommentar* (3rd ed, Cologne 2003) Vorbem zu den Art 56–60 EGV, paras 11–12; Müller (note 10) pp 190–197; Glaesner in: Schwarze (ed) *EU-Kommentar* (Baden-Baden 2001) Art 58 EGV, para 8; S Weber [1992] EuZW 561, 564–565; Glöckner [2000] EuR 592, 594–607; Haferkamp *Die Kapitalverkehrsfreiheit im System der Grundfreiheiten des EG-Vertrags* (Baden-Baden 2003) pp 161–206; agreeing in part Ohler *Europäische Kapital- und Zahlungsverkehrsfreiheit* (Berlin 2002) Art 56, paras 95–197.
18 Freitag [1997] EWS 186, 188; Fischer [2000] ZEuS 391, 400; Ohler [1996] WM 1801, 1802–1803; Ohler (note 17) Art 56, paras 114-117 has meanwhile changed his view.
19 Randelzhofer/Forsthoff (note 9) Art 43 EGV, para 114.
20 Kimms *Die Kapitalverkehrsfreiheit im Recht der Europäischen Union* (Frankfurt a M 1996) p 141.
21 Fischer [2000] ZEuS 391, 401–402; Freitag [1997] EWS 186, 190–191; Ohler [1996] WM 1801, 1804. Ohler has meanwhile changed his view, see Ohler (note 17) Art 56, paras 114–117. *Cf*

of capital and activities related to the movement of workers coincide in a single act. A case in point is the purchase of real estate by a migrant worker. If one wishes to assign the protection of this transaction exclusively to a single fundamental freedom, one has no recourse but to base this assignment on the motives of the migrant worker. According to this approach, the freedom of movement of workers would displace the provisions on free movement of capital, where the worker intends to use the real estate as a residence. If, on the other hand, it is intended as an investment, only the provisions regarding the movement of capital would be applicable.[22] This distinction is neither reasonable nor practicable because the reasons mentioned for the purchase are not mutually exclusive, but rather may be pursued simultaneously. Therefore, one should recognise that *eg* the purchase of real estate by a migrant worker may enjoy the protection of not only the freedom of movement of capital but also the freedom of movement of workers.[23] The doctrine of exclusivity should therefore be rejected. Rather, one should share the view that, in those cases where a capital movement is associated with a branch office, the provision of a service or the performance of an employment, the other respective affected fundamental freedom applies in addition to the freedom of movement of capital.[24] One of the consequences of a cumulative application is that the scope of protection of the more extensive freedom prevails. If one fundamental freedom merely prohibits discrimination (as is argued, for example, for the right of establishment and the freedom of movement of workers),[25] whereas the applicable concurrent fundamental freedom (such as the freedom of movement of capital) also includes non-discriminatory restrictions, then the (broader) prohibition on restrictions applies.

3. Crossing Borders

4   For a capital movement to enjoy the protection of Article 56 of the TEC (Article III-156 DC) it must cross a national border; purely domestic capital movements fall outside the scope of protection. The border crossing may occur in several ways. First, the capital (*ie* the proprietary rights) may change its location and thus cross the frontier. An obvious example is when cash is transported across the border.[26] Yet, other types of assets may also change their location. Claims against a debtor, for example, are considered to be located at the place where the debtor is resident.[27] If the debtor moves from country A to country B, the location of the claim moves across the border. The same applies to shares in a limited liability company (*Gesellschaft mit beschränkter Haftung, GmbH*), when the

---

also the (not particularly useful) differentiation proposed by Ress/Ukrow (note 1) Art 56 EGV, paras 28–31.
22 This is, for example, the view of Ohler [1996] WM 1801, 1803–1804, and Freitag [1997] EWS 186, 189. The Opinion of AG Geelhoed, ECJ *Reisch* [2002] ECR I-2157, paras 59–74, concerning the concurrence of capital movement and the provision of services, is similar.
23 On the freedom of movement of workers *cf* Art 9(1) Regulation 1612/68 (Regulation on the free movement of workers within the Community). In this regulation Art 39 TEC (Art III-133 DC) is more closely specified; the foreign worker shall enjoy all the rights and benefits accorded to the domestic workers in matters of housing, including ownership of the housing he needs.
24 References above in note 17.
25 On this matter see → § 9 paras 37 ff, and → § 10 paras 48 ff.
26 See the facts of the cases ECJ *Bordessa* [1995] ECR I-361, paras 32–35, and *Sanz de Lera* [1995] ECR I-4821, paras 40–48.
27 *Cf*, for example, sec 23(ii) of the *Zivilprozessordnung* (ZPO – German Code of Civil Procedure).

company's registered office is relocated from A to B. With regard to bearer instruments such as bearer shares, the instrument's location is the capital's location. Thus, physically transporting the bearer instrument across the frontier effectuates a cross-border capital movement. A security interest (such as a pledge or lien) in a piece of moveable property crosses the border when the property (*ie* the collateral) is transported into another country. The second possibility is that the owner of the asset changes. In this regard, a national border is certainly crossed when the seller of the asset transfers it to a purchaser who is resident in another country. One thinks for example of the conveyance of real estate between residents of different countries or of a transfer of ownership by way of cross-border inheritance. There is, however, another manner in which the transfer of assets may cross a national frontier. Such cases occur where the seller and the buyer are resident in the same country and the cross-border aspect results solely from the circumstance that the transferred asset is located in another country. For example, a seller living in Germany sells and conveys her real estate that is located in Austria to a purchaser who also lives in Germany; or a German debtor pledges securities he holds with a bank in Luxembourg to his German creditor. In this constellation, the transfer of assets remains restricted to a single country insofar as the asset is transferred from one resident to another. The freedom of movement of capital guaranteed by the TEC should nevertheless also provide protection in these cases. The object and purpose of this fundamental freedom is to open the borders for all assets. This includes a resident being able to dispose over an asset located in another country as easily as over a domestic asset.

The frontier which is crossed must be a frontier **between two Member States** or between a **Member State and a third country** (Article 56 TEC/Article III-156 DC). The freedom of movement of capital is thus the only fundamental freedom which protects not only commerce within the EC, but also commerce with third countries against unjustified restrictions (imposed by the Member States or the EC). For example, a Russian who purchases real estate located in Germany from an American is therefore able to invoke the protection provided by Article 56(1) of the TEC (Article III-156 DC) against German or EC legal provisions which restrict this transaction. The Article is intended to provide investors from third countries with the guarantee that they will be able to unlock their investment in the EU and repatriate the proceeds at any time.

4. Payments

Those capital transactions which are made as remuneration for commercial transactions enjoy a special legal status. The EC Treaty hives them off from capital movements and instead treats them as **payments** (Article 56(2) TEC/Article III-156 DC). The line of delineation is drawn by the purpose of the capital movement. If cash is transferred, a bank transfer effected, a cheque issued or a bill of exchange accepted in order to pay for a performance received (such as the delivery of goods, securities or the performance of a service), then the capital transfer is deemed a "payment".[28] Payments enjoy a special protection which goes beyond the protection provided for capital movements in general. Some of the grounds of restriction which exist for capital movements do not apply to payments.

---

28 ECJ *Luisi and Carbone* [1984] ECR 377, paras 21–22: "The physical transfer of bank notes may not therefore be classified as a movement of capital where the transfer in question corresponds to an obligation to pay…". From the literature see Ress/Ukrow (note 1) Art 56 EGV, para 174; Ohler (note 17) Art 56, para 320.

The reason for this betterment is that cross-border payments are often made for a performance that itself enjoys the protection of other fundamental freedoms (such as the freedom of movement of goods or services). This other freedom should not be rendered ineffectual or less effectual due to restrictions which are permitted for the freedom of capital movements (in Articles 57 TEC/Article III-157 DC and Article 59 TEC/Article III-159 DC), but not for the other fundamental freedom. This does not, however, mean that the protection provided by Article 56(2) of the TEC (Article III-156 DC) is limited to payments for a performance that falls within the scope of protection of another fundamental freedom. Rather, it applies to any and all cross-border payments.[29] For example, if the purchase price for the delivery of goods within Germany is to be paid to the seller's account with his bank in Switzerland, then the guarantees provided by Article 56(2) of the TEC (Article III-156 DC) apply. Payments which are made as consideration for cross-border trade in goods, services or capital, or for a performance that falls within the scope of establishment or movement of workers, enjoy double protection: the protection provided by the relevant fundamental freedom applicable to the underlying performance or activity (Articles 28–29 TEC/Article III-153 DC, Article 49 TEC/Article III-144 DC, Article 56(1) TEC/Article III-156 DC, Article 43 TEC/Article III-137 DC and Article 39 TEC/Article III-133 DC respectively), and the protection of Article 56(2) of the TEC (Article III-156 DC).[30]

II. Prohibition on Restrictions

7 The EC Treaty guarantees the free movement of capital and payments by prohibiting any (unjustified) **restriction** (Article 56(1) and (2) TEC/Article III-156 DC). This prohibition includes not only discriminatory legislation, which places greater restrictions (overt or covert) on cross-border capital movements or payments than on domestic capital movements or payments. Rather, it extends to measures which apply equally to cross-border and domestic capital movements and restrict them in equal measure. The prohibition applies where the measure "directly or indirectly, actually or potentially" (*Dassonville* formula) hinders capital movements or payments.[31] In contrast to the law of the movement of goods, there are no provisions in the law of capital movements or payments which are exempt from the prohibition on restrictions from the outset and thus would be *per se* permissible. This applies in the first place to export measures. According to the case-law of the ECJ, measures that restrict the export of goods do not interfere with the freedom of movement of goods (and thus do not require a justification) if the measure is equally applied, *ie* so long as they are equally applied to the marketing of domestic products.[32] This exception is already on shaky ground with the movement of goods.[33] There is no rea-

---

29 Haag in: Bieber/Epiney/Haag (eds) *Die Europäische Union* (6th ed, Baden-Baden 2005) § 15, para 37; Haferkamp (note 17) p 41.
30 Geiger (note 9) Art 56 EGV, para 5, and Ress/Ukrow (note 1) Art 56 EGV, para 183 for example present a different view: They argue that Art 56(2) TEC is *lex specialis*.
31 *Cf* ECJ *Dassonville* [1974] ECR 837, para 6. On the application of this formula to capital movements see Rohde *Freier Kapitalverkehr in der Europäischen Gemeinschaft* (Frankfurt a M 1999) pp 130–131.
32 An overview is given by Oliver/Jarvis *Free Movement of Goods in the European Community* (4th ed, London 2003) paras 6.81–6.90; → § 8 paras 32 ff.
33 See von Wilmowsky [1996] EuR 362, 363–368, for a critical assessment.

son to apply it *mutatis mutandis* to the freedom of capital movements and payments. Secondly, the sweeping exception of legislation pertaining to so-called "certain selling arrangements" is not able to provide a guide for the scope of protection of the freedom of movement of capital. Since the *Keck* decision, the ECJ has no longer applied the prohibition of Article 28 of the TEC to Member State sales and advertising restrictions, provided they are equally applied. They profit from a fiction: Independently from their actual effects, they are deemed not to impede trade in goods.[34] There is scarcely a justification for exempting this entire field already in the case of movement of goods.[35] This exemption is not able to satisfy the expectations placed in it and to simplify the monitoring of government interference in commerce, which is required by the Treaty's freedoms. Just as this case-law has not been applied to the other fundamental freedoms, it should also not be drawn upon to interpret the freedom of movement of capital.[36]

The prohibition on restrictions of Article 56 of the TEC (Article III-156 DC) **is directly applicable**: Without having to wait for an administrative act by a Member State or harmonising measures to be enacted by the EC, the courts and authorities must observe the freedom of movement of capital and may not apply inconsistent laws or regulations.[37] In this respect, the freedom of movement of capital is a latecomer. Whereas the other fundamental freedoms became directly applicable on 01 January 1970 after the agreed transition period, the freedom of movement of capital acquired this effect only much later, specifically on 1 July 1990. The Treaty article which mandated the free movement of capital in the original version of the EC Treaty, and which ceased to have effect at the end of 1993 and was replaced by Article 56 of the TEC (Article 67 TEC previous version), did not have direct effect. In contrast to the current Article 56 of the TEC (Article III-156 DC), it did not prohibit (unjustified) restrictions unambiguously, but rather only to the extent that they ran contrary to the "proper functioning of the common market". The ECJ interpreted this reservation to mean that the prohibition was dependent on the extent to which the national markets had been integrated. As the state of integration was in constant flux, the reservation was deemed to be too vague to be able to deduce the scope of the freedom of movement of capital directly from the Treaty.[38] It was therefore left to secondary Community law to determine the extent of liberalisation of capital movements. A prohibition on restrictions was first imposed by Directive 88/361/EEC (adopted in 1988), which no longer relied on the level of integration already achieved.[39] This prohibition on restrictions became directly applicable on 1 July 1990, when the deadline for

8

---

34 ECJ *Keck* [1993] ECR I-6097, para 16.
35 See the criticisms of, inter alia, Barnard *The Substantive Law of the EU* (Oxford 2004) pp 137–140, and von Wilmowsky [1996] EuR 362, 368–371.
36 *Cf* ECJ *Commission v United Kingdom* [2003] ECR I-4644, paras 45–47; *Commission v Spain* [2003] ECR I-4581, paras 58–62; also arguing against relying on the *Keck* case Fischer [2000] ZEuS 391, 404, Kimms (note 20) p 183. Glöckner [2000] EuR 592, 614–620, and Rohde (note 31) pp 131–132, for example, are of a different view. In more detail see Randelzhofer/Forsthoff (note 9) Vorbem zu den Art 39–55 EGV, paras 86–121.
37 ECJ *Sanz de Lera* [1995] ECR I-4821, paras 40–48 (Spanish legislation that subjected the export of cash and bearer cheques to prior approval).
38 ECJ *Casati* [1981] ECR 2595, paras 8–13 (Italian legislation requiring prior authorization for the export of cash).
39 Art 1(1)(i) Dir 88/361.

implementing the Directive expired.[40] The Treaty caught up with these developments of secondary law in 1993 by adopting the current Article 56 of the TEC (Article III-156 DC). (Since Article 56 TEC/Article III-156 DC largely corresponds to Article 1 of Directive 88/361, one may still consult the Directive for specific questions; some of the protected activities may be adduced in particular from Annex 1, the so-called nomenclature of capital movements. However, the Directive is not capable of stipulating the scope of the Treaty, nor do the classifications made there any longer have a meaning.)

9   Article 56(1) of the TEC (Article III-156 DC) generally prohibits (and therefore requires justification for) *inter alia*: import and export restrictions on cash, restrictions on the acquisition of shares in companies, restrictions on debt incurred in a foreign currency, channelling trade in securities or foreign exchange to certain legal persons, restrictions on taking out loans abroad (*eg* by requiring a cash deposit), restrictions on issuing bonds, disadvantaging foreigners in respect of real estate purchases. Due to the freedom of payments (Article 56(2) TEC/Article III-156 DC), the Member States are, for example, barred from prescribing certain types or modes of payment.[41]

10 The prohibition on restrictions set forth by Article 56 of the TEC (Article III-156 DC) is itself not without limitations. Measures by the Member States or the Community which restrict cross-border trade are not absolutely barred by virtue of Article 56 of the TEC (Article III-156 DC). Rather, they are subject to the **requirement of justification**: They must be suitable, necessary and adequate to promote a component of the **common welfare** (or general interest) to which the Treaty grants priority over unrestricted capital movements. With respect to the grounds of justification, one must distinguish between whether the restriction on capital movements applies within the Community or is in relation to third countries; for measures taken in the latter case, the EC Treaty provides additional grounds of justification.

III. Justification of Restrictions within the Community: The Subjects Protected by Article 58 of the TEC (Article III-158 DC) and the Mandatory Requirements

11 For measures which restrict cross-border capital movements or payments, not only with respect to third countries, but also within the Community, **two groups of grounds of justification** come into consideration. The **first group** consists of those subjects **codified in Article 58 of the TEC (Article III-158 DC)**. These include: taxes (on income from capital) ((1)(a)); national law and regulations; information regarding capital movements; and public policy or public security ((1)(b)). By citing "national laws and regulations" as a ground for intervention, the EC Treaty creates the impression that the Member States may restrict cross-border capital movements at their discretion, provided their measures are cast in the form of a law or regulation.[42] This understanding would nullify the prohibition

---

40 ECJ *Bordessa* [1995] ECR I-361, paras 32–35 (Spanish legislation requiring prior authorization for the export of cash and bearer cheques).

41 *Cf eg* the regulations of the former Belgo-Luxembourg Economic Union which prohibited Belgian and Luxembourg exporters from accepting cash, but rather required them to receive payment in the form of bank transfer or cheque; see the facts (not the decision which is outdated) of the case ECJ *Lambert* [1988] ECR I-4369.

42 This standpoint is expounded in Opinion AG Saggio, ECJ *Scientologie* [2000] ECR I-1335, para 18. He was of the opinion that the Member States retained more scope for action than they

on restrictions set forth in Article 56 of the TEC (Article III-156 DC). Since this would be consistent with neither the provision's integrating function nor the intentions of the Treaty authors, a prerequisite is that the relevant Member State provision is itself justified on a material basis and serves a concern of general interest that deserves priority over the freedom of commerce.[43] The concept of public policy is formed by the fundamental rules of a society, which also include the most important provisions of the criminal code.[44] Thus, restrictions on the movement of capital and payments to combat money laundering or the narcotics trade, for example, may be justified.[45] To protect "public security", a part of public policy, from internal and external threats, measures may be taken against *eg* capital movements of enemies of the constitution or terrorist groups. Capital movements which are associated with the establishment of a branch office may – above and beyond Article 58(1) of the TEC (Article III-158 DC) – also be restricted on those grounds that justify restrictions on the freedom of establishment (Article 58(2) TEC/Article III-158(2) DC). For transactions which represent not only a movement of capital but also the creation of an establishment, the catalogue of permissible restrictions on the movement of capital is thus supplemented by the grounds for restricting the right to establishment.[46]

Already early on, the ECJ committed itself to the interpretation that the codified grounds of justification (such as Article 30 TEC/Article III-154 DC, Article 39(4) TEC/Article III-133(4) DC, Article 45 TEC/Article III-139 DC, Article 46 TEC/Article III-140 DC, Article 55 TEC/Article III-150 DC and Article 58 TEC/Article III-158 DC) must be interpreted narrowly and that the subjects of protection are **exhaustively** listed. In order to be able to account for the numerous legitimate reasons for intervention which are not explicitly mentioned in the limitations of the fundamental freedoms, such as consumer or environmental protection, the ECJ had to create a **second group** of grounds of justification: interests which are part of the public welfare and which are to be valued higher than the interests of free commerce (the so-called "**mandatory requirements**"). The Court has thus adopted an inductive method and decides on a case-by-case basis which governmental regulatory interest deserves priority over free commerce and thus the recognition of being a "mandatory requirement". The attempt to deduce general criteria from this case-law has so far met with little success. Regarding the (widespread) understanding that

12

---

enjoyed in the case of the free movement of goods or persons, and were permitted to restrict the movement of capital by national provisions, "whatever nature they may be".

43 On the corresponding problem relating to public policy see ECJ *Prantl* [1984] ECR 1299, paras 32–33: Member State legislation does not fall within the ambit of "public policy" merely because it carries penal sanctions.

44 ECJ *Bouchereau* [1977] ECR 1999, paras 33–35; *Adoui* [1982] ECR 1665, para 8; *Scientology* [2000] ECR I-1335, para 17: "fundamental interest of society". Further references in Müller-Graff in: von der Groeben/Schwarze (eds) *Vertrag über die Europäische Union und zur Gründung der Europäischen Gemeinschaft, Kommentar* (6th ed, Baden-Baden 2003) Art 30 EGV, paras 49–50.

45 ECJ *Bordessa* [1995] ECR I-361, para 21.

46 Conversely, the same applies: A measure which is valid under the provisions of the free movement of capital restricts the freedom of establishment in a permissible manner (where the transaction enjoys the protection of these two fundamental freedoms) (see Art 43(2) TEC/Art III-137(2) DC). The interactive reservation clauses of Art 43(2) TEC (Art III-137(2) DC) and Art 58(2) TEC (Art III-158(2) DC) thus state that the grounds for limitations of the other respective Treaty chapter are applicable. *Cf* Kiemel (note 1) Art 56 EGV, para 19; Weber [1992] EuZW 561, 565.

solely "non-economic" regulatory purposes may represent a mandatory requirement,[47] it is true that protectionist measures with which the Member State seeks to shield its domestic enterprises from foreign competition cannot be justified. The Court generally describes this finding by stating that "[a] Member State cannot be allowed to avoid the effects of measures provided for in the Treaty by pleading the economic difficulties caused by the elimination of the barriers to intra-Community trade."[48] Yet, not every economic interest may be reproached as being protectionist. On the contrary, a number of "economic" regulatory interests have been recognised as justifying restrictions on the fundamental freedoms. One should also be sceptical of the widespread view that the mandatory requirements – in contrast to the codified grounds of justification – can only support those restrictions which apply indistinctly to domestic and foreign cases.[49] This distinction (distinctly – indistinctly applicable) can scarcely do justice to the complexity of the conflict between the Member State's regulatory power and economic integration. It makes little sense to ban the distinction between measures which apply indistinctly and those which apply distinctly from the prohibition side (by extending the prohibition on restrictions contained in the fundamental freedoms to measures applying indistinctly), only to endow this distinction with a primary function on the justification side. It is therefore not surprising that one repeatedly comes across judgments in which the ECJ finds that restrictions on the fundamental freedoms are justified by a mandatory requirement, although the restrictions apply distinctly and hinder cross-border commerce more than domestic commerce.[50] With respect to capital movements, price stability, the functioning of the capital markets and banking industry, consumer protection, environmental protection and urban and regional policy and urban renewal programmes count among the interests that may represent a mandatory requirement.

13 The extent to which the Member States and secondary Community legislation may restrict (cross-border) capital movements and payments without violating the prohibition of restrictions set forth in Article 56 of the TEC (Article III-156 DC) becomes clearer when one considers the **regulatory field** (such as tax law, corporate law, foreign trade and payments law, monetary law, real estate law, the law of loan guarantees) to which the measure belongs.

IV. Regulatory Fields

1. Tax Law: Capital Gains Tax

14 Taxes are a burden to trade. To the extent that cross-border trade is also hindered, tax legislation is subject to the scrutiny of the fundamental freedoms. Which of the fundamental freedoms applies depends on what is being taxed. The freedom of movement of capital

---

47 References in Müller-Graff (note 44) Art 28 EGV, para 204; Ress/Ukrow (note 1) Art 58 EGV, para 4.
48 *Cf eg* ECJ *Campus Oil* [1984] ECR 2727, para 35.
49 Settled case-law of the ECJ; references in Leible in: Grabitz/Hilf (eds) *Das Recht der Europäischen Union, Kommentar* (loose-leaf, Munich) Art 28 EGV, para 20.
50 See *eg* ECJ *Commission v Belgium* [1992] ECR I-305, paras 10–21 (indistinctly applicable tax regulations). *Cf* also the criticism of Oliver/Jarvis (note 32) paras 8.04–8.09; Müller-Graff (note 44) Art 28 EGV, paras 193–197; Leible (note 49) Art 28 EGV, para 20; von Wilmowsky [1992] EuR 414, 415.

is relevant where the transfer of, the holding of or the income from capital is subject to taxation.[51] One thinks, for example, of taxation on the purchase of real estate, securities, shares in companies or foreign currencies, the taxation of loans, and death duties. With regard to investment income, one thinks above all of taxation of interest on loans and distribution of profits to shareholders or partners (dividends). The justification of restrictions on the fundamental freedoms depends foremost on whether the tax rule is equally applicable or whether it contains different conditions for domestic trade and cross-border trade.

a) Non-Discriminatory Tax Legislation

If the tax restricts cross-border capital movement to the same extent as domestic capital movement (non-discriminatory tax), then there is no problem justifying it. Levying taxes to raise government revenue is recognised as a legitimate regulatory interest.[52] With respect to the freedom of movement of capital specifically, this is implied by Article 58(1) of the TEC (Article III-158(1) DC). By referring to specific aspects of taxation as justifications of restrictions, this provision expresses that levying taxes is, in principle, a permissible restriction on the movement of capital. (With regard to the other fundamental freedoms, this results from the *Cassis* decision, which cites fiscal supervision as an example of a "mandatory requirement".[53] This implies that raising government revenue also belongs to the national regulatory interests that justify restricting trade.) Accordingly, the ECJ held that the Austrian taxation of loans did not violate Article 56(1) of the TEC.[54] This tax (in the amount of 8 % of the amount of the loan) had to be paid by any borrower who was resident in Austria, whereas it was not material whether the lender is located in Austria or abroad. Thus, the cross-border credit business was burdened to the same extent as the domestic credit business. A controversial issue is whether Member States (or the Community) may levy a tax on purchases of foreign currencies (so-called Tobin tax) without violating Article 56(1) of the TEC (Article III-156 DC).[55] Since taxation of sales of goods and services (by the value-added tax) and of sales of real estate (by the land transfer tax) is consistent with the fundamental freedoms for goods, services and capital, the same should apply to a currency transaction tax. If raising government revenue represents a legitimate regulatory aim, then only discriminatory tax legislation will violate the fundamental freedoms.

b) Discriminatory Taxes

Case – Problem: (ECJ *Verkooijen* [2000] ECR I-4071)
V, who lived in the Netherlands, held shares of Petrofina NV, a Belgian stock corporation. A dividend in the amount of Gulden 2,337 (approximately EUR 1,060) was paid out on these shares in 1991. V declared this income on his (Dutch) tax return, expecting that the

---

51 See Schön *Gedächtnisschrift für Brigitte Knobbe-Keuk* (Cologne 1997) pp 743, 756–757.
52 See also Ohler [1996] WM 1801, 1807; Müller (note 10) pp 332–333.
53 ECJ *Cassis de Dijon* [1979] ECR 649, paras 8 and 14.
54 See the first part of the *Sandoz* judgment: ECJ *Sandoz* [1999] ECR I-7041, paras 17–27. (Regarding the second part see *infra* note 66).
55 With respect to this proposal see Tobin [1978] Eastern Economic Journal 153, 155: "The proposal is an internationally uniform tax on all spot conversions of one currency into another, proportional to the size of the transaction."

> income from dividends would remain tax free in the amount of the statutory exemption for income from shares (Gulden 2,000). However, pursuant to Article 47b of the Dutch law on income tax, the exemption applied only to those dividends which were derived from companies that had their registered office in the Netherlands. Since Pertofina NV had its registered office in Belgium, the Dutch tax authority did not apply the dividend exemption and subjected the entire amount of the income from the dividends to Dutch income tax. V brought suit against this decision. The highest Dutch court, the Hoge Raad, applied to the ECJ for a preliminary ruling regarding *inter alia* the question of whether limiting the tax exempt amount for dividends to domestic companies was consistent with the Treaty provisions on the free movement of capital.

aa) The Tax Reservation Clause of Article 58(1)(a) of the TEC (Article III-158(1)(a) DC)

17 Tax legislation is **discriminatory** where it restricts cross-border trade more than the Member State's domestic trade, either in law or in fact.[56] In those cases where the tax legislation interferes with *another* fundamental freedom (other than the freedom of movement of capital treated here) by hindering the intra-Community trade in goods, provision of services, the movement of workers or the establishment, the following legal rule has been developed: Discriminatory tax legislation is not permissible unless it is justified.[57] With respect to *capital movements*, the question arises whether discriminatory tax legislation is to be judged by different, less stringent standards. The chapter in the EC Treaty on capital movement contains a special provision on discriminatory tax legislation. Article 58(1)(a) of the TEC (Article III-158(1)(a) DC) stipulates that the Member States' tax legislation may distinguish on the basis of the taxpayer's residence and according to the place where their capital is invested *without* thereby violating the freedom of capital movement guaranteed by Article 56 of the TEC (Article III-156 DC). At first glance, the wording of this provision appears to permit discriminatory tax treatment on the basis of residence or the location of the capital investment even where this is *not* objectively justified. When this so-called tax reservation clause, which came into effect on 1 January 1994, was originally incorporated into the Treaty, its sponsors did in fact hope that it would permit the Member States to retain a number of discriminatory tax rules.[58] These expectations, however, were disappointed. The ECJ decided in 2000 that the tax reservation clause stipulated in Article 58(1)(a) of the TEC (Article III-158(1) DC) did not dispense with the requirement that a distinction made on the basis of residence of the taxpayer or the location of the investment must be objectively justified.[59] The tax reservation clause is itself subject to the

---

56 The question of when non-residents are, in fact, disadvantaged, is difficult to answer with regard to direct taxation; in more detail see the analysis of the ECJ's case-law by Schön (note 51) pp 743, 758–761.
57 See *eg* ECJ *Schumacker* [1995] ECR I-225, para 39 (freedom of movement of workers); *Wielockx* [1995] ECR I-2493, paras 23–27 (freedom of establishment); for an overview see Voß in: Dauses (eds) *Handbuch des EU-Wirtschaftsrechts* (loose-leaf, Munich) ch J, para 18–35.
58 The background has been described by Kiemel (note 1) Art 58 EGV, paras 12–14. In the Final Act of the Maastricht Treaty, the Conference of the Representatives of the Governments of the Member States affirmed that the reservation with respect to taxes will apply only with respect to the relevant provisions which existed at the end of 1993 (Declaration 7). Such declarations must be taken into account when interpreting the TEC. See however *infra* note 61.
59 ECJ *Verkooijen* [2000] ECR I-4071, paras 43–46; Opinion AG La Pergola on the same case, para 33; since then it has become settled case-law.

proviso contained in Article 58(3) of the TEC (Article III-158(3) DC), which prohibits arbitrary (*ie* objectively unjustifiable) distinctions. Consequently, distinctions made on the basis of the features set forth in the tax reservation clause (residence and location of the investment) also require an objective justification. An objective reason for the discriminatory tax rule must exist, and this reason has to be pursued in a suitable, necessary and adequate manner. The Court thus holds the tax reservation clause stipulated in Article 58(1)(a) of the TEC (Article III-158(1)(a) DC) to be declaratory only; it does not relax the requirements which apply to restrictions of the other fundamental freedoms.[60] Thus, contrary to the sponsors' intentions, the tax reservation clause does not permit additional interventions in capital movements, but rather only those which would be justified according to the principles applicable to restrictions of the other fundamental freedoms.[61]

bb) Grounds of Justification

Next we are confronted with the question of which "**mandatory requirements of the common welfare**" are capable of justifying tax legislation that burdens cross-border commerce more than domestic commerce. Indeed, it is all but clear whether such grounds of justification exist at all. The ECJ deems the "cohesion" (*ie* "coherence") of the national tax system as a mandatory requirement which is able to justify discriminatory taxes of cross-border commerce.[62] It is not, however, clear what is meant by "cohesion". This ground of justification has only been applied in one case so far, namely in an (unsuccessful) action brought by the Commission against Belgium because this state's income tax regulations treated certain domestic cases better than cross-border cases.[63] All other attempts by the Member States to defend discriminatory tax legislation by reference to the "cohesion" of their tax system have been unsuccessful.[64] One should therefore not accept "cohesion" as a justification for worse tax treatment of cross-border commerce. There is no justification for discriminatory tax legislation.[65]

18

---

60 Bachmann [1994] RIW 849, 850–851; Schön (note 51) pp 743, 763–768; Dautzenberg [1988] RIW 537, 540–542 have spoken out in favour of this interpretation; similarly Ohler [1996] WM 1801, 1807.
61 Therefore, neither can Declaration 7 (note 58) have any legal implications; Schön (note 51) pp 743, 768 note 113.
62 ECJ *Commission v Belgium* [1992] ECR I-305, paras 14–21; largely the same in content as ECJ *Bachmann* [1992] ECR I-249, paras 21–28; confirmed *inter alia* in ECJ *Verkooijen* [2000] ECR I-4071, para 43; from the literature see Dautzenberg [2000] StuB 720, 725–726.
63 The Belgian legislation required that the insurer have its registered office or a branch office in Belgium if the premiums of a life insurance policy should be deductible from taxable income; see note 62.
64 For further references see *eg* ECJ *Commission v Belgium* [2000] ECR I-7587, paras 31 and 33–36; Opinion AG Jacobs, ECJ *Commission v Belgium* [2000] ECR I-7587, paras 51–58 (Belgium's prohibition of the acquisition of bonds issued abroad); *Metallgesellschaft* [2001] ECR I-1727, paras 67–76 (taxation of dividends); *X and Y v Riksskatteverk* [2002] ECR I-10829, para 72 in conjunction with paras 52–59 (taxation of capital gains from the sale of stock); *Lenz* [2004] ECR I-7063, paras 34–39 (taxation of dividends); *Manninen* [2004] ECR I-7477, paras 40–48 (taxation of dividends); *Weidert und Paulus* [2004] ECR I-7359, paras 20–27 (statutory tax relief for shares in companies); see also *Bosal Holding BV* [2003] ECR I-9409, paras 29–32 (taxation of groups of companies).
65 See Ohler (note 17) Art 58, para 24. On the consequences for the German tax legislation relating to non-residents see Dautzenberg [2000] StuB 720, 726.

cc) Consequences

19 The **following discriminatory tax rules are in violation** of the freedom of movement of capital: the taxation of loans extended by foreign, but not domestic, lenders;[66] the more favourable taxation of interest that the taxpayer derives from debtors whose registered office or a branch office is located domestically;[67] the restriction of a tax incentive to shares in domestic companies;[68] the restriction of tax exemptions for dividends to those received from domestic companies;[69] the restriction of a land transfer tax exemption to transfers of real estate between the domestic subsidiaries of a corporate group;[70] less favourable taxation of capital gains from the sale of stock where the purchaser is a foreign legal entity.[71] Another violation of Article 56 of the TEC (Article III-156 DC) may lie in the tax credit system that some Member States employ in the taxation of dividends (as shareholder income). This system credits the (*pro rata*) corporate income tax paid by the *company* against the income tax, which the *shareholder* must pay for receipt of the dividend. What is problematic is that the tax credit is limited to domestic stock corporations: A person who holds shares in a foreign company and receives dividends therefrom cannot credit the corporate income tax paid abroad against his or her (domestic) tax return. There is no justification for this less favourable treatment (of the tax credit system in corporate income tax law) of foreign shares.[72] The incompatibility with the fundamental freedoms counts among the reasons why Germany abolished the tax credit system and replaced it with the "half income procedure" (*Halbeinkünfteverfahren*),[73] which no longer credits the corporate income tax paid by the company, but rather provides a tax exemption for half of the dividends received by the shareholder. This exemption also applies to dividends received from foreign companies.[74]

---

66 Second part of the *Sandoz* judgment: ECJ *Sandoz* [1999] ECR I-7041, paras 28–38.
67 ECJ *France v Commission* [2004] ECR I-2081.
68 ECJ *Weidert und Paulus* [2004] ECR I-7359. *Cf* also ECJ *Bosal Holding BV* [2003] ECR I-9409 (distinguishing between domestic and foreign subsidiaries when determining the taxable profit of the parent company; violation of the freedom of establishment).
69 ECJ *Verkooijen* [2000] ECR I-4071.
70 The judgment ECJ *Halliburton* [1994] ECR I-1137 was made on the basis of the freedom of establishment, but cross-border trade in real estate also falls within the scope of the freedom of movement of capital.
71 ECJ *X and Y v Riksskatteverk* [2002] ECR I-10829.
72 ECJ *Manninen* [2004] ECR I-7477, paras 25–55; *cf* also the decision of the Finanzgericht (First-Instance Fiscal Court) Cologne of 24 June 2004, [2004] GmbHR 1091. Knobbe-Keuk in: *Steuerrecht, Verfassungsrecht, Finanzpolitik: Festschrift für Franz Klein* (Cologne 1994) pp 347, 351–352, 358, and Rohde (note 31) pp 168–169 had already propounded a similar opinion; *cf* also the (in part outdated) overview presented by Saß [1993] DB 113, 115–117. A different opinion may be found in Schön (note 51) pp 743, 775–776.
73 See Pezzer [2000] StuW 144, 145–146.
74 See sec 3 No 40d in conjunction with sec 20(1) No 1 of the *Einkommensteuergesetz* (EStG – German Income Tax Law). *Cf* also the Austrian "half rate procedure" (*Halbsatzverfahren*), where the dividends derived from shareholdings are subject to a tax rate equal to half the tax rate applied to the tax payer's other income. In contrast to the German provisions, the Austrian legislation applied only to dividends derived from domestic companies. The Austrian legislation was to this extent inconsistent with Art 56 TEC; see ECJ *Lenz* [2004] ECR I-7063, paras 23–49; *cf* also the preliminary procedure question in ECJ *Schmid* [2002] ECR I-4573.

One encounters as yet unresolved issues when one attempts to extend the fundamental freedoms to double taxation of income. If, for example, a resident of State A receives income from a source in State B (such as from shares held in a company of State B, from leasing real estate in B or from employment in B), it may occur that both A and B tax this income. In those cases, where there is no bilateral agreement between A and B in place which would prevent double taxation, the question arises as to whether the fundamental freedoms prohibit double taxation. This is a case of discrimination: By taxing the income without regard to the taxes levied by the other state, more taxes are levied on the cross-border income than are levied on the same income derived from a domestic source. The measures taken by two states are thus responsible for the discrimination.[75] To remedy the discrimination, one of the states must take into account the measures taken by the other state and credit the taxes paid there. The difficulty now lies in assigning the roles: Which state deserves primary access to the taxable income, with the consequence that the other state is obliged to credit the taxes paid to the "primary" state?[76] Many scholars are still reluctant to derive such a ranking of jurisdiction for taxation from the fundamental freedoms.[77] In doing so, they capitulate in the face of a grave instance of discrimination. There is no reason for this reluctance. The "tax order" that would be established by the ECJ through the use of the prohibition of discrimination does not obviate the political decisions which the Member States or the Community may take with regard to this issue. The Member States or the Community are free to remedy the discrimination by another means (*ie* by establishing a different tax system), *eg* through a double taxation convention or an EC directive. Only when double taxation will be prohibited by an extensive use of the fundamental freedoms, enough pressure will be created to bring about positive harmonization (through negotiations under Article 293 TEC).

20

Case – Answer:
The provision of the Dutch law on income tax which restricts the exemption for income derived from capital investments to dividends derived from Dutch companies could violate Article 56(1) of the TEC (Article III-156 DC). This provision protects the movement of capital from unjustified restrictions both between the EU Member States and in relation to third countries. If shareholders receive dividends, there is a capital movement, because money is being assigned, without this being a payment for a performance on the part of the recipient (*ie* shareholder). Dividend payments which cross a national border fall within the scope of protection of Article 56(1) of the TEC (Article III-156 DC). The Dutch taxation of dividends derived from foreign companies restricts cross-border capital movements, but is nonetheless justified by the interest of the state in raising revenue. Only the rule which exempts dividends derived from domestic companies from taxable income up to a certain amount, but withholds this exemption for dividends derived from foreign companies, is problematic. Whether this unequal treatment is justified depends on how Article 58 of the TEC (Article III-158 DC) is to be interpreted. On the one hand, pursuant to Article 58(1)(a) of the TEC (Article III-158(1)(a) DC), the Member States are entitled to make a distinction according to the place of the investment when taxing income derived from capital investments. The Member States thus appear to have the right to tax income derived from divi

21

---

75 Schön (note 51) pp 743, 761–762.
76 This question has been aptly labelled the "final test" for the protection by the fundamental freedoms vis-à-vis national tax law; see Vanistendael [1996] CMLRev 255, 265.
77 For example Schön (note 51) pp 743, 773.

dends from foreign companies differently than such income from domestic companies. On the other hand, Article 58(3) of the TEC (Article III-158(3) DC) makes clear that tax law also prohibits any and all arbitrary discrimination. The strained relationship between the two statements of Article 58 of the TEC (Article III-158 DC) is resolved by the Court such that the tax reservation clause of (1) is to be interpreted in the light of prohibition of discrimination (3). Although the Dutch tax provision appears to be covered by the wording of Article 58(1)(a) of the TEC (Article III-158(1)(a) DC), it is thereby only permissible if there is an objective reason to deny the exemption for dividends paid by foreign companies. No such reasons are to be seen.[78] The exclusion of dividends paid by foreign companies from the exemption therefore violates Article 56(1) of the TEC (Article III-156 DC). It may no longer be applied by the Dutch tax authorities.

2. Company Law

a) Privatisation Law

22 The **privatisation of public companies** is often accompanied by measures by which the government attempts to retain influence over the company. The primary objective of these policies is to retain control over ownership of the company or over company policy (or over both). With regard to the **first case group**, some privatisation acts limit the number of voting shares that may be acquired in the company. If a person, for example, wished to invest in certain privatised companies in France or Great Britain (such as the French energy company Elf-Aquitaine or the British airport operator BAA plc), an investment in excess of a defined amount (*eg* 10 % or 15 %) required prior administrative approval. These restrictions on the freedom of movement of capital (and under certain circumstances the freedom of establishment) cannot be justified by the requirements of the common welfare; in particular, they do not further public policy or increase public security (Article 58(2)(b) TEC/Article III-158(1)(b) DC).[79] Legislation that does not limit the acquisition of shares but does limit the voting rights of the shares is equally unjustifiable. A case in point is the German privatisation of Volkswagen in 1960, which was accompanied by the limitation of the voting rights to 20 %.[80]

23 The **second case group** is formed by those governmental measures which serve to control the privatised company's management decisions. Some privatisation acts stipulate that certain transactions of the privatised company (such as the sale of important operations and subsidiaries) require prior approval by the government. Also belonging to this group is legislation which permits the government to fill a certain number of positions on the company's board of directors (or similar company bodies) independently of the number of shares held by the government.[81] That these measures are often found in the private

---

78 ECJ *Verkooijen* [2000] ECR I-4071, paras 47–62.
79 For details see ECJ *Commission v France* [2002] ECR I-4781, paras 50–51 (privatisation of Elf-Aquitaine); *Commission v Portugal* [2002] ECR I-4731, paras 43–53 (privatised undertakings in Portugal); *Commission v United Kingdom* [2003] ECR I-4644, paras 11, 44–50 (privatisation of British Airport Authority; restriction on the acquisition of shares carrying the right to more than 15 % of the votes).
80 See sec 2 of the *Gesetz über das Volkswagenwerk* (German Volkswagen Act); *Bundesgesetzblatt* (BGBl – German Official Federal Gazette) I 1960, 585; amended by BGBl I 1970, 1149.
81 See *eg* sec 4(1) of the German Volkswagen Act: The Federal Republic of Germany and Lower Saxony may each name two members of the (twenty member) supervisory board of Volkswagen

company's articles of association (and are thus cast in civil law, rather than in statutes and regulations) does not mean that the fundamental freedoms are not applicable. In terms of their effect, such measures remain a government approval procedure. The attendant restrictions on trade in shares of these companies are, however, seldom justified. A justification only comes into consideration in cases where the company is an integral part of public policy or public security (Article 58(1)(b) TEC/Article III-158(1)(b) DC). This is conceivable, for instance, in the case of energy or telecommunications companies: The government may intervene in their business operations if and to the extent that this is necessary to prevent a grave danger to the supply of their services.[82]

How the state exercises its influence is immaterial. Its legislation may be **directly** tied to the acquisition of shares or management decisions. However, the state may also **indirectly** intervene by retaining shares of the privatised company and vesting these with special membership rights (reservations of approval, veto rights, rights to fill positions of the governing bodies). The term "golden shares" is only applicable to the second mode of influence. The use of public law as well as civil law instruments (such as certain corporate-law powers granted by law) does not open any further scope for action for the state. If the measure restricts the (cross-border) trade in the shares of the privatised company, it must be justified by the overriding requirements of the common welfare.

b) Corporate Law

The memorandum and articles of association of a stock company contain *inter alia* provisions which limit or restrict trade in the company's stock. Here are a few examples: the requirement that stock may only be transferred with the consent of the company (*cf* section 68(2) *Aktiengesetz* – German Stock Corporation Act); limiting the voting rights of a shareholder who holds several shares to a maximum number (*cf* section 134(1)(ii) Stock Corporation Act); providing individual shareholders with multiple voting rights; authorising the company's executive board to take measures aimed at thwarting a tender offer (takeover bid) (*cf* section 33(2) *Wertpapiererwerbs- und Übernahmegesetz* – German Securities Acquisition and Takeover Act). The question of whether such clauses in the articles of association violate the guarantees provided by the EC Treaty for the freedom of cross-border capital movement (*ie* Article 56 TEC/Article III-156 DC) and must therefore be justified by the overriding requirements of the common welfare has not yet been answered. In contrast to the above section treating legislative privatisation measures, the rules

---

AG for as long as they hold shares in the corporation. While Lower Saxony holds shares in Volkswagen AG, the Federal Government does not.

82 These requirements have been deemed to be met by the Belgian legislation: The government of Belgium had retained the right to oppose the management decisions of those privatised companies which operate the lines and conduits for supplying gas and electricity in Belgium ("golden share"), see ECJ *Commission v Belgium* [2002] ECR I-4809, paras 48–55. In contrast, the right to veto the sale of certain subsidiaries by the oil company Elf-Aquitaine retained by the French government is not designed to guarantee energy supplies and therefore does not fall within the ambit of Art 58 TEC (Art III-158 DC); see ECJ *Commission v France* [2002] ECR I-4781, paras 52–53. Likewise, neither Spain's system of prior administrative approval for important business decisions of its privatised companies nor the UK's system of administrative approval for sale of airports by privatised British Airports Authority could be justified by reference to public security; ECJ *Commission v Spain* [2003] ECR I-4581, paras 71–84; *Commission v United Kingdom* [2003] ECR I-4644, paras 44–50.

under consideration here are not imposed by the state, but rather are agreed upon between private persons, namely the shareholders of the company. The TEC's prohibitions on restrictions and the requirements of justification, however, are addressed to Member States. At least in principle, the private economic actors (*ie* the citizens and companies) are the *beneficiaries* of the fundamental freedoms and are not restricted by them. (Autonomous private conduct is not regulated by the fundamental freedoms, but rather by the provisions on competition contained in Articles 81–85 TEC/Articles III-161-164 DC). If one uses this principle as a guide, then the articles of association of stock companies do not fall within the scope of Article 56 of the TEC (Article III-156 DC). The ECJ, however, has broken with this principle in some cases and subjected private (entrepreneurial) conduct to the prohibition on unjustified restrictions provided by the fundamental freedoms (so-called horizontal effect of the fundamental freedoms).[83] The degree to which the Court will extend this line of reasoning to corporate articles of association can scarcely be foreseen.[84]

3. Foreign Trade and Payments Legislation: Reporting Requirements

26 The EU Member States' foreign trade and payments legislation imposes comprehensive **reporting requirements** on the participants in cross-border capital and payment transactions. In **German law,** these are to be found in the *Außenwirtschaftsverordnung* (German Foreign Trade Regulation) and the *Bundesbankgesetz* (German Bundesbank Act). Reporting requirements do not prevent cross-border capital movements and payments, but they do burden them. Therefore, the question of their consistency with Article 56 of the TEC (Article III-156 DC) arises. The answer lies in Article 58(1)(b) of the TEC (Article III-158(1)(b) DC). Pursuant to this provision, the Member States are entitled to "lay down procedures for the declaration of capital movements for purposes of administrative or statistical information", which, according to the majority view, also applies to payments.[85] This provision does not, however, have the effect of permitting any reporting requirement whatsoever. Rather, only such information may be gathered as is needed by the public authorities to pursue requirements of the common welfare. The need for the information must be justified, *ie* must be supported by a legitimate regulatory interest. The condition is satisfied by, for example, such reporting requirements on payments with which crimes such as tax evasion, drug trafficking and the formation of terrorist organisations may be discovered.[86]

---

83 See generally on the horizontal effects of the fundamental freedoms → § 7 paras 45–46.
84 On likely consequences see Grundmann/Möslein (2003) ZGR 317, 350–364. *Cf* also the discussion in American constitutional law on the question as to whether or not non-mandatory State corporation law violates the interstate commerce clause of the US constitution, which guarantees the freedom of interstate commerce within the United States, where the State law hinders the transfer of shares in a company in order to make takeovers more difficult; see U.S. Supreme Court, *CTS v Dynamics*, 481 US (United States Reports) 69 (1987); see also Buxbaum/Hopt *Legal Harmonization and the Business Enterprise* (Berlin 1988) pp 130–154; Buxbaum (1987) 75 California Law Review 29; von Wilmowsky [1996] JZ 590, 592–593, 595–596.
85 Kiemel (note 1) Art 58 EGV, para 21; Rohde (note 31) pp 156–157. Ress/Ukrow (note 1) Art 58 EGV, para 33 present a different view.
86 *Cf* ECJ *Bordessa* [1995] ECR I-361, para 27.

It appears dubious whether the reporting requirements imposed by the German foreign trade and payments legislation are authorized by Article 58(1)(b) of the TEC (Article III-158(1)(b) DC). These reporting requirements apply to cross-border payments and cross-border holdings of property; they do not apply in domestic cases. By contrast, Article 58(1)(b) of the TEC (Article III-158(1)(b) DC) covers the declaration of "capital movements", *ie* measures which apply equally to both domestic as well as cross-border capital movements.[87] Reporting requirements which apply exclusively to cross-border capital movements may, however, be justified, in cases where the border crossing itself triggers a legitimate need for information. Nearly every country records the economic transactions between home and abroad in the so-called balance of payments in order to obtain knowledge of its external economic relations.[88] This balance of payments is calculated on the basis of the data which was gathered with the help of the reporting requirements. The test of compatibility with the fundamental freedoms therefore focuses on the question of which function the individual EU Member State's balance of payments still fulfils in the Economic and Monetary Union. The individual national balances of payments have become substantially less important since the launch of the third (and final) stage.[89] Since the transactions between the Member States of the Economic and Monetary Union no longer constitute foreign exchange transactions, *ie* exchanging domestic currency for foreign currency and *vice versa*, the individual national balances of payments (specifically the foreign exchange account) are no longer able to report on the change in monetary supply in the Economic and Monetary Union. National balances of payments in the European Economic and Monetary Union are therefore no longer capable of guiding the decisions on monetary policy (such as currency exchange rates and foreign exchange reserves).[90] For this, a balance of payments which is made from the perspective of the Economic and Monetary Union is necessary (and also sufficient). The hitherto unanswered question of whether the functional loss just described deprives the national reporting requirements relating to cross-border capital movements and payments between the Member States of the Euro zone of their justification requires closer examination. Furthermore, this examination would have to address the question whether the remaining functions of the national balances of payments (such as for the determination of the gross national product) are sufficient to justify the burdens coupled with the reporting requirements. A comparison to the German *Bundesländer* (federal states) could also provide insight into this issue; the *Bundesländer* do not need a balance of payments for their economic policies.

---

87 *Cf* Smits in: *Währung und Wirtschaft: Das Geld im Recht: Festschrift für Hahn* (Baden-Baden 1997) pp 245, 253.
88 For an introduction to foreign economic accounting see Stobbe *Volkswirtschaftliches Rechnungswesen* (8th ed, Berlin 1994) pp 236–247, and von Arnim *Volkswirtschaftspolitik* (6th ed, Neuwied 1998) pp 112–141.
89 In more detail see Rose/Sauernheimer *Theorie der Außenwirtschaft* (13th ed, Munich 1999) pp 31–37.
90 In more detail see *eg* Rose/Sauernheimer (note 89) pp 15–21.

4. Monetary Law

a) Monetary Policy

28 Some areas of capital movement, such as lending by credit institutions, are influenced by **monetary policy measures**. The ECB controls the amount of cash by its monopoly on issuing bank notes (Article 106 TEC/Article III-186 DC) and the amount of deposit money with the monetary policy instruments provided by Articles 18 to 20 of the Statute of the European System of Central Banks and of the European Central Bank (open market operations, credit operations, minimum reserves, other instruments).[91] Whether these measures are compatible with the Treaty provisions on the free movement of capital is scarcely discussed. In any case, they are justified by the requirements of the common welfare. By limiting the amount of money present in the Euro zone, they contribute to fighting inflation and maintaining price stability (Article 4(2) TEC/Article III-177(2) DC, Article 105(1) TEC/Article 185(1) DC, Article 2 Statute of the European System of Central Banks and of the European Central Bank).

b) Exchange Rate Policy

29 The freedom of capital movements entails that the exchange rate between the Euro and other currencies must be set by the free market. **Exchange rates set by the government and other interventions in the exchange rate** limit capital movement and thus require a justification by overriding requirements of the common welfare.[92] Justification is required in the following three cases: (i) where the Community concludes exchange rate agreements with third countries (*eg* within the framework of the IMF) pursuant to Article 111 of the TEC (Article III-326 DC); (ii) where the ECB intervenes in the currency markets pursuant to Article 105(2) of the TEC (Article III-185(2) DC) and Article 23 Statute of the European System of Central Banks and of the European Central Bank by acquiring and selling foreign exchange assets; (iii) where Member States which fall within the scope of an exception derogating from the Treaty pursuant to Article 124(2) of the TEC (Article III-200 DC). The only ground of justification is the maintainance of price stability (Article 105(1)(i) TEC/Article III-185(1)(i) DC). Thus, for example, intervention purchases by the ECB may become necessary if extensive capital exports threaten to erode the external value of the Euro and thereby fuel inflation.

---

91 For an overview of the ECB's monetary policy instruments see European Central Bank *The Single Monetary Policy in Stage Three* (Frankfurt a M 2000) pp 4–6, 14–24; Haug in: Schimansky/Bunte/Lwowski (eds) *Bankrechts-Handbuch* (2nd ed, Munich 2001) § 123, paras 68–74; Papathanassiou in: Schimansky/Bunte/Lwowski (eds) *Bankrechts-Handbuch* (2nd ed, Munich 2001) § 134, paras 70–109.

92 The assessment that a state-imposed split of the currency exchange (in one part with a fixed exchange rate and in a second part with a floating exchange rate) does not have the effect of restricting capital movements but merely constitutes an anomaly is hardly persuasive. Yet this is the position taken in Dir 88/361, Annex V, with respect to such measures imposed by the Belgo-Luxembourg Economic Union (see above note 41); *cf* ECJ *Lambert* [1988] ECR I-4369.

5. The Law of Real Estate Transactions

Trade in real estate is heavily regulated. Some restrictions have the effect that some classes of people are given preferential access to real estate. These restrictions face some difficulty in withstanding the "justification pressure" exerted on them by the guarantee of the freedom of capital movements provided by the EC Treaty. Yet not even the ECJ could always escape the concerns and fears which are unleashed in society when equal opportunity to acquire real property is provided.

a) Secondary Residences

In some Member States, the purchase of real estate is limited or prohibited if it is likely that the real estate will be used merely as a secondary residence. "Secondary residence" means that the house or apartment is used only for a few weeks during the year and remains unoccupied the rest of the time. Secondary residences are considered to be a problem when they are concentrated in a certain area, specifically in tourist areas. A variety of measures are employed to prevent the emergence of secondary residences in such areas.

aa) Measures

German urban development law intervenes in the development of condominiums. In tourist areas, the local authorities have the power to prohibit the formation of condominiums (section 22 of the *Baugesetzbuch* – German Federal Building Code).[93] It is immaterial whether the building – after the creation of the condominium – would actually have been used as secondary residence.[94] Austria, too has attempted to limit the spread of secondary residences by limiting the purchase of real estate. In contrast to Germany, however, all types of real estate are covered (*ie* not just condominiums) and the permit is based on the intended use: The required permit for the conveyance of the property is denied if it cannot be guaranteed that the buyer will not use the real estate as a secondary residence.[95] The question arises whether these restrictions on the purchase of real estate (and thus capital movements) are justified by mandatory requirements of the common welfare. Only then would they be consistent with Article 56(1) of the TEC (Article III-156 DC) and could thus be applied to purchases of real estate by foreigners (or more precisely: residents of other countries).

bb) Promoting the Common Welfare

Whether the restrictions imposed on secondary residences **promote the common welfare** (and not merely that of individual interest groups) has not yet been exhaustively examined.[96] The ECJ, for one, considers that it is conceivable that the measure may help to maintain "an economic activity independent of tourism", *ie* may operate to reduce depen-

---

93 For detailed commentary see *eg* Krautzberger in: Battis/Krautzberger/Löhr (eds) *Baugesetzbuch* (9th ed, Munich 2005), commentary on § 22.
94 *Bundesverwaltungsgericht* (BVerwG – German Federal Administrative Court) [1996] ZfBR 48, 50.
95 See the legislation of the Austrian states Tyrol (ECJ *Konle* [1999] ECR I-3099), Vorarlberg (ECJ *Salzmann* [2003] ECR I-4899) and Salzburg (ECJ *Reisch* [2002] ECR I-2157).
96 For the state of the discussion see Fischer [2000] ZEuS 391, 411; Glöckner [2000] EuR 592; Bachlechner [1998] ZEuS 519; Knapp [1999] EWS 409; Hammerl/Sippel [1992] RIW 883.

dency on tourism.[97] The Court is mistaken in this regard. If tourists are not able to spend their holiday in secondary residences, they will seek other accommodation, such as hotels. Measures against secondary residences merely redirect tourism into other channels without reducing it. The German legislation thus explicitly emphasises that the measures are aimed at *promoting* tourism (section 22(1) Federal Building Code). The aim is to retain a specific structure of the tourism industry: "the permanent residents leasing rooms and holiday apartments during the [tourist] season".[98] This also applies to Austria: Its restrictions on secondary residences are not applicable where the real estate is intended to be used as a hotel or vacation rental lodging. Thus, the limitations on secondary residences serve the commercial interests of a single group – the hotel industry – and not the common welfare. The other regulatory interest that the ECJ views as being promoted is more interesting: the maintenance of "a permanent population" and thus an intact social structure.[99] The greater the number of secondary residences, the more desolate the affected area becomes during off-season. This leads to a situation where districts are uninhabited for much of the year and a local social life therefore becomes impossible.[100] According to the majority view – which is not questioned here – the maintenance of a permanently inhabited district deserves to be recognised as a mandatory requirement.[101] In contrast, many other interests which are still brought forward as justifications of restrictions on secondary residences (such as preserving scarce farm land and reserving residential areas for the local population or the efficient use of expensive roads)[102] are hardly interests of the common welfare.[103]

cc) Principle of Proportionality

34 The measures taken to check secondary residences in areas characterised as centres of tourism must satisfy the **principle of proportionality**. In this regard, measures which subject the transfer of ownership of the affected real estate to preventive control (by a system

---

97 ECJ *Konle* [1999] ECR I-3099, para 40 (restrictions on the acquisition of ownership of holiday residences pursuant to the Tyrol *Grundverkehrsgesetz* (Tyrol Land Transfer Law)); confirmed in *inter alia* ECJ *Reisch* [2002] ECR I-2157, para 34 (*Salzburger Grundverkehrsgesetz* (Salzburg Land Transfer Law)).

98 *Oberverwaltungsgericht* (OVG – court of appeals in administrative law matters) Lüneburg [1983] ZfBR 238, 240.

99 ECJ *Konle* [1999] ECR I-3099, para 40. Furthermore see the (not legally binding) joint declaration on secondary residences, [1994] OJ C241/382 (Final Act concerning the conditions of accession of the Kingdom of Norway, the Republic of Austria, the Republic of Finland and the Kingdom of Sweden): "Nothing in the 'acquis communautaire' prevents individual Member States from taking national, regional or local measures regarding secondary residences, provided that they are necessary for land-use planning and environmental protection and apply without direct or indirect discrimination between nationals of the Member States in conformity with the 'acquis'."

100 On the dangers of a lack of social life see also OVG Lüneburg [1983] ZfBR 238, as well as BVerwG [1994] DVBl 1149, 1151 (disruption of the social infrastructure).

101 See above note 99. Doubts may arise from the fact that, in the final analysis, hotels and other lodging enterprises in whose favour the prohibition on secondary residences operates are also unoccupied in the off season.

102 Opinion AG La Pergola, ECJ *Konle* [1999] ECR I-3099, para 16; OVG Lüneburg [1983] ZfBR 238, 240; BVerwG [1994] DVBl 1149, 1151; *cf* also Bachlechner [1998] ZEuS 519, 520.

103 Also critical Glöckner [2000] EuR 592, 619–620.

of prior authorisation) are problematic. Consider first the Austrian provincial law (*Landesrecht*), which requires the prior authorisation of a land transfer authority (*Grundverkehrsbehörde*) for the conveyance of real estate. The authorisation is only granted if the authority concludes that the buyer will use the real estate as his or her principal residence. The ECJ held this prior authorisation procedure to be in violation of the principle of proportionality: It restricted the freedom of capital movement to a greater extent than is necessary.[104] Since the land transfer authority must make a prognosis as to the future use of the land, the law "allows the competent administrative authority considerable latitude which may be akin to a discretionary power". The exercise of a freedom guaranteed by the Treaty may not be subject to the discretion of the administrative authorities. Likewise, it is doubtful whether the German regulation (secion 22 *Baugesetzbuch*) could withstand scrutiny of its proportionality. The irrebuttable presumption made there, that, in areas characterised as tourist centres, any development of condominiums will lead to the spread of secondary residences, appears to be on shaky grounds. It is by no means a foregone conclusion that condominiums in tourist areas will not be used as primary residences.[105]

As an **alternative consistent with the Treaty** the ECJ suggests monitoring the actual use of the land and that "infringements ... may be penalised by a fine, by a decision requiring the acquirer to terminate the unlawful use of the land forthwith under penalty of its compulsory sale, or by a declaration that the sale is void resulting in the reinstatement in the land register of the entries prior to the acquisition of the property". In order to enforce such limitations of use, the Member States may require the owner to make disclosures as to the actual use of the property and, at the time when the property is purchased, to submit a declaration that the property will be used in compliance with the law.[106] On the basis of this case-law, it emerges that Member States which desire to prevent secondary residences should embark on this alternative course of action and impose and monitor use restrictions. Interventions in ownership structures, by contrast, run the risk of violating Article 56(1) of the TEC (Article III-156 DC) because they are either not suitable or not necessary. The ownership of a plot of land or a building is simply not related to its use (as a primary or secondary residence). If ownership of a plot of land or a residence is conveyed, restrictions on its use (imposed, for example, by local development plans) can be enforced against the new owner just as well.[107] Conversely, secondary residences can be created not only by acquiring ownership but also by lease. 35

dd) Denmark

Denmark does not face any of these problems. With respect to secondary residences it is exempted from observing the EC Treaty. Pursuant to a Protocol to the EC Treaty, it may 36

---

104 ECJ *Konle* [1999] ECR I-3099, paras 40–49 (Tyrol Land Transfer Law); ECJ *Reisch* [2002] ECR I-2157, paras 37–39 (Salzburg Land Transfer Law); ECJ *Salzmann* [2003] ECR I-4899, paras 45–52 – Salzmann (*Vorarlberger Grundverkehrsgesetz* (Vorarlberg Land Transfer Law)).
105 *Cf* also the fact situation in BVerwG [1996] ZfBR 48, 50.
106 On the requirement of a prior declaration on the part of the purchaser see ECJ *Reisch* [2002] ECR I-2157, paras 35–36; *Konle* [1999] ECR I-3099, paras 44–48.
107 This is comparable to the prohibitions on converting residences into office space. They are addressed to the respective owner of the real estate, and there is no attempt to enforce them by imposing restrictions on the transfer of the property.

permanently retain its legislation which was in force prior to 01 November 1993, notwithstanding its (likely) incompatibility with the EC Treaty.[108]

b) Agricultural Land

37   In many Member States, trade in **land belonging to the agricultural and forestry industry** is subject to special restrictions. These restrictions impose requirements pertaining to the individual farm or to the entire sector. Austrian provincial law offers examples of the first type. The land transfer laws of Tyrol and Vorarlberg attempt to reserve agricultural land for independent farmers: Only those who work the farm themselves and have the requisite professional expertise may purchase agricultural or forestry land. Furthermore, the purchaser must take residence on the premises. Finally, the purchase may not lead to the owner's property exceeding the size of a "small or medium-sized" agricultural business.[109] Whether or not this regulatory scheme promotes the common welfare is controversial. The ECJ agrees in principle: "Preserving agricultural communities, maintaining a distribution of land ownership which allows the development of viable farms and sympathetic management of green spaces and the countryside as well as encouraging a reasonable use of the available land" are objectives that belong to the common welfare.[110] The Court merely requires that exceptions must be made possible; the authorities may not require that the buyer personally operates the farm in every instance. This interpretation by the Court is hardly convincing. The interests of independent farmers cannot be equated with the common welfare.[111] The second type of regulation is to be found in Germany, among other places. The *Grundstücksverkehrsgesetz* (German Real Estate Transfer Act) attempts to bring about a certain (but not specifically described) structure of the affected agrarian sector with the aid of a system of prior approval. The approval for a sale of a plot of agrarian or forestry land may be denied, *inter alia,* if the intended sale would lead to an "unhealthy" distribution of land.[112] As regards this legislation, too, there are doubts as to whether it increases the public welfare. It is not apparent why state direction should be better able to bring about effective economic structures in the agricultural industry than the free market. Accordingly, the pre-emptive right of purchase pursuant to the *Reichssiedlungsgesetz* (German Reich Settlement Act) does not seem to be supported by any

---

108 See the Protocol on the acquisition of property in Denmark, [1992] OJ C191/68 (amendments to the Treaty of Maastricht). A protocol annexed to the Treaty forms an integral part thereof (Art 311 TEC). In its negotiations for accession to the EU Malta also demanded (unsuccessfully) that its restrictions on the acquisition of real property be permanently excepted from the provisions relating to the free movement of capital, COM (2001) 553 final, 10.
109 Tyrol: Sections 4, 6(1)(b) and (c) of the Tyrol Land Transfer Law of 1996, LGBl 1996 No 61; Vorarlberg: Sections 4, 5(1)(a) and (2)(d) of the Vorarlberg Land Transfer Law of 1993, LGBl 1993 No 61; also reprinted in ECJ *Ospelt* [2003] ECR I-9743.
110 ECJ *Ospelt* [2003] ECR I-9743, para 39 (see also paras 38–54); also propounded by some scholars, *eg* Schneider [2000] ZfV 16, 24.
111 Likewise Bachlechner [1998] ZEuS 519, 532–533.
112 Secs 2(1)(i), 9(1) No 1, 9(2) of the *Gesetz über Maßnahmen zur Verbesserung der Agrarstruktur und zur Sicherung land- und forstwirtschaftlicher Betriebe* (*Grundstücksverkehrsgesetz,* German Real Estate Transfer Act). An overview of this act is provided by Baur/Stürner *Sachenrecht* (17th ed, Munich 1999) § 27 II 1. Regarding the residential enterprises' right of pre-emption connected thereto see Stürner in: Soergel (ed) *Bürgerliches Gesetzbuch mit Einführungsgesetzen und Nebengesetzen, Kommentar Bd XVI* (13th ed, Stuttgart 2001) Vor § 1094, paras 22–24.

mandatory requirement either. (In contrast, zoning plans which specify certain uses – *eg* for agriculture – are justified.)

c) Real Estate Adjoining Land Frontiers and in Areas of Military Importance

Some Member States restrict the **acquisition of real estate adjoining land frontiers and in areas of military importance**.[113] External security (Article 58(1)(b) TEC/Article III-158(1)(b) DC) also numbers among the grounds for restricting (cross-border) capital movements. This is subject to the condition that the measure taken is suitable and necessary for the defence of the nation. Legislation which distinguishes between real estate buyers on the basis of nationality and makes the purchase of real estate more difficult or prohibits the purchase of real estate for foreigners only does not withstand this test. The conveyance of title to real property does not affect the ability to defend the nation. The Member States have the opportunity to use the property if it is needed for defence purposes, irrespective of who the owner is.[114]

38

6. Security Interests

a) Principles

Security interests (such as liens, pledges, mortgages, title retention clauses, ownership by way of security, assignment for security) are a form of capital. Although the freedom of movement of capital (Article 56(1) TEC/Article III-156 DC) guarantees both the cross-border creation and the cross-border mobility of security interests, a common market for security interests has thus far not been realised. Consider the following example: The security collateral (*ie* the object subject to a security interest) is transported from one Member State into another. The border-crossing into a new jurisdiction may function as a guillotine, severing all rights in the collateral completely. Similarly, the border-crossing may transform the security interest into another legal right under the new legal system, which could bring about losses of entitlements or gains of additional entitlements. This is attributable to mandatory rules of national civil law, which operate at two levels.[114] At the level of substantive law, it is property law (*ie* the law that governs real and personal property) which often restricts the creation of security interests. Thus, many Member States do not permit a seller's retention of title clause to extend to those assets, including claims, which take the place of the sold object after processing or resale. The requirement (for pledges) that the collateral provider may not retain possession of the collateral but rather must surrender it to the secured party[116] is a further restriction on creation. Finally, many jurisdictions place restrictions on the type of property which may be used as a collateral,

39

---

113 For references see Knapp [1999] EWS 409.
114 *Cf* ECJ *Albore* [2000] ECR I-5965, para 22: "The position would be different only if it were demonstrated, for each area to which the restriction applies, that non-discriminatory treatment of the nationals of all the Member States would expose the military interests of the Member State concerned to real, specific and serious risks which could not be countered by less restrictive procedures." It appears to be highly unlikely that equal treatment of foreigners will lead to such dangers.
115 In more detail see von Wilmowsky (note 11) pp 122–133, 94–122.
116 In German law see sections 1205–1206 of the *Bürgerliches Gesetzbuch* (BGB – German Civil Code).

the persons who serve as collateral providers or secured parties, or the type of claims that may be secured.[117] At the level of conflict of laws (*ie* those rules which determine what national law is to be applied in international cases), the cross-border creation and the cross-border mobility of security interests are restricted as well. In most European states, the law applicable to a security interest cannot be chosen by the parties of the security agreement. Rather, that country's law applies (mandatorily) in which the collateral is physically located (so-called **situs doctrine**). If the collateral is transported across a national border, the law applicable to the security interest automatically changes, thereby triggering legal losses (or legal gains) for the secured party. Because of its restrictive effects, the situs doctrine must be justified by (EC) "mandatory requirements" of the public welfare (if the doctrine shall be applied to security interests, the creation or mobility of which enjoys the protection of Article 56 TEC). If one embarks on this examination, one will arrive at the conclusion that the Member States' laws on security interests should change.[118] In principle, mandatory rules should give way to party autonomy at both levels. With regard to conflict of laws, the parties should be free to choose the applicable national law; at the level of substantive law they should be free to determine the content of the security interest (*ie* the entitlements, such as rights to preferential distribution and rights to dispose of the collateral). Party autonomy should only be restricted where this is necessary to achieve objectives of the common welfare, specifically: the transparency (or publicity) of the security interest (*eg* by registration), the protection of certain groups of creditors (namely such creditors who, like tort victims, should not be exposed to the competition for security interests), the proper functioning of insolvency proceedings, the protection of the market through good faith acquisition rules, and the protection of consumers as collateral providers.[119]

b) Example: Security Interests in a Foreign Currency

40 So far, only one question concerning security interests has been submitted to the ECJ: Do national rules which permit security interests to be created only in the national currency or in one of a set of currencies specified by national law violate Article 56(1) of the TEC (Article III-156 DC)?[120] Such requirements are, above all, imposed on security interests in real estate. If, for example, a land charge or a mortgage is to be created in Germany, the amount must be denominated in Euro, another currency of an EU Member State, Swiss francs or US dollars; otherwise no right *in rem* is created.[121] Other Member States impose

---

117 In addition, specifications relating to the currency in which the amount of the security interest may be set must also be counted among the restrictions relating to real property; see also the example in the following section.
118 See von Wilmowsky (note 11) pp 149–374.
119 The ECJ has recognised the transparency of security interests as a mandatory requirement; see ECJ *Trummer* [1999] ECR I-1661, para 30.
120 ECJ *Trummer* [1999] ECR I-1661 (suit to enter into the land register a mortgage, denominated in German marks, on a piece of real estate in Austria); ECJ *Westdeutsche Landesbank* [2001] ECR I-173 (action to recover damages brought by the Westdeutsche Landesbank against an Austrian notary who – prior to his country's accession to the EC – had caused a mortgage denominated in German Marks to be entered into an Austrian land register; the mortgage was therefore void).
121 Sec 28(ii) of the *Grundbuchordnung* (GBO – German Land Register Act) in conjunction with sec 1 of the *Verordnung über Grundpfandrechte in ausländischer Währung* (Regulation of 30 October 1997 on mortgages in foreign currencies), BGBl I 1997, 2683.

similar requirements, although the list of permitted currencies is sometimes shorter (only the domestic currency), sometimes longer (any of the currencies of the OECD or IMF members). The exclusion of other currencies may restrict the freedom of movement of capital.[122] Consider the case where the claim which is to be secured is denominated in another currency. Due to the limitation on the permitted currencies, it is not possible to create the mortgage in the same currency as the claim that is being secured. A collateralisation that is "currency congruent" and thus complete is thereby made more difficult, if not impossible.[123] If the claim and the security interest are not denominated in the same currency, the secured party carries the risk that its security interest will have less value than the secured claim as a result of subsequent currency fluctuations. There are no overriding requirements of the common welfare which justify these restrictions of the freedom of capital movements.[124] The free movement of capital guaranteed by the EC Treaty thus conflicts with provisions of civil law which limit the choice of currencies in which the security interest may be denominated. Such provisions cannot be applied to the creation of security interests which enjoy the protection of Article 56(1) of the TEC (Article III-156 DC). To this extent, all currencies must be permitted.[125]

V. Additional Restrictions With Regard to Third Countries

Since capital movements and payments that cross the **EU's external border** are protected by Article 56 of the TEC (Article III-156 DC) as well, they may only be restricted where the EC Treaty provides for an express or implied ground of justification. The grounds of justification treated thus far (Article 58 TEC/Article III-158 DC and the "mandatory requirements of the general interest") apply to measures which restrict capital movements and payments both within the Community and in relation to third countries. Moreover, the EC Treaty grants the Community and, in part, the Member States the power to impose greater restrictions on capital movements to or from third countries than on intra-Community capital movements or payments. By virtue of Articles 57, 59 and 60 of the TEC (Articles III-157, III-159 and III-160 DC), the external borders of the Community may be completely or partially sealed. *These* authorizations exist only in relation to third countries, not for capital movements or payments between the Member States. Furthermore, the grounds of justification set forth in Article 58 of the TEC (Article III-158 DC) and the "mandatory requirements of the general interest" which were developed to sup-

41

---

122 Schefold in: Schimansky/Bunte/Lwowski (eds) *Bankrechts-Handbuch* (2nd ed, Munich 2001) § 115, paras 318–333; Grothe *Fremdwährungsverbindlichkeiten* (Berlin 1999) pp 437, 445–449.
123 ECJ *Trummer* [1999] ECR I-1661, paras 25–26; Opinion AG La Pergola, ECJ *Trummer* [1999] ECR I-1661, para 12.
124 ECJ *Trummer* [1999] ECR I-1661, paras 29–31; Opinion AG La Pergola, ECJ *Trummer* [1999] ECR I-1661, paras 13–17; Opinion AG Leger, ECJ *Westdeutsche Landesbank* [2001] ECR I-173, paras 31–33; Grothe (note 122) pp 437, 445–449. For a different opinion see *eg* Rohde (note 31) pp 172–173 (justification by reference to "the purpose of the law, which lies in particular in protecting creditors by means of real property" – whatever that may mean (author's translation)). Whether consumer protection requires restrictions on the currency of the security interest is a question that can only arise in relation to consumers (as collateral providers).
125 Opinion AG La Pergola, ECJ *Trummer* [1999] ECR I-1661, para 16; Opinion AG Leger, ECJ *Westdeutsche Landesbank* [2001] ECR I-173, para 30; also in this way Fischer [2000] ZEuS 391, 414.

plement them may be construed differently in relation to third countries; thereby, additional grounds for restrictions in relation to third countries may be opened.

1. Restrictions Pursuant to Article 57 of the TEC (Article III-157 DC): No Justification Needed

42 The door that Article 56(1) of the TEC (Article III-156 DC) opens in principle for capital movements to and from third countries may be kept closed in accordance with Article 57(1) of the TEC (Article III-157 DC) or – once opened – slammed shut again pursuant to Article 57(2) of the TEC (Article III-157 DC). The most important areas of capital movements are covered: direct investments (such as shares in companies and shareholder loans),[126] investments in real estate, the acquisition of capital for establishing a branch office or subsidiary or for providing financial services, and the issuance of securities (such as stock and bonds). The other forms of capital movement (such as transferring cash across borders) do not fall within the scope of application. Article 57(1) of the TEC (Article III-157 DC) permits, first, the Community and the individual Member States to continue to apply those restrictions which existed on 31 December 1993 in respect of capital movements to or from third countries. Thus, very questionable protectionist measures have been grandfathered in which deny third country citizens and companies, for example, the acquisition of controlling interests in banks, insurance companies, media companies, air carriers and shipping companies.[127] Secondly, in the areas covered, the Community (not an individual Member State!) is authorised to restrict capital movements to or from third countries according to its discretion (Article 57(2) TEC/Article III-157 DC). The Council must decide unanimously (Article 57(2)(ii) TEC/Article III-157(2)(ii) DC). In contrast to all the other authorizations to restrict the fundamental freedoms, neither of the authorizations contained in Article 57 of the TEC (Article III-157 DC) are linked to any material conditions. Neither the continuation nor the imposition of restrictions must promote the common welfare.[128] The reason for this is that the Community should have a strong hand to play in negotiations with third countries for dismantling restrictions on capital movements: If the Community could not prevent or reverse the one-sided liberalisation brought about by Article 56 of the TEC (Article III-156 DC), it would lack the negotiating strength to force third countries to undertake reciprocal liberalisation measures.[129]

---

126 The TEC adopted the term "direct investment" from national accounting. Direct investments are recorded under *capital accounts/balance of capital movements*, a subclassification of a country's balance of payments. To distinguish it from its counterpart, portfolio investments, one follows the guidelines propounded by the IMF for its members, see International Monetary Fund (ed) *Balance of Payments Manual* (5th ed, Washington DC 1993); and the "nomenclature of capital movements" in Dir 88/361, Annex I. Commentaries: Rohde (note 31) pp 183–190; entry "Kapitalbewegungen, internationale II" in: Albers (ed) *Handwörterbuch der Wirtschaftswissenschaft* (Stuttgart 1988).
127 Regarding the measures still in force see Kiemel (note 1) paras 9–15; Honrath *Umfang und Grenzen der Freiheit des Kapitalverkehrs* (Baden-Baden 1998) pp 131–132.
128 However, the international obligations arising from OECD agreements, WTO regulations, and the EEA Agreement must be observed.
129 One could consider tying the authority under Art 57 TEC to the objectives set forth in this Article and to restrict it to such measures which are suitable, necessary and adequate to induce third countries to further liberalise capital movements on their end. Proposals in this direction

Freedom of Movement of Capital and Payments § 12 V 2

2. Restrictions Pursuant to Article 59 of the TEC (Article III-159 DC): Temporary Measures Only

Article 59 of the TEC (Article III-159 DC) authorises the Community to enact **temporary restrictions in relation to third countries**. In contrast to Article 57 of the TEC (Article III-157 DC), all forms of capital movement (including payments) may be restricted. Measures pursuant to Article 59 of the TEC (Article III-159 DC) are subject to the condition precedent that unusually extensive movements of capital to or from third countries cause, or threaten to cause, serious difficulties for the operation of economic and monetary union. The subjects of protection are all the components of the economic and monetary union. With respect to the economic union, which is limited to a "close" coordination of Member States' economic policies (Article 4(1) TEC/Article III-177(1) DC, Article 99 TEC/Article III-179 DC), this includes, for example, trade cycle policy, competition and regulatory policy and development area policy. The monetary union includes above all monetary policy and exchange rate policy, both of which have been transferred from the Member States to the Community pursuant to Article 4(2) of the TEC (Article III-177(2) DC) and Articles 105 to 124 of the TEC. The objectives of both the economic as well as the monetary union are stable prices, sound public finances and monetary conditions and a sustainable balance of payments (Article 4(3) TEC/Article III-177(3) DC). When capital flows from the Community to third countries or from third countries into the Community, different components of the economic and monetary union are affected, such as the exchange rate or the interest rate. These effects are wanted: They reflect the purpose of the free movement of capital, which is to ensure an optimal allocation of capital not only within the Community, but also in relation to third countries. These effects, therefore, cannot justify restrictions on capital movements or payments to or from third countries. Interventions are permissible only when capital movements lead to serious difficulties. Article 59 of the TEC (Article III-159 DC) is based on the idea that free capital movements at the Community's external borders may turn from a motor for economic benefits into the source of economic troubles. There is little guidance as to when this point is reached. Since the authority granted under Article 59 of the TEC (Article III-159 DC) has not yet been exercised, there is no case material which can be evaluated. Legal scholarship seeks refuge in scenarios which are necessarily rather opaque (such as "undesired interest rate developments", "currency instability", "heavy foreign exchange speculation", "extreme imbalance of balance of payments" and "overheated economic expansion")[130] and, in the end, do not provide an answer to the question of when the results of market processes are no longer acceptable. As an example of a specific economic difficulty, it at least imaginable that the ECB's foreign exchange reserves are exhausted.[131] But as long as the Euro's exchange rates are set by the market (*ie* without intervention by the ECB), such deficits in the foreign exchange account will not occur.[132]

43

If the situation described in Article 59 of the TEC (Article III-159 DC) should happen to occur, the Community may restrict capital movements, including payments, to or from

44

---

may be found in *eg* Ress/Ukrow (note 1) Art 57 EGV, para 12; and Kiemel (note 1) Art 57 EGV, para 20. Honrath (note 127) p 139, however, is sceptical.
130 See Honrath (note 127) pp 224, 227.
131 *Cf* Krämer in: Grabitz/Hilf (eds) *Das Recht der Europäischen Union, Kommentar* (loose-leaf, Munich) Art 119 EGV, para 8.
132 See Rose/Sauernheimer (note 89) pp 16, 20–21.

359

the third country for a period of no more than six months. In the event of a scarcity of foreign exchange, a moratorium, for example, may be imposed, whereby the "Euro-residents" will be barred from paying on foreign currency debts.[133] In this regard the Community must observe, however, the obligations it entered into under the OECD, the WTO and the IMF.[134]

3. Restrictions Pursuant to Article 60 of the TEC: Economic Sanctions

45 Capital movements and payments may, furthermore, be restricted in order to effect an **economic embargo** against a specific third country (Article 60 TEC).[135] The Community is responsible for deciding on the embargo. The Council (usually being composed of the ministers of economics and finance) decides with a qualified majority (Article 301 TEC). The Community must cooperate with another of the EU's pillars, namely the Common Foreign and Security Policy (CFSP). The Community may implement an embargo on capital movements and payments pursuant to Article 60 of the TEC only after the CFSP (through the Council of Ministers of Foreign Affairs) has adopted a decision to interrupt or to reduce, in part or completely, economic relations with that third country for reasons of policy (Articles 11 through 28 TEU). This occurs either through the adoption of a (thematic) "common position" (Article 15 TEU) or an (operative) "joint action" (Article 14 TEU), which as a rule require unanimity (Article 23 TEU).[136] Provided the Union has not taken any measures, a Member State may (for serious political reasons and in cases of urgency) take unilateral measures against a third country with regard to capital movements and payments (Article 60(2)(i) TEC). The Community may, however, review the individual Member State's measures and, where appropriate, decide to amend or abolish them (Article 60(2)(ii) TEC).

4. Broader Interpretation of Article 58 of the TEC (Article III-158 DC) and of the Mandatory Requirements

46 The **grounds of justification** specified in Article 58 of the TEC (Article III-158 DC) and the "**mandatory requirements of the general interest**" developed by the ECJ may justify restrictions on both intra-Community capital movements and capital movements to and from third countries. However, it is conceivable that the scope of a ground of justification depends on whether the relationship concerned is within the Community or with a third country. The interest a state has in an intervention may carry more weight in relation to third countries than in relations between the Member States.[137] One example are the requirements German civil law imposes on a surety where the surety is to serve as a security deposit for a payment obligation (*eg* in civil litigation, section 108 *Zivilprozessordnung* – German Code of Civil Procedure). Germany's *Bürgerliches Gesetzbuch* (Civil Code) permits only those guarantors who are resident in Germany (sections 232(2), 239(1) Civil

---

133 Schefold (note 122) § 117, para 35.
134 On these restrictions see Kiemel (note 1) Art 59 EGV, paras 15–16; Glaesner (note 17) Art 59 EGV, paras 6–8.
135 Art 60 TEC is *lex specialis* with respect to Art 301 TEC.
136 Schäfer [2002] BKR 1–3 reports on financial sanctions that have been taken.
137 Similarly Usher *The Law of Money and Financial Services in the European Community* (2nd ed, Oxford 2000) p 235.

Code). The courts have already held that this legal prerequisite may no longer be applied to guarantors from other EU Member States due to the lack of a justification.[138] The restriction of sureties to residents cannot be justified on grounds of public policy (Article 58(1)(b) TEC/Article III-158(1)(b) DC) because, pursuant to the European Civil Jurisdiction Convention, judicial decisions are as enforceable in other EU Member States as they are domestically. With regard to residents of third countries, the question is whether enforcement of the surety meets with significant difficulties: If it does, then there is a ground of justification for denying recognition of the guarantee.

VI. Conclusion

Freeing capital movements from unjustified restrictions (negative harmonisation) is the first step in developing a single EU-wide capital market and overcoming the fragmentation into diverse national markets. To deepen the integration process further, the remaining restrictions, *ie* those which are justified by the general interest, must be approximated (positive harmonisation). Integrated capital markets promise to raise economic welfare: By permitting the free market to operate, capital can be used for those investments which yield the greatest benefits.[139]

---

138 OLG Düsseldorf [1995] WM 1993; *cf* also ECJ *Commission v Italy* [2002] ECR I-1425, paras 36–40 (Italian law which required that a security deposit has to be provided by a credit institution which has its registered office or a branch office in Italy).
139 Ress/Ukrow (note 1) Art 56 EGV, paras 110–170 and Kiemel (note 1) Art 56 EGV, paras 59–78, for example, report on the measures taken to harmonise the legislation in force relating to the movement of capital.

§ 13
Prohibition of Discrimination Due to Nationality

Thorsten Kingreen

Leading cases: ECJ *Gravier* [1985] ECR 593; *Martínez Sala* [1998] ECR I-2691; *Bickel* [1998] ECR I-7637; *Grzelczyk* [2001] ECR I-9383.

Further reading: Epiney *Umgekehrte Diskriminierungen* (Munich 1995); Ettl *Der praktische Fall – Europarecht: Augen auf im Straßenverkehr* [2003] JuS 151; Plötscher *Der Begriff der Diskriminierung im Europäischen Gemeinschaftsrecht* (Berlin 2003); Rossi *Das Diskriminierungsverbot nach Artikel 12 EG-Vertrag* [2000] EuR 197; Schweitzer *Artikel 12 EGV – Auf dem Weg zum „allgemeinen" Gleichheitssatz* in: Arndt (ed) *Völkerrecht und deutsches Recht – FS Rudolf* (Munich 2001) pp 189; Updated annotations to Article 12 of the TEC: Epiney in: Calliess/Ruffert (eds) *Kommentar des Vertrages über die Europäische Union und des Vertrages zur Gründung der Europäischen Gemeinschaft* (2nd ed, Neuwied 2002); Holoubek in: Schwarze (ed) *EU-Kommentar* (Baden-Baden 2000); Lenz in: Lenz/Borchardt (eds) *EU- und EG-Vertrag* (3rd ed, Munich 2003); Streinz in: Streinz (ed) *EUV, EGV* (Munich 2003); Zuleeg in: von der Groeben/Schwarze *Kommentar zum Vertrag über die Europäische Union und zur Gründung der Europäischen Gemeinschaft* (6th ed, Baden-Baden 2003).

> **Case 1 – Problem** (ECJ *Hayes* [1997] ECR I-1711)
> 1
> The British citizen Hayes (H) sued the company Kronenberger (K) before the State Court of Saarbrücken for payment of the remainder of the purchase price of delivered component parts for processing and recycling facilities. K demanded that H provide a surety pursuant to the former § 110 of the *Zivilprozessordnung* (ZPO – Code of Civil Procedure). According to the former § 110 of the Code of Civil Procedure, foreigners who appear as a claimant before a German Court must provide a surety due to the costs of legal proceedings. This does not apply, however, if the state to which the claimant belongs does not demand a surety from a German national under the same circumstances. The State Court of Saarbrücken regarded this requirement to be fulfilled and granted the claim. K appealed to the regional Court of Appeal of Saarbrücken, which requested the ECJ to give a ruling on the question of whether the former § 110 of the Code of Civil Procedures violates Article 12(1) TEC.

I. Sources of Law and Systematic Classification

2 Through Article 12(1) of the TEC (Article I-4(2) DC), the law of the European Union prohibits **unequal treatment due to nationality**. This prohibition aims at both overcoming foreign status[1] and ensuring that citizens of the Union are treated as natives in every Member State. Article 12(1) of the TEC (Article I-4(2) DC) contains a specific principle of equality, as it forbids discrimination on grounds of only one differentiating criterion, namely nationality, and does not apply in every area of life, but only within the scope of application of the Treaty.[2] The express restriction that Article 12(1) of the TEC (Article I-4(2) DC) only applies "without prejudice to particular provisions of this Treaty" charac-

---

[1] Von Bogdandy in: Grabitz/Hilf (eds) *Kommentar zur Europäischen Union* (Munich 1994) Art 6 EGV, para 1.

[2] Therefore, the frequently-read term "general ban on discrimination" is misleading; concurrently Rossi [2000] EuR 197.

terises it as subordinate to the more specific discrimination prohibitions. Since "without prejudice to" means subject to,[3] Article 12(1) of the TEC (Article I-4(2) DC) "applies independently only to situations governed by community law in respect of which the Treaty lays down no specific prohibition of discrimination."[4] Therefore, Article 12 of the TEC (Article I-4(2) DC) is subsidiary to all provisions which incorporate the criterion of nationality[5], particularly the fundamental freedoms (→ §§ 8, 9, 10, 11, 12).[6] It is not, however, subsidiary to Article 141(1) of the TEC (Article III-214(1) DC), which forbids differentiation based on the criterion of gender.[7]

The prohibition on discrimination due to nationality in Article 12(1) of the TEC (Article I-4(2) DC) responds to *federal risk zones* which commonly arise because Member States tend to give preferential treatment to their own citizens compared to citizens from other Member States. Article 12(1) of the TEC (Article I-4(2) DC) states that affiliation to a Member State is irrelevant with regards to treatment in another Member State; it is therefore a *norm of transnational integration* (→ § 18 para 2). This sets it apart functionally from the *fundamental rights* of equality which serve to legitimize *(supra-) national* sovereignty.[8] In this respect, the repeated mention of the prohibition on discrimination in the charter of fundamental rights (Article II-81(2) DC) is superfluous and, in view of the differing addressees and restrictions, also not unproblematic.[9]   3

II. Structure of Review[10]

1. Scope of Protection

a) Personal Scope of Protection

Article 12(1) of the TEC (Article I-4(2) DC) protects all **natural** persons who are citizens of the European Union (Article 17 TEC/Article I-10 DC). As far as **legal** persons are concerned, the personal scope of protection is determined pursuant to Article 48 of the TEC (Article III-142 DC).[11]   4

It is uncertain whether and, if applicable, to what extent **third state nationals** are protected. Since Article 39(2) of the TEC (Article III-18(2) DC) and Article 43(1) of the TEC (Article III-137(1) DC) are expressly limited to Member State nationals, the lack of such a limitation in Art. 12(1) of the TEC (Article I-4(2) DC) could indicate that its scope of protection extends to third state nationals.[12] However, the special function of Article 12(1)   5

---

3 ECJ *Sagulo* [1977] ECR 1495, para 11; *Perfili* [1996] ECR I-161, para 11.
4 ECJ *Skanavi* [1996] ECR I-929, para 20.
5 Epiney in: Calliess/Ruffert (eds) *Kommentar des Vertrages über die Europäische Union und des Vertrages zur Gründung der Europäischen Gemeinschaft* (2nd ed, Neuwied 2002) Art 12 EGV, para 11.
6 *Cf* ECJ *Cowan* [1989] ECR 195, para 14; Holoubek in: Schwarze (ed) *EU-Kommentar* (Baden Baden 2000) Art 12 EGV, para 9; on the other hand, in favor of an ideal competition Schweitzer in: Arndt (ed) *Völkerrecht und deutsches Recht – FS Rudolf* (Munich 2001) pp 189 ff.
7 Von Bogdandy (note 1) para 58.
8 On the differentiation between norms of transnational integration and norms of supranational legitimation (→ § 18); *cf* further Rossi [2000] EuR 197, 209.
9 *Cf* Grabenwarter [2004] EuGRZ 563, 567 ff; Kingreen [2004] EuGRZ 570, 571 ff.
10 On the structure of review concerning rights of equality → § 18 paras 7 ff.
11 Von Bogdandy (note 1) para 32; → § 10 paras 62 ff.
12 Von Bogdandy (note 1) para 34.

of the TEC (Article I-4(2) DC) in relation to the internal market argues against this position. Unlike the fundamental rights of the Union, which, in principle, also apply to third state nationals (→ § 14 para 27), Article 12(1) of the TEC (Article I-4(2) DC) has no supranational integrating function. It is therefore not meant to supersede the national fundamental rights, which are no longer applicable to the extent that sovereignty has been transferred to the Union.[13] Like all provisions regarding the internal market, its function is rather to promote transnational integration and convey a qualified membership to citizens of the Union in every Member State compared to citizens of third states. This superior status, which is also expressed in the citizenship of the Union (Article 17 TEC/Article I-10 DC), would be nullified if third state nationals were to be granted the same rights through the Treaty.[14] However, it is possible to derogate from this general rule in individual cases if it is evident from the subject matter or a specific reference, particularly in a secondary law regulation, that third state citizens should also enjoy qualified protection from discrimination due to nationality.[15]

b) Material Scope of Protection

6   The material scope of protection of Article 12(1) of the TEC (Article I-4(2) DC) is limited to **"the scope of application of this Treaty"**. The meaning of this phrase is controversial:

According to the **ECJ**, the material scope of application of the Treaty only requires that a "situation ruled by community law"[16] exists or the case features "points of contact with some of the circumstances to which the law of the Community applies".[17] A positive competency of the Union is not required; in fact, merely indirect consequences on the exchange of goods and services within the Union are sufficient.[18] Accordingly, a situation connected to circumstances protected by one of the fundamental freedoms already falls within the Treaty's scope of application.[19] This broad understanding has been only slightly narrowed in earlier judgements of the ECJ by the comment that the "community law's current status of development"[20] is to be taken into account.

7   **Examples:** Provisions falling within the Treaty's scope of application are, *eg*, provisions which demand a minimum number of members of the nationality of the Member State for the establishment of an association[21]; furthermore, national rules of procedure which demand sureties for the costs of legal proceedings[22]. The same is true for provisions which govern entry to university courses (particularly registration and tuition fees[23]). However,

---

13 On the function of supranational integration see paras 1 ff.
14 Prevailing opinion, *cf* for instance Holoubek (note 6) paras 19 ff; Lenz in: Lenz/Borchardt (eds) *EU- und EG-Vertrag* (3rd ed, Munich 2003) Art 12 EGV, para 2; Streinz in: Streinz (ed) *EUV, EGV* (Munich 2003) Art 12, para 35.
15 Streinz (note 14) para 36.
16 ECJ *Cowan* [1989] ECR 195, para 10.
17 ECJ *Morson* [1982] ECR 3723, para 16.
18 ECJ *Hayes* [1997] ECR I-1711, para 17.
19 ECJ *Commission v Belgium* [1999] ECR I-3999, para 12.
20 ECJ *Lair* [1988] ECR 3161, para 15; *Brown* [1988] ECR 3205, para 18.
21 ECJ *Commission v Belgium* [1999] ECR I-3999, para 12.
22 ECJ *Hayes* [1997] ECR I-1711, para 17; *Saldanha* [1997] ECR I-5325, paras 16 ff; in addition Case 1.
23 ECJ *Gravier* [1985] ECR 593, para 31.

under the former development status of Union law, other means of financial support for studies (student loans) did not fall within the Treaty's scope of application, as education and social policies were regarded as matters of the Member States only.[24] Due to further developments in the law of the Union, the ECJ now regards this jurisdiction as outdated[25] (→ para 10).

The literature offers various suggestions to more closely define the term "the Treaty's scope of application."[26] In doing so, particular emphasis is placed on the competency provisions: areas which are accessible to community legislation due to a competency provision should also fall within the Treaty's scope of application,[27] whereas it is controversial whether this also applies to the cross-sectional competencies specifically pertaining to the internal market.[28] It is, however, dubious whether significant restrictions on the material scope of protection can be inferred from the competency provisions, for discriminations due to nationality usually emanate from the Member States and are, for the most part, encountered precisely in those areas in which the Union has no competency, such as in civil procedure law[29] or criminal (procedure) law[30]. As a matter of principle, competency provisions, when activated, can not be exempt from the consideration of applicable material standards.[31] Therefore, attempts to limit the scope of protection of subjective rights per competency provisions concerning the allocation of rights and duties are not helpful. Rather, all legislation of the Member States should fall within the Treaty's scope of application, unless something different results from the Treaty itself or the systematic interpretation of the Treaty.[32] This is the case *eg* for elections on regional and national levels, which, as can be deduced from Article 19(1) of the TEC (Article I-10(2) lit b; II-100 DC), do not fall within the Treaty's scope of application. Limiting the right to vote to nationals of the Member State does therefore not infringe Article 12(1) of the TEC (Article I-4(2) DC).

8

Due to the systematics of the Treaty, the so-called **reverse discrimination** also does not fall within the Treaty's scope of application. Reverse discrimination occurs when, within the sovereign territory of a Member State, different regulations apply in comparable circumstances because the Member State, due to community law requirements (mainly the fundamental freedoms), issues or upholds other provisions for domestic circumstances than for foreign circumstances.[33] If Article 12(1) of the TEC (Article I-4(2) DC) were applicable in these cases, the pertinent restriction of the fundamental freedoms, which has

9

---

24 ECJ *Lair* [1988] ECR 3161, para 14; *Brown* [1988] ECR 3205, para 17.
25 ECJ *Grzelczyk* [2001] ECR I-6193, para 35.
26 *Cf* the overview in Epiney (note 5) para 21.
27 Von Bogdandy (note 1) para 38; Zuleeg in: von der Groeben/Schwarze (eds) *Kommentar zum Vertrag über die Europäische Union und zur Gründung der Europäischen Gemeinschaft* (6th ed, Baden Baden 2003) Art 12 EGV, para 12.
28 In favour of this: von Bogdandy (note 1) para 38; dismissive: Zuleeg (note 27) para 12.
29 *Cf* correspondingly without discussion of the problem of competence ECJ *Hayes* [1997] ECR I-1711, para 17.
30 ECJ *Bickel* [1998] ECR I-7637, para 16.
31 Rossi [2000] EuR 197, 204. *Cf* for instance, also on the fundamental freedoms ECJ *Decker* [1998] ECR I-1831, para 23, in view of social policy; in addition also Kingreen [2001] NJW 3382, 3382.
32 Also similar Holoubek (note 6) para 31.
33 Lackhoff/Raczinski [1997] EWS 109, 110; in detail: Epiney *Umgekehrte Diskriminierungen* (Munich 1995) pp 17 ff.

been confirmed by the ECJ, would be transferred to circumstances with a cross-border element[34]: Article 12(1) of the TEC (Article I-4(2) DC) would reproduce for national circumstances the same effects the fundamental freedoms have on cross-border circumstances.[35] However, the fact that the fundamental freedoms are *leges speciales* compared to Article 12(1) of the TEC (Article I-4(2) DC), and are therefore concluding in this respect, speaks against this view. Therefore, the problem of reverse discrimination of nationals is dealt with at best through the national constitutional law (Article 3(1), 12(1) German Basic Law).[36]

10   Furthermore, at the "current development status of Union law", there will hardly be any cases which do not fall within the Treaty's scope of application. Particularly, the rights of participation effected by Union citizenship (Article 17 TEC/Article I-10 DC) and the right to freedom of movement (Article 18 TEC/Article I-10(2) lit a, II-105(1) DC) are responsible for this: Thus, due to Article 17(1) of the TEC (Article I-10 DC), the Treaty's scope of application is opened for every citizen of the Union who legally resides within the territory of another Member State. For instance, the right of equal access to social security systems is derived from this.[37] This provision of primary law concerns those who do not already enjoy protection from social discrimination on the basis of secondary Union law (Article 3 Directive 1408/71 and Article 7 II Directive/EEC 1612/68), *eg* students. Article 12(1) of the TEC (Article I-4(2) DC), fortified through Union citizenship, has therefore been developed by the ECJ into a social right to participate,[38] which, in this respect, complements the incomplete protection offered by secondary Union law; access to the social security system is henceforth stipulated in Article II-94(2) of the TEC (→ § 18 para 60). In addition, resulting from Article 12 in conjunction with Article 18 of the TEC (Article I-4(2) in conjunction with Article I-10(2) lit a, II-105(1) DC), all people who exercise their right to reside and move freely in another Member State enjoy an extensive right to equal treatment (for instance, the choice of the language used in criminal procedures).[39] Here, too, the participatory nature of Article 12(1) of the TEC (Article I-4(2) DC) is clearly revealed.

---

34 In addition Kingreen *Die Struktur der Grundfreiheiten des Europäischen Gemeinschaftsrechts* (Berlin 1999) pp 84 ff
35 *Cf* Hammerl *Inländerdiskriminierung* (Berlin 1997) pp 151 ff; Streinz (note 14) paras 58 ff.
36 *Cf* East Constitutional Court [2001] EuZW 219.
37 ECJ *Martínez Sala* [1998] ECR I-2691, para 57/62; *Grzelczyk* [2001] ECR I-6193, para 32; on this topic also Borchardt [2000] NJW 2057; Letzner [2003] JuS 118; Rossi [2002] JZ 351.
38 The right to participate, structured around the rights to equality, contains merely a claim to participation in already existing organisations (here: social benefits), but not an original claim to their establishment; *cf* differentiation between the derivative right to participate and the original right to governmental action Pieroth/Schlink *Grundrechte Staatsrecht II* (20th ed, Heidelberg 2004) paras 60 ff, 95 ff.
39 ECJ *Bickel* [1998] ECR I-7637, paras 14 ff.

2. Interference

Each discrimination on the basis of nationality constitutes an interference. 11

a) Addressees of the Norm

In any case, both the **Union** and the **Member States** are the addressees of the norm.[40] 12
Whether Article 12(1) of the TEC (Article I-4(2) DC) has any horizontal effect, however, is controversial.[41] The ECJ has not yet taken a stand on this matter; it does, however, view the free movement of persons as having direct horizontal effect at least within the area of private autonomous legislation (→ § 7 paras 45 ff). Opposing this view is the fact that by recognising this horizontal effect, the individual's right to non-discrimination against public authorities becomes a right against all fellow citizens. It is more appropriate to deal with cases of private abuse of power through either competition law (Articles 81 ff TEC/ Articles III-161 ff DC), or through Member States' duties to protect.[42]

b) Types of Interference

Article 12(1) of the TEC (Article I-4(2) DC) forbids "not only overt [direct][43] discrimination by reason of nationality but also all covert [indirect][44] forms of discrimination which, by the application of other criteria of differentiation, lead in fact to the same result."[45] 13

Direct discriminations are characterised by an express factual reference to the forbidden distinguishing criterion of nationality. 14

Examples: It constitutes direct discrimination if state museums charge their own nationals lower entry prices than other citizens of the Union[46]; the same applies if nationals from other Member States must pay additional registration and tuition fees to state universities.[47] 15

It is often problematic to determine whether an **indirect discrimination** exists because it is difficult to distinguish it from non-discriminating restrictions.[48] In a decision regarding this issue, the ECJ posed the question of whether "the large majority" of the cases ruled by the norm affect nationals of other Member States.[49] This argues for the assumption that, as with Article 141 of the TEC (Article III-214 DC) and the fundamental freedoms[50], what matters primarily is the actual effect a measure has, and therefore whether a particularly large number of the groups protected from discrimination are concerned. However, possibly coincidental repercussions of a measure cannot alone constitute discriminations on the basis of nationality. That is to say, Article 12(1) of the TEC 16

---

40 *Cf* only Holoubek (note 6) paras 21 ff.
41 Favouring a third-party effect: von Bogdandy (note 1) para 31 and, although deliberately, Rossi [2000] EuR 197, 216 ff; opposing this Holoubek (note 6) paras 26 ff und Streinz (note 14) para 39.
42 Nearer Kingreen (note 34) pp 195 ff.
43 Author's comment.
44 Author's comment.
45 ECJ *Boussac* [1980] ECR 3427, para 9; *Commission v Italy* [2002] ECR I-2965, para 15.
46 ECJ *Commission v Spain* [1994] ECR I-911, para 10.
47 ECJ *Commission v Belgium* [1994] ECR I-1593, para 19.
48 *Cf* the detailed analysis in Plötscher *Der Begriff der Diskriminierung im Europäischen Gemeinschaftsrecht* (Berlin 2003) pp 114 ff.
49 ECJ *Owens Bank* [1994] ECR I-117, para 16.
50 *Cf* for instance ECJ *Allué I* [1989] ECR 1591, para 12.

(Article I-4(2) DC) does not want to generally ban all inferior treatment of nationals of other Member States, but only that on the basis of nationality.[51] The deciding issue, therefore, is the substantive legal content of the possibly indirectly discriminating regulation: What matters is whether the measure in dispute *contains requirements which can typically only, or at least more easily, be fulfilled by natives rather than foreigners*, ie whether they are therefore specifically geared towards the inherently different positions of natives and foreigners. In other words, the addressee of the norm must be able to justify the proposed requirement with reasons other than nationality. If this line of argumentation succeeds, it will withstand the test of Article 12(1) of the TEC (Article I-4(2) DC) even if, in actual fact, more foreigners are concerned than natives.[52]

17   **Examples:** All regulations which, for instance, are linked the residence or a requirement of establishment are indirectly discriminating, as these requirements are usually more difficult for foreigners to fulfil than for natives.[53] Also constituting indirect discrimination is, for instance, the requirement of a native-licensed vehicle as a pre-condition for a preferential treatment by traffic law.[54] The same applies if a Member State makes the granting of social benefits conditional upon a formal residency permit, while natives must merely have a domicile or actual residence within the Member State.[55]

c) Justification

18   Although Article 12 of the TEC (Article I-4(2) DC) does not contain any express requirements for restrictions, it is nevertheless recognised that **indirect discriminations** due to nationality can be justified. In this process, the principle of **proportionality** is also activated: It is necessary to test whether the indirectly discriminating measure "is justified through objective circumstances"[56] and whether it is an adequate means to accomplish the objective it is aimed at.[57]

19   It is, however, unsettled whether **direct discriminations** can be justified. In the literature, Article 12(1) of the TEC (Article I-4(2) DC) is, in this respect, partly understood as an **absolute ban on discrimination** which is not open to justification. This understanding is derived from an interpretation of the wording "any discrimination" and the systematic circumstance that while the fundamental freedoms expressly offer means of justification, they are absent in Article 12(1) of the TEC (Article I-4(2) DC).[58] Yet these very same arguments should also argue against the possibility of justification of indirect discriminations, for an indirect discrimination is also a "discrimination" within the meaning of Article 12(1) of the TEC (Article I-4(2) DC). The jurisdiction of the **ECJ** is anything but consistent,[59] however, it seems to come down to the fact that direct discriminations can be

---

51 Von Bogdandy (note 1) para 18.
52 For this understanding of the particular principles of equality as bans on justification Pieroth/ Schlink (note 38) paras 447 ff, for the basic freedoms Kingreen (note 34) pp 143 ff.
53 ECJ *Sotgiu* [1974] ECR 153, para 11; *Commission v Luxemburg* [1993] ECR I-817, para 10.
54 ECJ *Commission v Italy* [2002] ECR I-2965, para 18.
55 ECJ *Martinez Sala* [1998] ECR I-2691, para 65.
56 *Cf* for instance ECJ *Mund & Fester* [1994] ECR I-467, para 17.
57 ECJ *Bickel* [1998] ECR I-7637, para 28.
58 Along these lines, for instance, von Bogdandy (note 1) para 23; Holoubek (note 6) para 55; Thümmel [1994] EuZW 242, 243.
59 *Cf* Plötscher (note 48) pp 131 ff.

justified, but must fulfil increased requirements in this respect. In a kind of parallelism to the incoherent jurisdiction towards the fundamental freedoms,[60] direct discriminations are only to be justified on the basis of the reasons for justification codified within the constitution, whereas for indirect discriminations, also other considerations of the public welfare come to bear.[61] The parallelism with the fundamental freedoms is generally plausible.[62] It is, however, incomprehensible why direct and indirect discriminations should be treated differently.[63] The ECJ's differentiation encourages covert protectionism, which cleverly disguises, rather than discloses, discriminations due to nationality. Furthermore, to a discriminated foreigner, it makes no difference whether he is discriminated against through a direct measure related to nationality, or through a different measure which, in the end, has the same effect as discrimination due to nationality. The dogmatically best way is uniformly linking up the test for justification with the constitutionally provided possibilities for restrictions, for instance, the aspects of "public order" in Article 39(3) of the TEC (Article III-133(3) DC) and Article 46(1) of the TEC (Article III-140(1) DC).

d) Legal Consequences of a Violation

In the event of a violation of Article 12(1) of the TEC (Article I-4(2) DC), it is **for the Member State to decide** whether the person who has thus far been discriminated against is to be treated the same as the person who has thus far been privileged, whether the incriminating regulation is to be extended to also affect the latter, or whether both are to be treated in another way altogether.

Case 1 – Answer:
The former § 110 of the Code of Civil Procedures could violate Article 12(1) TEC (Article I-4(2) DC).
(1) It is uncertain whether the former § 110 Code of Civil Procedures falls within the "Treaty's scope of application" in terms of Article 12(1) of the TEC (Article I-4(2) DC). In principle, due to a lack of Union competence, it is up to the Member State to regulate civil procedure law. However, this competence is not without limits; in particular, Article 12(1) of the TEC (Article I-4(2) DC) forbids discriminations in connection with economic activity. Although the former § 110 Code of Civil Procedures was not aimed at regulating commercial activity, it did have the effect that foreign business participants could not get access to the state courts as easily as those who were state nationals. As the law of the European Union guarantees these business participants the free movement of goods and services within the common market, access to the courts of a Member State in legal disputes which arise from the economic activity of the parties must also be available to them under the same conditions as those of the nationals of the state (ECJ *Hayes* [1997] ECR I-1711, para 14). The scope of protection is therefore affected.
(2) The scope of protection must be impaired. As Germany demands a surety from nationals of other Member States which it does not demand from its own nationals, direct discrimination is at hand.

---

60 Gundel [2001] Jura 79; Kingreen in: von Bogdandy (ed) *Europäisches Verfassungsrecht* (Berlin 2003) pp 631, 670 ff.
61 ECJ *Commission v Italy* [2003] ECR I-721, para 19, 21.
62 Rossi [2000] EuR 197, 212 ff.
63 Likewise also Epiney (note 5) para 42; Rossi [2000] EuR 197, 213 ff.

(3) It remains to be examined whether the discrimination is justified. Direct discriminations can also be justified from the reasons stated above (see above para 19). The requirement is that the former § 110 Code of Civil Procedures pursues a legitimate aim and is proportional. It is already doubtful whether the former § 110 Code of Civil Procedures is suitable, as the surety is not demanded from German claimants resident in a foreign country, despite the risk of enforcement which exists in these cases as well. Furthermore, it is disproportional to the aim it strives to achieve, as it also demands sureties from non-German claimants who are resident in Germany (ECJ *Hayes* [1997] ECR I-1711, para 24). The restriction can therefore not be justified. The former § 110 Code of Civil Procedures violates Article 12(1) of the TEC (Article I-4(2) DC).

Part IV: The Fundamental Rights of the European Union

§ 14
General Principles

Dirk Ehlers

Leading cases: ECJ *van Gend & Loos* [1963] ECR 1; *Costa v E.N.E.L.* [1964] ECR 584; *Stauder* [1969] ECR 419; *Internationale Handelsgesellschaft* [1970] ECR 1125; *Nold* [1974] ECR 491; *Familiapress* [1997] ECR I-3689; *Connolly* [2001] ECR I-1611; *Schmidberger* [2003] ECR I-5659; *Omega* [2004] ECR I-9609; BVerfG *Solange II* [1987] 3 CMLR 225; *Bananas Case* (2000) 102 BVerfGE 147.

Further reading: Beutler in: von der Groeben/Schwarze (eds) *Vertrag über die Europäische Union und Vertrag zur Gründung der Europäischen Gemeinschaft – Kommentar* (6th ed, Baden-Baden 2004) Art 6 EUV, paras 39 ff; Craig/de Búrca *EU law* (3rd ed, Oxford 2003) pp 317 ff; Kingreen in: Calliess/Ruffert (eds) *Kommentar des Vertrages über die Europäische Union und des Vertrages zur Gründung der Europäischen Union* (2nd ed, Neuwied 2002) Art 6 EUV, paras 16 ff; Kühling in: von Bogdandy (ed) *Europäisches Verfassungsrecht* (Heidelberg 2003) pp 583 ff; Meyer (ed) *Kommentar zur Charta der Grundrechte der Europäischen Union* (Baden-Baden 2003); Pechstein in: Streinz, Rudolf (ed) *EUV/ EGV Vertrag über die Europäische Union und Vertrag zur Gründung der Europäischen Gemeinschaft* (Munich 2003) Art 6 EUV, paras 8 ff; Pernice/Mayer in: Grabitz/Hilf *Das Recht der Europäischen Union* (loose-leaf, Munich) nach Art 6 EUV; Rengeling/Szczekalla *Grundrechte in der Europäischen Union* (Cologne/Berlin/Munich 2004); Stumpf in: Schwarze (ed) *EU-Kommentar* (Baden-Baden 2000) Art 6 EUV, paras 16 ff; Tridimas *The General Principles of EC Law* (2nd ed, Oxford 2006) pp 298–369; Weatherill *Cases and Materials on EU law* (7th ed, Oxford 2006) pp 66–87.

I. The Character and Position of the Fundamental Rights of the European Union within the Structure of International and National Law

1. The Notion of Fundamental Rights

A universally accepted or even just commonly employed **definition** of **fundamental rights** does not exist. For the purposes of this chapter they are understood as rights of (private) individuals against the exercise of public power which apply by virtue of international law or which are guaranteed on the highest level of a national law hierarchy. They bestow upon their beneficiaries a fundamental legal position vis-à-vis the state in the sense that their limitation must be justified. 1

The following paragraphs deal with the fundamental rights of the European Union. These rights concern not only the European Communities (*ie* the European Community and the European Atomic Energy Community), but also the European Union (*ie* the "roof" of the European Communities under public international law) in its supplementary policies as well as other forms of cooperation among the Member States. After the upcoming revision of the Treaties, the EU will be the legal successor of the present EC and EU – *ie* only one supranational organisation will remain – the European Union. Therefore, the term **fundamental rights of** "**the Union**" instead of "**the Community**" will be used throughout this chapter. The following presentation and discussion is based on the law as it stands today. Nevertheless, the fact that the Charter of Fundamental Rights of the Union will be put into force should not be left unconsidered. It will thus be referred to in addition to the current state of the law. 2

2. The Necessity of Guaranteeing Fundamental Rights on the EU Level

3   Up to now, the European treaties do not contain any binding written **catalogue of fundamental rights**, but only certain individual guarantees. Such a catalogue was not thought necessary at the time when the original treaties were concluded, as they were regarded as conventional agreements under international law. It soon became clear, however, that this perception was incorrect. Firstly, the EC treaties are not solely addressed to the Member States but in parts also to private individuals. Secondly, the Communities have been furnished with a wide range of law-making powers which directly affect the citizens of the Union. A limitation of such powers by way of fundamental guarantees securing the liberty and equality of individuals therefore seems to be indispensable.

4   The first impetus for recognising fundamental rights on the EU level came from the Member States. It was aimed at measuring the acts of the Communities against national fundamental rights provisions. On this basis, the *Corte Costituzionale* (Italian Constitutional Court)[1], the *Bundesverfassungsgericht* (German Federal Constitutional Court)[2] and other constitutional courts of the Member States[3] reserved for themselves the right to declare inapplicable such secondary EC legislation which they found to be in (qualified) conflict with national guarantees (para 14). The ECJ resisted these approaches from the very beginning, since they were incompatible with the doctrine of **supremacy of Community law** postulated and maintained by the Court without any exception.[4] Consequently, a solution could only be found by affording comprehensive and effective fundamental rights protection on the Community level itself. As the European treaties were not amended,[5] the ECJ – relying on its competence to ensure the observance of the law (Article 220 TEC/Article I-29(1)(ii) DC) – developed certain fundamental guarantees in form of unwritten general principles of law (→ § 1 paras 25 ff).[6] After the Court had established in *van Gend & Loos* (1963) that the EC treaties produce direct effects and create subjective rights of the individual even without any additional legislative measure under national law,[7] it expressly considered "fundamental human rights" for the first time in the *Stauder* judgment of 1969.[8] The breakthrough in recognising fundamental rights eventually occurred in the cases of *Internationale Handelsgesellschaft*[9] (1970) and *Nold*[10] (1974). Based on these decisions – and assisted by the critical jurisprudence of the German Federal Constitutional Court[11] – the fundamental rights of the Union have since been further shaped

---

1   Corte Costituzionale [1974] EuR 255, 262.
2   BVerfG *Solange I* [1974] 2 CMLR 540.
3   As to the current state of affairs *cf* Streinz in: Cremer (ed) *Tradition und Weltoffenheit des Rechts – FS Steinberger* (Berlin 2002) pp 1437, 1456 ff; Grabenwarter in: von Bogdandy (ed) *Europäisches Verfassungsrecht* (Heidelberg 2003) pp 283, 286 ff; French Conseil Constitutionnel, decision of 10 June 2004, *Journal officiel du 22 juin 2004*, p 11182.
4   *Cf* the seminal decision in ECJ *Costa v E.N.E.L.* [1964] ECR 584; see also Craig/de Búrca *EU law* (3rd ed, Oxford 2003) pp 319–320; Tridimas *The General Principles of EC Law* (2nd ed, Oxford 2006) pp 300–301.
5   *Cf*, however, the inclusion of citizen rights in the TEC (→ on this point see para 24 and § 20 para 11).
6   *Cf* Craig/de Búrca (note 4) pp 320–321.
7   ECJ *van Gend & Loos* [1963] ECR 3.
8   ECJ *Stauder* [1969] ECR 419, 424.
9   ECJ *Internationale Handelsgesellschaft* [1970] ECR 1125, para 4.
10 ECJ *Nold* [1974] ECR 491, para 13.
11 *Cf* BVerfG *Solange I* [1974] 2 CMLR 540.

General Principles   § 14 I 3

and strengthened. Nevertheless, they play a considerably smaller role in the considerations of both the ECJ and the CFI than the fundamental freedoms of the TEC (para 12). As far as known, no measures of the EC legislature – unlike administrative acts of the EC Commission – have yet been invalidated for a violation of fundamental rights.[12]

3. The Legal Foundation of the Fundamental Rights of the Union

Since the Charter of Fundamental Rights of the Union (paras 16 ff) is not yet legally binding, the fundamental rights of the Union are thus far based on individual treaty provisions, or have been developed by the ECJ as **general principles of law** under Article 220 of the TEC (Article I-29(1)(ii) DC). 5

Apart from the fundamental freedoms (para 12), the European treaties contain only a limited number of express **written rights** which primarily concern the guarantees of equal treatment as well as procedural and civic rights (Articles 18 ff, 255 TEC/I-9, I-10 DC). The written equality rights do not guarantee equality as such (see, however, para 21), but prohibit discrimination – either in specific cases (*eg* Articles 31, 72, 90, 294 TEC/Articles III-155, 237, 143 DC) or generally (Article 12 TEC/Art I-4(2) DC) – based on grounds of nationality. In addition, they protect against other forms of discrimination. For example, Article 141 of the TEC (Article III-214 DC) ensures male and female workers – with direct effect[13] – equal pay for equal work or work of equal value.[14] As far as written rights exist, they take priority over unwritten guarantees. 6

In the absence of express written guarantees, the recognition of fundamental rights of the Union rests on the **case-law** of the ECJ (and the CFI). The Court derives them largely from the **constitutional traditions** common to the Member States[15] and the international treaties for the protection of human rights[16]. As regards the latter source, the ECJ primarily draws upon the **European Convention for the Protection of Human Rights and Fundamental Freedoms** (ECHR) and the decisions of the European Court of Human Rights (ECtHR).[17] In addition to Articles 1–14 of the ECHR, this also comprises the guarantees contained in the Protocols, at least to the extent that they have been ratified by the Member States.[18] 7

Both the constitutional traditions common to the Member States and the ECHR do not represent sources of law, but only serve as a **subsidiary means for the determination of the general principles of EC law** from which the ECJ develops the fundamental rights of the Union in a process of comparative evaluation[19]. This leaves the Court a considerable 8

---

12 However, in the case of *ABNA* [2006] 1 CMLR 48, paras 83 ff, the ECJ held Directive 2002/2/EC of 28 January 2002, [2002] OJ L63/23, to be partially invalid in the light of the principle of proportionality. In view of this result, the Court found it unnecessary to further examine the compatibility of the Directive with fundamental rights (*cf* para 88 of the judgment).
13 ECJ *Defrenne II* [1976] ECR 455, paras 4 ff
14 *Cf* also Art 34(2)(ii) TEC
15 For the first time in ECJ *Internationale Handelsgesellschaft* [1970] ECR 1125, para 4. See also Craig/de Búrca (note 4) pp 327 ff, Tridimas (note 4) pp 301 ff.
16 For the first time in ECJ *Nold* [1974] ECR 491, para 13.
17 *Cf* the overview by Stumpf in: Schwarze (ed) *EU-Kommentar* (Baden-Baden 2000) Art 6 EUV, paras 20 ff.
18 More detailed Grabenwarter (2000) 60 VVDStRL 290, 328–329.
19 *Cf* Craig/de Búrca (note 4) pp 321, 325; Pernice [1990] NJW 2409, 2414; Beutler in: von der Groeben/Schwarze (eds) *Vertrag über die Europäische Union und Vertrag zur Gründung der Europäischen Gemeinschaft – Kommentar* (6th ed, Baden-Baden 2004) Art 6 EUV, para 63.

degree of latitude. It is, for example, immaterial for the determination of the common constitutional traditions whether a certain position is in fact shared by a majority of the Member States. Furthermore, neither the maximum[20], let alone the minimum level of fundamental rights protection in the Member States is decisive.[21] Rather, the Court adopts a position which, after a critical analysis of the different approaches ensuing from a comparative review, appears to offer the best solution.[22] In case of doubt, the ECJ takes guidance from the ECHR (also because it will often not be easy to actually ascertain the constitutional traditions common to the Member States, whereas the ECHR provides a uniform text ratified by all Member States and complemented by an extensive body of decisions).[23] Nonetheless, the reference to the common constitutional traditions – expressing the interlocking of the fundamental rights of the Union with domestic guarantees – plays an important role if the ECHR does not contain a certain guarantee[24] – *eg* the right to pursue a freely chosen occupation[25]. As to the effects the Charter of Fundamental Rights may have prior to entering into force see paras 16 ff.

9 After the adoption of a joint declaration by the European Parliament, the Council and the Commission concerning the protection of fundamental rights in 1977,[26] and after the European Parliament had made proposals in 1989 and 1994 for the adoption of a fundamental rights catalogue,[27] a provision was included in the Treaty of Maastricht (ex Article 5(2) TEU) according to which the Union (*ie* the European Communities, the Common Foreign and Security Policy (CFSP) and the Police and Judicial Cooperation in Criminal Matters (PJCCM) as the three pillars of the Union[28]) respects fundamental rights, as guaranteed by the ECHR and as they result from the constitutional traditions common to the Member States, as general principles of Community law.[29] Since the Treaty of Amsterdam, this provision is located in **Article 6(2) of the TEU** – supplemented by a corresponding extension of the ECJ's jurisdiction in Article 46(d) of the TEU. As a result, the entire Union is now expressly bound by fundamental guarantees.

10 The consequences for the EC are, however, rather limited. First of all, the provision in Article Article 6(2) of the TEU did not become part of the Community treaties and therefore only applies by virtue of the general rules of public international law.[30] Furthermore,

---

20 See, however, also ECJ *Nold* [1974] ECR 491, para 13, according to which the Court "cannot [...] uphold measures which are incompatible with fundamental rights recognized and protected by the Constitutions of [the Member States]". *Cf* also ECJ *AM & S* [1982] ECR 1575, para 18; *Hoechst* [1989] ECR 2859, para 19.
21 More detailed Tridimas (note 4) pp 311 ff.
22 See already Zweigert (1964) 28 RabelsZ 601, 611. *Cf* also Streinz *Europarecht* (6th ed, Heidelberg 2003) paras 362 ff.
23 *Cf* Craig/de Búrca (note 4) p 329.
24 *Cf* ECJ *Metronome Music* [1998] ECR I-1953, para 21; Günter *Berufsfreiheit und Eigentum in der Europäischen Union* (Heidelberg 1998) passim.
25 As to a partial guarantee – prohibition of forced labour – *cf* Art 4(2) ECHR (Art II-65(2) DC).
26 [1977] OJ C103/1.
27 *Cf* [1989] OJ C120/51; [1994] OJ C61/155. All of the abovementioned declarations and resolutions are primarily of political nature. They may have legal significance in the sense that they may contribute to the creation of customary international law within the meaning of Article 31(3)(b) of the Vienna Convention on the Law of Treaties. See, however, also ECJ *Hauer* [1979] ECR 3727, para 15; *Opinion 2/94* [1996] ECR I-1759, para 32.
28 *Cf* Art 1(3), Art 11 ff, 29 ff TEU.
29 For more details see Craig/de Búrca (note 4) p 318.
30 Contentious; *contra* Cirkel *Die Bindungen der Mitgliedstaaten an die Gemeinschaftsgrundrechte*

General Principles

the status of the constitutional traditions common to the Member States and the ECHR as mere subsidiary means for the determination of general principles of EC law has not changed. The **ECHR is not directly binding** on the Communities, since the Convention is only open to signatures of the members of the Council of Europe[31] (*ie* states[32]) and since the European Communities (presently) lack the competence to formally accede to the ECHR[33]. Not even a strict unilateral commitment to the ECHR (and the jurisprudence of the ECtHR generated thereunder) can be inferred from Article 6(2) of the TEU (since such a commitment would not be compatible with the obligation to merely "observe" fundamental rights, and with the concurrent commitment to the common constitutional traditions → § 2 para 9). Finally, the ECJ's competences in respect of fundamental rights obligations of the Communities have also been left unchanged (as can be seen in both Article 46(d) as well as Article 47 of the TEU). The substantive derivation and development of fundamental rights of the Union therefore (still) lies with the ECJ (and the CFI) on the basis of Article 220 of the TEC (Article I-29(1) DC).[34]

4. The Relation between the Fundamental Rights of the Union and other Fundamental Guarantees

The citizens of the Union are not only protected by the fundamental rights of the Union, but also by the fundamental freedoms of the TEC, the guarantees under the ECHR as well as domestic human rights provisions. This opens up the question of how the different guarantees relate to each other. **11**

a) The relation to the fundamental freedoms under the TEC

The fundamental freedoms guaranteed by the EC Treaty – comprising the free movement of goods (Articles 28, 29 TEC/Article III-153 DC; → § 8), workers (Article 39 TEC/Article III-133 DC; → § 9) and capital (Article 56 TEC/Article III-156 DC; → § 12), as well as the freedom of establishment (Article 43 TEC/Article III-137 DC; → § 10) and the freedom to provide services (Article 49 TEC/Article III-144 DC; → § 11) – serve as prohibitions of both discrimination and other unjustified interferences (→ § 7 paras 18 ff). They can therefore be regarded as special forms of the equal treatment guarantee and fundamental liberty rights in EU cross-border scenarios (*ie* fundamental rights of the Union in the wider sense). It remains to be seen if the category of the fundamental freedoms can eventually be discarded as a form of "eggshell"[35] in the evolution of the EU. This is at least not likely in the foreseeable future. It would also require further provisions on the fundamental rights as to their exact scope of application and limits in cases now covered **12**

(Baden-Baden 2000), p 27; Pechstein/Koenig *Die Europäische Union* (3rd ed, Tübingen 2000) para 117.

31 Art 59(1)(1) ECHR. *Cf*, however, the 14th Protocol to the ECHR of 13 May 2004 (not yet entered into force) by which Article 59 of the ECHR will be amended to include a right of accession for the EU.

32 *Cf* Article 4 of the Statute of the Council of Europe, ETS No 001.

33 *Cf* ECJ *Opinion 2/94* [1996] ECR I-1759, para 36; see, however, also Article I-9(2) of the DC which provides that the Union acceeds to the ECHR.

34 Likewise (as to the result) Herrnfeld (note 17) Art 46 EUV, para 16.

35 *Cf* Dreier in: Dreier (ed) *Grundgesetz* (Volume I, 2nd ed, Tübingen 2004) Vorb, para 49. For a clear distinction between fundamental freedoms and fundamental rights see Gebauer *Die Grundfreiheiten des EG-Vertrags als Gemeinschaftsgrundrechte* (Berlin 2004) pp 346 ff.

by the fundamental freedoms. By no means can the requirement of a cross-border element be abandoned in favour of applying the fundamental rights of the Union to any measure of the Member States; otherwise, the fundamental rights of the Union would extend beyond the (present) scope of EC law and would largely displace the domestic guarantees. A transfer of the **fundamental freedoms** into the body of fundamental rights of the Union would only constitute a formal change without any effect in substance. As part of primary EC law they enjoy equal rank and status. Where the same legal interest is protected both by the fundamental rights of the Union and the fundamental freedoms, the latter take precedence as the more particular and expressly recognised guarantees.[36] Article II-75(2) of the DC leads to a doubling of certain fundamental freedoms as fundamental rights under the Charter. The former remain, however, solely authoritative and continue to define the conditions and limits of the respective guarantee (Article II-112(2) DC).[37] The priority of the fundamental freedoms does not exclude a **concurrent application** of the **protective content** of the different types of guarantees. Where a certain conduct comes within the scope of protection of a fundamental freedom, any generally permissible restriction has to be scrutinised for fundamental rights compatibility because the limitations to the fundamental freedoms, as provided for by Community law, must themselves be "interpreted in the light of the general principles of law and in particular of fundamental rights [of the Union]".[38] In serving as limits to the restrictability of fundamental freedoms or as yardsticks for the interpretation of limitation provisions the fundamental rights of the Union amplify the guarantees accorded by the fundamental freedoms themselves and therefore contribute to the promotion of the common market and EU integration (→ § 7 para 94). On the other hand, there may also be tension (or **conflict**) between the fundamental rights of the Union and the fundamental freedoms under the EC treaty. This will be the case if (and to the extent to which) they protect different legal interests, *ie* where the exercise of a fundamental freedom is in breach of a fundamental right of the Union (for example, if the free movement of goods is used to transport publications infringing personality rights across intra-Community borders). This requires a proportionate balancing of the opposing legal interests when interpreting the limitation provisions. Since the fundamental rights of the Union may impose certain positive obligations (para 22), a Member State may even be obliged to restrict the exercise of a particular fundamental freedom.[39] The ECJ for a long time did not pay much regard to this dimension. A thorough consideration of the fundamental rights of the Union as general limits to the restrictability of the fundamental freedoms stood in contrast to an underdeveloped assessment of their own ability to limit those freedoms.[40] In the *Bosman*[41] decision which concerned the legality of the transfer system in European professional football, the ECJ accorded the guarantee of free movement of workers and employees (Article 39 TEC/

---

36 → § 7 para 15; *contra* Kingreen in: Calliess/Ruffert (eds) *Kommentar des Vertrages über die Europäische Union und des Vertrages zur Gründung der Europäischen Union* (2nd ed, Neuwied 2002) Art 6 EUV, para 81 with note 222; see now, however, Kingreen [2004] EuGRZ 570, 575.
37 Bernsdorff in: Meyer (ed) *Kommentar zur Charta der Grundrechte der Europäischen Union* (Baden-Baden 2003) Art 15, para 20; critical Kingreen [2004] EuGRZ 570, 574.
38 *Cf* ECJ *ERT* [1991] ECR I-2925, para 43; *Familiapress* [1997] ECR I-3689, para 24 = Case 1 (para 29). *Cf* generally Craig/de Búrca (note 4) pp 341–345; Tridimas (note 4) pp 323 ff.
39 *Cf* ECJ *Stichting* [1991] ECR I-4007, para 23.
40 Schindler *Die Kollision von Grundfreiheiten und Gemeinschaftsgrundrechten* (Berlin 2001) pp 125 ff.
41 ECJ *Bosman* [1995] ECR I-4921, para 92 ff.

Article III-133 DC) direct horizontal effect vis-à-vis the (private) football associations[42] without ever reaching the stage of considering the associations' right to freedom of association as guaranteed by Article 11 of the ECHR. In recent times, however, the ECJ has repeatedly recognised that the fundamental rights may serve as limits to the fundamental freedoms. In the *Schmidberger*[43] case, the Court tolerated the non-intervention of the Austrian authorities in a blockade of the Brenner motorway despite its limiting effect on the free movement of goods, because the demonstrators made use of their rights to freedom of expression and assembly guaranteed by Articles 10 and 11 of the ECHR (as well as the Austrian Constitution[44]). Similarly, in the *Omega* decision the ECJ held that the prohibition of so-called Laserdromes constituted an interference with the freedom to provide services, which was, however, justified by reason of preventing a violation of human dignity (as determined by the German courts).[45]

b) The Relation to the Guarantees under the ECHR

Since the ECHR is presently not a source of Community law, but only a subsidiary means for the determination of the fundamental rights of the Union (paras 7–8), the Convention does not create any direct obligations with regard to the European Communities. The ECJ seems nevertheless to be prepared to accept the leading role of the ECtHR in matters concerning the protection of fundamental rights.[46] Still, different understandings of fundamental rights cannot be ruled out (especially on issues the ECtHR has yet to decide). The **ECtHR** can indirectly influence Community law by holding the EC Member States – in their capacity as Convention States – responsible for domestic acts incompatible with the ECHR, even if they are based on Community law (→ § 2 paras 31–32). However, in its recent *Bosphorus* decision[47] the ECtHR developed a presumption that a State does not depart from the requirements of the ECHR when it does no more than implement legal obligations flowing from the membership of an organisation which protects the fundamental rights in a manner that can be considered comparable to the protection of the ECHR.[48] According to the ECtHR, this presumption can only be rebutted where the protection of Convention rights is manifestly deficient in the individual case.[49] The ECtHR found that the protection of fundamental rights guaranteed by EC law can be considered comparable to that of the Convention system[50] – a presumption which is susceptible to review in the light of any relevant changes[51]. Hence, it can be expected that, in the future, the ECtHR will refrain from scrutinising national measures against their consistency with the ECHR if these national measures fall inside strict obligations under EC law. On the other hand the ECtHR stressed that Member States remain fully responsible under the

13

---

42 → critical as to a direct horizontal effect of the fundamental freedoms § 7 para 46; see also → § 9 para 46.
43 ECJ *Schmidberger* [2003] ECR I-5659, paras 77 ff.
44 As to the relation between the fundamental rights of the Union and the national guarantees in this case *cf* Kadelbach/Petersen [2002] EuGRZ 213; Schorkopf [2004] ZaöRV 125, 133 ff.
45 *Cf* ECJ *Omega* [2004] ECR I-9609, para 40.
46 *Cf* Hoffmann-Riem [2002] EuGRZ 473, 478; Tridimas (note 4) p 343.
47 ECtHR *Bosphorus* (2006) 42 EHRR 1.
48 ECtHR *Bosphorus* (2006) 42 EHRR 1, paras 155–156.
49 ECtHR *Bosphorus* (2006) 42 EHRR 1, para 156.
50 ECtHR *Bosphorus* (2006) 42 EHRR 1, para 165.
51 ECtHR *Bosphorus* (2006) 42 EHRR 1, para 155.

Convention for all acts involving an exercise of State discretion provided for by EC law.[52] As a result, it will be a major issue for the ECtHR to decide whether or not a particular Community measure in fact provides such discretion. Where this question is answered in the affirmative the ECtHR will continue to reserve for itself the **final say** in matters concerning the protection of fundamental rights and freedoms. The overall consequence is that the fundamental rights of the Union are to be given a meaning compatible with the (older[53]) obligations of the Member States under the ECHR.[54] Conversely, Community law may also have an impact on the Convention. For example, the term "aliens" in Article 16 of the ECHR must be reduced to nationals from states outside the EU due to the permissible exercise of the rights guaranteed by Articles 10, 11 and 14 of the ECHR in connection with municipal elections (Article 19 TEC/Article I-10(2)(b) DC) and elections to the European Parliament (Article 190 TEC/Article I-10(2)(b) DC).[55] Furthermore, remedies available under Community law are to be regarded as "domestic" for the purposes of Article 35(1) of the ECHR.[56] The relation between the fundamental rights of the Union and the ECHR will evidently change if the Charter of Fundamental Rights enters into force (paras 16 ff) or if the Union even accedes to the ECHR (*cf* Article I-9(2) DC). Insofar as the Charter contains rights which correspond to rights guaranteed by the ECHR, the meaning and scope of those rights shall be the same as those laid down by the Convention – without preventing a more extensive protection (Article II-112(3) DC). No provision of the Charter is to be interpreted as restricting or adversely affecting the rights as guaranteed by the ECHR (Article II-113 DC). Therefore, the standard set by the **ECHR** always constitutes the **minimum level** of protection.[57] The reference to the ECHR does not seem to be meant to be static (*ie* referring only to the Convention law as it stands at the time when the Charter enters into force) but rather dynamic (*ie* including future amendments). Such dynamic references can be problematic[58] since the precise extent of the obligation concerned is unpredictable. In the present context, however, they may still be acceptable, as all Member States of the EU are at the same time Contracting States of the ECHR and are consequently involved in the future development of the Convention. As to problems of delineation *cf* para 19.

c) The Relation to National Fundamental Guarantees

14 Community law cannot be measured against domestic standards of the Member States. It is consequently not for the national courts to pronounce on the validity of acts of EC institutions. It is debatable whether this also holds true for the applicability of Community law within the respective domestic legal order. The answer largely depends on the doctrine of supremacy of Community law which the ECJ steadfastly maintains without any exception (para 4) to ensure the uniformity of the EC legal order. Acts of the Community can therefore only be scrutinised for compliance with the fundamental rights of the Union and not with national fundamental guarantees. The constitutional courts of the Member States have often taken a different view (para 4), even though most of them formulated

---

52 ECtHR *Bosphorus* (2006) 42 EHRR 1, para 157.
53 *Cf* Art 307(1) TEC (Art III-435(1) DC).
54 *Cf* Craig/de Búrca (note 4) pp 329–330; Grabenwarter (2000) 60 VVDStRL 290, 331.
55 Grabenwarter (2000) 60 VVDStRL 290, 333.
56 ECtHR *Dufay* App No 13539/88.
57 *Cf* Grabenwarter [2004] EuGRZ 563, 566.
58 See generally Schenke [1980] NJW 743.

General Principles   § 14 I 5

their reservations more cautiously than the *Bundesverfassungsgericht* (German Federal Constitutional Court). However, in all cases the acceptance of the supremacy of Community law comes with strings attached: For example, according to the *Solange* decisions[59] of the German Federal Constitutional Court, the Federal Republic of Germany may only transfer sovereign powers to the European Union within certain limits that are (now) laid down in Article 23(1) of the *Grundgesetz* (German Basic Law / Federal Constitution).[60] Where the Communities exercise powers that were never conferred upon them or where the rules of EC law violate inalienable standards of the Basic Law (Article 79(2) and (3)), Community legislation is – according to the Court – not applicable in Germany. Those inalienable standards include the general protection of fundamental rights. Article 23(1)(i) of the Basic Law, however, only requires an "essentially comparable" level of protection on the part of the EU, which the Federal Constitutional Court had already found to exist in its *Solange II* decision[61] of 1987.[62] As a consequence, the Court will only review acts of the Community if such a comparable level of protection is no longer guaranteed.

In contrast, national **measures implementing** or **applying Community law** must generally comply with fundamental rights standards imposed by the respective national legal order. Where, however, such measures are based on mandatory provisions of EC law, the doctrine of supremacy of Community law requires the non-application of conflicting domestic legislation – including domestic fundamental guarantees.[63]   **15**

5. Charter of Fundamental Rights of the Union

The fact that the European treaties lack a written collection of fundamental rights and that the ECJ therefore generally has to deduce and shape them on a case-by-case basis[64] has often been met with criticism. Demands were made for the creation of a catalogue of fundamental rights.[65] In reaction, the European Council (Article 4(2) TEU) in 1999 established a convention (chaired by the former German Federal President *Roman Herzog*) comprising national government representatives, the President of the Commission, as well as national and European parliamentarians to draft such a catalogue. At the European Council meeting in Nice on 7 December 2000, the **Charter of Fundamental Rights of the Union**[66] was 'solemnly proclaimed' by the European Commission, Parliament and Council. This proclamation, however, is not legally binding. During the meeting in Laeken on 15 December 2001, a constitutional convention (chaired by the former French President *Giscard*   **16**

---

59 BVerfG *Solange I* [1974] 2 CMLR 540; *Solange II* [1987] 3 CMLR 225.
60 Article 23 was inserted into the Basic Law in 1992.
61 BVerfG *Solange II* [1987] 3 CMLR 225.
62 *Cf* also BVerfG *Maastricht* (1993) 89 BVerfGE 155, 174–175; *Bananas Case* (2000) 102 BVerfGE 147.
63 As to the mere non-application (and not invalidity) of national legislation incompatible with Community law *cf* ECJ *Nimz* [1991] ECR I-297, para 19; BVerfG (1987) 75 BVerfGE 223, 244; (1992) 85 BVerfGE 191, 204.
64 *Cf* Borchardt *Die rechtlichen Grundlagen der Europäischen Union* (3rd ed, Heidelberg 2006) para 180 ff.
65 On the other hand, the present state of affairs is more flexible and open to future developments (Zuleeg [2000] EuGRZ 2000, 511). Furthermore, it cannot be denied that a written catalogue may indirectly lead to an extension of the competences of the Union (despite the provision in Art II-111(2) of the DC) and may have unitarising effects.
66 [2000] OJ C364/1; → more detailed § 20.

d'Estaing) was established and commissioned to draft a Constitution for Europe. The draft treaty, which had taken on the Charter of Fundamental Rights virtually unaltered and without any further discussions, was presented to the Intergovernmental Conference on 7 July 2003 and was signed – after various modifications which did not concern the Charter – on 29 October 2004. The Treaty, however, will not enter into force after it has been rejected by popular votes in France and the Netherlands. On its meeting of 21/22 June 2007 the European Council agreed on a new draft Treaty to be drawn up. Article 6 of the TEU on fundamental rights will be replaced with a text reading as follows: "The Union recognises the rights, freedoms and principles set out in the Charter of Fundamental Rights of 7 December 2000, as adapted on [●● 2007], which shall have the same legal value as the Treaties." In case of an adoption and ratification of the Reform Treaty the Charter of Fundamental Rights will – due to the cross reference in Article 6 – form part of primary Community law. The Charter – even at present – has certain **effects in advance**, since it combines the fundamental rights *acquis* developed in the Member States and can thus be considered as a concentrate of the common constitutional traditions.[67] While the CFI[68] and the Advocates General[69] have – on a regular basis – relied on the Charter as a subsidiary means for the determination of Community law, the ECJ has not taken a firm stand on the status of the Charter thus far.[70] However, the Reform Treaty is intended to provide for an opt-out clause with regard to the United Kingdom (*cf* the preface of this textbook). The courts of the United Kingdom shall not have the ability to find that the laws, regulations or administrative provisions, practices or action of the United Kingdom are inconsistent with the fundamental rights, freedoms and principles that the Charter of Fundamental Rights reaffirms. Furthermore, the opt-out clause determines that nothing in (Title IV) of the Charter creates justiciable rights applicable to the United Kingdom except in so far as the United Kingdom has provided for such rights in its national law. However, the European Union as well as all Member States must observe the general principles of Community law including the fundamental rights – as guaranteed by the European Convention for the Protection of Human Rights and Fundamental Freedoms and as they result from the constitutional traditions common to the Member States – when applying or implementing Community law. It can therefore not be assumed that the fundamental rights of the European Union will be of no relevance in the United Kingdom.

17   The Charter contains 54 Articles that are grouped in seven chapters headed **Dignity** (Articles II-61–65 DC), **Freedoms** (Articles II-66–79 DC), **Equality** (Articles II-80–86 DC), **Solidarity** (Articles II-87–98 DC), **Citizen Rights** (Articles II-99–106 DC), **Justice** (Articles II-107–110 DC) and **General Provisions** (Articles II-111–114 DC). The rights listed reaffirm the guarantees as they result, in particular, from the constitutional traditions and international obligations common to the Member States, the ECHR, the Social Charters adopted by the Union and by the Council of Europe and the case-law of the ECJ and of the ECtHR (Preamble of the Charter). Viewed from the entirety of the various sources of

---

67 Kingreen (note 36) Art 6 EUV, para 40 b.
68 *Cf* CFI *max mobil* [2002] ECR II-313, para 57.
69 *Cf*, for example, Opinion AG Alber, ECJ *TNT* [2001] ECR I-4109, para 94; Opinion AG Tizzano, ECJ *BECTU* [2001] ECR 4883, paras 26 ff.
70 In ECJ *Parliament v Council* [2006] ECR I-5769, para 38 the Court made reference to the Charter by pointing out its principal aim which is to reaffirm rights as they result, *inter alia*, from the constitutional traditions and international obligations common to the Member States. *Cf* also ECJ *Advocaten* C-303/05, paras 45 ff.

General Principles

law the Charter does not create – apart from minor exceptions – any new fundamental rights, but only visualises and systematises them. If one compares them with the guarantees of just one single source (*eg* only the ECHR), the Charter goes in parts considerably further (*eg* the prohibition of reproductive cloning of human beings pursuant to Article II-63(2)(d) DC, the right of access to free placement services pursuant to Article II-89 DC, the right to paid maternity leave pursuant to Article II-93(2) DC). At the same time, the Charter poses new questions (→ § 20):

For example, the Charter distinguishes between **rights** and **freedoms** on the one hand and **principles** (Article II-111 DC and the preamble) on the other, without always making clear, however, which guarantees fall into which category. Principles do not confer subjective rights to positive governmental action, but must be implemented through legislative and executive acts of the institutions, agencies and other bodies of the Union as well as of the Member States in exercising their respective competences. They are judicially cognisable only in the interpretation of such acts and in the ruling on their legality (Article II-112(5) DC). For example, national courts may invalidate domestic provisions that are contrary to the realisation of the principles. These include, *inter alia*, the protection of the environment (Article II-97 DC) and of consumers (Article II-98 DC). Other principles can be found in the "rights" of the elderly (Article II-85 DC) and the integration of persons with disabilities (Article II-86 DC). The guarantees of the Charter can, however, both confer rights and, at the same time, embody a certain principle. This probably holds true for the equality between women and men (Article II-83 DC), the protection of family and professional life (Article II-93 DC) as well as the entitlement to social security and social assistance (Article II-94 DC). Where the Charter calls for the respect of certain legal interests – *eg* Article II-82 of the DC: respect for cultural, religious and linguistic diversity – this usually means that those interests must be accorded sufficient weight in a balancing process with other (possibly conflicting) objectives.

18

Moreover, the Charter leads to **duplications** and even triplications in the protection of fundamental rights and freedoms.[71] For example, the right to freedom of movement (Articles I-10(2)(a), II-105 DC), the right to protection of personal data (Articles I-51, II-68 DC), the right of access to documents (Articles I-50(3), II-102 DC) or the right to vote and to stand as a candidate in elections (Articles I-10(2)(b), II-99 DC) are all guaranteed in multiple places of the Constitution. Problems of delineation can arise not only in relation to the fundamental freedoms (para 12) and the guarantees of the ECHR (para 13), but also because the **constitutional traditions common to the Member States** remain applicable as a subsidiary means for the determination of Community law (Articles I-9(3), II-112(4), II-113 DC). As can be inferred from the insertion of "in their respective fields of application", the mention in Article II-113 of the DC of the constitutions of the Member States is not to be taken as an exception to the doctrine of supremacy of Community law.[72] Should the ECJ derive new fundamental rights from the common constitutional traditions, the existing limitation provisions may not likewise be modified.[73] In any event, regard must be had to Article II-112(2) of the DC according to which the rights recognised by the Charter for which provision is made in other parts of the Treaties shall be exercised under the "conditions and within the limits" defined by these relevant parts.

19

---

71 *Cf* Grabenwarter [2004] EuGRZ 563, 567.
72 *Cf* Borowski (note 37) Art 53, para 5; Everling [2003] EuZW 225; *contra* Seidel [2003] EuZW 97.
73 *Cf* Grabenwarter [2004] EuGRZ 563, 569.

Moreover, the Charter does not establish any new power or task for the Union (Article I-111(2) DC). This is of particular importance where the Charter guarantees rights which the Union itself cannot restrict for lack of competence – *eg* the prohibition of the death penalty (Article II-62(2) DC) or the right to conscientious objection (Article II-70(2) DC) – and which therefore at present only have symbolic character.[74]

II. Functions of the Fundamental Rights of the Union

1. Guarantee of Liberty Rights

20 Just as the fundamental guarantees of the ECHR (→ *cf* § 2 para 13) the fundamental rights of the Union are primarily designed to accord the individual a certain **sphere of liberty**, *ie* the right to be free from unlawful interference as well as a right to reversal of such interferences where this remains possible. The liberty rights recognised by the ECJ exceed those guaranteed under the ECHR.[75] They concern the integrity of life and health (→ § 15 paras 9 ff), freedom of expression and association (→ § 15 paras 59 ff), freedom of religion (→ § 15 paras 47 ff) as well as the economic freedoms of the right to property (→ § 17) and the right to pursue a freely chosen occupation (→ § 16). In addition, the ECJ has in principle recognised a right to general freedom of action.[76] As discussed above (paras 16–17), the Charter of Fundamental Rights contains further guarantees and specifications: *eg* the right to conscientious objection (Article II-70(2) DC) or the provisions specifying the boundaries for limitations of the right to physical and mental integrity in the field of medicine and biology (Article II-63(2) DC). There are also some deliberate deviations from the text of the ECHR. For example, unlike Article 12 of the ECHR, Article II-69 of the DC does not inherently limit the right to marry and to found a family to men and women. Besides guarantees such as Article II-68 of the DC (protection of personal data) or Article II-73 of the DC (freedom of the arts and sciences) the Charter also goes beyond the ECHR in protecting the right to engage in work and to pursue a freely chosen occupation (Article II-75 DC → § 16) and the freedom to conduct a business (Article II-76 DC).

2. Guarantee of Equality Rights

21 Apart from the special written equality rights (para 6) and the prohibition of discrimination contained in the fundamental freedoms, the fundamental rights of the Union also comprise a **general right to equality before the law** (→ § 18 paras 11 ff).[77] This guarantee is not only defensive in character, but also confers on the individual a right to equal *preferential* treatment. It thus accords a (derivative) right to participation in granted benefits. Systematically somewhat misplaced in Title III, the Charter of Fundamental Rights also guarantees social rights or principles (Articles II-84 – II-86 DC) alongside the right to

---

74 *Cf* Borowski (note 37) Art 51, paras 42–43.
75 *Cf* the listing by Kingreen (note 36) Art 6 EUV, paras 93 ff; Stumpf (note 17) Art 6 EUV, paras 20 ff.
76 *Cf* ECJ *Rau* [1987] ECR 2289, paras 15 ff; see also ECJ *Hoechst* [1989] ECR 2859, para 19; *Dow Chemical* [1989] ECR 3137, para 16.
77 ECJ *Ruckdeschel* [1977] ECR 1753, para 7; *Edeka* [1982] ECR 2745, para 11; *Karlsson* [2000] ECR I-2737, para 39. *Cf* also Art II-80 ff DC.

equality before the law (Article II-80 DC) and the special prohibitions of discrimination (Articles II-81, II-83 DC).

3. Guarantee of Rights to Governmental Action / Positive Obligations

The fundamental rights of the Union may furthermore accord a **right to protection by the State,** *ie* they may impose on the State certain positive obligations.[78] While there is no clear jurisprudence on this issue yet, some decisions of ECJ can be interpreted to cautiously establish the concept of positive obligations (binding at least the Member States).[79] Such duties are also derived from the fundamental freedoms and from certain provisions of the ECHR (→ *cf* § 2 para 15; § 7 para 31). It should be borne in mind, however, that a positive obligation does not confer any new powers on the Union, but rather presupposes their prior existence (principle of parallelism between the competences of the EC and the protection of fundamental rights).[80] A duty under Community law to take governmental action can only exist if an appropriate competence has been conferred on the Community or if the Member States seek to impose limits on the fundamental freedoms (para 12). In principle, positive obligations do not require specific actions to be taken, but only call for effective measures to remedy the (potential) infringement of fundamental rights.[81] The Charter of Fundamental Rights contains a number of social guarantees (*eg* Articles II-90, 91(2), 93, 94, 95 DC) which are also designed to provide protection. In this context, the principle of parallelism between the competences of the EC and the protection of fundamental rights has not always been respected (para 20). Where protective measures of the Community come into consideration the principle of subsidiarity (Articles 5(2) TEC; I-11(3), II-111(1) DC) and proportionality (Article 5(3) TEC/Article I-11(4) DC) must be observed.[82]

22

Leaving aside the procedural guarantees (para 27), the fundamental rights of the Union used to hardly confer any **original rights to governmental action** – *ie* rights to the creation or allocation of previously inexistent institutions or first-time benefits. Again, the Charter of Fundamental Rights goes (in parts) further. For example, Article II-89 of the DC guarantees everyone the right of access to a free placement service. This must necessarily include the right to demand the setup of such a service.

23

4. Guarantee of the Citizens' Rights

Citizens' rights of the Union – especially the **right to vote** and to stand as a candidate in municipal elections and elections to the European Parliament, the right to freedom of movement and the right to petition – arise from Articles 18 ff of the TEC (Articles I-9, I-10, II-99 ff, III-123 ff DC). Pursuant to Article 255 of the TEC (Articles II-102, III-399

24

---

78 Critical Ruffert *Subjektive Rechte im Umweltrecht der Europäischen Gemeinschaft* (Heidelberg 1996) p 59.
79 *Cf* ECJ *Schmidberger* [2003] ECR I-5659, para 74; *Omega* [2004] ECR I-9609, para 35; more detailed Szczekalla *Die sogenannten grundrechtlichen Schutzpflichten im deutschen und europäischen Recht* (Berlin 2002) pp 459 ff.
80 Kingreen (note 36) Art 6 EUV, paras 46, 48; Lindner [2000] DÖV 543, 549; Pernice [2000] DVBl 847, 852; Schmitz [2001] JZ 833, 840.
81 Kühling in: von Bogdandy (ed) *Europäisches Verfassungsrecht* (Heidelberg 2003) pp 583, 603.
82 *Cf* the Protocol (No 30) on the application of the principles of subsidiarity and proportionality of 1997, annexed to the Treaty establishing the European Community.

DC), citizens of the Union (and other persons) have a right of access to documents. Moreover, the ECJ developed a right to good administration (now Article II-101 DC).[83] The Court tends to derive from the citizenship of the Union an obligation to equal treatment of nationals from other Member States in respect of access to social benefits (→ § 21 para 86).[84]

5. Guarantee of Procedural Rights

25 Procedural guarantees (→ see more detailed § 19) are of particular importance within the Community legal order. Over the years, the ECJ has recognised numerous procedural rights, *eg* the right to effective judicial protection[85], the right to be heard (not just before a court but also in administrative proceedings[86]) or the right not to be tried or punished twice for the same offence (*ne bis in idem*)[87]. Certain substantive fundamental guarantees may also require procedural safeguards (→ *cf* § 7 para 34). The procedural rights have to some extent been expressly codified in the treaties; however, they also partly overlap with the citizens' rights (*eg* Articles 21, 255 TEC/Articles I-10(2)(d), II-102, III-399 DC). They often go even beyond the (broadly interpreted) procedural guarantees of the ECHR. Contrary to Article 6(1)(i) of the ECHR (→ *cf* § 2 para 18), the right to an effective remedy and access to courts, for example, is not limited to disputes involving civil rights and obligations (see also Articles II-107 ff DC).[88]

6. The Objective Dimension of the Fundamental Rights of the Union

26 Finally, just as the fundamental freedoms (→ § 7 para 35) the fundamental rights of the Union have a certain objective dimension.[89] This dimension must in particular be observed in the enactment and application of secondary EC legislation. Furthermore, both the law of the Community and of the Member States must be interpreted **in conformity with the fundamental rights** of the Union. Again, it should be noted that the fundamental rights are unable to extend the competences of the Community (see also Article II-111(2) DC).

---

83 ECJ *Burban* [1992] ECR I-2253, para 12. See also CFI *Nölle* [1995] ECR II-2589, para 89; → § 20 para 11.
84 Critical as to the position of the Court Hailbronner [2004] NJW 2185.
85 See the ECJ's seminal decisions in *Johnston* [1986] ECR 1651, paras 17 ff, and *Heylens* [1987] ECR 4097, para 14.
86 ECJ *Hoffmann-La Roche* [1979] ECR 461, para 9; *Michelin* [1983] ECR 3461, para 17.
87 *Cf*, for example, ECJ *Gutmann* [1966] ECR 149; CFI *Limburgse* [1999] ECR II-931, paras 95–96. See also Article 4 of the 7th Protocol to the ECHR and Article 1 of the Convention between the Member States of the European Communities on Double Jeopardy of 25 May 1987, which has not yet entered into force.
88 *Cf* ECJ *Les Verts* [1986] ECR 1339, para 23.
89 *Cf* also Rengeling *Grundrechtsschutz in der Europäischen Gemeinschaft* (Munich 1993) pp 205 ff; Gersdorf (1994) 119 AöR 400, 402 ff.

III. Beneficiaries of the Fundamental Rights of the Union

1. Natural Persons

In consideration of Article 1 of the ECHR and the necessity to avoid areas devoid of fundamental rights protection when transferring sovereign powers to the Community, not only the citizens of the Union (Article 17(1)(ii) TEC/Article I-10(1) DC) but **all human beings** (under certain circumstances even the unborn life and already deceased persons) are in principle beneficiaries of the fundamental rights of the Union.[90] The Charter expresses this by employing phrases such as "everyone has the right" (Article II-62(1) DC) or "no one shall be" (Article II-62(2) DC). However, both the EC treaties and the subsidiary means for the determination of the general principles of Community law may require a different approach in certain cases. For example, it is self-evident that the citizens' rights (Articles 17 ff TEC/Articles II-99, II-100, II-104 ff DC) only apply to the citizens of the Union. Similarly, the fundamental freedoms only embrace persons from third countries under certain prerequisites.[91] In areas where the ECHR does not offer any protection (as, for example, in the case of freedom to pursue a freely chosen occupation) and where the majority of the Member States' constitutions confer a right only on their own citizens, the comparative and valuing process of determining the fundamental rights of the Union (para 8) may nevertheless result in an application to noncitizens of the Union.[92]

2. Entities with Legal Personality and Groups of Individuals

Entities with legal personality and groups of individuals can be beneficiaries of the fundamental rights of the Union if the **nature of the right** in question permits an application to non-natural persons.[93] Although the Court proceeds on a case-by-case basis, there are now numerous decisions[94] in which it has generally recognised that legal persons may invoke the fundamental rights (other than the strictly personal guarantees such as the right to life or personal integrity). Except for Article 48(2) (in conjunction with Article 55) of the TEC (Article III-142(2), 150 DC), commercial objectives do not have to be pursued. Legal persons are only sporadically mentioned in the Charter of Fundamental Rights (see Articles II-102, 103, 104 DC) – *eg* where the Charter sets out different requirements for the protection of natural and legal persons. This should not, however, be taken to imply that legal persons are barred from invoking the fundamental rights of the Union in all other circumstances. **State** organisations are not protected,[95] even where the State avails itself of private law patterns of organisation or if its actions are governed by private law (*eg* when entering into contracts of sale).[96] In contrast, the fundamental freedoms may also apply to (state)

---

90 *Cf* Borchardt (note 64) para 186; Rengeling/Szczekalla *Grundrechte in der Europäischen Union* (Cologne/Berlin/Munich 2004) § 4, para 344.
91 › § 7 para 41.
92 As to the fundamental right of the Union to freely choose and exercise an occupation *cf* Art II-75 DC (drawing distinctions between "everyone", "every citizen of the Union" and "nationals of third countries").
93 The ECJ apparently does not rely on this test. *Cf*, however, Rengeling/Szczekalla (note 90) § 5, para 390.
94 See, for example, ECJ *Internationale Handelsgesellschaft* [1970] ECR 1125, paras 4 ff; *National Panasonic* [1980] ECR 2033, paras 17 ff; *Schräder* [1989] ECR 2237, para 15.
95 Likewise Rengeling/Szczekalla (note 90) § 5, para 392.
96 → § 2 para 26.

entities governed by public law (as can be seen in Article 48(2) TEC/Article III-142(2) DC). Furthermore, such entities can rely on the procedural rights.[97] In case of mixed public-private organisations, EC law tends to regard the exercise of effective control as the decisive criterion.[98] This supports the view that – contrary to a widely held opinion in German law[99] – state-controlled enterprises with private shareholders are bound rather than protected by the fundamental rights of the Union. What remains unsolved is whether public entities such as state universities are protected at least in those activities that can be directly attributed to a sphere covered by a fundamental right. This should probably be answered in the affirmative.[100] Religious groups incorporated under public law[101] or public broadcasting organisations[102] should not (primarily) be attributed to the governmental sphere and consequently not be deprived of fundamental rights protection.

IV. Entities Bound by the Fundamental Rights of the Union

Case 1 – Problem: (ECJ *Familiapress* [1997] ECR I-3689)

29 The Heinrich Bauer-Verlag, a newspaper publisher established in Germany, publishes a weekly magazine which is also distributed in Austria. The magazine contains a number of crossword-puzzles. Readers sending in the correct solution are entitled to be entered in a draw for cash prizes. Unlike in Germany, such practices are contrary to competition law in Austria which aims to secure the competitiveness of smaller publishers and to maintain the diversity of the press. On this basis, an Austrian newspaper publisher seeks an injunction against the Bauer-Verlag enjoining the latter from selling in Austria publications offering readers the chance to take part in games for prizes. The Austrian court seized of the case has requested from the ECJ a preliminary ruling on the question whether Article 30 of the TEC is to be interpreted as precluding an application of legislation of Member State A prohibiting an undertaking established in Member State B from selling in Member State A a periodical produced in Member State B, where that periodical contains prize puzzle competitions or games which are lawfully organized in Member State B.

1. European Union and European Communities

30 Since the primary function of the fundamental rights is to limit the powers of the Union and the Communities respectively, the **institutions** of the European Union and the European Communities as well as their **bodies, offices and agencies**, even if legally autonomous, are addressees of the fundamental rights of the Union (*cf* Article II-111(1) DC).

---

97 See also ECJ *Netherlands v Commission* [1992] ECR I-565, paras 40 ff; Kingreen (note 36) Art 6 EUV, para 54.
98 As to the definition of public undertakings *cf* Article 2(i) of the Directive 80/723/EC on Transparency of Financial Relations between the Member States and Public Undertakings, [1980] OJ L195/35.
99 *Cf* Dreier (note 35) Art 1 III, para 70; Höfling in: Sachs (ed) *Grundgesetz* (4th ed, Munich 2007) Art 1, para 104; Ehlers in: Wurzel/Schraml/Becker (eds) *Rechtspraxis der kommunalen Unternehmen* (Munich 2005) B 41. *Contra* BVerfG-K, NJW 1990, 1783.
100 *Contra* Fink [2001] EuGRZ 193, 199–200, with reference to the ECJ's decision in *Hoechst* [1989] ECR 2859, para 17 (which, however, may not be generalised).
101 *Cf* Ehlers in: Sachs (ed) *Grundgesetz* (4th ed, Munich 2007) Art 140 GG/Art 137 WRV, para 23.
102 *Cf* Kühling (note 81) p 583, 612. As to their protection within the domestic legal order of the Member States *cf* Holznagel *Rundfunkrecht in Europa* (Tübingen 1996) pp 132 ff.

2. Member States of the European Union

Most of the **written fundamental rights** of the Union (in the wider sense) – as, for example, the principle of equal pay in Article 141(1) of the TEC (Article III-214(1) DC), the citizens' rights or the fundamental freedoms – are either expressly or implicitly addressed to the Member States and therefore directly bind them. In addition, the Member States must observe the requirements flowing from the protection of fundamental rights in the EC legal order when implementing Community law.[103] The following details apply: 31

The Member States are in particular **bound** by the fundamental rights of the Union when they implement Community law into their respective domestic legal order, directly apply Community law, or if they limit the fundamental freedoms through individual domestic measures.[104] Where a directive or a decision addressed to the Member States is to be **implemented** into national law, the Member States must use the discretion left to them in conformity with the fundamental rights of the Union.[105] Any act of secondary Community legislation which does not leave any choice as to form and method of implementation and which violates a fundamental right is void. An appropriate declaration may only be made by the ECJ,[106] which means that an action for annulment (Article 230 TEC/Article III-365 DC) must (or can) be brought. If the domestic authorities **apply** a regulation or a directly applicable directive / decision, they may not take any measures which the Communities would be barred from taking themselves by reason of being bound by the fundamental rights of the Union.[107] According to the jurisprudence of the ECJ[108] the Member States are required when implementing and applying Community rules to use their discretion in accordance with requirements flowing from the protection of fundamental rights in the Community legal order. Even where a directive or decision is not directly applicable, implementing acts of the Member States must stay within the limits of Community law and, consequently, the fundamental rights of the Union. Finally, the fundamental rights bind the Member States when restricting fundamental freedoms, since the limits to those freedoms must themselves be interpreted in the light of the fundamental rights of the Union (cf para 12).[109] 32

---

103 Settled case-law of the ECJ. Cf ECJ *Wachauf* [1989] ECR 2609, para 19; *ERT* [1991] ECR I-2925, para 43; *Karlsson* [2000] ECR I-2737, para 37. See also Craig/de Búrca (note 4) p 340.
104 Tridimas (note 4) pp 319 ff. As to the first two scenarios cf already Weiler in: Neuwahl et al (eds) *The European Union and Human Rights* (The Hague 1995) pp 51 (67 ff – agency situation). Cf also Craig/de Búrca (note 4) pp 340–341.
105 ECJ *Parliament v Council* [2006] ECR I-5769, paras 104–105. Likewise Kühling (note 81) pp 580, 608; contra Kingreen (note 36) Art 6 EUV, para 59.
106 See the seminal decision in ECJ *Foto-Frost* [1987] ECR 4199, paras 15 ff.
107 Cf Craig/de Búrca (note 4) p 340.
108 ECJ *Bostock* [1994] ECR I-955, para 16; *Duff* [1996] ECR I-569, para 29.
109 Cf the answer to Case 1 (para 38); → § 7 para 86. Critical Kingreen (note 36) Art 6 EUV, paras 61–62 with further references. According the ECJ's decision in *Herbert Karner* [2004] ECR

33 Pursuant to Article II-111(1) of the DC, the Charter of Fundamental Rights shall only apply to the Member States when they are "implementing Union law". Some commentators have expressed the view that the implementation of Union law does not include measures aimed at the **limitation** of **fundamental freedoms**.[110] However, the genesis of the relevant provisions rather points to a wider interpretation of Article II-111(1) of the DC along the lines of the above-mentioned jurisprudence of the ECJ.[111] Moreover, it is not linguistically impossible to speak of implementation where a Member States simply takes measures within the scope of application of EC law. On this basis, the Charter will not change the extent of the Member States' obligations under the fundamental rights of the Union.[112]

34 As regards the nature of the Member States' obligations under the fundamental rights of the Union, distinctions are sometimes made between **indirect** and **direct** obligations.[113] An indirect obligation would entail that while the Member States are not themselves bound by the fundamental rights the rules of Community law binding on the Member States would still have to be interpreted and applied in accordance with the fundamental rights of the Union. If, then, the Member States are required to observe fundamental rights either way, their obligation is always direct in character. The only question is whether the fundamental rights of the Union only provide for an objective standard which domestic public authorities must meet, or whether they also confer **subjective rights** on the individual. The guarantee of fundamental rights (and not just principles) includes the right to enforce the protected interests in a court of law. Hence, the fundamental rights accord their beneficiaries a cause of action. However, the national courts will probably only feel compelled to scrutinise national measures for compliance with the fundamental rights of the Union if the domestic system for the protection of fundamental rights does not come into operation or falls short of the standards guaranteed on the European level.[114]

3. Private Persons

35 While the ECJ has under certain prerequisites imposed an obligation on private individuals to respect the fundamental freedoms,[115] no similar development has yet occurred in relation to the fundamental rights of the Union. Subject to express provisions such as Article 141(1) of the TEC (Article III-214(1) DC) to the contrary, the fundamental rights (and the fundamental freedoms; → § 7 para 45–46) should not be interpreted to have any **direct horizontal effect**. Such an effect would turn the *rights* of individuals against an unfettered exercise of sovereign power into *obligations* vis-à-vis their fellow citizens and

---

I-3025, paras 43 ff, even a selling arrangement within the meaning of the ECJ's judgment in *Keck and Mithouard* (→ § 7 para 75) is to be tested for compliance with the fundamental rights of the Union. On this issue, see the appropriate criticism by Schaller [2005] JZ 193.
110 Cremer [2003] NVwZ 1452; Borowski (note 37) Art 51, para 29.
111 *Cf* Grabenwarter [2004] EuGRZ 563, 564–565.
112 Likewise Ranacher [2003] ZÖR 97; Griller in: Duschanek/Griller (ed) *Grundrechte für Europa* (Vienna 2002) pp 131, 132–133.
113 *Cf* Cirkel (note 30) pp 237–238.
114 *Cf* the answer to Case 1 (para 38) as well as ECJ *Schmidberger* [2003] ECR I-5659, para 74; *Omega* [2004] ECR I-9609, para 35.
115 See in particular ECJ *Angonese* [2000] ECR I-4139, paras 34 ff.

would thus lead to a far-reaching constraint on private autonomy. Where protection against unlawful interferences by private individuals seems necessary and appropriate, it can be achieved by according a right to protection by the state or the EC. The Charter of Fundamental Rights also does not mention private individuals in the provision determining its field of application (Article II-111 DC). However, some Articles have been worded in a way that could imply a direct horizontal effect (*eg* the prohibition of trafficking in human beings, Article II-65(3) DC, or the prohibition of child labour, Article II-92 DC).

Case 1 – Answer:
The request for a preliminary ruling is admissible pursuant to Article 234(1)(a) of the TEC (Article III-369(1)(a) DC). The cross-border distribution of the magazine is protected by Article 28 of the TEC (Article III-153 DC). The Austrian provisions prohibiting the sale of the magazine bear on the actual content of the product and are not concerned, as applied to the facts of the case, with a selling arrangement within the meaning of the ECJ's judgment in *Keck and Mithouard*. They therefore constitute measures of equivalent effect within the meaning of Article 28 of the TEC and interfere with the free movement of goods. The restriction of a fundamental freedom through national legislation which applies without distinction to all products can be justified by an overriding public-interest objective. Maintenance of press diversity may constitute such an overriding requirement. On the other hand, restrictions of the fundamental freedoms must be "interpreted in the light of the general principles of law and in particular of fundamental rights". According to the ECJ, the Member States are therefore bound by the fundamental rights of the Union when imposing limits on the fundamental freedoms. Consequently, the prohibition's simultaneous interference with the freedom of expression as protected by Article 10 of the ECHR and recognised by Community law must also be justified. It is for the national court to determine whether these conditions are satisfied. In any event, an outright prohibition of the distribution would constitute a disproportionate interference with the free movement of goods, since the aim of maintaining press diversity could be attained by measures less restrictive, but equally effective – for example, a note that readers in Austria do not qualify for the chance to win a prize. On this basis, a blanket prohibition of the distribution of the magazine would violate both the guarantee of free movement of goods as well as the fundamental right of the Union protecting freedom of expression.

V. Territorial and Temporal Scope of the Fundamental Rights of the Union

Both the territorial and temporal scope of the fundamental rights of the Union are determined according to **general principles** (*cf* also → § 7 paras 48–49). Similar to the guarantees under the ECHR (→ § 2 para 35) the fundamental rights of the Union may have extraterritorial effect, since any entity bound by them must also adhere to their standards abroad. Where new states join the Union the fundamental rights apply – subject to any specific agreement to the contrary – from the date of accession. In the course of the accession of the ten new Member States which joined the Union on 1 May 2004 transition periods were stipulated for certain fundamental freedoms under the TEC (→ § 7 para 49). These transition periods, however, do not concern the application of the fundamental rights of the Union.

VI. Guarantees of / Interferences with the Fundamental Rights of the Union

Case 2 – Problem: (ECJ *Hoechst* [1989] ECR 2859)

38 *Hoechst* – a German chemical company – brought an action under Article 230(4) of the TEC (Article III-365(4) DC) for the annulment of a Commission decision which had ordered (as per Article 14 of Regulation 17/62 – the precursor of Article 20 of Regulation 1/2003) an official search on the premises of *Hoechst* due to suspected anti-competitive practices.

39 As it has been demonstrated in the preceding chapters with regard to the guarantees of the ECHR (→ § 2 para 38) and the fundamental freedoms of the TEC (→ § 7 para 50) a measure can be scrutinised against its consistency with the fundamental rights of the Union by assessing whether the situation in question falls within the scope of protection (para 42), whether there is an interference with a fundamental right of the Union (para 44) and whether this interference is justified (paras 45 ff).[116] Where a violation of equality, procedural or citizens' rights is in question a different pattern may be adequate.

1. Scope of Protection of the Fundamental Rights of the Union

40 As regards the unwritten fundamental rights of the Union the judgments of the ECJ often lack a precise description of the scope of protection (*ie* the protected sphere). Normally, the ECJ immediately turns to the assessment of justification instead.[117] In contrast, the ECJ often elaborates on the scope of protection in cases in which it uses the ECHR as a point of reference – as it is normally the case today where the ECHR contains relevant guarantees (paras 7–8). The **personal scope of protection** of the fundamental rights of the Union includes all beneficiaries (paras 29–30). An abusive exercise of the fundamental rights is not protected (Article 17 ECHR, *cf* also Article II-114 DC). The Charter of Fundamental Rights of the European Union explicitly defines the scope of protection of its guarantees. In addition, the explanations[118] that were drawn up as a way of providing guidance in the interpretation of the Charter shall be given due regard by the courts of the Union and of the Member States (Article II-112(7) DC).[119] Where national measures are scrutinised for consistency with EU law recourse to the fundamental rights of the Union is not necessary if the subject matter in question is covered by secondary Community law. However, the relevant act of secondary Community legislation itself has to be measured against the fundamental rights of the Union.

Case 2 – Answer:

41 There appear to be no objections to the admissibility of the action for annulment under Article 230(4) of the TEC (Article III-365(4) DC) that was brought by *Hoechst*. It is well founded if the Commission decision in question violates (substantive) Community law – either because the decision lacks any (valid) legal basis (1.) or because its legal basis was applied in breach of EC law in the individual case (2.). 1. The Commission decision under

---

116 Likewise Kühling (note 81) pp 583, 614 ff; Rengeling/Szczekalla (note 90) § 7, para 506.
117 See the appropriate criticism raised by Nettesheim [1995] EuZW 106, 106–107; Huber *Recht der Europäischen Integration* (2nd ed, Munich 2002) p 103.
118 *Cf* the explanations which have been prepared by the Bureau of the Convention responsible for drafting the Charter of Fundamental Rights, CONV 828/1/03 REV 1 (18/07/2003).
119 *Cf* more detailed Dorf [2005] JZ 126, 130.

consideration was based on Article 14 of Regulation 17/62 which, *inter alia*, vests the Commission with the power to undertake official searches. The ECJ did not scrutinise Article 14 of Regulation 17 against its consistency with the inviolability of the home. According to the Court, business premises are not protected by this fundamental right of the Union. However, such a narrow concept of the inviolability of the home appears to be highly questionable (see *eg* ECtHR *Niemietz* (1993) 16 EHRR 97: business premises are protected by Article 8 of the ECHR). Nevertheless, the ECJ recognises that it follows from the constitutional traditions common to the Member States that any intervention by the public authorities in the sphere of private activities of any person, whether natural or legal, must have a legal basis that offers protection against arbitrary or disproportionate intervention. This requirement amounts to the recognition of a general freedom of action. In the view of the Court, Regulation 17 is consistent with such a guarantee. 2. The Commission also applied Article 14 of Regulation 17 in accordance with the fundamental rights of the Union. Hence, the action for annulment was dismissed.

2. Interferences with the Fundamental Rights of the Union

It may be disputable whether or not there is a need for the development of a precise dogmatic structure that closely defines interferences with equality, procedural or citizens' rights. Such a dogmatic structure is, however, indispensable with regard to fundamental liberty rights. The ECJ did not develop anything alike so far. It seems that the Court – like the ECtHR (→ *cf* § 2 para 41) – assumes a broad concept of 'interference' which may even include indirect effects on the individual's sphere of liberty which emanate from governmental action.[120] Nonetheless, as it has been demonstrated with regard to the fundamental freedoms (→ *cf* § 7 para 74), there must be a **sufficient link** between the governmental measure in question and the harmful effects that are experienced. Moreover, it seems that indirect effects need to cross a qualified threshold of perceptibility. **Secondary Community law** amounts to an interference before being implemented in the Member States if the duty to implement affects the exercise of the fundamental rights of the Union. The beneficiaries, however, may not judicially enforce their rights in these cases before the act of secondary Community law has been implemented (unless it is directly applicable). The question on whether or not one can speak of interferences in cases where only one out of several prescribed options for implementation affects the fundamental rights of the Union has not been settled so far.[121]

42

3. Justification of Interferences with the Fundamental Rights of the Union

There are some fundamental rights of the Union – *eg* the right to petition (Article 21 TEC/Article I-10(2)(d) DC) – an interference with which is not justifiable at all. However, according to the case-law of the ECJ the fundamental rights of the Union are in principle **"not absolute"**.[122] A comparative view on the ECHR reveals that the vast majority of its guarantees is not absolute either – most of the rights guaranteed by the ECHR are subject to restrictions (→ *cf* § 2 para 43). The same applies to the Charter of Fundamental Rights

43

---

120 *Cf* ECJ *Bosphorus* [1996] ECR I-3953, paras 22–23.
121 On this issue see Kühling (note 81) pp 583, 615.
122 ECJ *Schräder* [1989] ECR 2237, para 15; *Wachauf* [1989] ECR 2609, para 18; *Kühn* [1992] ECR I-35, para 16; *Germany v Council* [1994] ECR I-4973, para 78.

of the European Union. Instead of defining justifiable restrictions for every single fundamental right, the Charter provides for a so-called horizontal provision for restriction (Article II-112 DC). It allows for limitations on the exercise of the rights and freedoms recognised by the Charter as long as these limitations do not go beyond what is permissible under the ECHR (Article II-112(3) DC)[123] or with respect to the constitutional traditions common to the Member States (Article II-112(4) DC).[124] Where an interference with the fundamental rights of the Union is generally permissible, all formal (para 46) and substantive (para 47) requirements have to be satisfied and the general limits to the restrictability of rights and freedoms (paras 48 ff) must be observed.

a) Requirement of a Legal Basis

44 In its decision in *Hoechst*, the ECJ stated that in all the legal systems of the Member States any intervention by public authorities in the sphere of private activities of any person, whether natural or legal, must have a "legal basis" and be justified on the "grounds laid down by law". According to the Court, the need for such protection must be recognised as a general principle of Community law.[125] Consequently, any interference with the fundamental rights of the Union must have a **legal basis**. This principle has also found recognition in the Charter of Fundamental Rights of the Union according to which any interference with fundamental rights must be provided for by law (Article II-112(1)(i) DC). There is still ambiguity as to what precisely qualifies as a legal basis.[126] Where the **Communities themselves** are interfering with the fundamental rights of the Union, all interferences must be explicitly provided for within a regulation or directive[127]. In the absence of such secondary Community law restrictions need to have a basis in the Treaty itself. A legal basis is also required for **interferences by the Member States**. With respect to the ECHR, the decision on what qualifies as a legal basis is – at least to a certain extent – left to the Member States. In common law jurisdictions even unwritten (judge-made) law may be sufficient (→ § 2 para 46). It seems – not beyond any doubt – that this is also true with

---

123 As per Article II-112(3) of the DC the "meaning and scope" of the rights guaranteed by the Charter shall be the same as those laid down by the ECHR insofar as the guarantees of the Charter correspond to rights guaranteed by the Convention. In this context 'meaning and scope' not only refers to the scope of protection but also to the restrictability of the rights guaranteed by the ECHR. *Cf* the explanations which have been prepared by the Bureau of the Convention responsible for drafting the Charter of Fundamental Rights, CONV 828/1/03 REV 1 (18/07/2003) p 49; see also Uerpmann-Wittzack [2005] DÖV 152, 155; Weiß [2005] ZEuS 323, 330–331; *contra* Philippi *Die Charta der Grundrechte der Europäischen Union* (Baden-Baden 2002) pp 43–44. Guarantees 'correspond' to each other if their substance is protected both by the Charter and the Convention.
124 Where applicable, interferences with a fundamental right may not be justifiable for other reasons: *eg* any restrictions on human dignity (Article II-61 DC) are contrary to the respect for the essence of a fundamental right (Article II-112(1)(i) DC).
125 ECJ *Hoechst* [1989] ECR 2859, para 19.
126 The same applies to the fundamental freedoms (→ § 7 para 82). More detailed Weber [2000] NJW 537, 543; Wunderlich *Das Grundrecht der Berufsfreiheit und europäisches Gemeinschaftsrecht* (Baden-Baden 2000) p 187. See also Müller-Michaels *Grundrechtlicher Eigentumsschutz in der Europäischen Union* (Berlin 1997) p 48.
127 Where a directive does not have direct effect the national implementing measures (not the directive itself) might qualify as a legal basis for interferences.

regard to Community law. Not only Acts of Parliament qualify as a legal basis; any abstract provision that has been enacted by a branch of government and which is not only binding on a specified group of addressees can suffice. However, in the interest of the rule of law provisions for the restriction of fundamental rights must have the force of law.[128] Furthermore, they have to be generally accessible as well as sufficiently clear and precise in its terms to enable citizens to foresee its consequences.[129] The standards which apply to interferences with fundamental rights under domestic law (*eg* the requirement of an Act of Parliament) may possibly also apply to interferences with the fundamental rights of the Union.

b) Pursuance of Legitimate Objectives

The fundamental rights of the Union may only be restricted for reasons that correspond to "objectives of **general interest** pursued by the Community"[130] and the Member States respectively, or to the need to protect the rights and freedoms of others (*cf* Article II-112(1)(ii) DC). Effective consumer protection[131] and the maintenance of an undistorted competition[132], *inter alia,* represent such legitimate objectives in the field of economic rights. Where the standards of the ECHR apply, all restrictions must pursue a purpose prescribed in the Convention (Article 18 ECHR).

45

c) General Limits to the Restrictability of the Fundamental Rights of the Union

All restrictions on the fundamental rights of the Union are themselves subject to limits – *ie* the **general limits to the restrictability** of fundamental rights. Such general limits are the essence of a fundamental right, the principle of proportionality, the fundamental freedoms of the TEC and all other relevant provisions of primary Community law.

46

aa) The Essence of a Fundamental Right

According to the case-law of the ECJ, interferences with the fundamental rights of the Union may not impair the **very essence of those rights**.[133] A similar limit has been included in the Charter of Fundamental Rights of the Union (Article II-112(1)(i) DC). There is still ambiguity about whether or not it merely protects the common and universal essence of a fundamental right (in contrast to the individual – *ie* personalised – and situational – *ie* varying from case to case – essence of a right). However, the existing case-law is mostly interpreted as protecting the common and universal essence of fundamental rights.[134] However, adherence to the essence of a fundamental right of the Union does not require more than the preservation of all basic guarantees which emanate from the right in question. Hence, it is no longer of great significance beside the principle of proportionality.

47

---

128 *Cf* ECtHR *Silver* (1983) 5 EHRR 347, para 86.
129 *Cf* ECtHR *Sunday Times* (1979–80) 2 EHRR 245, para 47.
130 *Cf* ECJ *Wachauf* [1989] ECR 2609, para 18; *Karlsson* [2000] ECR I-2737, para 45.
131 ECJ *Keller* [1986] ECR 2897, paras 14–15.
132 ECJ *Hoechst* [1989] ECR 2859, para 25.
133 *Cf* for example ECJ *Wachauf* [1989] ECR 2609, para 18.
134 *Cf* Rengeling/Szczekalla (note 90) § 7 paras 445 ff.

bb) The Principle of Proportionality

48 It is settled case-law of the ECJ that interferences with the fundamental rights must be proportional in order to be justified.[135] Interferences are proportional if they are **suitable**, **necessary** and **adequate** (proportional *stricto sensu*) means for attaining the desired (legitimate) objective. In its judgments the ECJ often does not elaborate on all three components of the proportionality test.[136] Most notably, a critical appraisal of the adequateness of interferences with the fundamental rights is often rare. Furthermore – because of recognising a broad margin of appreciation on the part of Community institutions and national authorities – the ECJ generally employs rather low standards with regard to the principle of proportionality.[137] The Court often does not go beyond identifying a legitimate objective and characterising the measure in question as not being manifestly inappropriate having regard to this objective.[138] It is indispensable, however, to scrutinise interferences with fundamental rights for their necessity and adequateness. In addition, it appears to be intolerable to confine judicial review to the identification of manifest errors. On the other hand, one can hardly object to the ECJ's attempts not to unduly limit the political and legislative discretion of the Community institutions (*cf* also → § 7 para 96).

49 Particularly with regard to the review of EC regulations or directives, the ECJ employs a 'low-key proportionality test'.[139] This can be demonstrated by considering as an example the first decision of the ECJ on Regulation 404/93 on the common organisation of the market in bananas.[140] The Regulation drastically reduced the import of bananas from third countries into the Community. This reduction might constitute an infringement of the right to property and the freedom to pursue a trade or business of traders in third-country bananas. The ECJ rejected the view that the new import regime interferes with the right to property, because economic operators cannot claim a right to property in a certain market share.[141] As regards the freedom to pursue a trade or business, the Court understood the Regulation to constitute a proportional interference because it corresponded to objectives of general interest[142] and because it was not manifestly inappropriate

---

135 *Eg* ECJ *Wachauf* [1989] ECR 2609, para 18; *Germany v Council* [1994] ECR I-4973, paras 90 ff. See also Article 5(3) of the TEC. *Cf* also Tridimas (note 4) pp 141–142 (on the development of the principle of proportionality within the case-law of the ECJ).
136 However, according to Schwarze [2005] NJW 3459, 3465, in recent years the ECJ has put more emphasis on the proportionality test.
137 *Cf* the criticism raised by Nettesheim [1995] EuZW 106, 106–107; Huber [1997] EuZW 517, 521; Stein [1998] EuZW 261, 262; Pache [2001] EuR 475, 488–489; von Danwitz [2003] EWS 393, 394 ff. *Contra* von Bogdandy [2001] JZ 157, 161 ff.
138 ECJ *Schräder* [1989] ECR 2237, paras 20 ff; *Fedesa* [1990] ECR I-4023, paras 13 ff.
139 See, however, ECJ *ABNA* [2006] 1 CMLR 48, paras 83 ff, where the Court held that Directive 2002/2/EC of 28 January 2002, [2002] OJ L63/23, went manifestly beyond what was necessary to attain its objective and was therefore partially invalid in the light of the principle of proportionality.
140 ECJ *Germany v Council* [1994] ECR I-4973, paras 90 ff.
141 ECJ *Germany v Council* [1994] ECR I-4973, para 79; *cf* also ECJ *T Port* [1996] ECR I-6065, para 43 (cases of hardship must be taken into consideration).
142 Keeping in mind, however, the non-conformity of the import regime to WTO obligations, this view appears to be questionable. *Cf* WTO-Panel *WT/DS27/RW/ECU – Recourse to Art 21. 5 by Ecuador*.

having regard to this objective (*ie* organisation of the agricultural market). The ECJ did not rule out the possibility that the objectives of the Regulation could have been achieved by less restrictive measures. However, it took the view that it could not substitute its assessment for that of the Council as to the appropriateness of the measures adopted by the Community legislature if those measures had not been proved to be manifestly inappropriate for achieving the objective pursued. According to the ECJ, the applicant did not show that the Council had carried out such a "**manifestly erroneous assessment**". Consequently, the complaints of a breach of the right to property, infringement of the freedom to pursue a trade or business and failure to comply with the principle of proportionality were rejected as unfounded.

cc) The Fundamental Freedoms of the TEC / other Provisions of Primary Community Law

By reason of the doctrine of **uniformity of the Community legal order** the fundamental rights of the Union may only be restricted in a manner which conforms to primary Community law – most notably to the fundamental freedoms of the TEC.

50

4. Schematic Summary

A measure should be scrutinised against its consistency with the fundamental rights of the Union according to the following checklist:

51

I. Establishing a fundamental right of the Union
   1. Written Community law
   2. Article 6(2) of the TEU
      a) ECHR
      b) Constitutional traditions common to the Member States
   3. In the future: Charter of Fundamental Rights of the European Union
II. Scope of protection of the fundamental rights of the Union
   1. Subject matter of protection
      a) No secondary Community law that regulates the subject matter in question exhaustively while being consistent with primary Community law (if national measures are to be scrutinised)
      b) The conduct in question is protected by a fundamental right
      c) All other requirements for the application of the fundamental rights are met (in cases involving equality, procedural or citizens' rights)
      d) No abusive exercise of fundamental rights
   2. Personal scope of protection
      Beneficiaries of / entities bound by the fundamental rights of the Union
   3. Territorial scope of protection
      Extraterritorial effects of the fundamental rights of the Union
   4. Temporal scope of protection
      Corresponds to the date of accession to the Union
III. Interference with the fundamental rights of the Union
   1. Direct / indirect impact on the fundamental rights
   2. Sufficient link and perceptibility
IV. Justification of the interference
   1. Requirement of a legal basis which authorises to interfere with a fundamental right

a) Secondary Community law
   b) Statutory basis in national law
2. Pursuance of legitimate objectives according to the provisions of the ECHR
3. Pursuance of legitimate objectives according to other mandatory provisions
4. General limits to the restrictability of the fundamental rights of the Union
   a) Observance of the essence of a fundamental right
   b) Observance of the principle of proportionality
   c) Observance of the fundamental freedoms of the TEC and of all other provisions of primary Community law

VII. Judicial Protection

1. Judicial Protection of the Individual

52 Pursuant to Article 46(d) of the TEU the ECJ is vested with the judicial power to ensure that the fundamental rights are observed by the EU and its institutions. As regards measures by the Member States (or by private individuals) the jurisdiction of the Court emanates from Article 220 of the TEC (Article I-29(1)(ii) DC). EU law does not provide for any special type of proceedings in human rights matters (*eg* a complaint of unconstitutionality). Measures of the EC institutions are therefore only subject to review within the scope of the regular types of proceedings that are recognised in Community law (if all admissibility requirements are satisfied). Where an individual alleges that a **Community measure** violates the fundamental rights of the Union an **action for annulment** under Article 230(4) of the TEC (Article III-365(6) DC) has to be considered. However, the admissibility of such an action requires the Community measure in question to be a decision addressed to the claimant or to be a decision which, although in the form of a regulation or a decision addressed to another person, is of direct and individual concern to the claimant. Should the Community, in infringement of the fundamental rights, fail to act (*eg* in case of a failure to grant governmental protection) an **action for wrongful failure to act** as per Article 232 of the TEC (Article III-367 DC) may be admissible. On the other hand, the Community legal order still lacks a direct action for annulment brought by a natural or legal person against Community measures of general application – *ie* regulations[143] (as well as an action for the adoption of such measures). There is also no action for performance and no action for a declaratory judgment that can be brought by natural or legal persons. These shortcomings appear to be intolerable: One can only speak of fundamental rights as subjective rights if the protected interests of the individual can be enforced in a court of law (→ § 20 para 36). As it has been demonstrated above, judicial enforcement before the courts of the Community is not possible where secondary Community law of general application (directly) violates a fundamental right of the Union. According to the ECJ, these gaps have to be filled by remedies under national law. Although the national courts cannot rule on the validity of secondary Community legislation, they may (and sometimes must) request the ECJ to give a preliminary ruling pursuant to Article 234 of the TEC (Article III-369 DC) if they consider the Community measure in question to violate primary Community law. Fortunately, a future improvement of the judicial protection against Community measures of general application is

---

143 ECJ *Unión de Pequeños Agricultores* [2002] ECR I-6677; *Jégo-Quéré* [2004] ECR I-3425.

already arranged for: According to Article III-365(4) of the DC, any natural or legal person may institute proceedings against regulatory acts which are of direct concern to him or her and which do not entail implementing measures. Hence, the difficult demonstration of 'individual concern' will be dispensable in the future.

If a natural or legal person alleges that **national measures** violate the fundamental rights of the Union, he or she has to seek judicial protection in the domestic courts of the Member States. According to the principles developed in *Costanzo*[144] not only administrative authorities but also national courts are under an obligation to refrain from applying provisions of national law which conflict with the fundamental rights of the Union. Such cases necessarily involve some interpretation of the fundamental rights of the Union. Accordingly, national courts against whose decisions there is no judicial remedy under national law have to request the ECJ to give a preliminary ruling thereon pursuant to Article 234(3) of the TEC (Article III-369(3) DC).

53

2. Judicial Protection of the Institutions of the EC and the Member States

Where secondary Community law is incompatible with the fundamental rights of the Union, the institutions of the EC as well as the Member States can bring an action for annulment under Article 230(2) of the TEC (Article III-365(2) DC). In addition, the Commission is able to enforce the observance of the fundamental rights of the Union by the Member States by opening an **infringement procedure** as per Article 226 of the TEC (Article III-360 DC). The Member States have the same opportunity under Article 227 of the TEC (Article III-361 DC) if they are of the view that another Member State has violated the fundamental rights of the Union.

54

VIII. Other Forms of Protection of Fundamental Rights in the EU

Apart from the protection of fundamental rights against interferences by the Communities or the Member States (when implementing, applying or limiting EC law), there are other forms and levels of protection of fundamental rights in the EU.[145] As it has been mentioned above, Article 6(2) of the TEU obliges the Union as a whole – not only the Communities – to respect fundamental rights (para 9). The Charter of Fundamental Rights of the Union is intended to take on this function in the future. Furthermore, the **principle of homogeneity** enshrined in Article 6(1) of the TEU (Article I-2 DC) and its procedural protection in Article 7 of the TEU (Article I-58–59 DC) provide a basis for an effective protection of fundamental rights within all Member States of the Union.[146] Finally, the character of the European Union as a community of values (Article 1 ff TEU/Article I-1 ff DC) allows to make basic demands concerning the respect for human rights before entering into cooperation within the course of **EU foreign policy** (*eg* by means of association agreements[147]).[148] In order to provide for appropriate structures and

55

---

144 ECJ *Costanzo* [1989] ECR 1839, paras 32–33.
145 As to the different standards *cf* von Bogdandy [2001] JZ 157, 162 ff, 170.
146 *Cf* Schorkopf *Homogenität in der Europäischen Union* (Berlin 2000) pp 92–93.
147 *Cf* more detailed Hoffmeister *Menschenrechts- und Demokratieklauseln in den vertraglichen Außenbeziehungen der Europäischen Gemeinschaft* (Berlin 1998).
148 *Cf* the corresponding objective as formulated in Article 11(1) of the TEU (Article III-292(1) DC).

adequate resource allocations allowing the thorough definition of EU policy in relation to the protection of fundamental rights, the European Council on 13 December 2003 agreed to build upon the existing European Monitoring Centre on Racism and Xenophobia (EUMC) and to extend its mandate to become a Human Rights Agency. On 15 February 2007, the Council adopted its corresponding "Regulation establishing a European Union Agency for Fundamental Rights".[149] According to this new Council Regulation the agency is an independent centre of expertise on fundamental rights issues through data collection, analysis and networking. It shall advise the Union institutions and the Member States on how best to prepare or implement fundamental rights related Union legislation. The agency became operational on 1 March 2007.

---

149 Council Regulation (EC) 168/2007, [2007] OJ L53/1.

§ 15
Human Dignity, Fundamental Rights of Personality and Communication

Frank Schorkopf

The protection of human dignity, of personality and of communication exemplifies the peculiarities of both the development and the differentiation of fundamental rights' protection in the European Community. Induced by the elaboration of the Charter of Fundamental Rights, the protection of human dignity, including within its thematic scope the right to freedom from injury,[1] has only recently entered Community law as a normative principle. The ECJ recognises the protection of personality in several independent guarantees. These include the right to privacy, which is formed especially by Article 8 of the ECHR, the freedom of movement and the freedom of association. The majority of literature also regards the freedom of religion as one of the fundamental rights of Community law that protect the personality in a wider sense. The ECJ acknowledges the protection of communication exclusively within the scope of the traditional right of freedom of expression and its applications. Thus, the Court examines the freedom of opinion in the context of the Community's law of public service and the regulation of business publicity. The plurality of the media and the freedom of information derive their significance with respect to fundamental rights from their inclusion in the system of restrictions of the fundamental freedoms.

The **development of the protection of fundamental rights** on Community level ensues according to the circumstances of the cases the ECJ has to adjudicate. Correspondingly, the scope of the fundamental rights' guarantee relates to these individual cases. The further development and differentiation of the Community's protection of fundamental rights requires appropriate cases relevant to fundamental rights. The ECJ has already had numerous opportunities to express its opinion regarding the guarantees of the protection of personality and communication. In doing so, it makes concrete references to the corresponding provisions of the ECHR and the jurisdiction practice of the ECtHR, which seems to prove the thesis that there is a concordance in the respective scopes of protection provided by both systems of fundamental rights. Nevertheless it remains difficult to describe the current standards of fundamental rights detached from the individual cases in a case-oriented legal system based on precedents, in which also deliberate deviation from Convention practice occurs.[2] Enhancing the status of the Charter of Fundamental Rights by transforming it into a legally binding catalogue of fundamental rights might put an end to this insecurity with regard to the scope of the guarantees in the fu-

---

1 Moreover, the prohibition of torture and slavery, which is included in Articles II-64, 65 DC, is to be added to the content of this guarantee. Due to the lack of jurisdictional practice and points of contact in Community Law, these rights are not further dealt with in this chapter.

2 Differences in the extent of the guarantees of fundamental rights do exist concerning the protection from self-incrimination, *cf* ECJ *Orkem* [1989] ECR 3283, paras 29 ff; *Limburgse Vinyl Maatschappij* [2002] ECR I-8375, paras 274 ff on the one hand and ECtHR *Funke* (1993) 16 EHRR 297; *Saunders* (1997) 23 EHRR 313; *G. B. v Switzerland* (2002) 34 EHRR 265 on the other hand; as well as for the inviolability of the home, *cf* paras 21 ff.

ture.[3] The illustration of the protection of human dignity, personality and communication – understood in an all embracing sense – following hereafter is based on existing case material and is presented with a classic fundamental right's examination in mind. The chapter concludes with an outlook on emerging fundamental rights' guarantees in the fields of asylum, immigration and judicial co-operation under the headline "Freedom and Security".

I. Dignity of Man

Leading Cases: ECJ *Netherlands v Parliament and Council* [2001] ECR I-7079; *Omega* [2004] ECR I-9609.

Further Reading: Ackermann *Case C-36/02, Omega Spielhallen- und Automatenaufstellungs-GmbH v Oberbürgermeisterin der Bundesstadt Bonn* (2005) 42 CMLRev 1107; Jones *"Common Constitutional Traditions": Can the Meaning of Human Dignity under German Law Guide the European Court of Justice?* [2004] Public Law 167; Rau/Schorkopf *Der EuGH und die Menschenwürde* [2002] NJW 2448; Frahm/Gebauer *Patent auf Leben? – Der Luxemburger Gerichtshof und die Biopatent-Richtlinie* [2002] EuR 78.

1. Scope of Protection

a) Human Dignity

Case 1 – Problem: (ECJ *Netherlands v Parliament and Council* [2001] ECR I-7079)

3 The European Parliament and the Council issue a directive which obliges the Member States to protect biotechnological inventions under their national patent law. In particular, the directive lays down which elements of inventions that can be composed of plants, animals or the human body are patentable and which are not. It obliges the Member States to provide for the patentability of commercially applicable inventions for the production, treatment or use of biological material under certain conditions.
The Netherlands argue that this obligation to issue patents on animals, plants or human biological material violates Community law. They therefore ask the ECJ to declare the legally relevant act void. In their submission the Netherlands stipulate among other things that the directive infringes the dignity of man and the fundamental right of freedom from injury. They argue that the human body is the bearer of human dignity. They add that issuing patents for isolated living parts of the human body reduces them to mere objects. Furthermore, they raise concerns that the directive does not contain any provisions to ensure the uninfluenced consent of donor and recipient of the human material (*cf* Directive 98/44/EC).

4 Human dignity is the implied point of reference in the jurisdiction concerning the protection of fundamental rights on Community level. Nevertheless, until recently, the dignity of man hardly played an explicit role as an independent object of protection in the decisions of the Court of Justice. The landmark decision in the *Stauder* case is exemplary in this respect. In the initial proceedings the claimant argued that the concept of the purchase right for butter at a reduced price for recipients of public welfare infringes human dignity.[4] While the ECJ did not mention the concept of human dignity explicitly in the grounds for its decision, the Court made references to the "fundamental rights of the per-

---

3 → § 19 para 6.
4 ECJ *Stauder* [1969] ECR 419, 421.

son" and concluded that the purchase right did not require the name of the party entitled to be given.

In subsequent years the ECJ mentioned the dignity of man almost exclusively in connection with the **free movement of employees** and **Regulation 1612/68**. Its fifth recital reads: "Whereas the right of freedom of movement, in order that it may be exercised, by objective standards, in freedom and dignity, requires that equality of treatment shall be ensured in fact and in law in respect of all matters relating to the actual pursuit of activities as employed persons and to eligibility for housing."[5]

According to the continuing case law of the Court of Justice, Regulation 1612/68 is meant to safeguard the free movement of employees. The exercise of this right "in freedom and dignity" requires that the receiving state provides the best possible conditions for the integration of the employee's family.[6] To that end all obstacles for the mobility of employees are to be removed, particularly with regard to the right of the employee to let his family join him as well as to the conditions for the integration of his family in the receiving state. Therefore the employee and his family members are entitled to the same social privileges as nationals of the receiving state.

The concept of human dignity has hardly been mentioned in the Community's rules – apart from Regulation 1612/68 and Article 12 of the TV Without Frontiers Directive[7] ("Television advertising shall not prejudice respect for human dignity"). This might be attributed to the fact that the concept of human dignity is not known to the legal systems of all Member States as a *legal* principle. Since it had already found its manifest expression on Community level in the already acknowledged fundamental rights of freedom from injury and respect for privacy, formally acknowledging it as a fundamental right – or at least as a *legal* principle – it seemed to promise little more scientific insight. This conception has fundamentally changed, however, with the ECJ's decision in the case *Netherlands v Parliament and Council*.[8] In the grounds of this decision it says: "It is for the Court of Justice, in its review of the compatibility of acts of the institutions with the general principles of Community law, to ensure that the fundamental right to human dignity and integrity is observed."

The ECJ classifies both legal provisions as **general rules of Community law**.[9] Certainly a connection can also be drawn to the Charter, Article 1 of which reads (Article II-61 DC): "Human dignity is inviolable. It must be respected and protected". The Court has further developed these principles in the *Omega* case. In this preliminary ruling procedure from Germany, the Court had to answer the question whether national courts may refer to the findings of their own constitutional law to take measures which may contribute to the protection of public order in the respective Member States, but which interfere with fundamental freedoms at the same time. The original proceedings was based on an order of

---

5 Reg 1612/68.
6 ECJ *Di Leo* [1990] ECR I-4185, para 13; *Kaba* [2000] ECR I-2623, para 20.
7 Dir 89/552/EEC.
8 ECJ *Netherlands v Parliament and Council* [2001] ECR I-7079, para 70.
9 This differentiation between "compliance with the dignity of man" and the "fundamental freedom from injury" establishes no dogmatic difference. Rather, translations of the decision into other languages, especially the Dutch language of proceedings, show that the Court classifies the dignity of man as a fundamental right. Thus, expressly referring to Rau/Schorkopf [2002] NJW 2448 and to the differentiation in the German version, the AG Stix-Hackl in her opinion *Omega* [2004] ECR I-9609, para 90.

the city of Bonn which prohibited feigned acts of killing during a game because this business idea interfered with the public order, which includes the concept of the human dignity. In her opinion concerning the *Omega* case, Advocate General *Stix-Hackl* suggested to judge the relevant national measure on the basis of Community law on the one hand and, on the other hand, to interpret the Member State's ground of justification – the public order – according to the meaning and the consequence of human dignity in the Community's legal system.[10] The Court of Justice adopted this idea in its concise ruling and considered the interference with the free exchange of services caused by the forbidding disposition to be justified. It ruled that the scope of the notion of public order is not to be unilaterally determined by each Member State. Nevertheless the Member States have a margin of appreciation with regard to the specific circumstances in which they can refer to public order in a permissible way. According to the ECJ, the Community's legal system is undeniably aimed to guarantee the human dignity as a general legal principle; however, the national measure does not necessarily have to comply with a common opinion shared by all Member States on how to protect the fundamental right or legitimate interest in question.[11]

b) Freedom from Injury

9   The right to freedom from injury comprises **physical and mental integrity**.[12] In practice, a number of cases relevant to fundamental rights concern proceedings by civil servants of the Community claiming compensation for damages resulting from accidents during service.[13] In this context, jurisdiction has granted compensation for **immaterial damages** caused by actions of Community institutions.[14] Within the realms of medicine and biology, the scope of protection covers the right of a donor or recipient of human body parts to reach an uninfluenced decision while having comprehensive knowledge of the facts.[15]

10   The fundamental right to freedom from injury is not explicitly mentioned in the decision concerning the *Cowan* case.[16] However, since the ECJ declared the conduct of a Member State violating this fundamental right to be incompatible with Community law, this decision is nevertheless relevant for the issue at hand. The case concerned the legitimacy of discriminations relating to the granting of restitutions for victims of bodily harm. According to the ECJ, it is a necessary consequence of the freedom of movement granted by Community law that the life and limb of a person who resides in a Member State is protected in the same way as that of own nationals and the persons residing in this Member State. This entails a **prohibition of discrimination** towards the recipients of services as far as the protection from violence and the right to a victim's compensation laid down in national law is concerned.[17]

---

10 Opinion AG Stix-Hackl *Omega* [2004] ECR I-9609, paras 67 ff.
11 ECJ *Omega* [2004] ECR I-9609.
12 *Cf* Art II-63 DC.
13 ECJ *Lucaccioni* [1999] ECR I-5251; *Royale Belge SA* [1996] ECR I-5501; *Jänsch* [1987] ECR 4923; *Colmant* [1992] ECR II-469.
14 ECJ *Culin* [1990] ECR I-225, para 26.
15 ECJ *Netherlands v Parliament and Council* [2001] ECR I-7079, para 78.
16 ECJ *Cowan* [1989] ECR 195.
17 ECJ *Cowan* [1989] ECR 195, para 17; *cf* the Green Book of the Commission: Compensation for victims of offences, COM 2001, 536 final. The question of compensation is as well dealt with in

2. Interference

The dignity of man and the guarantees closely related to it are guaranteed both against interferences of Community institutions as well as against actions of the Member States. "Where a Member State relies on the provisions of the Treaty in order to justify national rules which are likely to obstruct the exercise of a freedom guaranteed by the Treaty, such justification, provided for by Community law, is to be interpreted in the light of the general principles of law and in particular of fundamental rights."[18]

The ECJ is not in charge of the investigation of an action relevant to fundamental rights if the subject of the investigation is a national rule which does not lie within the scope of Community law. However, from time to time the Court interprets this principle in a very strict manner and assumes its competence to jurisdiction in cases in which a connection of the facts of the case to Community law is untraceable for the spectator.[19]

3. Justification

The dignity of man in principle cannot be restricted, which means that any interference leads to a violation of this right.[20]

This "automatic" consequence results in delicate problems in preliminary rulings, because the legal investigation according to Community law has to distinguish between the different subjects of the cases and thus introduces a possibility for differentiation: If an act of the EC institutions violates the dignity of man, the action in question will be void. On the contrary, if a Member States' act is scrutinised with respect to the dignity of man, for example within the procedure for a preliminary ruling, such a clear-cut solution on the basis of the categories "valid or void" would unify the substance of the fundamental right in the whole European Union. This does not apply to the ethical core of the right but for its "ordinary meaning" in legal day-to-day life.

This problem was mirrored in the case *Omega*.[21] From the point of view of German authorities and courts, the planned commercial concept violates the dignity of man; in the United Kingdom, by contrast, at the time of the prohibition the shooting-game was not only proved in practice, but also ready to be exported by franchise contracts and patented technology. How can a contradiction in the evaluation of a case's substance be avoided if – on the one hand – the German prohibition is in accordance with Community law and – on the other hand – the same commercial concept, being "inimical to the dignity of man", is successfully practised in the United Kingdom at the same time? Would not a guarantee of the dignity of man by Community law have to provide the same protection in all Member States? To solve this problem, the Advocate General suggested taking the content of

---

the European Convention on the Compensation of Victims of Violent Crime of 24 November 1983, ETS No 116, in force as from 1 February 1988.

18 ECJ *Commission v Germany* [1992] ECR I-2575, para 23 referring to *ERT* [1991] ECR I-2925, para 43.
19 *Cf* ECJ *Carpenter* [2002] ECR I-6279 and *Austrian Broadcasting* [2003] ECR I-4989; *cf* more detailed paras 39 ff.
20 In spite of the provision for restriction in Article II-112 DC covering all rights and freedoms without any difference – and thus Article II-61 DC as well – the constructive emphasis on the dignity of man will remain – based on an appropriate interpretation – even after the entry into force of the Charter.
21 *Cf* para 8.

the guarantee of human dignity into consideration while applying the fundamental freedom at issue and the proportionality test.[22] By this approach, the relation between purpose and means is changed so substantially in favour of the dignity of man, that the limiting measures of the respective Member State will scarcely ever be disproportional. However, the unifying feature of this legal construction remains, just as the fact that a commercial concept can violate the dignity of man in one Member State and be successful in the market of another. It is therefore preferable to reduce the competence to scrutinise in Community law to an **abuse control** in the rare cases of a collision of the right for protection of human dignity and a fundamental freedom, and to concede a place in the *Community* law system to those features of a legal system which foster national identity (Article 6(3) TEU, Article I-5(1) DC).

Case 1 – Answer:

16 Concerning the Dutch invalidity suit following Article 230 of the TEC (Article III-365 DC), it is the ECJ's responsibility to secure control over the compliance of actions of the EC institutions with the general principles of Community law, such as to provide for the observance of the dignity of man and of the fundamental right to freedom from injury.
The observance of the dignity of man is generally secured by the provision in the directive determining that the human body in its separate phases of formation and development cannot be a patentable invention (Article 5(1) Dir). Parts of the human body as such are not patentable and their discovery cannot be protected. Only inventions which connect a natural part with a technical procedure enabling the isolation or reproduction of this part with regard to a commercial application can be the subject of a patent application. The result of work with sequences or parts of sequences of human genes can only lead to the granting of a patent if the application comprises a description of the new method of sequencing which led to the invention on the one hand, and of the intended commercial application on the other hand. Without such a commercial application, the work would not qualify as an invention, but as a mere discovery of a DNA-sequence, which is not patentable on its own. The directive thus only protects the result of a scientifically or technically inventive occupation. Biological data naturally occurring in the human body are only covered as far as they are necessary to carry out and make use of a particular commercial application. Finally, procedures to clone human beings, to change the genetic identity of a human being's germline and to use human embryos for industrial or commercial purposes are excluded from patentability as a violation of public order and public moral (Article 6 Dir). The directive thus conceptualises the patent right referring to living matter of human origin very narrowly in order to make sure that the human body really remains unavailable and inalienable and that human dignity is secured.
The fundamental right to freedom from injury cannot be invoked against a directive that only deals with the granting of patents and whose scope of applicability therefore does not cover events before and after the issue of a patent – be it research or the use of the patented products. Legal restrictions or interdictions that apply to the development or exploitation of patentable products are not affected by the issue of a patent (14th recital). The directive is not meant to replace restrictive provisions that are supposed to guarantee the respect for certain ethic standards beyond its scope of applicability. This includes the right of human beings to dispose over their bodies by consent while having full knowledge of the facts.
The question whether the right to freedom from injury, which in the scope of medicine and biology implies the uninfluenced consent of donor and recipient of parts of human origin

---

22 *Cf* opinion AG Stix-Hackl, ECJ *Omega* [2004] ECR I-9609, paras 103 ff.

in full knowledge of all circumstances, is generally raised in connection with the use of human parts, *eg* transplants. Therefore, solutions to the problems accompanying this are not to be searched for in the patent right of a special sector.

II. Protection of the Personality

Leading Cases: ECJ *Austrian Broadcasting* [2003] ECR I-4989; *Bosman* [1995] ECR I-4921; *X v Commission* [1994] ECR I-4737; *Commission v Germany* [1992] ECR I-2575; *Elliniki Radiophonia Tileorassi (ERT)* [1991] ECR I-2925; *Hoechst* [1989] ECR I-2859; *Dow Chemical* [1989] ECR 3137; *Cowan* [1989] ECR 195; *National Panasonic* [1980] ECR 2033; *AM & S* [1982] ECR 1575; *Commission v Germany* [1989] ECR 1263; *Prais* [1976] ECR 1589; *Stauder* [1969] ECR 419.

Further Reading: Ruffert *Die künftige Rolle des EuGH im europäischen Grundrechtsschutzsystem* [2004] EuGRZ 466; Spaventa *From Gebhard to Carpenter* (2004) 41 CMLR 743; Siemen *Grundrechtsschutz durch Richtlinien / Die Fälle Österreichischer Rundfunk ua und Lindqvist* [2004] EuR 306.

Legal Instruments: Directive 95/46 on the protection of individuals with regard to the processing of personal data and on the free movement of such data, [1995] OJ L281/31; Regulation 45/2001 on the protection of individuals with regard to the processing of personal data by the Community institutions and bodies and on the free movement of such data, [2001] OJ L8/1; Directive 2002/58 concerning the processing of personal data and the protection of privacy in the electronic communications sector (Directive on privacy and electronic communications), [2002] OJ L201/37.

1. Scope of Protection

a) Respect for the Private Life

Case 2 – Problem: *X v Commission* CFI [1992] ECR II-2195 and ECJ [1994] ECR I-4737
X has been admitted to a selection process for typists of the Commission. In spite of the fact that he had not passed the written examination, the Direction General for Personnel and Administration called upon him to undergo a medical examination with regard to a possible employment as a temporary public servant for a period of six months. X was subsequently examined by the medical examiner of the Commission. Clinical and lab examinations were conducted; however, X rejected the suggestion to undertake an HIV-test.
The medical examiner later informed X that he was not going to recommend his employment from a medical point of view. At the same time, he asked X to give him the name of his doctor in charge in order to inform him about the ascertained results. The Direction General for Personnel and Administration of the Commission then informed X that they had decided against employing him because he was not physically suitable. The evaluation of the medical results by X's doctor in charge shows that the medical examiner of the Commission had diagnosed an opportunistic infection, which indicates the last stage of AIDS ("full blown AIDS").
Further examinations within the administration proved that while X had not been subject to a concealed AIDS-test, a lab examination had been conducted to determine the lymphocytes T4/T8. This kind of examination is performed to judge the state of the immune system of the patient, not especially to find out about a viral or bacterial illness. Nevertheless, the test may substantiate the suspicion of an AIDS-infection. The action against the decision of the Commission connected with the motion of restitution of immaterial damages before the European Court of First Instance has not been successful. X appealed to the ECJ against this decision.

17

18 The **right to privacy** is the fundamental right with the greatest practical significance in connection to the protection of personality.[23] The ECJ derives the fundamental right from the common constitutional tradition of the Member States and explicitly refers to Article 8 of the ECHR.

19 The **special function** of Article 8 of the ECHR is particularly displayed in the subdivision of the scope of protection into different aspects of the guarantee of this fundamental right. The ECJ has explicitly named the right of protection of the confidentiality of medical information as an aspect of the right to privacy.[24] According to the system of the common European protection of fundamental rights, more aspects that lie within the realms of the right for the respect for private life can be identified. Among these are: Inviolability of the home[25], the confidentiality of lawyer's correspondence[26], the respect for family life[27] and the right to observance of secrecy concerning the state of health[28]. From a systematic point of view, the right to protection of personal data is also a feature of the respect for private life. The ECJ has not explicitly acknowledged an independent right of informational self-determination up to now. However, the law creating activities of the Community and the additions to primary law justify dealing with this right as an independent fundamental right here.[29]

20 By contrast, there is no such thing as a **general right of personality** on Community level. The ECJ uses a different terminology in its case-law, which is based on the system of the ECHR.

aa) Inviolability of the Home

21 The ECJ has acknowledged a fundamental right of inviolability of the home. The scope of protection covers **private residences** of individuals; however, the Court of Justice explicitly refuses to extend the scope of protection to companies.[30] This restriction is remarkable because the topic of the protection of business premises shows precisely that relation to commercial law whose frequent absence renders the development of a comprehensive catalogue of fundamental rights of the Community more difficult.[31]

22 The Court of Justice substantiates its opinion by pointing out that the legal systems of the Member States differ considerably regarding the manner and extent of the protection of business premises. An extension of the fundamental right to business premises can also not be derived from Article 8 ECHR. The scope of protection of this article only covers the "claim to respect for one's private and family life, for his home and for his correspond-

---

23 *Cf* ECJ *Commission v Germany* [1992] ECR I-2575, para 23 referring to ECJ *National Panasonic* [1980] ECR 2033; *X v Commission* [1994] ECR I-4737, para 17; *A v Commission* [1994] ECR II-179, para 48.
24 ECJ *Commission v Germany* [1992] ECR I-2575, para 23.
25 ECJ *Hoechst* [1989] ECR 2859; *Dow Chemical* [1989] ECR 3137 and 3165; *Roquette frères* [2002] ECR I-9011, paras 27 ff.
26 ECJ *AM & S* [1982] ECR 1575.
27 ECJ *Commission v Germany* [1989] ECR 1263.
28 ECJ *X v Commission* [1994] ECR I-4737.
29 *Cf* more detailed para 40.
30 ECJ *Hoechst* [1989] ECR 2859; *Dow Chemical* [1989] ECR 3137 and 3165.
31 *Cf* para 2 above.

ence," and only serves for the free development of one's personality. Furthermore, there is no pertinent jurisdiction of the ECtHR concerning this problem.[32]

This jurisdiction of the ECJ has been exposed to marked **criticism**. From a methodical point of view, the reference to "considerable differences" renders it impossible for the Member States' legal systems to extend the range of the guarantee of a Community's fundamental right by comparing and evaluating laws. In principal, this attempt of the ECJ results in determining the scope of the guarantee of a Community fundamental right according to a minimal standard.[33] Furthermore, some decisions of the ECtHR concerning Article 8 of the ECHR include business premises in the scope of this fundamental right. In the case *Chappell*, premises serving as private dwellings as well as business premises to the appellant had been searched by authorities. In this case, the Commission for Human Rights left open whether these business premises were covered by the term "dwelling".[34] Whereas the ECtHR included the premises of a lawyer's office into the scope of protection of Article 8 of the ECHR in the case *Niemitz*,[35] it explicitly stated in its recent decision in the case *Société Colas Est* that the scope of protection of Article 8 of the ECHR may as well cover business premises, business establishments and other company premises under certain circumstances.[36]

23

The grounds in both of the landmark cases of the ECJ concerning the fundamental right of the inviolability of the home do not contain any explicit statement concerning the requirements for a **justification** of an interference with the fundamental right. As the claimants were companies whose business premises had been searched, the scope of protection of the fundamental right was not even touched. However, the ECJ explicitly referred to the restrictions on Article 8(2) of the ECHR in another decision dealing with the interference with the extent of the guarantee of Article 8 of the ECHR.[37] Taking into consideration that this reference to possible restrictions of the fundamental rights of the Convention corresponds to a continuous holding of the Court of Justice, the decision in the case *National Panasonic* can be abstracted from the individual case and be generalised. In the administrative proceeding, which was the subject of the Court's scrutiny, the Commission had issued its decision based on Article 17 of the Regulation 17/62 – the First Antitrust Council Regulation.

24

According to this decision, an interference with the fundamental right of the inviolability of the home is justified if it has a **basis in law** on the one hand and if it represents a measure **necessary** for a democratic society on the other hand. This last requirement is qualified by the enumeration of admissible aims in Article 8(2) of the ECHR, whereby the interference needs to be "necessary for the national security, the public peace and order, the commercial welfare of the country, the defence of the public order and to prevent criminal offences, to protect health and morals or to protect the rights and freedoms of others".

25

---

32 ECJ *Dow Chemical* [1989] ECR 3137, paras 28 ff; *National Panasonic* [1980] ECR 2033, paras 19 ff.
33 *Cf* the criticism in Rengeling *Grundrechtsschutz in der Europäischen Gemeinschaft* (Munich 1993) p 121; but *cf* as well Everling [1990] EuR 195, 208.
34 ECtHR *Chappell* (1990) 12 EHRR 1 – *cf* as well the reference in Ress/Ukrow [1990] EuZW 499, 504, footnote 51 that the ECJ was in possession of the report of the Commission for Human Rights by the time of the court hearing in the Hoechst case.
35 ECtHR [1993] EuGRZ 65, 66.
36 ECtHR *Société Colas Est* (2004) 39 EHRR 373, paras 40–41.
37 ECJ *National Panasonic* [1980] ECR 2033, para 19.

26   Consequently, in the process of justifying an interference, the requirements of a statutory basis and the principle of **proportionality** are to be scrutinised. In spite of rejecting to include business premises in the scope of protection in the leading cases dealing with the fundamental right of inviolability of the home, the ECJ acknowledges a "protection against arbitrary and disproportional interferences" as a general principle of Community law. Ultimately, also these cases were scrutinized as to whether the measures of the Commission had a legal basis and whether they were in accordance with the principle of proportionality. Although the claimants were guaranteed a comparable level of protection, in the end it has to be stated that the protection of business premises nevertheless does not have a fundamental rights' foundation.

27   The **Rules for Antitrust Proceedings** (Council Regulation No 1/2003)[38] amended in 2003 refer to this fundamental rights' standard and aim to concretise it. Article 20 of this regulation (EC) 1/2003 authorises the Commission to fulfil its task to watch over the observance of the rules of competition in the Common Market and to carry out all necessary checks concerning enterprises and associations of enterprises. The employees of the Commission have the power (i) to enter all premises, real estate and means of transport, (ii) to check the accounts and all other business records, (iii) to make copies or extracts out of these, (iv) to put business premises and accounts or records under seal and (v) to demand oral declarations on the spot.

28   Hence the Commission has extensive powers of entry to collect evidence concerning possible violations of Community competition law. The Rules for Antitrust Proceedings therefore comprise numerous guidelines and procedural rules – for example the requirement of a judicial decree for the search (Article 21(3)) and a right to be heard (Article 27) – to guarantee the rights of the persons concerned.

29   Thus the Commission is obliged to name subject and purpose of the investigation to enable the company concerned to realise the extent of its duties to co-operate and, at the same time, to preserve their defence rights. The conditions for the Commission to exercise its powers of examination further depend on the procedure chosen, the attitude of the enterprise concerned and the participation of the national authorities.

30   Where the enterprises concerned take part in the examination, the employees of the Commission are authorised, inter alia, to see the records they asked for, enter the rooms they named and look at the content of the furniture. By contrast, they cannot violently get access to rooms or furnishings or force the employees of the enterprise to grant them access. Searches cannot be conducted without the consent of the responsible persons of the enterprise.

31   According to Article 17(6) Council Regulation No 1/2003, the Commission's civil servants are allowed to search for all sources of information necessary for the investigation even without the co-operation of the enterprise concerned, if the enterprise refuses to comply with the investigation. For this purpose, the national authorities are to be called in to grant the Commission the support necessary to fulfil its task. This support is stipulated for cases in which the enterprise explicitly refuses to comply, but it can also be demanded in advance. In this respect, it is the responsibility of each Member State to formulate conditions under which the national authorities have to grant the Commission support. The

---

38 These investigatory powers of the Commission apply as well for the merger control proceedings, Regulation (EC) 139/2004.

provisions for the proceedings which are suitable for the guarantee of the rights of the enterprises are determined according to the rules of national law, *ie* the Commission has to observe the procedural guarantees provided for in national law. However, according to the conception of Community law, the national authorities and courts (!) are not authorised to assess the necessity of the required investigation by the Commission and to ask for conveyance of the information contained in the Commission files in order not to endanger the investigation prerogative of the Commission and – this is to be suspected – to prevent the national authorities and courts from working together collusively. In this respect, the considerations of the Commission concerning factual and legal issues are only subject to a control of legitimacy by the ECJ (Article 20(8), 21(3) subparagraph 2 of the Council Regulation No 1/2003). After ascertaining the authenticity of the investigation decision, the national agencies are allowed to check whether the intended coercive measures are arbitrary or disproportional. The legal basis for investigative measures in rooms other than business premises, especially in private premises, modifies the elements of the provision – at least according to the wording – to the effect that a search warrant can only be executed after the approval of a Member States' court (Article 21(3) of the Council Regulation No 1/2003).

The **Charter of Fundamental Rights** guarantees the inviolability of the home in Article 7 (Article II-67 DC). The provision is modelled after Article 8 of the ECHR so that the rights guaranteed in Article 7 have the same meaning and importance as the rights in the ECHR do.[39] The remaining uncertainty with regard to the extent of the scope of protection is therefore not removed by the Charter.

32

bb) Protection of the Confidentiality of Lawyer's Correspondence

The ECJ developed the **principle of the confidentiality of the correspondence between lawyer and client** in connection with an administrative process of the Commission according to the Antitrust Regulation.[40] This principle, which the ECJ derived from a comparison between the legal provisions of the Member States, can be invoked when the correspondence takes place within the scope and interest of the right of defence of the client and if it comes from lawyers who are not bound to their client by a general contract for services.[41] The question whether this protection is to be extended to the correspondence between the top management of the enterprise and its legal department remains unsolved.

33

The decision of the ECJ does not contain a more extensive reference to fundamental rights. The **correspondence** is covered by the scope of protection of Article II-67 of the DC which is modelled after Article 8 of the ECHR. The term "correspondence" used there has been replaced with "communication" due to new developments in technology.

34

---

39 *Cf* Art II-112(3) DC.
40 ECJ *AM & S* [1982] ECR 1575; for the development and ratio of the decision see Temple Lang in: Hoskins/Robinson (eds) *A True European: Essays for Judge David Edward* (Oxford 2004) p 153.
41 ECJ *AM & S* [1982] ECR 1575, headnote 3 and para 21; CFI *Hilti* [1990] ECR II-163, para 13.

cc) Protection of the Confidentiality of Medical Information[42]

Case 2 – Answer:
35   Before he is employed, a temporary public servant is examined by a medical examiner of the Community institution according to Article 13 of the Conditions of Employment in order for the appointing authority to make sure that the applicant fulfils the qualifications for admission. The Conditions of Employment (Article 12(2)(d)) demand that someone can only be employed as a temporary public servant if he or she possesses the necessary physical fitness to exercise the official function.
The employment examination serves a legitimate interest of the Community organs: They have to be able to fulfil their tasks. But this interest does not justify examining the person concerned against his or her will. If the person concerned, after being informed, refuses to give his or her consent to an examination which is necessary to assess the physical fitness according to the medical examiner, the Community organs are not obliged to run the risk of employing him or her. However, according to the ECJ, the right to privacy requires to fully bear in mind the refusal of the person concerned. As X has explicitly refused to undergo an AIDS-test, this right was contrary to the administration making any test which was likely to ascertain this illness – the discovery of which X had rejected. The lymphocytes test in question was clue enough to enable the medical examiner to infer X's possible infection with the AIDS-virus from it.
The ECJ therefore overturned the challenged decision. As the case was ripe for judgement in the sense of Article 54(1) of the by-laws of the Court of Justice, the negative decision which had been communicated to X by the General Director for Personnel and Administration was overturned as well.

dd) Respect for Family Life

36   The right to the **respect for family life** is also part of the acknowledged fundamental rights of Community law. The ECJ has developed this fundamental right from the corresponding guarantee in Article 8 of the ECHR in connection with the right of abode of family members within the framework of the free movement of employees.[43] The facts forming the basis of the leading case concerned Article 10(3) of Regulation No 1612/68[44], which makes the right of abode of family members conditional on the fact that the employee has a dwelling which meets the regular requirements applying to native employees in the area he is employed. This regulation was contrary to a German provision which demanded that the families live in appropriate housing conditions for the whole duration of their stay, not only at the time of moving into the dwelling, to issue a residence permit for family members of migrant workers. According to the Court of Justice, Germany had violated its obligations resulting from the regulation. In the meantime, the fundamental right of the respect for family life has come to play a significant role concerning the interpretation of the fundamental freedoms and the law derived from them. The *Carpenter* case is – just as the quoted leading case – an example of this as it dealt with the Community law compatibility of the expulsion of the Philippine wife of a British national who rendered cross-frontier services.[45] The Court concluded in its preliminary ruling that Article 49 of the

---

42 *Cf* para 17 above.
43 ECJ *Commission v Germany* [1989] ECR 1263; *cf* the review of Watson [1989] ELRev 417 ff.
44 Reg (EEC) 1612/68.
45 ECJ *Carpenter* [2002] ECR I-6279, para 41.

TEC (Article III-144 DC) was to be interpreted in light of the fundamental right of the respect for family life. Therefore, as a matter of principle, the spouse of a person rendering services must not be expelled from the Member State of origin. The Court considers the refusal of entry into or the removal of a foreigner from the country that his close relatives live in to be an interference with the right of the respect for family life.[46]

In the literature discussing the protection of fundamental rights, it is predominantly held that the **protection of matrimony**, too, is acknowledged as a fundamental right of Community law.[47] The decision of the ECJ in the case *Grant*,[48] which is quoted in this context, contains an indirect definition of the term matrimony (life-time relationship between two persons of opposite sex).[49] However, the ECJ has acknowledged neither matrimony, nor "long-term relationships between persons of the same sex", nor "long-term relationships between persons of the opposite sex" as a fundamental right in the Union. The decision in the case *Eyüp*, which dealt with the family member status of the partner of a Turkish national entitled to association, remains an exception regarding the requirements of equity (ex aequo et bono).[50] With this case, the Court did not, however, acknowledge the equality of a long-term relationship between persons who are not married and matrimony.[51] The problems dealt with in this context also belong to the scope of application of the prohibition of discrimination on grounds of sex.[52]

37

The **Charter of Fundamental Rights** contains the right to get married and to start a family in Article 9 (Article II-69 DC), while Article 7 (Article II-67 DC) protects the right of respect for family life. Both rights are modelled after the guarantees in Article 12 and 7 of the ECHR.[53]

38

ee) Protection of Personal Data

Case 3 – Problem: (ECJ *Austrian Broadcasting Corporation* [2003] ECR I-4989)
Mrs N and Mr L, both of them top employees of the Austrian public broadcasting corporation (ORF), turned to Austrian courts to forbid their employer to convey data concerning their income to the Court of Auditors. According to Austrian law, the legal entities that are

39

---

46 ECJ *Orfanopoulos and Olivieri* [2004] ECR I-5257, para 97; *Akrich* [2003] ECR I-9607, paras 58 ff.
47 *Cf* Stumpf in: Schwarze (ed) *EU-Kommentar* (Baden-Baden 2000) Art 6 EUV, para 33; Kingreen in: Calliess/Ruffert (eds) *Kommentar des Vertrages über die Europäische Union und des Vertrages zur Gründung der Europäischen Gemeinschaft* (2nd ed, Neuwied 2002) Art 6 EUV, paras 107 ff.
48 ECJ *Grant* [1998] ECR I-621.
49 ECJ *Grant* [1998] ECR I-621, para 32.
50 ECJ *Eyüp* [2000] ECR I-4747, para 36.
51 This adjudication of the Court has remained a singular decision and has not been quoted again with regard to its explanations concerning family law; explicitly for a classification as a solution due to equity AG Colomer in his opinion of 10 June 2003, *KB/National Health Service* [2004] ECR I-541, para 60.
52 *Cf* Art 13 and 141 TEC (Art III-124 and III-214 DC) as well as 2001/51/EC: Council Decision of 20 December 2000 establishing a Programme relating to the Community framework strategy on gender equality (2001–2005), [2001] OJ L17/22; Council Directive 76/207/EEC of 9 February 1976 on the implementation of the principle of equal treatment for men and women as regards access to employment, vocational training and promotion, and working conditions as well as Council Directive 86/378/EEC of 24 July 1986 on the implementation of the principle of equal treatment for men and women in occupational social security schemes.
53 See McGlynn (2001) 26 ELRev 582, 585.

subject to the control of the Court of Auditors are obliged to inform the Court about the paid emoluments and retirement pensions as far as they exceeded the sum of € 82400 in the year 2000. Although the disclosure of the names of the persons concerned is not provided for by Austrian law, the Court of Auditors has followed the opinion in literature that deems this step necessary. The Court of Auditors includes the data concerning the income in its annual report, which is conveyed to the National Council, the Federal Council and the Land Parliaments and is made accessible to the public as well.

N and L were not successful in the lower instances, but in the trial of appeal they were heard with their argumentation that the Austrian practice of administration violates the Directive on Data Protection 95/46, which is directly applicable. The Supreme Court suspended the proceedings and presented the questions to the ECJ whether the Austrian provisions comply with Community law, especially with Directive 95/46, and if its provisions are directly applicable in a way that the parties can refer to them to prevent the application of compulsory provisions of national law.

40 In the landmark decision *Stauder* from 1969, the ECJ connected the individualisation of a citizen entitled to social welfare benefits with the "fundamental rights of the person".[54] In later decisions it stated that Community institutions are required to treat information confidentially that was given to them voluntarily, but with the request for maintenance of anonymity. This duty is a general principle which was partially laid down in Article 286 of the TEC (Article I-51 DC) in primary Community law.[55] The two examples show that the protection of **personal data** is by no means an idea which has entered Community law just recently, in the course of technical development and the corresponding adaptation of the fundamental rights' protection.

41 Legislation on Community level shows that the protection of personal data has meanwhile become a **fundamental right of the Union** with a specific scope of guarantee. According to the **Directive 95/46/EC**[56], the Member States have to ensure the natural person's right to the maintenance of private life in relation with the processing of personal data. The directive specifies the corresponding content of the guarantee in Article 8(1) of the ECHR and in the Convention of the Council of the European regarding the protection of individuals with regard to automatic processing of personal data, which has been ratified by all EU Member States.[57] Directive 2002/58/EC[58] clarifies and completes the aforementioned legislation with regard to the processing of personal data in the field of communication by electronic media. The Community as well as its organs and agencies are included in the obligation to data protection through Article 286 of the TEC (Article I-51 DC) according to the two directives. Regulation 45/2001[59] creates a "European Data Protection

---

54 ECJ *Stauder* [1969] ECR 419, especially para 7.
55 ECJ *Adams* [1985] ECR 3539, para 34.
56 *Cf* in detail the commentary by Brühmann in: Grabitz/Hilf (eds) *Das Recht der Europäischen Union* (Looseleaf, Munich) A 30.
57 Also *cf* ECJ *Fisher* [2000] ECR I-6751, paras 33 ff, stating that the Directive 95/46/EC adopted general principles which had already been acknowledged in the legal systems of the Member States. For the scope of applicability of the directive → (paras 41 and 45); for the Data Protection Group employed according to Art 29 of the directive see below note 83.
58 Directive on Data Protection for Electronic Communication (2002/58); explicitly referring to Art 7 and Art 8 of the Charter of Fundamental Rights for the European Union in the second recital.
59 [2001] OJ L8/1.

Supervisor" as an independent control authority, which is supposed to watch over the compliance with the data protection provisions with regard to the Community.[60] Article 1 of the regulation says: "In accordance with this regulation, [the institutions and bodies of the Community] shall protect the fundamental rights and freedoms of natural persons, and in particular their right to privacy with respect to the processing of personal data [...]."

The material provisions of this regulation are partially suited to **specify** the scope of protection of this fundamental right. Personal data may only be processed if (i) the processing is necessary to fulfil a task which is carried out in the public interest, or constitutes a legitimate execution of public authority according to primary or secondary Community law, or (ii) if the processing is necessary to obey a legal obligation of the person processing the data, or (iii) if the processing is necessary for the satisfaction of a contract or (iv) if the person concerned has given his consent without any doubt, or, finally, (v) if the processing is necessary to safeguard a vital interest of the person concerned. The processing of personal data revealing racial or ethnic origin, political opinion, religious or philosophic belief or union membership as well as the processing of data concerning health or sexual life is generally prohibited. Furthermore, the person concerned has the right not to be subjected to a decision which results in legal consequences or disturbs him or her considerably and which is only passed due to an automatic proceeding of data for the evaluation of single aspects of the person. The person concerned also has rights of information, including the right to demand the correction of incorrect data, as well as the right to ask for the blocking and extinction of data under certain conditions.

Limitations of the scope of protection are justified if they are necessary for: (i) the prevention, investigation, determination and prosecution of crimes, (ii) an important economic or financial concern of a Member State or the Community, (iii) the protection of the persons concerned or of the rights and freedoms of others, (iv) national or public security as well as the defence of the Member States, and (v) tasks of control, supervision and regulation which are permanently or temporarily connected to the execution of public authority in cases of the prosecution of criminal offences or the existence of a special concern. In the case of a limitation, the person concerned has to be informed about the main reasons for this restriction and instructed on his right to apply to the European Data Protection Supervisor.

Furthermore, the most recent jurisdiction of the Court of Justice reveals the **symbiotic relationship between the Community's data protection law and Article 8 of the ECHR**. Thus, according to the leading case *Austrian Broadcasting Corporation*, the provisions of the Data Protection Directive 95/46/EC, which are directly applicable, are to be interpreted in the light of the fundamental rights, especially the right of respect for the private life.[61] According to the opinion of the Court of Justice, a national provision concerning the processing of personal data therefore has to fulfil the standards of the provisions of secondary Community law, which are charged with fundamental rights. This results in a kind of fundamental rights' protection *by* directives.[62]

---

60 *Cf* the Decision No 1247/2002/EC of the European Parliament, of the Council and of the Commission of 1 July 2002 on the regulations and general conditions governing the performance of the European Data Protection Supervisor's duties, [2002] OJ L183/1.
61 ECJ *Austrian Broadcasting* [2003] ECR I-4989, para 68.
62 *Cf* Siemen [2004] EuR 306, 316; on the contrary critical Ruffert [2004] EuGRZ 466, 469.

Case 3 – Answer:

45 According to the Court of Justice, including data concerning the income in connection with the name of the recipient in a year's record fulfils the conditions of "processing of personal data" in the sense of the Directive 95/46. Passing on such data to third parties by the employer represents an interference with the private life in the sense of Article 8 of the ECHR which can only be justified if it has a basis in law, if one of the legitimate aims named in this article is pursued and if it is necessary in a democratic society to accomplish this aim.

Concerning the disclosure of the names, which was not provided for in the national law, the Austrian courts first have to check whether this proceeding complies with the requirement to be foreseeable. The requirement of a legitimate purpose, by contrast, is clearly fulfilled because the revelation was meant to ensure the economic and appropriate use of public funds by the administration and therefore focuses on the "economic welfare" of the country. With regard to necessity, the national courts have to check whether the publication of the names in connection with their income is necessary and whether it might be sufficient to inform the public only about the emoluments which are agreed upon by contract and other monetary benefits.

Should the Supreme Court deem the Austrian provision incompatible with the ECHR (!), it can also not be in compliance with the directive. However, should the court consider the provision necessary as well as adequate with regard to the pursued aim in favour of the common interest, it will have to check whether the requirement to be foreseeable is fulfilled.

Regarding the question of direct applicability of the directive, the Court stated that its provisions were so exact that an individual could rely on them in national courts to prevent the application of adverse provisions of internal law.

46 The development of the *acquis communautaire* with regard to data protection is taken up by the Charter of Fundamental Rights which contains a fundamental right of protection of personal data in Article 8. According to the comments drafted by the presiding committee of the Convent,[63] this fundamental right is based on the aforementioned provisions of primary and secondary Community law as well as on provisions of treaties of international law. Restrictions shall be possible in accordance with Article 52 of the Charter of Fundamental Rights (Article II-112 DC).

b) Freedom of Religion

47 The Community law does not contain a comprehensive fundamental rights' guarantee that comprises the freedom of thought, conscience and religion. This is not surprising because the scope of protection of this classic fundamental right hardly touches the sphere of EC competences and its relevance for the European Community is therefore not self-evident. An explicit Community competence with reference to religion only exists in connection with the prohibition of discrimination in Article 13 of the TEC (Article III-124 DC).

48 Nevertheless, one decision of the ECJ contains aspects concerning the law of religion which justify the assumption that the ECJ would acknowledge the freedom of religion as

---

63 These comments do not have any legal effect, but are meant to explain the provisions of the Charter in the light of the debates lead within the context of the negotiations about the Convention.

a fundamental right of Community law in an appropriate case.[64] In the case *Prais*[65], the ECJ had to decide on the action of an English woman of Jewish faith who had been invited to a application procedure for a post as a translator at the Council, but could not attend the actual appointment of the written examination due to religious beliefs. She was not allowed to participate on a later date of examination. The question disputed by the parties disputed was whether a new examination date should have been fixed. The ECJ stated with regard to the conduct of the Council: "if he [the employer] is informed about the obstacle caused by the faith on time, [he is obliged] to take all suitable steps to prevent the examination to take place on a day on which the applicant will not be able to turn up due to his or her religious belief […]."

However, neither the staff regulations for officials nor the mentioned fundamental rights obliged the appointing authority to prevent a conflict with a religious requirement they have not been informed about.[66]

49

In the ECJ's case-law, there are several more cases which have a relation to "religion or another form of philosophy of life".[67] However, the questions relevant to the issue are answered in connection with the provisions about the fundamental freedoms and the general prohibition of discrimination, respectively, so that there is no mention of a fundamental right of the freedom of religion in any decision.[68]

50

c) Freedom of Movement

The freedom of movement is a fundamental right of the employees and their families. Mobility within the Community is one of the means designated to improve the working and living conditions of the employee in order to facilitate his social advancement. At the same time, the Member States' demand for workforce is satisfied. All Member States are therefore obliged to grant all employees from other Member States the right to practice a profession of their choice within the Community.[69]

51

The freedom of movement requires the removal of all obstacles that interfere with the mobility of employees. This is particularly relevant with respect to the employee's right to let his family join him and to the conditions for the integration of his family in the receiving state.[70]

52

---

64 The freedom of religion is named as a fundamental right acknowledged by the ECJ by: Streinz *Europarecht* (6th ed, Heidelberg 2003) para 372; Stumpf in: Schwarze (ed) *EU-Kommentar* (Baden-Baden 2000) Art 6 EUV, para 25; according to Kingreen in: Calliess/Ruffert (eds) *Kommentar des Vertrages über die Europäische Union und des Vertrages zur Gründung der Europäischen Gemeinschaft* (2nd ed, Neuwied 2002) Art 6, para 114, the decision in the case *Prais* at least touches the issue of the freedom of religion.
65 ECJ *Prais* [1976] ECR 1589; cf the review by Hartley (1977) 2 ELRev 45.
66 ECJ *Prais* [1976] ECR 1589, paras 12/19.
67 ECJ *van Duyn* [1974] ECR 1337 (denial of entry for a follower of Scientology); *van Roosmalen* [1986] ECR 3097 (social insurance cover of a missionary); *Steymann* [1988] ECR 6159 (religious community as economic activity or service) and *Torfaen Borough Council* [1989] ECR 3851 (prohibition of sale on Sundays).
68 *Cf* in detail Heinig *Öffentlich-rechtliche Religionsgesellschaften* (Berlin 2003) p 380 and with examples of application pp 468 ff.
69 *Cf* the third recital of Reg 1612/68 and ECJ *Gül* [1986] ECR 1573, para 14.
70 *Cf* fifth recital of Reg 1612/68.

53   The fundamental right of the freedom of movement is connected to the fundamental freedom – of the same name – in Community law (Articles 39 TEC/Articles III-133 DC) and the secondary Community law implementing it, especially Regulation No 1612/68.[71] The conditions under which a limitation of the fundamental right may be justified emerge from this connection as well.[72] These limitations are based on the supposition that the persons entitled to fundamental rights are not able to secure their living for themselves and their families without governmental benefits. According to a more recent decision of the Court of Justice, there is no burden to the budget of the receiving state if the "sufficient financial means" are not raised directly by the entitled citizen of the Union, but are allocated by the parents for their child.[73]

54   With the Directive 2004/38 on the free movement of citizens of the Union and their family members, this legal status is going to change considerably.[74] This directive, which had to be implemented by the Member States until 30th April 2006, introduced a **right of permanent residence** (Article 16) which is not bound to conditions of residence any more after an uninterrupted stay of five years in the receiving Member State. The rights of the citizens and their family members, no matter of which nationality, were strengthened as well: The possibilities of the Member States to refuse to grant the right of residence or to withdraw this right with reference to public order have been restricted (Article 28).

d) Freedom of Association

55   The **freedom of association** also belongs to the fundamental rights which are protected by Community law. The ECJ has stated this explicitly in its decision in the case *Bosman* with reference to Article 11 of the ECHR.[75] The decision in the case *Confederation of German Trade Unions* from 1974 – which is often quoted in this context – also bears a certain thematic relation to this fundamental right.[76] The ECJ argued in this decision that officials are granted freedom of association according to Article 24a of the staff regulations for officials and that they are allowed to be members of trade unions or professional associations. However, the decision does not contain any reference to this right being tied to the category of fundamental rights.[77] The Charter of Fundamental Rights guarantees the freedom of assembly and association in Article 12 (Article II-72 DC).

---

71 There is a close relation to the right of respect for family life, *cf* again paras 36 ff above.
72 *Cf* para 36 above.
73 ECJ *Chen* [2004] ECR I-9925, para 29; *cf* as well the opinion of the First AG Tizzano in this case, paras 73 ff.
74 Dir 2004/38/EC of 29 April 2004 on the right of citizens of the Union and their family members to move and reside freely within the territory of the Member States amending Reg (EEC) 1612/68 and repealing Dirs 64/221/EEC, 68/360/EEC, 72/194/EEC, 73/148/EEC, 75/34/EEC, 75/35/EEC, 90/364/EEC, 90/365/EEC and 93/96/EEC.
75 ECJ *Bosman* [1995] ECR I-4921, para 79; following *Montecatini* [1999] ECR I-4539, para 137.
76 ECJ *Gewerkschaftsbund europäischer öffentlicher Dienst* [1974] ECR 917.
77 But *cf* Art 2 Reg 2679/98 of the Council, which formulates an escape clause according to which the regulation may not interfere with the execution of the national fundamental rights – especially the rights or freedoms of strike.

2. Interference

The fundamental rights to protection of the personality are safeguarded against interferences by Community institutions as well as actions of the Member States – the **general rules** apply.[78]

3. Justification

The **general rules** apply for the justification of an interference (→ § 14 paras 45 ff). Due to the special significance of the fundamental **right to privacy**, the following may be added: An interference with this fundamental right is justified under two conditions: First, the interference has to actually correspond to those aims of the Community that serve the public welfare. Secondly, it must "not be an unacceptable interference disproportional to the pursued purpose which attacks the rights thus guaranteed in their essence."[79] In more recent decisions, the ECJ has omitted a regular and general reference to the restrictions of Article 8(2) of the ECHR and the permissible aims of the limitation of a fundamental right enumerated there. Instead, the Court applies the quoted general formula for justification without losing sight of the material reservations for restrictions under the ECHR. Thus, the ECJ decided that the protection of public health and of human life belongs to the aims which may justify a limitation of the right to respect for private life. Accordingly, the responsible public authorities of a Member State are allowed to control the importation of pharmaceuticals which are available only on prescription in the importing state in the interest of public health. However, these controls have to be designed to meet the requirements which result from the protection of the fundamental rights.[80]

The cases *European Passenger Data*[81] dealt with the legitimacy of the ratification of a treaty[82] between the European Community and the United States of America concerning the conveyance and processing of passenger data. They show that there are constellations in Community law where an unjustified interference with a fundamental right[83] might not be removable because the Community has committed to a certain behaviour towards another state on the *level of international law* (*cf* Article 300(7) TEC).

---

78 See (para 11) and → § 14 paras 45 ff.
79 ECJ *Schräder* [1989] ECR 2237, para 15; *Commission v Germany* [1992] ECR I-2575, para 23.
80 ECJ *Commission v Germany* [1992] ECR I-2575, para 24.
81 ECJ *Parliament v Council* [2000] ECR I-2457 and *Parliament v Commission* [2006] ECR I-4721; *cf* the Grand Chamber order granting the European Data Protection Supervisor leave to intervene in theses cases, ECJ *Parliament v Council* [2005] ECR I-2457.
82 2004/496/EC: Council Decision of 17 May 2004 on the conclusion of an Agreement between the European Community and the United States of America on the processing and transfer of PNR data by Air Carriers to the United States Department of Homeland Security, Bureau of Customs and Border Protection, [2004] OJ L183/83.
83 Concerning the legal situation in the concrete cases see the opinion 4/2003 of the Data Protection Group according to Art 29 Dir 95/46/EC 13 June 2003, pp 5 ff and the opinion 2/2004 of 29 January 2004, p 6.

III. The Protection of Communication

Leading Cases: ECJ *Germany v Parliament and Council* C-380/03; ECJ *RTL Television* [2003] ECR I-12489; *Schmidberger* [2003] ECR I-5659; *Connolly* [2001] ECR I-1611; *Familiapress* [1997] ECR I-3689; *TV 10* [1994] ECR I-4795; *Ter Voort* [1992] ECR I-5485; *Elliniki Radiophonia Tileorassi (ERT)* [1991] ECR I-2925; *Gouda* [1991] ECR I-4007; *Commission v Netherlands* [1991] ECR I-4069; *Oyowe and Traore* [1989] ECR 4285; *Cinéthèque* [1985] ECR 2605; *VBVB und VBBB* [1984] ECR 19.

Further Reading: Agerbeek *Freedom of expression and free movement in the Brenner corridor* (2004) 29 ELRev 255; Gonzales *EC fundamental freedoms v human rights in the case C-112/00 Eugen Schmidberger v Austria* (2004) 31 Legal Issues of Economic Integration 219; Mann/Ripke *Überlegungen zur Existenz und Reichweite eines Gemeinschaftsgrundrechts der Versammlungsfreiheit* [2004] EuGRZ 125; Curtin *Citizen's fundamental right of access to EU information: an evolving digital passepartout* (2000) 37 CMLR 7; Hoffmeister *Art 10 EMRK in der Rechtsprechung des Europäischen Gerichtshofs für Menschenrechte 1994–1999* [2000] EuGRZ 358; Kühling *Die Kommunikationsfreiheit als europäisches Gemeinschaftsgrundrecht* (Berlin 1999) pp 110 ff; Simma/Weiler/Zöckler *Kompetenzen und Grundrechte: Beschränkungen der Tabakwerbung aus der Sicht des Europarechts* (Berlin 1999).

59 The **right of free expression** belongs to the fundamental rights whose observance is secured by the ECJ in settled case-law. The ECJ characterises the freedom of expression as "one of the substantial fundamental rights of a democratic society". By using this formula, the Court of Justice refers to the relevant guarantee of the ECHR and to the jurisdiction of the ECtHR. The right of free expression of opinion guaranteed in Article 10 of the ECHR and the relevant decisions of the ECtHR are the substantive basis of the Community law guarantee of protection of the freedom of expression and its specifications, *ie* the freedom of the press, of information and of broadcasting.[84] The decisions of the Strasbourg Court of Justice are of considerable significance because the ECJ jurisdiction still is and will most likely remain fragmentary. The ECJ is dependent upon factual circumstances relevant to fundamental rights for the development of its jurisdiction. Only in very few fields of the communication sector, the jurisdiction has condensed into a corpus of decisions that allows secured dogmatic statements about the fundamental rights' protection of communication on the level of Community law. The following explanations therefore concentrate on the leading cases in the relevant fields, *ie* the service regulations of the Community, freedom of the press and of broadcasting as well as business advertisement (commercial communication).

1. Scope of Protection

Case 4 – Problem: (ECJ *Connolly* [2001] ECR I-1611)[85]

60 The Commission official C was head of a section of the directorate for currency matters in the Commission's Directorate-General for Economy (DG II). Since 1991, C has submitted three draft essays about the application of currency theories, the development of the European currency system and the effects of the White Book about the future of Europe on the monetary system, in which he critically addressed the aforementioned topics. The superior refused to give C the consent which is necessary according to Article 17(2) of the staff regulations for officials. In April 1995, C asked for a holiday due to personal reasons for three months beginning in July 1995, which was granted by the Commission. During this holiday, C published a book with the title "The rotten heart of Europe. The dirty war for Europe's

---

84 *Cf* in detail Grabenwarter (2001) 60 VVDStRL 292, 325 with further references.
85 The decision of the Court of First Instance is published in *Connolly* [1999] ECR II-463, para 153.

money." C had not asked for consent to publish this book. At the beginning of September 1995, a series of articles about the book were published in the European and especially in the British press.

After beginning his work again in October 1995, disciplinary proceedings were instituted against him because of the violation of the obligations of the staff regulations for officials. He was charged with not having applied for consent before publishing his book. The content of the book was considered to be detrimental to the implementation of the economic and monetary union, which he was supposed to support by his work, as well as to the esteem and the reputation of the Commission. Furthermore, his whole behaviour detracted from the esteem of his office. After the having obtained the required opinion of the disciplinary council, C was removed from service without having been deprived of his right to a pension in January 1996.

The action for the repeal of the opinion of the disciplinary council and of his removal from service brought before the Court of First Instance was dismissed by judgement of the CFI in May 1999. C appealed to the ECJ against this decision in July 1999. He pleaded that the decision of the Commission to remove him from service due to the publication of the book violated his right of free expression of opinion. He argued that as an official of the EC, he was entitled to this right even in fields which are covered by the activities of Community institutions. The Court of First Instance had failed to appreciate the significance of the right of free expression of opinion in its decision.

a) Freedom of Expression

The right to free expression of opinion in its core content plays a considerable role on Community level – first of all – in the regulations for public service. The staff regulations for officials[86] (SR) impose duties on the officials which interfere with the scope of protection of this fundamental right. The decision in the case *Oyowe and Traore* is fundamental for the scope of these regulations against the background of the freedom of expression.[87] The claimants were staff members of an international non-profit association under Belgian law, which promoted the co-operation between the Community and the developing countries on behalf of the Commission. The claimants, who were also editors of the monthly published ACP-Courier, requested to be appointed as officials of the Commission. The Commission declined these applications, stating that as members of the editorial staff of the Courier, the claimants represented the special character of the ACP-States, which was not consistent with an official's duty of allegiance towards the Community. The ECJ rejected this argumentation of the Commission and explained in the crucial passage of the grounds: "Finally, it must be borne in mind that in any event the duty of allegiance to the Communities imposed on officials in the Staff Regulations cannot be interpreted in such a way as to conflict with freedom of expression, a fundamental right which

---

[86] Council Regulation (EC, ECSC, Euratom) No 2594/98 of 27 November 1998 amending Regulation (EEC, Euratom, ECSC) No 259/68 laying down the Staff Regulations of officials of the European Communities and the Conditions of Employment of other servants of the Communities.

[87] ECJ *Oyowe and Traore* [1989] ECR 4285 – the previous decisions ECJ *Fiddelaar* [1960] ECR 1077 and *Cowood* [1982] ECR 4625 already have a relation to the freedom of expression. But in both cases, the Court of Justice did not address the fundamental rights issue; at the time of the decision in the case of *Fiddelaar* the protection of fundamental rights was not yet acknowledged by the ECJ, in the case *Cowood* the violation of the freedom of expression challenged by the plaintiff was only included in the pleadings of a party.

the Court must ensure is respected in Community law, which is particularly important in cases, such as the present, concerning journalists whose primary duty is to write in complete independence of the views of either the ACP States or the Communities."[88]

62 As is customary in public service regulations, an official's **general duty of allegiance** is clearly defined by particular obligations. In this context, the interdiction according to Article 17(2) of the SR, not to publish texts – neither alone nor in co-operation with others – which are related to the activities of the Community without the consent of the appointing authority, has given rise to several guiding decisions of the ECJ.

63 In the *Connolly* case, the ECJ interpreted Article 17(2) of the SR in conformity with the fundamental rights. The power of the institutions to decline the consent to the publication of an official created the basis for a serious interference with the freedom of expression. As this is one of the substantial foundations of a democratic society, the provision was to be interpreted restrictively. Accordingly, the consent may only be refused if the publication is likely to cause a serious damage to the concerns of the Community.[89] The appointing authority is therefore obliged to weigh the concerned interests when applying the provision. In doing so, it has to consider, on the one hand, the concerns of the official to express opinions orally or in writing which are different from that of the Community institution and are a minority opinion. On the other hand, it has to consider the degree of the interference of Community interests which would result from the intended expression of opinion. In this weighing process, however, only a "real threat of a serious interference with the interests of the Community set forth on the basis of concrete, objective circumstances" can be taken into consideration.

64 The official has to be informed about these circumstances at the time of the **refusing decision**, at the latest at the time of the decision with which a possible complaint is turned down. This should allow the Community judge to be able to check the legality of the decision which refuses to consent to the publication. Moreover, the concerned official has to be informed so that he is able to judge the correctness of the decision himself.

65 The decisions in the case *Cwik* show that these criteria are interpreted restrictively and that the Community institutions are only granted a very **narrow margin of appreciation**. In the original proceedings, the CFI held that the claim made by the Commission official *Cwik* was justified and overturned the decision of the Commission to refuse the consent to the publication of a lecture. At an earlier time, the claimant had been given the consent of his superiors to lecture on the "economic and political fine tuning" of the economic and monetary union during the 5th International Congress for Economic Culture. The consent had been given with several added remarks that urged for a more "classic presentation" and pointed to the dangers of "fine tuning". After the claimant had given his lecture, he asked for the consent to the publication of the manuscript. The superior official obtained several opinions of qualified staff members and eventually declined the consent, because the opinions expressed by Cwik were not consistent with the line of the Commission. The CFI overturned this decision, referring to the importance of the freedom of expression.[90]

66 The ECJ confirmed the legal argumentation of the CFI, which had held that more factors should have been considered in the specific case. First, the claimant did not have any

---

88 ECJ *Oyowe and Traore* [1989] ECR 4285, para 16.
89 ECJ *Connolly* [2001] ECR I-1611, para 53.
90 CFI *Cwik* [2000] ECR II-713, para 66.

supervisory power, secondly, his manuscript was written for a specialised public audience, and thirdly, the Commission had already committed itself to a point of view at the time in question.[91] The pleadings of the Commission reproduced in the grounds of the ECJ show that the principles developed in the *Connolly* case had been acknowledged by the Commission, but had been understood and applied in a very broad sense. Consequently, the decision in the *Cwik* case has defined the fundamental rights' protection of the freedom of expression of Community officials more precisely.

Another decision by the ECJ dealt with the compatibility of the official's **obligation to act with restraint** with the right of free expression towards the superior. The ECJ ruled that the obligation to act with restraint specified in Article 12 and 21 of the SR must not be interpreted restrictively if an official exercised the right he is entitled to according to Article 43(2) of the SR by adding his own remarks to an assessment he was informed about. "Accordingly, an official cannot be considered to have failed to meet that requirement unless he uses seriously insulting language or language which seriously undermines the respect due to the reporting officer."[92]

Case 4 – Answer:
In the decision to remove C from service, the appointing authority ascertained a violation of Article 17(2) of the SR. C had not asked for the consent to publish his work. However, he should have recognised that this consent would be declined for the same reasons the consent to the publication of a few essays of a comparable content had been declined before. Finally, C had seriously interfered with the concerns of Community through his behaviour and had injured the image and esteem of the Commission. The ECJ therefore rejected the plea of a violation of the freedom of expression so that the action brought by C was not successful.

The requirement of a previous consent to a publication serves the justified purpose that a text relating to the activities of the Community must not interfere with its concerns, especially the esteem and the appearance of a Community institution. Article 17(2) of the SR is not disproportional when measured against the aim of the protection of the general public interest. It cannot be inferred from the provision that the rules about the previous consent entitle the institution concerned to the execution of an unrestricted censorship. The previous consent to the publication is only necessary where the text which the official in question means to publish is related to the activities of the Community. Additionally, the provision does establish a complete publication ban, which would affect the very essence of the right of free expression. Article 17(2) of the SR renders the granting of the consent to publication to a general policy. That is to say, the consent may only be refused if the intended publication is likely to interfere with the concerns of the Community. Because the refusing decision can be challenged according to Articles 90 and 91 of the SR, the official concerned can have the measure of the Community institution reviewed by a Community judge. Besides, the formality prescribed by Article 17(2) of the SR serves as prevention. The provision can prevent the interests of the Community from being threatened. Furthermore, the consent procedure can help to avoid the imposition of a disciplinary penalty on the official by the Community institution after the publication of a text likely to interfere with the concerns of the Community.

Considering all these arguments, the violation of Article 17(2) of the SR might not have been stated in the decision of C's removal from service if the concerns of the Community

---

91 ECJ *Cwik* [2001] ECR I-10269, paras 14 and 23.
92 ECJ *Economic and Social Committee v E* [1999] ECR I-8877, para 15.

> had not been threatened in any way. Therefore, the consequence the Commission attributed to this provision does not seem to go beyond the pursued purpose and does not violate the freedom of expression.

b) Freedom of the Press and Broadcasting

69 The freedom of the press and broadcasting is a specification of the freedom of expression. The jurisdiction on this guarantee started with the decision of the ECJ in the case "Flemish Books".[93] The ruling was prompted by a decision of the Commission based on Council Regulation No 17. In this decision, the Commission declared an agreement between Flemish and Dutch publisher and bookseller associations to be incompatible with Article 81(1) of the TEC (Article III-161 DC). The agreement provided for a vertical control of prices and exclusive rights of sale. The claimants were of the opinion that the Commission's decision violated the freedom of expression. They argued that a system of a vertical price control supported the diversity of the published titles, ensured the publication of works which are hard to sell and that without such a system, the publishing industry would be dependent on state subsidies. The ECJ rejected this argumentation. The claimants had not pointed out an actual connection between the Commission's decision and the freedom of opinion. Nevertheless, the grounds explicitly say that the ECJ considers the freedom of press – the term "freedom of publishing" is used in the grounds – to be guaranteed both for the publisher as well as for the distributing companies.[94]

70 In recent times, the fundamental rights' aspects of **book price fixing** have gained more attention because the Commission has instituted a pre-trial proceeding under competition law against the cross-boarder control of prices of book trade in Germany and Austria as well as in Switzerland.[95]

71 The significance of the freedom of broadcasting on the Community level is reflected by the **TV Without Frontiers Directive**.[96] In its eighth recital, the directive explicitly acknowledges that the broadcasting and distribution of television services are specific manifestations in Community law of a more general principle, namely the freedom of expression as enshrined in Article 10(1) of the ECHR. Community law provides for the free movement of services regardless of their cultural or other content. Furthermore, there are no restrictions for citizens of other Member States who are resident in a Member State different from the one of the beneficiary. National law concerning the broadcasting of TV signals therefore has to secure that broadcasting is performed in the light of Article 10 of the ECHR and any limitations have to meet the standards set forth in Article 10(2) of the ECHR and Article 46(1) of the TEC (Article III-140(1) DC). In its decision in the case *Elliniki Radiophonia Tileorassi* (ERT), the Court of Justice acknowledged that the limitations are to be judged by reasons of public order, security and health, taking the

---

93 ECJ *VBVB and VBBB* [1984] ECR 19.
94 ECJ *VBVB and VBBB* [1984] ECR 19, para 34.
95 *Cf* Blanke/Kitz [2000] JZ 118; Everling *Buchpreisbindung im deutschen Sprachraum und Europäisches Gemeinschaftsrecht* (Baden-Baden 1997); see the Commission's press release IP/02/461 of 22 March 2002.
96 Dir 89/552/EEC [1989] OJ L298/23 as amended by Dir 97/36/EC [1997] OJ L202/60; for the planned revision *cf* European Commission, Communication on the future of European regulatory audiovisual policy, COM (2003) 784 final.

freedom of opinion guaranteed in Article 10 of the ECHR into account.[97] In its decision in the case *RTL Television,* the Court of Justice considered the interference with Article 10 of the ECHR due to measures against excessive advertising to be justified. The protection of the viewers as consumers as well as their interest to have access to programmes of good quality was a legitimate aim.[98] The limitation of the number of advertising blocks did not aim at the content of the message, affected all producers and they could generally determine the time of the interruption. Therefore, the limiting measures the directive provides for were deemed to be proportional.[99]

c) Commercial Communication

A third field of the Community's right of free expression can be summarised by the keyword **commercial communication**. This means all forms of communication "seeking to promote either products, services or the image of a company or organisation to final consumers and/or distributors."[100] The term comprises all forms of advertisement, of direct marketing, sponsoring, sales promotion and public relations.

The ECtHR[101] and the Human Rights Committee under the International Covenant on Civil and Political Rights[102] have acknowledged that the transmission and reception of opinions, messages or ideas for commercial purposes fall into the scope of protection of the right of free expression. Nevertheless, these forms of the right of free expression are not protected to the same extent as the expression of opinions on political or social matters. The ECJ has however not yet explicitly commented on this question.

The proceedings on the legitimacy of the so-called Directive on Advertising Tobacco Products[103] provided an occasion to decide about the extent of the fundamental rights' protection of the "commercial speech". The directive prohibited all forms of advertising for and sponsoring of tobacco products in the Community. The prohibition comprised both direct and indirect advertising, *eg* by diversifying products. Germany had instituted an action for annulment against the legislative measure. It submitted *inter alia* that the directive violated Article 10 of the ECHR because the companies concerned were no longer able to inform the public about their products.

In his opinion, AG Fennelly argued that information of commercial nature should also be protected by Community law. Although such information does not contribute to the

72

73

74

75

---

97 ECJ *ERT* [1991] ECR I-2925, paras 45 ff – for the link with the TV-Directive also *cf* the opinion of the AG Lenz in this case, paras 49 ff.
98 ECJ *RTL Television* [2003] ECR I-12489, paras 70 ff. In this context the ECJ has referred to earlier decisions stating that certain aims of cultural policy may justify the limitation of the free movement of services by the Member States. Among these aims are the protection of the consumer against excessive commercial advertising and the maintenance of a certain programme quality. *Cf* ECJ *Stichting* [1991] ECR I-4007, para 27; *ARD* [1999] ECR I-7599, para 50.
99 ECJ *RTL Television* [2003] ECR I-12489, para 72.
100 *Cf* the Green paper from the Commission, Commercial Communications in the Internal Market, COM (96) 192 final, p 2 and the following document COM (98) 121 final.
101 See ECtHR [1996] EuGRZ 392; *Groppera Radio AG* (1990) 12 EHRR 321; *Colman* (1994) 18 EHRR 119; *Casado Coca* (1994) 18 EHRR 1, paras 35 ff; *VGT Verein gegen Tierfabriken* (2002) 34 EHRR 159.
102 Communications No 359/1989 and 385/1989 *Ballantyne Davidson McIntyre*, decision from 31 March 1993, CCPR/C/47/D/359/1989 and 385/1989/Rev 1.
103 Dir 98/43 EC.

§ 15 III 1   Frank Schorkopf

accomplishment of social aims in a liberal democratic society in the same way as political, journalistic, literary or artistic opinions do, he argued that the fundamental rights are not merely respected for their instrumental social function, but also because they are essential to autonomy, dignity and the development of personality.[104] It is further said in the opinions: "[I]ndividuals' freedom to promote commercial activities derives not only from their right to engage in economic activities and the general commitment, in the Community context, to a market economy based upon free competition, but also from their inherent entitlement as human beings to freely express and receive views on any topic, including the merits of the goods or services which they market or purchase."

76   In its decision, the ECJ declared the Tobacco Advertising Directive to be invalid because it was based on an improper legal foundation. Therefore, it did not have to scrutinise the further causes of action. However, the Community's regulation concerning tobacco advertising, which has been controversial for years, remains significant for the freedom of expression even after the widely noticed decision on the Tobacco Advertising Directive. After the so-called Directive on Tobacco Products entered into force, especially the question of the negative freedom of opinion is being discussed.

77   The Directive on Tobacco Products[105] has altered and summarised two existing legal instruments. The Labelling Directive[106] in its final version required that health warnings regarding the tar and nicotine quantities are to be specified on the packaging of tobacco products and that, additionally, a warning label is to be printed on the unit packets of tobacco products. Apart from that, a binding limiting value has been fixed for the maximum tar yield of cigarettes by the Directive 90/239/EEC for the first time. The Directive on Tobacco Products not only tightens the requirements for information and warning labels on the packaging of tobacco products. In addition, the space reserved for the warnings on the packaging will be enlarged, new labels will be introduced and it will become possible to apply photos and pictures to the packages. It is remarkable that according to Article 5(8) of the Directive, it is left to the discretion of the Member States whether the packaging must contain a reference to the authority issuing the warning according to national law.[107] Based on this regulation it can be concluded that, according to Community law, the warning labels do not necessarily have indicate that the health warnings are an opinion of Member State authorities.[108] Taking into consideration that the Community legislator always aims to comply with the fundamental rights standard, this provision indicates how the scope of the negative freedom of expression is being understood.

78   Another decision to be named in connection with the freedom of information is the *Grogan* case. The preliminary proceeding dealt with the Irish prohibition to spread information in other Member States about hospitals that carry out abortions. The ECJ refused to scrutinise the Irish measure by the standards of the Union's fundamental rights. The behaviour of the defendant students spreading such information contrary to the Irish pro-

---

104 Opinion AG Fennelly [2000] ECR I-8419, paras 154 ff referring to ECtHR *Handyside* (1979–80) 1 EHRR 737, para 49.
105 Dir 2001/37/EC.
106 Dir 89/662/EEC, as amended by Dir 92/41/EEC.
107 Art 5(8) reads as follows: "Member States may stipulate that the warnings referred to in paragraphs 2 and 4 are to be accompanied by a reference, outside the box for warnings, to the issuing authority."
108 *Cf Bundesverfassungsgericht* (BVerfG – German Federal Constitutional Court) (1997) 95 BVerfGE 173, 181 concerning the German implementation act of the Labelling Directive.

hibition and the medical services in other Member States were "too loosely" connected to fall into the scope of application of the freedom of services.[109] By contrast, AG van Gerven claimed in his opinion that the freedom of services comprised the right to obtain information about service-rendering companies established in other Member States without hindrance in the own Member State. The AG considered such an interpretation of the Community law to comply with Article 10 of the ECHR.[110]

d) Freedom of Information

The process of informing oneself, *ie* the access, the receipt and passing on, the saving and processing of data, is the basis for exercising a freedom of expression in a broader sense. The tendencies in the European Union to establish an independent freedom of information[111] are met with a lukewarm response. The envisaged scope of protection – as far as it is not already comprised by the freedom of opinion – is already covered by the guarantee of the **right of access to data**[112] specific to Community law. Within the field of the Union's fundamental rights, no room should be given to further increase the subjectivity of the idea of transparency.

79

e) Freedom of Assembly

The *Schmidberger* case dealt with the legal evaluation of a blockade caused by a demonstration of environmental activists and which lasted several hours. The Court of Justice closely examined the requirements for legitimate restrictions of the freedom of opinion and assembly.[113] Referring to Article 11 of the ECHR, the Court assumed in its decision that the freedom of assembly was a general principle of Community law.[114] The decision particularly emphasises that the right to assemble peacefully is a feature of the collectively exercised freedom of expression.

80

2. Interferences

The right of free expression is protected against interferences by the Community institutions. Furthermore, the ECJ also judges measures of the Member States by the standard of the Community's fundamental right if a national regulation falls into the scope of application of Community law. If the jurisdiction of the Court of Justice is invoked in a preliminary proceeding, it provides the national court with all the criteria of interpretation needed to determine whether the provision at issue is compatible with the Community's fundamental rights.[115] This explicitly also applies to the case that a Member State

81

---

109 ECJ *Grogan* [1991] ECR I-4685, paras 24 and 31, in this context *cf* the decision of the ECtHR *Open Door* (1993) 15 EHRR 244.
110 Opinion AG van Gerven, ECJ *Grogan* [1991] ECR I-4703, para 19.
111 *Cf* in particular Art II-71(1) DC and Curtin (2000) 37 CMLRev 7.
112 In this context *cf* the Report from the Commission on the implementation of the principles in EC Regulation No 1049/2001 regarding public access to European Parliament, Council and Commission documents, COM (2004) 45 of 30 January 2004 pp 6 ff.
113 ECJ *Schmidberger* [2003] ECR I-5659, paras 77 ff; Agerbeek (2004) 29 ELRev 255 ff.
114 The Court had already acknowledged the existence of the freedom of assembly as a general principle of law in the case ECJ *Montecatini* [1999] ECR I-4539, para 137.
115 ECJ *ERT* [1991] ECR I-2925, para 42; *Cinéthèque* [1985] ECR 2605, para 26.

refers to the exception provisions[116] to justify a national measure restricting a fundamental freedom. Therefore, the exception provisions of the TEC only apply to the national regulation in question if it complies with the Union's fundamental rights.

82 The interference with communication in the EU by intelligence agencies of Member States and, above all, foreign states presents interesting and often neglected problems. Whereas the investigating activities of the Member States are subject to the categories of Community law,[117] this is not the case – for the moment – when it comes to foreign espionage activities. A temporary committee of the European Parliament addressed the existence of a global **interception system for private and commercial communication** in the fifth legislative period. It reached the conclusion that, among others, Article 8 of the ECHR only permitted interferences in order to protect national security. The provisions on which the interference is based have to be laid down in national law and be accessible to the public and they must clearly define the circumstances and conditions under which state power may conduct them.[118]

3. Justification

83 In principle, the justification of interferences with the right of free expression is subject to the general rules. Therefore, the explanations given in the context of the general fundamental rights' principles apply.[119] The ECJ adopts the content of the restriction laid down in Article 10(2) of the ECHR to a considerable extent, just as it did when determining the scope of protection: The fundamental right can be subject to formal provisions, conditions, restrictions or threat of punishment. These have to have a basis in law and have to be necessary for a democratic society. The interferences have to be indispensable for the interest of national security, territorial integrity or public security, the maintenance of order or the prevention of crimes, to protect health or morale, a good reputation or the rights of others, to prevent the spreading of confidential information or to keep up the authority and impartiality of jurisdiction. The ECJ interprets these restrictions strictly because it understands the adjective "indispensable" to mean an imperative necessity for society. The Member States have discretion concerning the decision whether such a necessity is in hand. However, the restriction has to be in the right proportion to the pursued legitimate aim. Furthermore, the reasons the national authorities refer to for its justification have to be applicable and sufficient.[120]

84 Apart from these principles of justification for restrictions of the freedom of opinion derived from the ECHR, the ECJ has developed additional requirements for the determination of the legitimate purpose by making the right of free expression itself a criterion of

---

116 *Cf* Arts 30, 46 and 55 TEC.
117 Detailed information concerning the coordinated intelligence measures of the EU Member States is provided by the working document by the rapporteur Schmid in the temporary EP-Committee about the system for the interception of private and commercial communications, Doc-No PE 294.997, 4.
118 Resolution of the EP on the existence of a global Interception System for private and economic communication (interception system Echelon) of 5 September 2001, [2002] OJ C72E/221. In this context also confer the report of the rapporteur Schmid of 11 July 2001 which is detailed and full of material, A5-0264/2001 final.
119 → § 14 paras 45 ff.
120 ECJ *Connolly* [2001] ECR I-1611, paras 40 ff.

the weighing process. The relevant decisions respectively deal with the Dutch law to regulate the spreading of radio- and TV-programmes, radio and TV fees and State aids for press organs (Mediawet). The law provides for different restrictions of the freedom of services, especially concerning advertising and the content of the programmes. These also apply to the operators of radio and TV in other Member States that transmit programmes into the Netherlands. The Dutch government argued that the provisions of Mediawet should protect the needs of the different social, cultural, religious and intellectual movements in the Netherlands. In principle, the Court of Justice accepted this argumentation. The maintenance of a pluralistic broadcasting system, which is supposed to be guaranteed by the Dutch policy, is – according to the opinion of the ECJ – connected with the freedom of expression. Therefore, such a cultural policy can be an imperative reason of public interest which justifies a limitation of the freedom of services.[121] To summarise: The Member States' measures to protect the variety of the media, which are claimed to be based on the freedom of expression, are suitable to justify a limitation of the freedom of services.

The ECJ has extended this jurisdiction in its decision in the case *Familiapress*. The maintenance of the variety of the media can be an **overriding requirement** which also justifies a limitation of the free movement of goods.[122] However, where a Member State relies on an "overriding requirement", such justification must "also be interpreted in the light of general legal principles of law and, in particular, of the fundamental rights."[123] This interpretation is added to the scrutiny of the general principle of proportionality. The ECJ has already emphasised the necessity of such a balancing process in the case *Ter Voort*[124] in which, among other questions, it had to decide about the compliance of a directive with the freedom of expression. The requirements immanent to exercise the freedom of opinion have to be weighed against the requirements which result from the legitimate aim pursued with the legal act.[125] According to the established case-law of the ECJ, provisions of national law "must be proportionate to the objective pursued, and that objective must not be capable of being achieved by measures which are less restrictive of intra-Community trade."[126]

IV. Freedom and Security – Outlook

Further Reading: Council *The Hague Programme: strengthening freedom, security and justice in the European Union* OJ 2005 C 53/1; European Commission *Area of Freedom, Security and Justice: Assessment of the Tampere programme and future orientations* COM (2004) 401 final, of 2 June 2004, Guild *Crime and the EU's constitutional future in an area of freedom, security, and justice* (2004) 10 ELRev 218; Schmitt von Sydow, *Liberté, démocratie, droits fondamentaux et État de droit* [2001] 2 Revue du droit de l'Union européenne 285 ff; Wollenschläger *Das Asyl- und Einwanderungsrecht der EU* [2001] EuGRZ 354.

---

121 ECJ *Commission v Netherlands* [1991] ECR I-4069, para 30; *Stichting* [1991] ECR I-4007, paras 22 ff; *Veronica Omröp Organisatie* [1993] ECR I-487, para 9; *TV 10* [1994] ECR I-4795, paras 18 ff.
122 ECJ *Familiapress* [1997] ECR I-3689, para 18.
123 ECJ *Familiapress* [1997] ECR I-3689, para 24.
124 ECJ *Ter Voort* [1992] ECR I-5485.
125 ECJ *Ter Voort* [1992] ECR I-5485, para 38.
126 ECJ *Familiapress* [1997] ECR I-3689, para 19 referring to ECJ *Pall* [1990] ECR I-4827, para 12; *Mars* [1995] ECR I-1923, para 15.

86 In October 1999, the Tampere European Council adopted a programme which provides for political guidelines, specific aims and a time table. This is supposed to realise the freedom of movement for persons in the Union, to provide for the personal security of the citizens and to guarantee an easy access to the judiciary by ensuring a mutual acknowledgement of court decisions in the whole Union. This dynamic project, whose first phase has been completed on 1st May 2004[127], encroaches upon several very delicate fields of fundamental rights. These may be sketched out as policy of asylum, of visa, of refugees and immigration, deportation of foreigners and extradition of own nationals as well as general prosecution of crimes and execution of sentences.

87 If the developments in the fields of internal politics and the judiciary are added to the reflections about fundamental rights' protection in the Union, it becomes clear why the **Charter of Fundamental Rights** contains a right to freedom and security (Article II-66 DC), a right to asylum (Article II-78 DC) as well as guarantees concerning the protection in the case of deportation, expulsion and extradition (Article II-79 DC).

88 However, these guarantees anticipate an ensuing state of integration for the future rather than having a sound basis in the *acquis communautaire*. A right to freedom and security is linked to the *habeas corpus*-guarantee and could secure the physical freedom of movement following Article 5 of the ECHR.[128] Because the Community does not have a competence for measures limiting the freedom of movement even in the preliminary investigation of competition law, the question of the significance of Community law for this right is open for the time being. The asylum policy of the Community is based on the principle that the material law of asylum in the Member States remains unaffected, which means that there is no law of asylum of the Community. Therefore, the endeavours of the EC concentrate on creating common minimum standards for a co-ordinated European law of asylum.[129] In this context it is also noteworthy that the granting of asylum for a citizen of the Union by an EU-Member State has been generally ruled out by a protocol to the Treaty of Amsterdam.[130] In the field of the law of extradition, national measures

---

127 *Cf* the working document from the Commission (SEK (2004) 693 of 2 June 2004), annex to the Communication from the Commission Area of Freedom, Security and Justice: Assessment of the Tampere programme and future orientations (COM (2004) 401 final of 2 June 2004); the judicial-political programme of the following years is contained in the "Hague Programme" of the Council, [2005] OJ C53/1.

128 *Cf* Bernstorff in: Meyer (ed) *Charta der Grundrechte* (Baden-Baden 2001) Art 6, para 11.

129 The legal instruments in this field are Directive 2003/9/EC of 27 January 2003 laying down minimum standards for the reception of asylum seekers; Regulation (EC) 343/2003 establishing the criteria and mechanisms for determining the Member State responsible for examining an asylum application lodged in one of the Member States by a third-country national, amended by Regulation (EC) 407/2002 of 28 February 2002 laying down certain rules to implement Regulation (EC) 2725/2000 concerning the establishment of "Eurodac" for the comparison of fingerprints for the effective application of the Dublin Convention; Directive 2001/55/EC of 20 July 2001 on minimum standards for giving temporary protection in the event of a mass influx of displaced persons and on measures promoting a balance of efforts between Member States in receiving such persons and bearing the consequences thereof.

130 According to the protocol to the EC-Treaty on the granting of asylum for nationals of Member States of the EU, the assumption that as far as the EU-Member States themselves are concerned they are considered safe countries of origin is omitted under the following conditions: If the person applying for asylum comes from a country that has declared a state of emergency according to Article 15 of the ECHR or if a proposal according to Article 7(2) of the TEU has been

issued in compliance with the framework order about the European Warrant of Arrest will accelerate the proceedings.[131] The fact that the decision whether a request for extradition is granted is made subject to further legal regulation may not deceive about the fact that the competence is still with the Member States. The (general) acknowledgement of judiciary acts of other Member States, which also increasingly occurs in extradition law, can result in a perceivable reduction of fundamental rights' protection of the individual, and with that, a loss of freedom.[132]

In their public statements, the Community institutions show that the great importance of measures to create an "area of freedom, security and justice" has been recognised. In this context, the European Council has adopted the establishment of an Office for Human Rights[133] during its conference in December 2003. Apart from that, the Commission brought up the increased application of Article 7 of the TEU[134] (Article I-59 DC). However, it is doubtful whether these two are suitable mechanisms to protect the subjective rights of the citizens in the individual case. Instead of improving the effective protection of individual rights in the Community courts, the steps considered by the Community institutions are based on international – political – strategies for the protection of human rights.

89

---

initiated against the Member State concerned in the framework of the sanction proceeding; further cf the protocol declaration of the Member States.

131 This is shown by the Report of the Commission about the European Warrant of Arrest and the conditions of surrender between the Member States of 23 February 2005, COM (2005) 53 final 6. The facts of the case underlying the order of the Second Senate of the BVerfG of 24 November 2004 [2004] EuGRZ 667 show what ensues from an acceleration of the extradition proceedings.

132 This is exemplified by the facts of the case underlying the order of the First Chamber of the Second Senate of the BVerfG of 3 March 2004 [2004] EuGRZ 321. The Chamber overruled the order of the competent Higher Regional Court which had declared the extradition of the complainant to Italy for the execution of the sentence permissible. The complainant had been sentenced to an eight years' imprisonment in absence.

133 The office shall be created by extending the European Monitoring Centre on Racism and Xenophobia, cf Presidency Conclusions, Brussels European Council of 12 and 13 December 2003, 27: „In the same context, the Representatives of the Member States meeting with in the European Council, stressing the importance of human rights data collection and analysis with a view to defining Union policy in this field, agreed to build upon the existing European Monitoring Centre on Racism and Xenophobia and to extend its mandate to make it a Human Rights Agency to that effect."

134 Communication from the Commission to the Council and the European Parliament, COM (2003) 606 final of 15 October 2003; in this context cf Schorkopf in: Grabitz/Hilf Recht der Europäischen Union (Loose-leaf Munich) Art 7 EUV, para 53; Schmitt von Sydow [2001] 2 Revue du droit de l'Union européenne 285 ff.

§ 16
The Right to Pursue a Freely Chosen Occupation

Matthias Ruffert

Leading cases: ECJ *Nold* [1974] ECR 491; *Germany v Council (Bananas)* [1994] ECR I-4973, paras 64 ff.

Further reading: Borrmann *Der Schutz der Berufsfreiheit im deutschen Verfassungsrecht und im europäischen Gemeinschaftsrecht* (Berlin 2002); Glos *Die deutsche Berufsfreiheit und die europäischen Grundfreiheiten* (Frankfurt am Main 2003); Günter *Berufsfreiheit und Eigentum in der Europäischen Union* (Heidelberg 1998); Ruffert in: Calliess/Ruffert (eds) *EUV/EGV, Das Verfassungsrecht der Europäischen Union mit Europäischer Grundrechtecharta, Kommentar* (3rd ed, Munich 2007) Art 15 GRCh; Wunderlich *Das Grundrecht der Berufsfreiheit im Europäischen Gemeinschaftsrecht* (Baden-Baden 2000).

I. Scope of Protection

1. Function, Significance and Sources of the Right to Pursue a Freely Chosen Occupation in EU Law

1   Together with the guarantee of property (→ § 17), the **right to pursue a freely chosen occupation** is the central economic fundamental right. Following the understanding of German constitutional law, which may be considered in a way that transcends jurisdictional barriers, this fundamental right guarantees the freedom to earn one's living by a steady occupation, *ie* the economic side of the "pursuit of happiness" of American origin. However, in every legal system governed or influenced by fundamental rights, the exact content and restrictions of that guarantee can only be determined in view of its historically shaped economic constitution.[1] The level of protection of the fundamental right to pursue a freely chosen occupation is dependent upon factual and legal structures which were created prior to constitutional law. This holds even more true for a system of fundamental rights without a written, binding catalogue of fundamental rights. In Community law, the fundamental right to pursue a freely chosen occupation is developed by various fundamental normative decisions which are not easily to be reconciled and which obstruct the effective guarantee of the fundamental right.

2   The first and most important starting point is the objective of the **internal market**. The fundamental freedoms and the harmonisation of legal systems both aim to establish private autonomy within the whole area of the Community, *ie* the free development of economic entities in the Community.[2] The fundamental freedoms help to promote this goal by demanding a justification for those national regulations which limit transnational economic activities such as trade in goods, dependent occupation, services, establishment,

---

1 *Cf* Pitschas *Berufsfreiheit und Berufslenkung* (Berlin 1983) pp 249 ff, 253 ff; Uber *Freiheit des Berufs* (Hamburg 1952) pp 113 ff; Papier in: Benda/Maihofer/Vogel (eds) *Handbuch des Verfassungsrechts* (2nd ed, Berlin 1994) § 18, paras 5 ff, 34–36; Scholz in: Maunz/Dürig, *Grundgesetz Kommentar II* (loose-leaf, Munich 1981) Art 12, paras 78–80.
2 Müller-Graff in: von der Groeben/Schwarze (eds) *Kommentar zum Vertrag über die Europäische Union und zur Gründung der Europäischen Gemeinschaft* (6th ed, Baden-Baden 2003–2004) Vor Art 30–37 EGV, para 3.

and movement of capital.³ By means of harmonisation, obstacles are minimised which are due to the legitimate national regulation of the Member States in the interest of common welfare. Moreover, competition policy shall prevent infringements of economic liberty caused by the concentration of private power in certain areas of the market. Finally, this protection of transnational economic activity is accompanied by the monetary union. Since the Treaty of Maastricht, the economic constitution of the Community has been consistently and expressly devoted to the principle of an open market economy with free competition (Article 4(1), 98(ii) TEC/Article III-178 DC).⁴ This orientation is further strengthened by the involvement in the World Trade Organisation (WTO, Article 11(1) Agreement establishing the WTO), which also aims at the reduction of trade barriers, although individual economic entities cannot derive individual rights from WTO-law (yet). Elements of the right to pursue a freely chosen occupation are also guaranteed by some important human rights instruments;⁵ above all, the Charter of Fundamental Rights of the European Union (EU-Charter) guarantees the right to pursue a freely chosen occupation in its Article 15(1) (Article II-75(1) DC), and entrepreneurial freedom in its Article 16 (Article II-76 DC) – having recourse to Community law and national laws and practices.⁶ All in all, the whole of the fundamental decisions of European law as described are an ideal breeding ground for a far reaching guarantee of the right to pursue a freely chosen occupation.

Since the soil for the right to pursue a freely chosen occupation seems so secure, none of the leading cases of the ECJ concerning that right had to deal with subjects already mentioned. The overwhelming jurisprudence regarding that right concerns the **Common Agricultural Policy (CAP)**.⁷ This is the second starting point for the factual-normative framework of the guarantee of the right to pursue a freely chosen occupation in Community law. At the heart of the CAP are the European market organisations according to Article 34(1)(ii)(c) of the TEC (Article III-228(1)(c) DC). The total public regulation of agricultural markets as achieved by the market organisations through fixed prices, interventions and the attribution of reference quantities is principally irreconcilable with a comprehensive and overriding guarantee of private economic activity as contained in the right to pursue a freely chosen occupation.⁸ The same is true – with modifications – for the regulated coal and steel markets following the ECSC-Treaty⁹. This breach in the

3

---

3 *Cf* Feger [1987] RdA 13, 16; Notthoff [1995] RIW 541, 544 ff.
4 See Schliesky *Öffentliches Wirtschaftsrecht* (2ⁿᵈ ed, Heidelberg 2003) pp 22 ff; Hatje in: von Bogdandy *Europäisches Verfassungsrecht* (Heidelberg 2003) pp 683, 692 ff, but consider Rengeling *Grundrechtsschutz in der Europäischen Gemeinschaft* (Munich 1993) p 27.
 The wording in Article I-3 III of the Draft Constitution is weaker at first sight: "The Union shall work for [...] a social market economy, highly competitive and aiming at full employment and social progress [...]".
5 Universal Declaration of Human Rights (GA Res 217A (III), GAOR, 3ʳᵈ Sess, Part I, p 71): Art 12 (right against arbitrary interference), Art 23 No 1 (right to work, to free choice of employment, to just and favourable conditions of work and to protection against unemployment); International Covenant on Economic, Social and Cultural Rights (UNTS 993, 3): Article 6(1) (right to earn one's living through freely chosen work), Art 7(c) (equal opportunity of vocational promotion). *Cf* Stadler *Die Berufsfreiheit in der Europäischen Gemeinschaft* (Munich 1980) pp 100 ff.
6 *Cf* Tettinger [2001] NJW 1010, 1014.
7 *Cf* Günter *Berufsfreiheit und Eigentum in der Europäischen Union* (Heidelberg 1998) p 18.
8 *Cf* Kluth [2001] JURA 371.
9 Leading case: ECJ *Nold* [1974] ECR 491, para 14.

system has led to the fact that the ECJ has so far never quashed a Community regulation in the framework of the CAP for violating the right to pursue a freely chosen occupation. The Court argued that particularly in the framework of a Common Market Organisation, the right to pursue a freely chosen occupation is subject to limitations.[10] Concentrating on the problem of the CAP particular to Community law also detracts attention from the basic collision between the right to pursue a freely chosen occupation on the one hand and non-economic as well as social aspects of the common good on the other hand.

4 This – wrongly – reduces the weight of the third starting point. As an **economic fundamental right**, the right to pursue a freely chosen occupation is closely linked to social guarantees. The inability to integrate social questions in the phrasing of fundamental rights and basic freedoms, which can be explained historically, has not only led to delaying the introduction of the guarantee of property into the ECHR until the additional protocol of 1952. It also resulted in the failure to include the right to pursue a freely chosen occupation in the ECHR[11] – except for the prohibition of forced and obligatory labour, which only concerns a partial aspect (similar to Article 12(2) of the *Grundgesetz* [German Basic Law])[12] and does not protect the right to pursue a freely chosen occupation in general. Nevertheless, we have to consider single guarantees in the European Social Charter (1961), which, though not expressly mentioned in Article 6(2) of the TEC, is part of common European tradition of fundamental rights (see Article 136(1) TEC; Article III-209(1) DC), albeit only with respect to its relative bindingness according to Article 20(1) of the Social Charter.[13] The guarantees thus touched upon (right to work, just, safe and healthy working conditions, fair wages, creation of coalitions, collective agreements, protection of the youth, protection of female workers, vocational counselling, vocational training, social security in the widest sense) are evidently linked to the idea of social fundamental rights. The Charter of Fundamental Rights of the European Union is oriented in this direction. Its Article 15(1) (Article II-75(1) DC) is not limited to the fundamental right to pursue a freely chosen occupation in its classical sense, but it contains over and above "a right to work". Third state nationals are granted the right to work on the same conditions as Union citizens as long as they have a legal title of access to the labour markets in the Member States. These guarantees are accompanied by a number of social rights:[14] hear-

---

10 ECJ *Schräder* [1989] ECR 2237, para 15; *Zuckerfabrik Süderdithmarschen* [1991] ECR I-415, para 73; *Germany v Council* [1994] ECR I-4973, para 78; *SMW Winzersekt* [1994] ECR I-5555, para 22; *Fishermen's Organisations* [1995] ECR I-3115, para 55; *Affish* [1997] ECR I-4315, para 42.
11 Golsong in: Mosler/Bernhardt/Hilf (eds) *Grundrechtsschutz in Europa* (Berlin 1977) pp 7, 9; Bartsch [1979] EuR 105, 109; Partsch in: Bettermann/Neumann/Nipperdey (eds) *Die Grundrechte I/1* (Berlin 1966) pp 235, 351; Frowein in: Isensee/Kirchhof (eds) *Handbuch des Staatsrechts Bd VII* (Heidelberg 1992) § 18, para 24; Borrmann *Der Schutz der Berufsfreiheit im deutschen Verfassungsrecht und im europäischen Gemeinschaftsrecht* (Berlin 2002) pp 150 ff.
12 *Stadler* (note 5) pp 105 ff. The European Commission on Human Rights (EuCommHR) refrained from interpreting this provision as a general guarantee of the right to pursue a freely chosen occupation; cf EurCommHR, App No 1468/62, *Iversen v Norway* (1963) 6 Yearbook of the European Convention on Human Rights 278, 328; critical Partsch (note 11) pp 347 ff.
13 Birk in: Richardi/Wlotzke (eds) *Münchener Handbuch zum Arbeitsrecht I* (2nd ed, Munich 2002) § 17, para 94; Gomien/Harris/Zwaak *Law and practice of the European Convention on Human Rights and the European Social Charter* (Strasbourg 1996) p 379; Blumenwitz [1989] NJW 621, 624; → § 5 paras 49 ff.
14 *Cf* only Mahlmann [2000] ZEuS 419, 432 ff.

ings for workers (Article 27; Article II-87 of the DC), collective bargaining and measures (Article 28; Article II-88 of the DC), job management (Article 29; Article II-89 of the DC), protection against unjustified dismissal (Article 30; Article II-90 of the DC), just and appropriate conditions of work (Article 31; Article II-91 of the DC), prohibition of child labour and protection of the youth (Article 32; Article II-92 of the DC), protection of motherhood (Article 33; Article II-93 of the DC). Even beyond social political decisions and aims,[15] a balance must be found between the right to pursue a freely chosen occupation and common values, such as in the areas of environmental, health and consumer protection[16] as well as when coordinating the access to professions in the internal market.[17]

Against this background, the guarantees of the right to pursue a freely chosen occupation in the national legal systems are to be considered as sources of legal insight (→ § 14 para 9).[18] All written constitutions of Member States contain that fundamental right.[19] The *Common Law* of England, too, guarantees the right to pursue a freely chosen occupation using various synonyms – *right to work, right to earn a living, interest in pursuing a livelihood*[20] –, and even without a written fundamental right, the exercise of a profession is less densely regulated in England than in continental Europe in the interest of economic entities.[21] Similarly, the freedom to pursue a freely chosen occupation is guaranteed in many important new Member States.[22]. In France, free entrepreneurship (*liberté d'entreprendre*) is derived from Article 4 of the Declaration of Rights of Man and Citizens, the right to do anything which is not detrimental to somebody else.[23] The general principle of

5

---

15 In that sense ECJ *SAM Schiffahrt und Stapf* [1997] ECR I-4475, paras 72 ff.
16 Environmental protection: ECJ *ADBHU* [1985] ECR 531, para 13; *Marshall* [1990] ECR I-4071, para 28; Consumer Protection: *Keller* [1986] ECR 2897, para 14; *SMW Winzersekt* [1994] ECR I-5555, para 25; Protection of public health: *Affish* [1997] ECR I-4315, para 43.
17 Penski/Elsner [2001] DÖV 265, 272; following Bleckmann *Europarecht* (6th ed, Cologne et al 1997) para 590.
18 Having recourse only to them Penski/Elsner [2001] DÖV 265, 271.
19 Art 23(3) No 1 Constition of the Kingdom of Belgium; § 74 Constitutional Act of the Kingdom of Denmark; § 18 Constitution of Finland; Art 5(1) and 22 Constitution of Greece; Art 4 and 41 Constitution of the Italian Republic; Art 11(5) Constitution of the Grand Duchy Luxembourg; Art 19(3) Constitution of the Kingdom of the Netherlands; Art 6(1) Austrian Basic Law on the General Rights of Nationals 1867 (*cf* Art 149(1) Constitution of the Republic of Austria); Art 47(1), 61(1) Constitution of the Portuguese Republic; Art 35(1), 38 Spanish Constitution 1978. However, the single provisions are heterogeneous in their scope and content: Günter (note 7) p 223. Doubtful – without a comprehensive legal comparison – Besselink (1998) 35 CMLR 629, 636 ff note 9, and – following him – Penski/Elsner [2001] DÖV 265, 270.
20 *Cf* Wunderlich *Das Grundrecht der Berufsfreiheit im Europäischen Gemeinschaftsrecht* (Baden-Baden 2000) pp 46 ff with many references to the relevant jurisprudence. As to the nature of the guarantees Günter (note 7) pp 52 ff as well as Stadler (note 5) pp 323 ff. Similarly, there is an unwritten right derived from Art 40(3) No 1 and 2 Irish Constitution (*right to earn a living*); *cf* Günter (note 7) pp 70 ff; Stadler (note 5) pp 282 ff.
21 Ehlermann in: Fröschle (ed) *Rechenschaftslegung im Wandel, Festschrift für Wolfgang Dieter Budde* (Munich 1995) pp 157, 171; following him Wunderlich (note 20) p 45.
22 Bulgaria: Art 48(3) Constitution 1991; Poland: Art 65 Consitution 1997; Romania: Art 38 Constitution 1991; Czech Republic: Art 26 Charta of Fundamental Rights 1991.
23 *Cf* Wunderlich (note 20) pp 52 ff. In its decision No 98–401 DC of 10 June 1998, the Conseil constitutionnel declared the shortening of working hours by law constitutional (Loi d'orientation

liberté du commerce et de l'industrie is derived from two revolutionary statutes from 1791 which are still valid.[24] Nevertheless, it has to be considered that the effective guarantee of those two freedoms is negatively affected by the fact that the constitutional and administrative Courts grant a broad scope of discretion to the legislator and the authorities and reduce their control of proportionality. The intensity of control, however, tends to be higher with respect to the *liberté du commerce et de l'industrie* than with respect to the *liberté d'entreprendre*.[25] – In Germany, a similar development is taking place. Article 12(1) of the Basic Law guarantees all Germans the right to chose one's profession, place of work and place of vocational training freely; the prohibitions of forced labour in Article 12(2) and Article 12(3) of the Basic Law have only attained limited significance. In the context of the reservation of regulation in Article 12(1) (ii) of the Basic Law, the *Bundesverfassungsgericht* (BVerfG – German Federal Constitutional Court) has sometimes granted the legislator an extremely far reaching scope of discretion and has not scrutinised the choice of the common goods which may limit the fundamental right.[26] More recently, the BVerfG has developed further dimensions of the right to pursue a freely chosen occupation out of Article 12(1) of the Basic Law. The participative right derived from Article 12(1), Article 3(1) of the Basic Law is relevant for the admission of an individual applicant to University.[27] As for the positive obligation to protect this freedom, the BVerfG in individual cases transcends the legal protection of the right to pursue a freely chosen occupation and, politically motivated, tries to balance the socially conflicting positions (employee – employer) without having been given any competence to do so by a legislative decision, and without a constitutional basis or dogmatic reasons.[28]

6   As the normative basis is not entirely homogeneous, reaching a decision in favour of a certain **concept of protection** tends to become a political question. The underlying understanding of economic policy considerably influences the determination of the concrete mode of protecting the right to pursue a freely chosen occupation, be it in describing the scope of protection, be it on the level of restrictions and their justification or on the level of functions of the fundamental right. It is not the task of a Community jurist to make that decision, but he can work to elucidate its normative basis. Under this premise, the following explanations emanate from the necessity to construe the content of the freedom to pursue a freely chosen occupation in accordance with the national constitutions as well as with Article 15(1) (Article II-75(1) DC) and Article 16 (Article II-76 DC) of the Charter of Fundamental Rights of the European Union, and to give it the appropriate strength in order to balance it justly on the level of justification of restrictions with other aspects of the common good, be they of social or another matter. Social rights should not be derived directly from the right to pursue a freely chosen occupation: A right to work was purposefully excluded from the Charter (2000)[29] and is included in the European Social Charter in

---

et d'incitation relative à la réduction du temps de travail), as the legislator had taken into account the "Right to Work" in the preamble of the Constitution of 1946.
24 Günter (note 7) p 75; Stadler (note 5) pp 265 ff; Wunderlich (note 20) pp 54 ff.
25 In detail Wunderlich (note 20) pp 152 ff.
26 Cf for the scope of discretion of the legislator Manssen in: von Mangoldt/Klein/Starck (eds) *Grundgesetz I* (5th ed, Munich 2005) Art 12, para 125.
27 BVerfG (1973) 33 VerfGE 303.
28 Ruffert *Vorrang der Verfassung und Eigenständigkeit des Privatrechts* (Tübingen 2001) pp 434 ff, 462 ff.
29 Grabenwarter [2001] DVBl 1, 5; Schmitz [2001] JZ 833, 841; Tettinger [2001] NJW 1010, 1014. In

a considerably relativised form. The motives against its introduction, *ie* the danger of weakening the fundamental rights because they cannot be realised and the necessity of a scope of discretion of the legislator in this area, are only too well known. Singular social guarantees are contained in the chapter of the Charter titled "Solidarity". Furthermore, essential rights of protection are contained in the social provisions of the TEC and, above all, in the secondary law created on its basis: equality of the sexes, work protection, appropriate working conditions, to name only a few of them.[30] The "right to work" in Article 15(1) (Article II-75(1) DC) of the Charter cannot be read as the entitlement to a concrete employment.[31] Nevertheless, it is not without content. Notwithstanding the limited legal status of the Charter as it stands, it prohibits infringements by the state or any other public entity upon independent work, thereby increasing the necessity to justify public regulation of the choice and exercise of a career. In a social political context, the provision regulates the explicit, though not entirely justiciable task for those the Charter is addressed to (Article 51 EU-Charter, Article II-111 DC) to create the real possibility to exercise a profession, *ie* to aim at full employment (in this sense also Article 125 ff TEC, Article III-203 ff DC[32]).

Given that the dimension of the right **directed against public authorities** is chosen as a starting point, the planned economy organisation of markets according to the CAP is the real anachronism. Whether the CAP will survive the near future is questionable at the very least. Until now, the majority of cases available for the analysis of the right to pursue a freely chosen occupation are cases from the field of agricultural law.

2. Subject Matter of Protection

Case 1 – Problem: ECJ *Rau* [1987] ECR 2289
Within the framework of a common market organisation for milk and milk products, the commission decides to distribute 900 tons of butter from intervention stocks in packages of 250 g for free together with a package of trademark butter of the same weight. The measure's purpose is to gain knowledge about the consumers' behaviour when the price of butter declines. Last but not least, the "mountain of butter" is to be reduced. M is a large producer of margarine. He objects to the decision, arguing that it constitutes an infringement of the principle of free choice of profession, freedom of activity and the freedom of competition.

---

addition, only a few Member States link the social guarantee with the fundamental right (Belgium, Netherlands, Luxemburg, Italy, Spain, Portugal, Greece, Finland); *cf* the references in note 19.
30 Birk (note 13) § 19, paras 86 ff.
31 Likewise Grabenwarter [2001] DVBl 1, 5; Ruffert in: Calliess/Ruffert (eds) *EUV/EGV, Das Verfassungsrecht der Europäischen Union mit Europäischer Grundrechtecharta, Kommentar* (3rd ed, Munich 2007) Art 15 GRCh, paras 3, 6;→ § 19 para 8. It also does not appear to be possible to deduce a right to promote small and medium enterprises from Art 16 (Art II-76 DC) as developed by Tettinger [2001] NJW 1010, 1014.
32 *Cf* Krebber in: Calliess/Ruffert (note 31) Art 125 EGV, para 8 (with differentiations).

a) Content and Single Guarantees

9 The scope of protection of the fundamental right to pursue a freely chosen occupation has yet to be defined abstractly by the ECJ.[33] However, such a definition can be derived from a comprehensive view of the jurisprudence as well as the Charter as a source of law.

10 According to this, the right to pursue a freely chosen occupation in Community Law contains a comprehensive guarantee of freedom of **economic activity**.[34] This is emphasised by the guarantees of the Charta, which not only contains the right to work and to pursue a freely chosen or accepted profession (Article 15(1) EU-Charter, Article II-75(1) DC), but also the freedom to operate a business (Article 16 of the EU-Charter, Article II-76 of the DC). Last but not least, the Charter makes it clear that this is an independent guarantee and not merely a specification derived from the freedom of activity in general.[35]

11 The characteristic feature of the activities protected under this guarantee is the **aim to earn one's living**. This feature is also to be found in the jurisdiction which describes the scope of application of the fundamental freedoms related only to economic activity. However, the ECJ does not formulate particularly strict requirements and subsumes any activity which has an economic connotation whatsoever under the relevant fundamental freedom.[36] The **duration of the activity** is only relevant insofar as the term "occupation" used in the Charter in all its languages (Beruf/profession/profesión/professione/profissão/beroep/erhverv) suggests more than a singular or short term activity. The freedom of entrepreneurship goes beyond that; hence, the issue of duration is less important here than when interpreting the term of occupation (Beruf) in Article 12(1) of the Basic Law.[37] Parallel to the freedom of movement for workers, a *de minimis*-rule is to be inferred.[38] By contrast, the legality of the activity is irrelevant. The legitimacy and prohibition of vocational activity are questions of limitations and their justification.[39]

12 The **single guarantees** which have so far been formulated in the jurisprudence of the Court can be attributed to this comprehensive guarantee of economic activity. Especially the freedom of trade is considered to be a protected fundamental right by the ECJ.[40] The freedom of contract with respect to the vocational activity is also attributed to that right, though not in an entirely consistent manner.[41] In this context, the Court in singular cases

---

33 *Cf* Wunderlich (note 20) p 105.
34 Expressly: ECJ *Finsider* [1985] ECR 2857, para 23.
35 Another view was taken by Schilling [2000] EuGRZ 3, 12. Wunderlich (note 20) pp 106 ff (similarly Günter (note 7) p 23) proves that the individual forms of economic activity are part of the jurisprudence on the freedom to chose one's occupation freely and that they do not contain particular guarantees (which is made clear *eg* in CFI *Atlanta* [1996] ECR II-1707, para 63). Taking recourse to the jurisprudence of the BVerfG distinguishing the general freedom of activity and the freedom of occupation should be avoided (see Stadler (note 5) pp 36 ff).
36 *Cf* Birk (note 13) § 19, para 11, to the broad concept of worker of the ECJ; → § 9 paras 5 ff.
37 Here, the requirements are fairly low already, *cf* Wieland in: Dreier (ed) *Grundgesetz Kommentar I* (2nd ed, Tübingen 2004) Art 12, para 55.
38 *Cf* Brechmann in: Calliess/Ruffert (note 31) Art 39 EGV, para 9.
39 On this note Penski/Elsner [2001] DÖV 265, 271. Distinguishing Wunderlich (note 20) pp 72 ff. With a different tendency Steindorff [1982] NJW 1902, 1904.
40 ECJ *Nold* [1974] ECR 491, para 14; *ADBHU* [1985] ECR 531, para 9. As AG *Stix-Hackl* states correctly in her opinion from 20 January 2004, this is only about terminology and not about different guarantees (ECJ *Di Lenardo and Dilexport* [2004] ECR I-6911, para 110).
41 *Cf Ruffert* (note 28) pp 297 ff with further references.

assumes an independent guarantee,[42] but rightly considers the free choice of the (business) partner of contract to be part of the right to pursue a freely chosen occupation.[43] The right also includes the freedom of competition.[44] Given the importance of free competition in EC law, reluctant phrases in ECJ judgements should not be overestimated, at least at the level of protection.[45]

All in all, the union right to pursue a freely chosen occupation guarantees **"economic activity" in all its aspects**.

b) Delimitation from Other Community Law Guarantees

aa) The Protection of Property

In its jurisprudence, the Court does not always differentiate between **the protection of property** and the protection of the right to pursue a freely chosen occupation.[46] With respect to the sources of legal insight, this is not convincing in terms of legal methodology (Article 1 of the 1st Prot ECHR; Article 295 TEC; Article III-425 DC).[47] Legal literature predominantly differentiates according to the rough terms protection of existing positions/protection of chances of acquisition, which are taken from German constitutional law.[48] If the independence of the Community legal system is not ignored, drawing this parallel is unobjectionable. The protection of property is pertinent – where appropriate in combination with the protection of the right to pursue a freely chosen occupation – where a case is about the use of a place or means of production. The right to pursue a freely chosen occupation alone is relevant when duties or prohibitions are related to activity, not substance. The Court does not scrutinise taxes and similar duties with respect to the right of property.[49] If one follows this line of thought, a test with respect of right to pursue a freely chosen occupation is necessary in these cases.[50]

bb) Other Fundamental Rights

There are difficulties of delimitation with respect to the Community law fundamental rights of **communication** (in particular the freedom of expression; → § 15 paras 59 ff) in the area of commercial advertisements. It is most convincing to address the matter in a differentiated way which, for the sake of utmost protection, leaves both guarantees to

---

42 Only allusively in ECJ *Sukkerfabriken Nykøbing* [1979] ECR 1, para 20; *Spain v Commission* [1999] ECR I-6571, para 99.
43 ECJ *Neu* [1991] ECR I-3617, para 13.
44 ECJ *Rau* [1987] ECR 2289, para 15; as well as ECJ *Metronome Music* [1998] ECR I-1953, para 28.
45 Rather different Wunderlich (note 20) p 109.
46 ECJ *Duff* [1996] ECR I-569, para 30; *Bosphorus* [1996] ECR I-3953, paras 21 ff; *SAM Schiffahrt und Stapf* [1997] ECR I-4475, paras 72 ff; *Metronome Music* [1998] ECR I-1953, para 21. Questionable as well ECJ *Hauer* [1979] ECR 3127, para 32. *Cf* Beutler in: von der Groeben/ Schwarze (eds) *Kommentar zum Vertrag über die Europäische Union und zur Gründung der Europäischen Gemeinschaft* (6th ed, Baden-Baden 2003–2004) Art F, para 57.
47 Penski/Elsner [2001] DÖV 265, 267. As to the protection of property see → § 16.
48 Kingreen (note 31) Art 6 EUV, para 131; followed by Wunderlich (note 20) p 127.
49 Kingreen (note 31) Art 6 EUV, para 146.
50 Like here Penski/Elsner [2001] DÖV 265, 271, and – for German constitutional law – Hohmann [2000] DÖV 406. Thus, the approach is correct in: ECJ *Schräder* [1989] ECR 2237, para 15.

coexist side by side if the commercial advertisement contains a valuing expression of opinion.[51] In Germany, the Benetton-jurisprudence shows which problems the exclusion of the freedom of communication would have caused for commercial advertising[52]. The concept represented here is in line with the jurisprudence of the ECtHR that sees commercial advertising as an activity under Article 10 of the ECHR and thus does not exclude it from the scope of application of the ECHR, which does not contain a fundamental right to pursue a freely chosen occupation.[53]

16 There are no serious problems in relation to the Union fundamental right of **association**, which is recognised by the ECJ following Article 11 of the ECHR.[54] Collisions between the right to pursue a freely chosen occupation (eg of an employee) and the freedom of association of another (eg employer) are to be balanced on the level of justification. Concerning a positive duty to protect which may be derived to a limited extent from the right to pursue a freely chosen occupation, one must bear in mind that the freedom of coalition, which is linked to the freedom of association, contains a particular mechanism to protect workers' rights.[55]

17 Finally, the fundamental right to pursue a freely chosen occupation is a liberty right and thus applicable alongside **Community equality rights**. This is true for the particular prohibition of discrimination in Article 34(2) of the TEC[56] (Article III-228(2) DC) as well as for the general principle of equality as a general principle of law.[57] The relationship to Article 12 of the TEC (Article I-4(2) DC) is pursuant to the principles as established for the fundamental freedoms (→ paras 21 ff). There is no conflict with Article 141 of the TEC (Article III-214 DC) and the secondary law promulgated in that context, as this area of the law does not contain fundamental rights in the strict sense, but only particular regulations for the design of national law which, under certain circumstances, can have a direct effect. The same is true for measures under Article 13 of the TEC (Article III-124 DC) which, in order to be valid, on the contrary have to be proportionate with respect to the fundamental freedom to pursue a freely chosen occupation.[58]

---

51 Opinion AG Fennelly, ECJ *Germany v Parliament and Council* [2000] ECR I-8419, paras 152 ff (the ECJ did not take up the fundamental rights aspect); critically Hilf/Frahm [2001] RIW 128, 133; Hatje *Wirtschaftswerbung und Meinungsfreiheit* (Baden-Baden 1993) p 62; Perau *Werbeverbote im Gemeinschaftsrecht* (Baden-Baden 1997) pp 269 ff; of different opinion Wunderlich (note 20) pp 129 ff. For a comprehensive analysis of economic advertising Kühling *Die Kommunikationsfreiheit als europäisches Gemeinschaftsgrundrecht* (Berlin 1999) pp 464 ff.
52 BVerfG (2001) 102 BVerfGE 347, 359 ff.
53 Wunderlich (note 20) pp 59 ff; Callies [1996] EuGRZ 293.
54 ECJ *Bosman* [1995] ECR I-4921, para 79.
55 Richardi in: Richardi/Wlotzke (eds) *Münchener Handbuch zum Arbeitsrecht I* (2nd ed, Munich 2002) § 10, para 31.
56 ECJ *Leukhardt* [1989] ECR 1991, para 19; *Marshall* [1990] ECR I-4071, paras 19 ff; *Zuckerfabrik Süderdithmarschen* [1991] ECR I-415, paras 66 ff; *Kühn* [1992] ECR I-35, para 18; *Germany v Council* [1994] ECR I-4973, paras 64 ff.
57 ECJ *SMW Winzersekt* [1994] ECR I-5555, paras 30 ff; *Fishermen's Organisations* [1995] ECR I-3115, paras 44 ff; *Affish* [1997] ECR I-4315, paras 41 ff; *SAM Schiffahrt und Stapf* [1997] ECR I-4475, paras 50 ff; CFI *Atlanta* [1996] ECR II-1707, paras 41 ff, 59 ff. Cf Stadler (note 5) p 36.
58 The following directives are to be tested here: Council Directive 2000/43/EC of 29 June 2000, [2000] OJ L180/22, implementing the principle of equal treatment between persons irrespective of racial or ethnic origin; Council Directive 2000/78/EC of 27 November 2000, [2000] OJ L303/16 establishing a general framework for equal treatment in employment and occupation.

cc) Legitimate Expectations

According to the jurisprudence of the ECJ, the **protection of legitimate expectations** is a general principle of law that exists alongside the fundamental rights.[59] However, confidence in a given regulatory structure could also be relevant within the fundamental right to pursue a freely chosen occupation.[60] In particular, the ECJ opposes the idea that single economic entities can have trust in the continuity of certain regulations of a European market organisation adopted within the framework of CAP; hence it does not consider economic losses caused by the modification of the market order, which withdraws advantages it had granted before, to be interferences with the right to pursue a freely chosen occupation.[61]

The general incongruity of **market organisations shaped in a planned economy style** on the one hand and the guarantee to pursue a freely chosen occupation on the other hand has been pointed out above. On the level of the scope of protection, this contrast can only be overcome if economic activity in terms of the fundamental right also includes such activities that are influenced or even generated by the market organisations. If economic entities are established within a highly regulated market, the level of protection of the right to pursue a freely chosen occupation is also determined by the regulative structure as it exists.[62] This does not, however, amount to an absolute protection of existing positions: Necessary reforms in the agricultural policy will always lead to intrusions in economic positions which then have to be justified by the common good objectives behind the respective reform.[63]

The situation is completely different if considerable losses are caused by the introduction of a European market organisation, as was the case with the banana market in 1993.[64] Such cases are not about the confidence of market participants in a certain regulatory structure, but about taking away a generally existing freedom by public – Community – law.[65] Since a high level of regulation remote from the market is to be expected in the agricultural sector due to Article 32(3) with annex I of the TEC (Article III-236(3) with annex I of the DC), limitations of the legal position of economic entities may only be recognised at the level of justification.

c) The Relationship with the Fundamental Freedoms

Those fundamental freedoms that have been given the character of prohibitions of limitation in the jurisprudence of the ECJ are having the effect of a special **right to pursue a freely chosen occupation of Community citizens**,[66] which brings up the question of their

---

59 Calliess in: Calliess/Ruffert (note 31) Art 6 EUV, para 26.
60 The fundamental right is applied alongside with the test of legitimate expectations: ECJ *Kühn* [1992] ECR I-35, paras 13 ff.
61 ECJ *Eridania* [1979] ECR 2749, para 22; *Rau* [1987] ECR 2289, para 18.
62 Similarly Günter (note 7) p 19; Penski/Elsner [2001] DÖV 265, 271 ff, 275; with the same tendency Priebe in: Dauses (ed) *Handbuch des Europäischen Wirtschaftrechts* (loose-leaf, Munich 1999) para 290. For economic subjects outside a concrete market organisation Hilf/Willms [1989] EuGRZ 189, 191.
63 Like here Wunderlich (note 20) p 118.
64 Like here Günter (note 7) p 22. With a different starting point Wunderlich (note 20) pp 117 ff.
65 Thus, the ECJ applies the test of the fundamental right to pursue a freely chosen occupation: ECJ *Germany v Council* [1994] ECR I-4973, paras 78 ff.
66 *Cf* ECJ *Heylens* [1987] ECR 4097, para 14; Explicitely: Pernice *Grundrechtsgehalte im Gemein-*

relationship to the general fundamental right. This relationship cannot be determined according to the addressee of the right, since under Community law, the Member States can be under a duty to protect the Community fundamental rights[67] and at the same time the Community can be under a duty to protect the fundamental freedoms.[68] Rather, the relationship between both forms of the guarantee follows from the paramount importance of the objective to create an internal market within the whole of Community law. In order to effectively establish transnational freedom of contract, the fundamental freedoms must be construed as *leges speciales*.[69] This also holds true if one follows a position in legal literature which considers the fundamental freedoms to be equality rights.[70] The objective of the guarantee, which is to destroy obstacles in transnational economic activities, is in principle not changed by this shift of perspective.

22 This finding of a relationship of **speciality** between the right to pursue a freely chosen occupation and the fundamental freedoms reflects the current situation of the European legal system. Accordingly, Article 15(2) of the EU-Charta takes up the relevant fundamental freedoms.[71] Without these fundamental freedoms and the dynamic accorded to them by the ECJ via supremacy and direct effect, the integration of Europe would not have been imaginable. On a higher level of integration it can be considered to substitute the fundamental freedoms with a general right to pursue a freely chosen occupation so that intrusions into transnational economic activity would only be a particular form of interference. However, the right to pursue a freely chosen occupation would then have to provide a similar level of protection as the fundamental freedoms do at the moment. The perspective on the relationship between Community and national public power would change considerably as well.

Case 1: Answer

23 The production of margarine is an economic activity, hence it falls within the scope of protection of the right to pursue a freely chosen occupation in its special form of the freedom of entrepreneurship. Though the ECJ does not consider the economic position which stems from market organisations to be protected, this line of argumentation should be given up for the sake of the right to pursue a freely chosen occupation of companies which are active

---

schaftsrecht (Baden-Baden 1979) pp 174 ff; Riegel (1977) 102 AöR 410, 430 ff. Too far Borrmann (note 11) pp 229 ff: identity between fundamental freedoms and the right to pursue a freely chosen occupation.

67 For the right to pursue a freely chosen occupation ECJ *Duff* [1996] ECR I-569, paras 28 ff.
68 Fundamentally Schwemer *Die Bindung des Gemeinschaftsgesetzgebers an die Grundfreiheiten* (Frankfurt am Main 1995). Singular references from the jurisprudence of the ECJ and the opinions of the AGs Wunderlich (note 20) pp 93 ff; → § 13 paras 28 ff.
69 Wunderlich (note 20) p 104. Of different opinion Stadler (note 5) p 66: Fundamental freedoms as a particular guarantee to free movement.
70 Explicitly Kingreen *Die Struktur der Grundfreiheiten des Europäischen Gemeinschaftsrechts* (Berlin 1999); with differentiations Hoffmann *Die Grundfreiheiten des EG-Vertrags als koordinationsrechtliche und gleichheitsrechtliche Abwehrrechte* (Baden-Baden 2000) pp 29 ff.
71 Against Grabenwarter [2001] DVBl 1, 5, one should not – with respect to the wording – dispense with the requirement of a transnational relation. The text refers to the fundamental freedoms with the respective requirements, *cf* the explanations by the Bureau of the Convention responsible for drafting the Charter of Fundamental Rights, CONV 49 from 11 October 2000, Dok Charte 4473/00, p 17.

in the scope of CAP. Thus, it has to be checked whether the interference with the scope of protection of the right to pursue a freely chosen occupation can be justified by the aim of a measure, here: the analysis of the effects of a certain form of marketing.

3. Personal Scope of Protection

a) Union Citizens

All **Union citizens** are bearers of the fundamental right to pursue a freely chosen occupation. The Charter makes clear that the common European guarantee does not differentiate between independent or dependent activities, even though the fundamental right is limited to independent activity in some Member States and the ECJ has only ruled on independent activity until now.[72] The mere existence of the free movement of workers expresses the protection of dependent activity in Community law as a matter of principle without any doubt. Only members of the civil service are, for a lack of Community competence, excluded from that freedom (Article 39(4) and Article 45 (with 55) TEC; Article III-133(4), Article III-139 with Article III-150 DC) and are therefore outside the personal scope of the right to pursue a freely chosen occupation.[73]

b) Legal Persons

As a short glance in the EU-Charta shows, it would be far fetched to deprive private **legal persons** from the personal scope of the right to pursue a freely chosen occupation, because entrepreneurship (Article 16 EU-Charter; Article II-76 DC) must also be granted to companies if that guarantee shall be an effective one. In the jurisprudence of the Court this is beyond question.

As far as legal persons are concerned, if they are a bearer of public power – in German law: public legal persons – a more differentiated view is required. The argument of confusion (*ie* the bearer and the addressee of a fundamental right must not be identical) clearly applies at least in cases where a legal subject constituted at Community law level is concerned (*eg* an independent agency[74]). By contrast, when dealing with a legal person that is backed by Member State public power, we have to consider that the guarantee of fundamental rights positions is not meant to rearrange the allocation of competences between the Community and its Member States in a way that is not in accordance with the Treaty. An entitlement of these legal persons with respect to the fundamental right therefore cannot be justified. This is also true for state or state dominated public or mixed economy companies as the precise normative prohibitions of primary Community law (Articles 16, 81–82, 86, 87–89 TEC; Articles III-122, III-161, III-162, III-166, III-167, III-169 DC) will not be overcome by an unwritten freedom.[75]

---

72 Like here: Kingreen in: Calliess/Ruffert (eds) *Kommentar zu EU-Vertrag und EG-Vertrag* (2nd ed, Neuwied 2002) Art 6 EUV, para 132; Wunderlich (note 20) p 111.
73 Stadler (note 5) p 344; Wunderlich (note 20) p 120.
74 See for the competence of their formation Calliess in: Calliess/Ruffert (note 31) Art 7 EGV, paras 25 ff.
75 Different view taken by Notthoff *Novellierungsversuche des Energiewirtschaftsrechts vor dem Hintergrund grundrechtlicher Normen* (Frankfurt am Main 1994) pp 241 ff; Tettinger in: Bauer (ed) *Europarecht, Energierecht, Wirtschaftsrecht: Festschrift für Bodo Börner zum 70. Geburtstag* (Cologne 1992) pp 625, 637 ff; Wunderlich (note 20) pp 122 ff; as well Bleckmann/Pieper in:

c) Third State Nationals (including Legal Persons)

27 Another question regarding the personal scope of protection is the status of third state nationals, in particular from the perspective of German constitutional law, which guarantees the right to pursue a freely chosen occupation only for Germans.[76] The answer to this question, which has not been dealt with by the ECJ until now, is given by Article 15(3) EU-Charter (Article II-75(3) DC):[77] In general, nationals of third countries are not given access to the internal market by primary law or a provision of the EU-Charter. This is in compliance with public international law, because market access as granted by Article XIV of the GATS is only guaranteed by a system of sector specific positive lists.[78] However, *if* third state nationals may work legally in the area of the Member States, they are granted the same rights as Union citizens. The dividing line between the personal entitlement to the fundamental right and its absence is thus not congruent with the borders of the Community, but follows the legality of economic activity in the area of the Community.[79] This concept may breach Member States' traditions, especially because the Union fundamental right to pursue a freely chosen occupation primarily binds the Community and only binds the Member States within the scope of application of Community law.

II. Infringement

Case 2 – Problem: ECJ *SMW Winzersekt* [1994] ECR I-5555
28 Theo Trierweiler (T) is a winegrower in the Mosel valley and produces sparkling wine following the "méthode champenoise", *ie* by shaking the bottles manually to create the sparkling effect. This method is more expensive than others (*eg* the production of sparkling wine in metal tanks), and consequently T has the indication "méthode champenoise" printed on the bottle-labels. A council regulation prohibits the use of that indication for sparkling wine which does not originate from Champagne (France). T feels that is an interference with his right to pursue a freely chosen occupation.

29 First of all, infringements of the right to pursue a freely chosen occupation may occur in the form of **normative regulations**. In this context, one should refrain from transferring the three steps theory (Drei-Stufen-Theorie) from German constitutional law to Community law.[80] The ECJ has only vaguely indicated the difference between regulating the choice of

---

Dauses (ed) *Handbuch des Europäischen Wirtschaftrechts* (loose-leaf, Munich 1999) Vol I, paras 137 ff. The argument of equal treatment in competition is not valid due to the particular public law obligations of public and mixed (public and private) undertakings.

76 Kingreen in: Calliess/Ruffert (note 31) Art 51 GRCh, para 52; Ruffert in: Callies/Ruffert (note 31) Art 15 GRCh, paras 7 ff; similarly Lenz in: Lenz *EU- und EG- Vertrag* (3rd ed, Cologne 2003) Art 220, para 34. Of different opinion Bleckmann/Pieper (note 75) Vol I, para 139 with further references; Beutler (note 2) (ex-) Art F EUV, para 79. Penski/Elsner [2001] DÖV 265, 265, refer that problem to the level of restrictions.
77 See already Art 137(3), 4th indent of the TEC (after Nice: Art 137 I(g) TEC); to this Krebber (note 2) Art 137, para 15.
78 *Cf* Art XVI ff GATS ([1994] OJ L336/184); to this Koehler *Das Allgemeine Übereinkommen über den Handel mit Dienstleistungen (GATS)* (Berlin 1999) pp 116 ff.
79 Even further Wunderlich (note 20) pp 123 ff.
80 But see *Notthoff* [1995] RIW 541, 543.

a profession and its exercise.[81] Detached from the German fundamental rights dogmatic, infringements of varying intensity can be coped with by a differentiated test of proportionality which considers how far bearers of the right are excluded from the exercise of a certain profession. While the three-step-concept may thus develop heuristic functions, it does not establish dogmatic categories in a binding manner. Normative regulations can also interfere in an indirect manner – which activates the duty to justify[82] – *eg* if the competitive position of an economic subject is impaired.

On this basis, **non-normative infringements** are possible as well, such as the payment of subsidies to a competitor or warnings or recommendations expressed by Community institutions. Furthermore, competition of public companies caused by Community law (see Article 16 TEC/Article III-122 DC and Article 36 EU-Charter/Article II-96 DC: Access to services of common economic interest) may interfere with the right to pursue a freely chosen occupation of private economic entities. Such interferences have not yet found their way into the jurisprudence of the ECJ because the overall dominance of agricultural law creates most of the problematic cases. Finally, the difference between direct and indirect interferences is of such limited use that it should not be considered in greater detail. Every infringement, whether vocationally specific or not, has to be justified.

Case 2: Answer
The production and marketing of sparkling wine is an economic activity that falls within the scope of the right to pursue a freely chosen occupation. The duty to design the label in a certain way interferes with the freedom to pursue one's occupation because the marketing of sparkling wine is regulated in a limiting way. However, the duty is not disproportionate: It is aimed at consumer protection, and it does not appear that the council overlooked a less intrusive means when exercising its legislative discretion. The essence of the right to pursue a freely chosen occupation is not touched upon because the core of the exercise of the profession remains intact.

III. Justification

Case 3: Problem: ECJ *Metronome Music* [1998] ECR I-1953
Under Article 1 (1) of the Directive 92/100 ([1992] OJ L346/6), the Member States are obliged to provide a right to authorise or prohibit the renting and lending of originals and copies of copyrighted works. In Germany, the directive has been duly transposed into domestic law. The "Metronome Musik GmbH", the record label of the pop group "Die Ärzte" ("The Physicians"), files a motion in the competent county Court for a preliminary injunction against the "Music Point Hokamp GmbH", which commercially rents out compact discs, to prevent them from renting out the CD "Planet Punk". In the preliminary reference procedures before the ECJ, the Music Point Hokamp GmbH asserts an interference with its right to pursue a freely chosen occupation.

---

81 ECJ *Hauer* [1979] ECR 3727, para 32; *Commission v Germany* [1986] ECR 2519, para 27; *Keller* [1986] ECR 2897, para 9; *SMW Winzersekt* [1994] ECR I-5555, para 24. Therefore going too far Penski/Elsner [2001] DÖV 265, 271; Stadler (note 5) pp 345 ff, and – showing this tendency – Bleckmann/Pieper (note 75) Vol I, para 86; on the contrary, the position taken here is shared by Kingreen in: Calliess/Ruffert (note 72) Art 6 EUV, para 139; Wunderlich (note 20) pp 112 ff.
82 Ruffert in: Calliess/Ruffert (note 31) Art 15 GRCh para 11; Wunderlich (note 20) pp 113 ff.

1. Restrictions of the Right to Pursue a Freely Chosen Occupation

33 Restrictions of the right to pursue a freely chosen occupation can be formulated in a way that is consistent with the jurisprudence of the ECJ, a comprehensive view of the national legal systems, the ECHR and the EU-Charter (Article 52(1) EU-Charter, Article II-112(1) DC). Accordingly, restrictions are admissible if they can be based upon a statutory prohibition, if they aim at realising the common good (including the rights of others), if they are proportionate and if they do not infringe upon the essential content of the right to pursue a freely chosen occupation.[83]

2. Requirements for a Restriction of the Right to Pursue a Freely Chosen Occupation in Conformity with Community Law

a) Legal Basis

34 Restrictions of the right to pursue a freely chosen occupation need a **legal basis**.[84] This requirement links the fundamental rights to the principle of limited competence.[85] Until now, this issue has not been developed in jurisprudence, as no case of an interference without a legal basis has been presented to the courts.[86] Community law in general has to be construed as to not infringe the right to pursue a freely chosen occupation.[87]

b) Realisation of the Common Good

35 **The requirement to realise the common good** is fulfilled in most cases before the ECJ due to the aims of the CAP (Article 33(1) TEC; Article III-227(1) DC). Beyond this, a strict orientation towards those Community objectives which have expressly been codified (Article 2 TEC; Article I-3 DC) or other Community law norms is necessary.[88] If a prohibition is not meant to fulfil a Community objective – even if the Community institutions allege this – it infringes upon the right to pursue a freely chosen occupation.[89] In addition, there are duties of the Community under public international law.[90] Fundamental rights of others, which are guaranteed as general principles of law, can only be protected in the framework of an existing Community competence (→ § 14 para 47). Common values which only arise from the common European constitutional tradition are not meant to justify actions of the Community institutions and are thus only relevant in the

---

83 ECJ *Keller* [1986] ECR 2897, para 8; *Schräder* [1989] ECR 2237, para 15; *Marshall* [1990] ECR I-4071, para 27; *Zuckerfabrik Süderdithmarschen* [1991] ECR I-415, para 73; *Kühn* [1992] ECR I-35, para 16; *Germany v Council* [1994] ECR I-4973, para 78; *Fishermen's Organisations* [1995] ECR I-3115, para 55; *Affish* [1997] ECR I-4315, para 42; *SAM Schiffahrt und Stapf* [1997] ECR I-4475, para 72; *Metronome Music* [1998] ECR I-1953, para 21; CFI *Dubois et Fils* [1998] ECR II-125, para 74. *Cf* already ECJ *Nold* [1974] ECR 491, para 14.
84 ECJ *Hoechst* [1989] ECR 2859, para 19; Penski/Elsner [2001] DÖV 265, 272.
85 Wunderlich (note 20) p 186.
86 *Cf* Wunderlich (note 20) pp 185 ff.
87 ECJ *Neu* [1991] ECR I-3617, para 12.
88 ECJ *Metronome Music* [1998] ECR I-1953, para 23: Art 30, 151 TEC (Art III-154, III-280 DC); Rengeling (note 4) p 216. In her tendency more restrictive Wunderlich (note 20) p 197.
89 Opinion of AG Fennelly, ECJ *Germany v Parliament and Council* [2000] ECR I-8419, para 151.
90 ECJ *Metronome Music* [1998] ECR I-1953, para 25.

area of Member State activity.[91] Consequently, the wording used by the ECJ whereby the limitation of the right to pursue a freely chosen occupation could be derived from its social function is misleading.[92] The correct piece of information to be derived from this statement is that there is no fundamental right which can be exercised irrespective of the rights of others, the whole of a legal system and the pursuit of legitimate social-political aims. It would be wrong to transform the right to pursue a freely chosen occupation into a 'serving freedom' that can only be exercised in a socially desirable way.[93]

c) Guarantee of the Essential Content

The uttermost limit for restrictions of the fundamental right to pursue a freely chosen occupation is the guarantee of its essential content (→ § 14 para 49). This general limit to the restrictability of rights and freedoms can be drawn from the continuous jurisprudence of the ECJ[94] and has been introduced into the EU-Charter for all fundamental rights (Article 52(1) (i) EU-Charter; Article II-112(1) DC). To preserve the independent status of the guarantee of the essential content, as was last but not least expressed in the EU-Charter, it should be reviewed separately from the principle of proportionality. There are correct indications of this in the recent jurisprudence of the ECJ.[95] However, the area of the fundamental right to pursue a freely chosen occupation which requires absolute protection is hardly discernable in the framework of the CAP.

36

d) The Principle of Proportionality

The **principle of proportionality** has been developed in the jurisprudence of the ECJ both as an independent principle and as a principle in the framework of fundamental rights.[96] In the context of the right to pursue a freely chosen occupation, the proportionality test is necessary and is regularly undertaken by the ECJ.[97] The relevant criteria to be balanced are the right to pursue a freely chosen occupation on the one hand and the principle legitimating the restriction on the other hand. The test follows the three step pattern: suitability, necessity and appropriateness. Within the test of proportionality, the less severe inter-

37

---

91 As reluctant as here Wunderlich (note 20) pp 190 ff. Günter (note 7) pp 23 ff differentiates between Member State and Community common aims but does not consider the aspect of competence.
92 ECJ *Schräder* [1989] ECR 2237, para 15; *Kühn* [1992] ECR I-35, para 16; *Germany v Council* [1994] ECR I-4973, para 78; *SMW Winzersekt* [1994] ECR I-5555, para 22; *Affish* [1997] ECR I-4315, para 42; *SAM Schiffahrt und Stapf* [1997] ECR I-4475, para 72; *Metronome Music* [1998] ECR I-1953, para 21; ECJ *Di Lenardo and Dilexport* [2004] ECR I-6911, para 82; *Spain and Finland v Parliament and Council* [2004] ECR I-7789, para 52; CFI *Dubois et Fils* [1998] ECR II-125, para 74. *Cf* already ECJ *Nold* [1974] ECR 491, para 14; *Hauer* [1979] ECR 3727, para 32.
93 Too far-reaching Wunderlich (note 20) p 195. Like here already Meier [1974] DVBl 674.
94 *Cf* above note 83.
95 ECJ *Marshall* [1990] ECR I-4071, para 28; *Germany v Council* [1994] ECR I-4973, paras 81 ff; *SMW Winzersekt* [1994] ECR I-5555, para 24; *cf* Günter (note 7) pp 29 ff.
96 Linked together in ECJ *Fishermen's Organisations* [1995] ECR I-3115, paras 55 ff; *Affish* [1997] ECR I-4315, paras 29 ff. *Cf* Emmerich-Fritsche *Der Grundsatz der Verhältnismäßigkeit als Direktive und Schranke der EG-Rechtsetzung* (Berlin 2000) pp 399 ff; Penski/Elsner [2001] DÖV 265, 273.
97 *Cf eg* ECJ *Schräder* [1989] ECR 2237, para 18; *Zuckerfabrik Süderdithmarschen* [1991] ECR I-415, para 76; *Bosphorus* [1996] ECR I-3953, paras 23 ff.

ference of rules regarding the exercise of a profession – as compared with limitations to the choice of a profession – can be considered, without postulating that Community law should be adapted to German fundamental rights dogmatic.

38   In its effort to conserve CAP rules which are structurally in contrast with free economic activity, and thus with the right to pursue a freely chosen occupation (see above paras 1–2), the ECJ has often only superficially examined the potential infringement of the fundamental right and has often shown disrespect for the individual interest behind the protection of the fundamental right at stake.[98] This is particularly clear when considering the **scope of control**. In general, the Community institutions are granted a broad scope of discretion and prognosis by the ECJ which is even broader with respect to measures of economic policy, in particular within the framework of CAP.[99] According to this standard of control, only those measures which are evidently inapt[100] or evidently unnecessary[101] can be considered as not consistent with Community law, which until now has not been the case in any instance of the Court's jurisprudence on the right to pursue a freely chosen occupation. This broad scope of discretion and prognosis shall even be granted to Member States' authorities which are involved in the implementation of Community law.[102]

39   Consequently, the strong criticism of this broad scope of discretion and prognosis, which was voiced primarily after the banana market judgement[103], but also with respect to other judgements, is not without justification.[104] The standard of control may not be reduced in a way that would render the test of proportionality futile. In a way, the Court takes up a concept of legal protection here which is above all oriented towards the **conservation of a functioning administration** without effective judicial influence.[105] However, fixing the standard of control is not possible by means of abstract, universal formulae. Nonetheless, the standard of evidence has to be replaced by a standard of control which demands differentiated requirements of plausibility and consistent reasoning of the Community legislator. In this context, the inclusion of special provisions for cases of hardship on the level of necessity, as already adopted by the Court, is important.[106] The standards of fundamental rights protection on Community level and on the level of the Basic Law are only equivalent because the BVerfG, too, grants the legislator a broad scope of discretion in economic matters.

---

98 *Eg* ECJ *Duff* [1996] ECR I-569, para 30; Günter (note 7) pp 26 ff; Pernice in: Grabitz/Hilf (eds) *Das Recht der Europäischen Union* (loose-leaf, Munich 1999) Art 164 EGV, para 62 b.
99 ECJ *Leukhardt* [1989] ECR 1991, para 19; *Germany v Council* [1994] ECR I-4973, paras 89 ff; *SMW Winzersekt* [1994] ECR I-5555, para 21; Streinz in: Streinz (ed) *Vertrag über die Europäische Union und Vertrag zur Gründung der Europäischen Gemeinschaft* (Munich 2003), GR-Charta (EU-Charter) Art 15, para 5, speaks of a hardly restricted discretion.
100 ECJ *Germany v Council* [1994] ECR I-4973, para 94; *SMW Winzersekt* [1994] ECR I-5555, para 22.
101 ECJ *SMW Winzersekt* [1994] ECR I-5555, para 27.
102 ECJ *Fishermen's Organisations* [1995] ECR I-3115, paras 57 ff.
103 ECJ *Germany v Council* [1994] ECR I-4973.
104 *Berrisch* [1994] EuR 461, 466 ff; Everling (1996) 33 CMLR 401, 419 ff; id (1998) 162 ZHR 403, 417 ff; Heitsch [1997] EuGRZ 461, 467; Hohmann [1995] EWS 381; Huber [1997] EuZW 517, 521; Kokott (1996) 121 AöR 599, 607 ff; Nettesheim [1995] EuZW 106; Pauly [1998] EuR 242, 256 ff; Penski/Elsner [2001] DÖV 265, 273 ff; Stein [1998] EuZW, 262 ff; Storr (1997) 36 Der Staat 546, 565 ff. Differently assessed by Dony [1995] CDE 461, 486, 491.
105 Breuer Contribution to the discussion (2002) 61 VVDStRL 430.
106 ECJ *T Port* [1996] ECR I-6065, paras 26 ff; thereto Wunderlich (note 20) pp 211 ff.

Case 3: Answer
The commercial renting out of CDs is an economic activity which falls within the scope of application of the right to pursue a freely chosen occupation. If this activity is forbidden by Community law, the acting Community institutions interfere with the scope of protection. This is also true if the prohibition stems from a directive in cases where national law – as in the given case – is predetermined by the directive to the extent that the infringement cannot be attributed to the Member State alone. The interference can nevertheless be justified having recourse to the common good of the protection of intellectual property. This requirement is embedded in Article 30 of the TEC (Article III-154 DC) as well as in Article 151(2) (4th indent) of the TEC (Article III-280(2)(d) DC), which promotes artistic creation. Furthermore, public international legal duties of the Community derived from TRIPS can also back the argumentation. Given the evident danger of illegal copying, the regulation is not disproportionate, and as a licence to rent can be negotiated with the bearer of the copyright, the option to rent is not permanently excluded. Hence, the guarantee of essential content is not touched upon.

40

§ 17
The Fundamental Right to Property

Christian Calliess

Leading cases: ECJ *Hauer* [1979] ECR 3727; *Germany v Council (Bananas)* [1994] ECR I-4973; *Generics* [1998] ECR I-8001; *Nitrates Directive* [1999] ECR I-2603.

Further reading: Günter *Berufsfreiheit und Eigentum in der Europäischen Union* (Heidelberg 1998); Kingreen in: Calliess/Ruffert (eds) *Kommentar des Vertrages über die Europäische Union und des Vertrages zur Gründung der Europäischen Union* (2nd ed, Neuwied 2002) Art 6 EUV; Müller-Michaels *Grundrechtlicher Eigentumsschutz in der Europäischen Union* (Berlin 1997); Rengeling *Die wirtschaftsbezogenen Grundrechte in der Europäischen Grundrechtscharta* [2004] DVBl 453; Meyer (ed) *Charta der Grundrechte der Europäischen Union* (2nd ed, Baden-Baden 2006) Art 17.

I. The Position and Relevance of the Fundamental Right to Property in Community Law

1 **The fundamental right to property** under Community law has found its explicit expression in Article II-77 of the DC of the signed, yet still inoperative European Constitution. Article II-77(1) of the DC taken over from the Charter of Fundamental Rights of the European Union (→ *cf* § 20) reads: "Everyone has the right to own, use, dispose of and bequeath his or her lawfully acquired possessions. No one may be deprived of his or her possessions, except in the public interest and in the cases and under the conditions provided for by law, subject to fair compensation being paid in good time for their loss. The use of property may be regulated by law insofar as is necessary for the general interest." This scope of protection is explicitly extended by the wording of Article II-77(2) of the DC: "Intellectual property shall be protected."

2 In **European multi-level constitutionalism**[1], which continues to possess a strong economic focus resulting from the fact that it originated in the European Economic Community (EEC), the fundamental right to property is considered to be one of the cardinal fundamental rights. The TEC currently in force already recognises protected property as it is safeguarded in the Member States, since Article 295 of the TEC (Article III-425 DC) guarantees the inviolacy of the rules governing the system of property ownership in the Member States and Article 30 of the TEC (Article III-154 DC) permits an exception from the fundamental freedom of the free movement of goods, *inter alia*, for the purpose of protecting intellectual and commercial property. However, these provisions do not imply any property guarantee in the sense of a subjective right against impairments of property through the Community.[2]

---

1 *Cf* Pernice (2001) 60 VDStRL 148; Calliess in: Calliess/Ruffert (eds) *Kommentar des Vertrages über die Europäische Union und des Vertrages zur Gründung der Europäischen Union* (2nd ed, Neuwied 2002) Art 1 EUV, paras 17 ff.

2 For detailed remarks on Art 295 TEC (with a negative conclusion) see Thiel [1991] JuS 274; likewise Kingreen in: Calliess/Ruffert (eds) *Kommentar des Vertrages über die Europäische Union und des Vertrages zur Gründung der Europäischen Union* (2nd ed, Neuwied 2002) Art 295 EGV, para 4; Müller-Michaels *Grundrechtlicher Eigentumsschutz in der Europäischen Union* (Berlin 1997) pp 34 ff.

With regard to the interaction between Article III-425 of the DC, which is coextensive with the provision of Article 295 of the TEC currently in force, and the guarantee of the fundamental right to property according to Article II-77 of the DC, it is necessary to distinguish between the **right to property** and the **rules governing the system of property ownership**. While the determination of the rules governing the system of property ownership is up to the Member States according to Article III-425 of the DC, the right to property as a Union fundamental constitutional right is concretised within the context of Community law in Article II-77 of the DC. Therefore, Article III-425 of the DC does not influence the ECJ's competence to determine the substance and the limits of the Community right to property in accordance with Article II-77 of the DC.

As is the case in German Constitutional law, the fundamental right to property at the Community level, too, is characterised by the fact that its **scope of protection** is determined by legal norms. Unlike, eg, in the case of the freedom of opinion, its subject matter of protection first needs to be normatively created by the legislator (within certain limits defined by a core area circumscribed by the terms private usefulness and institutional guarantee). Property, therefore, is a creation of the legal system(s).[3] On the same note, Article 295 of the TEC (Article III-425 DC) confirms that the definition of the actual scope of property, and consequently of the scope of protection of the fundamental right to property, is **jointly** determined within multilevel constitutionalism by the legal systems of the Member States and the norms of Community law. Therefore, as suggested by Article II-77(1) of the DC, property as it is protected by Community law is composed of the norms of both national and European law. Even though Article 17 of the Charter of Fundamental Rights of Nice[4], which itself forms the basis of Article II-77 of the DC, was worded following Article 1 of the 1st Prot ECHR, the ECHR jurisdiction on Article 1 of the 1st Prot ECHR (→ for details see § 5 paras 3 ff) plays only a subordinate role in the determination of the scope of protection. With regards to the scope of protection determined by legal norms, the ECHR is unable to contribute anything beyond the interpretation of the wording of Article 1 of the 1st Prot ECHR, since the ECHR lacks its own legislator capable of shaping the concept of property.

II. The Derivation and Dogmatic Structure of the Fundamental Right to Property under Community Law

Case 1 – Problem: (ECJ *Hauer* [1979] ECR 3727)
In June 1975, German winemaker Liselotte Hauer filed an application for permission to grow grape-vines on her estate in Bad Dürkheim. She was refused such permission by the federal state of Rhineland-Palatinate, *inter alia* on the grounds that the newly adopted EC Regulation 76/1162 on Measures Designed to Adjust Wine Growing Potential to Market Requirements[5] prohibited any new planting of grape-vines over a longer period. In her lawsuit before the administrative court, the winemaker *inter alia* asserted that one of the reasons why she could not comply with the provisions of the EC Regulations was that they

---

3 Ehlers (1992) 51 VVDStRL 211, 214 ff.
4 On the legally binding nature of the Charter see Alber [2001] EuGRZ 349 with further references.
5 Reg 76/1162.

constituted a breach with the fundamental rights of free exercise of profession and protection of property standardised in Articles 12 and 14 of the *Grundgesetz* (GG – German Basic Law). The administrative court then referred the matter to the ECJ, asking for a preliminary ruling.

Case 1 – Answer:

6   Before the express regulation in Article II-77 of the DC, the ECJ's judgment in the *Hauer* case[6] was fundamental for the protection of property under Community law. This case marked the first time that the ECJ asserted "its own claim with regard to the verbalisation of Community-specific dogmatics of property".[7] Although it is an older decision, it is particularly suited to illustrate the ECJ's methodical approach to deriving the right to property and determining its limits – an approach that continues to carry considerable weight in multilevel constitutionalism.

7   In a first examination step (para 14 of the judgment), the Court of Justice refers to its judgment in the *Internationale Handelsgesellschaft* case[8] and stresses that the assessment of the question of a potential infringement of fundamental rights through an action of the Community organs can by no means be different from an assessment within the framework of Community law itself. According to the ECJ, "the introduction of special criteria for assessment stemming from the legislation or constitutional order of a particular Member State would, by damaging the substantive unity and efficacy of Community law, inevitably lead to the destruction of the unity of the Common Market and jeopardize the cohesion of the Community". It is interesting that in its first examination step, the ECJ mainly focuses on the retention of the *acquis communautaire* rather than the protection of individual fundamental rights.

8   It is not until the second examination step (para 15 of the judgment) that the ECJ, under reference to the already mentioned judgments in the *Internationale Handelsgesellschaft* and the *Nold*[9] cases, emphasises that "fundamental rights form an integral part of the **general principles of law**, the observance of which it [the Court of Justice] ensures." In this respect, the Court of Justice is "bound to draw inspiration from the constitutional traditions common to the Member States." The obligation expressed by the word "bound" is toned down again by the phrasing "to draw inspiration from." Consequently, the ECJ must closely examine the way in which the fundamental right to property is guaranteed in the constitutions of the Member States. However, the ECJ is merely "bound to draw inspiration" from them and is therefore not bound to the specific peculiarities of the fundamental rights in the constitutions of the Member States. On the other hand, it is precisely the constitutional traditions of the Member States that offer a suitable starting point for determining the European content of the fundamental right to property. This is especially true because the (main) Community legislator, the Council of Ministers, is composed of representatives of the national governments, who should not be given the

---

6 ECJ *Hauer* [1979] ECR 3727.
7 Beutler [1980] EuR 130, 134.
8 ECJ *Internationale Handelsgesellschaft* [1970] ECR 1125.
9 ECJ *Nold* [1974] ECR 491.

opportunity to use the Council of Ministers as a means to circumvent the legislative limits prescribed by the national fundamental rights. However, exactly which standard of property is meant to be protected under European law? In this respect, there is wide agreement these days that with regard to content, neither a minimum nor a maximum standard of fundamental rights protection is realisable within the Community in practice. On the one hand, the common minimum standard leads to a low degree of protection capable of challenging the supremacy of Community law at the national level.[10] On the other hand, a desirable maximum standard is very difficult to enforce in view of the respective different concepts of fundamental rights of the individual Member States. In order to solve this problematic issue, the method resorted to for obtaining and concretising the European fundamental rights is that of **evaluation by legal comparison**. Even though the ECJ has not yet explicitly named the method used for developing general principles of law and, therefore, fundamental rights, the final motions of the Advocates General[11] and the statements in the relevant literature[12] still reveal the necessity of finding, through "evaluation by legal comparison", the "best solution" for Community law on the basis of national and international guarantees of fundamental rights. The ECJ's starting point is the conclusion that the general principles of law need to blend in with the objectives and structures of EC law.[13] Consequently, the ECJ is inclined to adopt the view that in case of a divergence between the norms of the national legal systems, the legal system to be preferred is the one with the norm that matches best the objectives and structures of EC law.

In a third step (paras 17–19 of the judgment), the ECJ then uses this dogmatic basis to **review the European fundamental right to property**: "The right to property is guaranteed in the Community legal system in accordance with the ideas common to the constitutions of the Member States, which are also reflected in the first protocol to the European Convention for the Protection of Human Rights." Interestingly, however, instead of starting its examination with a reference to constitutional traditions of the Member States, the ECJ first of all examines Article 1 of the 1st Prot ECHR. Referring to Article 1(2) of the 1st Prot ECHR, the Court of Justice then concludes its examination by stating that while the Protocol did authorise restrictions to the use of property in principle, these were limited "to the extent to which they are deemed 'necessary' by a State for the protection of the 'general interest'". Meanwhile, however, according to the ECJ, this provision does not yet allow for a sufficiently definite answer to the question raised by the submitting administrative court. On the one hand, this shows that in a certain (non-legal) way, the ECJ feels bound to the ECHR despite the fact that (so far) the EC has not acceded to it ($\rightarrow$ § 2 para 30; § 14 para 13). Yet on the other hand, it is made clear – especially by the concluding sentence – that the ECJ takes up the ECHR as a mere starting point for its examination of fundamental rights. The ECHR is just a "first obstacle" to be overcome by the community measure with a view to the protection of fundamental rights. Addi-

9

---

10 *Cf* the Solange case-law of the *Bundesverfassungsgericht* (BVerfG – German Federal Constitutional Court), (1974) 37 BVerfGE 271, 285 = *Solange I* [1974] 2 CMLR 540; (1986) 73 BVerfGE 339, 387 = *Solange II* [1987] 3 CMLR 225; Ress/Ukrow [1990] EuZW 499, 504.
11 Opinion AG Gand, ECJ *Firma Kampffmeyer* [1967] ECR 361, 367; Opinion AG Roemer, ECJ *Zuckerfabrik Schöppenstedt* [1971] ECR 987, 990; *Werhahn* [1973] ECR 1254, 1258, 1273; Opinion AG Warner, *van de Roy* [1976] ECR 352.
12 Ress/Ukrow [1990] EuZW, 499, 500, 502 ff with further references.
13 *Cf*, for example, ECJ *Internationale Handelsgesellschaft* [1970] ECR 1125, para 4.

tional demands to the protection of fundamental rights may be posed by the constitutional traditions as a "second obstacle". In the *Hoechst* case at the latest, however, the ECJ unambiguously declared these two sources of legal insight to have equal priority,[14] an assessment which is supported by the wording of Article 6(2) of the TEU (Article I-9(3) DC).

10   In a *fourth examination step* (paras 20–22 of the judgment), the ECJ then **compares the constitutions of the Member States** with respect to the elaboration of the right to property: "Therefore, in order to be able to answer that question, it is necessary to also consider the indications provided by the constitutional rules and practices of the ... Member States. One of the first points to emerge in this regard is that those rules and practices permit the legislature to control the use of private property in accordance with the general interest." This reference to all Member States and their practices makes it clear that the ECJ also includes the unwritten British constitution as well as those constitutions not expressly dealing with this problem. After having made concrete reference to three explicit constitutional provisions, the ECJ then states that in each and every Member State, the social function of the right to property has been expressed concretely in numerous legislation acts: "Thus in all the Member States there is legislation on agriculture and forestry, the water supply, the protection of the environment and town and country planning, which imposes restrictions, sometimes appreciable, on the use of real property. More particularly, all the wine-producing countries of the Community have restrictive legislation, albeit of differing severity, concerning the planting of vines, the selection of varieties and the methods of cultivation. In none of the countries concerned are those provisions considered to be incompatible in principle with the regard due to the right of property." The ECJ uses the result of the comparative analysis for stating that the property-limiting content of Regulation 76/1162 constitutes a restriction existing in the Member States and approved as legitimate in an identical or similar form.

11   Finally, in its fifth and sixth examination steps (paras 23–30 of the judgment), the ECJ examines in a manner that complements the previous examination a) "whether the restrictions introduced by the provisions in dispute in fact correspond to objectives of general interest pursued by the Community" and b) "whether, with regard to the aim pursued, they constitute a disproportionate and intolerable interference with the rights of the owner, impinging upon the very substance of the right to property". In doing so, the ECJ refers to the **principle of proportionality**. As a general legal principle – based on the legal systems of the Member States – the principle of proportionality is acknowledged in the ECJ's permanent legislation as an unwritten element of Community law. From now on, the principle of proportionality is also expressly fixed in Article 5(3) of the TEC (Article I-11(4) DC).[15] With a view to the specific case, the ECJ then examines whether the measure in question serves common welfare. In doing so, it holds the measure to a European standard. With reference to the Preamble of the regulation and the general objectives of the respective policy, in this case the agricultural policy, the ECJ finds that the measure serves the common welfare. In respect of the thus determined common welfare concern (containment of surpluses, advancement of wine quality), the

---

14 ECJ *Hoechst* [1989] ECR 2859, paras 13 ff; *cf* Ress/Ukrow [1990] EuZW 499, 501.
15 For detailed remarks see Calliess *Subsidiaritäts- und Solidaritätsprinzip in der Europäischen Union* (2nd ed, Baden-Baden 1999) pp 116 ff with further references.

ECJ then reaches a positive result in its following very short and dogmatically diffuse proportionality test, which draws no clear line between suitability, necessity and adequacy.

III. The European Fundamental Right to Property in Detail

1. The Scope of Protection of the Fundamental Right to Property

> **Case 2 – Problem:** (ECJ *Germany v Council* [1994] ECR I-4973)
> Regulation 93/404 introduced a common organisation of the market in bananas. According to the provisions contained therein, bananas from the so-called ACP States associated with the EU through development politics as well as those bananas grown within the EU including its overseas territories shall form the largest portion of the banana market, while for bananas imported from third countries, Community quotas shall be introduced and divided among the importers. Germany raised an action for annulment against the banana market regulation in accordance with Article 230 of the TEC (Article III-365 DC), one of its reasons being that for those importers who had so far been importing large-scale amounts of bananas from Central America, the deprivation of market shares associated with the import quotes represented an infringement of their fundamental right to property.

12

Article II-77 of the DC protects not only material property rights,[16] but also non-material objects such as private rights to claim[17] and – as pointed out by Article II-77(2) of the DC – intellectual property rights (copyrights, patent rights, publishing rights and other trademark rights).[18]

13

However, in light of the fact that its scope of protection is determined by legal norms, property in Community law is a **product** of the legal system and, therefore, its contents are determined by the legislation, especially in civil law (first and foremost of the Member States).[19] The question as to whether the property guarantee also covers the business interests of an established and running enterprise as a whole (*ie* beyond the protection of the resources contained therein) remains open.[20] This is not really a problem if one is aware of the fact that ultimately, the protection of the business enterprise can reach no further than the protection of its foundations, which after all are already individually protected by the fundamental right to property. Consequently, in any case, the stock of the enterprise must

14

---

16 Rengeling [2004] DVBl 453, 459; *cf* Bernsdorff in: Meyer (ed) *Charta der Grundrechte der Europäischen Union* (2nd ed, Baden-Baden 2006) Art 17 GR-Charta, paras 1 ff; Streinz in: Streinz (ed) *EUV/EGV. Vertrag über die Europäische Union und Vertrag zur Gründung der Europäischen Gemeinschaft* (Munich 2003) Art 17 GR-Charta, paras 6 ff; already ECJ *Hauer* [1979] ECR 3727, paras 17 ff; for detailed remarks see Günter *Berufsfreiheit und Eigentum in der Europäischen Union* (Heidelberg 1998) pp 33 ff.
17 *Cf* Müller-Michaels (note 2) p 66 on Art 1 Prot 1 ECHR.
18 Already in ECJ *Metronome Music* [1998] ECR I-1953, paras 21 ff; *Günter* (note 16) pp 34 ff; on Art 1 Prot 1 ECHR; Riedel [1988] EuGRZ 333, 334.
19 Kingreen (note 2) Art 6 EUV, para 142.
20 According to Rengeling [2004] DVBl 453, 460; Wetter *Die Grundrechtscharta des Europäischen Gerichtshofes* (Frankfurt 1998) pp 145 ff with reference made to ECJ *Biovilac* [1984] ECR 4057, paras 21 ff, as well as Thiel [1991] JuS 274, 279.

be affected.[21] According to present legislation, capital as such, *eg* in the form of obligations in cash, does not fall under property protection.[22] While initially, the ECJ still left it open whether the protection of property also covers legal positions under public law (*eg* social contributions),[23] it has now affirmed this in its more recent jurisdiction, provided that such positions are at least in part also based on personal contributions of the beneficiary.[24] This requirement is missing with regard to commercial advantages in consequence of market-regulating measures, such as the allocation of reference quantities within the framework of a common organisation of the market.

15 According to the current legislation, the protection of property under Community law also does not cover purely commercial interests or prospects, the incertitude of which is an intrinsic characteristic of commercial activity,[25] such as *eg* a specific market share.[26] Admittedly, the determination of the scope, for instance in the case of Community competition-regulating measures (*eg* specification of production quotas and marketing rules) is problematic. At the least, the fundamental right to property is impaired whenever the use of production sites and facilities of the respective business enterprise is immediately affected, as is *eg* the case with steel production quotas.[27] The case is different with measures only pertaining to the marketing of a product, but not concerning the use of property at the production sites and facilities as such (*eg* minimum price regulations[28]).[29] Finally, the fundamental right to property also includes the so-called right of continuance and free disposition, thereby protecting the trust of the owners in the continuity of the legal positions created by the legislator, by virtue of which the owners are able to make use of their property.[30] These are the legal positions referred to by the ECJ as "vested rights",[31] which are in turn to be distinguished from mere expectations and chances of profit. They presuppose an element of trust based on measures taken by the Community or the Member States.[32] In the ECJ's judgment, however, such an element of trust is impossible to achieve where decisions of the Community organs may be changed at their discretion (especially within the scope of application of the market regulations).[33] The relativisation

---

21 Müller-Michaels (note 2) pp 39 ff; ECJ *Valsabbia* [1980] ECR 907, para 90 seems to lean towards this view as well.
22 Explicit remarks in ECJ *Zuckerfabrik Süderdithmarschen* [1991] ECR I-415, para 74; ambiguous ones, however, in ECJ *Schräder* [1989] ECR 2237, paras 15 ff; for a critical view see Günter (note 16) pp 40 ff and Schilling [1991] EuZW 310.
23 ECJ *Testa* [1980] ECR 1979, para 22; *Rönfeldt* [1991] ECR I-323; for an opinion against an inclusion see AG Darmon in the Opinion to that decision.
24 ECJ *von Deetzen* [1991] ECR I-5119, para 27; *Bostock* [1994] ECR I-955, para 19; *Country Landowners Association* [1995] ECR I-3875, para 14; CFI *O'Dwyer* [1995] ECR II-2071, para 99.
25 ECJ *Nold* [1974] ECR 491, para 14; *Valsabbia* [1980] ECR 907, para 89.
26 ECJ *Germany v Council* [1994] ECR I-4973, para 79.
27 Kingreen (note 2) Art 6 EUV, para 149 under reference to ECJ *Metallurgiki Halyps* [1982] ECR 4261, para 13 and ECJ *Hoogovens Groep* [1985] ECR 2831, para 29.
28 ECJ *Valsabbia* [1980] ECR 907, para 90.
29 Günter (note 16) p 39.
30 Kingreen (note 2) Art 6 EUV, para 150.
31 ECJ *Elz* [1976] ECR 1097, paras 18, 20; *Eridania* [1979] ECR 2749, para 22.
32 ECJ *Kühn* [1992] ECR I-35, paras 14 ff.
33 ECJ *Eridania* [1979] ECR 2749, para 22; *Faust* [1982] ECR 3745, para 27; *Kühn* [1992] ECR I-35, para 13; *Germany v Council* [1994] ECR I-4973, para 79.

of property protection this brings about, however, is not unproblematic. After all, the scope of protection must not depend on whether the trust in the future use might be breached by the actions of the Community or the Member States. What must be decisive in this respect is the weight of the interest vis-à-vis the property, which is to be checked within the context of the justification of the encroachment.[34]

Case 2 – Answer:
In the provisions of the banana market regulation, the ECJ could not detect any impairment of the scope of protection of the fundamental right to property, because no business participant could claim a property right to a market share which they had owned at any point before the introduction of the common organisation of the market.[35] According to this judgment, a market share "constitutes only a momentary economic position exposed to the risks of changing circumstances".[36] Moreover, a business participant can claim no vested right, nor even a justified trust in the perpetuation of an existing situation, as long as the Community organs were acting within the limits of their lawful discretion.[37]

16

2. Impairment of the Scope of Protection

Case 3 – Problem: (ECJ *Olive Oil* [1984] ECR 3881)
EC Regulation 81/71 facilitated the purchase – at an extremely attractive fixed price – of olive oil which had been bought up by the Italian encroachment office S in fulfilment of its obligations under the Common Agricultural Policy in the course of encroachment measures, and which the EC had already repeatedly and unsuccessfully offered for sale on the market. Apparently, the designated fixed price was so attractive that the buyers had to be drawn by lot among the numerous prospective clients. Winner of this lottery drawing and therefore chosen as buyer was B. Now having become aware of the fact that the buyers, due to the non-market-driven fixed prices for the olive oil, could expect to make extraordinarily high profits, S and the EC Commission first of all delayed the delivery of the merchandise. The Commission then decreed Regulation 81/2238, by effect of which Regulation 81/71 – and consequently also the basis for the claim of B to the delivery of the acquired olive oil – were revoked due to alterations of the market conditions and in order to avoid serious disturbances of the market in the interest of a superior public agenda/interest. By way of Regulation 81/2239, the olive oil was offered once more; however, this time not at a fixed price but to the highest bidder at a predetermined minimum selling price. The drawn buyers, ie also B, were granted a right of pre-emption. B raised a plea of nullity against Regulation 81/2238.

17

According to Article II-77 of the DC, **encroachment** is defined as the withdrawal of an ownable item or the subjection of its use, disposition or utilisation to certain restrictions.[38] This definition is based on the hitherto existing case-law of the ECJ. The ECJ itself had adopted the ECHR's concept of property encroachment (*cf* Article 1 of the 1st Prot

18

---

34 Kingreen (note 2) Art 6 EUV, para 150; also Besse [1996] JuS 396, 400 ff; Huber [1997] EuZW 517, 521; Nettesheim [1995] EuZW 106.
35 ECJ *Germany v Council* [1994] ECR I-4973, para 79.
36 ECJ *Germany v Council* [1994] ECR I-4973, para 79.
37 ECJ *Germany v Council* [1994] ECR I-4973, para 80.
38 Rengeling [2004] DVBl 453, 460; Dupp/Grzeszick in: König/Rieger/Schmitt (eds) *Europa der Bürger* (Frankfurt 1998) pp 111, 119.

ECHR) which the aforementioned ECHR *Hauer* case had been based on. The sharpest possible encroachment, namely property withdrawal, comprises – following the ECHR's specifications – both the formal expropriation through law or on the basis of law and other property restrictions factually affecting the owner in the same way as a formal expropriation (de facto expropriation).[39] To be distinguished are restrictions not (and not even partially) withdrawing property as such, but merely imposing a temporal, territorial or factual limitation on its disposability.[40]

19   With a view to the legislative definition of the fundamental right to property, in respect of measures taken by the legislator, one has to differentiate between **property-constituting** and **property-impairing** norms; that is to say, not every legal regulation concerning property automatically represents an encroachment. As already mentioned earlier, in European multi-level constitutionalism, national property may also be co-developed, co-limited and co-expanded through Community rules[41]. Insofar, the general and obligation-neutral regulation of property use through the Community legislator does not constitute any property encroachment as long as it does not extend to legal positions created by previous property-constituting provisions and does not diminish the authority contained therein.[42]

20   Commensurate with the property guarantee of the ECHR and the implementation of the fundamental right to property in the individual Member States, Article II-77(1)(iii) of the DC, too, provides the legislator with the authorisation to regulate the utilisation of private property for the sake of the collective interest. Accordingly, the property guarantee under Community law cannot claim unlimited validity either, but must be perceived in view of its societal function.[43] Consequently, also in Community law, the guarantee of property is complemented by the principle of **social duteousness**. Its societal function at the same time also serves as a justification for and limitation of the restrictions imposed on property utilisation. A property encroachment may take place either directly through the regulation of an individual case, *ie* concretely and individually, or in principle also through a norm, *ie* abstractly and generally. However, if the criticised measure affects the complainant in the same way as anyone else, that is to say, if it does not distinguish the claimant in any way, the Court of Justice tends to reject an encroachment.[44] This makes the assessment of merely indirectly burdening measures problematic: changes in the external competition conditions brought about by Community measures (*eg* low-price intervention sales of skimmed-milk powder to the disadvantage of other market participants)[45] or the abolition of previously provided marketing options[46] have so far not been qualified as encroachments by the ECJ. On the other hand, however, the negative effects of sanctioning measures on the affected trade participants constitute an encroachment

---

39 ECtHR *Sporrong and Lönnroth* (1983) 5 EHRR 35, para 63; for detailed remarks see Gelinsky *Der Schutz des Eigentums gemäß Art. 1 des Ersten Zusatzprotokolls zur Europäischen Menschenrechtskonvention* (Berlin 1996) pp 56 ff.
40 On the problem of differentiation *cf*, for example, Müller-Michaels (note 2) pp 74 ff.
41 *Cf* already Pernice *Grundrechtsgehalte im Europäischen Gemeinschaftsrecht* (Baden-Baden 1979) p 185.
42 Kingreen (note 2) Art 6 EUV, para 153.
43 ECJ *Schräder* [1989] ECR 2237, para 15; *Generics* [1998] ECR I-7976, para 79.
44 ECJ *SMW Winzersekt* [1994] ECR I-5555, para 23.
45 ECJ *Biovilac* [1984] ECR 4057, para 22; *Zuckerfabrik Bedburg* [1987] ECR 49, paras 25 ff.
46 ECJ *France and Ireland* [1996] ECR I-795, para 64.

according to the ECJ.[47] Therefore, in cases where indirect effects of the respective State-controlled measures lead to a direct restriction of the use, disposition or utilisation of property, this is perfectly sufficient for assuming an encroachment; a subsistence threat is not required.[48] In addition, it remains to be examined whether the measure also interferes with the freedom to choose an occupation.

So far, there is no ECJ legislation with regard to **property divestment**.[49] There is some uncertainty as well regarding the level of intensity an encroachment must reach before it is considered an expropriation under Community law. In other words, it is still unclear within the context of the Community right to property whether, in addition to the divestment of property on the basis of a mandatory measure, it might also be appropriate to classify other property restrictions imposed as a direct result of a Community measure and unacceptable for individual owners as so-called de facto expropriations. An aggravating aspect in this context is the fact that as a general rule, the ECJ only starts to analyse the impact and measure of an encroachment within the framework of the proportionality test.[50] However, one may conclude from the ECJ's elaborations in the *Hauer* judgment that no "act depriving the owner of his property" exists at least as long as "he remains free to dispose of it or put it to other uses which are not prohibited". Against this background, the disputed grape-vine growing prohibition turns out to be no more than an utilisation restriction, because, after all, the owner continued to be free to dispose of her real property.[51] Therefore, apparently, the decisive aspect for the ECJ is the purpose of the measure, *ie* its intent rather than its effect, so that it must be aimed at permanently depriving owners of their rights in the form of the property item itself, the right of disposition or all utilisation possibilities. In the final analysis, the ECJ appears to want to follow a formal point of view.[52]

Case 3 – Answer:
The action for annulment raised by B in accordance with Article 230(4) of the TEC (Article III-365(4) DC) is admissible. In particular, B is directly and individually affected by the suspension of the original Regulation 81/71 effected by Regulation 81/2238,[53] since this voids B's claim to delivery of the purchased olive oil. Within the context of the reasonable grounds of the claim, it is necessary first of all to verify whether B may in fact assert any infringement of the fundamental right to property considered a part of the Community legal system in accordance with Article 6(2) of the TEU (Article II-77(1) DC). It remains to be seen whether B has already gained ownership of the olive oil, since also property-asset related subjective rights under public law are already to be regarded as property if legal positions resembling those of owners are created thereby. B is entitled to such vested right in the form of his claim for delivery of the oil against the encroachment authority resulting

---

47 ECJ *Bosphorus* [1996] ECR I-3953, paras 22 ff.
48 Kingreen (note 2) Art 6 EUV, para 152; von Milczewski *Der grundrechtliche Schutz des Eigentums im Europäischen Gemeinschaftsrecht* (Frankfurt 1994) p 78.
49 The same conclusion is reached by Streinz (note 16) Art 17 GR-Charta, para 10.
50 Müller-Michaels (note 2) p 47.
51 ECJ *Hauer* [1979] ECR 3727, para 19.
52 *Cf* ECJ *Booker Aquavulture Ltd* [2003] ECR I-7411.
53 For corresponding detailed remarks see Cremer in: Calliess/Ruffert (eds) *Kommentar des Vertrages über die Europäische Union und des Vertrages zur Gründung der Europäischen Union* (2nd ed, Neuwied 2002) Art 230 EGV, paras 27 ff and 44 ff.

from the public law contract. The deprivation of this legal position brought about by the contested provision no longer ranges within the scope of the societal restriction of property, but is to be regarded as an expropriation due to the fact that it constitutes a total deprivation of B's vested claim. However, according to Article 1 of the 1st Prot ECHR and the legal systems of the Member States (*cf* now Article II-77(1)(iii) DC), such an encroachment requires a legal basis, may be undertaken only in the interest of public welfare and must provide an indemnification regulation. While B was granted a right of pre-emption as a way of compensation, this was offered at far more unfavourable conditions than those provided for in the original contract. Therefore, this right of pre-emption is unsuitable as a compensation for the expropriation or as a substitute for an indemnification regulation.[54]

23 Already at this point, a decisive dogmatic weakness of the hitherto existing protection of property under Community law is revealed: Due to the inadequate standardisation of the conditions for the restriction of property rights, the examination of property impairments is usually shifted to the level of the justification of the contested measure.[55] Thus, a virtual **escape into the proportionality test** is taking place, which is detrimental to the development of European dogmatics of property differentiated into scope of protection, limitations and justification. One can only hope – and this is to be assumed – that the ECJ will refine and specify its dogmatics of property on the basis of Article II-77 of the DC.

3. Justification

Case 4 – Problem: (ECJ *Nitrates Directive* [1999] ECR I-2603)
24 Farmer B "fertilises" his fields and pastures with liquid manure. This type of commonly practiced "fertilisation" is a contributing reason for the sometimes high nitrate values present in water, which pose a risk to human health. The EC is trying to preclude this risky practice with its Nitrates Directive 91/676, according to which "Member States shall [...] designate as vulnerable zones all known lands in their territory" which drain into waters contaminated with nitrates (the respective norm is a nitrates concentration of 50 mg/l) and "which contribute to pollution". For these, national action programmes need to be set up, which, *inter alia*, must provide for temporal and quantitative restrictions on the application of fertilisers onto agricultural lands. B is contesting these action programmes before the administrative court. He argues that, on the one hand, his lands have been specified as vulnerable zones although not only agriculture but also other emission sources are contributing to the transgression, and that, on the other hand, the respective regulations constitute a disproportionate interference with his fundamental right to property and also an infringement of the polluter-pays principle. The administrative court submits these questions to the ECJ, asking for a preliminary decision.

Case 5 – Problem: (ECJ *Bosphorus* [1996] ECR I-3953)
25 In 1992, F, a Turkish aircraft charter company, leased aircrafts from the State-owned Yugoslavian aircraft company JAT. One of these aircrafts was seized by Irish authorities at Dublin

---

54 *Cf* the respective Opinion by AG Lenz in ECJ *Olive Oil* [1984] ECR 3900, 3911 ff; the ECJ itself, in *Olive Oil* [1984] ECR 3881, paras 12 ff, already deals with the illegality of the regulation before examining the expropriation.
55 Such is the criticism voiced by Schilling [1991] EuZW 311.

Airport under the Community provision sanctioning Yugoslavia, according to which the authorities of the Member States were entitled to seize Yugoslavian-owned aircrafts. F, on the other hand, asserted its rights arising from the leasing contract: Since neither F's headquarters were in Yugoslavia, nor did F conduct any activities in that country, the sanction not only infringed their property rights, but was also obviously unnecessary and disproportionate because the owner of the aircraft in question had already been punished by the freezing of leasing rates which had been paid by the plaintive aircraft company into blocked accounts.

According to the wording of Article II-77(1)(ii) of the DC, when examining whether a measure is justified, one needs to distinguish between the divestment of property as the strongest form of property encroachment and the restriction of its utilisation.[56]

Under Community law – and also in view of Article II-77 of the DC and Article 1(2) of the 1st Prot ECHR – an **expropriation** is first of all only admissible if it is provided for by the law and if it is carried out for the benefit of the public (→ for details, see § 5 paras 35 ff). An expropriation is legally provided for if it is permitted by one of the legal acts mentioned in Article I-33 of the DC (comparable to Article 249 TEC currently in force). At first glance, the Community lacks the legislative competence to carry out expropriations (cf in particular Article III-425 DC)[57]. Nevertheless, in some fields (eg agriculture), the EC has been granted competences extensive enough for them to have a potential impact on individual property positions and also – in particular cases – to reach the level of (at least a factual) property divestment.[58] The concept of public benefit essentially corresponds to the concept of general interest in Article 1(1)(ii) of the 1st Prot ECHR.[59] With a view to the judicature of the Member States, this shall also include the divestment of property in favour of private parties provided that at the same time, this aids the furtherance of the public agenda.[60] Whether or not the justification of a property divestment also requires a statutory indemnification regulation has not yet been ultimately resolved. Looking at Article II-77(1)(ii) of the DC, this is – in contrast to the wording of Article 1 of the 1st Prot ECHR – the case. The ECJ's current jurisdiction on the Community fundamental right to property is still vague in this respect: on the one hand, restrictions of production which are demanded due to the economic situation, which constitute an impairment to the profitability and substance of a company and which therefore are of an expropriating nature have not been regarded as a violation of the right to property.[61] On the other hand, the ECJ has pointed out that it "would be incompatible with the requirements of the protection of fundamental rights" if a Community rule had "the effect of depriving the lessee, without compensation, of the fruits of his labour and of his investments".[62] Moreover, the ECJ is checking the Community's liability for a potential property infringement in other cases under the aspect of non-contractual liability according to Article

---

56 Likewise Art 1 Prot 1 ECHR; for basic remarks see ECJ *Hauer* [1979] ECR 3727, para 19.
57 Müller-Michaels (note 2) pp 46 ff.
58 Cf ECJ *Booker Aquavulture Ltd* [2003] ECR I-7411. von Milczewski (note 48) p 30.
59 Peukert in: Frowein/Peukert *Europäische Menschenrechtskonvention* (2nd ed, Kehl 1996) Art 1 1. ZP EMRK, paras 51 ff; → § 5 para 38.
60 ECtHR *James* (1986) 8 EHRR 123, paras 40 ff.
61 ECJ *Metallurgiki Halyps* [1982] ECR 4261, para 13; *Hoogovens Groep* [1985] ECR 2831, para 29.
62 ECJ *Wachauf* [1989] ECR 2609, para 19.

288(2) of the TEC (Article III-431 DC).[63] The CFI, too, has so far left it open "whether there is any general principle of law by virtue of which the Community would be obliged to compensate a person who has been subject to a measure expropriating his property or restricting his freedom to enjoy his right to property [...]". In any case, the Court does consider an indemnification obligation for expropriating measures the Community organs themselves conduct "conceivable"[64]. Despite all those unresolved issues, it may be concluded from the constitutional traditions of the Member States as well as from the legislation (Article I-7(3) DC) concretising Article 1 of the 1st Prot ECHR, confirmed by Article II-77(1)(ii) of the DC, that the property guarantee and the respective applicable basic principle of proportionality directly result in an indemnification obligation. Consequently, property divestments in the form of formal expropriations must be disproportionate and therefore unlawful already in the absence of an indemnification regulation. In respect to the factual expropriations – which are the first ones to come into consideration due to the limited competences of the EU – a statutorily provided indemnification is no justification prerequisite according to Article II-77(1)(ii) of the DC. Nevertheless, it may be concluded from the case-law of the ECJ regarding the basic principle of the protection of confidence. that an indemnification claim resulting from Article 288(2) of the TEC (Article III-431 DC) comes into consideration.[65]

28 According to the settled case-law of the ECJ, mere **restrictions to the exercise of the right to property** are legitimate only "provided that any restrictions in fact correspond to objectives of general interest pursued by the Community and do not constitute in relation to the aim pursued a disproportionate and intolerable interference, impairing the very substance of the rights guaranteed".[66] According to the wording of Article II-77 of the DC and Article 1(2) of the 1st Prot ECHR, utilisation restrictions must "only" meet the requirement of being necessary to safeguard the general interest. However, this is to be seen in conjunction with the general barrier regulation of Article II-112 of the DC, so that the formula of the ECJ is confirmed also in respect of its essence, and therefore to its full extent.

29 With regard to the **justification** of utilisation restrictions, the ECJ orients itself towards two key points, between which the respective proportionality test mediates. To begin with, the Court examines the utilisation restriction in view of its non-profit objective. For this purpose, in addition to making use of the regulations of the corresponding legal act, it also resorts to the reasonable considerations. The ECJ then needs to examine whether the thus determined objective pursued with the respective measure is in the interest of public welfare. This examination is carried out by means of the treaty provisions, normally *eg* according to Article 2 of the TEC (Article I-3 DC), and also pursuant to the specific provisions in the various Community policy fields. Accordingly, the issues recognised by the ECJ as relevant general interests in its case-law on the protection of property include *eg*

---

63 ECJ *Biovilac* [1984] ECR 4057, paras 11, 21; *Zuckerfabrik Bedburg* [1987] ECR 49, paras 25 ff.
64 CFI *Dubois et fils* [1998] ECR II-125, para 57.
65 Kingreen (note 2) Art 6 EUV, paras 162 ff under reference to ECJ *CNTA* [1975] ECR 533, para 44; *Mulder* [1992] ECR I-3061, paras 12 ff; for remarks that expressly leave this question open see CFI *Dubois et fils* [1998] ECR II-125, para 57; *cf* Müller-Michaels (note 2) p 59.
66 Settled case-law. Only *cf* ECJ *Metronome Music* [1998] ECR I-1953, para 21; *Generics* [1998] ECR I-7976, para 79.

consumer protection,[67] health and environmental protection[68] as well as the Community's objectives regarding its agricultural commodity market policies in accordance with Article 33 of the TEC (Article III-227 DC) – an issue of high significance for the hitherto existing legal practice.[69] Moreover, in the *Metronome* case, the ECJ substantiated the justification of the introduction of an exclusive lending right for compact discs effected in the Community as a consequence of copyright-related considerations with a reference to Article 30 of the TEC (Article III-154 DC), which – according to the ECJ – safeguards the protection of the copyright in works of literature and art as an element of industrial and commercial property.[70] Taking an additional look at the case-law of the ECHR in accordance with Article 6(2) of the TEU (Article I-9(3) DC), it becomes obvious that at the end of the day, all measures undertaken in pursuance of legitimate political objectives, regardless of whether they pertain to economic, social or other fields of public concern, serve general interests.[71] The second key point concerns the infringement of the essence of property.

The essence is touched upon if a property-restricting Community measure led to a divestment of the property as such or of the right to its free utilisation,[72] or if the restriction in question made it virtually impossible for the affected owner to pursue his economic activities.[73] On the other hand, the essence is left untouched if the measure affects "only the arrangements governing the exercise of that right and do not jeopardize its very existence",[74] and does "not affect the possibility for the operators in question to engage" in other ways of utilising their property.[75] Therefore, the safeguard of the essential content corresponds with the safeguard of the core of property.[76] An encroachment into this essence is evaluated by the ECJ on the basis of the overall extent to which the rights of the owner are restricted.[77] These restrictions must not constitute an encroachment which is disproportionate and unacceptable with a view to their intended purpose. Another aspect to be considered in this context is the social function of property,[78] which enjoys particular protection wherever it serves the safeguard of personal liberty. Correspondingly, however, the legislator's freedom to act increases to the extent to which property bears a social relation,[79] as is *eg* the case within the framework of a common organisation

---

67 ECJ *SMW Winzersekt* [1994] ECR I-5555, para 20.
68 ECJ *Nitrates Directive* [1999] ECR I-2603, para 56; Tomuschat in: Ossenbühl (ed) *Eigentumsgarantie und Umweltschutz* (Heidelberg 1990) pp 47 ff.
69 ECJ *Leukhardt* [1989] ECR 1991, para 20; *Germany v Council* [1994] ECR I-4973, para 82; *SMW Winzersekt* [1994] ECR I-5555, para 21.
70 Evidence given in Müller-Michaels (note 2) p 49.
71 ECtHR *James* (1986) 8 EHRR 123, para 45 on the insofar corresponding concept of "public interest" in Art 1(1)(ii) Prot 1 ECHR.
72 ECJ *Biovilac* [1984] ECR 4057, para 22.
73 ECJ *Generics* [1998] ECR I-7976, para 85.
74 ECJ *SMW Winzersekt* [1994] ECR I-5555, para 24.
75 ECJ *Kühn* [1992] ECR I-35, para 17.
76 Also *cf* Müller-Michaels (note 2) pp 52 ff.
77 A somewhat more detailed examination of the presence of interferences with the essence was *eg* carried out in the judgments of the ECJ *von Deetzen* [1991] ECR I-5119, para 29; *Kühn* [1992] ECR I-35, para 17.
78 ECJ *Hauer* [1979] ECR 3727, para 20.
79 Kingreen (note 2) Art 6 EUV, para 155.

of the market.[80] With regard to these criteria, the relevant literature correctly points out that the ECJ tends towards a relative understanding of what constitutes the essence, according to which only disproportionate encroachments infringe the essence of a fundamental right. However, if this is in fact the case, the guarantee of essence loses its independent function vis-à-vis the principle of proportionality.[81]

Case 4 – Answer:

30 Within the context of the preliminary ruling according to Article 234 of the TEC (Article III-369 DC), the ECJ does not carry out the proportionality test within the framework of the concrete examination of fundamental rights (in this case, the right to property), but rather conducts an abstract test beforehand, as is often the case. Later, when the Court examines the fundamental right to property, it merely refers to the proportionality test in respect to its results.[82] Since this procedure does not hold the relation between regulation objective and regulation encroachment to the examination standard of the principle of proportionality, it cannot extract a concrete content for the decision of the individual case and therefore cannot effectively develop its controlling power. Thus, the ECJ's conclusion is hardly surprising, according to which the provisions of the Nitrates Directive are sufficient for providing the Member States with the legislative freedom they need in order to bring about a proportionate implementation.[83] In order for the examination (of the polluter-pays principle, the fundamental right to property and the justification of the encroachment[84]) to be compliant with the respective dogmatic and more convincing in its overall result, the review should have been conducted the other way round: First of all, the ECJ would have had to examine and – as was in fact the case – affirm the existence of an encroachment into the real property of B through the fertilisation restrictions. Within the context of its proportionality test, the ECJ should then have concretely related this encroachment to the regulation objective of health and environmental protection, and thereafter, it should have put the regulation to the test of its suitability, necessity and adequacy. It is interesting to see how the ECJ treats B's reference to the polluter-pays principle: In the ECJ's opinion, it is sufficient "to state that the Directive does not mean that farmers must take on burdens for the elimination of pollution to which they have not contributed". It was for the Member States "to take account of the other sources of pollution when implementing the Directive and, having regard to the circumstances, are not to impose on farmers costs of eliminating pollution that are unnecessary". Contrary to the prevailing opinion,[85] the ECJ hereby explicitly regards the polluter-pays principle specific to environmental law as a concept of the principle of proportionality and refers to the elaborations already existing in that field.[86]

31 What is remarkable is that the ECJ, within the context of its concrete **proportionality test**, places a relatively high importance on the Community objectives. Thus, *eg* the property-relevant Community acts in the field of agricultural policies are merely subjected to a significantly limited proportionality test by the ECJ, who does not wish to put its own politi-

---

80 ECJ *Hauer* [1979] ECR 3727, para 23; *Schräder* [1989] ECR 2237, para 15; *Germany v Council* [1994] ECR I-4973, para 78; *Irish Farmers Association* [1997] ECR I-1809, para 27.
81 Kingreen (note 2) Art 6 EUV, para 76; of different opinion Müller-Michaels (note 2) p 53.
82 ECJ *Nitrates Directive* [1999] ECR I-2603, paras 46–50, 57.
83 ECJ *Nitrates Directive* [1999] ECR I-2603, para 50.
84 ECJ *Nitrates Directive* [1999] ECR I-2603, paras 51 ff.
85 *Cf* Calliess (note 1) Art 174 EGV, paras 34 ff.
86 ECJ *Nitrates Directive* [1999] ECR I-2603, paras 51 ff.

The Fundamental Right to Property   § 17 III 3

cal considerations in the place of the decisions made by the legislative organs. A good example of this practice are the elaborations in the *Banana* judgment: "The Court's review must be limited in that way in particular if, in establishing a common organization of the market, the Council has to reconcile divergent interests and thus select options within the context of the policy choices which are its own responsibility." The European Court of Justice continued that, while it could not be excluded that "other means for achieving the desired result were indeed conceivable", it still did not deem itself authorised to "substitute its assessment for that of the Council as to the appropriateness or otherwise of the measures adopted by the Community legislature if those measures have not been proved to be manifestly inappropriate for achieving the objective pursued".[87] Therefore, the Community legislator's wide discretionary power regarding the organisation of the common market is formative for the implementation of the proportionality test: the necessity and adequacy of the measure was only examined in very few decisions, and even where this is the case, the examinations do not go beyond a very rudimentary form of testing. Mostly, the proportionality test was concluded after the suitability check. If the ECJ, under the heading "adequate proportion", exceptionally does carry out a comparative evaluation of legal interests, such consideration is limited to the examination of the merit of the objective pursued by the encroachment and fails to deal with the degree and intensity of the individual concern.[88] This leads to a considerable – at least in comparison to the German legal practice[89] – decrease of the control density regarding fundamental rights,[90] and as a result, there has not been a single case to date in which invoking the fundamental right to property was successful. The wide discretionary scope granted to the Community legislator by the ECJ with regard to the choice of political objectives, as well as the decrease of the standard of control this brought about, is – sometimes heavily – criticised by the majority of opinions voiced in the relevant literature.[91]

Case 5 – Answer:
The Court of Justice came to the conclusion that the sanction measure in question had indirectly property-infringing effects and therefore damnified F, who was not responsible for the situation that had lead to the order of the sanctions. However, the significance of the objectives pursued with the regulation could in itself justify substantial negative consequences for certain business participants. In the face of an objective which is so fundamental for the

32

---

87 ECJ *Germany v Council* [1994] ECR I-4973, paras 89–91, 94; *SMW Winzersekt* [1994] ECR I-5555, para 21; *Schräder* [1989] ECR 2237, para 21.
88 Only exemplarily, *cf* ECJ *Hauer* [1979] ECR 3727, paras 23 ff; *Germany v Council* [1994] ECR I-4973, paras 64 ff; *SMW Winzersekt* [1994] ECR I-5555, paras 20 ff.
89 For a contrasting view see Kischel [2000] EuR 380, who tries to provide evidence for the presumption that the control of the German Federal Constitutional Court does not take priority over the control of the ECJ.
90 For detailed – and differentiated – corresponding remarks see von Bogdandy [2001] JZ 157, 163 ff; on control density in community law in general see Herdegen/Richter in: Frowein (ed) *Die Kontrolldichte bei der gerichtlichen Überprüfung von Handlungen der Verwaltung* (Berlin 1993) p 209; Schwarze in: Schwarze/Schmidt-Aßmann (eds) *Das Ausmaß der gerichtlichen Kontrolle im Wirtschaftsverwaltungs- und Umweltrecht* (Baden-Baden 1992) p 211.
91 *Cf*, for example, Nettesheim [1995] EuZW 106, 107; Huber [1997] EuZW 517; Stein [1998] EuZW 261; for differentiating remarks see von Bogdandy [2001] JZ 157, 163 ff; Zuleeg [1997] NJW 1201 and Kischel [2000] EuR 380.

international community and also serves the common welfare, an objective aimed at terminating the state of war in the region as well as the massive violations of human rights and of humanitarian public international law in the Republic of Bosnia and Herzegovina, the confiscation of the aircraft in question, which is owned by a person based or active in Yugoslavia, could not be regarded as inadequate or disproportionate.[92]

IV. Conclusion

33 Through Article II-77 of the DC, the content and scope of the Community fundamental right to property have gained a clearer outline.[93] All the same, the scope of protection of fundamental rights will continue to be difficult to determine in the future, and its outline will continue to be marked by case-law. Nevertheless, thanks to the catalogue of fundamental rights now put down in writing, it remains to be hoped that the ECJ will address the lack of methodical transparency criticised in the relevant literature[94] and give greater acuity to its case-law regarding fundamental rights. However, one needs to bear in mind in this respect that with regard to the elucidation of fundamental rights, the ECJ's approach is not all that different from the procedures of the national constitutional courts.[95] Thus, *eg*, the German Federal Constitutional Court, too, had to outline the scope of the fundamental right to property according to Article 14 of the Basic Law within the context of a still developing legal practice.[96] Consequently, the problem up to now was less the clear determination of the fundamental rights' scopes of protection through the ECJ,[97] but rather the proportionality test, which the ECJ – possibly because of the vagueness of the scope of protection – has so far been reaching fairly rapidly in its procedure of review. Quite rightly, time and again – most recently with a view to the already mentioned *Banana* and *Sparkling Wine* judgments – there has been articulate criticism in this respect. In both cases, the ECJ simply adopted the arguments brought forth by the Community legislator to justify the encroachment into fundamental rights without any further critical evaluation from a constitutional law point of view. However, not every consideration regarding the political convenience of a measure can justify an encroachment into fundamental rights. Therefore, before considering the common welfare issues asserted by the Council, the ECJ should first of all examine them in view of their factual validity as well as their substantiality and importance for constitutional law. The wide discretionary scope granted to the Council by the ECJ with regard to the choice of political objectives and the resulting limitation of the standard of control to "clearly disproportionate" impairments of fundamental rights which transgress the "limits of discretion" of the Council are hardly compatible with the previous Article 220 of the TEC (replaced by Article I-29(1) DC) and Article 6(2) of the TEC (Article I-9(3)

---

92 ECJ *Bosphorus* [1996] ECR I-3953, paras 22 ff.
93 With a view to property rights *cf* the overview given in Rengeling/Szczekalla *Grundrechte in der Europäischen Union* (Cologne/Berlin/Munich 2004) pp 627 ff; Thiel [1991] JuS 274, 278 ff.
94 Streinz *Bundesverfassungsgerichtlicher Grundrechtsschutz und Europäisches Gemeinschaftsrecht* (Baden-Baden 1989) pp 384 ff; different view by Nettesheim [1995] EuZW 106, 107.
95 Rengeling/Szczekalla (note 93) pp 627 ff with further references.
96 *Cf* Ehlers (1992) 51 VVDStRL 211, 214 ff; Wendt *Eigentum und Gesetzgebung* (Hamburg 1985).
97 Likewise Nettesheim [1995] EuZW 106, 107.

DC).⁹⁸ Another alarming aspect is the fact that the individual fundamental rights related interests of affected parties are left un-reviewed within the examination of the encroachment. No proper balancing of the interests of the individual against those of the common welfare takes place. Rather, the Court of Justice generally leaves the decision whether an objective is compliant with the Community's general welfare and whether the chosen measure constitutes the mildest suitable measure, which must still be proportionate to the objective pursued, to the legislative discretion of the competent Community organ.⁹⁹

---

98 Such is the justified criticism voiced by Nettesheim [1995] EuZW 106, 107; similarly Huber [1997] EuZW 517; Stein [1998] EuZW 261; for a differentiating view see von Bogdandy [2001] JZ 157, 163 ff; Zuleeg [1997] NJW 1201 and Kischel [2000] EuR 380.
99 Pernice/Mayer in: Grabitz/Hilf (eds) *Das Recht der Europäischen Union* (loose-leaf, Munich) Art 220 EGV, para 62 c.

§ 18
Basic Rights of Equality and Social Rights

Thorsten Kingreen

I. Rights to Equality

Further reading: Kingreen *Theorie und Dogmatik der Grundrechte im europäischen Verfassungsrecht* [2004] EuGRZ 570; Kischel *Zur Dogmatik des Gleichheitssatzes in der Europäischen Union* [1997] EuGRZ 1; Rengeling/Szczekalla *Grundrechte in der Europäischen Union* (Cologne 2004) paras 867 ff; Sattler *Allgemeiner Gleichheitssatz und spezielle Gleichheitssätze in der Rechtsprechung des Europäischen Gerichtshofs* in: Ipsen (ed) *Recht – Staat – Gemeinwohl – FS Rauschning* (Cologne 2001) pp 51 ff.

1. Overview and System

1 The law of the European Community contains a **multitude of laws** on equality. On the one hand, the guarantees for equality are extended to the actions of the organs of the Union as *basic rights of the Union,* as the Member States, being states under the rule of law, can only transfer national jurisdiction bound by the basic rights to the Union (*supranational legitimation*); on the other hand, as well as containing a demand directed at the Member States to refrain from discrimination due to nationality, they contain a *conditio sine qua non* for fair competition and the integration of national markets (*transnational integration*), which is professed in Article 2 and Article 14(2) of the TEC (Article I-4(2), III-130(2) DC).[1] The law of the European Union, therefore, has two levels of subjective public rights to equality:[2] rules concerning transnational integration and rules concerning supranational legitimation:

a) The concept of Transnational Integration

2 Norms of transnational integration respond to the danger, inherent in every federal system, of a Member State trying to influence the competition with other Member States through the preferential treatment of its members; to put it simply: they respond to federal risk zones. The **equal treatment of all citizens of the Union** is achieved by stating that affiliation to one Member State is irrelevant with regards to treatment in another Member State. They therefore stand for the primary historical creation idea of the European project, the common market, and, at their core, the basic freedoms directed against protectionism in Member States (→ *cf* § 7 para 1) as well as the general ban on discrimination on the basis of nationality contained in Article 12 of the TEC (Article I-4, III-123 DC) (→ cf § 13).

b) The concept of Supranational Legitimation

3 Rules concerning supranational legitimation, on the other hand, have the function of **limiting the exercise of jurisdiction**: they satisfy the need for legitimation produced by the Euro-

---

1 *Cf* Chalmers (1994) 19 ELR 385, 397: "*The non-discrimination principle is central to any market philosophy.*"
2 Kingreen [2004] EuGRZ 570, 573 ff.

pean legal system, which takes precedence over national law and which has direct validity (→ *cf* § 14 para 4). Only there rules are treated within the context of the basic rights of the Union in this chapter. Just like many constitutions of the Member States, the law of the European Union recognises a general principle of equality as well as specific principles of equality:

The **general principle of equality** (Article II-80 DC) protects against *any improper differ-* 4 *entiation in all areas of life* by measures of the Community in cases where it has taken the place of the Member States. The addressee of the norm is therefore primarily the Community; it could, however, also be the Member States, according to the general principles valid for the basic rights of the Union (→ *cf* § 14 paras 31 ff), but only if they are implementing Community law (*cf* also Article II-111(1)(i) DC).

The general principle of equality is supplemented by specific *principles of equality* 5 which guarantee equality *only in certain areas of life* and/or *according to certain criteria*. The historically oldest specific principle of equality is Article 34(2)(ii) of the TEC (Article III-228(2)(ii) DC).[3] According to this, all discrimination between manufacturers and consumers inside a common market organisation is to be excluded. **Specific principles** are now to be found above all in the Charter of Fundamental Rights (Article II-81, 83–87 DC; → paras 17 ff).

Article 141(1) of the TEC (Article III-214(1) DC) has a special position with its postu- 6 late, directed at the Member States, of **equal pay for men and women** doing the same or equivalent work. Historically, it is connected with transnational integration: its entry into the treaties goes back substantially to the endeavours of France, which already recognised this kind of regulation at the time of the Community's establishment and feared competition disadvantages compared to other Member States, in which the right to equal remuneration was not standardised.[4] Article 141(1) of the TEC (Article III-214(1) DC) does not, however, refer to the forbidden differentiation criterion of nationality, *ie* the crossing of borders, but to gender, and therefore to a criterion which bears no specific relation to the realisation of the common market. In practice, the regulation has therefore developed into a basic right which promotes more than merely the prevention of competition falsifications.[5] In contrast to Article II-83 DC, it is not, however, a standard for the actions of the Union[6] (*ie* Community law implementing measures of the Member States), but is solely addressed to the Member States.

2. Norm Structure and Structure of Review

Rights to equality possess a norm structure differing from that of the civil rights and 7 liberties. While the civil rights and liberties merely refer to the vertical relationship between citizens and the state, the **horizontal perspective** comes in through the rights to equality. The bipolar relationship between citizens and the state concerning civil rights and liberties is expanded into a tripolar or even multipolar relation with regard to the

---

3 *Cf* ECJ *Germany v Council* [1994] ECR I-4973, para 62.
4 *Cf* Langenfeld *Die Gleichbehandlung von Mann und Frau im Europäischen Gemeinschaftsrecht* (Baden Baden 1990) p 30.
5 Express qualification of a "basic right", for instance in ECJ *Deutsche Post* [2000] ECR I-929, para 56.
6 On the binding of the Community to the principle of equality of gender: ECJ *Razzouk* [1984] ECR 1509, para 17.

principle of equality through the inclusion of comparative facts: it is not the intensity of the burden which is decisive, but the inequality of the imposition.

8   It is unresolved which consequences ensue for the **structure of review**. While this issue, up until now, has scarcely been discussed regarding Community law, a two-stage-test is mostly favoured for the principles of equality within German constitutional law: in a first step, a case of discrimination in comparable circumstances is established, while the matter of its constitutional justification is treated in a second step. This deviation from the test for civil rights and liberties is based on the assumption that the three-step "scope of protection-intrusion-justification" (→ cf § 14 para 39) which is practised for these rights does not adequately reflect the norm structure of the principle of equality: The three-level structure represents the liberal principle of distribution, which opposes the unlimited guarantee of freedom which generally precedes state access with a principally limited state authority for intrusions into this sphere.[7] This rule-exception model cannot be transferred to the principle of equality which, moreover, knows no scope of protection and, therefore, no interference therewith.[8]

9   This confrontation arguably overemphasises the differences which certainly exist[9]: After all, the rights to equality also protect certain patterns of human behaviour from unfounded interference by the state;[10] the difference is simply that an interference does not arise from the restriction alone, but from the equal or unequal treatment. The principle of distribution is also valid: The sovereign institution does not have to justify itself less for the unequal treatment of (by Community standards) constitutionally substantially similar circumstances (and respectively for the equal treatment of substantially different circumstances) than for an intrusion into the scope of protection of a civil right. Correspondingly, the principle of proportionality, which was originally tailored towards curtailments on freedom, is also increasingly applied in the test for justification of an equal or unequal treatment[11] as well as in the context of the Community laws on equality.[12] However, the classical formula "Scope of protection – damage/intrusion – justification" promises a benefit of efficiency primarily for those principles of equality the scope of application of which is limited in personal or objective terms.[13] Here it is sensible in the interest of problem solving and for the purpose of clarifying matters of competition to initially broach the issue of the protected sphere within the issue of discrimination.[14] On the other hand, in cases concerning the general principle of equality and the specific principles of equality, in which the particularities do not result from the limitation to a certain sphere or person subgroup, but from the limitation to individual differentiation criteria (which are systematically assigned to the level of interference), a two-stage test makes more sense.

---

7   *Cf* for instance, Böckenförde [1974] NJW 1529, 1537; Schlink [1984] EuGRZ 457, 467.

8   *Cf* only Bryde/Kleindiek [1999] Jura 36, 37; Dreier in: Dreier (ed) *Grundgesetz Kommentar Bd I* (2nd ed, Tübingen 2004) paras 151 ff; Pieroth/Schlink *Grundrechte Staatsrecht II* (20th ed, Heidelberg 2004) paras 430, 501.

9   *Cf* for instance, on the problem of reservation of statute in rights of equality Jarass [1995] AöR 345, 375 ff.

10 Huster *Rechte und Ziele* (Berlin 1993) pp 225 ff; Jarass [1995] AöR 345, 361 ff, 365 ff.

11 Pieroth/Schlink (note 8) paras 438 ff.

12 *Cf* Rengeling/Szczekalla *Grundrechte in der Europäischen Union* (Cologne 2004) paras 878 ff.

13 → under paras 17 ff for Article 141 TEC (Art III-214 DC).

14 *Cf* for instance, for the basic freedoms § 7 paras 47 ff as well as Kingreen *Die Struktur der Grundfreiheiten des europäischen Gemeinschaftsrechts* (Berlin 1999) pp 75 ff.

Differences between rights to civil liberty and rights to equality exist in the **legal consequences**: Whereas an interference with the right to freedom must simply be suppressed, the unequal treatment of two groups can be remedied in various ways: the first group can be treated as the second group, the second group as the first group, or both can be treated in a new, third way.[15]

3. The General Principle of Equality

Leading cases: ECJ *Ruckdeschel* [1977] ECR 1753; *Moulins Pont-à-Mousson* [1977] ECR 1795; *Edeka* [1982] ECR 2745; *Karlsson* [2000] ECR I-2737.

Further reading: Hölscheidt in: Meyer (ed) *Charta der Grundrechte der Europäischen Union* (2nd ed, Baden-Baden 2006), Art 20 GrCh; Kingreen in: Calliess/Ruffert (eds) *Kommentar des Vertrages über die Europäische Union und des Vertrages zur Gründung der Europäischen Union* (2nd ed, Neuwied 2002), Art 6 EUV, paras 174 ff; Mohn *Der Gleichheitssatz im Gemeinschaftsrecht* (Strasbourg 1990); Pernice/Mayer in: Grabitz/Hilf (eds) *Das Recht der Europäischen Union* (loose-leaf, Munich) nach Art 6 EUV, paras 161 ff; Streinz in: Streinz (ed) *EUV/EGV. Vertrag über die Europäische Union und Vertrag zur Gründung der Europäischen Gemeinschaft* (Munich 2003) Art 20 GrCh.

The general principle of equality has for a long time been recognised by the ECJ as a **basic right of the Union**[16] and henceforth also finds itself in Article II-80 DC. It is, however, not derived from the subsidiary means for the determination of rules of law referred to in Article 6(2) of the TEU (→ *cf* hereunto § 14 para 9), like the right to freedom, but is mostly placed in a rather unclear connection with Article 34(2)(ii) of the TEU (Article III-228(2)(ii) DC).[17] This is also due to the fact that a multitude of decisions affect common market regulations in the field of agriculture. Nevertheless, it would be methodically more consistent to resort to the classical subsidiary means for the determination of rules of law in this regard as well.[18]

As regards content, the general principle of equality forbids treating "like cases differently, thereby subjecting some to disadvantages as opposed to others without such differentiation being justified by the existence of substantial objective differences."[19]

a) Discrimination

A discrimination exists if comparable circumstances are handled differently or if dissimilar circumstances are treated in the same way.[20]

The **test** for discrimination begins with the *formation of comparison groups*.[21] In doing so, the standard of comparison is established which gives the principle of equality its con-

---

15 Pieroth/Schlink (note 8) para 479.
16 *Cf* firstly ECJ *Ruckdeschel* [1977] ECR 1753, para 7; detailed proof in Kingreen in: Calliess/Ruffert (eds) *Kommentar des Vertrages über die Europäische Union und des Vertrages zur Gründung der Europäischen Union* (2nd ed, Neuwied 2002), Art 6 EUV, para 170.
17 *Cf* the summary in Kingreen (note 16) para 170 .
18 The general principle of equality is guaranteed in Art 14 ECHR and in all constitutions of the Member States (*cf* Kingreen (note 16) para 170).
19 Thus already ECJ *Klöckner-Werke* [1962] ECR 615, although without deriving from the basic right to a general principle of equality.
20 *Cf* for instance ECJ *Spain v Commission* [1993] ECR I-3923, para 37; *SMW Winzersekt* [1994] ECR I-5555, para 30.
21 Mohn *Der Gleichheitssatz im Gemeinschaftsrecht* (Strasbourg 1990) pp 52 ff; Example from case-law: ECJ *Karlsson* [2000] ECR I-2737, paras 39 ff.

crete substance: It decides what is similar and what is dissimilar. The comparison requires at least two sets of circumstances which are similar in terms of certain conditions and features, but for which dissimilarities remain [22]. The comparability requires a benchmark (*tertium comparationis*) which forms the common preamble under which the persons and groups of person to be compared become exclusively and completely apparent.[23] According to the ECJ, interchangeability is an important criterion in the comparability of products.[24] This depends particularly upon the behaviour of the consumer. The aspect of competition between the two products, which is also occasionally considered, is also closely connected therewith.[25]

If comparable sets of circumstances exist, it then needs to be established whether a **discrimination** exists.[26] The function of the principle of equality as a rule concerning supranational legitimation (→ above paras 3 ff) implicates, however, that in this respect not all discriminations are relevant: If transnational cases are being specifically disadvantaged in comparison with domestic circumstances (so-called federal risk zone), the prohibition on discrimination and the basic freedoms are pertinent. The discrimination of domestic circumstances in comparison with transnational circumstances (so-called reversed discrimination), does not, however, fall within the scope of application of Community law,[27] but is to be measured, if necessary, against the national principle of equality.[28] No discrimination exists in relation to another set of circumstances which has been handled in a legally incorrect manner (*no equality in injustice*).[29]

b) Justification

14 The ECJ's **test for justification** is extremely inconsistent, overall lacking dogmatic guiding principles. In particular, the substantial requirements for discrimination differ from case to case.[30] While the ECJ particularly emphasises the Community organs' broad scope for judicial evaluation in the area of agricultural policy,[31] in other decisions a substantial analysis of the reasons which legitimate the differentiation is demanded.[32] The re-establishment of competition equality is, for instance, recognised as an important reason for differential treatment.[33]

---

22 *Cf* Kirchhof in: Isensee/Kirchhof (eds) *Handbuch des Staatsrechts Bd V* (Heidelberg 1992) § 124, paras 6 ff.
23 Heun in: Dreier (ed) *Grundgesetz Kommentar Bd I* (2nd ed, Tübingen 2004) Art 3, para 23; Pieroth/Schlink (note 8) paras 431 ff.
24 ECJ *Ruckdeschel* [1977] ECR 1753, para 7; *Moulins Pont-à-Mousson* [1977] ECR 1795, paras 14, 17.
25 For instance negated in ECJ *Koninklijke Scholten-Honig* [1978] ECR 1991, paras 28, 32.
26 Mohn (note 21) pp 103 ff.
27 ECJ *Moser* [1984] ECR 2539, paras 14 ff.
28 Austrian Constitutional Court [2001] EuZW 219.
29 ECJ *Witte* [1984] ECR 3465, para 15; *Ahlström Osakeyhtiö* [1993] ECR I-1307, para 197.
30 *Cf* in addition Hölscheidt in: Meyer (ed) *Charta der Grundrechte der Europäischen Union* (2nd ed, Baden-Baden 2006) Art 20, para 16; Pernice/Mayer in: Grabitz/Hilf (eds) *Das Recht der Europäischen Union* (loose-leaf, Munich) Art 6 EUV, para 164.
31 ECJ *WuidArticle* [1990] ECR I-435, para 13
32 *Cf* for instance ECJ *Ruckdeschel* [1977] ECR 1753, para 7; *Moulins Pont-à-Mousson* [1977] ECR 1795, paras 14, 17.
33 ECJ *T Port* [1998] ECR I-1023, para 81.

What is unclear is the significance of the principle of proportionality within the scope of the test for equality.[34] Proposals for a **test of proportionality** have arisen in several judgements of the ECJ.[35] It has even been said in the literature that the ECJ consistently tests the proportionality of the differentiation.[36] As far as evidence exists for this, it only refers to decisions involving Article 34(2)(ii) of the TEU (Article III-228(2)(ii) DC). In terms of the general principle of proportionality, there is, on the other hand, no generalised assertion[37] from which conclusions could be deduced with regards to whether and, if applicable, in which cases the ECJ supports the integration of the principle of proportionality into the test for equality.

15

c) Legal Consequences of a Violation

It is a matter for the Member States to determine whether the person who has thus far been discriminated against is to be treated as the person who has thus far been privileged, whether the encumbering regulation should also extend to the latter, or whether they are both to be treated in a third way.

16

4. Specific Principles of Equality

Specific principles of equality are to be found in Articles II-81, 83–86 of the DC as well as in Article 141 of the TEC (Article III-214 DC). Article II-82 of the DC does not contain a basic right, but a basic principle in terms of Article II-112(5) of the DC.[38] It could thereby influence the test of individual basic rights of the Union, such as freedom of religion (Article II-70 1st sentence DC), freedom of expression (Article II-71 DC), freedom of art (Article II-73 1st sentence DC) and the law on non-discrimination (Article II-81 DC), on the justification level in that it only permits such intrusions which the law of diversity protects.

17

Substantially, the specific principles of equality produce an "increase in the minimal standard of equality, which is based solely on the general principle of equality."[39] For certain areas of life (for instance, equal pay in employment law, Article 141 TEC/Article III-214 DC) and/or in regard to certain forbidden criteria of differentiation (particularly those named in Article II-81(1) DC), the specific principles of equality contain special provisions in relation to the general principle of equality, which override it within the scope of its range.

18

---

34 For a discussion on the so-called "new formula" of the German Federal Constitutional Court *cf* for instance Brüning [2001] JZ 669; Kischel [1997] EuGRZ 1, 5 ff, approves a dependence upon this case law.
35 ECJ *Edeka* [1982] ECR 2745, para 13.
36 *Cf* for instance Huber [1997] EuZW 517, 520; Pernice/Mayer (note 30) para 164; Zimmerling in: Lenz/Borchardt (eds) *EU- und EG-Vertrag* (3rd ed, Munich 2003) Art 6 EUV, para 71.
37 However, *cf* in turn ECJ *Edeka* [1982] ECR 2745, para 13, where the impression is given that the test for proportionality is an element of control of arbitrariness.
38 Hölscheidt (note 30) Art 22 para 16.
39 Thus for the relationship of the rights to equality in the Basic Law: Sachs in: Isensee/Kirchhof (eds) *Handbuch des Staatsrechts Bd V* (Heidelberg 1992) § 126, para 16.

a) Non-Discrimination, Article II-81 of the DC

Further reading: Hölscheidt in: Meyer (ed) *Charta der Grundrechte der Europäischen Union* (2nd ed, Baden-Baden 2006) Art 21GRCh; Rengeling/Szczekalla *Grundrechte in der Europäischen Union* (Cologne 2004) paras 890 ff; und Streinz in: Streinz (ed) *EUV/EGV. Vertrag über die Europäische Union und Vertrag zur Gründung der Europäischen Gemeinschaft* (Munich 2003).

19   The law on **non-discrimination** forbids direct and indirect discrimination on the basis of any characteristics mentioned in Article II-81 DC. These are, according to the test for discrimination, to be tested at the level of justification. Here the question arises of whether discriminations on the basis of these frowned-upon characteristics are at all open to justification.[40] On the one hand, the general rules on limitations in Article II-112(1) of the DC are also valid here; on the other hand, Article II-81 of the DC speaks apodictically of a prohibition. In its case-law concerning discrimination on grounds of gender (→ paras 48 ff) or nationality (→ § 12 paras 17 ff), the ECJ appears to act on the assumption of a possibility of justification if an objective reason is existent. It is necessary to differentiate in this respect: For several characteristics (such as age), objective reasons for differentiations are self-evident, whilst they are virtually unimaginable with respect to other characteristics (such as race, skin colour). At any rate, a justification can only be considered if the discrimination is unavoidable for the protection of other rights protected by the constitution; in consequence, it requires a stricter test of proportionality.[41]

20   The basic right is **supplemented** by Article 13 of the TEC (Article III-124 DC). This establishes a Union competence to take necessary measures in order to combat discrimination.[42] The Union has particularly used this to introduce two anti-discrimination directives.[43]

b) Equality of Men and Women, Article 141(1) of the TEC (Article III-214(1) DC), Article II-83 of the DC

Leading cases: ECJ *Defrenne II* [1976] ECR 455; *Defrenne III* [1978] ECR 1365 ; *Bilka* [1986] ECR 1607; *Barber* [1990] ECR 1889.

Further reading: Bieback *Die mittelbare Diskriminierung wegen des Geschlechts* (Baden-Baden 1997); Haverkate/Huster *Europäisches Sozialrecht* (2nd ed, Neuwied 1999) paras 657 ff; Langenfeld *Die Gleichbehandlung von Mann und Frau im Europäischen Gemeinschaftsrech* (Baden-Baden 1990); Rengeling/Szczekalla *Grundrechte in der Europäischen Union* (Cologne 2004) paras 916 ff. Updated annotations to Article 141 of the TEC (Article III-214 DC): Coen in: Lenz/Borchardt (eds) *EU- und EG-Vertrag* (3rd ed, Munich 2003); Eichenhofer in: Streinz (ed) *EUV/EGV. Vertrag über die Europäische Union und Vertrag zur Gründung der Europäischen Gemeinschaft* (Munich 2003); Krebber in: Calliess/Ruffert (eds) *Kommentar des Vertrages über die Europäische Union und des Vertrages zur Gründung der Europäischen Union* (2nd ed, Neuwied 2002); Rebhahn in: Schwarze (ed) *EU-Kommentar* (Baden-Baden 2000); Rust in: von der Groeben/Schwarze (eds) *Kommentar zum Vertrag über die Europäische Union und zur Gründung der Europäischen Gemeinschaft* (6th ed, Baden-Baden 2003); Schlachter in: Dieterich (ed) *Erfurter Kommentar zum Arbeitsrecht* (6th ed, Baden-Baden 2006); Stein-

---

40 Hölscheidt (note 30) Art 21, para 29.
41 Rengeling/Szczekalla (note 12) para 912; *c* for Art 3(3)(1) Basic Law for instance also Osterloh in: Sachs *Grundgesetz Kommentar* (3rd ed, München 2003) Art 3 para 254.
42 Epiney in: Calliess/Ruffert (eds) *Kommentar des Vertrages über die Europäische Union und des Vertrages zur Gründung der Europäischen Union* (2nd ed, Neuwied 2002) Art 13 EGV para 1.
43 Streinz in: Streinz (ed) *EUV/EGV. Vertrag über die Europäische Union und Vertrag zur Gründung der Europäischen Gemeinschaft* (Munich 2003) Art 13 paras 21 ff.

Basic Rights of Equality and Social Rights §18 I 4

meyer in: Fuchs (ed) *Kommentar zum Europäischen Sozialrecht* (3rd ed, Baden-Baden 2003). – About Article 23 ECHR (Article II-83 DC): Hölscheidt in: Meyer *Charta der Grundrechte der Europäischen Union* (2nd ed, Baden-Baden 2006); Streinz in: Streinz (ed) *EUV/EGV. Vertrag über die Europäische Union und Vertrag zur Gründung der Europäischen Gemeinschaft* (Munich 2003).

Case 1 – Problem: (ECJ *Grant* [1998] ECR I-621)
South-West Trains Ltd (SWT), an English SEQ test c railway company, offers its employees and their relatives fare reductions. An affidavit was released which stated that non-married life partners could also get the benefit of these reductions, provided that the people concerned had been in a "serious relationship" for at least two years. However, the provisions in the employment contract applied only to partners of a different sex, and not for same sex partnerships. For this reason, SWT refused to grant the fare reductions to the female life partner of one of their employees, Lisa Grant (G). Consequently, G sued SWT before the Industrial Tribunal of Southampton. The tribunal presented the question to the ECJ of whether the actions of SWT violate Article 141(1) of the TEC (Article III-214(1) DC).

21

Case 2 – Problem: (ECJ *Lewark* [1996] ECR I-243)
The claimant, Mrs Lewark (L), is employed for 30 hours a week in the nursing department of B's dialysis centre, which is located in Germany, and belongs to the works council there, which consists of three members. Her working hours are split equally over four days a week. There are 21 employees in the nursing department of the dialysis centre; 7 men and 14 women. While all but one of the men are employed full-time, 10 of the 14 women are employed part-time. L is the only member of the works council who is employed part-time. From 11 to 15 November 1996, on the basis of a decision by the works council and with the approval of B, L took part in a training course required for her work in the works council. She also attended this course on 13 November, when she was not supposed to work at B's centre due to her part-time employment. According to § 37(2), (7) of the Works Constitutions Act, members of the works council have the right to take part in training events without a reduction in pay. However, further to this, L demands from B compensation for the 7 hours she spent at the training course on what would normally have been her day off. She argues that no special sacrifice can be demanded from her in comparison with the members of the works council who are employed full-time. She views B's refusal as a discrimination forbidden by Article 141(1) of the TEC (Article III-214(1) DC). After both the Labour Court and the Regional Labour Court had granted the action, the Federal Labour Court presented to the ECJ the question of whether Article 141(1) of the TEC (Article III-214(1) DC) prevents the national legislator from protecting the members of the works council only from such losses in income which they would otherwise suffer due to loss of working hours on account of their participation in the works council.

22

Apart from Article II-81(1) of the DC, a ban on **discrimination due to gender** also appears in Article II-83 of the DC and in Article 141(1) of the TEC (Article III-214(1) DC). While the ban in Articles II-81, 83 of the DC covers all areas of life, Article 141(1) of the TEC (Article III-214(1) DC) limits itself to the postulate for equal pay for men and women performing the same or equivalent work. Differences also exist in terms of the addressee: while Articles II-81, 83 DC bind the Union and bind the Member States only when they implement Union law (Article II-111(1)(i) DC), Article 141(1) of the TEC (Article III-214(1) DC) is directed at the Member States alone. The binding of the Member States to Union law therefore limits itself to the area of equal pay in employment law if the Member States are not implementing Union law; on the other hand, the binding of the Union is not, in this respect, unlimited. This difference can be explained by the fact that the

23

473

§ 18 I 4   Thorsten Kingreen

historically older Article 141(1) of the TEC (Article III-214(1) DC) has transnational integrational roots (→ para 6) and is furthermore supplemented by the Member State guarantees as national norms of legitimation, while Articles II-81, 83 of the DC have functions of supranational legitimation in terms of actions of the Union.

24 The following representation limits itself to **Article 141 of the TEC** (Article III-214 DC), which was shaped, up until now, by the practice of jurisdiction. In its first paragraph, the article contains the basic right to non-discrimination on the basis of gender. Paragraph 2 defines the term "remuneration"; paragraph 3 contains a basic principle of authorisation for measures which aim to guarantee the application of the principles of equal opportunities and equal treatment for men and women; and in paragraph 4, there is a preliminary clause, directed at the Member States, for certain measures of "positive discrimination".

aa) Scope of Protection

25 The scope of protection of Article 141(1) of the TEC (Article III-214(1) DC) covers the remuneration paid to employees.

(1) Personal Scope of Protection

26 The limitation of the personal scope of protection for **employees** results from the definition of remuneration in paragraph 2. According to the definition in Article 39 of the TEC (Article III-133 DC; → cf § 9 paras 5 ff), an employee is "each person who, for a certain period of time, renders a service to another, according to their instructions, for which he receives payment in return."[44] All those who are dependently employed within EU territory are protected; this includes, therefore, not only citizens of the Union, but also third state nationals.[45]

27 **Public-law employment status** is also covered,[46] even in the core sovereign areas. This follows from a systematic comparison with Article 39 of the TEC (Article III-133 DC), which excludes such occupations from the regulation's scope of application in its fourth paragraph. This would be unnecessary if they were to not fall under the definition of employee in terms of Article 39(1) of the TEC (Article III-133(1) DC). Therefore, according to the case-law of the ECJ, police officials[47], for instance, and members of the armed forces[48] are also employees.

The employee does not also have to be the recipient of the benefit. In fact, a third person, who is not an employee himself, can rely on Article 141(1) of the TEC (Article III-214(1) DC) if the remuneration claim has its roots in a working relationship, as is the case eg with widows' pensions.[49]

---

44 ECJ *Lawrie-Blum* [1986] ECR 2121, para 17; cf also the summary of the essential elements of the meaning of remuneration in Rust in: von der Groeben/Schwarze (eds) *Kommentar zum Vertrag über die Europäische Union und zur Gründung der Europäischen Gemeinschaft* (6th ed, Baden-Baden 2003) Art 141 EGV, paras 380 ff.
45 Langenfeld (note 4) pp 43 ff.
46 ECJ *Gerster* [1997] ECR I-5253, paras 17 ff.
47 ECJ *Johnston* [1986] ECR 1651, paras 26 ff, for the consistent meaning of employee in Dir 76/207, [1976] OJ L39/40.
48 ECJ *Kreil* [2000] ECR I-69, para 18.
49 ECJ *Ten Oever* [1993] ECR I-4879, paras 12 ff; *K B v National Health Service* [2004] ECR I-541, para 27.

(2) Material Scope of Protection

In material terms, Article 141(1) of the TEC (Article III-214(1) DC) guarantees equality with regard to the *remuneration* awarded to employees. Furthermore, *ultra vires* bans on discrimination, which are not limited to remuneration, can arise from secondary law.

As a result of the legal definition of **remuneration** in Article 141(2) of the TEC (Article 214(2) DC), not only basic pay and minimum wage fall within the objective scope of protection, but also all other gratuities which imply a working relationship and which are based on an employee-employer relationship[50] (overtime and bank holiday bonuses, shift premiums, all types of gratification). Remuneration is therefore *every reward attributable to the employer that is connected to the rendered work,* irrespective of its legal basis.[51] Therefore, the rewards do not need to be rooted in individual or collective contracts of employment, but can also have been paid on the basis of legal regulations[52] or even voluntarily.[53]

Examples: For instance, according to the decision of the ECJ, Christmas bonuses[54], continued remuneration in the case of illness[55], transitional money[56] as well as severance pay and payment of damages in the case of termination of employment[57], payment to members of works councils during external training[58] and even fare reductions for rail officials after entry into retirement[59] fall under the term remuneration.

Article 141 of the TEC (Article III-214 DC) requires a "close connection between the type of employment service and the level of remuneration".[60] Therefore, *other conditions* which do not concern remuneration for performed work do not fall within the objective scope of protection, not even when they actually have a financially detrimental effect.[61] The general Directive on Equal Treatment 76/207,[62] which covers both dependently employed and self-employed persons, affords protection from other discriminations concerning employment law.[63] With regards to the differentiation between remuneration covered by Article 141(1) o the TEC (Article III-214(1) DC) and other employment conditions that fall under Article 2(1) of the Directive 76/207, which is difficult in individual cases, particularly due to the absent third party effect of Article 2(1) of the Directive

---

50 *Cf* for instance Rebhahn in: Schwarze (ed) *EU-Kommentar* (Baden-Baden 2000) Art 141 EGV, para 11.
51 *Cf* Krebber in: Calliess/Ruffert (eds) *Kommentar des Vertrages über die Europäische Union und des Vertrages zur Gründung der Europäischen Union* (2nd ed, Neuwied 2002) Art 141 EGV, para 25.
52 *Cf* already ECJ *Defrenne II* [1976] ECR 455, para 40.
53 *Cf* recapitulatory, for instance, ECJ *Seymour-Smith* [1999] ECR I-623, para 15; *Lewen* [1999] ECR I-7243, para 19.
54 ECJ *Lewen* [1999] ECR I-7243, para 21.
55 ECJ *Rinner-Kuhn* [1989] ECR 2743, para 7.
56 ECJ *Kowalska* [1990] ECR I 2591, para 11.
57 ECJ *Commission v Belgium* [1993] ECR I-673, paras 12 ff; *Seymour-Smith* [1999] ECR I-623, paras 24 ff.
58 ECJ *Bötel* [1992] ECR I-3589, paras 13 ff; *Lewark* [1996] ECR I-243, paras 22 ff.
59 ECJ *Garland* [1982] ECR 359, paras 5 ff.
60 ECJ *Seymour-Smith* [1999] ECR I-623, para 34.
61 Fundamentally ECJ *Defrenne III* [1978] ECR 1365, para 21.
62 Directive of the council of implementation of the principle of equal treatment of men and women in view of access to employment, to vocational training and to occupational promotion, as well as in respect of working conditions from 9 February 1976, [1976] OJ L39/40.
63 ECJ *Commission v Germany* [1985] ECR 1459, para 24.

76/207[64], but which is very important, the ECJ differentiates as follows: it approves the necessary connection to payment of remuneration if the formation of an employment condition "quasi-automatically" has an effect on the level of remuneration, but denies it if the condition of employment only establishes the possibility of an influence on the remuneration.[65]

33 **Example:** One provision of the collective wage agreement for state employees used to calculate the period of service for promotion into a higher earnings group, which treated part-time and full-times employees unequally as there were often detrimental effects for the women employed part-time, fell under the definition of remuneration in Article 141(2) of the TEC (Article III-214(2) DC), as promotion into the next group happened automatically.[66] On the other hand, a provision of the Bavarian career plan arrangement for civil servants which calculated the period of service differently for part-time and full-time employees did not regulate a remuneration in terms of Article 141(2) of the TEC (Article III-214(2) DC), but was only the result of having been registered in a promotion list, which did not establish a right, but only the possibility of a promotion.[67] The ECJ differentiates correspondingly in the event of a termination of employment: compensation due to unfair dismissal is to be measured by Article 141 of the TEC (Article III-214 DC), while the requirements of reintegration of the employee are to be reviewed according to Directive 76/207.[68] The ECJ also measures other actions in connection with the establishment of employment by Article 2(1) of the Directive 76/207 and not by Article 141(1) of the TEC (Article III-214(1) DC), in particular, the allocation of quotas for women in civil service[69] and the restriction on women's entry into the weapon's division of the Federal Armed Forces.[70]

34 Furthermore, Article 141(1) of the TEC (Article III-214(1) DC) covers only those services which are at least indirectly attributable to the employer. The **attributability** poses particular difficulties with respect to the assessment of *old-age pension schemes*. The ECJ differentiates as following: while pension schemes of the employing company fall under Article 141 of the TEC (Article III-214 DC), Directive 79/7[71] alone, and not Article 141 of the TEC (Article III-214 DC), should apply for the national general pension system. Due to the fact that the ban on discrimination in Article 4(1) of the Directive 79/7 has no horizontal effect[72], and because of the preliminary clauses provided for in Article 7 of the Directive 79/7, which afford to the Member States deviations from the law of non-discrimination not provided for in Article 141(1) of the TEC (Article III-214(1) DC) (particularly concerning Member State regulations which favour women, although sometimes only putatively, in particular in connection with retirement entry age)[73], the differentiation

---

64 On the third party effect of Art 141(1) TEC (Art III-214 DC) *cf* para 50.
65 ECJ *Nimz* [1991] ECR I-297, para 9; *Gerster* [1997] ECR I-5253, paras 24 ff.
66 ECJ *Nimz* [1991] ECR I-297, para 9; *cf* further ECJ *Bilka* [1986] ECR 1607, paras 24 ff; *Kowalska* [1990] ECR I-2591, para 13.
67 ECJ *Gerster* [1997] ECR I-5253, paras 23 ff.
68 ECJ *Seymour-Smith* [1999] ECR I-623, paras 25 ff, 37 ff.
69 ECJ *Kalanke* [1995] ECR I-3051, paras 12 ff; *Marschall* [1997] ECR I-6363, paras 21 ff; *Badeck* [2000] ECR I-1875, paras 13 ff; *Abrahamsson* [2000] ECR I-5539, paras 40 ff.
70 ECJ *Kreil* [2000] ECR I-69, paras 10 ff.
71 Directive of the council on the gradual implementation of the principle of equal treatment of men and women within the area of social security from 12 December 1978, [1979] OJ L6/24.
72 On the third party effect of Art 141(1) TEC (Art III-214 DC) under para 50.
73 *Cf* Haverkate/Huster *Europäisches Sozialrecht* (Baden-Baden 1999) paras 729 ff.

has significant practical meaning, but sometimes causes considerable friction due to the interlocking of company and general pension schemes.[74]

With regard to **pension schemes**, whether they can be attributed to the employer depends decisively on the *occupational basis of the pension payment*. This significantly depends on the employer's influence on the pension scheme. The fact that a pension scheme is based on a legal obligation, independent from the parties' agreement in the employment contract, can therefore be an important indication against an occupational basis. However, this alone is not deciding, as the employer's reason for contribution is, in principle, irrelevant, as long as it is effected in connection with the employment relationship.[75] The fundamental concepts in the determination of an occupational basis are, therefore, not "occupation-based" versus "required by law", but "occupation-based" versus "general (social-) national".[76] An occupational basis for the pension contribution exists if the employer himself finances the complete contribution, or part thereof, in some cases even after deducting the amount from the employer's own salary, and retains an influence over the determination of the type and extent of the contribution to be paid.[77] However, the less the modalities of the contributory payment and of the contributions themselves are formed through the concrete employment relationship, and the stronger the financial investment of the public hand and the influence of general socio-political considerations are[78] (which can particularly manifest themselves in solidary reallocation and in the inclusion of the unemployed), the less the system is connected to the employment relationship, with the result that the occupational basis of the pension contribution is to be denied.[79] This is the case, for instance, for the payment of the social security contributions required by law.[80] However, if the pension contribution has an occupational basis, the concrete function of the private occupational pension scheme within the Member State's social security system is irrelevant. It is, therefore, not challenged by the fact that the private occupational pension scheme substitutes wholly, or in part, the national statutory social security scheme.[81] 35

bb) Interference

Every discrimination on the basis of gender regarding remuneration for the same or equal work by the Member State or by a private employer constitutes an **interference**. 36

(1) Addressees of the Norm

In addition to the **Member States**, **private persons** are also norm addressees of Article 141(1) of the TEC (Article III-214(1) DC), which is problematic[82]; consequently, the 37

---

74 Krebber (note 51) Art 141 EGV, para 72.
75 ECJ *Beune* [1994] ECR I-4471, paras 24, 26; *Lewen* [1999] ECR I-7243, para 20; Steinmeyer in: Fuchs (ed) *Kommentar zum Europäischen Sozialrecht* (3rd ed, Baden-Baden 2003) Art 141 EGV, paras 25 ff; Rebhahn (note 50) Art 141 EGV, para 14.
76 Steinmeyer (note 75) Art 141 of the TEC para 27.
77 Fundamentally: ECJ *Barber* [1990] ECR I-1889, paras 22 ff; Steinmeyer (note 75) Art 141 EGV, para 33.
78 ECJ *Barber* [1990] ECR I-1889, para 23; further Coen in: Lenz/Borchardt (eds) *EU- und EG-Vertrag* (3rd ed, Munich 2003) Art 141 EGV, para 9.
79 *Cf* the catalogue of criteria in Steinmeyer (note 75) Art 141 EGV, paras 32 ff.
80 ECJ *Defrenne I* [1971] ECR 445, paras 7, 12.
81 ECJ *Barber* [1990] ECR I-1889, para 28; *Coloroll Pension Trustees* [1994] ECR I-4389, para 71.
82 → § 13 para 12.

§ 18 I 4   Thorsten Kingreen

parties to a collective labour agreement are bound by it.[83] On the other hand, the Community is not bound by Article 141(1) of the TEC (Article III-214(1) DC), but by Article II-83 of the DC (→ para 23).

(2) Comparison Groups

38 The determination of discrimination begins with the formation of **comparison groups**.[84] This requires a benchmark formed by the general heading under which the persons who have been treated differently fall. This benchmark is given in Article 141 of the TEC (Article III-214 DC) as "the same or equal work". The law of the Union does not explain how the equality of the work is to be ascertained; however, in the interests of the consistent applicability of Article 141 of the TEC (Article III-214 DC), there must be some uniform criteria, particularly as the understanding of this term in the Member States varies considerably.[85] The Commission has, therefore, developed an elaborate classification system[86] which can aid with the definition, but which is not legally binding. Individual declarations can also be found in the decisions of the ECJ: According to these, the equality or similarity of the work depends neither on the subjective assessment of the employee, nor on that of the employer.[87] Instead, the objective circumstances are decisive, such as the type of work, the educational requirements, and the conditions of employment.[88] No equal or equivalent work exists if the same activity is performed by employees with different levels of training.[89]

39 Furthermore, comparability is, as with every principle of equality, only given if both cases fall within the **area of competence** of the body responsible for the different treatment.[90] This does not mean that only employees of one employer can be compared with each other, for discriminations can also stem from legal norms or collective agreements, which can cover a multitude of employees from different employers. However, the discrimination must "be attributed to one and the same source"; otherwise "there is no body which is responsible for the inequality and which could restore equal treatment".[91]

(3) Types of Interference

40 Article 141(1) of the TEC (Article III-214(1) DC) prohibits direct and indirect discriminations on the basis of gender.

(a) The Prohibited Differentiation Criterion of Gender

41 Article 141 of the TEC (Article III-214 DC) is only applicable to discriminations based on the **gender** of the employee. This includes such circumstances which can only occur with a

---

83 ECJ *Lewen* [1999] ECR I-7243, para 26; lately: ECJ *Sass* [2004] ECR I-11143, para 25.
84 *Cf* generally Pieroth/Schlink (note 8) paras 431 ff.
85 *Cf* Schlachter in: Dieterich (ed) *Erfurter Kommentar zum Arbeitsrecht* (3rd ed, Munich 2003) Art 141 EGV, para 9.
86 COM(1994) 6 final and COM(1996) 336 final.
87 Rebhahn (note 50) Art 141 EGV, para 15.
88 ECJ *Royal Copenhagen* [1995] ECR I-1275, paras 32 ff.
89 ECJ *Angestelltenbetriebsrat der Wiener Gebietskrankenkasse* [1999] ECR I-2865, paras 20 ff.
90 *Cf* generally Jarass in: Jarass/Pieroth (eds) *Grundgesetz Kommentar* (7th ed, Munich 2004) Art 3, para 4a.
91 ECJ *Lawrence* [2002] ECRI-7325, para 18.

Basic Rights of Equality and Social Rights §18 I 4

member of that sex, particularly pregnancy and birth.[92] Discriminations due to same-sex orientation are not covered.[93]

(b) Direct Discriminations

A **direct** discrimination exists if a measure connected to pay is explicitly linked to gender.[94] 42

Example: For instance, a direct discrimination exists if maternity leave is not counted in the period of employment in respect of the granting of bonuses[95], and also if parenting leave is only considered in the pensions of mothers.[96] 43

(c) Indirect Discriminations

In practice, the most common and most difficult cases are those of **indirect** discriminations. Their existence is determined following Article 2(2) of the Directive 97/80 (the so-called burden of proof directive)[97]. According to this, an indirect discrimination exists when provisions, criteria and procedures, seemingly formulated to be gender neutral, in fact disadvantage a significantly high proportion of one gender.[98] It therefore suffices that a rule formulated to be gender neutral predominantly works to the disadvantage of one gender. In order to calculate these actual effects, the absolute figures of the concerned employees of one gender may not be applied; rather, the number of people of one gender concerned at any one time must be placed in relation to the total number of employees of this sex, and within each group, the percentage of people concerned must be determined.[99] Article 4 of Directive 97/80 diverts the burden of proof onto the defendant, namely the employer or the Member State. Accordingly, persons who consider themselves aggrieved by discrimination on the basis of gender must only establish the credibility of the facts which indicate the existence of discrimination. This can be achieved particularly with the help of official or non-official statistics. It is then for the defendant to prove that no discrimination occurred. 44

Example: An indirect discrimination on the basis of gender is presumed if part-time employees are placed in a worse position than full-time employees, as the number of women who are employed part-time is typically higher than the number of men.[100] Therefore, for instance, payment of a lower hourly rate for part-time employees[101] and the exclusion of part- 45

---

92 Rebhahn (note 50) Art 141 EGV, para 21.
93 *Cf* ECJ *Grant* [1998] ECR I-621, para 47; partly opposite Rebhahn (note 50) Article 141 EGV para 21; *cf* in addition Case 2.
94 Rebhahn (note 50) Art 141 EGV, para 23; Schlachter (note 85) Art 141 EGV, para 14.
95 ECJ *Lewen* [1999] ECR I-7243, para 42.
96 ECJ *Griesmar* [2001] ECR I-9383, para 67.
97 Directive of the council over the burden of proof in discriminations on the basis of gender from 15 December 1997, [1998] OJ L14/6.
98 *Cf* ECJ *Dilku* [1986] ECR 1607, para 29, *Lewark* [1996] ECR I-243, para 28, *Geister* [1997] ECR I-5253, para 30.
99 ECJ *Seymour-Smith* [1999] ECR I-623, paras 58 ff; also in addition Steinmeyer (note 75) Art 141 EGV, paras 63 ff and Rust (note 44) Art 141 EGV, para 459.
100 Additionally covered Biermann *Die Gleichbehandlung von Teilzeitbeschäftigten bei entgeltlichen Ansprüchen* (Berlin 2000) pp 162 ff; Saunders *Gleiches Entgelt für Teilzeitarbeit* (Heidelberg 1997) pp 29 ff.
101 ECJ *Jenkins* [1981] ECR 911, para 13.

time employees from entry into a working health care system[102] were regarded as discriminations. The ECJ also extends the ban on discrimination very widely to the requirements which must be fulfilled in order to enjoy the protection of a norm:[103] A discrimination, therefore, also exists if the national law makes the granting of a benefit (here: surviving dependents' pension) dependent on the fact that the people concerned are married, but the possibility of entry into marriage has been refused to them due to a change of sex. On the other hand, the employer is not obliged to compensate for all family-based disruptions of the occupational career.[104] Referring to an age group shall also not be considered to be an indirect discrimination.[105]

46 The jurisdiction of the ECJ, notwithstanding its mostly persuasive socio-political findings, is dogmatically dissatisfying, as it ultimately promotes statistics to a method of interpretation by **focusing on the actual effects** of a law.[106] Basic rights are individual rights; the question of whether basic rights are infringed can therefore not depend on whether the individual belongs to a certain group (here: women), and whether others, possibly even many others, within this group are affected, especially if it is unclear where the percentage boundaries should lie.[107] This is particularly problematic for persons who do not belong to the group which is mainly affected, but who are nevertheless affected by the detrimental results, such as men who work part-time due to parenting. They can not claim sexual discrimination regarding the detrimental effects of their interrupted occupational careers, as the law mainly affects women and not men. Ultimately the ECJ is concerned with the practical effect: employment conditions and occupationally political conditions which are linked to parenting rather than gender, which in reality, however, mostly effect women, should be reviewed on their objective justification.

47 At least within the scope of the test for justification, the ECJ is moving away from the exclusive test of actual effects and asking whether the rejected provision (which statistically affects more women than men) is justified through objective factors which have nothing to do with sexual discrimination.[108] Here, the understanding of Article 141(1) of the TEC (Article III-214(1) DC) is reminiscent of a **ban on justification** which obliges the addressees of the norm to justify the differentiation without recourse to the forbidden differentiation criterion of "gender".[109] If this justification succeeds, it will sustain even if, as a result, it concerns more persons of one sex than another.[110] The ban on justification thereby combines the matter of discrimination with the test for its constitutional justification, particularly regarding the aim of the discrimination.

---

102 ECJ *Bilka* [1986] ECR 1607, paras 29 ff.
103 ECJ *K.B. v National Health Service* [2004] ECR I-541, para 30; in this respect critical Classen [2004] JZ 513.
104 ECJ *Bilka* [1986] ECR 1607, paras 29 ff.
105 ECJ *Danfoss A/S* [1989] ECR 3199, paras 24 ff; critical Krebber (note 51) Art 141 EGV, para 45.
106 Less critical Schlachter (note 85) Art 141 EGV, para 16, 19, which interprets the statistics as a method of reducing the requirement of proof for the gender dependency of a discrimination.
107 Therefore rather speculative Rust (note 44) Art 141, para 459.
108 *Cf* for instance, ECJ *Kirsammer-Hack* [1993] ECR I-6185, para 32.
109 *Cf* for Art 3(2) Basic Law Pieroth/Schlink (note 8) paras 447 ff.
110 Also for Art 3(2) Basic Law Pieroth/Schlink (note 8) para 453.

cc) Justification

Article 141 of the TEC (Article III-214 DC) contains **no express provisions on limitations**. Nonetheless, it is recognised that discriminations due to gender can also be justified. In doing so, one must differentiate between direct and indirect discriminations: while indirect discriminations are generally justifiable, some argue that direct discriminations cannot be justified at all[111], or only under heightened conditions.[112] This differentiation is not convincing,[113] as it is irrelevant for the individual whether he is burdened through express ties to the group to which he belongs, or through characteristics typically displayed by this group.[114]   48

The **justification test** consists of the identification of a legitimate aim of the discrimination, which must also be recognised by the treaties, and the test of proportionality of the measure: Thus, the ECJ regards discriminations by employers as justified if they (1) correspond to an "actual corporate need" and (2) are practical and necessary to achieve the aim.[115] This is particularly the case where this claim is supported by the substantiated argument that jobs, or the continuity of the business, could be secured through this measure. Differences in laws and wage agreements can be justified through occupational and socio-political aims if they are suitable and necessary to achieve the aim.[116] Since the Community lacks competence to a large extent in social-political matters, the Member States have a wide scope for decision-making in this respect.[117]   49

Example: The aim of facilitating minor employment can justify an exemption from the obligation to contribute to social insurance.[118] The protection of small and medium-sized businesses, which is also recognised in Article 137(2)(i) lit b) of the TEC (Article III-210 DC), can justify exemptions from national consumer protection laws.[119] General statements claiming that certain measures provide employment are not, however, sufficient.[120]   50

dd) Legal Consequences of a Violation

According to general principles, the affected law/measure is not to be applied in the case of a violation Article 141(1) of the TEC (Article III-214(1) DC). It is necessary to differentiate between the time before and the time after the national measure/law has been conformed according to the decision of the ECJ: 51

Until the coming into force of a new national law, the employee has a claim resulting directly from Article 141 of the TEC (Article III-214 DC) to payment of the remuneration granted to the favoured gender.[121] This claim in principle also includes past working hours; however, due to reasons of legal certainty and in order to avoid disproportionate

---

111 Classen [1996] JZ 621, 624.
112 So Rebhahn (note 50) Art 141 EGV, para 24.
113 → cf § 13 para 19.
114 As here Kischel [1997] EuGRZ 1, 4 ff.
115 ECJ *Bilka* [1986] ECR 1607, para 36.
116 ECJ *Rinner-Kühn* [1989] ECR 2743, para 14.
117 ECJ *Nolte* [1995] ECR I-4625, para 33.
118 ECJ *Nolte* [1995] ECR I-4625, para 31.
119 ECJ *Kirsammer-Hack* [1993] ECR I-6185, paras 32 ff.
120 ECJ *Seymour-Smith* [1999] ECR I-623, para 76.
121 ECJ *Nimz* [1991] ECR I-297, para 21; near Nicolai [1996] ZfA 481, 485 ff.

encumbrances, it does not extend to work done before 8 April 1976.[122] With regard to company pensions, the temporal effect is even limited to work completed after 5 May 1990 if no legal steps were taken previously to secure the claims.[123] However, this shall only apply to the benefits themselves, not to the requirements for access to an occupational pension scheme.[124]

As soon as a new law/measure which implements the decision of the ECJ comes into force, it alone is decisive. According to the principles pertaining to the legal consequences of a violation against principles of equality[125], the new law must not necessarily extend the privilege which has so far been granted to one sex to the other sex as well; rather, it is equally admissible to abolish altogether the privilege that the favoured sex has enjoyed up until now.[126] Article 141(1) of the TEC (Article III-214(1) DC) only acts with regard to equal treatment, not to the level on which this occurs.

Case 1 – Answer:
The refusal by SWT to grant the fare reductions to G's life partner could be a violation of Article 141(1) of the TEC (Article III-214(1) DC).
(1) Firstly, it is debatable whether the personal scope of protection is affected, as the benefit is not to be granted to employee G, but rather to her lifetime partner. However, the assumption is correct that the employee does not have to also be the recipient of the benefit. Rather, a third person, who is not an employee himself, can rely on Article 141(1) of the TEC (Article III-214(1) DC) if the claim for remuneration originates from an employment relationship (ECJ *Ten Oever* [1993] ECR 4879, paras 12 ff). As the fare reductions are offered on the basis of G's employment contract with SWT, they stem from an employment relationship. The objective scope of protection is also affected, as the fare reduction is another remuneration within the meaning of Article 141(2) of the TEC (Article III-214(2) DC; ECJ *Grant* [1998] ECR I-621, para 13 = *Ehlers* JK 99, EGV Art 119/1).
(2) The scope of protection must have been interfered with. Article 141(1) of the TEC (Article III-214(1) DC) also obliges private persons. SWT is, therefore, a capable addressee of the norm. An interference has conceivably occurred in the form of a direct discrimination. However, it is questionable which comparison groups are to be formed. One could compare a man who lives together with a woman with a woman who lives with a woman, as is the case with G. They are treated unequally, as only the man living with a woman may enjoy the pleasure of the benefit. The reference point of the comparison would be living together with a woman. However, these are not the correct groups of comparison, for the formation of comparison groups depends mainly on the aim of the measure/law (*cf* generally Gubelt in: von Münch/Kunig *Grundgesetz-Kommentar Bd I* (loose-leaf Munich) Article 3, para 17). The rule concerning the fare reductions does not differentiate between men and women, but rather between heterosexual and homosexual life partnerships. Comparison groups are therefore employees living with a partner of a different sex, and those living with a partner of the same sex. Although these groups are treated unequally, this discrimination is based neither the gender of G, nor on that of her partner, but on sexual orientation (dissenting opinion AG Elmer, ECJ *Grant* [1998] ECR I-621, paras 19 ff). The question of whether discriminations on the basis of sexual orientation fall under Article 141(1) of the

---

122 ECJ *Defrenne II* [1976] ECR 455, paras 74 ff.
123 ECJ *Barber* [1990] ECR I-1889, paras 43 ff.
124 Near Rebhahn (note 50) Art 141 EGV, para 37.
125 *Cf* above para 10.
126 ECJ *Coloroll Pension Trustees* [1994] ECR I-4389, para 30.

TEC (Article III-214(1) DC) is controversial (*cf* in addition the proof in *Szczekalla* [1998] EuZW 215, 216). The evaluation of this matter does not depend on the fact that homosexual life partnerships do not fall under the basic right of marriage, henceforth protected under Article II-69 of the DC (therefore problematic in this respect ECJ *Grant* [1998] ECR I-621, paras 32 ff). After all, the fare reductions are not only granted to married couples and are therefore not connected to the marital status, but rather to actual cohabitation. However, there is a systematic argument against the inclusion of sexual orientation: "gender" and "sexual orientation" are explicitly differentiated between in both Article 13(1) of the TEC (Article III-124(1) DC) and in Article II-81(1) of the DC in the Charter of Fundamental Rights. This would be unnecessary if "sexual orientation" was covered by the term "gender". The refusal of SWT to grant the fare reductions to G's life partner is, therefore, no discrimination on the basis of gender, and therefore does not constitute a violation of Article 141(1) of the TEC (Article III-214(1) DC).
Furthermore, G can also not invoke Article 13(1) of the TEC (Article III-124(1) DC) against SWT's refusal. This provision is formulated as a norm of authorisation which requires an action of the council but contains no particular primary law right to equality (Epiney in: Calliess/Ruffert (eds) *Kommentar des Vertrages über die Europäische Union und des Vertrages zur Gründung der Europäischen Union* (2nd ed, Neuwied 2002) Art 13 EGV, para 1; dissenting opinion Holoubek in: Schwarze (ed) *EU-Kommentar* (Baden-Baden 2000) Art 13 EGV, para 7).

Case 2 – Answer:
§ 37(2), (7) of the Works Constitutions Act, which limits the compensation payment of wages to the time in which the member of the works council should have been working, could constitute a violation of Article 141(1) of the TEC (Article III-214(1) DC).
(1) The scope of protection must be affected. It is problematic whether or not the claim to the wages during the training course is "remuneration" within the meaning of Article 141(2) of the TEC (Article III-214(2) DC). The payment by the employer is wage compensation, not remuneration for holding an office in the works council, which is an honorary office that is by nature unpaid. One can therefore doubt whether the wage compensation should be qualified as remuneration which is to be paid on the basis of performance due to an employment contract (Wiese in: Fabricius/Kraft/Wiese/Kreutz/Oetker (eds) *Betriebsverfassungsgesetz* (6th ed, Neuwied 1998) § 37, para 55; differentiating Kort [1997] RdA 277, 281 ff). The ECJ on the other hand emphasises the fact that the legal concepts and qualifications of the national law are irrelevant for the application of Article 141(1) of the TEC (Article III-214(1) DC). The wage compensation does not arise from the employment contract, but is granted on the basis of the existence of a working relationship, for only employees of the company can be members of the works council (ECJ *Lewark* [1996] ECR I-243, paras 20 ff).
(2) The scope of protection must then have been interfered with. The addressee in this case is the Federal Republic of Germany as a Member State which has to take responsibility for the (possibly) inadequate wage compensation provision of § 37(2), (7) of the Works Constitutions Act. An interference might have occurred in the form of an indirect discrimination. It is doubtful, however, whether this is a case of unequal treatment, for the loss in wages, which is marginal in absolute numbers, for part-time employees compared to full-time employees is merely a logical consequence of their differing working hours. However, the training course demands a sacrifice of free time from part-time employees which full-time employees do not have to bear (thus the arguments of AG Jacobs ECJ *Lewark* [1996] ECR I-243, para 26). However, this sacrifice of free time is not, strictly speaking, remuneration.

Nevertheless, the ECJ assumes – on the basis of its premise that wage compensation constitutes remuneration according to § 37(2), (7) of the Works Constitutions Act – a discrimination, as the part-time members of the Works Council receive a lower amount of total pay than the full-time members for the same number of hours (ECJ *Lewark* [1996] ECR I-243, paras 25 ff). This discrimination is based on gender, as the proportion of women amongst part-time employees as well as amongst part-time members of the Works Council is, percentage-wise, significantly lower than the figures for men (ECJ *Lewark* [1996] ECR I-243, paras 28 ff).
(3) This discrimination could be justified. This requires that the Member State can show a legitimate aim for the discrimination, and that the aim is proportional. In this case, sociopolitical aims could justify the discrimination. The fact that an office in the works council is by nature unpaid demonstrates the will of the German legislature to value the independence of the works council more than economic incentives for accepting such a position. The Federal Employment Court, which is competent to test the proportionality, also regarded the rule as proportionate (ECJ *Lewark* [1996] ECR I-243, para 38) (BAG (1997) 85 BAGE 224, 231 ff): the independence of the works council is guaranteed through the principle of the honorary post. It is prohibited for the member of the works council to increase his wage through the assignment of free time for the execution of his works council duties, and thereby to attain an advantage which other employees of the company are not able to achieve. The discrimination is also necessary, for the award of claims for remuneration would challenge the principle of honorary posts completely, not only in view of the training course. § 37 II, VII Works Constitution Act therefore does not violate Article 141(1) of the TEC (Article III-214(1) DC).

c) Rights of Children (Article II-84 DC); Rights of Old People (Article II-85 DC); Integration of Persons With Disabilities (Article II-86 DC)

Further reading: Annotations to Article 24-26 ECHR (Article II-84-86 DC): Hölscheidt in: Meyer *Charta der Grundrechte der Europäischen Union* (2nd ed, Baden-Baden 2006); Rengeling/Szczekalla *Grundrechte in der Europäischen Union* (Cologne 2004), paras 916 ff; Streinz in: Streinz (ed) *EUV/EGV. Vertrag über die Europäische Union und Vertrag zur Gründung der Europäischen Gemeinschaft* (Munich 2003).

54 Articles II-84–86 of the DC emphasise three groups as particularly needing protection (**children**, **elderly people** und **persons with disabilities**). That is rather innovative: while the protection of disabled persons is included in at least a few national texts on the basic rights, children are mostly accorded merely a knee-jerk protection through the rights of their parents or of the family, and the particular need for protection of elderly people is mainly reduced to the security of the pension scheme.[127] The practical meaning of the basic rights has not been very significant up to now, but could increase, as the Union has an independent competence within the field of protection from discrimination in Article 13(1) of the TEC (Article III-124 DC). The Union's competences in the field of economical and working life (for instance in employment policy, Article 125 TEC/Article III-203 and in industry policy, Article 157 TEC/Article III-279 DC) can also, in this respect, bring about areas of conflict with regard to basic rights.

55 Externally, Articles II-84–86 of the DC are not recognisable as **rights to equality**. Children, old people and disabled persons are already protected against discriminations

---

127 *Cf* Hölscheidt (note 30) Art 24 paras 6 ff, Art 25 para 3, Art 26 paras 2 ff.

through the characteristics "age" (which also refers to children[128]) and "disability" in Article II-81(1) of the DC. However, as far as the functions of the basic rights are concerned, the guarantees in Articles II-84–86 of the DC evidently exceed the guarantees concerning rights for equality (→ § 14 paras 18 ff): they partly contain particular **rights to freedom** (*eg* Article II-84(1)(ii), (iii) DC as *leges speziales* to Article II-71(1) DC), but are also partly formulated as derivative **rights to participation** (Article II-85 DC: "participation in social and cultural life"; Article II-86 DC: "participation in community life") and as original rights to governmental action (Article II-84(1)(i) DC: "claim to protection and public welfare").[129]

II. Social Rights

Further reading: Bernsdorff *Soziale Grundrechte in der Charta der Grundrechte der Europäischen Union* [2001] VSSR 1; Kingreen in: Calliess/Ruffert (eds) *Kommentar des Vertrages über die Europäische Union und des Vertrages zur Gründung der Europäischen Union* (2nd ed, Neuwied 2002) Art 6 EUV, paras 180 ff; Pernice/Mayer in: Grabitz/Hilf (eds) *Das Recht der Europäischen Union* (loose-leaf Munich) Art 6 EUV, paras 193 ff; Pitschas *Europäische Grundrechte-Charta und soziale Grundrechte* [2000] VSSR 207; Rengeling/Szczekalla *Grundrechte in der Europäischen Union* (Cologne 2004) paras 990 ff; Riedel in: Meyer (ed) *Charta der Grundrechte der Europäischen Union* (Baden-Baden 2006) Article 27–38; Streinz in: Streinz (ed) *EUV/EGV. Vertrag über die Europäische Union und Vertrag zur Gründung der Europäischen Gemeinschaft* (Munich 2003) Article 27–38.

1. Solidarity and Social Rights

Chapter IV of the Charter of Fundamental Rights of the European Union is titled **"Solidarity"**. Following chapters II and III, which guarantee freedom and equality, chapter IV addresses the third motto of the French Revolution, brotherliness, which is closely connected through historical ideas.[130] Social philosophy paraphrases solidarity as the necessity of a qualified, and thereby also exclusive, connectivity, which is significantly based on the waiver of individual interests and rights in favour of the community united in solidarity and the community's aim.[131] However, solidarity is also a term which is used often in law, particularly in social law. It also finds wide application within European law, where it is by no means limited to social policy.[132] Within the scope of chapter IV of the Charter of Fundamental Rights, in addition to the norms of occupational and social law reference (Articles II-87–94 DC), there are provisions whose connections with solidarity are not revealed at first glance, for instance concerning the protection of health, the

56

---

128 Meyer *Das Diskriminierungsverbot des Gemeinschaftsrechts als Grundsatznorm und Gleichheitsrecht* (Frankfurt/Main 2002) pp 72 ff.
129 On the differentiation between derivative rights to participate and original rights to governmental action: Murswiek in: Isensee/Kirchhof *Handbuch des Staatsrechts Bd V* (loose-leaf Heidelberg) § 112, para 2, as well as under para 59.
130 Wildt *Solidarität – Begriffsgeschichte und Definition heute* in: K Bayertz (ed) *Solidarität* (Frankfurt/Main 1998) pp 202–203.
131 *Cf* for evidence Kingreen *Das Sozialstaatsprinzip im europäischen Verfassungsverbund. Gemeinschaftsrechtliche Einflüsse auf das deutsche Recht der gesetzlichen Krankenversicherung* (Tübingen 2003) pp 244 ff.
132 *Cf* for instance, the "Solidarity in the world" in the preamble of the DC and the "mutual solidarity" (Art III-294(2) DC) in *the Common External and Security Policies*.

environment and consumers (Article II-95 2nd sentence, 97, 98 DC). In this context, solidarity evidently serves as a generic term in order to proclaim a common responsibility for public rights which could not be realised in a free competition of powers; this interpretation is also indicated by the repeated mention of vital services in Article II-96 DC.[133] The relation of solidarity to the basic rights has, however, scarcely been examined to date. There are two possible starting points in this regard: one connected to the concept of solidarity (*cf* para 57), and one of a legal-theoretical nature which differentiates between basic rights and basic principles (*cf* para 58):

57 One can differentiate **solidarity** as the basic principle of a voluntary integration from the **principle of solidarity** as a legal principle of a forced integration.[134] The basic rights protect the freedom of *solidarity*, for instance in the general freedom of association (Article II-72 DC), but also through several of the rights guaranteed in chapter IV: These are the freedom of collective action, guaranteed in Article II-88 of the DC, and protection of the family, guaranteed in Article II-93 of the DC, which both protect communities characterised by the principle of voluntary integration. On the other hand, the *principle of solidarity* is an element of forced integration linked with obligatory effects of redistribution (for instance, with an obligatory social insurance system)[135], and as such stands in a conflicted relationship with the freedom of the individual protected in the basic rights to decide with whom he wants to be solidly united (for instance, he may choose not to be a member of a social health care system, but rather to insure himself privately against illness). This enforcement of solidarity is an interference with the basic rights which needs justification. In this respect, chapter IV also offers approaches: by professing the necessity of access to social security systems (Article II-94 DC) and to services of general economic interest (vital services, Article II-96 DC), it points to constitutional positions which counter-balance the freedom conveyed by the basic rights to escape the enforcement of solidarity.[136]

58 From a legal-theoretical perspective, chapter IV contains a differentiation which is not to be found in other chapters of the Charter of Fundamental Rights. Specifically, it includes **basic principles** in addition to basic rights.[137] *Basic rights* are subjective-public rights which place individuals in a situation where they can demand a certain behaviour from an official in pursuit of their own interests.[138] On the other hand, *basic principles* do not generate subjective rights; rather, in the understanding of the constitutional treaty (Article II-52(5) DC[139]), they are authorisations to act which the Union and the Member States can use within the scope of their competences and, if applicable, use in order to restrict the rights to freedom. The difference between basic rights and basic principles has is of fundamental importance for the scope of the provisions in chapter IV. However, it has still

---

133 *Cf* already Art 16 TEC (Art III-122 DC).
134 Kingreen (note 131) pp 253 ff.
135 Explicitly, for instance § 1 *Sozialgesetzbuch V* (SGB V – German Social Insurance Code): *"Krankenversicherung als Solidargemeinschaft"*.
136 Therefore, also *cf* ECJ *Poucet and Pistre* [1993] ECR 637, para 18.
137 In addition Rengeling/Szczekalla (note 12) paras 993 ff. The differentiation between basic rights and basic principles should largely correspond to the German differentiation between basic rights and basic principles, *cf* in addition, for instance, Sommermann *Staatsziele und Staatszielbestimmungen* (Tübingen 1997), pp 415 ff.
138 *Cf* for instance, Maurer *Allgemeines Verwaltungsrecht* (15th ed, Munich 2004) § 8, para 2.
139 The provision was first included by the constitutional convention.

hardly been clarified what a basic rights and basic principles are. The interpretations of these notions are based on the wording and genesis of the provisions:[140]

- According to their wording ("Right to", "claim to", "must be guaranteed", "are guaranteed"), Articles II-87–91, 93, 94(2), 95 1st sentence of the DC grant subjective-public rights, and are therefore basic rights. Article II-92 of the DC is not formulated as a right, but as a Member State duty to protect. However, in the meantime it is also recognised by Community law that subjective public claims to the guarantee of protection result from the state duties to protect;[141] therefore, the basic rights character of Article II-92 of the DC cannot be questioned. It is not completely clear what is meant by the phrase "recognises and regards", which appears in several norms (Article II-94(1), (3), 96 DC). Norms worded in this manner can also be found outside of chapter IV, where they serve as foundations of subjective-public rights.[142] The equivalent is argued for Article II-94(1), (3) DC.[143] On the other hand, according to the commentaries on the chairmanship of the Convention for Fundamental Rights (which was enhanced by the new Article II-52(7) DC), no new rights were to be established through Article II-96 of the DC.[144]

- Articles II-95 2nd sentence, 97, 98 of the DC undoubtedly contain basic principles. They oblige the Member States and the Union respectively, within the scope of their competences, to respect the aims mentioned within. As they are not basic rights, they will not be analysed further in the following account of the social rights.

2. Typology of Social Rights

Insofar as chapter IV of the Charter of Fundamental Rights contains basic rights (→ para 58), one can speak, in a very general sense, of **social rights**;[145] this ties in with earlier European proclamations of the basic rights.[146] For many Member States, for Germany as well as for Great Britain and the Scandinavian countries, for instance, social basic rights are new constitutional ground; this explains why chapter IV is the most controversial of the whole Charter.[147] According to the traditional understanding of basic rights, brought to light in the Human Rights declarations of the 18th and 19th centuries, they are first and foremost civil rights which protect the freedom of the individual from state interference; furthermore, there are political rights to participation, most notably the right to vote. On the other hand, social basic rights broach the issue of virtual freedom, *ie* the actual conditions that the state has to create so that the freedom concerned in the basic rights can in fact be exercised; in this respect, they are owed to the further development of

---

140 Also *cf* with the following the commentaries on Article 27–36 of the Charter of Fundamental Rights (Article II-87-96 DC) by Riedel in: Meyer *Charta der Grundrechte der Europäischen Union* (2nd ed, Baden-Baden 2006).
141 *Cf* Kingreen (note 16) Art 6 EUV, paras 47 ff.
142 *Cf* with Article 26 of the Charter of Fundamental Rights (Article II-86 DC), for instance Hölscheidt (note 30) Art 26, paras 11 ff.
143 Riedel (note 140) Art 34, para 21.
144 Also Riedel (note 140) Art 36, paras 12 ff.
145 Pernice/Mayer (note 30) Art 6 EUV, paras 193 ff; Riedel (note 140) Vorbem Art 27 ff, paras 31 ff.
146 *Cf* for instance Zuleeg [1992] EuGRZ 329.
147 Riedel (note 140) Vorbem Art 27 ff, paras 1 ff.

the liberal state under the rule of law to the social state under the rule of law. That alters the view of the state, which now no longer appears as an adversary, but as a guarantor of freedom. Also linked to social basic rights is the fear that the normative force of the basic rights is being endangered by unrealistic promises in the form of claims, for instance to work and domicile, as these can only be granted "within the realms of possibility".[148] Moreover, this view conjures up the danger that social basic rights could promote constitutional law to be the only binding standard to measure what is socially just, thereby shifting the discourse concerning the social balance in society from Parliament to the courts.[149]

60   The legitimate objections against social basic rights understood in this manner are not, however, concerned with Articles II-87 ff of the DC. This is demonstrated by apportioning the basic rights according to their functions, *ie* how the basic rights can affect the relationship between the individual and the state. It is crucial to be aware that social basic rights, in their conceptual blurriness, do not occupy one certain basic rights' function (namely that of the right to governmental action) but ultimately act as a collective term for all basic rights with socio-political implications; accordingly, the dogmatic significance of classification as a "social basic right" is low. Therefore, if the basic rights in chapter IV are run through a distributor, differentiated according to the functions of the basic rights, it becomes clear that the voiced criticism does not concern the social basic rights themselves, but merely one individual function of the basic rights, namely the **original right to governmental action**.[150]

- Articles II-87 ff of the DC partially codify a social minimum standard, which they also position against state interference. Such classical rights to defence and protection are guaranteed by Article II-88 of the DC with the freedom of coalition, furthermore Article II-87 of the DC with the co-determination of employees, Article II-90 of the DC with protection from unfair dismissal, Article II-91 of the DC with the guarantee of just and adequate working conditions, and Article II-92 of the DC with the protection of children and young people. In all cases respectively, the minimum standard in respect of the social state, which is guaranteed in every Member State, is either being protected from any sovereign access or, as the case may be, active protection by the sovereign is being demanded in order to safeguard this minimum standard. This social minimum standard establishes, as is the case with the rights to freedom, the scope of protection of the basic right in which the state is interfering when it curtails it, or if the state does not undertake extensive measures of protection for its safekeeping. In this respect, the minimum standard contains social rights to defence and a guarantee of protection, which follow the common review trilogy of "scope of protection-interference-justification".
- Furthermore, the basic rights of chapter IV contain *rights to participation*, which are structured as rights to equality. Rights to participation guarantee equal entry into already existing social systems, such as to employment services (Article II-89 DC), to systems of social security (Article II-94 DC), to health care (Article II-95 2nd sentence

---

148 Formulation of BVerfG (1972) 33 BVerfGE 203, 333.
149 *Cf* for instance Murswiek (note 129) § 112, paras 49 ff, with further references on the discussion in Germany.
150 On the "necessity of clear terminology" within this context, also Haverkate/Huster (note 73) paras 645 ff.

DC) and to services of general economic interest (Article II-96 DC). Each refusal of entry therefore constitutes a discrimination requiring justification, which can be tested according to the structure of review recommended for rights to equality (*cf* paras 7 ff).

– Original rights to governmental action, which contain claims to the creation of not yet existing provisions and precautions, or the rendering of vital services, are to be differentiated from the derivative rights to participation.[151] They alone are subject to the objections outlined above. The criticism of the notion of social basic rights is therefore ultimately based on the resistance against original rights to governmental action. However, not every social right is such a right to governmental action; on the contrary, chapter IV in fact contains no such right: Articles II-75, 89, 90 of the DC do not, for instance, guarantee a right to employment, but only a right to work, a right of entry to a job service monopoly, and protection from unfair dismissal. Instead of a right to a residence, Article II-94(3) of the DC guarantees only "support for the residence", and only guarantees this according to the requirements of the national provisions. At best, one might regard the claim to legal aid concerning court costs according to Article II-107(3) of the DC, which is to be found outside chapter IV, as a social right to governmental action. However, this is a right which is indispensable to the perception of the basic rights to legal protection and which has moreover been recognised in the case-law of the ECHR for a long time.

---

151 *Cf* on the differentiation between a right to participate and a right to governmental action Pieroth/Schlink (note 8) paras 60 ff.

§ 19
Judicial and Procedural Fundamental Rights

Jörg Gundel

Leading cases: ECJ *Union de Pequeños Agricultores* [1997] ECR I-6677; *Oleificio Borelli* [1991] ECR I-6313; *TU-München* [1991] ECR I-5469; *Zuckerfabrik Süderdithmarschen* [1991] ECR I-415; *Factortame* [1990] ECR I-2433.

Literature: Schwarze *Rechtsstaatliche Grundsätze für das Verwaltungshandeln in der Rechtsprechung des Europäischen Gerichtshofs* in: Colneric (ed) *Une communauté de droit – Festschrift für Gil Carlos Rodríguez Iglesias* (Berlin 2003) pp 147–148; Lais *Das Recht auf eine gute Verwaltung unter besonderer Berücksichtigung der Rechtsprechung des Europäischen Gerichtshofs* [2002] ZEuS 447; Pache *Das Europäische Grundrecht auf einen fairen Prozeß* [2001] NVwZ 1342; Haibach *Die Rechtsprechung des EuGH zu den Grundsätzen des Verwaltungsverfahrens* [1998] NVwZ 456; Lenaerts *Sanktionen der Gemeinschaftsorgane gegenüber natürlichen und juristischen Personen* [1990] EuR 17.

I. Overview

1. Relevance of Judicial and Procedural Fundamental Rights in Community Law

1 The judicial and procedural fundamental rights have clearly been **modelled following the ECHR,** which offers a broad field of guarantees in this area – in contrast to the field of the economic fundamental rights – with its Articles 5–7 of the ECHR[1]. These procedural guarantees have a varying influence on Community law. For instance, the classic judicial fundamental rights, such as Article 5 (right to liberty), Article 6(2)–(3) (presumption of innocence, guarantees in criminal trials) and Article 7 of the ECHR (*nulla poena sine lege*) have played a less important role, since the relation of Community law to criminal law has been quite indistinct so far. However, this is presently changing due to the rapidly developing cooperation in the area of Justice and Home Affairs (JHA)[2]. But also in the classic fields of Community law, these guarantees are of importance.[3] This is the case, for instance, regarding the question of whether the non-implementation of EC directives can constitute obligations for individuals to the extent that failure to follow them can result in criminal liability.[4]

---

1 → § 6.
2 See representative the Council Framework Decision of 13 June 2002 on the European arrest warrant and the surrender procedures between Member States, [2002] OJ L190/1; for its fundamental human rights difficulty see Vennemann [2003] ZaöRV 103, 104; Wouters/Naert (2004) 41 CMLRev 909, 923, 924 and BVerfG [2004] EuGRZ 667 (interim measure).
3 As for example the activity of the European Anti-Fraud Office (OLAF), on this *eg* Mager [2000] ZEuS 177, 178; Haus [2000] EuZW 745, 746; particularly to the procedural rights of the person concerned Gleß/Zeitler (2001) 7 ELJ 219, 220. To the basic acknowledgement of the *nulla poena* principle in Community law see already ECJ *Kirk* [1984] ECR 2689, para 22: 'The prohibition of the retroactive effect of criminal statutes, as established in Article 7 of the European Convention on Human Rights, is a common legal maxim in all legal orders of the Member States, and constitutes a common legal principal which the Court has to ensure.' This guarantee is now also to be found in Article II-109(1) DC (see forthwith para 4).
4 Such a 'reverse vertical direct effect' of directives at the expense of the individual and in favour of the prosecuting state has been rightly rejected by the ECJ, (for a criminal case see) ECJ

However, it is the rights to a fair trial and an effective remedy as contained in Article 6(1) (→ § 6 paras 34–35) and Article 13 of the ECHR (→ § 6 para 63 ff) which take centre stage in Community law. Specifications of these rights can be found in various individual guarantees, such as the right to be heard, the right of the concerned person to access records, to be told the grounds for an encumbering decision, and to receive a ruling within a reasonable time. Thus, the primary aspect is to develop a legal framework to ensure that administrative proceedings of Community institutions and national authorities, which are undertaken to enforce Community Law, are in accordance with the rule of law, and subsequently to guarantee an effective judicial control of these administrative actions through the Community jurisdiction and (as far as the proceedings have been implemented by national authorities) domestic courts.

2. Sources of Community Law Procedural Fundamental Rights

a) General Principles as Original Link

Technically, the procedural human rights of Community law have so far been seen as an implementation of **general principles of Community Law**,[5] even though the ECJ now increasingly refers directly to the provisions of the ECHR. Regarding this formal independence of the guarantee, the question consistently arises to which extent the interpretation of the ECtHR has to be taken into account for the general principles of Community law that exist in parallel.[6] At the same time, the application as general principles does offer a flexibility which is not always ensured within the scope of the ECHR. For example, it is irrelevant for the application of the right to a fair trial as a general principle of Community law whether the scope of application of Article 6(1) of the ECHR (civil and criminal matters) is affected.[7] The Community law procedural fundamental rights are applicable in the administrative procedure[8] as well as in the following administrative court procedure.[9]

Despite the wording of Article 6(2) of the TEU, which names the ECHR as the only common international treaty source of the general principles beside the common constitutional traditions of the Member States, the Community Law is not limited to the safeguard of the rights guaranteed therein. In fact, the ECJ has already referred to the proce-

---

Kolpinghuis [1987] ECR 3969. In later decisions, the ECJ has held that the interpretation of national law in the light of the directives must not lead to a sharpening of criminal law; ECJ *Luciano Arcaro* [1996] ECR I-4705, para 42; *Inquiries against X* [1996] ECR I-6609, para 25 (screen workstations); most recently ECJ *Berlusconi* [2005] ECR I-3565; for the further development of the ECJ jurisdiction on non-implemented directives see Gundel [2001] EuZW 143; Jarass/Beljin [2004] EuR 714.

5 This formal independence from the ECHR is emphasised *eg* in CFI *Mannesmannröhren-Werke* [2001] ECR II-729, paras 59, 60; *Mayr Melnhof* [1998] ECR II-1751, para 311. On the mechanism of the general principles still authoritative Lecheler *Der Europäische Gerichtshof und die allgemeinen Rechtsgrundsätze* (Berlin 1971); recently again Lecheler [2003] ZeuS 337.

6 As an example see Case 1 (freedom of testimony) and para 35 (right to be heard on the opinions of the Advocates General in the proceedings before the ECJ).

7 *Cf* hereto below para 17.

8 Already ECJ *Hoffmann-La Roche* [1979] 461, para 9; later CFI *Enso Española* [1998] ECR II-1875, para 80.

9 The right to a fair trial in Article 47 CFR (Article II-107 DC) does not limit the scope of application as does Article 6 ECHR, see para 6.

dural guarantees of the ICCPR[10]; furthermore, it has recognised procedural fundamental rights which were based in the Member States' legal systems. A specific implementation of a procedural guarantee may be acknowledged even if it is to be found only in the legal system of one Member State.[11]

b) Codification through the Charter of Fundamental Rights

5   The Charter of Fundamental Rights of the European Union ($\to$ § 20), which has so far only been solemnly proclaimed without being legally binding, will gain legal force and become the main direct legal source once the Constitutional Treaty has been ratified. Nevertheless, the ECJ has already referred to it as 'a source of interpretation' for the general principles.[12] First of all, procedural rights are contained in its chapter on the citizen's rights (Articles II-99–106 DC). There, the new comprehensive 'right to good administration' (Article II-101 DC) is to guarantee a fair administrative proceeding[13]; specific implementations are exemplarily ('particularly') listed in Article II-10 of the DC.[14] Moreover, there is the right of access to documents of the institutions (Article II-102 DC)[15] as well as the right to refer to the Ombudsman (Article II-103 DC)[16] and the right to petition to the European Parliament (Article II-104 DC). Further guarantees are listed in the following chapter of the judicial rights (Articles II-107–110 DC), which according to Articles 6 and 13 of the ECHR generally ensure the right of effective access to an impartial tribunal (Article II-107(1),(2) DC) as well as the guarantees in criminal proceedings already known to the ECHR, such as the presumption of innocence (Article II-108 DC).

6   Compared to the procedural guarantees of the **ECHR**, the CFR and its systematical coverage of the procedural rights are an improvement inasmuch as for the first time, a

---

10 See ECJ *Orkem* [1989] ECR 3283, para 31 (presumption of innocence) and Art 14g ICCPR (freedom of testimony).
11 See ECJ *AM & S* [1982] ECR 1575, see also Mattfeld [1983] EuR 40 to the confidentiality 'legal privilege' of the correspondence between lawyer and client (this protection, different from German law, is also given when the client is in possession of the documents); on the scope of this guarantee *eg* Rethorn in: Köbler/Heinze/Hromadka (eds) *Europas universale rechtsordnungspolitische Aufgabe im Recht des dritten Jahrtausends – Festschrift für Söllner* (Munich 2000) pp 893, 894; Kapp/Roth [2003] RIW 946; Kapp/Roth [2003] ZPR 404; Seitz [2004] EuZW 231.
12 For example CFI *max-mobil* [2002] ECR II-313, para 48; but see also CFI [2001] *Mannesmannröhren-Werke* ECR II-729 = [2001] EuZW 345 with annotations by Pache: There is no reference to acts of law prior to the proclamation; on this subject see Cavicchi [2002] RIDPC 599.
13 More detailed Bauer *Das Recht auf eine gute Verwaltung im europäischen Gemeinschaftsrecht* (Frankfurt aM 2002); see also Bullinger in: Eberle (ed) *Der Wandel des Staates vor den Herausforderungen der Gegenwart-Festschrift für Brohm* (Munich 2002) pp 25 ff; Zito [2002] RIDPC 425; Michelet [2002] AJDA 949, Lais [2002] ZeuS 447. The ECJ used in its prior case-law the 'principle of orderly administration'; *cf* Usher (1985) 38 Current Legal Problems 269.
14 See below para 10.
15 See below para 21.
16 The institution of the Ombudsman has had an important impact on the further development of the procedural guarantees, first on the establishment of the right of access to Community documents (see below paras 21 f), moreover through the development of an 'European Codex for good administration', which further distinguishes the right of good administration, but is not legally binding (see *eg* Hill [2002] DVBl 1316, 1318–1319; Harden [2001] RMUE 573, 614 ff); to the role of the Ombudsman *eg* Yeng-Seng [2003] RevMC 326, 331 ff; Yeng-Seng [2004] RTDH 527 ff.

clear line of distinction is drawn between the rights in the *administrative procedure* (Article II-101 DC) and the right of judicial control and a fair *judicial* trial (Article II-107 DC). Additionally, the problematic limitation of the guarantees to civil and criminal matters (despite the otherwise largely identical wording) is avoided.[17] However, it is disadvantageous that according to the explicit wording of Article II-101 of the DC, the rights in the administrative procedure are merely granted to protect against the Community institutions.[18] This becomes obvious in the textual comparison with the generally worded Article II-107 of the DC. Insofar as the procedural enforcement of Community law is incumbent upon the Member States, one must therefore fall back on the general principles.[19] All in all, by abstaining from textual innovations, the CFR confines itself to clarifying and systematically bringing together procedural guarantees which either have already been standardized in other areas[20] or have been developed by the judiciary.

c) The Relevance of Secondary Legislation

Guarantees of proceedings or procedural rights are also often contained in **secondary legislation**.[21] Partly, the existing status according to the primary legislation is only declaratively repeated or further specified; partly, secondary legislation contains independent amendments. With a view to the procedural fundamental rights, the following only deals with such procedural provisions which can be traced back to the Treaty's text or general legal principles.[22]

7

3. Obligors

The procedural fundamental human rights primarily bind the **Community institutions** (see below II., paras 10 ff). The Community legislation is not allowed to choose procedural regulations which would violate those rights. The Community executive has to observe the

8

---

17 *De lege ferenda eg* Flauss [2001] AJDA 1060, 1062; Hotellier [2001] SZIER 175, 193–194 plead for the abandonment of this objective limitation of Art 6 ECHR, following the model of the CFR.
18 Hereto Stelkens [2004] ZEuS 129, 137–138; Lais [2002] ZEuS 447, 457–458; critically Heringa/Verhey (2001) 8 MJ 11, 30.
19 See Magiera in: Meyer-Ladewig (ed) *Konvention zum Schutz der Menschenrechte und Grundfreiheiten –Handkommentar* (Baden-Baden 2003) Art 41, para 9; for the obligation of the Member States in this case see para 38. Since on the other hand Art II-101 DC 'affirms' the current judisdiction for procedural requirements on Community institutions *and* Member States, there should be no differences as regards content. So CFI *max-mobil* [2002] ECR II-313, para 48; see also Stelkens [2004] ZEuS 129, 138.
20 This applies *eg* to the justification requirement for Community acts of law (Art 253 TEC), which is now listed in Art II-101(2) DC as part of the right to good administration.
21 See *eg* Regulation of the Council 2988/95 of 18 December 1998 about the Protection of the Communities' Financial Interests, which sets a general framework for the pronouncement of administrative sanctions for the safeguard of these interests, thereby also effecting the protection of the individual; see ECJ *Gisela Gerken* [2004] ECR I-6369, paras 40 ff (to Art 2(2)(ii) of the Reg: retroactivity of milder sanctions); *Herbert Handlbauer GmbH* [2004] ECR I-6171.
22 A borderline case in this regard is the right of access to Community documents (see below para 21), which since the Treaty of Amsterdam has been stipulated in Art 255 TEC (Art III-399 DC), but is actually specified in secondary legislation. The question of whether this right can already claim the status of a legal principal is controversially discussed. In the CFR it can be found in Art II-102 DC.

rights of the concerned parties while implementing administrative proceedings. Moreover, access to the Community tribunals as well as the judicial proceedings are also subject to these requirements. Therefore, administrative decisions, as for instance in Commission antitrust suits, have to be reached within a reasonable time;[23] accordingly, the excessive duration of the proceedings would be classified as an infringement of fundamental procedural rights in a subsequent judicial review.[24]

9   The **Member States, too,** are bound by the Community fundamental procedural rights. The procedural requirements obligate the Member States' authorities and courts when they act within the scope of application of Community law (see below III., paras 40 ff). Furthermore, the implementation of Community law has created forms of cooperation between the Community administration and the Member States' authorities which cause specific problems for the realisation of fundamental procedural rights (see below IV., paras 55 ff).

II. Fundamental Procedural Rights in Relation to the Community Institutions

1. Fundamental Procedural Rights in Relation to the Community Administrative Organs

a) Individual Rights

10   The most important procedural rights of the administrative process are exemplarily ('particularly') listed in Article II-101(2) of the DC: The right to a fair and public hearing before the decree of an unfavourable measure, the right of access to the relevant documents. Furthermore, the obligation to state the reasons for legal actions, which is already mentioned in the primary legislation (Article 253 TEC/Article III-397 DC), also belongs to the fundamental procedural rights. Although this applies to all actions of Community law, it serves a special purpose in the case of adversarial decisions of the Community institutions. That is to say, first, the concerned parties are informed about the reasons (of the decision) and second, it allows for a judicial control.[25]

11   The ECJ jurisdiction[26] had already clarified that **the right to be heard** prior to unfavourable administrative decisions has to be guaranteed even without the existence of an express secondary provision.[27] As a necessary element of the right to a fair hearing, the

---

23 CFI *Limburgse Vinyl Maatschappij* [1999] ECR II-931, paras 120 ff; *SCK and FNK* [1997] ECR II-1739, para 56; prior ECJ *Guérin Automobiles* [1997] ECR I-1503 paras 37–38.
24 For the first time on the duration of proceedings before the ECJ see ECJ *Baustahlgewebe* [1998] ECR I-8417; on this Hartwig [1998] EuGRZ 369; Toner (1999) 36 CMLRev 1345; Pallaro [2000] DCSI 493; further ECJ *Limburgse Vinyl Maatschappij* [2002] ECR I-8375, paras 206 ff; → § 6 paras 49 ff for the case-law of the ECtHR.
25 This double function of the justification is highlighted *eg* in the case-law of access to Community documents (see below para 20) CFI *JT's Corporation Ltd.* [2000] ECR II-3269, para 64 with further verifications; CFI *van der Wal* [1998] ECR II-545, para 63; for the justification of objection recovery of state-aids CFI *EPAC* [2000] ECR II-2267, para 34; the justification is also important in competition decisions, see CFI *Enso Española* [1998] ECR II-1875, paras 109–110.
26 See also the overviews of the ECJ case-law about the principles of the administrative decisions in Haibach [1998] NVwZ 456; Gassner [1995] DVBl 16.
27 Emphatically ECJ *Fiskano* [1994] ECR I-2885, para 39; *Lisrestal* [1996] ECR I-5373, para 21; CFI *Eyckeler and Malt* [1998] ECR II-401, para 76; *Primex Produkte* [1998] ECR II-3773, para 59.

judicature has also accepted the accessory right of access to documents[28] of the concerned party.[29] In order to be able to effectively express its point of view, the party has to know the documents which have been used to its disadvantage.[30]

The right to use one's own language when communicating with Community institutions is a specific Community fundamental procedural right which is granted to the citizens only in relation to the Community institutions.[31] This right has been incorporated into primary legislation as a specification of Union citizenship by the Treaty of Amsterdam. Nowadays, it is to be found in Article 21(3) of the TEC (Article I-10(2)(d) DC) (→ § 21 para 69) as well as in Article 41(4) of the CFR (Article II-101(4) DC),[32] which oblige the Community institutions to communicate with the EU citizen in the official Community language he has chosen. However, it is questionable how long the Community will afford itself this luxury of omnilinguality, which on the hand is expensive, but which on the other hand seems indispensable for the Community's legitimation.[33]

Nevertheless, the Court has rightly been reluctant to recognise further **unwritten fundamental procedural rights**. Thus, it refused to acknowledge an unwritten claim of an instruction on legal remedies available, which according to the TEC is not a requirement for

---

28 On this *eg* CFI *LR AF* 1998 [2002] ECR II-1705, para 169 ff; *ICI* [1995] ECR II-1847; *Cimenteries CBR* [1992] ECR II-2667; *Hercules Chemicals* [1991] ECR II-1711; see for the literature Erlandsson [1998/1] LIEI 139; Louis [1998] CDE 47; de Bronett [1997] WuW 383; Levitt (1997) 34 CMLRev 1413.

29 The Commission has summarised the principles for the application of this right (in the wake of the ECJ case-law) in the Official Journal, [1997] OJ C23/3; now it is explicitly regulated in Art 27(2) Reg 01/03 (see to this further below note 37); see on this Nowak [2004] DVBl 272, 275–276.

30 Hence, the ECJ concluded in *Musique Diffusion* [1983] ECR I-1825, para 30 that the tribunal is not allowed to use incriminating material to which the concerned party had not been able to express his opinion to his detriment. However, this does not apply absolutely, but is to be reconciled with the rights of other involved parties. In an anti-trust suit, *eg*, it can therefore be necessary to protect trade secrets of the concerned parties against the inspection of a third party (*eg* the claiming competitor).

31 This right does not apply in relation to Member States' authorities, for whose actions naturally the official language of the state of residence is to be used. However, an exception can be found in Art 84(4) Reg 1408/71, which is concerned with the field of social systems: 'The authorities, institutions and tribunals of one Member State may not reject claims or other documents submitted to them on the grounds that they are written in an official language of another Member State.' See on this provision and individual further exceptions de Witte in: Dinstein/Tabory (eds) *The Protection of Minorities and Human Rights* (Brill 1992) pp 277, 290–291; for an example of an application, see ECJ *Teresa Guerra* [1967] ECR 294 (on a statement of claim in Italian language before a Belgian tribunal).

32 On the principles of the secondary legislation in the language regime of the Community see Oppermann [2001] ZEuS 1; Oppermann [2001] NJW 2663; for the future development Nabli [2004] CDE 197; Van der Jeught [2004] JTDE 129; Yvon [2003] EuR 681.

33 The principle of omnilinguality does not apply in relation to the independent agencies of the EC (*ie* bodies and agencies of the Community as units with their own legal personality), which are not mentioned in Art 21 TEC (Art I-10(2)(d), Art III-128 DC) see CFI *Christina Kik* [2001] ECR II-2235; critically Gundel [2001] EuR 764 (the restricted language regime of the EC trademark agency in Alicante, which only uses the languages of the five biggest Member States); this restriction is accepted by the ECJ and affirmed in its decision ECJ *Kik* [2003] ECR I-8283.

the end of respite in the case of an action for annulment of Community acts (Article 230(5) TEC/Article III-365(6) DC: generally two months).[34]

14 If the Community institutions have violated one of those guaranteed rights in the administrative procedure, the ECJ can declare the decision reached in this procedure **void** due to an infringement of an essential form requirement (Article 230(2) 2nd Alternative TEC/Article III-365(2) DC). The allocation on this cause of action means at the same time that the violation's (potential) impact on the decision's content is decisive for the success of the action. That is to say that only such infringements which could have had an effect in the concrete case[35] can be classified as a violation of an 'essential form requirement'.[36]

b) Particularly: Procedural Rights in Anti-Trust Proceedings

15 The most important direct area of applicability for fundamental procedural rights against Community institutions is the EC-Anti-Trust Law, which so far the Commission itself, above all, has been directly enforcing against the concerned business participants. Even after the decentralisation of the cartels' supervision through Regulation 01/03,[37] where this task had been shifted to a large extent to the Member States' authorities, in individual cases it is still the Commission that has the right of direct access regarding anti-trust violations.[38]

16 In this area, which is at least similar to criminal law, not only the 'general procedural guarantees' apply. Moreover, the question arises whether other specific guarantees, such as the prohibition of double punishment in criminal proceedings for the same criminal offence, exist.[39]

---

34 ECJ *Guérin Automobiles* [1999] ECR I-1441, para 15 (affirmation of CFI *Guérin Automobiles* [1998] ECR II-253, para 161); criticising this decision Martínez Soria [2001] EuR 682, 694 with further evidence. The ECJ held in this case that although such an obligation of instruction exists in most of the Member States, it is only part of the ordinary or "simple law", *ie* law ranking under constitutional law.
35 See recently CFI *Mannesmann-Röhrenwerke* [2001] ECR II-729, para 55, according to which 'the rights of the defence are infringed by virtue of a procedural irregularity only in so far as that irregularity had a definite impact on the possibilities for the undertakings implicated to defend themselves'. This is comparable to § 46 *Verwaltungsverfahrensgesetz* (VwVfG / German Administrative Procedures Law), see Kahl (2004) 95 VerwArch 1, 22 ff. Procedural infringements have an effect particularly in areas where the Community institutions have a margin of appreciation, see *eg* CFI *Primex Produkte* [1998] ECR II-3773, paras 60, 71.
36 Actually, there is a deviating arrangement of the wording of Art 230(2) TEC. It is not an infringement (seen from an abstract point of view) of an 'essential procedural requirement' that is necessary, but an 'essential infringement' (in the concrete case) of a form requirement; so rightly Booß in: Grabitz/Hilf (eds) *Das Recht der Europäischen Union* (loose-leaf, Munich 2001) para 103 to Art 230 TEC (Art III-365 DC).
37 The Council Reg 01/03 of 16 December 2002 on the Implementation of the rules on competition laid down in Art 81 and 82 of the EC Treaty. This replaces the Council Reg No 17 of 6 February 1962 (First Implementation Regulation of Art 81and 82 of the Treaty).
38 See on the regulation of competences Art 4 ff of the Reg 01/03 (note 37); on the procedural rights after the reform *eg* Meyer/Kuhn [2004] WuW 880; on the basis of the prior law Weiß [1997] EWS 253; Zampini [1999] RevMC 628.
39 See Art II-101 DC; → § 6 para 58 f on the prohibition to be punished twice in criminal proceedings pursuant to Art 4 Prot 7 ECHR; on the EC-Anti-Trust law see Ameye (2004) 25 ECLR

Case 1 – Problem: (ECJ *Orkem* [1989] ECR I-3283)
While conducting investigations due to the suspicion of inadmissible price-fixings, the Commission requests information from the X-AG, which is located in Germany. Since the X-AG does not react to this request, the Commission issues a formal decision, according to which the X-AG
(1) must disclose which other business companies had been present at a meeting of leading executives of the X-AG with different, currently unknown, competitors
(2) must disclose which fixings or other violations of Article 81 of the TEC (Article III-161 DC) were made at this meeting or in the aftermath.
The X-AG claims that it doesn't have to reply to those inquiries, since the disclosure of this information would constitute an inadmissible pressure to self-incriminate. Is this true?

The principle of the right to a fair trial, which for the ECHR is laid down in Article 6 of the ECHR, applies also in the Commission's anti-trust law investigations. This applies regardless of whether these proceedings are to be classified as civil or criminal law matters according to Article 6 of the ECHR[40]. The Community tribunals have so far not had to decide on this question[41], since this proceeding requirement as a general principle of Community law is applicable regardless of the classification.[42]

Case 1 – Answer:
An absolute right to avoid self-incrimination does not exist in Community law. Thus, the *'nemo-tenetur'* principle only applies for (natural) persons in criminal proceedings, but not for legal persons threatened with a competition fine.[43] Although the guarantee to a fair trial, which is applicable here as well, does not compel the acceptance of an absolute right to silence, it nevertheless restricts the Commission's right to interrogate.
Therefore, the X-AG has to answer the request (1), even though this might provide information for the investigators which in the end gives evidence for a breach of competition law

---

332, 339–340 and ECJ *Walt Wilhelm* [1969] ECR 1, paras 10–11; CFI *Tokai Carbon and others* [2004] ECR II-1181, paras 130 ff: A parallel punishment according to national and EC-Competition law is not per se forbidden due to different points of focus. However, for reasons of equity, an imposed sanction must have a moderating effect.

40 For the requirements of the application of Art 6 I ECHR see the article itself; → § 6 paras 28.
41 Thus *eg* CFI *SCK and FNK* [1997] ECR II-1739, para 56 on the right of adopting a Commission decision within a reasonable time: 'Accordingly, without there being any need to rule on the question whether Article 6(1) of the European Convention on Human Rights is, as such, applicable to administrative proceedings before the Commission relating to competition policy, it is necessary to consider whether, in this case, in the proceedings preceding the adoption of the contested decision, the Commission breached this general principle of Community law.' Arguably rightly, the CFI held in *Enso Española* [1988] ECR II-1875, para 56 that the Commission cannot itself be described as a 'tribunal' within the meaning of Art 6(1) ECHR when implementing Competition law, even though the procedural guarantees might already apply at this stage; likewise ECJ *Musique Diffusion* [1983] ECR I-1825, para 7; *van Landewyck ('Fedetab')* [1980] ECR 3225, para 80; for disciplinary procedures of the Commission ECJ *N.* [1998] ECR I-4871.
42 See also Pache [2001] NVwZ 1342; Pache [2000] EuGRZ 601, 603.
43 ECJ *Orkem* [1989] ECR 3283, para 31. Alike the German constitutional law BVerfG (1996/1997) 95 BVerfGE 220, 241–242; denying this sure enough Weiß [1998] JZ 289–290; Weiß [1999] NJW 2236–2237.

and results in the imposition of an administrative fine. By contrast, the reply to question (2) would not only provide evidence, but demands an evaluation of the facts by the company which would amount to a plea of guilty. The obligation to answer those questions violates the right to a fair trial, as has also been held by the ECJ.[44]

20 The solution offered by the Community tribunals is not unproblematic since the ECtHR has granted an absolute right to silence in a similar case on the basis of Article 6 of the ECHR.[45] Being aware of this judisdiction the CFI has affirmed a more restrictive interpretation in the scope of application of Community law.[46]

c) An Independent Procedural Right: The Right to Access of Community Institutions' Documents

21 Lately, a further specific procedural area has been developed: The right to access of Community institutions' documents. Independent rights of information, which are to be distinguished from the right to access of documents (deriving from the right to a fair trial), were initially established in 1990 by the Environmental Directive[47] in relation to the Member States' authorities.[48] On Community level, the right to access records was stipulated within the rules of procedure of the Council[49] and the Commission,[50] without being restricted to the environmental field. With the accession of the Scandinavian Member States Sweden and Finland, which have a distinct tradition in the transparency of administrative actions[51], the discussion about the right to information has become more

---

44 ECJ *Orkem* [1989] ECR 3283, paras 38 ff.
45 ECtHR *Funke* (1993) 16 EHRR 297, paras 41, 44 ff (custom proceedings), hereto Philippi [2000] ZEuS 97, 114 ff; see also ECtHR *Saunders* (1997) 23 EHRR 313, para 71 (investigations of the broke-exchange supervision); to these decisions of the ECtHR and the consequences for the Community Law see also Riley (2000) 25 ELRev 264, 270 ff; but restricting to the exclusion of an obligation of self-incrimination the latest case-law of the ECtHR, see ECtHR *Allen* (2002) 35 EHRR CD 289; *Weh* (2005) 40 EHRR 890, paras 39 ff.
46 CFI *Mannesmannröhren-Werke* [2001] ECR II-729, para 70 ff (legally binding after the cancellation of the former appeal C-190/01), see the consideration in CFI *Mannesmannröhren-Werke* [2001] ECR II-729, paras 311–312; critically hereto Schohe [2002] NJW 492–493. This discrepancy can be possibly explained by the fact that in the cases of the ECtHR (note 45) only natural persons have been affected. The plaintiffs in the case of *Mannesmannröhren-Werke* rightly pointed out that Art 6 ECHR does not distinguish between natural and legal persons, see para 45 of the decision. However, one could think to affirm a criminal proceeding according to Art 6 ECHR only if a natural person is affected.
47 Council Directive 90/313 of 7 June 1990 'on the freedom of access to information on the environment'; on this Hatje [1998] EuR 734; Wilsher (2001) 7 EPL 671; meanwhile it has been replaced by Dir 03/4 of the European Parliament of 28 January 2003; see eg Nowak [2004] DVBl 272, 273–274.
48 On the incomplete implementation by the German Environment Information Law see ECJ *Commission v Germany* [1999] ECR I-5087.
49 Council Decision of 20 December 1993 on public access to Council documents, [1993] OJ L340/43.
50 Commission Decision of 8 February 1994 on public access to Commission documents, [1994] OJ L46/58.
51 For Sweden see Österdahl (1998) 23 ELRev 336 ff; Ragnemalm in: *Scritti in Onore di Mancini* (Vol II, Milan 1998) pp 809, 812 ff.

intense on Community level, too. Article 255 of the TEC (Article III-399 DC) (→ § 21 paras 71 ff),[52] which was incorporated by the Treaty of Amsterdam and served as the basis for Regulation 1049/01,[53] now guarantees these rights to access also in relation to the Community institutions. Furthermore, the Regulation lays down the restrictions and the reasons for a refusal (for example the protection of public security or international relations).

The **right to information,** which is now also codified in primary legislation, has led to an extensive judisdiction[54] that is consistently enforcing this right against the very restrictive (contrary to public assertions) practice of the Community institutions.[55] Accordingly, the existing reasons for rejection have to be construed narrowly[56] and the rejection of access has to be justified in a way which reveals the reason for this denial.[57] Moreover, the justification has to be related to each concerned document.[58] However, the CFI has also clarified that this right only guarantees access to existing documents, but does not establish a general right to information in relation to the Community institutions.[59]

22

---

52 However, the provision is not directly applicable and does not question the limitations and exclusions which already apply, see CFI *David Petrie* [2001] ECR II-3677, paras 34 ff. Regarding the question if the principle of transparency has to be accepted as a general principle of Community law; see *eg* Broberg (2002) 27 ELRev 194; Nowak [2004] DVBl 272, 279280.
53 Reg 1049/01 of the EP and the Council of 30 May 2001 'public access to EP, Council and Commission documents' hereto *eg* Wägenbauer [2001] EuZW 680; Partsch [2001] NJW 3154; Peers (2002) 21 YEL 385; Feral (07/2001) Europe 5; Schauss [2003] JTDE 487; de Leeuw (2003) 28 ELRev 324 Alberti [2003] RIDPC 55; Bartelt/Zeitler [2003] EuR 487; Heitsch *Die Verordnung über den Zugang zu Dokumenten der Gemeinschaftsorgane im Lichte des Transparenzprinzips* (Berlin 2003) pp 63 ff.
54 See the synopsis at Jann in: Funk (ed) *Der Rechtsstaat vor neuen Herausforderungen – Festschrift für Adamovich* (Vienna 2002) pp 241 ff; Kröger in: Schweizer (ed) *Festschrift für Druey* (Zurich 2002) pp 817 ff; Kadelbach (2001) 38 CMLRev 179; Davis (2000) 25 ELRev 303; Tomkins (1999/2000) 19 YEL 217; Österdahl (1999) 36 CMLRev 1059; Dyrberg (1999) 24 ELRev 157; Castenholz *Informationszugangsfreiheit im Gemeinschaftsrecht* (Baden-Baden 2004); monographic Riemann *Die Transparenz der Europäischen Union* (Munich 2004); Meltzian *Das Recht der Öffentlichkeit auf Zugang zu Dokumenten der Gemeinschaftsorgane* (Berlin 2005).
55 See the admission of a partial access to documents by CFI *Hautala* [1999] ECR II-2489, affirmed by ECJ *Hautala* [2001] ECR I-9565; CFI *Kuijer* [2000] ECR II-1959; *Mattila* [2001] ECR II-2265, paras 66 ff (affirmed by ECJ *Mattila* [2004] ECR I-1073, paras 30 ff), whereas the Community organs have maintained an 'all-or-nothing' solution. On the adequate consideration of the perceivable interest of the applicants on the information in demand see CFI *BAT* [2001] ECR II-2997, para 42 ff; *Carvel and Guardian Newspapers Ltd* [1995] ECR II-2765, para 67 ff.
56 CFI *BAT* [2001] ECR II-2997, para 40 ff; *Denkavit* [2000] ECR II-3011, para 45; *Bavarian Lager* [1999] ECR II-3217, para 39; ECJ *Netherlands and van der Wal* [2000] ECR I-1, para 27.
57 CFI *Interporc* [1998] ECR II-2289, para 112; *WWF UK* [1997] ECR II-313, para 66; de Leeuw (1997) 3 EPL 339.
58 CFI *Svenska Journalistförbundet* [1998] ECR II-2289, para 112; *JT's Corporation Ltd* [2000] ECR II-3269, para 64–65; diminishing CFI *Mattila* [2001] ECR II-2265, para 87 ff.
59 CFI *KL Meyer* [1999] ECR II-3273, para 35.

2. Procedural Rights before the Community Tribunals

a) Access to the Community Tribunals

aa) **Direct** and **Indirect** Access to the Community Tribunals

23   The guarantee of an effective judicial protection by the Community judiciary is firstly related to the question of the possibility of an access to the court. In principle, an effective judicial review of incriminating decisions by Community institutions belongs to the general principles of Community law.[60]

24   According to the Treaties' conception and the current jurisdiction, individuals regularly gain access to the Court in an 'indirect' way, that is to say, through the national tribunals and the preliminary rulings subject to Article 234 of the TEC (Article III-369 DC). In general, it is for the national courts to decide when to refer a question. However, according to Article 234(3) of the TEC (Article III-369 DC), the national courts of last instance are obliged to refer the question if there is a serious problem of interpretation.[61] If the court wants to assume the invalidity of secondary legislation, it is obliged to refer no matter which position it has in the stages of appeal.[62] However, the individual cannot enforce this referral by Community law. There is no non-submission complaint to the ECJ[63]; thus, the Community law relies on the domestic courts for the correct application.[64] The only existing indirect sanction, though under very restricted requirements, is the possibility of Community Law liability for court decisions.[65]

bb) Admissible Actions of Annulment of Individuals against **Decisions** Addressed to Them

25   This concept of indirect access also applies where individuals ask for the review of the validity of Community institutions' acts. A direct access to the Community tribunals without further requirements is opened by Article 230(4) of the TEC (Article III-365(4) DC) only to those applicants who challenge a decision of Community institutions which is addressed to them. This is the case, for example, for the addressee of a Commission administrative fine decision in competition matters. For these admissible actions of indivi-

---

60 Thus, again for Commission competition decisions, CFI *Enso Española* [1998] ECR II-1875, para 60.
61 On the restriction of the referral obligation by the 'acte clair-doctrin' see ECJ *CILFIT* [1982] ECR 3415.
62 On this and on the exception for provisional measures see below paras 51 ff.
63 Corresponding considerations can be found *eg* in Allkemper *Der Rechtschutz des einzelnen nach dem EG Vertrag* (Baden-Baden 1995) pp 209–210 with further annotations.
64 Various Member States offer the possibility to reprove violations of the referral obligation of the last judicial instance subject to Art 234(3) TEC (Art III-369 DC) under reference to the *national* fundamental right of the legal judge; see for Art 101(1)(ii) GG BVerfG (1987) 75 BVerfGE 223, later *eg* BVerfG [2001] JZ 923; BVerfG [2002] NJW 1486; for Austria likewise VerfGH Vienna [1996] EuGRZ 529. However, there is no demand for the opening of this additional instance by Community law. In Member States where such a possibility does not exist, the parties of the initial proceeding have the alternative of a complaint to the ECtHR on the grounds of a violation of the obligation to refer. The arbitrary violation of such an obligation can furthermore be rebuked as a breach of Art 6 ECHR (fair trial), see ECtHR *Dotta* App No 38399/97; *Predil Anstalt* App No 31993/96; *Canela Santiago* App No 31993/96 and hereto Flauss [2000] RFDC 843, 850.
65 See hereto ECJ *Köbler* [2003] ECR I-10239.

duals, nowadays the CFI is the initial court instance established by the SEA to disburden the ECJ and also, by creating an additional trial court,[66] to improve individual judicial protection.[67]

According to Article 230(5) of the TEC, the addressees of such a decision have to bring their action of annulment within two months. If this does not happen, the decision becomes final and absolute and consequently binding for the addressee.[68] However, neither the Treaties nor the secondary legislation provide for an instruction on legal remedies which informs the concerned person about his possibility (and obligation) to challenge the decision. Moreover, the ECJ itself did not consider such an instruction a necessary requirement for a fair trial.[69] Nevertheless, in specific exceptional cases one can assume an excusable error of the plaintiff which would foreclose the failure to observe the time-limit.[70]

cc) Individual Actions against General **Provisions of Secondary Legislation**

Where the measure in question is a decision not addressed to the plaintiff subject to Article 230(4) of the TEC (Article III-365(4) DC), the plaintiff has to be affected 'directly and individually' by this measure. According to the judisdiction, in order to demonstrate individual concern, the applicant must be able to show that the decision affects him 'by reason of certain attributes which are peculiar to [him] or by reason of circumstances in which [he is] differentiated from all other persons' and hence, can be distinguished 'individually' just as in the case of the person addressed.[71] Due to this restrictive interpretation, actions of annulment against normative acts of law have regularly been dismissed. Thus, as a rule, regulations or directives could not be directly reviewed by individuals.[72]

However, from the point of view of an effective judicial protection, the literature has already demanded for a long time a broader interpretation of Article 230(4) of the TEC (Article III-365(4) DC) in favour of the admissibility of direct actions of individuals against EC-Regulations.[73] So far, the judisdiction has opposed such an interpretation,

---

66 Third recital of the Council Decision establishing a Court of First Instance of the European Communities [1988] OJ L319.
67 See retrospectively Azizi [2002] ÖJZ 41, 44 ff; Lenaerts [2000] CDE 323; from the date of origin Müller-Huschke [1989] EuGRZ 214; Cruz Vilaça/Pais Antunes in: *Mélanges Boulouis* (Paris 1991) pp 47 ff.
68 See for the scope of this binding effect eg ECJ *Assi Domän* [1999] ECR I-5363, paras 57–58.
69 ECJ *Guérin Automobiles* [1999] ECR I-1441, para 15; confirmed by CFI *Guérin Automobiles* [1998] ECR II-253, para 161; in this particular case the plaintiff brought a suit against the 15 Member States before the ECtHR which was dismissed on procedural grounds, see ECtHR *Guérin* App No 25201/94.
70 See *eg* CFI *Pitsiorlas* [2001] ECR II-717, para 22; ECJ *Pitsiorlas* [2003] ECR I-4837, paras 20 ff.
71 Settled case-law since ECJ *Plaumann* [1963] ECR 213, 214.
72 On this Gundel (2001) 92 VerwArch 81. By contrast, the requirements for Community decisions (also including the decisions addressed to the Member States) related to third parties can be fulfilled in most cases; see with further verifications Mager [2001] EuR 661, 673 ff.
73 Critically on the restrictive interpretation *eg* Bleckmann in: Erichsen (ed) *System des verwaltungsgerichtlichen Rechtsschutzes – Festschrift für Menger* (Cologne/Munich 1985) pp 872, 873–874, 882; von Danwitz [1993] NJW 1108, 1111ff; Allkemper (note 53) pp 64; Reich in: Micklitz/Reich (eds) *Public Interest Litigation before European Courts* (Baden-Baden 1996) pp 3 ff; Schockweiler [1996] JTDE 1, 8; Jacobs in: *Mélanges Schockweiler* (Baden-Baden 1999) pp 197, 203 ff; Dutheil de la Rochère [2000] RevMC 223, 224–225.

because an effective judicial protection is guaranteed by the national courts through the preliminary rulings (Article 234 TEC/Article III-369 DC).[74] Nevertheless, the Court, referring to the character of the EC as a legal community, has established the principal that there must always be the possibility of a judicial enforcement of legal positions established by the Community.[75] Direct access to Community courts in order to provide a complete judicial protection has so far only been extended in such cases which were not concerned with the protection of individual rights, but with the relationship among the Community institutions. In the categories of the German constitutional proceedings, this would rather be assigned to the *Organstreitverfahren*.[76] In cases which are related to individuals, secondary legislation can be reviewed through the 'indirect access' of proceedings before national courts and the preliminary rulings. However, this solution is questioned time and again in cases where the indirect review proves to be difficult.

29 **Case 2 – Problem:** (CFI *Jégo-Quéré* [2002] ECR II- 2365)
A new released EC Regulation stipulates that in the deep sea fishing industry, only nets with a certain minimum mesh size are allowed to be used. A, who owns several fishing vessels which would be affected by this change, is worried that he will catch less fish with this type of net, and that the regulation will therefore have a significant adverse effect on his business. Therefore, he considers the Regulation to be disproportional. He brings suit before the CFI and argues that since his interests are affected to a considerable degree, the principle of effective legal protection demands that he should be qualified as 'individually concerned' and his action should therefore be admissible. He maintains that it would not be reasonable for him to have validity of the prohibition reviewed before the national courts by consciously violating the measure and taking on criminal proceedings. Moreover, there are no other actions which could be challenged before the domestic courts.
Is the action for annulment admissible?

30 **Case 2 – Answer:**
Since A's action does not challenge a decision which is addressed to him, it is only admissible if he is directly and individually concerned by the measure, Article 230(4) of the TEC (Article III-365(4) DC).
Since there were no additional legal acts necessary to specify A's obligation, the criterion of direct concern was fulfilled in the present case. However, according to the current interpretation of Article 230(4) of the TEC (Article III-365(4) DC), individual concern exists only when the situation of the plaintiff is comparable to that of an addressee of a decision. He has to be distinguishable from other potential plaintiffs. In the case of generally applicable legal acts, this requirement regularly cannot be fulfilled. This would also apply to A's action.

---

74 On the current situation Gundel (2001) 92 VerwArch 81; last ECJ *La Conqueste SCEA* [2002] ECR I-1179, para 47 (confirming CFI *La Conqueste SCEA* [2001] ECR II-181).
75 So *eg* ECJ *Les Verts* [1986] ECR 1339, para 23.
76 See initially the acceptance of a right of action for the Parliament for the defence of its rights against the wording of the Treaty by ECJ *Parliament v Council* [1990] ECR I-2041, para 23, which had been codified in Art 230(3) TEC (Art III-365(3) DC) (Maastricht-version); the Treaty of Nice had qualified the Parliament as a privileged applicant of Art 230(2) TEC (Art III-365(3) DC). Similarly for the capacity to be a defendant ECJ *Les Verts* [1986] ECR 1339, para 23 (restitution of the expenses for the election campaign); CFI *Martinez, de Gaulle and others v Parliament* [2001] ECR II-2823, paras 47 ff (acceptance of groups as parliamentary parties in the EP).

Judicial and Procedural Fundamental Rights § 19 II 2

He is affected by the measure in the same way as any other economic operator who decides to work in this area.[77]
However, the CFI[78] overruled this interpretation in the present case and held that in cases where actions before national courts are not adequate protection against national measures, the criterion of an effective legal protection as guaranteed in Article 6 and 13 of the ECHR as well as in Article II-107 of the DC has to be interpreted in such a way that a significant tangency of the plaintiff's interests would be sufficient.

However, speaking against this reorientation is the fact that an indirect review before the national courts cannot only be achieved through criminal proceedings, which would indeed be unacceptable, but also by way of a preventive declaratory action against the responsible national authority.[79] Since legal protection can thus be guaranteed by the Member States' legal systems (which are obliged to offer these possibilities[80]), there is no need to interpret Article 230(4) of the TEC (Article 365(4) DC) in such a way which consequently would eliminate the admissibility requirement of individual concern. The ECJ also pointed out these limits as determined by the wording of the provision and confirmed its judisdiction in spite of the criticism of the CFI.[81] However, in the draft for the Constitution, the current text of Article 230(4) of the TEC (Article II-365(4) DC) is amended through a provision of a 3rd alternative[82] which – albeit restricted to implementing measures[83] – abandons the criterion of the individual concern, thereby opening the way to direct action.

31

---

77 CFI *Jégo-Quéré* [2002] ECR II-2365, para 38 (reversed by ECJ *Jégo-Quéré* [2004] ECR I-3425); to this decision as well Cassia [2002] RevMC 547; Jaqué [2002] AJDA 476.
78 CFI *Jégo-Quéré* [2002] ECR II-2365, paras 45, 49 under reference of the final Opinion of AG Jacobs to ECJ *Unión de Pequeños Agricultores* [2002] ECR I-6677.
79 See *eg* ECJ *SMW Winzersekt* [1994] ECR I-5555 (request for a preliminary ruling by the VG Mainz [1994] ZLR 153 with annotations by Koch). The Tobacco-Regulation was presented to the ECJ in the same way. While the actions for annulment of the producers had been dismissed (CFI *Salamander AG* [2000] ECR II-2487), the simultaneous reference of an English court (hereto Seidel [1999] EuZW 369) was negotiated together with an action for annulment of the German government and became superfluous only due to the latter's success, see ECJ *Imperial Tobacco* [2000] ECR I-8599. Also the validity of the Tobacco-Regulation has been reviewed through such a validity reference (ECJ *BAT* [2002] ECR I-11453). The German action for annulment, however, was dismissed due to expiry of the time limit (ECJ *Germany v Parliament and Council* [2002] ECR I-4561).
80 On this Temple Lang (2003) 28 ELRev 102; Gundel (2001) 92 VerwArch 81, 105 ff.
81 ECJ *Unión de Pequeños Agricultores* [2002] ECR I-6677, paras 44–45, see also Braun/Kettner [2003] DÖV 59, Malferrari/Lerche [2003] FWS 254, Rengeling in: Hansmann (ed) *Umweltrecht und richterliche Praxis – Festschrift für Kutscheidt* (Munich 2003) pp 93 ff; Röhl [2003] Jura 830; Usher (2003) 28 ELRev 575; Giliaux [2003] CDE 177; Mehdi [2003] RTDE 23. Later also ECJ *Bactria Industriehygiene* [2003] ECR I-15105, para 58; *Rothley and others* [2004] ECR I-3149, paras 46 ff; ECJ *Jégo-Quéré* [2004] ECR I-3425, paras 29 ff; the CFI has yielded to this viewpoint, see CFI *VVG* [2002] ECR II-3239, para 39; *Vannieuwenhuyze-Morin* [2003] ECR II-1997, paras 27 ff.
82 See Cremer [2004] EuGRZ 577; Mayer [2004] DVBl 606; Varju (2004) 10 EPL 43; Schwarze (2004) 10 EPL 285.
83 The wording 'legal acts with regulation character' seems at first glance to go further, but the terminology is already adapted to the Constitutional Treaty, so that the future 'European laws'

32   An **extension of the direct legal protection,** which at first sight seems to be favourable for the citizens, could also have adversarial consequences. If the concerned party does not use the possibility of an action for annulment against a known Community legal act, a subsequent indirect review, as for instance in the proceedings of a preliminary ruling, would be denied according to the ECJ *Textilwerke Deggendorf* case-law.[84] This preclusion rule, which is used by the Court to prevent circumventions of the time-limit of Article 230(5) of the TEC (Article III-365(6) DC), has so far only been important for individual measures, such as for decisions of the Commission against Member States ordering the reversed transaction of unlawfully granted national state-aids.[85] If the principal judicial review (*Normenkontrolle*) is opened by an extensive interpretation of Article 230(5) of the TEC (Article III-365(6) DC), the question of whether the corresponding '*Deggendorf-*Rule' should be extended to such cases arises as well.[86]

b) Guarantees in Proceedings before the Community Tribunals

33   The fundamental procedural rights also play a significant role for the 'how' of the legal protection before the Community tribunals. Recent discussions in this context concern the comparison between the practice of the ECJ with the requirements of the ECHR as well as those of the national constitutional laws.

aa) Lawful Judge

34   The lawful judge guarantee also applies to the Community tribunals.[87] As far as the jurisdiction of the courts is concerned, no problems arise. The primary focus of the discussion concerned the appointment of the lawful judge in the composition of the judge's bench in 'overstaffed' councils, such as the five-judge-chambers of the ECJ[88] to which up to seven judges can be assigned, although only five judges make the decision. After the *Bundesver-*

(so far: regulations) and the 'European framework laws' (so far: directives) are not included; for further questions of classification see Cremer [2004] EuGRZ 577, 579.

84 So first ECJ *Textilwerke Deggendorf* [1994] ECR I-833; on this Pache [1994] EuZW 615; Hoskins (1994) 31 CMLRev 1399; later ECJ *Eurotunnel* [1997] ECR I-6315, paras 26 ff; *Acrington Beef* [1996] ECR I-6699, paras 15–16; see further ECJ *Wiljo* [1997] ECR I-585, paras 15 ff; for the development of the case-law see Jaeger in: *Mélanges Schockweiler* (Baden-Baden 1999) pp 233, 235.

85 Thus the facts in the *Textilwerke Deggendorf* decision. A state-aid beneficiary who comes to know about an unfavourable Commission decision (for him) has to make use of the possibility to bring action of Art 230(4) TEC (Art III-365(4) DC), since he fulfils the conditions of the direct and individual concern. If he fails to do so, he will be precluded from claiming the unlawfulness of the Commission decision for the reversed transaction in the following national proceeding. For an application of this rule see BGH [2004] WM 693.

86 See Gundel (2001) 92 VerwArch 81, 97–98; Köngeter [2002] NJW 2216, 2218. AG Jacobs maintains that this rule cannot be extended to legal acts with a normative character ('general actions'), see para 65 of his Opinion to ECJ *Unión de Pequeños Agricultores* [2002] ECR I-6677. In fact, the Court had applied them to EC-regulations as long as they could exceptionally (in the field of anti-dumping regulations) be challenged with a direct action by individuals, see ECJ *Nachi Europe* [2001] ECR I-1197, paras 30ff, hereto Moloney (2002) 39 CMLRev 393.

87 Generally on this subject Grzybek *Prozessuale Grundrechte im Europäischen Gemeinschaftsrecht* (Baden-Baden 1993) pp 76 ff.

88 On the various panels of ECJ judges see Middeke in: Rengeling (ed) *Handbuch des Rechtsschutzes in der Europäischen Union* (2nd ed, Munich 2003) § 3, paras 18 ff.

fassungsgericht (BVerfG – German Federal Constitutional Court)[89] placed high demands for the German jurisdiction on the abstract determination of the appointment of the responsible judges in a concrete case, the German literature requested a corresponding appointment practice for the Community tribunals, too.[90] Initially, the ECJ rejected their suggestion to that effect on the grounds that a manipulation of the bench had not been obvious in the concrete case.[91] However, in the aftermath it was decided that for each judicial year, an order is to be issued according to which the judges of the overstaffed chambers are to be employed.[92]

bb) Right to be heard

Furthermore, the right to be heard is guaranteed before the Community tribunals. Thus, the parties have to know the entire procedural matter to be able to express their point of view on it. 35

Recently, following the case-law of the ECtHR, the position of the Advocate General at the ECJ has been questioned under this aspect. At the end of the proceedings, the AG submits a public, but not binding decision proposal to the ECJ which nonetheless points the way to the decision in many cases (Article 49 of the Statute of the Court of Justice, Article 59 of the Rules of Procedure of the Court of Justice). However, the ECtHR, with reference to corresponding institutions of the national procedural orders under the aspect of a fair trial and the equilibrium of arms, demands that the concerned parties must have the possibility to express their point of view on these decision proposals. Consequently, these proposals should not be the 'last word' before the judicial decision-finding.[93] 36

However, one can doubt if this judisdiction can actually be applied to the ECJ. This is *inter alia* questioned because the Advocate Generals, different from the situation in the cases decided by the ECtHR, are themselves members of the court.[94] Therefore, their opinions could be considered as the beginning of the final judicial decision-finding, to which the parties make no further contribution.[95] The ECJ believes that the requirement of a fair trial is fulfilled as long as the oral proceedings can be reopened, if in the opinion of the Court the final proposals reveal new aspects and hence require a parties' statement.[96] 37

---

89 See BVerfG (1996/1997) 95 BVerfGE 322.
90 See *eg* Mößlang [1996] EuZW 69, reciprocating Wichard [1996] EuZW 305–306; see also Stotz [1995] EuZW 749.
91 See ECJ *Gaal* [1995] ECR I-1031.
92 See [1998] OJ C299/1; in the meantime, the procedure has been regulated in the new amended Art 11c Rules of Procedure of the Court of Justice [2003] OJ L147/17.
93 From the ECtHR case-law see ECtHR *Vermeulen* (2001) 32 EHRR 313; ECtHR *Lobo Machado* (1997) 23 EHRR 79; ECtHR *Reinhardt and Slimane-Kaïd* (1999) 28 EHRR 59; *Kress* App No 39594/98.
94 This difference is emphasized by Tridimas (1997) 34 CMLRev 1349, 1380.
95 ECJ *Emesa Sugar* [2000] ECR I-665, para 14. 'It does not form part of the proceedings between the parties, but rather opens the stage of deliberation by the Court. It is not therefore an opinion addressed to the judges or to the parties which stems from an authority outside the Court [...]. Rather, it constitutes the individual reasoned opinion, expressed in open court, of a Member of the Court of Justice itself ...'; similar paras 94 ff of the Opinion of AG Colomer, ECJ *Kaba* [2000] ECR I-2219.
96 Thus ECJ *Emesa Sugar* [2000] ECR I-665, para 18 with different examples of past decisions (not published in the official collection); ECJ *Deutsche Telekom* [2000] ECR I-743, paras 22 ff; *VBA*

cc) Right to a Decision within Reasonable Time

38 An effective legal protection also requires that the judicial decision is reached within **reasonable time**. In this context, for example, the prohibition of an overlong duration of the proceedings as laid down in Article 6 of the ECHR becomes relevant, which the ECJ also recognises as a binding requirement for its own work.[97]

39 The legal protection system of Community law relies to a great extent on the cooperation between the Community tribunals and the national courts in the preliminary rulings proceedings. This gives rise to the structural problem that the duration of the procedure might be extended precisely by the preliminary rulings procedure. However, even the ECtHR itself, when reviewing Article 6 of the ECHR, has conceded that such extensions are to be accepted in the interest of an efficient preliminary rulings procedure.[98]

III. Requirements of Community Procedural Fundamental Rights for Member States

1. Applicability of Procedural Fundamental Rights to Member States' Actions

40 In principle, the Community fundamental rights serve to set boundaries for the Community institutions, whereas the fundamental freedoms (not exclusively, but mainly) are addressed to the Member States.[99] Nevertheless, **according to settled case-law,** the Community fundamental rights – and thus also the procedural fundamental rights – in specific constellations apply to the **Member States as well** (→ § 14 paras 31 ff).

41 To begin with, this is the case in constellations where Member States are responsible for the enforcement of Community law. From a Community law point of view, it should be irrelevant for the application of the Community fundamental rights standard whether this right is enforced by the Community institutions themselves, or has generally been delegated to the Member States, as is the case in most areas.[100] Hence, the Member States' 'procedural autonomy'[101] in implementing Community Law is restricted in this respect. This universal statement regarding the scope of the Union's fundamental rights is of significant importance for the Community procedural fundamental rights. Since Community law is mainly enforced by the Member States, the procedural guarantees, such as the the

---

[2000] ECR-I 2135, paras 63–64; hereto Lawson (2000) 37 CMLRev 983; Schilling [2000] ZaöRV 395; earlier already Schilling [1999] ZeuS 75, 79.

97 ECJ *Baustahlgewebe* [1998] ECR I-8417 (to a procedural duration before the ECJ of 5 $^1/_2$ years).

98 ECtHR *Pafitis and Others* (1999) 27 EHRR 559, para 95 (on this critically Peukert in: *Mélanges Ryssdal* (Cologne 2000) pp 1107, 1118–1119); likewise recently ECtHR *Koua Poirrez* (2005) 40 EHRR 34, para 56.

99 On the different structure and task of Community fundamental human rights and fundamental freedoms see as well Lecheler *Einführung in das Europarecht* (2nd ed, Munich 2003) pp 219 ff, 224.

100 For the application of Community fundamental rights in this area see eg ECJ *Bostock* [1994] ECR I-955, para 16; *Wachauf* [1989] ECR 2609; *HZA Hamburg Jonas* [1988] ECR I-2355, para 22: '... and that all national authorities responsible for applying Community law are bound to observe the general principles of Community law.' Regarding the more narrow wording of Art II-101 DC, which should not be regarded as a concluding provision, see above para 5.

101 On this principle eg Rodríguez Iglesias [1997] EuGRZ 289; for the parallel limitations of the autonomy of Art 10 TEC (Art I-5(2) DC) see paras 39 ff.

right to be heard[102] or the guarantee of a fair trial, must also apply here.[103] Partly, this area in fact represents the only immediate field of application for these guarantees.[104]

Furthermore, according to ECJ case-law, the Community fundamental rights also apply to cases where Member States interfere with **legal positions** which have been granted to the individual by Community law. Insofar as this is the case, as for instance with national restrictions of fundamental freedoms[105] or the equal treatment of both genders in working life[106], the Community procedural fundamental human rights hence apply as well, particularly the right of an effective judicial review.[107] Therefore, the expulsion of an EU citizen by a Member State, which interferes with his freedom of movement, has to be judged by Community procedural rights.[108] However, this settled case-law is questioned through the wording of Article II-111(1) of the DC, which only mentions the enforcement, but not the restriction of Community law by the Member States. Hence, the provision could be regarded as a limitation of the existing legal position.[109] Nevertheless, it seems quite unlikely that the ECJ will follow this approach.

42

Thus, the actions of the Member States do not fall into the field of application of the EU citizen rights as far as there is no correlation with a position regulated by Community law.[110]

43

---

102 See notably *eg* ECJ *Krombach* [2000] ECR I-1935, paras 26, 42.
103 See on the derivation of the inadmissability of improperly obtained evidence ECJ *Steffensen* [2003] ECR I-3735, paras 72 ff.
104 This applies *eg* for the *nulla-poena* principle as long as the EC has no competence to enact the '*Kernstrafrecht*' (basic criminal law). Therefore, the establishment of the *nulla poena*-principle in Art II-109 DC insofar does not affect the already non-competent Community legislator, but means that individual violations of Community law can be sanctioned under consideration of this principle by the national legislator and the domestic criminal courts (see already above note 3).
105 ECJ *Heylens* [1987] ECR 4097, para 14 (acceptance of vocational qualifications of other Member States).
106 ECJ *Johnston* [1986] ECR 1651, para 18 (review of an exclusion of the rule of equal access to work through national courts).
107 See ECJ *Heylens* [1987] ECR 4097, para 14; *Johnston* [1986] ECR 1651, para 18 with explicit reference to Art 6 and 13 ECHR; see further ECJ *Piercarlo Bozetti* [1985] ECR I-2301, para 17: '... it is for the legal system of each Member State to determine which court has jurisdiction to hear disputes involving individual rights derived from Community law, *but at the same time the Member States are responsible for ensuring that those rights are effective protected in each case.*' (emphasised by the author).
108 By contrast, according to the ECtHR's case-law, Art 6 ECHR is not applicable in expulsion proceedings, because these are neither civil nor criminal proceedings, see ECtHR *Maaouia* (2001) 33 EHRR 1037, para 35; → § 6 para 35.
109 '[T]his Charter [is] addressed to the institutions, bodies, offices and agencies of the Union ... *and to the Member States only when they are implementing Union law*.' (emphasised by the author); on this question see Cremer [2003] NVwZ 1452; Mager [2004/1] EuR Beih 41, 53 ff.
110 For such a case ECJ *Kremzow* [1997] ECR I-2629, para 16, dealing with a referral concerning procedural guarantees in homicide proceedings. The mere fact that the accused would be hindered in his freedom of movement by the execution of his prison sentence is insufficient to assume an adequate connection; similarly ECJ *Grado and Bashir* [1997] ECR I-5531.

2. Parallel Guarantees of Procedural Rights through Fundamental Freedoms

44 In this area, the Community fundamental rights guarantees **overlap** with the provisions of the fundamental freedoms. Therefore, the prohibition of discrimination on the grounds of nationality (Article 12 TEC/Article I-4(2), III-123 DC) can require that EU citizens are granted the same language privileges in court that members of a national minority of the concerned state are entitled to.[111] Likewise, the obligation to pay a security for legal costs must not be connected with the nationality of another Member State.[112] Accordingly, citizens of other Member States (within the scope of application of Community law) must not be treated worse compared to nationals in matters of procedural law already due to the fundamental freedoms. Therefore, one can find procedural guarantees also in secondary legislation which were enacted to the fundamental freedoms related to the free movement of persons.[113] Moreover, in the field of the free movement of goods, the ECJ has derived specific requirements for the Member State's administrative proceedings directly from the fundamental freedom itself.[114]

3. Parallel Guarantee of Procedural Rights through the Requirement of Equal and Effective Protection (Article 10 TEC/Article I-5(2) DC)

a) Strengthening of Procedural Rights through the Requirement of Effectiveness

45 Particularly in the area of the Member State's enforcement of Community law, the individual procedural fundamental rights often correspond with the general requirements of an equal and effective implementation of Community law, which the ECJ derived from Article 10 of the TEC (Article I-5(2) DC). These two principles demand on the one hand, that Community law is not implemented under less favourable conditions than the existing legal positions based in national law (**principle of equality**)[115], and on the other hand,

---

111 See ECJ *Mutsch* [1985] ECR 2681: Art 39 TEC (Art III-133 DC) claims to allow a German employee to use the German language in a criminal proceeding before a Belgian court, when members of the German-speaking minority in Belgium are entitled with this right. Likewise to Art 12 TEC ECJ *Bickel and Franz* [1998] ECR I-7637, on this also Hilpold [2000] JBl 93; Bultermann (1999) 36 CMLRev 1325. The ECHR minimum standard guarantees only the right to consult an interpreter.
112 See ECJ *Hayes* [1997] ECR I-1711 (on the former version of § 110 *Zivilprozessordnung* (ZPO – German Code of Civil Procedure) = [1999] ZEuP 964 with annotations by Kubis (*Verstoß gegen Art 12 EGV*); likewise ECJ *Data Delecta* [1996] ECR I-4661 (hereto Streinz/Leible [1998] IPRax 162); ECJ *Saldanha* [1997] ECR I-5325 (hereto Ehricke [1999] IPRax 311).
113 See *eg* the procedural guarantees in Art 8–9 of Dir 64/221 regarding to the effects of nationals of other Member States; regarding the requirements see ECJ *Orfanopoulos and Olivieri* [2004] ECR I-5257, paras 101 ff; *Yiadom* [2000] ECR I-9265; *Shingara and Radiom* [1997] ECR I-3343; O'Neill (1998) 35 CMLRev 519; ECJ *Gallagher* [1995] ECR I-4253; on the Member State's obligation to inform the concerned person about the reasons for its expulsion as stated in Art 6 of the Dir, see already ECJ *Rutili* [1975] ECR I-1219, para 33.
114 Thus on the Member States' requirements for the admission proceedings for food additives deriving from the free movement of goods ECJ *Greenham and Abel* [2004] ECR I-1333, para 35 with annotations by Streinz and Jarvis (2004) 41 CMLRev 1395: 'This proceeding has to be easily accessible and be terminated in reasonable time; if it leads to a rejection, this denying decision has to be open for an appeal within a judicial proceeding.'
115 This aspect has been primarily characterised as rule of non-discrimination. However, this characterisation can lead to misunderstandings and confusion since in this case, it is not meant

that these positions, irrespective of such a comparison, have to be enforced under a certain minimum standard of effectiveness (**principle of effectiveness**).[116]

Therefore, one can derive from the principle of equality that for claims of Community law, as for instance for motions of reimbursement of unlawful Community law fees, the applying time limits must not be shorter than those provided by national law.[117] Accordingly, it arises from the principle of effectiveness that judicial protection must be available in each case. Furthermore, its conditions must be reasonable, that is to say the procedural rules of the Member States 'must not render virtually impossible or excessively difficult the exercise of rights'.[118] Hence, generally the time limits of the proceedings must not be too narrow. Procedural preclusion rules have to be applied in such a way that they do not thwart an effective enforcement of the concerned (legal) position.[119] Furthermore, those rules of evidence are inadmissible which would render the exercise of rights excessively difficult[120], irrespective of whether they also apply to the rights of national law. Finally, the need for a Community liability against violations of Community law, as elaborated by the Court, is also derived from the principle of effectiveness. This Community liability is necessary if the enforcement of Community law cannot be guaranteed in a different way.[121]

46

b) In particular: Right to Legal Protection through National Courts

The principle of effectiveness particularly requires, parallel to Article 6 and 13 of the ECHR, the possibility of access to a court. Here the Court initially formulated that the Community law does not require the creation of new unknown remedies, but only the security of legal protection as laid down by national law.[122] However, this statement, which guaranteed only equal protection and did not consider the principle of a minimum

47

---

as a discrimination of a person on the grounds of nationality, but according to the 'origin' of the right. Hence, the ECJ lately uses the term of equality, see eg ECJ *Roquette frères* [2000] ECR I-10465; in other current decisions also the notion of *'Äquivalenzgrundsatz'* (principle of equivalence) can be found, see ECJ *Ansaldo Energia* [1998] ECR I-5025, paras 27, 29; *Edis* [1998] ECR I-4951, para 34; *Dilexport* [1999] ECR I-579, para 25.

116 See eg Schmidt-Aßmann *Festgabe 50 Jahre BVerwG* (Cologne 2003) pp 487, 489. For the specific area of the protection of the financial interests of the Community, the ECJ's systematisation has been reflected in the text of the Treaty: Pursuant to Art 280(4) TEC (Art I-53(7) DC) it is required to '[afford an] *effective* and *equivalent* protection' of the Community interests in the Member States (emphasized by the author).

117 For such a case see ECJ *Deville* [1988] ECR I-3513; *Barra* [1988] ECR I-355; see as well ECJ *Edis* [1998] ECR I-4951, paras 21 ff.

118 So eg ECJ *Dilexport* [1999] ECR I-579, para 25; *Ansaldo Energia* [1998] ECR I-5025, paras 27; *Jeunehomme* [1988] ECR I-4517, para 17.

119 See ECJ *Peterbroeck* [1995] ECR I-4599; ECJ *van Schijndel* [1995] ECR I-4705; on both decisions von Danwitz [1996] UPR 323; Heukels (1996) 33 CMLRev 337; Prechal (1998) 35 CMLRev 681; Cahn [1998] ZEuP 969; most recently Mas [2002] ÖJZ 161.

120 See ECJ *Les Fils du Jules Bianco* [1988] ECR I-1099, paras 12–13; *San Giorgio* [1983] ECR-I 3595, para 14; last ECJ *Weber's Wine World* [2003] ECR I-11365, paras 110 ff; see on this Gundel in: *Festschrift Götz* (Göttingen 2005) pp 191 ff.

121 Thus the starting point of the ECJ case-law to the Member States liability of the citizens for breaches of Community law as derived from the requirements of Art 10 TEC (Art I-5(2) DC), see ECJ *Francovich* [1991] ECR I-5357.

122 ECJ *Rewe* [1981] ECR 1805, para 44.

standard of effectiveness, has not been repeated. Instead, in its later decisions the ECJ has explicitly required that new remedies be provided if this proves necessary for the effective implementation of Community law.[123] *Prima facie* for the German law, these requirements seem to be secured anyway by the guarantee of Article 19(4) of the *Grundgesetz* (GG – German Basic Law). Nevertheless, the example of legal protection for the award of public contracts has shown that also in the German judicial protection order, no different from other Member States, it might become necessary to adapt the law. It is noteworthy that in Germany this area was only regulated reluctantly following the provisions of the EC-Remedies-Directive[124].[125]

> **Case 3 – Problem:** (Conseil d'Etat (F), Assemblée du contentieux 5 March 1999 – *Président de l'Assemblée Nationale* [1999] AJDA 460)[126]
>
> 48 The administration of the Parliament of Member State X concludes a contract for the installation of the room electronics of the plenary hall. According to the Member State's law, the decisions of the Parliament are not open to judiciary review. The inferior competitor Y, who despite his more favourable offer has not been considered, nevertheless appeals to the administrative court. There, he claims that the contract has been concluded under breach of the directive on the awarding of public work contracts.[127]
> Is this action admissible?

49 Parallel to the principle of effectiveness, also the Community fundamental rights standard applies within Community law. Therefore, the right to legal protection against measures of national authorities which interfere with legal positions as guaranteed by Community law applies for two reasons: one, because it is necessary for an effective enforcement of Community law, and two, because it results from the human rights standard of the ECHR (Articles 6, 13 ECHR). This double function becomes especially apparent, for example, in the guarantee of interim relief against national law which violates Community law.[128] The

---

123 See *eg* ECJ *Factortame* [1990] ECR I-2433 for the obligation of national courts to guarantee interim relief also in the case of unlawful Community statute law; lately *eg* ECJ *Safalero* [2003] ECR I-8679, paras 50, 56; *Connect Austria* [2003] ECR I-5197, para 35.

124 Dir 89/665 of 21 December 1989 on the coordination of the laws, regulations and administrative provisions related to the application of review procedures on the award of public supply and public work contracts within the scope of the award of public supply- and construction assignments.

125 The incorporation of the provisions in §§ 97 ff of the *Gesetz gegen Wettbewerbsbeschränkungen* (GWB – German Competition Act), which took place with effect from 1 January 1999; on this and on the previously approved 'budgetary solution' *eg* Martin-Ehlers [1998] EuR 2774; Pietzcker (1998) 162 ZHR 427.

126 Case formed after Conseil d'Etat (F), Assemblée du contentieux 5 March 1999 – *Président de l'Assemblée Nationale* [1999] AJDA 460, see also Bergeal [1999] RFDA 333 with submissions by governmental commissar.

127 Dir 93/37 on the coordination of the award of public work contracts (in the mean time displaced by Dir 04/18 on the coordination of procedures for the award of public work contracts, public supply contracts and public services).

128 ECJ *Factortame* [1990] ECR I-2433; directly to this decision also Smith [1992] EuZW 308; Toth (1990) 27 CMLRev 573; Barav/Simon [1990] RevMC 591. For the requirements on national procedural law to this question and the effects on German law see as well Kadelbach [1999] *KritV* 378; Hauser [2000] VBLBW 377; Sommermann in: Grupp (ed) *Planung-Recht-Rechtschutz – Festschrift für Blümel* (Berlin 1999) p 523; Schoch [1997] DVBl 289.

same is true, for instance, for national procedural time-limits which are so short that they render virtually impossible or excessively difficult the citizens' exercise of their guaranteed Community rights.[129] However, as a matter of principle, the limitation of material rights through national procedural time-limits is admissible.[130]

Case 3 – Answer:
Y's action is admissible aberrant from national law. The principle of the minimum standard of effectiveness requires, parallel to the Articles 6, 13 of the ECHR, the possibility to claim the violation of Community law positions before national courts. For the public work contracts area, this additionally follows from the secondary legislation.[131] Opposing principles of national procedural law, such as judicial immunity for actions of the parliaments, have to give way to the supremacy of Community law. Accordingly, in the present case, the French *Conseil d'Etat* did not preclude a judicial review of *'actes du parlement'*, as was settled case-law, but held the action to be admissible.[132]

50

c) Conflicts between Procedural Guarantees and the Principle of Effectiveness

In individual cases, the Community law principle of effectiveness can also become a burden for the Community citizens and **conflict** with their protection interest.[133] Hence, it is ambivalent in this respect. For instance, where decisions are to be promptly carried out,

51

---

129 This affects particularly the reimbursement of national charges and fees which were imposed under breach of Community law and the subsequent granting of benefits which were unlawfully denied under Community law respectively; for the first group of cases see Gundel (note 120).
130 Thus most recently ECJ *Kühne & Heitz* [2004] ECR I-837. Also, when reviewing administrative actions of Community institutions, the ECJ emphasises the fact that preclusive time limits establish legal security by, *eg* the period for filing an action of Art 230(5) TEC (Art III-365(6) DC) and the binding effect of an administrative act after the time limit has expired, so *eg* ECJ *Assi Domän* [1999] ECR I-5363, paras 57 ff. In ECJ *Emmott* [1991] ECR I-4269, para 21 the ECJ, relying on a particularly far-reaching derivation from the principle of effectiveness, held that national time limits do not begin to run prior to the implementation of the EC directive upon which the claim rests. However, this position was subsequently tempered by the Court in favour of an individual review of each case, see ECJ *Fantask* [1997] ECR I-6783, hereto Gundel [1998] NVwZ 910; Notaro (1998) 35 CMLRev 1385.
131 Art 1 of Dir 89/665 (note 124). The directives regulating the awarding of a contract also apply to the public contracts of national parliaments, see ECJ *Commission v Belgium* [1998] ECR I-5063 (work contract of the Flemish regional parliament).
132 In the decision of the *Conseil d'Etat*, this connection – as is frequently the case – is not mentioned. The necessity of Community law to change the jurisdiction becomes clear in the final submissions of the governmental commissar, [1999] RFDA 333, 338.
133 So *eg* in the case of the reimbursement of aids granted in violation of Community law, see ECJ *Alcan* [1997] ECR I-1591, para 37 = [1997] EuZW 276 with annotations by Hoenicke: The same principle which allows citizens to retrieve fees unlawfully imposed by the Community in spite of national preclusion time limits leads to the conclusion that profits/increase in fortune gained in violation of Community law cannot be defended by invoking the national preclusion time limit of § 48(4) VwVfG. The *Tafelwein*-decision burdens the EU-Market-Citizens in a similar way regarding the possibility of interim measures of the authorities, whereas the *Factortame*-decision (ECJ *Factortame* [1990] ECR I-2433), relying on the same idea, is to the citizens' advantage.

§ 19 III 3   Jörg Gundel

the principle of effectiveness can require that the remedy against negative decisions does not have a suspending effect as provided by national law.[134]

52 However, insofar as such conflicts exist, the ECJ has found **balancing solutions**. This becomes particularly clear in the review of the validity of secondary legislation. The principle according to which the Member States' courts cannot declare secondary Community legislation void by themselves, but rather have to refer questions about its validity to the ECJ (absolute right of the ECJ to reject Community law, *Verwerfungsmonopol*)[135], is characterised by the idea of an effective implementation of Community law. This applies to national courts independently of their position in the stages of appeal and thus goes even further than the wording of Article 234(3) of the TEC (Article III-369 DC). Nevertheless, since the outcome of the preliminary ruling has to be awaited first, there have been concerns that this could foil an effective legal protection of the citizen against unlawful Community law. However, the ECJ confronted these concerns by allowing the national courts to issue interim measures if at the same time they comply with their obligation to refer the question to the Court.[136] An interim 'suspension' of the application of secondary law is therefore accepted if the ECJ is given the opportunity to have the concluding and final binding word in the respective question of validity. This judicially developed compromise apparently manages to create a successful balance[137] between the requirements of an effective enforcement of Community law and an effective legal protection of the individual.[138]

53 The ECJ has also found a similar balanced solution in another constellation in which the need for legal security was confronted with the requirement for an effective legal protection. Since the beginning of the 80's, the ECJ has called upon its competence to limit the temporal application of its decisions in preliminary proceedings as well.[139] If the Court makes use of this possibility, as for example when declaring secondary legislation void or interpreting Community law in a way which results in national law breaching Community law, it becomes binding not before the decree of its decision. In principle, one cannot object to this limitation, even though such a moderation of legal consequences is only mentioned for the action of nullity (Article 231(2) TEC/Article III-366 DC) in the Treaty. This moderation is a result of the ECJ's constitutional function.[140]

---

134 ECJ *Commission v Germany* [1990] ECR I-2879; hereto *eg* Vedder [1991] EWS 10; von Stülpnagel [2001] DÖV 932.
135 So firstly ECJ *Foto-Frost* [1987] ECR 4199.
136 So ECJ *Zuckerfabrik Süderdithmarschen* [1991] ECR I-415; ECJ *Atlanta II* [1995] ECR I-3799; *Atlanta I* [1995] ECR I-3761; Voss [1996] RIW 417; for later use cases ECJ *Krüger GmbH* [1997] ECR I-4517; *Affish* [1997] ECR I-4315.
137 Pietzcker in: Hermann (ed) *Recht im Wandel. Beiträge zu Strömungen und Fragen im heutigen Recht – Festschrift 150 Jahre Heymanns Verlag* (Cologne/Munich 1995) pp 623, 633 talks about a 'Solomonic solution'.
138 By contrast, in interim proceedings the recent jurisdiction of the BVerfG grants to the special courts the (preliminary) right to dismiss law (*'Normverwerfungskompetenz'*) and regards referrals pursuant to Art 100(1) GG to be inadmissible at this stage, see BVerfG (1992) 86 BVerfGE 382, 389 as well as OVG NW [1992] NVwZ 1226; OVG Berlin [1992] NvWZ 1227 (An exception has to be made where principle proceedings are not provided; see for submission by judges on their own motion regarding such a case BVerfG (1983) 63 BVerfGE 131). For the comparison of ECJ and BVerfG-case-law on this question see Pietzcker (note 137) pp 623.
139 For the development of the judiciary see *eg* Weiß [1995] EuR 377; Everling in: Baur (ed) *Europarecht, Energierecht, Wirtschaftsrecht – Festschrift für Börner* (Cologne/Munich 1992) p 57.
140 For the corresponding provision for the decision of the BVerfG see § 79 of the *Bundesverfas-*

Judicial and Procedural Fundamental Rights § 19 IV 1

54 However, by generally applying this solution also to the plaintiffs of the initial proceeding, this limitation of legal consequences finally led to the outcome that the plaintiffs lost their action's victory again.[141] Initially, the Court put up with this 'harshness'. Later, however, it developed the principle for such cases that the plaintiffs of the initial proceeding as well as all concerned persons who appealed simultaneously, judicially or non-judicially, prior to the decree of the ECJ's decision are to be excluded from the limitation of retroactivity.[142] Otherwise the plaintiff would be deprived of his right of effective judicial protection[143] against breaches of Community law.

IV. Particular Problems in 'Tiered' Proceedings und 'Mixed' Decisions between National Authorities and EC-Commission

1. The 'Tiered' Proceeding

a) The Phenomenon

55 **Tiered proceedings**[144] are a specific form of the implementation of Community law in which the citizen at first only deals with the 'implementing' Member States' authorities, while the ultimate decision is made in the background by the Community institutions. This arrangement raises problems especially for the compliance with procedural guarantees, but also for the legal protection against already taken decisions.

56 By this arrangement, as it can be found for instance in the EC-customs law, the national authorities accept the application of the concerned person and are 'usually' entitled to an independent decision. Only in certain cases of doubt they are obliged to refer the facts to the Commission which then makes a definite decision which the national bodies have to enforce against the applicant. Similar arrangements are to be found regarding the administration of Community aids, as for example the EC-social fund. Here, the national authorities have jurisdiction over the continuous administration and the surveillance of the application of funds; however, the binding decision as to whether the aid will be definitely awarded or the funding must even be reclaimed instead is made by the Com-

---

sungsgerichtsgesetz (BVerfGG – German Federal Constitutional Court Act); this corresponds to the fact that the extension of the ECJ's competences was not controversially discussed in the German literature, whilst in the French literature and the administrative judiciary this competence of the ECJ, primarily under reference to the exceeding of the judicial functions, has not been accepted. However, in France a subsequent constitutional review of laws is not otherwise known. This makes the necessity of such a provision quite obvious; see Gundel *Die Einordnung des Gemeinschaftsrechts in die französische Rechtsordnung* (Berlin 1997) p 276; see also the comparative jurisprudence advices at Isaac [1987] CDE 444.

141 Thus the objection of the Italian *Corte constitutionale* 21 April 1989 No 232/89 – *Fragd Spa.*, *Riv Dir Int* [1989] 103; the Italian constitutional court thereby claimed the right to a 'final review' corresponding to the '*Solange*-judiciary' of the BVerfG (to this *eg* Lecheler (note 99); *cf* also Lecheler [2001] JuS 120); to the controversy Azzena [1992] Riv Trim Dir Pubbl 688.
142 Thus programmatically ECJ *Roquette frères* [1994] ECR I-1445, paras 26 ff; however, the Court has refused to extend this balancing solution retroactively to already decided dissenting cases, see ECJ *Roquette frères* [1989] ECR I-1553.
143 So ECJ *Roquette frères* [1994] ECR I-1445, para 27.
144 On this *eg* Sydow (2001) 34 DV 517; detailed Nehl *Europäisches Verwaltungsverfahren und Gemeinschaftsverfassung* (Berlin 2002) pp 41, 81, 413.

513

mission.¹⁴⁵ This arrangement has the advantage for the Community institutions that they still have the power to decide doubtful cases without being confronted with the mass of unproblematic cases.

b) Endangerment of Rights in Administrative Proceedings

57   However, this proceeding arrangement is not only advantageous. It also leads to an endangerment of the concerned person's procedural rights, because the externally competent body and the actually deciding body are not the same. Hence, the right to be heard could be impaired if additional arrangements are not made.

58   The ECJ initially accepted these deficiencies and maintained that a direct guarantee of the right to be heard is not provided by secondary legislation.¹⁴⁶ Since its leading *TU-München*-decision of 1991¹⁴⁷, however, it has in fact been demanding the particular protection of the right to be heard. In this ruling it was also clarified that this requirement cannot depend on the arrangements made by secondary legislation.

59   Subsequent judgments held several times that this could lead to the fact that the Commission cannot only rely on the communication with the intermediary Member States authorities for its decision, but that the concerned person has to be directly granted the right to make a statement, even though such a direct contact is not provided for in secondary legislation.¹⁴⁸ This is necessary, for example, when the Commission wants to derogate to the detriment of the concerned persons from the assessment of the facts¹⁴⁹ or when an aspect is considered relevant for the decision on which the applicant has not been able to express his point of view.¹⁵⁰ Furthermore, in such cases the Commission has to allow the applicant to access the records as part of the right to be heard.¹⁵¹ In the end, the Commission has adjusted to these requirements.¹⁵²

---

145 For the allocation of the tasks *eg* ECJ *DAFSE* [2001] ECR I-673; before ECJ *Mediocurso* [2000] ECR I-7183 (partial reversal of CFI *Mediocurso* [1998] ECR II-3477).
146 Thus ECJ *Nicolet* [1986] ECR 2049, paras 13 ff; *Nicolet* [1988] ECR 1557, paras 13–14.
147 See particularly ECJ *TU-München* [1991] ECR I-5469; later ECJ *Fiskano* [1994] ECR I-2885, para 39; CFI *France-Aviation* [1995] ECR II-2841; *Eyckeler and Malt* [1998] ECR II-401, paras 74 ff; *Primex Produkte* [1998] ECR II-3773, paras 57 ff; on this Lecheler/Gundel *Übungen im Europarecht* (Berlin/New York 1999) pp 97 ff.
148 See most recently regarding the customs law CFI *Kaufring* [2001] ECR II-1337; to this ruling Heselink [2001] ZfZ 321–322.
149 Thus in the *Kaufring* case (note 148): Here the national authorities assumed that the mistake was not noticeable for the importers, whereas the Commission reached the opposite estimation; similar the facts of CFI *Eyckeler and Malt* [1998] ECR II-401; *Primex Produkte* [1998] ECR II-3773.
150 Thus in the case ECJ *TU-München* [1991] ECR I-5469; see para 38 of the Opinion of AG Jacobs.
151 Emphatically CFI *Eyckeler and Malt* [1998] ECR II-401, paras 79 ff; *Primex Produkte* [1998] ECR II-3773, paras 62–63.
152 Initially, the Commission tried to limit the effects of the ECJ jurisdiction on its administrative practice by demanding that the applications as forwarded by the national authorities must include an attached declaration in writing of the applicant, in which he affirms that he has not completely expressed his point of view on the submitted facts (Art 87(1)(i) Commission-Reg 2454/93 laying down provisions for the implementation of Council-Reg 2913/92 establishing the Community Customs Code in the version of the Commission-Reg 12/97). However, subsequently the CFI has held that this amendment can only constitute an improvement in the first procedural stage before the national authorities, but cannot secure the required right to be heard

In this context, the ECJ has also applied on Community law the compensations 60
mechanism as already known in national law. According to this, in areas in which the control of the contents of the decision is limited by margins of administrative appreciations, the control of compliance with the procedural rights is of particular importance.[153]

c) Difficulty of Legal Protection

The gradation of competences in the decision making process also leads to problems in 61
securing a complete legal protection. If the concerned person wants to challenge the final decision of the national authorities, the national court must always refer to the ECJ if it believes that the underlying decision of the Commission breaches Community law.[154] Although this may give rise to delays, a review remains possible. The situation is different where the concerned person already knew the interlocutory judgment of the Commission. In this case, he has to proceed directly against this decision to prevent the finally binding effect of the administrative decision.[155] If, however, he comes to know about the Commission's decision only during the proceeding against the closing decision of the national authority, the initiation of a further proceeding would not be reasonable for him. Furthermore, in these cases there is no danger of circumvention of the time limit of Article 230(5) of the TEC (Article III-365(6) DC).[156]

2. Problems of Judicial Protection in 'Mixed Decisions'

Besides the cases in which the Commission makes the decision in the background and it is 62
then merely enforced by the national administrations, situations exist as well where the Community and the national authorities respectively make decisions in their own competence. This is relevant in arrangements regarding Community aids.

---

under the aspects which the Commission would consider important in the second stage, see CFI *Eyckeler and Malt* [1998] ECR II-401, paras 84–85; *Mehibas Dordtselaan* [2000] ECR II-15, paras 44 ff. It was not until the Commission-Reg 1677/98 regarding the change of the implementation of the Customs' Code-Reg that a provision corresponding to the jurisdiction was incorporated: 'Where, at any time in the procedure ..., the Commission intends to take a decision unfavourable towards the person concerned by the case presented, it shall communicate its objections to him/her in writing, together with all the documents on which it bases those objections. The person concerned by the case submitted to the Commission shall express his/her point of view in writing within a period of one month from the date on which the objections were' (Art 872a DVO Customs-Code, parallel to this Art 906a DVO Customs Code).

153 See eg Schwarze in Colneric (ed) *Une communauté de droit – Festschrift für Gil Carlos Rodríguez Iglesias* (Berlin 2003) pp 147, 160, 162–163; Kahl (2004) 95 VerwArch 1, 9f; clearly ECJ *TU-München* [1991] ECR I-5469. Here the ECJ's case-law has developed into a more intensified control of Commission's decisions under the effect of several referrals of the *Bundesfinanzhof* (BFH – German Federal Tax Court).
154 The underlying decision ECJ *Foto-Frost* [1987] ECR 4199 is concerned with such a proceeding from the custom area.
155 On this also Lecheler/Gundel (note 147) p 95.
156 Lecheler/Gundel (note 147) p 96; to this background the '*Textil-Deggendorf*' judiciary see above note 31. However, opposing Nehl (note 144) p 429, who always demands the performance/implementation of the direct action (but does also note that this does not correspond to the practice of the ECJ).

§ 19 IV 2   Jörg Gundel

63 **Case 4 – Problem:** (ECJ *Oleificio Borelli* [1992] ECR I-6313)
X submits an application for the funding of an agricultural project from the EC-regional aid fund. According to the relevant EC-regulation, the application is to be submitted to the national authority, which then has to forward it to the Commission. The Commission, however, can approve the application only if the Member State has also decided to promote the project (and thus bears half of the financing).
In the case of X, the Member State refused such an aid. Hereupon, the EC-Commission also rejected the application although all further conditions for an approval were met. X brings action before the CFI against this Commission decision. He claims that the denying decision of the national authority breaches Community law. The Commission should have taken this into account and thus reach a positive decision about the aid. This was the only way to secure the observance of Community law, because pursuant to national procedural law, the national authority's decision alone as an interlocutory judgement is not regarded to be judicially reviewable.

64 The **particularity** of these cases lies in the fact that (part-)decisions, as made by the national authorities, cannot be reviewed before the Community tribunals. The ECJ excludes such a control of national administrative measures within an action of annulment against Commission decisions because this assessment of Member State's action is exclusively provided in the proceeding for breaches of Community law (Articles 226, 227 TEC/Article III-360 DC).[157]

65 Nevertheless, the Community guarantee of an effective and complete legal protection requires that the judicial control of the governmental decision is ensured according to the standard of Community law. Thus, this review is a matter for the national courts, which are responsible for the general control of the authorities when they are applying Community law.[158] They can or respectively must refer questions about the interpretation of underlying Community law to the ECJ (Article 234(3) TEC/Article III-369 DC).

Case 4 – Answer:
66 X's action against the rejecting Commission decision is admissible. However, insofar as this decision shows any deficiencies, the CFI/ECJ are going to dismiss it as ungrounded. Neither the Commission nor the ECJ will review the lawfulness of the Member State's decision. In fact, this control is for the Member States. This applies also, when the national procedural law considers these decisions to be dependent actions of preparation (and hence not reviewable on their own). The Member State's legal systems are obliged by Community law to guarantee the admissibility of appropriate actions. Although the Court has also in this case confirmed the right of complete legal protection, it has been determined to be an obligation of the Member States.

---

157 See already ECJ *Triveneta Zuccheri* [1990] ECR I-1083, paras 16 ff; ECJ *CT Control BV and JCT Benelux BV* [1993] ECR I-3873, paras 55 ff. Such reviews are only admissible in the proceedings against the Member States for failure to fulfil their obligations.
158 ECJ *Oleificio Borelli* [1992] ECR I-6313, paras 13 ff; on this *eg* García de Enterría (1993) 13 YEL 19; Galetta in: Magieria/Sommermann (eds) *Verwaltung in der Europäischen Union* (Berlin 2001) 63, 76 ff; Nehl (note 144**Fehler! Textmarke nicht definiert.**) p 432; alike *eg* ECJ *La Conqueste SCEA* [2002] ECR I-1179, para 47.

Nevertheless, while the lawfulness of the national authority decision is reviewed before the competent courts, the rejecting decision of the Commission will become binding after the time has expired, Article 230(5) of the TEC (Article III-365(6) DC).[159] If the national remedy is successful in the end, this constitutes a new situation of facts, so that the Commission can decide about the aid anew without being bound to the prior decision. Consequently, also in these cases the legal protection against each part of the decision is guaranteed. However, the way to this protection is extremely intricate and complicated.

67

V. Summary

The judicial and procedural fundamental rights are based to a large extent on the guidelines of the ECHR which have been adopted in the Charter of Fundamental Rights of the European Union. Among these, the guarantees of fair trial and an effective legal protection, from which numerous derivations (the right to be heard, legal protection within reasonable time etc) result, take centre stage. These guarantees are complemented and occasionally strengthened through the principles of equal and effective implementation of Community law in the Member States (Article 10 TEC/Art I-5 II DC). In other constellations they have to be harmonised with the principle of effectiveness, which can also work against the individual's procedural position. Different from other fundamental rights of Community law, which primarily bind the Community legislator, the procedural fundamental rights act above all as limitations of the Member States' authorities and courts, which enforce Community law.

68

---

[159] This could also not be prevented by a parallel action of annulment against the decision of the Commission. As in the case of *Borelli*, it would have to be dismissed as being unfounded.

§ 20
The Charter of Fundamental Rights of the European Union

Christian Calliess

Leading cases: CFI JFE *Engineering Corp* [2004] ECR II-2501; ECJ *Jégo-Quéré* [2002] ECR I-2365; CFI *max.mobil* [2002] ECR II-313; ECJ *BECTU* [2001] ECR I-4881 including the opinion of AG Tizzano

Further reading: Alber *Die Selbstbindung der europäischen Organe an die Europäische Charta der Grundrechte* [2001] EuGRZ 349; Calliess *Ansätze zur Subjektivierung von Gemeinwohlbelangen im Völkerrecht – Das Beispiel des Umweltschutzes* [2000] ZUR 246; Cremer *Der vorprogrammierte Verfassungskonflikt* [2000] NVwZ 1452; Grabenwarter *Die Charta der Grundrechte für die Europäische Union* [2001] DVBl 1; Grabenwarter *Auf dem Weg in die Grundrechtsgemeinschaft?* [2001] EuGRZ 563; Kingreen *Theorie und Dogmatik der Grundrechte im europäischen Verfassungsrecht* [2004] EuGRZ 570; Mager *Die Bedeutung der Grundrechte für das Binnenmarktziel* [2004] EuR 41; Pernice *Eine Grundrechte-Charta für die Europäische Union* [2000] DVBl 847; Schorkopf *Nationale Grundrechte in der Dogmatik der Grundfreiheiten* [2004] ZaöRV 64, 125; Stein in: Cremer (ed) *Tradition und Weltoffenheit des Rechts – Festschrift für Helmut Steinberger* (Berlin 2002) p 1425; Rengeling/Szczekalla *Grundrechte in der Europäischen Union, Charta der Grundrechte und Allgemeine Rechtsgrundsätze* (Cologne 2004).

I. Introduction

1 The Charter of Fundamental Rights is the first **written catalogue of fundamental rights** in primary Community law. It is included in the signed but not yet operational European Constitution as Chapter II. A written catalogue of fundamental rights was more than necessary to remedy the protection of fundamental rights based purely on case-law, which became unacceptable for a confederation [1] (Article 6(1) TEU/Article I-2 DC) based on the rule of law [2]. In accordance with Article 164 of the Treaty of the European Economic Community (today Article 220 TEC/Art I-29(1) DC), the ECJ further developed the fundamental rights on the foundation of and by comparing the constitutional traditions common to the Member States and the ECtHR.[3] Although this approach has been confirmed explicitly in Article 6(2) of the TEU [4], the scope of protection of fundamental rights remained hard to specify, since the ECJ still had to develop them in a process constantly perfecting itself.[5] Due to the unspecific scope of the content and the restrictions of

---

1 *Cf* Calliess in: Calliess/Ruffert (eds) *Kommentar des Vertrages über die Europäische Union und des Vertrages zur Gründung der Europäischen Union* (2nd ed, Neuwied 2002) Art 1 EUV, paras 17 ff.
2 Stein in: Cremer (ed) *Tradition und Weltoffenheit des Rechts – Festschrift für Helmut Steinberger* (Berlin 2002) p 1429 f; likewise Alber/Widmaier [2000] EuGRZ 497, 499 ff; von Bogdandy [2001] JZ 157, 166 ff; Santer in: Heusel (ed) *Grundrechtecharta und Verfassungsentwicklung in der EU* (Cologne 2002) pp 13, 14; Mertin in: Heusel (ed) *Grundrechtecharta und Verfassungsentwicklung in der EU* (Cologne 2002) pp 55, 57.
3 *Cf* more detailed Rengeling *Grundrechtsschutz in der Europäischen Gemeinschaft* (Munich 1993) pp 223 ff; Kingreen in: Mager [2004] EuR 41, 44.
4 Overview by Kingreen in: Calliess/Ruffert (eds) *Kommentar des Vertrages über die Europäische Union und des Vertrages zur Gründung der Europäischen Union* (2nd ed, Neuwied 2002) Art 6 EUV, paras 27 ff and 84 ff; Dörr in: Dörr/Lenz (eds) *Europäischer Verwaltungsrechtsschutz* (Baden-Baden 2006), paras 497 ff.
5 Instructive Ress/Ukrow [1990] EuZW 499, 502 ff; Streinz *Bundesverfassungsgerichtlicher Grundrechtsschutz und EG-Recht* (Passau 1989) pp 401 ff; affirmative von Bogdandy [2001] JZ 157, 167 ff.

the fundamental rights, the ECJ tended to rush quickly to the proportionality test. Nevertheless, the court stressed its limitations to further develop the law as opposed to the Community legislator.[6] Compared to German standards, this leads to a decreased level of controlling fundamental rights.[7] In many cases, the test of justification ended with the determination of the legitimate aim and the conclusion that the measures taken to realise the aim were not manifestly inappropriate (*Evidenzkontrolle*). With a view to the margin of appreciation of the Community legislator, the ECJ rarely tested the necessity and adequacy.[8]

Against this backdrop, the protection of fundamental rights **did not meet the standards of the rule of law** in several ways. Firstly, the protection of fundamental rights provided through the ECJ seemed insufficient: One aspect is the question of certainty of the law, since in each case the ECJ first had to "find" and develop the fundamental right in question. This meant that the fundamental right was not visible to the bearer of this right – contrary to the principles of transparency and citizen-friendliness laid down in Article 1(2) of the TEU (Article I-1(1) DC).[9] The effectiveness of the protection of fundamental rights also proved to be insufficient. The ECJ understands itself as "the motor of integration". In light of this understanding, the ECJ paid less attention to an extensive proportionality test[10] and instead promoted the integration and therefore the preservation of the legislative act rather than the protection of the individual.[11] Additionally, the aforementioned insufficiency was compensated only by "judge-made law". Although "judge-made law" is known in every legal system within the European Union, it is usually used only to compensate rules that were unintentionally left incomplete by the legislation.[12] Taking into account the standard of European integration and the power of the institu-

2

---

6 Kingreen (note 4) Art 6 EUV, paras 74 ff; instructive and with a view towards the strict case-law of the ECJ concerning the fundamental freedom von Bogdandy [2001] JZ 157, 165 ff, and doubtful concerning the competence of the ECJ to take a powerful role within the political process, 166 ff.
7 More detailed and differentiating von Bogdandy [2001] JZ 157, 163 ff; concerning the surveillance within the Community law in general Herdegen/Richter in: Frowein (ed) *Die Kontrolldichte bei der gerichtlichen Überprüfung von Handlungen der Verwaltung* (Berlin 1993) pp 209 ff; Magiera *Grundrechtsgeltung und Grundrechtswirklichkeit in der Europäischen Union* in: Bauer/Huber/Niewiadomski (eds) *Ius Publicum Europaeum – Referate und Diskussionsbeiträge des XII. Deutsch-Polnischen Verwaltungskolloquiums* (Stuttgart 2002) pp 21 ff; Kühling *Grundrechte* in: von Bogdandy (ed) *Europäisches Verfassungsrecht* (Berlin 2003) pp 583, 586 ff.
8 *Cf* as an example ECJ *Germany v Council* [1994] ECR I-4973, paras 94 ff; critical Nettesheim [1995] EuZW 106; Huber [1997] EuZW 517; Stein [1998] EuZW 261; differentiating von Bogdandy [2001] JZ 157, 163 ff; different opinion Zuleeg [1997] NJW 1201 and Kischel [2000] EuR 380, who tries to prove that the protection provided is not comparable to the one provided by the *Bundesverfassungsgericht* (BVerfG – German Federal Constitutional Court).
9 *Cf* more detailed Callies (note 1) Art 1 EUV, paras 27 ff and 34 ff with further references.
10 Common wordings are *eg* "In correspondence with the goals of the Community...", "not obviously inappropriate" and "does not inflict with the essence of the fundamental right".
11 Stein (note 2) pp 1431 ff; von Bogdandy [2001] JZ 157, 165 ff; more detailed Dehousse *The European Court of Justice* (Basingstoke 1998) pp 36 ff; different opinion Zuleeg [2000] EuGRZ 511, 512 ff.
12 *Cf* Stein in: Reinhart (ed) *Richterliche Rechtsfortbildung – Festschrift der Juristischen Fakultät zur 600-Jahr-Feier der Universität Heidelberg* (Heidelberg 1986) pp 619 ff.

tions, an insufficient protection of the fundamental rights is rarely unintentional.[13] These deficits have been remedied by the written catalogue of fundamental rights.

3   The **Charter of Fundamental Rights of the European Union**[14] is based on a mandate of the European Council formed during the EU-summit in Cologne in June 1999.[15] The Charter was "ceremonially proclaimed" at the beginning of the summit of Nice dated 7 December 2000.[16] According to the mandate, however, it was determined that the draft, which was to be provided by December 2000, should only be ceremonially proclaimed first and then the Charter should subsequently be included in the contract, thereby becoming legally binding. Although the Charter never did come into force, it proved to be an important step towards the European Constitution. As Chapter II, the Charter was incorporated into the European Constitution nearly unchanged by the European Convent.[17]

II. Contents and Restrictions of Fundamental Rights

Case 1 – Problem:
4   A resides in the Spanish town of S. 30 meters away from A's residence, B, a big local manufacturer of batteries, put a waste treatment plant into operation. Although B does not possess the necessary permit in accordance with Spanish or European law (IVU-Dir 96/61), S implicitly acquiesces his actions. Chemicals which result from the production of the batteries are also treated at the plant. After a while, A and her family suffered serious medical conditions. A suspected these to be the result of the emissions of the facility. A's attempts to receive information from the local authorities about the hazardousness of the emissions and her attempts to enforce the ratification procedure as well as measures to protect her and her family's health were not successful. A brings an action before the national court relying on Article II-97 of the DC.

1. Overview of the Fundamental Rights Guaranteed by the Charter

5   In the version of the DC, the Charter is divided into several titles following the preamble. Title I is named "Dignity", Title II is called "Freedoms", Title III "Equality", Title IV "Solidarity", Title V "Citizenship Rights", Title VI "Justice" and Title VII "General Provisions".

6   Just like the *Grundgesetz* (GG – German Basic Law), the first provision of the **catalogue of fundamental rights** incorporated in the DC contains the guarantee of human dignity[18] in Article II-61 of the DC. Human dignity is to be respected and protected. This

---

13 Stein (note 2) pp 1430 ff.
14 Text with comments in [2000] EuGRZ 554 ff.
15 SN 150/99, Annex IV; printed – just as other documents concerning the development of the Charter – in: Deutscher Bundestag (ed) *Die Charta der Grundrechte der EU, Zur Sache 1/2001* (Berlin 2001) p 71; concerning the genesis of the Charter Meyer/Engels in: Deutscher Bundestag (ed) *Die Charta der Grundrechte der EU, Zur Sache 1/2001* (Berlin 2001) pp 7 ff.
16 Concerning the genesis Geiger in: Heusel (ed) *Grundrechtecharta und Verfassungsentwicklung in der EU* (Cologne 2002) pp 17, 19; concerning the proclamation and its legal effects Alber [2001] EuGRZ 349 ff.
17 [2004] OJ C310, 1.
18 *Cf* Poscher [2004] JZ 756; Schmidt [2002] ZEuS 631.

already points out the two crucial functions of the protection of fundamental rights, namely the defensive function that aims at the omission of governmental actions and the protective function that aims at governmental interference in order to protect the individual against interferences by third parties.[19] The protective function has found recognition both in the case law of the ECtHR and, and least rudimentarily, in the case law of the ECJ.[20] Article II-61 of the DC is followed by the right to life in Article II-62(1) of the DC. The right to integrity of the person is laid down in Article II-63 of the DC, which then is specified by criminal law and administrative law provisions, such as the prohibition of the death penalty and torture in Article II-62(2) of the DC[21] and Article II-64 of the DC. The latter seem surprising since the European Union has only peripheral competences in cross-border crime investigation and the administration of penal justice (*cf* Article 34(2) TEU).[22] Article II-63(2) of the DC also contains four significant provisions, three of them stating prohibitions whereas one states a precept to regulate interferences with human rights in connection with medicine and biology. These guarantees derive from the Convention on Human Rights and Biomedicine.[23] Noteworthy is the prohibition on reproductive cloning on human beings as well as the prohibition on using the human body and its parts as a source of financial gain.[24] On the one hand, these aspects can be derived from national constitutional law[25], or, as the ECJ points out with reference to Dir 98/44 on the protection of biotechnological inventions[26], from the concept of human dignity and physical integrity recognised in Community law. Nevertheless, this explicit provision draws attention to the challenges posed by new biotechnological developments. For example, a clear line is drawn in matters regarding the highly controversial[27] cloning of human beings. This means that therapeutic cloning of human beings can be legally admissible in some ways.[28] At the same time, however, the provision provides for a strict governmental control, especially in view of the possibility of reproductive cloning.

Title II essentially repeats the freedoms laid down in the **ECHR**. The right to liberty was extended by the right to security (Article II-66 DC). Further rights mentioned are the respect for private and family life (Article II-67 DC), the freedom of thought, conscience and religion (Article II-70 DC), the freedom of expression and information (Article II-71 DC) and the freedom of assembly and association (Article II-72 DC). The right to marry and the right to found a family in Article II-69 of the DC deviate from Article 12 of the ECHR inasmuch as the right to found a family has been disconnected from the right to marry. Also, the explicit reference to "men and women" was not included in the provision. The wording of the provision and the reference to national law enable the national legislation to recognise alternative forms of partnership, and also homosexual relationships, as

7

---

19 *Cf* more detailed Calliess *Rechtsstaat und Umweltstaat* (Tübingen 2001) pp 307 ff and 437 ff.
20 *Cf* Calliess [2001] ZUR 246, 249 ff with further references; → *cf* § 2 para 9; § 13 para 20.
21 Schmitz [2001] JZ 833, 842.
22 Concerning this development von Bubnoff [2001] ZEuS 165, 171, in which the Charter could have a guiding position.
23 (1997) 36 ILM 817.
24 *Cf* von Bubnoff [2001] ZEuS 165, 190 ff.
25 *Cf* Benda [2001] NJW 2147; Herdegen [2001] JZ 773; Frankenberg [2000] KJ 325.
26 ECJ *Netherlands v Parliament and Council* [2001] ECR I-7079, paras 69 ff; more detailed Calliess/Meiser [2002] JuS 426.
27 Overview given by Herdegen [2001] JZ 773; Frankenberg [2000] KJ 325.
28 *Cf* Taupitz [2001] NJW 3433.

a basis for founding a family and creating one's life.[29] The following provisions are not yet included in the ECHR. The protection of personal data, although protected by means of the ECtHR's established case law concerning Article 8 of the ECHR (→ cf § 3 para 3), is explicitly mentioned in Article II-68 of the DC. The right to conscientious objection is recognised in Article II-70(2) of the DC, the freedom of arts and sciences in Article II-73 of the DC[30] and the right to asylum in Article II-78 of the DC.[31] The right to asylum does not extend the protection of Article 63(1) of the TEC[32] and thus does not grant a title.

8 The **economical rights** contained in the ECHR are stated in Article II-75 of the DC to Article II-77 of the DC.[33] In Article II-75(1) of the DC, the right to pursue a freely chosen occupation, which is not limited to EU-citizens, is guaranteed. Moreover, the provision promotes the "right to work", which is usually categorised as a social right. In accordance with Article II-89 of the DC, the "right to work" is meant to be an alternative to the "right to be employed", which can not be demanded within a social and free market (cf Article I-4 III DC) (→ cf § 15 para 6).

9 In respect to the citizens of the European Union, Article II-75(2) of the DC adds the **fundamental freedoms** as stated in the TEC to the aforementioned rights. This raises the question whether the incorporation of the fundamental freedoms into the Charter abolishes the element of border crossing, which is inherent to the application of the fundamental freedoms.[34] Moreover, it is questionable if the fundamental freedoms are meant to be prohibitions of limitations situated at the same level as the fundamental rights. This might be prevented by the cross-reference of Article II-112(2) of the DC. In Article II-76 of the DC, the freedom to conduct business, which "is accepted by Community and national law"[35], is explicitly recognised. The right to property is guaranteed in Article II-77 of the DC.

10 Article II-80 of the DC contains – in accordance with the constitutional traditions common to the Member States – the **general principle of equality**. The general principle of equality is put into concrete terms by the **specified rules of non-discrimination** laid down in Article II-81 and II-83 of the DC, which in turn correspond with Article 12, 13 and 141 of the TEC as well as with Article 14 of the ECHR. Article II-82 of the DC applies to the respect of cultural, linguistic and religious diversity. The provision is the result of the battle for the inclusion of the explicit protection of minorities – and is systematically misplaced in Title III. Article II-84 of the DC is inspired by the United Nation's Convention on the Rights of the Child and provides for protection and care of every child as well as

---

29 Critical concerning the content Tettinger [2001] NJW 1010, 1012 ff, who describes Art 9 as a "pale formula" and finds fault with the decision to leave the definition of marriage and family to the national legislation.
30 Tettinger [2001] NJW 1010, 1012 ff; Schmitz [2001] JZ 833, 842.
31 Cf more detailed Mahlmann [2000] ZEuS 419, 428 ff; misleading Grabenwarter [2001] DVBl 1, 5, who speaks of the fundamental right of asylum; cf also von Bogdandy [2001] JZ 157, 161 ff.
32 Cf Brechmann in: Calliess/Ruffert (eds) *Kommentar des Vertrages über die Europäische Union und des Vertrages zur Gründung der Europäischen Union* (2nd ed, Neuwied 2002) Art 63 EUV, paras 3 ff with further references.
33 Cf more detailed Schwarze [2001] EuZW 517, 518 ff.
34 Cf Grabenwarter [2001] DVBl 1, 5 ff.
35 Tettinger [2001] NJW 1010, 1014 ff – "at least indirectly" – derives a component promoting the middle classes from this.

for the right to maintain a relationship to both of its parents.[36] In light of the systematics of the Charter and the EU's competence, the provision is questionable.

The **EU citizenship rights** proclaimed in Title V correspond with the rights contained in the TEC. As an example, the right to vote and to stand as a candidate for the election of the European Parliament in Article II-99 of the DC, the right to vote and to stand as a candidate for municipal elections in the state of residence in Article II-100 of the DC, the freedom of movement and of residence in Article II-105 of the DC, the right to diplomatic and consular protection in Article II-106 of the DC and, corresponding to Article 255 of the TEC[37], the right of access to documents in Article II-102 of the DC can be named. Recently, the right to good administration in Article II-101 of the DC was added, which comprehends the procedural rights, such as the right to be heard and the right to have one's affairs handled impartially, fairly and within a reasonable time by the institutions and bodies of the EU. It also includes the obligation for the administration to give reasons for its decisions, the right to state liability as well as – contrary to the aforementioned Article II-102 of the DC – the right of each person to access his or her files. Until these rights were incorporated in the Charter, they were scarcely and only disjointedly mentioned in the TEC or acknowledged only by judge-made law[38]. 11

Title VI, containing **procedural rights**, is essentially based on the guarantees contained in Article 6 and 13 of the ECHR[39]. The most striking development is the extension of the scope of protection of Article 6 of the ECHR[40] and of the corresponding constitutional traditions common to the Member States. While both Article 6 of the ECHR and the constitutional tradition common to the Member States limit the protection to civil and criminal procedures, Article II-107(2) of the DC enunciates a general entitlement to a public hearing similar to Article 19(4) of the German Basic Law.[41] 12

The most controversial[42] Title IV of the Charter named **Solidarity** contains a merger of social and economic rights[43], which derives from primary Community law as well as from the law of the Member States. Protective provisions concerning employment are provided in Article II-92 (protection in case of unjustified dismissal), Article II-91 (just and fair work conditions), Article II-92 (prohibition of child labour and protection of young people at work) and Article II-93(2) of the Charter (prohibition from dismissal for a reason relating to maternity). The right to social benefit and participation is stated in Article II-89 (right to access to a job placement service), in Article II-94 (social security and so- 13

---

36 More positive Tettinger [2001] NJW 1010, 1013 ff.
37 For further details *cf* Wegener in: Calliess/Ruffert (eds) *Kommentar des Vertrages über die Europäische Union und des Vertrages zur Gründung der Europäischen Union* (2nd ed, Neuwied 2002) Art 255 EGV, paras 6 ff as well as Calliess (note 1) Art 1 EUV, paras 34 ff.
38 Martinez *Die Kodizes der guten Verwaltungspraxis* [2001] EuR 682; Lais [2002] ZEuS 447; Bauer *Das Recht auf gute Verwaltung im Europäischen Gemeinschaftsrecht* (Frankfurt aM 2002).
39 More detailed Lenz in: Heusel (ed) *Grundrechtecharta und Verfassungsentwicklung in der EU* (Cologne 2002) p 109.
40 More detailed Tonne *Effektiver Rechtsschutz durch staatliche Gerichte als Forderung des Europäischen Gemeinschaftsrechts* (Cologne 1997) pp 147 ff.
41 Grabenwarter [2001] DVBl 1, 8 ff; *cf* also Calliess [2002] NJW 3577.
42 *Cf* Bernsdorff [2001] VSSR 1, 2 ff with further references; Koskinen in: Heusel (ed) *Grundrechtecharta und Verfassungsentwicklung in der EU* (Cologne 2002) p 83.
43 Positively as to the result *cf* Tettinger [2001] NJW 1010, 1014 ff, who, however, with justification, still demands "dogmatic efforts of structuring".

cial assistance) and in Article II-95 (health care) of the Charter. Albeit systematically incorrect and problematic as regards competences, Article II-74 of the DC guarantees the right to education and to compulsory lessons free of charge.[44] The recognition of access to services of general economic interest as provided by national law and practices in order to promote the social and territorial cohesion of the Union in Article II-96 of the DC seems to be an awkward provision within a catalogue of fundamental rights. The provision was included upon request of the French government presumably aiming on limiting the effects of Article 86 of the TEC that enables the European Commission to evaluate governmental and governmentally supported services and social services only on the criteria of competition. Nonetheless, this provision, in view of Article III-122 of the DC (former Article 16 TEC), is superfluous and, given the systematic context, a bizarre idea. The inclusion of the public policies in Article II-95(ii) (health care), Article II-97 (environmental protection) and Article II-98 of the DC (consumer protection) also seems superfluous. These provisions are mere reiterations of Article III-278(1) of the DC (former Article 152 TEC), Article III-233(2) of the DC (former Article 174 and Article 6 TEC) and Article III-235 of the DC (former Article 153 TEC). Almost all of these "rights"[45], which had been demanded by the literature in order to establish a comprehensive policy of fundamental rights,[46] extend the competence of the EU[47].

2. The Restrictions within the Charter of Fundamental Rights

14 Strikingly and contrary to the ECHR (→ cf § 2 paras 43 ff) or to the German Basic Law, only few fundamental rights of the Charter contain provisions for restriction. This is caused by the intention to keep the Charter as short as possible, since the inclusion of restrictions would have doubled the content.[48] Instead, the Charter in Article II-112 of the DC and II-113 of the DC contains a general and highly complex **provision for restrictions**, which is correctly called the "Achilles' heel" of the protection of fundamental rights.[49] The reason for the complexity of the provision lies in the fact that Article II-112 and Article II-113 of the DC do not only serve as provisions for restrictions, they also help to examine the scope of protection and they are supposed to resolve conflicts between the different sources of law. Thus, these articles simultaneously resolve the relations between the Charter and the law of the European Union, the protection of fundamental rights provided by the Member States' constitutions and by the ECHR.[50]

---

44 Blank *Soziale Grundrechte in der Europäischen Grundrechtscharta* (Frankfurt aM 2002); further – with partly critical opinion – Bernsdorff [2001] VSSR 1, 20 ff with further references.
45 For further possibilities of understanding *cf* Bernsdorff [2001] VSSR 1, 8 ff; von Bogdandy [2001] JZ 157, 160 ff.
46 Alston/Weiler in: Alston (ed) *The EU and Human Rights* (Oxford 1999) pp 3 ff with, in parts, far-reaching consequences, *cf* pp 14, 60 ff; about this predominantly critical and, in the end rightly, differentiating von Bogdandy [2001] JZ 157.
47 Different opinion Alston/Weiler (note 46) pp 21; correctly von Bogdandy [2001] JZ 157, 161 ff.
48 *Cf* Kenntner [2000] ZRP 423; as to the minor changes within the context of the Constitutional Convent Hirsch in: Schwarze (ed) *Der Verfassungsentwurf des Europäischen Konvents* (Baden-Baden 2004) pp 111, 116 ff.
49 Thus Kenntner [2000] ZRP 423.
50 For further details *cf* Grabenwarter in: Cremer (ed) *Tradition und Weltoffenheit des Rechts – Festschrift für Helmut Steinberger* (Berlin 2002) pp 1135 ff.

Article II-112 of the DC defines the premises and the general limits to the restrictability of rights and freedom as well as the horizontal scope of the fundamental freedom by means of a specific provision for restriction. In this respect, Article II-112(1)(i) of the DC, on the one hand, states the formal requirement of a statutory basis. The term of law is mentioned again in Article I-33 of the DC, including the European law and the European skeleton laws, which are comparable to the known categories of regulation and directive set out in Article 249 of the TEC.[51]

A further limit to the restrictability of rights and freedoms in Article II-112(1)(i) of the DC is the principle of essence and the proportionality test set out in Article II-112(1)(ii) of the DC. According to Article II-112(1)(ii) of the DC, restrictions can only be admissible if they are necessary and genuinely meet objectives that serve common welfare recognised by the Union or if they serve the protection rights and freedoms of the individual. This wording connects the restrictions of Article 8 to Article 11 of the ECHR and the ECJ's case law.[52]

The general provision for restriction, however, is limited – in connection with Article II-113 of the DC – by two **most-favoured-nation clauses**. According to Article II-112(2) of the DC, the rights of the Charter deriving from the Community Treaties or from the TEU shall be exercised within the restrictions set out in the respective treaties. This might lead to a shortfall of the fundamental rights provided for by the Member States' constitutions and the ECHR. This danger is to be avoided by Article II-112 and Article II-113 of the DC:[53] Pursuant to Article II-112(3)(i) of the DC, the rights of the Charter corresponding to those of the ECHR have to contain the same scope of protection[54]. By means of this reference, the restrictions and the level of protection provided for by the ECHR is set out as the standard of fundamental rights protection[55], in case the Community law does not include an even more beneficial provision. Hence, the fundamental-rights protection of the ECHR was incorporated as a minimum standard (*cf* Art II-113 DC)[56]. Admittedly, it will not be easy in a given instance to judge if the rights in question do in fact correspond. Also, the exact significance of meaning and scope will be hard to identify.[57] According to the explanation of the Presidency, the provisions do not need to be identical. An approximate similarity of content is sufficient, which must, of course, be expressed in the wording (a scope of protection developed by judge-made law does, by contrast, not suffice). The term "corresponding" is to be understood in a way that the provisions must apply to the same factual situation.[58] Article II-112(3)(ii) of the DC – deviating from Article II-112(3)(i) of the DC – makes an exception if Union law provides for a more extensive

---

51 As to the former legal position in more detail *cf* Ruffert in: Calliess/Ruffert (eds) *Kommentar des Vertrages über die Europäische Union und des Vertrages zur Gründung der Europäischen Union* (2nd ed, Neuwied 2002) Art 249 EGV, paras 14 ff, 38 ff and 43 ff with further references.
52 As to that in more detail Kingreen (note 4) Art 6 EUV, paras 69 ff.
53 For further details as to the entire problem *cf* Grabenwarter (note 50) pp 1139 ff.
54 Overview in Borowsky in: Meyer (ed) *Charta der Grundrechte* (2nd ed, Baden-Baden) Art 52, para 32.
55 Grabenwarter [2001] DVBl 1; for further details *cf* Molthagen *Das Verhältnis der EU-Grundrechte zur EMRK* (Hamburg 2003).
56 Corresponding explanations of the Convent's president, CONVENT 49 CHARTE 4473/00 [2000] EuGRZ 559; alike Fischbach (2000) 12 RUDH 7, 8; Krüger/Polakiewicz [2001] EuGRZ 92, 99.
57 On the same problem *cf* Grabenwarter [2001] DVBl 1.
58 For further details *cf* Grabenwarter (note 50) pp 1139 ff.

protection. Finally, according to Article II-113 of the DC, nothing in this Charter is to be interpreted as restricting or adversely affecting human rights and fundamental freedom; this provision will be examined later on. Ultimately, this system of restrictions shall ensure that the most extensive protection provided for by one of the three legal systems will always be applied.[59]

18   The general horizontal system of restrictions is completed by **special vertical restrictions**, which refer to the legislative competence of the Member States. An example is Article II-112(6) of the DC that promotes the exercise of fundamental rights under reserve of "national laws" or even "customs". This causes a double restriction, perforating the uniform restriction provided by Article II-112(1) of the DC. Naturally, these vertical restrictions, which focus on the legal systems of the Member States, are detrimental to the aim of guaranteeing a uniform protection of fundamental rights and the Charter thus misses one of its primary goals.[60]

3. Comment

19   Especially the vertical restrictions describe one of the Charter's central problems: The Charter establishes fundamental rights beyond the legislative competences of the Union. The "axiom of parallelism of competences and protection of fundamental rights"[61], and thus the character of fundamental rights as provisions allocating negative competences to governmental action, was disregarded.[62] The Convent evidently succumbed to the temptation[63] to include fair and good rights in the Charter that hardly serve any need, since both EU and EC lack the competence to endanger these rights (*cf* the right to marry and to found a family stated in Article II-69 DC, that consequently refers to the law of the Member States; similar are the Articles II-74, 84 and 89 DC). The same is true for some rights to benefit and participate provided for by the Charter. To some extent, rights are granted without the Union having the competence to redeem them (*cf* the right to access preventive health care and the right to benefit from medical treatment in Article II-85 DC). Article II-85 DC itself contradicts Article III-278 VII DC (similar to the former Article 152 TEC)[64] and solves this contradiction only by reference to the laws and customs of the Member States.[65]

20   Possibly, this disrespect of the parallelism of **competence** and **protection of fundamental rights** is based on noble motives – in particular with regard to the development of the Charter by means of ensuring a broad participation of the public (for example, anyone was able to send suggestions via the internet regarding fundamental rights to be included).

---

59 Sceptical in case of fundamental rights relations between different legal systems – without good reason – Grabenwarter (note 50) pp 1140 ff, who does not realise that the restrictions do not refer to the fundamental rights relations between the different legal systems in general but are applied only if one single fundamental right is protected by all of the legal systems.
60 Magiera [2000] DÖV 1017, 1026 ff.
61 *Cf* appropriate Pernice [2000] DVBl 847, 852 ff.
62 Ehmke (1963) 20 VVDStRL 53, 89 ff.
63 Raising doubts Pernice [2000] DVBl 847, 852 ff.
64 Critical Bernsdorff [2001] VSSR 1, 22 ff; *cf* concerning the reach of the competence Wichard in: Calliess/Ruffert (eds) *Kommentar des Vertrages über die Europäische Union und des Vertrages zur Gründung der Europäischen Union* (2nd ed, Neuwied 2002) Art 152 EGV, paras 9 ff.
65 Although critical in detail rather positive (no "systematic suggestions") Bernsdorff [2001] VSSR 1, 17 ff.

This applies all the more to the discussion of the Charter's contents that sometimes became politically independent in a way that the actual aim of the Charter – to effectively bind the Union to the fundamental rights – was lost sight of, which gave way to a general debate about the updating and modernising of the catalogue of fundamental rights that was no longer limited to the European level.[66]

In view of the Charter's legally binding nature within the DC, however, it would have 21 been preferable to refer, at first, only to those fundamental rights that were already acknowledged by the ECJ in its case law,[67] therefore **the general principles of law** developed under consideration of the constitutional traditions common to the Member States and the consented guarantees of the ECHR. Taking this as a basis, existing gaps could have been filled in view of the Union's competences and by means of further fundamental rights. Corresponding to the dynamic increase of European competences, for example in the area of inner and outer security, the catalogue of fundamental rights will have to increase, too.[68] The Convent, which – as it was said – worked under pressure of time, failed to reflect the required parallelism of competence and protection of fundamental rights to a sufficient extent and, as a result of that, got tangled up in the jungle of competences. This can be seen clearly if one takes a closer look at the different wordings used to guarantee different fundamental rights (for example "the Union acknowledges and regards according to the Community law and the legal provisions and traditions of the Member States"). The citizens of the Union, however, to whom the fundamental rights should actually have been made "visible" by means of the Charter, will – contrary to the principles of transparency and citizen-friendliness – not be able to distinguish between enforceable and non-enforceable rights.[69]

Furthermore, it is to be criticized that – in particular under the title of "**Solidarity**" – 22 contrary to the provisions of the European Council in Cologne[70], which in view of concerns as to the exceeding of competences only wanted "true" fundamental rights to be included in the Charter, determinations of "state's and Union's aims" having the appearance of fundamental rights are included in the Charter. In particular those guarantees showing a mere objectively-legal effect and imposing an obligation only on the Union bodies, which grant no rights to the individual,[71] neither have a conceptual nor a systematic legitimacy in the catalogue of fundamental rights. Moreover – and in this respect, the concerns of the European Council in Cologne are unfounded anyway – they are completely unnecessary as a mere repetition of legally binding provisions from the remaining European constitutional law[72].

---

66 Cf Bernsdorff [2001] VSSR 1; also Tettinger [2001] NJW 1010, 1012 ff.
67 Cf Kingreen (note 4) Art 6 EUV, paras 93 ff, providing a catalogue of unwritten fundamental rights albeit by the ECJ accepted; also Griller in: Duschanek/Griller (eds) *Grundrechte für Europa* (Vienna 2002) pp 131, 132.
68 Pernice [2000] DVBl 847, 852 ff.
69 Stein (note 2) pp 1426 ff.
70 Cf note 14.
71 Fundamental concerning the fundamental aims of states policy Sommermann *Staatsziele und Staatszielbestimmungen* (Tübingen 1997) pp 358 ff.
72 Different Grabenwarter [2004] EuGRZ 563, 565, who considers the fundamental aims of state policy to be "orders to optimise"; cf further Schwarze [2004] EuR 535, 561.

§ 20 II 3

Christian Calliess

23 In case so-called **modern fundamental rights** are to be included in the Charter, as intended in view of today's challenges and for which some arguments might be found,[73] one look at the thorough discussion as to possibilities and limits of its wording would have been enough to find a concept and wording of fundamental rights that is able to live up to the expectations. So instead of repeating the provisions set out in Articles I-3(2) and III-233 of the DC with awkward wording in Article II-97 of the DC[74], it would have been less far-fetched to establish a procedural fundamental right to environmental protection[75]. In the course of a discussion held both in national[76] and in international contexts[77], three components of a procedural fundamental right to environmental protection have emerged: A right to the citizens' participation in administrative decisions pertaining to the environment, a right to appropriate access to the court as well as – as a necessary prerequisite for exercising both other rights – a right to obtain information regarding the environment.[78] With these contents, such a procedural fundamental right to environmental protection is reflected both in the Principle 10 of the Declaration of Rio[79] and – recently – in the UN-ECE Convention on Access to Information, Public Participation in Decision-Making and Access to Justice in Environmental Matters, which was passed at the conference of the Ministers of the Environment in Aarhus, Denmark, dated 23 June to 25 June 1998 (the so-called Aarhus Convention) and signed by all Member States of the EU.[80] Its Article 1 states: "In order to contribute to the protection of the right of every person of present and future generations to live in an environment adequate to his or her health and well-being, each Party shall guarantee the rights of access to information, public participation in decision-making, and access to justice in environmental matters in accordance with the provisions of this Convention." From a procedural fundamental right to environmental protection that meets these criteria, concrete procedural rights may be derived, which enable the affected person to enforce his needs and interests pertaining to environmental protection. For the legislature and administration, these procedural provisions contain certain requirements as to the structuring of proceedings which ensure the legal position of the individual, for example in the permit procedure for a facility. A possible wording of Article II-97 of the DC, in accordance with the applicable legal situation, could have been the following: "Each individual is entitled to a clean and healthy environment as well as its preservation and protection. This is guaranteed by means of the rights

---

73 *Cf* Calliess [2000] ZUR 246.
74 Art II-97 DC reads as follows: "A high level of environmental protection and the improvement of the quality of the environment must be integrated into the policies of the Union and ensured in accordance with the principle of sustainable development."
75 Apparently affirmative concerning the content of the fundamental rights of this provision Hirsch (note 48) pp 111, 124; as said here Grabenwarter [2004] EuGRZ 563, 565.
76 *Cf eg* Kloepfer *Zum Grundrecht auf Umweltschutz* (Berlin 1978) pp 24 ff, who understands them as a concept of participation. More accurate is his connection to the "status activus processualis". *Cf* further Brönneke [1993] ZUR 153, 157 ff, whose approach leads to a procedural conception of the right to environmental protection. *Cf* further Calliess (note 20) pp 463 ff.
77 *Cf* only Ruffert *Subjektive Rechte im Umweltrecht der Europäischen Gemeinschaft* (Heidelberg 1996) pp 18 ff.
78 Ruffert (note 77) pp 23 ff; Krämer [1998] EuGRZ 285, 291 ff with further references.
79 [1992] ILM 874, 878 ff; more detailed to the Declaration of Rio published in (1993) 21 UTR 411; Schröder (1996) 34 ArchVR 251 as well as Ruffert [1993] ZUR 208.
80 *Cf* Scheyli (2000) 38 ArchVR 217; further Wegener in: Cremer/Fisahn (eds) *Jenseits der marktregulierten Selbststeuerung – Perspektiven des Umweltrechts* (Berlin 1997) pp 83, 192 ff.

to information, participation in the administrative procedure and effective access to the court". Such a wording faces the concerns that have been raised – with justification – against a material fundamental right of environmental protection designed as a claim to state performance (*Leistungsrecht*),[81] but at the same time, effectively accommodates the requirements of a limited subjectification (*Subjektivierung*) of environmental protection as a common interest.[82] Even if – as it is said – the convent for fundamental rights was subject to increased time pressure while working on the title "Solidarity", this empty homage to environmental protection, unnecessary in view of the former provisions of the TEC, unsystematic in terms of a catalogue of fundamental rights and obviously owed to political expectations alone, should have been omitted. One should to do it properly or not at all. This criticism also applies both to the consumer protection set out in Article II-98 of the DC as well as – in the end – the health protection established in Article II-95(ii) of the DC accordingly.

Case 1 – Answer:
At first, it should be examined whether there is a fundamental right in the DC that A can refer to for protection. The following subject matters of protection may be considered: "environment" and "health". The DC contains neither a material nor a procedural fundamental right of environmental protection. The environmental protection provided for in Article II-97 of the DC is designed as an "aim of the Union"; therefore, it cannot grant any subjective rights and thus is no fundamental right. The same is true mutatis mutandis for Article II-95(ii) of the DC, Article II-95(i) of the DC, which on the one hand contains a right (to performance), but on the other hand is not applicable as regards contents. However, Article II-63(i) of the DC (physical and mental integrity includes health) – in the dimension of protection of fundamental rights set out in paragraph 1 – may be considered. In view of the ECtHR's case law, it seems obvious that environmental protection may be asserted as a partial guarantee of certain other fundamental rights. Accordingly, the Strasbourg court for human rights – in the *López Ostra* case – surprisingly derived a claim to protection against the ecological damage of third parties not from the right to live pursuant to Article 2(1)(i), but from the right to the respect of private and family life guaranteed by Article 8 of the ECHR; this applies "even if the health of the person affected is not seriously endangered."[83] By the state's toleration of facilities which damage the environment, the governmental bodies disregarded the balance between the economic interest of the municipality (in the case: S) and the rights of the complainant (in the case: A) from Article 8 of the ECHR. In its decision in the *Guerra* case[84], the ECtHR then derived a complainant's claim to information pertaining to the environment from Article 8 of the ECHR as otherwise, they could not judge the dangerousness of the neighbouring facility and take the appropriate steps.[85] These approaches of the ECtHR, which emphasise the protective dimension of fundamental rights, can – as is proven by the hitherto existing case law of the ECJ regarding Article 28 of the TEC[86] (Article III-153 DC) – in fact be transferred to Article II-63(1) of the DC; therefore, A can refer to it.

---

81 *Cf* in contrast to this Kotulla [2000] KJ 22, who tries to refute these objections.
82 *Cf* more detailed Calliess [2000] ZUR 246, 253 ff; similar Müller FAZ (7 September 2000) p 16.
83 ECtHR *López Ostra* (1995) 20 EHRR 277 (paras 51, 58 of the decision).
84 ECtHR *Guerra* (1998) 26 EHRR 357.
85 In detail Schmidt-Radefeldt *Ökologische Menschenrechte* (Baden-Baden 2000) pp 116 ff and 148 ff.
86 ECJ *Commission v France* [1997] ECR I-6959, paras 32 ff; *cf* Szczekalla [1998] DVBl 219, 221 ff.

III. On the Area of Application of the Charter of Fundamental Rights of the European Union

25 The Charter's **area of application** is determined by Article II-111(1) of the DC of the European Constitution: "The provisions of this Charter are addressed to the institutions, bodies, offices and agencies of the Union with due regard to the principle of subsidiarity and to the Member States only when they are implementing Union law. They shall therefore respect the rights, observe the principles and promote the application thereof in accordance with their respective powers and respecting the limits of the powers of the Union as conferred on it in the other Parts of the Constitution." The term "bodies" as used in Article I-18(2) of the DC refers to the European Parliament, the European Council, the Council of Ministers, the European Commission as well as the ECJ.[87] Although the original version of the Charter did not apply to them, now institutions, authorities and agencies are also included in the area of application of Article II-111(1) of the DC to fill possible gaps in the commitment to the fundamental rights. It is, however, questionable what may be inferred from the mention of the principle of subsidiarity. After all, the principle of subsidiarity pursuant to Article I-9(3) of the DC (former Article 5 TEC) only governs the application of already existing competences, but not the allocation of new competences.[88] In the end, the only reasonable interpretation is[89] that the statement of Article II-111(2) of the DC shall only be emphasised, according to which the Charter neither creates new powers or tasks for the Community and the Union, nor changes the powers and tasks already set out in the treaties.[90]

26 The limitation of the Charter's application in Article II-111(1) of the DC to "the Member States only when they are **implementing Union law**" is misleading. At first glance, the wording might correspond with the case law of the European Court of Justice, according to which the Member States have to respect the fundamental rights of the Union where they restrict existing rights when implementing Union law.[91] It is clear that this includes indirect execution[92] and the implementation of Union law in the national law.[93] Moreover, the ECJ declared that the Member States are under obligation to observe the European fundamental rights when they act within the framework of exceptional provisions concerning the fundamental rights.[94] This extended scope of Union law is characterized by the formula of the Union law's area of application.[95] The differing interpretation of the terms "implementation" in accordance with Article II-111 of the DC and

---

87 Concerning the original version Stein (note 2) pp 1433 ff; Borowsky (note 54) Art 51, paras 18 ff.
88 Cf Calliess *Subsidiaritäts- und Solidaritätsprinzip in der EU* (2nd ed, Baden-Baden 1999) pp 62 ff.
89 Concerning further possibilities of understanding Stein (note 2) pp 1433 ff.
90 In the same way Borowsky (note 54) Art 51, paras 22 ff.
91 ECJ *Wachauf* [1989] ECR 2609; *Klensch* [1986] ECR 3477.
92 ECJ *Wachauf* [1989] ECR 2609; *Klensch* [1986] ECR 3477; *Bostock* [1994] ECR I-955; *Duff* [1996] ECR I-569, 610, para 29; *Graff* [1994] ECR I-3361, 3379, para 17; *Belgocodex* [1998] ECR I-8153, 8175, para 26; *Karlsson* [2000] ECR I-2737.
93 ECJ *Inquiries against X* [1996] ECR I-6609; Jürgensen/Schlünder (1996) 121 AöR 200, 208 ff.
94 ECJ *ERT* [1991] ECR I-2925; *Familiapress* [1997] ECR I-3689; Cirkel *Die Bindung der Mitgliedstaaten an die Gemeinschaftsgrundrechte* (Berlin 2005) pp 78 ff and 98 ff; Chwolik-Lanfermann *Grundrechtsschutz in der Europäischen Union* (Frankfurt aM 1994) pp 78; Kokott (1996) 121 AöR 599, 604; concerning possible conflicts Cremer [2003] NVwZ 1452.
95 ECJ *ERT* [1991] ECR I-2925, 2964, para 42; similar *Demirel* [1987] ECR 3719, 3754, para 28; *Grogan* [1991] ECR I-4685, 4741, para 31.

"application" of Community law in the case law of the ECJ may lead to difficulties in the area of European protection of fundamental rights. For if Article II-111 of the DC is not construed in view of the case law, as is advocated by some in the literature, legal acts of the Member States which limit fundamental freedoms would fall out of the target spectrum[96].

Although the unambiguous wording of Article II-111 of the DC, by means of using the word "only", points towards a restrictive interpretation qualifying the case law of the ECJ[97], on the other hand, it is to be considered that the case law of the ECJ in matters of fundamental rights was not supposed to immediately become obsolete due to the impact of the Charter of fundamental rights of the European Union. Above all, this is provided for by the protective clause set out in Article II-113 of the DC, which is geared towards a minimum standard based on the provisions of the ECHR and the constitutional traditions common to the Member States for the purpose of safeguarding the former level of protection in the area of application of Union law. Since the ECJ has developed its case law pertaining to the fundamental rights from these very sources[98], the protection of individual rights hitherto guaranteed by Union law is part of the minimum standard which in no case may be affected[99]. By interpreting Article II-111 of the DC while considering these requirements, it is to be concluded that fundamental rights shall be interpreted in view of the ECtHR's former case law, but without considering its choice of terms. This approach entails, however, that the fundamental rights are compulsory for the Member States in the context of the enforcement of exceptions to the fundamental freedoms.

Within the framework of an **indirect execution**[100] of Community law, the European fundamental rights completely replace the guarantees of fundamental rights. This applies mutatis mutandis in case of partially open provisions, so that no national fundamental rights shall be used for interpretation[101].

When **implementing Community law** in national law, only the community act of secondary law is to be measured against the European fundamental rights[102]. On the other hand, the national act of implementation is exclusively controlled by the Member States' com-

---

96 Likewise Cremer [2003] NVwZ 1452, 1453; similar Kingreen [2004] EuGRZ 570, 573; concerning the interpretation of Art 51 of the Charter of Fundamental Rights Borowsky (note 54) Art 51, para 29; Calliess [2001] EuZW 261, 266 ff.
97 Ranacher (2003) 58 ZöR 21, 98; concerning the genesis of Art II-51 DC Hirsch (note 48) pp 111, 116 ff; De Burca (2001) 26 ELRev 126, 136 ff; Grabenwarter [2001] DVBl 1, 3.
98 ECJ *Hauer* [1979] ECR 3727; *Internationale Handelsgesellschaft* [1970] ECR I-1125; *Nold* [1974] ECR 491; opinion AG Roemer, ECJ *Zuckerfabrik Schöppenstedt* [1971] ECR I-987, 990; opinion AG Roemer, ECJ *Werhahn* [1973] ECR I-1254, 1258, 1273; opinion AG Warner, ECJ *van de Roy* [1976] ECR I-352.
99 Likewise the Presidency of the Constitutional Convent CHARTE 4487/00, Convent 50 of 11 October 2000; adopting the Presidency of the Constitutional Convent CONV 828/1/03 REV 1 of 18 July 2003; in detail Grabenwarter [2004] EuGRZ 563; Ranacher (2003) 58 ZöR 21, 99; de Witte [2001] MJ 81, 85; Hummer *Der Status der "EU-Grundrechtecharta": politische Erklärung oder Kern einer europäischen Verfassung?* (Bonn 2002) pp 76 ff; Mahlmann [2000] ZEuS 419, 437; Vranes [2002] JBl 630, 635.
100 Concerning the term Jarass *Grundfragen der innerstaatlichen Bedeutung des EG-Rechts* (Cologne 1994) pp 97 ff; Magiera [1998] DÖV 173, 176.
101 ECJ *Bostock* [1994] ECR I-955, 16 ff; *Demirel* [1987] ECR 3719, 3754, para 28; apparently different Pernice [1990] NJW 2409, 2417 "double constitutional loyalty"; Wetter *Die Grundrechtscharta des Europäischen Gerichtshofes* (Frankfurt aM 1998) pp 94 ff.
102 ECJ *Hauer* [1979] ECR 3727; *Nold* [1974] ECR I-491, 507, paras 12 ff.

mitment to fundamental rights[103]. Insofar as the Union law determines the contents of an [act of] implementation, these will not be applicable[104]. If a secondary act is repealed by the ECJ, it loses its determining effect. As a result, national fundamental rights will become completely applicable again. Finally, insofar as valid secondary law allows for a certain leeway for construction, European fundamental rights will shine through[105].

30   An analysis of the case law reveals that the ECJ assumes a commitment to European fundamental rights in the enforcement of exceptions of the fundamental freedoms[106]. As a result, European fundamental rights combined with fundamental freedoms can influence the legal systems of the Member States. To be more precise, the fundamental rights can have an effect on the construction of the facts of a fundamental freedom[107] or its general limit to its restrictability[108] and are established in the Member States' legal systems via the fundamental freedoms. The implications of this implied triple commitment of national law to national and European fundamental rights as well as to the European fundamental freedoms are clear: The European fundamental rights have a radiating effect on the fundamental freedoms, which in turn limit national law. By means of the thus developed material situation, European fundamental rights, combined with fundamental freedoms, can reach far into the competences of the Member States. Metaphorically, one might call this a second layer of fundamental rights which is covering the Member States' level[109].

31   Due to the different **levels of fundamental rights**, there is certainly a danger of undermining the carefully balanced interlocking of Union and national law[110]. If fundamental

---

103 Ruffert [1995] EuGRZ 518, 523 with further references; Ruffert (note 51) Art 249 EGV, para 71; Jürgensen/Schlünder (1996) 121 AöR 200, 208, 213 ff; Hilf [1988] EuR 1; Kingreen/Störmer [1993] EuR 263, 281; Kingreen (note 4) Art 6 EUV, para 59; Störmer (1998) 123 AöR 541, 568; Schilling [2000] EuGRZ 3, 34 ff; Rengeling *Grundrechtsschutz in der Europäischen Gemeinschaft* (Munich 1993) pp 190 ff; different: Wetter (note 101) pp 94 ff; Szczekalla in: Rengeling (ed) *Handbuch des europäischen und deutschen Umweltrechts* (2nd ed, Cologne 2003) § 12 para 31; Temple Lang [1991/2] LIEI 23, 28 ff.
104 BVerfGE *Solange II* [1987] 3 CMLR 225, 339 ; BVerfG Maastricht [1994] 1 CMLR 57, 89, 155; BVerfG (2001) 102 BVerfGE 147; Ruffert [1995] EuGRZ 518, 523 ff; Sensburg [2001] NJW 1259; Lecheler [2001] JuS 120, 123; Limbach [2001] NJW 2913.
105 ECJ *Commission v Council* [1983] ECR 4063, para 15; *Klensch* [1986] ECR 3477, para 21; *Rauh* [1991] ECR I-1647, para 17; *Herbrink* [1994] ECR I-223; *Murphy* [1988] ECR 673, para 11.
106 Kadelbach/Petersen [2003] EuGRZ 693, 698; Weber [2003] DVBl 220, 223; different opinion Cremer [2003] NVwZ 1452, 1454; Mager [2004] EuR 41, 54.
107 ECJ *Keck* [1993] ECR I-6097; *Wurmser* [1989] ECR 1105, para 11; *Aragonesa* [1991] ECR I-4151, para 13; *Commission v Germany* [1989] ECR 229, para 16; Gellermann [2000] DVBl 509, 516; detailed Feiden *Die Bedeutung der „Keck"-Rechtsprechung im System der Grundfreiheiten* (Berlin 2003) pp 27 ff.
108 ECJ *Familiapress* [1997] ECR I-3689, para 27; similar *Carpenter* [2002] ECR I-6279, paras 40 ff; *Omega* [2004] ECR I-9609; on the criticism Mager [2003] JZ 204, 206; Kingreen/Störmer [1993] EuR 263, 281 ff; Cremer [2003] NVwZ 1452, 1453; Langenfeld/Zimmermann [1992] ZaöRV 259, 303; Kühling [1997] EuGRZ 296, 299 ff; Wetter (note 101) pp 85; concerning the consequences Ruffert [1995] EuGRZ 518, 528 ff; Coppel/O'Neill (1992) 29 CMLR 669, 678; Kingreen [2004] EuGRZ 570, 576.
109 Kingreen [2004] EuGRZ 570, 572.
110 Kanitz/Steinberg [2003] EuR 1013, 1025 ff; Kingreen [2004] EuGRZ 570, 573; Cremer [2003] NVwZ 1452, 1454; Cremer [2004] NVwZ 668, 669; Schorkopf (2004) 64 ZaöRV 125, 138.

freedoms are enriched with fundamental rights content[111], the ECJ, by means of an expansive understanding of European fundamental freedoms under the influence of fundamental rights, could take a dominant position within the general system of the protection of fundamental rights[112].

These tendencies would be further intensified in case the ECJ – as has happened in two cases so far – should combine obligations to protect fundamental freedoms with modifications of fundamental rights. Since in these cases, the Member States are obliged to act if the fundamental freedoms are restricted[113], they would have to enforce exceptions to the fundamental freedoms even if national guarantees of fundamental rights would actually prohibit an intervention[114]. Explicitly, there would be a danger of Member States' constitutions being modified under the influence of European fundamental rights[115]. It is questionable whether this line of development is compatible with the provisions of Article II-111(2) of the DC, which determines that no new competences and powers shall accrue due to the Charter of fundamental rights of the European Union.

IV. On the Legally Binding Nature of the Charter of Fundamental Rights of the European Union prior to the European Constitution Coming into Effect

Case 2 – Problem: (ECJ *BECTU* [2001] ECR I-4881)
BECTU is an English union with approximately 30 000 members which are [professionally] active in the area of broadcasting, TV, movie and entertainment. Its members are mostly employed on the basis of short-term contracts – often less than thirteen weeks with the same employer – so that a large number of members are not able to fulfil the requirements for a paid annual holiday set out in the applicable English working hours act. According to BECTU, the persons affected are denied the right to such a holiday as well as remuneration in its place for the simple reason that they, although working regularly, worked successively for several different employers. Therefore, BECTU is of the opinion that the working hours act is an incorrect implementation of Article 7 of Directive 93/104/EC of 23 November 1993 concerning certain aspects of the organisation of working time. This Directive grants the claim in dispute to any employee. Moreover, the minimum working time which was demanded by the working hours act was in objection to Article II-91(2) of the DC. The English court having jurisdiction refers these questions to the ECJ for a preliminary decision. What will be the opinion of the Advocate General?

The Charter of Fundamental Rights of the European Union cannot bind the ECJ – neither as a mere ceremonial declaration nor as an incorporated part of the European Constitution, which is not yet in effect. As the Charter was also not included besides the other **sources of fundamental rights** named in Article 6(2) of the TEU during the summit of Nice, the ECJ was not legally obliged to consider [the Charter] when interpreting fundamental

---

111 ECJ *Familiapress* [1997] ECR I-3689, para 27; *Carpenter* [2002] ECR I 6279, paras 40 ff; *Omega* [2004] ECR I-9609.
112 Concerning the corresponding tendencies Ruffert [2004] EuGRZ 466, 468; Mager [2003] JZ 202, 204, 207; Schorkopf (2004) 64 ZaöRV 125, 131 ff; *eg* for a broad point of departure ECJ *Läärä* [1999] ECR I-6067, paras 31, 35 and 36; *Zenatti* [1999] ECR I-7289, paras 29, 33 and 34.
113 ECJ *Commission v France* [1997] ECR I-6959, para 29; *Schmidberger* [2003] ECR I-5859.
114 Mager [2004] EuR 41, 46.
115 Schorkopf (2004) 64 ZaöRV 125, 138.

rights. This, however, does not prevent the ECJ from consulting the Charter of Fundamental Rights of the European Union to confirm or, respectively, clarify a result obtained in accordance with the former Article 6(2) of the TEU[116]. However, only the CFI[117] and several Advocates General have made use of this possibility[118]. This is supported by the fact that the Charter – despite the aforementioned deficiencies, in particular in spite of its contents which exceed the scope of its powers – predominantly formulates a catalogue of fundamental rights that – at least in its core and arranged by the ECHR, TEU and TEC, the ECJ's case law as well as other European agreements – already belongs to legally binding standard within the European protection of fundamental rights. Insofar, the rights contained in the Charter "only" represent a – unquestionably important – visualisation, confirmation and affirmation of applicable law. Moreover, the Charter, in its principal part, is designed to be legally applicable. This is confirmed especially by the aforementioned provisions of Article II-111 ff. DC which only make sense if the Charter is binding. Furthermore, in former cases the ECJ proceeded in a similar way when it referred to the declaration of fundamental rights of the Community institutions dated 1977[119] in its grounds, *eg* in the *Hauer* case.[120] The recent opinions of several Advocates General confirm these considerations.

Case 2 – Answer:

35 In view of the question concerning whether and when paid holiday is being granted pursuant to the Directive, which was admissibly referred to the ECJ in accordance with Article 234 of the TEC (Art III-369 DC), the Advocate General could refer to Article II-91(2) of the DC, which grants the right to a paid annual holiday to any employee. This confirms that a general right to a paid annual holiday exists in the EU. Referring to the fact that the Charter – apart from the European Council's ceremonial declaration in Nice – has also been approved by the European Parliament, Council and Commission and, partly, goes back to an express mandate of national parliaments, the Advocate General would have to emphasise that the Charter cannot be ignored in proceedings relevant to fundamental rights. Accordingly, Advocate General *Tizzano* explains:
"Even more important to me, however, seems the fact that this claim has been ceremonially declared in the Charter of Fundamental Rights of the European Union ... Indeed, the Charter of the Fundamental Rights of the European Union was not awarded ... any authentic normative effect, *ie* it is a mere formal [construction] without any independent binding effect. Even though no reference shall be made to the already commenced, thorough debate on the effects the Charter could develop in any case in other forms and ways, attention shall be drawn to the fact that it mostly contains determinations which clearly recognise rights already established elsewhere. Additionally, one can read in the preamble: This Charter confirms ... (these rights). Therefore I am of the opinion that in a legal dispute about the nature and scope of a fundamental right, the corresponding determinations in the Charter and, in particular, its obvious purpose to serve as a relevant standard, as far as their provisions allow, for all persons acting in the Community – Member States, bodies, natural and juristic

---

116 Affirming Grabenwarter [2001] DVBl 1, 11 ff.
117 *Eg* CFI *Gonnelli and AIFO v Commission* T-231/02 (order of 2 April 2004).
118 *Cf eg* opinion AG Tizzano, ECJ *Queen v Secretary of State* [2001] ECR I-4881, paras 26 ff; *in detail* Alber [2001] EuGRZ 349, who itemises all references (even those still unpublished) and comments them on pp 351 ff.
119 [1977] OJ C103, 1.
120 ECJ *Hauer* [1979] ECR 3727, para 15.

persons – cannot be ignored. In this regard, therefore, I am of the opinion that the Charter represents the most qualified and definite confirmation of the fact that the claim to be granted paid annual holiday is indeed a fundamental right."[121] In this way, Article II-91(2) of the DC confirms and supports the result obtained beforehand by construing the Directive. This confirming and supporting effect therefore constitutes a bridge to the indirect or, respectively, "soft" binding nature of the Charter of Fundamental Rights of the European Union. The ECJ, however, did not pay any attention to the Charter of the Fundamental Rights of the European Union in its relating judgments[122] – as in any other judgment issued so far[123].

In view of the citizen's **possibilities to legal protection** to enforce the fundamental rights granted by means of a binding Charter, it may not be ignored that a Community law equivalent of the constitutional complaint is not established by the TEC. Apart from the nullity suit pursuant to III-365(4) of the DC (former Article 230(4) TEC), citizens are therefore not granted the possibility to obtain legal protection directly from the ECJ. Article III-365(4) of the DC, however, requires either an individual and concrete decree within the meaning of Article I-32(1)(iv) of the DC (comparable to former decisions pursuant to Article 249(4) TEC), or that an individual person is directly and individually affected by a general and abstract legal act[124]. While the criterion of directness pursuant to Article III-365(4) of the DC has been adopted without any changes from Article 230(4) of the TEC and shall merely exclude persons who are only possibly affected[125], individuality can only be affirmed where the relevant legal act is of a decisive nature for the complainant[126]. Moreover, the case law of the ECJ, which is not uniform in terms of the subject matter and the right of action and therefore unclear as to its result, has mostly interpreted the prerequisites of the former Article 230(4) of the TEC restrictively so far.[127] Therefore, the courts of the Member States are awarded a particular protective function by acting as a "European judge" within the predominant Community law's scope of application, and as such bear responsibility for the application of the Union law in accordance with the Charter of Fundamental Rights. Apart from the preliminary ruling procedure pursuant to Article III-369 of the DC (former Article 234 TEC), they ensure the legal protection of the citizens in cooperation with the ECJ. In view of the uniform application of the Community law and the ECJ's monopoly on dismissal, at least the national court having final jurisdiction must refer to the ECJ questions relevant to Union law, which includes questions regarding the compatibility of a provision with the (binding) Charter of fundamental rights of the European Union. The efficiency of the protection of Fundamental Rights is admittedly called into question if a national court does not consider it necessary to refer a question of legal force (*Gültigkeitsfrage*) to the ECJ. According to

36

---

121 Opinion AG Tizzano, FCJ *Queen v Secretary of State* [2001] ECR I-4881, paras 26 ff.
122 ECJ *BECTU* [2001] ECR I-4881.
123 For this and concerning the possibilities of the ECJ so far Alber [2001] EuGRZ 349, 351 ff.
124 Cremer [2004] EuGRZ 577; Mayer [2004] DVBl 606.
125 Cremer in: Calliess/Ruffert (eds) *Kommentar des Vertrages über die Europäische Union und des Vertrages zur Gründung der Europäischen Union* (2nd ed, Neuwied 2002) Art 230 EGV, para 46.
126 Cremer (note 125) Art 230 EGV, paras 48 ff.
127 In detail Cremer (note 125) Art 230 EGV, paras 27 ff and 44 ff; concerning new decisions Calliess [2002] NJW 3577 ff.

German law, orders of reference can be enforced only if the limits of arbitrariness are exceeded in cases where the right to one's lawful judge is denied.[128] It is this situation which gives reason to think about a direct access to the ECJ in case of an infringement of fundamental rights from the Charter, such as, for example, in form of a fundamental rights complaint complementing Article III-365(4) of the DC.[129] This applies even more if one considers the close connection of efficiency between the material safeguarding of fundamental rights on the one hand and ways of enforcement on the other hand, which can only be provided by special forms of proceedings of the constitutional court.[130]

Case 1 – Answer (continued):

37　In view of the fact that the Charter of the Fundamental Rights of the European Union is still not legally binding, A can refer (as already clarified by the example in case 2) to Article II-63(1) of the DC only for confirmation or, respectively, support of a fundamental right already applicable within Union law in accordance with Art 6(2) of the TEU. Insofar, at first, the emphasis is placed on the fact that the ECtHR has derived a partial guarantee concerning the environment, including protection obligations of the state, from Article 8 of the ECHR.[131] The situation is more difficult regarding the Member States' constitutional law. The relevant partial guarantees of fundamental rights which protect the environment, primarily conveyed by means of an obligation to protect, are only to be found in the dogmatics of Germany[132], Austria[133] and – in a similar way, but making certain distinctions – France[134]. Even if partial guarantees of fundamental rights protecting the environment are only to be found in three Member States, this does not mean that these are excluded from EU law. After all, the concept of judging comparative law requires that a solution be sought which is ideal both for the structure and the aims of Union law.[135] The fact that guarantees of fundamental rights protecting the environment in their scope of protection fit into the structure and aims of the Union law is proved not only by the Community's objective of environmental protection in the former Articles 174(1) and (2) of the TEC (Art III-233 DC), according to which the environmental policy shall contribute to the "protection of the environment" and the "protection of human health" on a "high standard of protection"[136], but also by the state's obligation to protect the fundamental freedom developed by the ECJ

128　BVerfG (1988) 75 BVerfGE 223, 233 ff; critical von Danwitz [1993] NJW 1111, 1114; further de Witte (note 46) pp 859, 877, 889 ff.
129　Continuing in so far Reich [2000] ZRP 375, 377 ff, who proposes – as an alternative to a Charter of Fundamental Rights (*cf* pp 375, 378) for Art 6 TEU only – a supplementation of Art 230 TEC by a para 6 (the proposing of a phrasing on p 378).
130　Pernice [2000] DVBl 847, 858 ff; Tettinger [2000] NJW 1010, 1015 ff; Mahlmann [2000] ZEuS 419, 440 ff each with further references.
131　Likewise in Case 1 – Answer in the 1st part.
132　*Cf* Isensee in: Isensee/Kirchhof (eds) *Handbuch des Staatsrechts Bd V* (Heidelberg 1992) § 111, paras 86 ff; Calliess (note 20) 312 ff and 437 ff; Unruh *Zur Dogmatik der grundrechtlichen Schutzpflichten* (Berlin 1996).
133　*Cf* Feik in: Grabenwarter/Thienel (eds) *Kontinuität und Wandel der EMRK* (Kehl 1998) pp 205 ff with further references and with an elucidation of the orientation conditioned by constitutional law along the ECTR and the ECtHR's case law as well as the German Constitution; further Szczekalla in: Rengeling (eds) *Handbuch zum europäischen und deutschen Umweltrecht Bd I* (Cologne 1998) § 12, para 20 with further references.
134　Classen [1987] JöR 29, 30 ff; Ruffert (note 77) pp 52 ff.
135　Ress/Ukrow [1990] EuZW 499, 502 ff; Ruffert (note 77) pp 29 ff, 60 ff.
136　*Cf* Calliess (note 1) Art 174 EGV, paras 7 ff.

(at first for Article 28 TEC/Article III-153 DC)[137]. Against this backdrop, Article II-63(1) of the DC may be understood as a confirmation and support of a Union fundamental right, determined pursuant to Article 6(2) of the TEU, which grants A a right to state protection against emissions, including a relating right to information. Furthermore, the case would have to be within the area of application of the Charter of Fundamental Rights of European Union determined in Article II-112(1) of the DC. This is the case, because, in view of the applicable Directive 96/61/EC on integrated pollution prevention, (at least also) the "implementation of Union law" is in question. As a result of that, the Spanish court having jurisdiction in the present case is bound by Article II-63(1) of the DC. A, however, can only obtain legal protection in the context of the submission proceedings pursuant to Article 234 of the TEC (Article III-369 DC). A nullity suit pursuant to Article 230(4) of the TEC (Art III-365 DC) – such as a possible fundamental rights complaint – is out of the question since the infringement of a fundamental right does not result from a measure of the Community's organs, but from a state's measure.

Provided that the Charter gains binding nature as a part of the European Constitution, another basic problem will arise which in polemic terms could be described as[138] an "**inflation of the protection of fundamental rights**"[139]. This problem is best dealt with by means of a reasonable integration into the complex system of European protection of fundamental rights, consisting of national constitutional courts as well as the courts of Luxemburg and Strasbourg[140]. The inclusion of the Charter in the European constitutional law combined with the European Constitution will bring about clarity on the EU level. As a result, the ECJ and the European Court will obtain a normative basis for their case law. 38

At the same time, Article I-7(2) of the DC makes it clear that the Union intends to integrate itself into the Strasbourg system of protecting human rights by joining the ECHR[141]. Contrary to the former legal situation, when joining the ECHR failed due to the fact that the EU lacked legal personality[142], Article I-6 of the DC expressly declares that the Union now posses such a personality. Even the technical problems connected with the joining now seem to be solvable.[143] As a result, the Strasbourg court now stands prepared to solve individual "accidents" in the protection of fundamental rights not only on the national but also on Community level. The decision *Matthews*[144], in particular, proves that the ECtHR has already embarked on a new road. 39

---

137 ECJ *Commission v France* [1997] ECR I-6959, paras 32 ff; also Szczekalla [1998] DVBl 219, 221 ff.
138 Stein (note 2) pp 1425 ff, 1435 ff with reference to Weiler [2000] 6 ELJ 95.
139 Term *cf* Trechsel [1998] ZFuS 371.
140 *Cf* also Ress in: Haller (ed) *Staat und Recht – Festschrift für Günther Winkler* (Vienna 1997) pp 897 ff with further references.
141 Stein (note 2) pp 1435 ff.
142 ECJ *Opinion 2/94* [1996] ECR I-1759.
143 In detail Alber/Widmaier [2000] EuGRZ 497, 507 ff; Philippi [2000] ZEuS 97, 124 ff.
144 *Cf* at this point Bröhmer [1999] ZEuS 197; Ress [1999] ZEuS 219; interesting in this context is that the ECtHR did not reject the App Nr 566 72/00 (Senator-Lines) à limine, but instead delivered it to the 15 EU Member States (*cf* [2000] EuGRZ 334).

V. The European Agency for Fundamental Rights

40 To ensure the coherence and convergence of the European protection of fundamental rights, it seems to be reasonable against this backdrop to institutionally accompany and safeguard the further development of fundamental rights by means of a **European agency**. Therefore, the representatives of the Member States gathered in the European Council in Brussels, and passed a resolution on 12 and 13 December 2003, according to which the mandate of the European Monitoring Centre for Racism and Xenophobia is to be expanded and the centre is to be transformed into an agency for fundamental rights[145]. This new agency shall – according to the slightly vague wording – give both the Community bodies and the Member States the required means to enable them to create concepts and implement measures in order to fulfil their obligations to protect fundamental rights. The agency therefore shall be an interface which facilitates the contact between several participants in the area of fundamental rights, enables the development of synergies and promotes the dialogue between all parties involved. In view of the competences of other European bodies, in particular the ECJ and the ECtHR, it is not intended to establish a possibility to file complaints or petitions with the agency[146].

41 To date, however, no decision has been made as to the question whether the scope of action of the agency of fundamental rights only extends to the EU law's area of application within the meaning of Article II-111(1) of the DC or if, additionally, it shall prepare information and analysis about the compliance with values and fundamental principles of the state pursuant to Article I-2 of the DC[147]. From the perspective of a coherent system for the protection of fundamental rights, the second option has the advantage that the agency could intervene and give warning in preliminary stages of concrete infringements of fundamental rights to protect the values and principles set out in Article I-2 of the DC.

42 Likewise, no decision has yet been made as to the question whether the future scope of tasks of the Agency of fundamental rights shall be focused on certain Community measures or, respectively, policies of the Union, or if it rather shall follow in a more extensive sense the fundamental rights of the Charter of Fundamental Rights of the European Union[148]. In any case, when deciding on the areas of responsibility it should be considered that the principle of parallelism of the Community's competence and protection of fundamental rights has not been kept up strictly throughout the Charter of Fundamental Rights of the European Union. In case of a further area of responsibility it should therefore be avoided to have the agency of fundamental rights being active outside of the Union's competences. A proposal for a possible decree was (to be) provided in the year 2005[149].

---

145 Notification of the Commission through the Agency of Fundamental Rights of 25 October 2004, COM (2004) 693 final, 3.
146 COM (2004) 693 final, 4.
147 COM (2004) 693 final, 6.
148 COM (2004) 693 final, 8.
149 COM (2004) 693 final, 4.

VI. Prospect

Considering all of the above, it is to be concluded that the Charter of Fundamental Rights of the European Union is not actually unnecessary but – in exceeding its function to make the European fundamental rights visible to the citizens for the purpose of transparency and citizen-friendliness – closes a gap in applicable Union law which was no longer acceptable in view of the status of integration and in terms of the rule of law. In case, however, the Charter obtains a legally binding nature with the DC, as it is intended, deficits existing in the aforementioned areas could lead to problems and disputes between the EU and its Member States.

Part V: Citizenship Rights in Europe

§ 21
European Citizenship Rights*

Stefan Kadelbach

Leading cases: ECJ *Micheletti* [1992] ECR I-4239; *Martínez Sala* [1998] ECR I-2691; *Bickel and Franz* [1998] ECR I-7637; *Grzelczyk* [2001] ECR I-6193; *D'Hoop* [2002] ECR I-6191; *Baumbast* [2002] ECR I-7091; *Garcia Avello* [2003] ECR I-11613; *Collins* [2004] ECR I-2703; *Trojani* [2004] ECR I-7573; *Orfanopoulos and Oliveri* [2004] ECR I-5257; *Bidar* [2005] ECR I-2119; *Schempp* [2005] ECR I-6421.

Further reading: Weiler in: Weiler (ed) *The Constitution of Europe* (Cambridge 1999) pp 324–357; Kostakopoulou *Ideas, Norms and European Citizenship* (2005) 68 MLR 233–267; Szyszcak *Current Developments: European Union law – Citizenship and human rights* (2004) 53 ICLQ 493–501; von Bogdandy/Bitter in: Rodríguez Iglesias/Kadelbach/Gaitanides (eds) *Europa und seine Verfassung – Festschrift für Manfred Zuleeg* (Baden-Baden 2005) pp 309–322.

I. Introduction

Citizenship of the Union appears at the beginning of Part Two of the TEC, thus occupying a prominent position (Articles 17–22 TEC/Articles I-10 and III-123 to III-129 DC). **Two developments** find expression in Union citizenship. First, European integration, which had its origins in selected sectors of the economy and quickly turned into a comprehensive process of economic integration, has gone beyond its purely economic orientation.[1] Second, it had become necessary to expand the fundamental freedoms by supplementing them with fundamental human rights, because the Community has the power to take measures that directly interfere, or authorise to interfere, in subjective interests, as is particularly the case for agricultural law, customs regulation and competition law.[2]

Yet the **exercise of governmental power** in the Union requires not only the counterbalance of fundamental human rights, but also legitimacy through the citizens of the Union. If interventions in the economy for reasons of public interest and the distribution of all kinds of community subsidies are not to remain a concern of the governments, then there must be an active European citizenry. The preamble to the 1957 EEC Treaty already made reference to this, when it set "an ever closer union among the peoples of Europe" as an objective. Article 1(2) of the TEU (Article I-1(1) DC) suggests that this goal has not yet been achieved, as it states that decisions should be taken "as closely as possible to the citizen" in the "ever closer union among the peoples of Europe". In a democratic community, the citizens themselves, mediated by institutions and procedures, should stand behind

---

* The author owes thanks to Messrs Joseph Windsor and David Barthel for translation.
1 Even the EEC was a community not only of its Member States, but also of its citizens, *cf* ECJ *van Gend & Loos* [1963] ECR 3, 25; *EEA* [1991] ECR I-6079, para 21.
2 *Cf* in more detail Oppermann in: Hailbronner (ed) *Staat und Völkerrechtsordnung – Festschrift für Karl Doehring* (1989) pp 713, 722.

the decisions. Yet in the European Union, the key decisions are taken by the Member States' representatives, whose democratic legitimacy flows from their respective national parliaments. The European Parliament's powers are not comparable to those of a national representative assembly. While this situation may suffice from the perspective of constitutional law,[3] it is unsatisfactory from a civil society perspective. Citizenship of the Union should therefore help to bridge the gap that arises through this form of legitimacy and create another identity and loyalty, which complements national citizenship.[4] Article 2 point 3 of the TEU thus sets the "strengthen[ing of] the protection of the rights and interests of the nationals of its Member States through the introduction of a citizenship of the Union" as an objective of the Union. The new Treaty establishing a Constitution for Europe was explicitly prepared on behalf of the citizens and States of Europe (Article I-1(1) DC).

3 This chapter shall first retrace the path that has led the EC to Union citizenship (II.). Then the relationship to the precondition of Member State citizenship (Article 17(1)(ii) TEC/Article I-10(1)(i) DC) and the status of national citizenship shall be examined (III.). The individual rights of Union citizenship (IV.) can then better be assessed in their importance (V.).

II. Union Citizenship as a Matter of the European Union

1. From Market Citizen to Union Citizen

4 Union citizenship is the result of political initiatives, legislative activity and judicial development. It originated within a market society limited to economic freedoms. To the extent that the TEC, in its original form, provided certain classes of persons with rights, the beneficiaries were active participants in the economic process.[5] The legal positions created were tied to employment, goods and capital. Individuals were holders of rights – levelled against the Member States – as "**market citizens**".[6]

5 More comprehensive **civil rights** in the traditional sense began to develop at the end of the 60s, when liberty rights against the Community itself were created in order to counterbalance emerging Community powers.[7] At about the same time, Community legislation infiltrated the field of social rights. In particular as a result of the freedom of movement of workers, a comprehensive system of entitlements soon developed on the basis of secondary law, providing an equal legal status for workers from other Member States on a

---

3 Judgment of the *Bundesverfassungsgericht* (BVerfG – German Federal Constitutional Court) *Maastricht* [1994] 1 CMLR 57.
4 *Cf* Oppermann *Europarecht* (3rd ed, Munich 2005) § 4, para 53; Hilf in: Grabitz/Hilf (eds) *Das Recht der Europäischen Union* (27th instalment, Munich 2005) Art 17 EGV, para 1.
5 However, the Commission was already of the opinion in 1962 that individuals were not to be considered merely as "production factors", but rather as bearers of rights and freedoms, see [1962] OJ p 2118.
6 Ipsen/Nicolaysen [1964] NJW 339, 340; Ipsen *Europäisches Gemeinschaftsrecht* (Tübingen 1972) pp 187, 250 ff, 742–743; critical of the value of the rights of the "market citizen" from an economic perspective Nienhaus in: Hrbek (ed) *Bürger und Europa* (Baden-Baden 1994) pp 29 ff.
7 In 1969, the ECJ took the first step with ECJ *Stauder* [1969] ECR 419 and *Internationale Handelsgesellschaft* [1970] ECR 1125; on the protection of fundamental rights by the ECJ see Pernice [1990] NJW 2409; on the relationship between fundamental rights and citizenship of the Union see O'Leary (1995) 32 CMLRev 519.

non-discriminatory basis.[8] Typifying this process, European coordinating social legislation accords employees from EC Member States and their dependents equal access to social insurance benefits. European employment law is also counted among the social rights, as is the health protection legislation enacted in the fields of environmental law and consumer protection law, which, to a greater or lesser extent, were enacted as a consequence of the freedom of movement of goods.[9]

In the course of time, freedom of movement, residence and social rights lost their close connection to trade in goods and services. The obligation to include migrant workers in the host nation's social system, originally imposed to facilitate mobility, was detached from the requirement of an employment contract.[10] The prospects of **political participation** reveal another dimension of those rights, not motivated by the objective of the common market. For instance, Article 138(3) of the EEC Treaty (now Article 190(4) TEC/Article III-330(1) DC) guarantees political participation by mandating elections to the European Parliament by direct universal suffrage.

Therefore, the demand to combine these elements of civil, social and democratic rights of the citizens of Europe into a single, independent status was only logical.[11] Since the summit of the Heads of Government (intergovernmental conference) in The Hague in 1969, initiatives have been commenced with the goal of creating a **"Europe of citizens"** which fosters identity. This process included proposals by the Commission regarding the introduction of the rights to vote and stand for public office (*ie* electoral rights) at the municipal level,[12] a report presented in 1975 by the Belgian prime minister *Leo Tindemans* containing proposals for new individual rights,[13] the "Charter of Fundamental Rights" of the European Union, developed by the European Parliament,[14] the introduction of direct elections to the European Parliament[15] and the creation of a passport union with a standardised passport.[16]

New impulses came from the (draft) Treaty on European Union, under the leadership of *Altiero Spinelli*, which in 1984 introduced the concept of **citizenship of the Union** into the Community for the first time.[17] The European Council in Fontainebleau thereupon resolved to prepare community measures "to strengthen and promote its identity and its

---

8 Evans (1982) 45 MLR 496; Everling [1990] EuR Supp 1 pp 81 ff; O'Leary *The Evolving Concept of Community Citizenship* (The Hague 1996) pp 65 ff; Laubach *Bürgerrechte für Ausländer und Ausländerinnen in der Europäischen Union* (Baden-Baden 1998) pp 21 ff; Becker [1999] EuR 522; → § 9 paras 19 ff.
9 Reich *Bürgerrechte in der Europäischen Union* (Baden-Baden 1999) pp 207 ff, 262 ff, 391 ff; see also Arts 27–38 Charter of Fundamental Rights of the European Union [2001] OJ C364/1.
10 Evans (1984) 32 AJCL 679, 689 ff.
11 Grabitz *Europäisches Bürgerrecht* (Cologne 1970); *cf* also Tomuschat (1973) 33 ZaöRV 379; Randelzhofer in: Randelzhofer (ed) *Gedächtnisschrift Grabitz* (Munich 1995) pp 580 ff; see also Magiera [1987] DÖV 221; Magiera [1987] ZRP 331; Marias in: Marias (ed) *European Citizenship* (Maastricht 1994) pp 1, 3 ff.
12 Commission of the European Communities, Towards a Europe for Citizens, Bull EC 7–75, pp 5, 23 ff.
13 Bull EC Supplement 1–76, pp 29 ff.
14 [1975] OJ C179/30; *cf* Zuleeg in: von Münch (ed) *Staatsrecht – Völkerrecht – Europarecht – Festschrift Schlochauer* (Berlin 1981) pp 983 ff.
15 [1976] OJ L278/1; the first direct elections were held on this basis in 1979.
16 [1981] OJ C241/1, with later additions [1995] OJ C200/1.
17 [1984] OJ C77/33, Art 3.

image both for its citizens and for the rest of the world."[18] The *Adonnino* working group subsequently incorporated most of the rights which were later included as European Citizenship Rights of the TEC in its 1985 report.[19]

9   Above and beyond the area of political recommendations, European citizenship soon established itself as a **legal institution** which superseded market citizenship. In the case-law of the ECJ, tourists were recognised as within the scope of the so-called passive freedom of services. Students were entitled access to educational facilities and grants solely on the basis of the general prohibition on discrimination (now Article 12 TEC/Articles I-4(2) and III-123 DC).[20] The 1987 'Erasmus' Decision of the Council concerning student exchange was the first legal act to refer to a "Europe for citizens".[21] A short time later, the Commission propounded the first legislative proposals for municipal elections.[22] The Council enacted three Directives concerning the right of foreign residency for persons not gainfully employed.[23]

2. TEC Stipulations Relating to Union Citizenship

10   With the Treaty of Maastricht in 1992, Union citizenship was finally incorporated into **primary Community law**, not coincidentally simultaneously with the rechristening of the EEC as the European Community.[24] The Treaty of Amsterdam supplemented these provisions with the right of European citizens to information in their own language (Article 21(3) TEC/Articles I-10(2)(d) and III-128 DC).[25] With the Charter of Fundamental Rights of the European Union of 7 December 2000, which was also later incorporated into the Treaty establishing a Constitution for Europe as part II, Union citizenship was again expanded.[26]

---

18 Bull EC Supplement 7–85, p 5 (no 6).
19 Reports of the ad hoc Committee on a People's Europe to the European Council, Bull EC Supplement 7–85, pp 9 ff, 19 ff.
20 On tourism see ECJ *Luisi and Carbone* [1984] ECR 377, para 16; *Cowan* [1989] ECR 195, para 17; on vocational education see *Gravier* [1985] ECR 593, paras 19 ff; on "vocational citizens" see Oppermann in: Nicolaysen/Quaritsch (eds) *Lüneburger Symposion für Ipsen* (1988) pp 87, 91.
21 [1987] OJ L166/20; *cf* ECJ *Commission v Council* [1989] ECR 1425, para 29.
22 Bull EC Supplement 7–86; the proposed directive ([1988] OJ C246/3) was tabled due to the upcoming introduction of citizenship of the Union; *cf* in more detail Magiera [1988] EA 475; de Lobkowicz [1989] DÖV 519.
23 With respect to the right of residence for people who are not economically active Dir 90/364, [1990] OJ L180/26; for the right of residence for pensioners Dir 90/365, [1990] OJ L180/28; for the right of residence of students Dir 90/365, [1990] OJ L180/30 which was annulled by the ECJ for incorrect basis of jurisdiction (ECJ *Parliament v Council* [1992] ECR I-4193) and replaced by Dir 93/96, [1993] OJ L317/59; the legislative acts relating to residence have meanwhile been consolidated into one Dir, see Dir 2004/38 on the right of citizens of the Union and their family members to move and reside freely within the territory of the Member States, [2004] OJ L158/77, to be implemented by 30 April 2006.
24 An initiative of Spain marked the beginning, see Council document SN 3940/90 of 24 September 1990, *cf* in more detail Solbes Mira [1991] RMC 168; for historical documents see Laursen/Vanhoonacker (eds) *The Intergovernmental Conference on Political Union* (Maastricht 1992); see also Closa (1992) 29 CMLRev 1137, 1153 ff.
25 Arts 17–21 EC/Arts I-10, III-125 to III-129 DC correspond to what were Articles 8–8e of the Maastricht version.
26 Arts 39–46 of the Charter of Fundamental Rights, Arts II-99–106 DC.

At first glance, the provisions of the TEC on Union citizenship look like an unfinished mosaic. Article 17(2) of the TEC (Article I-10(1)(i) DC) sets nationality of a Member State as the only condition. The individual rights specified thereafter do not appear to have much to do with each other and seem to offer little that is new: freedom of movement (Article 18 TEC/Article I-10(2)(a) DC), the electoral rights in municipal and European Parliament elections in the Member Sate of residence (Article 19 TEC/Article I-10(2)(b) DC), diplomatic and consular protection (Article 20 TEC/ Article I-10(2)(c) DC) as well as the rights to petition and information (Article 21 TEC/Articles I-10(2)(d) and III-128 DC). In Articles 41 and 42 (Articles II-101 and II-102 DC) the Charter of Fundamental Rights adds the "right to good administration", developed by the ECJ, and the right to access to documents (Article 255 TEC/Articles II-102 and III-399 DC). **11**

The complete picture, however, only becomes clear in light of the interrelation of the EC Treaty's Articles on Union citizenship. Article 17(2) of the TEC (Article I-10(2)(i) DC) states that citizens of the Union shall enjoy "the rights conferred by this Treaty and shall be subject to the duties imposed thereby." Thus, European civil rights are not exhaustively specified in Articles 18 to 21 of the TEC (Articles I-10(2), III-125 to III-128 DC), but rather arise out of the totality of legal relations between the individual and the Community based on the Treaty.[27] The European Council had already emphasised in Rome in 1990 that European citizenship would have to include social and economic as well as civil rights.[28] These include not only the fundamental freedoms, but also fundamental human rights and the general prohibition on discrimination, regardless of whether or not they have their basis in the nationality of a Member State.[29] The rights granted under secondary law and the right to legal protection by a court of law define the status of Union citizenship even further.[30] It thus comprises a great number of rights guaranteed by the Treaty or secondary law in addition to rights developed by case-law. The special meaning of Articles 17–21 of the TEC (Article I-10 DC) lies in the fact that they specify the non-economic rights – the right of residence (Article 18 TEC/Article I-10(2)(a) DC), the right to participate in elections (Article 19 TEC/Article I-10(2)(b) DC) and the right to diplomatic and consular protection (Article 20 TEC/Article I-10(2)(c) DC) – which apply *exclusively* to Union citizens. **12**

The **provisions relating to Union citizenship**, which are to be found in Part Two of the Treaty, thus only set the framework of a comprehensively designed system of rights. The ECJ's jurisdiction did not yet extend to the subject matter of the second and third pillars (then Article L TEU, now amended as Article 46 TEU) when the Maastricht Treaty entered into force. Consequently, the fact that Union citizenship derives from the TEC and not, as with the fundamental human rights, from the TEU (Article 6 TEU/Articles I-2, I-5(1) DC), brings the rights associated with it under the jurisdiction of the ECJ. Union citizenship cannot be an intergovernmental concern. **13**

Its prominent place in the TEC, its importance for the identity of the Union and its objective of strengthening the rights of individuals all speak for the direct applicability of **14**

---

27 Haag in: von der Groeben/Schwarze (eds) *Vertrag über die Europäische Union und Vertrag zur Gründung der Europäischen Gemeinschaft – Kommentar* (6th ed, Baden-Baden 2004) Art 17 EGV, para 10.
28 Bull EC Supplement 2-91.
29 Third Commission Report on Citizenship of the Union, (2001) COM 506 final pp 2–3, 23 ff.
30 Everling [1992] ZfRV 241, 243 ff, 251 ff; Oppermann (note 4) § 4, para 54.

the rights set forth in Articles 18 to 21 of the TEC (Article I-10(2) DC).[31] Nonetheless, some of these provisions contain reservations (Articles 18(1), 19(1)(ii), 19(2)(ii) TEC/Articles I-10(2)(a) and I-10(2)(iii), Articles I-10(2)(b) and I-10(2)(iii) DC), empower the Council to enact legislation (Articles 18(2), 19(1)(ii), (2)(ii) TEC/Article III-126 DC) or contemplate further agreements between the Member States (Article 20(ii) TEC/Article I-10(2)(c) DC). It therefore remains to be seen whether the substantive rights are sufficiently safeguarded. In the final analysis, the answer depends on the interpretation of the individual guarantees.[32]

15   While **legal persons** cannot as such be bearers of European citizenship rights, just as it is not possible for them to be bearers of civil rights, specific rights can nevertheless be applied to legal persons of civil law *mutatis mutandis*, to the extent that they are suitable.[33] Thus, they are explicitly mentioned in the right to petition (Articles 21, 194, 195 TEC/Articles I-10(2)(d), III-334 and III-335 DC). Legal persons are, in light of the relevant practice under international law, of course entitled to consular and diplomatic protection (Article 20 TEC/Article I-10(2)(c) DC).[34]

16   Union citizenship is thus designed to be **comprehensive** and **open** for future changes.[35] It is flexible and subject to change, as is integration itself. Yet it has a firm core, as is evidenced by the exception of this area from closer cooperation (Article 11(1) TEC). It follows from Articles 19(1), (2) and 20(i) of the TEC (Article I-10(2)(b), (2)(c) DC) that equality of the Union's citizens is a fundamental principle. Agreements on closer cooperation necessarily lead to discriminations which are contradictory to the principle of equality.[36]

III. Nationality, National Citizenship and Citizenship of the Union

17   Article 17 of the TEC (Article I-10 DC) employs three different terms to describe the relationship of the individual to the public entity above him. According to Article 17(1)(ii) of the TEC (Article I-10(1)(i) DC), every person holding the *nationality* of a Member State is a *citizen of the Union*. Citizenship of the Union complements, but does not replace *national citizenship* (Article 17(1)(iii) TEC/Article I-10(1)(ii) DC). How, then, do Union citizenship, nationality and national citizenship interact?

---

31 Opinion AG La Pergola, ECJ *Martínez Sala* [1998] ECR I-2691, para 20.
32 Kluth in: Calliess/Ruffert (eds) *Kommentar des Vertrages über die Europäische Union und des Vertrages zur Gründung der Europäischen Gemeinschaft* (2nd ed, Neuwied 2002) Art 17 EGV, para 12.
33 Monar/Bieber *Die Unionsbürgerschaft* (Baden-Baden 1995) p 77.
34 Haag (note 27) Art 20 EGV, para 9; Kluth (note 32) Art 20 EGV, para 20; Szczekalla [1999] EuR 325–326; arguing in the contrary Monar/Bieber (note 33) p 36; Hilf (note 4) Art 20 EGV, para 8.
35 Pursuant to Art 22(1) TEC/Art III-129 DC the Commission shall report every three years on the developments; for 1993 see the First Report, (1993) COM 702 final; for the period 1994–96 see the Interim Report, (1997) COM 230 final; for the period 1997–2000 the Third Report (note 29); for the period 2001–2004 the Fourth Report, (2004) COM 695 final.
36 Kaufmann-Bühler in: Lenz/Borchardt (eds) *EU- und EG-Vertrag Kommentar* (3rd ed, Cologne 2003) Vorbem Art 17–22 EGV, para 4.

1. Nationality and National Citizenship

The concepts of "nationality" and (national) "citizenship" are related, but have different legal meanings.[37]

Nationality is described as a legal relationship which places the individual under the sovereign jurisdiction of a State. It can equally well be described as a feature or status of a person.[38] There is no substantive difference. What is decisive is that the concept of nationality describes the formal legal affiliation of a person with a State. It has a meaning under international and national law.

From the perspective of **international law**, nationals are those persons to whom the State is entitled to grant rights and upon whom it may impose obligations, irrespective of their place of residency. Furthermore, nationality is the basis for the State's right to exercise diplomatic and consular protection abroad and the duty to permit entry into its own territory. States have the power to regulate the conditions for the grant and loss of nationality as an expression of their sovereignty, but this power is subject to limits imposed by international law. Thus, provisions regarding nationality may not encroach on the sovereignty of other States over their own citizens. Furthermore, other States are not bound to recognise the attribution of nationality if it is merely formal, *ie* exists only *de jure*.[39] Thus, the legal status of nationality must correspond to a real social bond with a public entity. In light of this, nationality has the function of delimiting the scope of sovereignty between States and identifying an exclusive relationship between the individual and the State.

From the point of view of **national public law**, the meaning of nationality varies according to the respective constitution. It is not, of itself, bound to specific rights and duties.[40] While the *Grundgesetz* (German Basic Law) attaches a number of rights and duties to German nationality, this is but one of various conditions which must be met in order to trigger *eg* the right to vote (Article 38(2) Basic Law) or compulsory military service (Article 12a Basic Law).

In contrast, **(national) citizenship** is the embodiment of the rights and obligations which constitute a person's affiliation with a State and society.[41] It traces its origins back to the Enlightenment ideas of freedom, equality and brotherhood and implies civil, social and political rights. The so-called active status, the right to vote and to be elected, is the criterion of exclusion. Since time immemorial, a large part of the population has been excluded from political participation on the basis of age, education, gender, social class or,

---

37 In German law, a distinction is made between *Staatsbürgerschaft* and *Staatsangehörigkeit*; the English and French terms (citizenship/nationality and citoyenneté/nationalité respectively) do not wholly correspond, but are largely congruent, see Gosewinkel (1995) 21 Geschichte und Gesellschaft, 533, 544–545.
38 On the argument between the "status theory" and the "legal relationship theory" see Makarov *Allgemeine Lehren des Staatsangehörigkeitsrechts* (2nd ed, Stuttgart 1962) pp 21 ff; Kimminich in: Dolzer/Vogel/Grasshoff (eds) *Bonner Kommentar zum Grundgesetz* (Heidelberg 2003) Art 16, paras 4 ff.
39 ICJ *Liechtenstein v Guatemala (Nottebohm)* [1955] ICJ Reports 4, 23; see also ECJ *Commission v Belgium* [1980] ECR 3881, para 10: nationality as a relationship of special bond to the State, with reciprocal rights and duties.
40 *Cf* Randelzhofer in: Maunz/Dürig (eds) *Grundgesetz* (45th instalment Munich 2005) Art 16, para 9; Grawert (1984) 23 Der Staat 178, 182 ff.
41 Preuß (1995) 1 ELJ 267, 269 ff.

indeed, due to nationality. In the public communities of antiquity, as in the cities of the Middle Ages, political rights constituted the difference between citizenship and lesser forms of affiliation.[42] The Enlightenment and the French Revolution changed none of this.[43] In contrast, the important role played by social rights in the purely factual possibility of free development of personality only becomes clear retrospectively in the context of the industrial age, which brought new problems of social inequality with it. Against this background, social rights, in addition to political rights, become an essential element of citizenship.[44] Only the bearer of all freedoms and social and political rights is a citizen.

23   The connection between nationality and citizenship lies in the fact that **full citizenship** is reserved for nationals. This was more clearly seen in the 19th century than today. In Germany, even freedoms were bound to nationality after the 1848–49 revolution,[45] and the like holds true for social welfare.[46] Increasingly, however, not only freedoms, but also social welfare entitlements became separated from nationality and instead were made dependent on residency.[47] Political rights have been an exception. They still make up the decisive element for citizenship, as is evident from Article 33(1) and (3) of the Basic Law. The former stipulates that all Germans have the same political rights and duties, and the latter distinguishes between civil rights (*bürgerliche Rechte*) and political rights (*staatsbürgerliche Rechte*). The German Federal Constitutional Court also adheres to this tradition, when it assumes that the people, from whom all State authority must be derived (Article 20(2) of the Basic Law), must be the German people, comprising all German nationals.[48]

24   The concept of **citizenship of the Union** used in the TEC is not comparable to nationality, nor is it intended to be.[49] Instead, it intentionally orients itself towards the idea of citizenship. The implication is not an assertion of sovereignty over persons; rather, the Union conceives of individuals as bearers of rights and duties (Article 17(2) TEC/Article I-10(2)(1) DC). The political rights of participation held against the Community (Articles 19(2), 21 TEC/Articles I-10(2)(b), I-10(2)(d), III-128 DC) form the basis of a legal position which is similar to the status of active citizenship. How far this parallel goes has to be seen in light of the specific rights (see IV. below).

---

42 Eder in: Molho/Raaflaub/Emlen (eds) *City-States in Classical Antiquity and Medieval Italy* (Stuttgart 1991) pp 169 ff; Isenmann *Die deutsche Stadt im Spätmittelalter 1250–1500* (Stuttgart 1988) pp 93 ff.
43 Lamoureux in: Colas/Emeri/Zylberberg (eds) *Citoyenneté et nationalité* (Paris 1991) pp 55 ff; Brubaker *Citizenship and Nationhood in France and Germany* (Cambridge 1992) pp 21 ff.
44 Marshall *Citizenship and Social Class* (Cambridge 1950); Dahrendorf in: van Steenbergen (ed) *The Condition of Citizenship* (Cambridge 1994) pp 10, 13.
45 Oestreich *Geschichte der Menschenrechte und Grundfreiheiten im Umriss* (2nd ed, Berlin 1978) pp 81 ff; Grawert *Staat und Staatsangehörigkeit* (Berlin 1973) pp 195–196; even today the civil rights pursuant to Art 8, Art 9(1), Art 11 and Art 12(1) Basic Law are granted only to Germans.
46 Fahrmeir (1997) 40 The Historical Journal 721, 726 ff.
47 Noiriel *Le creuset français* (Paris 1988) pp 110 ff; Hollifield *Immigrants, Markets and States* (Cambridge 1992) pp 223 ff.
48 BVerfG (1991) 83 BVerfGE 37, 59.
49 *Cf* Hobe (1993) 32 Der Staat 245; Closa (1995) 32 CMLRev 487, 488 ff, 515 ff.

2. Nationality as a Condition for Citizenship of the Union

Case 1 – Problem: (ECJ *Micheletti* [1992] ECR I-4239)
M was born in Argentina, the son of Italian parents. M has both Italian as well as Argentine nationality. After successfully completing dentistry studies in Argentina, he wished to establish himself as a dentist in Spain and, to this end, submitted his Italian passport. The Spanish authorities recognised the diploma on the basis of a Treaty between Spain and Argentina. However, they rejected the application to establish a practice on the basis of Article 9 of the *Codigo Civil*. Pursuant thereto, in the case of dual citizenship, where neither citizenship is Spanish, priority shall be given to that citizenship where the person had his habitual residence before his entry into Spain. In the case of M, this meant that priority was given to the Argentine citizenship. M took legal action. The competent court, the Tribunal Superior de Justicia de Cantabria, submitted the question to the ECJ, asking whether the provisions of the TEC relating to citizenship are consistent with provisions of national law which deprive nationals of Member States rights granted on the basis of the Treaty, solely on the grounds that the person in question also has the nationality of a third State and had heretofore been a resident thereof.

25

Article 17(1)(ii) of the TEC (Article I-10(1)(i) DC) stipulates that every person who holds the **nationality** of a Member State shall be a **citizen of the Union**. Terms which are used in the TEC are, as a rule, to be interpreted in their specific meaning under Community law, ie are to be construed autonomously. This can even be the case where a legal term refers to something which falls within the regulatory scope of a Member State, as with the term "*public policy*" within the meaning of Articles 30, 39(3), 46 of the TEC (Articles III-154, III-133 III, III-140 DC). Thus, Article 17(1)(ii) of the TEC (Article I-10(1)(i) DC) could also have a specific meaning under Community law with respect to the term *citizenship*, which would have to be interpreted in light of the effective exercise of the rights of Union citizenship, in particular the fundamental freedoms. The historical context and the placement of Article 17(1)(ii) of the TEC (Article I-10(1)(i) DC) in the Treaty, however, speak against this reading.

26

Even before the Treaty of Maastricht entered into force, some of the Member States reserved the exclusive power to regulate citizenship. On ratifying the Treaty of Rome, Germany declared that Article 116 of the Basic Law – the constitutional provision which governs who holds German nationality – was also applicable for the purposes of Community law.[50] Great Britain also is exceptional, as it distinguishes between nationality in a narrower sense and membership in the Commonwealth. In a unilateral declaration on acceding to the EC in 1972, Great Britain defined the term *British subject* for the purposes of Community law differently than for the purposes of national and international law. Thus, a citizen of the Union is now whoever is a British subject, possesses an unrestricted right of residency or holds citizenship on the grounds of a relationship to Gibraltar.[51]

27

The "Declaration on nationality of a Member State", which was attached to the Final Act of the Treaty of Maastricht, later stipulated that wherever the TEC refers to nationals of the Member States, the question of whether an individual possesses the nationality of a Member State shall be settled solely by reference to the national law of the Member

28

---

50 [1957] BGBl II-764.
51 [1972] OJ L73/196; [1973] C64/10; [1983] C23/1; the declaration is consistent with Community law, see ECJ *Kaur* [2001] ECR I-1237.

State concerned.[52] Therefore, the Member States have sole authority to set the conditions for nationality and the loss thereof.[53] Thus, the totality of Member State provisions on nationality defines who is a citizen of the Union.

29 As a result of this **distribution of authority**, Union citizenship can be more easily acquired in some Member States than in others. This can be particularly unfortunate where it leads to unequal duties in different Member States.[54] The individual national models and the practice of naturalisation vary significantly. Demands, especially by the European Parliament, to harmonise certain conditions for the acquisition and loss of nationality[55] do not have any political chance for success in the foreseeable future. Waiving the authority to define autonomously who is a national would decisively change the quality of the Member States and the status of the Union. However, all Member States are subject to the obligation of loyal cooperation (Article 10 TEC/Article I-5(2) DC) in this area as well. This obligation prohibits making naturalisation as simple as to render a common immigration policy (see Article 63 TEC) practically impossible or to significantly obstruct it.[56]

30 Nationality and Union citizenship are inseparable pursuant to Article 17(1)(ii) of the TEC (Article I-10(1)(i) DC). **Foreign nationals of third States** or **stateless persons** are not able to acquire Union citizenship independently.[57] Consequently, the concept of Union citizenship, for the time being, does not incorporate the philosophical idea that citizens of a public entity are those who desire to live within a common political and legal order.[58] Nor can citizenship of the Union be waived without at the same time forfeiting one's nationality.[59]

Case 1 – Answer

31 The Spanish court's preliminary reference to the ECJ for its interpretation is unquestionably admissible pursuant to Article 234(1) of the TEC (Article III-369(a) DC). Pursuant to Article 43 of the TEC (Article III-137 DC), M can assert his right to establishment if he is a national of a Member State. Pursuant to the declaration on Article 17(2)(ii) of the TEC (Article I-10(1)(i) DC), it is not Community law, but rather national law, which governs. Thus, M holds the nationality of a Member State if he has effectively acquired Italian nationality. Of this there is no question; in particular, the circumstance that M also holds Argen-

---

52 Final Act of the Treaty on European Union (on nationality of a Member State), Part III 2nd Declaration; see also Conclusions of the European Council in Edinburgh, Bull EC 12–92, pp 26 ff.
53 ECJ *Micheletti* [1992] ECR I-4239, paras 10, 14; O'Leary (1992) 12 YEL 353, 364 ff; Jessurun d'Oliveira (1993) 30 CMLRev 623; Ruzié (1993) 97 RGDIP 107.
54 For details on the case involving a Spanish/Argentine dual national who desired to establish himself in Italy see de Groot in: Coen (ed) *Europa '93 auf dem Weg zur Europäischen Union. Festschrift Albert Bleckmann* (Herne 1993) pp 87, 94–95.
55 European Parliament, [1991] OJ C326/205; see also de Groot *Staatsangehörigkeit im Wandel* (Cologne 1989) pp 23 ff; O'Leary (1992) 12 YEL 353, 383–384; Sauerwald *Die Unionsbürgerschaft und das Staatsangehörigkeitsrecht in den Mitgliedstaaten der Europäischen Union* (Frankfurt aM 1996) pp 120 ff, 156 ff.
56 Hatje in: Schwarze (ed) *EU-Kommentar* (Baden-Baden 2000) Art 17 EGV, para 4; naturalisation of immigrants is a matter of common concern of the EU institutions, see the Communication of the Commission with respect to immigration, integration and employment, COM (2003) 336 final.
57 Commission, Third Report (note 29) p 8 note 4.
58 *Cf* Meehan *Citizenship and the European Community* (London 1993) pp 123 ff; Habermas in: van Steenbergen (ed) *The Condition of Citizenship* (Cambridge 1994) pp 20, 23; Closa (1995) 32 CMLRev 487, 488 ff, 507 ff.
59 *Bayerischer Verwaltungsgerichtshof* (Bavarian High Administrative Court) [1999] NVwZ 197.

tine nationality in accordance with the principle of *jus soli* is not problematic. He therefore has dual nationality. However, pursuant to the principles of general public international law, Spain may be entitled not to recognise his Italian citizenship as effective. International law stipulates that a genuine, real connection must exist between the State and the individual. One may question this in the case of M, since M has never lived in Italy. These rules of customary international law are superseded by the TEC's more specialised provisions, which are limited to the legal order of the Union. The Declaration on the Treaty of Maastricht, according to which Member State law alone governs, expresses the Union States' reciprocal recognition, without reservation, of law on nationality. Therefore Spain may not fail to recognise Italian citizenship in derogation of Italian law, unless Italian law makes an orderly immigration policy impossible. There is no evidence of this. Spain must therefore grant M the right to establish a dental practice.[60]

This decision has a number of consequences for the treatment of **persons with multiple nationalities**.[61] It is clear that M cannot be denied the right to establishment nor any of the other rights contingent upon citizenship of the Union in Germany. But the question remains, how persons holding nationality in two Member States are to be treated. Since all rights pursuant to the TEC arise from citizenship in a Member State, such persons may not be discriminated against as nationals, for example, where the fundamental freedoms more greatly benefit foreign nationals of the Union. Thus, so-called domestic discrimination is exceptionally *im*permissible here, even when the other EU nationality is not effective.[62] Dual nationals who hold the nationality of a Union State and a third country have a similar status, provided a treaty between the Community and the third State grants rights corresponding to the fundamental freedoms. This is the case with the Member States of the European Economic Area and Turkey.[63]

32

3. Citizenship of the Union as a Complement to National Citizenship

Citizenship of the Union is contingent on citizenship of a Member State of the Union. Union citizenship within the Union is to fulfil a role parallel to national citizenship in the Member States. Union citizenship does not compete with national citizenship, but rather is intended to **complement** it (Article 17(1)(iii) TEC/Article I-10(1)(ii) DC). Thus, Union citizenship is meant "to give the effect of multiple levels".[64] The question therefore arises as to who the addressee of the rights of Union citizenship actually is.

33

---

60 The answer reflects the current legal situation.
61 *Cf* in detail Zimmermann [1995] EuR 54, 64 ff.
62 On being a national of an EU Member State as a substantive condition ECJ *Matteucci* [1988] ECR 5589; for a case concerning German/French nationality ECJ *Gullung* [1988] ECR 1, paras 11 ff; in general Wölker in: Groeben/Schwarze (eds) *Vertrag über die Europäische Union und Vertrag zur Gründung der Europäischen Gemeinschaft – Kommentar* (6th ed, Baden-Baden 2004) Vorbem Art 39–41 EGV, paras 46 ff; on domestic discrimination see below notes 66, 78, 163.
63 *Cf* in more detail Arts 28, 31 and 36 of the EEA Treaty; a Treaty with Switzerland on free movement, [2002] OJ L114/6, entered into force 1 July 2002; on privileged status of Turkish citizens ECJ *Sürül* [1999] ECR I-2685; on the right of establishment of Polish, Bulgarian and Czech nationals pursuant to the transitional provisions prior to accession see ECJ *Gloszczuk* [2001] ECR I-6369, paras 30 ff, *Kondova* [2001] ECR I-6427, paras 30 ff and *Barkoci and Malik* [2001] ECR I-6557, paras 30 ff.
64 Commission, Third Report (note 29) p 8; a key feature of Union citizenship is thus its being "additional", see Closa (1992) 29 CMLRev 1137; O'Keefe in: O'Keefe/Twomey (eds) *Legal Issues*

34 The first addressee is the **Union**, in particular where it acts within the so-called first pillar, the Community. The goal of a clearer definition of the individual's legal status finds expression in the rights relating to European elections, petition, information and access to documents (Articles 19, 21, 255 TEC/Articles I-10(2)(b), I-10(2)(d), III-128, III-399 DC). Thus, in relation to the Union, describing citizenship of the Union as a legal relationship or legal status is unproblematic.[65]

35 Furthermore, the **Member States** are also addressees of most of the obligations arising out of Union citizenship. This applies to the freedom of movement (Article 18 TEC/ Article I-10(2)(a) DC), electoral rights in municipal elections (Article 19(1) TEC/Article I-10(2)(b) DC) and diplomatic and consular protection (Article 20 TEC/Article I-10(2)(c) DC). The right to stand as a candidate for the European Parliament (Article 19(2) TEC/Article I-10(2)(b) DC) also requires the respective Member State's cooperation. According to their wording, these rights are addressed to the receiving Member State where the national of another Member State resides or is seeking residence. Moreover, the question arises as to whether Union citizenship imposes obligations on a Member State regarding its own nationals. True to its case-law on so-called domestic discrimination, the ECJ has so far rejected extending European citizenship rights to a Member State's own nationals, instead permitting stricter regulation.[66] This question arises, however, only in relation to the freedom of movement and the general prohibition on discrimination (Articles 18 and 12 TEC/Articles I-10(2)(a), Art I-4(2), III-123 DC). The other rights are, according to their wording and purpose, addressed not to the home State but either to other States (Articles 19(1), (2), 20 TEC/ Articles I-10(2)(b), I-10(2)(c) DC) or only to the Union (Articles 21, 255 TEC/Articles I-10(2)(d), III-128, III-399 DC). The problem will therefore be revisited below in connection with the respective rights.

36 Union citizenship therefore creates a **special status for the individual** *vis-à-vis* the Union and at the same time the Member States, complementing national citizenship. The nature of this status will now be described.

IV. European Citizenship Rights

1. Freedom of Movement

a) Legal Scope

37 The right of Union citizens pursuant to Article 18 of the TEC (Article I-10(2)(a) DC) to move and reside freely within the territory of the other Member States is central to the status of Union citizenship, because it is the precondition for all the other rights. The importance of Article 18 of the TEC (Article I-10(2)(a) DC) lies in its expansion of individual rights with economic aims into a general right to move freely within Europe, without the requirement of a specific justification. The **fundamental freedoms** are thus the more specialised guarantees with respect to the freedom of movement, because, above and

---

of the Maastricht Treaty (London 1994) pp 87, 102–103; Hailbronner/Renner *Staatsangehörigkeitsrecht* (2nd ed, Munich 1998) introduction para 50, for parallels to the *Indigenat* in 19th century Germany; similarly Hobe (1993) 32 Der Staat 245, 258–259.

65 Kluth (note 32) Art 17 EGV, para 6; similarly Kaufmann-Bühler (note 36) Vorbem Art 17–22 EGV, para 3.

66 ECJ *Uecker* [1997] ECR I-3171, para 23; for an opposing view see O'Leary (1995) 32 CMLRev 519, 528–529; Borchardt [2000] NJW 2057, 2059; Toner (2000) 7 Maastr JECL 158, 169–170; see also above note 62 and below notes 78, 163.

beyond the right provided by Article 18 of the TEC (Article I-10(2)(a) DC), they grant the right to economic participation.[67] In contrast, the **prohibition on discrimination** set forth in Article 12 of the TEC (Articles I-4(2), III-123 DC) is, as a more general provision, subsidiary to the freedom of movement. As will be seen, it can, however, in conjunction with Article 18 of the TEC (Article I-10(2)(a) DC), give rise to a comprehensive entitlement.[68]

According to the ECJ's case-law, Article 18 of the TEC (Article I-10(2)(a) DC) is **directly applicable**.[69] The fact that Article 18 of the TEC (Article I-10(2)(a) DC) only grants the rights to free movement "subject to the limitations and restrictions laid down in this Treaty and by the measures adopted to give it effect" appears to speak against this interpretation. However, this case-law is in line with the van *Gend en Loos* rationale; accordingly, if a provision of primary law is to be directly applicable, it must be clearly formulated, unconditional and not require an act of transformation.[70] The wording of Article 18 of the TEC (Article I-10(2)(a) DC) grants everyone "the right" to move freely. If the restrictions are contained in "this Treaty" itself, then it follows that the right itself is also guaranteed by the Treaty. A systematic comparison with other provisions reveals a difference from Article 19 of the TEC (Article I-10(2)(b) DC). Article 19 of the TEC (Article I-10(2)(b) DC and III-126 DC) grants electoral rights subject to detailed arrangements to be adopted at a later time. In contrast, pursuant to Article 18(2) of the TEC (Article I-10(2)(a) DC), the Council "may" adopt provisions to facilitate the rights specified in Article 18(1) of the TEC (Article I-10(2)(a) DC), but is not required to do so, which would not make sense if the provision were not directly applicable. Furthermore, the Treaty objective of extending the civil rights of the citizens, which also finds expression in the charge to the Council to adopt measures to facilitate the exercise of the freedom of movement (Article 18(2) TEC/Article I-10(2)(a) DC), speaks rather for than against direct applicability.

38

Rights contained for a long time in secondary Community law are thus raised to the level of the EC Treaty and have become a **fundamental right**,[71] the exercise of which, however, is regulated in greater detail by secondary law. Above all, constitutional policy motivates this legislative technique. Substantively the scope of protection of Article 18 of the TEC (Article I-10(2)(a) DC) coincides with the still valid provisions that existed before the Maastricht Treaty entered into force in 1993. Thus, university students admitted to a foreign educational institution also have a right to reside for the duration of their course of study.[72] However, the provisions of secondary law must be interpreted in light of the objectives of Article 18 of the TEC (Article I-10(2)(a) DC), since this is now on a higher level.

39

---

67 *Cf* in more detail ECJ *Skanavi* [1996] ECR I-929, para 22.
68 This is similar to German law, where entitlements are derived from civil rights contained in the Basic Law, such as the freedom of profession, in conjunction with the principle of equality and the social welfare clause contained in Article 20 of the Basic Law, *cf* Jarass/Pieroth (eds) *Grundgesetz* (8th ed, Munich 2006) Art 12 paras 59–60, 66 ff.
69 ECJ *Baumbast* [2002] ECR I-7091, para 84; see also Pernice in: Colneric et al (eds) *Une communauté de droit – Festschrift Gil Carlos Rodríguez Iglesias* (Berlin 2003) pp 177, 187; Magiera in: Streinz (ed) *EUV/EGV* (Munich 2003) Art 18, para 11; arguing against direct effect Pechstein/Bunk [1997] EuGRZ 547.
70 Established case-law since ECJ *van Gend & Loos* [1963] ECR 3, 25–26.
71 See also Art 44 of the Charter of Fundamental Rights of the European Union.
72 ECJ *Raulin* [1992] ECR I-1027.

b) Scope of Protection

40 Only **Union citizens** hold the fundamental right of free movement. Family members, who are nationals of third States, which are not privileged States pursuant to a Community treaty, have a right to freedom of movement and residency pursuant only to secondary law.[73] The right to move freely is addressed against the Member States. In this regard, the question of whether the Union citizen's own State can be the addressee of claims becomes even more urgent than before.[74] It becomes relevant to the extent that the freedom of movement of nationals is more restricted under domestic law than would be permissible for nationals of other Member States.[75] Nationals enjoy the protection of the personal fundamental freedoms against their own State only if they are prevented from travelling to the territory of another Member State.[76] Purely domestic cases which do not contain a cross-border element, on the other hand, do not fall within the scope of protection.[77] It would be hierarchically contradictory, were the subsidiary safeguard, Article 18 of the TEC (Article I-10(2)(a) DC), to afford greater protection. Thus, the nature of Article 18 of the TEC (Article I-10(2)(a) DC) as a fundamental human right does not add anything to the legal situation. Yet one should speak of a fundamental human right only if all the Union's citizens within the scope of Community law are equally entitled to the right. However, even after the introduction of the current Article 18 of the TEC (Article I-10(2)(a) DC), the ECJ has held fast to its case-law.[78] Consequently, the complete scope of the right to freedom of movement emerges only in conjunction with the relevant national law.[79] However, Member States may not restrict the freedom of movement of their nationals if they desire to cross national borders within the Union.[80]

41 Thus, the **subject matter of protection** includes the exit of one and entry into another Member State as well as movement, residency and temporary stays. To this extent, Article 18 of the TEC (Article I-10(2)(a) DC) contains a prohibition on restrictions. This right may not be subject to any substantive or time-related restrictions; in particular, restrictions for only non-nationals are prohibited. As a prohibition on discrimination, Article 18 of the TEC (Article I-10(2)(a) DC) also operates as a protective right against the State. But identity checks remain permissible under national law in order to ensure that the per-

---

[73] Art 45(2) of the Charter of Fundamental Rights of the European Union.
[74] Kluth (note 32) Art 18 EGV, para 8; Hatje (note 56) Art 18 EGV, para 6; Borchardt [2000] NJW 2057, 2059; sceptical Everling in: Hrbek (ed) *Bürger und Europa* (Baden-Baden 1994) pp 49, 52, 56.
[75] On travelling restrictions for members of *Sinn Fein* in British case-law see Toner (2000) 7 Maastr JECL 158, 161.
[76] ECJ *Singh* [1992] ECR I-4265, para 19.
[77] *Cf* in more detail ECJ *Saunders* [1979] ECR 1129, para 11; *Werner* [1993] ECR I-429, para 17.
[78] ECJ *Uecker* [1997] ECR I-3171, para 23.
[79] Constitutions which grant the freedom of movement usually reserve this right for their own nationals, see Art 11(1) German Basic Law; Art 5(4) of the Greek, Art 16 of the Italian, Art 44 of the Portuguese and Art 19 of the Spanish constitutions; section 44(2) of the Danish constitution makes a reservation relating to the acquisition of real property by foreigners, which is permitted in accordance with a protocol to the Treaty. In Belgium, Ireland, Luxemburg, the Netherlands and Sweden, the freedom of movement within the respective country is not guaranteed by the constitution. Only section 7 of the Finnish constitution expressly requires equal treatment of nationals and foreigners who legally reside in Finland.
[80] ECJ *Elsen* [2000] ECR I-10409, paras 34–35.

son claiming the right actually bears it.[81] Foreigners may be required to furnish proof of legal residency, provided nationals have a similar duty to prove their identity.[82]

Furthermore, the right to freedom of movement in conjunction with Article 12 of the TEC (Articles I-4(2), III-123 DC) forms the basis of a broad **claim to non-discriminatory treatment of non-nationals**, which can also establish a derivative right to benefits.[83] The potential scope can hardly be estimated. Some commentators propose a substantive restriction, such that there must be a connection to the right to reside.[84] Thus, EU foreigners may not be discriminated against, for example, in the acquisition of real property, be it an industrial facility or a holiday residence, unless otherwise provided for in the Treaties or the Acts of Accession. However, there is no bright line to be drawn between measures relating to residency and measures relating to other subject matters.

The scope of protection is intended to be **comprehensive**. It is limited only by the conditions in Article 18(1) of the TEC (Article I-10(2)(a) DC). The implicit restrictions on the objective elements include above all the requirements to prove adequate means of support and adequate health insurance, both of which are permissible under secondary law.[85] It follows that secondary law and the related case-law still govern the circumstances under which the national of another EU State who does not find employment or has become unemployed may be deported.[86] The same applies to tourists who for whatever reason run out of money. In neither case does Article 18 of the TEC (Article I-10(2)(a) DC) foresee an expansion of the legal status.

42

43

c) Interferences and Restrictions

The same analysis of conceivable interferences applies to the **personal freedoms** as well. They may take the form of restrictions, in particular measures related to rights of entry and residence, but may also appear in the form of discrimination, which arises when foreign EU nationals or a Member State's own nationals cross an internal border.

44

The right to reside and the freedom of movement may only be infringed if the TEC or secondary law so provides. As with the fundamental freedoms, they can be restricted primarily for **purposes of public policy**. Thus, conviction for a crime, for instance, may lead to the termination of the right to residency; of course, this is subject to strict conditions, as is the case with restrictions on the free movement of workers, the freedom of establishment or the freedom to provide services. As with the fundamental freedoms, the principle of proportionality must be observed. The crimes must be of a certain gravity and the infringement on the freedom of movement must remain reasonable.[87]

45

---

81 ECJ *Wijsenbeek* [1999] ECR I-6207.
82 ECJ *Commission v Germany* [1998] ECR I-2133.
83 *Cf* in more detail ECJ *Martinez Sala* [1998] ECR I-2691, paras 32, 82.
84 Kluth (note 32) Art 18 EGV, para 5; in contrast Hilf (note 4) Art 18 EGV, para 7.
85 For details see Art 7 of the new freedom of movement directive Dir 2004/38/EC (note 23).
86 On the largely unsettled question of the status of those seeking employment see Randelzhofer/Forsthoff in: Grabitz/Hilf (eds) *Das Recht der Europäischen Union* (27th instalment, Munich 2005) Art 39 EGV, paras 54 ff, 134 ff.
87 *Cf* the case of an Italian tourist who was barred from entering Greece for life upon a conviction for possession of illegal narcotics, ECJ *Calfa* [1999] ECR I-11, paras 15 ff; the judgement was grounded solely on the impossibility of a future exercise of the fundamental freedoms, without mentioning the freedom of movement of the citizens of the Union; critical of the judgement

46 **Measures under secondary community law** which relate to the regulation of the freedom of movement will have to be based on Article 18(2) of the TEC (Article I-10(2)(a) DC) to a large degree in the future. However, Article 18(2) of the TEC (Article I-10(2)(a) DC) may not lead to further restrictions, but may only facilitate the freedom of movement. Newly enacted secondary law points in that direction.[88]

2. Political Rights

a) Electoral rights

aa) Common principles

47 Pursuant to Article 19 of the TEC (Article I-10(2)(b) DC, cf also II-99, II-100, III-126 DC), citizens of the Union who reside in a Member State of which they are not nationals have the right to vote and to stand as a candidate in municipal elections (Article 19(1) TEC/Article I-10(2)(b) DC) and in elections to the European Parliament (Article 19(2) TEC/Article I-10(2)(b) DC) in the Member State of residence.[89] The two **electoral guarantees** have different relationships to Union law.

48 The **municipal electoral rights** are seen as an expression of the European freedom of movement. They are intended to remedy disadvantages caused when a person chooses to reside in another Member State. Their objective is to establish equality in local elections, as already achieved at the national level. They therefore set no criteria relating to the nature and content of how public opinion is to be influenced. From a constitutional perspective, the close link between the political rights to vote and to stand for public office is severed in certain areas in favour of a more open concept of sovereignty in the Union.

49 In contrast, on the subjective side, the **European electoral rights** mirror the democratic dimension of the Union's institutional law. They take a pan-European view of electoral rights; the electorate is not differentiated according to nationality. The goal is to promote a common political identity for citizenship of the Union. The new Draft Constitution tries to do justice to this: whereas Article 189 of the TEC states that the European Parliament consists "of the peoples of the States brought together in the Community", the new Constitutional Treaty refers to the Union's citizens (Articles I-20(2), I-46(2) DC).

50 Both electoral guarantees of Article 19 of the TEC (Article I-10(2)(b) DC) are linked to the **place of residency**. The Member States determine the meaning of the term "residency" and the conditions under which it may be established.[90] However, the principle of residency is not to be interpreted restrictively. For instance, a voter must be allowed to vote in the country of origin if she or he so requests; any other interpretation of Article 19 of the TEC (Article I-10(2)(b) DC) would contradict the overriding objective of Articles 17 to 22 of the TEC (Article I-10, III-125 to III-129 DC), namely, to extend Union citizens'

Becker [1999] EuR 522, 532; Reich (2001) 7 ELJ 3, 12; see now ECJ *Orfanopoulos and Olivieri* [2004] ECR I-5257, paras 66 ff.
88 The new Dir 2004/38/EC (note 23) is considered as expanding on existing free movement rights, see Commission, Forth Report (note 35) p 6.
89 The historical roots can be traced back to 1972, see Bieber [1978] EuGRZ 203, 204.
90 Haag (note 27) Art 19 EGV, para 8; Oliver (1996) 33 CMLRev 473, 482-483, 493; Degen [1993] DÖV 749, 756 bases his opposing view on a judgement of the ECJ relating to the meaning of residency for taxation purposes (the country of "normal residence", see ECJ *Ryborg* [1991] ECR I-1943, para 28).

European Citizenship Rights   § 21 IV 2

rights.[91] However, the right to vote and stand for election in European elections may, in sum, be exercised only once in a given election. Member States may, for example, enact legislation to regulate the right to vote for persons with multiple residences.[92] To the extent that voting more than once is not permitted, the Member States must take measures to prevent abuse.[93] In contrast, it is possible to stand simultaneously as a candidate in more than one European municipal election. Moreover, the Member States may set further conditions, provided they are consistent with the principle of equality, *ie* either are necessary due to the fact that the affected Union citizen is a foreigner or they must apply equally to the relevant Member State's own nationals. It is therefore permissible to require Union citizens to be entered on the electoral roll.[94] However, re-registration may not be required for each election if the Member State's own nationals are not subject to such a requirement. Furthermore, requirements relating to the minimum age, minimum period of residency, obligation to register, etc., which apply equally to everyone, of course remain in force. Where voting is compulsory, as is the case in Belgium, for example, this can be imposed on all Union citizens; however, there is then no obligation to be entered on the electoral roll.[95]

The **secondary community law** enacted pursuant to Article 19 of the TEC (Article I-10(2)(b) DC) authorises the Member States to provide for exceptions where warranted by problems specific to a Member State (Article 19(1)(ii), (2)(ii) TEC/Article III-126 DC). Thus, Member States in which the proportion of foreign Union citizens exceeds 20 % may temporarily restrict the right to vote of foreign Community voters in favour of its own nationals, provided that the principle of proportionality is observed.[96]   **51**

In addition to the rights to vote and stand for election, Article 19 of the TEC (Article I-10(2)(b) DC) covers **political rights** that are related to the electoral rights. The electorate therefore has a right to information and to participate in election campaigns. For candidates, related rights are attached to the right to stand for election, such as the right to participate in election campaigns, the right to equal access to State-run media as well as the right to exercise the mandate, in the event the candidate wins the election. Furthermore, the European Charter of Fundamental Rights confirms in Article 11 (Article II-71 DC) the freedom of expression and information and in Article 12 (Article II-72 DC) the freedom of assembly and association.   **52**

bb) Municipal electoral rights (Article 19(1) TEC/Article I-10(2)(b) DC, cf also II-100 DC)

Every Union citizen residing outside his or her Member State of nationality has the right to vote and stand as a candidate at **municipal elections** under the same conditions as local nationals. Union citizens are thus granted the right to participate in forming domestic public opinion in the Member States at the lowest level.   **53**

---

91 Kaufmann-Bühler (note 36) Art 19 EGV, para 2.
92 Art 4 of Dir 93/109, [1993] OJ L329/34 (hereinafter "European Election Dir"); Art 3 of Dir 94/80, [1994] OJ L368/38 (hereinafter "Municipal Election Dir").
93 Arts 11 and 13 European Election Dir; Art 10 Municipal Election Dir.
94 Art 9 European Election Dir; Art 7 Municipal Election Dir.
95 *Cf* in more detail Art 7(2) Municipal Election Dir.
96 *Cf* in more detail Art 14(1) European Election Dir with respect to Luxemburg; Art 12(1) Municipal Election Dir for Luxemburg and some of the municipalities of Belgium; for more detail see Silvestro [1993] RMC 612, 613.

54   The figures on migration at the beginning of the 1990s, when this provision was adopted, reveal its practical significance. At that time, 5 million of the approximately 325 million citizens in the European Community resided outside their country of origin; 1.3 million nationals of other Member States lived and worked in Germany; and approximately 290,000 German citizens resided abroad in other Member States.[97] The ratios have hardly changed since then.[98] A change of residency across borders generally meant a loss of municipal electoral rights.[99]

55   It was necessary to amend the **German Basic Law** in order to implement Union citizens' municipal electoral rights.[100] Pursuant to Article 28(1)(ii) of the Basic Law, the people must be represented at the municipal level. According to the German Federal Constitutional Court and most legal scholars, Article 20(2) of the Basic Law, which enshrines the principle of people's sovereignty, refers to the German people.[101] Thus, the electoral rights in connection with election to public office are subject to the condition of German nationality. In regard to elections to municipal representative bodies, this linkage, however, does not fall within the scope of the perpetuity clause of the German Basic Law (Article 79(3) of the Basic Law),[102] which protects the essential parts of the Constitution from amendment. This is largely due to the fact that the municipal representative bodies are not considered to belong to the legislative, but rather the executive branch.[103] The municipal electoral rights for Union citizens therefore found a sufficient constitutional basis in the newly introduced Article 28(1)(iii) of the Basic Law.[104] Details are set forth in the Municipal Election Directive, without which Article 19(1) of the TEC (Article I-10(2)(b) DC) could not become effective.[105] Its implementation, which has since been completed, falls within the jurisdiction of the *Länder*.

---

97 Degen [1993] DÖV 749.
98 Commission Third Report (note 29) p 18; see also Commission report on the application of the Municipal Election Dir, COM (2002) 260.
99 In Spain and France, citizens who were resident abroad were granted the right to vote in municipal elections, as was the case in Greece and Italy, though the voter had to cast the ballot in person. On the other hand, only Denmark, Ireland, the Netherlands and Sweden had granted all foreigners the right to vote in municipal elections, subject to specified requirements. Other Member States granted this right on the basis of reciprocity (*eg* Spain and Finland) or for the nationals of certain other States (*eg* Great Britain and Portugal).
100 On the constitutional amendments in France see Kovar/Simon [1993] CDE 285, 304 ff; on the constitutional amendments in Spain see Lopez Castillo/Polakiewicz [1993] EuGRZ 277; on the constitutional amendments in Portugal see Lopes Marinho in: Laursen/Vanhoonacker *The Ratification of the Maastricht Treaty* (1994) pp 231 ff; otherwise relating to the implementation in the Union States Hasselbach [1997] ZG 49, 64 ff.
101 BVerfG (1991) 83 BVerfGE 37 (Electoral rights of foreigners in Schleswig-Holstein); BVerfG (1991) 83 BVerfGE 60 (Hamburg); see also Huber [1989] DÖV 531; but see Zuleeg in: Zuleeg (ed) *Ausländerrecht und Ausländerpolitik in Europa* (Baden-Baden 1987) pp 153 ff; Bryde [1989] JZ 257.
102 BVerfG (1991) 83 BVerfGE 37, 59; BVerfG [1998] NVwZ 52; see also Papier in: Magiera (ed) *Das Europa der Bürger in einer Gemeinschaft ohne Binnengrenzen* (Berlin 1990) pp 27 ff; Karpen [1989] NJW 1012, 1016.
103 BVerfG (1984) 65 BVerfGE 283, 289.
104 BVerfG [1998] NVwZ 52.
105 Note 92.

§ 21 IV 2

56 The **Municipal Election Directive** sets forth the scope of protection of Article 19(1) of the TEC (Article I-10(2)(b) DC). Pursuant to Article 2(1)(b) of this Directive, "municipal elections" means "elections by direct universal suffrage to appoint the members of the representative council and, where appropriate, under the laws of each Member State, the head and members of the executive of a basic local government unit." The Annex to the Municipal Election Directive stipulates what that means to federal States such as Germany and Austria which have constituent states that are also municipal entities, such as the cities of Berlin, Bremen, Hamburg and Vienna.

57 The **right to stand for election** is subject to special conditions. For elected candidates who are nationals of another Union State, Article 19(1) of the TEC (Article I-10(2)(b) DC) derogates from Article 39(4) of the TEC (Article III-133(4) DC), which permits the Member States to fill key positions in public service with their own nationals only. However, the Municipal Election Directive also limits the scope of protection in this regard. Member States may provide that only their own nationals may hold the office of the directly elected head, deputy or member of the governing college of the executive of a basic local government unit. This derogation from the principle of equal treatment can be traced back to a French initiative. France has used the authorisation in its constitution, because the municipal elections there are also decisive for the composition of the Senate, which participates in the exercise of national sovereignty.[106] Bavaria and Saxony have also made use of this authorisation.[107] In light of the fact that Article 19(1)(ii) of the TEC (Article III-126 DC) restricts derogations to cases of special conditions specific to a Member State, it appears doubtful whether this reservation is consistent with higher Community law.[108] Nevertheless, the Commission as well as the German and French courts assume that the provision is admissible under primary law.[109]

58 **Other municipal means of democratic participation**, such as referenda, lie outside the scope of Article 19(1) of the TEC (Article I-10(2)(b) DC), because they are not concerned with elections, but with decisions on specific issues.[110] The wording of Article 19 of the TEC (Article I-10(2)(b) DC) and the Municipal Election Directive does not cover these forms of participation. Many of the *Länder* permit Union citizens to vote in such referenda. The question was raised, however, whether Article 28(1)(iii) of the Basic Law, which only speaks of "elections", permits this. The homogeneity clause of Article 28(1)(i) of the Basic Law stipulates that the basic principles of the constitutional order on the federal and *Land* levels correspond. If one assumes that the respective meanings of "the people" in Article 20(2) and Article 28(1)(ii) of the Basic Law are identical (the latter provision is merely a territorial restriction), then Article 28(1)(iii) of the Basic Law appears to be an

---

106 Compare Art 88(3)(ii), Art 24 and Art 3 of the French constitution.
107 Art 36(1) *Bayerisches Wahlgesetz* (Bavarian Electoral Act); sec 46 *Sächsiche Gemeindeordnung* (Saxon Municipalities Act).
108 Wollenschläger/Schraml [1995] BayVBl 385, 388 believe these provisions to be inconsistent with Community law; Hasselbach [1997] ZG 49, 56 ff; Pieroth/Schmülling [1998] DVBl 365, 367–368; but see Gundel [1999] DÖV 353, 358.
109 See the proposal's motives in (1994) COM 38 final p 29; *Bayerischer Verfassungsgerichtshof* (Bavarian Constitutional Court) [1997] BayVBl 495; the German Federal Constitutional Court declined to accept the complaint of unconstitutionality, relying on Art 101(1)(ii) Basic Law, due to a failure to apply to the ECJ, see BVerfG [1999] NVwZ 293; not critically discussed by the French Conseil constitutionnel, CC no 92–308 DC, Rec S 55 (Maastricht I).
110 Hilf (note 4) Art 19 EGV, para 15; Hatje (note 56).

exception which is to be restrictively interpreted. Since it does not explicitly mention such referenda and initiatives, it would then exclude foreign Union citizens from participating in them.[111] But this argument is not conclusive. Article 28(1)(iii) of the Basic Law must be understood in conjunction with Article 23(1) of the Basic Law, proclaiming membership in the European Union as a constitutional principle and thus opening the structure of the German State for the purposes of Union citizenship. At the municipal and district levels the principle of homogeneity is thus derogated from for this purpose in any case. Furthermore, the very peculiarities of municipal democracy allow for the extension of Union citizens' rights to initiatives and referenda without hindrances.[112]

59   **Interference:** Since Article 19(1) of the TEC (Article I-10(2)(b) DC) prohibits both discrimination and obstruction to the exercise of these rights, a Member State encroaches on them when it erects obstacles to the exercise of electoral rights or treats Union citizens less favourably than its own nationals.

60   **Restrictions:** A justification for interference can only be based on the Municipal Election Directive. If one follows the view that the Directive's reservation permitting the Member States to fill key municipal positions with their own nationals only is illegal under Community law,[113] then exclusion of candidates from other Union States would be a breach of Article 19(1) of the TEC (Article I-10(2)(b) DC). Provided the implementation acts remain within the scope of the Directive, the infringement is attributable to the European Community. Since this question concerns the annulment of a legislative act by the Council, it can only be determined by the ECJ (Articles 230, 234(1)(b) TEC/Articles III-365, III-369(b)).

cc) Electoral rights to the European Parliament (Article 19(2) TEC/Article I-10(2)(b) DC, cf also II-99 DC)

61   It is a natural consequence of the establishment of direct **elections to the European Parliament** that the rights to vote and to stand for election are bound to Union citizenship. Until direct elections to the European Parliament were introduced, there was only the incomplete procedural provision on the Treaty level (now Article 190 TEC/Articles I-20, III-330 DC). Although the right to vote in elections to the European Parliament has existed since universal suffrage was introduced in 1976,[114] the details governing the exercise of this right were and are largely left to the Member States. Moreover, until the Maastricht Treaty entered into force, this right was generally reserved to the Member State's own nationals, not because the European Parliament exercised sovereign powers, but rather because there were no uniform regulations governing election procedures.

---

111 According to the Federal Minister of the Interior in a circular to the *Länder* dated 30 January 1995, unpublished; see also Scholz in: Maunz/Dürig (eds) *Grundgesetz* (45th instalment Munich 2005) Art 28, paras 41–42.
112 See Hailbronner/Renner (note 64) Einl para 62; Laubach (note 8) pp 78 ff; those who see the German people as "Europeanized" by virtue of Art 28(1)(iii) Basic Law come to the same result, see *eg* Hobe [1994] JZ 191, 193 and Engelken [1996] DÖV 737, as do those who view residency as the criterion for membership in the local "community of legitimacy", see Schmidt-Jortzig *Kommunalrecht* (Stuttgart 1982) pp 39–40.
113 See above note 108.
114 Council Decisions 76/787, [1976] OJ L278/1 and 2002/772, [2002] OJ L283.

Scope of protection: In terms of the personal scope of protection, according to its wording Article 19(2) of the TEC (Article I-10(2)(b) DC) benefits only Union citizens residing in a Member State the nationality of which he or she does not possess. Although European electoral rights form the basis of a direct claim under Community law to political participation, the wording of Article 19(2) of the TEC (Article I-10(2)(b) DC) does not include citizens residing in their own State. Nonetheless, they must also have a right under public law to participate in the elections, since it is not the intent of Article 19(2) of the TEC (Article I-10(2)(b) DC) to privilege citizens residing abroad. Furthermore, elections to the European Parliament are subject to Article 3 of the 1st Prot ECHR. Pursuant thereto, the member States are obligated to hold free elections by secret ballot, "under conditions which will ensure the free expression of the opinion of the people in the choice of the legislature." The scope of protection of Article 19(2) of the TEC (Article I-10(2)(b) DC), which is not of itself directly applicable, is regulated in detail by the European Election Directive, which is in turn to be transformed by national statutory law. The European Election Directive still does not create a standardized election procedure, but rather limits itself to the issues related to the right to vote, such as the requirement of registration and the exclusion of multiple voting and candidacies. By and large, Article 19(2) of the TEC (Article I-10(2)(b) DC) and the relevant secondary community law have meanwhile been properly implemented in national law.[115]

This right is **interfered** with when a Union citizen is prevented from participating in an election or participation is unreasonably obstructed by conditions which do not apply to nationals or do not affect nationals with the same severity.

Restrictions: The European Election Directive not only regulates electoral rights; it also authorises the Member States to impose restrictions. This applies, for example, to the deprivation of electoral rights in the country of origin, which the host State is bound to recognise.

Remarkably, the legal concept of the "**people**" is changed by attaching electoral rights to residency. An Italian residing in Germany belongs to the German people for the purposes of European elections, and participates in determining who occupies Germany's seats in the European Parliament (Article 190(2) TEC). This consequence in fact moves the principle of national voting contingents of the Member States towards the objective of a European legitimising constituency for those fields which fall within the Union's jurisdiction.[116] However, the importance of Article 19(2) of the TEC (Article I-10(2)(b) DC) and its implementing legislation lies in its subjective components,[117] which correspond to the right to vote on the national level. The value of both participatory rights depends on the powers of the respective parliament. They should, therefore, correspond with each

---

115 Commission, Third Report (note 29) p 17; Fourth Report (note 35) p 11
116 The equality of the vote pursuant to the German Basic Law is not affected, cf BVerfG [1995] EuGRZ 566.
117 Cf Kovar/Simon [1993] CDE 285, 307. The declared objective of increasing voter participation, however, has so far not been achieved. The Union citizens' interest in European elections is marginal, above all in Germany and France, where 63 % of the eligible voters live. Voter participation by those who are eligible to vote and do not live in their home countries is approximately 9 % across Europe, though the trend is slightly upwards. In Germany only 2.1 % of the Union citizens eligible to cast a ballot actually registered to vote for the 1999 election, whereas in France the percentage was approximately 4.9 %; cf in more detail the Commission, Third Report (note 29) p 18, note 31.

other; European citizenship rights must be supplemented by participatory rights to the extent that the (national) citizen has lost influence in his or her Member State due to the national parliament's loss of powers.[118]

b) The right to petition (Articles 21 and 194 or 195 TEC/Articles I-10(2)(d), III-128 and III-334 or III-335 DC, cf also II-104 DC)

66 Pursuant to Article 21(1) of the TEC (Articles I-10(2)(d), III-128 DC), every Union citizen has the **right** in accordance with Article 194 of the TEC (Article III-334 DC) **to petition** the European Parliament. Its importance for Union citizenship becomes clear when one recalls that the right to petition fulfils the function of creating a bond between the citizen and the people's representatives in constitutional States. Along with the electoral rights, it opens another, albeit marginal, opportunity to actively participate in political events and is intended to facilitate integration.[119] At the same time, it offers citizens the opportunity to pursue their interests and rights outside administrative and court proceedings, of course without a right to set one's own conditions for petitioning. Depending on how strongly this aspect of legal protection is emphasised, national constitutions recognise this right for foreigners as well. Article 194 of the TEC (Article III-334 DC) also follows this model. In contrast to Article 21, Article 194 of the TEC (Articles I-10(2)(d), III-128 DC and III-334 DC) does not have any independent meaning and grants the right to petition not only to Union citizens, but to all persons who reside in a Member State.[120]

67 Whereas the right to petition Parliament is rather political in nature, legal protection is in the foreground with the right to apply to the **Ombudsman** (Articles 21(2) and 195 TEC/Articles I-10(2)(d), III-128 and III-335 DC, cf also II-103 DC). The two procedures are not mutually exclusive. The Ombudsman has the task of investigating complaints concerning maladministration in the activities of the Community institutions or bodies within her or his jurisdiction. The Ombudsman conducts inquiries, seeks opinions, and submits reports. Thus, the institution of the Ombudsman is a form of control over the administration, which should increase the transparency of the conduct of the Community's administrative bodies. The standard of review is good administrative practice, which is further secured by way of an individual right (Article 42 of the Charter of Fundamental Rights/Articles II-101 to II-103 DC).[121]

68 The **subject matter of protection** of the right to petition is specified in Articles 194 and 195 of the TEC (Articles III-334 and III-335 DC). With respect to the Parliament, which has created a Committee of Petitions,[122] it refers to all matters that come within the Community's fields of activities, and with respect to the Ombudsman furthermore to matters relating to Police and Judicial Cooperation in Criminal Matters (Article 41(1) TEU). The European Parliament's practice extends the right to petition beyond the jurisdiction of the Community to all matters that come within the European Union's fields of activity.[123] The petitioner must be directly affected. While the practice is liberal in this regard, nonetheless

---

118 Everling [1992] ZfRV 241, 255–256.
119 *Cf* Bauer in: Dreier (ed) *Grundgesetz* (Vol I, 2nd ed, Tübingen 2004) Art 17, para 12.
120 As here Art 17 German Basic Law, Art 28 Belgium, Art 10 Greece, Art 27 Luxemburg and Art 8 Dutch constitutions.
121 Guckelberger [2003] DÖV 829, 835–836.
122 Annex VI Title XVII of the Rules of Procedure of the European Parliament, [1999] OJ L202/1.
123 Rule 174 of the Rules of Procedure of the European Parliament.

many petitions are rejected as inadmissible.[124] Every person has the right to have his or her petition accepted, reviewed and answered. On the other hand, there is no right to remedial action even if a request is recognised as valid. The right to petition is therefore only encroached upon if a petition is not accepted, not reviewed or not answered. In this case, the petitioner is able to bring an action for failure to act before the CFI (Article 232 TEC/ Article III-367 DC). Specific restrictions are foreign to Community law, although collisions with the fundamental rights, such as third parties' rights of personality, are conceivable.

c) Right to information (Article 21(3) TEC/Article I-10(2)(d) DC)

The right to apply to any institution of the Community (Article 7 TEC/Articles I-19, I-30 to 32 DC) or the Ombudsman in one of the languages specified in Article 314 of the TEC (Article IV-448(1) DC) and to receive an answer in the chosen **language** (Article 21(3) TEC/Article I-10(2)(d) DC) supplements the right to petition. The primary objective of the rule is to permit each Union citizen to use his or her native language, even if this is non-binding within the framework of Article 314 of the TEC (Article IV-448(1) DC). The subject matter of protection includes every form of inquiry, request for information, applications without a specific form, opinions and petitions. On the other hand, it is not entirely clear to what extent there is a right to a specific answer. The Union objective of being as close to the citizens as possible and the principle of transparency (12th recital of the Preamble and Article 1(2) TEU, Article 255 TEC/Article III-399 DC) speak against understanding Article 21(3) of the TEC (Article I-10(2)(d) DC) as solely providing a guarantee for the use of the relevant language. Not only must an answer be given, it must also take the inquiry into account. More complex questions may be answered by referring to the relevant documents (see Article 255 TEC/Article III-399 DC).[125] The specific content depends on the nature of the inquiry as well as the interests of third parties and the Member States which the competent authority is bound to protect. The obligation to maintain confidentiality (Article 287 TEC/Article III-430 DC) thus operates to restrict the right to an answer.

d) Right to access documents (Article 255 TEC/Articles II-102, III-399 DC)

The right to access to documents of the Community institutions (Article 255 TEC, Article 42 of the Charter of Fundamental Rights, Article II-102, III-399 DC) is closely related to the guarantees provided by Articles 19 and 21 of the TEC (Articles I-10(2)(b) and I-10(2)(d) DC). This **right to information** is, on the one hand, a condition for participating in the public debate; on the other hand it offers a means of public control over the administration.[126] The effectiveness of this right depends, above all, on the voluntary co-operation of the Community's institutions and bodies, but meanwhile has been raised to

---

124 In the European Parliament's legislative period 1997–2000 only 54 % were admissible, cf Commission, Third Report (note 29) pp 20–21; to judge by the figures cited, the numerical value is rather small (958 in the legislative period 1999/2000), and the trend downward is continuing.
125 On Article 21's related right to information, see Kaufmann-Bühler in: Schwarze (ed) *EU-Kommentar* (Baden-Baden 2000) Art 21 EGV, para 2.
126 Österdahl (1998) 23 ELRev 336; Curtin (2000) 37 CMLRev 7; Kadelbach in: Schmidt-Aßmann/ Hoffmann-Riem (eds) *Verwaltungskontrolle* (Baden-Baden 2001) pp 205, 220–221; on the relation to Union citizenship ECJ *Interporc* [2003] ECR I-2125, para 39.

the level of constitutional law and is governed more specifically by a Regulation enacted on the basis of Article 255(2) of the TEC (Article III-399 DC).[127]

71   **Scope of protection:** As with the rights pursuant to Article 21 of the TEC (Article I-10(2)(d) DC), the beneficiaries are not only Union citizens. The addressees of this right are the Parliament, the Council and the Commission and the committees established by or assisting them.[128] Substantively it provides a right to access, upon request, to documents within the possession of the Community institution. A special interest does not need to be demonstrated. The access may be provided by reference to the official place where the information can be found, by sending copies or by electronic transmission.

72   **Restrictions:** Only the reasons for confidentiality specified in the Regulation may be brought forward to deny a request. According to the established case-law of the CFI and ECJ, these are, as exceptions, to be interpreted restrictively.[129] They include overriding public interests such as public security, defence and military matters, international relations and financial, monetary or economic policy, and the right to privacy and integrity of the individual, in particular in accordance with Community legislation on data protection.[130] In addition, access is to be denied where disclosure would undermine the protection of Community interests, in particular court proceedings or inspections, investigations or audits. Finally, there is no right to access to documents of a preliminary nature or such information which may only be disclosed with the prior consent of the Member State.

3. Right to Diplomatic and Consular Protection
(Article 20 TEC/Article I-10(2)(c) DC)

a) Purpose and effect of the provision

73   Article 20 of the TEC (Article I-10(2)(c), III-127 DC, cf also II-106 DC) guarantees every Union citizen the **consular and diplomatic protection** of the other Member States in countries where the given Member State has no representation. This provision does not introduce a claim to protection against the Union itself. Cooperation in diplomatic and consular representation which is already permissible under international law,[131] however, forms an integral part of the Common Foreign and Security Policy (Article 20 TEU/ Article III-306 DC). Article 20 of the TEC (Article I-10(2)(c) DC) thus expresses the Member States' common responsibility for all Union citizens.

74   In Article 20(ii) of the TEC (Article I-10(2)(c), III-127 DC), the Member States have agreed to undertake the international negotiations required to secure this protection. The resultant intergovernmental discretion means that Article 20 of the TEC (Article

---

127 Reg 1049/2001/EC regarding public access to European Parliament, Council and Commission documents [2001] OJ L145/43; in detail de Leeuw (2003) CMLRev 324.
128 On comitology procedures see CFI *Rothmans International* [1999] ECR II-2463.
129 Kadelbach (2001) 38 CMLRev 179.
130 Art 4(1) of Reg 1049/2001 (note 127) in conjunction with Dir 95/46/EC on the protection of individuals with regard to the possession of personal data and on the free movement of such data, [1995] OJ L281/31 and the national laws of implementation; concerning data protection in Europe see Hatje in: Magiera/Sommermann (eds) *Verwaltung in der Europäischen Union* (Berlin 2001) pp 193, 205 ff.
131 Art 8 of the Vienna Convention on Consular Relations of 24 April 1963, UNTS 596, 261 (hereinafter "Vienna Convention"); see also Art 2(3) of the European Consular Convention of 11 November 1967, ETS No 61, which applies between six of the Union States.

I-10(2)(c) DC) is not, as such, directly applicable.[132] The representatives of the governments in the Council have therefore resolved upon common regulations specifying this right in greater detail in several Decisions,[133] which require adoption by national law. This has thus far not occurred.[134] As these Decisions are not subject to the jurisdiction of the ECJ, a direct effect via this avenue is foreclosed.[135] The rights promised by Article 20 of the TEC (Article I-10(2)(c) DC) thus remain without legally binding effect. In addition to the measures internal to the Union, the consent of the relevant third State with respect to which the diplomatic and consular protection is to be exercised is required. The consent may, in a specific case, be tacit.[136] The validity of the right to protection, on the other hand, does not depend on this.

b) Scope of protection

Consular protection primarily encompasses a State's own nationals, ships and airplanes abroad by consular administrative activity, such as issuing identity papers, exercising notary and registry functions, protecting interests in inheritance, guardianship and wardship matters, representation before a court, the transmission of documents and dealing with requests for legal aid.[137] By contrast, diplomatic protection involves the assertion of the interests of a State's nationals or legal persons after another State breaches international law. In particular, diplomatic protection is triggered by failure to meet those standards of customary international law safeguarding foreigners in terms of life, personal integrity, personal freedom, property or due process of law.[138]

Diplomatic protection in the technical sense could previously only be exercised by the injured party's State, aside from certain narrow exceptions, which are not of interest here. According to the prevailing understanding, this proceeding concerns a claim between the affected States, rather than a claim of an individual.[139] Yet the wording of Article 20 of

---

132 Closa (1995) 32 CMLRev 487, 502–503; taking a different view Everling in: Hrbek (ed) *Bürger und Europa* (Baden-Baden 1994) pp 49, 62; Ruffert (1997) 35 AVR 459, 471–472; Szczekalla [1999] EuR 325, 327–328.
133 See Decision 95/553 regarding protection for citizens of the European Union by diplomatic and consular representations, [1995] OJ L314/73, in force since 3 May 2002, see Commission, General Report; on the activities of the EU in 2002 para 513; Decision on the practical arrangements to be made by consular officials, unpublished; Decision 96/409 on the establishment of an emergency travel document, [1996] OJ L168/4, which has been criticised due to its restrictive content, see Ruffert (1997) 35 AVR 459, 466 ff, who considers this secondary community law to be in violation of higher Community law.
134 As per 30 September 2006, the German Act on consular officials, their tasks and powers, [1974] BGBl I-2317 has not been modified with respect to Art 20 TEC.
135 Kluth (note 32) Art 20 EGV, paras 16–17 takes a different view.
136 On the procedure to date in such cases see Art 8 Vienna Convention (note 131), which requires an "appropriate notification" and is subject to the proviso that the receiving State does not object.
137 See the list in Art 5 Vienna Convention (note 131), furthermore §§ 1–17 Consular Act (note 134).
138 Hailbronner in: Graf Vitzthum (ed) *Völkerrecht* (3rd ed, Berlin 2004) pp 187 ff.
139 Three levels of claims must thus be distinguished: the claim for restitution by the injured party against the responsible State pursuant to its domestic law; the claim for reparation under international law by the injured party's State of origin against the breaching State; and finally a possible claim of the injured party against his own State for diplomatic protection, which is governed by the domestic law of that State.

the TEC (Article I-10(2)(c) DC) prevents it from being interpreted in the sense of international law; a State's exercise of diplomatic protection does not depend on its having representation in the breaching State, nor must this occur *on* the latter's territory (Article 20(i) TEC/Article I-10(2)(c) DC). The German version misleadingly refers to diplomatic and consular protection. Versions of the EC Treaty in other languages (Article 314 TEC/ Article III-448(1) DC) make clear that the Article guarantees "protection by diplomatic or consular authorities" (French: "protection de la part des autorités diplomatiques et consulaires").[140] Article 20 of the TEC (Article I-10(2)(c) DC) thereby embraces two forms of protection which are not always clearly distinguishable in practice. First, it ensures consular protection. The reference to diplomatic representation accounts for the fact that embassies can also perform consular tasks.[141] Second, Article 20 of the TEC (Article I-10(2)(c) DC) goes beyond mere consular protection to include measures associated with diplomatic protection under international law. If necessary, such measures may need to be carried out within the third State, such as making legal declarations, transferring documents, official exertions for the release of incarcerated persons, assistance in the exhaustion of legal remedies, etc.

77   The **protective purpose** of Article 20 of the TEC (Article I-10(2)(c) DC) is therefore to provide protection to the nationals of other Union States in foreign countries on the same conditions as the nationals of that State. This was foreseen primarily for acute emergencies, such as the loss of identification and travel documents.[142] In view of the phenomenon of mass tourism to foreign lands, this provision is of significant practical importance. When the Maastricht Treaty entered into force, there were only five countries in which all Union States were represented; in 17 countries, merely two of the then 15 Union States were represented.[143] The relevance of Article 20 of the TEC (Article I-10(2)(c) DC) will continue to grow in the future since the provision makes the reduction of existing embassies and consulates possible. The personal scope of protection is determined by citizenship of the Union and, for legal persons, whether they belong to a Union State under that State's private law.[144] International law imposes certain restrictions in this regard, however. For example, the nationality must be effective. In cases of dual nationality where the applicant is seeking protection against a State of which he or she is also a national, diplomatic protection was long considered to be out of the question and is in any event problematic where the effective nationality is that of the allegedly breaching State.

78   Protection by a State other than the home State is **subsidiary**. If the home State maintains representation, it has priority. Another Union State may not become engaged with-

---

140 This was also the intention of the States which prevailed in the Treaty negotiations, see Jiménez Piernas (1993) 20 Revista de las Instituciones Europeas 9, 18; Weyland in: Marias (ed) *European Citizenship* (Maastricht 1994) pp 63, 64; on point, in this sense, Ruffert (1997) 35 AVR 459, 465, 472, 476; another view can be found in Haag (note 27) Art 20, EGV para 6; Hatje (note 56) Art 20, EGV, para 9; Hilf (note 4) Art 20, para 15; see also Stein in: Ress/Stein (eds) *Der diplomatische Schutz im Völker- und Europarecht* (Baden-Baden 1996) pp 97 ff.
141 Art 3(ii) Vienna Convention (note 131); see also Art 3(2) of the Vienna Convention on Diplomatic Relations of 18 April 1961, UNTS 500, 95.
142 See the "Guidelines for the Protection of Unrepresented EC Nationals by EC Missions in Third Countries", published as document 7142/94, PESC 161, COCON 2 of the General Secretary of the Council dated 24 May 1994; Art 5(1) Decision 95/553 (note 133).
143 Commission, Second Report (note 35) p 11.
144 See above note 34.

European Citizenship Rights § 21 IV 3

out its consent, nor does the person seeking protection have the right to choose. However, in cases of acute danger, effective action must be possible. If another Union State maintains a consulate in a remote province and the home State does not, the former is obliged to render the assistance required, to the extent possible in cooperation with the home State, if the authorities of the home State are not able to be reached in a timely manner.

c) Interferences and restrictions

The rights of the Union citizens relate to **equal treatment** and thus do not extend further than those of nationals of the Member State obliged to render assistance. Different levels of protection are thereby maintained. Thus the right is only encroached upon where the Member State does not treat the Union citizen as well as it treats its own nationals. 79

Restrictions are imposed by international law, the provisions foreseen in Article 20(ii) of the TEC (Article III-127 DC), and the domestic law of the Member States, to which the "same conditions" clause of Article 20 of the TEC (Article I-10(2)(c) DC) refers. Under German law, the individual only has a right to the exercise of discretion without legal error, which is derived from the protective function of the German Basic Law's fundamental human rights.[145] Such restrictions flow from other constitutionally recognised interests. However, whereas foreign policy may justify broad discretion on the part of the German Federal Foreign Office (*Auswärtiges Amt*) in the performance of strictly *diplomatic* protection, such considerations play a much smaller role in *consular* affairs, so that the right to protection may then relate to specific measures. This right is then infringed when the measures are not taken. 80

d) Judicial protection

Article 20 of the TEC (Article I-10(2)(c) DC) contains certain peculiarities regarding **legal protection** before a court. As long as the Member States do not take sufficient implementing measures, Article 20 of the TEC (Article I-10(2)(c) DC) does not provide any effective guarantees. The question of its actionability is therefore currently largely of a theoretical nature. However, if one is of the view that Article 20 of the TEC (Article I-10(2)(c) DC) is directly applicable, then actions for breach thereof may be brought before national courts. Independently of the question of direct effect, actions for damages pursuant to the principles of Member State liability for failure to properly implement European law are conceivable[146] as far as the Member States have not implemented Article 20 of the TEC (Article I-10(2)(c) DC) and pertinent secondary law. 81

---

145 BVerfG (1976) 40 BVerfGE 141, 177–178; BVerfG (1976) 41 BVerfGE 126, 182; BVerfG (1981) 55 BVerfGE 349, 364–365; BVerfG [1992] NJW 3222, 3223; furthermore *Bundesverwaltungsgericht* (BVerwG – German Federal Administrative Court) (1982) 62 BVerwGE 11, 14; in detail Hofmann *Grundrechte und grenzüberschreitende Sachverhalte* (Heidelberg 1993) pp 107 ff.
146 ECJ *Brasserie du pêcheur* [1996] ECR I-1029.

4. Citizenship of the Union and the Prohibition on Discrimination (Article 12 TEC/Articles I-4(2), III-123 DC)

82 **Case 2 – Problem:** (cf ECJ *Martínez Sala* [1998] ECR I-2691)
S was born in 1956 and is a Spanish national. Since 1968 she has lived in Germany, where she has held various jobs. Since 1989 she has received welfare benefits. Until 1984, she had received residency permits, since then, however, she has been given only certificates stating that she has applied to extend the residency permit. In January 1993, she applied for a child-raising allowance in the *Land* of Bavaria for her daughter, who was born that month. The relevant statute[147] entitles any person who has a child for whom he or she is the legal guardian or custodian to such support, provided such child lives in the same household and the legal guardian raises the child himself or herself and is not employed or not employed full-time. Bavaria rejected the application due to the fact that S had no valid residency permit. Pursuant to the statute, the applicant must have his or her habitual residence in Germany and foreigners must have a valid residency permit. Pursuant to Regulation (EEC) 1612/68, all workers who are nationals of the Member States enjoy the same social and tax benefits as national workers. Pursuant to Regulation (EEC) 1408/71, the requirement of equal treatment includes services to families. The competent regional administrative court for social security and related matters (*Landessozialgericht*) doubts whether these provisions are applicable to S. The court would like to know whether the refusal of the child-raising allowance is consistent with the EC Treaty.[148]

a) The relationship between the principle of equality and European citizenship rights

83 Most of the European citizenship rights aim to establish equality of nationals of other Union States with the host State's own nationals. The **prohibition on discrimination on the basis of nationality**, which is anchored in Article 12 of the TEC (Articles I-4(2), III-123 DC) as a general principle, is therefore directly related to Union citizenship.[149] Although it may be enlightening that the same basic legal considerations underpin European citizenship rights and the general prohibition on discrimination, the relationship between Articles 17 to 21 of the TEC (Article I-10 DC) and Article 12 of the TEC (Articles I-4(2), III-123 DC) must be examined more closely.

84 Article 12 of the TEC (Articles I-4(2), III-123 DC) stipulates that "without prejudice to any special provisions contained [in this Treaty], any discrimination on the grounds of nationality shall be prohibited." The prohibition on discrimination, thus, protects within the EC Treaty's scope of application, but special provisions establishing equality remain

---

147 *Gesetz über die Gewährung von Erziehungsgeld und Erziehungsurlaub* (BerzGG), [1985] BGBl I-2154; the child-raising allowance, regardless of its amount, is not tied to financial need.
148 On family benefits see Art 4(1)(h) of Reg 1408/71 on the application of social security schemes to employed person, to self-employed persons and to members of their families moving within the Community, [1971] OJ L149/2 in the version of [1999] OJ L38/1; this provision also applies to family aid, see ECJ *Hoever and Zachow* [1996] ECR I-4895; on the attribution of the concept of social benefits pursuant to Art 7(2) of Reg 1612/68 on freedom of movement for workers within the Community ([1968] OJ L257/2 in the version of [1992] OJ L245/1) see ECJ *Commission v Luxemburg* [1993] ECR I-817, para 21.
149 Shaw (1997) 3 EPL 413, 425 ff. The Commission therefore also includes in its report on Union citizenship the initiatives undertaken by the Union – authorised by Art 13 TEC – against discrimination on bases other than nationality, see Third Report (note 29) pp 4, 26 ff; on the legislation previously enacted see Baer [2001] ZRP 500.

unaffected. The provisions relating to Union citizenship belong to the "scope of application" of Article 12 of the TEC (Articles I-4(2), III-123 DC). On the other hand, Article 17(2) of the TEC (Article I-10(2)(i) DC) refers to "the rights conferred by this Treaty [...] and the duties imposed thereby," which also includes Article 12 of the TEC (Articles I-4(2), III-123 DC).[150] The ECJ drew from this the conclusion that Union citizens legally residing in the territory of another Member State may rely upon Article 12 of the TEC (Articles I-4(2), III-123 DC) in all matters covered by the EC Treaty.[151] This concept has far-reaching consequences.

b) Scope of Entitlements on the grounds of European citizenship rights based on Article 12 of the TEC (Articles I-4(2), III-123 DC) in conjunction with Article 18 of the TEC (Article I-10(2)(a) DC)

Social rights under Union law have depended on the recipient having been employed at a certain time in the relevant Member State or being a dependent of such a person. The same has been true for Union citizens who are students, are seeking employment or are retired. In its recent case-law, the ECJ has separated the entitlements within the framework of social security and similar government benefits from residency permits based on the fundamental freedoms. Instead, the ECJ refers to Union citizenship and now focuses solely on legal residency.[152] In this regard, it does not depend on whether Article 18 of the TEC (Article I-10(2)(a) DC) itself already grants the Union citizen such a right to reside.[153] According to the decision's underlying reasoning, the residency permit was not based in Community law, but rather in German law, pursuant to which the application itself permits temporary residence for the duration of the administrative proceedings.

The reservations of Article 18 of the TEC (Article I-10(2)(a) DC), which restrict its scope of protection, are not, however, without effect on account of this. As already mentioned, a Directive permits conditioning the right to reside, above and beyond the scope of the fundamental freedoms, on adequate means of support and health insurance. Therefore, the Member States are not prevented from linking measures terminating the right to reside to the receipt of social assistance.[154] The direct effect of Article 18 of the TEC (Article 10(2)(a) DC) does not affect this consequence. The crucial point is that Union citizens who legally reside in the territory of another Member State may not be treated

85

86

---

150 ECJ *Martínez Sala* [1998] ECR I-2691, para 62.
151 ECJ *Martínez Sala* [1998] ECR I-2691, para 63.
152 ECJ *Martínez Sala* [1998] ECR I-2691, para 63.
153 Germany had an obligation towards Spain pursuant to the European Convention on Social and Medical Assistance not to repatriate the claimant subsequent to her unemployment, see Art 6 European Convention on Social and Medical Assistance of 11 December 1953, which was concluded within the framework of the Council of Europe and to which Germany and Spain acceded. Germany made the reservation that it was not obliged to grant to the nationals of the other Contracting Parties social assistance under the Federal Social Assistance Act at the same level as for nationals, see Annex II, No 2. On nationality as a criterion for different treatment in German social and social assistance law see Zuleeg [1987] NJW 2193, 2197–2198; Hailbronner [1992] VSSR 77; Kokott in: Hailbronner (ed) *Die allgemeinen Regeln des völkerrechtlichen Fremdenrechts* (Heidelberg 2000) pp 25 ff.
154 Borchardt [2000] NJW 2057, 2059–2060 wants to limit such measures to cases of abuse, *ie* if the right to reside is exploited to receive greater benefits; more narrowly Randelzhofer/Forsthoff (note 86) Art 39 EGV, para 193.

worse than nationals. They have, with this restriction, a **right to equal treatment with respect to social services**.[155]

87 The ECJ further developed this line of reasoning in its *Grzelczyk* decision. A French student was studying at a Belgian university. He had provided for his own needs for three years, but in the fourth year he was unable to do so due to his examinations. The ECJ decided that he was entitled to receive the subsistence level aid under Belgian law pursuant to Articles 12 (Articles I-4(2), III-123 DC) and 17 of the TEC (Article I-10 DC). Since in this case he was only subsequently and temporarily indigent, his right to reside could not be automatically revoked due to his claiming social assistance.[156] In the *D'Hoop* case, the ECJ decided that a Belgian woman who had completed her degree in France had a right to a readjustment allowance granted to graduates on the same conditions as nationals.[157] The result of this case-law is that not only discrimination on the basis of nationality is prohibited, but also discriminatory treatment due to a change of residency.

88 The linkage between Union citizenship and the prohibition on discrimination also has consequences **outside the field of social law**. An important example is the right to proceedings in the Union citizen's native language. In *Bickel and Franz*, the ECJ had to decide the question of whether German and Austrian criminal defendants had a right to have the criminal proceedings, which had been commenced in the Italian region of Trentino-Alto Adige, conducted in German. Since the Italian law of this province granted such a right to the members of the German-speaking community in this region, the Court held that the refusal to grant this right to German-speaking Union citizens, who were not Italian nationals and not resident in the province of Bolzano, was a breach of Article 12 of the TEC (Articles I-4(2), III-123 DC).[158] The fact that criminal law is not within the Treaty's scope of protection (cf Article 12 TEC/Articles I-4(2), III-123 DC) was not dispositive.[159] The Court saw the necessary connection to Community law not only in the (passive) right to services but also in the right to free movement pursuant to Article 18 of the TEC (Article I-10(2)(a) DC). Once this connection had been established, the discriminatory treatment of German-speaking Union citizens as opposed to Italian nationals needed an objective and reasonable justification. The minority rights of the German-speaking community in Trentino-Alto Adige were insufficient, since a prohibition on the extension of their language right to others did not affect them. Furthermore, it was not argued that extending

---

155 The *Sala* case-law could result in the Member States being more restrictive with regard to unemployed Union citizens, see O'Leary (1999) 24 ELR 68, 78; Toner (2000) 7 Maastr JECL 158, 179–180.
156 ECJ *Grzelczyk* [2001] ECR I-6193, paras 34 ff, reversing ECJ *Brown* [1988] ECR 3205, according to which, under the state of Community law at that time, granting subsistence aid to students did not fall within the scope of now Art 12 TEC; with respect to unemployment aid ECJ *Collins* [2004] ECR I-2703; to basic social assistance ECJ *Trojani* [2004] ECR I-7573; to student's grants ECJ *Bidar* [2005] ECR I-2119; for a comment on that line of decisions see von Bogdandy/Bitter in: Rodríguez Iglesias/Kadelbach/Gaitanides (eds) *Europa und seine Verfassung – Festschrift für Manfred Zuleeg* (Baden-Baden 2005) pp 309 ff.
157 ECJ *D'Hoop* [2002] ECR I-6191; criticising this decision Kanitz/Steinberg [2003] EuR 1013, 1016 ff; but see also Reich/Harbacevica [2003] CMLRev 615, 627–628.
158 ECJ *Bickel and Franz* [1998] ECR I-7637, paras 16, 23 ff.
159 Similarly, in the *Schempp* Case, where income tax law was at issue, the fact that the TEC does not provide powers for direct taxes alone was no obstacle to apply Articles 12 and 18 TEC, see ECJ *Schempp* [2005] ECR I-6421.

European Citizenship Rights   § 21 IV 4

the right to proceedings in the defendants' native language would lead to any particular difficulties. Consequently, the discriminatory treatment was not justified.[160]

The prohibition on discrimination imposed by Article 12 in conjunction with Article 18 of the TEC (Articles I-4(2), III-123 with Article I-10(2)(a) DC) thus creates a **blanket clause**. For the ECJ, "Union citizenship is destined to be the fundamental status of nationals of the Member States, enabling those who find themselves in the same situation to enjoy the same treatment in law irrespective of their nationality, subject to such exceptions as are expressly provided for."[161] It appears that there is no field which does not fall within its scope, as long as legal residence is the only condition for the national law's applicability.[162] However, generalisations must be treated with caution. Linking Article 18 of the TEC (Article I-10(2)(a) DC) with the principle of equality of Article 12 of the TEC (Articles I-4(2), III-123 DC) does not lead to the wholesale granting of equal status to all Union citizens as such. In particular, the linkage does not promote the – legally and politically desirable – elimination of domestic discrimination.[163]

89

c) Justification of discrimination

To recapitulate, illegal discrimination occurs where a national of a Member State is legally resident in another Member State and meets all other relevant conditions for the benefit of a right given to nationals, but is nonetheless deprived of that right. Such discrimination, however, may be **justified** for objective, reasonable purposes. The purpose must pursue a goal recognised under Union law and be proportional to this end (→ cf § 17 paras 31–32).

90

Case 2 – Answer:
I. Admissibility: The regional administrative court for social security and related matters will apply for a preliminary decision to the ECJ permissible under Article 234 of the TEC (Article III-369 DC), enquiring about the interpretation of the EC Treaty. II. Legal grounds: 1. Article 7(2) of Regulation 1612/68 on freedom for movement of workers within the Community grants workers who are nationals of another Member State "the same social and tax advantages as national workers." Pursuant to Article 2 of Regulation 1408/71 on the application of social security schemes, workers, self-employed persons, and students as well as their family members and heirs are entitled to those benefits which fall within the Regulation's scope of application. S would therefore in any case be entitled to receive the child-raising allowance if she could be classified as a worker. In this regard it must be borne in mind that there is no standardised definition of the term "worker" under Community law. a) For the purposes of Article 39 of the TEC (Article III-133 DC) in conjunction with Regulation

91

---

160 The consequence of this precedent is *not*, as Hilpold [2000] JBl 93, 99 assumes, that the authorities are now required to grant every Union citizen the right to use the language of his choice. If, for example, a Finnish Union citizen, whose legal proceeding is before a court in Trentino-Alto Adige, wishes to have the proceedings conducted in German, this wish need not be granted under Union law – as long as Italians whose native language is not German but who speak German better than Italian (for example, because their native language is Slovenian) do not have a right to proceedings conducted in German at their request. In this regard, the right to an interpreter free of charge pursuant to Art 6(3)(a), (e) ECHR is pertinent.
161 ECJ *Grzelczyk* [2001] ECR I-6193, para 31.
162 On a case concerning the right to the use of a name ECJ *Garcia Avello* [2003] ECR I-11613.
163 → § 7 para 20.

1612/68, a worker is a person who provides services for another during a certain period of time and at their instruction, and for which she or he receives compensation as consideration. A person may be a worker even before the commencement of employment, eg while seeking employment, or after the employment relationship has been terminated. However, the details necessary to qualify S as a worker according to these criteria are missing. b) A worker within the meaning of Article 42 of the TEC (Article III-136 DC) in conjunction with Regulation 1408/71 (now replaced by Regulation 883/2004), which is intended to guarantee access to social services, is a person who is insured by law or is voluntarily insured against a risk within the framework of a system of social security; it does not depend on whether an employment relationship is in place. In this case as well, the necessary details are absent. 2. Thus the crucial issue is whether a provision of Community law prevents a Member State from conditioning the allowance to a national of another Member State on that national's furnishing a formal residency permit. This requirement could be a breach of Article 12 of the TEC (Articles I-4(2), III-123 DC), which prohibits discrimination on the basis of nationality within the scope of application of the EC Treaty. The prohibition on discrimination is applicable to persons who are in a situation which is governed by Community law.[164] Substantively, the payment of child-raising allowances falls within the scope of application of secondary law (Article 4(h) of Regulation 1408/71, today Article 3(1)(j) of Regulation 883/2004) and thus the EC Treaty. It is questionable, however, whether S nevertheless falls within the personal scope of application if she is not a worker within the meaning of Articles 39 ff of the TEC (Article III-133 DC). At this point, the ECJ refers to today's Article 17(2) of the TEC (Article I-10(2)(i) DC), which is linked to the status of the Union citizens and their rights conferred by the EC Treaty, which includes the prohibition on discrimination contained in Article 12 of the TEC (Articles I-4(2), III-123 DC) (para 62). Consequently, the issue of whether nationals and foreigners from EU Member States were treated differently must be examined. Since the requirement of a residence permit only has a declaratory effect under national law, the requirement of a specific permit was discriminatory. No objective, reasonable purpose justifies the discrimination. S may therefore not be excluded from receiving the child-raising allowance.

V. Concluding Remarks

92   There are different appraisals as to the reach of the consequences of Union citizenship. Whereas some have levelled the criticism that Articles 17 to 21 of the TEC (Article I-10 DC) are more symbolic in nature and did not introduce any substantive changes beyond the rights already existing under Community law,[165] others reacted positively to the regulatory framework granting individual rights, which are independent of economic rights and which occupy a central position in the EC Treaty, as a first step towards constitutionalising a European citizenship.[166] Such differences of opinion continue to exist.[167] The result varies according to the point of reference. An analysis based on positive law and its reali-

---

164 ECJ *Cowan* [1989] ECR 195, para 10.
165 Jessurun d'Oliveira in: Dehousse (ed) *Europe after Maastricht: An ever closer Union?* (Munich 1994) pp 126, 135 ff; O'Leary *European Union Citizenship. The options for reform* (London 1996) pp 44 ff; Weiler in: Winter et al (eds) *Reforming the Treaty on European Union. The Legal Debate* (The Hague 1996) pp 57, 65 ff.
166 O'Keefe (note 64) p 107.
167 See de Búrca in: *Referate für den Ersten Europäischen Juristentag* (Baden-Baden 2001) pp 39, 66–67.

sation will reach different conclusions than a perspective oriented towards the parallels to national citizenship.[168]

Looking at the provisions set forth in the EC Treaty, the implementing measures and the ECJ's case-law is like admiring an unfinished painting: 93

Currently, the promise of **diplomatic** and **consular protection** under Community law must be deemed nearly meaningless (Article 20 TEC/Article I-10(2)(c) DC). The Member States understand it merely as a right to consular assistance, the exercise of which is already permitted under applicable international law. 94

With regard to the **freedom of movement** (Article 18 TEC/Article I-10(2)(a) DC), Union citizenship has added little to the pre-existing secondary law. Nonetheless, for the first time there is a standardised basis for the different forms of the right to reside, which will effect a seamless right to mobility within Europe. Article 18(2) of the TEC (Article I-10(2)(a) DC), as a basis for secondary law, has already begun to produce a certain unifying effect. 95

The right to **petition** and **information** (Article 21 TEC/Article I-10(2)(d) DC) primarily refers to other provisions of the EC Treaty and thereby confirms the already existing state of affairs. The right to access to documents (Article 255 TEC/Article III-399 DC) sets further accents, since it had previously been unknown in the legal orders of some Member States. While all of these rights are typical positive civil rights, they are only of a subsidiary nature in terms of political decision-making. 96

The **rights to vote** and stand as a candidate at the municipal and European levels in the Member State of residence (Article 19 TEC/Article I-10(2)(b) DC) allow for further consideration of the legitimacy of sovereign power. Voting rights on both levels have legally expanded the notion of active citizenship in the context of legitimising entities. Although the notion previously differed based on the Member States, nationality no longer makes a legal difference for legitimacy in the Union. Nonetheless, the real importance of this provision is currently marginal. However, the Treaty establishing a Constitution for Europe, which emphasises the role of civil society and foresees referenda (Article I-47 DC), demonstrates the serious endeavours to increase the Union citizens' political participation. 97

Finally, the link between Union citizenship and the **general prohibition on discrimination** (Article 12 TEC/Articles I-4(2), III-123 DC) established by the ECJ's case-law has had significant effects. The ECJ applies the principle of national treatment, which can be seen in Articles 18, 19 and 20 of the TEC (Articles I-10(2)(a), (b) and (c) DC), to social and cultural rights beyond black letter law. Even though these rights are not original, but are rather contingent upon legal residence in a Member State,[169] they testify, as do the political rights, to the fact that the purely economic purpose of the rights guaranteed to the individual under Community law has been overcome. 98

Most importantly, then, the Treaty provisions on Union citizenship continue to **eliminate legal distinctions based on nationality**. Disadvantages which are caused by leaving the home State are to be counterbalanced. In certain fields, the Member States are obliged to grant rights to which their own nationals have a claim to other Union citizens. Union citi- 99

---

168 Shaw (1998) 61 MLR 295, 297 ff.
169 Closa (1995) 32 CMLRev 487, 508 concludes that the social rights provided under Community law form a break with the free market; however, the Member States are not thereby encouraged to create new policies of social intervention.

zenship defines an additional citizenship status beyond borders. For this reason, Article 17(1)(iii) of the TEC (Article I-10(1)(ii) DC) makes clear that citizenship of the Union complements national citizenship.[170]

100   The **further potential** which is assumed to go hand-in-hand with Union citizenship becomes evident in a direct comparison with national citizenship. Like national citizenship, Union citizenship is a sort of collective term for those rights which in their totality confer a status. Freedom of movement, political rights and diplomatic protection were long reserved to a State's own nationals. Therefore, from this point of view, the guarantees offered by Articles 17 to 21 of the TEC (Article I-10 DC) are particularly symbolic. The social rights as well are at least historically the rights of nationals,[171] so that the case-law extending them to other Union citizens follows the intent of Articles 17 to 21 TEC (Article I-10 DC). Also in line with Union citizenship's complementary function is the idea of an electorate based only on Union citizenship and place of residence, as is the case for the European Parliament (Article 19(2) TEC/Article I-10(2)(b) DC).[172]

101   Union citizenship, despite these parallels, is qualitatively not, and is not meant to be, comparable to national citizenship with its comprehensive scheme of rights and duties. Yet the rights it brings together eloquently express the shared responsibility of the Union and Member States for the individual citizen.

---

170 Similarly BVerfG (1994) 89 BVerfGE 155, 184: Union citizenship creates a long-term legal bond between the Member States' nationals – a bond that, while not as strong as that within a State, still legally and bindingly expresses the current level of existential commonness.
171 Note 46.
172 On the connection to the Union's legitimacy see Preuß (1995) 1 ELJ 267, 276 ff; Weiler in: Weiler (ed) *The Constitution of Europe* (Cambridge 1999) pp 324, 344 ff. Whether there is a "European people" behind this pan-European subject of legitimacy depends on the perspective, which is not necessarily related to the purely legal conception of Union citizenship. On identity-building factors such as the nation, a people, language, culture, history, myth, etc see Grimm [1995] JZ 581, 587 ff; for a critical assessment of a concept of a people based on Union citizenship see Augustin *Das Volk der Europäischen Union* (Berlin 2000) pp 41 ff, 63 ff; *cf* also Hrbek (note 6) pp 119, 130, according to whom there is a partial European identity, which has established itself alongside the European identity; see also the debate between Korioth (2003) 62 VVDStRL 117, 151–152 and von Bogdandy, (2003) 62 VVDStRL 156, 168 ff.

Table of Cases
Decisions of the European Court of Human Rights

Decision	Application Number	Cited at (§ – para)
A v United Kingdom (1999) 27 EHRR 611	25599/94	§ 2–59
Abdulaziz (1985) 7 EHRR 471	9214/80; 9473/81; 9474/81	§ 2–16
Adam	43359/98	§ 2–41
AGOSI (1987) 9 EHRR 1	9118/80	§ 5–22, 28, 31, 43
Ahmed (1997) 24 EHRR 278	25964/94	§ 4–31
Ahmed (2000) 29 EHRR 1	22954/93	§ 2–43
Airey (1979–80) 2 EHRR 305	6289/73	§ 2–21; § 6–66
Akdivar (1997) 23 EHRR 143	21893/93	§ 2–64
Aksoy (1997) 23 EHRR 553	21987/93	§ 6–26, 65
Albert and Le Compte (1983) 5 EHRR 533	7299/75; 7496/76	§ 4–84
Allen (2002) 35 EHRR CD 289	76574/01	§ 19–20
Allenet de Ribemont (1995) 20 EHRR 557	15175/89	§ 6–44
Amann (2000) 30 EHRR 843	27798/95	§ 3–3, 6
Amuur (1996) 22 EHRR 533	19776/92	§ 6–46, 21
Ankerl (2001) 32 EHRR 1	17748/91	§ 6–39
Arslan (2001) 31 EHRR 264	26432/94	§ 4–32
Artico (1981) 3 EHRR 1	6694/74	§ 2–64
Asan Rushiti (2001) 33 EHRR 1331	28389/95	§ 6–44
Ashingdane (1985) 7 EHRR 528	8225/78	§ 6–17, 37
Assanidze (2004) 39 EHRR 653	71503/01	§ 2–69
Atlan (2002) 43 EHRR 833	36533/97	§ 6–40
Autronic AG (1990) 12 EHRR 485	12726/87	§ 2–13; § 4–18, 21, 54
B v Austria (1991) 13 EHRR 20	11968/86	§ 6–9, 27
B v France (1994) 16 EHRR 1	13343/87	§ 3–8
Baghli (2001) 33 EHRR 799	34374/97	§ 3–7, 12, 25, 30
Baischer (2003) 37 EHRR 964	32381/96	§ 6–46
Banković	52207/99	§ 2–35; § 3–51
Barberà (1994) Série A, Vol 285-C	10590/83	§ 2–69
Barfod (1991) 13 EHRR 493	11508/85	§ 4–27, 49
Barthold (1985) 7 EHRR 383	8734/79	§ 2–32; § 4–3, 8, 31, 46
Beckles (2003) 36 EHRR 162	44652/98	§ 6–43
Belchev	39270/98	§ 6–24
Belgian Linguistics Case (1979–80) 1 EHRR 252	1474/62; 1677/62; 1691/62; 1769/63; 1994/63; 2126/64	§ 2–14
Belilos (1988) 10 EHRR 466	10328/83	§ 2–39
Beyeler (No 2) (2003) 36 EHRR 46	33202/96	§ 5–32, 37–38, 42
Bizzotto App No 22126/93	22126/93	§ 6–19
Bladet Tromsø (2000) 29 EHRR 125	21980/93	§ 4–47, 50
Bodén (1988) 10 EHRR 36	10930/84	§ 6–34
Borgers (1993) 15 EHRR 92	12005/86	§ 3–75; § 6–39

Decisions of the European Court of Human Rights

Decision	Application Number	Cited at (§ – para)
Bosphorus (2006) 42 EHRR 1	45036/98	§ 1–18; § 2–32, 37, 66–67; § 14–13
Bouamar (1989) 11 EHRR 1	9106/80	§ 6–7, 16, 29
Bowman (1998) 26 EHRR 1	24839/94	§ 4–31
Boyle and Rice (1988) 10 EHRR 425	9659/82; 9658/82	§ 6–63, 65
Bozano (1987) 9 EHRR 297	9990/82	§ 6–6, 9
Brand	49902/99	§ 6–19
Brandstetter (1993) 15 EHRR 378	11170/84; 12876/87; 13468/87	§ 6–40
Brannigan (1994) 17 EHRR 539	14553–14554/89	§ 6–30
Brogan (1989) 11 EHRR 117	11209/84; 11234/84; 11266/84; 11386/85	§ 6–25–26, 31
Broniowski (2005) 40 EHRR 495	31443/96	§ 5–32, 54
Buckley (1997) 23 EHRR 101	20348/92	§ 2–18
Buldan	28298/95	§ 6–66
Burghartz (1994) 18 EHRR 101	16213/90	§ 3–73
Cantoni RJD 1996-V, 1614	17862/91	§ 2–32
Casado Coca (1994) 18 EHRR 1	15450/89	§ 4–8, 31, 33, 46, 96; § 15–73
Castells (1992) 14 EHRR 445	11798/85	§ 4–30, 40
Cha'are Shalom Ve Tsedek	27417/95	§ 3–31–32, 67
Chahal (1997) 23 EHRR 413	22414/93	§ 6–20, 28
Chappell (1990) 12 EHRR 1	10461/83	§ 15–23
Chassagnou (2000) 29 EHRR 615	25088/94; 28331/95; 28443/95	§ 2–14; § 4–76; § 5–48, 57
Ciliz	29192/95	§ 3–9, 18, 24, 27–28
Cisse	51346/99	§ 4–60, 63
Ciulla (1991) 13 EHRR 346	11152/84	§ 6–7, 11
Civet (2001) 31 EHRR 871	29340/95	§ 2–64
Clooth (1992) 14 EHRR 717	12718/87	§ 6–27
Coëme	32492/96	§ 2–27
Colman (1994) 18 EHRR 119	16632/90	§ 15–73
Comingersoll (2001) 31 EHRR 772	35382/97	§ 2–69
Condron (2001) 31 EHRR 1	35718/97	§ 6–43
Corigliano (1983) 5 EHRR 334	8304/78	§ 6–48
Costello-Roberts (1994) 19 EHRR 112	13134/87	§ 2–34; § 6–65
Cruz Varas (1992) 14 EHRR 1	15576/89	§ 2–56
Cyprus v Turkey (2002) 35 EHRR 731	25781/94	§ 2–54, 15; § 3–51, 62; § 4–13
D v United Kingdom (1997) 24 EHRR 423	30240/96	§ 3–38
Dahlab	42393/98	§ 3–31, 36, 70
Dalia (2001) 33 EHRR 625	26102/95	§ 2–64
De Becker (1979–80) 1 EHRR 43	214/56	§ 2–36
De Cubber (1985) 7 EHRR 236	9186/80	§ 6–37
De Haes (1998) 25 EHRR 1	19983/92	§ 4–49

Decisions of the European Court of Human Rights

Decision	Application Number	Cited at (§ – para)
De Jong (1986) 8 EHRR 20	8805/79; 8806/79; 9242/81	§ 6–13
De Moor (1994) 18 EHRR 372	16997/90	§ 6–40
De Wilde (1979–80) 1 EHRR 373	2832/66; 2835/66; 2899/66	§ 6–29
Demir (2001) 33 EHRR 1056	21380/93; 21381/93; 21383/93	§ 6–26
Denmark v Turkey	34382/97	§ 2–54
Desmots	41358/98	§ 2–27
Deumeland (1986) 8 EHRR 448	9384/81	§ 6–34, 48
Deweer (1979–80) 2 EHRR 439	6903/75	§ 6–36
Diennet	18160/91	§ 6–36, 46
Dombo Beheer (1994) 18 EHRR 213	14448/88	§ 6–39
Döring	37595/97	§ 5–11
Dotta	38399/97	§ 2–27; § 19–24
Dragan	33743/03	§ 2–23
Drozd (1992) 14 EHRR 745	12747/87	§ 2–35
Dudgeon (1982) 4 EHRR 149	7525/76	§ 2–32; § 3–8
Dufay	13539/88	§ 14–13
Eckle (1983) 5 EHRR 1	8130/78	§ 6–48, 51
Editions Périscope (1992) 14 EHRR 597	11760/85	§ 6–34, 48
Edwards (2002) 35 EHRR 487	46477/99	§ 6–66
Eisenstecken (2002) 34 EHRR 860	29477/95	§ 2–39
Elsholz (2002) 34 EHRR 1412	25735/94	§ 3–9, 24, 28–29
Engel (1979–80) 1 EHRR 647	5100/71; 5101/71; 5102/71; 5354/72	§ 4–33, 70; § 6–6, 9–10, 29
Erdagöz (2001) 32 EHRR 443	21890/93	§ 6–13
Ergi v Turkey (2001) 32 EHRR 388	23818/94	§ 3–52, 65
Ezeh and Conners (2004) 39 EHRR 1	39665/98; 40086/98	§ 6–36
Ezelin (1992) 14 EHRR 362	11800/85	§ 4–2, 57, 61, 63, 67, 94
Fayed (1994) 18 EHRR 393	17101/90	§ 6–37
Feldek	29032/95	§ 4–1
Ferrazzini (2002) 34 EHRR 1068	44759/98	§ 6–35
Fischer (1995) 20 EHRR 349	16922/90	§ 6–46
Fischer	37950/97	§ 6–58
Fogarty (2002) 34 EHRR 302	37112/97	§ 2–43
Former King of Greece et al v Greece (2001) 33 EHRR 516	25701/94	§ 5–8, 32, 37, 43, 47–48
Fox (1991) 13 EHRR 157	12244/86; 12245/86; 12383/86	§ 6, 12–13, 23, 31
Fredin (No 1) (1991) 13 EHRR 784	12033/86	§ 5–11, 38
Fredin (No 2)	18928/91	§ 6–46
Fressoz and Roire (2001) 31 EHRR 28	29183/95	§ 4–50
Funke (1993) 16 EHRR 297	10828/84	§ 6–43; § 15–2; § 19–20
G.B. v Switzerland (2002) 34 EHRR 265	27426/95	§ 15–2

Decisions of the European Court of Human Rights

Decision	Application Number	Cited at (§ – para)
G.K. v Poland	38816/97	§ 6–27, 30
Garaudy RJD 2003-IX	65831/01	§ 2–40
Garcia Alva (2003) 37 EHRR 335	23541/94	§ 6–30
Gaskin (1990) 12 EHRR 36	10454/83	§ 4–11, 26
Gaygusuz (1997) 23 EHRR 364	17371/90	§ 5–7, 17; § 9–25
Ghiban	11163/03	§ 2–23
Girardi	50064/99	§ 6–51
Glasenapp (1987) 9 EHRR 25	9228/80	§ 4–43
Golder (1979–80) 1 EHRR 524	4451/70	§ 4–33
Goodwin (1996) 22 EHRR 123	17488/90	§ 4–50
Goodwin (2002) 35 EHRR 447	28957/95	§ 3–8, 11
Görgülü	74969/01	§ 3–28
Gradinger	15963/90	§ 6–58
Grams	33677/96	§ 3–64
Granger (1990) 12 EHRR 469	11932/86	§ 2–64
Grigoriades (1999) 27 EHRR 464	24348/94	§ 4–30
Groppera Radio AG (1990) 12 EHRR 321	10890/84	§ 2–48, 63; § 4–7, 54–56; § 15–73
Guérin	25201/94	§ 19–26
Guerra (1998) 26 EHHR 357	14967/89	§ 2–11; § 3–7; § 4–11; § 20–24
Gustafsson (1996) 22 EHRR 409	15573/89	§ 4–85, 88, 93
Guzzardi (1981) 3 EHRR 333	7367/76	§ 6–6, 12, 14, 18
H v Belgium (1988) 10 EHRR 399	8950/80	§ 6–40, 46
H.L.R. (1998) 26 EHRR 29	24573/94	§ 3–41
Haase (2005) 40 EHRR 430	11057/02	§ 3–29
Håkansson and Sturesson (1991) 13 EHRR 1	11855/85	§ 5–37; § 6–46
Halkin Emeği Partisi (2003) 36 EHRR 59	22723/93, 22724/93; 22725/93	§ 4–79
Handyside (1979–80) 1 EHRR 737	5493/72	§ 2–48; § 4–1, 7, 29, 34, 52; § 5–36, 40, 43; § 15–75
Hashman and Harrup (2000) 30 EHRR 241	25594/94	§ 4–9, 25
Hatton (2002) 34 EHRR 1	36022/97	§ 2–16; § 3–19
Hatton (2003) 37 EHRR 611 (Grand Chamber)	36022/97	§ 3–19, 28
Heaney RJD 2000-XII	34720/97	§ 6–43
Hennig	41444/98	§ 6–48
Hentrich (1994) 18 EHRR 440	13616/88	§ 5–37, 44
Herczegfalvy (1993) 15 EHRR 437	10533/83	§ 2–46; § 6–17
Hiro Balani (1994) 19 EHRR 566	18064/91	§ 6–40
Hirst (2004) 38 EHRR 825	74025/01	§ 2–17
Hirst	40787/98	§ 6–30
Holy Monasteries (1995) 20 EHRR 1	13092/87; 13984/88	§ 5–5, 44, 47
Hornsby (1997) 24 EHRR 250	18357/91	§ 2–64
Hornsby RJD 1998-II (Just Satisfaction)	18357/91	§ 2–69

Decisions of the European Court of Human Rights

Decision	Application Number	Cited at (§ – para)
Horvat	51585/99	§ 6–66
Hristov	35436/97	§ 6–30
Hubner	34311/96	§ 6–60
Iatridis (2000) 30 EHRR 97	31107/96	§ 2–64; § 5–37
Ignaccolo-Zenide (2001) 31 EHRR 212	31679/96	§ 3–18
Ilaşcu (2005) 40 EHRR 1030	48787/99	§ 2–16, 28, 35
Ilowiecki (2003) 37 EHRR 546	27504/95	§ 6–26–27
Immobiliare Saffi (2000) 30 EHRR 756	22774/93	§ 5–27
Informationsverein Lentia (1994) 17 EHRR 93	13914/88; 15041/89; 15717/89; 15779/89; 17207/90	§ 4–26, 55
Ireland v United Kingdom (1979–80) 2 EHRR 25	5310/71	§ 2–19, 27, 41, 44; § 6–11
J.G. v Poland	36258/97	§ 6–24
Jacubowski (1995) 19 EHRR 64	15088/89	§ 4–46
Jahn	46720/99	§ 5–23–24, 37, 47, 53–54
James (1986) 8 EHRR 123	8793/79	§ 2–7; § 5–32, 37–39, 43, 45, 47, 49–51; § 6–64; § 17–27, 29
Jéčius RJD 2000-IX, 237	34578/97	§ 2–59
Jersild (1995) 19 EHRR 1	15890/89	§ 4–33, 45
K.-F. (1998) 26 EHRR 390	25629/94	§ 2–18, 50
K.-H.W. v Germany (2003) 36 EHRR 1081	37201/97	§ 6–53
Kaya (1998) 28 EHRR 1	22729/93	§ 6–66
Kemmache (No 1 and 2) (1992) 14 EHRR 520	12325/86; 14992/89	§ 6–26–27
Kemmache (No 3) (1995) 19 EHRR 349	17621; 91	§ 6–8, 13
Keus (1991) 13 EHRR 700	12228/86	§ 6–22, 31
Khan (2001) 31 EHRR 1016	35394/97	§ 3–13; § 6–40
Kind	44324/98	§ 2–18
Kjeldsen (1979–80) 1 EHRR 711	5059/71; 5920/72; 5926/72	§ 2–13; § 4–4
Klass et al (1979–80) 2 EHRR 214	5029/71	§ 3–6; § 6–63, 65
Klein (2002) 34 EHRR 415	33379/96	§ 6–48
Kleine Staarmann	10503/83	§ 5–14
Knauth	41111/98	§ 3–3
König (1979–80) 1 EHRR 170	6232/73	§ 6–34, 48
König	39753/98	§ 6–29
Kormacheva	53084/99	§ 6–49
Kosiek (1987) 9 EHRR 328	9704/82	§ 4–13
Koua Poirrez (2005) 40 EHRR 34	40892/98	§ 19–39
Krastanov (2005) 41 EHRR 1137	50222/99	§ 6–49
Kreps	34097/96	§ 6–27
Kress	39594/98	§ 19–36
Kreuz	28249/95	§ 6–37
Kruslin (1990) 12 EHRR 547	11801/85	§ 2–46

Decisions of the European Court of Human Rights

Decision	Application Number	Cited at (§ – para)
Kudla (2002) 35 EHRR 198	30210/96	§ 2–18; § 6–66
Kuśmierek	10675/02	§ 6–52
Kutzner (2002) 35 EHRR 653	46544/99	§ 3–25
Labita	26772/95	§ 6–24
Laumont (2003) 36 EHRR 625	43626/98	§ 6–8
Lawless (No 2) (1979–80) 1 EHRR 13	332/57	§ 2–44
Lawless (No 3) (1979–80) 1 EHRR 15	332/57	§ 6–5, 11
Le Compte et al (1982) 4 EHRR 1	6878/75 ; 7238/75	§ 4–73, 84; § 6–36, 46
Leander (1987) 9 EHRR 433	9248/81	§ 4–11; § 6–65
Lehideux and Isorni (2000) 30 EHRR 665	24662/94	§ 4–33
Letellier (1992) 14 EHRR 83	12369/86	§ 6–26–27
Lietzow	24479/94	§ 6–30
Lingens (1986) 8 EHRR 407	9815/82	§ 4–1, 11, 27, 30, 45, 48
Lislawska	37761/97	§ 6–50
Lithgow (1986) 8 EHRR 329	9006/80; 9262/81; 9263/81; 9265/81; 9266/81; 9313/81; 9405/81	§ 5–8, 37, 49–51; § 6–37, 64
Lobo Machado (1997) 23 EHRR 79	15764/89	§ 19–36
Loizidou (1995) 20 EHRR 99	15318/89	§ 2–19
Loizidou (1997) 23 EHRR 513	15318/89	§ 1–6; § 2–35; § 3–51
López Ostra (1995) 20 EHHR 277	16798/90	§ 2–41; § 3–7, 19, 27; § 20–24
Luberti (1984) 6 EHRR 440	9019/80	§ 6–17, 29
Lüdi (1993) 15 EHRR 14	12433/86	§ 3–6
Luedicke (1979–80) 2 EHRR 149	6210/73; 6877/75; 7132/75	§ 3–74
Lukanov (1997) 24 EHRR 121	21915/93	§ 6–5, 7
Maaouia (2001) 33 EHRR 1037	39652/98	§ 6–35; § 19–42
Magee (2001) 31 EHRR 822	28135/95	§ 6–43
Malone (1985) 7 EHRR 173	8691/79	§ 3–6
Maltzan et al (2006) 42 EHRR 92	71916/01; 71917/01; 10260/02	§ 2–28
Mansur (1995) 20 EHRR 535	16026/90	§ 6–26
Manzoni	19218/91	§ 6–48
Marckx (1979–80) 2 EHRR 330	6833/74	§ 2–63; § 5–19
markt intern (1990) 12 EHRR 161	10572/83	§ 4–8, 17, 31, 46, 96
Mathieu-Mohin (1988) 10 EHRR 1	9267/81	§ 2–17, 43
Matthews (1999) 28 EHRR 361	24833/94	§ 1–17; § 2–22, 30, 32, 64
Matwiejczuk	37641/97	§ 6–27
McCann et al (1996) 21 EHRR 97	18984/91	§ 3–58
Mehemi (2000) 30 EHRR 739	25017/94	§ 3–7, 12, 30
Monnell (1988) 10 EHRR 205	9562/81; 9818/82	§ 6–9
Morel (2001) 33 EHRR 1118	34130/96	§ 6–37
Morsink	48865/99	§ 6–19

Decisions of the European Court of Human Rights

Decision	Application Number	Cited at (§ – para)
Moustaquim (1991) 13 EHRR 802	12312/86	§ 2–48
Müller (1991) 13 EHRR 212	10737/84	§ 4–14, 15, 17, 53
Muller	21802/93	§ 6–27
Müller	6849/72	§ 5–15
Murray (1995) 19 EHRR 193	18731/91	§ 6, 11–13, 23
Murray (1996) 22 EHRR 29	14310/88	§ 6–43
N.F. v Italy (2002) 35 EHRR 106	37119/97	§ 4–78
National Union of Belgian Police (1979–80) 1 EHRR 578	4464/70	§ 4–75, 86
Neumeister (1979–80) 1 EHRR 136 (Just Satisfaction)	1936/63	§ 2–69
Neumeister (1979–80) 1 EHRR 91	1936/63	§ 6–26
NEWS Verlags GmbH & Co. KG (2001) 31 EHRR 246	31457/96	§ 4–18
Nielsen (1989) 11 EHRR 175	10929/84	§ 6–16
Niemietz (1993) 16 EHRR 97	13710/88	§ 2–25; § 3–4–5, 13, 24–25; § 14–41
Nikitin (2005) 41 EHRR 149	50178/99	§ 6–59
Nikolova (2001) 31 EHRR 64	31195/96	§ 6–24, 30
Norris (1991) 13 EHRR 186	10581/83	§ 3–8
Nuray Şen (No 2)	25354/94	§ 6–66
O'Hara (2002) 34 EHRR 812	37555/97	§ 6–13, 26
Oberschlick (1998) 25 EHRR 357	11662/85	§ 4–1, 30, 45
Observer (1992) 14 EHRR 153	13585/88	§ 2–20; § 4–1, 17, 24, 32, 42
Öcalan (2003) 37 EHRR 238	46221/99	§ 3–57; § 6–6
Öcalan (2005) 41 EHRR 985 (Grand Chamber)	46221/99	§ 2–69; § 3–57
Odièvre (2004) 38 EHRR 871	42326/98	§ 3–8, 27, 67
Oğur (2001) 31 EHRR 912	21594/93	§ 3–52, 59, 64
Olbertz	37592/97	§ 5–11
Oliveira	25711/94	§ 6–58
Open Door (1993) 15 EHRR 244	14234/88; 14235/88	§ 2–6; § 4–42; § 15–78
Osman (2000) 29 EHRR 245	23452/94	§ 2–16
Otto-Preminger-Institut (1995) 19 EHRR 34	13470/87	§ 4–15, 31, 52
Özdep (2001) 31 EHRR 674	23995/94	§ 4–77
Özgür Gündem (2001) 31 EHRR 1082	23144/93	§ 4–17
Öztürk (1984) 6 EHRR 409	8544/79	§ 6–36
Pafitis and Others (1999) 27 EHRR 559	20323/92	§ 19–39
Pammel (1998) 26 EHRR 100	17820/91	§ 2–18
Papachelas (2000) 30 EHRR 923	31423/96	§ 5–34, 49
Papamichalopoulos (1996) 21 EHRR 439	14556/89	§ 2–69
Paskhalidis et al	20416/92	§ 6–34
Pauger (1998) 25 EHRR 105	16717/90	§ 6–46
Pellegrin (2001) 31 EHRR 651	28541/95	§ 6–34

Decisions of the European Court of Human Rights

Decision	Application Number	Cited at (§ – para)
Pérez (1996) 22 EHRR 153	16462/90	§ 6–29
Petra (2001) 33 EHRR 105	27273/95	§ 3–15, 21
Philis (1991) 13 EHRR 741	12750/87; 13780/88; 14003/88	§ 6–37
Philis (No 2) (1998) 25 EHRR 417	19773/92	§ 6–52
Piermont (1995) 20 EHRR 301	15773/89; 15774/89	§ 2–44
Pierre-Bloch (1998) 26 EHRR 202	24194/94	§ 6–35
Pine Valley (1993) 16 EHRR 379	12742/87	§ 5–55, 59
Plattform „Ärzte für das Leben" (1991) 13 EHRR 204	10126/82	§ 4–59, 62
Podbielski	27916/95	§ 6–52
Poiss (1988) 10 EHRR 231	9816/82	§ 6–51
Poiss (1991) 13 EHRR 414 (Just Satisfaction)	9816/82	§ 5–34
Posti & Rahko (2003) 37 EHRR 158	27824/95	§ 3–69
Powell and Rayner (1990) 12 EHRR 355	9310/81	§ 4–26; § 6–65
Predil Anstalt	31993/96	§ 19–24
Pretto (1984) 6 EHRR 182	7984/77	§ 6–51
Pretty (2002) 35 EHRR 1	2346/02	§ 2–14; § 3–3, 50
Prince Hans-Adam II of Liechtenstein	42527/98	§ 5–10
Probstmeier	20950/92	§ 2–18
Quinn (1996) 21 EHRR 529	18580/91	§ 6–7
Rachevi	47877/99	§ 6–52
Radio ABC (1998) 25 EHRR 185	19736/92	§ 4–55
Raimondo (1994) 18 EHRR 237	12954/87	§ 5–38–39
Randall	44014/98	§ 6–43
Rees (1987) 9 EHRR 56	9532/81	§ 2–21; § 3–11
Refah Partisi (2002) 35 EHHR 56	41340/98; 41342/98; 41343/98; 41344/98	§ 1–12; § 2–68
Refah Partisi (2003) 37 EHRR 1	41340/98; 41342/98; 41343/98; 41344/98;	§ 4–72, 79
Reid (2003) 37 EHRR 211	50272/99	§ 6–19
Reinhardt and Slimane-Kaïd (1999) 28 EHRR 59	23043/93; 22921/93	§ 19–36
Reinmüller	69169/01	§ 6–44
Rekvényi (2000) 30 EHRR 519	25390/94	§ 2–46
Remli (1996) 22 EHRR 253	16839/90	§ 2–70; § 6–37
Ribitsch (1996) 21 EHRR 573	18896/91	§ 3–42
Rowe and Davis (2000) 30 EHRR 1	28901/95	§ 6–40
Ruiz-Mateos (1993) 16 EHRR 505	12952/87	§ 6–40
S W v United Kingdom Série A Vol 335-B	20166/92	§ 6–56
S.A. Jacquers Dangeville RJD 2002-III	36677/97	§ 2–27
Şahin (2005) 41 EHRR 109	44774/98	§ 3–37
Sakik (1998) 26 EHRR 662	23878/94; 23879/87; 23880/93; 23881/87; 23882/87; 23883/87	§ 6–26
Salman (2005) 41 EHRR 8	21986/93	§ 3–40, 52–53, 59, 64

Decisions of the European Court of Human Rights

Decision	Application Number	Cited at (§ – para)
Santiago	31993/96	§ 19–24
Saunders (1997) 23 EHRR 313	19187/91	§ 6–43; § 15–2; § 19–20
Schenk (1991) 13 EHRR 242	10862/84	§ 6–44
Schiesser (1979–80) 2 EHRR 417	7710/76	§ 6–24
Schmautzer (1996) 21 EHRR 511	15523/89	§ 2–39
Schmidt (1994) 18 EHRR 513	13580/88	§ 2–7; § 3–66
Schmidt and Dahlström (1979–80) 1 EHRR 632	5589/72	§ 4–83
Schöps	25116/94	§ 6–30
Schouten (1995) 19 EHRR 432	19005/91; 19006/91	§ 6–34
Schuler-Zgraggen (1993) 16 EHRR 405	14518/89	§ 6–46
Schwabe	13704/88	§ 4–45
Scollo (1996) 22 EHRR 514	19133/91	§ 2–69
Scott (1997) 24 EHRR 391	21335/93	§ 6–26
Sekanina (1994) 17 EHRR 221	13126/87	§ 6–44
Selmouni (2000) 29 EHRR 403	25803/94	§ 3–40, 42, 45
Senator Lines GmbH (2004) 39 EHRR 13	56672/00	§ 2–33
Serves (1999) 28 EHRR 265	20225/92	§ 6–43
Sibson (1994) 17 EHRR 193	14327/88	§ 4–85
Sidiropoulos (1999) 27 EHRR 633	26695/95	§ 4–78
Sigurjonsson (1993) 16 EHRR 462	16130/90	§ 4–76, 88
Silver (1983) 5 EHRR 347	5947/72 6205/73, 7052/75, 7061/75 7107/75, 7113/75, 7136/75	§ 6–64; § 14–44
Slivenko (2004) 39 EHRR 490 (Grand Chamber)	48321/99	§ 6–20
Smirnova (2004) 39 EHRR 450	46133/99; 48183/99	§ 6, 50–51
Smith & Grady (2000) 29 EHRR 493	33985/96; 33986/96	§ 3–8, 68
Soering (1989) 11 EHRR 439	14038/88	§ 2–35; § 3–41, 54; § 5–8, 20, 32, 34
Sommerfeld (2004) 38 EHRR 756	31871/96	§ 3–28
Sporrong and Lönnroth (1983) 5 EHRR 35	7151/75; 7152/75	§ 5–8, 20, 32, 34; § 6–66; § 17–18
Stafford (2002) 35 EHRR 1121	46295/99	§ 6–9
Steel (1999) 28 EHRR 603	24838/94	§ 4–9, 25, 37; § 6–8
Société Colas Est (2004) 39 EHRR 373	37971/97	§ 2–25; § 15–23
Stögmüller (1979–80) 1 EHRR 155	1602/62	§ 2–64; § 6–13, 26–27
Streletz, Kessler and Krenz (2001) 33 EHRR 751	34044/96; 35532/97; 44801/98	§ 1–12; § 2–16, 18; § 6–55, 57
Sunday Times (1979–80) 2 EHRR 245	6538/74	§ 2–46; § 3–22; § 4–11, 17, 36; § 14–44
Sunday Times (No. 2) (1992) 14 EHRR 229	13166/87	§ 4–17
Süssmann (1998) 25 EHRR 64	20024/92	§ 6–49

583

Decisions of the European Court of Human Rights

Decision	Application Number	Cited at (§ – para)
Swedish Engine Drivers' Union (1979–80) 1 EHRR 617	5614/72	§ 2–7; § 4–83, 86
Sylvester (2003) 37 EHRR 417	36812/97; 40104/98	§ 3–28
T.P. and K.M. v United Kingdom (2002) 34 EHRR 42	28945/95	§ 6–66
Tammer (2003) 37 EHRR 857	41205/98	§ 4–31
Tekdağ	27699/95	§ 6–66
Tekin (2001) 31 EHRR 95	22496/93	§ 2–43
Tele 1 Privatfernsehgesellschaft MBH (2002) 34 EHRR 181	19182/91	§ 4–55
Tepe (2004) 39 EHRR 29	27244/95	§ 6–66
The Socialist Party (1999) 27 EHRR 51	21237/93	§ 4–74
Thorgeirson (1992) 14 EHRR 843	13778/88	§ 4–17, 29–30, 40, 45
Thynne, Wilson and Gunnel (1991) 13 EHRR 666	11787/85; 11978/86; 12009/86	§ 6–31
Tolstoy Miloslavsky (1995) 20 EHRR 442	18139/91	§ 4–43
Tomasi (1993) 15 EHRR 1	12850/87	§ 6, 26–27
Tomé Mota RJD 1999-IX, 402	32082/96	§ 2–64
Toth (1992) 14 EHRR 551	11894/85	§ 6–26–27
Tre Traktörer AB (1991) 13 EHRR 309	10873/84	§ 5–8, 11
Tsirlis (1998) 25 EHRR 198	19233/91; 19234/91	§ 6–31
Tyrer (1979–80) 2 EHRR 1	5856/72	§ 1–12; § 2–21; § 3–41
Unabhängige Initiative Informationsvielfalt (2003) 37 EHRR 710	28525/95	§ 4–45, 49
United Communist Party of Turkey (1998) 26 EHRR 121	19392/92	§ 4–2, 74, 79
Van der Leer (1990) 12 EHRR 567	11509/85	§ 6, 22–23
Van der Tang (1996) 22 EHRR 363	19382/92	§ 6, 26–27
Van Droogenbroeck (1982) 4 EHRR 443	7906/77	§ 6–29
Van Kück (2003) 37 EHRR 973	35968/97	§ 3–3, 71; § 6–38
Van Marle (1986) 8 EHRR 483	8543/79; 8674/79; 8675/79; 8685/79	§ 5–11
Vereinigung demokratischer Soldaten Österreichs (1995) 20 EHRR 56	15153/89	§ 4–30
Vereniging Weekblad Bluf! (1995) 20 EHRR 189	16616/90	§ 4–50
Vermeulen (2001) 32 EHRR 313	19075/91	§ 19–36
VGT Verein gegen Tierfabriken (2002) 34 EHRR 159	24699/94	§ 4–17; § 15–73
Vittorio	44955/98	§ 6–6
Vo (2005) 40 EHRR 259	53924/00	§ 2–24; § 3–49
Vogt (1996) 21 EHRR 205	17851/91	§ 4–43, 77, 79, 90
Von Hannover (2005) 40 EHRR 1	59320/00	§ 2–1; § 3–3, 27; § 4–31

Decisions of the European Court of Human Rights

Decision	Application Number	Cited at (§ – para)
Von Maltzan (2006) 42 EHRR 92	71916/01; 71917/01; 10260/02	§ 5–54
Vos	10971/84	§ 5–14
W v Switzerland (1994) 17 EHRR 60	14379/88	§ 6–26–27
W v United Kingdom (1988) 10 EHRR 29	9749/82	§ 3–28
Waite (2000) 30 EHRR 261	26083/94	§ 1–16; § 2–32; § 6–37
Wassink	12535/86	§ 6–31
Weber (1990) 12 EHRR 508	11034/84	§ 4–17; § 6–36
Weeks (1988) 10 EHRR 293	9787/82	§ 6–9, 28
WEH (2005) 40 EHRR 890	38544/97	§ 6–43; § 19–20
Wemhoff (1979–80) 1 EHRR 55	2122/64	§ 6–9, 26
Wiesinger (1993) 16 EHRR 258	11796/85	§ 5–38, 44
Wille (2000) 30 EHRR 558	28396/95	§ 4–23, 27
Wingrove (1997) 24 EHRR 1	17419/90	§ 4–15, 31, 52
Winterwerp (1979–80) 2 EHRR 387	6301/73	§ 6–5, 7, 17, 29–30
Wohlmeyer Bau GmbH	20077/02	§ 6–52
Worm (1998) 25 EHRR 454	22714/93	§ 2–65; § 4–36
Wynne (No 2) (2004) 38 EHRR 864	67385/01	§ 6–31
X and Y v The Netherlands (1986) 8 EHRR 235	8978/80	§ 2–16, 75; § 3–8, 23, 26, 68
X v The Netherlands	4130/69	§ 5–14
X v United Kingdom (1982) 4 EHRR 188	7215/75	§ 6–17, 22–23
X v United Kingdom (1983) 5 EHRR 192	7215/75	§ 6–5
Yağci (1995) 20 EHRR 505	16419/90; 16426/90	§ 6–26
Yankov (2005) 40 EHRR 854	39084/97	§ 6–24
Young, James and Webster (1982) 4 EHRR 38	7601/76; 7806/77	§ 2–34; § 4–57, 77, 83, 85
Z et al v United Kingdom (2002) 34 EHRR 97	29392/95	§ 2–16; § 6–66
Zannouti	42211/98	§ 6–27
Zumtobel (1994) 17 EHRR 116	12235/86	§ 6–37

Decisions of the European Court of Justice

Decision	Case Number	Cited at (§ – para)
Abrahamsson [2000] ECR I-5539	C-407/98	§ 18–33
Acrington Beef [1996] ECR I-6699	C-241/95	§ 19–32
Adams [1985] ECR 3539	145/83	§ 15–40
ADBHU [1985] ECR 531	240/83	§ 16–4, 12
Adoui [1982] ECR 1665	115/81	§ 9–12, 48; § 12–11
Advocaten	C-303/05	§ 14–16
AETR [1971] ECR 263	22/70	§ 1–34
Affish [1997] ECR I-4315	C-183/95	§ 16–3, 4, 17, 20, 33, 37; § 19–52
Agegate [1989] ECR 4459	3/87	§ 9–9
Ahlström Osakeyhtiö [1993] ECR I-1307	89/85	§ 18–13
Akrich [2003] ECR I-9607	C-109/01	§ 15–36
Albore [2000] ECR I-5965	C-423/98	§ 12–2, 38
Alcan [1997] ECR I-1591	C-24/95	§ 19–51
Allué I [1989] ECR 1591	33/88	§ 9–39; § 13–16
Allué II [1993] ECR I-4309	C-259/91; C-331/91	§ 9–21, 39, 51
Almelo [1994] ECR I-1477	C-393/92	§ 8–8
Alpine Investments [1995] ECR I-1141	C-384/94	§ 1–47; § 7–57, 77, 96; § 8–41; § 11–31, 41
AM & S [1982] ECR 1575	155/79	§ 14–8; § 15–19, 33; § 19–4
AMID [2000] ECR I-11619	C-141/99	§ 10–36, 38
Angestelltenbetriebsrat der Wiener Gebietskrankenkasse [1999] ECR I-2865	C-309/97	§ 18–38
Angonese [2000] ECR I-4139	C-281/98	§ 1–49; § 7–21, 42; § 8–20; § 9–46, 51, 55; § 11–45; § 14–35
Anker [2003] ECR I-10447	C-47/02	§ 9–27
Annibaldi [1997] ECR I-7493	C-309/96	§ 1–30
Ansaldo Energia [1998] ECR I-5025	C-279/96	§ 19–45, 46
Antonissen [1991] ECR I-745	C-292/89	§ 9–15
Apple and Pear Development Council [1983] ECR 4083	222/82	§ 7–43
Aragonesa [1991] ECR I-4151	C-1/90	§ 8–58, 59, 91; § 20–30
Arblade [1999] ECR I-8453	C-369/96; C-376/96	§ 7–24; § 9–35
ARD [1999] ECR I-7599	C-6/98	§ 15–71
Asscher [1996] ECR I-3089	C-107/94	§ 7–21; § 9–9; § 10–51
Assi Domän [1999] ECR I-5363	C-310/97	§ 19–26, 49
ASTI [1991] ECR I-3507	C-213/90	§ 9–37
Atlanta I [1995] ECR I-3761	C-465/93	§ 19–52
Atlanta II [1995] ECR I-3799	C-466/93	§ 19–52
Austrian Broadcasting [2003] ECR I-4989	C-465/00	§ 15–12, 39, 44
Ayaz [2004] ECR I-8765	C-275/02	§ 9–32

Decisions of the European Court of Justice

Decision	Case Number	Cited at (§ – para)
B & Q [1992] ECR I-6635	C-169/91	§ 7–73
Bachmann [1992] ECR I-249	C-204/90	§ 9–22, 51; § 12–18
Bactria Industriehygiene [2003] ECR I-15105	C-258/02	§ 19–31
Badeck [2000] ECR I-1875	C-158/97	§ 7–13; § 18–33
Banks [2000] ECR I-2005	C-178/97	§ 9–35
Barber [1990] ECR I-1889	262/88	§ 18–35, 51
Barkoci and Malik [2001] ECR I-6557	C-257/99	§ 10–8; § 21–32
Barra [1988] ECR I-355	309/85	§ 19–46
Barth [2004] ECR I-6483	C-502/01	§ 9–39
BASF [1999] ECR I-6269	C-44/98	§ 7–74; § 8–45
Basset [1987] ECR 1747	402/85	§ 8–77
BAT [2002] ECR I-11453	C-491/01	§ 19–31
Bauhuis [1977] ECR 5	46/76	§ 7–85
Baumbast [2002] ECR I-7091	C-413/99	§ 1–48; § 7–4; § 9–29; § 21–38
Baustahlgewebe [1998] ECR I-8417	C-185/95	§ 1–30; § 19–8, 38
Baxter [1999] ECR I-4809	C-254/97	§ 10–50
Bayer [1988] ECR 5249	65/86	§ 8–19
BECTU [2001] ECR I-4881	C-173/99	§ 20–33, 35
Beentjes [1988] ECR 4635	31/87	§ 7–22
Belgium v Spain [2000] ECR I-3123	C-388/95	§ 8–48, 77, 82
Belgocodex [1998] ECR I-8153	C-381/97	§ 20–26
Berlusconi [2005] ECR I-3565	C-387/02; C-391/02; C-403/02	§ 19–1
Bernini [1992] ECR I-1071	C-3/90	§ 9–11, 29
Bettray [1989] ECR 1621	344/87	§ 9–4
Beune [1994] ECR I-4471	C-7/93	§ 18–35
Bickel and Franz [1998] ECR I-7637	C-274/96	§ 13–8, 10, 18; § 19–44; § 21–88
Bidar [2005] ECR I-2119	C-209/03	§ 7–11; § 21–87
Biehl [1990] ECR I-1779	175/88	§ 9–22
Bilka [1986] ECR 1607	170/84	§ 18–33, 44, 45, 49
Biovilac [1984] ECR 4057	59/83	§ 17–14, 20, 27, 29, 27
Birden [1998] ECR I-7747	C-1/97	§ 9–13
Bleis [1991] ECR I-5627	C-4/91	§ 7–51; § 9–27
Blesgen [1982] ECR 1211	75/81	§ 8–36
Bluhme [1998] ECR I-8033	C-67/97	§ 8–45, 75, 83
Bond van Adverteerders [1988] ECR 2085	352/85	§ 11–20
Booker Aquaculture Ltd [2003] ECR I-7411	C-20/00	§ 17–21, 27
Bordessa [1995] ECR I-361	C-358/93	§ 12–2, 4, 8, 11, 26
Bosal Holding BV [2003] ECR I-9409	C-168/01	§ 12–18, 19
Bosman [1995] ECR I-4921	C-415/93	§ 1–47; § 7–1, 24, 45, 46, 78; § 8–20; § 9–7, 42, 46, 50, 51;

587

Decisions of the European Court of Justice

Decision	Case Number	Cited at (§ – para)
		§ 10–21; § 11–45; § 14–12; § 15–55; § 16–14, 37; § 17–20, 25, 32
Bosphorus [1996] ECR I-3953	C-84/95	§ 14–42; § 16–14, 37; § 17–20, 25, 32
Bostock [1994] ECR I-955	C-2/92	§ 14–32; § 17–14; § 19–41; § 20–26, 28
Bötel [1992] ECR I-3589	C-360/90	§ 18–31
Bouchereau [1977] ECR 1999	30/77	§ 7–85; § 9–48; § 11–59; § 12–11
Boukhalfa [1996] ECR I-2253	C-214/94	§ 7–48
Boussac [1980] ECR 3427	22/80	§ 13–13
Bozkurt [1995] ECR I-1475	C-434/93	§ 9–32
Brasserie du pêcheur [1996] ECR I-1029	C-46/93	§ 21–81
Broede [1996] ECR I-6511	C-3/95	§ 7–96; § 10–21, 27
Broekmeulen [1981] ECR 2311	246/80	§ 7–21
Brown [1988] ECR 3205	197/86	§ 9–17, 5; § 13–6, 7; § 21–87
Buchner [2000] ECR I-3625	C-104/98	§ 7–49
Burban [1992] ECR I-2253	C-255/90	§ 14–24
Burbaud [2003] ECR I-8219	C-285/01	§ 9–42
Burmanjer [2005] ECR I-4133	C-20/03	§ 7–90
Cabour [1998] ECR I-2055	C-230/96	§ 7–47
Calfa [1999] ECR I-11	C-348/96	§ 9–2, 47, 55; § 10–57, 58; § 12–12; § 21–45
Campus Oil [1984] ECR 2727	72/83	§ 8–63, 65, 74; § 9–48; § 11–59; § 12–12
Canal Satélite [2002] ECR I-607	C-390/99	§ 7–57; § 8–92, 93; § 11–54
Carpenter [2002] ECR I-6279	C-60/00	§ 7–25; § 8–13; § 11–54; § 15–12, 36; § 20–30, 31
Casagrande [1974] ECR 773	9/74	§ 9–29
Casati [1981] ECR 2595	203/80	§ 1–41; § 12–8
Cassis de Dijon [1979] ECR 649	120/78	§ 1–46; § 7–7, 63, 74, 78; § 8–56, 58, 79, 88, 91; § 10–3, 24, 34, 67, 69; 12–15
Centros [1999] ECR I-1459	C-212/97	§ 7–1, 24, 58; § 10–24, 34, 67, 69
Chen [2004] ECR I-9925	C-200/02	§ 15–53
CILFIT [1982] ECR 3415	283/81	§ 19–24
Cinéthèque [1985] ECR 2605	60/84	§ 8–80; § 15–81

Decisions of the European Court of Justice

Decision	Case Number	Cited at (§ – para)
Ciola [1999] ECR I-2517	C-224/97	§ 7–21, 78, 90; § 8–60; § 11–40
Clean Car [1998] ECR I-2521	C-350/96	§ 7–4, 21, 39, 45; § 9–28, 39, 46, 55
Clinique [1994] ECR I-317	C-315/92	§ 8–39
CMC Motorradcenter [1993] ECR I-5009	C-93/92	§ 7–74; § 8–45
CNTA [1975] ECR 533	74/74	§ 17–27
CO.NA.ME. [2005] ECR I-7287	C-231/03	§ 7–34
Colim [1999] ECR I-3175	C-33/97	§ 7–22
Collins [1993] ECR I-5145	C-92/92	§ 7–11
Collins [2004] ECR I-2703	C-138/02	§ 9–15; § 21–87
Coloroll Pension Trustees [1994] ECR I-4389	C-200/91	§ 18–35, 51
Commission v Austria [2004] ECR I-8291	C-465/01	§ 7–18; § 9–37
Commission v Belgium [1980] ECR 3881	149/79	§ 7–62; § 9–27; § 21–20
Commission v Belgium [1988] ECR 5445	42/87	§ 9–29
Commission v Belgium [1992] ECR I-305	C-300/90	§ 12–12, 18
Commission v Belgium [1992] ECR I-4431	C-2/90	§ 8–8, 60, 61, 80
Commission v Belgium [1992] ECR I-6757	C-211/91	§ 11–59
Commission v Belgium [1993] ECR I-6295	C-37/93	§ 9–37
Commission v Belgium [1993] ECR I-673	C-173/91	§ 18–31
Commission v Belgium [1994] ECR I-1593	C-47/93	§ 13–15
Commission v Belgium [1997] ECR I-1035	C-344/95	§ 9–15
Commission v Belgium [1998] ECR I-5063	C-323/96	§ 19–50
Commission v Belgium [1999] ECR I-3999	C-172/98	§ 13–6, 7
Commission v Belgium [2000] ECR I-1221	C-355/98	§ 9–55; § 10–46; § 12–23
Commission v Belgium [2000] ECR I-3123	C-388/95	§ 8–92
Commission v Belgium [2000] ECR I-7587	C-478/98	§ 12–18
Commission v Belgium [2002] ECR I-4809	C-503/99	§ 7–57; § 12–23
Commission v Council [1983] ECR 4063	218/82	§ 20–29
Commission v Council [1989] ECR 1425	242/87	§ 21–9
Commission v Denmark [1988] ECR 4607	302/86	§ 8–80, 83
Commission v Denmark [2003] ECR I-9693	C-192/01	§ 8–85
Commission v France [1986] ECR 1725	307/84	§ 9–27; § 10–35
Commission v France [1991] ECR I-659	C-154/89	§ 11–63
Commission v France [1996] ECR I-1307	C-334/9994	§ 7–57
Commission v France [1997] ECR I-6959	C-265/95	§ 1–50; § 7–28; § 8–16, 19; § 20–24, 32, 37
Commission v France [1998] ECR I-5325	C-35/97	§ 7–49; § 9–17
Commission v France [1998] ECR I-6197	C-184/96	§ 8–45, 92
Commission v France [2000] ECR I-1049	C-169/98	§ 9–39
Commission v France [2000] ECR I-11499	C-55/99	§ 8–86

589

Decision	Case Number	Cited at (§ – para)
Commission v France [2002] ECR I-4781	C-483/99	§ 7–1; § 12–23, 22
Commission v Germany [1979] ECR 2555	153/78	§ 8–52
Commission v Germany [1985] ECR 1459	248/83	§ 18–32
Commission v Germany [1986] ECR 2519	116/82	§ 16–29
Commission v Germany [1986] ECR I-3755	205/84	§ 10–30, 31, 35
Commission v Germany [1987] ECR 1227	178/84	§ 7–1; § 8–75, 85, 86, 88
Commission v Germany [1989] ECR 1263	249/86	§ 15–19, 36
Commission v Germany [1989] ECR 229	274/87	§ 8–22, 59, 85, 91; § 20–30
Commission v Germany [1989] ECR 3997	186/88	§ 8–28
Commission v Germany [1990] ECR I-2879	217/88	§ 19–51
Commission v Germany [1992] ECR I-2575	C-62/90	§ 8–71; § 15–11, 18, 19, 57
Commission v Germany [1992] ECR I-3141	C-195/90	§ 7–12
Commission v Germany [1994] ECR I-2039	C-317/92	§ 7–95
Commission v Germany [1994] ECR I-3303	C-131/93	§ 8–92
Commission v Germany [1998] ECR I-2133	C-24/97	§ 21–41
Commission v Germany [1998] ECR I-6871	C-102/96	§ 8–54
Commission v Germany [1999] ECR I-5087	C-217/97	§ 19–21
Commission v Germany [2002] ECR I-9977	C-325/00	§ 8–19
Commission v Greece [1988] ECR 1637	147/86	§ 7–37
Commission v Greece [1991] ECR I-1361	C-205/89	§ 7–85; § 8–57
Commission v Greece [1991] ECR I-727	C-198/89	§ 11–67
Commission v Greece [1995] ECR I-1621	C-391/92	§ 8–40
Commission v Greece [1996] ECR I-3285	C-290/94	§ 7–62
Commission v Greece [1998] ECR I-1095	C-187/96	§ 9–21, 51
Commission v Greece [2001] ECR I-7915	C-398/98	§ 8–63
Commission v Ireland [1981] ECR 1625	113/80	§ 7–85, 90; § 8–17, 28, 60
Commission v Ireland [1982] ECR 4005	249/81	§ 7–43; § 8–19
Commission v Ireland [1997] ECR I-3327	C-151/96	§ 7–57
Commission v Italy [1982] ECR 2187	95/81	§ 8–57
Commission v Italy [1987] ECR 2625	225/85	§ 9–27
Commission v Italy [1990] ECR I-4285	67/88	§ 8–91
Commission v Italy [1996] ECR I-2691	C-101/94	§ 7–34; § 10–58

Decisions of the European Court of Justice

Decision	Case Number	Cited at (§ – para)
Commission v Italy [2001] ECR I-4923	C-212/99	§ 9–39
Commission v Italy [2001] ECR I-541	C-162/99	§ 9–37
Commission v Italy [2002] ECR I-1425	C-279/00	§ 12–46
Commission v Italy [2002] ECR I-2965	C-224/00	§ 13–13, 17
Commission v Italy [2002] ECR I-305	C-439/99	§ 10–52
Commission v Italy [2003] ECR I-513	C-14/00	§ 8–88
Commission v Italy [2003] ECR I-721	C-388/01	§ 7–5, 21, 90; § 13–19
Commission v Luxemburg [1993] ECR I-817	C-111/91	§ 13–17; § 21–82
Commission v Luxembourg [1994] ECR I-1891	C-118/92	§ 9–21
Commission v Luxembourg [1996] ECR I-3207	C-473/93	§ 9–27
Commission v Netherlands [1991] ECR I-4069	C-353/89	§ 8–80; § 15–84
Commission v Portugal [2002] ECR I-4731	C-367/98	§ 7–1; § 10–21; § 12–22
Commission v Spain [1994] ECR I-911	C-45/93	§ 7–21, 78; § 10–21; § 13–15
Commission v Spain [1994] ECR I-923	C-375/92	§ 11–46
Commission v Spain [1998] ECR I-6717	C-114/97	§ 9–37; § 10–41, 42, 44, 45, 46; § 12–7, 23
Commission v Spain [2003] ECR I-4581	C-463/00	§ 7–96; § 12–7, 23
Commission v Spain [2003] ECR I-459	C-12/00	§ 8–88
Commission v United Kingdom [1983] ECR 203	124/81	§ 8–22
Commission v United Kingdom [1988] ECR 547	261/85	§ 8–92
Commission v United Kingdom [1992] ECR I-5785	C-279/89	§ 9–38
Commission v United Kingdom [2003] ECR I-4644	C-98/01	§ 12–7, 22, 23
Compassion in World Farming [1998] ECR I-1251	C-1/96	§ 8–54
Conegate [1986] ECR 1007	121/85	§ 8–74, 91
Conforama [1991] ECR I-997	C-312/89	§ 7–73
Connect Austria [2003] ECR I-5197	C-462/99	§ 19–47
Connolly [2001] ECR I 1611	C-274/99	§ 15–60, 63, 83
Consorzio del Prosciutto di Parma [2003] ECR I-5121	C-108/01	§ 8–92
Corsica Ferries [1989] ECR 4441	C-49/89	§ 11–20
Corsica Ferries [1994] ECR I-1783	C-18/93	§ 11–47
Costa v E.N.E.L. [1964] ECR 1141	6/64	§ 2–33; § 7–9; § 11–7; § 14–4
Costanzo [1989] ECR 1839	103/88	§ 7–9; § 14–53

591

Decisions of the European Court of Justice

Decision	Case Number	Cited at (§ – para)
Country Landowners Association [1995] ECR I-3875	C-38/94	§ 17–14
Cowan [1989] ECR 195	186/87	§ 7–69; § 13–2, 6; § 15–10; § 21–9, 91
Cowood [1982] ECR 4625	60/82	§ 15–61
Cristini [1975] ECR 1085	32/75	§ 9–23
CT Control BV and JCT Benelux BV [1993] ECR I-3873	C-121/91	§ 19–64
Culin [1990] ECR I-225	343/87	§ 15–9
Cullet [1985] ECR 305	231/83	§ 8–60, 63
Cwik [2001] ECR I-10269	C-340/00	§ 15–66
D'Hoop [2002] ECR I-6191	C-224/98	§ 1–48; § 21–87
DAFSE [2001] ECR I-673	C-413/98	§ 19–56
Daily Mail [1988] ECR 5483	81/87	§ 7–21; § 10–67
DaimlerChrysler [2001] ECR I-9897	C-324/99	§ 7–7
Danfoss A/S [1989] ECR 3199	109/88	§ 18–45
Dansk Supermarked [1981] ECR 181	58/80	§ 8–19
Dassonville [1974] ECR 837	8/74	§ 1–46; § 7–24, 72; § 8–33; § 12–7
Data Delecta [1996] ECR I-4661	C-43/95	§ 19–44
De Agostini [1997] ECR I-3843	C-34/95	§ 7–63; § 8–41, 43, 60; § 11–63, 66
de Groot [2002] ECR I-11819	C-385/00	§ 9–22
de Lasteyrie du Saillant [2004] ECR I-2409	C-9/02	§ 7–4; § 10–38, 52, 53, 59
Deak [1985] ECR 1873	94/84	§ 9–29
Decker [1998] ECR I-1831	C-120/95	§ 1–44; § 7–89; § 8–53, 60, 65, 80, 83; § 13–8
Defrenne I [1971] ECR 445	80/70	§ 18–35
Defrenne II [1976] ECR 455	43/75	§ 7–13; § 14–6; § 18–30, 51
Defrenne III [1978] ECR 1365	149/77	§ 18–32
Delhaize [1992] ECR I-3669	C-47/90	§ 8–77
Deliège [2000] ECR I-2549	C-51/96	§ 9–7
Demirel [1987] ECR 3719	12/86	§ 10–7; § 20–26, 28
Denkavit [1984] ECR 2171	15/83	§ 7–44
Denkavit [1991] ECR I-3069	C-39/90	§ 8–54, 91
Deutsche Milchkontor [1994] ECR I-2757	C-426/92	§ 8–74
Deutsche Post [2000] ECR I-929	C-270/97	§ 18–6
Deutsche Telekom [2000] ECR I-743	C-50/96	§ 19–37
Deutscher Apothekerverband [2003] ECR I-14887	C-322/01	§ 1–46
Deville [1988] ECR I-3513	240/87	§ 19–46

Decisions of the European Court of Justice

Decision	Case Number	Cited at (§ – para)
Di Lenardo and Dilexport [2004] ECR I-6911	C-37/02	§ 16–12, 35
Di Leo [1990] ECR I-4185	C-308/89	§ 9–29, 37; § 15–6
Diatta [1985] ECR 567	267/83	§ 9–29
Dilexport [1999] ECR I-579	C-343/96	§ 19–45, 46
DocMorris [2003] ECR I-14887	C-322/01	§ 7–7, 17, 22, 77, 85; § 8–42
Donà [1976] ECR 1333	13/76	§ 7–45
Dow Chemical [1989] ECR 3137	97/87	§ 14–20; § 15–19, 21, 22; § 16–14, 21, 38
Du Pont de Nemours Italiana [1990] ECR I-889	21/88	§ 7–87
Duff [1996] ECR I-569	C-63/93	§ 14–32; § 16–14, 21, 38; § 18–15; § 20–26
Economic and Social Committee v E [1999] ECR I-8877	C-150/98	§ 15–67
Edeka [1982] ECR 2745	245/81	§ 14–21; § 17–15; § 18–15
Edis [1998] ECR I-4951	C-231/96	§ 19–45, 46
EDSrl [1999] ECR I-3845	C-412/97	§ 8–45, 48
EDV-systems [1989] ECR 4035	3/88	§ 11–33
EEA [1991] ECR I-6079	C-1/91	§ 21–1
Elsen [2000] ECR I-10409	C-135/99	§ 21–40
Elz [1976] ECR 1097	56/75	§ 17–15
Emesa Sugar [2000] ECR I-665	C-17/98	§ 1–30; § 19–37
Emmott [1991] ECR I-4269	C-208/90	§ 19–49
Ergat [2000] ECR I-1487	C-329/97	§ 9–32
Eridania [1979] ECR 2749	230/78	§ 16–18; § 17–15
ERT [1991] ECR I-2925	C-260/89	§ 1–30, 38; § 7–94; § 8–71; § 14–12, 31; § 15–11, 71, 81; 20–26
Eurotunnel [1997] ECR I-6315	C-408/95	§ 19–32
Evans [1995] ECR I-563	C-324/93	§ 8–62, 63, 65
Exportur [1992] ECR I-5529	C-3/91	§ 8–77
Eyüp [2000] ECR I-4747	C-65/98	§ 9–32; § 15–37
Factortame [1990] ECR I-2433	C-213/89	§ 7–9, 34; § 19–47, 49, 51
Factortame [1991] ECR I-3956	C-221/89	§ 10–17, 20, 24
Familiapress [1997] ECR I-3689	C-368/95	§ 7–63, 89, 94; § 8–39, 52, 59, 71, 83; § 14–12, 29; § 15–85; § 20–26, 30, 31
Fantask [1997] ECR I-6783	C-188/95	§ 19–49
Faust [1982] ECR 3745	52/81	§ 17–15

Decisions of the European Court of Justice

Decision	Case Number	Cited at (§ – para)
Fedesa [1990] ECR I-4023	331/88	§ 14–48
Ferlini [2000] ECR I-8081	C-411/98	§ 9–19
Fernández de Bobadilla [1999] ECR I-4773	C-234/97	§ 9–39, 55
Fiddelaar [1960] ECR 1077	44/59	§ 15–61
Finalarte [2001] ECR I-7831	C-49/98	§ 9–35
Finsider [1985] ECR 2857	63/84	§ 16–10
Fisher [2000] ECR I-6751	C-369/98	§ 15–41
Fishermen's Organisations [1995] ECR I-3115	C-44/94	§ 16–3, 17, 33, 37, 38
Fiskano [1994] ECR I-2885	C-135/92	§ 19–11, 58
Foster [1990] ECR I-3313	C-188/89	§ 7–43
Foto-Frost [1987] ECR 4199	314/85	§ 14–32; § 19–52, 61
France and Ireland [1996] ECR I-795	C-296/93	§ 17–20
Francovich [1991] ECR I-5357	C-6/90	§ 19–46
Gaal [1995] ECR I-1031	C-7/94	§ 19–34
Gallagher [1995] ECR I-4253	C-175/94	§ 19–44
Garcia Avello [2003] ECR I-11613	C-148/02	§ 8–13; § 21–89
Garland [1982] ECR 359	12/81	§ 18–31
Gebhard [1995] ECR I-4165	C-55/94	§ 1–47; § 7–24, 57, 96; § 9–51; § 10–18, 21, 26, 27, 40, 59; § 11–34
Geddo [1973] ECR 865	2/73	§ 8–22
Generics [1998] ECR I-7976	C-368/96	§ 17–20, 28, 29
Geraets-Smits [2001] ECR I-5473	C-157/99	§ 7–1, 91
Germany v Commission [2004] ECR I-2081	C-344/01	§ 12–19
Germany v Council [1994] ECR I-4973	C-280/93	§ 14–43, 48, 49; § 16–3, 17, 20, 33, 35, 36, 38, 39; § 17–12, 15, 16, 29, 31; § 18–5; § 20–1
Germany v Parliament and Council [2000] ECR I-8419	C-376/98	§ 16–15, 35
Germany v Parliament and Council [2002] ECR I-4561	C-406/01	§ 19–31
Gerster [1997] ECR I-5253	C-1/95	§ 18–27, 32, 33, 44
Gewerkschaftsbund europäischer öffentlicher Dienst [1974] ECR 917	175/73	§ 15–55
Gisela Gerken [2004] ECR I-6369	C-295/02	§ 19–7
Givane [2003] ECR I-345	C-257/00	§ 9–3
Gloszczuk [2001] ECR I-6369	C-63/99	§ 10–8; § 21–32
Gourmet International [2001] ECR I-1795	C-405/98	§ 7–76; § 8–25, 41, 42, 43
Grado and Bashir [1997] ECR I-5531	C-291/96	§ 19–43

Decisions of the European Court of Justice

Decision	Case Number	Cited at (§ – para)
Graf [2000] ECR I-493	C-190/98	§ 7–24, 74, 78; § 9–43
Graff [1994] ECR I-3361	C-351/92	§ 20–26
Graffione [1996] ECR I-6039	C-313/94	§ 8–39
Grant [1998] ECR I-621	C-249/96	§ 1–38; § 3–10; § 15–37; § 18–21, 41; § 21–9
Gravier [1985] ECR 593	293/83	§ 13–7; § 21–9
Greenham and Abel [2004] ECR I-1333	C-95/01	§ 19–44
Griesmar [2001] ECR I-9383	C-366/99	§ 18–43
Groener [1989] ECR 3967	379/87	§ 9–39, 55
Groenveld [1979] ECR 3409	15/79	§ 8–48
Grogan [1991] ECR I-4685	C-159/90	§ 11–20; § 15–78; § 20–26
Grzelczyk [2001] ECR I-6193	C-184/99	§ 1–48; § 7–11, 49; § 9–2; § 10–49; § 13–7, 10; § 21–87, 89
Guérin Automobiles [1997] ECR I-1503	C-282/95	§ 19–8
Guérin Automobiles [1999] ECR I-1441	C-153/98	§ 19–13, 26
Guiot [1996] ECR I-1905	C-272/94	§ 7–24
Gül [1986] ECR 1573	131/85	§ 15–51
Gullung [1988] ECR 1	227/85	§ 21–32
Gutmann [1966] ECR 149	18/65	§ 14–25
Haag II [1990] ECR I-3711	C-10/89	§ 8–17
Halliburton [1994] ECR I-1137	C-1/93	§ 12–19
Hauer [1979] ECR 3727	44/79	§ 14–9; § 16–14, 39, 35; § 17–5, 6, 13, 21, 26, 29, 31; § 20–27, 29, 34
Hautala [2001] ECR I-9565	C-353/99	§ 19–22
Hayes [1997] ECR I-1711	C-323/95	§ 13–6, 7, 8, 21; § 19–44
Hedley Lomas [1996] ECR I-2553	C-5/94	§ 7–95; § 8–53, 55
Heijn [1984] ECR 3263	94/83	§ 8–31
Heinonen [1999] ECR I-3599	C-394/97	§ 8–92
Henn and Darby [1979] ECR 3795	34/79	§ 8–28
Hennen Olie [1990] ECR I-4625	302/88	§ 7–43
Herbert Handlbauer GmbH [2004] ECR I-6171	C-278/02	§ 19–7
Herbert Karner [2004] ECR I-3025	C-71/02	§ 14–32
Herbrink [1994] ECR I-223	C-98/91	§ 20–29
Hermès [1998] ECR I-3603	C-53/96	§ 10–10
Heylens [1987] ECR 4097	222/86	§ 7–34; § 16–21; § 19–42
Hochstrass [1980] ECR 3005	147/79	§ 7–11

595

Decisions of the European Court of Justice

Decision	Case Number	Cited at (§ – para)
Hocsman [2000] ECR I-6623	C-238/98	§ 9–3
Hoechst [1989] ECR 2859	46/87	§ 1–30; § 2–25; § 3–13; § 7–82; § 14–8, 20, 28, 38, 44, 45; § 15–19, 21; § 16–34; § 17–9
Hoever and Zachow [1996] ECR I-4895	C-245/94	§ 9–26, 37; § 21–82
Hoffmann-La Roche [1978] ECR 1139	102/77	§ 8–77
Hoffmann-La Roche [1979] ECR 461	85/76	§ 14–25; § 19–3
Hoogovens Groep [1985] ECR 2831	172/83	§ 17–15, 27
Houtwipper [1994] ECR I-4249	C-293/93	§ 7–96
Humbel [1988] ECR 5365	263/86	§ 11–20
Hünermund [1993] ECR I-6787	C-292/92	§ 7–43; § 8–43
HZA Hamburg Jonas [1988] ECR I-2355	170/86	§ 19–41
Ideal Standard [1994] ECR I-2789	C-9/93	§ 8–17
Imperial Tobacco [2000] ECR I-8599	C-74/99	§ 19–31
INAIL [2002] ECR I-691	C-218/00	§ 9–7
Inquiries against X [1996] ECR I-6609	C-74/95	§ 19–1; § 20–26
Inspire Art [2003] ECR I-10155	C-167/01	§ 7–1, 4, 58, 96; § 10–67, 69, 72
Internationale Handelsgesellschaft [1970] ECR 1125	11/70	§ 1–29; § 2–9; § 7–9; § 14–4, 7, 28; § 17–7, 8; § 20–27; § 21–5
Interporc [2003] ECR I-2125	C-41/00	§ 21–70
Irish Farmers Association [1997] ECR I-1809	C-22/94	§ 17–29
Jägerskiöld [1999] ECR I-7319	C-97/98	§ 8–8
Jänsch [1987] ECR 4923	277/84	§ 15–9
Jany [2001] ECR I-8615	C-268/99	§ 7–4; § 9–12, 33; § 10–8, 23; § 11–36
Jégo-Quéré [2004] ECR I-3425	C-263/02	§ 14–52; § 19–30, 31
Jenkins [1981] ECR 911	96/80	§ 18–45
Jeunehomme [1988] ECR I-4517	123/87	§ 19–46
Johnston [1986] ECR 1651	222/84	§ 1–30; § 7–34; § 18–27; § 19–42
K.B. v National Health Service [2004] ECR I-541	C-117/01	§ 3–11; § 18–28
Kaba [2000] ECR I-2623	C-356/98	§ 9–2, 23, 29; § 15–6
Kaba II [2003] ECR I-2219	C-466/00	§ 9–29
Kalanke [1995] ECR I-3051	C-450/93	§ 7–13; § 18–33
Kapasakalis [1998] ECR I-4239	C-225/95	§ 9–19
Karlsson [2000] ECR I-2737	C-292/97	§ 14–21, 31, 45; § 16–4, 29, 33; § 18–13; § 20–26
Kaske [2002] ECR I-1261	C-277/99	§ 9–26

Decisions of the European Court of Justice

Decision	Case Number	Cited at (§ – para)
Kaur [2001] ECR I-1237	C-192/99	§ 9–28; § 21–27
Keck [1993] ECR I-6097	C-267/91	§ 1–46; § 7–74, 75; § 8–37; § 9–43; § 10–54; § 11–55; § 12–7; § 20–30
Keller [1986] ECR 2897	234/85	§ 14–45; § 16–4, 29, 33
Kemikalieinspektionen [2000] ECR I-5681	C-473/98	§ 8–92
Kempf [1986] ECR 1741	139/85	§ 9–5, 10
Kenny [1978] ECR 1489	1/78	§ 9–38
Khalil [2001] ECR I-7413	C-95/99	§ 9–28
Kieffer [1997] ECR I-3629	C-114/96	§ 7–44
Kik [2003] ECR I-8283	C-361/01	§ 19–12
Kirk [1984] ECR 2689	63/83	§ 19–1
Kirsammer-Hack [1993] ECR I-6185	C-189/91	§ 18–47, 50
Klensch [1986] ECR 3477	201/85	§ 20–16, 29
Klöckner-Werke [1962] ECR 615	17/61	§ 18–12
Knoors [1979] ECR 399	115/78	§ 7–21
Köbler [2003] ECR I-10239	C-224/01	§ 19–24
Kohl [1984] ECR 3651	177/83	§ 7–85
Kohll [1998] ECR I-1931	C-158/96	§ 1–44; § 7–1, 88, 89; § 11–20, 62, 63
Kolpak [2003] ECR I-4135	C-438/00	§ 9–31
Kolpinghuis [1987] ECR 3969	80/86	§ 19–1
Kondova [2001] ECR I-6427	C-235/99	§ 21–32
Koninklijke Scholten-Honig [1978] ECR 1991	125/77	§ 18–13
Konle [1999] ECR I-3099	C-302/97	§ 12–2, 32, 33, 34, 35
Kowalska [1990] ECR I-2591	C-33/89	§ 18–31, 33
Kraus [1993] ECR I-1663	C-19/92	§ 7–24; § 9–42, 51; § 10–1
Kreil [2000] ECR I-69	C-285/98	§ 1–44; § 7–13; § 18–27, 33
Kremzow [1997] ECR I-2629	C-299/95	§ 7–20; § 19–43
Krombach [2000] ECR I-1935	C-7/98	§ 19–41
Krüger GmbH [1997] ECR I-4517	C-334/95	§ 19–52
Kühn [1992] ECR I-35	C-177/90	§ 14–43; § 16–18, 33, 35; § 17–15, 29
Kühne [2001] ECR I-9517	C-269/99	§ 7–34
Kühne & Heitz [2004] ECR I-837	C-453/00	§ 19–49
Kurz [2002] ECR I-10691	C-188/00	§ 9–32
Kus [1992] ECR I-6781	C-237/91	§ 9–32
Kuusijaevi [1998] ECR I-3419	C-275/96	§ 9–26
La Conqueste SCEA [2002] ECR I-1179	C-151/01	§ 19–28, 65
Läärä [1999] ECR I-6067	C-124/97	§ 7–90; § 20–31

Decisions of the European Court of Justice

Decision	Case Number	Cited at (§ – para)
Lair [1988] ECR 3161	39/86	§ 9–17; § 13–6, 7
Lambert [1988] ECR I-4369	128/87	§ 12–9, 29
Lauder [2000] ECR I-117	C-220/98	§ 8–89
Lawrence [2002] ECRI- 7325	C-320/00	§ 18–39
Lawrie-Blum [1986] ECR 2121	66/85	§ 9–5, 27; § 18–26
Lebon [1987] ECR 2811	316/85	§ 9–23
Leclerc [1995] ECR I-179	C-412/93	§ 8–41, 43
Lehtonen [2000] ECR I-2681	C-176/96	§ 7–24, 45; § 9–7, 49
Lenz [2004] ECR I-7063	C-315/02	§ 12–18
Les Fils du Jules Bianco [1988] ECR I-1099	331/85	§ 19–46
Les Verts [1986] ECR 1339	294/83	§ 14–25; § 19–28
Leukhardt [1989] ECR 1991	113/88	§ 16–17, 38; § 17–29
Levin [1982] ECR 1035	53/81	§ 9–5, 8
Lewark [1996] ECR I-243	C-457/93	§ 18–22, 31, 44
Lewen [1999] ECR I-7243	C-333/97	§ 18–30, 31, 35, 37, 43
Limburgse Vinyl Maatschappij [2002] ECR I-8375	C-238/99	§ 15–2; § 19–8
Lisrestal [1996] ECR I-5373	C-32/95	§ 19–11
Loi Evin [2004] ECR I-6613	C-262/02	§ 7–96; § 11–65; § 12–6
Lucaccioni [1999] ECR I-5251	C-257/98	§ 15–9
Luciano Arcaro [1996] ECR I-4705	C-168/95	§ 19–1
Luisi and Carbone [1984] ECR 377	286/82	§ 9–1; § 11–25; § 12–6; 21–9
Lütticke [1966] ECR 293	57/65	§ 7–12
MacQuen [2001] ECR I-837	C-108/96	§ 7–96; § 9–39
Manghera [1976] ECR 91	59/75	§ 7–12
Manninen [2004] ECR I-7477	C-319/02	§ 12–18, 19
Marchandise [1991] ECR I-1027	C-332/89	§ 7–73
Mars [1995] ECR I-1923	C-470/93	§ 7–66; § 8–39; § 15–85
Marschall [1997] ECR I-6363	C-409/95	§ 7–13; § 18–33
Marshall [1990] ECR I-4071	370/88	§ 16–4, 17, 33, 36
Martínez Sala [1998] ECR I-2691	C-85/96	§ 9–2, 23; § 13–10, 17; § 21–14, 42, 82, 84
Masgio [1991] ECR I-1119	C-10/90	§ 9–43
Mathot [1987] ECR 809	98/86	§ 8–13
Matteucci [1988] ECR 5589	235/87	§ 9–23; § 21–32
Mattila [2004] ECR I-1073	C-353/01	§ 19–22
Mazzoleni and ISA [2001] ECR I-2189	C-165/98	§ 7–24
Mediocurso [2000] ECR I-7183	C-462/98	§ 19–56
Meeusen [1999] ECR I-3289	C-337/97	§ 9–9, 18; § 10–48, 49
Meints [1997] ECR I-6689	C-57/96	§ 9–17, 39

Decisions of the European Court of Justice

Decision	Case Number	Cited at (§ – para)
Melkunie [1984] ECR 2367	97/83	§ 8–85, 86
Mengner [1995] ECR I-4741	C-444/93	§ 9–3, 10
Merida [2004] ECR I-8471	C-400/02	§ 9–23, 39
Metallgesellschaft [2001] ECR I-1727	C-397/98	§ 12–18
Metallurgiki Halyps [1982] ECR 4261	258/81	§ 17–15, 27
Metronome Music [1998] ECR I-1953	C-200/96	§ 14–8; § 16–12, 14, 32, 33, 35; § 17–13, 28
Meyhui [1994] ECR I-3879	C-51/93	§ 7–44; § 8–18
Micheletti [1992] ECR I-4239	C-369/90	§ 7–37; § 21–25, 28
Michelin [1983] ECR 3461	322/81	§ 14–25
Molenaar [1998] ECR I-843	C-160/96	§ 9–26
Montecatini [1999] ECR I-4539	C-235/92	§ 15–55, 80
Morson [1982] ECR 3723	35/82	§ 13–6
Moser [1984] ECR 2539	180/83	§ 7–20; § 18–13
Moulins Pont-à-Mousson [1977] ECR 1795	124/76	§ 18–13, 14
Mulder [1992] ECR I-3061	C-104/89	§ 17–27
Muller [1986] ECR 1511	304/84	§ 8–85, 86
Müller-Fauré [2003] ECR I-4509	C-385/99	§ 7–1, 89, 91; § 11–64
Mund & Fester [1994] ECR I-467	C-398/92	§ 13–18
Murphy [1988] ECR 673	157/86	§ 20–29
Musique Diffusion [1983] ECR I-1825	100/80	§ 19–11, 18
Mutsch [1985] ECR 2681	137/84	§ 9–23; § 19–44
N. [1998] ECR I-4871	C-252/97	§ 19–18
Nachi Europe [2001] ECR I-1197	C-239/99	§ 19–32
National Panasonic [1980] ECR 2033	136/79	§ 14–28; § 15–18, 22, 24
Nazli [2000] ECR I-957	C-340/97	§ 9–32
Netherlands and van der Wal [2000] ECR I-1	C-174/98	§ 19–22
Netherlands v Commission [1992] ECR I-565	C-48/90	§ 14–28
Netherlands v Parliament and Council [2001] ECR I-7079	C-377/98	§ 15–3, 7, 9; § 20–6
Neu [1991] ECR I-3617	C-90/90	§ 16–12, 34
Nicolet [1986] ECR 2049	203/85	§ 19–58
Nicolet [1988] ECR 1557	43/87	§ 19–58
Nimz [1991] ECR I-297	C-184/89	§ 7–9; § 14–15; § 17–15; § 18–32, 33, 51
Ninni-Orasche [2003] ECR I-13187	C-413/01	§ 9–5
Nitrates Directive [1999] ECR I-2603	C-293/97	§ 17–24, 29, 30
Nold [1974] ECR 491	4/73	§ 1–30; § 2–9; § 14–4, 7, 8; § 16–3, 12, 33, 35; § 17–15; § 20–27, 29

599

Decisions of the European Court of Justice

Decision	Case Number	Cited at (§ – para)
Nolte [1995] ECR I-4625	C-317/93	§ 18–49, 50
O'Flynn [1996] ECR I-2617	C-237/94	§ 7–22, 89; § 9–38, 50
Oebel [1981] ECR 1993	155/80	§ 8–36
ÖGB [2000] ECR I-10497	C-195/98	§ 9–39
Olazabal [2002] ECR I-10981	C-100/01	§ 9–48
Oleificio Borelli [1992] ECR I-6313	C-97/91	§ 19–63, 65
Olive Oil [1984] ECR 3881	232/81	§ 17–17, 22
Omega [2004] ECR I-9609	C-36/02	§ 3–39; § 7–57, 85, 92; § 10–23; § 14–12, 22, 34; § 15–8; § 20–30, 31
Oosthoek [1982] ECR 4575	286/81	§ 7–73
Orfanopoulos and Olivieri [2004] ECR I-5257	C-482/01	§ 15–36; § 19–44; § 21–45
Orkem [1989] ECR 3283	374/87	§ 15–2; § 19–4, 17, 19
Ortscheit [1994] ECR I-5243	C-320/93	§ 7–95; § 8–54
Ospelt [2003] ECR I-9743	C-452/01	§ 12–37
Owens Bank [1994] ECR I-117	C-129/92	§ 13–16
Oyowe and Traore [1989] ECR 4285	100/88	§ 15–61
Öztürk [2004] ECR I-3605	C-373/02	§ 9–32
Paletta I [1992] ECR I-3423	C-45/90	§ 9–26
Pall [1990] ECR I-4827	C-238/89	§ 15–85
Parfums Christian Dior [2000] ECR I-11307	C-300/98	§ 10–10
Parliament v Commission [2006] ECR I-4721	C-318/04	§ 15–58
Parliament v Council [1990] ECR I-2041	70/88	§ 19–28
Parliament v Council [1992] ECR I-4193	C-295/90	§ 21–9
Parliament v Council [2005] ECR I-2457	C-317/04	§ 15–58
Parliament v Council [2006] ECR I-5769	C-540/03	§ 1–37; § 14–16, 32
Parodi [1997] ECR I-3899	C-222/95	§ 12–2
Pastoors [1997] ECR I-1	C-143/95	§ 8–83
Peralta [1994] ECR I-3453	C-379/92	§ 7–74; § 8–45; § 10–47, 54, 59, 60
Perfili [1996] ECR I-161	C-177/94	§ 13–2
Peterbroeck [1995] ECR I-4599	C-312/93	§ 19–46
Pfeiffer [1999] ECR I-2835	C-255/97	§ 7–89; § 10–47, 54, 59, 60
Piercarlo Bozetti [1985] ECR I-2301	179/84	§ 19–42
Pinna [1986] ECR 1	41/84	§ 9–38
Pitsiorlas [2003] ECR I-4837	C-193/01	§ 19–26
Plaumann [1963] ECR 213	25/62	§ 19–27
Pokrzeptowicz-Meyer [2002] ECR I-1049	C-162/00	§ 9–33
Portugaia Construções [2002] ECR I-787	C-164/99	§ 7–78; § 9–35; § 12–11

Decisions of the European Court of Justice

Decision	Case Number	Cited at (§ – para)
Portugal v Council [1999] ECR I-8395	C-149/96	§ 10–10
Poucet and Pistre [1993] ECR 637	C-159/91	§ 18–57
Prais [1976] ECR 1589	130/75	§ 15–48, 49
Prantl [1984] ECR 1299	16/83	§ 8–33, 45; § 12–11
Preussen Elektra [2001] ECR I-2099	C-379/98	§ 7–90; § 8–8, 60
Punta casa [1994] ECR I-2355	C-69/93	§ 1–46
Ramrath [1992] ECR I-3351	C-106/91	§ 9–51
Rau [1987] ECR 2289	133/85	§ 14–20; § 16–8, 12, 18
Rauh [1991] ECR I-1647	C-314/89	§ 20–29
Raulin [1992] ECR I-1027	C-357/89	§ 9–10, 17; § 21–39
Ravil/Bellon [2003] ECR I-5053	C-469/00	§ 8–92
Razzouk [1984] ECR 1509	75/82	§ 18–6
Reed [1986] ECR 1283	59/85	§ 9–23
Reisch [2002] ECR I-2157	C-515/99	§ 12–3, 32, 33, 34, 35
Reisebüro Broede [1996] ECR I-6511	C-3/95	§ 11–63
Rewe [1981] ECR 1805	158/80	§ 19–47
Rewe [1984] ECR 1229	37/83	§ 7–44
Reyners [1974] ECR 631	2/74	§ 7–61; § 10–1, 45
Richardt [1991] ECR I-4621	C-367/89	§ 8–74; § 9–48
Rinner-Kühn [1989] ECR 2743	171/88	§ 9–10; § 18–31, 49
Roders [1995] ECR I-2229	C-367/93	§ 7–49
Rönfeldt [1991] ECR I-323	C-227/89	§ 9–26; § 17–14
Roquette frères [1989] ECR I-1553	20/88	§ 19–54
Roquette frères [1994] ECR I-1445	C-228/92	§ 19–54
Roquette frères [2000] ECR I-10465	C-88/99	§ 19–45
Roquette frères [2002] ECR I-9011	C-94/00	§ 2–25; § 15–19
Rothley and others [2004] ECR I-3149	C-167/02	§ 19–31
Rousseau [1987] ECR 995	168/86	§ 8–13
Royal Bank of Scotland plc [1999] ECR I-2651	C-311/97	§ 10–50, 51
Royal Copenhagen [1995] ECR I-1275	C-400/93	§ 18–38
Royal Pharmaceutical Society [1989] ECR 1295	266/87	§ 7–43
Royale Belge SA [1996] ECR I-5501	C-76/95	§ 15–9
Royer [1976] ECR 497	48/75	§ 9–3, 24
RTL Television [2003] ECR I-12489	C-245/01	§ 15–71
Ruckdeschel [1977] ECR 1753	117/76	§ 14–21; § 18–11, 13, 14
Ruhrkohlen-Verkaufsgesellschaft [1960] ECR 857	36/59	§ 1–25
Rush Portuguesa [1990] ECR I-1417	C-113/89	§ 9–35
Rutili [1975] ECR I-1219	36/75	§ 19–44
Ryborg [1991] ECR I-1943	C-297/89	§ 21–50
Sacchi [1974] ECR 409	155/73	§ 11–38

601

Decisions of the European Court of Justice

Decision	Case Number	Cited at (§ – para)
Safalero [2003] ECR I-8679	C-13/01	§ 19–47
Säger [1991] ECR I-4221	C-76/90	§ 7–89, 96
Sagulo [1977] ECR 1495	8/77	§ 13–2
Saint-Gobain [1999] ECR I-6161	C-307/97	§ 10–35, 51
Saldanha [1997] ECR I-5325	C-122/96	§ 13–7; § 19–44
Salzmann [2003] ECR I-4899	C-300/01	§ 12–32, 34
SAM Schiffahrt und Stapf [1997] ECR I-4475	C-248/95	§ 16–4, 14, 17, 33, 35
San Giorgio [1983] ECR-I 3595	199/82	§ 19–46
Sandoz [1983] ECR 2445	174/82	§ 8–86
Sandoz [1999] ECR I-7041	C-439/97	§ 12–15, 19
Sanz de Lera [1995] ECR I-4821	C-163/94	§ 12–4, 8
Sass [2004] ECR I-11143	C-284/02	§ 18–37
Saunders [1979] ECR 1129	175/78	§ 21–40
Savas [2000] ECR I-2927	C-37/98	§ 10–7
Schempp [2005] ECR-I 6421	C-403/03	§ 21–88
Schindler [1994] ECR I-1039	C-275/92	§ 7–57, 90, 97; § 8–9, 52; § 11–57
Schmidberger [2003] ECR I-5659	C-112/00	§ 7–31, 86; § 8–15, 16; § 14–12, 22, 34; § 15–80; § 20–32
Schnitzer [2003] ECR I-14847	C-215/01	§ 11–34
Scholz [1994] ECR I-50	C-419/92	§ 9–20
Schöning [1998] ECR I-47	C-15/96	§ 7–78; § 9–21, 39, 40
Schräder [1989] ECR 2237	265/87	§ 7–96; § 14–28, 43, 48; § 15–57; § 16–3, 11, 33, 35, 37; § 17–14, 20, 29, 31
Schumacher [1989] ECR 617	215/87	§ 7–95
Schumacker [1995] ECR I-225	C-279/93	§ 9–22; § 10–51; § 12–17
Schutzverband [1983] ECR 127	109/82	§ 8–60
Schutzverband gegen unlauteren Wettbewerb [2000] ECR I-151 C-254/98		§ 7–89; § 8–42, 45, 60, 80; § 12–2, 11
Scientologie [2000] ECR I-1335	C-54/99	§ 7–85; § 12–2, 11
Sehrer [2000] ECR I-4585	C-302/98	§ 9–39, 41
Semeraro [1996] ECR I-2975	C-418/93	§ 7–74; § 8–45; § 10–7
Sevince [1990] ECR I-3461	C-192/89	§ 9–32; § 10–7
Seymour-Smith [1999] ECR I-623	C-167/97	§ 18–30, 31, 32, 33, 44, 50
Sgarlata [1965] ECR 279	40/64	§ 1–25
Shingara and Radiom [1997] ECR I-3343	C-65/95	§ 19–44
Simmenthal II [1978] ECR 629	106/77	§ 7–7
Singh [1992] ECR I-4265	C-370/90	§ 10–15, 38; § 21–40
Sirdar [1999] ECR I-7403	C-273/97	§ 7–13

Decisions of the European Court of Justice

Decision	Case Number	Cited at (§ – para)
Skanavi [1996] ECR I-929	C-193/94	§ 7–11; § 13–2; § 21–37
Smits [2001] ECR I-5473	C-157/99	§ 10–54
SMW Winzersekt [1994] ECR I-5555	C-306/93	§ 16–3, 4, 17, 28, 29, 35, 36, 38; § 17–20, 29, 31; § 18–13; § 19–31
Sodemare [1997] ECR I-3395	C-70/95	§ 10–31
Sotgiu [1974] ECR 153	152/73	§ 7–22; § 9–21, 38; § 13–17
Spain and Finland v Parliament and Council [2004] ECR I-7789	C-184/02	§ 16–35
Spain v Commission [1993] ECR I-3923	C-217/91	§ 18–6
Spain v Commission [1999] ECR I-6571	C-240/97	§ 16–12
Spotti [1993] ECR I-5185	C-272/92	§ 9–21
Stauder [1969] ECR 419	29/69	§ 1–26, 28; § 14–4; § 15–4, 40; § 21–5
Steen I [1992] ECR I-341	C-332/90	§ 7–20; § 9–19
Steen II [1994] ECR I-2715	C-132/93	§ 7–20
Steffensen [2003] ECR I-3735	C-276/01	§ 19–41
Steinhauser [1985] ECR I-1819	197/84	§ 10–48
Steymann [1988] ECR 6159	196/87	§ 9–7; § 10–21, 31; § 11–28; § 15–50
Stichting [1991] ECR I-4007	C-288/89	§ 14–12; § 15–71, 84
Sukkerfabriken Nykøbing [1979] ECR 1	151/78	§ 16–12
Sürül [1999] ECR I-2685	C-262/96	§ 9–32; § 21–32
Svensson [1995] ECR I-3955	C-484/93	§ 7–57; § 12–3
Sydhavnens [2000] ECR I-3743	C-209/98	§ 8–60
T Port [1996] ECR I-6065	C-68/95	§ 14–49; § 16–39
T Port [1998] ECR I-1023	C-364/95	§ 18–14
t'Heukske [1994] ECR I-2199	C-401/92	§ 8–40
Taghavi [1992] ECR I-4401	C-243/91	§ 9–29
Ten Oever [1993] ECR I-4879	C-109/91	§ 18–28
Ter Voort [1992] ECR I-5485	C-219/91	§ 15–85
Teresa Guerra [1967] ECR 294	6/67	§ 19–12
Terhoeve [1999] ECR I-345	C-18/95	§ 9–36, 40
Testa [1980] ECR 1979	41/79	§ 17–14
Textilwerke Deggendorf [1994] ECR I-833	C-188/92	§ 19–32
Thetford [1988] ECR 3585	35/87	§ 8–77
Thévenon [1995] ECR I-3813	C-475/93	§ 9–26
Thijssen [1993] ECR I-4047	C-42/92	§ 10–45
Torfaen Borough Council [1989] ECR 3851	145/88	§ 7–73; § 8–36; § 15–50
Triveneta Zuccheri [1990] ECR I-1083	347/87	§ 19–64
Trojani [2004] ECR I-7573	C-456/02	§ 1–48; § 9–2; § 21–87

Decisions of the European Court of Justice

Decision	Case Number	Cited at (§ – para)
Trummer [1999] ECR I-1661	C-222/97	§ 12–2, 39, 40
TU-München [1991] ECR I-5469	C-269/90	§ 19–58, 59, 60
TV 10 [1994] ECR I-4795	C-23/93	§ 10–30; § 15–84
Überseering [2002] ECR I-9919	C-208/00	§ 7–1; § 10–61, 69, 72; § 11–6, 51, 62, 63
Uecker [1997] ECR I-3171	C-64/96	§ 21–35, 40
Unión de Pequeños Agricultores [2002] ECR I-6677	C-50/00	§ 7–34; § 14–52; § 19–30, 31, 32
Valsabbia [1980] ECR 907	154/78	§ 17–14, 15
van Bennekom [1983] ECR 3883	227/82	§ 8–86
van Binsbergen [1974] ECR 1299	33/74	§ 1–47; § 7–24; § 10–30; § 11–6, 51, 62, 63
van der Veldt [1994] ECR I-3537	C-17/93	§ 8–88
van Duyn [1974] ECR 1337	41/74	§ 7–85; § 9–1, 48; § 15–50
van Gend & Loos [1963] ECR 3	26/62	§ 1–43; § 7–7, 12; § 14–4; § 21–1, 38
van Harpegnies [1998] ECR I-5121	C-400/96	§ 8–75, 92
van Landewyck ('Fedetab') [1980] ECR 3225	209/78	§ 19–18
van Roosmalen [1986] ECR 3097	300/84	§ 15–50
van Schaik [1994] ECR I-4837	C-55/93	§ 7–57
van Schijndel [1995] ECR I-4705	C-430/93	§ 19–46
van Wesemael [1979] ECR 35	110/78	§ 11–63, 67
Vanacker [1993] ECR I-4947	C-37/92	§ 7–7
Vander Elst [1994] ECR I-3803	C-43/93	§ 9–35
VBA [2000] ECR-I 2135	C-266/97	§ 19–37
VBVB and VBBB [1984] ECR 19	262/80	§ 15–69
Verkooijen [2000] ECR I-4071	C-35/98	§ 12–16, 17, 18, 19, 21
Veronica Omröp Organisatie [1993] ECR I-487	C-148/91	§ 8–80; § 12–2; § 15–84
Vestergaard [1999] ECR I-7641	C-55/98	§ 7–21, 90
Vlassopoulou [1991] ECR I-2357	C-340/89	§ 7–34, 96; § 9–55; § 10–52
von Deetzen [1991] ECR I-5119	C-44/89	§ 17–14, 29
Vougioukas [1995] ECR I-4033	C-443/93	§ 9–26
VT4 [1997] ECR I-3143	C-56/96	§ 10–31
Wachauf [1989] ECR 2609	5/88	§ 1–38; § 14–31, 34, 45, 47, 48; § 17–27; § 19–41; § 20–26
Wählergruppe [2003] ECR I-4301	C-171/01	§ 9–32
Walrave [1974] ECR 1405	36/74	§ 1–49; § 7–45, 48; § 8–20; § 9–7, 46

Decisions of the European Court of Justice

Decision	Case Number	Cited at (§ – para)
Walt Wilhelm [1969] ECR 1	14/68	§ 19–16
Watson [1976] ECR I-1185	118/75	§ 10–1
Watts [2006] ECR I-4325	C-372/04	§ 7–91
Weber's Wine World [2003] ECR I-11365	C-147/01	§ 19–46
Weidert und Paulus [2004] ECR I-7359	C-242/03	§ 12–18, 19
Werner [1993] ECR I-429	C-112/91	§ 21–40
Westdeutsche Landesbank [2001] ECR I-173	C-464/98	§ 12–40
Wielockx [1995] ECR I-2493	C-80/94	§ 10–51; § 12–17
Wijsenbeek [1999] ECR I-6207	C-378/97	§ 9–24, 55; § 21–41
Wiljo [1997] ECR I-585	C-178/95	§ 19–32
Witte [1984] ECR 3465	188/83	§ 18–13
WuidArticle [1990] ECR I-435	267/88	§ 18–14
Wurmser [1989] ECR 1105	25/88	§ 20–30
X and Y v Riksskatteverk [2002] ECR I-10829	C-436/00	§ 12–18, 19
X v Commission [1994] ECR I-4737	C-404/92	§ 15–17, 18, 19
Yiadom [2000] ECR I-9265	C-357/98	§ 9–2, 24; § 19–44
Yves Rocher [1993] ECR I-2361	C-126/91	§ 7–73; § 8–45
Zenatti [1999] ECR I-7289	C-67/98	§ 7–96; § 9–54; § 20–31
Zuckerfabrik Bedburg [1987] ECR 49	281/84	§ 17–20, 27
Zuckerfabrik Süderdithmarschen [1991] ECR I-415	143/88	§ 16–3, 17, 33, 37; § 14–17; § 19–52
Zurstrassen [2000] ECR I-3337	C-87/99	§ 9–22, 51

Table of Model Cases

I. Decisions of the European Court of Human Rights

Decision	Application Number	Cited at (§ – para)
AGOSI (1987) 9 EHRR 1	9118/80	§ 5–22
Amuur (1996) 22 EHRR 533	19776/92	§ 6–4
Bladet Tromsø (2000) 29 EHRR 125	21980/93	§ 5–47
D v United Kingdom (1997) 24 EHRR 423	30240/96	§ 3–38
Gaygusuz (1997) 23 EHRR 364	17371/90	§ 5–7
Guerra (1998) 26 EHRR 357	14967/89	§ 2–11
Gustafsson (1996) 22 EHRR 409	15573/89	§ 4–82
Handyside (1979-80) 1 EHRR 737	5493/72	§ 5–36
Jahn	46720/99	§ 5–26
James (1986) 8 EHRR 123	8793/79	§ 5–45
K-F (1998) 26 EHRR 390	25629/94	§ 2–50
K.-H.W. v Germany (2003) 36 EHRR 1081	9749/82	§ 6–53
Matthews (1999) 28 EHRR 361	24833/94	§ 2–22
Müller (1991) 13 EHRR 212	10737/84	§ 4–14
Pine Valley (1993) 16 EHRR 379	12742/87	§ 5–55
Refah Partisi (2003) 37 EHRR 1	41340/98; 41342/98; 41343/98; 41344/98	§ 4–72
Schmidt (1994) 18 EHRR 513	13580/88	§ 3–66
Sporrong and Lönnroth (1983) 5 EHRR 35	7151/75; 71527/75	§ 5–20
Stankov (1998) 26 EHRR 103	29221/95; 29225/95	§ 4–58
Steel (1999) 28 EHRR 603	24838/94	§ 4–37
von Hannover (2005) 40 EHHR 1	59320/00	§ 2–1
Wille (2000) 30 EHRR 558	28396/95	§ 4–23

II. Decisions of the European Court of Justice

Decision	Case Number	Cited at (§ – para)
Alpine Investments [1995] ECR I-1141	C-384/93	§ 11–41
Angonese [2000] ECR I-4139	C-281/98	§ 7–42
Austrian Broadcasting Corporation [2003] ECR I-4989	C-465/00	§ 15–39
BECTU [2001] ECR I-4881	C-173/99	§ 20–33
Belgium v Spain [2000] ECR I-3123	C-388/95	§ 8–82
Bettray [1989] ECR 1621	344/87	§ 9–4
Bleis [1991] ECR I-5627	C-4/91	§ 7–51
Bosphorus [1996] ECR I-3953	C-84/95	§ 17–25
Carpenter [2002] ECR I-6279	C-60/00	§ 11–54
Commission v France [1997] ECR I-6959	C-265/95	§ 7–28
Commission v Spain [1998] ECR I-6717	C-114/97	§ 10–41

Decisions of the European Court of Justice

Decision	Case Number	Cited at (§ – para)
Connolly [2001] ECR I-1611	C-274/99	§ 15–60
DocMorris [2003] ECR I-14887	C-322/01	§ 7–17
Erich Ciola [1999] ECR I-2517	C-224/97	§ 11–40
Evans [1995] ECR I-563	C-324/93	§ 8–62
Factortame [1991] ECR I-3956	C-213/89	§ 10–17
Familiapress [1997] ECR I-3689	C-368/95	§ 14–29
Gebhardt [1995] ECR I-4165	C-55/94	§ 10–18
Germany v Council [1994] ECR I-4973	C-280/93	§ 17–12
Gourmet International [2001] ECR I-1795	C-405/98	§ 8–25
Grant [1998] ECR I-621	C-249/96	§ 18–21
Hauer [1979] ECR 3727	44/79	§ 17–5
Hayes [1997] ECR I-1711	C-323/95	§ 13–1
Hoechst [1989] ECR 2859	46/87	§ 14–38
Jégo-Quéré [2002] ECR II-2365	C-263/02	§ 19–29
Kohll [1998] ECR I-1931	C-158/96	§ 7–88
Lehtonen 2000] ECR I-2681	C-176/96	§ 9–49
Lewark [1996] ECR I-243	C-457/93	§ 18–22
Loi Evin [2004] ECR I-6613	C-429/02	§ 11–65
Luisi and Carbone [1984] ECR 377	286/82	§ 11–25
Mars [1995] ECR I-1923	C-470/93	§ 7–66
Martínez Sala [1998] ECR I-2691	C-85//96	§ 21–82
Meeusen [1999] ECR I-3289	C-337/97	§ 9–18
Metronome Music [1998] ECR I-1953	C-200/96	§ 16–32
Micheletti [1992] ECR I-4239	C-369/90	§ 21–25
Müller-Fauré [2003] ECR I-4509	C-385/99	§ 11–64
Netherlands v Parliament and Council [2001] ECR I-7079	C-377/98	§ 15–3
Nitrates Directive [1999] ECR I-2603	C-293/97	§ 17–24
Oleificio Borelli [1992] ECR I-6313	C-97/91	§ 19–63
Olive Oil [1984] ECR 3881	232/81	§ 17–17
Omega [2004] ECR I-9609	C-36/02	§ 7–92
Orkem [1989] ECR I-3283	2374/87	§ 19–17
Pfeiffer [1999] ECR I-2835	C-255/97	§ 10–47
Rau [1987] ECR 2289	133/85	§ 15–8
Schindler [1994] ECR I-1039	C-275/92	§ 11–57
Schmidberger [2003] ECR I-5659	C-112/00	§ 8–15
SMW Winzersekt [1994] ECR I-5555	C 306/93	§ 16-28
Terhoeve [1999] ECR I-345	C-18/95	§ 8–36
Tourist Guide [1991] ECR I-682, I-718, I-735	C-375/92	§ 11 58
Überseering [2002] ECR I-9919	C-208/00	§ 10–61
Verkooijen [2000] ECR I-4071	C-35/98	§ 12–16
X v Commission [1994] ECR I-4737	C-404/92	§ 15–17

607

III. Decisions of National Courts

Decision	Cited at (§ – para)
Bundesverfassungsgericht (GER) (2004) 111 BVerfGE 307	§ 2–73
Bundesverwaltungsgericht (GER) (1993) 91 BVerwGE 327	§ 5–62
Conseil d'Etat (F), Assemblée du contentieux 5 March 1999 – *Président de l'Assemblée Nationale* [1999] AJDA 460	§ 19–48
High Court (England and Wales) *Venables & Thompson v News Group Newspapers* [2001] 1 All ER 908	§ 2–73

Index

(§, para)

abortion § 3, 49, 52 ,
access
    to documents § 21, 70 ff
    to documents of Community Institutions
      § 19, 5, 20–21
    to an independent and impartial tribunal
      § 6, 37 ff; § 20, 12
    to records § 19, 2, 11, 59
accession to the ECHR (see ECHR)
acquired rights § 5, 8
advertising, restrictions on § 11, 65
agricultural Policy § 16, 3, 18
    market organisations § 16, 3, 19–20
allegiance, duty of (for government officials)
    § 15, 61–62
anonymous births § 3, 8
applicability, direct § 7, 7, 9, 49, 99; § 11, 6; § 12, 8
application for employment § 9, 15
arrest
    apprehension of minors § 6, 16
    conditions of arrest § 6, 6, 19
    convictions § 6, 7 ff
    duration of pre-trial custody
      § 6, 26–27
    right of compensation payment for
      deprivation of liberty § 6, 31
    right of judicial review of remand in custody
      § 6, 28 ff
assembly, freedom of § 4, 2, 57–71, 78, 81, 89, 92; § 15, 80
association agreements § 9, 31–32
association, freedom of § 4, 1–3, 70, 72–96; § 15, 55
asylum § 15, 88

Bachmann-judgement § 12, 18
Bananas case § 16, 39; § 17, 31
beneficiaries (see ECHR; fundamental rights of the European Union; fundamental freedoms)
biotechnology § 20, 6
birth, anonymous § 3, 8
broadcasting, television and film, freedom of
    § 4, 2, 20, 21, 26, 33, 44, 54–56
burden of proof § 3, 42, 46, 52
business premises § 3, 13

capital
    term § 12, 2
Cassis de Dijon case-law § 7, 63, 74, 78, 89–90; § 8, 37, 56, 58, 79–80; § 12, 15
certain selling arrangements § 8, 37 ff
CFSP
    economic embargo pursuant to Art 60 TEC
      § 12, 45
Charter of Fundamental Rights of the Union
    § 1, 35 ff; § 14, 3, 16 ff, 20 ff, 27–28, 33, 35, 40, 51, 55
    legal force § 1, 36–37; § 14, 16; § 20, 26
    provisions on restriction § 14, 43–44, 46; § 20, 14
    scope of protection § 20, 25
child custody § 3, 12, 18, 28
children, parental education of § 3, 31
citizenship § 21, 22 ff
citizenship of the Union § 7, 4, 7, 11, 14, 20; § 9, 2; § 21
    addressees § 21, 33 ff
    beneficiaries § 21, 15
    history § 21, 4 ff
    minority rights § 21, 88 ff
    nationality as a condition § 21, 25 ff
    prohibition of discrimination § 21, 37, 83 ff
    scope § 21, 10 ff
    social rights § 21, 85 ff
closed shop § 4, 77, 85
coherence (of the national tax system) § 12, 18
collective organisations § 11, 45
communication § 3, 6
    commercial § 15, 72 ff
Community law § 7, 1, 7, 9–10, 15, 20, 25, 30, 34, 48, 50, 56, 58, 82, 84 ff, 93 ff, 102, 104
    direct effect § 7, 7, 46
    execution § 20, 26
    precedence in application of secondary
      Community law § 7, 9, 102
    primary § 7, 10, 15, 44, 87, 93–94
    principle of uniformity § 7, 94
    secondary § 7, 7, 24, 35, 44, 46, 54, 81, 84–85, 95–96; § 8, 2, 18, 53, 55; § 9, 3
    supremacy of Community law § 7, 9, 95
company law § 4, 74; § 12, 25
comparative evaluation, process of § 14, 8; § 17, 8

609

Index

compensation for disadvantaging of women § 3, 70
competition law
  Council Regulation No 1/2003 § 15, 27 ff
  proceedings § 19, 8, 15 ff
complaint, right to an effective § 6, 63 ff
conditions of work and employment § 9, 21
conscience, freedom of § 3, 31 ff
constitutional traditions common to the Member States § 14, 7–8; § 17, 8
consular protection, right to § 21, 73 ff
continuance and free disposition, right of § 17, 15
correspondence § 3, 3, 5–6, 14–15
Costa ENEL case-law § 7, 9; § 14, 4
Council of Europe § 2, 5
  Committee of Ministers § 1, 11
  Parliamentary Assembly § 1, 23
covert discrimination (see fundamental freedoms)
criminal litigation, rights of the defendant § 6, 41 ff
cross-border scenario (see fundamental freedoms)
customs
  tariff, common § 8, 2
  union § 8, 2

Dassonville formula § 7, 24, 27, 72, 74–75, 79; § 8, 33 ff, 46, 48, 94; § 12, 7
data protection § 3, 3; § 15, 39 ff
death penalty § 3, 54 ff
demonstration, freedom of § 4, 60–63, 68–69
deportation of aliens, procedural guarantees § 6, 62
deprivation of liberty § 6, 3 ff
diplomatic protection, right to § 21, 73 ff
direct investments § 12, 42
direction of another person (performance of services under) § 9, 9
Directive 88/361/EEC § 12, 8
discretion / margin of appreciation § 16, 38–39
  by the Member States § 8, 86 ff
discrimination, prohibition of § 3, 66 ff (see also fundamental freedoms)
  general principle of equality § 18, 11 ff
  – differences to civil rights § 18, 7 ff
  – formation of comparison groups § 18, 13
  – legal consequences of a violation § 18, 16
  – norm structure § 18, 7 ff
  – principle of proportionality § 18, 15
  specific principles of equality § 18, 17 ff
  – equality of men and women, § 18, 21 ff

– integration of persons with disabilities, § 18, 54
– relation to the general principle of equality § 18, 18
– rights of children, § 18, 54
– rights of elderly people, § 18, 54
– typology, § 18, 2 ff
dividends, taxation of § 12, 19
Drittwirkung (see fundamental rights of the European Union, fundamental freedoms)
duration of court proceedings, adequate § 2, 18; § 6, 48 ff, 66

ECB § 12, 28, 29
ECHELON § 15, 82
economic activity § 9, 7
Economic and Monetary Union
  balance of payments § 12, 27
  economic troubles § 12, 43
economic constitution of the Community § 16, 2
economic embargo (see embargo)
effect, direct § 7, 7, 13, 43, 49
effects § 7, 11, 23–24
  of the prohibition of discrimination § 7, 11, 23
  of the prohibition of limitation § 7, 24
effet utile § 19, 45 ff
embargo (economic embargo)
  movement of capital § 12, 45
employment law § 16, 4
entities bound (by fundamental rights) (see ECHR; fundamental rights of the Union; fundamental freedoms)
environmental protection § 3, 7, 19, 26
  fundamental right to § 20, 23
equality of arms, principle of § 6, 39
essence of a fundamental right (see fundamental rights of the European Union)
establishment, freedom of § 10
  company statute § 10, 64
  country of origin principle § 10, 3 ff
  definition § 10, 20 ff
  delineation from the freedom to provide services § 10, 19–21, 26 ff, 31–32, 34
  destination principle § 10, 3 ff, 19
  economic activity § 10, 20, 24
  and the freedom of establishment under international public law § 10, 6
  and CFSP § 10, 9 ff
  incorporation theory § 10, 64 ff
  indirect discrimination § 10, 50–51
  international company law § 10, 66 ff
  legal persons § 10, 16, 34 ff, 62 ff

610

Index

open discrimination § 10, 50
primary establishment § 10, 33–34
prohibition of restriction § 10, 5, 52 ff
real seat / head office theory § 10, 64 ff
reverse discrimination § 10, 39
secondary establishment § 10, 33, 35–36
European Central Bank § 12, 28, 29
European citizenship rights § 7, 18; § 20, 11
European Convention for the Prevention of Torture and Inhuman or Degrading Treatment or Punishment § 1, 20
European Convention for the Protection of Human Rights and Fundamental Freedoms, fundamental rights of the ECHR § 2, 1 ff
accession of the EC/EU § 1, 33 ff; § 20, 38–39
applicability § 2, 39
Article 8 of the ECHR § 15, 18 ff, 23–24, 34, 36
Article 10 of the ECHR § 15, 59 ff, 71
beneficiaries § 2, 22 ff
– legal persons under private law and other groups of individuals § 2, 25
– legal persons under public law § 2, 25–26
– natural persons § 2, 22 ff
– citizens of the Contracting States § 2, 22
– nationals of third countries § 2, 22
entities bound by the Convention Rights § 2, 27 ff
– Convention States of the Council of Europe § 2, 27–28
– European Community § 2, 30; § 14, 11
– private persons § 2, 34
functions § 2, 11 ff
– civic rights § 2, 17
– defensive or liberty rights § 2, 13
– equal treatment and equality before the law § 2, 14
– procedural rights § 2, 18
– rights to governmental action / positive obligations § 2, 15–16
history and development § 1, 5 ff
horizontal effect (Drittwirkung) § 2, 6, 34
individual application/ individual complaint § 1, 8, 11–12; § 2, 53, 56 ff
interference § 2, 41–42
interpretation § 2, 21, 43, 55, 64
judicial protection § 2, 50 ff
– individual application § 2, 52, 56 ff
– capacity to be party to proceedings § 2, 59
– capacity to take legal action § 2, 59
– content of complaint § 2, 65–66

– exhaustion of domestic remedies § 2, 64
– legal standing § 2, 63
– time-limit § 2, 65
– inter-state cases § 2, 53
language § 2, 5, 57, 64, 71
means for the interpretation of the fundamental rights of the European Union § 1, 44 ff; § 14, 8, 13
obligation to international organisations § 1, 16 ff
principle of proportionality § 2, 14, 44, 48
protocols to the ECHR § 1, 10, § 2, 5–6, 13–14, 21–22, 27, 39, 48, 58, 71
– 1st § 2, 5, 13, 15, 17, 21, 24, 26, 35–36, 42, 46–47
– 3rd § 2, 5
– 4th § 2, 5, 13, 23, 35, 46
– 6th § 2, 5, 13, 35, 39
– 7th § 2, 3, 5, 14–15, 18, 23, 34–35, 46; § 6, 62
– 11th § 2, 51
– 12th § 2, 5, 14
– 13th § 2, 39
– 14th § 2, 5, 9, 30, 52, 55, 66–67
rank and status of the ECHR within the domestic legal orders § 2, 6 ff
rank within the German legal order § 1, 14
relation to the fundamental rights of the European Union § 2, 9; § 14, 13
requirement of a legal basis § 2, 3, 39, 43, 46; § 3, 21 ff, 35, 45, 57
restriction of Convention Rights
– general provisions § 2, 44
– inherent Convention limitations § 3, 45
– specific provisions § 2, 45 ff
right to governmental protection § 2, 16, 68
scope of protection § 2, 35–36
– personal (see beneficiaries)
– subject matter of protection § 2, 62
– temporal § 2, 36
– territorial § 2, 35
treaty establishing a Constitution for Europe § 2, 9, 30, 33
European Court of Human Rights § 2, 5, 7, 16, 24, 43 ff, 53–54
European Data Protection Supervisor § 15, 41–42
European Parliament, rules governing the election to § 21, 61 ff
European Passenger Data § 15, 58
European Social Charter § 1, 19; § 5, 62 ff; § 16, 4, 6
European Warrant of Arrest § 15, 88

611

Index

euthanasia § 3, 50
evidence
   hearing of evidence § 6, 38, 42–43
   the principle of equality of arms § 6, 39–40
   right to be heard § 6, 40
exchange rate policy § 12, 29
expression, freedom of § 4, 1–9, 16, 26–28, 30, 39, 52, 57; § 15, 61 ff, 76–77
expropriations § 5, 23 ff; § 17, 18, 27
   compensation § 5, 30, 33, 45 ff; § 17, 27
   – of foreign nationals § 5, 46
   – leeway for the determination of the amount § 5, 50
   – necessary level of the compensation § 5, 49
expulsion and deportation measures § 3, 7, 17, 30, 33, 41, 44, 47

Factortame case-law § 10, 17, 25
family
   members § 9, 29
   life § 3, 9 ff; § 15, 36 ff
federal community, situations hazardous to § 13, 3; § 18, 2
foreign relations (of the EC) § 1, 39
foreign trade and payments legislation § 12, 26–27
foreseeability of a legal basis for an interference § 3, 22
   criminal law, rules of § 6, 54, 56
form requirements, essential § 19, 14
free movement of services § 15, 71, 78, 84
   comprehensive prohibition of interferences § 11, 50
   cross-boarder element § 11, 26
   definition § 11, 19
   delineation
   – from the freedom of establishment § 11, 34
   – from the free movement of capital § 11, 37
   – from the free movement of goods § 11, 38
   – from the freedom of movement for workers § 11, 36
   direct applicability § 11, 6
   direct discriminations § 11, 46
   exception of Article 45 of the TEC § 11, 33
   freedom to provide services § 11, 27
   freedom to receive services § 11, 28
   general limits § 11, 66
   indirect discriminations § 11, 47

   liberalisation under secondary legislation § 11, 11
   modification of the prohibition of interferences § 11, 55
   the new strategy for the internal market § 11, 13
   obligors § 11, 43
   personal scope of protection § 11, 15
   principle of proportionality § 11, 66
   remuneration § 11, 20
   requirement of residency in the host state § 11, 48
   restrictions
   – explicit written § 11, 59
   – unwritten § 11, 62
   structure of the freedom to provide services in Community Law § 11, 4
   subject matter of protection § 11, 18
   territorial scope of protection § 11, 14
freedom and security § 15, 86 ff
freedom of movement
   within the community § 15, 51 ff; § 21, 37 ff
   of the employees § 15, 5–6, 36, 51 ff
freedom of movement for workers
   relation to the free movement of capital § 12, 3
freedom of occupation § 3, 5; § 5, 47
   delineation from the fundamental freedoms § 16, 21 ff
   interferences § 16, 30
freedom of the press and broadcasting § 4, 2, 17–22; § 15, 69 ff
fundamental freedoms
   beneficiaries § 7, 16, 21, 36 ff, 99
   – companies § 7, 38–39
   – legal persons
   – governed by private law § 7, 38
   – governed by public law § 7, 38
   – natural persons
   – nationals of the Member States § 7, 37
   – non-EU citizens § 7, 41
   cross-border scenario/situation § 7, 6, 15, 19 ff, 27, 37, 47, 55, 58, 69, 77, 91, 97, 98; § 8, 13; § 9, 19; § 11, 26; § 12, 4–5, 39
   delineation § 7, 10 ff, 57
   – from each other § 7, 57; § 11, 34 ff; § 12, 3
   – from the fundamental rights of the Union § 7, 15; § 14, 12
   – from the general prohibition of discrimination § 7, 11
   – from specific prohibitions of discrimination § 7, 12–13

Index

direct applicability § 7, 7, 9, 49
direct internalisation § 7, 7
discrimination § 7, 11, 13, 19 ff, 24 ff, 30, 33–34, 45, 47, 68 ff, 72, 75, 78, 89 ff, 96, 98; § 9, 37 ff; § 16, 17
– the concept of § 7, 22, 69
– covert § 7, 22, 24, 69, 78, 90, 98
– direct § 7, 22, 24, 70; § 8, 28, 60–61, 79; § 11, 46
– indirect § 7, 22, 24, 70; § 8, 29, 31, 79; § 11, 47
– overt § 7, 22, 24, 69, 78, 90–91, 96, 98
– reporting requirements in cross-border capital and payment transactions § 12, 26–27
– standard of comparison § 7, 20
– tax legislation § 12, 16–21
entities bound by the fundamental freedoms § 7, 7 ff, 16, 42 ff, 67, 93, 98
– European Communities § 7, 43–44, 67, 103–104
– Member States § 7, 7, 37, 43, 48, 94, 104
– private persons § 7, 45, 46
exception to the scope of protection § 7, 59 ff; § 9, 27; § 11, 33
functions
– equality rights § 7, 19 ff
– liberty rights § 7, 24–25
– objective dimension of the fundamental freedoms § 7, 35
– procedural rights § 7, 34
– rights to governmental action § 7, 28 ff
– subjective rights of the individual § 1, 42–43
general limits to restrictability § 7, 80, 92 ff, 98; § 9, 52 ff; § 11, 66
– fundamental rights of the Union § 7, 86, 94–95, 98
– other provisions of primary Community law § 7, 94
– principle of proportionality § 7, 96
interference § 7, 15, 66 ff, 74, 80 ff
justification § 7, 15, 22, 27, 46, 50, 58, 61, 63, 73, 78 ff, 84, 87, 89–90, 94, 97–98; § 8, 51 ff
obligation to protect § 1, 49
prohibition of discrimination § 1, 44 ff; § 3, 64 ff; § 21, 37, 83 ff
– general § 7, 11, 13, 19, 25, 45
– specific § 7, 11, 19 ff, 23 ff, 30, 69
prohibition of inferior treatment § 7, 12, 19, 21, 69

prohibition of limitation § 1, 44 ff; § 7, 24 ff, 33–34, 72, 78, 89; § 9, 41
– the concept § 7, 24–25
– differentiation between discrimination and limitation § 7, 78
– free movement of capital § 12, 7–10
restrictions § 7, 1, 3, 11, 16, 19, 24, 27, 31, 40–41, 46, 61, 63, 72, 74, 76, 78, 81 ff, 86, 89–90; 94 ff, 98 § 8, 32 ff
– on exports § 8, 47–48
restrictions / authorisation to restrict § 7, 16, 50, 61, 80, 83 ff, 88 ff, 98
– unwritten § 7, 88 ff
– written § 7, 83 ff
requirement of a legal basis § 7, 82
requirements, mandatory § 7, 63, 74, 79, 89 ff, 93–94, 96; § 9, 50
– agricultural industry § 12, 37
– capital movements to and from third countries § 12, 46
– "coherence" of the national tax system § 12, 18
– enforcement (of a surety) abroad § 12, 46
– maintenance of "a permanent population" § 12, 33
– price stability § 12, 28–29
– restrictions on secondary residences § 12, 33
– security interests § 12, 39
– social structure § 12, 33
– statistical information § 12, 26–27
– tax revenue § 12, 15
reverse discrimination § 7, 20; § 21, 37 ff, 40, 83 ff, 89
scope of protection § 7, 16, 50 ff, 98
– personal § 7, 37 ff; § 9, 28–29; § 16, 24 ff
– subject matter of protection § 7, 53 ff; § 9, 5; § 11, 18
– temporal § 7, 49
– territorial § 7, 48; § 11, 14
supremacy of the fundamental freedoms § 7, 9
term § 1, 40
Fundamental Rights of the European Union § 2, 32; § 8, 70 ff; § 14, 1 ff
beneficiaries § 14, 27–28
– legal persons § 14, 28
– natural persons § 14, 27
– citizens of the Member States § 14, 27
– nationals of third countries § 14, 27
Charter of Fundamental Rights of the Union § 14, 16 ff
competence § 14, 4–5, 24, 28

613

constitutional traditions common to the Member States (see subsidiary means for the determination of the fundamental rights of the Union)
delineation § 14, 12 ff
– from the fundamental freedoms § 7, 15, 25, 31, 82, 86, 93 ff, 98; § 14, 12
– from the fundamental rights of the ECHR § 14, 13
– from national guarantees § 14, 14–15
ECHR (see subsidiary means for the determination of the fundamental rights of the Union)
entities bound by the fundamental rights of the Union § 1, 33; § 14, 30 ff
– European Union / European Communities § 1, 35; § 14, 30
– Member States § 1, 34; § 14, 31 ff
– private persons § 14, 35
essence of a fundamental right § 14, 47; § 16, 36; § 17, 11, 28; § 20, 16
functions § 14, 20 ff
– equality rights § 14, 21
– European citizenship rights § 14, 24
– liberty rights § 14, 20
– objective dimension § 14, 26
– procedural rights § 14, 25
– rights to governmental action / positive obligations § 14, 22–23
fundamental rights of the Union as general limits to restrictability § 7, 93 ff; § 14, 12
general limits to restrictability § 14, 46 ff
horizontal effect (Drittwirkung) § 14, 35
interferences with § 14, 42
judicial protection § 14, 52 ff
justification § 14, 43 ff
legal foundation § 14, 5 ff
level of review § 14, 4; § 16, 38–39; § 17, 31; § 20, 1
necessity of guaranteeing fundamental rights on the EU level § 14, 3–4
notion § 14, 1–2
principles of Community law, general § 7, 10, 15, 82, 94; § 14, 5
principle of proportionality § 14, 48–49
prohibition of discrimination, general § 14, 6, 21
prohibition of discrimination, specific § 14, 6
right to governmental protection § 14, 22
requirement of a legal basis § 7, 82; § 14, 44; § 20, 15
restrictions § 14, 43 ff

schematic summary of the stages of fundamental rights scrutiny § 14, 51
scope of protection § 14, 40
scope of protection § 14, 37
– personal (see beneficiaries)
– subject matter of protection § 14, 40
– temporal § 14, 37
– territorial § 14, 37
source of law § 14, 5, 7–8
subsidiary means for the determination of the fundamental rights of the Union § 14, 8, 10, 13, 16, 19, 27
– constitutional traditions common to the Member States § 14, 7–8
– ECHR § 14, 7–8, 10, 13

GATS § 11, 10
Gebhard **case-law** § 10, 18, 40
general limits to the restrictability (see fundamental rights of the European Union; fundamental freedoms)
general principles of Community law § 7, 10, 15, 82; § 14, 5 ff (see also fundamental rights of the European Union)
goods § 8, 8 ff
governmental action, rights to § 7, 29 ff
derivative rights to governmental action § 7, 30
original rights to governmental action § 7, 33
governmental protection, right to § 3, 26–27, 33, 62 ff; § 7, 31, 94; § 14, 12, 22, 35, 52
grounds for an encumbering decision, duty to give § 19, 2, 10, 22

Habeas-Corpus-doctrine § 6, 28; § 15, 88
harmonisation of Member States' laws § 7, 35
movement of capital § 12, 20, 47
headscarf § 3, 31, 35
health and life, confidentiality of § 8, 75
heard, right to be § 19, 10
home, protection of § 3, 13; § 15, 21 ff
horizontal effect (see fundamental rights of the European Union, fundamental freedoms)
Human
dignity § 3, 39, 45; § 15, 3 ff; § 20, 6
rights protection, international § 1, 1
Human Rights Act (United Kingdom) § 1, 13

identity
national § 15, 15
sexual § 3, 8
import restrictions § 8, 22 ff, 32, 36, 39

Index

industrial and commercial property, protection of § 8, 17, 77
information
  freedom of § 4, 2, 6, 10–13, 17, 54; § 15, 79
  right to § 6, 22–23; § 21, 70
innocence, presumption of § 6, 1, 44; § 19, 5
integrity
  physical § 3, 39
  physical and mental § 15, 9–10
intellectual property § 5, 18
interference with a fundamental right (see ECHR; fundamental rights of the European Union; fundamental freedoms)
internal market § 7, 1, 19, 25, 39, 44, 90
  goal of § 16, 2
  movement of capital § 12, 1, 47
internalisation, direct § 7, 7
internet § 4, 22
interpretation
  autonomous § 3, 24
  dynamic § 3, 41

job-seeking § 9, 15
judicial protection § 7, 16, 34, 99 ff
  effective § 6, 2, 48; § 19, 2, 23 ff, 54, 61 ff
  interim measures § 19, 47, 49, 51
justification (of interferences) (see ECHR; fundamental rights of the European Union; fundamental freedoms)

***Keck*-formula** § 7, 27, 74 ff, 98; § 8, 30, 36 ff; § 12, 7
  impact on the freedom to provide services § 11, 55
killing, repressive § 3, 58
knowledge of one's own descent § 3, 8

lawful judge § 19, 24, 34
lawyer's correspondence, confidentiality of § 15, 33
legal persons (see ECHR; fundamental rights of the European Union; fundamental freedoms – beneficiaries)
legal remedies, instruction on § 19, 13
legitimate expectations, protection of § 16, 18
liberty rights § 20, 7
life § 3, 48 ff
  unborn § 3, 49
limitation (see fundamental freedoms)

mandatory requirements (see fundamental freedoms)

margin of appreciation § 3, 25, 48; § 4, 16, 34, 44, 46, 52–53, 79
market
  access § 8, 41
  citizen § 21, 4
marketing of a product § 8, 40
marriage § 3, 9, 11
  protection of matrimony § 15, 37–38
***Matthews* case-law** § 20, 39
measures having equivalent effect
  to export restrictions § 8, 47 ff
  to import restrictions § 8, 22 ff
media § 4, 4, 9, 11, 17–22, 26, 29, 56
  diversity of § 15, 73–74, 85
medical information, protection of § 15, 9, 35
military operations (out of area) § 3, 51, 61
minimum reserves § 12, 28
minority protection § 1, 21
misjudgement, compensation for § 6, 61
monetary law § 12, 28–29
monetary policy § 12, 28
morals, protection of § 4, 16, 34, 44, 52–53, 65
mortgage § 12, 40
municipal electoral rights § 21, 53 ff

national treasure § 8, 76
nationality § 21, 18 ff, 26 ff
ne bis in idem § 6, 58–59; § 19, 16
nemo tenetur § 6, 43; § 19, 17 ff
noticeability § 8, 45
nulla poena sine lege [principle of no crime without a law] § 6, 54 ff; § 19, 2, 41

occupation § 16, 11
open market operations § 12, 28
origin, country of, principle § 11, 13
OSCE § 1, 2
overt discrimination (see fundamental freedoms)

parallelism between the competences of the EC and the protection of fundamental rights § 14, 22; § 20, 20
payments
  balance of § 12, 27, 43
  freedom of § 12, 6
personal data, protection of § 15, 39 ff, 58
personality, free development of § 3, 3
persons, free movement of § 9, 1
petition, right to § 21, 66 ff
***Pfeiffer* case-law** § 10, 47, 60
police custody § 3, 40, 42, 53
policy, public (see public policy)

615

political parties   § 4, 43, 72, 77, 79–80
posting of workers directive   § 11, 12
preliminary ruling, duty to file a request for
    § 19, 24, 52, 64–65
price fixing (books)   § 15, 69–70
prisoners   § 3, 15
private life   § 3, 3 ff
    respect for   § 15, 17 ff
privatisation of public companies   § 12, 22–24
procedural rights   § 2, 12, 14–15, 18, 20, 38, 69;
    § 7, 18, 34
product-related measures   § 7, 76
prohibition of discrimination   § 1, 44 ff; § 3,
    66 ff; § 21, 37, 83 ff
    due to gender   § 18, 20 ff
    general   § 7, 11, 45
    due to nationality   § 13; § 14, 6
    – direct discriminations   § 13, 14–15
    – indirect discriminations   § 13, 16–17
    – reverse discrimination of nationals   § 13, 9
    – right of equal access to social security
      systems   § 13, 10
    – scope of application of this treaty   § 13,
      6 ff
    remuneration   § 18, 29 ff, 53
    – justification of direct discriminations
      § 18, 42–43
    – justification of indirect discriminations
      § 18, 44 ff
    – regarding the assessment of old-age
      pension schemes   § 18, 34 ff
    specific   § 7, 19 ff, 23, 30, 78
prohibition of limitation   (see fundamental
    freedoms)
property
    claims under public law   § 5, 13 ff
    expectations and prospects of acquisitions
      § 5, 10
    expropriation   § 5, 24; § 17, 21
    goodwill   § 5, 11
    interferences
    – equitable balance of interests   § 5, 44
    – justification   § 5, 35 ff
    – legality of restrictions   § 5, 37
    – margin of appreciation   § 5, 36 ff, 43
    – national peculiarities   § 5, 53
    – proportionality   § 5, 41 ff
    – public interest   § 5, 38
    right
    – beneficiaries   § 5, 9
    – interferences   § 5, 20 ff; § 17, 18
    – measures concerning restrictions on use
      § 5, 27 ff

    – miscellaneous encroachments   § 5, 32 ff
    – prohibition of discrimination   § 5, 57
    – restrictions on the use of property   § 17,
      28
    – scope of protection   § 5, 7 ff
    – social function of   § 17, 10, 29
    rules governing the system of property
      ownership   § 17, 2
    social responsibility   § 17, 20
proportionality, principle of   § 3, 25, 30, 59–60,
    70; § 7, 96; § 11, 66; § 8, 72, 82 ff; § 12, 34–35;
    § 14, 48–49; § 16, 37; § 17, 31
protection by the State, right to   § 14, 22; § 20, 13
protection of one's religion / belief   § 3, 31, 34
public policy   § 7, 32, 46, 85–86, 89; § 9, 12
    free movement of capital   § 12, 11, 22–23
    freedom of movement for workers   § 9,
      47–48
public procurement law, judicial protection in the
    field of   § 19, 47–48
public security   § 7, 32, 46, 85–86, 89
    defence of the nation   § 12, 38
    free movement of capital   § 12, 11, 22–23,
      38
    freedom of movement for workers   § 9,
      47–48
public trial   § 6, 45 ff
punishment, possible sanctions and seriousness
    § 6, 36

quality of products   § 8, 39

racial discrimination   § 3, 39
real estate
    agriculture   § 12, 37
    free movement of capital   § 12, 32
    military importance   § 12, 38
    prior approval   § 12, 37
    protection through the free movement of
      capital   § 12, 4
    restrictions on real estate transactions   § 12,
      30–38
    secondary residences   § 12, 31–36
    spectrum of capital movement   § 12, 2
    urban development law   § 12, 32
reasonable time, right to a decision within   § 19,
    2, 8, 38–39
relationship, unmarried long-term   § 3, 9 ff
religion   § 4, 58, 72
    freedom of   § 3, 31 ff; § 15, 47 ff
remuneration received in return   § 9, 10
reporting requirements in cross-border capital and
    payment transactions   § 12, 26–27

Index

reputation, protection of § 4, 19, 30, 31, 48, 51
requirements, mandatory (see fundamental freedoms)
res judicata of administrative decisions § 19, 26, 61, 67
resident rights § 9, 24; § 21, 37 ff
restrictions (see ECHR; fundamental rights of the European Union; fundamental freedoms)
restrictions on exports
  capital movement § 12, 7
  quantitative § 8, 47
reverse discrimination (see fundamental freedoms)
right of succession § 5, 19
right to be heard § 6, 40; § 19, 11, 35, 41, 57 ff
rights to governmental action § 7, 18, 28 ff; § 14, 22–23
  derivative § 7, 30
  original § 7, 33; § 14, 23

sales-related measures § 7, 76
scenario, cross-border (see fundamental freedoms)
scope of protection (see ECHR; fundamental rights of the European Union; fundamental freedoms)
secondary Community law (see Community law)
secondary residences § 12, 31–36
sectoral exceptions (see fundamental freedoms)
security
  interests § 12, 39–40
  right to § 6, 6
  systems, social § 9, 25
security interests § 12, 39–40
self-defence § 3, 63
self-determination
  over personal data § 3, 3
  sexual § 3, 8, 26
services, directive on § 11, 11
sex § 3, 8–11, 68, 70
shares in companies § 12, 2, 9, 22, 23, 25
situs doctrine § 12, 39
slaughtering according to Muslim or Jewish rites § 3, 31–32
social rights § 5, 62 ff; § 16, 4; § 18, 56 ff; § 21, 83 ff
  original right to governmental action, § 18, 60
  rights to participation, § 18, 60
Solange decisions of the *Bundesverfassungsgericht* § 14, 4, 14
solidarity § 18, 56–57

state aids, prohibition of § 7, 87
  relation to the fundamental freedoms 7, 87
state trade monopolies § 8, 4
statutory basis, requirement of (see ECHR; fundamental rights of the European Union; fundamental freedoms)
subjective rights
  fundamental freedoms § 7, 8, 35
  supranational norms of legitimation § 18, 3 ff
  transnational norms of integration § 18, 2
subsidiarity, principle of § 20, 25
surety § 12, 46

tax law
  coherence of the national tax system § 12, 18
  corporate income tax § 12, 19
  credit business § 12, 15
  discriminatory taxes § 12, 16–21
  double taxation § 12, 20
  free movement of capital § 12, 14–21
  mandatory requirements (of the common welfare) § 12, 15, 18
  non-discriminatory tax § 12, 15
  purchase of foreign currencies § 12, 15
  residence § 12, 17
  taxation of dividends § 12, 19
  tax reservation clause of Art 58(1)(a) TEC § 12, 17
  Tobin tax § 12, 15
third countries
  free movement of capital § 12, 5, 41–46
thought, protection of § 3, 31 ff
'tiered' proceedings § 19, 55 ff
Tobacco
  Products, Directive on § 15, 76–77
  Advertising, Directive on § 15, 74 ff
Tobin tax (see tax law)
torture § 3, 39 ff
trade union rights § 4, 2, 75, 76, 77, 80–93
transitory periods following the enlargement of the EU § 11, 9
treatment
  degrading § 3, 39, 41
  inhuman § 3, 39, 41
Treaty Establishing a Constitution for Europe, consequences of § 1, 51; § 14, 2
trial
  fair § 2, 18, 27; § 3, 74–75; § 6, 38 ff; § 19, 3, 18, 24, 26, 36
  right to use one's own language § 19, 12, 44
tribunal, independent and impartial § 6, 37

617

TV Without Frontiers Directive § 15, 71

Überseering **case-law** § 10, 61, 72

waiver

right to an impartial tribunal § 6, 37
right to non-in camera proceedings § 6, 46
work, right to § 16, 6
worker § 9, 6
WTO § 16, 2